THE
ANNUAL REGISTER
Vol. 248

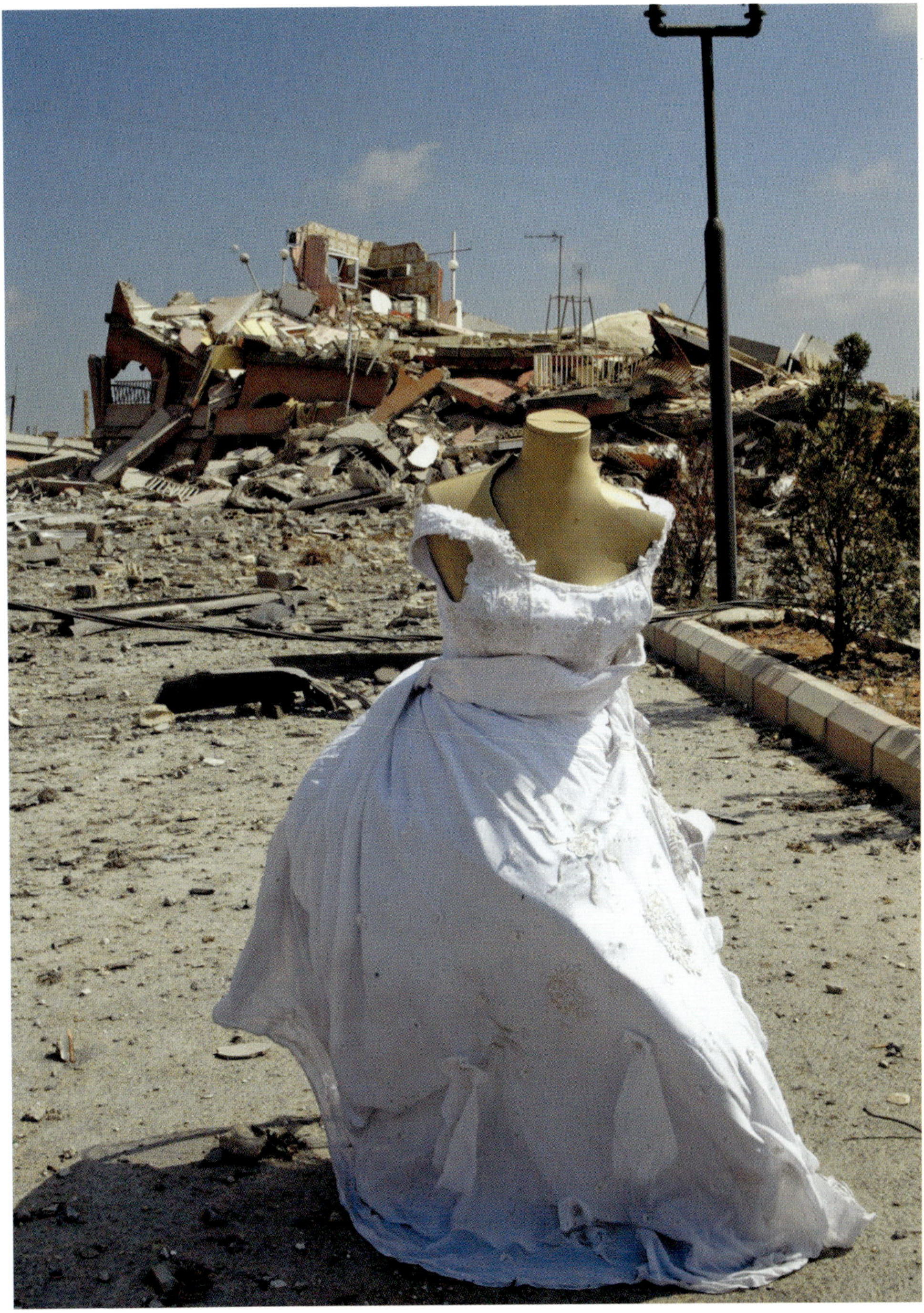

War Torn (31 July): A mannequin adorned with a wedding dress stands abandoned in the Lebanese town of Qana, where at least 28 people (including 16 children) were killed a day earlier in an Israeli air raid. (REUTERS/Sharif Karim).

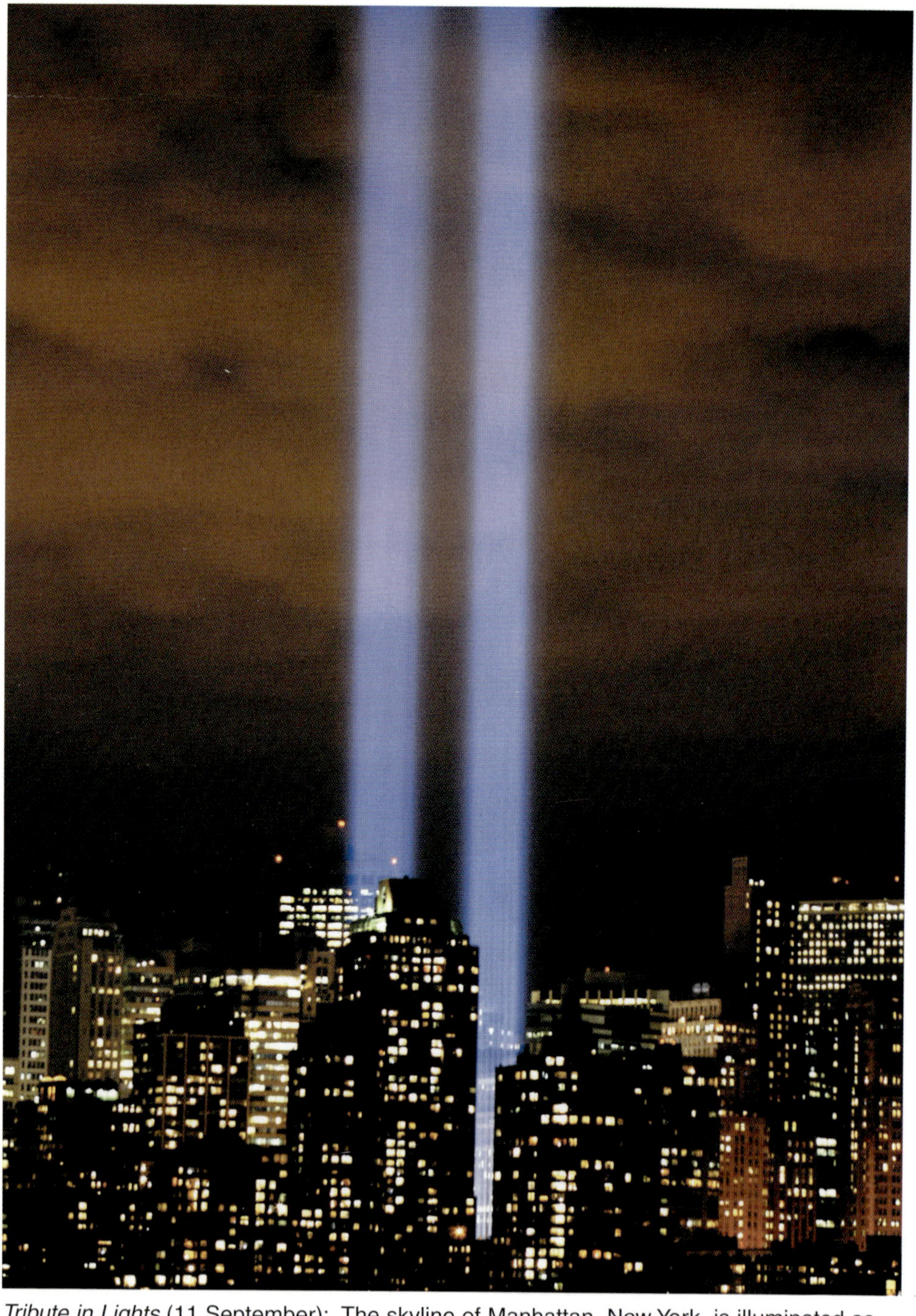

Tribute in Lights (11 September): The skyline of Manhattan, New York, is illuminated as the fifth anniversary of the 11 September 2001 attacks on the World Trade Centre is observed. (REUTERS/Gary Hershorn).

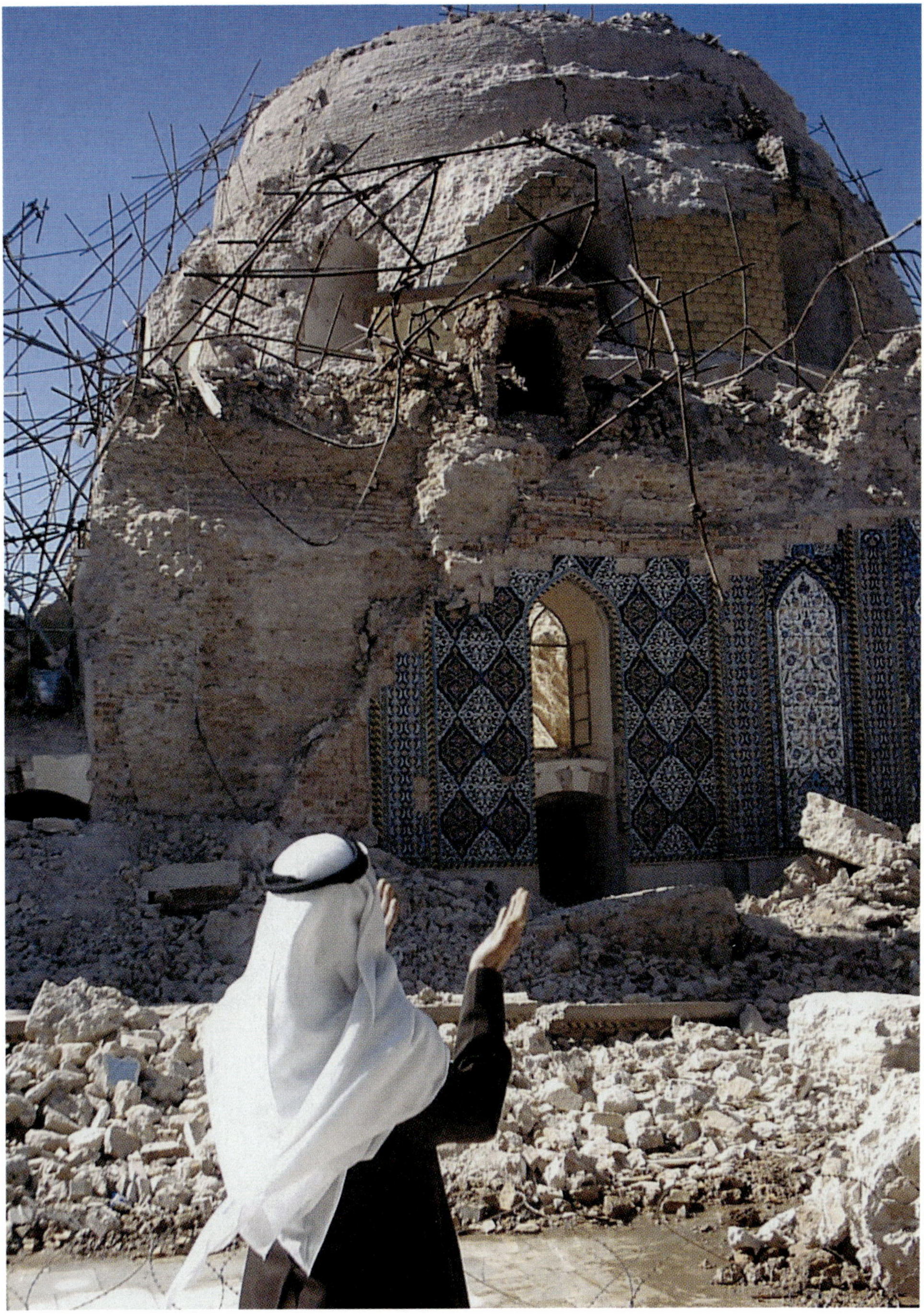

Sectarian Hatred (24 February): An Iraqi Shi'ite prays in front of the revered al-Askariya shrine in Samarra, Iraq, two days after it was severely damaged by a bomb thought to have been planted by al-Qaida. (REUTERS/Stringer).

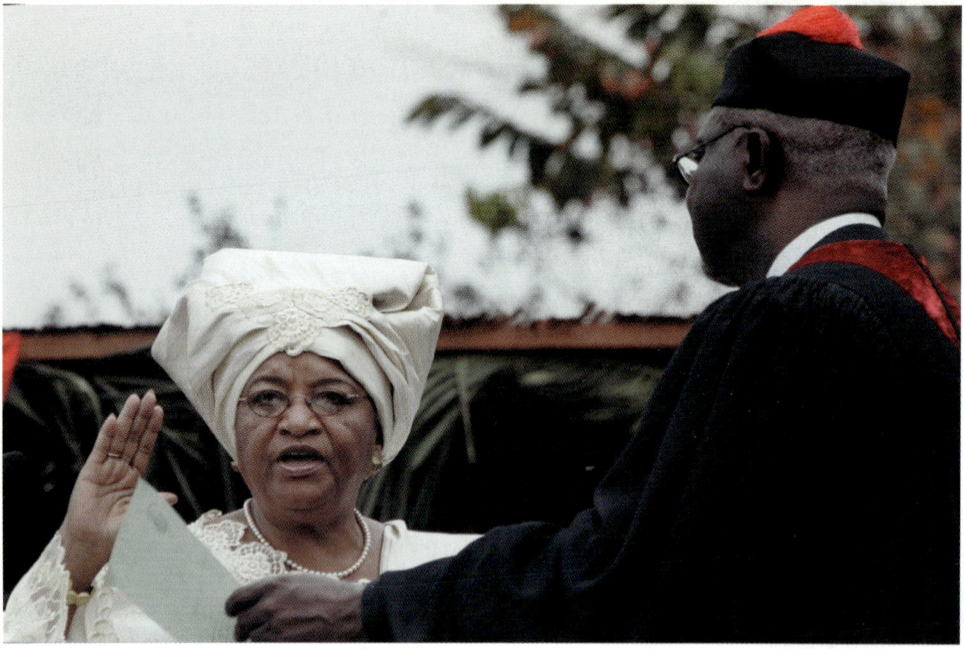

Embracing the Future (16 January): Ellen Johnson-Sirleaf, Africa's first elected female head of state, is sworn in as the new president of Liberia during a ceremony in Monrovia. (REUTERS/Jason Reed).

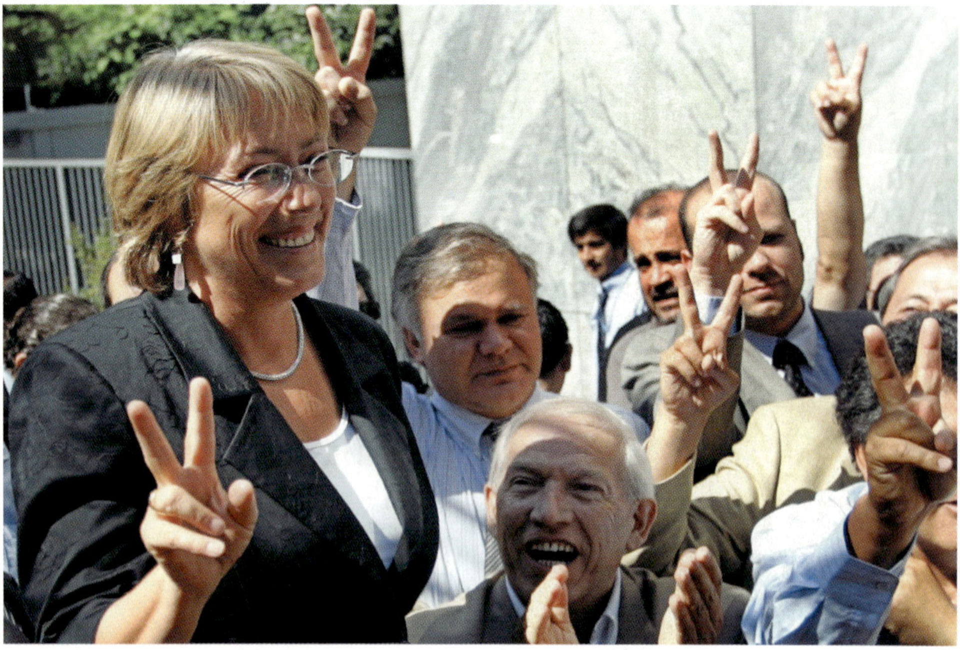

Overcoming the Past (12 January): Socialist candidate Michelle Bachelet, a former victim of Chile's military dictatorship, campaigns in Santiago en route to her election as the country's first woman president. (REUTERS/Jorge Silva).

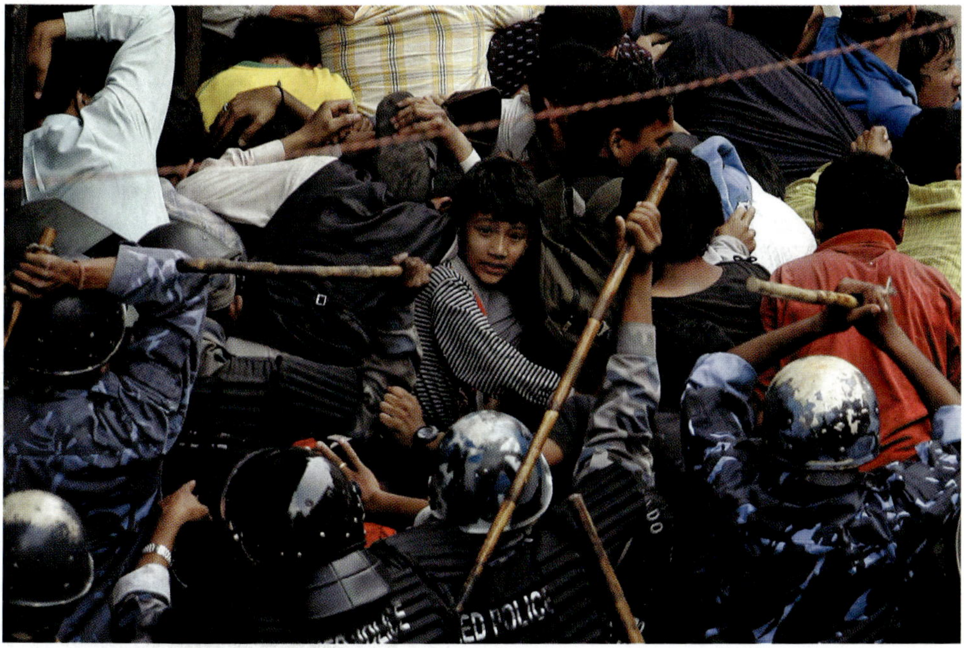

Tide of Change (22 April): Riot policemen beat pro-democracy demonstrators in Nepal's capital, Kathmandu, prior to the fall of the dictatorial government of King Gyanendra. (REUTERS/Adrees Latif).

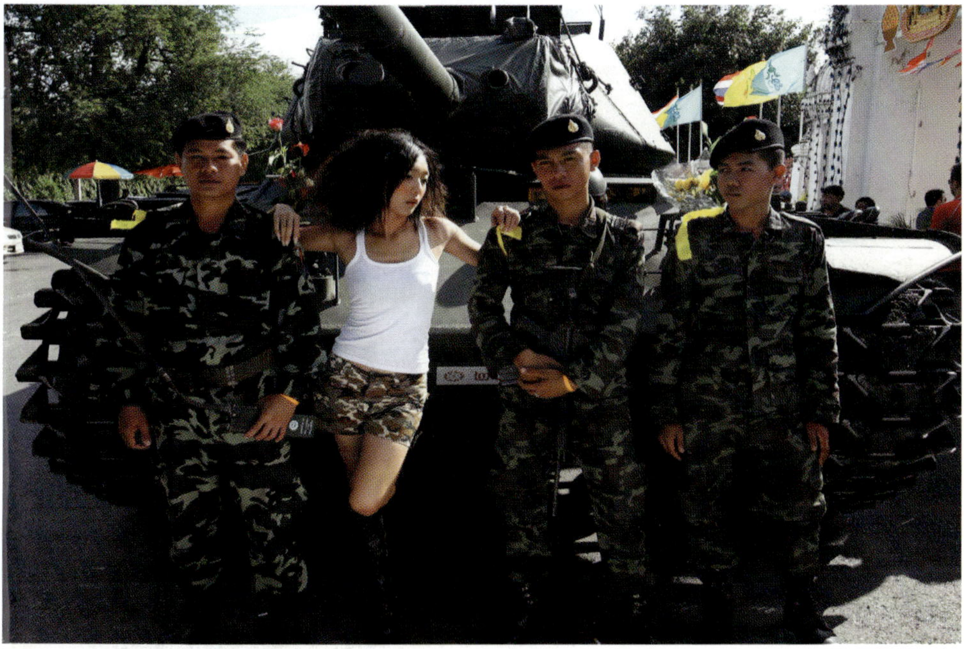

Welcomed Intervention (21 September): A Thai fashion student poses with soldiers in Bangkok following a bloodless, and largely popular, coup by the army. (REUTERS/Darren Whiteside).

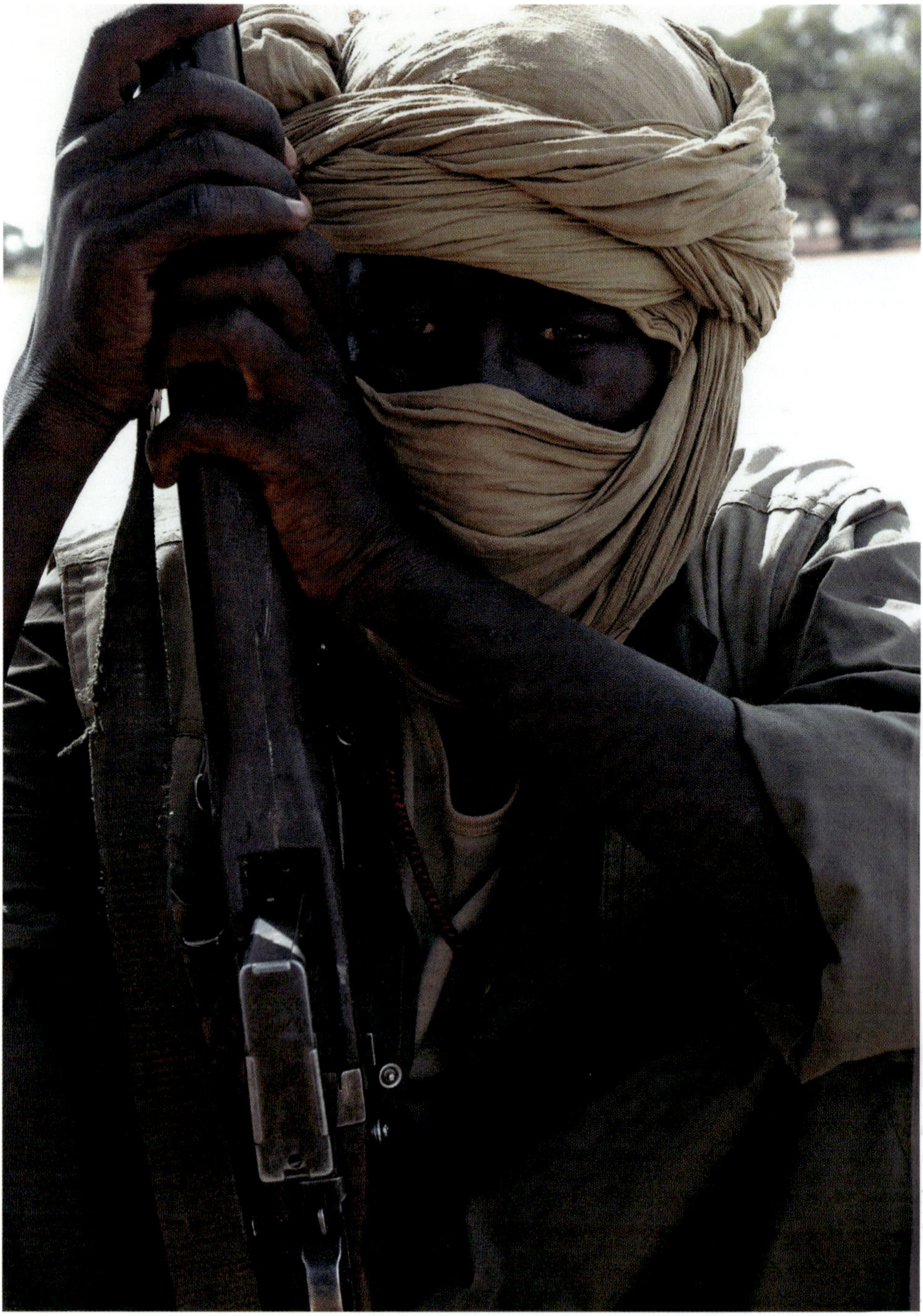

Continuing Conflict (28 August): A rebel with the National Redemption Front, an alliance of groups opposed to the Darfur peace agreement, waits at an outpost in Umm Sidir, northern Darfur. (REUTERS/Candace Feit).

THE ANNUAL REGISTER

World Events 2006

Edited by
D.S. LEWIS

Deputy Editor
WENDY SLATER

FIRST EDITED IN 1758
BY EDMUND BURKE

ProQuest
Start here.

THE ANNUAL REGISTER: World Events 2006
Published by ProQuest
7200 Wisconsin Ave.
Bethesda, MD 20814
United States of America and
4640 Kingsgate, Cascade Way
Oxford Business Park South
Oxford, OX4 2ST, England

ISBN: 978-1-60030-070-7 / ISSN 0266-6170

British Library Cataloguing in Publication Data
The Annual Register—2006
1. History—Periodicals
909.82'8'05 D410

Library of Congress Catalog Card Number: 4-17979

Set in Times Roman by
NEW AGE GRAPHICS, Silver Spring, MD, USA

Printed in the USA by
THE SHERIDAN BOOKS, Chelsea, MI, USA
Jacket design: John Moss

CONTENTS

CONTRIBUTORS

PREFACE	**D.S. Lewis,** PhD, Editor, *The Annual Register*
EXTRACTS FROM PAST VOLUMES	**Philip M.H. Bell,** Senior Research Fellow, University of Liverpool
PART I	
HISTORICAL OVERVIEW	**Anatol Lieven,** PhD, Senior Research Fellow, The New America Foundation, Washington DC
PART II	
UNITED KINGDOM	**Harriet Jones,** MSc, PhD, Senior Research Fellow, Institute of Contemporary British History
UNITED KINGDOM ECONOMY	**Michael Kandiah**, MA, PhD, Lecturer in Contemporary British History and Director of the Oral History Programme, Centre for Contemporary British History, Institute of Historical Research, University of London
SCOTLAND	**Charlotte Lythe,** MA, Honorary Research Fellow in Economic Studies, University of Dundee
WALES	**Gwyn Jenkins,** MA, Director of Collection Services, The National Library of Wales, Aberystwyth
NORTHERN IRELAND REPUBLIC OF IRELAND	**Alan Greer,** PhD, Reader in Politics & Public Policy, University of the West of England, Bristol
GERMANY, AUSTRIA, SWITZERLAND	**Dan Hough,** PhD, Lecturer in Politics, University of Sussex
FRANCE	**Martin Harrison,** Professor of Politics, University of Keele
ITALY	**Mark Donovan,** PhD, Senior Lecturer in Politics, Cardiff University of Wales; Editor, *Modern Italy*
BELGIUM, NETHERLANDS, LUXEMBOURG	**Martin Harrison** (see France)
DENMARK, ICELAND, NORWAY, SWEDEN, FINLAND	**Mary Hilson,** PhD, Lecturer in Contemporary Scandinavian History, University College, London
EUROPEAN MINI-STATES	**Martin Harrison** (see France)
SPAIN, GIBRALTAR	**William Chislett,** Former correspondent of *The Times* in Spain (1975-78) and the *Financial Times* in Mexico (1978-84); author of three books on Spain for the Elcano Royal Institute (2002, 2003 and 2005)
PORTUGAL	**Martin Eaton,** BA, PhD, FRGS/IBG, Reader in Human Geography, University of Ulster at Coleraine
MALTA	**Dominic Fenech,** BA, DPhil, Professor of History, University of Malta
GREECE	**Susannah Verney,** PhD, Lecturer in Department of Political Science and Public Administration, University of Athens; editor, *South European Society and Politics*
CYPRUS	**Robert McDonald,** Writer and broadcaster on Cyprus, Greece and Turkey

TURKEY	**A.J.A. Mango,** BA, PhD, Orientalist and writer on current affairs in Turkey and the Near East
PART III	
POLAND	**Frances Millard,** PhD, Professor in the Department of Government, University of Essex
ESTONIA, LATVIA, LITHUANIA	**David J. Galbreath,** PhD, Lecturer in Politics and International Relations, University of Aberdeen.
CZECH REPUBLIC, SLOVAKIA	**Sharon Fisher,** MA, Analyst specialising in East European political and economic affairs, Global Insight
HUNGARY	**Daniel Izsak,** BA, Journalist; Former European Affairs Specialist & Desk Editor, BBC World Service
ROMANIA	**Gabriel Partos,** South-East Europe Analyst, BBC World Service
FORMER YUGOSLAV REPUBLICS BULGARIA, ALBANIA	**Othon Anastasakis,** MA, PhD, Director, South East European Studies Programme, St Antony's College, Oxford
RUSSIA, WESTERN CIS	**Wendy Slater,** MA, PhD, former Lecturer in Contemporary Russian History, UCL; Deputy Editor, *The Annual Register*
CAUCASUS	**Elizabeth Fuller,** BA, Caucasus Analyst, Radio Free Europe/Radio Liberty, Prague
PART IV	
UNITED STATES OF AMERICA	**James D. Miller,** PhD, Associate Dean, Department of History, Carleton University, Ottawa
CANADA	**David M.L. Farr,** MA, DPhil, LLD, Emeritus Professor of History, Carleton University, Ottawa
MEXICO, CENTRAL AMERICA	**Peter Clegg,** MSc, PhD, Lecturer in Politics, University of the West of England, Bristol
ARGENTINA, BRAZIL, SOUTH AMERICA	**Kurt Perry,** Freelance writer specialising in Latin America
CARIBBEAN	**Peter Clegg** (see Mexico, Central America)
PART V	
ISRAEL, PALESTINE, IRAQ	**Darren Sagar,** MA, Freelance writer specialising in Middle Eastern and South-East Asian affairs
EGYPT, JORDAN, SYRIA, LEBANON	**David Butter,** MA, Chief Energy Analyst, Economist Intelligence Unit; Editor *Business Middle East*; Editor ViewsWire Middle East
SAUDI ARABIA, YEMEN, ARAB GULF STATES	**James Gavin,** BA, contributing editor, *Gulf States Newsletter*
SUDAN	**Ahmed Al-Shahi,** MLitt, DPhil, Former lecturer in Social Anthropology, University of Newcastle Upon Tyne
LIBYA, TUNISIA, ALGERIA, MOROCCO, WESTERN SAHARA	**R.I. Lawless,** PhD, Emeritus Reader in Modern Middle Eastern Studies, University of Durham; Research Associate, Queen Elizabeth House, University of Oxford.
PART VI	
HORN OF AFRICA	**Guy Arnold,** Writer specialising in Africa and North-South affairs

KENYA, TANZANIA, UGANDA	**William Tordoff,** MA, PhD, Emeritus Professor of Government, University of Manchester
NIGERIA, GHANA, SIERRA LEONE, THE GAMBIA, LIBERIA	**Guy Arnold,** (see Horn of Africa)
FRANCOPHONE AFRICA	**Kaye Whiteman,** Former publisher, *West Africa*
CAPE VERDE, SÃO TOMÉ AND PRÍNCIPE	**Christopher Saunders,** DPhil, Professor in Department of Historical Studies, University of Cape Town

PART VII

DEMOCRATIC REPUBLIC OF CONGO, BURUNDI & RWANDA, MOZAMBIQUE	**Colin Darch,** PhD, Senior Information Specialist, African Studies Library, University of Cape Town
GUINEA BISSAU, ANGOLA, ZAMBIA, MALAWI	**Christopher Saunders** (see Cape Verde etc.)
ZIMBABWE	**R.W. Baldock,** BA, PhD, Managing Director, Yale University Press; writer on African affairs
BOTSWANA, LESOTHO, NAMIBIA, SWAZILAND, SOUTH AFRICA	**Elizabeth Sidiropoulos,** BA Hons, MA, Director of Studies, South African Institute of International Affairs (SAIIA), Johannesburg; and **Terence Corrigan,** BA, Researcher, SAAIIA

PART VIII

IRAN	**Keith McLachlan,** BA, PhD, Emeritus Professor, School of Oriental and African Studies, University of London
AFGHANISTAN	**Matthew Cann,** BA, Freelance writer specialising in Central Asia
CENTRAL ASIAN REPUBLICS	**Shirin Akiner,** PhD, Lecturer in Central Asian Studies, School of Oriental and African Studies, University of London
INDIA, PAKISTAN, SRI LANKA, BANGLADESH, NEPAL, BHUTAN	**David Taylor,** PhD, Senior Lecturer in Politics with reference to South Asia, School of Oriental and African Studies, University of London
MAURITIUS, SEYCHELLES, COMOROS, MALDIVES, MADAGASCAR	**Malyn Newitt,** BA, PhD, JP, Charles Boxer Professor of History, Department of Portuguese, King's College, London

PART IX

BURMA (MYANMAR), THAILAND, MALAYSIA, BRUNEI, SINGAPORE, VIETNAM, CAMBODIA, LAOS	**Stephen Levine,** PhD, Professor and Head of School of History, Philosophy, Political Science and International Relations, Victoria University of Wellington
INDONESIA, EAST TIMOR, PHILIPPINES	**Norman MacQueen,** BA, MSc, DPhil, Head of Department of Politics, University of Dundee
CHINA, HONG KONG, TAIWAN	**Phil Deans,** BA, PhD, Professor of International Affairs, Temple University, Tokyo
JAPAN	**Ian Nish,** PhD, Emeritus Professor of International History, London School of Economics and Political Science
NORTH AND SOUTH KOREA	**J.E. Hoare,** PhD, Consultant on East Asia; former chargé d'affaires in Pyongyang
MONGOLIA	**Phil Deans** (see China, Hong Kong, Taiwan)

PART X	
AUSTRALIA	**James Jupp,** AM, MSc (Econ), PhD, FASSA, Director, Centre for Immigration and Multicultural Studies, Australian National University, Canberra
PAPUA NEW GUINEA	**Norman MacQueen** (see Indonesia etc.)
NEW ZEALAND, PACIFIC ISLAND STATES	**Stephen Levine** (see Burma etc.)
PART XI	
UNITED NATIONS	**David Travers,** BA, Lecturer in Politics and International Relations, Lancaster University; Specialist Advisor on UN to House of Commons' Foreign Affairs Committee
DEFENCE ORGANISATIONS	**Paul Cornish,** PhD, Peter Carrington Chair in International Security and Head of International Security Programme, Chatham House, London
ECONOMIC ORGANISATIONS	**Paul Rayment,** MA, Former Director of the Economic Analysis Division of the UN Economic Commission for Europe, Geneva
COMMONWEALTH	**Derek Ingram,** Consultant Editor of *Gemini News Service*; author and writer on the Commonwealth
FRANCOPHONIE	**Kaye Whiteman,** (see Francophone Africa)
COMMUNITY OF PORTUGUESE-SPEAKING COUNTRIES	**Martin Eaton** (see Portugal)
NON-ALIGNED MOVEMENT AND GROUP OF 77	**Peter Willets,** PhD, Professor of Global Politics, Department of Sociology, The City University, London
ORGANISATION OF THE ISLAMIC CONFERENCE	**Darren Sagar** (see Israel, Palestine etc.)
EUROPEAN UNION; COUNCIL OF EUROPE	**Michael Berendt,** Expert on affairs of the European Union
ORGANISATION FOR SECURITY AND CO-OPERATION IN EUROPE; EUROPEAN BANK FOR RECONSTRUCTION AND DEVELOPMENT	**Michael Kaser,** MA, DLitt, DSocSc, Emeritus Fellow of St Antony's College, Oxford, and Honorary Professor University of Birmingham
OTHER EUROPEAN ORGANISATIONS	**Martin Harrison** (see France etc.)
AMERICAN AND CARIBBEAN ORGANISATIONS	**Peter Clegg** (see Latin America, Caribbean)
ARAB ORGANISATIONS	**Darren Sagar** (see Israel, Palestine etc.)
AFRICAN ORGANISATIONS AND CONFERENCES	**Christopher Saunders** (see Guinea Bissau etc.)
EURASIAN ORGANISATIONS	**Shirin Akiner** (see Central Asia)
ASIA-PACIFIC ORGANISATIONS	**Darren Sagar** (see Israel, Palestine etc.)
PART XII	
THE INTERNATIONAL ECONOMY	**Paul Rayment** (see Economic Organisations)
PART XIII	
MEDICAL, SCIENTIFIC AND INDUSTRIAL RESEARCH	**Neil Weir,** FRCS, Consultant otolaryngologist and **Lorelly Wilson,** Honorary Teaching Fellow, University of Manchester

INFORMATION TECHNOLOGY	**Kristian Saxton,** CEO of software consultancy, Aethernet
ENVIRONMENT	**Tim Curtis,** Regional Editor, *Keesing's Record of World Events*; writer on international affairs

PART XIV

INTERNATIONAL LAW	**Christine Gray,** MA, PhD, Fellow in Law, St John's College, Cambridge
EUROPEAN COMMUNITY LAW	**N. March Hunnings,** LLM, PhD, Editor, *Encyclopedia of European Union Law: Constitutional Texts*
LAW IN THE UK	**Jonathan Morgan,** MA, Fellow in Law, Christ's College, Cambridge
LAW IN THE USA	**Robert J. Spjut,** ID, LLD, Member of the State Bars of California and Florida

PART XV

RELIGION	**Revd Dr Mark Chapman**, Vice Principal, Ripon College Cuddesdon, Oxford; **Miri Freud-Kandel**, MA, PhD, Lecturer in Modern Judaism, Oxford Centre for Hebrew and Jewish Studies, Junior Research Fellow, Wolfson College, Oxford; **Peter Oppenheimer**, MA, President, Oxford Centre for Hebrew and Jewish Studies; **Shaunaka Rishi Das**, Director, Oxford Centre for Hindu Studies, Oxford; **Timothy Winter**, MA, Sheikh Zayed Lecturer in Islamic Studies, University of Cambridge

PART XVI

OPERA	**Rodney Milnes,** OBE, Hon. RAM; Chief Opera Critic, *The Times*, 1992-2002
MUSIC	**Francis Routh,** Composer and author; founder director of the Redcliffe Concerts
BALLET & DANCE	**Jane Pritchard,** Curator of Dance, the Victoria and Albert Museum of Performing Arts, London
THEATRE	**Matt Wolf,** London theatre critic of *The International Herald Tribune* and Bloomberg News and contributing editor and chief critic for the new theatre.com website
CINEMA	**Derek Malcolm,** Cinema critic, *The Guardian*
TV & RADIO	**Raymond Snoddy,** Freelance journalist specialising in media issues, writing for the *Independent*
VISUAL ARTS	**Anna Somers Cocks,** Editor, *The Art Newspaper*
ARCHITECTURE	**Jay Merrick,** Architecture correspondent, *The Independent*; writer for *New Statesman*, *Blueprint*, *Monument*, and *ArtReview*; and novelist
LITERATURE	**Alastair Niven,** OBE, Principal, Cumberland Lodge; formerly Director of Literature, British Council

PART XVII SPORT	**Paul Newman,** Chief Sports Feature Writer, *The Independent*
PART XVIII DOCUMENTS AND REFERENCE	**AR editorial staff**
PART XIX OBITUARY	**James Bishop,** Former Editor of *The Illustrated London News* and Foreign News Editor of *The Times*
PART XX CHRONICLE OF 2006	**Wendy Slater** (see Russia)
MAPS AND DIAGRAMS	**Richard Lear,** Galecrest

ACKNOWLEDGMENTS

THE editor gratefully acknowledges his debt to a number of individuals and institutions for their help with sources, references and documents. Acknowledgment is also due to the principal sources for the national and IGO data sections (showing the situation at end 2006 unless otherwise stated), namely the World Bank Group website, the *Financial Times* (London), *Keesing's Record of World Events* (Keesing's Worldwide), the FCO website (for UK Overseas Territories), National Statistics (for UK populations), and National Statistics, Republic of China (for Taiwan). Whilst every effort is made to ensure accuracy, the Board and the bodies which nominate its members, the editors, and the publisher disclaim responsibility for any opinions expressed or the accuracy of facts recorded in this volume.

GNI per capita at PPP is a measure of Gross National Income that allows a standard comparison of real price levels between countries by using the PPP (Purchasing Power Parity) rate. At the PPP rate, one international dollar has the same purchasing power over domestic GNI that the US dollar has over US GNI. PPP GNI per capita is PPP GNI divided by mid-year population

ABBREVIATIONS AND ACRONYMS

AC	Arctic Council
ACP	African, Caribbean and Pacific states associated with EU
ACS	Association of Caribbean States
ADB	Asian Development Bank
AL	Arab League
ALADI	Latin American Integration Association
AMU	Arab Maghreb Union
ANZUS	Australia-New Zealand-US Security Treaty
APEC	Asia-Pacific Economic Co-operation
ASEAN	Association of South-East Asian Nations
AU	African Union
Benelux	Belgium-Netherlands-Luxembourg Economic Union
BSEC	Black Sea Economic Co-operation
Ancom/CA	Andean Community of Nations
Caricom	Caribbean Community and Common Market
CBSS	Council of the Baltic Sea States
CE	Council of Europe
CEEAC	Economic Community of Central African States
CEFTA	Central European Free Trade Agreement
CEI	Central European Initiative
CENSAD	Community of Sahel-Saharan States
CIS	Commonwealth of Independent States
COMESA	Common Market of Eastern and Southern Africa
CPLP	Community of Portuguese-Speaking Countries
CSTO	Collective Security Treaty Organisation
CWTH	The Commonwealth
DRC	Democratic Republic of Congo
DR-CAFTA	Dominican Republic-Central American Free Trade Agreement
EAC	East African Community
EBRD	European Bank for Reconstruction and Development
ECB	European Central Bank
ECO	Economic Co-operation Organisation
ECOWAS	Economic Community of West African States
EEA	European Economic Area
EEC	Eurasian Economic Community
EFTA	European Free Trade Association
EU	European Union
G-8	Group of Eight
G-7	Group of Seven
G-77	Group of 77
GCC	Gulf Co-operation Council
GDP	Gross domestic product
GNI	Gross national income
HIPC	Heavily Indebted Poor Countries
HIV/AIDS	Human Immunodeficiency Virus/Acquired Immune Deficiency Syndrome
IBRD	International Bank for Reconstruction and Development
IDA	International Development Association
IEA	International Energy Agency

IGAD	Inter-Governmental Authority on Development
IGO	Inter-governmental organisation
IMF	International Monetary Fund
IPCC	UN Intergovernmental Panel on Climate Change
IOC	Indian Ocean Commission
ISP	Internet service provider
MDG	Millennium Development Goals
Mercosur	Southern Common Market
NAFTA	North American Free Trade Agreement
NAM	Non-Aligned Movement
NASA	the US National Aeronautics and Space Administration
NATO	North Atlantic Treaty Organisation
NC	Nordic Council
NGO	Non-governmental organisation
OAPEC	Organisation of Arab Petroleum Exporting Countries
OAS	Organisation of American States
OECD	Organisation for Economic Co-operation and Development
OECS	Organisation of Eastern Caribbean States
OIC	Organisation of the Islamic Conference
OIF	International Organisation of Francophonie
OPEC	Organisation of the Petroleum Exporting Countries
OSCE	Organisation for Security and Co-operation in Europe
PACE	Parliamentary Assembly of the Council of Europe
PC	Pacific Community
PFP	Partnership for Peace
PIF	Pacific Islands Forum
PPP	Purchasing power parity
PRGF	Poverty Reduction and Growth Facility
SAARC	South Asian Association for Regional Co-operation
SADC	Southern African Development Community
SCO	Shanghai Co-operation Organisation
SELA	Latin American Economic System
UAE	United Arab Emirates
UEMOA	West African Economic and Monetary Union
UK	United Kingdom of Great Britain and Northern Ireland
UNESCO	United Nations Educational, Scientific and Cultural Organisation
USA	United States of America
WHO	World Health Organisation
WMO	UN World Meteorological Organisation
WTO	World Trade Organisation

PREFACE

GLOBAL warming was once again a key theme of the year. Certainly there was no shortage of indications of the growing speed at which the planet's temperature appeared to be rising. Amid a plethora of statistics and projections, the authoritative Stern Review (the summarised conclusions of which are included in this volume) gave a dispassionate but chilling prediction of the disastrous consequences attendant upon the current trend of carbon emissions.

There was also clear evidence of the constraints on the world's only remaining superpower to determine specific outcomes, not the least of which was in Iraq. US troops continued to suffer heavy casualties and yet were unable to stem the tide of steadily worsening violence as the country slid inexorably into civil war. The long shadow of Saddam Hussein was removed at the end of the year as the former dictator ascended the gallows amid scenes of sectarian hatred which epitomised the seemingly intractable ethnic and religious divisions within the country. His death was but one of many during a year in which Sunni terrorists and Shi'ite death squads tortured and killed with an appalling ruthlessness which ratcheted up the body count on a daily basis.

In his speech to commemorate the fifth anniversary of the terrorist attacks of 11 September 2001, the transcript of which appears in this volume, US President George W. Bush professed his continuing belief in eventual victory. Domestic public opinion turned increasingly against the war, however, and in the mid-term elections in November the Democrats won control of Congress. This year's volume includes the executive summary of the report of the bipartisan Iraq Study Group, which acknowledged the "grave and deteriorating" situation in Iraq and, in seeking a viable exit strategy, recommended that Syria and Iran—hitherto pariah states—be invited to assist in establishing security within the shattered country. The current volume of *The Annual Register* also carries the conclusions of the US National Intelligence Estimate assessment of global terrorism, which stated that the war in Iraq was increasing support for the "global jihadist movement", thereby making terrorist attacks upon the USA more likely.

The global jihadist movement—an incidental effect of which was the continued erosion of civil liberties in the wake of a universal increase in security measures—was fuelled by the incomprehension and intolerance that divided the Judaeo-Christian and Islamic worlds. This division was evident in the protests over a group of seemingly unremarkable satirical cartoons—including some which caricatured the Prophet Mohammed—which were published in late 2005 in a newspaper in Denmark. In 2006, these drawings, the reproduction of which in some European media was justified on the grounds of freedom of speech, led to violent protests by outraged Muslims in a host of countries. The response seemed to many secular observers to be grotesquely disproportionate to the catalyst.

"Disproportionate" was also a term widely applied to Israel's military assault upon Lebanon in response to provocations by Hezbullah. The five-week war in July and August inflicted massive damage on Lebanon's infrastructure and destabilised its (pro-Western) government, but failed in its objective of destroying Hezbullah. The sight of the impressive Israeli army, hitherto the epitome of rapid mobile warfare, floundering in an attritional struggle against a well-armed and disciplined guerrilla force was a reminder of a key tenet of modern warfare: sophisticated weapons systems could not be guaranteed to deliver victory. It also handed Hezbullah a huge propaganda triumph across the Arab world and undermined the Israeli government of Ehud Olmert which had been elected with a mandate to make further withdrawals from the occupied Palestinian territories.

With the Palestinians moving away from their tradition of secular politics by electing in January a government dominated by the Islamist organisation, Hamas, which had been an enthusiastic exponent of suicide bombing, prospects for any settlement of the Middle East's core conflict between Israelis and Palestinians seemed more remote. Indeed, some analysts began to talk of an "arc of crisis" encompassing Iraq, Iran, Syria, Lebanon, Israel and Palestine. With the Taliban resurgent in Afghanistan, it seemed possible that this arc could broaden in the coming years.

Iran continued to develop its nuclear programme in 2006, increasing the perception that the country remained the greatest beneficiary of the war in Iraq. Its president's insistence—in a speech announcing the successful enrichment of uranium (the transcript of which may be read in this volume)—that the project was solely for peaceful purposes did little to quell the international disquiet that surrounded a programme which he presented to the world as a patriotic triumph. North Korea, too, continued with its nuclear ambitions and caused international outrage in October by conducting what it claimed was a nuclear test. Both countries were subjected to UN sanctions (the relevant UN resolutions are contained within this volume) but they were sanctions which lacked any real bite. The USA condemned the conduct of both states but was unable to force them to desist with their nuclear aspirations.

The limits of US power were also apparent outside the Middle East. In Darfur, where more than 200,000 people had been killed in the last three years, the slaughter continued, in part because the very concept of Western intervention had been discredited in the aftermath of the Iraq war. Effective UN action against Sudan's government was also consistently blocked by China, even though by the end of the year the conflict had spilled into neighbouring Chad. China's self-declared "strategic partnership" with Africa—based on a rapacious quest for oil and raw materials to fund its extraordinary economic growth—offered Africa's governments an alternative to involvement with the West, in that it proffered aid and trade without inconvenient demands for democratic reform or good governance. In November China—which was on course soon to become Africa's largest lender and its most significant trading partner—hosted a summit of 48 African countries in Beijing. It was a clear reminder of the changing balance of the present as well as being a portent of the future.

D.S. Lewis
Aquitaine, May 2007

EXTRACTS FROM PAST VOLUMES

225 years ago

1781. *The Surrender of Lord Cornwallis at Yorktown, October.* Such was the issue of the Virginian war. The loss of Lord Cornwallis's army was too heavy a blow to be soon or easily recovered. It was evident, that it must entirely change the nature of the war on the side of Great Britain; and that it could no longer be carried on offensively by land, at least to any considerable extent. Indeed, the surrender at York Town may be considered as the closing scene of the whole continental war in America.... [When] we consider the effect this revolution may have on the political state of the whole human race, we shall in every respect find it extraordinary.

200 years ago

1806. *The death of Pitt, 22 January.* Thus died William Pitt, in the 47th year of his age, after having enjoyed greater power and popularity, and held the first place in the government of his country, for a longer course of years, than any former minister of England. It is not our province to enter at large into his character and merits. That he was a person of the most rare and splendid qualities, a powerful orator, a skilful debater, an expert and enlightened financier, his greatest enemies must admit.... But, whether the appellation of illustrious statesman has been justly applied to him, is a question on which men may reasonably differ.

175 years ago

1831. *The death of Bolivar, December 1830.* He was enthusiastic in the great cause of throwing off the yoke of the mother country; he was therefore trusted, and worthy of being entrusted. Probably no other native could so successfully have kept together, till the contest was over, the materials with which he had to operate.... But his qualities as a statesman to govern the country during peace, fell infinitely below his qualifications to secure her independence by war. His political institutions were founded on vague and hazy ideas, whose origin was to be sought any where but in experience. Even in his own time the building was falling in pieces around him.

150 years ago

1856. *The United States.* The question of slavery has long been felt to be one of the most momentous affecting the future destinies of the United States. It is the dark cloud on the horizon, which threatens the approaching storm. Between the Northern and the Southern States there is on this subject an irreconcilable difference of opinion....

125 years ago

1881. *Afghanistan.* The change of Government and policy was marked by Lord Hartington's first despatch, dated May 21, addressed to the new Viceroy, Lord Ripon. The first object of the Home Government was therein declared to be 'the speedy withdrawal of the greater part of the troops now engaged in Afghanistan, and the ultimate withdrawal of the whole from positions beyond our own frontier'; and the restoration of a friendly independent state on the north-western frontier of India.

100 years ago

1906. *Earthquake at San Francisco.* The great earthquake at San Francisco began at 5.13 a.m. (local time) on April 18, and was followed during the day by several shocks of more or less violence. The damage done to the city, though considerable, was small in comparison with that due to the fire which followed, whereby property to the estimated value of 40,000,000 *l.* sterling was destroyed. From a geological point of view the earthquake was remarkable for its capriciousness and the rotatory character of the movement. The better class residences on the hills were but little affected, while the low-lying portions were almost all destroyed.

75 years ago

1931. *The Manchurian crisis, September.* On a report (which was denied by the Chinese) that a portion of the South Manchurian Railway track had been destroyed by soldiers from the Petaying barracks near Mukden, Japanese troops in the neighbourhood were mobilised, the barracks were attacked and taken, the arsenal and aerodrome at Mukden seized, and the city itself occupied.... All these steps were taken by the military authorities on their own initiative, without consulting the Government in Tokio. The latter did not venture to disown them....

50 years ago

1956. *The Hungarian rising.* The country, naturally, saw only that the hated Soviet tyranny had returned. The fighting which followed the treacherous Russian *coup* was on a scale and of an intensity far exceeding that of the preceding week. The Soviets employed heavy artillery and bombers, and their troops, many of whom were Asians, used their arms ruthlessly and indiscriminately. The Hungarian freedom fighters, most of whom were of young or even of tender age, fought back with the reckless courage of fury and despair, while the workers and miners backed the combatants by a general strike of extraordinary completeness.

25 years ago

1981. *Music.* Pop music continued unabated (called by Anthony Burgess, in an article in *The Times*, 'a moronic sub-art'), and one well-known group defied its obituary notice of 1978 by reappearing in 1981 for another American tour. The Rolling Stones, with a reformed, middle-aged Mick Jagger, presented themselves to a new generation of teenagers, yet unborn when the Stones first hit the pop music trail.

THE ANNUAL REGISTER

FOR THE YEAR 2006

I THE YEAR IN REVIEW

A few decades from now, the most significant developments in 2006 may be seen to have been related to global warming: even clearer evidence that it was occurring, and a greater awareness of its dangers, even in the USA. In the shorter term, however, the most important development will most probably be seen as the further decline of US global power, reflected not only in the growing disaster in Iraq, but also in the USA's inability decisively to influence events elsewhere in the world.

US difficulties were worsened by the continuing disarray of the European Union (EU) and the North Atlantic Treaty Organisation (NATO). Efforts to mobilise greater real European military support for US efforts in Afghanistan met only very limited success, while with the impending accession to the EU of Romania and Bulgaria west Europeans appeared to have reached the limit of their appetite for further enlargement, especially with regard to Turkey. By contrast, both China and Russia grew visibly stronger and more assertive during the course of 2006.

In Latin America, the wave of electoral successes for populist and nationalist movements continued, and most of these had anti-US agendas, or at least rhetoric. In Mexico, the left-wing candidate, Andrés Manuel López Obrador, was very narrowly defeated in the July 2006 presidential elections, but suspicions of vote-rigging and his party's subsequent rejection of the results and disruption of the Mexican legislature dealt a blow to Mexico's new democracy. In Thailand, meanwhile, democracy was suspended in September by a military coup against the autocratic and corrupt prime minister, Thaksin Shinawatra.

Within the USA, the most important factor influencing domestic politics and external policy was the war in Iraq. On 22 February, the bombing by Sunni terrorists of the revered Shi'ite al-Askariya shrine in Samarra led to savage Shi'ite reprisals against Sunni civilians, and a severe overall worsening in communal violence. Throughout the year, monthly totals for civilian deaths from bombings and death squads continued to increase. The last day of 2006 saw the total of US dead in that war reach the highly symbolic figure of 3,000, more people than had been killed in the al-Qaida attacks on the USA of 11 September 2001. In consequence of these figures, and the effects on recruitment, training, and morale of repeated deployments, 2006 saw increasing warnings by senior US military figures that the two wars, in Iraq and Afghanistan, risked "breaking the US army". This concern was echoed even more publicly and forcefully by some of their UK military counterparts.

Fears over the direction and cost of US strategy were increased by a serious deterioration of the situation in Afghanistan, with a surge in Taliban attacks and dire warnings from NATO commanders that unless the West succeeded in improving the security situation and bringing real development within the next year, the war in Afghanistan might become unwinnable. The Taliban drew much of its support from ethnic kinsfolk among the Pashtuns of neighbouring Pakistan, leading to worsened relations between the Afghan and Pakistani governments. The US administration for its part found itself in an extremely difficult situation, privately agreeing that the Taliban enjoyed safe havens in Pakistan, but unwilling to put too much pressure on the Pakistani administration of General Pervez Musharraf for fear of bringing about its collapse, and drastically weakening the US position in the entire region.

The importance of Pakistan both as a threat and a source of assistance in the "war on terror" was emphasised in August when the UK police and intelligence forces announced that with the help of the Pakistani authorities they had foiled an attempt by British-Pakistani Islamists to blow up several transatlantic airliners in suicide bomb attacks, using explosives disguised as beverages.

The effect of the Iraq casualty figures on US public opinion was diminished by the absence of conscription, meaning that the losses were suffered by limited and generally underprivileged sections of the population, not by the elites. Less important than the casualty figures themselves was the fact that it seemed to more and more US citizens that these lives were being lost in a war that should never have been launched, and in which there was no longer any real hope of victory. Month after month, the rhetoric of the administration of US President George W. Bush about the USA winning the struggle was belied by continued attacks on US troops and increasingly savage violence between Iraq's ethno-religious communities. The death in June of the leader of al-Qaida in Iraq, Abu Musab al-Zarqawi, touted by the Bush administration as a great victory, turned out to have no appreciable effect on the worsening course of events. The same seemed likely to be the case with the execution of Saddam Hussein on 30 December.

In October, the Johns Hopkins University school of public health published a survey estimating that some 655,000 Iraqis had been killed since the US invasion of Iraq in 2003. This figure was many times the US and Iraqi official estimates (although the US administration's ability to counter this claim was weakened by the fact that, as a matter of policy, the US military had not collected figures for civilian deaths, even of those killed directly by US troops). The Johns Hopkins survey was widely criticised as based on an inadequate sample. However, in the debate over this issue it became apparent that even if the figure of 655,000 was exaggerated, the numbers of Iraqi casualties were almost certainly considerably higher than had previously been thought. The fighting and terrorism in Iraq also produced a massive flow of refugees to neighbouring states and within the country, with Human Rights Watch estimating the number of Iraqi refugees in Jordan alone at up to 750,000.

By December, a CBS television poll in the USA showed 50 per cent of respondents saying that the USA should begin to end its involvement in Iraq immediately. Seventy-five per cent expressed disapproval of Bush's handling of the war. The political impact of the war was seen in the November 2006 US mid-term elections to Congress (the bicameral legislature), in which the Democrats won majorities in both the House of Representatives (the lower house) and—by a margin of only one seat—in the Senate, for the first time in 12 years. The San Francisco Democratic representative, Nancy Pelosi, became the first woman speaker of the House of Representatives. Control of the Senate, however, remained in doubt, as the sudden illness of South Dakota Democratic senator Tim Johnson made it seem possible that the Republican governor of the state would nominate a Republican to succeed him, and restore the Republican majority.

According to opinion surveys, disillusionment with the Bush administration's conduct of the war in Iraq was the single most important factor in persuading people to vote against the Republicans. Bush admitted in the wake of the vote that his party had "taken a thumping". An immediate result of the elections was the resignation of Defence Secretary Donald Rumsfeld, widely blamed (including within the US military) for US failures in Iraq, and especially for failure to plan for the consequences of the overthrow of Saddam Hussein's regime.

Rumsfeld was replaced by former CIA director Robert Gates. Regarded as a moderate figure and a safe pair of hands, his nomination sailed through the Senate without significant Democratic opposition. Some worried commentators, however, drew attention to his record at the CIA of distorting intelligence on the Soviet Union and going along with the Reagan administration's illegal "Iran-Contra" strategy in the 1980s (the covert sale of arms to Iran to fund the anti-communist Contra guerrillas in Nicaragua). They worried that Gates would not be strong or courageous enough to stand up to the remaining hawks in the administration, grouped around Vice-President Dick Cheney.

Second in importance among the reasons US citizens gave for voting against the Republicans was concern over ethical questions. The year began with the resignation of Tom "The Hammer" DeLay, Republican leader in the House of Representatives, due to his involvement in a series of scandals. As the year went on, the developing criminal process against former lobbyist Jack Abramoff was a potent source of further Republican embarrassment. Abramoff's criminal activities included corrupt links with a number of leading Republican congressional representatives, as well as White House officials. (His list of clients also included some Democrats, but far fewer, since as their party was out of power they had far fewer favours to bestow on Abramoff in return.) Concern about Republican ethics received a tremendous boost in the weeks immediately before the Congressional elections from revelations concerning Republican Representative Jack Foley, who turned out for years to have been sending improper messages to teenage (male) congressional pages (high-school pupils temporarily employed by Congress).

Shortly after the elections, the bipartisan Iraq Study Group (ISG), headed by former Secretary of State James Baker and former (Democratic) Representative Lee Hamilton, published an eagerly-awaited report on the war. Its most important and radical recommendation concerned the need for the USA to open direct negotiations with Iran and Syria, in an effort to forge a regional agreement on limiting the Iraqi conflict and restricting the involvement of neighbouring states on opposite sides. The Baker-Hamilton Commission also took the (by US standards) radical step of declaring the Israeli-Palestinian conflict to be a major source of destabilisation in the Middle East, and urging new US steps towards its solution as part of a new US strategy in the region.

Unfortunately, but predictably, these recommendations were ignored both by the Bush administration and by the great majority of the leadership of the Democrats. Instead, as the year ended Bush appeared prepared to modify his Iraq strategy in only two regards: through a reshuffle of the civilian and military command of the operation, and through a temporary "surge" of some tens of thousands of new troops intended to improve the security situation in the Iraqi capital, Baghdad. This idea received the backing of the leading Republican presidential candidate for 2008, Senator John McCain, but was greeted with muted dismay by other Republican leaders, who increasingly saw a continuation of the war as disastrous for their party's future electoral chances.

Bush's "surge" idea was, however, opposed by much of the US high command and denounced by leading retired US military figures. Emboldened by this and by their victory in the Congressional elections, more and more leading Democrats began to call for an early withdrawal of troops from Iraq, or at least for a fixed timetable for withdrawal. Nonetheless, the Democrats' ability to take a strong stand on Iraq continued to be diminished by their inability to suggest a concrete and effective alternative strategy to the failed approaches of the Bush administration, as demonstrated by their silence concerning key aspects of the Baker-Hamilton report. The bulk of the Democratic leadership remained too tied to Israel, too afraid of being labelled traitors, and too committed to US dominance of the Middle East to contemplate radical new approaches to the region.

Throughout 2006, the difficulties faced by the USA in the Middle East were both reflected and magnified by Israel's conflicts. The year saw intense pressure by the US administration, backed up by the west Europeans, on the newly-elected Hamas government of the Palestinian territories either to recognise Israel or to leave office. Western hostility to Hamas was increased by a stream of (mostly ineffective) rocket attacks on Israel from the Hamas-controlled Gaza Strip.

In June, Israel launched a massive military operation against Hamas after an Israeli solider was captured. The Hezbullah organisation in Lebanon announced that they would help their "Palestinian brothers", and in July ambushed an Israeli patrol near Shtula, northern Israel, killing three Israeli soldiers and capturing two. It was widely assumed in the West—though without firm evidence—that the Hezbullah attack had been encouraged by Iran and/or Syria, as a way of demonstrating their resilience in the face of US pressure.

Israel, backed by the USA, responded to the Hezbullah attack with a massive attack on Lebanon, intended to smash Hezbullah as a military organisation and send a strong signal to Syria and Iran of Israel's power and their impotence. In this position, the USA and Israel were initially backed by the UK, leading to a new wave of British criticism of the government of Prime Minister Tony Blair as excessively subservient to the Bush administration. The war was eventually brought to an end on 14 August when the UN succeeded in cobbling together an international force, headed by France, to patrol southern Lebanon and prevent Hezbullah attacks on Israel and Israeli Defence Forces (IDF) attacks on Lebanon.

The Israeli operation proved a serious mistake, which inflicted more than 1,200 Lebanese civilian deaths, but failed to destroy Hezbullah's military strength. Hezbullah rocket attacks on northern Israel continued throughout the war, inflicting 39 Israeli civilian casualties. The IDF lost 119 men. The Israeli military suffered a severe blow to its prestige, reinforcing still further the lesson of the Iraq and Afghan wars, that even overwhelming firepower and technological superiority may prove impotent in the face of determined resistance by guerrilla fighters backed by the local population.

The Israeli coalition government of Ehud Olmert suffered a particular blow, as it was blamed by many Israelis for bungling the operation. The year began with Olmert's Kadima party, founded and headed by the legendary Ariel Sharon, riding high in the polls and seemingly set to dominate Israeli politics for the foreseeable future. But after Prime Minister Sharon suffered a massive stroke in early January and was removed from power, Olmert proved unable to consolidate his own authority, and the end of the year saw him almost a lame-duck premier.

By contrast, Hezbullah at the end of the year was still very much the leading military force in Lebanon, and in control of its own Shi'ite areas. Its prestige was boosted still further by the speed, efficiency, and honesty with which it conducted efforts to reconstruct the areas devastated by Israeli bombardment. December 2006 saw massive demonstrations in the Lebanese capital Beirut and elsewhere calling for a strengthened Hezbullah and Shi'ite role in the Lebanese government. The only positive result for the USA from this debacle was that the growth in Iranian power encouraged the Sunni autocracies of Saudi Arabia and the Gulf states to go on looking to the USA for protection.

At the end of the year, Hamas, backed by Iran and Syria, was still in power in the Gaza Strip and dominated the Palestinian cabinet, but thanks to Western support, the Palestinian president, Mahmoud Abbas, and his Palestine Liberation Organisation (PLO) continued to dominate the West Bank. The rivalry between the two organisations led to growing clashes towards the end of the year, including assassinations and armed riots.

Iran meanwhile pushed ahead with its uranium enrichment programme, while also continuing to promise that this was for exclusively civilian purposes. In December the USA finally succeeded in putting together a UN Security Council resolution imposing sanctions on Iran, but it seemed unlikely that it would have much effect. December did, however, bring a hopeful sign with the heavy defeat of the party of the radical Iranian president, Mahmoud Ahmadinejad, in elections to local councils and the Assembly of Experts (the national council of clerics responsible for selecting the supreme leader). The biggest winners were moderate conservative forces led by the former president, Ali Akbar Hashemi Rafsanjani. However, to exploit this opportunity for a deal with Iran would still have required the US administration radically to change its policy, and of this there was no sign. The US bipartisan establishment seemed incapable either of making its will prevail in Iran, or of abandoning an evidently failed strategy. Indeed, the last weeks of 2006 saw greatly heightened Bush administration rhetoric against Iran, raising fears of an impending US attack.

The year was therefore a very bad one for the USA in the Middle East. US backing for Israel in its Lebanese operation diminished still further US prestige in the region. The official Bush administration strategy (backed by the Democrats) of spreading democracy and freedom came even more to seem an exercise in Orwellian doublespeak. Secretary of State Condoleezza Rice's description of the suffering of Lebanese and Iraqis as "the birth pangs of a new Middle East" was generally regarded in the region (and elsewhere) as both intellectually ridiculous and morally obscene.

The US inability to develop a new strategy in the Middle East and the "war on terror" was closely linked to the continued limitations on thought and debate concerning the region within the USA itself. This related above all to the severe restrictions on criticism of Israel—and the role of the Israeli lobby in the USA—in US politics and the US mainstream media. Thus, during the Lebanese war, when public opinion in almost every other country in the world (including close US allies such as the UK) was strongly critical of Israel, the US Senate and House of Representatives voted by overwhelming majorities resolutions unconditionally supportive of Israeli actions, and this was backed up by most of the US media. Towards the end of the year, former President Jimmy Carter published a book criticising Israel's treatment of the Palestinians as akin to apartheid, but his work was promptly swamped by a wave of ferocious criticism, including in such ostensibly liberal journals as the *New York Times* and *Washington Post*.

Elsewhere in the world, US power and influence suffered from the colossal financial, military, and political distraction represented by the Iraq war. However, even without this distraction, it was likely that the USA would have encountered serious limits to its ambitions. For what the heralds of the USA's status as "the sole superpower" in a "unipolar world" had forgotten was that (to paraphrase the late speaker of the US House of Representatives, Tip O'Neill) all geopolitical and military power is in the end local: that is to say, power that can be brought to bear in a particular place, or on a particular issue.

Power is also always not absolute but relative: that is to say, relative to the power of another state or states in the given region. Thus, militarily speaking, the USA in 2006 remained the only possessor of aircraft carrier battle groups, but these proved wholly useless in the slums of Baghdad and Fallujah. Similarly, the fact that the USA possessed global reach to a vastly greater degree than China or Russia did not diminish the fact that Russia was more powerful than the USA in eastern Ukraine, and China more influential than the USA in North Korea.

The limitations on US ability to influence developments in the Far East were demonstrated in October, when North Korea conducted a small (and possibly botched) underground nuclear test. In the past, US leaders, and Republican politicians in particular, had threatened the most drastic responses should this happen. In fact, all the Bush administration was able to do in response was to go to the Chinese government with a request that they agree to impose tougher sanctions on North Korea. Since they were themselves angered by North Korea's action, the Chinese government did agree to increased pressure. Restrictions on Chinese supplies of heating oil brought a moderation in North Korean rhetoric, and an apparent private promise not to conduct further tests.

The whole episode symbolised the rising power of China vis a vis the USA in the region, a power which was nevertheless expressed in a cautious fashion and chiefly through multilateral regional institutions like the Shanghai Co-operation Organisation. Elsewhere in the world, however, China continued its drive to secure access to supplies of raw materials and energy, signing agreements with Sudan, Algeria, and other states, and causing increased talk in the USA (and to a lesser extent Europe) about the possibility of future struggles, and even conflicts, over scarce resources. Throughout the year, the USA exerted heavy pressure on China to revalue its currency in order to reduce Chinese exports to the USA, but without significant results.

Inside China, the central leadership under President Hu Jintao demonstrated its continued grip by moving decisively against the Communist Party leadership in Shanghai, removing and imprisoning several senior officials for corruption. However, 2006 saw a growing number of demonstrations, sometimes violent, against local authorities in the countryside. These often stemmed from peasant anger at the seizure of land by local Communist officials, and led to increased stress by the central government on the need to redistribute wealth to China's impoverished interior provinces and to the countryside.

In the former Soviet Union, Russia's possession of large amounts of natural resources (including 13 per cent of the world's oil production) contributed to a notable revival of Russian influence. This reflected a continuation of strong Russian economic growth (around 6.5 per cent in 2006), an inability on the part of the USA to spend really large sums in order to spread US influence, and a faltering of prospects for further EU enlargement.

The year began with a Russian decision to cut off gas supplies to Ukraine, after the failure of negotiations aimed at raising prices towards global market levels. Since the collapse of the Soviet Union, Russia had been providing Ukraine and other former Soviet republics with heavily subsidised energy, as part of its strategy of maintaining a sphere of influence in the region. As a result of the Ukrainian "Orange revolution" of 2004, Ukraine appeared to have taken a decisive step away from Russia and towards membership of the West, and so the Russian government saw no need to continue the subsidy. A compromise was soon reached which essentially split the difference between the existing price and the world market price.

The affair increased fears in western European countries that their growing dependence on Russian energy supplies would also make them vulnerable to

Russian political pressure. These fears tended to ignore the fact that the dependence was mutual, since Europe also provided by far the greatest market for Russian gas, and Russia could not create alternative markets without the construction of immensely costly pipelines from Siberia to the Far East. The gas issue, however, contributed to wider fears concerning Russia, which were heightened in November when Alexander Litvinenko, a former KGB officer in the pay of Boris Berezovsky, the exiled Russian magnate and bitter enemy of the administration of Russia's President Vladimir Putin, was assassinated by radioactive poisoning in London.

Widely remarked in Russia, but not in the West, was the fact that the Russian annual energy subsidy to Ukraine (between 3 and 5 billion US dollars per year) considerably exceeded the total of all Western aid to Ukraine in the decade to 2006. This reflected a fundamental weakness in the West's professed strategy of integrating Ukraine: namely a profound unwillingness to make the sacrifices necessary to do so. Ukrainians saw that the "Orange revolution" had not in fact led to a radically new policy on the part of the EU, or even significantly eased freedom of movement for Ukrainians, whereas millions of Ukrainians continued to work legally in Russia and send back remittances which made a significant contribution to the Ukrainian economy (as also those of Moldova, Georgia, Armenia, and Azerbaijan).

The Ukrainian legislative elections of March saw the "pro-Russian" Party of the Regions, led by former Prime Minister (and failed presidential candidate in 2004) Viktor Yanukovych, emerge with a plurality. There followed months of political turmoil before a coalition government was eventually formed in August with Yanukovych as premier. As a result, US plans to offer Ukraine a NATO "membership action plan" at the NATO summit in Riga (the Latvian capital) in November were put on indefinite hold. At the same time, the course of events in Ukraine did not mean that that country was simply sinking back under Russia's control: Yanukovych made a point during his first months in office of visiting Brussels, Washington DC, and other western capitals to stress his government's commitment to economic reform and closer ties to the West.

In private, EU officials declared candidly that they were not prepared even to think seriously about future prospects for Ukrainian membership. This was hardly surprising, as the year saw an intensifying crisis in relations between the EU and Turkey over the accession process for that country. Ostensibly, the chief blocking factors were Turkish trade sanctions against the (Greek) Republic of Cyprus, and Turkish failure to make greater progress with regard to human rights and the independence of the judiciary. In the background to EU pressure over these issues, however, lay the deep unwillingness of many western Europeans (including large majorities in France, Germany, and elsewhere) to contemplate EU membership for a large and growing Muslim country.

Fears of Turkish immigration were increased by the larger than expected flow of immigrants to western Europe from new member states like Poland, although if previous experience was anything to go by, these would soon be assimilated and pose no significant long-term problem. In the long term, western European tolerance of immigration and support for further EU enlargement would both be largely determined by the state of the western European economies. The year saw hopeful signs from this point of view, with the German economy—by far Europe's biggest—recovering after years of semi-stagnation to achieve a respectable growth rate of 2.4 per cent, contributing to overall EU growth of 2.6 per cent.

The world economy as a whole also grew strongly in 2006, by an estimated 5.1 per cent of GDP, well ahead of world population growth of some 1.14 per cent. China and India both continued their spectacular growth, at 10.4 and 9.2 per cent of GDP respectively, and were accompanied by newer Asian success stories like Vietnam. The US economy also did well, at 3.3 per cent growth. Latin America by contrast saw only lacklustre growth rates, and sub-Saharan Africa continued to limp along at the bottom of world indices for development. This was despite steep rises in the prices of many raw materials, brought about above all by the growing appetite of China. In 2006, Chinese oil consumption reached 7.35 million barrels per day, up from 6.86 million barrels in 2005, and more than one-third of the US figure of 20.67 million barrels.

The extent and nature of world economic growth led to both short-term and long-term fears concerning its sustainability. Short-term fears focused on trade and fiscal imbalances, above all relating to the USA. The growing US trade deficit with China (which rose from US$201 billion in 2005 to US$213 billion in 2006) led to fears that the new Democrat-controlled US Congress might take steps towards protectionism, and that China's retaliation would undermine first the dollar and then the entire US and world economies. Widespread concern was also expressed concerning the faltering US property market, in which so much US personal and corporate wealth had become tied up. A majority of economists predicted an impending economic downturn, but differed greatly about its likely extent.

The longer term concern related to the environmental consequences of the present level and nature of global economic growth, and in particular of China's booming consumption of fossil fuels and emission of greenhouse gases. The year saw a plethora of evidence of accelerating global warming. The USA experienced the hottest year since records began, and most of western Europe saw its warmest winter on record. Worldwide, 2006 was only slightly cooler than 2005, which remained the hottest year ever recorded. Several reports told of glaciers and ice sheets retreating even faster than previously predicted.

In October, the UK government published the report of a commission headed by Sir Nicholas Stern, former chief economist at the World Bank. This stated that carbon emissions had already increased the average global temperature by 0.5 degrees Celsius, and that if present trends of emission growth continued, there was a more than 75 per cent chance of temperatures rising by up to 3 degrees Celsius, and a 50 per cent chance of their rising by 5 degrees Celsius. The results of the first figure would be disastrous floods and droughts in the developing world, and a drop in global GDP of up to 3 per cent. A rise of 5 degrees would run a very strong risk of melting the polar ice caps and drowning many of the world's greatest cities, thereby creating population movements on an unmanageable scale. The report argued that to take immediate action to stabilise emissions would cost no more than 1 per cent of global GDP, whereas to continue "business as usual" could eventually cost up to 20 per cent. It described global warming as "the greatest and most wide-ranging market failure ever seen".

The Stern report came under predictable attack from US energy and motor industry executives and lobbyists. However, earlier in the year there were signs of the beginnings of a shift in attitudes to energy conservation and greenhouse gas emissions even within the US Republican party, driven in part by concern over the security of oil supplies from the Middle East. In August, California Governor Arnold Schwarzenegger signed a law setting the target of a 25 per cent reduction in the state's emissions by 2020. The new Democratic majority in Congress also vowed to take stronger action to encourage energy conservation and curb emissions. However, the record of many Congressional Democrats was not encouraging, and public support remained lacklustre. In November, California voters rejected proposition 87, establishing a new tax on oil in order to fund alternative energy, by 54 per cent to 45 per cent.

Outside Iraq and sub-Saharan Africa, 2006 was therefore not a bad year, especially by the lugubrious standards of so much of human history. Most countries experienced peace and growing—though very unevenly distributed—prosperity. There were reasons to fear, however, that it would be seen in hindsight as a fair year which yet was pregnant with future disasters.

II WESTERN AND SOUTHERN EUROPE

UNITED KINGDOM—SCOTLAND—WALES—NORTHERN IRELAND

UNITED KINGDOM

CAPITAL: London AREA: 245,000 sq km POPULATION: 60,203,000
OFFICIAL LANGUAGES: English; Welsh in Wales POLITICAL SYSTEM: multiparty monarchy
HEAD OF STATE: Queen Elizabeth II (since Feb '52)
RULING PARTY: Labour Party (since May '97)
HEAD OF GOVERNMENT: Tony Blair, Prime Minister (since May '97)
MAIN IGO MEMBERSHIPS (NON-UN): NATO, CWTH, EU, OSCE, CE, PC, OECD, G-8
CURRENCY: pound sterling (end-'06 US$1=£0.51220, €1=£0.67590)
GNI PER CAPITA: US$37,600, US$32,690 at PPP ('05)

WITH hindsight, it became clear that 2006 was the last year of the ancien regime of Prime Minister Tony Blair. His commitment in September to leave office within a year meant that the spotlight would henceforward focus on his likely successor, Chancellor of the Exchequer Gordon Brown. Although the new Conservative leader, David Cameron, was relatively effective in his attempts to rejuvenate his party's image, there were no solid indications that this could be turned into an early election victory. The more interesting questions concerned the Blair legacy: which policies would be maintained and which would be abandoned when Brown took over? In domestic terms, it seemed reasonable to assume that the project to modernise the UK's public services and institutions would continue, although it was not clear whether the model for change would be the same. On the foreign policy front, the increasingly public rift—between senior politicians, military leaders, and civil servants on the one hand, and Downing Street on the other—over the UK's support for US foreign policy, in what US President George W. Bush and his administration termed the "war on terror", made it an odds-on bet that a Brown government would look very different indeed.

POLITICS. Labour suffered a crushing defeat at the by-election in Dunfermline and West Fife in February, when the Liberal Democrats overturned a 11,500 majority (see p. 28). The result was especially embarrassing for Gordon Brown, whose own Scottish constituency of Kircaldy and Cowdenbeath bordered Dunfermline and who had visited four times during the campaign. It was also David Cameron's first important contest since assuming the Conservative leadership. For the Liberal Democrats the win was vital to restoring political confidence after months of turmoil. Labour's loss was ascribed largely to local issues, however, such as a proposed toll rise for the Forth road bridge, and the closure of the Lexmark computer printer plant with the loss of 700 jobs. The defeat heartened critics of Gordon Brown within the party, and jeopardised the "dual premiership" strategy that had begun to emerge as the Brown camp prepared for a smooth transition following Blair's eventual resignation. Senior allies of Blair attempted in vain, however, to identify a potential candidate of sufficient substance to challenge Brown, who had spent the first weeks of the year attempting to craft an image as a national leader and appropriate heir to the Blairite agenda.

Labour's defeat in Dunfermline was compounded in May when local elections led to substantial losses in London and the south-east. The party was not helped by a disastrous fortnight before polling day during which a combination of scandals and ministerial mismanagement dominated the news. Labour came third in terms of the share of the vote, with 26 per cent, losing control of 19 councils and 298 seats. Blair responded with an immediate and far-reaching cabinet reshuffle, designed to reassert his authority and to overshadow the bad news. Charles Clarke lost his job at the home office, following the controversy over foreign prisoners (see pp. 16-17), and returned to the backbenches. John Reid was moved from defence to replace him. Foreign Secretary Jack Straw was demoted to the post of leader of the Commons, replacing Geoff Hoon, who in turn replaced Douglas Alexander as Europe minister. Margaret Beckett became the first woman to serve as foreign secretary, an appointment that raised eyebrows in Whitehall as she was thought to be unprepared for such a demanding and sensitive role. David Miliband was promoted to Beckett's old position at the department of the environment, food and rural affairs. Ruth Kelly was moved from the department of education, taking over John Prescott's brief covering housing and regional policy at a new department for communities and local government. Although remaining in the post of deputy prime minister, Prescott was stripped of most of his powers and the office of the deputy prime minister was scrapped. Alan Johnson replaced Kelly at education, and Douglas Alexander took over the transport brief from Alistair Darling, who became the new trade secretary. If Brown's supporters had hoped for a reshuffle designed for a "stable and orderly transition" they were disappointed: this was a cabinet poised to deliver on several key Blair objectives during his final months in office. In the face of renewed calls from the Brown camp to name a departure date from Number 10, the prime minister was defiant.

The popular perception of Blair and his allies as dishonest and corrupt was not helped by continued episodes of "sleaze", from which Brown was largely successful in distancing himself. At the beginning of March, the secretary of culture, media and sport, Tessa Jowell, announced that she was separating from husband David Mills, a corporate lawyer, following two weeks of press revelations over their personal finances. Cabinet Secretary Sir Gus O'Donnell accepted Jowell's assurances that she had had no knowledge that money alleged to have been a "bribe" from Italy's prime minister, Silvio Berlusconi (see p. 48), had been used by her husband to help pay off a mortgage on their London home. While Jowell was supported by cabinet and backbench colleagues, the incident underscored the extent of the financial and ethical gap between ordinary Labour voters and the party leaders. At the end of April, it was the turn of John Prescott to be in the firing line, when his former mistress and diary secretary, Tracey Temple, sold her story to the *Mail on Sunday* for £250,000. Prescott's apparent enjoyment of the perks of office would continue to be a source of embarrassment, especially his acceptance of corporate hospitality from US billionaire Philip Anschutz, for while the scandals might have led other ministers to resign, Prescott's unique position as honest broker between Blair and Brown made him irreplaceable.

Far more serious was the scandal that surfaced in March, when it was revealed that a group of backers had loaned the Labour party nearly £14 million before the 2005 election, without the knowledge of its treasurer, Jack Dromey. Unlike donations, loans did not have to be declared, enabling donors to remain anonymous; the fact that most of those named had been put forward for working peerages by Blair suggested the possibility that Labour had raised money by offering honours. Moreover, the Conservatives were revealed also to have relied upon loans in the same period, a substantial proportion of which had come from foreign lenders, who were ineligible to donate funding under UK law. Downing Street responded initially by appointing Sir Hayden Phillips, former permanent secretary at the department for constitutional affairs, to report on the future of party funding in liaison with the parties.

Blair's attempts to contain the situation were undermined when three complaints were brought under the Honours (Prevention of Abuses) Act 1925, by MPs led by the Scottish Nationalist, Angus MacNeil. Scotland Yard announced on 21 March that an investigation was being launched by the Metropolitan Police specialist crimes directorate. On 13 April headteacher Des Smith, who had until January advised the body that found sponsorship for the "city academies" touted as the flagship secondary school initiative by Blair, was arrested for allegedly having suggested that sponsors could expect to be rewarded with honours. He was released on police bail. On 12 July Blair's close friend and party fundraiser Lord Levy was arrested, as was the biotechnology millionaire and party donor Sir Christopher Evans on 20 September; both were bailed without charge. It emerged that the police had questioned a number of government ministers as well as other prominent figures, including former Conservative leader Michael Howard. As speculation mounted in the autumn over whether criminal charges would be brought, pressure was brought on the attorney general, Lord Goldsmith, to distance himself from taking responsibility for that decision, because his close political links to Blair suggested a conflict of interest. In a letter to MPs on 16 November, acting Assistant Commissioner John Yates, who was leading the investigation, reported that it had turned up "significant and valuable material" and that "considerable progress continues to be made". There had been 90 interviews so far, with people from all three parties but including almost all of the members of the cabinet in the months before the 2005 election. On 14 December Downing Street announced that Blair had been questioned by police. It was expected that a dossier of evidence would be sent to the Crown Prosecution Service early in 2007. Meanwhile, the Phillips report into the reform of party funding was delayed by the failure of the major parties to reach an agreement, and had not been published by the end of the year.

These developments contributed to dissatisfaction within the Labour party over Blair's continuing refusal to give a clear answer on the question of his departure. Humiliating by-election defeats on 29 June at Blaenau Gwent (see pp. 30-31) and Bromley and Chislehurst did not help. The situation came to a head on 6 September, a fortnight before the party conference in Manchester, when seven government members—all at one time loyal Blairites, among them a junior defence minister, Tom Watson—resigned in protest at the prime minister's refusal to name a departure date. Downing Street responded by openly backing a statement from David Miliband that it would be reasonable to assume that there would be a "stable and orderly" transition, leading to a new leader being in place by the Labour conference in 2007. This was a substantial concession, but Brown remained unhappy at the failure to make public a detailed timetable, and also at continued criticism in the press from figures close to Blair. Following a series of apparently heated meetings between the two men, Blair was forced publicly to declare that he would not be prime minister in a year's time. Downing Street staff were reportedly authorised by Blair himself to use the word "blackmail" to describe Brown's actions; and, interviewed in the *Daily Telegraph*, Charles Clarke launched an extraordinary attack in which he accused Brown of being a "control freak" with "psychological" issues. "Stable and orderly" was not the impression being given to the country. However, by the year's end Brown had clearly strengthened his position, and no significant rival had emerged. It seemed unlikely that he would face any serious opposition for the leadership, and that the real contest would be between those colleagues lining up to run for the deputy leadership contest, set for May 2007.

David Cameron performed well during his first full year as leader, largely due to the talent of his well-paid marketing guru, Steve Hilton. His determination to re-brand the Conservative party found him often at odds with grassroots Tories and senior rightwing figures such as Lord Tebbit. But this tension was an inevitable part of the task of dragging the Conservatives back towards the political mainstream, and there was broad acceptance in the party that his strategy was "good politics". With many senior Labour figures questioning Brown's commitment to the Blairite New Labour agenda, it was smart for Cameron to portray himself as the natural heir to the prime minister, and he consistently stressed the extent to which he agreed with Blair on many issues. "Built to last", a document launched at the end of February, set out the broad values of his "modern, compassionate Conservatism" in terms vague enough to be unobjectionable to anybody on any wing of any party. Its major planks included encouraging enterprise, fighting social injustice, meeting environmental threats, providing first-class social services, ending global poverty, protecting the country, empowering people and communities, and being open, meritocratic and forward-looking. This was followed up by a roadshow of consultation meetings around the country with party members between March and July. By avoiding commitment to specific details of policy, this exercise enabled Cameron to focus on the construction of a new language of Conservatism, such as the "responsibility revolution" that he promised to deliver. But by April there was growing concern within the party that the spin surrounding Cameron made him seem superficial to voters. This was unsurprising, given stunts such as a dogsled trip in April to a glacier on Spitsbergen in order to highlight his commitment to tackling global warming; only days later it was revealed in the press that his publicised bike trips to the office were often followed by a car carrying his papers and a change of shoes.

The strong showing in the local elections in May were a better gauge of disaffection with Blair than of a Conservative revival. Disturbingly, the Conservatives came perilously close to losing the traditionally safe seat of Bromley and Chislehurst in the 29 June by-election caused by the death of Eric Forth, where their 13,000-seat majority was slashed to only 633 by the Liberal Democrats. The constituency had weeks before rejected Cameron's selection "A-list"—his attempt at making the party appear more inclusive by encouraging the selection of more women and minority ethnic candidates—in favour of local party activist Bob Neill.

During the second half of the year, Cameron made a few strategically chosen policy commitments designed to embed the party's new image, and proposals began to emanate from his policy review groups. In June he promised to give same-sex commitment ceremonies equal status with marriage under any future tax policies. In July he turned the party's image on crime on its head by calling for more measures to combat the causes of crime and anti-social behaviour in what became known as his "hug-a-hoodie" speech. In August his transport policy review group proposed a radical programme of steep price rises on air travel and gas-guzzling cars, to be offset by reductions in other taxes. He consciously distanced himself from the Thatcher years by denouncing her policies on the apartheid in South Africa. The taxation review led by Shadow Chancellor George Osborne proposed to scrap inheritance tax on people's main family home. At his speech to the party conference in Bournemouth on 1 October, Cameron stressed the importance of "sticking to the plan", of not rushing into early policy commitments and of being patient. But the party's recovery was not quick enough for many Conservatives, and polling data suggested that there was still a long way to go before the party would stand a realistic chance of victory at a general election. The question hanging over Cameron was whether his party's right wing would continue to give his approach the benefit of the doubt without clearer indications that it was working.

Cameron's move to the centre was bad news for the Liberal Democrats, preoccupied in the early months of the year with a leadership crisis prompted by the resignation of Charles Kennedy on 8 January. Kennedy, who 48 hours earlier had publicly admitted that he was an alcoholic, had lost the support of the parliamentary party. The contest that followed was marred by further scandal when Shadow Home Secretary Mark Oaten, running as a moderniser candidate, dropped out of the race and resigned from his position following revelations of a six-month affair with a male prostitute. Simon Hughes, party president who was popular on the left, was subsequently discredited when *The Sun* newspaper effectively outed him as bisexual after his denials that he was gay. This left Chris Huhne as the only effective challenger to acting leader Sir Menzies Campbell. When the results were announced at the beginning of March, Campbell won by a larger majority than expected. At 64 he was by far the oldest party leader, and critics were unconvinced that he had the charisma to lead the party in the next election. His management of the party organisation was praised; radical and imaginative proposals, like the plan released in August to cut the basic rate of income tax by 2p, offset by £8 billion worth of new environmental taxes, meant that the Liberal Democrats had a clear and attractive set of policies; but Campbell's parliamentary performance was weak and his visibility with the public low.

GOVERNING MULTICULTURAL BRITAIN. There continued to be a high level of public anxiety about immigration, in spite of the fact that record numbers of Britons had moved abroad in recent years; emigration figures had risen by 30 per cent since the 1990s, with approximately 350,000 people departing annually. Moreover, there was ample evidence that the influx of eastern European workers since EU enlargement had benefited UK economic performance substantially. The new arrivals were taking low paid work and plugging gaps in sectors of the market such as catering and agriculture. The fact that the majority were young, without dependents, meant that they eased the pensions burden and helped keep interest rates low. However, it became clear that the government had vastly underestimated the numbers of eastern Europeans who would come, and there was widespread dismay when home office minister Tony McNulty admitted in August that an estimated 600,000 people had come to work in the UK from eight east European countries which joined the EU in 2004, more than 20 times the number predicted. If this had benefited the economy by driving down wage rates, it had done so at the expense of low paid British workers, a serious potential threat to social cohesion. The prospect of a new wave of immigration prompted by the accession to the EU of Bulgaria and Romania in January 2007 was unsurprisingly controversial. In October Home Secretary John Reid announced a package of transitional control orders on lower-skilled Bulgarian and Romanian workers, a maximum of 19,750 of whom would initially be able to work only in the food processing and agricultural sectors, unless other firms could provide convincing evidence of labour shortages. Self-employed workers, such as plumbers or carpenters, however, would not face restrictions.

It became increasingly obvious in 2006 that the government lacked basic administrative control over immigration processes. At the end of April, an official inquiry into the foreign population within Britain's prisons identified major failings in how the Immigration and Nationality Directorate and the Prison Service were handling deportations. An acute shortage in trained staff meant that around 1,000 foreign prisoners who should have been deported upon release were still at liberty in the UK, and it was clear that a number had gone on to commit serious crimes. In May further evidence of incompetence emerged when David Roberts, the civil servant responsible for removing illegal immigrants, told the parliamentary home affairs committee that he did not have "the faintest idea" of the numbers involved. Although by definition, those who had escaped detection could not be counted, his candid remarks fed public fears of an immigration system that was out of control. In the same month *The Observer* newspaper gave credence to allegations that had been published in *The Sun* in January, when it revealed that a senior immigration official had been caught on videotape seeking sex from an 18-

year old female asylum seeker in exchange for helping with her case. Scotland Yard confirmed that police were investigating a large-scale "cash-for-asylum" racket among low paid immigration officials; corruption was said to be endemic. In July, the crossbench peer Lady Mar, a lay member of the Immigration Appeal Tribunal, resigned in protest at the "incompetence" she had encountered there.

On 25 July John Reid, Clarke's replacement as home secretary, announced a series of measures designed to restore confidence in the system that he had declared "not fit for purpose" shortly after taking office in May. Promising to introduce electronic border controls as the cornerstone of the reforms, he admitted that these would not be fully running until 2014. Among other measures he proposed were new targets for processing asylum claims, the introduction of biometric identity cards for foreign nationals resident in the UK by 2008, the introduction of biometric visas so that airlines could be penalised for carrying passengers not entitled to enter the country, new measures to crack down on the employment of illegal immigrants, and new resources for the enforcement and surveillance of points of entry. He rejected calls for a regularisation or amnesty for the more than 250,000 illegal immigrants already in the country, thought by many critics to be an essential step in fixing the system. Reid's proposals lacked substance and there was little evidence that the culture of incompetence was changing.

While administrative bungling exacerbated public anxiety about immigration, it was the terrorist threat to the UK that was the key issue undermining the British multicultural consensus. Although there was no serious terrorist incident in 2006, high profile arrests were made as the counterterrorist agencies continued to uncover plots and networks of activity. There continued to be disagreement, as well, over the extent to which existing legislation gave the state sufficient powers to control the problem. Existing capabilities were clearly frustrating to the authorities.

February saw frantic attempts by the government to negotiate the deportation of a group of suspected terrorists as it grew increasingly unlikely that they could be successfully brought to trial under current circumstances. In October, it was revealed that two of the 15 suspects under highly restrictive control orders had evaded the authorities and were missing. In June, during a police raid at a house in Forest Gate, east London, Mohammed Abdul Kahar was shot and wounded. He and his brother were arrested but later released without charge, and no suspicious items were found on the premises. The detention of terrorist suspect Rashid Rauf in Pakistan was the trigger for a police swoop at a number of addresses on 10 August, where they arrested 21 people and claimed to have successfully thwarted an alleged plot to smuggle liquid bombs reportedly onto as many as ten transatlantic flights. Searches uncovered bomb-making materials and suicide video notes from some of those arrested. In November admitted terrorist Dhiren Barot was given a life sentence for planning a series of attacks in the UK, for which he had been arrested in 2004.

In all, by the end of 2006 around 400 people in the UK had been charged with terrorist offences since the 11 September 2001 attacks on the USA, of whom

215 had been convicted and another 100 were awaiting trial. In November Dame Eliza Manningham-Buller, director-general of MI5, the UK's security service, warned that the agency had identified a further 30 major terrorist plots being planned in Britain, and revealed that 1,600 individuals were being investigated for their involvement.

There were signs that significantly higher levels of immigration, combined with revelations about institutional failure and the continued threat of terrorism, were beginning to break down the UK's traditionally liberal attitude towards multiculturalism and ethnic diversity. Controversy focused on Muslim communities in particular. Launching the Commission on Integration and Cohesion on 24 August, Communities Secretary Ruth Kelly questioned whether multiculturalism was now encouraging segregation in British society. She called for a "new, honest debate" about extremism and argued that it was not racist to discuss immigration and asylum. She stated that Britain had moved away from a "near uniform consensus on the value of multiculturalism" and was facing challenges which she hoped that the new Commission would address. The delayed launch had first been announced by Blair in the wake of the London bombings of 7 July 2005 (see AR 2005, pp. 14-16).

On 20 September Reid was heckled by protesters as he made a speech warning Muslim parents in east London that fanatics were "looking to groom and brainwash your children for suicide bombing". On 5 October Jack Straw provoked anger and indignation among broad sections of the Muslim community when, writing in a local newspaper in his Blackburn constituency, he revealed that he asked female Muslim visitors to his surgery to remove the full veil, or niqab. He argued that the niqab was "such a visible statement of separation and difference" that it threatened positive community relations. On 15 October Shadow Home Secretary David Davis accused Muslim leaders of encouraging "voluntary apartheid" by sealing themselves off into separate societies. On 17 October Blair weighed in, when he publicly backed a school in West Yorkshire which had suspended assistant teacher Aishah Azmi for refusing to remover her niqab in the presence of men. Describing the veil as a "mark of separation" which made non-Muslims feel "uncomfortable" he added that there was an issue apparent throughout Europe about how Islam "comes to terms and feels comfortable with" the modern world. On 19 October, Azmi lost the discrimination test case she had brought against her employers; but she was awarded £1100 for victimisation in the way the dispute was handled, and the employment tribunal rebuked ministers for commenting on the case while it was still sub judice.

Meanwhile, the government decided in mid-October to give local councils the power to force newly founded faith schools to admit 25 per cent of pupils who were not of that faith. Interpreted by some as being targeted at Muslim schools, the move proved to be highly controversial with Roman Catholic and Jewish institutions. Education Secretary Alan Johnson was forced to climb down on 26 October, announcing that he would no longer try to force a quota. To these debates was added the incident, also occurring in October, when British Airways banned a Christian employee from wearing a small cross. Nadia Eweida was told to remove the necklace because it contravened the company's uniform policy. Eweida's objections were backed by the Muslim Council of Britain as "an expression of private religious belief", and British Airways backed down over fears that the policy would affect ticket sales.

What had started as a debate about integration and multiculturalism had, in only a few weeks, broadened into a wider one about the role of religious belief in society. Writing in *The Times* on 27 October, Archbishop of Canterbury Rowan Williams argued that politicians should not only not interfere with a Muslim woman's right to wear a veil, but that it was "politically dangerous" to construct a social ideal in which no visible signs of religion would be seen. His comments reflected concern among all religious groups that there was growing support for the idea that Britain should adopt a secular model comparable to France. Speaking to an invited audience at Downing Street at the beginning of December, Blair reiterated that Muslims had a "duty to integrate" into British society and to respect the country's core values of democracy, tolerance, and respect for the law. "For the first time in a generation," he declared, "there is an unease, an anxiety, even at points a resentment that our very openness, our willingness to welcome difference, our pride in being home to many cultures, is being used against us; abused, indeed, in order to harm us." He indicated that in the past, government grants had been awarded too freely to groups representing different religions and ethnicities, and that in the future such funding would stipulate the promotion of integration as well as support for distinctive cultural identity. In response Muhammad Abdul Bari, secretary general of the Muslim Council of Britain, stated that while he welcomed Blair's positive remarks on multiculturalism and integration, "It was disappointing to see that the PM continues to see the phenomenon of terrorism as a clash of values rather than being prepared to examine whether some of our misguided policies in the Middle East have contributed to gravely exacerbating the threat from extremist groups."

OTHER DOMESTIC NEWS. The department of education faced criticism in January when it was revealed that a registered sex offender had been given a job as a PE teacher in a Norwich school, in spite of the government's 2004 pledge urgently to implement the recommendations of the inquiry into the Soham murders (in which two girls had been murdered by the caretaker of their local school, see AR 2003, p. 31) led by Sir Michael Bichard. Although Education and Skills Secretary Ruth Kelly bore the brunt of popular blame, it was a leadership failure at senior police levels that accounted for the continued inability to devise a single national database with which to screen applicants for jobs working with vulnerable adults and children.

In February the government suffered its second defeat in the House of Commons since 1997, when its controversial race and religious hatred bill was rejected on two votes. Critics had claimed that it was unnecessary and would threaten basic freedom of speech. The defeat was due to miscalculation on the part of the Labour whips, who failed to bring home MPs campaigning in the Dunfermline by-election. Embarrassingly, the second ballot was lost by a single vote, which would have been saved had the prime minister attended. Coming soon after the defeat in November 2005 over 90-day detentions for terror suspects (see AR 2005, p. 17), this was another sobering message to the government, which was facing a number of controversies on other legislative issues.

The bill authorising the introduction of compulsory identity (ID) cards was one of these, and the government was defeated a total of five times in the House of Lords before reaching a compromise on 29 March. Under the new plans, although everyone applying for or renewing their passport would have their biometric information and other identity details placed on the national identity register, anyone applying for a passport before January 2010 would be able to opt out of having an ID card. This might have ended the parliamentary wrangle, but the scheme was still facing a number of problems. In July a series of leaked emails suggested that officials feared that the scheme would be a failure due to unrealistic pressure to meet a 2008 introduction date. With so much evidence of administrative failure in other branches of the home office, pressure was mounting on the government to scrap the scheme altogether in order to focus resources on dealing with immigration and crime. Home office estimates that the scheme would cost £5.4 billion to set up and run were greeted with scepticism, given the history of cost overruns on other large government technical projects. Scepticism increased in December, when John Reid announced that the computer database behind the scheme would be an amalgamation of existing IT networks rather than one built from scratch. Blair continued to defend the scheme, insisting that it was essential on modernising grounds and dismissing arguments that it would erode civil liberties.

The government's education reform proposals were a further source of division. The proposal to encourage the formation of "trust schools", independent of local authorities and backed by business or faith communities, divided both cabinet and the parliamentary party. In February Blair made a series of concessions on his education reforms in an attempt to defuse the revolt ahead of the publication of the bill. The concessions were designed to overcome fears that the reforms would benefit middle-class pupils disproportionately by introducing selection. When publication of the revised bill failed to persuade enough rebels to drop their opposition, Blair relied upon Conservative support for the bill to pass its second reading in the Commons on 15 March, when 51 Labour MPs rebelled. Further concessions enabled the bill easily to pass its third reading on 24 May, but still reliant upon opposition support, with 46 Labour backbenchers continuing to vote against. By the end of the year, however, only 60 schools had expressed an interest in setting up trusts and it was by no means clear that the reforms would be taken up in significant numbers.

The government was accused in February of burying evidence of a serious financial crisis in the National Health Service (NHS), in spite of the fact that spending on healthcare had risen by around one-third in real terms since 1997. The combined deficit for the 28 strategic health authorities in England for the financial year to the end of March was predicted to be as high as £750 million. Corrective measures ordered by Health Secretary Patricia Hewitt were alleged to be significantly damaging the quality of patient care. Sir Nigel Crisp, permanent secretary at the department of health and chief executive of the NHS in England, warned at the end of February that persistent overspending was threatening the government's programme for improving services. Wards had been closed and treatment delayed, in efforts to contain the scale of the problem; but costs had risen primarily due to factors such as rising staff salaries and increased pharmaceutical costs. Crisp's departure was announced on 7 March; the prime minister denied that he had been sacked for having failed to exercise sufficient financial control of the expanding service. Hewitt was jeered while delivering an address to the Royal College of Nurses at the end of April in which she defended the reform programme. In October, it was confirmed that the final deficit for the financial year ending 31 March was £547 million. Official figures showed that there were more than 900 compulsory redundancies in the NHS between April and September, although around 20,000 posts had been cut in total. Speaking in December, Blair appealed to NHS managers and doctors to support the reform programme. His words reflected well-founded frustration: while all the evidence showed clearly that reforming the structure of healthcare would improve the service and save lives, the government had failed to communicate these issues effectively to the public.

Preparations began in 2006 for the 2012 London Olympic games, but there were signs of controversy by the end of the year. In his March budget, Gordon Brown delighted officials at UK Sport when he announced £200 million of additional funding for athletes, an amount that would enable athletes to be funded in every sport represented at the games. However, concerns began to focus on the rising costs of the games when David Higgins, chief executive of the Olympic Delivery Authority, warned that the infrastructure budget alone might treble. Authority Chairman Jack Lemley underlined these concerns by stressing that the project was "a marathon, not a sprint". A series of revisions to plans for the east London site were unveiled in June in an attempt to rein in costs; but in October, the project suffered a serious setback with Lemley's sudden resignation. The US consultant, hired for his reputation for delivering projects on time and within budget, was said to have been unable to cope with the workload in view of a heart problem. Lemley himself claimed that he left because he feared that disagreements among politicians were serious enough to make his goals unachievable. In November London mayor Ken Livingstone warned that the revised budget would reach £5 billion—more than double the original estimate—and it emerged that the treasury was advocating a contingency fund to deal with a potential overspend of 60 per cent on construction work. Only days later, the London assembly warned that costs might rise to as much as £8 billion.

In November, Blair's last Queen's speech was dominated by proposals to combat terrorism and crime. A total of six bills being prepared by the home office included measures to raise the penalty for carrying a knife, to improve the way offenders were managed, to give law enforcement agencies new powers to combat serious and organised crime, to provide the Immigration Service with further powers to police the country's borders, to provide for trials without juries in serious fraud cases, and to reform the tribunal service. Other proposals included measures to allow older and disabled people to travel without charge on buses at off-peak times; to replace the troubled Child Support Agency with a new streamlined body; to replace incapacity benefits with a tougher employment and support allowance; and to give local authorities greater powers to combat housing fraud. A climate change bill would establish an independent body to work with the government on meeting carbon emissions reduction targets. There were also proposals for a national road pricing scheme, under which drivers would have to pay to use certain routes, and proposals to strengthen power and leadership in local government.

The question of how to replace the UK's Trident nuclear weapons system, due to become obsolete from 2020, was raised by Blair's promise that a decision would be made before the next election. Except that there was no real decision to be made, as there was clearly never any doubt in Whitehall that it was essential to maintain Britain's status as a nuclear power, even if this meant spending huge sums on developing a weapons system that was only likely to be meaningful in symbolic terms. This was one of those issues over which a small group of establishment figures in Whitehall was really in control, a point that was not lost on Gordon Brown, who in June passed an important test with the mandarins when he unexpectedly announced his commitment to retaining the nuclear deterrent. Blair's launch of a "debate" on the issue in November was in reality a publicity exercise designed to persuade the majority of voters to support a decision that had already been taken.

News in the final weeks of the year was dominated by the bizarre and disturbing story surrounding the London murder of former Russian KGB officer Alexander Litvinenko, who had been granted asylum status in 2001. An opponent of the Russian president, Vladimir Putin, he had been investigating the 7 October murder in Moscow of Russian investigative journalist Anna Politkovskaya, an outspoken critic of the Chechen war (see pp. 107-08). So far as the facts could be established by the end of the year, Litvinenko had met two Russians at a London hotel on 1 November, both former KGB officers. Later the same day, he had lunch with Italian academic Mario Scaramella and was handed papers identifying Politkovskaya's murderers and other potential assassination targets. Feeling unwell, he was taken to a hospital in north London, where he died on 23 November, after dictating a letter in which he blamed Putin for his murder. Tests revealed that Litvinenko had been poisoned by the radioactive isotope, polonium 210. As police retraced his steps in the days and weeks that followed, it emerged that 12 people who had come into contact with him had tested positive for low levels of polonium 210, and traces of the substance had been found at 13 different sites in London and on three aircraft. It was also revealed that German authorities had found traces of polonium 210 at several locations in Hamburg visited by Dmitry Kovtun, one of the men whom Litvinenko had met on the day he was poisoned. A team of Scotland Yard detectives flew to Moscow in connection with the investigation, returning before Christmas, but the mystery of Litvinenko's death remained unsolved at the end of the year (see p. 108).

THE UK AND WORLD AFFAIRS. In Iraq, where the UK provided the leadership of the multi-national division (south-east) which included troops from eight other countries, there were some 7,100 UK troops serving by the end of the year, down from approximately 8,500 in January. There were 28 British deaths in total during 2006, bringing the total number of UK fatalities since the start of the campaign to 127. According to the ministry of defence, 685 UK military and civilian personnel were flown out of Iraq on medical grounds in 2006, approximately 30 of whom were classed as seriously or very seriously injured.

In a speech to the Foreign Press Association on 7 February, then Defence Secretary John Reid set out the conditions under which coalition forces could complete the handover of security in Iraq. Predicting that there would be significantly fewer UK troops in the country in a year's time, he made it clear that this would depend upon the extent to which Iraqis could assure their own security. The first indication of this came on 13 March, when Reid announced that the UK presence would be reduced by around 800 personnel following the next roulement of British forces in May. Speaking during a visit to the Iraqi capital, Baghdad, a few days later, he denied that civil war was imminent, and claimed that significant progress continued to be made. On 19 June Iraqi Prime Minister Nouri al-Maliki was able to announce that the control of security in Muthanna province would be handed over to the Iraqi security forces in July; Najaf province was handed over in December.

Basra was a different matter. In February shocking video footage emerged, appearing to show British soldiers beating a group of Iraqi teenagers in 2003 in an army compound where they had been dragged following a riot in Amara, north of Basra province. Four soldiers were arrested in the days that followed, but the incident served to increase friction with local people and the increasingly powerful Shi'ite militias. The provincial council in Basra suspended relations with the UK, a move that included the ending of co-operation with the UK consulate and the cessation of joint patrols between British and Iraqi security forces. On 6 May five UK personnel were killed when a Lynx helicopter crashed in Basra city. An angry crowd soon gathered and several army vehicles were set alight as crowds tried to prevent British troops trying to reach the blazing wreckage. In another incident, in September, Corporal Donald Payne became the first British soldier ever to be convicted of a war crime as he pleaded guilty to the systematic abuse of prisoners at a detention centre in Basra in 2003. Six others pleaded not guilty in an episode which led to the death of hotel receptionist Baha Mousa and the sustained abuse of a number of others over a period of 36 hours. Proceedings were still under way as the year ended.

These revelations belied the myth that the operation in Basra was a relative success story. The newly appointed defence secretary, Des Browne, negotiated a series of undertakings from the Iraqi government during his June visit, on the delivery of a new security plan for the province. There continued to be serious concerns, however, about levels of corruption within the Iraqi police service in Basra. "Operation Sinbad", with the objective of rooting out police corruption, was launched in September. A major operation was carried out on 25 December to curtail the activities of a rogue police unit known as the "serious crimes unit", which was notorious for collaborating with criminal militias to murder and kidnap local people and troops. The unit's compound was completely destroyed in the action, and more than 100 prisoners, many with signs of torture, were rescued, while seven gunmen were killed.

British hostage Norman Kember, and his two Canadian colleagues, were freed on 23 March after a rescue mission led by the SAS into one of the most dangerous parts of Baghdad. Kember, 74, a Christian peace activist, was widely criticised when he pointedly failed to thank the men who had rescued him.

British troops had a tough year in Afghanistan, where the UK assumed a leading role in the International Security Assistance Force (ISAF), a NATO-led, UN-authorised mission in the south, to which 35 other countries also contributed forces. Around 5,600 UK service personnel were deployed there by the year's end. In January it was announced that a 3,300-strong UK task force would be deployed to the south of the country in 2006, spearheading an international effort to extend the authority of the Afghan government to those regions. Worries for the safety of the troops were well founded as conditions deteriorated alarmingly in Helmand province, a volatile, opium-producing region, and soldiers became embroiled in a long series of fierce engagements with Taliban fighters. Of the 44 British service personnel killed since the start of operations in Afghanistan in November 2001, 40 died in 2006; a further 256 were evacuated on medical grounds. Early indications suggested that the incidence of psychological illness, or combat stress, among troops serving in Afghanistan was significantly higher than had been the case in Iraq. In July it was announced that the numbers deployed in the south would rise to 4,500 by the autumn, a reflection of the difficulties involved in operations there in an area four times the size of Wales.

By the early autumn, there was increasing alarm at the plight of British troops in southern Afghanistan. A growing number of relatives spoke of their concern over the degree of stress and exhaustion that soldiers were suffering. Supplies and rations to the remote region were reported to be erratic. Ageing or inadequate equipment was also compromising the safety of the troops; 20 alone had died as a result of the failure to replace lightly-armoured Land-Rovers, which were vulnerable to roadside bombs. The refusal of other members of the NATO alliance to supply reinforcements to ISAF left the UK little choice but to put more troops and helicopters on standby for deployment, an offer that was made in September during talks between NATO chiefs in Warsaw. There was deep frustration at the refusal of allies, such as Spain and Germany, to deploy troops in the south. At the end of September bitter recriminations broke out between factions of the RAF and infantry, provoking fears that morale was on the point of collapse.

By October, a growing sense of dismay was apparent among senior military officers and civil servants involved in defence and foreign affairs over UK policy in the Middle East and Afghanistan. In an astonishing move, General Sir Richard Dannatt, the newly appointed chief of the general staff, gave an interview to the *Daily Mail* in which he called for withdrawal from Iraq on the grounds that the UK presence there was exacerbating UK security problems around the world.

Field Marshal Sir Peter Inge, a former head of Britain's armed forces (chief of the general staff 1992-94), warned that British strategy lacked a clear sense of focus and direction, and that its policies on Iraq and Afghanistan seemed to be tied to a US administration that had lost credibility. A week later General the Lord Guthrie, former chief of the defence staff (1997-2001), condemned the decision to send an already overstretched UK army into southern Afghanistan as "cuckoo". By the end of the year this pressure was clearly having an effect. Gordon Brown, on his first visit to Iraq in November, stated that British troops could begin withdrawing within "a few months", an early indication that the government was beginning to rethink its strategy there. Blair flew to Washington DC to give evidence to the bipartisan Iraq Study Group on 14 November, but at this stage there were more important players putting pressure on the administration of US President George W. Bush.

In July there emerged signs of tension within the British government's normally supine relationship with the Bush administration, over the diplomatic response to Israel's military campaign against Hezbullah militants in Lebanon (see pp. 197-203). At the G-8 summit in St Petersburg, Blair initially attempted to act as a bridge between Bush's support for the campaign and European condemnation of it by calling on all sides to show restraint. He expressed misgivings over the extent of Israel's response to Hezbullah in a telephone call to Israeli Prime Minister Ehud Olmert, but he gave the general impression that the UK was prepared to tolerate the escalating violence. This caused a major rebellion inside the cabinet. During a visit to the Lebanese capital, Beirut, on 22 July, foreign office minister Kim Howells was openly critical of Israeli tactics. Former Foreign Secretary Jack Straw also voiced his opposition. In the 27 July cabinet meeting, it was reported that minister after minister urged Blair to break with the US administration and publicly criticise Israel. Bush's apology for having failed to ask permission for a plane carrying bombs bound for Israel to land at Prestwick airport near Glasgow did little to impress ministers as their rift with Blair over Middle Eastern policy began to harden.

Blair took the view that the Lebanon crisis was part of a larger picture, at the heart of which lay the problem of Israel and Palestine. He believed that quiet diplomatic efforts by the USA, the UK, and France to broker a ceasefire would be more effective in this wider context, and pressed Bush to consider reviving negotiations between Israel and Palestine once hostilities ceased. In a speech to the World Affairs Council in Los Angeles on 1 August, Blair called for the formation of an "arc of moderation" to counter the "arc of extremism" in the Middle East encompassing Gaza, southern Lebanon, Syria, Iraq, Iran, and Afghanistan. The key to that challenge, he argued, was the revival of the Israel-Palestine peace process. At a joint news conference with Olmert in Israel on 9 September, there were some indications that the Israeli line on restarting the process was softening, but critics remained deeply sceptical that the British prime minister would have any significant influence on this issue during his final months in office. This was confirmed in December, during Blair's end-of-year tour of the Middle East, where there was little evidence that his views were taken seriously.

THE ECONOMY IN 2006. The December report of the IMF to the Treasury, the British finance ministry, stated that the UK's economic performance had been "impressive". Unsurprisingly, therefore, the chancellor of the exchequer, Gordon Brown, proudly declared in his December pre-budget report that 2006 had seen "the tenth consecutive year of economic growth". Indeed, the British economy had been recording year-on-year growth since 1992. In June 2006 the Office of National Statistics (ONS) announced that it had been under-estimating the UK's GDP over the past few years. The revised method of calculations estimated that GDP growth in 2006 had been 2.9 per cent, the fastest pace in two years and better than the chancellor's target of 2.75 per cent. Additionally, despite exceptionally high government borrowing in May, it appeared that Brown was broadly on track to keep to his so-called "golden rule" of maintaining a balanced national budget over an economic cycle.

Even so, it was not obvious that the British economy would necessarily perform so well. For the UK's central bank, the Bank of England, the control of inflation had been consistently difficult. The Bank's target was the maintenance of the consumer price index (CPI), the government's measurement of the level of inflation, broadly within the 2 per cent range. At the start of the year CPI was recorded at 1.7 per cent, but through the year it pushed upwards, peaking in December at 3 per cent, a figure higher than anticipated or thought to be desirable. In large part, this was the result of a combination of external factors, in particular a broad increase across import prices and, during the first half of 2006, a surge in the price of crude oil and natural gas, the most obvious cost for the UK economy of the Iraq war. During this period, petrol prices in the UK edged ever closer to the symbolic £1 per litre. Although the value of crude oil subsequently fell dramatically, domestic petrol prices did not contract accordingly and nor did domestic utility bills. Escalating energy costs also contributed to generally higher transport costs, with further inflationary pressures. The Automobile Association estimated that motorists had an additional £50 added to their expected annual running costs. The retail price index (RPI), which included housing costs such as mortgage payments, rose to 4.4 per cent in December, the highest since December 1991, and up from 3.9 per cent in November. RPI was a measure that more closely reflected the cost of living, which indicated that most households' experience of inflation was higher than the CPI rate suggested.

Adding to the financial burdens on most households were the increases in mortgage payments, the result of two successive hikes in the Bank of England's interest rates. The first of these came in August, which took the rate to 4.75 percent, and then in November, when the rate rested at 5 per cent.

Personal indebtedness in the UK, already the highest in the EU, continued to rise. At the end of the year the Bank of England estimated that the total amount of money owed by people living in the UK was £1,278 billion. Of this amount, around £1,066 billion was in the form of mortgages. The rest, defined as consumer credit, was in the form of debts to credit cards, bank overdrafts, and other forms of borrowing, and was growing at the slowest rate since 1994. Credit card debt fell by £1.8 billion, while mortgage lending rose by £66.8 billion, a 20 per cent increase from the previous year. Partly this was because the strong housing market encouraged homeowners to release equity. Equity release was more attractive because of comparably high repayment costs on credit card debt and because there were fewer 0 per cent interest rate deals being offered to new credit card customers. According to Datamonitor, a business research firm, the credit card business had reached saturation point in the UK.

The housing market, which was expected to dampen after the two interest rate rises, remained surprisingly robust. According to the Halifax bank and Nationwide building society—two of the UK's largest mortgage lending institutions—house prices had increased by around 10 per cent over the year. Halifax's survey of regional house prices in the last quarter of the year showed the fastest growth in Northern Ireland, where prices jumped 44.1 per cent compared to the same period a year earlier, three times as fast as in Scotland where prices rose by 16 per cent. The Nationwide's survey showed that London house prices rose by 11.3 per cent. Property analysts estimated that people were extending themselves up to their financial limit in order to cover their mortgages.

The growth of real disposable incomes was only 1.3 per cent in the final quarter of the year, the weakest rise in household budgets since 2004. Retailers estimated that consumers had been squeezed by a greater tax burden than before, with direct and indirect taxes cumulatively taking nearly one-quarter of household income, considerably higher than when the Labour government came to office in 1997. Research by the supermarket group, Asda, suggested that the average family had just £150 a month to spend. Consequently, most retailers were expecting the worst Christmas sales for a quarter of a century, and this prompted some retailers to begin aggressive price-cutting, which was met with mixed results. For instance, the retail chain Debenhams' pre-Christmas "2 day sale" was reported by them to have been a "near disaster".

In fact, overall retail sales over the Christmas period turned out to be surprisingly strong. The volume of retail sales between October and December was 1.4 per cent higher than in the previous three months. The highest growth came from non-store (Internet and mail order) retailing, at 3.8 per cent, the highest for this sector for a year and a half. Compared with the same period in 2005, the volume of total sales in the three months to December 2006 went up 3.6 per cent. The retail sectors that performed solidly were the department store chains with established reputations, like John Lewis, which revealed that it had performed well before Christmas and had broken all records on the first day of its post-Christmas sale with a taking of £18 million. Most retailers reported that luxury brands and designer label goods had also sold extremely well during both the pre- and post-Christmas periods.

As in previous years, most of the UK's external balances, aside from the trade in services, were in deficit. The balance of payments current account deficit for the third quarter of 2006 was £9.4 billion, up from the £8.3 billion gap in the second quarter. The surplus on trade in services was £2.4 billion in October, the same as in September. During 2006 the value of the pound sterling remained high compared with the US dollar, nearly reaching the US$2 mark in November, the highest rate for 14 years. While sterling/euro rates were not as favourable, this provided no real respite for the manufacturing sector, with overall manufacturing productivity declining a couple of percentage points compared to the previous year.

Nevertheless, UK corporate profitability was generally high, particularly in the service sectors (with banks making record profits, derived largely from their overseas activities) and the oil and gas extraction companies. The London stock exchange retained its international position, with shares in the stock market company surging more than 124 per cent over the year amid takeover offers from the US exchange, Nasdaq.

British unemployment rates edged upwards, ending 2006 at 5.5 per cent, unchanged over the previous quarter but up by 0.6 per cent over the year. Average regular earnings (that is, earnings excluding bonuses) were up 3.7 per cent in the year, with pay in the private sector rising marginally faster, 3.9 per cent, than in the public sector at 3.1 per cent. If bonuses were included in the calculations, private sector earnings were stronger, a rise of 4.2 percent, against a public sector earnings rise of 3.2 per cent. Around £9 billion in bonuses was awarded to top earners in the City of London, the UK's financial centre. About the same amount in bonuses was paid to all other high earners. The Trades Union Congress (TUC) estimated that since 2000 the pay of British executives had risen 17 times faster than that of employees.

The UK attracted labour from the eight eastern European states that had acceded to the EU in 2004. According to the home office minister, Tony McNulty, nearly 600,000 migrants came from these countries, the largest numbers (62 per cent) coming from Poland (see p. 76). This raised fears about the ability of the economy to absorb such a large number of workers. However, studies by the home office found that these migrants were not proving to be a strain on the welfare system, and other studies showed that they were performing jobs that were not being filled or were creating new jobs. According to McNulty, "These are economically productive individuals who are making significant contributions to our economy." That this could happen with such comparative ease was indicative of the strength of the UK economy in 2006.

SCOTLAND

CAPITAL: Edinburgh AREA: 78,313 sq km POPULATION: 5,094,800
OFFICIAL LANGUAGES: English & Gaelic POLITICAL SYSTEM: devolved administration within UK
HEAD OF STATE: Queen Elizabeth II (since Feb '52)
RULING PARTIES: Labour & Liberal Democrats (since May '99)
HEAD OF GOVERNMENT: Jack McConnell (Labour), First Minister (since Nov '01)

THE only by-election in Scotland during the year to the UK Parliament at Westminster was caused by the death of Rachel Squire, who had been elected in 2005 as Scottish Labour MP for the Dunfermline and West Fife constituency. Unexpectedly, the seat was captured in February by the Scottish Liberal Democrats, with a swing of 16 per cent from Scottish Labour and 9 per cent from Scottish Conservatives (see p. 11). To add to the Labour party's embarrassment, Gordon Brown, the chancellor of the exchequer, was a resident in the constituency. Otherwise, there were few changes in the Scottish political scene. The Scottish National Party (SNP) held the Moray Scottish Parliament seat which had been vacated by the death in March of Margaret Ewing. In local council elections the SNP won two seats from Scottish Labour, but lost one to the Scottish Conservatives; and the Scottish Liberal Democrats and an independent candidate each gained one seat from Scottish Labour. Opinion polls towards the end of the year showed rising support for Scottish independence, giving the SNP some hopes for victory in the Scottish Parliament elections due in 2007.

The development of windfarms was a recurrent theme during the year. The Black Law windfarm in Lanarkshire opened in January: with 42 turbines it was the largest onshore windfarm in the UK. Approval was granted in April for a 140-turbine farm at Whitelee, near Glasgow; this was expected to be the largest onshore windfarm in Europe. In December work started on construction of the UK's largest offshore windfarm, with 60 turbines, in the Solway Firth. The Scottish executive had set targets that 18 per cent of electricity generated in Scotland by 2010, and 40 per cent by 2020, would come from renewable sources, and these developments were significant in this context.

Also recurrent during the year were land buy-outs by local communities. The most important of these was the community purchase of the South Uist Estate, an area of more than 36,000 hectares containing about 5 per cent of all Scottish crofts. The estate comprised most of the island of South Uist, together with most of Benbecula and all of Eriskay, all three islands being in the Outer Hebrides. In a separate buy-out, significant parts of north Lewis (also in the Outer Hebrides) became community property.

Proceedings of the Scottish Parliament were disrupted from early March to early May by structural repairs. The repairs became necessary after a beam in the roof of the debating chamber swung out of position when a strut at one end came loose. Various temporary measures ensured that parliamentary business could continue while the chamber roof was inspected and the beams checked and made secure. It appeared that the cost of the repairs would fall on the Parliament itself rather than insurers or contractors, despite the newness of the controversial building which had been completed only in 2004 (see AR 2004, p. 29; AR 2005, p. 461).

After considerable debate, the Scottish Parliament decided in November to make St Andrew's day (30 November) a bank holiday in Scotland. (St Andrew was the patron saint of Scotland.) The eventual legislation was, however, more limited in scope than its sponsors had hoped, and came down to little more than an exhortation to Scottish employers to grant a holiday on that day in lieu of some other day's holiday. Since the Scottish clearing banks had decided in 1996 to harmonise their closing days with those in England and Wales, it appeared unlikely that Scottish banks would close on this new "bank holiday".

The ban on smoking in public places in Scotland became effective on 26 March. Despite concerns expressed, there did not appear to be any immediate negative effect on sales in most bars and public houses, and in some the smoke-free atmosphere increased custom. More problematic was the implementation of the ban in other public places. For example, in hospitals it was accepted that facilities would have to be provided for in-patients who were smokers, but perhaps not for staff and visitors.

On 1 April free bus travel within Scotland became available to those over 60 and the disabled. Previously, such arrangements had operated within some local authority areas, but the new scheme was Scotland-wide.

The annual negotiations in the EU fisheries council about the limits on fishing permitted for the following year were of major concern to the Scottish fishing and fish-processing industries. The shortage of certain fish, especially cod, in the North Sea, led to pressure on the EU Commission for a complete ban on catching such species, but the eventual deal agreed in December represented a compromise between environmental arguments and the case for maintaining the viability of the industries. There were cuts in the quotas of fish that could be caught and the permitted number of days that each boat could spend at sea in the main North Sea fisheries, but some increase in quotas for the Atlantic fisheries to the west of Scotland.

Two popular visitor attractions in Glasgow reopened, in both cases after a major three-year refurbishment. In July, the Kelvingrove museum reopened and within four months, 1.8 million visitors had taken advantage of the new layout which enabled more material to be exhibited in a much more modern format. In November restoration was completed on the Kibble Palace, a huge Victorian greenhouse in the city's Botanic Gardens. In Edinburgh the most unusual event was the CowParade, from May to July, in which 94 variously decorated fibreglass cows were scattered throughout the city. Sixty-two of the models were auctioned in September, raising over £252,200 for charity.

WALES

CAPITAL: Cardiff AREA: 20,755 sq km POPULATION: 2,958,600
OFFICIAL LANGUAGES: Welsh & English POLITICAL SYSTEM: devolved administration within UK
HEAD OF STATE: Queen Elizabeth II (since Feb '52)
RULING PARTY: Labour (since May '03)
HEAD OF GOVERNMENT: Rhodri Morgan (Labour), First Secretary (since Feb '00)

FOR Welsh politicians this was a year of anticipation for major changes due in 2007, in what was described by First Minister Rhodri Morgan as the development of Wales as a "small, smart confident nation".

The new Welsh Assembly building, the Senedd, was opened on 1 March, St David's day. Despite criticism of its £67 million cost, it provided a fitting symbol to Wales's new self-confidence and the building itself, designed by Sir Richard Rogers, won several design and environmental awards. Despite its new surroundings, Labour's minority government in the National Assembly continued to struggle to deliver its programme against a backdrop of a fall in the party's popularity. This was exemplified for the second year running by the voters of Blaenau Gwent. Peter Law, the Welsh Assembly member and Westminster (UK Parliament) member for Blaenau Gwent, following his sensational victory in the 2005 UK general election, died on 25 April after a long illness (see AR 2005, p. 28-29). Labour's inability to repair the wounds of the previous year, exacerbated by its heedless decision in elevating its defeated candidate in 2005, Maggie Jones, to the House of Lords, led to the decision of Law's widow Trish Law and his agent Dai Davies to stand for the two seats, at Cardiff and Westminster respectively, in by-elections which were arranged for the same day, 30 June. Labour spent a total of £112,000 on its campaign, as opposed to less than £14,000 by its independent opponents, and cabinet ministers were sent to the constituency, including Gordon Brown but, significantly, not Tony Blair. However, Labour's Owen Smith was defeated by the local candidate Davies, and Trish Law comfortably won the Assembly seat. As in the previous year's general election, this was seen as victory for local interests over unresponsive central authority.

At Westminster the result of the Blaenau Gwent by-election, together with other issues, increased the pressure on the prime minister, Tony Blair, and some Welsh members of Parliament were among those who were involved in moves to oust him. Despite its small contingent of three MPs, Plaid Cymru was often in the news as a result of its attacks on government policy over Iraq and the alleged selling of honours (see pp. 13-14). At the same time the leader of the Welsh Liberal Democrats, Lembit Opik, was drawing attention to himself because of his misjudgements over the Liberal Democrat leadership and for his colourful personal life. Under the new leadership of David Cameron and his equivalent in Wales, Nick Bourne, the Conservative party, which had been in the past implacably opposed to devolution, emphasised its new approach of developing the Welsh Assembly to serve better the needs of Wales, rather than undermining it. In December Welsh MP Ann Clwyd, a consistent supporter of government policy over the Iraq war, failed to retain her position as vice-chair of the parliamentary Labour party.

The Government of Wales Act finally received royal assent on 25 July. This would have major consequences on the way Wales was to be governed, although its measures fell far short of those recommended by the Richard commission on which it was founded. It allowed for the creation, after the Assembly elections in May 2007, of an executive body, the Welsh Assembly government, separate from the legislative body, the National Assembly, and with the power to draw up its own legislation (see AR 2005, pp. 29-30).

It was also a year of protests relating to the National Health Service (NHS). Cancer patient, Jayne Sullivan held a personal sit-in in the Assembly foyer in February because the Assembly's health minister, Brian Gibbons, had not approved the drug herceptin for use by women in the early stages of breast cancer. The sit-in lasted for seven days and the drug was made available in June. There were also protests in Aberystwyth, Llandudno, Builth Wells, and Haverfordwest in opposition to proposals to downgrade hospital services. Wales's ambulance service was in constant flux, with no fewer than four chief executives being in post at some stage during the year. Upon his resignation, one of these, Roger Thayne, alleged that as many as 500 lives were being lost annually because of the inefficiency of the service, and an inquiry by the auditor general for Wales found that problems in the service were "long-standing and severe".

There was good and bad news for the Welsh economy during the year, together with a degree of uncertainty. The success of business parks, such as Celtic Springs near Newport which employed over 1,000 workers, was counterbalanced by the closure of factories in Ebbw Vale, Waunarlwydd, and Bynea. The campaign to keep open the Burberry factory in the Rhondda involved Hollywood celebrities who appealed for the company to reverse its plans to move the manufacture of the famous clothing brand abroad. There was uncertainty in Broughton, Flintshire, where 7,000 workers were employed at the Airbus aeroplane factory, because of delays in the A380 superjumbo project. There were also concerns in south Wales, because the steel company Corus, which employed over 8,000 workers in the area, was subject to takeover bids by two multinational corporations.

In December the Assembly budget for 2007-08 was finally passed after a lengthy wrangle. The £14 billion budget had been rejected by the opposition in October leading to a period of negotiations between the opposition parties and Labour's minority Assembly government, specifically over spending on education. In early December it became clear that, whereas some adjustments to the budget had been made, no agreement had been reached, but the opposition parties were split over tactics. Whereas the Conservatives and the Liberal Democrats were prepared to vote down the budget—a situation which might have led to a coalition of opposition parties taking over from Labour—Plaid Cymru was less willing to engage in a political gamble, with Assembly elections less than six months away. In the event Plaid Cymru abstained on the budget vote, amid accusations of cowardice by the other opposition parties, but it was seen by many as a mature and responsible approach whereby political advantage was sacrificed in the interests of good government.

Although politicians sought to raise awareness of the serious issues facing Wales, they were unable to receive the same attention as that achieved by a personable, Welsh-speaking, teenager from Blaenau Ffestiniog, Glyn Wise, who captured the public's imagination as a result of his appearance in the popular television series *Big Brother*.

NORTHERN IRELAND

CAPITAL: Belfast AREA: 18,843 sq km POPULATION: 1,724,400
OFFICIAL LANGUAGES: English, Irish & Ulster Scots POLITICAL SYSTEM: devolved administration within UK
HEAD OF STATE: Queen Elizabeth II (since Feb '52)
RULING PARTIES: Democratic Unionist Party (DUP), Sinn Féin (SF), Social Democratic and Labour Party (SDLP), & Ulster Unionist Party (UUP)
HEAD OF GOVERNMENT: Peter Hain (Labour), Secretary of State for Northern Ireland (since May '05)

AGAINST the background of ongoing talks to restore devolution, there were several notable firsts in cross-community dialogue during the year. In April three Democratic Unionist Party (DUP) members became the party's first life peers and the DUP sent a delegation to a meeting of the British-Irish Inter-Parliamentary Body for the first time. Former Ulster Unionist leader David Trimble also entered the House of Lords. The leaders of the Roman Catholic Church had their first formal meetings with the Protestant Orange Order (June) and with DUP leader Ian Paisley (October). In May the nationalist Social Democratic and Labour Party (SDLP) held discussions with the Orange Order, and in October Sinn Féin had its first meeting with a Church of Ireland delegation led by Archbishop Robin Eames, who retired as All Ireland Primate at the end of the year.

At the end of January the government launched a fundamental review of spending for 2007-09 and a drastic cut in the number of quangos was announced in March, both measures intended to allow resources to be redirected to front-line services. In education, controversy continued over the retention of (selective) grammar schools and around the future of the integrated education sector. December saw the publication of a review carried out by Sir George Bain, whose radical recommendations for rationalisation of the school system and the possible closure of some schools were strongly criticised by the Catholic bishops. Substantial investment was announced for deprived loyalist areas of inner city Belfast and for the road network, and in October Chancellor of the Exchequer Gordon Brown outlined details of a £50 billion funding package that would follow the restoration of power-sharing. At the end of October work began on the demolition of the notorious Maze prison to make way for a proposed new sports stadium.

At the beginning of the year the Northern Ireland secretary, Peter Hain, tried to pressure the parties into resuming power-sharing negotiations by repeatedly referring to "public anger" at the payment of salaries to assembly members "for jobs they refuse to do". The year began inauspiciously when widespread opposition forced the government to drop legislation that would have allowed "on the run" paramilitaries to return to Northern Ireland and remain free under a special licence. Political progress was linked closely to the reports of the Independent Monitoring Commission (IMC), especially about IRA decommissioning (see AR 2005, pp. 32-33). The IMC indicated that the IRA was committed to the political path, but it voiced some reservations about continued intelligence gathering and the involvement of senior IRA figures in criminal activity. Its September report noted progress on security "normalisation", including the removal of the last British army watchtowers in south Armagh. In October the Queen attended a ceremony in Belfast to mark the disbandment in 2007 of the home service battalions of the Royal Irish Regiment (RIR). A £250 million redundancy package for RIR members, announced in March, was criticised by Sinn Féin but for unionists generous severance packages were considered essential to the restoration of confidence in the political process.

The qualified findings of the IMC reports dashed hopes of an early agreement on a return to devolution. At the DUP conference in February, Ian Paisley reiterated that he would not share power with Sinn Féin if the IRA remained "in business". Nevertheless the government saw a "sea change" in the IRA's behaviour and detected enough progress to allow the resumption of political talks in early February. However the process remained beset by a lack of trust, and throughout the year the DUP maintained its refusal to enter face-to-face talks with Sinn Féin until IRA criminality had ended. An attempt in February to instigate a "parallel rather than separate talks" scheme collapsed in acrimony with Sinn Féin accusing the UK government of rigging the process so that the DUP would not have to engage with it directly.

After a deadline was missed for agreement on legislation to allow policing to be devolved to the Assembly, UK Prime Minister Tony Blair and his Irish counterpart Taoiseach Bertie Ahern unveiled an 11-paragraph British-Irish plan at Navan Fort, in County Armagh, on 6 April, overshadowed by the murder two days earlier of Denis Donaldson, the ex-Sinn Féin official at the centre of the 2002 spy-ring affair (see AR 2005, p. 33). The "take-it-or-leave-it" blueprint, dubbed "plan A", envisaged recalling the Assembly in May, but if it failed to elect a power-sharing executive by 24 November then the Assembly would be scrapped and "plan B" introduced, involving enhanced north-south co-operation. In April former Alliance party deputy leader Eileen Bell was named as presiding officer for the Assembly, and the "immovable" November deadline was enshrined in legislation passed through Parliament in May.

On 22 May, Ian Paisley refused to accept nomination by Sinn Féin as first minister and the Assembly adjourned after just 12 minutes. As a result Hain set up a preparation for government committee, composed of delegates from the main parties. After its first meeting ended in failure when it could not agree on a chairperson, Hain appointed two senior figures, from the DUP and Sinn Féin, to chair the committee. However little progress was made, so in October the governments convened three days of talks in Scotland. The St Andrews agreement unveiled by Blair and Ahern set out another sequence of moves and deadlines that would lead to the restoration of devolution by 26 March 2007. Under the deal—described as amendments to the 1998 Belfast agreement—the parties had to confirm acceptance of the timetable by 10 November. Following the passage of Westminster legislation to give effect to the agreement, the Assembly was to nominate a DUP first minister and a Sinn Féin deputy first minister on 24 November. Although all parties agreed to proceed on the basis of the St Andrews agreement, a lack of trust continued to dog the process. A scheduled meeting between the DUP and Sinn Féin on 21 October was postponed after the DUP insisted that the proposed first and deputy first ministers should take an oath upon their nomination in support of the police. However Hain confirmed that Sinn Féin would not have formally to declare support for policing until it assumed its ministerial posts in 2007.

As the Assembly met on 24 November, proceedings were wrecked when notorious loyalist Michael Stone tried to storm the building. The following day his early release from prison under the Belfast agreement was suspended and he was formally charged with attempted murder and possession of explosives. Before the disruption Sinn Féin had nominated Martin McGuinness as deputy first minister, but the DUP refused to nominate a first minister. However the speaker deemed that Paisley had satisfied the criteria for nomination; and in a subsequent statement Paisley clarified that he would be willing to become first minister in a power-sharing executive, provided that Sinn Féin met certain conditions.

Attention for the rest of the year focused on how to break the deadlock over policing, with the formation of a small sub-group of the preparation for government committee. The difficulties centred on how to balance Sinn Féin's endorsement of the police with a commitment by the DUP that it would enter a power-sharing executive and agree to the devolution of powers over policing and justice. This severely tested the party management skills of the respective leaderships. Internal tensions became evident within the DUP, with MEP Jim Allister signalling his "grave difficulties" with the St Andrews deal and others continuing to oppose power-sharing with Sinn Féin. In December MP William McCrea insisted that the timetable for devolution was unrealistic because it would not allow "a credible testing time of the so-called republican conversion to democracy".

At Sinn Féin's annual conference (Ard Fheis) in February a resolution that opposed joining the policing board until "a timetable for British withdrawal" had been set was defeated. The leadership stressed that support for policing would have to involve the transfer of powers to the Assembly and all-Ireland institutions. Accordingly it refused to make nominations for its two seats on the reconstituted policing board appointed by Hain in March. Difficulties were compounded by the announcement that the UK's security agency, MI5, would be given responsibility for national security throughout the UK.

On 19 October a meeting of Sinn Féin's national executive agreed to launch a wide consultation on the St Andrews agreement. In late December party leader Gerry Adams embarked on a crucial series of moves designed to pave the way for the policy shift, following "considerable progress" in a series of negotiations with the UK government, including discussions on the future role of MI5. On 29 December a meeting of Sinn Féin's national executive decisively backed a motion to convene a special Ard Fheis on policing. Tensions within the wider republican family were evident, highlighted when senior Sinn Féin leaders revealed that they had received threats from dissident republicans. However, the year ended with a renewed crisis in the political process when Paisley tempered his welcome for the moves on policing with the caveat that he would await further developments to see whether there had been "delivery in both word and deed", and Sinn Féin responded by complaining about the failure of the DUP to respond positively to its initiative.

REPUBLIC OF IRELAND—GERMANY—FRANCE—ITALY—BELGIUM—THE NETHERLANDS—LUXEMBOURG

REPUBLIC OF IRELAND

CAPITAL: Dublin AREA: 70,000 sq km POPULATION: 4,151,000
OFFICIAL LANGUAGES: Irish & English POLITICAL SYSTEM: multiparty republic
HEAD OF STATE: President Mary McAleese (since Nov '97)
RULING PARTIES: coalition of Fianna Fáil (FF) & Progressive Democrats (PD)
HEAD OF GOVERNMENT: Bertie Ahern (FF), Prime Minister/Taoiseach (since June '97)
MAIN IGO MEMBERSHIPS (NON-UN): EU, OSCE, CE, OECD, PFP
CURRENCY: euro (end-'06 £1=€1.47970, US$1=€0.75780)
GNI PER CAPITA: US$40,150, US$34,720 at PPP ('05)

THE political atmosphere grew increasingly frenetic as the parties geared up for the general election due in spring 2007. The Labour party continued negotiations with Fine Gael on a joint manifesto and reshuffled its front bench in April, giving ex-leader Ruairi Quinn a more prominent role. In September Michael McDowell took over the leadership of the Progressive Democrats following the resignation of Mary Harney, who continued as minister for health while McDowell took over as tanaiste (deputy prime minister). In a cabinet reshuffle in February Fianna Fáil's Mary Wallace joined the government as minister in the agriculture department; Pat "the Cope" Gallagher moved to transport, and John Browne switched from agriculture to the department of communications, marine and natural resources. In December, Seán Haughey was appointed minister of state for education following the resignation of Síle de Valera.

At the beginning of the year the governing coalition and the Fine Gael/Labour alternative were neck-and-neck in the opinion polls, but by May the opposition led by nine percentage points. However, support for the governing parties increased substantially in the autumn and they ended the year well ahead, with a poll in November putting the combined support for the government at 43 per cent, with 35 per cent for Fine Gael/Labour. Fianna Fáil was boosted in April by the first military commemoration of the 1916 rising for 35 years, although the pluralist character of modern Ireland was highlighted when the taoiseach, Bertie Ahern, and the president attended ceremonies to mark the 90th anniversary of the battle of the Somme on 1 July.

In September a political storm erupted after Ahern confirmed a press report that he had accepted payments from businessmen in the early 1990s, which he described as "loans" made to cover the costs of his divorce settlement. In an effort to defuse the crisis he repaid more than €90,000 (including "interest") and in October he apologised to the Dáil and the Irish people for a "misjudgement" that he now regretted. The affair created tensions between the coalition partners, but opinion polls indicated that while most people thought that Ahern had been wrong to accept the money, only one-third considered the issue a resignation matter; moreover there was an increase in his personal approval ratings and in support for the government generally.

Socio-economic issues dominated the policy agenda and the government worked closely with the UK to restore devolution in Northern Ireland (see p. 34). Tensions remained over allegations of collusion, and in June Ahern strongly criticised the British government for failing to set up a full public inquiry into the 1989 murder of Belfast solicitor Pat Finucane. In February, a planned "love Ulster" march by loyalists in Dublin failed to materialise when republican protesters clashed with gardaí (police), prompting criticism from across the political spectrum of the attempt to "discredit democratic protest".

After five months of negotiations, a new partnership agreement, "toward 2016", was concluded between the state and the "social partners" (employers, trade unions, the agri-food industry, and the community sector). GDP growth of 5 per cent and buoyant public finances allowed an increase of €4 billion in planned expenditure for 2007, focused on the established priorities of health, education, justice, social welfare, and crime-fighting. Tax changes in the December budget included a 1 per cent reduction in the top rate of income tax and a doubling of mortgage interest relief for first-time house buyers.

Mandatory minimum sentences for gun offences and the introduction of a firearms amnesty were announced in March, followed in December by further measures to tackle organised crime, including the strengthening of the police force and the newly created Garda Reserve. In May emergency legislation had to be rushed through the Dáil after the Supreme Court sparked a political crisis by overturning the 1935 law on statutory rape.

The government continued to press the UK to close the Sellafield nuclear site despite an adverse ruling over its campaign by the European Court of Justice. In the face of violent local opposition the government maintained support for the construction by Shell of the Corrib gas pipeline (see AR 2005, p. 34). Several government-sponsored enquiries focused on topics such as child abuse in the Dublin archdiocese, the retention of children's organs by hospitals, and the investigation into the Dublin and Monaghan bombings of 1974. The most sensational revelation came at the end of the year when the report of the Moriarty tribunal severely criticised former Taoiseach Charles Haughey for misappropriating funds and accepting payments from businessmen during his political career. Such payments had allowed Haughey, who had been given a state funeral in June following his death at the age of 80 (for obituary see p. 581), to live a life "vastly beyond the scale of what he earned as a public representative".

GERMANY

CAPITAL: Berlin AREA: 357,000 sq km POPULATION: 82,485,000
OFFICIAL LANGUAGE: German POLITICAL SYSTEM: multiparty republic
HEAD OF STATE: President Horst Köhler (since July '04)
RULING PARTIES: "grand coalition" between Christian Democratic Union/Christian Social Union (CDU/CSU) and Social Democratic Party (SPD)
HEAD OF GOVERNMENT: Angela Merkel (CDU), Chancellor (since Oct '05)
MAIN IGO MEMBERSHIPS (NON-UN): NATO, EU, OSCE, CE, CBSS, AC, OECD, G-8
CURRENCY: euro (end-'06 £1=€1.47970, US$1=€0.75780)
GNI PER CAPITA: US$34,580, US$29,210 at PPP ('05)

For once, politics and economics did not dominate German life throughout 2006: a sporting event did. Germany hosted the football World Cup for the first time as a unified country and, for a month through June and July, the world's gaze turned on the Federal Republic to watch the "beautiful game's" best artisans battle it out up and down the land.

To the surprise of many Germans, the world very much liked the look of what it saw. The DFB (German Football Association) not only organised a wonderful sporting occasion, but they also instituted a public relations exercise for their country of which any marketing agency would have been exceptionally proud (see p. 512). The German team played attractive football, losing heroically to Italy in the semi-final, and worries about hooliganism by a minority of so-called supporters came to nothing. "Citizens of the world" really were, as the tournament slogan claimed, "welcome as guests at their friend's place!" Germans themselves—much to the surprise of many media commentators— also enjoyed supporting their team. A genuine feel-good factor swept through the country during the balmy summer months, and a newly discovered sense of non-confrontational patriotism oozed through the nation. Even Chancellor Angela Merkel appeared to be gripped by football fever, leaping out of her seat in Borussia Dortmund's Westfalenstadion as Oliver Neuville scored a last minute winner in a nail-biting encounter with neighbouring Poland.

These positive feelings of pride did much to make life for Merkel's "grand coalition" of Christian Democrats (CDU) and Social Democrats (SPD) more straightforward than it perhaps might have been. Merkel had taken office in late 2005 claiming that her government would continue reforming Germany's welfare state and revitalising the still stuttering economy. The resignation in March of Matthias Platzeck as leader of the SPD—the junior partner in Merkel's grand coalition—due to ill health did little to change the balance of power within the national government. His replacement, Kurt Beck, remained outside government (just as Platzeck had been), and he continued critically to support Merkel in her attempt to reform and renew some of the key pillars of Germany's institutional framework—namely, the relationship between the Bundestag and the Bundesrat (the lower and upper chambers of the national legislature), and the division of competencies between the national and regional levels in Germany's federal system—as well as some of the most costly parts of the welfare state.

Yet even though the public appeared to be more interested in football than politics, Merkel's government ended 2006 as unpopular as the administration of

Gerhard Schröder which had preceded it. Both Merkel's CDU and Beck's SPD struggled to register 30 per cent in opinion polls, and although Merkel's personal popularity remained reasonably high there was little evidence that Germans had any faith in her government actually to implement its reforming agenda. Germany's traditionally downbeat media also appeared less than satisfied with the fruits of Merkel's first full year in office. This was perhaps even more surprising when one considered that economic growth in 2006 was a thoroughly respectable 2.7 per cent (the highest it had been since 2000); 700,000 fewer people were registered unemployed (9.8 per cent of the population); and Germans seemed more enthusiastic about the future than they had been for many years. Indeed, economic growth in 2006 was built on much increased domestic demand rather than on exports (which only contributed 0.7 of a percentage point). German consumers had enough confidence to spend a little of their savings and the corresponding boost to the economic recovery was not insignificant. Net borrowing was also down, enabling Germany—for the first time since 2001—to meet the Maastricht Treaty's criterion of a maximum budget deficit of 3 per cent of GDP.

A drop in Merkel's popularity was, of course, always likely; at the end of 2005 she was very much in her honeymoon period in office, talking eloquently about what her government would do and generally calming everyone down after the dramatic last few months of Gerhard Schröder's premiership. When she attempted to shape policy herself, critical voices were almost certain to emerge, and emerge they did. Merkel's promise that she would "under-promise and over-deliver" did not seem to be worth much when her two most expansive reform projects for the year were unveiled: health and federalism. Policy differences soon appeared between the CDU and the SPD, and also between national and regional politicians within both parties (but particularly the Christian Democrats), and much of Merkel's reform agenda was watered down by bickering politicians.

Merkel's trumpeted healthcare reform was the best example of this. The reform was supposed to rein in spiralling costs by encouraging more competition within the system as well as introducing a national health fund. Debates about the practical viability of such a fund were soon overtaken by party political discussions, as it became clear that the concept only existed as a bridge between the widely differing expectations of the two coalition partners: the Social Democrats insisted that contributions to the fund be linked in some way to individual earnings; the Christian Democrats preferred a flat rate contribution. The compromise that both parties eked out tried to do both things, linking contributions to income levels and including the option of a flat rate charge on top of this. Germany's richer states—Bavaria, Baden-Wüurttemberg, and Hesse—also balked at the thought of their contributions rising steeply, and their (Christian Democrat) minister presidents all became increasingly vocal in their criticisms of the compromise. Given not just the controversy of the proposed new arrangements but also the complexity of the model itself, the grand coalition opted officially to reach agreement on the key points of the reform but also to postpone its implementation until January 2009. This, clearly, was to be an argument for another day.

Other reforms, however, were more successful. The retirement age was raised to 67, and concerted efforts were made to cut subsidies in order to tackle Germany's budget deficit. A somewhat controversial anti-discrimination reform was passed, and a number of new benefits for working parents were introduced.

The first part of the government's federalism reform was completed, even if the more prickly second part—centred on the much more controversial financial aspect of Germany's new federal framework—was to be finalised only in 2007. The reform was certainly wide-ranging, involving more than 20 changes to the federal constitution. It had also been a long time coming (discussions about such a reform started more than four years previously) and the speed and ease with which a number of national and regional politicians agreed the final reform package was in itself remarkable. The upper house of parliament, the Bundesrat, representing Germany's 16 federal states (Länder), would lose the right of veto on approximately 60 per cent of all legislation (the figure was likely to drop to between 30 and 40 per cent, depending on how the new law actually functioned in practice) theoretically making it easier for federal governments to implement their policy programmes. In return for these major concessions by the German states, the central government in Berlin was forced to relinquish powers in sectors such as education, the prison system, shopping and restaurant laws, and the civil service. The most controversial of these was certainly education, an area where the federal government would find it exceptionally difficult to influence any policy outcomes in future.

One of the more surprising discussions about federal/regional competencies came towards the end of 2006 as politicians tried to emulate countries such as Ireland, Italy, and the UK by pushing through a national ban on smoking in public places. This relatively uncontroversial measure had to be shelved when it ran up against some unexpected constitutional barriers. More specifically, the federal government overlooked the fact that it did not have the constitutional right to implement a ban in places such as restaurants, bars, and night clubs. Restaurant law, the government only belatedly realised, was a regional policy competence, not a national one. Despite claims by some in the medical profession that the powerful tobacco lobby was also influencing the government's attitude, it was nevertheless clear that the complicated nature of the federal system worried many politicians and that there might indeed be other—as yet undiscovered—reasons why a national law might fall under any prospective constitutional challenge. Reluctantly, the main substance of the proposals was dropped altogether in late 2006, as the coalition agreed to ban smoking in federal government buildings, at train stations, and in trains themselves. This compromise did not stop the media from almost unanimously criticising the weakness of Merkel's government. Regional politicians were also in the firing line as it became clear that their willingness to defend their own right to act was much more important to them than agreeing a common line and acting independently in their regions to achieve it. It was possible, however, that 2007 would see the regions implement a much more wide-ranging law (that would include all public buildings) than the federal government felt able to propose, even if the bans were likely to remain regionally nuanced.

In terms of foreign policy, 2006 saw Merkel row back from the more confrontational stances taken by Gerhard Schröder's regime and look to take more responsibility in international peacekeeping missions. Strong misgivings in the media and by members of the parliamentary opposition could not prevent 780 German troops from being sent to the Democratic Republic of Congo (DRC) as the backbone of a 2,000-strong EU peacekeeping mission to ensure stability during the DRC's elections (see pp. 259-60). Afghanistan, and the role of German troops there, also caused much public head scratching before, in September 2006, the federal parliament opted to extend Germany's mission until October 2007.

Increasing public disquiet with the performance of the federal government was not apparent in elections in 2006; although five out of 16 German states had elections to their regional parliaments, there were no federal polls (federal elections or elections to the European Parliament in Brussels). Moreover, three of the state elections took place in March 2006 when Merkel was still enjoying her honeymoon period, and the two polls in September were in sparsely populated Mecklenburg-Western Pomerania and the small state of Berlin; Merkel's CDU was in opposition in both. Local factors also played a not inconsiderable role in the campaigns, ensuring that the unpopularity of the two parties in national government did not figure as large as it might otherwise have done.

The Christian Democrats had been in political disarray in Berlin for a number of years and they were given little hope of ousting the governing coalition of SPD and Left Party (Linkspartei, LP). The LP was the main loser of this particular election as its share of the vote fell from 22.6 to 13.4 per cent. Despite this, the strong performance of the SPD under the charismatic leadership of Klaus Wowereit enabled the red-red coalition to carry on much as it had done before. The results of the poll in Mecklenburg-Western Pomerania saw the CDU perform worse than in 2002, but the 10 percentage point drop for the SPD left the Social Democrats with a coalition conundrum. If they opted to carry on governing with the Left Party as they had been doing since 1998, their parliamentary majority would have been a wafer thin single vote. A "grand coalition" with the CDU, on the other hand, would give them a clear working majority of seven seats. They opted for the latter course. The main talking point in Mecklenburg-Western Pomerania was, however, the entry of the far-right National Democrats into the regional parliament for the first time, polling 7.3 per cent of the vote and sending six deputies to sit in the state parliament.

Although Merkel's grand coalition attempted to implement a number of much needed reforms during 2006, the year was clearly dominated not by politics but by the preparations for, execution of, and positive feedback from the football World Cup. Germany's steady economic progress also helped to depoliticise a considerable portion of the year, mainly as Germans began to feel a little more relaxed about themselves and their future. Only in the autumn and winter of 2006 did the normality of everyday life return. The year to come, with Germany's presidencies of the EU and G-8 due in 2007 and the federal government's attempts to continue reforming Germany's institutions might, however, be decidedly different.

FRANCE

CAPITAL: Paris AREA: 552,000 sq km POPULATION: 60,743,000
OFFICIAL LANGUAGE: French POLITICAL SYSTEM: multiparty republic
HEAD OF STATE: President Jacques Chirac (UMP), since May '95
RULING PARTY: Union for a Popular Movement (UMP) (since Nov '02)
PRIME MINISTER: Dominique de Villepin (since June '05)
MAIN IGO MEMBERSHIPS (NON-UN): NATO, EU, OSCE, CE, OECD, G-8, PC, Francophonie
CURRENCY: euro (end-'06 £1=€1.47970, US$1=€0.75780)
GNI PER CAPITA: US$34,810 (incl DOMs), US$30,540 at PPP ('05)

FOR 2006, President Jacques Chirac promised stabilisation of the public finances, a new generation of nuclear power stations, complete electrification of the rail network, a European Internet search engine to challenge Google, aid to small businesses, legal reforms, and advances in European integration. This was a strikingly ambitious agenda from a man whose term had 16 months to run. Progress was inevitably partial and uneven. All the while, the approach of the 2007 presidential election was rarely far from the minds of politicians and commentators, who scrutinised every turn of events for their electoral implications. How closely this engaged the wider public was another matter.

After protracted internal debates a poll of Socialist party members in November produced a sweeping victory for Ségolène Royal. The little known president of the Poitu-Charentes regional council, she challenged far more experienced male contenders, promising a "new politics" involving listening to the people. Exactly what that implied in policy terms remained unclear, not least because the unity of the left was fragile. However, she would be the first female candidate for the presidency with a realistic chance of victory. On the right the struggle was even more bitter. Chirac did not rule out a third term, although his age—74—and events worked against him. Such support as he initially had waned to vanishing point during the year. The remaining contenders were the prime minister, Dominique de Villepin, and the minister of the interior, Nicolas Sarkozy. Their increasingly venomous rivalry coloured the conduct and outcome of almost every important issue.

In France wise politicians have always needed to have an eye not only on the electoral calendar but also on "the street", which has so often been the graveyard of reform. Yet in February, with little or no consultation, the prime minister launched a controversial first employment contract. Aimed at reducing high youth unemployment, it would allow employers to dismiss workers under 26 at will at any time during their first two years. However, what de Villepin saw as an incentive to employers was viewed elsewhere as subverting "the French model", with its cherished tradition of job security. Widespread student protests followed. Many universities were occupied, demonstrations spread to every large town. National one-day strikes ensued, with the initial specific objections swelling into a wider demonstration of popular disaffection with the political elite. De Villepin stood his ground, offering only minor concessions. Eventually, in an unprecedented intervention, Chirac ruled that the Law on Equality of Opportunities, though approved by Parliament and cleared by the Constitutional Council, must not be implemented before a new bill was carried reducing the period to one year and requiring employers to give reasons for dismissals. This was not only a humiliation for de Villepin but also put paid to any hope of other reforms until after the election.

De Villepin's commitment to "economic nationalism" in the face of globalisation faced several challenges. A threat to block Mittal Steel's takeover bid for Arcelor SA—which had important steel-making plants in France—failed after a four-month struggle. When the Italian energy company ENEL was preparing to bid for Gaz de France (GDF), the government swiftly intervened to safeguard French independence in terms of energy by brokering a merger between GDF and the Franco-Belgian energy group, Suez. However, the terms were disputed, the unions were alarmed about jobs and consumers about prices, while the European Commission had concerns about competition. Also, the deal would reduce the state's share in GDF from 80 per cent to 34 per cent in contravention of its pledge not to privatise. The cabinet was divided and it took several months to secure sufficient backing from government supporters in the National Assembly (the lower chamber of the bicameral Parliament). Then, a successful legal rearguard action by the unions delayed a final decision into 2007, with the risk that the issue might collapse or become caught up in the presidential election. All the while, France was at odds with Germany over the leadership of the troubled Airbus project's parent company, EADS, with ministers pressing for a greater French role in ownership and management, effectively overturning the original 1999 agreement between the two countries. Finally, in December, criticising the European Central Bank, de Villepin called for a return to "national sovereignty" over interest rates.

Meanwhile, the economy was happier than for several years. Initially it grew rapidly, though it flagged in the third quarter, ensuring that the year's 2.6 per cent target would not be met. Unemployment fell as promised, from 9.7 to 8.6 per cent, responding to government subsidised job-creation schemes and demographic factors. Inflation, at 1.5 per cent, was below the EU average. In his 2007 budget Finance Minister Thierry Breton envisaged reducing the national debt from 66.6 per cent of GDP to 63.6 per cent, reducing state expenditure and stabilising the budget deficit at 2.5 per cent of GDP. Some €3.8 billion would be cut from income tax; taxes on small business would also be reduced, and the development aid budget raised to 0.5 per cent of GDP. For all this, awareness of the need for change coupled with the seeming impossibility of achieving it nurtured a sentiment of "déclinisme", one of those moods of gloomy introspection to which France was periodically prone.

No year would be complete without political scandals. In July a total of 38 people received modest sentences in an affair centred on the Paris city hall during the period when Chirac was mayor. Later, eight politicians and officials were convicted of putting phantom voters on the electoral register in 1989, again while Chirac was mayor. (As president, Chirac was immune from investigation but could, conceivably, face investigation after leaving office.) However, what set the chattering classes really alight was a freshly discovered scandal, the Clearstream affair, which broke in April. It arose from an anonymous letter falsely listing Sarkozy, among others, as holding secret accounts with the Clearstream bank in Luxembourg, possibly fed by kickbacks from the sale of frigates to Taiwan. For

Sarkozy, this was a smear by de Villepin or his allies. (Whether Chirac, who detested Sarkozy, was also deeply involved, remained unclear.) De Villepin initially denied ordering a senior intelligence officer to investigate the affair, but later had to admit that he had done so. One of the alleged originators of the list, who was an old friend of the prime minister, was forced to resign as a vice-president of EADS. As the year ended, de Villepin was questioned for 17 hours by examining magistrates over his role in the affair. He declared himself "the victim of slanders and lies". As with almost any classic French political scandal the truth remained elusive. There was no doubt, though, that the affair had further envenomed the relationship between Sarkozy and de Villepin, whose hopes of becoming the presidential candidate of the right had vanished. On the very day that he was questioned, Sarkozy had effectively been chosen as candidate at a party congress in Bordeaux. The year ended with Sarkozy and Royal neck and neck in the polls and 30 or so others also hoping to stand, including the formidable veteran Jean-Marie Le Pen on the far right.

Immigration and law and order remained highly contentious. Sarkozy took a hard line on both, allegedly in a bid to attract former Le Pen voters. He introduced "selective immigration", discriminating in favour of workers with skills identified as important to France, making it more difficult for family members to join them, and requiring them to sign an "integration contract" committing them to respect "the French way of life". They would not now automatically be eligible for permanent residence by living in France for 10 years. Meanwhile, Sarkozy pressed ahead with the expulsion of undocumented immigrants, with some 25,000 deported during the year. However, opposition from teachers, parents, and humanitarian organisations forced him to agree that most families with children in school would be spared. Meanwhile, the first anniversary of the 2005 November riots (see AR 2005, pp. 41-42) passed with fewer disturbances than had been feared. Even so, in December, the Assembly adopted a bill supported by Sarkozy toughening punishments on young offenders. Many of the problems of the deprived suburban estates had as yet to be otherwise addressed.

Not all developments were so contentious. There was legislation on equal opportunities, including tackling age discrimination in employment, proposals to develop renewable energy, a new law on takeover bids, a programme for social housing, and measures to counteract avian influenza. From February 2007 (2008 for cafes and restaurants) smoking would be banned in public places. And, in June, a long cherished dream of Chirac's was realised with the opening of the musée du Quai Branly, dedicated to non-Western art from Oceania, Asia, Africa, and the Americas.

Few new proposals fleshed out Chirac's vision of "a more democratic, more stable and more effective" EU. Hopes of reviving the Franco-German "motor" bore little fruit, while an attempt to abolish the national veto over cross-border policing and judicial co-operation over crime and terrorism failed. There was no sign of change in the public mood that brought rejection of the proposed EU constitution in 2005 (see AR 2005, pp. 368-69). Opposition to Turkish membership of the EU hardened and this (plus awareness that a large Armenian diaspora had votes) underlay the Assembly's vote in October, by 106 to 19 with many abstentions, to criminalise denial of the Armenian massacres in the Ottoman empire in 1915 (see p. 76). An angry Turkish response forced Chirac to express regrets. In February, a damning report by the Council of Europe's human rights commissioner criticised the French legal system, detention conditions, treatment of members of ethnic minorities, and failures to tackle abuses by the police.

It emerged in February that the French nuclear strike force had been modified to increase its range and accuracy; Chirac declared that France would be prepared to use her nuclear weapons against any new threat or state-sponsored terrorist attack. Earlier, agreement was reached with the UK to share the cost of constructing new aircraft carriers. However, an attempt to have the old aircraft carrier, Clemenceau, dismantled in India turned into a fiasco. India refused to accept the ship and it had to be towed back from the Indian Ocean to lie rusting in harbour at Brest.

When Israel invaded Lebanon in July, France challenged the US and British line by speedily demanding action to stop the fighting (see pp. 197-203). After offering a mere 200 troops to the expanded UN Interim Force in Lebanon (UNIFIL), mindful of heavy French losses during a previous role there (see AR 1983, p. 131), Chirac eventually committed 2,000 troops. By now, military resources were becoming stretched, with this new commitment added to those in the Balkans, Afghanistan, and Africa. France joined the international condemnation of Iran's nuclear ambitions but again broke ranks with the USA and its allies by opposing sanctions. In May, a new agency, Cultures France, was created to enhance French cultural influence abroad, and in December a new 24-hour television news channel, France 24, was launched to achieve another longstanding dream of Chirac to convey distinctively French perceptions of the world.

ITALY

CAPITAL: Rome AREA: 301,000 sq km POPULATION: 57,471,000
OFFICIAL LANGUAGE: Italian POLITICAL SYSTEM: multiparty republic
HEAD OF STATE: President Giorgio Napolitano (since May '06)
RULING PARTIES: the Union alliance, comprising Democrats of the Left (DS), La Margherita alliance, and others including Communists and Greens
HEAD OF GOVERNMENT: Romano Prodi (the Union), Prime Minister (since May '06)
MAIN IGO MEMBERSHIPS (NON-UN): NATO, EU, OSCE, CE, CEI, OECD, G-8
CURRENCY: euro (end-'06 £1=€1.47970, US$1=€0.75780)
GNI PER CAPITA: US$30,010, US$28,840 at PPP ('05)

THE winter of 2005-06 was dominated by the election campaign which led to the narrowest of defeats for Prime Minister Silvio Berlusconi in the 9-10 April vote and the return to government of Romano Prodi and his left-wing alliance, now known as the Union. In June, a referendum saw Italians reject, by 62 to 38 per cent, a major constitutional reform which had been pushed through Parliament by the former government. The election led to changed emphases in both domestic and international affairs, the latter seeing an end to Italy's apparently unconditional support for the USA and a preference for action in accord with the UN and the European Union. By early December, Italy had ended its military presence in Iraq whilst the government's left wing was urging withdrawal also from Afghanistan in favour of the expanded UN commitment in Lebanon, UNIFIL, which Italy had strongly promoted. Over the summer, meanwhile, public attention had turned to sport, with the football World Cup ending in victory for Italy, notwithstanding that a series of major football scandals had suggested that widespread match-fixing might have undermined the ability of Italian footballers actually to play well.

The election was preceded by electoral reform in December 2005, pushed through Parliament against the protests of the opposition, as had been the constitutional reform (see AR 2005, p. 44). In the event, the reform backfired. Thus, despite gaining a slightly larger share of the national vote in the Senate (the upper house), the government won fewer seats, partly because the left unexpectedly won four of the six new overseas constituencies; whilst in the Chamber of Deputies (the lower house), the opposition's extraordinarily narrow victory (less than 25,000 out of some 40 million votes cast) was translated into 54 per cent of the seats (340 of 630) thanks to the majority bonus system designed to secure effective government.

The campaign was rancorous, punctuated by two ministerial resignations and, in the wake of the result, Prime Minister Berlusconi did not hesitate to dispute the outcome, alleging widespread electoral fraud. In December, both houses of the new Parliament decided to conduct major partial vote recounts, apparently spurred into action by a film which, ironically, alleged vote fraud by the previous government, rather than the then opposition. In sum, the political climate continued routinely to be described as "poisonous", or similar. The new President of the Republic, Giorgio Napolitano, like his predecessor, urged both government and opposition to seek reciprocal legitimation, but his words appeared to fall on deaf ears. Indeed, Napolitano himself, a distinguished former Communist who had been elected as one of the first actions of the new Parliament, gained his appointment by the vote of the new majority, ending the recent practice of bipartisan election to that office.

The new government comprised nine parties including, on the one hand, two communist parties and a Green party which, together, constituted a rather traditional (or "radical") socialist bloc and, on the other, some rather conservative centrist forces, so that the coalition promised to be difficult to manage. This was especially true in the Senate where the government had a majority of just two (158 to 156) elected senators, plus the support, for opportunist reasons, of a Latin American independent. The narrowness of this majority meant that the vote of the seven life senators would be decisive on several occasions. Given the government's weakness in Parliament and the pressing need for structural reform of the public administration as well as of major socio-economic institutions (most notably, public pensions), the opposition hoped that an early government crisis would lead to the formation of a government of national unity. This did not happen either immediately or over the passage of the budget in the autumn.

Prodi appointed an international financial technocrat, Tommaso Padoa-Schioppa, as his economics minister and "TPS", as he became known, stated his priority to be fiscal discipline, implicitly criticising the previous government which had allowed the country's national debt—the third largest in the world, after Japan and Greece—to rise for the first time in 11 years, in 2005, to 108 per cent. The principal means for achieving this in the first instance were measures against tax evasion, and in fact tax incomes for 2006 were far higher than predicted. This, together with the relatively positive state of the world economy, meant that the new government benefited from more favourable economic circumstances in its "honeymoon period" than had its predecessor in 2001. This did not mean that it would be able to do more than briefly postpone the structural reforms urged on it by the IMF and other bodies, not least the international ratings agencies, so that the continued survival of the government through 2007 was far from certain, particularly given the explicit opposition of the left-wing parties and the major trade union confederation, the CGIL (General Confederation of Italian Workers), to cuts in workers' pensions.

In the international sphere, one major issue for government cohesion—the deployment in Iraq—had been resolved by the former government itself pledging to withdraw Italian troops before the year was out; but Italy's role in Afghanistan continued to be a point of friction within the government. To some extent it was the credibility of the new foreign minister and former prime minister (1998-2000), Massimo D'Alema, with both the left and the USA, that prevented foreign policy becoming a destabilising factor for the government. At a more structural level what mattered was the narrowness of the majority and the left's determination not to repeat the disaster of 1998 when it had brought down Prodi's first government to the ultimate advantage, in the 2001 election, of the right.

Other international embarrassments nevertheless existed, not least with the USA. Thus in June, Rome public prosecutors requested that New York State national guardsman, Mario Lozano, be charged with the murder of the Italian military intelligence officer, Nicola Calipari, in Baghdad (see AR 2005, pp. 46; 191); and in July, Milan public prosecutors sought the extradition of 26 alleged CIA agents, charged with the "extraordinary rendition", or abduction, of the Egyptian imam, Abu Omar, from Milan in 2003 (see AR 2005, p. 46). In fact, several Italian officials were also accused of involvement in the kidnapping including, eventually, Nicolo Pollari, the head of SISMI (military intelligence). In November, Pollari, together with the head of the civilian intelligence agency (SISDE) and the head of CESIS, the intelligence co-ordinating body, were all replaced. The move came as the government exerted its authority in the wake, also, of revelations about an illegal domestic espionage operation—carried out from within Telecom Italia and apparently linked to SISMI—and the existence of a semi-independent unit within SISMI which, under the Berlusconi government, had targeted the then opposition, disseminating disinformation and apparently even hypothesising the use of violence against some of its leading figures.

The government's initial popularity, boosted by early liberalisation measures in favour of consumers which targeted professional monopolies such as pharmacists, lawyers, and taxi companies rapidly fell away in the autumn. Its ratings were undermined in particular by a mass pardon (backed by the opposition's Forza Italia and the Christian Democrat UDC) that released more than 20,000 convicted prisoners in an effort to end the humanitarian crisis caused by prison overcrowding.

Other notable early government measures related to the Berlusconi government's massive infrastructure programme and judicial reform. Major transport projects, not least the Messina Strait bridge, were scrapped, largely because of a lack of funding but also because of environmentalist opposition. Environmental concerns became a major issue in the north-west of Italy and risked delaying, at least, the construction of the Lyon-Turin stretch of the pan-European high-speed rail route from Lisbon to Kiev. The controversial judicial reform, named after the former justice minister, Roberto Castelli, envisaged major revisions to the Italian magistracy, and especially sought to reinforce the separation of personnel between its prosecution and judicial functions. Many saw it as an attempt to emasculate the judiciary, substantially undermining its independence of Parliament and government. The new justice minister, Clemente Mastella, revised several aspects of the regulation before it came into force, but failed to satisfy many critics of the legislation.

The opposition, as well as the government, was internally divided and Berlusconi remained a controversial figure. Renewed charges were brought against him, of tax fraud and illegal share dealing with regard to Telecinco, Spain's leading television channel, and of bribery with regard to the tax consultant, David Mills, husband of UK cabinet minister Tessa Jowell (see p. 12). Meanwhile, in May his close friend and colleague, Cesare Previti, was given a definitive six-year sentence by the Court of Cassation for the IMI-SIR case (bribing judges to give the Mondadori publishing house to Berlusconi); albeit in November the same court annulled Previti's conviction in the SME case (bribing judges to influence the sale of the food processing giant of that name) on the grounds of territorial incompetence.

The UDC, now released from the coalition constraint, moved increasingly to distance itself from Berlusconi and the House of Freedom alliance, theorising the existence of two oppositions, one populist and one—itself—moderate. It thus chose not to participate in the large anti-tax, anti-government demonstration held in Rome on 2 December. The success of that demonstration encouraged Berlusconi and the leader of the National Alliance, Gianfranco Fini, to speed up preparations for the much-discussed merger of their parties, creating a Freedom Party, in all likelihood to be federated with the Northern League. That party's leader, Umberto Bossi, however, remained keen to retain his strategic independence, even hypothesising collaboration with the government in order to achieve some of the objectives that had been denied him by the referendum defeat, such as greater independence for those regions—primarily Lombardy and the Veneto—with the means to benefit from it. Party merger was also on the agenda for the two main government parties, the quasi-Catholic Margherita and the Democrats of the Left (DS), which sought to reduce the fragmentation of the left and to reinforce the reformist or moderate component of the Union by forming a single Democratic party. Opposition to the merger was strong, however, as socialists and Catholics each sought to retain their distinct identities, so that no full merger was envisaged before the 2009 European elections.

Centrists in both camps opposed these attempts to reinforce the new bipolar structuring of Italian politics, and nearly everyone agreed that further electoral reform was needed to encourage the aggregation of homogenous blocs. Yet no one agreed who exactly comprised these, and few thought that the fragmented and deeply divided parliamentary forces would be able to agree on a new system, even under the pressure of the referendum movement which was seeking to mobilise public opinion, once again, against the existing electoral system.

BELGIUM, THE NETHERLANDS, AND LUXEMBOURG

Belgium

CAPITAL: Brussels AREA: 33,000 sq km POPULATION: 10,471,000
OFFICIAL LANGUAGES: French, Flemish & German POLITICAL SYSTEM: multiparty monarchy
HEAD OF STATE: King Albert II (since Aug '93)
RULING PARTIES: Flemish Liberals and Democrats (VLD), Socialist Party-Walloon (PS), the Reform Movement (MR), and Social Progressive Alternative Party (SPA)/Spirit Party
HEAD OF GOVERNMENT: Guy Verhofstadt (VLD), Prime Minister (since July '99)
MAIN IGO MEMBERSHIPS (NON-UN): NATO, EU, Benelux, OSCE, CE, OECD, Francophonie
CURRENCY: euro (end-'06 £1=€1.47970, US$1=€0.75780)
GNI PER CAPITA: US$35,700, US$32,640 at PPP ('05)

The Netherlands

CAPITAL: Amsterdam AREA: 41,000 sq km POPULATION: 16,329,000
OFFICIAL LANGUAGE: Dutch POLITICAL SYSTEM: multiparty monarchy
HEAD OF STATE: Queen Beatrix (since April '80)
RULING PARTIES: Christian Democratic Appeal (CDA) forms minority coalition with People's Party for Freedom and Democracy (VVD) (since July '06)
HEAD OF GOVERNMENT: Jan Pieter Balkenende (CDA), Prime Minister (since July '02)
MAIN IGO MEMBERSHIPS (NON-UN): NATO, EU, Benelux, OSCE, CE, OECD
CURRENCY: euro (end-'06 £1=€1.47970, US$1=€0.75780)
GNI PER CAPITA: US$36,620, US$32,480 at PPP ('05)

Luxembourg

CAPITAL: Luxembourg AREA: 3,000 sq km POPULATION: 457,000
OFFICIAL LANGUAGE: Letzeburgish POLITICAL SYSTEM: multiparty monarchy
HEAD OF STATE: Grand Duke Henri (since Oct '00)
RULING PARTIES: coalition of the Christian Social People's Party (CSV/PCS) and the Luxembourg Socialist Workers' Party (LSAP/POSL) (since July '04)
HEAD OF GOVERNMENT: Jean-Claude Juncker (CSV/PCS), Prime Minister (since Jan '95)
MAIN IGO MEMBERSHIPS (NON-UN): NATO, EU, Benelux, OSCE, CE, OECD, Francophonie
CURRENCY: euro (end-'06 £1=€1.47970, US$1=€0.75780)
GNI PER CAPITA: US$65,630, US$65,340 at PPP ('05)

ONE evening in December BELGIUM'S French language broadcaster, RTBF, broke into its programme on La Une (channel 1) with "breaking news" that Flanders (the Dutch-speaking north) had declared independence; Belgium as such had ceased to exist, the King and Queen had fled, and Flemish crowds were dancing in the streets. It was, of course, a hoax, but one that, however briefly, deceived many people. It did so because the tensions between Flanders and French-speaking Wallonia were so sustained and intense that a split no longer seemed incredible. Uproar followed: "in very poor taste", sniffed the prime minister's spokesman; "irresponsible" said ministers. Some people hoped that the programme might jolt people into a recognition of what they had in common. Only the separatists of the Vlaams Belang (VB) party approved.

Earlier incidents had already exacerbated relations between Flemings in the richer north and Walloons in the poorer south. In April, the minister-president of the Flemish region, Yves Leterme, declared Belgium an "accident of history", with "no intrinsic value"; Dutch and French speakers had nothing more in common than "the king, the national football team and certain brands of beer". In September, Merchtem, in Flanders, banned French in its schools. In municipal elections in October, when the coalition supporting the government of Guy Verhofstadt fared badly, the separatist (and anti-immigration) vote increased in many towns. The result in Antwerp was hailed with some relief because the Socialists outpolled VB, but even there the VB vote increased.

One event that did unite the country was the disappearance in June of two young girls in Liège; they were subsequently found murdered. This stirred painful memories of an earlier national trauma over the killings of another two girls, also in Liège, in 1996 and the subsequent lurid trial of the murderer for a total of six abductions and four murders (see AR 1996, p. 55; AR 2004, p. 50). Coincidentally, the government announced the introduction of electronic identity cards for all children under 12.

The economy had an improved year, with industrial production reviving, employment rising (though still well above the eurozone average), lower inflation, and higher real incomes. However, exports were disappointing and, late in the year, a four-week strike and sit-in failed to stop the car manufacturer Volkswagen from transferring production of the Golf model from its Forest plant to Germany, with the loss of some 2,000 jobs.

Since taking office in 2003, the coalition government of Jan Peter Balkenende in THE NETHERLANDS had been working to revitalise a stagnating economy, with tax cuts, curbs in social welfare programmes, and greater investment in education and training. It had been attacked by the opposition as making the poor pay for economic recovery, and polls regularly charted its unpopularity. Accordingly there was no great surprise when the municipal elections in March showed substantial opposition gains, particularly by the Labour party (PvdA) and the Socialists (SP), although local issues were also important in many seats. The elections were also noteworthy for the growing participation of Turkish immigrants, some 350 of whom were candidates. In Amsterdam, PvdA, which had been swept aside in 2002 by followers of the anti-immigrant campaigner Pim Fortuyn, now won the highest vote and more seats than they had held before 2002.

Immigration and security now seemed less salient than previously. Nevertheless, they could still be troublesome. In January the combative immigration and integration minister, Rita Verdonk, caused uproar by suggesting that Dutch should be the only language spoken in the streets. In May, a Somali-born MP for the People's Party for Freedom and Democracy (VVD), who had been under police protection after criticising the treatment of women within Islam (her own religion until 2002 when she became an atheist), was shown to have lied to obtain asylum. Ayaan Hirsi Ali resigned her seat and moved to the USA. Verdonk controversially threatened to remove Hirsi Ali's Dutch citizenship. Though Verdonk relented, the small Democrats 66 (D66) party withdrew from the government in protest, precipitating the latter's collapse, the creation of a caretaker administration, and a general election in November.

Despite Verdonk's proposal to ban the burka in public places, immigration was a secondary issue in the election campaign, although all the larger parties favoured a tougher line on immigration. It featured in the issue of the 26,000 asylum seekers who had been refused but who had continued to remain in the Netherlands for more than five years: should they be expelled, or amnestied and given residence permits? However, most attention focused on the economy, though environmental issues also drew attention. For the governing Christian Democratic Appeal (CDA), the government's reforms had been so successful that they needed not be pushed much further. The conservative liberal VVD wanted to press on, however, to make the economy more competitive. The opposition campaigned for the reversal of some measures and greater attention to healthcare and the poor. Whatever the objective merits of these differing positions, between March and November the sentiment appeared to have grown that the economy was coming right: GDP was growing at around 2.7 per cent, inflation was low, personal consumption had picked up, exports were buoyant and unemployment was down a full percentage point. The September budget projected a budget surplus in 2007, cuts in taxes on business, a drop of 55,000 in unemployment, and rising disposable incomes.

With the polls suggesting that many voters made up their minds at the last moment, the trend of March was reversed. On a turnout of 80.1 percent, the CDA did relatively well, winning 41 seats in the 150-seat second chamber—a loss of only three seats—while the main opposition parties, the PvdA, VVD, and D66, all lost ground. The Socialists came second with 25 seats, a gain of 16. Several new parties also gained representation, including the Party for the Animals (PvdD) with two seats, becoming the first animal rights group to enter a European parliament. One party that was not successful was the newly formed Party for Neighbourly Love, Freedom and Diversity whose paedophiliac tendencies roused protests. A court ruling resting on freedom of assembly and expression allowed it legal existence. However, it failed to secure sufficient expressions of support to field candidates.

Meanwhile, the new parliament was very finely divided and negotiations to assemble a fresh coalition proved particularly protracted. After Verdonk renewed her rejection of an amnesty for the failed asylum seekers, the prime minister bowed to protests and relieved her of responsibility for immigration. Extraditions were suspended. However, the caretaker government was still in place as the year ended.

One other controversial issue arose in December. The government decided to award medals to the Dutch UN peacekeepers who in 1995 had so signally failed to protect the Muslim enclave of Srebrenica in the worst atrocity of the Yugoslav civil war. Defence Minister Henk Kamp said it had been difficult for them and "we want to support them". A report criticising the Dutch government for allowing troops to become "unwittingly" complicit in the Srebrenica massacre had led, in 2002, to the resignation of the then government (see AR 2002, p. 65).

Mittal Steel's unsolicited €18.6 billion bid for the larger steelmaker, Arcelor SA, in January presented a major political problem. With its headquarters in LUXEMBOURG, Mittal was the country's largest private employer and the Grand Duchy had a 5.6 per cent stake in it. The prime minister, Jean-Claude Juncker, depicting Mittal as mere asset strippers, vowed to fight the bid. The government even prepared legislation (of uncertain validity) allowing Arcelor to mount a "poison-pill" defence. Juncker's government was no happier when Arcelor accepted an alternative US$16 billion offer from a Russian company, Severstal. A shareholder revolt followed in which, after much acrimony and many twists and turns, Mittal prevailed. Juncker was obliged to acquiesce, claiming that assurances from Mittal now made this an "acceptable" "marriage of equals".

Still not reconciled to the French and Dutch rejection of the EU constitution (see AR 2005, p. 369), the government looked with little success for ways of resuming progress towards closer integration. There were some signs that opinion in this most "European" of EU members might be becoming slightly less wholehearted, with 27 per cent indicating in an end-of-year poll that the country had not benefited from membership, compared with only 20 per cent in 2005.

Otherwise the government's main preoccupations were the liberalisation of energy markets and energy supplies and the continuing threat of avian influenza. While economically Luxembourg was in important respects stronger than some of her neighbours, there were problems with structural unemployment, rapidly rising public expenditure, and inadequate long term healthcare provision for an aging population.

DENMARK—ICELAND—NORWAY—SWEDEN—FINLAND—AUSTRIA—SWITZERLAND—EUROPEAN MINI-STATES

NORDIC COUNTRIES

Denmark

CAPITAL: Copenhagen AREA: 43,000 sq km POPULATION: 5,418,000
OFFICIAL LANGUAGE: Danish POLITICAL SYSTEM: multiparty monarchy
HEAD OF STATE: Queen Margrethe II (since Jan '72)
RULING PARTIES: Liberal Party (V) in coalition with Conservative People's Party (KF)
HEAD OF GOVERNMENT: Anders Fogh Rasmussen (V), Prime Minister (since Dec '01)
MAIN IGO MEMBERSHIPS (NON-UN): NATO, EU, NC, CBSS, AC, OSCE, CE, OECD
CURRENCY: Danish krone (end-'06 £1=DKr11.0297, US$1=DKr5.64920)
GNI PER CAPITA: US$47,390, US$33,570 at PPP ('05)

Iceland

CAPITAL: Reykjavík AREA: 103,000 sq km POPULATION: 295,000
OFFICIAL LANGUAGE: Icelandic POLITICAL SYSTEM: multiparty republic
HEAD OF STATE: President Ólafur Ragnar Grímsson (since Aug '96)
RULING PARTIES: Independence Party (IP) & Progressive Party (PP)
HEAD OF GOVERNMENT: Geir H. Haarde (IP), Prime Minister (since June '06)
MAIN IGO MEMBERSHIPS (NON-UN): NATO, EFTA/EEA, NC, AC, OSCE, CE, OECD
CURRENCY: Icelandic krona (end-'06 £1=IKr136.301, US$1=IKr69.8100)
GNI PER CAPITA: US$46,320, US$34,760 at PPP ('05)

Norway

CAPITAL: Oslo AREA: 324,000 sq km POPULATION: 4,618,000
OFFICIAL LANGUAGE: Norwegian POLITICAL SYSTEM: multiparty monarchy
HEAD OF STATE: King Harald V (since Jan '91)
RULING PARTIES: coalition of Labour Party (AP), Socialist Left Party (SV), and Centre Party (Sp)
HEAD OF GOVERNMENT: Jens Stoltenberg (AP), Prime Minister (since Oct '05)
MAIN IGO MEMBERSHIPS (NON-UN): NATO, EFTA/EEA, NC, CBSS, AC, OSCE, CE, OECD
CURRENCY: Norwegian krone (end-'06 £1=K12.2098, US$1=K6.25360)
GNI PER CAPITA: US$59,590, US$40,420 at PPP ('05)

Sweden

CAPITAL: Stockholm AREA: 450,000 sq km POPULATION: 9,024,000
OFFICIAL LANGUAGE: Swedish POLITICAL SYSTEM: multiparty monarchy
HEAD OF STATE: King Carl XVI Gustav (since Sept '73)
RULING PARTIES: Alliance for Sweden coalition, consisting of Moderate party (MP), Liberal party (FpL), Centre party (CP), and Christian Democrats (KdS)
HEAD OF GOVERNMENT: Fredrik Reinfeldt (MP), Prime Minister (since Oct '06)
MAIN IGO MEMBERSHIPS (NON-UN): EU, NC, CBSS, AC, PFP, OSCE, CE, OECD
CURRENCY: Swedish krona (end-'06 £1=K13.3588, US$1=K6.84200)
GNI PER CAPITA: US$41,060, US$31,420 at PPP ('05)

Finland

CAPITAL: Helsinki AREA: 338,000 sq km POPULATION: 5,245,000
OFFICIAL LANGUAGE: Finnish POLITICAL SYSTEM: multiparty republic
HEAD OF STATE: President Tarja Halonen (SSDP) (since Feb '00)
RULING PARTIES: Centre Party (KESK) in coalition with Social Democratic Party (SSDP) and Swedish People's Party (SFP) (since April '03)
HEAD OF GOVERNMENT: Matti Vanhanen, Prime Minister (since June '03)
MAIN IGO MEMBERSHIPS (NON-UN): EU, NC, CBSS, AC, PFP, OSCE, CE, OECD
CURRENCY: euro (end-'06 £1=€1.47970, US$1=€0.75780)
GNI PER CAPITA: US$37,460, US$31,170 at PPP ('05)

IN DENMARK, the year was dominated by a crisis over the publication in a national newspaper of 12 cartoons depicting the Prophet Mohammed. The affair had wider repercussions throughout the Nordic region and beyond.

The cartoons were originally published in September 2005 in the newspaper *Jyllands-Posten.* According to the paper's cultural editor, Flemming Rose, the drawings were intended to provoke a public debate about religious tolerance, self-censorship, and freedom of expression in a society that, like most of the rest of Europe, now had a significant Islamic minority population. In October 2005, the ambassadors of 11 mostly Muslim countries wrote to the Danish prime minister, Anders Fogh Rasmussen, citing the publication of the cartoons as merely one example of the derogatory treatment of Muslims in Denmark, and requesting a meeting. This was refused by the government, though the Danish foreign minister met his Egyptian counterpart in November. A criminal case was brought against *Jyllands-Posten* but it was rejected by the public prosecutor in Viborg in a decision published on 7 January 2006.

The dispute erupted into a full-scale crisis suddenly at the end of January. It seemed that this was partly due to the actions of a group of Danish imams who had toured the Middle East during the previous autumn with the intention of drawing attention to the cartoons. Some Muslims objected more or less strongly to the cartoons, partly on the grounds that they went against the teachings of many branches of the Muslim faith that proscribed the depiction of the Prophet Mohammed in any form, and partly because some of the cartoons were felt to portray a particularly negative stereotype of Islam. The cartoon that was perhaps singled out for most criticism showed a bearded man wearing a turban in the form of an ignited bomb. As news about the cartoons spread beyond Denmark, it quickly became clear that they were provoking strong views among Muslims and non-Muslims alike. On 26 January Saudi Arabia recalled its ambassador to Denmark and urged a boycott of Danish goods, which primarily affected the large Swedish-Danish dairy company Arla. This was followed by some diplomatic sanctions from the governments of Syria, Kuwait, and Libya, and large demonstrations throughout the Middle East where protesters burned the Danish flag. Fogh sought to distance himself personally from the cartoons, but refused to issue a formal apology, stating that it was not appropriate for the government to take responsibility for the actions of the free press. The editor of *Jyllands-Posten* apologised for having caused offence to Muslims, but defended his decision to publish the cartoons.

The affair took on a wider significance when the French newspaper *France Soir* republished the cartoons on 31 January. It was followed the next day by other newspapers throughout Europe (although not in the UK). The editors of these papers argued that they had republished the cartoons in order to defend the principles of freedom of expression and of the press. Opponents claimed that their actions were simply inflammatory. The international situation now worsened. Three Danish embassies—in Syria, Lebanon, and Iran—were burned in arson attacks and the Danish foreign ministry advised Danish citizens to avoid travel to the Middle East.

From the middle of February, however, the crisis subsided as quickly as it had flared up. On 15 March the director of public prosecutions in Denmark, Henning Fode, upheld the earlier decision not to bring criminal proceedings against *Jyllands-Posten.* In his statement he noted that freedom of expression should not be regarded as an absolute right, and that the Danish constitution did in fact contain two clauses restricting freedom of expression in order to protect religious and other groups from scorn and degradation, but he did not feel that these had been violated in this case.

At least 139 people died as a result of the cartoons crisis, mostly in violent protests in Nigeria, Libya, Pakistan, and Afghanistan. The whole affair was marked by the expression of extreme opinions on both sides: by radical Muslims who saw the cartoons as further evidence of the hostility of the West towards Islam, and by those arguing that freedom of expression should be regarded as an absolute, and who sometimes expressed their views in anti-Islamic terms. These issues had resonances far beyond Denmark. The whole affair had to be seen in the context of the continuing debate in Europe about multiculturalism, integration, religious tolerance, and secularism (see pp. 18-19; 51; 477-79), and also the continuing repercussions of the so-called "war on terror". Danish troops continued to see action in both Iraq and Afghanistan in 2006 as allies of the US-British forces.

In Denmark itself, there were fears of a new crisis in October, when video footage was circulated showing members of the right-wing Danish People's Party youth group holding a competition to draw caricatures of Mohammed at their summer camp. The prime minister intervened quickly to condemn the competition and the video. However, towards the end of the year there seemed to be a general feeling that the crisis had had the positive effect of promoting a much more open debate about integration and the position of Denmark's Muslim minority than had perhaps hitherto been the case. It was suggested that many Danish Muslims had become more politically and socially engaged as a result of the crisis, which was thought to be a good thing. In December, it was reported in the Danish press that the cartoons crisis had actually helped to project a more nuanced picture of Denmark and Danish society in many Muslim countries, though the Egyptian government in particular remained strongly critical of the Danish government's response to the affair and its intervention in Iraq.

There was also a Nordic dimension to the affair which strained intra-Nordic relations. In NORWAY the Christian journal *Magazinet* published the cartoons early in

January, but the Norwegian government sought to defuse the crisis by issuing a formal apology later in the month. Even so, the Norwegian embassy in the Syrian capital, Damascus, was set on fire and completely destroyed by demonstrators. The cartoons did not appear in print in either FINLAND or Sweden, but they did cause controversy when they appeared on the Internet in both countries. This caused the Finnish prime minister, Matti Vanhanen, to issue a hasty statement—too hasty, according to his critics—regretting the publication of the cartoons on the website of the right-wing group Suomen Sisu, and apologising for offence caused to the religious sentiments of Finnish Muslims. The Finnish foreign minister, Erkki Tuomioja, had also publicly criticised the Danish government for its failure to apologise.

Meanwhile in SWEDEN the cartoons appeared on the website of the right-wing party, Sweden Democrats, in mid-February, but the site was closed following the intervention of officials at the foreign ministry. Initially the foreign minister, Laila Freivalds, denied knowing anything about her department's intervention, but she later admitted that she had indeed sanctioned it. She was forced to resign, although in fact she had been in trouble for many months over her department's handling of the 2004 tsunami crisis (see AR 2005, pp. 51-52). The government as a whole had received strong criticism on the tsunami affair from the parliamentary constitutional committee during its hearings in January, and Freivalds looked likely to face a vote of no-confidence had she continued in office.

Freivalds' resignation was just one of several difficulties to beset Sweden's governing Social Democratic Labour party (SAP) as it prepared for a general election in September. The chair of the party's youth wing was accused of drunk and disorderly behaviour and using racist language to a security guard, and a prominent municipal politician in Malmö was accused of taking bribes (though was later acquitted). The prime minister, Göran Persson, was alleged to have broken labour laws in the construction of his grand new manor house, which was itself seen as inappropriately opulent for a social democratic politician. Many commentators suggested that these difficulties were all symptoms of a party that had been too long in office. In the government's favour was the strong state of the Swedish economy, which recorded a growth rate of 5.6 per cent in the second quarter of 2006. But unemployment remained stubbornly high, especially among young people and ethnic minorities.

The election resulted in victory for the four party centre-right Alliance for Sweden, and the Social Democrats were defeated for only the third time since they first came to power in 1932. The clear winner was the conservative Moderate party (MP), led by Fredrik Reinfeldt, who became the new prime minister. Elected party leader following the MP's heavy defeat in 2002, Reinfeldt had repositioned his party as the New Moderates, abandoning neo-liberalism for a centrist position as the defender of the welfare state. Among his coalition partners the Centre party also made strong gains, while the Christian Democrats and the Liberal party lost seats, the latter having been implicated in an electoral scandal involving hacking into the Social Democrats' internal computer system. In a development that many regarded as worrying, the anti-immigration Sweden Democrats made strong gains in southern parts of the country, leaving them with 2.93 per cent of the vote and only 60,000 votes short of parliamentary representation.

Persson announced his intention to resign as SAP leader immediately following the election, leaving the question of his successor to be decided in the spring of 2007. Reinfeldt's new government had a shaky first month in office when two of its ministers were forced to resign: the trade minister, Maria Borelius, for admitting that she had employed illegal domestic labour; and the culture minister, Cecilia Stegö Chilò, whose portfolio included public sector broadcasting, when it turned out that she had not paid her television licence since 1990. These resignations overshadowed the government's first budget, which included proposals to reform the unemployment benefits system (the so-called a-kassa), proposals which resulted in unofficial strike action by some trade unions in November.

FINLAND'S presidential election in January resulted in the return of the incumbent, the Social Democrat Tarja Halonen. The contest was much closer than predicted, however, and went to a second round run-off between Halonen and the National Coalition challenger Sauli Niinistö. The long-running question of NATO membership, to which Halonen remained opposed, dominated the campaign.

There was also an unexpected change of government in ICELAND. In June, the prime minister Halldór Ásgrímsson resigned, following losses in the local elections by his Progressive party the previous month. He was replaced by the foreign minister, Geir H. Haarde, leader of the Independence party. The government continued to be formed, as before, of a coalition between the Independence and Progressive parties, though the distribution of ministerial portfolios changed.

The most important event of the year in Iceland was probably the unilateral announcement by the USA in March that it would be closing its airbase and withdrawing its troops by September. This followed several years of negotiations between the two countries over the long-term future of an arrangement which had endured since World War II; but the US announcement nonetheless took the Icelanders by surprise. The abandonment of the American town at Midnesheidi, near the Keflavik airport, led to the loss of several hundred Icelandic jobs, and although US aircraft had had little role to play in actively defending Icelandic territory, they had made a valuable contribution to search and rescue operations over the years. Despite the US withdrawal, the 1951 bilateral defence agreement remained in force for the time being, but it seemed likely that the future of Icelandic defence policy would have to be more closely aligned to NATO or even the EU in the future.

Iceland attracted international attention following the announcement in October of its decision to resume commercial whaling after a ban that had lasted 17 years. The Icelandic ministry of fisheries insisted that the hunting of limited numbers of minke and fin whales was sustainable, but many environmentalists disagreed, arguing that whaling was also unnecessary and inhumane. Norway's ministry of fisheries and coastal affairs increased its quota for the permitted hunting of minke whales by 250 to 1,052 for 2006, which drew a formal protest from 11 states, including the UK, when the whaling season began in May.

As in the rest of the world, the weather continued to make the news in the Nordic countries in 2006. The summer brought further evidence of retreating glaciers and melting sea ice in the Arctic north. This was followed by an autumn which was the warmest on record in Denmark, and which brought heavy rainfall and severe floods to western Sweden. In December, this led to the sudden collapse of a section of the E6 motorway, the main route between Sweden and Norway.

The Winter Olympic Games in Turin were a great disappointment for the Norwegian team, which won only two gold medals, and only three medals overall in the cross-country skiing events which they had dominated in 2002. The Swedes were the highest ranked Nordic team with seven gold medals, including a win over Finland in the men's ice hockey final.

In a rather different context, the Finnish hard rock band Lordi, dressed as monsters in outlandish costumes, won the Eurovision song contest in May. It was the first time Finland had won the competition in over 40 years of trying.

AUSTRIA

CAPITAL: Vienna AREA: 84,000 sq km POPULATION: 8,211,000
OFFICIAL LANGUAGE: German POLITICAL SYSTEM: multiparty republic
HEAD OF STATE: Federal President Heinz Fischer (since July '04)
RULING PARTIES: Social Democratic Party (SPÖ) in coalition with the People's Party (ÖVP)
HEAD OF GOVERNMENT: Wolfgang Schüssel (ÖVP), Federal Chancellor (since Feb '00; replaced Jan '07 by Alfred Gusenbauer, SPÖ)
MAIN IGO MEMBERSHIPS (NON-UN): EU, OSCE, CE, PFP, OECD
CURRENCY: euro (end-'06 £1=€1.47970, US$1=€0.75780)
GNI PER CAPITA: US$36,980, US$33,140 at PPP ('05)

AUSTRIAN politicians experienced a turbulent 2006. Chancellor Wolfgang Schüssel's right-wing government began the year in positive vein, taking over the European Union's six-month rotating presidency on 1 January. Schüssel's government was not able to use this as a springboard to success in the parliamentary elections of 1 October, however, and although his party—the Austrian People's Party (ÖVP)—eventually, after protracted negotiations, returned to share power with the Social Democrats (SPÖ), Schüssel's long and illustrious career in politics drew abruptly to a rather undignified close.

Austria's presidency of the EU began with a rather clichéd summit entitled "The Sound of Europe". It took place in Salzburg, where the famous film (*The Sound of Music*) had been shot and which was also Mozart's birthplace (the 250th anniversary of his birth was enthusiastically celebrated in 2006). Although the Austrian EU presidency set itself some rather lofty goals—mainly in the area of job creation and fostering economic competitiveness—it was its adept crisis management that would remain longer in the memory. More specifically, the Austrian presidency skilfully handled the energy crisis that occurred when Russia's gas company, Gazprom, started to flex its muscles in an attempt to raise European energy prices (see pp. 106; 400-02).

The main event in Austria in 2006 was undoubtedly the national election and, especially, its messy and bitter fallout. The previous coalition of the ÖVP and the far-right Alliance for the Future of Austria (BZÖ) was punished at the polls in October, with the ÖVP winning 66 seats in the Nationalrat (the lower house of the bicameral legislature) compared with 68 won by the opposition SPÖ. All indicators pointed to a "grand coalition", the type of government that had governed Austria for most of its post-war history. Negotiations between the People's Party and the Social Democrats appeared to be going well until the ÖVP took umbrage at the SPÖ's decision to vote with the Greens and the far-right Freedom Party (FPÖ) in favour of parliamentary investigations into two scandals: the procurement process for Austria's controversial Eurofighter jets, and alleged government failures in the supervision of a number of banks. Schüssel, who was leading negotiations for the ÖVP, promptly broke off coalition talks, declaring that they would only be resumed after the potentially embarrassing probes were completed. Eventually a compromise solution was found which enabled Schüssel to save face and, after a full three months of negotiations, SPÖ leader Alfred Gusenbauer to take over the chancellorship from January 2007.

The causes for the somewhat surprising election result—Austria continued to perform well economically and Schüssel, although never loved, was widely respected—kept analysts busy. The Social Democrats had led in most opinion polls until April/May 2006. Subsequently, however, the trade union movement (which supported the SPÖ), the Österreichischer Gewerkschaftsbund, was engulfed by the scandal surrounding its bank, BAWAG PSK. One theory suggested that, by continuing to focus their campaign on the scandal right up to election day, People's Party officials may have alienated centrist voters by overplaying the negative campaigning.

Despite the pessimism of many Austrians, the country's economy remained one of Europe's strongest. Growth remained in excess of 3 per cent, the budget deficit was a highly respectable 1.1 per cent of GDP, and unemployment stood at a fraction over 5 per cent. Inflation, furthermore, was a perfectly respectable 1.6 per cent. The new government had a sound base on which to build in 2007.

SWITZERLAND

CAPITAL: Berne AREA: 41,000 sq km POPULATION: 7,441,000
OFFICIAL LANGUAGES: German, French, Italian & Rhaeto-Romanic POLITICAL SYSTEM: multiparty republic
RULING PARTIES: Coalition of Swiss People's Party (SVP/UDC), Social Democratic Party (SPS/PSS), Radical Democratic Party (FDP/PRD) and Christian Democratic People's Party (CVP/PDC)
HEAD OF GOVERNMENT: Moritz Leuenberger (SPS/PSS), 2006 President of Federal Council and Minister of Environment, Transport, Energy, and Communications
MAIN IGO MEMBERSHIPS (NON-UN): OECD, OSCE, CE, EFTA, PFP, Francophonie
CURRENCY: Swiss franc (end-'06 £1=SFr2.38930, US$1=SFr1.22370)
GNI PER CAPITA: US$54,930, US$37,080 at PPP ('05)

In early 2005 it was not unheard of for Swiss politicians to paint a gloomy picture of Switzerland's economic prospects. Economic reforms were urgently needed, and if they did not quickly materialise Switzerland could, so some rather influential forces argued, be the sick man of Europe within 25 years. Yet by the end of 2006 one wondered what all the fuss was about. The economy was booming (even without any noticeable reforms) and, controversial referendums on immigration aside, a relatively quiet political year had gone by. The budget enjoyed a healthy surplus (around SFr900 million) and economic growth remained robust at just under 3 per cent, although this was likely to fall during 2007.

Christoph Blocher, Switzerland's right-wing justice minister—always at the centre of Swiss party politics—finally managed to make a mark in an area of particular interest to his Swiss People's Party (SVP): asylum and immigration. A referendum held on 26 September saw 68 per cent of voters agree to tighten laws in this area, making it more difficult for asylum seekers and other foreigners to claim residence in Switzerland. This result reversed a narrow defeat for similar policies in a 2002 poll, when just over half of those who voted had rejected a proposal to clamp down on alleged abuses of the asylum system by alleged bogus asylum seekers. (Blocher claimed that two-thirds of all applications were in this category.) The success of the 2006 initiative arose from, amongst other factors, the support for the new law of two other right-wing parties in the government.

Other laws on the status of foreigners in Switzerland were also updated in 2006. The new legislation demanded that foreigners make a concerted effort to integrate into Swiss society, a requirement that had previously been confined to those who were actively seeking to obtain citizenship. The SVP also sought—ultimately unsuccessfully—to block a package of aid from Switzerland worth SFr1 billion for the eight new EU member-states in central and eastern Europe. On 26 November the programme was approved with the backing of 53 per cent support in the referendum. The money was to be distributed over the next five years.

EUROPEAN MINI-STATES

Andorra

CAPITAL: Andorra la Vella AREA: 445 sq km POPULATION: 66,000
OFFICIAL LANGUAGE: Catalan POLITICAL SYSTEM: multiparty monarchy (co-principality)
HEADS OF STATE: President Jacques Chirac of France & Bishop Joan Enric Vives of Urgel (co-princes)
RULING PARTIES: National Andorran Coalition, dominated by Liberal Party of Andorra (PLA)
HEAD OF GOVERNMENT: Albert Pintat Santolària (PLA), President of Executive Council (since May '05)
MAIN IGO MEMBERSHIPS (NON-UN): CE, OSCE
CURRENCY: euro (end-'06 £1=€1.47970, US$1=€0.75780)
GNI PER CAPITA: US$10,726 or more ('05 est), -

Holy See (Vatican City State)

CAPITAL: Vatican City AREA: 0.44 sq km POPULATION: 783 ('05 est)
OFFICIAL LANGUAGES: Italian & Latin POLITICAL SYSTEM: non-party papacy
HEAD OF STATE: Pope Benedict XVI (since April '05)
HEAD OF GOVERNMENT: Cardinal Tarcisio Bertone, Secretary of State (since Sept '06)
MAIN IGO MEMBERSHIPS (NON-UN): OSCE
CURRENCY: euro (end-'06 £1=€1.47970, US$1=€0.75780)
GNI PER CAPITA: equivalent to population of Rome

Liechtenstein

CAPITAL: Vaduz AREA: 160 sq km POPULATION: 34,000
OFFICIAL LANGUAGE: German POLITICAL SYSTEM: multiparty monarchy
HEAD OF STATE: Prince Hans Adam II (since Nov '89)
RULING PARTIES: coalition of the Progressive Citizen's Party (FBP) and the Patriot Union (VU) (since April '05)
HEAD OF GOVERNMENT: Otmar Hasler, Prime Minister (since April '01)
MAIN IGO MEMBERSHIPS (NON-UN): EFTA/EEA, OSCE, CE
CURRENCY: Swiss franc (end-'06 £1=SFr2.38930, US$1=SFr1.22370)
GNI PER CAPITA: US$10,726 or more ('05 est), -

Monaco

CAPITAL: Monaco-Ville AREA: 1.95 sq km POPULATION: 33,000
OFFICIAL LANGUAGE: French POLITICAL SYSTEM: non-party monarchy
HEAD OF STATE: Prince Albert II (since April '05)
RULING PARTY: the Union for Monaco (UNAM) (since Feb '03)
HEAD OF GOVERNMENT: Patrick Leclercq, Minister of State (since Jan '00)
MAIN IGO MEMBERSHIPS (NON-UN): OSCE, Francophonie
CURRENCY: euro (end-'06 £1=€1.47970, US$1=€0.75780)
GNI PER CAPITA: US$10,726 or more ('05 est), -

San Marino

CAPITAL: San Marino AREA: 60.5 sq km POPULATION: 28,000
OFFICIAL LANGUAGE: Italian POLITICAL SYSTEM: multiparty republic
HEADS OF STATE AND GOVERNMENT: Captains-Regent Antonio Carattoni and Roberto Giorgetti (for six months, from Oct '06)
RULING PARTIES: Christian Democratic Party (PDCS) in coalition with Party of Socialists and Democrats (PSD)
MAIN IGO MEMBERSHIPS (NON-UN): OSCE, CE
CURRENCY: euro (end-'06 £1=€1.47970, US$1=€0.75780)
GNI PER CAPITA: US$44,607 ('05), -

UNLIKE his predecessor in the HOLY SEE, Pope Benedict XVI would not be a globetrotter. Perhaps this was just as well since his first ventures abroad were attended by controversy. A warm reception in his native Bavaria in May was overtaken by controversy over his quoting a medieval ruler's condemnation of Islam as "evil and inhumane", thereby generating Muslim anger and bringing a later visit to Turkey into question (see p. 475). In Poland, some criticised a failure squarely to address the responsibility of Catholics over the Holocaust. In Spain, where Church and government were at loggerheads over marriage, abortion, the role of the Church in education, and the proposed beatification of Catholic "martyrs" of the civil war, the prime minister failed to attend the pope's valedictory mass. Visiting Turkey in November, Benedict XVI was at pains to heal the earlier breech, not without success, and meditated side by side with the grand mufti of Istanbul at one of Islam's greatest places of worship, the Blue Mosque. He spoke of his hope that, together, they would find "the means and paths of peace for the good of humanity".

Meanwhile, a changing of the guard was underway at the Holy See. Cardinal Tarcisio Bertone became secretary of state—roughly, head of government—a genial man with a human touch and love of football. One cardinal who had been implicated in shady financial dealings was pointed towards retirement. Another senior churchman was ordered to retire to a "life of prayer and penitence" after allegations of child abuse, signalling a tougher Vatican stance on the issue. The pope also chided the Roman Rota (the Holy See's appeals court) for the pain that its cumbersome bureaucracy caused those who sought annulment of their marriage, although there were no hints of change in policy on divorce.

In his first encyclical, *Deus caritas est*, Benedict surprised those who had dubbed him "God's rottweiler" with his gentleness and warmth about erotic love. However, he also warned against the danger of Christian charitable activities prejudicing the Church's essential mission by being sucked into the orbit of parties and government. He also called for modern music to be barred in the mass, and stem cell researchers were threatened with excommunication. His predecessor had created record numbers of saints; Benedict stressed the need for greater caution. Finally, his Easter sermons, inveighing against the decadence of the modern world, extending even to the Church, were impeccably conservative.

In July, LIECHTENSTEIN celebrated its 200th anniversary as a state. Thanks to modern measuring techniques it also grew—a whole 0.5 sq km—to 160 sq km.

In January Prince Alois von und zu Liechtenstein chided the government for its lack of progress with its reform programme. The government's immediate priorities were balancing the budget without raising taxes and reducing public expenditure, reform of company law, and the competitiveness of its finance sector. It adopted EU requirements on disclosure by companies, restructured social welfare contributions, and revised the system of allocating funds to local authorities, all the while maintaining its cost-cutting approach and aiming to be in current account surplus in 2007. The economy remained buoyant but the launching of a new labour market service to fight unemployment, especially among the young, reflected a determination not to become complacent.

Although MONACO was among the most intensively developed spots on earth, new projects in 2006, such as a harbour enlarged to take the largest yachts and the extension of the tiny principality's area by reclaiming land from the Mediterranean, would make it even more so. Yet it was an uneasy year for the government. Prince Albert II's economic and financial adviser became implicated in a controversial land deal. Although exonerated by an enquiry, he was subsequently shunted into a lesser post. In November, the director of Prince Albert's cabinet, Jean-Luc Allavena, abruptly left his post after only 14 months, together with the head of media relations, amid much talk of disharmony among the prince's team of advisers.

The unmarried prince acknowledged paternity of a 14-year-old daughter, Jazmin Grace Rotolo, arising from an affair with a waitress in 1991. (A son by a Togolese air stewardess had been acknowledged in 2005, see AR 2005, p. 59.) The Prince remained unmarried but Charlene Wittstock, an Olympic swimming champion from South Africa, was acknowledged as his official companion. In April he became the first head of state to reach the North Pole on foot, to draw attention to the effects of global warming.

In San Marino elections to the Grand and General Council of Sammarinese on 4 June brought substantial changes in the 60-strong unicameral legislature, with several additional parties gaining representation. On a slightly reduced turnout of 71.8 per cent, the Christian Democrats won the most votes but nevertheless lost four of their 25 seats. The big winners were the Socialists, with 20 seats, a gain of five. The Popular Alliance lost heavily, with seven seats (from 12), the Unified Left won five, and the New Socialist Party three. Four other parties won one seat each.

SPAIN—GIBRALTAR—PORTUGAL—MALTA—GREECE—CYPRUS—TURKEY

SPAIN

CAPITAL: Madrid AREA: 506,000 sq km POPULATION: 44,708,964 (National Statistics Institute, Jan '06
OFFICIAL LANGUAGE: Spanish POLITICAL SYSTEM: multiparty monarchy
HEAD OF STATE: King Juan Carlos (since Nov '75)
RULING PARTY: Spanish Socialist Workers' Party (PSOE)
HEAD OF GOVERNMENT: José Luís Rodríguez Zapatero, Prime Minister (since April '04)
MAIN IGO MEMBERSHIPS (NON-UN): NATO, EU, OSCE, CE, OECD
CURRENCY: euro (end-'06 £1=€1.47970, US$1=€0.75780)
GNI PER CAPITA: US$25,360, US$25,820 at PPP ('05)

The influx of illegal immigrants, coupled with growing public concern and criticism by some EU governments of Spain's policies, forced the Spanish Socialist Workers' party (PSOE) government to clamp down. Against a backdrop of dramatic pictures in the media of the bodies of immigrants washed up on beaches as a result of crossing the Atlantic in small boats, opinion polls showed that Spaniards viewed immigration as the country's second biggest problem after unemployment.

Spain's 4.8 million international migrants, legal and illegal—the 10th largest number in the world—accounted for 11 per cent of Spain's population, according to the UN population division. In 1990, Spain was not even among the top 20 recipient countries.

The government's extraordinary regularisation in 2005 turned some 560,000 illegal immigrants into legal ones and encouraged others to enter Spain during 2006. The more than 31,000 sub-Saharans who arrived in fishing boats in the Canary Islands was four times higher than the number arriving between 2002 and 2005. In regularising immigrants' status, the government did not consult other EU Schengen treaty countries which allowed passport-free travel, and in neighbouring France the interior minister (and presidential hopeful), Nicolas Sarkozy, chastised Spain for encouraging clandestine immigration. The Spanish government sought help during 2006 from the EU to stem the human tide, and stepped up deportations.

The main political development was the ceasefire, declared on 22 March by the terrorist group Basque Homeland and Freedom (ETA), and broken on 30 December when a car bomb at Madrid's airport injured 29 people and killed two, the group's first fatalities since 2003. Prime Minister José Luis Rodríguez Zapatero immediately suspended the peace process which had got nowhere. ETA, which had killed more than 800 people in 38 years of fighting for an independent Basque country, sought to "promote a democratic process in the Basque country...in which our rights are recognised". The government had little to offer ETA other than legalising Batasuna, its political wing, which continued its street violence, and transferring some of the more than 500 convicted ETA prisoners nearer to their homes. Zapatero was also severely constrained by failing to win the support of the right-wing Popular party (PP) for the peace initiative. Its leader, Mariano Rajoy Brey, said that the government had no right to try to negotiate with ETA until the group had laid down its arms.

The PP made the Socialists' anti-terrorist policy the focal point of its permanent state of aggressive confrontation with the government. The PP had still not come to terms with losing power in the 2004 election, which came three days after Muslim terrorists killed 191 people on crowded Madrid commuter trains (see AR 2004, pp. 64-65). The PP still tried to establish some links between the Islamists and ETA, even though prosecutors and police declared that only radical Muslims were involved in the 2004 attacks. Political life was very polarised.

Catalonia, one of Spain's richest regions, won its battle for greater self-government, but its new statute of autonomy did not go as far as its parliament wanted. The charter, a blueprint for other regions seeking more self-rule, gave Catalonia a greater share of the taxes raised in its region but not the control over them that was sought nor the right to decide what proportion should be transferred to the central government. It extended the region's powers to include an independent judiciary, control over regional transport, and infrastructure services. The PP said that the charter was unconstitutional and called for a nationwide referendum on the issue. The only referendum held was in Catalonia where the "yes" vote won 73.9 per cent and the "no" vote 20.7 per cent. The pro-independence Catalan Republican Left (ERC), part of the coalition government along with the Catalan Socialists (PSC) and Greens—United Left, expressed its discontent with the watered down version of the original text by casting blank votes.

The new charter inflamed passions across the political spectrum, rattled some sabres in the armed forces, pitted the PSC against the Socialist-run central government, and led to the collapse of the coalition government in Catalonia after the ERC walked out. José Montilla Aguilera, the industry minister in the central government, replaced Pasqual Maragall i Mira, the region's outgoing Socialist premier, as the Socialists' candidate in November's early elections. The Convergence and Union (CiU) party again won the most seats in the 135-member Catalan parliament, but not enough to govern alone and stop a return of the three-way coalition, headed by the Socialists who won five fewer seats than in 2003.

Internationally, Spain increased the number of its peacekeeping troops in Afghanistan from around 500 to 750; and its contribution of up to 1,100 troops to the UN Interim Force in Lebanon (UNIFIL) was the fifth largest. The government's willingness to play a significant role in the world's hot spots went some way towards easing tensions with the US administration caused by the withdrawal of Spain's 1,300 peacekeeping troops from Iraq in 2004 (see AR 2004, p. 64). Another factor that smoothed relations with the USA was Spain's decision not to sell 12 military aircraft to the avowedly anti-US government of President Hugo Chávez Frías of Venezuela. The US administration's ban on the re-export of US technology in the aircraft meant that EADS-CASA (the Spanish branch of the European aerospace company, EADS) had to substitute these parts, and it concluded that it was not commercially viable to do so.

The economy grew by close to 4 per cent, the 13th straight year of stronger growth than the eurozone average. The Madrid stock market's rise of 32 per cent was the highest in Europe. The booming construction sector, the engine of the economy (Spain's housing starts of around 800,000 a year were more than France, Germany, and the UK combined), was the source of several major corruption scandals. The most serious of these led the central government to dissolve the city government of Marbella and put it in the hands of administrators after the mayor and three town councillors were imprisoned on charges of profiteering from the property boom in the jet-setting resort. Police seized or embargoed more than €2.4 billion in property, helicopters, thoroughbred horses, artwork, and antique guns. The courts were awash with corruption cases, many of them involving Socialist and PP mayors. Miloon Kothari, a UN special advisor, said that Spain's housing market suffered from "unbridled speculation" and an "extreme" level of corruption. Spain's score in Transparency International's corruption league worsened in 2006 and the country had the dubious distinction of accounting for 26 per cent of the total number of €500 notes in circulation in the eurozone, although most Spaniards had never seen one. The notes were commonly used in "black money" transactions.

In a bid to reduce the EU's highest level of short-term contracts (affecting one in every three salaried workers in Spain), the government, employers, and trade unions agreed to ban the constant rolling over of these contracts. Under the new employment law, any employee who had held two or more temporary contracts totalling more than 24 months, within a 30-month period, automatically had the right to be given a permanent contract.

Sparks flew in the electricity sector after Germany's Eon launched a €37 billion takeover bid for Endesa, Spain's largest power company. The German initiative stymied the government's plans to create a national champion in the energy sector with a lower bid for Endesa by the Barcelona-based Gas Natural. The government was forced to lift most of the 19 conditions imposed on Eon, in return for agreeing to the takeover, after these were roundly condemned as illegal by the European Commission. The Commission opened two separate infringement procedures against the Spanish government: one for breaching internal market rules and one for violating the Commission's exclusive power to rule on big, pan-European mergers.

Spanish companies continued to invest heavily abroad. In the UK, Ferrovial bought BAA, the airports group, for €14.8 billion, and Agbar acquired Bristol Water for €237 million. Iberdrola, Spain's second-largest electricity company, launched a €17.2 billion bid for Scottish Power which would create Europe's third-biggest integrated power utility. In the USA, BBVA, Spain's second-largest bank, purchased two banks in Texas (Texas Regional Bancshares and State

National Bancshares) for US$2.6 billion; Grupo Santander, Spain's largest banking group, paid US$651 million for 90 per cent of Drive Financial, a Texas-based vehicle financing company; and Ebro Puleva, the largest Spanish food group, acquired New World Pasta for €282 million. BBVA also entered the Chinese market, paying €501 million for 5 per cent of Citic Bank, China's seventh-largest lender, and €488 million for 15 per cent of the Hong Kong-listed Citic International Financial Holdings.

On the religious front, the government agreed a new financing deal for the Roman Catholic church. Taxpayers, as of 2007, were able voluntarily to donate to the church more of their yearly tax declarations, but the government stopped making an annual contribution to cover the shortfall between the church's expected income and expenditure. The percentage contribution by taxpayers rose from 0.52 per cent to 0.7 per cent of income. The church was also no longer exempted from paying VAT. The accord was a timid and belated first step towards the self-financing commitment agreed after the death of General Francisco Franco Bahamonde, who ruled Spain from 1939 to 1975. The church enjoyed many privileges under his regime, and still received more than €5 billion per year from the state, mainly for schools. The government also made Catholic religion classes voluntary in schools receiving public funds, to the church's fury.

In a further bid to lay to rest the ghosts of the Franco era, the government approved a draft law to compensate all victims of the 1936-39 civil war and the dictatorship that followed. It did not annul tens of thousands of summary death sentences handed down by the regime, but it did ban the far right from holding rallies at Franco's grave in the Valley of the Fallen outside Madrid, and recommended the removal of Francoist symbols from public buildings.

GIBRALTAR

CAPITAL: Gibraltar AREA: 6.5 sq km POPULATION: 28,779
OFFICIAL LANGUAGE: English POLITICAL SYSTEM: semi-autonomous UK overseas territory
HEAD OF STATE: Queen Elizabeth II
GOVERNOR-GENERAL: Sir Francis Richards (since May '03)
RULING PARTY: Gibraltar Social Democrats (GSD)
HEAD OF GOVERNMENT: Peter Caruana, Chief Minister (since May '96)
CURRENCY: Gibraltar pound, at a par with UK pound (end-'06 US$1=£0.5220)
GNI PER CAPITA: US$27,900 ('00), -

In Gibraltar, the UK and Spain reached an historic agreement on 18 September to improve transport and telecommunication links and ease border crossings. It was the first deal under the tripartite forum established in 2004 to air longstanding grievances, which until then had been dealt with through megaphone diplomacy (see AR 2004, p. 67). Spain, however, did not drop its sovereignty claim. The key agreement was joint use of the Rock's airport by Spain and Gibraltar, with the building of a terminal that straddled the border zone. Flights from Spain to Gibraltar began on 16 December.

The UK also agreed to top up the pensions of some 6,000 Spaniards who had worked in Gibraltar's Royal Navy dockyards and lost their jobs when Spain's

General Francisco Franco Bahamonde closed the border in 1969. It was not fully opened until 1985.

A further rapprochement in relations meant that the Spanish flag would fly on the Rock for the first time since 1954 when Franco had closed the Spanish consulate in a fit of rage over a visit by Queen Elizabeth II. The flag would fly at a branch of the Cervantes Institute, Spain's institution for the learning of Spanish and the promotion of culture, which was being built.

The accord showed that Spain's switch to a pragmatic charm offensive had paid dividends. Shortly beforehand, however, the Spanish government failed to undermine British sovereignty over Gibraltar when it was unable to persuade EU judges to prevent the Rock voting as part of a UK European Parliament constituency. The European Court of Justice ruled that there was no reason under EU law why Gibraltar should not be part of the south west constituency of the European Parliament.

Gibraltarians approved a new constitution on 30 November which gave the Rock greater autonomy. The new charter was approved by 60.2 per cent of those who voted and rejected by 37.7 per cent. Turnout was 60.4 per cent, much lower than the last referendum in 2002 when some 85 per cent of the electorate of around 20,000 turned out to vote 99 per cent against sharing sovereignty with Spain (see AR 2002, p. 84). The new constitution did not alter the UK's sovereignty over Gibraltar.

PORTUGAL

CAPITAL: Lisbon AREA: 92,000 sq km POPULATION: 10,557,000
OFFICIAL LANGUAGE: Portuguese POLITICAL SYSTEM: multiparty republic
HEAD OF STATE: President Aníbal Cavaco Silva (PSD) (since March '06)
RULING PARTY: Socialist Party (PS)
HEAD OF GOVERNMENT: José Sócrates (PS), Prime Minister (since March '05)
MAIN IGO MEMBERSHIPS (NON-UN): NATO, OECD, EU, OSCE, CE, CPLP
CURRENCY: euro (end-'06 £1=€1.47970, US$1=€0.75780)
GNI PER CAPITA: US$16,170, US$19,730 at PPP ('05)

THE year began with voters going to the polls on 22 January to elect a new president. In a remarkable political comeback, former Prime Minister Aníbal Cavaco Silva fought off the challenge of two Socialist candidates, Manuel Alegre and Mário Soares. Securing 51 per cent of the vote was enough to gain Silva a narrow victory and made him the first centre-right politician to fill the post since Portugal's revolution in 1974. Defeat for the Socialist party (PS)-supported candidates also meant that a first period of cohabitation between the PS Prime Minister José Sócrates and the Social Democratic (PSD)-supported Silva had been created. While the position was largely ceremonial, Portuguese presidents had the power to dissolve the Assembly of the Republic (unicameral legislature) and appoint prime ministers. Silva replaced Jorge Sampaio who had served the maximum of two five-year terms (from March 1996). On 15 May Sampaio relocated to New York to fulfil his appointment as the UN secretary-general's special envoy to stop tuberculosis.

In the meantime Silva was sworn into office on 3 March, and in his presidential address vowed to work with the PS government, claiming to "know by my own experience the value of co-operation among government bodies". Most commentators concluded that Silva had won on the back of his experience as a prime minister between 1985 and 1995. In 2006, the Portuguese economy continued to stagnate, interest rates grew, and the government was forced to negotiate a turbulent path through recession. It was, therefore, inevitable that Silva's training as an economist—if not his rather austere image—persuaded the electorate to support the "strongest" candidate. Significantly, there were 3.3 million abstentions and just 2.7 million voted in favour of the president, reflecting a general disillusionment with the state of Portugal's domestic politics.

This air of pessimism was compounded by major police investigations into corruption among construction companies, some of the largest ever drugs seizures, the prolonged Casa Pia trial into sexual abuse at a children's home (see AR 2004, p. 69), and ongoing governmental attempts at reform. On 31 March, a programme for restructuring central public administration, reducing the number of civil service bodies from 518 to 332, was presented to the Assembly. The minister of finance, Fernando Teixeira dos Santos, claimed that none of the 573,000-strong public service work force would be made redundant, but many would be expected to become mobile and undergo special retraining in order to move to a new job.

Described as the most significant public reform of the last 30 years, it was not surprising that the bill provoked widespread opposition. Disruption came on 6 July when three main trade unions representing public administration workers organised a 24-hour strike. In response, on 7 July the government reaffirmed its commitment to reducing staffing costs by almost €1 billion in 2006-07. On 20 July the Assembly of the Republic approved legislation on the mobility scheme, and on 9 November public sector workers escalated their action by embarking on a two-day nationwide strike. Large-scale disruption occurred, with hundreds of schools and hospitals closed and rubbish lying uncollected in many areas. The government's position, however, remained entrenched and dos Santos reaffirmed a commitment to cutting costs in the "unsustainable" and "expensive" public administration. These measures were seen as integral to tackling Portugal's budget deficit and reducing it from 4.6 per cent in 2006 to a projected 3.7 per cent in 2007, thus bringing the country into line with limits contained in the EU's Stability and Growth Pact.

A further blow to the country's economy came on 11 July when General Motors (GM) Europe announced the closure of its Opel Combo van-manufacturing plant at Azambuja on the outskirts of Lisbon. Once again, the news was greeted with dissent and a series of lightning strikes was called, culminating in a three-day walkout by employees on 5 September. The opposition proved fruitless and compensation packages were negotiated to soften the blow of redundancy. Final shutdown occurred in December, directly affecting around 1,200 workers as well as provoking losses in sales of up to €100 million. Production was transferred to GM's much larger plant at Zaragoza in Spain, allegedly in order to take advantage of lower labour costs.

The summer brought some relief as the country united behind its bid to win the football World Cup in Germany. Utilising a mixture of youth and experience, and after fractious and controversial but winning encounters with the Netherlands and England, Portugal reached the semi-final stage. A sporadically entertaining game was lost 0-1 to the eventual runners-up, France (see p. 512).

While the country's annual scourge of forest fires was not as catastrophic as in previous years (see AR 2005, p. 65), conflagrations still flared. Tragically, six firefighters were killed when surrounded by flames on the outskirts of the village of Famalicao near Guarda. The incident occurred on 9 July when temperatures soared in excess of 40 degrees Celsius and Portugal was forced to issue health warnings over extreme levels of ultraviolet radiation. In contrast, a weakened hurricane Gordon narrowly missed the Azores Islands on 20 September and heavy rainfall wrought autumnal floods, power cuts and general havoc in Tomar and Santarém on 19 November.

As the year drew to an end Portugal's restrictive abortion laws were again bought into focus with the announcement of a referendum to be held on 11 February 2007 (see AR 2005, p. 65). Abortions were only allowed in Portugal in cases of rape, foetal abnormality, or if a woman's life was in danger. However, with up to 10,000 women each year requiring medical treatment after illegal back street abortions, the PS government supported calls for women to be allowed the right to terminate a pregnancy within the first 10 weeks. On 30 November, President Silva agreed to hold a public vote on the issue. Amid intensive media debate, hopes were high that a clear message would be delivered and the results of the last ballot in 1998, when the move to relax the law was ruled invalid because of a low turnout (see AR 1998, p. 97), might be clarified.

MALTA

CAPITAL: Valletta AREA: 316 sq km POPULATION: 404,000
OFFICIAL LANGUAGES: Maltese & English POLITICAL SYSTEM: multiparty republic in British Commonwealth
HEAD OF STATE: President Edward Fenech Adami (since March '04)
RULING PARTY: Nationalist Party (PN)
HEAD OF GOVERNMENT: Lawrence Gonzi, Prime Minister (since March '04)
MAIN IGO MEMBERSHIPS (NON-UN): CWTH, OSCE, CE, EU
CURRENCY: Maltese lira (end-'06 £1=ML0.63520, US$1=ML0.32540)
GNI PER CAPITA: US$13,590, US$18,960 at PPP ('05)

The state of the economy, the financial situation, and the country's progress towards adopting the euro were the dominant issues of the year. After an extended period of minimal economic growth, 2006 saw some hesitant improvement. Although the loss of jobs in traditional manufacturing areas continued to cause concern, there was significant new investment and promises of investment in higher technology industries and services, such as pharmaceuticals, information and communications technology, and financial services. This somewhat arrested the trend of creeping unemployment, which was, however, abetted by a worrisome downturn in the vital tourism sector. With the exception of the cruise liner trade, where record arrivals raised hopes of Malta's becoming a hub and a regular port of call for Mediterranean cruises, tourist arrivals dropped considerably during 2006. The decline impelled the government finally to tackle the problematic issue of low-cost airlines by allocating financial assistance for that purpose, under growing pressure from the tourism lobby. This enabled the government to reach an agreement with Ryanair and other low-cost airlines to start operating in Malta on a limited number of routes. Air Malta, the national carrier, already dogged by high fuel prices and insufficient revenue, now faced stronger competition.

With the prospect of a general election on the horizon, the Nationalist (PN) government and the Labour (MLP) opposition redoubled their claims, respectively, that economic recovery was in full swing, or that it was mere window dressing and manipulation of statistics. On the country's finances, which for years had been the biggest weakness of the administration, the government's claim that it had succeeded in bringing down the budget deficit to a manageable level—meeting the convergence criteria set out in the 1991 Maastricht Treaty to be eligible to join the eurozone—was countered by the opposition's charge that the tax burden had risen unacceptably. Meanwhile, fuelled by rising oil prices, inflation was a growing concern not just because it hit the cost of living and that of production, but because it raised questions as to whether Malta would be allowed to adopt the euro as planned in January 2008. By the end of the year, however, the inflation rate, too, began moving towards the required parameters. The opposition, which had been critical of what it called the government's haste to adopt the euro, dropped its criticism in the face of charges that deep down it remained eurosceptic, having lost the last election on an anti-EU membership platform (see AR 2003, p. 85). In what was seen as an election budget, the government's estimates for 2007 radiated optimism and cut direct taxes.

Apart from EU-related issues, the country's foreign relations continued to turn mostly on the unceasing flow of irregular cross-Mediterranean migration, in whose trajectory Malta lay. Despite more talks, the Euro-North African co-operative mechanism that had been contemplated the previous year to deal with migration did not materialise (see AR 2005, pp. 66-67). In August, the EU's external border security agency, Frontex, extended its operations to the Mediterranean to help principally Malta, Italy, and Spain intercept and send back immigrant boatloads.

GREECE

CAPITAL: Athens AREA: 132,000 sq km POPULATION: 11,089,000
OFFICIAL LANGUAGE: Greek POLITICAL SYSTEM: multiparty republic
HEAD OF STATE: President Karolos Papoulias (since March '05)
RULING PARTY: New Democracy (ND)
HEAD OF GOVERNMENT: Kostas Karamanlis, Prime Minister (since March '04)
MAIN IGO MEMBERSHIPS (NON-UN): NATO, EU, OSCE, CE, BSEC, OECD
CURRENCY: euro (end-'06 £1=€1.47970, US$1=€0.75780)
GNI PER CAPITA: US$19,670, US$23,620 at PPP ('05)

THE erosion of human rights and the infringement of national sovereignty by foreign security service activity on Greek soil had already become issues in 2005, following the alleged abduction and interrogation of 28 Pakistanis by UK and Greek undercover agents. These were to remain key themes in 2006.

The event of the year was a press conference held on 2 February. Following a newspaper leak, three government ministers revealed a major telephone tapping scandal affecting the highest echelons of government. It was announced that around 100 mobile telephones from the Vodafone network had been followed, including lines used by the prime minister and cabinet members, the leadership of the police, and foreign ministry officials. The bugging had continued for a year and a half, beginning during the heightened security alert preceding the August 2004 Olympic Games but continuing afterwards. Describing the system of "shadow" mobile phones through which the listening operation had taken place, the minister of public order pinpointed their geographical location in the neighbourhood of the US embassy. However, he claimed that the secret government inquiry had been unable to proceed further, as Vodafone had dismantled the interception software before informing the prime minister in March 2005. Greece's Authority for Information and Communication Security (ADAE) immediately began an investigation and reported that the "shadow" telephones had made calls to Maryland, USA, home of the National Security Agency. Subsequent hearings in Parliament's institutions and transparency committee suggested that the telephone tapping affair was only a small part of a massive foreign surveillance operation during the Olympic Games.

An additional twist concerned the mysterious death, just before Vodafone decided to inform the government, of Kostas Tsalikidis, a software expert employed by the company. In November, the government majority in the institutions and transparency committee refused to allow testimony from the Tsalikidis family, who did not accept the coroner's verdict of suicide, and rejected an opposition demand for the establishment of a parliamentary commission of inquiry into the telephone tapping. The following day, ADAE imposed a €76 million fine on Vodafone for violating the legislation on communications security.

In the case of the Pakistanis (see AR 2005, p. 69), a May report by the public prosecutor supported the abduction claims, suggesting that the Greek secret service was responsible. With the minister for public order famously describing mutual kidnapping as the Pakistanis' national sport, the government rejected calls for a parliamentary investigation.

The year's third major scandal was of a different nature, revealing both the malfunctioning of the market economy and the abuse of government power. Following the discovery that the major milk marketing companies had formed a trust to keep producer payments low and consumer prices high, the general director of the government's competition committee was caught seeking a bribe from one of the companies in return for reducing its fine. The close connections among the protagonists and leading government figures resulted in the case becoming known as "the scandal of the chums".

The January announcement of a new round of constitutional revision just five years after the last suggested that the basic state-citizen contract had become vulnerable to repeated amendment by transient parliamentary majorities. There were no plans for the separation of church and state, while particularly controversial proposals included changing the articles guaranteeing constitutional protection of forestland and the public character of higher education.

Education policy had already become the main front of opposition to government reform plans. Proposals for higher-education reform sparked student sit-ins, with all universities in Greece under occupation throughout the June examination period. In September schoolteachers began a six-week strike in protest at the underfunding of education. Both rounds of protest included a series of major demonstrations, whose policing became a major issue, particularly following the publication of photographs of police awaiting demonstrators with knuckledusters.

The 25th anniversary of Greece's entry to the European Community was not marked by any special celebration. The economy had been under EU surveillance since 2005, following the previous year's recalculation of the budget deficit as almost double the limit of 3 per cent of GDP permitted to eurozone members under the EU's Stability and Growth Pact (see AR 2005, p. 68). The country's financial credibility suffered further damage in September, when the government announced an upward readjustment of GDP by 25 per cent, based on the inclusion of para-economic activities such as smuggling and prostitution. Acceptance of the new figure implied reduction of the budget deficit below the 3 per cent level. It also meant that Greece would in future be entitled to lower receipts from the EU budget while qualifying to pay a higher contribution.

Given the year's travails, October's local government elections—occurring at the vulnerable midpoint of the government's term—could easily have been a government rout. Instead the governing New Democracy party kept two of the three major municipalities while winning 30 out of 54 prefectures. The result confirmed the finding of opinion polls throughout the year that the socialist official opposition was not deemed a credible alternative.

In foreign affairs, a central Greek aim—to use Turkey's accession negotiations with the EU to force Turkish recognition of the Republic of Cyprus—appeared to have become official EU policy (see pp. 75-76; 405-06). In bilateral Greek-Turkish relations, the purchase of a majority share in the Turkish Finansbank by the Commercial Bank of Greece encouraged predictions of a new era of economic co-operation. In May a collision between two Greek and Turkish fighter planes over the Aegean resulted in the death of the Greek pilot. Indicative of the changed climate, the incident did not result in a protracted nationalist outburst.

Two cases of violence against immigrant children by fellow pupils generated intense debate about integration, racism, and youth ethics. In June five boys admitted killing 11-year-old Georgian-born Alex Meshiesvili, missing since February, but then retracted their confessions. In November the response of the local community following the gang rape of a 16-year-old Bulgarian girl in a school toilet forced the victim to leave the island of Evia, her home for the previous 10 years.

CYPRUS

CAPITAL: Nicosia AREA: 9,250 sq km (3,555 sq km in TRNC) POPULATION: 1,048,373: 784,301 Greek Cypriots and others (end '05 est); TRNC 264,172 (May '06 census)

OFFICIAL LANGUAGES: Greek &Turkish POLITICAL SYSTEM: separate multiparty republics: Republic of Cyprus (recognised by UN), Turkish Republic of Northern Cyprus (TRNC—recognised only by Turkey)

HEAD OF STATE AND GOVERNMENT: President Tassos Papadopoulos (since Feb '03) in Republic of Cyprus; President Mehmet Ali Talat (since April '05), Ferdi Sabit Soyer (CTP), Prime Minister (since April '05) in TRNC

RULING PARTIES: Democratic Party (DIKO), Communist Party (AKEL), & Socialist Party of Cyprus (EDEK) form cabinet in Republic of Cyprus; Republican Turkish Party (CTP) & Freedom Party (OP) form coalition in TRNC

MAIN IGO MEMBERSHIPS (NON-UN): Republic of Cyprus: EU, OSCE, CE, CWTH; TRNC: OIC (observer)

CURRENCY: Cyprus pound (end-'06 £1=C£0.85540, US$1=C£0.43810); Turkish new lira in TRNC (end-'06 £1=TL2.75000, US$1=TL1.40850)

GNI PER CAPITA: US$16,510, US$22,230 ('05 est, based on regression); TRNC: US$10,200

AFTER a hiatus of nearly two years, the UN resumed efforts to restart settlement talks on the divided island. On 28 February, the secretary-general, Kofi Annan, met the Greek Cypriot president, Tassos Papadopoulos, in Paris and secured agreement to recommence (after legislative elections in May) negotiations at "technical level" with a view to preparing the ground for a formal relaunch of diplomatic initiatives. On 8 July, Papadopoulos and the Turkish Cypriot president, Mehmet Ali Talat, held a three-hour session with the UN undersecretary-general for political affairs, Ibrahim Gambari. They agreed to the preparation of discussions on "substantive issues" towards a "bi-communal, bizonal settlement based on political equality".

Negotiators—Tassos Tzionis for the Greek Cypriots and Rashid Pertev for the Turkish Cypriots—met on 31 July with the secretary-general's new special representative for Cyprus, Michael Moller, and exchanged preliminary lists of topics. By the end of the year the negotiators had met on some 20 occasions; however, so far as could be determined (the meetings were subject to a strict press blackout), no progress had been achieved. Annan, who had devoted an inordinate amount of his 10-year term of office seeking to resolve the Cyprus problem, commented ruefully in his final report on the mission of the UN Force in Cyprus (UNFICYP): "I cannot but regret the continued stalemate in the political process and the missed opportunities."

EU relations were dominated by efforts to end the continuing economic embargo of the Turkish Republic of Northern Cyprus (TRNC) while, at the same time, finessing efforts by the government of Turkey to link full implementation of the additional protocol to its customs union agreement with the opening of direct trade with the northern territory. The additional protocol, signed in July 2005 (see AR 2005, p. 71), had extended the terms of Turkey's customs union agreement with the EU to the 10 enlargement states (of which Cyprus was one). Turkey had coupled its signature with a unilateral declaration saying that it would not open its ports and airports to vessels and aircraft from the Republic of Cyprus until such time as there was a federal settlement on Cyprus in which the Turkish Cypriots were represented, and until international trade was permitted directly with the north.

On 24 January the Turkish foreign minister, Abdullah Gul, launched amid considerable fanfare an "action plan" providing for the opening of Turkey's ports and airports to Cypriot planes and ships in exchange for the opening to international traffic of the northern Cypriot ports of Famagusta, Kyrenia, and Karavostassi, and Ercan airport near Nicosia. The Greek Cypriots refused and accused Turkey of demanding "exchanges for meeting binding obligations" under the additional protocol.

The European Commission concurred that there could be no linkage between Turkey's implementation of the additional protocol and the opening of trade with northern Cyprus. Nonetheless, the Turkish government, facing elections in 2007 and fearful of a nationalist backlash if it conceded, continued to refuse access to Cypriot planes and vessels, causing the government of the Republic to threaten to veto further progress in Turkey's EU accession negotiations. The Finnish government, which held the presidency of the EU during the latter half of 2006, tried to broker a deal which would have allowed Famagusta port to be opened to direct trade for two years under EU auspices. As an inducement to the Greek Cypriots, it proposed that Varosha, the deserted tourist suburb of Famagusta, should be transferred from Turkish military control to UNFICYP administration. The Greek Cypriot government insisted, however, that for the deal to be acceptable Famagusta port would have to be opened to Greek as well as Turkish Cypriot traders and that Greek Cypriot owners of properties in Varosha would have to be allowed to reclaim and resettle them. Ultimately the EU Commission intervened to suggest that eight of Turkey's 35 negotiating chapters under the acquis communautaire (free movement of goods; right of establishment and freedom to provide services; financial services; agriculture and rural development; fisheries; transport; customs union; and external relations) should be suspended until such time as Turkey implemented the additional protocol in full. The government of Cyprus joined in consensus acceptance of this proposal during the foreign ministers council on 11 December (see pp. 75-76; 405-06).

On the domestic political front, elections for the House of Representatives (the unicameral legislature of the Republic of Cyprus) on 21 May saw the two main political parties—the communist Progressive Party of Working People (AKEL) and the conservative Democracy Rally (DISY)—lose considerable electoral support, though they still emerged as the largest blocs in the 56 seat Assembly, each with 18 representatives. The centre-right Democratic Party (DIKO) and the socialist Movement for Social Democracy (EDEK) each increased their vote and secured respectively 11 and five seats. AKEL, DIKO, and EDEK, which formed the government coalition (the executive and legislature were separate in Cyprus), formed a voting alliance to take control of the Assembly, with DISY assuming the leading role in the opposition. In the wake of the election, President Papadopoulos changed seven of his 11 ministers (though he kept the party balance in government constant at four ministries for AKEL, three for DIKO, two for EDEK, and two independent). In October Papadopoulos stood down as the leader of DIKO (though he remained as president) and was replaced by a former aide, Marios Karoyian.

In two by-elections held in the TRNC on 25 June the pro-settlement Republican Turkish Party (CTP)—the leading partner in the then coalition government—increased its seats to 25 in the 50 member Assembly. Shortly, thereafter, the prime minister, Ferdi Sabit Soyer, dissolved his uneasy coalition with the rejectionist Democrat Party (DP) and on 23 September formed a fresh coalition with the newly founded Reform Party (OP), which consisted of four assemblymen who had defected from the DP and another rejectionist party, the National Unity Party (UBP). The new coalition government consisted of seven ministers from the CTP and three from OP with the post of deputy prime minister and foreign minister held by OP leader, Turgay Avci.

TURKEY

CAPITAL: Ankara AREA: 775,000 sq km POPULATION: 72,636,000
OFFICIAL LANGUAGE: Turkish POLITICAL SYSTEM: multiparty republic
HEAD OF STATE: President Ahmet Necdet Sezer (since May '00)
RULING PARTY: Justice and Development Party (AKP) (since Nov '02)
HEAD OF GOVERNMENT: Recep Tayyip Erdogan, Prime Minister (since March '03)
MAIN IGO MEMBERSHIPS (NON-UN): NATO, OSCE, OECD, CE, OIC, ECO, BSEC
CURRENCY: new lira (end-'06 £1=TL2.75000, US$1=TL1.40850)
GNI PER CAPITA: US$4,710, US$8,420 at PPP ('05)

NEGOTIATIONS on Turkey's accession to the European Union, which began in October 2005 (see AR 2005, p. 72), were suspended in December on eight of the 35 chapters into which they had been divided. Moreover, none of the other chapters was to be closed until Turkey opened its harbours and airfields to the Republic of Cyprus, which was recognised internationally—except by Turkey—but whose authority extended in fact only over the southern two-thirds of the island inhabited by Greek Cypriots. Commenting upon this decision, which was reached by the EU foreign ministers on 11 December and approved by the full Council of the EU at its meeting in Brussels on 14-15 December, Finland's foreign minister, Erkki Tuomioja, speaking for the presidency, claimed that it amounted to an "encouragement to Turkey", and that nobody doubted the possibility of Turkey joining the EU once it had met all the criteria. An unofficial offer by Turkey to give partial access to Cypriot ships and aircraft, provided the Turkish part of the island (recognised by Turkey as the Turkish Republic of Northern Cyprus, the TRNC) were allowed to communicate directly with the outside world, was rejected by the Greek Cypriots (see pp. 73-74).

The EU was also critical of the prosecution in Turkey of writers accused of "insulting the Turkish identity". The cases, instigated by nationalist lawyers against novelists Orhan Pamuk and Elif Shafak, were dismissed by the courts. Turkish public opinion was sharply divided when Orhan Pamuk was awarded the Nobel prize for literature on 12 October. The president of the republic, Ahmet Necdet Sezer, failed to congratulate him, but Pamuk was entertained by the Turkish embassy in Stockholm, the capital of Sweden, when he received the prize in December.

Responding to the complaint made by the EU Commission in its annual report that the pace of reforms had slowed down, Turkey's chief EU negotiator, Minister of State Ali Babacan, said on 29 December that Turkey would press on with domestic reforms and that a schedule would be drawn up to this effect to cover the period to 2013. Earlier EU statements had suggested that 2014 was the earliest possible date for Turkey's accession. Ali Babacan added that the speed of the accession process would depend on Europe's readiness to accept Turkey's membership.

An acrimonious break was thus avoided and Turkey's political dialogue with the EU was set to continue. However, as expectations of achieving EU membership in the foreseeable future were disappointed, surveys showed that popular support for it fell in Turkey from above 70 to below 40 per cent. Relations with Europe suffered also as a result of votes in European parliaments recognising the massacres of Armenians in the Ottoman empire in 1915 as a crime of genocide. On 5 September the Turkish prime minister, Recep Tayyip Erdogan, declared that Turkey would disregard a non-binding recommendation by the European Parliament that recognition of the Armenian genocide should be a condition of EU membership. There was widespread outrage in Turkey when the French National Assembly (the lower chamber of that country's bicameral legislature) voted on 12 October to make denial of the Armenian genocide a punishable offence in France, a country which was, in any case, seen in Turkey as the main opponent of Turkey's accession to the EU (see pp. 44-45). On 15 November the commander of the Turkish land forces, General Ilker Basbug, declared that the Turkish army had broken off all military links with France.

Although the USA was even less popular than the EU, relations at the official level improved. On 5 September Turkey's Grand National Assembly (the unicameral legislature) authorised the despatch of a contingent of Turkish troops to Lebanon to serve in the reinforced UN Interim Force in Lebanon, UNIFIL. In December Turkey decided to take part in the production phase of the US-led F-35 Joint Strike Fighter (JSF) in preference to the Eurofighter. The presence in northern Iraq of the main base of the militants of the radical Kurdish nationalist PKK (Kurdistan Workers Party), listed as a terrorist organisation both in the USA and the EU, continued to be the main irritant in US-Turkish relations. However, tension on the subject was reduced on 28 August when the USA appointed General (retd) Joseph Ralston, former NATO supreme commander in Europe, to co-ordinate action against the PKK with Turkish and Iraqi authorities. In October the PKK commander Murat Karayilan said that his organisation had ended "violent action" inside Turkey. His statement followed an appeal for an unconditional cessation of violence by the Democratic Society Party (DTP), the main legal vehicle for Kurdish nationalism within Turkey. The number of terrorist incidents decreased thereafter, although mines laid by the PKK in south-eastern Turkey continued to cause casualties. In all, close on 100 members of the security forces lost their lives in terrorist attacks. They included 15 soldiers and policemen killed in one week in mid-July, when a US warning to Turkey to desist from an operation against PKK bases in northern Iraq coincided with the Israeli onslaught—which enjoyed US support—against Hezbullah in Lebanon (see pp. 197-203). Prime Minister Erdogan and Foreign Minister Abdullah Gul exchanged visits with their opposite numbers in Iran, Syria, and other Muslim countries. While these initiatives met with US understanding, there was unease at the official visit to Syria by President Sezer in April, at a time when the Syrian regime was under pressure for its alleged involvement in the murder of the former Lebanese prime minister, Rafiq Hariri in April 2005 (see AR 2005, pp. 181-83).

While the PKK mounted hit-and-run attacks on the security forces in south-eastern Turkey, an offshoot of the organisation, the Freedom Falcons of Kurdistan (TAK), targeted Mediterranean tourist resorts. On 28 August, three people were killed and almost 40 injured in Antalya, and injuries were also caused by bomb explosions in Marmaris and Mersin. On 20 April, the public prosecutor in the eastern Turkish town of Van, Ferhat Sarikaya, was dismissed after he had drawn up an indictment against members of the security forces accused of throwing a bomb at a bookshop owned by PKK sympathisers in the town of Semdinli, near the border with Iraq. The prosecutor's indictment had quoted charges that the commander of land forces, General Yasar Buyukanit, had condoned illegal undercover operations against the PKK when he served in south-eastern Turkey. However, a campaign against Buyukanit, whose robust secularist views made him unpopular with members of the ruling Justice and Development Party (AKP), failed to stop his promotion to the senior military post of chief of the general staff in August.

Prime Minister Erdogan's refusal to interfere with the normal promotion pattern helped to defuse the tension between secularists and Islamists which had been exacerbated by the murder on 17 May of Mustafa Yucel Ozbilgin, a judge of the Council of State (the supreme administrative tribunal), after that court had barred the promotion of a schoolteacher for wearing a Muslim headscarf. Government ministers were taunted at the judge's funeral in Ankara, which was attended by military commanders, senior civil servants, and opposition politicians. During the funeral, Turkey's veteran social-democratic politician, Bulent Ecevit, who as prime minister had ordered Turkish troops to land in Cyprus in July 1974, suffered a brain haemorrhage from which he died on 5 November (for obituary see p. 576).

Ecevit's funeral occasioned another large-scale secularist demonstration against the AKP government. The political debate grew more lively as the country prepared for presidential elections in April and parliamentary elections in November 2007. Erdogan refused to advance the date of legislative elections to allow a new parliament to choose the successor to staunchly secularist President Sezer; nor would he reveal whether he would stand for the presidency himself, a prospect which worried Turkish secularists.

The economy grew above target by 5-6 per cent, according to provisional figures. In the first 11 months of the year exports rose by 16 per cent to US$85 billion and imports by 17 per cent to US$137 billion. During the same period the number of foreign visitors dropped by 6 per cent to 20 million, and net revenue from tourism amounted to US$17 billion. The increase in the deficit in the external current account in the first nine months of the year to US$28 billion, or 8.5 per cent of GNP, was the main cause for concern. Foreign direct investment rose in the same period to US$12.5 billion. To ensure an adequate inflow of short-term capital, the Central Bank raised its rate of interest on advances from 25 to 29 per cent over the year. The parity of the Turkish currency fell from TL1.35 to TL1.41 to the US dollar, while consumer prices rose by nearly 10 per cent over the year. The index of the Istanbul stock exchange (ISE) fell slightly from 40,000 to 39,000 year-on-year. In December, the IMF declared itself satisfied with the performance of the Turkish economy and released a further credit facility of US$1.1 billion. Economic progress was symbolised by the opening of new international terminals at the airports of Ankara and Izmir.

III CENTRAL AND EASTERN EUROPE

POLAND—BALTIC STATES—CZECH REPUBLIC—SLOVAKIA—HUNGARY—ROMANIA—BULGARIA

POLAND

CAPITAL: Warsaw   AREA: 323,000 sq km   POPULATION: 38,165,000
OFFICIAL LANGUAGE: Polish   POLITICAL SYSTEM: multiparty republic
HEAD OF STATE: President Lech Kaczynski (PiS) (since Dec '05)
RULING PARTIES: Law and Justice (PiS) forms coalition with Self-Defence (SRP) and League of Polish Families (LPR)
HEAD OF GOVERNMENT: Jaroslaw Kaczynski (PiS), Prime Minister (since July '06)
MAIN IGO MEMBERSHIPS (NON-UN): NATO, OSCE, CE, CEI, CBSS, OECD, Francophonie, EU
CURRENCY: zloty (end-'06 £1=Zl5.66760, US$1=Zl2.90280)
GNI PER CAPITA: US$7,110, US$13,490 at PPP ('05)

THE year 2006 saw prolonged political turbulence arising from the continuing uncertainties prompted by the outcome of the September 2005 elections (see AR 2005, pp. 75-76). Negotiations between the leading parliamentary party, Law and Justice (PiS), and its once-preferred coalition partner, Civic Platform (PO), broke down definitively, and the PO became the main party of opposition to PiS's minority government under Prime Minister Kazimierz Marcinkiewicz. The threat of premature elections was a recurring theme, and the form of the government changed several times as PiS continued its efforts to ensure a majority.

In the first phase, PiS secured a parliamentary majority for Marcinkiewicz's administration through informal bargaining with two radical parties hitherto regarded as unacceptable partners, the populist Self-Defence (SRP) and the nationalist-clerical League of Polish Families (LPR). In February these three parties agreed a stabilisation pact, including support for a wide-ranging legislative programme. In May they established a formal coalition government, with SRP leader Andrzej Lepper and LPR leader Roman Giertych entering government as deputy prime ministers, and additionally ministers of agriculture and education, respectively. Chronic tensions were apparent from the outset, however, with Prime Minister Marcinkiewicz uneasy at the choice of coalition partners, and the SRP and LPR pressing hard for increased budget expenditure whilst experiencing internal dissension and defections amongst their parliamentary deputies. In June Marcinkiewicz attracted criticism for dismissing Minister of Finance Zyta Gilowska, who was widely viewed as a guarantor of fiscal stability, following allegations that she had co-operated with the communist-era security services (she was subsequently vindicated by the Lustration Court). In July the government changed again as Jaroslaw Kaczynski—the leader of PiS and twin brother of President Lech Kaczynski—took over as prime minister.

As prime minister, Kaczynski could not dispel continuing conflicts. On 22 September the shape of the government changed again, with Lepper's dismissal for "loutish behaviour" and the reinstatement of Gilowska. The exchange of invective following the removal of SRP personnel reached a peak with the televising of secretly filmed tapes showing PiS leaders receptive to the demands of SRP deputy, Renata Beger, postulated in exchange for switching her party allegiance to PiS. Kaczynski dismissed all allegations of impropriety on the grounds that these were "normal political negotiations" and condemned the release of the tapes as a "provocation". Indeed, PiS appeared to be engaged in a systematic attempt to poach SRP and LPR members in order to maintain support for the government. Yet the government's majority could not be assured. Talk of new elections resurfaced and PiS seemed briefly amenable to this prospect. However on 16 October the SRP returned to the coalition and Lepper regained his former ministerial posts.

In local government elections in November PiS broadly maintained its position, but it lost badly to the PO in the large cities, including the symbolic presidency of Warsaw. Changes in the local government electoral law that provided opportunities for parties to aggregate their votes proved less effective than PiS had anticipated. Its junior partners, the SRP and LPR, did badly, especially the LPR. Third place in the local elections went to the alliance of the Left and Democrats which brought together the once powerful but now much depleted Democratic Left Alliance (SLD); Polish Social Democracy (SDPL), which had split from the SLD in early 2004; and the Democratic party (PD), essentially the remnants of the former Freedom Union (UW), which had failed to cross the electoral threshold in 2005. The position of PiS within the coalition was strengthened, but the Kaczynski government as a whole was further weakened by a series of "sex-for-jobs" and sexual harassment accusations made against SRP deputies in December.

PiS's determination to command a parliamentary majority stemmed from the crusading impulse of the Kaczynski twins to eliminate the "system" (uklad), a putative web of corruption, intrigue, and informal relations between "liberals" and "ex-communists" said to have dominated Poland's transformation since 1989. From the start of the year PiS began to take control of key posts in the state administration and to pursue a legislative programme to secure the fundamental "cleansing" and restructuring of the state. By the end of the year the Ombudsman, the Institute of National Memory (dedicated to investigating Nazi and Soviet atrocities committed in Poland), the Tribunal of State (the judicial body ruling on constitutional compliance by senior officials), and the reconstituted National Broadcasting Council were effectively in PiS's hands, along with an important element of the Constitutional Tribunal. Key legislation included the establishment of a new Anti-Corruption Bureau with wide-ranging policing powers; a new lustration law, extending the notion of collaborators of the former communist regime; and a new civil service law that rejected the notion of an impartial civil service, appointed and promoted on strict meritocratic criteria. The Military Intelligence Service (WSI), deemed complicit in major corruption, was abolished.

Throughout 2006 membership of the EU brought continuing economic benefits to Poland. The economy remained strong, with an estimated annual growth rate of 5.5 per cent. The government took advantage of this to increase a number of social benefits, although it was much criticised for failing to inaugurate a fundamental reform of the public finances. Its convergence programme aimed to meet the criteria of the EU's Stability and Growth Pact by 2009 and to enter the eurozone in 2011, but many regarded its premises as highly optimistic. There was also anxiety about the lack of a clear "European strategy" and about Poland's capacity to absorb EU funds. PiS was regarded in most circles as "eurosceptic", while its two governing partners were overtly so, with the SRP demanding renegotiation of the accession treaty, and the LPR favouring outright withdrawal from the EU.

Other external issues affected the governing coalition, not least the SRP's opposition to the presence of Polish troops in Iraq. Poland's poor relations with Germany barely improved (see AR 2005, p. 76), despite the efforts of German Chancellor Angela Merkel. In July President Kaczynski reacted badly to his satirical treatment by a small German newspaper, and he missed a scheduled Weimar triangle summit with Merkel and French President Jacques Chirac. Relations with Russia deteriorated further, including a Russian prohibition of Polish meat imports. In November Poland vetoed the negotiating mandate for the European Commission to begin discussions on an expanded EU-Russia economic agreement (see p. 403). This was popular at home, but the lack of prior consultations with EU partners gave credence to the view that Poland was the EU's "new awkward partner".

ESTONIA—LATVIA—LITHUANIA

Estonia

CAPITAL: Tallinn AREA: 45,000 sq km POPULATION: 1,345,000
OFFICIAL LANGUAGE: Estonian POLITICAL SYSTEM: multiparty republic
HEAD OF STATE: President Toomas Hendrik Ilves (ESDP) (since Sept '06)
RULING PARTIES: coalition of the Estonian Reform Party (ER), the Estonian People's Union (ERL), and the Estonian Centre Party (EK)
HEAD OF GOVERNMENT: Andrus Ansip (ER), Prime Minister (since April '05)
MAIN IGO MEMBERSHIPS (NON-UN): OSCE, CE, PFP, BC, CBSS, EU, NATO
CURRENCY: kroon (end-'06 £1=K23.1511, US$1=K11.8575)
GNI PER CAPITA: US$9,100, US$15,420 at PPP ('05)

Latvia

CAPITAL: Riga AREA: 65,000 sq km POPULATION: 2,300,000
OFFICIAL LANGUAGE: Latvian POLITICAL SYSTEM: multiparty republic
HEAD OF STATE: President Vaira Vike-Freiberga (since July '99)
RULING PARTIES: People's Party (TP) leads four-party coalition
HEAD OF GOVERNMENT: Aigars Kalvitis (TP), Prime Minister (since Dec '04)
MAIN IGO MEMBERSHIPS (NON-UN): OSCE, CE, PFP, BC, CBSS, EU, NATO
CURRENCY: lats (end-'06 £1=L1.03320, US$1=L0.52920)
GNI PER CAPITA: US$6,760, US$13,480 at PPP ('05)

Lithuania

CAPITAL: Vilnius AREA: 65,000 sq km POPULATION: 3,415,000
OFFICIAL LANGUAGE: Lithuanian POLITICAL SYSTEM: multiparty republic
HEAD OF STATE: President Valdas Adamkus (since July '04)
RULING PARTY: Lithuanian Social Democratic Party (LSDP) heads minority coalition
HEAD OF GOVERNMENT: Gediminas Kirkilas (LSDP), Prime Minister (since July '06)
MAIN IGO MEMBERSHIPS (NON-UN): OSCE, CE, PFP, BC, CBSS, Francophonie, EU, NATO
CURRENCY: litas (end-'06 £1=L5.10900, US$1=L2.61670)
GNI PER CAPITA: US$7,050, US$14,220 at PPP ('05)

In terms of themes such as the European Union, relations with Russia, and domestic political squabbles and rivalries, it appeared that little changed in the Baltic states of Estonia, Latvia and Lithuania during 2006. However, the nature of the Baltic states' relationship with all three topics did develop over the year. In 2005, both Estonia and Lithuania had anticipated joining the eurozone in 2007. For different reasons, both countries failed to satisfy the European Commission and European Central Bank in 2006 that they would be ready to adopt the euro. The Russian Federation remained a topic of discussion in the Baltic region, whether because of the geo-political considerations in the western former Soviet states about Russia's dominance of the region, or because of the proposed German-Russian north European gas pipeline which would cross the Baltic Sea from Russia to Germany, bypassing the Baltic states and potentially compromising their energy and environmental security. Finally, Baltic domestic politics was dominated by elections, government squabbles, and the fallout from the political instability of 2005 (see AR 2005, pp. 78-79).

Estonia in 2006 was primarily dominated by the issue of the EU as well as by the turmoil of domestic politics. Relations with the EU concerned market competition and Estonia's possible entrance into the Schengen treaty area. As well as Latvia and Lithuania, Estonia was sent a warning letter by the European Commission in April over the failure to deregulate its energy market, only to be hit in November by a fine worth €45.6 million for stockpiling sugar. In 2006, Estonia's efforts to enter the visa-free Schengen zone become more pronounced. According to the then Estonian president, Arnold Ruutel, the key problem facing entry was the lack of border guard personnel, especially in Estonia's north-east region of Ida-Virumaa. The Estonian government had hoped that, in preparation for joining Schengen, border controls with neighbouring EU member-states would be removed as early as 2007. However, due to technical problems with a new computer database, the Estonian government feared that it would not be able to enter Schengen until 2008 (rather than 2007). Nevertheless, the EU's Schengen evaluation committee issued a positive report in October, praising Estonia's efforts such as the integrated maritime surveillance system. Finally, despite the problems with the European Commission and entry into Schengen, on 9 May the Estonian Riigikogu (unicameral legislature) ratified the treaty providing for an EU constitution.

Estonian domestic politics lost a senior statesman and gained a dynamic new president in 2006. Former Estonian President Lennart Meri died in Tallinn on 14 March, aged 76, after a prolonged battle with brain cancer (for obituary see p. 587). When the Soviet Union occupied Estonia in 1944, Meri and his family were deported to Siberia, only to find their way back to Soviet Estonia. Although trained as a historian, he became an actor and later produced radio plays. By the late Soviet period, he became heavily involved in the Estonian independence movement, becoming minister of foreign affairs within the Estonian Popular Front (the opposition) and eventually creating Estonia's post-Soviet ministry of foreign affairs. In 1992, Meri became president of an independent Estonia until 2001. He was known for his multi-lingual diplomatic skills, as well as his broad knowledge of, and appreciation for, Estonian and European culture.

Meri's two successors as president competed for the Estonian presidency in 2006. When the Riigikogu proved unable to elect a new president in August, after the Centre Party and People's Union had essentially boycotted the vote, an electoral college was established to decide between the incumbent, Arnold Ruutel, and Toomas Hendrik Ilves, a member of the European Parliament. Following considerable political wrangling within the electoral college, Ilves was eventually declared the winner with 174 votes against 162. The choice meant that, at least for a short time, all three Baltic presidencies would be held by former North American citizens, as Ilves was a former US citizen, Latvia's Vaira Vike-Freiberga a former Canadian national, and Lithuania's Valdas Adamkus a former US passport holder.

While LATVIA geared up for its own presidential race (due in 2007), the outgoing incumbent was attempting to become the next UN secretary-general. In this contest, however, Vike-Freiberga, came third, following overwhelming support within the UN Security Council for the South Korean candidate, Ban Ki-moon. Amongst the candidates for the 2007 presidential contest there were at least two worthy names: a former foreign minister, Sandra Kalniete, and a prominent academic, Zaneta Ozolina.

Latvia held a general election for the Saeima (unicameral legislature) in October, which resulted in the return of the governing coalition, a first for post-Soviet Latvia. The election was won by the People's Party, which had dominated the Latvian legislature since 1999, and held several key ministerial posts (including prime minister and foreign minister) in the previous administration. New Era (JL)—the People's Party's biggest centre-right rival—came in with 18 seats, as opposed to 23 for the People's Party. New Era's leader, Einars Repse, had resigned in 2005 as defence minister, following an investigation by the state corruption bureau (see AR 2005, p. 79). Thus, understandably, the two big centre-right parties were unable to come to an agreement over forming a governing coalition. The coalition eventually consisted of the People's Party (TP), Latvia First Party (LPP), the Greens and Farmers Union (ZZS), as well as the nationalist alliance Fatherland and Freedom (TB-LNNK).

LITHUANIA had experienced a tumultuous year in 2004, with the impeachment of the incumbent president (see AR 2004, p. 83). The year 2006 was equally turbulent. The government had expected to adopt the euro in 2007 but in May 2006 the European Commission and the European Central Bank decided that Lithuania could not satisfy the convergence criteria for Economic and Monetary Union. The inflation rate at the time was 2.7 per cent, only slightly above the required 2.6 per cent. In October, the European commissioner for economic and monetary affairs, Joaquín Almunia, encouraged the European Commission and European Central Bank not to rewrite the rules for euro adoption in the new member-states, stating that inflation in Lithuania looked to remain high for several years to come.

Intrigue remained a key theme in Lithuanian domestic politics. In April the New Union-Social Liberals (NS-SL) withdrew from the four-party coalition government after Arturas Paulaskas, the party leader, was removed as speaker of the Seimas (the unicameral legislature) amid accusations of corruption. The Lithuanian Social Democratic Party (LSDP), the Labour Party (DP), and the Farmers and New Democracy Union (VNDPS) opted to continue as a three-party coalition under Prime Minister Algirdas Brazauskas (LSDP), commanding a narrow majority. In May, state security forces raided the headquarters of the DP on suspicion that it had received funding from the Russian secret service and bribes for supporting the procurement of EU funds. The DP's leader, Russian-born Viktor Uspaskich, was in Russia when the raid occurred. The DP, already weakened by the defection of seven anti-Uspaskich legislators, withdrew from government, a move which signalled the collapse of the coalition. In the negotiations which followed, the Social Democrats and Conservatives were expected to construct a broad "rainbow coalition". However, the Social Democrats pulled out of talks with the Conservatives, choosing instead to form a centre-left minority coalition government. The new administration consisted of the Social Democrats, the National Farmers' Union, the Civil Democracy party, and the Liberal Centrists. Despite their exclusion, the Conservatives promised "silent support" for the minority government. Yet the political imbroglio was not over. The year ended with the investigation and removal of the director of the state security department, Arvydas Pocius, on suspicion of corruption and having leaked classified materials. After a Seimas vote, Pocius submitted his resignation to the president on 22 December.

Thus, the bulk of events in the Baltic states in 2006 concerned European and domestic politics. Yet the Baltic states continued to make a significant international impact in relation to their relatively small size. In June, Latvian President Vike-Freiberga addressed a joint-session of the US Congress (the bicameral legislature). In October, Britain's Queen Elizabeth II visited Estonia. In November, Latvia's capital, Riga, hosted the NATO summit (see pp. 378-79), bringing the leaders of 26 member-states to the Baltic region. In 2006, all three Baltic states reaffirmed their commitment to the wars in Afghanistan and Iraq, leading the US national security adviser, Steve Hadley, to tell reporters at the NATO summit that the Baltic states were "punching above their weight" in the two war zones.

CZECH REPUBLIC

CAPITAL: Prague AREA: 79,000 sq km POPULATION: 10,196,000
OFFICIAL LANGUAGE: Czech POLITICAL SYSTEM: multiparty republic
HEAD OF STATE: President Vaclav Klaus (ODS) (since Feb '03)
RULING PARTIES: Civic Democratic Party (ODS) negotiating coalition with Christian Democratic Union-Czech People's Party (KDU-CSL) & Green Party (SZ)
HEAD OF GOVERNMENT: Mirek Topolanek (ODS), Prime Minister (since Sept '06)
MAIN IGO MEMBERSHIPS (NON-UN): NATO, OSCE, CE, CEI, OECD, Francophonie, EU
CURRENCY: koruna (end-'06 £1=Kor40.6677, US$1=Kor20.8291)
GNI PER CAPITA: US$10,710, US$20,140 at PPP ('05)

THE Czech Republic underwent considerable political turmoil during 2006, as the 2-3 June parliamentary elections resulted in a stalemate. With the lower house, the Chamber of Deputies, evenly divided between left and right, the country was without a stable government throughout the second half of the year, as the various parties struggled to reach agreement on the formation of a new coalition government.

The June elections put an end to eight years of leadership by the Social Democratic party (CSSD). In the four years prior to the elections, the CSSD had ruled the country in coalition with two junior partners from the centre-right: the Christian Democratic Union (KDU-CSL) and the Freedom Union (US-DEU). Under the leadership of Prime Minister Jiri Paroubek, the CSSD managed to regain popular support, after recording less than 10 per cent approval ratings in 2005, when the party was plagued by scandals (see AR 2005, p. 81).

In the June elections both the CSSD and its chief rival, the right-wing the Civic Democratic Party (ODS), won higher than expected levels of support. The ODS was the election winner, with 35.4 per cent of the vote and 81 seats in the 200-seat Chamber, while the CSSD finished second, with 32.3 per cent and 74 seats. Only three additional parties won sufficient voter backing to enter the legislature: the Communists (with 12.8 per cent of the vote and 26 seats); the KDU-CSL (with 7.2 per cent and 13 seats); and the Greens (with 6.3 per cent and 6 seats). As expected, the US-DEU failed to pass the 5 per cent threshold.

The ODS's electoral success was widely seen as a pyrrhic victory, however, as the party's chances of forming a stable centre-right government were considered extremely slim. After the elections, President Vaclav Klaus asked ODS leader Mirek Topolanek to form the next government. Topolanek first tried to establish a coalition with the KDU-CSL and the Greens, but with a combined total of only 100 seats it soon became clear that such a coalition would not succeed, especially after the CSSD and Communists joined forces in blocking the appointment of a new chairman for the Chamber of Deputies. By early August, the nascent coalition had disintegrated. Instead, the ODS started talks with the CSSD, aimed at forming an ODS-led minority government which would serve until new parliamentary elections could be called. However, divergent policy aims complicated the negotiations between the two rivals, and political tensions heightened further after senior ODS officials alleged that the previous CSSD-led government had used telephone tapping against political opponents and journalists. The ODS and CSSD even had difficulties agreeing on a date for fresh elections, as the latter wanted to delay them as long as possible, based on falling popularity levels. Indeed, while Paroubek had served the CSSD well prior to the elections, his post-election behaviour reduced the party's public support.

When put to the test on 3 October, Topolanek's first cabinet failed to win a parliamentary vote of confidence, with even some KDU-CSL deputies withdrawing their backing. Following Topolanek's initial failure, the appointment of a new candidate for prime minister was delayed until after the elections to the Senate (the upper house) and local governments, held in late October. The ODS won a stunning victory in these, giving the party an absolute majority in the Senate. Based on these results, President Klaus opted in early November to allow Topolanek a second attempt at forming a government. This time Topolanek initially reached out to the CSSD, indicating that the ODS would likely form a joint cabinet with the CSSD and KDU-CSL. CSSD support was especially crucial in pushing forward the state budget for 2007, which was the most important bill requiring parliamentary approval in the second half of the year.

The Chamber of Deputies duly passed the budget bill on 13 December with backing from 149 deputies, including most representatives of the CSSD, ODS, and KDU-CSL. After securing CSSD support for the budget, Topolanek surprised observers by announcing later the same day that he was ending coalition negotiations with the CSSD. Instead, the ODS resumed talks with the KDU-CSL and the Greens, with the hope of gaining the additional backing of several rebel CSSD representatives who had left their party following the elections. Thus, the Czech Republic ended 2006 without a stable government, as the parliamentary vote of confidence in Topolanek's second cabinet was put off until early 2007.

On the economic front, the country performed well in 2006, with strong GDP growth, falling unemployment rates, relatively low inflation, and a foreign trade surplus. The main problem related to fiscal challenges, as the 2002-06 CSSD-led government had delayed much needed reforms, particularly in regard to the healthcare and pension systems. Economists sharply criticised the budget for 2007, since the public finance deficit was expected to reach 4 per cent of GDP, far above the EU's convergence criteria for entry to the eurozone. By September 2006, fiscal concerns had led politicians and economists from across the spectrum to acknowledge that the Czech Republic's adoption of the euro would be delayed beyond the previous target date of January 2010.

SLOVAKIA

CAPITAL: Bratislava AREA: 49,000 sq km POPULATION: 5,387,000
OFFICIAL LANGUAGE: Slovak POLITICAL SYSTEM: multiparty republic
HEAD OF STATE: President Ivan Gasparovic (since June '04)
RULING PARTIES: Direction-Social Democracy Party (Smer-SD), Slovak National Party (SNS), and People's Party-Movement for a Democratic Slovakia (LS-HZDS) form ruling coalition
HEAD OF GOVERNMENT: Robert Fico (Smer-SD), Prime Minister (since July '06)
MAIN IGO MEMBERSHIPS (NON-UN): OSCE, CE, PFP, CEI, OECD, EU, NATO
CURRENCY: Slovak koruna (end-'06 £1=K50.8180, US$1=K26.0278)
GNI PER CAPITA: US$7,950, US$15,760 at PPP ('05)

THE year 2006 represented a turning point for Slovakia, as parliamentary elections on 17 June brought a shift in the country's political leadership, bringing to a close Mikulas Dzurinda's period of almost eight years as prime minister. After the elections, Dzurinda's centre-right cabinet was replaced by a coalition of left-leaning and populist/nationalist parties under the leadership of Prime Minister Robert Fico. Few analysts viewed the new coalition positively. Nevertheless, the economy continued to perform well during the second half of the year, as the Fico cabinet left in place most of the pro-business policies that had been enacted during the previous term.

In the years prior to the elections, Dzurinda had headed a centre-right cabinet which consisted of four parties: the Slovak Democratic and Christian Union

(SDKU), the Christian Democratic Movement (KDH), the Party of the Hungarian Coalition (SMK), and the Alliance of the New Citizen (ANO). While the 2002-06 government brought the country into the European Union and made remarkable progress in enacting reforms, the four parties had problems maintaining their alliance. Personality conflicts and disputes over religious and social issues contributed to declining cohesion, culminating in the KDH's exit from the ruling coalition in February in protest at Dzurinda's refusal to approve a treaty with the Vatican which would have allowed medical staff to refuse to perform abortions or carry out fertility treatment on religious grounds. Thus, the parliamentary elections had to be brought forward by three months from their scheduled September date.

Slovakia's surging economy was not enough to bring victory for Dzurinda's SDKU in the June elections. Instead, Fico's Direction-Social Democracy (Smer-SD), was the clear election winner, with 29.2 per cent of the vote and 50 seats in the 150-member Narodna Rada (unicameral legislature). Although finishing a somewhat distant second, the SDKU still achieved a better than expected 18.3 per cent of the vote and won 31 seats. Next came the SMK and the Slovak National Party (SNS), both of which secured just under 12.0 per cent of the vote and 20 seats. Only two other groups surpassed the 5 per cent threshold required for parliamentary representation: former Prime Minister Vladimir Meciar's party, the People's Party-Movement for a Democratic Slovakia (LS-HZDS), and the KDH. With around 8.5 per cent of the vote each, the HZDS and KDH secured 15 and 14 seats, respectively. ANO failed to enter the Narodna Rada.

Most analysts anticipated that Smer-SD would form a government with the KDH and SMK, both of which were internationally respected parties which would have helped boost Fico's image abroad. Another possibility was a government involving Dzurinda's SDKU, the SMK, and the KDH, together with the HZDS, an option that would have put Smer-SD and the SNS in opposition. However, the enactment of either was complicated by the KDH's stance. The party was divided internally over whether to participate in a government led by Smer-SD, particularly since the SDKU would then have been in opposition, where it could have attracted dissatisfied KDH voters. The second scenario was even less attractive to the KDH: while Dzurinda would have co-operated with Meciar of the HZDS as a way of preventing Fico from undoing the reforms of the 2002-06 term, the KDH viewed any alliance with Meciar as immoral, given his responsibility for Slovakia's direction during the 1990s. Although some had hoped that the HZDS would elect a new leader after the elections, paving the way for a centre-right government, Meciar remained chairman.

As the KDH continued its internal debate over whether to take part in a Smer-SD-led cabinet, Fico surprised observers by announcing on 28 June that his party would establish a government with Meciar's HZDS and the nationalist SNS. International financial markets responded to that news with considerable anxiety, as both the HZDS and SNS had served in government during 1992-98, a period characterised by economic cronyism, international isolation, and limited adherence to the rule of law. Still, President Ivan Gasparovic appointed the new government on 4 July.

The Narodna Rada approved the Fico cabinet's policy manifesto on 4 August. While the manifesto was quite vague in its approach towards economic policy, it did propose populist tax reforms. In the end, however, the state budget law for 2007 enacted only limited fiscal changes from the 2002-06 term, as the Fico government appeared uneasy about taking steps that would contribute to a decline in international confidence in the Slovak economy.

Fico learned a key lesson shortly after the June elections, when he suggested a possible delay in Slovakia's entry into the eurozone. That statement—combined with his decision to form a cabinet with the HZDS and SNS—contributed to a sharp decline in the koruna during June and July. Only after the National Bank of Slovakia (NBS) had spent several billion US dollars-worth of foreign currency reserves to prop up the domestic currency on international financial markets did Fico concede, promising to maintain the January 2009 target date for eurozone accession which had been set by Dzurinda's government. By August, the koruna resumed its strengthening trend, reaching record highs against the euro in subsequent months. In fact, the koruna appreciated so rapidly that the NBS had to intervene against the currency in December.

GDP growth accelerated sharply in 2006, recording record high levels, thanks in part to surging automotive sales connected with the launch of a new Slovak-based manufacturing plant by PSA Peugeot Citroen. The country's labour situation also experienced improvement as unemployment fell to its lowest levels in years. Even in the fiscal arena, the country recorded unexpectedly good results: despite Fico's pre-election spending promises, Slovakia's budget deficit was well below the original target.

HUNGARY

CAPITAL: Budapest AREA: 93,000 sq km POPULATION: 10,088,000
OFFICIAL LANGUAGE: Hungarian POLITICAL SYSTEM: multiparty republic
HEAD OF STATE: President Laszlo Solyom (since Aug '05)
RULING PARTIES: coalition of Hungarian Socialist Party (MSzP) & Alliance of Free Democrats (SzDSz)
HEAD OF GOVERNMENT: Ferenc Gyurcsany (MSzP), Prime Minister (since Sept '04)
MAIN IGO MEMBERSHIPS (NON-UN): NATO, OSCE, CE, CEI, PFP, OECD, EU
CURRENCY: forint (end-'06 £1=Ft371.987, US$1=Ft190.523)
GNI PER CAPITA: US$10,030, US$16,940 at PPP ('05)

FOLLOWING a year in which Hungary increasingly lived on borrowed money, 2006 was time for a reality check. The country experienced political turmoil, with a general election in the spring and in autumn the worst street violence in Budapest since the failed uprising of 1956 against Soviet rule (see AR 1956, pp. 253-60). Economic growth slowed to 3.8 per cent, while inflation jumped to 6.4 per cent as austerity measures were introduced to reduce ballooning budget and current account deficits. Unemployment also continued to grow, reaching 7.4 per cent. Political instability and the worsening economic climate seemed to confirm views of Hungary's status as the "laggard" of the new EU countries (see AR 2005, p. 85).

The year was dominated by Hungary's "dreadful politicians", a term coined by *The Economist.* General and local elections were held, the fifth since the end of communism in 1989. Despite a budget deficit of around 10 per cent of GDP—the highest in the EU—and relatively sluggish growth compared with other European emerging markets, both government and opposition downplayed the problems and contested the election promising higher public spending and further tax cuts. The volatility of the forint signalled the market's view on such election manifestos. The European Commission tactfully gave the government until September to submit a revised economic programme on how to join the eurozone.

On 9 and 23 April, Hungarians re-elected the incumbent government, for the first time since the fall of communism. In Hungary's 386-seat unicameral legislature, the National Assembly, the governing coalition secured a 54 per cent majority. The Hungarian Socialist party (MSzP), led by Prime Minister Ferenc Gyurcsany, took 190 seats; its coalition partner, the Alliance of Free Democrats (SzDSz), 20 seats. The opposition Fidesz-Hungarian Civic Alliance, led by former Prime Minister Viktor Orban, secured 164 seats, together with its ally, the Christian Democrats (KDNP). The Hungarian Democratic Forum (MDF) won 11 seats.

By June, the government was forced to acknowledge the need for austerity measures and said, with a whiff of post-victory nonchalance, that measures to restore the budgetary balance "won't hurt" ordinary Hungarians. By the autumn, however, the government had announced tuition fees in higher education; redundancies in the public sector; VAT, income tax, and utility price increases; and the introduction of contributory healthcare payments.

In what many saw as adding insult to injury, on a taped admission leaked to the press on 17 September the prime minister told a closed meeting of fellow party delegates that the government had "screwed up" and "lied morning, noon and night" about the state of the economy in order to hold onto power. He added that their only achievement in the last four years was to be re-elected. Despite this revelation, Gyurcsany refused to resign saying that he meant to break with the "policy of half-truths and lies of the last 16 years".

The leaked tape led to more than a month of demonstrations, mainly by extreme right-wing groups, with more moderate Fidesz supporters joining crowds of around 10,000 protesters. Rioting started on 18 September when a fringe group, including football hooligans, stormed the state television headquarters when their petition was not read out on air, throwing bottles and cobblestones, setting fire to cars, and damaging the building. There were 150 people injured, 102 of whom were police officers. Police clashed with rioters during the following nights at other locations, using teargas and water cannons. The protesters claimed to be taking part in a "moral revolution" and compared the rioting to the 1956 uprising.

Calm returned temporarily ahead of the municipal elections on 1 October, when Fidesz won a majority in all but one of 19 county councils, but failed again to take the capital, Budapest, and to replace the city's high profile mayor of 16 years, Gabor Demszky of the SzDSz. Fidesz and around 50,000 protesters claimed that the government had lost its legitimacy and should resign. Gyurcsany, however, strengthened his position after winning a vote of confidence in the National Assembly on 6 October.

Instead of a sombre, uplifting commemoration, with dignitaries from at least 47 countries in attendance, the 50th anniversary of the 1956 uprising on 23 October saw some of the worst street violence in Budapest. At one point rioters drove a T-34 tank from an open-air exhibition into a police cordon. The police response, according to critics, was heavy-handed with reports of officers beating up handcuffed rioters and bystanders. Rioting and demonstrations ceased as Fidesz initiated a referendum about government policies to be held in spring 2007. The political crisis—increasingly a duel between Gyurcsany and Orban, who had lost two consecutive elections and was frequently accused of using populist and nationalist rhetoric—showed no signs of abating, despite growing public demand for at least a basic level of co-operation and dialogue. Political commentators described the situation as a "cold civil war".

Ironically, the only good-spirited commemoration of 1956 was held four months early by the US president, George W. Bush, in Budapest, because he was unable to attend in October. In his open-air speech on 22 June, with the Hungarian capital and an approaching summer storm providing dramatic background, Bush said that Hungary represented "the triumph of liberty over tyranny". Iraqis, he said, would take inspiration and "draw hope" from Hungary's success. However, Hungary's president, Laszlo Solyom, nudged Bush by reminding him that "every step and measure" should be "in line with international law" when fighting terrorism.

Relations with Russia continued to improve. With two summits (28 February in Budapest and 18 September in Sochi, Russia) high on symbolism, Prime Minister Gyurcsany and Russia's president, Vladimir Putin, announced plans to develop an energy hub in Hungary with Russian involvement.

Once EU enthusiasts, Hungarians joined the ranks of the most eurosceptic countries: in a Eurobarometer (EU public opinion) poll only 41 per cent said that membership "benefited" Hungary, a dramatic drop of 11 per cent from 2005. Despite widespread pessimism and a rather disappointing year, Hungarians retained some confidence in their purchasing power as they turned to their credit cards for comfort: all national retail records were broken during the pre-Christmas period.

ROMANIA

CAPITAL: Bucharest AREA: 238,000 sq km POPULATION: 21,632,000
OFFICIAL LANGUAGE: Romanian POLITICAL SYSTEM: multiparty republic
HEAD OF STATE: President Traian Basescu (PD) (since Dec '04)
RULING PARTIES: coalition of the Justice and Truth Alliance (DA: comprising National Liberal Party (PNL) & Democratic Party (PD)) and Hungarian Democratic Union of Romania (UDMR)
HEAD OF GOVERNMENT: Calin Popescu-Tariceanu (PNL), Prime Minister (since Dec '04)
MAIN IGO MEMBERSHIPS (NON-UN): OSCE, CE, CEI, PFP, CEFTA, BSEC, Francophonie, NATO
CURRENCY: new leu (end-'06 £1=NL4.97080, US$1=NL2.54600)
GNI PER CAPITA: US$3,830, US$8,940 at PPP ('05)

FOR Romania, 2006 was a year of anticipation, with its people's aspirations finally confirmed when the European Commission recommended in September that

Romania (along with Bulgaria, see p. 93) should be allowed to join the European Union, on schedule, on 1 January 2007. The need to press ahead with reforms to meet the EU's entry requirements helped preserve the governing coalition in spite of the growing alienation between its two main parties. Meanwhile, for many Romanians there were signs of moderate prosperity as the surge in economic growth continued.

The issue of Romania's EU accession date dominated much of the political calendar. This arose from the accession treaties that Romania (and Bulgaria) had concluded in 2005, which allowed for their EU membership to be delayed by one year if they failed to meet the entry conditions on time (see AR 2005, pp. 88; 90). Romania suffered something of a setback in May when the European Commission's report on its progress put off making a recommendation until the last moment—the monitoring report due in the autumn—notwithstanding the fact that it was judged to have overtaken Bulgaria in the key areas of tackling corruption and organised crime.

In the end matters turned out well for both candidate countries when the European Commission's report, published on 26 September, recommended that they should be admitted to the EU, without delay, at the beginning of 2007. However, the Commission advised the EU's existing member states, which adopted its recommendations in December, to apply a number of so-called "safeguard clauses" in the initial period of membership. There was to be further monitoring to ensure that reforms were carried out. For Romania, this was to mean the possibility that other EU members would not recognise the judgments, and execute the warrants, issued by its courts. It would also involve the withholding of some farm subsidies until a properly administered system for their distribution was put in place. In addition, a ban on the exports of some Romanian food products was to remain in force until acceptable standards of health and hygiene were achieved.

There was further disappointment for Romania (and Bulgaria) when almost all of the EU's older and more prosperous member states announced that they would keep in place for at least two years restrictions on the employment of citizens from the accession countries. Nevertheless, these aspects of "second-class membership" were overshadowed for most Romanians by the fact that their country was now finally considered worthy of joining the club of developed European states.

The determination of Romania's politicians to avoid contributing to a delay in joining the EU helped keep the governing coalition—the Justice and Truth Alliance (DA)—in place, in spite of the severe strains it suffered on several occasions. Relations between President Traian Basescu and Prime Minister Calin Popescu-Tariceanu went from bad to worse, reflecting the growing antagonism between the president's Democratic Party (PD) and the prime minister's National Liberals (PNL). Matters appeared to come to a head at the end of June when Tariceanu proposed—without prior consultations with his coalition allies—that Romania should pull its 900-strong forces out of Iraq because of the mounting human and financial costs. His move was rebuffed by the

Supreme Defence Council, chaired by Basescu, who declared that it would be against Romania's national interests. Although the prime minister appeared to be trying to capitalise on growing concern over the continued deployment in Iraq, his gambit failed. Opinion polls suggested that the vast majority of respondents supported the strongly pro-USA president who argued that Romania could not turn its back on its international commitments and endanger its national security.

Basescu and Tariceanu were also at odds over the campaign to combat corruption, which the president was pursuing with relentless energy. Among the prominent figures charged with various offences were two of the prime minister's close business associates: Dinu Patriciu, chief executive of Rompetrol, the country's second-largest oil company; and Deputy Prime Minister Gheorghe Copos, who stepped down in June. Copos's small Conservative party left the governing coalition at the end of the year, thereby further weakening the government. Although the anti-corruption drive was welcomed at home and abroad (not least by the EU), Basescu's opponents suggested that some of the charges were politically motivated. His supporters countered by claiming that Tariceanu was trying to hinder a number of investigations.

Apart from the indictments issued against some of his associates, Tariceanu was also weakened by the emergence of a breakaway faction within the PNL. Led by two former party chairmen, Theodor Stolojan and Valeriu Stoica, the new grouping established good relations with Basescu. This appeared to serve the president's goal of recruiting fresh adherents to the PD from across the political spectrum, ahead of possible early elections in which a resurgent PD might stand separately from the PNL.

One issue upon which Basescu and Tariceanu agreed without hesitation was in declining to send peacekeeping forces to Lebanon as part of the expanded UN Interim Force in Lebanon (UNIFIL) (see pp. 197-203). Earlier, Basescu reaffirmed Romania's backing for US policy on Iraq and Afghanistan when he met US President George W. Bush in Washington DC in late July. During the year Romania continued to deny allegations that it might have provided the USA with a secret detention facility for questioning suspected international terrorists (see pp. 408-10).

Avian influenza made an unwelcome return in May. By early June officials had confirmed 125 cases of the H5N1 strain of the virus, including at locations in the capital, Bucharest. Although the outbreak of the disease was brought under control after a few weeks, the EU extended its ban on poultry imports from Romania to cover the whole country.

Once again the economy performed well. The growth in GDP bounced back to above 7 per cent, helped by strong domestic demand which reflected a continuing spending spree; the annual inflation rate fell to 5 per cent. Although Romania remained among Europe's poorer countries, more and more of its citizens were enjoying at least some degree of prosperity.

BULGARIA

CAPITAL: Sofia AREA: 111,000 sq km POPULATION: 7,741,000
OFFICIAL LANGUAGE: Bulgarian POLITICAL SYSTEM: multiparty republic
HEAD OF STATE: President Georgi Purvanov (since Nov '01)
RULING PARTIES: coalition of the Bulgarian Socialist Party (BSP), the National Movement Simeon II, and the Turkish Movement for Rights and Freedoms (DPS)
HEAD OF GOVERNMENT: Sergei Stanishev (BSP), Prime Minister (since Aug '05)
MAIN IGO MEMBERSHIPS (NON-UN): OSCE, CE, PFP, CEI, CEFTA, BSEC, Francophonie, NATO
CURRENCY: lev (end-'06 £1=L2.90180, US$1=L1.50540)
GNI PER CAPITA: US$3,450, US$8,630 at PPP ('05)

THIS was the final year of preparations for Bulgaria, along with Romania (see p. 91), to become a member of the European Union by 1 January 2007. It was not a particularly welcoming year for another round of EU enlargement, following the addition of ten new member states in 2004, eight of them from central and eastern Europe (see AR 2004, pp. 390-92), and the club was suffering from post-enlargement fatigue and constitutional blues. Like Romania, Bulgaria was much poorer than other EU member states, with GDP per capita of about 33 per cent of the EU average. In addition, most existing members were worried about the level of preparedness of the two countries to join the EU, and harboured particular fears related to waves of immigration from the two states. On top of that, the European Commission repeatedly indicated the poor state of administration in Romania and Bulgaria, and the level of corruption and organised crime (see p. 404). Some critics claimed that the EU had rushed to commit to the accession of the two states, despite their lack of readiness to become members.

As a result, during the final months before accession, the two countries were subject to strict monitoring to ensure that they made more progress in the fight against corruption and organised crime. Most of the 15 older (pre-2004 enlargement) EU member states put in place restrictions on the free movement of workers from the two new members after 1 January 2007. Also Bulgaria was expected to make more effort to combat organised crime, the most serious of the EU's concerns. It was also agreed that both countries would have to report every six months on progress in fighting corruption; and that by March 2007 they would have established agencies to handle millions of euros-worth of EU agricultural subsidies, or risk losing one-quarter of the cash. Both would also face food export bans, due to the prevalence of animal diseases, while Bulgarian planes could be banned from flying into EU airspace until the country improved its air safety standards.

Bulgaria had experienced a more difficult post-communist transition to democracy and a market economy than had the other central European and Baltic countries. Its economy reached a low point in 1997, yet since 2001 it had grown consistently, with unemployment falling sharply from around 20 per cent to 9.9 per cent in 2005, and inflation being brought under control. Annual GDP growth in 2006 reached 5.8 per cent; but incomes and living standards remained low when compared with those of the other EU countries.

In October 2006, the Bulgarian president, Georgi Purvanov won a second five-year term, beating his nationalist opponent, Volen Siderov of Attack party. The centre-right candidate, Constitutional Court chairman Nedelcho Beronov, was relegated to a poor third, because of divisions between several parties and personalities which had allowed Siderov to emerge as Purvanov's main challenger. The Attack party leader had repeatedly claimed that ethnic minorities such as Turks and Roma should not be allowed into the Bulgarian government, and demanded that the government revise its privatisation deals and tackle organised crime. Voter turnout was particularly low—at 35 per cent in the first round and 41.21 per cent in the second—taken by some commentators to be a sign of widespread anger with the political establishment.

ALBANIA—BOSNIA & HERZEGOVINA—CROATIA—MACEDONIA—SLOVENIA—SERBIA—MONTENEGRO

ALBANIA

CAPITAL: Tirana AREA: 29,000 sq km POPULATION: 3,130,000
OFFICIAL LANGUAGE: Albanian POLITICAL SYSTEM: multiparty republic
HEAD OF STATE: President Gen. (retd) Alfred Moisiu (since June '02)
RULING PARTIES: Democratic Party of Albania (PDS)-led coalition (since Sept '05)
HEAD OF GOVERNMENT: Sali Berisha (PDS), Prime Minister (since Sept '05)
MAIN IGO MEMBERSHIPS (NON-UN): OSCE, PFP, CE, CEI, BSEC, OIC, Francophonie
CURRENCY: lek (end-'06 £1=AL183.613, US$1=AL95.2700)
GNI PER CAPITA: US$2,580, US$5,420 at PPP ('05)

ON 12 June, Albania signed a stabilisation and association agreement (SAA) with the European Union, a remarkable step towards the integration of Albania into the EU bearing in mind the extent of the country's exclusion and isolation during the communist era. The signing of the agreement was the most important political event of Albania's difficult 15-year post-communist transition, as the country tried to recover politically and economically in the demanding European environment. Albania began its SAA negotiations in January 2003 followed by 11 rounds of political and technical talks between EU representatives and Albanian officials. The 500-page agreement set out a series of political, economic, legal, and judicial reforms that Albania was committed to implement before it could join the EU.

The SAA had yet to be ratified, as was customary, by all 25 member states (and from January 2007 by 27 member states), a process expected to take two to three years. In the meantime, an interim agreement would regulate commercial matters between Albania and the EU until the SAA entered into force. The signing of the SAA reflected the EU's recognition of Albania's progress towards democracy and the rule of law, and the constructive and non-inflammatory policy of the Albanian government towards the separatist Albanian-populated Kosovo region of Serbia (see pp. 101-02). However, the EU retained serious concerns over political infighting between the Albanian government and the opposition, the protection of minorities, weaknesses in law implementation, poor infrastructure, the grey economy, and the trafficking of drugs and people.

Despite annual economic growth of around 6 per cent, Albania continued to be among the most problematic transition countries. It remained among the poorest countries in Europe, with officially registered unemployment at just under 15 per cent, and 25 per cent of the population living below the poverty line. Remittances from Albanians working in other countries, principally Greece and Italy, were vital to the national economy. According to some estimates, around 20 per cent of the total labour force worked abroad.

BOSNIA & HERZEGOVINA

CONSTITUENT REPUBLICS: Federation of Bosnia & Herzegovina (FBiH); and Republika Srpska (RS, Serb Rebublic)
CAPITAL: Sarajevo AREA: 51,129 sq km POPULATION: 3,907,000
OFFICIAL LANGUAGES: Bosnian, Croatian, Serbian POLITICAL SYSTEM: multiparty republic
HEADS OF STATE: Haris Silajdzic (Party for Bosnia-Herzegovina, SBiH), Bosniak; Nebojsa Radmanovic (Party of Independent Social Democrats, SNSD), Serb; Zeljko Komsic (Social Democratic Party, SDP), Croat (since Nov '06)
PRESIDENTS OF REPUBLICS: FBiH: Niko Lozancic (Croatian Democratic Union, HDZ) (since Jan '03); RS: Milan Jelic (SNSD) (since Oct '06)
PRIME MINISTERS: Republic of Bosnia & Herzegovina: Adnan Terzic (Party of Democratic Action, SDA) (since Dec '02); FBiH: Ahmet Hadzipasic (SDA) (since Feb '03); RS: Milorad Dodic (SNSD) (since Feb '06)
MAIN IGO MEMBERSHIPS (NON-UN): OSCE, EBRD, CE, CEI, PFP
CURRENCY: marka (end-'06 £1=M2.90150, US$1=M1.50530)
GNI PER CAPITA: US$2,440, US$7,790 at PPP ('05)

IN January, the German politician, Christian Schwarz-Schilling replaced Lord (Paddy) Ashdown in the post of the high representative of the international community in Bosnia & Herzegovina. Ashdown stepped down after four years in power. Schwarz-Schilling arrived with the intention of being more of an "adviser" than an "international ruler", in contrast to Ashdown, who was often criticised—particularly by Bosnian Serbs—for relying too heavily on his powers to force through legislation and dismiss elected officials. Schwarz-Schilling announced that he was there to oversee a transition to home rule, hoping to see the office of the high representative dissolved by June 2007. When he took over, there had been some progress regarding the establishment of central state institutions, and Bosnia's stabilisation and association talks with the European Union; yet major challenges lay ahead, including improving the country's economy—still operating at only at 60 per cent of its pre-war level—streamlining the country's hugely complex and expensive bureaucratic structure, strengthening central authorities and national institutions, and implementing reforms in fields such as defence and education.

To the dismay of the high representative and the international community, the package of constitutional amendments which had been proposed in 2005 to change the Dayton constitution failed to gain the required two-thirds majority in Bosnia's lower house of parliament (the House of Representatives) when it was put to the vote in April. This package of reforms had aimed to strengthen the central government and simplify the numerous and complex central and local administrations in Bosnia & Herzegovina. Had it succeeded, it would have represented the first major formal overhaul of the constitution since the 1995 Dayton peace accords (see AR 1995, pp. 126-27; 559-62). The amendments would have transferred more powers to central government from the two entities that comprised Bosnia & Herzegovina: the Serb dominated Republika Srpska (RS), and the Croat and Bosniak (Muslim) Federation of Bosnia & Herzegovina (FBiH). This change was seen as necessary in order to phase out international supervision and to facilitate the incorporation of the country into Western structures, such as NATO and the EU.

Support for the constitutional amendments came predominantly from the Bosniak Party for Democratic Action (SDA) and the Social Democrats (SDP). Some Serbian parties had also agreed to them, albeit more reluctantly. But staunch opposition came from new Muslim and Croat parties, which were advocating the immediate abolition of Republika Srpska (RS). One such player was the Party for Bosnia & Herzegovina (SBiH), whose leader, Haris Silajdzic, was a prominent political figure and wartime Bosnian prime minister (1993-96). He chose to make a strong political comeback with his opposition to the constitutional amendments, claiming that they were dangerous in that they cemented the entity system and, with it, the RS. At the other end of the political spectrum, the radical Serbian parties from RS and some non-governmental groups were similarly opposed, fearing that the constitutional changes would gradually weaken the Serbian entity.

Without an amended constitution, and with the nationalist parties on the rise, the country held general elections in October 2006, in which 55 per cent of eligible voters went to the polls to elect representatives to the House of Representatives and to the parliaments of Bosnia's two entities (the House of Representatives of the FBiH, and the People's Assembly of RS). In addition, direct elections were held for the three members of the Bosnian presidency, and, in RS, for the entity's president and vice presidents. The electoral campaign was heated, with some Serb politicians calling for an independence referendum in RS and with the Muslim vote divided between Silajdzic's SBiH, and the SDA. All in all, a total of 36 parties, eight coalitions, and 12 independent candidates contested the elections.

In November, the three members of the collective presidency were sworn in: Serb Nebojsa Radmanovic of the Independent Social Democrats (SNSD), Bosniak Haris Silajdzic, and Croat Zeljko Komsic of the Social Democrats (SDP) would rotate as presidency chairman over their four-year term. The parties also agreed that the new prime minister of Bosnia & Herzegovina—to assume office in January 2007—would be Nikola Spiric, a Bosnian Serb professor of finance and a former parliamentarian from the Alliance of Independent Social Democrats (SNSD). The outgoing prime minister, Adnan Terzic of the Muslim Party of Democratic Action (SDA), was thus the first prime minister since the end of the war in 1995 to serve a full four-year term.

Political developments in Republika Srpska were marked by the rising star of Milorad Dodik, the RS prime minister, whose party, the SNSD, achieved a decisive victory in the October elections. Dodik declared his government's priorities to be economic development, decentralisation, the continued existence of the RS police, co-operation with the UN war crimes tribunal (the International Criminal Tribunal for the Former Yugoslavia, ICTY), and progress towards joining Euro-Atlantic structures. The sweeping victory for Dodik's SNSD came after a campaign of unrelenting nationalism in which he repeatedly threatened to call an independence referendum, should the autonomy of Republika Srpska be compromised. Similarly, in the Muslim-Croat Federation (FBiH), ethnonationalist parties did quite well, with the Bosniak SBiH and the Croatian Democratic Union (HDZ) leading the way.

During 2006, Bosnia continued talks with the EU directed towards the signing of a stabilisation and association agreement (SAA), under the shadow of insufficient co-operation with the ICTY, a problematic public administration, inadequate measures against corruption, and an incomplete reform of the police service. In its November report, the European Commission remarked that progress had slowed and a number of important issues remained to be tackled before negotiations for an SAA could be concluded. The Commission called for constitutional reform to ensure a better functioning of the state, and for the implementation of the police reform, which was being held back largely by the Bosnian Serbs. It also mentioned the need for greater co-operation with the ICTY to arrest major war crimes suspect, Radovan Karadzic. However, like Serbia and Montenegro, Bosnia & Herzegovina finished the year as a member of the NATO Partnership for Peace, with a view to eventual full membership of NATO.

CROATIA

CAPITAL: Zagreb AREA: 57,000 sq km POPULATION: 4,444,000
OFFICIAL LANGUAGE: Croatian POLITICAL SYSTEM: multiparty republic
HEAD OF STATE: President Stipe Mesic (since Feb '00)
RULING PARTIES: Croatian Democratic Union (HDZ) in coalition with the Croatian Social Liberal Party (HSLS) and the Democratic Centre (DC)
HEAD OF GOVERNMENT: Ivo Sanader (HDZ), Prime Minister (since Dec '03)
MAIN IGO MEMBERSHIPS (NON-UN): OSCE, CE, CEFTA, CEI, PFP
CURRENCY: kuna (end-'06 £1=K10.9039, US$1=K5.58470)
GNI PER CAPITA: US$8,060, US$12,750 at PPP ('05)

CROATIA enjoyed a substantial comparative advantage vis-a-vis the other western Balkan countries: it was the most prosperous economically, the most politically stable, and had the most advanced relationship with the EU. The arrest of the Croatian war crimes suspect most wanted by the International Criminal Tribunal for the Former Yugoslavia (ICTY) at The Hague, General Ante Gotovina, in December 2005—after four years on the run and under enormous pressure from the EU (see AR 2005, p. 94)—led to a remarkable normalisation of Croatia's relations with the international community.

Although there was no formal timetable for accession, EU officials believed that Croatia could become a member of the union by the end of the decade, provided that it was successful in addressing problems in the judiciary, its public administration, its fight against corruption, its handling of its ethnic Serb population, and its disputes with neighbouring Italy and Slovenia. The European Commission reacted strongly to the Croatian government's plans in December to go ahead with implementing an amended ecological and fisheries protection zone (ZERP), which would restrict fishing in a 72-km wide zone along Croatia's Adriatic coast, arguing that Croatia should refrain from activating such a zone unilaterally without consulting the two EU member states most affected by the move, Italy and Slovenia. Croatia had originally declared the protected zone in October 2003 (see AR 2003, p. 117).

Croatia's Yugoslav and post-Yugoslav wartime past continued to affect its political establishment and society. In October, the police arrested six former soldiers on suspicion of having committed war crimes against ethnic Serbs. The six were accused of detaining and killing Serbian civilians in the town of Osijek, in eastern Croatia, in late 1991 and early 1992. In November, a member of Croatia's unicameral legislature (the Sabor), Branimir Glavas, was also arrested on suspicion of war crimes after the Sabor lifted his immunity from prosecution. He was suspected of ordering the torture and killing of ethnic Serb civilians in Osijek. Later in the month, more than 20,000 people gathered to commemorate the 15th anniversary of the fall of the eastern Croatian town of Vukovar to the Serb-dominated federal Yugoslav army, the JNA, during the war in 1991. The three-month siege and bombardment of Vukovar was a particularly brutal episode during the Croatian war of independence from Yugoslavia (see AR 1991, pp. 167-74).

In addition, the consequences of Yugoslavia's disintegration continued to reverberate in Croatia's disputes with Slovenia. These concerned principally their maritime border in the Piran bay; and the repayment of Croatian clients' deposits in the former Yugoslav Ljubljanska Banka (in Slovenia). Croatia was pressing for the repayment of individual losses, and rejected Slovenia's proposal to deal with the bank issue as part of the broader succession process among former Yugoslav states.

MACEDONIA

CAPITAL: Skopje AREA: 26,000 sq km POPULATION: 2,034,000
OFFICIAL LANGUAGE: Macedonian POLITICAL SYSTEM: multiparty republic
HEAD OF STATE: President Branko Crvenkovski (since May '04)
RULING PARTIES: Internal Macedonian Revolutionary Organisation-Democratic Party for Macedonian National Unity (VMRO-DPMNE) heads coalition
HEAD OF GOVERNMENT: Nikola Gruevski, (VMRO-DPMNE), Prime Minister (since Aug '06)
MAIN IGO MEMBERSHIPS (NON-UN): OSCE, PFP, CE, CEFTA, CEI, Francophonie
CURRENCY: Macedonian denar (end-'06 £1=D90.6905, US$1=D46.4496)
GNI PER CAPITA: US$2,830, US$7,080 at PPP ('05)

SINCE the 2001 Ohrid agreement, which ended the violence between government forces and ethnic Albanians (see AR 2001, pp. 137-39), Macedonia had been seen to co-operate—more than any other western Balkan country—in the implementation of the agreement aimed at greater decentralisation in the Albanian-dominated areas. By and large, Macedonia was regarded by the international community as the most accommodating and successful example of multi-ethnic co-existence within the western Balkans. A number of constitutional amendments and laws had been enacted, strengthening the rights of the Albanian communities (see AR 2004, p. 100). Yet, despite some advances, Macedonia was one of the most impoverished countries in Europe, with a very weak economy and a very large informal sector. Much of the population complained that the reform policies had done little to create jobs or boost wages; and the 2006 elections proved that certain political parties were ready to stir up inter-ethnic tension, and that extremist language still found resonance with some voters.

In July, the country underwent national elections to the Sobranje (the unicameral legislature), which resulted in a change of government. Nikola Gruevski, leader of the formerly nationalist, centre-right Internal Macedonian Revolutionary Organisation-Democratic Party for Macedonian National Unity (VMRO-DPMNE), came first in the elections with 32.5 per cent of the national vote, followed by the Social Democratic Union (SDSM) of the former prime minister, Vlado Buckovski. The VMRO-DPMNE was last in power in 2001, during the ethnic Albanian revolt which threatened to plunge the country into civil war. While the elections and the transfer of power were conducted democratically, the pre-electoral period was marred by violence and intimidation. According to the Organisation for Security and Co-operation in Europe (OSCE), there were almost daily instances of low-level violence during the campaign, such as armed clashes between party activists and attacks on campaign offices in Albanian areas. After prolonged consultations, the VMRO-DPMNE formed a coalition government, including representatives of four other parties: the Democratic Party of Albanians (DPA), the New Social Democratic Party (NSDP), the Socialist Party (SPM), and the Liberal Party (LPM). The coalition agreed to continue dialogue to overcome disputes between the ruling and opposition blocs and to ensure reform, focusing primarily on the restructuring of the education sector and some of the Sobranje's regulations.

The European Union had played a pivotal role in Macedonia's development. The EU's firm approach since 2001 and its ample resources—including a police mission—provided a successful example of crisis management. In December 2005, the EU offered formal candidate status to Macedonia (with the nomenclature of "former Yugoslav Republic of Macedonia", under pressure from Greece, see AR 2005, p. 96). However, the EU did not offer a timetable for the start of accession talks. This reflected, on the one hand, the EU's willingness to reward Macedonia for its progress with the Ohrid agreement and, on the other, its hesitation to engage with a largely unprepared country. In its November annual report, the European Commission praised the overall progress in the implementation of the Ohrid agreement, yet expressed its concerns over the pre-election irregularities, the new government's apparent predisposition towards making politically and ethnically motivated appointments, the inefficiency of the judiciary, the lack of political will to fight corruption, and the considerable size of the informal sector in the economy.

SLOVENIA

CAPITAL: Ljubljana AREA: 20,000 sq km POPULATION: 1,998,000
OFFICIAL LANGUAGE: Slovene POLITICAL SYSTEM: multiparty republic
HEAD OF STATE: President Janez Drnovsek (since Dec '02)
RULING PARTIES: coalition of the Slovenian Democratic Party (SDS), New Slovenia-Christian People's Party (Nsi), the Slovenian People's Party (SLS), & the Democratic Party of Pensioners of Slovenia (DeSUS)
HEAD OF GOVERNMENT: Janez Jansa (SDS), Prime Minister, since Dec '04
MAIN IGO MEMBERSHIPS (NON-UN): OSCE, CE, CEI, Francophonie, EU, NATO
CURRENCY: tolar (end-'06 £1=T348.689, US$1=T182.395)
GNI PER CAPITA: US$17,350, US$22,160 at PPP ('05)

SLOVENIA'S diplomacy had consistently aimed to turn the country away from the former Yugoslavia—from which it had seceded in 1991—and to enter the European Union. Having achieved this goal in 2004 in one of the most remarkable post-communist transitions, Slovenia subsequently sought a more prominent international role. In January 2006, the Slovenian government decided to send soldiers to Iraq to help train Iraqi security forces, in what was a remarkable shift from its previous approach. This policy reversal instantly sparked an intense debate, with the opposition parties calling the decision risky and the government defending this very small contribution toward stabilisation efforts in Iraq. Overall, the Slovenian public was opposed to the idea of sending troops to Iraq, being highly critical of the motives behind the US-led invasion of that country. While all the governing coalition parties supported the move, the main opposition parties—the Liberal Democrats (LDS) and the Social Democrats (SD)—condemned it in the strongest terms.

For his part, the president of Slovenia, Janez Drnovsek, appeared particularly motivated to engage in foreign affairs by unveiling a peace plan for the Darfur region of Sudan. Closer to home, he also proposed initiatives to resolve a Slovenian-Croatian border dispute and presented a proposal for the final status of Kosovo, a proposal which put the country at odds with Serbia. In January, the president had established a civil society group—the Movement for Equality and Development—leaving open the possibility that the movement might compete in local elections, though only as a list of candidates rather than a party. Before establishing the movement, Drnovsek left the opposition LDS, which he had led for more than a decade.

During 2006 Slovenia was on a fast track to becoming the first new EU member state from central and eastern Europe to introduce the euro. In February, Joaquín Almunia, the European commissioner for economic and monetary affairs, argued that Slovenia met all criteria for euro adoption, with an inflation rate at 2.7 percent, public debt at 30 per cent of GDP, and the budgetary deficit at 1.8 per cent, and in July the European Commission gave the green light for Slovenia to introduce the euro by January 2007 (see p. 407). The country would thereby become Europe's first former communist state to adopt the euro as its currency, and the 13th country in the eurozone.

Only three months after assuming leadership of the government's key body for co-ordinating wide-ranging economic reform, the development minister, Joze

Damijan, resigned in March over what most believed was a difference of opinion with the prime minister, Janez Jansa, over the scope of the reforms. Damijan was considered an economic liberal who favoured the extensive withdrawal of the state from the economic sphere as well as the liberalisation of public services. The centre-right government's push towards structural reform, set out in a blueprint adopted in November 2005, was aimed at making Slovenia more competitive globally, fostering faster economic growth, and providing the foundation for a stable pension system.

SERBIA

CAPITAL: Belgrade AREA: 88,316 sq km POPULATION: 7,440,769 (excl Kosovo)
OFFICIAL LANGUAGE: Serbian POLITICAL SYSTEM: multiparty republic
HEAD OF STATE: President Svetozar Marovic (DPS) (since March '03)
RULING PARTIES: Democratic Party of Serbia (DSS) and Serb Renewal Movement/New Serbia (SPO-NS)
PRESIDENTS OF REPUBLICS: Boris Tadic (President of Serbia, since July '04); Fatmir Sejdiu (President of Kosovo, since Feb '06)
HEAD OF GOVERNMENT: Vojislav Kostunica (DSS), Prime Minister (since March '04)
MAIN IGO MEMBERSHIPS (NON-UN): OSCE (suspended), CE, CEI, EBRD, PFP
CURRENCY: dinar (end-'06 £1=D117.675, US$1=D60.2705)
GNI PER CAPITA: US$3,280 ('05, Serbia & Montenegro, excl Kosovo), -

THE year 2006 was a critical one for developments in Serbia, in regard to the country's relationships with Montenegro, Kosovo, and the European Union. It was the year when Montenegro became an independent state (see pp. 104-05); when supervised negotiations began over the final status of Kosovo; and when the EU froze its association talks with Serbia as a result of non-co-operation with the International Criminal Tribunal for the former Yugoslavia (ICTY) in The Hague over the arrest of former Bosnian Serb commander General Ratko Mladic. These developments affected Serbian domestic politics, already operating under the shadow of rising nationalism and a precarious governing coalition. It was also the year when former Yugoslav President and war crimes indictee Slobodan Milosevic died in his cell in The Hague.

Kosovo was by far the most difficult and nationally sensitive problem in Serbia. Relations between Serbia and its majority Albanian-populated province had reflected the uneasy relationship between Serbian and Kosovo Albanian nationalisms since the early 20th century. This culminated in the dramatic events of the 1999 NATO intervention in Kosovo (see AR 1999, pp. 138-43), and the region's subsequent cloudy status as an international protectorate under UN supervision and administration, whilst officially remaining part of Serbia. Based on the October 2005 decision of the UN Security Council, it was agreed that discussions should be launched in 2006 with the aim of concluding an agreement by the end of the year. The task of mediating between the sides through shuttle diplomacy was assigned to the former president of Finland, Martti Ahtisaari, who had helped to broker the ceasefire between NATO and Serbia in 1999. When negotiations started, the two sides were locked in intractable opposition: Kosovo Albanians were seeking full independence; Serbia wanted "more than autonomy, less than independence" for Kosovo, and demanded that Serbia retain sovereignty, a single seat at the UN, and control of the external borders. Apart from the nationally sensitive significance of Kosovo as the traditional birthplace of the Serbian state, which weighed heavily in the minds of most Serbs, the Serbian government was particularly worried over the fate of the minority Serbian population in Kosovo, which lived in precarious conditions. Out of the estimated population of 2 million in Kosovo, there were 200,000 remaining Serbs, about half of whom lived in enclaves protected by NATO troops. More than 220,000 Serbs and other minority populations had left Kosovo since 1999, with fewer than 15,000 having returned, according to UN sources. Kosovo Albanians, on the other hand, who made up 90 per cent of the population and retained negative historical memories of Serb domination, absolutely rejected any possibility of continuing to live under Serbian sovereignty.

In view of such wide differences, the talks started from a minimum set of commonly agreed principles including: (i) no partition of Kosovo; (ii) no return to the situation as it was before March 1999; (iii) no union of Kosovo with neighbouring states; and (iv) protection of minorities. Moreover, Ahtisaari's strategy was to begin the talks on technical issues in order to find some common ground between the two sides and eventually to tackle the central question of the status of Kosovo. In February 2006, talks began with an agenda covering local government reform and decentralisation, the preservation of cultural sites, and human rights. All discussions proved exceptionally difficult, with some minimum agreement on the question of cultural issues (the protection of Serbian Orthodox churches and monasteries), but with the issue of local government being the most contentious. The two sides disagreed significantly over how much power should be held locally: Serbian officials insisted that ethnic Serbs in Kosovo should be allowed to run affairs in their communities, link up with other Serbian areas, and enjoy special ties to Serbia; and Kosovo Albanians rejected these conditions as a form of partition of the province along ethnic lines.

The six-nation contact group—the UK, France, Germany, Italy, Russia, and the USA—which was overseeing the negotiations, was divided, with the UK and the USA speaking more explicitly about independence for Kosovo and Russia gradually becoming more reluctant to accept full independence without Serbian consent. In November, Ahtisaari decided to delay his recommendation for a final status for Kosovo until after the outcome of the Serbian elections of January 2007. This decision was largely influenced by the adoption of a new constitution in Serbia following the country's split with Montenegro. In the first new constitution since the days of Milosevic, Serbia declared, among other things, that Kosovo was an integral part of the country.

Developments in The Hague were another source of controversy. In March 2006, the former Yugoslav president, Slobodan Milosevic, died in his cell at the ICTY detention centre as his trial for war crimes, crimes against humanity, and genocide, was nearing its end (see p. 463; for obituary see p. 588). A Dutch investigation concluded that he had died of a heart attack, dismissing claims by his supporters that he had been poisoned. He was buried in his Serbian home town, Pozarevac, but the Serbian government refused to allow a state funeral. His death was received with mixed reactions of relief and regret, joy and sorrow: relief because the much-hated dictator had finally passed away; regret because he did not live long enough to receive punishment; joy because he died discredited and alone in a prison cell; and sorrow from those who still supported him and considered him a national hero.

Justice remained to be done in regard to the trials of the other Serbian political figures who were associated with the wars in former Yugoslavia. Four months after the death of Milosevic, six former senior political and military leaders of Serbia and Yugoslavia went on trial in The Hague, charged with crimes committed in Kosovo. They included the former president, Milan Milutinovic, nominally the second most important person after Milosevic; the former deputy prime minister of Yugoslavia, Nikola Sainovic; the former chief-of-staff of the Yugoslav army, the JNA, General Dragoljub Ojdanic; and the former army generals Nebojsa Pavkovic, Sreten Lukic, and Vladimir Lazarevic. However, the leader of the Serbian Radical Party (SRS), Vojislav Seselj, refused to attend the start of his trial in The Hague, demanding the right to choose his own reserve defence lawyer and to be allowed unrestricted visits from his wife. He was accused by prosecutors of having formed a paramilitary group responsible for alleged atrocities in Croatia, Bosnia, and the Vojvodina region of Serbia. His ultra-nationalist SRS dominated the Serbian National Assembly (unicameral legislature) and was fiercely opposed to independence for Kosovo.

The international community remained deeply disappointed with the failure to arrest war crimes and genocide suspect Ratko Mladic. The ICTY and its prosecutor, Carla del Ponte, repeatedly accused the Serbian government of co-operating insufficiently on the issue. This prompted the EU to freeze its stabilisation and association agreement (SAA) talks with Serbia in early May 2006. On this question, Serbian political parties and the population were divided: many regarded Mladic as a national hero but others grew tired of Serbia being held hostage over the fate of a single former general. The leader of the G17 Plus party, Miroljub Labus, resigned as Serbia's deputy prime minister in the coalition government of Prime Minister Vojislav Kostunica soon after the association talks with the EU were interrupted, and in October G17 Plus quit the governing coalition in protest at the lack of any subsequent progress. Yet despite international reservations over the failure to apprehend Mladic, NATO in December took the major decision to admit Serbia into its Partnership for Peace, thus launching a new period of co-operation between Serbia and NATO.

MONTENEGRO

CAPITAL: Podgorica AREA: 13,812 sq km POPULATION: 650,575
OFFICIAL LANGUAGE: Serbian (Montenegrin) POLITICAL SYSTEM: multiparty republic
HEAD OF STATE: President Filip Vujanovic
RULING PARTIES: Democratic Party of Socialists (DPS) and Social Democrats (SDP) form governing coalition
HEAD OF GOVERNMENT: Zeljko Sturanovic (DPS), Prime Minister (since Nov '06)
MAIN IGO MEMBERSHIPS (NON-UN): OSCE, EBRD, PFP
CURRENCY: euro (adopted unilaterally)
GNI PER CAPITA: n/a

ON 21 May Montenegro—a country of just over 650,000 people—declared independence for the second time in its modern history. In 1878, Montenegro had first achieved independence, which lasted until the end of World War I. In 1918, Montenegro became part of the Kingdom of Serbs, Croats and Slovenes; in 1945, one of the republics of the Socialist Federal Republic of Yugoslavia; in 1992 part of the Federal Republic of Yugoslavia (the Serb-dominated "rump Yugoslavia", following the independence of Bosnia & Herzegovina, Croatia, Macedonia, and Slovenia); and in 2002 a constituent state of what came to be called—for a brief four-year period—Serbia & Montenegro. This latter, stillborn, state was created through EU pressure, on the understanding that there would be a referendum in 2006 to decide upon the fate of the union (see AR 2002, pp. 123-24).

In May, Montenegro duly held its referendum with 55.53 per cent of voters voting in favour of independence and 44.57 per cent against. In order to make the outcome of the referendum as legitimate and acceptable as possible, the EU had insisted upon the existence of a qualified majority based on 55 per cent approval and a minimum turnout of 50 per cent plus one voter. Both sides—pro-and anti-independence—agreed to the terms and the referendum was held under EU supervision. The turnout was as high as 86.3 per cent with a large number of the Montenegrin diaspora choosing to vote. Prior to the poll, the Montenegrin population was divided, with Serb politicians, Orthodox church leaders, and Montenegrins from the mountainous inland regions largely opposing secession, and ethnic Montenegrins and Albanians from the coastal areas in favour of independence. The prime minister of Montenegro, Milo Djukanovic, had been a staunch champion of independence, arguing that an independent Montenegro would have a stronger economy and a better chance of faster accession to the EU. Following the vote, on 3 June Montenegro formally declared independence from its union with Serbia in a peaceful and orderly way (for declaration see pp. 559-60).

In September 2006, during the first general election since independence, the governing coalition won an absolute majority but Prime Minister Djukanovic stepped down and was succeeded by his Democratic Party of Socialists (DPS) ally, Zeljko Sturanovic. Djukanovic had been the longest serving prime minister of the Balkans, taking office in 1991 having started his political career alongside Yugoslav President Slobodan Milosevic but breaking ranks in 1997 and becoming an ardent supporter of Montenegrin independence. During his last years in power, his name was associated with revelations by an Italian magistrate that he was allegedly involved with cigarette smuggling.

In line with earlier agreements between the two states, Serbia became the successor state of Serbia & Montenegro, while the independent Montenegro applied for membership of the EU, other international organisations, and the UN. The latter application was granted in June, thus making the new state the 192nd member of the UN. With the independence of Montenegro, Serbia lost direct access to the Adriatic coast and became a landlocked country with special rights of access to the sea. Serbia also inherited the legal claim to the UN-administered province of Kosovo (see pp. 101-02). Concerning the division of state assets, Serbia, as the successor country, inherited most government buildings, diplomatic missions, and army property, but, naturally, lost the union's navy. For their part, the Montenegrins were given favourable treatment regarding the use of hospitals, universities, and other services in the Serbian capital, Belgrade, as a result of the limited capacity and small size of their own new country.

Following its independence, Montenegro drew up with the EU a separate mandate for talks aimed at the conclusion of a stabilisation and association agreement (SAA), potentially leading to eventual accession to the club. EU officials, however, complained about Montenegro's poor administrative capacity and its modest results in tackling corruption and organised crime. The EU also recommended that the country adopt a new constitution in line with European standards, strengthen its fledgling institutions, sustain the pace of reforms, and continue co-operation with the International Criminal Tribunal for the Former Yugoslavia (ICTY), in order to further negotiations. In December 2006, NATO admitted Montenegro to its Partnership for Peace pre-membership programme.

RUSSIA, WESTERN CIS AND THE CAUCASUS

RUSSIA

CAPITAL: Moscow AREA: 17,075,000 sq km POPULATION: 143,151,000
OFFICIAL LANGUAGE: Russian POLITICAL SYSTEM: multiparty republic
HEAD OF STATE: President Vladimir Putin (since May '00)
RULING PARTY: United Russia party
HEAD OF GOVERNMENT: Prime Minister Mikhail Fradkov (since March '04)
MAIN IGO MEMBERSHIPS (NON-UN): CIS, APEC, OSCE, G-8, CE, PFP, CBSS, BSEC, AC
CURRENCY: rouble (end-'06 £1=R51.3690, US$1=R26.3100)
GNI PER CAPITA: US$4,460, US$10,640 at PPP ('05)

It was a year in which Russia demonstrated greatly increased self-assuredness in the international arena, founded upon its control of energy supplies. Nevertheless, it was not clear that the country would be able to sustain the spectacular energy-based economic growth that was the basis for its new-found international confidence.

Energy policy dominated Russia's international relations. It was the world's second-largest oil producer and the largest producer and exporter of natural gas. As chairman of the G-8 (Group of 8: the G-7 most advanced industrialised economies plus Russia) for the first time in 2006, Russia chose energy security as a theme of the G-8 summit, held in St Petersburg, Russia's second city, in July. However, Russia's claim to be a reliable supplier of energy had been fatally undermined in January when its state-owned gas monopoly, Gazprom, carried out a threat to cut off gas supplies to Ukraine in a dispute over pricing (see p. 113). Gazprom's decision sharply to raise the price of natural gas for former Soviet countries including Ukraine, Moldova, Armenia, Georgia, the Baltic states, and even Belarus (see p. 111), was seen as a bullying attempt to draw those countries back into its orbit. US Vice-President Dick Cheney in May castigated Russia for using its energy supplies as "tools of intimidation and blackmail". Russia's energy minister, Viktor Khristenko, pointed out, however, that Russia had moved towards market-based pricing mechanisms and needed to stop subsidising those countries that continued to benefit from prices of around US$50 per 1,000 cubic metres (tcm) of gas when the global market price in 2006 had risen to around US$230.

The interruption in energy supplies to Ukraine had consequences for the European economies further downstream of the pipelines: Germany, Austria, Poland, Hungary, and Slovakia all reported a drop in gas supplies in January. An alarmed European Union attempted to co-ordinate its energy policy to lock Russia into maintaining supplies (see pp. 400-03), but Gazprom proved adept in concluding bilateral agreements with individual countries and Russia repeatedly rejected the EU's demands that it ratify the 1998 energy charter treaty, which would have allowed reciprocal access by energy suppliers to distribution pipelines in Europe and Russia. Russian officials also suggested that Gazprom would look for markets other than Europe if the EU frustrated its plans to expand into gas distribution networks there. The Russian president, Vladimir Putin, in September told the "Valdai group" of Russia experts and academics that Russia aimed to increased exports of oil and gas to Asia from 3 per cent of its production to 30 per cent in 10 to 15 years' time. However, there was an element of bluster in the Russian approach: most of Russia's gas had to be exported to Europe, because the pipelines ran that way. A major investment in infrastructure would be needed if other parts of the world were to supplant Europe as Russia's principal market. The security of energy supplies to Europe from Russia was in fact under greater threat from the lack of investment in that country's new energy fields and infrastructure, according to analysts. In March, separate reports from the International Energy Agency (IEA, the energy policy adviser to its 26 member-countries) and from the Organisation of the Petroleum Exporting Countries (OPEC) warned that gas and oil supplies from Russia were at risk in future from inefficient production, transport, and distribution facilities. A leaked report from Russia's industry and energy ministry, reported in the Russian business daily *Vedomosti* in November, predicted a possible shortfall of 46.6 billion cubic metres of gas in 2015 (annual production in 2005 was 600 billion cubic metres).

Despite these worries, Gazprom's apparently unstoppable rise continued. The world's third-largest corporation by market capitalisation had demonstrated a "seemingly insatiable appetite" for buying up assets outside its core business, according to a report in November from the Organisation for Economic Co-operation and Development, the OECD. Gazprom also announced in October that it would develop the vast Shtokman field without foreign partners, and at the end of the year Gazprom also took control of the Sakhalin II oil and gas field project in Russia's far east, buying out the foreign partners (Royal Dutch Shell and two Japanese corporations) that owned the project. Sakhalin II was due to come on stream in 2008. Symbolising Gazprom's dominance, in December the design was revealed for the company's new headquarters in St Petersburg. In a competition boycotted by the Russian Union of Architects, the winning design, from UK-based architects RMJM, was a modernist, twisting glass needle, 396-metres high, to be placed in the heart of the UNESCO-listed 18th-century city.

Other international energy projects came under pressure during the year from their Russian partners, proving that Russia was far from the enfeebled state of the 1990s when production sharing agreements had been negotiated, such as Sakhalin II, that gave Russia a share of the profits only once the foreign investors had recouped their costs. State owned businesses were closely entwined with the political establishment: Gazprom's board chairman, Dmitry Medvedev, was Russia's first deputy prime minister, for example. This incorporation of state power with major state businesses was unique amongst G-8 countries, and indicated an ongoing policy by the Russian state of seizing control of strategic assets.

The year also saw Russia make final payments in August to liquidate its US$21.3 billion debt to the Paris Club of sovereign creditors well before the deadline, and in July introduce full convertibility of the rouble six months ahead of schedule.

Nevertheless, a number of reports in 2006 questioned whether Russia really was the economic powerhouse that these developments implied. In December, the IMF concluded that GDP growth—projected to increase at 6.5 per cent in 2006-07, the same rate as 2005—was "running close to potential" and that structural reforms and more investment, particularly in the natural monopolies, would be needed for long term growth. The Russian authorities, according to the report, agreed that structural reforms (outside the banking sector) were "behind schedule", but argued that "high oil prices and robust growth make it difficult to mobilize political support for reforms". Similarly, the OECD's survey of Russia in 2006 said that the country's recent "impressive" economic performance needed improved transparency and a reining back of the state's expansion into strategic sectors if it were to be sustained. The most immediate problems were linked to corruption, however. The World Bank and the non-governmental corruption monitoring organisation, Transparency International, both rated Russia poorly in terms of accountability and control over corruption.

Weak observance of the rule of law was spectacularly demonstrated in 2006 with a series of contract killings. The two most prominent victims were Andrei Kozlov, the deputy chairman of the Russian Central Bank, who was involved in banking sector reforms to combat money laundering; and Anna Politkovskaya, an internationally-renowned journalist, murdered at the entrance of her apartment building in Moscow in October. Politkovskaya was a prominent critic of Russia's conduct of the war in Chechnya, although she also criticised human rights violations by the Chechen rebels. Her 2004 book, *Putin's Russia* (which was not published in Russia), had warned that the Putin presidency was undermining civil society. Much of the speculation about who had ordered her murder focused on the Russian-backed Chechen prime minister, Ramzan Kadyrov, who had openly called for Politkovskaya's death. Two days before her murder, Kadyrov had turned 30, making him eligible to stand as Chechnya's president, and some conspiracy theories suggested her murder was a "birthday present" for the Chechen president.

The Chechen war, now in its seventh year, continued with little sign of abating. Although the Russian authorities claimed that Kadyrov's government had the situation under control, in November a commander of Russian forces in Chechnya, Colonel-General Yevgeny Baryaev, said that young Chechens continued to join the rebel formations and that the Russian army continued to shell the mountainous areas where they were hiding. "There are no grounds to relax", said Baryaev, "either for the power structures, the law-enforcement bodies or the local authorities." This admission was a more honest portrayal of the situation than the triumphalism that accompanied the death, in July, of Chechen rebel leader Shamil Basayev, in what the Russian authorities claimed was a special operation but Chechen rebels said was an accident. Basayev had been responsible for a number of atrocities that took the Chechen war to civilians in Russia. These included the theatre siege in Moscow in 2002, and the siege of the school in Beslan, North Ossetia, in 2004 (see AR 2002, pp. 129-30; AR 2004, pp. 108-09).

The extent to which the Russian authorities had compounded the casualties from these incidents was still unclear. In December, the official commission investigating the Beslan atrocity released its report, and unsurprisingly exonerated the federal authorities from blame. However, one of the members of the commission (an explosives expert, Yury Savelyev) had earlier claimed publicly that the chaotic handling of the siege had contributed to the death toll, which in August officially rose to 332 when one of the hostages died of her injuries. The sole surviving hostage-taker to be captured, Nur-Pasha Kulayev, was convicted in May of terrorism, hostage-taking and murder.

The most bizarre Russian assassination, however, came at the end of the year in the UK, when Alexander Litvinenko, a defector from Russia's Federal Security Service, the FSB, died in a London hospital on 23 November of what turned out to be poisoning with the radioactive substance, polonium-210. Litvinenko had fled to the UK in 2000 and been granted asylum in 2001. He became a close associate and employee of the exiled Russian former oligarch, Boris Berezovsky, an opponent of Putin. In a statement released after his death, Litvinenko accused Putin of killing him. Investigations begun by the British and Russian police—although with little collaboration between the two services—failed to produce any clear lead as to who might have administered the radioactive substance to Litvinenko. Traces of polonium-210 were found in locations in London and in aircraft used by Russian contacts of Litvinenko whom he met in London; two of these men were hospitalised in Moscow at the end of the year with suspected radiation poisoning (see p. 22; for obituary of Litvinenko see p. 585).

The Litvinenko case and other high-profile assassinations highlighted international concerns over human rights in Russia. Commentators struggled for terms to describe its political system: "managed democracy" was one; "ersatz democracy" was another. *The Economist* suggested in October that Russia was "heading towards fascism", because of the increasing state corporatism and the mounting racist attacks directed against members of ethnic minorities from former Soviet republics who manned the retail business. In August, a racially-motivated bombing killed 11 people in a market in Moscow; in September, the town of Kondopoga in Karelia, on the Finnish border, was the scene of race riots in which Russians attacked Caucasian-owned businesses; and there were reprisals against Georgian businesses and ethnic Georgians living in Russia after Georgia arrested four Russian intelligence officers in September (see p. 118). This was in addition to individual racist attacks in Russia's cities—St Petersburg being particularly prone—in which 54 people died in 2006 (compared with 36 in 2005), according to the racist monitoring group, Sova.

Kremlin ideologists, however, had a different term for the new Russian reality: the concept of "sovereign democracy", coined by presidential aide Vladislav Surkov in a speech in February to activists of the ruling party, Unified Russia. Dismissed by Putin's critics (both domestic and international) as a euphemism for nascent totalitarianism, "sovereign democracy" in a more nuanced interpretation represented Russia's ambitions to regain its great-power status and become an alternative ideological and geopolitical pole to the West, an aim presented in Putin's 2005 state of the nation address (see AR 2005, pp. 101-02). The standards of liberal democracy were not part of this scenario.

BELARUS—UKRAINE—MOLDOVA

Belarus

CAPITAL: Minsk AREA: 208,000 sq km POPULATION: 9,776,000
OFFICIAL LANGUAGES: Belarusian & Russian POLITICAL SYSTEM: multiparty republic
HEAD OF STATE AND GOVERNMENT: President Alyaksandr Lukashenka (since July '94)
RULING PARTIES: Non-party supporters of President Lukashenka
PRIME MINISTER: Syarhey Sidorski (since Dec '03)
MAIN IGO MEMBERSHIPS (NON-UN): CIS, OSCE, PFP, CEI, NAM
CURRENCY: Belarusian rouble (end-'06 £1=BR4,128.92, US$1=BR2,142.00)
GNI PER CAPITA: US$2,760, US$7,890 at PPP ('05)

Ukraine

CAPITAL: Kyiv (Kiev) AREA: 604,000 sq km POPULATION: 47,111,000
OFFICIAL LANGUAGE: Ukrainian POLITICAL SYSTEM: multiparty republic
HEAD OF STATE: President Viktor Yushchenko (since Jan '05)
RULING PARTY: Party of Regions (PRU)
HEAD OF GOVERNMENT: Viktor Yanukovych (PRU), Prime Minister (since Aug '06)
MAIN IGO MEMBERSHIPS (NON-UN): CIS, OSCE, CE, PFP, BSEC, CEI
CURRENCY: hryvna (end-'06 £1=H9.86280, US$1=H5.05150)
GNI PER CAPITA: US$1,520, US$6,720 at PPP ('05)

Moldova

CAPITAL: Chisinau (Kishinev) AREA: 34,000 sq km POPULATION: 4,206,000
OFFICIAL LANGUAGE: Moldovan POLITICAL SYSTEM: multiparty republic
HEAD OF STATE: President Vladimir Voronin (since April '01)
RULING PARTY/IES: Communist Party of Moldova (PCM)
HEAD OF GOVERNMENT: Vasile Tarlev (PCM), Prime Minister (since April '01)
MAIN IGO MEMBERSHIPS (NON-UN): CIS, OSCE, CE, PFP, BSEC, CEI, Francophonie
CURRENCY: leu (end-'06 £1=ML25.3819, US$1=ML13.0000)
GNI PER CAPITA: US$880 (excl data for Transdniester republic), US$2,150 at PPP ('05)

BELARUS experienced a turbulent year in which the pro-democracy opposition failed to remove incumbent president Alyaksandr Lukashenka in the presidential elections, but nevertheless succeeded in attracting international attention through courageous protest against Lukashenka's dictatorship.

The elections, held on 19 March, were condemned by the opposition as rigged and criticised by international observers as neither free nor fair. Lukashenka won 83 per cent of the vote. There were numerous instances of intimidation of both the domestic opposition and international observers, including those from the Organisation for Security and Co-operation in Europe (OSCE). Observers from the Russian-dominated Commonwealth of Independent States (CIS), however, praised the elections as "free, open and transparent". On the evening of 19 March, protests began in central Minsk against the results, and continued for four days with numbers fluctuating from a few hundred people, who maintained an overnight vigil in freezing temperatures, to several thousand. The improvised camp set up by the protesters was forcibly dismantled by police on the night of March 23-24, with Belarusian television claiming that "alcohol, used syringes, and pornography" had been discovered there. On March 25, the two principal opposition candidates in the presidential election—Alyaksandr Milinkevich, the former rector of the Belarusian state university, and Alyaksandr Kazulin—addressed a rally of their supporters in Yanki Kupala square in Minsk. Kazulin then urged the crowd to march to a remand centre where some of those arrested at the previous rallies were being held. This march, however, was violently dispersed by the police and Kazulin himself was arrested.

In July, Kazulin was sentenced to five-and-a-half years in prison on charges of hooliganism and disturbing the peace. He went on a hunger strike in October, which he broke after 53 days, having succeeded in drawing the attention of the international community to Belarus's plight when the USA's ambassador to the United Nations raised the issue on 12 December at a closed-door session of the Security Council, much to Russia's disgruntlement. Milinkevich, meanwhile, served a brief prison sentence in the spring and was subject to repeated harassment throughout the year. In December, he received the European Parliament's Sakharov prize for freedom of thought, and dedicated it to "all those Belarusians who are struggling for freedom, all those who came to the square this spring to defend their dignity, all those who were and still are imprisoned, those who were expelled from universities and who were fired from their job".

International condemnation of the Belarusian authorities for their actions against the opposition included an entry-visa ban and asset freeze imposed in the spring on Lukashenka and other senior officials by the EU and the USA. In addition, the UN human rights rapporteur on Belarus, Adrian Severin, said in a report delivered in September, that the country was manifesting signs of being a dictatorship. He also warned that the Belarusian economy could not sustain the "protectionist, paternalist social policy" that he said the government was deploying to reward compliance with its repression of civil and human rights.

Some indication that Belarus might indeed suffer economic problems came from the unlikely quarter of Russia at the end of the year, when Russia more than doubled the price of gas which it supplied to Belarus. Agreement on a new price was reached only on 31 December, narrowly averting the threat of an interruption to gas supplies to Belarus. Crucially, the agreement also involved the sale of a 50 per cent stake in Belarus's gas distribution pipeline network to Russia's state-controlled gas monopoly, Gazprom. Russia also decided to start imposing duty on its crude oil exports to Belarus—hitherto duty-free—as of January 2007. The decision was expected to cause a significant shortfall in the Belarusian budget.

Political stability eluded UKRAINE for most of 2006, as power drained away from the president, Viktor Yushchenko, the leader of the 2004 "Orange revolution" (see AR 2004, pp. 113-15). In August, after protracted negotiations, Yushchenko's rival in the 2004 presidential elections, Viktor Yanukovych, became prime minister, and by the end of the year he appeared to have consolidated his authority.

On 26 March Ukraine held elections to the Verkhovna Rada, the unicameral 450-seat legislature. The elections were particularly significant in that they were the first to take place after constitutional amendments, agreed as part of the 2004 presidential election crisis, had transferred some presidential powers to the legislature. The new Verkhovna Rada would have the right to nominate ministers, including the prime minister; only the ministers of foreign affairs and defence, the prosecutor general, and the head of the security service would be nominated by the president and subject to approval by the legislature. The elections were also the first to form the legislature entirely through proportional representation, single-mandate districts having been abolished as part of the constitutional changes.

The elections, in which 67.7 per cent of the electorate went to the polls, were won by the Party of Regions, led by Yanukovych. Taking 32.14 per cent of the vote, it was allocated 186 seats. The "orange" forces which had forced Yanukovych to relinquish the presidency after the rigged elections of October 2004 were disunited and their potential supporters split between President Yushchenko's Our Ukraine bloc, which took almost 14 per cent of the vote and 81 seats, and the Yuliya Tymoshenko bloc—led by the eponymous, glamorous "orange princess" and former prime minister—which came second to the Party of Regions with 22.29 per cent of the vote and 129 seats.

Squabbling between Tymoshenko's supporters and the pro-presidential Our Ukraine group had destroyed the first "orange" government in 2005, forcing Tymoshenko out of office, to be replaced as prime minister by technocrat Yury Yekhanurov (see AR 2005, pp. 106-07). However, after the strong performance of the Party of Regions in the March legislative elections, it seemed that a revived "orange" alliance would be cobbled together in order to prevent the possibility of a Yanukovych government. In June, the "orange" forces agreed that Our Ukraine would nominate Petro Poroshenko as speaker of the Verkhovna Rada whilst the Yuliya Tymoshenko bloc would nominate Tymoshenko as prime minister. However, this alliance collapsed almost as soon as it had been formed when the junior partner—the Socialist party of Ukraine (SPU), which had won 33 seats in the elections—withdrew. The SPU argued that the agreement to appoint Poroshenko and Tymoshenko to the leading posts threatened political stability because of the known rivalry between them. The SPU decided to throw in its lot with the Party of Regions and the Communists (21 seats) and form a new "anti-crisis coalition" in the Verkhovna Rada which, on 18 July, formally proposed Yanukovych as prime minister.

This move introduced a renewed period of fraught negotiations between the Party of Regions and President Yushchenko. The deal to make Yanukovych prime minister was reached only at the last moment—the deadline by which the president had to endorse the nominee for prime minister or call fresh elections—and involved a "declaration of national unity" that the "anti-crisis coalition" signed with Our Ukraine, although that party was not formally admitted to the coalition. Announcing the agreement, Yushchenko said that his decision to endorse Yanukovych's candidacy proved that "I understand the whole complexity in the east and the west of Ukraine." Yanukovych's power-base, and the principal body of support for his Party of Regions, lay in the Russian-speaking eastern regions of the country.

The composition of the new cabinet, formed in August, was determined by quotas allocated to the various parties, with the president nominating the ministers of defence and foreign affairs (as provided for by the constitutional amendments introduced in 2006), and, by special agreement, the interior minister. Our Ukraine took five other portfolios. The Yuliya Tymoshenko bloc announced that it was moving into "uncompromising opposition" to Our Ukraine and the government.

Disunity swiftly reappeared, however, as it became clear that the new prime minister would not accept direction from the president, even over the thrust of Ukraine's foreign policy. Symbolically, the first foreign visit made by Prime Minister Yanukovych was to Russia, whilst in September, on a visit to Brussels, he distanced his government from the declared intentions of the Yushchenko presidency to take Ukraine into a closer relationship with—and eventual membership of—NATO, the WTO, and the EU. In October, relations between president and prime minister broke down as Our Ukraine announced that it would not, after all, join the "anti-crisis coalition" and pulled four of its ministers out of the government (one of whom later withdrew his resignation).

By November, there was open hostility between the Verkhovna Rada and the president, as the legislature sought to dismiss Foreign Minister Boris Tarasyuk, and the president stood firm against the removal of this close ally. Although at the end of the year the situation remained unresolved—Tarasyuk continued to act as foreign minister on the president's instruction, whilst finding himself barred from cabinet meetings—the hapless minister eventually resigned on 30 January 2007.

The main points of contention between President Yushchenko and Prime Minister Yanukovych thus seemed to be over foreign policy. Nevertheless, there were signs that the policy disagreements were less substantive than they appeared, and that the dispute was really a power struggle between a weakened president and an increasingly powerful prime minister. On a December visit to the USA (which Tarasyuk was rumoured to have tried to prevent), the Ukrainian prime minister insisted that membership of NATO and the EU were the long-term goals of his administration, but that public scepticism towards these bodies in Ukraine—and particularly in his constituency in the east—was a significant obstacle. He also emphasised that he was committed to transparency in government and to maintaining good relations with Russia, "as equal partners". Yanukovych pointed out that Russia was more than "just a market for our products and a supplier of energy resources"; there were, he said, "historic factors, cultural, family-related, and geopolitical ones" that influenced Ukraine's relations with its neighbour, although these relations needed to be based "upon our own national interests and priorities, primarily economic ones".

Relations with Russia were indeed vital for Ukraine, as demonstrated at the start of the year when a dispute over the price of natural gas supplied from Russia resulted in a three-day interruption in Ukraine's gas supply, prompting great alarm in other European countries downstream of the gas piped through Ukraine. By imposing sharp increases in the price of its gas (and the Turkmen gas supplied through Russian pipelines), Russia was giving notice that it was no longer prepared to subsidise the economies of Ukraine and other former Soviet states which were, after all, moving towards becoming market economies. The complex gas price deal reached in January committed Ukraine to paying a relatively modest increase; in October the price was raised again. The main damage from the affair was to Russia whose reliability as an energy supplier was viewed with greater suspicion in the West after it carried out its threat to turn off the taps to Ukraine (see pp. 106; 400-01). In Ukraine, the economy in general was relatively buoyant. An IMF report released in January 2007 noted that "Ukraine's economy has proven resilient over the last year in the face of higher energy prices and domestic political uncertainties".

In MOLDOVA the separatist Russian-speaking region, the self-proclaimed Transdniester republic, continued to thwart attempts by the international community to resolve its status. Like the two separatist regions in Georgia—Abkhazia and South Ossetia (see p. 117)—Moldova's Transdniester was a so-called "frozen conflict" arising from the fragmentation of the Soviet Union. A referendum held in the region on 17 September saw 78.6 per cent of the 390,000 registered voters casting their ballots in a two-part plebiscite in which 97.2 per cent voted in favour of independence and future attachment to Russia, whilst 94.9 per cent voted against rejecting independence for Transdniester and rejoining Moldova. The latter, as well as the EU and the USA refused to acknowledge the ballot as legitimate; Russia, however, welcomed the referendum's result, with President Vladimir Putin warning that the conflict was no different from the drive towards independence by the Kosovo region of Serbia, which was attracting considerable international support (see pp. 101-02). Critics accused Russia of seeking to use the separatist movement in the Transdniester republic to destabilise the Moldovan government, which was seeking closer ties with the West.

Whilst the referendum had little international legitimacy, it was instrumental in ensuring the overwhelming re-election on 10 December of the incumbent president of Transdniester, Igor Smirnov with 82.4 per cent of votes cast, giving him a fourth consecutive term in office.

Moldova's government, meanwhile, struggled to balance its economic dependence upon Russia with its desire to integrate further with western Europe (see AR 2005, pp. 108-09). In January, after a brief interruption in supplies, a compromise deal was reached over the price of natural gas from Russia, which was demanding prices closer to international rates from Moldova, as it was of other former Soviet republics such as UKRAINE, Georgia, and even BELARUS (see above and p. 106). However, the deal did not prevent Russia in March from imposing a ban on meat and wine imports from Moldova on health and quality grounds. As some 80-90 per cent of Moldovan wine was exported to Russia, representing 10 per cent of Moldova's GDP, the ban caused significant damage to the Moldovan economy. Russia announced in November that it would lift the ban, but without specifying when. According to the IMF, the ban and the gas price rise would cause a 2-3 per cent fall in Moldova's economic growth in 2006-07. In May the IMF approved a three-year credit arrangement, under its poverty reduction and growth facility, giving Moldova an amount equivalent to SDR80.08 million, but it warned in its first review, released in January 2007, that "the main risks to the program come from possible further deterioration in trade relations with Russia connected with the Transnistria dispute."

ARMENIA—GEORGIA—AZERBAIJAN

Armenia

CAPITAL: Yerevan AREA: 30,000 sq km POPULATION: 3,016,000
OFFICIAL LANGUAGE: Armenian POLITICAL SYSTEM: multiparty republic
HEAD OF STATE: President Robert Kocharian (since Feb '98)
RULING PARTIES: Republican Party of Armenia (NHK) heads coalition with Armenian Revolutionary Federation (Dashnak/HHD)
PRIME MINISTER: Andranik Markarian (since May '00)
MAIN IGO MEMBERSHIPS (NON-UN): CIS, CE, OSCE, PFP, BSEC, CEI
CURRENCY: dram (end-'06 £1=D704.056, US$1=D365.250)
GNI PER CAPITA: US$1,470, US$5,060 at PPP ('05)

Georgia

CAPITAL: Tbilisi AREA: 70,000 sq km POPULATION: 4,474,000
OFFICIAL LANGUAGE: Georgian POLITICAL SYSTEM: multiparty republic
HEAD OF STATE: President Mikheil Saakashvili (since Jan '04)
RULING PARTY: National Movement-Democratic Front (since March '04)
PRIME MINISTER: Zurab Noghaideli (since Feb '05)
MAIN IGO MEMBERSHIPS (NON-UN): CIS, CE, OSCE, PFP, BSEC
CURRENCY: lari (end-'06 £1=L3.34810, US$1=L1.71480)
GNI PER CAPITA: US$1,350, US$3,270 at PPP ('05 est, based on regression)

Azerbaijan

CAPITAL: Baku AREA: 87,000 sq km POPULATION: 8,388,000
OFFICIAL LANGUAGE: Azeri POLITICAL SYSTEM: multiparty republic
HEAD OF STATE: President Ilham Aliyev (since Oct '03)
RULING PARTY: New Azerbaijan Party (YAP)
PRIME MINISTER: Artur Rasizade (since Oct '03)
MAIN IGO MEMBERSHIPS (NON-UN): CIS, CE, OSCE, PFP, BSEC, OIC, ECO
CURRENCY: new manat (end-'06 £1=NM1.68650, US$1=NM0.87490)
GNI PER CAPITA: US$1,240, US$4,890 at PPP ('05)

DOMESTIC politics in all three South Caucasus states in 2006 were largely overshadowed by the ongoing search for solutions to the conflicts in Nagorno-Karabakh, Abkhazia, and South Ossetia and, in the case of Georgia, by spiralling tensions in relations with Russia.

In ARMENIA, the speaker of the National Assembly (unicameral legislature), Artur Baghdasarian, stepped down on 22 May following a public polemic with President Robert Kocharian over whether Armenia should join NATO. Deputy Speaker Tigran Torosian was elected to succeed Baghdasarian on 1 June. Baghdasarian's Orinats Yerkir party left the coalition government, in which it was replaced by the small pro-presidential United Labour Party, which had six National Assembly mandates. The Prosperous Armenia party, founded by wealthy businessman Gagik Tsarukian, attracted tens of thousands of new members, emerging as the main challenger to the ruling Republican Party of Armenia (HHK) in the legislative elections due in May 2007. Defence Minister Serge Sarkisian, regarded as a potential successor to President Kocharian when the latter's second and final term ended in 2008, joined, and was immediately elected to a leading position in the HHK in July. In late November, two members of an association representing former combatants in the Karabakh war, Zhirayr Sefilian and Vartan Malkhasian, were arrested on charges of plotting a coup d'etat prior to the 2007 parliamentary ballot. A senior tax official was killed by a car bomb in Yerevan on 6 September, and two village mayors were shot dead in August and December.

Following their defeat in elections to the Milli Mejlis (unicameral legislature) in November 2005 (see AR 2005, pp. 111-12), some opposition parties in AZERBAIJAN decided against either fielding candidates in the 13 May repeat elections in 10 constituencies or participating in the new Milli Mejlis. Opposition candidates failed to win any of those 10 seats. The opposition Azerbaijan National Independence party split into two, while the Musavat party was rent by protracted infighting. The ruling New Azerbaijan party (YAP) won most seats in elections to local councils on 6 October.

Former senior interior ministry official Gadzhi Mamedov went on trial on charges of masterminding several murders and abductions, and in testimony in July accused the former economic development minister, Farkhad Aliyev (who was under arrest), of the March 2005 killing of opposition journalist Elmar Huseynov (see AR 2005, p. 112). Several opposition journalists were assaulted and beaten in 2006. In late November, the opposition Azerbaijan Popular Front party and three opposition media outlets were evicted from the premises they rented in central Baku, and the popular independent television channel ANS was shut down, but allowed to resume broadcasting two weeks later following widespread international condemnation of the ban.

In GEORGIA, the opposition Democratic Front faction boycotted Parliament for several months, beginning in April, to protest over the perceived harassment of one of its deputies. The party was then trounced by the ruling United National Movement in the 5 October local elections. President Mikheil Saakashvili steadfastly ignored repeated opposition calls for the resignation of his close associate, Interior Minister Vano Merabishvili, four of whose subordinates were sentenced in July for the January murder of a young banker. Saakashvili dismissed his minister for conflict resolution, Giorgi Khaindrava, on 21 July, shortly after Khaindrava argued that Merabishvili should have resigned over the killing. The interior ministry's role in and handling of unrest in a Tbilisi prison on 27 March in which seven prisoners died was also widely criticised. Saakashvili did, however, dismiss the hawkish defence minister, Irakli Okruashvili, in November, appointing him instead as minister of economic development. Okruashvili resigned from that post after only one week.

Interior ministry troops were deployed in late July to the Kodori gorge, which straddled western Georgia and the separatist unrecognised Republic of Abkhazia to apprehend renegade local official Emzar Kvitsiani, whom the Georgian authorities accused of plotting a coup. Kvitsiani eluded capture, but former senior security official Irakli Batiashvili was arrested on charges of colluding with him, and remained in pre-trial detention as of the end of 2006. So too did 12 supporters of fugitive former National Security Minister and Justice party chairman Igor Giorgadze, who were arrested on 7 September on charges of conspiring to overthrow the Georgian leadership.

Armenian President Kocharian and his Azerbaijani counterpart Ilham Aliyev met three times—on the outskirts of Paris on 10-11 February, in Bucharest on 5 June, and in Minsk on 28 November—to discuss approaches to resolving the Nagorno-Karabakh conflict. According to Azerbaijani Foreign Minister Elmar Mammadyarov, the two sides had narrowed the points of difference between them, but had not reached total agreement on a framework peace plan drafted by the Minsk group of the Organisation for Security and Co-operation in Europe (OSCE), details of which were made public in late July. On 10 December, Armenian voters in the unrecognised Nagorno-Karabakh Republic overwhelmingly endorsed a new constitution in a referendum dismissed by the international community as not legally valid.

Georgian and Abkhaz representatives met for the first time in five years under the auspices of the UN in Tbilisi, the Georgian capital, on 15 May, but hopes of galvanising the deadlocked peace talks, and specifically for the signing of a non-aggression pact, crumbled four weeks later when President Saakashvili appointed his moderate negotiator in those talks, Irakli Alasania, as ambassador to the UN. The Abkhaz authorities suspended peace talks in late July after the botched Georgian incursion into the Kodori gorge (see above), and later said that they would return to the negotiating table only when Georgia complied with a 13 October UN Security Council resolution calling for the withdrawal of unauthorised Georgian forces still in Kodori.

The leaders of the unrecognised Republic of South Ossetia rejected all Georgian peace overtures and repeatedly accused Georgia of planning a new attack. South Ossetian National Security Council Secretary Oleg Alborov and two teenagers were killed in separate bomb blasts in Tskhinvali, the capital of South Ossetia, on 9 and 14 July. South Ossetia's president, Eduard Kokoity, was re-elected for a second term on 12 November, while South Ossetia's Georgian population elected Dmitry Sanakoyev as their "president" in a separate ballot. The international community declined to recognise either ballot as valid, and similarly rejected the simultaneous referendum in which Ossetians overwhelmingly registered support for their republic's unrecognised "independent" status.

ARMENIA maintained its cordial relations with Russia, and in return for ceding control of further state assets secured a two year postponement of the anticipated steep rise in the price of imported Russian gas. Construction of a pipeline intended to import gas from Iran was almost complete by year's end. President Kocharian visited Tehran in July. AZERBAIJAN and GEORGIA, similarly faced with a 100 per cent increase in the price of imported Russian gas, sought to diversify supplies to reduce their dependence on Russia, reaching agreement in late December on sharing Turkey's quota for 2007 of gas from Azerbaijan's offshore Shah Deniz field. The South Caucasus pipeline that was to transport that gas from Baku via Tbilisi to Erzerum in eastern Turkey was commissioned in late December.

All three countries signed agreements in Brussels on 14 November cementing their accession to the EU's new neighbourhood programme. On 22 September, NATO formally invited Georgia to begin an "intensified dialogue", the penultimate stage prior to qualifying for a formal invitation to join the alliance. Azerbaijani President Aliyev and Georgian President Saakashvili paid state visits to the USA in late April and July respectively. Georgian Prime Minister Zurab Noghaideli also visited Washington DC in November to solicit more US investment and support for Georgia's pro-Western foreign policy.

GEORGIA'S relations with Russia reached an all-time low. Saakashvili blamed Moscow for explosions in late January which cut supplies of electricity and natural gas to Georgia. In late March, Russia banned imports of Georgian wine and mineral water on quality grounds, a ban which Saakashvili denounced as politically motivated. On 15 February, the Georgian Parliament criticised as ineffective the Russian peacekeeping forces deployed in South Ossetia and accused Russia of seeking to annex that region; and on 18 July it called for the withdrawal of Russian peacekeepers from both South Ossetia and Abkhazia and their replacement by an international contingent.

On 27 September, the Georgian authorities arrested four Russian servicemen in Tbilisi and accused them of espionage. As a result of intercession by the EU and the OSCE, the four were handed over to the OSCE in Tbilisi on 2 October and deported to Russia. On 3 October, Russia nonetheless imposed a total transport blockade on Georgia and began selectively deporting Georgian citizens currently living and working in Russia. Russia's president, Vladimir Putin, who met Saakashvili in June in an unsuccessful bid to defuse bilateral tensions, would not agree to a similar one-on-one meeting in late November.

ARMENIA and AZERBAIJAN again boasted double-digit economic growth in 2006, with GDP increasing by an estimated 13.5 per cent in Armenia, despite stagnating industrial output that fuelled the foreign trade deficit, and by a record 34 per cent in Azerbaijan during the first eight months of the year. The Baku-Tbilisi-Ceyhan export pipeline for Azerbaijan's Caspian oil was formally inaugurated on 13 July (see AR 2005, pp. 74; 113). On the basis of 8.4 per cent GDP growth in January-November, officials in GEORGIA predicted annual growth of 10-11 per cent.

IV THE AMERICAS AND THE CARIBBEAN

UNITED STATES OF AMERICA

CAPITAL: Washington, DC AREA: 9,364,000 sq km POPULATION: 296,497,000
OFFICIAL LANGUAGE: English (de facto); Spanish widely used POLITICAL SYSTEM: multiparty republic
HEAD OF STATE AND GOVERNMENT: President George W. Bush, Republican, since Jan '01
RULING PARTY: Congress is controlled by the Democrats
MAIN IGO MEMBERSHIPS (NON-UN): NATO, OSCE, OECD, G-8, OAS, NAFTA, APEC, AC, CP, PC, ANZUS, DR-CAFTA
CURRENCY: US dollar (end-'06 £1=US$1.95250, €1=$1.31960)
GNI PER CAPITA: US$43,740, US$41,950 at PPP ('05)

THE war in Iraq and the "war on terror" dominated much of the nation's public life during what President George W. Bush predicted in January would be a "decisive year". The year's predominant domestic issues—the state of the economy and illegal immigration—also proved to be inextricably bound up with questions of the USA's relations to the world beyond its borders. Elections in November to Congress (the bicameral legislature), and the campaigns that preceded them, provided the major venues for public discussion of the economic, cultural, military, diplomatic, and political challenges facing the country.

ECONOMY. In January the Senate (the upper house of Congress) confirmed President Bush's choice to replace Alan Greenspan—a "legend" according to the president—who was retiring after almost two decades as chairman of the Federal Reserve, the country's central bank. Educated at Harvard and the Massachusetts Institute of Technology, Ben Bernanke had been a professor of economics at Princeton and a member of the Federal Reserve's board of governors before becoming the chairman of the president's council of economic advisers in June 2005. Bernanke was a popular choice with both domestic financial institutions and international investors. In his annual state of the union address, delivered on 31 January, the president touted what he saw as the successes of the economy, while stressing the priorities of "keeping America competitive" and maintaining the nation's leadership in the global economy. "We will choose to build our prosperity by leading the world economy...or shut ourselves off from trade and opportunity", insisted Bush, positing a choice between his policies and those of the protectionists and centralisers who favoured "walling off our economy", concentrating "more power in Washington and raising taxes". His proposals included making previous tax cuts permanent, reducing the cost of healthcare, and opening more international markets to US products.

Financial indicators sent mixed messages to those seeking to assess the state of the country's economy. The stock market offered one area of rapid growth, with the Dow Jones index breaking through the 12,000 point mark, exceeding even the highs of the dot.com Internet investment bubble of the late 1990s. Investors nostalgic for those heady days were doubtless cheered by the fact that, by the year's end, US$500 could buy an adventurous investor one entire share in the Internet search engine company Google Inc.. After a long period of rising prices, the housing market slowed down significantly while interest rates rose. The rate of inflation fell to 2.6 per cent, its lowest level since 2003. The unemployment rate ended the year at 4.5 per cent, down from 4.7 per cent in January, with jobs growing in several areas of the economy, including healthcare and food services. That much of the growth came in service rather than manufacturing industries did little to allay fears that better-paying, skilled jobs were being "outsourced" to countries in Asia and South America, or just disappearing altogether. The automobile manufacturing giants Ford and General Motors, for example, announced plans for substantial job and plant reductions over the coming years in an effort to deal with escalating losses in the face of stiff overseas competition.

The rising cost of oil was one factor contributing to consumers' declining appetite for US-made cars. Prices rose significantly in the first half of the year, from just over US$60 per barrel to almost US$80 by the summer, with average national prices for a gallon of gasoline breaking the US$3 barrier in August. Prices then began to fall and by December had returned to the levels at which they began the year. Nevertheless, the steep summer rise challenged long-standing popular assumptions that cheap fuel was a national birthright and intensified fears of global vulnerability for a nation that consumed about one-quarter of the world's oil, two-thirds of it imported. The ex-oilman in the White House acknowledged these concerns when, to the surprise of many, the president announced in January that the country was "addicted to oil". Bush proposed an extended and expensive period of national rehabilitation that included an "advanced energy initiative" intended to increase funding for research into alternative fuels, such as solar, wind, and "safe nuclear" energy, as well as hydrogen and ethanol for transportation. "By applying the talent and technology of America" in these areas, Bush insisted, "this country can dramatically improve our environment, move beyond a petroleum-based economy, and make our dependence on Middle Eastern oil a thing of the past." There were some signs that energy users were adjusting their behaviour in response to rising prices by opting for smaller, more fuel-efficient cars over larger, low-mileage vehicles.

The popularity of foreign-made cars contributed to the country's continuing trade deficit, which reached over US$700 billion by November, on track to break the existing record—set in 2005—of US$717 billion. The significant decline of the US dollar over much of the year against many currencies, including the euro and the pound sterling, helped to make US exports more competitive in certain markets. The dollar declined much less against the currencies of the major Asian economic powers, Japan and China. The trade deficit with China alone stood at well over US$200 billion by the year's end. The national debt reached approximately US$8,500 billion in 2006, with a record proportion of it owed to other countries and foreign banks.

May saw a decisive moment in the long-running Enron scandal when, after a trial lasting more than three months, Ken Lay and Jeffrey Skilling—former executives of the energy company—were found guilty on multiple counts of fraud and conspiracy (see AR 2002, p. 147). Lay died of a heart attack several weeks later, while on vacation in Aspen, Colorado. He was 64 (for obituary, see p. 585). In September, Skilling was sentenced to 24 years in prison.

DIPLOMATIC AFFAIRS. Questions of energy policy and the country's dependence on foreign oil took on particular urgency not only because of the precarious state of affairs in the Middle East, but also as a consequence of the USA's deepening diplomatic differences with major oil producers, Venezuela and Iran. Already strained relations with the leftist government of Venezuela's president, Hugo Chávez Frías, continued to deteriorate (see pp. 180-81; AR 2005, pp. 166-67). In May, President Bush announced that the USA would stop selling military supplies to Venezuela. Addressing the UN General Assembly in September, one day after Bush had done so, Chávez explained to his audience that "the devil came here yesterday", and it "smells of sulphur still today." Reverting to a more conventional leftist critique of US foreign policy, the Venezuelan leader went on to insist that "the American empire is doing all it can to consolidate its hegemonistic system of domination, and we cannot allow him to do that. We cannot allow world dictatorship to be consolidated." One USA-Venezuela deal that did go ahead was Chávez's plan to supply cut-price heating oil to poor residents of Massachusetts and New York, through an arrangement between the Venezuelan government-controlled Citgo Petroleum Corporation and non-profit organisations in those states. Supplies began to arrive in November.

President Mahmoud Ahmadinejad of Iran, a Chávez ally, also continued his rhetorical and diplomatic jousting with President Bush. Tensions in relations between Iran and the USA continued around the issues of Iran's nuclear programme and its providing of training and supplies to Shi'ite militias in Iraq. Throughout the year Iran sparred with the USA, the UN, and the International Atomic Energy Agency (IAEA) over the development of its nuclear programme and its refusal to co-operate with IAEA inspectors (see pp. 280-82). Negotiations between Iran and both the IAEA and several European countries made little progress. In July a UN Security Council resolution (1696 (2006)) called on Iran to stop the enrichment of uranium or face sanctions. In the face of Iranian resistance to these demands, the UN Security Council unanimously approved limited sanctions in December (resolution 1737 (2006)). (For text see pp. 542-48). The Bush administration also accused Iran, as well as Syria, of aiding and abetting insurgents crossing their borders into Iraq, charges that both countries repeatedly denied. The administration continued to reject calls that it negotiate directly with Syria and Iran in order to solicit their assistance in bringing greater order to Iraq.

In November the Senate, by a vote of 85 to 12, gave strong support to an agreement negotiated between President Bush and India's Prime Minister Manmohan Singh that would allow the USA to provide India with nuclear fuels and technology for its civilian nuclear power programme (see pp. 300-01). The vote reflected the US priority of nurturing an increasingly influential India as an ally and as a customer, with Senator Richard Lugar, Republican chair of the foreign relations committee, describing the pact as "one more important step toward a vibrant and exciting relationship between our two great democracies". The deal did have its critics. They argued that providing supplies for its civilian programme allowed India to devote other resources to its nuclear weapons programme, which—unlike the civilian one—would still remain beyond international inspection. They argued that making this exemption to non-proliferation policies would allow India to produce more weapons, encourage regional rivals Pakistan and China to do the same, and, more generally, send a mixed message to the world at a time when the USA was also making strenuous efforts to prevent countries such as Iran and North Korea from developing nuclear weapons. The Senate bill still remained to be reconciled with the version adopted by the House of Representatives (the lower chamber of Congress), which was passed in July by a vote of 359 to 68.

North Korea's nuclear programme continued to be a major focus of US concern. In July missile tests in the Sea of Japan brought widespread condemnation and prompted a unanimous UN Security Council resolution (1695 (2006)) calling on North Korea to stop such testing and to resume negotiations about the future of its nuclear programme. In October, the underground testing of a North Korean nuclear weapon prompted even greater international concern and the unanimous passage of UN Security Council resolution 1718 (2006) banning the sale of materials that could be used to make weapons of mass destruction and sanctioning the inspection by other countries of goods bound for or leaving North Korea (for texts see pp. 552-58). Bush described the weapons test as "a threat to international peace and security" but also re-stated his commitment to seeking, along with nations neighbouring North Korea, a multilateral diplomatic solution to the problem. North Korean representatives, however, continued to insist on direct negotiations between their country and the USA.

As well as his June visit to Iraq (see below), President Bush visited Afghanistan in March, where he was welcomed by his counterpart Hamid Karzai who told him that Afghans "owe a great, great deal in this country's rebuilding—peace, democracy, the strong steps toward the future—to your support, to your leadership, to the American people, and to the way you have given your hand to the Afghan people." Bush also visited India and Pakistan on his March trip, where he discussed the USA's strengthening relations with those countries.

Later that month he visited Mexico where he met President Vicente Fox Quesada, as well as Canada's new Prime Minister, Stephen Harper. In July he visited Germany on his way to Russia for the annual G-8 summit. He attended the November NATO summit in Latvia, a recent addition to the alliance. The same month Bush visited Vietnam for the Asia-Pacific Economic Co-operation (APEC) meeting, also making stops in Indonesia and Singapore.

The president hosted numerous foreign leaders during the year, including those of Australia, Brazil, China, Germany, Israel, Italy, Lebanon, and Turkey. In June President Bush accompanied Japan's Prime Minister Junichiro

Koizumi, a devotee of Elvis Presley, to the late singer's Graceland mansion in Memphis, Tennessee. Bush thanked Priscilla Presley and her daughter, Lisa Marie Presley, for hosting this "unusual experience" while an overwhelmed Koizumi, more than once breaking into the songs of his musical hero, thanked the president "very much for treating me nice". Another unusual experience occurred in May during a visit to Washington DC by UK Prime Minister Tony Blair—more of a Beatles man—when both leaders acknowledged that the occasional regrettable mistake had indeed been made during the invasion and subsequent occupation of Iraq.

SOCIETY AND CULTURE. The world of international affairs continued to intersect with the realms of celebrity and philanthropy. Africa continued to attract the attention of the rich and famous. Actor George Clooney became the most public figure to speak out on behalf of the people of Darfur as they faced attack from the Sudanese government and its allies (see pp. 217-19). In May the multi-tattooed actor, Angelina Jolie, travelled to Namibia with her fellow performer and new beau, Brad Pitt, for the birth of their baby, Shiloh Nouvel Pitt-Jolie, bringing more attention to the southern African country than it had received since the USA and the Soviet Union were pumping it full of military hardware in the heyday of the Cold War. Singing star Madonna became embroiled in controversy when she sought to adopt a Malawian toddler named David Banda amid conflicting reports as to whether or not the boy's father approved of his departure for a life of mansions and paparazzi in the West (see pp. 268-69). Undeterred by criticism, Madonna exhorted other members of the fortunate classes to follow her example. June brought good news for those required to remain in sub-Saharan Africa when the fabulously wealthy investment guru, Warren Buffett, announced that he would be giving 85 per cent of his billions to philanthropic foundations, most of it to the one run by the fabulously wealthy computer magnate, Bill Gates, and his wife, Melinda Gates. This unprecedented pact between, according to *Forbes* magazine, the world's two richest people augured well for the many programmes run by the Gates foundation, including those that addressed children's health in Africa. In the face of such generosity it was, perhaps, considered impolite to dwell on the oddities of a global economic system—often praised for its free-functioning rationality—that would enable two people to amass combined personal fortunes worth 50 times the GDP of the country that little David Banda was leaving behind.

Back home, celebrities, especially musicians, also did their bit to aid the reconstruction of New Orleans, an iconic city in the history of music. As rebuilding proceeded, the continuing impact of Hurricane Katrina—which had smashed the Gulf Coast in August 2005 (see AR 2005, pp. 121-24)—only occasionally came to national attention. It did so in January when President Bush visited Mississippi and Louisiana to see and discuss reconstruction efforts on the Gulf Coast. This was the first of several presidential visits over the course of the year. In February a congressional report on the response to, and the aftermath of, the catastrophe took 600 pages to argue that "Katrina was a national failure, an abdication of the most solemn obligation to provide for the common welfare. At every level—individual, corporate, philanthropic, and governmental—we failed to meet the challenge that was Katrina." The report was especially unsparing in its criticisms of the department of homeland security and its head, Michael Chertoff. Describing a federal response characterised by "fecklessness, flailing and organizational paralysis", the report maintained that "a blinding lack of situational awareness and disjointed decision making needlessly compounded and prolonged Katrina's horror." Chertoff, for his part, rejected criticisms that his department, which contained the Federal Emergency Relief Agency (FEMA), had neglected preparation for natural disasters because of its preoccupation with readying itself for possible terrorist attacks. The president proclaimed 29 August a national day of remembrance of Hurricane Katrina. Fortunately, the 2006 hurricane season was mercifully mild with no major storm system reaching the US coasts.

It was a year of extreme and destructive weather nonetheless. March brought massive wildfires to Texas, while both early spring and autumn were marked by violent storms and tornadoes in the South and Midwest. Spring also brought heavy rains and flooding to both coasts, with New England experiencing its worst flooding in decades. Summer brought extended heatwaves, resulting in numerous deaths, particularly among the elderly. The scorching summer and a milder than usual start to winter helped to make 2006 the USA's warmest year on record. There were man-made disasters, too. In early January a group of 13 miners was trapped underground by an explosion in a coal mine in Sago, West Virginia. Twelve of the men died, a tragedy compounded by an erroneous report claiming that all but one of them had been found alive. Their relatives' joy turned to anger several hours later when it emerged that only one man had survived. Grieving relatives directed their ire at officials from the mine's owners, International Coal Group. In October a vast arson fire in Cabazon, California, destroyed homes and land and took the lives of five firefighters attempting to bring it under control.

As well as those made briefly famous by their death, many of the already famous and influential died in 2006. The world of food lost Robert Baker, inventor of the chicken nugget. The world of Reds lost two of its own, actor Aaron "Red" Buttons and basketball coach and executive Arnold "Red" Auerbach. Two prominent Texas politicians—Senator Lloyd Bentsen and Governor Ann Richards—and two influential and controversial members of the Reagan administration—Jeane Kirkpatrick, academic and UN ambassador, and Caspar Weinberger, former defence secretary—passed away. The creators of two very different icons of World War II died: Iva Toguri D'Aquino, known (falsely) as the radio propagandist "Tokyo Rose", and photographer Joe Rosenthal, who was turned down for military service due to his poor eyesight but nevertheless maintained his focus long enough to capture for history the US Marines' raising of the star-spangled banner on Iwo Jima. Famous economists Milton Friedman and John Kenneth Galbraith drew their last graph. Civil rights leader, Coretta Scott King, and feminist author of the culture-changing *The Feminine Mystique*,

Betty Friedan, also passed away. Authors Mickey Spillane and William Styron, poet Stanley Kunitz, playwright Wendy Wasserstein and historian Lawrence W. Levine died, while the arts community lost Robert Altman, film director; Joseph Barbera, legendary cartoon producer; actors Maureen Stapleton and Glenn Ford, opera director Sarah Caldwell, and dancer and choreographer Katherine Dunham. Female sporting pioneers Ann Calvello, the roller derby legend also known as "the meanest mama on skates", and stock car racer Louise Smith died. So too did two world champion boxers: heavyweight Floyd Patterson and featherweight Willie Pep. It was a year of loss for US music with the death of a number of its great and influential figures, including country music songwriter Marijohn Wilkin, who co-wrote classics such as *Long Black Veil* and *One Day at a Time*, singers and musicians Wilson Pickett, Gene Pitney, Billy Preston, Lou Rawls, Anita O'Day, Buck Owens, and—on 25 December, Christmas day, the self-proclaimed "godfather of soul", James Brown. Brown famously said of those who styled themselves after him, "I taught them everything they know, but not everything I know." As Brown "lay in state" at the Apollo theatre in Harlem, fans danced in memoriam in the streets. (For Bentsen, Richards, Kirkpatrick, Weinberger, Friedman, Galbraith, Friedan, Spillane, Styron, Altman, Patterson, and Brown see Obituary).

On 26 December, Gerald R. Ford, 38th president of the USA, died. Appropriately understated but heartfelt praise came from all corners of the political world for a man widely deemed as surpassingly decent and genuinely bipartisan in the often indecent and overly partisan world of Washington politics. Memorials to Ford, arguably downplaying the furore created at the time by his pardoning of his predecessor, Richard M. Nixon, credited him with easing the country's path away from the divisive crises of the Vietnam war and the Watergate scandal and towards a restoration of unity and the hope of national renewal (for obituary see p. 577).

NATIONAL SECURITY. If interviews conducted in his final months but not released until after his death were any guide, Ford was one of the growing number of Republicans who had come to harbour doubts about the conduct of the war in Iraq. Whatever his occasional acknowledgements of errors in its conduct, President Bush continued to insist that there was no alternative to perseverance and victory in Iraq, and to present the conflict in Iraq as part of a larger struggle in which security at home was inseparably bound up with the pursuit of freedom and the vigorous prosecution of the "war on terror" beyond the nation's borders. "Abroad", the president proclaimed in his January state of the union speech, the USA remained "committed to an historic, long-term goal—we seek the end of tyranny in our world". Acknowledging that there were those who would "dismiss that goal as misguided idealism", Bush maintained that global altruism and national self-interest were harmonious goals, insisting that "every step toward freedom in the world makes our country safer." The USA stood ready "once again", the president proclaimed, to "accept the call of history to deliver the oppressed and move this world toward peace".

In Bush's view, Iraq remained the "the central front" in this larger battle to spread freedom and to defeat those who "rage and fight against it". As in 2005, political developments and increasing violence continued to proceed in an uneasy symbiosis, with the balance—in the eyes of most observers—increasingly tilting away from compromise and order towards bloodshed and chaos. The results of Iraq's elections in December 2005 were announced on 20 January. The United Iraqi Alliance, a coalition of Shi'ite parties, won the most seats—128—but not enough to give it the two-thirds majority required to control the Council of Representatives (the unicameral legislature) under the new constitutional arrangements (see AR 2005, pp. 186-88). The Kurdistan Alliance and the Iraqi Consensus Front, a Sunni coalition, were the next largest blocs in the new assembly. After intense negotiations a new government took office in May, under the leadership of Prime Minister Nouri al-Maliki, a compromise choice of the Shi'ite parties, and President Jalal Talabani, a Kurdish leader (see pp. 205-06).

The intense conflicts and lengthy negotiations that shaped the formation of the new government pointed to the depths of political and sectarian divisions which also found expression in many acts of extreme violence. In this respect, the year began in distressing and familiar fashion from the perspective of the USA and its coalition and Iraqi allies. Over 100 Shi'ite pilgrims in Karbala and 50 men applying for jobs in the police force in Ramadi were killed in early January. Similar kinds of attacks persisted throughout the year. A Pentagon (US department of defence) report at the end of the year estimated that the average number of attacks aimed at both military and civilian targets had risen to almost 1,000 per week. The nature of the violence reflected the inter-related threats facing efforts to create a stable Iraq. Attacks by insurgent groups such as al-Qaida in Iraq were aimed at elements (such as the police) of the emerging Iraqi state. The intensifying attacks carried out by Shi'ite and Sunni militias on members of the rival communities indicated a deepening sectarian divide. The high levels of violence and disorder afflicting certain parts of the country also took their toll on efforts to reconstruct Iraq's society and economy. While there were some improvements—in agriculture, for example—oil production had still not returned to pre-war levels, and unemployment and inflation rates remained very high.

June brought a moment of good news for the Bush administration when US forces killed the leader of the al-Qaida Organisation for Holy War in Iraq, Abu Musab al-Zarqawi (see p. 208). The same month Bush made his first visit to Iraq's capital, Baghdad, since November of 2003. He met the new prime minister and his cabinet and "assured them that we'll keep our commitment". He "also made it clear to them that in order for us to keep our commitment and be successful, they themselves have to do some hard things", such as curtailing the militias, further developing the country's own security services, and making the compromises necessary to win over more Sunnis to the political process. As the year progressed, neither the killing of Zarqawi nor the creation of a new government had an appreciable impact on the levels of carnage and chaos blighting daily life in Iraq. US casualties continued to rise. December proved the deadliest month of the year for US forces, with over 100 servicemen and women killed. The last day of the year saw the US death toll since the beginning of the conflict surpass 3,000 while combat casualties numbered more than 22,000.

The escalating violence, and the seeming unwillingness or inability of either the Iraqi or US government to deal with it, proved to be central elements in the debate over war policy that dominated political life back in the USA. While the president's public pronouncements continued to emphasise the role of outside insurgents in generating the violence and unrest, others focused increasingly on the sectarian violence dividing Iraqis themselves. Pentagon officials, speaking in November at the release of the Pentagon's quarterly report to Congress, acknowledged that the insurgents, through actions such as the bombing of Samarra's al-Askariya shrine in February (see p. 207), had achieved a major "strategic success" in fomenting sectarian violence that had "escalated at an unbelievably rapid pace". According to the report, the foreign insurgents' activities now provided the "backdrop" to the increasingly violent Sunni-Shi'ite battle for "religious, political and economic influence". Critics of the war agreed that it was now this "civil war" that presented the major, perhaps insuperable, barrier to the USA's achieving victory—however modestly redefined—in Iraq.

Opinion polls and opinion makers charted the growing dissatisfaction with the US government's handling of the war. Among the harshest, and most surprising, of the critics, were some of the neo-conservative thinkers and pundits who had been the strongest proponents of going to war. Some now distanced themselves from the manner in which it was being conducted. Kenneth Adelman, who had served in the Reagan administration and more recently on the defence policy board, an advisory committee to the department of defence, admitted that he had greatly overestimated the competence of a "national security team" that he claimed had "turned out to be among the most incompetent teams in the post-war era. Not only did each of them, individually, have enormous flaws, but together they were deadly, dysfunctional." Emboldened by growing public criticism of the war and of the president's apparent intransigence in the face of that criticism, Democratic party leaders resolved to make the war in Iraq a central issue of the midterm elections.

As public attention and political debate focused on Iraq, Afghanistan remained something of a forgotten front in the "war on terror". There was growing evidence of a resurgence in the Taliban's influence as economic reconstruction failed to have the desired results and opium production increased dramatically in areas where the Taliban or tribal warlords held sway. Taliban attacks on government and NATO targets increased in number and sophistication, and NATO units engaged in heavy fighting with Taliban forces at various times throughout the year (see pp. 283-85). Afghanistan attracted greater attention as the year progressed, with most observers agreeing that, from the US perspective, the situation was worsening considerably. Nevertheless most attention remained on the administration's conduct of the war in Iraq, helping to ensure that it would be the dominant issue in the November elections.

POLITICS. Other issues that had preoccupied the political classes in 2005 slipped from public attention. Conflicts over judicial interests and ideologies subsided as the battles over Supreme Court nominees concluded quietly at the end of January when the Senate voted 58 to 42 to confirm Samuel Alito's appointment to the Supreme Court (see AR 2005, pp. 116-17). The question of who had revealed to the media that Valerie Plame was a CIA agent had been a major story in 2005 (see AR 2005, pp. 117-18), but no longer gripped Washington DC. I. Lewis "Scooter" Libby, former chief-of-staff to Vice-President Dick Cheney, had been indicted in 2005 but had still not gone on trial. Meanwhile the investigation into presidential advisor Karl Rove's role in the matter concluded without any indictment. Both Rove and Robert Novak, the journalist who had first written of Plame's status, acknowledged that Rove had been one of Novak's sources. In July Plame and her husband Joseph Wilson sued Cheney, Libby, and Rove, accusing them of conspiring to punish Wilson for his criticism of the president's rationale for invading Iraq. Interest was briefly revived in August, when Richard Armitage, former deputy secretary of state to Colin Powell, was finally revealed as Novak's original source. Armitage claimed to have "inadvertently" divulged Plame's status to the columnist.

As pundits looked forward to Libby's trial, it was the likely testimony of the vice-president, whose low public profile seemed much of the time in an inverse relationship to his inside influence, that aroused their anticipation. Cheney attracted further unwelcome attention in February when he accidentally shot a friend and Republican party supporter, Harry Whittington, while they hunted for quail on a south Texas ranch. Whittington recovered, but the incident briefly aroused questions of why news of a serious accident involving the vice-president was not released for almost a day, and then by the owner of the ranch to a local news outlet in Corpus Christi rather than to the national media.

Of the major policy issues raised by President Bush at the start of his second term, the reform of social security had largely slipped from public sight by 2006. The president did call for the establishment of a bipartisan commission to investigate the impact of the country's aging population—particularly the retirement of the "baby boom" generation—on social security, and the healthcare schemes for the elderly (Medicare) and the poor (Medicaid). The resort to such a commission itself reflected a retreat from the more ambitious agenda of the previous year in the face of intense opposition and unease, even among his own supporters.

Illegal immigration was one issue that increased in visibility during 2006. It proved challenging to politicians in both parties, eager to appease supporters in favour of tougher border and immigration controls, while not wishing to alienate potential supporters among a Latino population growing in political influence. That influence was on display on 1 May, when protests and boycotts—collectively entitled "a day without immigrants"—were held in towns and cities across the country. Marchers numbered in the hundreds of thousands in Chicago and Los Angeles, although they were far fewer in most other places and overall numbers were less than organisers had predicted.

Both major parties remained divided on the issue. Bush continued to encourage Congress to pass legislation allowing for both a guest worker programme to tackle the issue of the estimated 11 million illegal immigrants already in the country, and for a tougher set of measures to ensure better border security in the future. He argued that only this dual approach could take account of the economic indispensability of immigrant labour while addressing public concern regarding the nation's porous southern border. His own party was divided on the issue. Some, like Senator John McCain of Arizona, supported a guest worker programme, as did many Democrats. Various kinds of guest worker plan were proposed, but most included provisions through which illegal immigrants would identify themselves for registration, be allowed to work for a period of years, and, by meeting various other requirements, eventually be allowed to apply for legal residency or citizenship. Other Republicans, mindful of present public opinion on the issue and past proposals which granted amnesty to illegal immigrants but did not secure the border, refused to support the president's two-pronged approach. Republicans, such as Senator Johnny Isakson of Georgia, demanded that the borders be secured before any amnesty or guest worker programme be considered. They called for the hiring of more border guards, greater surveillance of the border regions, a crackdown on employers who hired illegal workers, and, in some cases, the construction of a wall along parts of the border.

The Senate eventually passed a bill in May which combined guest worker and security elements. Its bipartisan supporters, led by Senators McCain and Edward Kennedy of Massachusetts, acknowledged that it was unlikely to find favour in the House of Representatives, which had already passed a security-only bill in December 2005 that called for making illegal immigration a felony and for building a 1,125 km fence along the border. The unresolved issue of illegal immigration and its social and cultural as well as economic consequences for the country would prove to be one of the more contentious issues in the autumn election campaigns.

The odour of corruption permeated the fabric of the nation's politics in 2006. Several scandals linked the corporate world to the political world by way of influential lobbyists. The year began with lobbyist Jack Abramoff pleading guilty to various charges, including conspiracy to bribe government officials and tax evasion. In return for the plea he offered to provide evidence against members of Congress and other government officials said to have been the beneficiaries of gifts and hospitality in return for legislative favours.

Among those affected by the Abramoff investigation was former House majority leader Tom DeLay, the Republican congressman from Texas, who had participated in a golfing trip to St Andrews, Scotland, with Abramoff in 2000. In addition, two of DeLay's former aides who later went to work for Abramoff, Michael Scanlon and Tony C. Rudy, pleaded guilty to charges relating to illegal activities involving the high-profile lobbyist. DeLay himself had resigned as leader in September 2005, after being indicted by a Texas court on conspiracy charges relating to political fundraising. DeLay vehemently denied the accusations, but as pressure mounted from various investigations and from some of his own colleagues, with opinion polls showing him facing a tough fight in November, he announced in April that he would not run for re-election.

Spooked by the attention being given to tales of corporate influence and congressional greed, both Democrats and Republicans began the year seeking to outdo each other in their zeal to introduce lobbying reform. House Speaker Dennis Hastert of Illinois declared the need to "regain the trust of the American people", while many others promised sweeping legislation to address the problem. As the immediate panic subsided, so too did congressional enthusiasm for legislation. Bills were proposed in both House and Senate, but disagreement as to whether they went too far or not far enough prevented progress. By the end of the congressional session, the promised comprehensive legislation had not yet materialised.

A steady stream of unseemly stories nevertheless ensured that corruption remained a prominent issue, with one survey revealing that over 80 per cent of respondents believed that it was common for lobbyists to bribe members of Congress. In March a former Republican congressman, Randy "Duke" Cunningham of California, pleaded guilty to fraud, tax evasion, and conspiracy to commit bribery, crimes which had brought him millions of dollars in gifts in return for helping companies win government contracts. In May, the FBI, which suspected him of taking bribes, searched the Capitol Hill office of a Louisiana Democratic congressman, William Jefferson. A search of his home uncovered US$90,000 in cash stored in a freezer. Politicians on both sides raised questions about whether the raid—the first of its kind in US history—violated the separation of powers between the legislative and executive branches, but most also agreed that there were, on the face of it, few legitimate reasons to keep so much cash in with the frozen peas and the ice cream. Jefferson's insistence that he had done nothing wrong appeared to satisfy the constituents in Louisiana's second district, who helped him to a comfortable victory in a run-off election in December. Congressman Jefferson's supporters notwithstanding, the public appeared to have all the evidence it needed of graft's insidious and pervasive reach, with large numbers of voters citing corruption as a major election issue.

MIDTERM ELECTIONS. Political corruption and government incompetence and lack of accountability were among the key issues framing both Republican and Democratic midterm election campaigns. Illegal immigration, with its implications for the country's economy and culture, aroused strong passions and disagreements, within as well as between parties. Cultural issues loomed less large than in the 2004 election, but still proved important. So, too, did broad questions of national security, which prompted extensive debate. Over everything else, however, the war in Iraq cast its gloomy shadow. As the campaign began,

Democratic hopes were high that they could overturn the Republicans' 29-seat majority in the House of Representatives. With only one-third of the Senate seats up for election, and fewer than one-third of those seriously in play, there were fewer expectations that the Democrats could win the six seats necessary to become the majority part in the Senate.

The Democrats fought a disciplined campaign, designed to focus on the pressing problems facing the country, and on what they argued was Republican unwillingness to address them. With the Republicans in control of the executive and both chambers of the legislative branch, and with two recent Republican appointees to the highest court of the judicial branch, the Democrats made much of the claim that this dominance had, in fact, contributed to the corruption and incompetence of which so many voters complained. They argued that those dissatisfied with the current state of affairs at home and abroad should vote for a change of congressional leadership in Washington DC.

Republican candidates, for their part, tended to fight more localised campaigns, hoping to benefit from a voting pattern that had often favoured incumbents in previous elections: namely that voters' intense dissatisfaction with Congress as a whole nevertheless coexisted alongside approval of their own representative's performance. Many candidates distanced themselves from policies—especially relating to Iraq and illegal immigration—favoured by the president, whose campaigning presence was rarely welcomed except in the most staunchly Republican areas. Nevertheless, during the campaign long-running issues came together with particular events to work against that hope in many electoral districts.

Congressional corruption regained a high profile. Republican Representative Bob Ney of Ohio pleaded guilty in September to a variety of charges relating to his acceptance of gifts, such as vacations, from Jack Abramoff. Ney joined DeLay's aides and two officials from the Bush administration—Roger Stillwell, an official at the interior department, and David Safavian, a White House procurement official—in pleading guilty to illegal behaviour involving dealings with Abramoff. More damaging to the Republican election effort was the revelation in late September that Florida Representative Mark Foley had exchanged sexually explicit e-mails and instant messages with former congressional (male) pages (teenage high-school pupils temporarily employed by Congress). As the House voted to refer the matter to its ethics committee, and House Speaker Hastert called for federal and state investigations into the matter, Foley resigned on 29 September and several days later checked himself into an alcohol rehabilitation programme, where he remained throughout the election campaign. A picture emerged from the scandal of a Republican leadership that had known about Foley's indiscretions but had failed to take decisive action to deal with him, seemingly more concerned about avoiding the political fallout should Foley's predilections become public knowledge than with addressing a serious ethical problem in its midst. The frantic buck-passing that followed the public disclosure of Foley's behaviour only heightened public perceptions of a Republican leadership failing to meet its responsibilities. While widespread public cynicism regarding the ubiquity of political corruption harmed both parties, it disproportionately affected the Republican party at the November polls.

Illegal immigration was the issue that proved most divisive for the parties, both internally and in competition with each other. On the Democratic side, many agreed with House Minority Leader Nancy Pelosi's support for a plan offering illegal immigrants a "pathway to earned legalisation and citizenship" provided that they met a variety of requirements, such as paying back taxes and learning English. This position placed those Democrats closer to the president on the issue than to more conservative Democrats, who criticised Bush and his Republican supporters for being too soft on immigration. Nick Lampson, for example, the successful Democratic candidate for the Texas seat vacated by former Majority Leader DeLay, spoke out against "a guest worker programme for people who broke our law to come here".

As an election issue, illegal immigration also presented Republicans with a dilemma. On the one hand, the hardline attitude reflected by Colorado Representative Tom Tancredo's description of illegal immigration as a "scourge" appealed to many Republican loyalists. On the other hand, the perception that the party was strong on increasing border security but unwilling to consider accommodating existing illegal immigrants risked alienating Latino voters, a group to which Republicans had, with some success, been trying to appeal. On 26 October, with the election looming and nervous Republicans pleading for him to do so, President Bush signed into law the Secure Fence Act, based on the House bill's demand for a border fence. "The American people demand border security", declared Republican Senator Bill Frist of Tennessee, a leading proponent of the security-first approach, "and this Republican Congress and president are committed to achieving operational control of the border through an enforcement-first approach." Democratic critics saw the bill as an eve-of-election ploy designed to placate popular demand for restrictions on illegal immigration. Making the best of a bill that aroused anger across Latin America and did not accord with his own wishes, President Bush insisted that the legislation represented one step towards comprehensive immigration reform.

Republican efforts to inject cultural or moral issues into the campaign proved less successful than they had in previous elections. Indeed the campaign's most prominent ethical question—whether or not the federal government should fund stem cell research using human embryos—worked in the Democrats' favour. In July, Bush had exercised the first veto of his presidency when he refused to sign a bill that would have provided federal funding for embryonic stem cell research. During the election campaign the issue took centre stage because of an advertisement run by Missouri Democratic candidate for the Senate, Claire McCaskill. The advertisement showed actor Michael J. Fox, clearly showing the symptoms of the Parkinson's disease from which he suffered, endorsing McCaskill because of her support of research that many believed could find a cure for ailments such as Parkinson's. The issue received further publicity when conservative talkshow host Rush Limbaugh criticised Fox, insinuating that he was acting or "off his meds" (medication) while also mimicking the actor's jerky, twitchy body movements. Limbaugh's intervention brought even more unwelcome attention for conservatives to an issue on which polls showed a two-to-one margin in public support for federal funding of stem cell research.

In a twist on the usual campaign plot, national security proved a liability for the Republicans, while Democrats pushed to keep military matters to the forefront of public debate. Republicans sought to present themselves as the only safe option when it came to the security of the homeland in a time of terror. As election day approached and polls presented ever bleaker pictures of Republican prospects, President Bush went so far as to suggest of his opponents that "however they put it, the Democrat approach in Iraq comes down to this: The terrorists win and America loses." Yet the ongoing conflict and chaos in Iraq, and perhaps, just as importantly, the president's seeming reluctance to acknowledge just how badly the war was going, did much to undercut such claims. They appeared to have limited resonance beyond diehard Republicans, as public discontent with the conduct of the war grew. Many Republicans sought to turn the debate to other topics, made uneasy by President Bush's insistence that victory was closer than almost anyone else, candidate or voter, believed. They were also troubled by the administration's seeming indifference to those concerns. When, in the week before the election, Vice-President Cheney insisted that it would be "full speed ahead" in Iraq regardless of the election results, he encapsulated in a few short words the growing public impression that the White House was not only oblivious to the problems with its current war policy but also indifferent to the growing public unease about that policy.

For the most part, the Democratic leadership and candidates presented a united front on the war, criticising what they saw as profound errors in its conduct and the president's stubborn refusal to change strategy in the face of mounting violence and declining hopes for political stability. They remained somewhat vague on alternatives, generally supporting a phased withdrawal of US troops that would not place the troops on the ground in any greater danger than they already faced. This cautious position did not sit well with many of the party's grassroots supporters, who demanded withdrawal from Iraq as soon as possible. The strained relations between party stalwarts and leaders, particularly those who had voted in October 2002 to support the use of force against Iraq, were best illustrated in the primary contest for the Democratic nomination in Connecticut for Senate. The incumbent, Senator Joseph Lieberman, one of the few remaining Democratic supporters of the president's war policy, lost to anti-war candidate Ned Lamont, a political newcomer. Lieberman then chose to run as an independent Democrat in the Senate election, which he won with the support of many independent voters and the Republican party, which effectively endorsed his candidacy.

Yet with a clear majority of citizens holding the belief that it had not enhanced the country's security, the Iraq war generally proved to be a winning issue for the Democrats, with polls showing that four out of five of those who disapproved of the war voted Democratic. The Senate race in Virginia offered a striking example of the centrality of the war to the election, as well as of the success of the Democrats' strategy of running conservative candidates in conservative areas. Republican George Allen, a previous governor of the state and frequently mentioned as a presidential prospect for 2008, was seeking a second term. James Webb, the Democratic candidate, was a veteran of the Vietnam war and had served as secretary of the navy in the Reagan administration. New to electoral politics, Webb had received strong backing in the Democratic primary from national party leaders intent upon finding a candidate capable of challenging a popular incumbent in a conservative-leaning state. Webb held to conservative positions on issues such as support for gun ownership rights and the death penalty, but was outspoken in his criticism of the conduct of the war. He called for the troops, who included his own son serving in the Marines, to be brought home and wore his son's combat boots on the campaign trail to symbolise what he argued was a position that supported troops being asked to fight an unwinnable war. Allen continued to express his support for the war, and he was also hurt by a comment aimed at a Webb aide at a rally, which was interpreted as an ethnic slur. Although Webb's margin of victory was very small, it was a victory that few had considered likely at the beginning of the campaign.

Allen was one of six Republican incumbents to lose their Senate seats. In Rhode Island, Ohio, and Pennsylvania the Democrats won fairly comfortably in the end, especially in the Pennsylvania contest in which incumbent Rick Santorum, a powerful figure in the Senate, lost by 58 to 41 per cent to challenger Robert Casey, Jr. The Democrats also won tight races in Missouri, where Democrat Claire McCaskill benefited from the stem cell controversy (see above), and in Montana, where incumbent Republican Conrad Burns—another politician tainted by his connections to Abramoff—lost to conservative Democrat John Tester. All Democratic incumbents up for re-election won, including Robert Byrd of West Virginia, who was set for a record-breaking ninth term, having first come to the Senate in 1958. Those incumbents, plus the six seats won from the Republicans, combined with the support of Lieberman and of Bernie Sanders, the new Independent socialist senator from Vermont, who both intended to caucus with the Democrats, gave the Democrats a majority of 51 to 49 seats in the new Senate to be sworn in on 3 January 2007.

The Democrats' margin of victory in the House of Representatives proved greater than even many of their most optimistic supporters had dared to predict. Many moderate Republicans lost their seats, but the Democrats made gains in "red" states (those which had consistently leaned Republican in recent times), as well as in those "blue" states where their strength was traditionally greater. Three Republicans lost their seats in Indiana, while prominent Republican incumbents went down to defeat in states such as North Carolina, Kentucky, Kansas, Texas, and Florida. Among the Democratic gains was the Florida seat vacated by the scandal-plagued Mark Foley shortly before the election. Democrats also picked up the open Ohio seat previously occupied by the disgraced Robert Ney. Every Democratic incumbent in the House was re-elected, making this the first election in history in which no sitting Democratic representative or

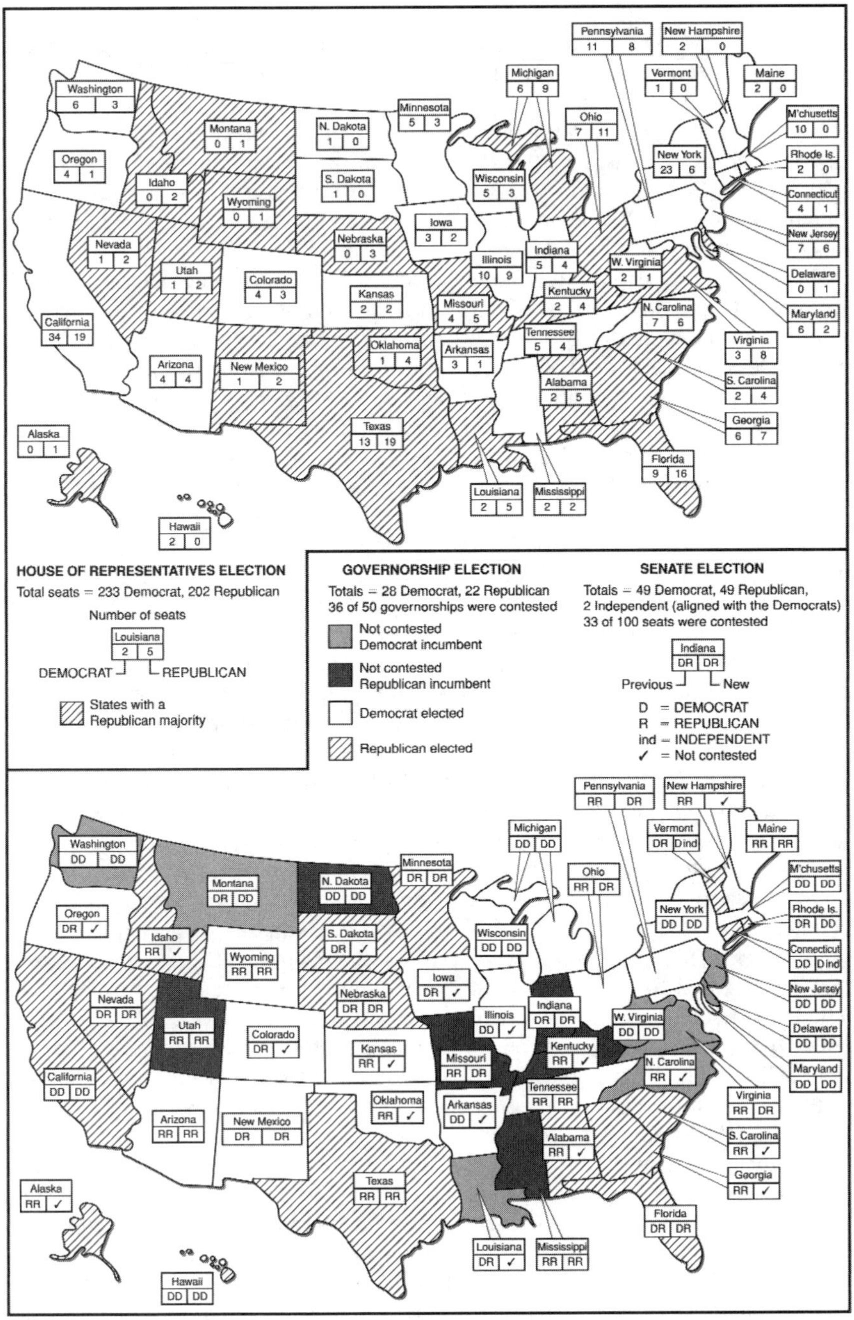
Pennsylvania 11 8
New Hampshire 2 0
Michigan 6 9
Vermont 1 0
Maine 2 0
Washington 6 3
Minnesota 5 3
Ohio 7 11
M'chusetts 10 0
Montana 0 1
N. Dakota 1 0
Oregon 4 1
New York 23 6
Rhode Is. 2 0
Idaho 0 2
S. Dakota 1 0
Wisconsin 5 3
Connecticut 4 1
Wyoming 0 1
Iowa 3 2
New Jersey 7 6
Nevada 1 2
Nebraska 0 3
Indiana 5 4
Illinois 10 9
W. Virginia 2 1
Delaware 0 1
Utah 1 2
Colorado 4 3
Kansas 2 2
Kentucky 2 4
Maryland 6 2
California 34 19
Missouri 4 5
N. Carolina 7 6
Tennessee 5 4
Virginia 3 8
Oklahoma 1 4
Arkansas 3 1
Arizona 4 4
New Mexico 1 2
Alabama 2 5
S. Carolina 2 4
Georgia 6 7
Texas 13 19
Alaska 0 1
Florida 9 16
Louisiana 2 5
Mississippi 2 2
Hawaii 2 0
HOUSE OF REPRESENTATIVES ELECTION
Total seats = 233 Democrat, 202 Republican
Number of seats
Louisiana 2 5
DEMOCRAT
REPUBLICAN
States with a Republican majority
GOVERNORSHIP ELECTION
Totals = 28 Democrat, 22 Republican
36 of 50 governorships were contested
Not contested Democrat incumbent
Not contested Republican incumbent
Democrat elected
Republican elected
SENATE ELECTION
Totals = 49 Democrat, 49 Republican,
2 Independent (aligned with the Democrats)
33 of 100 seats were contested
Indiana DR DR
Previous
New
D = DEMOCRAT
R = REPUBLICAN
ind = INDEPENDENT
✓ = Not contested
Pennsylvania RR DR
New Hampshire RR ✓
Michigan DD DD
Vermont DR Dind
Maine RR RR
Washington DD DD
Minnesota DR DR
Ohio RR DR
M'chusetts DD DD
Montana DR DD
N. Dakota DD DD
Oregon DR ✓
New York DD DD
Rhode Is. DR DD
Idaho RR ✓
S. Dakota DR ✓
Wisconsin DD DD
Connecticut DD Dind
Wyoming RR RR
Iowa DR ✓
New Jersey DD DD
Nevada DR DR
Nebraska DR DR
Indiana DR DR
Illinois DD ✓
W. Virginia DD DD
Delaware DD DD
Utah RR RR
Colorado DR ✓
Kansas RR ✓
Kentucky RR ✓
Missouri RR DR
N. Carolina RR ✓
Maryland DD DD
California DD DD
Tennessee RR RR
Virginia RR DR
Oklahoma RR ✓
Arkansas DD ✓
Arizona RR RR
New Mexico DR DR
Alabama RR ✓
S. Carolina RR ✓
Georgia RR ✓
Texas RR RR
Alaska RR ✓
Florida DR DR
Louisiana DR ✓
Mississippi RR RR
Hawaii DD DD

senator was defeated. Democrats picked up 31 seats, emerging with a majority of 233 to 202. "The American people, with their votes yesterday, placed their trust in the Democrats. We will honour that trust. We will not disappoint", declared Nancy Pelosi, insisting that her party "will make this the most honest, ethical and open Congress in history". Pelosi herself was in line to become the first ever female speaker of the House when the 111th Congress convened in 2007. Other firsts included representatives Keith Ellison of Minnesota, the first Muslim elected to Congress, and Hank Johnson of Georgia and Mazie Hirono of Hawaii, the first Buddhists elected to Congress.

The Democrats also did well at the state level, winning gubernatorial races in Arkansas, Colorado, New York, Ohio, and Massachusetts, all states in which the Republican incumbent was retiring; and in traditionally Democratic Maryland, where Democrat Martin O'Malley defeated incumbent Robert Ehrlich, who had been the state's first Republican governor in almost 40 years. There was success for Republicans in some states, including Florida where Charlie Crist, the state's attorney general, defeated Democratic candidate, Jim Davis, in the fight to succeed Republican Jeb Bush (brother of the president), who was leaving the term-limited office. In California, Republican Arnold Schwarzenegger won re-election, his popularity resting in part on his championing of policies with strong appeal to independents and moderate Democrats. With every Democratic incumbent winning, the Democrats emerged with a majority of the country's governorships (28 to 22) for the first time since 1995.

The electorate had held the Republicans accountable for the perceived failures of commission and omission relating to corruption, the economy, immigration, and national security. At a time of national crisis, the House, under Republican leadership, had convened for fewer days than in any congressional session since World War II. The Senate's attendance record was little better. At a time of multiple scandals, the House ethics committee was virtually moribund. While hurting Democrats too, this disgust with Washington politics fell more heavily on the Republicans as the party in power. It did not help that their greatest failings came in areas such as moral values and national security where they traditionally claimed greatest superiority over their opponents. Exit polls suggested that six in 10 of the 40 per cent of voters who considered corruption an "extremely important" issue voted for the Democrats. Of the similar percentage of the electorate who considered terrorism "extremely important" most favoured the Republicans, but only by a margin—7 per cent—that indicated the Republicans' significantly diminished superiority on that issue. Most damaging of all, a substantial portion of the electorate had made of the election what the Republicans had tried to prevent it from becoming: a referendum on the causes and conduct of the war in Iraq and on the performance of the president leading the war effort. "There's no doubt that Iraq is a big piece of why people want change", claimed Representative Rahm Emanuel of Illinois, who, as chairman of the Democratic congressional campaign committee, received much of the credit for the Democrats' winning strategy. "The economy is also there", he went on, "how Congress works is there. But Iraq is your first piece of evidence in the case you make for change." Many on both sides agreed with his assessment that, more than any other issue, Iraq had caused the Republicans' downfall. And public opinion on the conduct of the war could not be separated from the public's opinion of the country's commander-in-chief. Those same exit polls showed that over one-third of voters cast their ballot to express their opposition to President Bush.

The day after the election, Bush acknowledged that he was "obviously disappointed with the outcome of the election and as the head of the Republican party, I share a large part of the responsibility". Yet despite the Republicans receiving what the president himself described as "a thumping", most post-election analysis cautioned against reading a decisive ideological realignment, from conservative to liberal, into the results. The Democrats had clearly been successful in attracting moderate and independent swing voters, but they had done so in part by running moderate candidates on a platform that mostly consisted of broadly popular policies. Despite their grand haul of seats, the Democrats' 52 per cent share of the popular vote hardly signalled a landslide. Evidence suggested that dissatisfaction with the Republicans, rather than enthusiasm for the Democrats, was the decisive factor for many voters. Most interpreters of the national mood predicted that the Democrats would be judged just as severely if their management of the nation's business in the 111th Congress proved to be no more ethical or effective than that of the Republicans in the 110th Congress.

Whatever its other consequences, the election seemed to obliterate any remaining assumptions that Iraq war policy could continue on the same course. Almost immediately after the election, President Bush offered evidence that he had "got the message" regarding public dissatisfaction with that policy when he accepted Secretary of Defence Donald Rumsfeld's resignation. Bush announced Rumsfeld's successor as Robert Gates, a former director of the CIA and president of Texas A&M university. Gates was confirmed with a minimum of fuss and questioning, the only headline from the hearings being his view that the USA was not winning the war in Iraq. The White House promptly disagreed with the assessment of its new defence secretary.

Gates had been a member of the innocuously entitled Iraq Study Group (ISG), a cross-party collection of Washington worthies, such as Democrats Vernon Jordan and Leon Panetta and Republicans Sandra Day O'Connor and Edwin Meese. The US Congress established the ISG in March to examine events in Iraq and to propose potential strategies for success. Chaired by Republican James Baker and Democrat Lee Hamilton, the ISG submitted its report—entitled *The Iraq Study Group Report: The Way Forward—A New Approach*—in December (for summary see pp. 539-41). Describing the situation in Iraq as "grave and deteriorating", the report recommended 79 changes to existing strategy, including less emphasis on combat missions and more on training Iraqi forces; greater stress on fighting counterinsurgents rather than policing sectarian conflicts between Sunnis and Shi'ites; a gradual reduction of US troops; and greater diplomatic engagement with Syria and Iran. Critics on the right dubbed the ISG the "Iraq surrender group", dismissing its recommendations as dangerous and unrealistic. By contrast, those who favoured a change in policy spoke approvingly of the report.

Incoming chair of the House intelligence committee, Congressman Silvestre Reyes of Texas, endorsed the report as evidence that "President Bush's policy of 'stay the course' is not working" and that the Democrats' proposals "to begin redeploying US troops and to switch the mission of US forces from combat to training and support" offered the best way forward. Reyes's credibility, not to mention his suitability for his new post, was called into question soon afterwards, however, when he proved unable to distinguish between Sunnis and Shi'ites, mistakenly suggesting that al-Qaida was made up predominantly of the latter, during an interview with the *Congressional Quarterly*.

In the wake of the elections, some Republicans spoke in strong terms of the need for a change of course. Speaking in the Senate in early December, a clearly pained Senator Gordon Smith of Oregon, acknowledged that "I, for one, am at the end of my rope when it comes to supporting a policy that has our soldiers patrolling the same streets in the same way, being blown up by the same bombs day after day." Previously a strong supporter of the war who had spoken against withdrawing troops, Smith now declared current policy "absurd. It may even be criminal." The president said he would give the ISG report careful consideration, while managing to give the impression that he probably would not. As it became increasingly clear that he did not intend to incorporate any of its more important recommendations into his re-assessment of policy in Iraq, the report slipped from view.

The ISG's report did, however, contribute to the strengthening consensus that maintaining the status quo in Iraq was no longer sustainable. Some 70 per cent of respondents to an opinion poll conducted soon after the report's release expressed their disapproval of the president's conduct of the war in Iraq, while 60 per cent of them went so far as to say that the war was not worth fighting. In a sense, however, with its 79 recommendations, the report also reflected the indecision among politicians and the public alike when it came to choosing between alternative options, all of which were replete with their own dangers. Even as everyone concurred on the need for change, division and indecision continued to characterise the debate as to what the "way forward" should look like. Few leading figures called for immediate withdrawal. Many of those calling for redeployment or withdrawal—including the ISG—did not argue for it to happen immediately, whilst those insisting on a timetable for withdrawal often remained imprecise about how such a schedule should be established or implemented. Those like Republican senators John McCain of Arizona and Lindsey Graham of South Carolina, who insisted that withdrawal would mean defeat for the USA and a more dangerous world for everyone, called for more troops to be sent. As the president himself appeared to be leaning towards that option, other Republicans such as Colin Powell—his former secretary of state—publicly questioned its advisability. Yet others questioned whether the further deployment of perhaps tens of thousands of additional troops was feasible, given the Iraq Study Group's estimate that two-thirds of US-based army units were not ready to be deployed because of shortages of personnel, training, and equipment. Some leading generals, as well as retired generals like Powell, warned that US land forces were close to breaking point given the many demands being made on them around the world. In a December press conference Bush expressed his support for expanding the size of the US Army and Marine Corps, and promised to call for those measures in the new year.

A December of many deaths drew to a close with the hanging of former Iraqi President Saddam Hussein (see pp. 203-205). President Bush hailed the former tyrant's trial and execution as "an important milestone on Iraq's course to becoming a democracy that can govern, sustain, and defend itself, and be an ally in the War on Terror". Like many others, however, the president was offended by the manner of the execution, as Saddam went to his death to the accompaniment of taunts from some of the Shi'ite executioners and observers present. Through the marvel of modern technology, sounds and images of the execution, captured on a mobile phone, were soon available to anyone with an Internet connection. Most telling of all, perhaps, when it came to how far events in Iraq had moved on since the invasion, was that few observers believed that Saddam's death would have any appreciable effect on current developments there. As the year that he had predicted in January would be "decisive" drew to a close, Bush postponed, until the new year, his decision on what changes he would make to his Iraq war policy. He did warn, however, that "difficult choices and additional sacrifices" lay ahead.

CANADA

CAPITAL: Ottawa AREA: 9,971,000 sq km POPULATION: 32,271,000
OFFICIAL LANGUAGES: English & French POLITICAL SYSTEM: multiparty system in British Commonwealth
HEAD OF STATE: Queen Elizabeth II (since Feb '52)
GOVERNOR-GENERAL: Michaëlle Jean (since Sept '05)
RULING PARTY: Conservative Party of Canada (CPC)
HEAD OF GOVERNMENT: Stephen Harper, Prime Minister (since Feb '06)
MAIN IGO MEMBERSHIPS (NON-UN): NATO, OECD, OSCE, G-7, OAS, NAFTA, APEC, CP, AC, CWTH, Francophonie
CURRENCY: Canadian dollar (end-'06 £1=C$2.28500, US$1=C$1.17030)
GNI PER CAPITA: US$32,600, US$32,220 at PPP ('05)

CANADA experienced another spell of minority government in 2006, following 11 years of a stable Liberal party administration. This had been led by Jean Chrétien who was succeeded as leader of the party and prime minister by his colleague, Paul Martin. Martin took over the post in December 2003, and called an election a year later to validate his position. The Liberal Party lost ground in the campaign and emerged in a minority position. Martin hung on to power through the next year before being defeated in the House of Commons (the lower chamber of the bicameral Parliament). Another election, held in January 2006, brought the chief opposition party, the Conservative Party of Canada (CPC), to power but also in a minority position. It governed throughout 2006.

There were several reasons for the downfall of the Liberal administration. One was the fatigue which tends to settle over administrations which have been too long in power. The Liberals were seen as enjoying "a culture of entitlement", rewarding their friends with government posts and contracts. They were also believed to be devoid of fresh policy initiatives. But the chief mark against them was a scandal in Quebec—the province which had been a power base for the party for generations—involving Liberal maladministration of funds allocated to promote the image of a united Canada, after the narrow defeat in 1995 of a referendum proposing sovereignty for Quebec (see AR 2005, pp. 129-30). There was anger throughout the country over Liberal misbehaviour and the displeasure was especially strong in Quebec which felt a sense of humiliation. The Martin government failed to defend itself effectively in the election of January 2006 and gave up office.

In the meantime, a merger of conservative political forces had been brought about by Stephen Harper, a young political analyst and former MP from Alberta. Harper took over the leadership of a movement which expressed western discontent with the influence of the two large central provinces in the federation, Ontario and Quebec. He succeeded in merging his Alliance party with the historic Progressive Conservative Party, a party of national standing, to create the CPC. Of the 308 seats in the House of Commons, the Liberals had held 133 before the January election; their share fell to 102. The CPC, which had controlled 99 seats before the election, saw its representation rise to 125 seats. The principal gain was in Ontario, where the Conservatives emerged as the dominant party. The party also gained unexpectedly in Quebec, taking 10 seats in the province for the first time. The separatist party, the Bloc Québécois, lost votes across the province, although it retained 51 of the 75 Quebec ridings. It was in mixed French- and English-speaking constituencies that the Conservatives made their gains, taking seats from Liberal incumbents. Canada's socialist party, the New Democratic Party (NDP), under a new leader, Jack Layton, also made gains in the election, increasing its number of seats from 19 to 29.

Stephen Harper's Conservatives, while fiercely castigating the Liberals for their role in the Quebec scandal, stressed traditional conservative values in the campaign. They emphasised the need to give more powers to the provinces in the Canadian federation, since education and health were the responsibilities of this level of government. In their view government expenditures should be reduced and budgets balanced. They proposed a strengthening of Canada's armed forces, to give the country more influence in a world menaced by international terrorism.

Harper, at the age of 46, was sworn in as Canada's 22nd prime minister on 6 February. His cabinet was composed of 26 members, nine from the four western provinces, nine from Ontario, and five from Quebec. The two most important positions in the administration were given to Peter MacKay from Nova Scotia, who was named minister for foreign affairs, and James Flaherty from Ontario, who was appointed minister of finance. There were two controversial choices. A member of the appointed Senate (the upper chamber of Parliament), from Montreal, was brought into the cabinet, since the CPC did not have an elected member from that major city. A Liberal cabinet member from Vancouver, who had dealt with the file on the softwood lumber dispute with the USA (see below), was induced to change parties and take on the same responsibility in the new Conservative cabinet.

The new government's first priority was the drafting of an accountability act, designed to reform government procedures in order to avoid the errors of the Quebec advertising scandal. A range of new officials was appointed to supervise financial practices and ensure ethical conduct among ministers and officials. The activities of lobbyists were closely scrutinised and changes were instituted in the sensitive area of contributions to political parties. The ambitious new act received formal approval on 12 December.

Two other CPC campaign promises were accomplished more easily. The federal goods and services tax of 7 per cent was reduced by one percentage point from 1 July. A child support programme, which the Conservatives had promised as a substitute to a Liberal plan, gave families Can$100 per month for each child under six years of age.

The Canadian economy benefited markedly from high energy prices in 2006. At the beginning of the year it was reported that Canada had achieved a surplus on international trade and investment of Can$30.2 billion for the previous 12 months, the first time that this condition had occurred. Canada's energy resources were considerable, the tar sands of northern Alberta, for instance, being second only to the oil reserves of Saudi Arabia. The tar sands were undergoing rapid exploitation with much of their oil production flowing south to the USA. Canada also possessed significant energy reserves in conventional oil and gas fields, in hydro-electric power and in uranium deposits. Activity in the energy fields brought the Canadian dollar, in its relationship with its US counterpart, to its highest level in 28 years. The IMF projected economic growth for Canada of 3 per cent for 2006. Employment was in a healthy state and the consumer price index remained stable.

With these favourable economic conditions the Conservative government's first budget, issued on 2 May, stressed expenditure. Over the next three years tax cuts and concessions amounting to Can $26 billion were announced. These concessions benefited middle class tax payers but also gave relief to users of public transport. Large expenditures were promised to buy transport aircraft, supply vessels, and armoured vehicles for the Canadian armed forces and plans were instituted to increase the size of these forces.

Canada increased its military commitments abroad. In 2002 the government had sent a force to assist in stabilisation and reconstruction in Afghanistan. It was based in Kabul. In 2005 it was announced that the size of the contingent would be increased to 2,300 and that it would move to the Kandahar region, an area in which the Taliban was strongly represented (see p. 282). In early 2006 the disposition was complete and the force engaged itself in active military operations under the NATO command structure. Parliament held two sessions to discuss the mission of the Afghan force. At the first of these, on 10 March, there was a general consensus that Canada had a responsibility to assist in the pacification of Afghanistan. The second session was held on 17 May, by which time there was a more widespread realisation of the costs of the operation.

Although the mission received support in the House, this was not as strong as in the first debate. Nevertheless the Harper government announced that it would extend the term of the Afghan mission to February 2009.

Harper and his colleagues changed Canada's traditionally balanced position towards the Palestinian-Israeli conflict. For many years the country had attempted to steer a middle course between supporting Israel and seeking to help Palestians achieve self-determination. Funds had been provided for a number of projects in both Israel and Palestine. However, when Hamas emerged as the winner of the general election in the Palestine National Authority (the PNA—see p. 186), the Canadian government, on 30 March, cut off official support to the PNA on the grounds that its assistance could be diverted to terrorist activities. Canada was the first Western country to take this decision. Following Israel's attack upon southern Lebanon in July (see pp. 197-203), Harper assumed a pro-Israeli stance and described the ferocious assault upon Lebanese settlements as a "measured response". This comment disturbed many Canadians who felt it marked an unfortunate change from Canada's even-handed attitude towards the conflict.

A major commercial dispute with the USA was settled as part of an effort by the Harper government to restore more harmonious relations with the administration of President George W. Bush. In 2001 the US commerce department had imposed duties on the export of Canadian construction lumber to the USA, a trade valued at Can$50 billion annually. In spite of the duties, Canadian softwood lumber had captured about one-third of the US market. Over the years the duties had been appealed against to panels under the WTO and the North American Free Trade Agreement (NAFTA) but the USA had ignored outcomes favourable to Canadian interests.

Prime Minister Harper discussed the problem with President Bush on several occasions, with the result that on 27 April a preliminary deal was announced. This arrangement gave Canadian lumber exports unlimited access to the USA, with the proviso that if prices fell below an agreed level Canada would be obliged to levy a tax on its exports or submit to a quota system. The disposition of Can$5 billion collected under the duties and partly distributed to US lumber firms had been a major item in the dispute. The preliminary agreement required the USA to repay Can$4 billion of this sum to Canadian lumber companies. The deal was approved by Parliament, and went into force on 12 October, thereby ending a major irritant in the largest bilateral trade flow in the world.

MEXICO AND CENTRAL AMERICA

MEXICO—GUATEMALA—EL SALVADOR—HONDURAS—NICARAGUA—COSTA RICA—PANAMA

MEXICO

CAPITAL: Mexico City AREA: 1,958,000 sq km POPULATION: 103,089,000
OFFICIAL LANGUAGE: Spanish POLITICAL SYSTEM: multiparty republic
HEAD OF STATE AND GOVERNMENT: President Felipe Calderón (PAN) (since Dec '06)
RULING PARTIES: National Action Party (PAN)
MAIN IGO MEMBERSHIPS (NON-UN): OAS, SELA, ALADI, ACS, APEC, NAFTA, OECD
CURRENCY: Mexican peso (end-'06 £1=MP21.0157, US$1=MP10.7638)
GNI PER CAPITA: US$7,310, US$10,030 at PPP ('05)

PRESIDENTIAL and legislative elections held on 3 July and their aftermath dominated events during the year. In the presidential election, Felipe Calderón, candidate of the centre-right National Action Party (PAN), won against long-time favourite Andrés Manuel López Obrador from the centre-left Party of the Democratic Revolution (PRD). Roberto Madrazo, representing the once dominant Party of the Institutional Revolution (PRI), finished third with 22 per cent of the vote.

However Calderón's margin of victory was only 244,000 votes or 0.58 per cent of all votes recorded. In response, López Obrador questioned the veracity of the result and requested Mexico's independent Federal Election Tribunal (TRIFE) to investigate the ballot process. In doing so López Obrador outlined a long list of alleged election law violations. A part of the problem was that the counting process took three days, and for much of that time López Obrador was ahead, which created the impression that victory would be his. However, election observers from the EU said that they saw no major irregularities. Indeed, TRIFE ruled against a full recount, and instead ordered a checking of votes from 9 per cent of polling stations where it decided there had been problems. The decision caused López Obrador to attack the tribunal, claiming that it was not independent but rather served the interests of the PAN. As the PRD candidate was laying out his case to TRIFE, his supporters protested against the election result. On 16 July, hundreds of thousands demonstrated in Mexico City and elsewhere. Other rallies took place subsequently; in addition, a camp of supporters was established in Zócalo, Mexico City's historic central square, and along the Reforma, one of the city's main roadways.

On 5 September, after two months of bitter legal argument, TRIFE confirmed that Calderón had won a majority of votes in the election. The final margin of victory was put at 233,831 votes or 0.56 per cent. The tribunal concluded that while there had been some irregularities, they were not enough to invalidate the vote. In response López Obrador rejected TRIFE's verdict, dismissed calls for him to recognise Calderón's victory, and began a campaign of "civil resistance". A high profile example occurred just before the final confirmation of the results, when on 1 September the president's annual state of the union address to Congress (the bicameral legislature) was cancelled for the first time in Mexico's history, after members of the PRD occupied the podium and prevented outgoing President Vicente Fox Quesada from speaking. Later in the month López Obrador held a "national democratic convention" and declared himself president-elect, while in mid-November he swore himself in as the "legitimate president of Mexico". However, despite López Obrador's continued high profile, his intractable position led to a decline in his support amongst former voters and the left-wing press. Also, the encampment in Zócalo and the Reforma was disbanded. López Obrador's last throw of the dice came on 1 December when PRD members attempted to prevent Calderón's inauguration. But the attempt failed and Calderón took the oath.

In his inaugural speech, Calderón set out the priorities for his first three months in office, which included tackling crime and poverty, and job creation. He also promised to expand existing welfare programmes and launch a universal healthcare scheme for children. Through these policies Calderón attempted to unite a very polarised country after a very divisive election. The policies also represented an attempt to bring together a Congress that his party did not control. In legislative elections held at the same time as the presidential contest—and the results of which were not questioned—the PAN, for the first time in its history, became the largest party in both houses, with 206 seats in the 500-seat Chamber of Deputies (the lower house) and 52 out of 128 seats in the Senate (the upper). However, these numbers were not sufficient to give the party an overall majority. The PRD became the Congress's second-largest party with 127 seats in the Chamber of Deputies and 29 senators. The PRI did as badly in the congressional elections as it had in the presidential ballot, losing seats in both chambers.

Away from national politics the situation in the southern Mexican state of Oaxaca was tense. Months of protests against the state governor, Ulises Ruiz of the PRI, began in May when teachers handed in a document calling for improvements to the education system. The teachers received no response, so went on strike. The protest widened when the city centre was occupied from 22 May. In response, local police attempted to remove the protesters on 14 June, but clashes ensued and at least four demonstrators were killed. A few days later the Popular Assembly of the Peoples of Oaxaca (APPO) was formed, which included more than 100 grassroots organisations, including unions, indigenous and peasant groups, and women's movements. APPO organised several large-scale demonstrations, attacking the governor for not only doing little to meet the teachers' demands, but also for electoral fraud, corruption, and authoritarianism. Furthermore, APPO demonstrators occupied radio stations and public buildings, and erected barricades in areas under their control, which had the effect of paralysing much of the city. In spite of such opposition, the governor refused to resign and on 28 October President Fox sent federal forces to retake the city centre. This they did, but the protests continued.

CENTRAL AMERICA

Guatemala

CAPITAL: Guatemala City AREA: 109,000 sq km POPULATION: 12,599,000
OFFICIAL LANGUAGE: Spanish POLITICAL SYSTEM: multiparty republic
HEAD OF STATE AND GOVERNMENT: President Oscar Berger (GANA) (since Jan '04)
RULING PARTIES: Grand National Alliance (GANA), composed of the Reform Movement (MR) and the National Solidarity Party (PSN), in coalition with the National Union for Hope (UNE) and the National Advancement Party (PAN)
MAIN IGO MEMBERSHIPS (NON-UN): OAS, SELA, CACM, ACM, ACS, NAM, DR-CAFTA
CURRENCY: quetzal (end-'06 £1=Q14.9948, US$1=Q7.68000)
GNI PER CAPITA: US$2,400, US$4,410 at PPP ('05 est, based on regression)

El Salvador

CAPITAL: San Salvador AREA: 21,000 sq km POPULATION: 6,881,000
OFFICIAL LANGUAGE: Spanish POLITICAL SYSTEM: multiparty republic
HEAD OF STATE AND GOVERNMENT: President Antonio Elías (Tony) Saca (ARENA) (since June '04)
RULING PARTIES: Nationalist Republican Alliance (ARENA) in coalition with the National Conciliation Party (PCN) (since March '03)
MAIN IGO MEMBERSHIPS (NON-UN): OAS, SELA, CACM, ACS, DR-CAFTA
CURRENCY: Salvadorian colón (end-'06 £1=C17.0879, US$1=C8.75200)
GNI PER CAPITA: US$2,450, US$5,120 at PPP ('03-'05)

Honduras

CAPITAL: Tegucigalpa AREA: 112,000 sq km POPULATION: 7,205,000
OFFICIAL LANGUAGE: Spanish POLITICAL SYSTEM: multiparty republic
HEAD OF STATE AND GOVERNMENT: President Jose Manuel "Mel" Zelaya Rosales (since Jan '06)
RULING PARTY: Liberal Party of Honduras (PLH) (since Jan '06)
MAIN IGO MEMBERSHIPS (NON-UN): OAS, SELA, CACM, ACS, NAM, DR-CAFTA
CURRENCY: lempira (end-'06 £1=L36.8916, US$1=L18.8950)
GNI PER CAPITA: US$1,190, US$2,900 at PPP ('05 est, based on regression)

Nicaragua

CAPITAL: Managua AREA: 130,000 sq km POPULATION: 5,487,000
OFFICIAL LANGUAGE: Spanish POLITICAL SYSTEM: multiparty republic
HEAD OF STATE AND GOVERNMENT: President Daniel Ortega Saavedra (FSLN) (since Nov '06)
RULING PARTY: Sandinista National Liberation Front (FSLN)
MAIN IGO MEMBERSHIPS (NON-UN): OAS, SELA, CACM, ACS, NAM, DR-CAFTA
CURRENCY: gold córdoba (end-'06 £1=C35.1636, US$1=C18.0100)
GNI PER CAPITA: US$910, US$3,650 at PPP ('05)

Costa Rica

CAPITAL: San José AREA: 51,000 sq km POPULATION: 4,327,000
OFFICIAL LANGUAGE: Spanish POLITICAL SYSTEM: multiparty republic
HEAD OF STATE AND GOVERNMENT: President Oscar Arias Sánchez (since May '06)
RULING PARTY: National Liberation Party (PLN)
MAIN IGO MEMBERSHIPS (NON-UN): OAS, SELA, CACM, ACS
CURRENCY: colón (end-'06 £1=C1,011.86, US$1=C518.250)
GNI PER CAPITA: US$4,590, US$9,680 at PPP ('03-'05)

Panama

CAPITAL: Panama City AREA: 76,000 sq km POPULATION: 3,232,000
OFFICIAL LANGUAGE: Spanish POLITICAL SYSTEM: multiparty republic
HEAD OF STATE AND GOVERNMENT: President Martín Torrijos Espino (PRD) (since Sept '04)
RULING PARTIES: New Nation alliance (PN) composed of the Democratic Revolutionary Party (PRD) and the Popular Party (PP)
MAIN IGO MEMBERSHIPS (NON-UN): OAS, SELA, NAM, DR-CAFTA
CURRENCY: balboa (end-'06 £1=B1.95250, US$1=B1)
GNI PER CAPITA: US$4,630, US$7,310 at PPP ('05 est, based on regression)

GUATEMALA saw a significant landmark on 29 December: the 10th anniversary of the signing of a peace accord that brought to an end the 36-year civil war (see AR 1996, p. 177). But not all those involved in the accord took part in the official events marking its anniversary. Former guerrilla group Guatemalan National Revolutionary Unity (URNG), which became a political party in 1998, did not participate, citing its disappointment over the lack of progress in dealing with violence and injustice in society. Indeed, the anniversary of the peace accord coincided with the release of figures highlighting the worsening brutality in the country. Homicides increased (again) by 5.4 per cent in 2006 to 5,629, according to figures released by the interior ministry. This was an average of 15.5 murders per day. Commenting on the numbers, human rights procurator Sergio Morales said that "proportionally there are more people being killed now than during the civil war" and that the current level of violence was "scandalous". In an attempt to address the worsening security situation the government signed an agreement with the UN on 12 December to establish an independent commission to investigate and dismantle illegal armed groups operating within the country, and to prosecute the powerful individuals—some believed to be state actors—who ran them. The agreement needed legislative approval, which had not been given by the end of the year. In a separate measure, in April the government introduced a citizen security squadron (incorporating 2,400 soldiers) to patrol crime blackspots in the capital, Guatemala City, and elsewhere.

In other developments, Guatemala's hopes of becoming a non-permanent member of the UN Security Council in 2007 and 2008 ended after a bitter and inconclusive contest with Venezuela. After 47 rounds of voting for Latin America and the Caribbean's non-permanent seat, in which Guatemala led Venezuela in 46 rounds (they tied once), neither country was able to secure the required two-thirds majority in the General Assembly. With no likely end to the stalemate, the two countries agreed in early November to drop their candidacies in favour of PANAMA (see p. 362). More positive international news came in July when Guatemala formally joined the US-Dominican Republic-Central American Free Trade Agreement (DR-CAFTA) (see AR 2005, p. 135).

Campaigning for the March mid-term elections in EL SALVADOR was halted temporarily after the sudden death of Schafik Handal, leader of the leftist opposition Farabundo Martí National Liberation Front (FMLN). Handal, one of the five guerrilla leaders who had led the FMLN during the country's 12-year civil war, died in late January. Responding to what he termed a "moment of mourning", President Antonio Elías "Tony" Saca announced the suspension of campaigning until the funeral had been held. When the results of the elections were announced, the president's centre-right Nationalist Republican Alliance (ARENA) had increased its representation in the Legislative Assembly (the unicameral legislature) from 27 to 34 seats, thereby finishing as the largest party but not achieving an overall majority. The FMLN, meanwhile, received a degree of sympathy from the voters following the death of Handal and not only recovered the seats which it had lost to defections over the past year but went on to add one to the 31 which it had won in 2003 (see AR 2005, p. 136). A range of smaller centre-right and centre-left parties secured the remaining seats.

As ARENA lacked an overall majority in the Assembly, it faced a difficult legislative period. However, Saca was able to pass the 2007 budget with relative ease after enacting revenue-raising measures which avoided the need to issue bonds partially to finance the budget. By doing this only an absolute majority of 43 votes was required in the Assembly, rather than a qualified majority of 56 votes.

Internationally, EL SALVADOR sent its seventh contingent of troops to Iraq, despite the death of two Salvadorean soldiers there in July.

HONDURAS President Manuel Zelaya received little goodwill after his January inauguration, with growing social unrest and widespread calls for a more pro-active leadership style. In Zelaya's first seven months alone there were more than 140 separate protests. Most serious was a strike by 60,000 teachers demanding salary increases. In one protest outside the presidential palace, clashes between teachers and police left several people injured. Although the government offered to open talks with the teachers, it had limited room for manoeuvre to meet their demands for higher wages because of its strict fiscal policy, which was overseen by the IMF. Protests were also held against controversial ownership laws that allowed foreign companies to control 34 per cent of every Honduran mine. The influential Roman Catholic church supported these protests at a time when the government was attempting to persuade foreign companies to invest in the country. Some of the demonstrations took on a more political hue, with the governing Liberal party blaming the opposition National party for initiating the rise in social unrest, while the opposition used its votes in the National Congress (the unicameral legislature) to block government legislation that would have curbed street protests.

President Zelaya also had to cope with a very difficult security situation, with high levels of violent crime, kidnapping, and burglary. In reply the government brought in the military to strengthen police action. The authorities hoped to employ private security firms to work alongside government forces, but this proposal was dropped after protests from opposition groups, which feared that it would lead to vigilante-style justice by non-government agents.

NICARAGUA saw the return of Daniel Ortega Saavedra as leader, after November's presidential election. Ortega, of the Sandinista National Liberation Front (FSLN), who had led Nicaragua through left-wing revolution and a civil war before being voted out of office in 1990, won 38.1 per cent of the vote, defeating the second-placed candidate, Eduardo Montealegre of the Nicaraguan Liberal Alliance (ALN), by 9 per cent.

Ortega won the presidency at the first attempt because, under Nicaraguan electoral law, any candidate who gained 35 per cent of the vote and was at least 5 per cent ahead of the second-placed candidate secured outright victory. Thus, while the total number of votes for all the conservative candidates was greater than Ortega's 38.1 per cent, the right's unwillingness to join forces gave Ortega victory. The failure of the right to unite came despite attempts by the USA, through their ambassador in Nicaragua, Paul Trivelli, to close the divisions. Also Oliver

North—a key figure in securing funds for the right-wing Contra rebels during the civil war—visited Nicaragua on 23 October and cautioned against an Ortega win.

In reply Ortega made every effort to reassure Nicaragua and the international community of his moderate programme. Prior to the election he chose as his running mate a former Contra and supported a very restrictive abortion law. He had once favoured abortion rights, but changed his stance after strongly embracing Roman Catholic values. After his victory Ortega pledged no change in economic policy and a "respectful relationship" with the USA. Ortega's efforts to overcome his Marxist past seemed to pay off when the US state department cautiously welcomed Ortega's success and said that it would look to establish "positive relations" with the government.

After a manual recount Oscar Arias Sánchez of the National Liberation Party (PLN) won the presidency of Costa Rica after an election was held on 5 February. In the closest presidential race for 50 years, former president Arias defeated Otton Solis of the Citizen's Action party by 40.9 per cent to 39.8 per cent, making the margin between the two men just over 18,000 votes. Arias was the clear favourite prior to the vote but his strong support for the controversial US-Dominican Republic-Central American Free Trade Agreement (DR-CAFTA) cut into his advantage. The lack of a clear political consensus on DR-CAFTA and the minority position of the PLN in the unicameral legislature (the Congress) meant that Costa Rica was the only signatory country not to have ratified the trade agreement by the end of the year.

In other news the president announced in August that he was moving the country's embassy in Israel from Jerusalem back to Tel Aviv, as a step towards correcting an error that "harms us internationally and deprives us of any form of friendship with the Arab world and the Islamic civilisation". Arab countries had severed relations with Costa Rica after it moved its embassy to Jerusalem in 1982.

In a referendum held in Panama on 22 October more than 78 per cent of voters supported a proposal to widen the Panama Canal. The National Assembly (unicameral legislature) and the president had already backed the project. The plans to expand the canal involved the construction of a third set of locks alongside the existing facilities to speed transit through the waterway and allow for the passage of larger ships. The final scheme was decided upon after six years of discussion, which considered more than 100 studies. In the referendum campaign the government emphasised the likely benefits of the project for ordinary Panamanians as well for businesses and banks: for example, the creation of 7,000 direct construction jobs and 35,000 support jobs, and the use of new canal revenues to fund social development programmes. The government also stated that the project would cost US$5.25 billion, but that it would not be financed through taxation, but rather via increased toll charges. Those campaigning for a "no" vote argued that the official costing was highly optimistic (they put the figure at around US$10 billion) and suggested that the project would leave Panama with very high levels of debt and would encourage corruption. The Panama Canal Authority set an ambitious completion date of 2014, the centenary of the inauguration of the original canal.

THE CARIBBEAN

CUBA—JAMAICA—DOMINICAN REPUBLIC AND HAITI—WINDWARD & LEEWARD ISLANDS—BARBADOS—TRINIDAD & TOBAGO—THE BAHAMAS—GUYANA, BELIZE AND SURINAME—UK DEPENDENCIES—NETHERLANDS ANTILLES AND ARUBA—US DEPENDENCIES

CUBA, JAMAICA, DOMINICAN REPUBLIC AND HAITI

Cuba

CAPITAL: Havana AREA: 115,000 sq km POPULATION: 11,269,000
OFFICIAL LANGUAGE: Spanish POLITICAL SYSTEM: one-party republic
HEAD OF STATE AND GOVERNMENT: President Fidel Castro Ruz (since Jan '59)
RULING PARTY: Cuban Communist Party (PCC)
MAIN IGO MEMBERSHIPS (NON-UN): OAS (suspended), ALADI, ACS, SELA, NAM
CURRENCY: Cuban peso (end-'06 £1=Cub1.95250, US$1=Cub1.0000)
GNI PER CAPITA: US$876-US$3,465 ('05 est), -

Jamaica

CAPITAL: Kingston AREA: 11,000 sq km POPULATION: 2,657,000
OFFICIAL LANGUAGE: English POLITICAL SYSTEM: multiparty system in British Commonwealth
HEAD OF STATE: Queen Elizabeth II
GOVERNOR-GENERAL: Kenneth Octavius Hall (since Feb '06)
RULING PARTY: People's National Party (PNP)
HEAD OF GOVERNMENT: Portia Simpson Miller (PNP), Prime Minister (since March '06)
MAIN IGO MEMBERSHIPS (NON-UN): OAS, SELA, ACS, Caricom, ACP, CWTH, NAM
CURRENCY: Jamaican dollar (end-'06 £1=J$130.838, US$1=J$67.0120)
GNI PER CAPITA: US$3,400, US$4,110 at PPP ('05)

Dominican Republic

CAPITAL: Santo Domingo AREA: 49,000 sq km POPULATION: 8,895,000
OFFICIAL LANGUAGE: Spanish POLITICAL SYSTEM: multiparty republic
HEAD OF STATE AND GOVERNMENT: President Leonel Fernández Reyna (PLD) (since Aug '04)
RULING PARTIES: Dominican Liberation Party (PLD)-led alliance
MAIN IGO MEMBERSHIPS (NON-UN): OAS, SELA, ACS, ACP, NAM, DR-CAFTA
CURRENCY: Dominican Republic peso (end-'06 £1=DP65.2608, US$1=33.4250)
GNI PER CAPITA: US$2,370, US$7,150 at PPP ('03-'05)

Haiti

CAPITAL: Port-au-Prince AREA: 28,000 sq km POPULATION: 8,528,000
OFFICIAL LANGUAGE: French POLITICAL SYSTEM: multiparty republic
HEAD OF STATE: President René Préval (Lespwa) (since May '06)
RULING PARTIES: Lespwa (Hope)-led coalition
HEAD OF GOVERNMENT: Jacques Edouard Alexis, Prime Minister (since June '06)
MAIN IGO MEMBERSHIPS (NON-UN): OAS, SELA, Caricom, ACS, ACP, Francophonie, NAM
CURRENCY: gourde (end-'06 £1=G72.0454, US$1=G36.9000)
GNI PER CAPITA: US$450, US$1,840 at PPP ('05 est, based on regression)

In CUBA the health of President Fidel Castro Ruz was the major issue of concern. At the end of July Castro underwent emergency stomach surgery, causing him to delegate powers to a number of senior figures under the overall direction of his brother, Defence Minister Raúl Castro Ruz. This was the first time in his 47-year tenure that Castro had relinquished power. His last public appearance had been on 26 July. Despite expectations that he would resume power in December, this did not happen. Furthermore, Castro's continued illness prevented him from attending a military parade in Havana in early December that was organised to mark his 80th birthday. The gravity of Castro's condition remained uncertain: some Western diplomats claimed that he had cancer and was close to death (the Cuban authorities denied this), while participants in a US congressional visit to Cuba (the biggest such group to visit the island since Castro came to power) declared that he was recovering, but that he would not resume command. In recognising the new political dynamic in Cuba, the communist regime made every attempt to project a united front, describing Raúl Castro as the "guardian" of the Cuban revolution, stressing the central role of the military, and emphasising the importance of continuity when Fidel died. However, Raúl Castro also expressed a readiness to "resolve at the negotiating table" the dispute with the USA and, after initial hostility, the US administration indicated that dialogue might be possible.

In JAMAICA Portia Simpson Miller became the country's first female prime minister after winning the presidency of the governing People's National Party (PNP). Following a bruising and divisive campaign, Simpson Miller defeated the national security minister, Peter Philips, in the 25 February ballot to replace outgoing PNP president and Jamaica's prime minister, Percival J. Patterson. Simpson Miller (formerly local government minister) was sworn into office on 30 March.

In October, the government was accused of impropriety after accepting a US$470,000 donation from a Netherlands-based oil trader. Even though Simpson Miller denied any wrongdoing, the money was returned and Information Minister Colin Campbell, who was at the centre of the scandal, resigned.

Legislative elections held on 16 May in the DOMINICAN REPUBLIC gave a sizeable victory to President Leonel Fernández Reyna's Dominican Liberation Party (PLD). The result meant that the PLD secured a majority of seats in both the Chamber of Deputies and the Senate (the lower and upper houses of the bicameral National Congress, the legislature). Despite gaining control of Congress, a result that indicated substantial popular support for his economic reform programme, Fernández was forced to withdraw several tax increases unveiled in November after political and civil society groups condemned them. The proposals led to threats of strikes and contributed to a large fall in the president's approval rating. Instead he announced plans to reduce spending in order to meet the government's budget commitments.

René Préval won the delayed presidential election in HAITI (see AR 2005, p. 141) on 7 February after electoral authorities divided the blank votes cast proportionally among the candidates. That gave Préval 51 per cent and a first round victory. Préval was Haiti's first elected president since the uprising that forced Jean-Bertrand Aristide out of office in 2004 (see AR 2004, p. 150).

Elections for the National Assembly (the bicameral legislature) also took place on 7 February, but most contests were not settled until a second round was held in April. Although Préval's Lespwa (Hope) party fell short of the majority needed to choose the next prime minister and appoint a cabinet, he received the backing of several smaller parties. Consequently Préval's choice for prime minister, Jacques Edouard Alexis, was ratified by the Assembly in May.

After Préval's election, a period of relative calm prevailed in Haiti, but this was broken in July when 21 people were massacred in the shanty town of Grand Ravine. By the end of the year, the president and government were under increasing pressure for failing to deal with a worsening security situation, despite their attempts to negotiate with groups implicated in the violence. Indeed, criticism came to a head in mid-December when armed gangs abducted 30 schoolchildren in a series of incidents in the suburbs of Port-au-Prince. The ability of the authorities to deal with the crisis was undermined by concerns over the health of President Préval. On 10 December Préval, 63, revealed that he was undergoing tests in CUBA. He had been in remission for prostate cancer for five years, but there were fears that it had returned. He went back to Havana for further tests on 26 December.

WINDWARD AND LEEWARD ISLANDS

Antigua & Barbuda

CAPITAL: St John's AREA: 440 sq km POPULATION: 81,000
OFFICIAL LANGUAGE: English POLITICAL SYSTEM: multiparty system in British Commonwealth
HEAD OF STATE: Queen Elizabeth II
GOVERNOR-GENERAL: Sir James B. Carlisle (since June '93)
RULING PARTY: United Progressive Party (UPP)
HEAD OF GOVERNMENT: Baldwin Spencer, Prime Minister (since March '04)
MAIN IGO MEMBERSHIPS (NON-UN): OAS, OECS, Caricom, ACS, ACP, CWTH, NAM
CURRENCY: East Caribbean dollar (end-'06 £1=EC$5.27160,US$1=EC$2.7000)
GNI PER CAPITA: US$10,920, US$11,700 at PPP ('05)

Dominica

CAPITAL: Roseau AREA: 48,400 sq km POPULATION: 72,000
OFFICIAL LANGUAGE: English POLITICAL SYSTEM: multiparty republic in British Commonwealth
HEAD OF STATE: President Nicholas Liverpool (since Oct '03)
RULING PARTY: Dominica Labour Party (DLP)
HEAD OF GOVERNMENT: Roosevelt Skerrit, Prime Minister (since Jan '04)
MAIN IGO MEMBERSHIPS (NON-UN): OAS, ACS, OECS, Caricom, ACP, CWTH, NAM, Francophonie
CURRENCY: East Caribbean dollar (see above)
GNI PER CAPITA: US$3,790, US$5,560 at PPP ('05)

St Christopher (Kitts) & Nevis

CAPITAL: Basseterre AREA: 260 sq km POPULATION: 48,000
OFFICIAL LANGUAGE: English POLITICAL SYSTEM: multiparty system in British Commonwealth
HEAD OF STATE: Queen Elizabeth II
GOVERNOR-GENERAL: Sir Cuthbert Sebastian (since Jan '96)
RULING PARTY: St Kitts-Nevis Labour Party (SKNLP)
HEAD OF GOVERNMENT: Denzil Douglas, Prime Minister (since July '95)
MAIN IGO MEMBERSHIPS (NON-UN): OAS, ACS, Caricom, OECS, ACP, CWTH, NAM
CURRENCY: East Caribbean dollar (see above)
GNI PER CAPITA: US$8,210, US$12,500 at PPP ('05)

St Lucia

CAPITAL: Castries AREA: 616 sq km POPULATION: 166,000
OFFICIAL LANGUAGE: English POLITICAL SYSTEM: multiparty system in British Commonwealth
HEAD OF STATE: Queen Elizabeth II
GOVERNOR-GENERAL: Perlette Louisy (since Sept '97)
RULING PARTY: United Workers' Party (UWP)
HEAD OF GOVERNMENT: Sir John Compton (UWP), Prime Minister (since Dec '06)
MAIN IGO MEMBERSHIPS (NON-UN): OAS, ACS, OECS, Caricom, ACP, CWTH, NAM, Francophonie
CURRENCY: East Caribbean dollar (see above)
GNI PER CAPITA: US$4,800, US$5,980 at PPP ('05)

St Vincent & the Grenadines

CAPITAL: Kingstown AREA: 390 sq km POPULATION: 119,000
OFFICIAL LANGUAGE: English POLITICAL SYSTEM: multiparty system in British Commonwealth
HEAD OF STATE: Queen Elizabeth II
GOVERNOR-GENERAL: Freddy Ballantyne (since Sept '02)
RULING PARTY: Unity Labour Party (ULP)
HEAD OF GOVERNMENT: Ralph Gonsalves, Prime Minister (since April '01)
MAIN IGO MEMBERSHIPS (NON-UN): OAS, ACS, OECS, Caricom, ACP, CWTH, NAM
CURRENCY: East Caribbean dollar (see above)
GNI PER CAPITA: US$3,590, US$6,460 at PPP ('05)

Grenada

CAPITAL: St George's AREA: 344 sq km POPULATION: 107,000
OFFICIAL LANGUAGE: English POLITICAL SYSTEM: multiparty system in British Commonwealth
HEAD OF STATE: Queen Elizabeth II
GOVERNOR-GENERAL: Sir Daniel Williams
RULING PARTY: New National Party (NNP)
HEAD OF GOVERNMENT: Keith Mitchell, Prime Minister (since June '95)
MAIN IGO MEMBERSHIPS (NON-UN): OAS, SELA, ACS, Caricom, OECS, ACP, CWTH, NAM
CURRENCY: East Caribbean dollar (end-'06 £1=EC$5.27160, US$1=EC$2.7000)
GNI PER CAPITA: US$3,920, US$7,260 at PPP ('05)

The issue of crime and how to deal with it was of concern to several Windward and Leeward Islands countries. In ST VINCENT & THE GRENADINES the personal aide and press secretary to Prime Minister Ralph Gonsalves was murdered on 6 March. In response the government asked for assistance from the UK and Barbados in solving the case. Later in March ST KITTS & NEVIS appealed to the UN Security Council for co-operation and assistance to "prevent, combat and eradicate the illicit trade in small arms and light weapons in all its aspects". It was the first time that a representative from St Kitts & Nevis had addressed the Security Council. ST LUCIA, meanwhile, called on the People's Republic of China to assist in dealing with its growing crime problem. And in May, DOMINICA signed a mutual prison transfer agreement with the UK to allow prisoners to serve sentences in their home countries.

In the political arena the prime minister of ANTIGUA & BARBUDA, Baldwin Spencer, met Iranian President Mahmoud Ahmadinejad on 17 September in Havana, the Cuban capital, which hosted the year's Non-Aligned summit (see pp. 396-97). According to reports, Spencer "lauded Iran's progress and development" and "voiced his country's strong enthusiasm for co-operating with Iran at bilateral and multilateral levels".

Three months later, the United Workers Party (UWP), led by Sir John Compton, unexpectedly won St Lucia's general election. The UWP took 11 of the 17 seats in the House of Assembly (the lower house of the bicameral Parliament). Compton, 82, had previously led St Lucia for 29 years, first from 1964 to 1979, and then from 1982 to 1996. He came out of retirement in 2005 to resume leadership of his party (see AR 2005, p. 143).

Meanwhile, in GRENADA, three of the 17 people convicted of involvement in the killing of former Prime Minister Maurice Bishop in 1983 were released early from prison for good behaviour; and in Dominica the government established diplomatic relations with Algeria as part of its policy to improve links with developing countries.

With regard to economic matters, Dominica received US$1.8 million from the IMF after it completed the seventh and last review of the country's performance under its three-year poverty reduction and growth facility (PRGF) arrangement, which was first approved in December 2003. This brought total disbursements to US$11.6 million. Grenada, meanwhile, signed a three-year PRGF with the IMF, worth about US$15 million. The IMF also praised Antigua & Barbuda for its "strong start" in addressing the country's "deep-rooted economic problems". There was less good news for St Lucia where banana exports fell to a record low in 2005 as more farmers left the industry because of increased competition and the region's declining level of preferential treatment in the key European market.

BARBADOS, TRINIDAD & TOBAGO, THE BAHAMAS

Barbados

CAPITAL: Bridgetown AREA: 430 sq km POPULATION: 270,000
OFFICIAL LANGUAGE: English POLITICAL SYSTEM: multiparty system in British Commonwealth
HEAD OF STATE: Queen Elizabeth II
GOVERNOR-GENERAL: Sir Clifford Husbands
RULING PARTY: Barbados Labour Party (BLP)
HEAD OF GOVERNMENT: Owen Arthur, Prime Minister (since Sept '94)
MAIN IGO MEMBERSHIPS (NON-UN): OAS, SELA, ACS, Caricom, ACP, CWTH, NAM
CURRENCY: Barbados dollar (end-'05 £1=Bd$3.85520, US$1=Bd$2.0000)
GNI PER CAPITA: US$3,466-US$10,725 ('05 est), -

Trinidad & Tobago

CAPITAL: Port of Spain AREA: 5,128 sq km POPULATION: 1,305,000
OFFICIAL LANGUAGE: English POLITICAL SYSTEM: multiparty republic in British Commonwealth
HEAD OF STATE: President Max Richards (since Feb '03)
RULING PARTY: People's National Movement (PNM)
HEAD OF GOVERNMENT: Patrick Manning (PNM), Prime Minister (since Dec '01)
MAIN IGO MEMBERSHIPS (NON-UN): OAS, SELA, ACS, Caricom, ACP, CWTH, NAM
CURRENCY: Trinidad & Tobago dollar (end-'06 £1=TT$12.2873, US$1=TT$6.29330)
GNI PER CAPITA: US$10,440, US$13,170 at PPP ('05)

The Bahamas

CAPITAL: Nassau AREA: 14,000 sq km POPULATION: 323,000
OFFICIAL LANGUAGE: English POLITICAL SYSTEM: multiparty system in British Commonwealth
HEAD OF STATE: Queen Elizabeth II
GOVERNOR-GENERAL: Arthur Dion Hanna (since Feb '06)
RULING PARTY: Progressive Liberal Party (PLP)
HEAD OF GOVERNMENT: Perry Christie, Prime Minister (since May '02)
MAIN IGO MEMBERSHIPS (NON-UN): OAS, SELA, ACS, Caricom, ACP, CWTH, NAM
CURRENCY: Bahamian dollar (end-'06 £1=B$1.95250, US$1=B$1)
GNI PER CAPITA: US$10,726 or more ('05 est), -

THE Permanent Court of Arbitration, based in The Hague, settled the long-running maritime border dispute between BARBADOS and TRINIDAD & TOBAGO after a ruling in April. The ruling created a single maritime boundary situated almost midway between the two countries, and called on both sides to work out an agreement covering fishing rights. Although the ruling rejected the boundary claims put forward by each country, both claimed victory because the judgment secured their key maritime interests.

In other news from TRINIDAD & TOBAGO, the government announced in March plans to bring in UK police officers to help curb escalating crime. In April, the former prime minister (1995-2001), leader of the opposition Basdeo Panday was jailed for two years after being found guilty of deliberately failing to declare a London bank account. He was later released on bail on health grounds, pending an appeal. Following the verdict, Kamla Persad Bissessar replaced Panday as leader of the opposition United National Congress. Meanwhile, in September, the country's hopes for a significant expansion in oil and gas production suffered a setback after the failure of the deep-water well, Ibis Deep.

In March the government of THE BAHAMAS allowed two Cuban dentists held in the country for nearly a year to travel to the USA. The two were detained after a boat carrying them and 16 other migrants stalled in Bahamian waters in April 2005. In the intervening period, the US government, the governor of Florida, Jeb Bush, and some members of Florida's congressional delegation had called on the Bahamas to release the two. In addition, Cuban-American groups staged several protests and called for tourists to boycott the Bahamas. When the two Cubans were freed, however, the Bahamas government denied all suggestions that it was responding to US pressure. Also in March, the judicial committee of the UK Privy Council (which was the court of final appeal for the Bahamas) ruled against the country's mandatory death penalty.

GUYANA, BELIZE, AND SURINAME

Guyana

CAPITAL: Georgetown AREA: 215,000 sq km POPULATION: 751,000
OFFICIAL LANGUAGE: English POLITICAL SYSTEM: multiparty republic
HEAD OF STATE: President Bharrat Jagdeo (since Aug '99)
RULING PARTY: People's Progressive Party-Civic (PPP-C)
PRIME MINISTER: Samuel Hinds (since Dec '97)
MAIN IGO MEMBERSHIPS (NON-UN): OAS, SELA, AP, ACS, Caricom, ACP, CWTH, NAM
CURRENCY: Guyanese dollar (end-'06 £1=G$370.966, US$1=G$190.000)
GNI PER CAPITA: US$1,010, US$4,230 at PPP ('05 est, based on regression)

Belize

CAPITAL: Belmopan AREA: 23,000 sq km POPULATION: 292,000
OFFICIAL LANGUAGE: English POLITICAL SYSTEM: multiparty system in British Commonwealth
HEAD OF STATE: Queen Elizabeth II
GOVERNOR-GENERAL: Sir Colville Young
RULING PARTY: People's United Party (PUP)
HEAD OF GOVERNMENT: Said Musa, Prime Minister (since Aug '98)
MAIN IGO MEMBERSHIPS (NON-UN): OAS, SELA, ACS, Caricom, ACP, CWTH, NAM
CURRENCY: Belize dollar (end-'06 £1=Bz$3.81670, US$1=Bz$1.98000)
GNI PER CAPITA: US$3,500, US$6,740 at PPP ('05)

Suriname

CAPITAL: Paramaribo AREA: 163,000 sq km POPULATION: 449,000
OFFICIAL LANGUAGE: Dutch POLITICAL SYSTEM: multiparty republic
HEAD OF STATE: President Ronald Venetiaan (since Aug '00)
RULING PARTIES: New Front for Democracy (NF) coalition supported by the A-Combination (A-Com) coalition
HEAD OF GOVERNMENT: Vice-President Ram Sardjoe (since Aug '05)
MAIN IGO MEMBERSHIPS (NON-UN): OAS, SELA, AP, ACS, Caricom, ACP, OIC, NAM
CURRENCY: Surinam dollar (end-'06 £1=S$5.35950, US$1=S$2.74500)
GNI PER CAPITA: US$2,540 ('05), -

INCUMBENT Bharrat Jagdeo won the presidential election in GUYANA held on 28 August, while his People's Progressive Party/Civic (PPP/C) increased its representation in the National Assembly (unicameral legislature). In a break with the past, the elections were peaceful and the results accepted by the opposition. Such calm was surprising, given events prior to the vote. On 22 April, Guyana's agriculture minister, Satyadeow Sawh, was shot dead in his home, along with his brother and sister. The murders, committed by masked gunmen in military fatigues, led Jagdeo to claim that they could form "part of a sinister plan to impact the outcome of the upcoming...elections". He later criticised the security forces for their apparent impotence in dealing with this and other violent crimes. In the weeks immediately preceding the election, gunmen killed five people after storming the offices of one of Guyana's leading newspapers, several military-styled camps were discovered, and objections were raised by opposition parties regarding the delay in the elections from the constitutionally due date of 4 August to 28 August.

Meanwhile, in a 25 May address on the 40th anniversary of independence, Jagdeo stated that the biggest threat to the security of Guyana "comes from the enemy within", focusing in particular on the drug barons and armed gangs operating in the country. This view seemed to be supported by the US state department's 2006 International Narcotics Control Strategy Report, which warned that the illicit drugs trade was "corrupting Guyanese society on a dangerous scale" and breeding violent armed groups "who threaten Guyana's fragile democracy". However, the PPP/C's approach in dealing with alleged drug dealers was undermined by the party's reluctance to meet a request from the USA for the extradition of Guyanese businessman and PPP/C supporter, Shaheed "Roger" Khan. A US grand jury had indicted Kahn in April for conspiring to import cocaine into the USA, but it was not until late June that Kahn was arrested (in Trinidad) and taken to the USA. President Jagdeo then suggested that Khan might have been a victim of US extraordinary rendition.

In BELIZE concerns over the economy dominated the year. In a statement on 29 August the IMF claimed that the Belizean economy had reached a "critical juncture", and warned about the potentially destabilising effects of the very high levels of public debt and balance of payments deficits. Aware of the growing crisis, the government of Belize introduced several measures in an attempt to correct the imbalances, including spending cuts and tax rises. In addition, it announced that an attempt would be made to undertake a debt restructuring agreement with external commercial creditors. Belize's ratio of debt to GDP was 90 per cent, with debt interest payments alone consuming 27 per cent of fiscal revenue. In a report released in October, the IMF welcomed the measures enacted by the government, but warned that large fiscal and balance of payments deficits were likely to persist, and that medium-term stability would only be secured with the introduction of a disciplined and credible reform programme.

In other developments in Belize, the opposition United Democratic Party won a landslide victory in local elections held in March. This marked the first major electoral defeat in a decade for Prime Minister Said Musa's People's United Party, and indicated public dissatisfaction with the government's performance.

Also in March, Belize, Guatemala, and Honduras began talks to settle their claims to a maritime area in the Gulf of Honduras that was part of a long running boundary dispute.

In January high-ranking officials of the SURINAME military were implicated in illegal arms deals with Brazilian drugs gangs. A Brazilian congressional investigation heard testimony alleging their involvement. In the previous three years, munitions, heavy arms, and hand grenades had been stolen from Surinamese army depots and police stations. Then in April, Surinamese authorities uncovered an illegal arms trade ring between Suriname and Guyana.

In other developments, torrential rainfall in May caused serious flooding in the interior of the country. At least three deaths were reported, as well as the destruction of 150 villages. Despite the internal problems the government received some good news when it was reported that the economy had expanded by 5 per cent in 2005, in part due to the global commodity boom and increased gold and bauxite mining output.

UK OVERSEAS TERRITORIES

Anguilla

CAPITAL: The Valley AREA: 96 sq km POPULATION: 12,200 ('03 est)
OFFICIAL LANGUAGE: English POLITICAL SYSTEM: semi-autonomous UK overseas territory
GOVERNOR-GENERAL: Andrew George (since July '06)
RULING PARTIES: Anguilla National Alliance (ANA) & Anguilla Democratic Party (ADP) form United Front coalition
HEAD OF GOVERNMENT: Osbourne Fleming (ANA), Chief Minister (since March '00)
MAIN IGO MEMBERSHIPS (NON-UN): Caricom (associate), OECS (assoc.)
CURRENCY: East Caribbean dollar (end-'06 £1=EC$5.27160, US$1=EC$2.7000)
GDP PER CAPITA: US$7,736 ('03 est), -

Bermuda

CAPITAL: Hamilton AREA: 53 sq km POPULATION: 65,000
OFFICIAL LANGUAGE: English POLITICAL SYSTEM: semi-autonomous UK overseas territory
GOVERNOR-GENERAL: John Vereker
RULING PARTY: Progressive Labour Party (PLP)
HEAD OF GOVERNMENT: Ewart Brown (PLP), Prime Minister (since Oct '06)
MAIN IGO MEMBERSHIPS (NON-UN): Caricom (obs.)
CURRENCY: Bermudian dollar (end-'06 £1=Bm$1.95250, US$1=Bm$1)
GDP PER CAPITA: US$63,222 ('03 est), -

British Virgin Islands

CAPITAL: Road Town AREA: 153 sq km POPULATION: 27,000 ('05 est)
OFFICIAL LANGUAGE: English POLITICAL SYSTEM: semi-autonomous UK overseas territory
GOVERNOR-GENERAL: David Pearey (since April '06)
RULING PARTY: National Democratic Party (NDP)
HEAD OF GOVERNMENT: Orlando Smith, Chief Minister (since June '03)
MAIN IGO MEMBERSHIPS (NON-UN): OECS (assoc.), Caricom (assoc.)
CURRENCY: US dollar (end '06 £1=1.95250)
GDP PER CAPITA: US$38,643 ('03), -

Cayman Islands

CAPITAL: George Town, Grand Cayman AREA: 259 sq km POPULATION: 45,000
OFFICIAL LANGUAGE: English POLITICAL SYSTEM: semi-autonomous UK overseas territory
GOVERNOR-GENERAL: Stuart Jack (since Nov '05)
RULING PARTY: People's Progressive Movement (PPM)
HEAD OF GOVERNMENT: Kurt Tibbetts (since May '05)
MAIN IGO MEMBERSHIPS (NON-UN): Caricom (obs.)
CURRENCY: Cayman Island dollar (end-'06 £1=CI$1.67600, US$1=CI$0.85840)
GDP PER CAPITA: US$36,271 ('05), -

Montserrat

CAPITAL: Plymouth AREA: 102 sq km POPULATION: 4,483 (est)
OFFICIAL LANGUAGE: English POLITICAL SYSTEM: semi-autonomous UK overseas territory
GOVERNOR-GENERAL: Deborah Barnes-Jones (since May '04)
RULING PARTIES: Montserrat Democratic Party (MDP), New People's Liberation Movement, and independent coalition
HEAD OF GOVERNMENT: Lowell Lyttleton Lewis (MDP), Chief Minister (since June '06)
MAIN IGO MEMBERSHIPS (NON-UN): OECS, Caricom, ACS
CURRENCY: East Caribbean dollar (see above)
GDP PER CAPITA: EC$20,231 ('04)

Turks & Caicos Islands

CAPITAL: Cockburn Town AREA: 430 sq km POPULATION: 32,000 ('06 census est)
OFFICIAL LANGUAGE: English POLITICAL SYSTEM: semi-autonomous UK overseas territory
GOVERNOR-GENERAL: Richard Tauwhare (since July '05)
RULING PARTY: Progressive National Party (PNP)
HEAD OF GOVERNMENT: Michael Misick (PNP), Premier (since Aug '03)
MAIN IGO MEMBERSHIPS (NON-UN): Caricom (assoc.), ACS (assoc)
CURRENCY: US dollar (end-'06 £1=1.95250)
GDP PER CAPITA: US$13,506 ('03 est), -

THE place of ANGUILLA, BERMUDA, BRITISH VIRGIN ISLANDS, CAYMAN ISLANDS, MONTSERRAT, and TURKS & CAICOS in UK government foreign policy was highlighted in a white paper published in March entitled "Active diplomacy for a changing world: The UK's international priorities". The document listed the maintenance of security and good governance in the UK Overseas Territories as one of the nine strategic international priorities for the UK over the next 10 years. The March white paper updated a 2003 white paper on the UK's international priorities, "Partnership for progress and prosperity". Specific aims of the 2006 document included: the maintenance of a proper balance between rights and responsibilities in the constitutional relationship between the UK and the Overseas Territories; to manage the impact of new international obligations affecting the Territories; and to minimise the vulnerability of small island territories to economic change and international crime, and help increase their preparedness to deal with natural and other disasters.

Some of the guiding principles of the white paper could be seen in the Turks & Caicos Islands with the introduction of a new constitution in August, which led the governor to make significant changes to the responsibilities of his key ministers. Premier (formerly chief minister) Michael Misick, Deputy Premier (formerly deputy chief minister) Floyd Hall, and Minister of Home Affairs Galmo Williams were put in charge of the conduct of business for external affairs, defence, and internal security (including the police force), and the regulation of international financial services. The Turks & Caicos were accepted as an associate member of the Association of Caribbean States in March.

In other developments, in Montserrat Lowell Lewis and his Montserrat Democratic Party won the 31 May general election, despite winning only one of the nine seats contested. Lewis was granted victory after both the former ruling party, the New People's Liberation Movement, which won three seats, and an independent candidate offered him their support. Meanwhile the British Virgin Islands banned smoking within enclosed public spaces and within 50 ft (15.24 m) of any public space under a law passed in November. The Tobacco Products Control Act also placed restrictions on the packaging, advertising, and distribution of tobacco.

NETHERLANDS ANTILLES AND ARUBA

Netherlands Antilles

CAPITAL: Willemstad (Curaçao) AREA: 800 sq km POPULATION: 183,000
OFFICIAL LANGUAGES: Dutch, Papiamento & English POLITICAL SYSTEM: autonomous dependency of the Netherlands
GOVERNOR-GENERAL: Fritz Goedgedrag (since July '02)
RULING PARTIES: Antillean Restructuring Party (PAR) heads coalition
HEAD OF GOVERNMENT: Emily de Jongh-Elhage (PAR), Prime Minister (since March '06)
CURRENCY: Netherlands Antilles guilder (end-'06 £1=AG3.49490, US$1=AG1.79000)
GNI PER CAPITA: US$10,726 or more ('05 est), -

Aruba

CAPITAL: Oranjestad AREA: 193 sq km POPULATION: 101,000
OFFICIAL LANGUAGE: Dutch POLITICAL SYSTEM: autonomous dependency of the Netherlands
GOVERNOR-GENERAL: Olindo Koolman
RULING PARTY: People's Electoral Movement (MEP)
HEAD OF GOVERNMENT: Nelson O. Oduber (MEP), Prime Minister (since Sept '01)
CURRENCY: Aruba guilder (end-'06 £1=AG3.45040, US$1=AG1.79000)
GNI PER CAPITA: US$10,726 or more ('05 est), -

THE constitutional status of the smaller territories of the NETHERLANDS ANTILLES was finalised in October. The previous December it had been agreed that Bonaire, Sint Eustatius, and Saba would become Kingdom Islands, but the specific details of the arrangements were left open for further discussion (see AR 2005, p. 149). On 11 October it was agreed that the three territories would become part of the Netherlands, with a status similar to that of a normal Dutch municipality. This was possible under article 134 of the Dutch constitution, which also gave the populations of the islands a right to vote in Dutch and European parliamentary elections. Also under the agreement, the Dutch government retained its financial supervision over the islands, while each territory was required to maintain a balanced budget. No decision was reached on when the islands would attain their new status, but the October agreement marked the beginning of the end of the Netherlands Antilles as a single state within the Kingdom of the Netherlands (the Netherlands, Netherlands Antilles, and Aruba).

Subsequently, on 3 November, the two larger territories within the Netherlands Antilles—Curaçao and Sint Maarten—signed an agreement with the Dutch government to become autonomous islands within the Kingdom, a similar status to that of ARUBA. Underpinning the agreement was an understanding that Curaçao and Sint Maarten would govern themselves except on matters of defence, foreign policy, and law enforcement. On signing the agreement, the Netherlands Antilles prime minister, Emily de Jongh-Elhage, described it as "historic" and predicted "that the bonds will be closer, not only between the islands, but also the European part of the Kingdom".

Earlier in the year, tensions between the Netherlands, the NETHERLANDS ANTILLES, and ARUBA, on the one hand, and Venezuela on the other, came to the fore. In a speech to the Netherlands parliament in March, Dutch Defence Minister Henk Kamp accused Venezuela's President Hugo Chávez of having designs on those parts of the Antilles which lay off the Venezuelan coast. Although Kamp later backtracked and played down the likelihood of a Venezuelan invasion of Aruba, Bonaire, and Curaçao, Antillean Prime Minister Elhage also expressed concern about a possible Venezuelan attack. In response, the Venezuelan government strongly denied having any such intention. Nevertheless, some leading politicians in Venezuela had in the past demanded the creation of "Bolivarian" cells on the islands to press for independence from the Netherlands and reunification with Venezuela, and Chávez had called for the Caribbean to be "decolonised" and had suggested that Aruba, Bonaire, and Curaçao could be used by the USA as a springboard for an invasion of his country.

US DEPENDENCIES

Puerto Rico

CAPITAL: San Juan AREA: 9,103 sq km POPULATION: 3,911,000
OFFICIAL LANGUAGES: Spanish & English POLITICAL SYSTEM: multiparty system in US Commonwealth
GOVERNOR-GENERAL: Anibal Acevedo Vilá (PPD)
RULING PARTY: New Progressive Party (PNP)
CURRENCY: US dollar (end-'05 £1=1.95250)
GNI PER CAPITA: US$10,726 or more ('05 est), -

US Virgin Islands

CAPITAL: Charlotte Amalie AREA: 342 sq km POPULATION: 115,000
OFFICIAL LANGUAGE: English POLITICAL SYSTEM: semi-autonomous overseas territory of the USA
GOVERNOR-GENERAL: Charles Turnbull (Democratic Party)
GOVERNOR-GENERAL ELECT: John deJongh (Democratic Party)
RULING PARTY: Democrats
CURRENCY: US dollar (end-'06 £1=1.95250)
GNI PER CAPITA: US$10,726 or more ('05 est), -

PUERTO RICO suffered a partial government shutdown when it ran out of money on 1 May, two months before the end of the fiscal year. The crisis forced the closure of schools and numerous public agencies, which meant that thousands of government workers had to apply to the state for financial assistance. Serious divisions between Governor Aníbal Acevedo Vilá and the opposition-dominated legislature over the country's previous two budgets had meant that neither had been passed, forcing the government to borrow money repeatedly from the Government Development Bank in order to cover its financial commitments. On this occasion, the government failed to find sufficient funds to meet its obligations. However, normal government resumed two weeks later after a compromise deal was arrived at between the governor and the legislature for a series of temporary measures to cover government expenditure until the end of the fiscal year on 30 June.

The shutdown and efforts to overcome it concentrated the minds of all politicians on the island's parlous financial state, and on 25 June the country's first budget in two years was passed, to cover the 2006-07 financial year. The budget included measures to rein in public debt through spending cuts and a restructuring of the tax system.

In a separate development, the US government indicted a Puerto Rican utility company, the Puerto Rico Aqueduct and Sewer Authority, for "environmental crimes", and agreed a deal for the company to pay a record US$9 million fine for polluting US waters and violating the Clean Water Act.

Government officials in the US Virgin Islands (USVI) reacted angrily to an article in *The Economist*, published in September, that criticised the territory's lack of preparedness for a terrorist attack. The USVI homeland security director, Mel Vanterpool, described the article as "disparaging" and "ridiculous". The article claimed that the USVI was a prime target for terrorists because of government corruption, unprotected borders, weak infrastructure, and poorly trained and inadequately staffed emergency services. The article also criticised the territory's social, economic, and cultural condition.

In November, meanwhile, John deJongh was elected governor after winning a runoff election. He would assume office on 1 January 2007.

SOUTH AMERICA

BRAZIL—ARGENTINA—PARAGUAY—URUGUAY—CHILE—PERU—BOLIVIA—ECUADOR—COLOMBIA—VENEZUELA

BRAZIL

CAPITAL: Brasília AREA: 8,547,000 sq km POPULATION: 186,405,000
OFFICIAL LANGUAGE: Portuguese POLITICAL SYSTEM: multiparty republic
HEAD OF STATE AND GOVERNMENT: President Luiz Inácio "Lula" da Silva (since Jan '03)
RULING PARTIES: Workers' Party (PT) heads coalition
MAIN IGO MEMBERSHIPS (NON-UN): OAS, ALADI, SELA, Mercosur, AP, CPLP
CURRENCY: real (end-'06 £1=R4.13860, US$1=R2.14700)
GNI PER CAPITA: US$3,460, US$8,230 at PPP ('05)

The mensalão ("monthly payment") corruption scandal (see AR 2005, pp. 151-53) continued to dominate politics in Brazil in 2006, but did not deter voters from re-electing President Luiz Inácio "Lula" da Silva for a second consecutive four-year term in October.

It was announced in June that da Silva would seek a second term, and it was widely anticipated that he would secure re-election in the first round of voting on 1 October, after opinion polls had, throughout the campaign, indicated that he would win. Da Silva's victory was secured, however, only in a second round run-off vote after he won 48.6 per cent of the first round vote, whilst Geraldo Alckmin, the candidate of the Brazilian Social Democratic Party (PSDB) and da Silva's closest rival, secured 41.6 per cent. Under the terms of Brazil's constitution, a candidate was required to poll more than 50 per cent of the vote to win the election on the first round. Da Silva's failure to win outright was widely regarded by analysts as a reflection of disquiet amongst the electorate over the mensalão scandal and other allegations of corruption, which had plagued his administration since June 2005. When the second round of voting was held on 29 October, da Silva defeated Alckmin by a comfortable margin, winning 60.83 per cent to Alckmin's 39.17 per cent. Voter turnout was 83.2 per cent in the first round and 81 per cent in the second, according to the Superior Electoral Court (TSE), meaning that over 100 million people had participated in each round. During his victory speech in Sao Paulo, Brazil's largest city, on 29 October, da Silva pledged that his government would prioritise Brazil's "most needy" people during its second term in office.

Several senior politicians, including many ruling Workers' Party (PT) officials, were dismissed from office or resigned in 2005 after being implicated in the mensalão scandal. The most senior member of da Silva's government to leave office in 2006 over the scandal was Finance Minister Antonio Palocci, who was forced to resign on 27 March after being accused of violating banking secrecy laws by seeking information from a state-owned bank about a witness who had testified against him during congressional hearings. Palocci was replaced on 27 March by Guido Mantega, a former budget and planning minister and president of the state-run Brazilian Development Bank (BNDES). In April, Palocci was charged by the police with receiving illegal payments from a company with local government contracts, when he was a city mayor in the state of Sao Paulo in 2001 and 2002. The final report of a congressional inquiry into the scandal was published in June, and concluded that 79 people, including Palocci, should face criminal charges for their alleged wrongdoing. The report also suggested that the money used to settle a US$13,000 debt, which had been incurred by da Silva during his 2002 presidential election campaign, may have been raised illegally by PT officials.

In other developments connected to the mensalão scandal, former PT secretary general Silvio Pereira, who resigned in July 2005 after admitting his role in the corruption, claimed in May that da Silva had known about a plan by PT officials to raise R1 billion in donations from companies in exchange for government contracts. The claim was published in an interview published on 7 May in the daily newspaper *O Globo*, but just three days later Pereira distanced himself from the comments attributed to him, telling a congressional committee that he no longer knew what was "true and what was not".

On 15 September, just weeks before the first round of voting in the presidential elections, the PT became embroiled in a new corruption scandal, when two men, allegedly hired by the party, were arrested in possession of almost US$800,000, which was, according to the police, due to be exchanged for information implicating da Silva's closest political rivals—including Alckmin—in wrongdoing. The PT president, Ricardo Jose Ribeiro Berzoini, resigned from his post on 6 October after being implicated in the suspected attempt to mount a smear campaign. The alleged "dirty tricks" plan came to light shortly after the publication of a congressional commission of inquiry report on 10 August, which called for the expulsion of 72 legislators for participating in a corruption ring and the embezzlement of public health funds. According to the inquiry, an ambulance manufacturing company had offered financial and other inducements to 69 deputies and three senators, in exchange for their agreement to include funds in the federal budget to buy at inflated prices ambulances which were later bought by local health authorities. The scandal, which had surfaced in May, was dubbed "operation leech" by the Brazilian media.

In an attempt to reduce the risk of corruption in an election year, the Chamber of Deputies (the lower chamber of Congress, the bicameral federal legislature) on 9 February approved a measure limiting the amount of money that candidates could spend on election campaigns. In August, however, da Silva was fined some R900,000 after the TSE ruled that he had violated electoral legislation by prematurely engaging in election campaign advertising. (It was illegal under Brazilian electoral law to begin campaign advertising before the start of the official election campaign.) The TSE ruled that a booklet presenting a review of the government's activities—1 million copies of which had been commissioned by da Silva in January—was akin to an election campaign leaflet, meaning that he had breached the law.

Many analysts considered the greatest challenge of da Silva's second term to be the passage through Congress of a series of economic reforms, which had been hindered by the revelations of corruption, the congressional public inquiries, and the crumbling congressional support that had followed. In elections to the Chamber of Deputies, in which all 513 seats were contested on 1 October, under a system of proportional representation, the PT won 83 seats, whilst the Brazilian Democratic Movement Party (PMBD) won 89, more than any other party. In elections to the 81-seat Senate (the upper chamber), also held on 1 October and in which 27 seats (one-third) were contested, the PT secured two seats, increasing its overall representation to 11.

The results of the legislative elections meant that the PT would be forced to work with coalition partners in both chambers to achieve the majority which was required to approve da Silva's legislative agenda. The PMBD voted on 30 November to join the coalition government. This was regarded as a significant success for da Silva, who was also thought to have negotiated an alliance involving the Brazilian Socialist Party (PSB) and the Communist Party of Brazil (PCB). PT leaders announced in December that da Silva was eager for his coalition partners to reach an agreement over the presentation of a single candidate for the presidency of the Chamber of Deputies, a position commanding significant authority over the legislative agenda.

Da Silva, who was due to be inaugurated for his second term in January 2007, was regarded as Brazil's "best" ever president, according to the results of a survey which was published in December by the research institute Datafolha. Some 35 per cent of the survey's respondents had voted for da Silva, many of them expressing strong support for his education and economic policies, whilst disapproving of his policies on healthcare, job creation, and—perhaps unsurprisingly—fighting corruption.

Congress on 18 April approved Brazil's budget for 2006, which included estimated revenue of some R456 billion and estimated expenditure of R406.9 billion.

The budget also included plans to increase GDP by 4.5 per cent and limit inflation to 4.5 per cent. In December, however, the Central Bank announced that it was forecasting inflation to reach 3.1 per cent in 2006, whilst economic growth was expected to reach 3 per cent. The lower forecasts signalled that the Bank would continue to reduce interest rates in 2007, according to many analysts. The Bank had on 29 November reduced Brazil's interest rate to 13.25 per cent from 13.75 per cent, the 12th consecutive rate reduction, making this the longest period of rate cuts in the country's history. Meanwhile Brazil's unemployment rate in 2006 reached its lowest point in January, when it stood at 9.2 per cent.

During a closed meeting on 14 December the leaders of the Senate and the Chamber of Deputies agreed with party leaders to increase the salaries paid to legislators by 90.7 per cent with effect from 1 February 2007. The decision, which caused widespread controversy and discontent, would have increased the monthly salary of a legislator from R12,847 to R24,500. In the face of public criticism of the pay rise, however, the Supreme Court on 19 December ruled that it was unconstitutional because it had not been approved by a majority vote in both chambers of Congress. Legislators announced on 20 December that a vote on the matter would be delayed until February 2007. The sharp contrast between rich and poor in Brazil was highlighted on 27 December, when da Silva signed into law a bill increasing the minimum wage from April 2007 by 8.5 per cent to R380 per month, less than 2 per cent of the salary proposed for legislators. It was thought that more than 27 million Brazilians earned a wage equivalent to (or less than) the minimum, meaning that the increase would cost around R1 billion.

Violent social unrest—some of it due to prison conditions, some as a result of protests over land—was a significant theme of the year. On 10 September Ubiratan Guimaraes, a former military police colonel who was in 2001 sentenced to 638 years in prison for using "excessive force" in October 1992 to suppress an uprising which killed at least 111 inmates of Carandiru prison (see AR 2001, p. 204), was found dead at his home in Sao Paulo. Guimaraes, whose conviction was overturned in February after a court ruled that he had merely obeyed orders issued by his superiors, had been shot dead, prompting the police to investigate both his girlfriend and the First Command of the Capital (PCC) gang as possible perpetrators. Violent uprisings occurred frequently in Brazil's notoriously overcrowded prisons. In 2006, however, inmates were also blamed for orchestrating violence on the streets in Sao Paulo. In May, more than 200 people were killed in the city, including 123 suspected gang members, 23 prisoners, 31 police officers, and seven other public officials, after imprisoned leaders of the PCC gang were transferred to a remote, maximum security prison. It was thought that the imprisoned gang leaders, who were angered by the prison transfers, had used mobile telephones to order gang members in Sao Paulo to retaliate by initiating attacks on police officers throughout the city, including the use of machine guns and hand grenades.

A new wave of attacks was launched in Sao Paulo in August, during which at least six gang members were killed and 28 others were arrested. Television journalist Guilherme Portanova and his assistant Alexandre Coelho Calado were kidnapped by gang members on 12 August, highlighting the influence that gang members wielded from their prison cells. Coelho Calado was released the same day with a videotape recording, in which a PCC member condemned Brazil's prison system and demanded improved conditions. Portanova was released on 14 August after the video was broadcast on national television, as demanded by his captors. Evidence emerged in November that police officers had executed "dozens of suspects" during the violence in May, although a local government official said that there was no evidence indicating that the police had operated a "death squad".

At least seven inmates died during a riot on 22 March at the Jundai prison, about 30 km west of Sao Paulo, which began after inmates were angered by the transfer of some prisoners to another prison. Two guards and an inmate were also killed on 19 December, at the Laudemir Neves prison in the city of Foz do Iguacu, near Brazil's border with Paraguay and Argentina, during an uprising by inmates who were demanding improved conditions. The Laudemir Neves prison was built to house only 350 inmates but was thought to hold at least 800. Gang violence linked to the illegal drugs trade also erupted in December, in the slum areas (favelas) of the city of Rio de Janerio, during which at least 19 people were killed. On 28 December seven of the victims burned to death after armed men attacked a bus and set it alight, prompting the local authorities to deploy more than 20,000 police officers in an attempt to suppress further outbreaks of violence.

Violent clashes over land had increased during da Silva's first term in office, according to a report published on 30 November by a coalition of human rights groups. The report said that 1,690 violent land disputes had taken place in 2006, representing an increase over 2002 of more than 80 per cent. The report strongly criticised da Silva for failing to deliver on his pledges to redistribute more land to the urban poor. The government was also criticised in a separate report (entitled "Conflicts in the countryside—Brazil 2005") published in April by Brazil's Pastoral Land Commission (CPT). The report revealed that 64 people had died—including 38 through assassination—in 2005 as a result of land conflicts, and urged da Silva's administration to do more to prevent land-related violence.

In June, more than 500 members of the Movement for Liberation of the Landless (MLST), a former faction of the Landless Workers' Movement (MST), invaded the Chamber of Deputies to protest against the slow pace of redistribution of land. Most of the activists were arrested after violent clashes with security guards, who were trying to prevent the protesters from reaching the main debating chamber. Seven of the arrested protesters were charged with attempted murder after a security guard suffered serious injuries. In the first eight months of 2006, the MST staged 180 farm invasions, before declaring a moratorium on further protests pending completion of the presidential election.

The government declared three days of national mourning after Brazil suffered its worst aviation disaster on 29 September when a Boeing 737-800, operated by the Brazilian low-cost airline Gol, which was en-route from Manaus to Brasilia, crashed in a dense jungle area in the Amazonian state of Mato Grosso, killing all 154 people aboard. It was thought that the disaster occurred after a mid-air collision with a small executive jet, in which one of the Boeing's wings was clipped and damaged. Remarkably, the executive jet later landed safely. The authorities on 8 December charged the two pilots of the small jet (US citizens Joseph Lepore and Jan Paladino) with "exposing an aircraft to danger".

ARGENTINA

CAPITAL: Buenos Aires AREA: 2,780,000 sq km POPULATION: 38,747,000
OFFICIAL LANGUAGE: Spanish POLITICAL SYSTEM: multiparty republic
HEAD OF STATE AND GOVERNMENT: President Nestor Kirchner (since May '03)
RULING PARTY: Justicialist Party (PJ)
MAIN IGO MEMBERSHIPS (NON-UN): OAS, SELA, ALADI, Mercosur
CURRENCY: peso (end-'06 £1=AP5.93610, US$1=AP3.07950)
GNI PER CAPITA: US$4,470, US$13,920 at PPP ('05)

IN Argentina, the country's "dirty war" era (1976-83) dominated the political agenda in 2006, some 30 years after the 1976 coup that overthrew the government of President Isabel Martínez de Perón and led to the installation of a military junta (see AR 1976, pp. 80-81).

The government made clear its intentions on 23 March, the eve of the 30th anniversary of the 1976 coup, when it was announced that Nestor Kirchner, the current president, had signed a decree to make public previously secret military documents relating to the "dirty war" era. On 24 March Kirchner publicly urged the country's courts to annul the presidential pardons granted in 1989-90 by former President Carlos Saúl Menem (1988-99) to hundreds of military officers charged with torture and murder during the "dirty war" era. In September a judge ruled that the pardons granted to General Jorge Rafael Videla, former dictator of Argentina; José Alfredo Martínez de Hoz, a former economy minister; and General Albano Eduardo Harguindeguy, a former interior minister, all of whom had held office in the period 1976-81, were unconstitutional. The rulings followed an investigation into human rights abuses committed during the "dirty war", including the abduction of two businessmen in 1976-77, and opened the possibility that the three men would face trials on charges related to crimes against humanity.

In June former police officer Miguel Osvaldo Etchecolatz, 77, became the first former official to face trial in Argentina since the Supreme Court had ruled in June 2005 that two amnesty laws enacted in 1986-87 were unconstitutional (see AR 2005, pp. 155-56). Etchecolatz was on 19 September convicted of kidnapping, torturing, and murdering six people during the "dirty war" era and sentenced to life in prison. Julio Hector Simon (also known as "Turco Julian"), another former police officer, was the first former official to be convicted of human rights violations, since the amnesty laws were overturned, when he was sentenced on 4 August to 25 years in prison for the kidnapping and torturing in 1978 of two political activists and for the abduction of their eight-month-old daughter.

A judge in Uruguay on 7 December authorised the extradition to Argentina of six Uruguayan former military and police officers, who were wanted in Argentina for their alleged role in the disappearance in 1976, and presumed murder, of Argentinian citizen María Claudia García. The authorities in Argentina believed that the six men had participated in "Operation Condor", a reputed conspiracy by South American leaders in the 1970s and 1980s to crush leftist political opponents (see p. 180).

President Kirchner's determination to address the crimes committed during the "dirty war" was again evident in June when he announced that his government had enacted the "Law of National Defence", limiting Argentina's armed forces to protecting the country against foreign aggression and reducing the powers of military commanders. The law was originally approved in 1988, but subsequent administrations had failed to enact the legislation, which was finally signed at a ceremony in Buenos Aires on 12 June by Defence Minister Nilda Garré. On 15 December Kirchner urged the judiciary to increase the pace of its investigations into crimes committed during the "dirty war" era to avoid further "delays" and to ensure that the families of victims knew "what really went on".

A report published by the World Bank in December warned that there were signs of "overheating" in Argentina's economy, which had grown by almost 9 per cent each year since the country's economic collapse in 2001 (see AR 2001, pp. 204-07). The report portentously suggested that a "harsh...correction" was likely unless the government gradually slowed the growth rate.

The Supreme Court on 27 December issued a landmark ruling upholding a government decree of January 2002, which had forcibly converted billions of US dollars of savings into devalued pesos. The Court ruling ordered banks to repay depositors in local currency the total value of deposits originally held in US dollars. In effect, this ruling judged the 2002 decree constitutional and brought to an end some 50,000 lawsuits from disgruntled depositors; it also meant that banks were forced to repay depositors at a rate of 3.08 pesos to the US dollar, equivalent to the current market rate of the peso and intended to restore the dollar value of the deposits. The rate of compensation was calculated by using a currency conversion rate of 1.40 pesos to the US dollar (the market rate of the peso when it was devalued by some 40 per cent on 7 January 2002), which was adjusted for inflation and included an annual interest rate of 4 per cent, to be applied retroactively.

The country's budget for 2007, which was approved by the Senate (the upper chamber of the bicameral federal legislature) on 13 December, included spending plans amounting to US$39.7 billion and forecast economic growth of 4 per cent. Following Argentina's deal in June 2005 to restructure the country's nearly US$100 billion of foreign debt (see AR 2005, p. 154), the government in January completed early repayment of its entire outstanding obligations to the IMF, amounting to SDR6.656 billion. During his state of the nation address on 1 March, President Kirchner said that the deal to restructure Argentina's foreign debt had achieved an "unprecedented saving" of US$67 billion and restored economic freedom to the country. Economy Minister Felisa Miceli on 18 December presented the government's proposals for restructuring Argentina's debt with the Paris Club of 19 sovereign creditor countries, which amounted to around US$6.3 billion.

The historically strong relationship between Argentina and Uruguay became strained in 2006 by a dispute over the construction of two paper pulp mills in the Uruguayan city of Fray Bentos, near the Uruguay river which formed the border between the two countries. The authorities in Argentina argued that the construction project "posed a serious threat to the ecosystem" of the river, thereby contravening the Statute of the River Uruguay, a treaty which Argentina and Uruguay signed in 1975. Argentina took the dispute to the International Court of Justice (ICJ) in an attempt to halt the project, but the court on 14 July rejected Argentina's complaints (see p. 461).

Argentina's relations with Iran also soured in 2006 when public prosecutors in Argentina issued international arrest warrants in November against the former Iranian president, Ali Akbar Hashemi Rafsanjani (1989-97), and seven of his officials for allegedly masterminding a bomb attack in July 1994 on a Jewish community centre in Buenos Aires (see AR 2004, p. 165). The attack killed 85 people and injured more than 200 others, making it the country's worst ever terrorist incident. According to the authorities in Argentina, the former Iranian officials had, in 1993, ordered guerrillas from Hezbullah, the Lebanese-based Shi'ite Muslim movement, to carry out the attack. In 2005, Argentinian investigators had identified an alleged Hezbullah member as the suicide bomber (see AR 2005, p. 156). The Iranian authorities angrily rejected the charges, describing them as a "Zionist plot".

The vexed question of the Falkland Islands (Islas Malvinas), which complicated relations with the UK, surfaced frequently in 2006 some 24 years after the British defeat of General Leopoldo Galtieri's ill-fated military invasion of the islands (see AR 1982, pp. 7-21). President Kirchner on 1 March reiterated that his government "unwaveringly upheld" its "claims of sovereignty" over the archipelago, whilst Foreign Minister Jorge Taiana in June accused the UK of rejecting Argentina's calls for a resumption of talks on sovereignty and asked the UN to intervene. Also in June, Congress (the bicameral legislature) established a special commission to promote internationally Argentina's sovereignty claims over the islands and the government announced a temporary suspension of several defence co-operation agreements with the UK.

The apparent hardening of Argentina's policy on the Falkland Islands in 2006 came ahead of presidential elections, which were due to be contested in October 2007. As the year ended Kirchner had not declared whether he would seek re-election in 2007, but former president Carlos Menem, who collapsed in September during a speech at a political rally in the town of La Calera, confirmed on 13 December that he would stand.

In other developments, Aníbal Ibarra, the mayor of Buenos Aires, who had been suspended from duty in October 2005, was dismissed from his post on 7 March at the end of an investigation which found him guilty of failing to enforce safety standards that might have prevented a fire at a nightclub in the city in December 2004, which killed 194 people (see AR 2004, p. 163).

The provincial Supreme Court in Buenos Aires on 7 August ruled to grant an abortion to a mentally disabled rape victim who was four months pregnant. The ruling overturned two previous judgments by lower courts which had rejected the woman's request for an abortion on the grounds that it was unconstitutional. Abortion was illegal in Argentina except when a woman's life was endangered by pregnancy or when a woman who was mentally incapable had been raped.

PARAGUAY—URUGUAY—CHILE—PERU—BOLIVIA—ECUADOR—COLOMBIA—VENEZUELA

Paraguay

CAPITAL: Asunción AREA: 407,000 sq km POPULATION: 6,158,000
OFFICIAL LANGUAGE: Spanish POLITICAL SYSTEM: multiparty republic
HEAD OF STATE AND GOVERNMENT: President Nicanor Duarte Frutos (PC) (since Aug '03)
RULING PARTIES: Colorado Party (PC), supported by Authentic Radical Liberal Party (PLRA)
MAIN IGO MEMBERSHIPS (NON-UN): OAS, ALADI, SELA, Mercosur
CURRENCY: guarani (end-'06 £1=G10,094.2, US$1=G5,170.00)
GNI PER CAPITA: US$1,280, US$4,970 at PPP ('05 est, based on regression)

Uruguay

CAPITAL: Montevideo AREA: 177,000 sq km POPULATION: 3,463,000
OFFICIAL LANGUAGE: Spanish POLITICAL SYSTEM: multiparty republic
HEAD OF STATE AND GOVERNMENT: President Tabaré Vázquez (EP-FA), since March '05
RULING PARTY: Progressive Encounter-Broad Front (EP-FA)
MAIN IGO MEMBERSHIPS (NON-UN): OAS, ALADI, SELA, Mercosur
CURRENCY: peso Uruguay (end-'06 £1=UP47.7277, US$1=UP24.4450)
GNI PER CAPITA: US$4,360, US$9,810 at PPP ('05)

Chile

CAPITAL: Santiago AREA: 757,000 sq km POPULATION: 16,295,000
OFFICIAL LANGUAGE: Spanish POLITICAL SYSTEM: multiparty republic
HEAD OF STATE AND GOVERNMENT: President Michelle Bachelet (since March '06)
RULING PARTIES: Concertación coalition composed of Party for Democracy (PPD), Socialist (PSC), Christian Democratic (PDC), & Social Democratic Radical (PRSD) parties
MAIN IGO MEMBERSHIPS (NON-UN): OAS, ALADI, SELA, APEC, NAM, Mercosur
CURRENCY: Chilean peso (end-'06 £1=Ch1,049.83, US$1=Ch537.700)
GNI PER CAPITA: US$5,870, US$11,470 at PPP ('05)

Peru

CAPITAL: Lima AREA: 1,285,000 sq km POPULATION: 27,968,000
OFFICIAL LANGUAGES: Spanish, Quechua, Aymará POLITICAL SYSTEM: multiparty republic
HEAD OF STATE AND GOVERNMENT: President Alan García Pérez (APRA) (since July '06)
RULING PARTIES: Union for Perú (UPP) largest party in Congress; Peruvian Aprista Party (APRA) holds presidency
MAIN IGO MEMBERSHIPS (NON-UN): OAS, APEC, ALADI, SELA, CA, AP, NAM
CURRENCY: new sol (end-'06 £1=S6.22740, US$1=S3.18950)
GNI PER CAPITA: US$2,610, US$5,830 at PPP ('05)

Bolivia

CAPITAL: La Paz and Sucre AREA: 1,099,000 sq km POPULATION: 9,182,000
OFFICIAL LANGUAGES: Spanish, Quechua, Aymará POLITICAL SYSTEM: multiparty republic
HEAD OF STATE AND GOVERNMENT: President Evo Morales (MAS) (since Jan '06)
RULING PARTY: Movement Towards Socialism (MAS)
MAIN IGO MEMBERSHIPS (NON-UN): OAS, ALADI, SELA, AG, CA, NAM, Mercosur
CURRENCY: boliviano (end-'06 £1=B15.4112, US$1=B7.99500)
GNI PER CAPITA: US$1,010, US$2,740 at PPP ('05)

Ecuador

CAPITAL: Quito AREA: 284,000 sq km POPULATION: 13,228,000
OFFICIAL LANGUAGE: Spanish POLITICAL SYSTEM: multiparty republic
HEAD OF STATE AND GOVERNMENT: President Alfredo Palacio (since April '05)(since Jan '03)
PRESIDENT ELECT: Rafael Correa Delgado (MPAIS/PS-FA)
RULING PARTY: Institutional Renewal Party of National Action (PRIAN)
MAIN IGO MEMBERSHIPS (NON-UN): OAS, ALADI, SELA, AG, CA, NAM
CURRENCY: sucre (end-'06 £1=S48811.3, US$1=S25000.0)
GNI PER CAPITA: US$2,630, US$4,070 at PPP ('05)

Colombia

CAPITAL: Santa Fe de Bogotá AREA: 1,139,000 sq km POPULATION: 45,600,000
OFFICIAL LANGUAGE: Spanish POLITICAL SYSTEM: multiparty republic
HEAD OF STATE AND GOVERNMENT: President Alvaro Uribe Vélez (Colombia First, PC) (since Aug. '02)
RULING PARTIES: Party of the "U" (UP), Colombian Conservative Party (PCC), and Radical Change (CR)
MAIN IGO MEMBERSHIPS (NON-UN): OAS, ALADI, SELA, AG, CA, ACS, NAM
CURRENCY: Colombian peso (end-'06 £1=Col4,330.92, US$1=Col2,218.20)
GNI PER CAPITA: US$2,290, US$7,420 at PPP ('05 est, based on regression)

Venezuela

CAPITAL: Caracas AREA: 912,000 sq km POPULATION: 26,577,000
OFFICIAL LANGUAGE: Spanish POLITICAL SYSTEM: multiparty republic
HEAD OF STATE AND GOVERNMENT: President Hugo Chávez Frías (since Feb '99)
RULING PARTY: Fifth Republic Movement (MVR)
MAIN IGO MEMBERSHIPS (NON-UN): OAS, ALADI, SELA, CA, ACS, OPEC, NAM
CURRENCY: bolívar (end-'06 £1=Bs6,662.65, US$1=Bs3,412.46)
GNI PER CAPITA: US$4,810, US$6,440 at PPP ('05)

THE year was marked by the deaths of General (retd) Augusto Pinochet Ugarte, the dictator of CHILE in 1973-90, and of General Alfredo Stroessner Matiauda, the dictator of PARAGUAY in 1954-89, both of whom had viciously opposed democracy in the region. Many of the former dictators' opponents celebrated their demise, despite the fact that neither man had faced justice for any of the crimes which had been committed in their name (for obituaries see pp. 590-91; 599). The year was also defined by the holding of democratic elections, in which more than 75 million people in five of the region's countries (including Chile) exercised the right to vote for a leader of their choice, thus highlighting a stark contrast with the era of oppression symbolised by dictators such as Pinochet and Stroessner.

Pinochet, who had spent the last 16 years of his life fighting a series of human rights, fraud, and corruption charges, died of heart failure on 10 December (one week after suffering a heart attack) at a military hospital in the Providencia area of Santiago. Pinochet, 91, was described in many media reports as a "polarising" figure in CHILE, a charitable reference to the sharp divide that existed between his supporters, who claimed that he had saved the country from the "scourge of communism" by leading an armed coup in 1973 against elected President Salvador Allende, and his opponents, who condemned him as a savage dictator responsible for the death of at least 3,000 dissidents and the torture of some 28,000 others. The government rejected requests for a full state funeral (an honour normally bestowed upon former presidents) and declared that there would be no official period of mourning to commemorate Pinochet's life. The former dictator was cremated at an undisclosed location during a private ceremony on 12 December, hours after a funeral service was held at a military college in the Las Condes area of Santiago, where he had trained as a young soldier. An estimated 60,000 people, most of whom were supporters of Pinochet, flocked to the college to view the former dictator's casket. There was a series of violent clashes involving Pinochet's supporters, his opponents, and the police, during which at least 65 people were injured, leading the police to use water cannon and tear gas to disperse the crowds. Pinochet's grandson, Captain Augusto Pinochet Molina, was on 13 December discharged from the army, after strongly criticising the judges who had been investigating his grandfather.

In a letter published before his death, which was revealed to the public on 24 December, Pinochet said he had been "proud of the enormous action" that he took "to stop Marxist-Leninism assuming total power" in Chile, referring to the coup which he had led against Allende. In the letter, which was widely published in newspapers around the world, he also said that "different methods of military control, like temporary detentions, official exile and execution by court martial were necessary".

Stroessner died from pneumonia on 16 August at a hospital in Brasilia, the capital of Brazil, where he been living in exile since he was overthrown by a military coup in February 1989. Stroessner, who had himself seized power in a coup in May 1954, contracted pneumonia after undergoing surgery for a hernia. During his 34-year period of rule Stroessner used a near-permanent state of siege and suspended many civil liberties, prompting hundreds of opposition leaders to flee PARAGUAY. It was also believed that at least 900 political opponents had disappeared under Stroessner's dictatorship as part of "Operation Condor", under which leftist political opponents of regimes in South America were killed or abducted.

Another South American leader to die in 2006 was Valentín Paniagua Corazao. He had been elected interim president of PERU by Congress (the bicameral legislature) in November 2000, after President Alberto Kenyo Fujimori fled to Japan (see AR 2000, p. 172). Paniagua, 70, fell seriously ill with a respiratory infection in August and died on 16 October at a hospital in Lima.

ELECTORAL DEVELOPMENTS. New leaders emerged in presidential elections contested in CHILE, PERU, and ECUADOR, whilst voters in COLOMBIA and VENEZUELA overwhelmingly re-elected the incumbent presidents for a further term. The left-wing forces, which had in recent years scored notable electoral victories in the region, continued to consolidate their position in 2006, including a victory for the left-leaning Michelle Bachelet Jeria, who became the first woman in history to be elected president of Chile. Bachelet, the candidate of the Socialist Party of Chile (PSC), a faction of the ruling Concertación coalition, won just over 53 per cent of the second round vote, which was held on 15 January, following an inconclusive first round contest on 11 December 2005 (see AR 2005, p. 159). Her only rival, Sebastián Piñera Echenique of the National Renewal party (RN), secured just over 46 per cent. During her victory speech, Bachelet, 54, pledged to increase prosperity and improve social justice in CHILE. After her inauguration ceremony on 11 March, Bachelet, who had herself been a victim of torture during the era of Pinochet's dictatorship, said she wanted "a government in which citizens will have an active participation, a government at the service of people".

A new left-wing leader also emerged in ECUADOR, where Rafael Correa Delgado, a former finance minister, won the second round of voting in presidential elections held on 26 November, after a late surge in support for his candidacy. Correa won more than 56 per cent of the vote, whereas Alvaro Fernando Noboa Pontón, his only second round rival, secured 43.33 per cent. During the election campaign Correa described the National Congress (the Ecuadorean unicameral legislature) as a "sewer" of corruption, pledged to call a national referendum on the formation of a constituent assembly to rewrite the country's constitution, and vowed to sever Ecuador's ties with international financial institutions, such as the IMF and the World Bank. On 28 November Correa warned foreign oil companies in Ecuador that he planned to increase the share of crude oil due to the state, and indicated that he might also increase the proportion of oil revenues that foreign companies were obliged to pay to the state above a certain level of income in Ecuador.

Correa's Country Alliance (MPAIS) refused to field candidates in the legislative elections contested on 15 October, meaning that he would be required to govern without direct congressional support when his term in office commenced in January 2007. Noboa's Institutional Renewal Party of National Action (PRIAN) won 27 seats in the 100-seat legislature, whilst the January 21 Patriotic Society Party (PSP) secured 21 seats.

Ecuador's former president, Colonel Lucio Gutiérrez, who was removed from office in April 2005 (see AR 2005, p. 160), was prevented from contesting the election after he was stripped of his political rights for two years when an electoral court ruled in May that he had violated laws by failing to report campaign contributions in 2002. An appeal against the ruling was rejected by the Constitutional Court on 18 October.

Correa's plans for the oil industry in Ecuador, which was the country's largest source of export income, led some observers to compare him with President Hugo Chávez Frías of VENEZUELA, who secured a new term in office in presidential elections contested on 3 December. Chávez's re-election, which granted him a new six-year mandate, was secured with more than 62 per cent of the vote.

Manuel Rosales Guerrero, the candidate of the opposition A New Time (UNT) party and Chávez's nearest rival, won almost 37 per cent of the vote. After the results of the election were announced by the National Electoral Council (CNE) on 5 December, Chávez told his supporters that they had voted for a "socialist project to construct a profoundly different Venezuela" and for a "profound consciousness", adding that he wished to continue steering the country towards its ongoing "democratic, social, political, economic, and moral revolution".

It was announced after the election that Chávez's Movement for the Fifth Republic (MVR) party was dissolving to form the "United Socialist Party of Venezuela". Chávez's coalition, which was headed by the MVR, included more than 20 smaller parties, among them the Communist Party of Venezuela (PCV), Fatherland For All (PPT), We Can (PODEMOS), and Popular Venezuelan Unity. It was thought that many—if not all—of the smaller coalition parties would also dissolve to join the newly formed "United Socialist Party of Venezuela". Rosales and Julio Borges Junyent, the leader of the Primero Justicia party, had on 12 December called on all opposition parties to unite.

A presidential election contested in Peru also required the calling of a second round of voting after no candidate secured more than half of the total valid votes cast in the first round, which was held on 9 April. Peruvian Aprista Party (APRA) candidate and former president (1985-90), Alan García Pérez, won the second round on 4 June by securing just over 52 per cent of the vote, whereas his second round opponent, Lt-Col (retd) Ollanta Humala Tasso, the Union for Peru (UPP) candidate, won just over 47 per cent. Some analysts believed that many people voted for García because they feared Humala's radical leftist policies more than they feared re-electing García, whose first term in office had ended in 1990 in economic crisis, pervasive corruption, and escalating guerrilla violence. Humala, although very popular in rural areas of Peru, found his second round campaign overshadowed by a perceived alliance with Chávez, a leader who was unpopular amongst many Peruvian voters.

In legislative elections to Peru's 120-seat National Congress held simultaneously with the presidential contest, Humala's UPP won 45 seats, whilst García's APRA trailed in second-place with 36 seats. During his inauguration speech on 28 July, García pledged to fight against poverty, outlining a plan to invest some US$1.6 billion in poor rural areas to help improve healthcare and education and to strengthen the public infrastructure. Garcia also announced that he was more than halving his presidential salary.

In Colombia, incumbent President Alvaro Uribe Vélez, the candidate of the Colombia First (PC) party, won an historic landslide victory in presidential elections contested on 28 May after winning just over 62 per cent of the vote. Uribe's closest rival, Carlos Gaviria Díaz of the leftist Alternative Democratic Pole (PDA), secured some 22 per cent of the vote. Uribe's victory was historic in that it was the first occasion in Colombia's recent history that a sitting president had been re-elected, following a Constitutional Court ruling in November 2005 that allowed a second consecutive presidential term (see AR 2005, p. 159).

Uribe's tough security policies to confront Colombia's civil war were popular amongst a majority of voters, and many opinion polls had widely predicted that he would win re-election. Uribe's ability to defeat the country's leftist guerrilla groups and reintegrate into society the demobilised fighters of the right-wing paramilitary organisation, the United Self Defence Forces of Colombia (AUC), were deemed by most analysts to be the greatest challenges of his second term.

OTHER POLITICAL DEVELOPMENTS. Hugo Chávez of VENEZUELA was one of several foreign dignitaries to attend the presidential inauguration of Evo Morales—the first indigenous person to be elected head of state in BOLIVIA—in a ceremony which took place on 22 January in La Paz, the capital. Morales had been elected in the first round vote in December 2005 (see AR 2005, pp. 158-59). Ricardo Lagos, the then president of CHILE, also attended the ceremony, marking the first official visit to Bolivia by a Chilean president since 1955, and indicating a warming of relations between the two countries, which had fought two wars against each other in the 19th century.

During his inaugural speech, Morales vowed that his government would put an end to "injustice" and "inequality" in BOLIVIA. Morales's Movement Towards Socialism (MAS) party on 2 July won 137 seats in elections to a 255-seat constituent assembly. During his election campaign in 2005 Morales had pledged to create the assembly in order to rewrite Bolivia's 1994 constitution. The election pledge was fulfilled when the assembly convened on 6 August for a period of one year in the southern city of Sucre. Morales described the main purpose of the assembly as an opportunity to redefine Bolivia and to overcome "centuries of discrimination" against its indigenous peoples. On 17 November the MAS-dominated assembly approved a measure allowing constitutional reforms to be decided by a simple majority instead of a two-thirds majority, provoking near universal condemnation amongst opposition legislators, some of whom began a hunger strike in protest. Attempts by the opposition to overturn the vote, including the holding of protest rallies and the calling of a series of strikes, failed on 17 November when the Constitutional Court rejected its complaints. The court's judgment meant that the ruling MAS had secured the authority to rewrite individual articles of Bolivia's constitution, although the opposition retained the ability to veto the final draft, which still required the approval of a two-thirds majority.

Morales on 1 May fulfilled another electoral pledge when he issued a decree requiring foreign-owned energy companies to relinquish control of their natural gas fields to the state, warning that they must enter into new operating contracts with the government within 180 days or cease trading in BOLIVIA. Under the decree, foreign energy companies would be paid to operate the installations and the state would regain control of one of Bolivia's most precious natural resources. The move was expected to increase the government's energy revenue to some US$780 million during 2007. According to a report published in December by the Bolivian Hydrocarbons Chamber, an organisation representing Bolivia's energy sector, the country was expected to increase its oil and gas exports in 2006 by 56.9 per cent compared with 2005. Energy exports represented almost 50 per cent of Bolivia's total exports. International concerns over the announcement prompted Morales on 15 May to address the European Parliament in Strasbourg, where he attempted to reassure European legislators that foreign-owned energy companies operating in Bolivia had not been "expropriated" or "expelled" from the country. Despite international opposition to the plan, several foreign-owned energy companies on 26-27 October signed new contracts, under which majority control of their Bolivian operations was ceded to the state. The new contracts were signed into law by Morales on 3 December.

Morales' legislative agenda provoked further discord in November when the opposition controlled Senate (the upper chamber) approved a land reform bill that allowed the state to expropriate land which had been obtained illegally or which did not serve productive economic or social functions. The bill, which also allowed the state to redistribute expropriated land to poor rural communities, had been strongly opposed by opposition legislators who attempted to prevent its passage by boycotting the Senate. Morales responded by threatening to pass the bill by presidential decree, prompting three opposition legislators to break ranks by attending the chamber and voting in favour of the reforms. Almost 90 per cent of the productive land in Bolivia was owned by just 50,000 families, while some 3 million poor people shared the rest, according to some estimates. Morales had announced in June that he would redistribute some 20 million hectares of land, which was equivalent to some 20 per cent of Bolivia's territory, over a five year period. As the year ended, Morales' approval rating had reached 67 per cent, according to an opinion poll published in *La Razon*, a Bolivian newspaper.

The government in VENEZUELA on 1 April took control of seven oil fields that were operated by foreign oil companies under service contracts. Five of the fields were surrendered to the state voluntarily in accordance with Venezuela's hydrocarbons law, which Chávez had enacted in November 2001 and which required all oil production in the country to be undertaken by companies in which the state had majority ownership. In accordance with the law, service contracts for the five fields were cancelled on 31 March and replaced by joint venture contracts with Petroleos de Venezuela (PDVSA), the state-owned oil company. The government took control of the remaining two oil fields without the agreement of the foreign oil companies operating the installations after they failed to meet the deadline for the formation of a joint venture company with PDVSA. The National Assembly (the Venezuelan unicameral legislature) on 16 May approved an amendment to the hydrocarbons law, increasing the oil royalties paid by foreign energy companies operating in Venezuela from 16.67 per cent to 33.3 per cent. Chávez also announced plans to increase the rate of income tax payable by four foreign oil companies which operated oil installations in Venezuela's eastern Faja region, near the Orinoco river, to 50 per cent (from 34 per cent). The government said that the new taxes would increase state revenue by an estimated US$1.3 billion, which would be "redistributed to benefit our people".

In other developments in VENEZUELA, the National Assembly on 7 March voted to approve changes to the design of the country's national flag. The new design included an additional star, to represent the Guayana region of Venezuela, and changes to the coat of arms which appeared in the upper left corner of the flag. The new coat of arms included the addition of tropical fruits, flowers, a bow and arrows, and a machete; and a white horse that had formerly appeared facing towards the right was changed to face towards the left, in what was an apparent gesture to Chávez's left-wing political credentials.

The international media watchdog, Reporters Without Borders, on 31 December condemned an announcement made by Chávez (on 28 December), in which he threatened to revoke the licence of Radio Caracas Televisión (RCTV), Venezuela's oldest commercial television station. The media watchdog urged the government to review its broadcast media policies, calling on it to create an independent body to oversee the assignment and renewal of broadcasting licences. Chávez said that RCTV, which frequently broadcast material that was critical of the government, was "in the service of those who make coups against the people, against the nation, against national independence and against the dignity of the republic", referring to its alleged role in supporting the 2002 coup which temporarily removed Chávez from power (see AR 2002, pp. 198-210). RCTV officials indicated that they would file a legal appeal against the decision, arguing that its licence was not due to expire until 2012.

Nicanor Duarte Frutos, the president of PARAGUAY, on 21 August announced a number of new ministerial appointments, including that of Rubén Ramírez Lezcano as foreign affairs minister. Immediately after his appointment, Ramírez Lezcano announced that that the improvement of Paraguay's relations with Mercosur, the South American Common Market, would be his main priority. Duarte also announced (in November) a major reshuffle of senior military posts.

The first legal abortion in COLOMBIA was performed in August on an 11-year-old girl who had been raped by her stepfather. Leaders of the Roman Catholic church in Colombia condemned the operation, although Cardinal Alfonso López Trujillo, president of the Vatican's pontifical council for the family, on 30 August denied that the Vatican would excommunicate the doctors who had performed the operation. The Constitutional Court in Bogota, the Colombian capital, had on 10 May ruled in favour of legalising abortion in cases where a woman's life or health was endangered, when the pregnancy was the result of rape, or if the foetus was unlikely to survive outside the womb. Prior to the ruling, women who had an abortion in Colombia faced up to four years in prison. A new law prohibiting the smoking of tobacco in schools, hospitals, government offices, buses, and other public places, took effect in CHILE on 14 August. The law included a provision to impose a US$30 fine on people who defied the public smoking ban. The legislation also imposed limits on tobacco advertising and requirements on tobacco manufacturers to increase the amount of space devoted to the health warnings that were emblazoned on tobacco products.

DRUGS, TERRORISM, AND CIVIL CONFLICT. The cultivation of coca, which was the raw ingredient used in the illicit process of cocaine production, was a contentious issue in the region, principally because the US government feared that it would increase the flow of illegal drugs to the USA and elsewhere. Coca was, however, also used for traditional (and legal) purposes, including chewing, cooking, and for use as a natural remedy for minor ailments, and was an important part of the region's economy and culture.

In BOLIVIA, President Morales announced on 3 October to the Six Federations union of coca growers that he proposed to impose a new tax on the cultivation of coca crops grown for legal and traditional purpose, explaining that the revenue raised would be used to regulate and legitimise its production. In PERU, which was the world's second-largest producer of coca (the world's largest being COLOMBIA), the USA spent more than US$100 million per year as part of its attempts to eradicate the country's illicit coca production. In October, President García promised George W. Bush, the US president, that he would develop programmes in Peru to replace coca with alternative crops, but on 19 December he openly advocated the use of the coca leaf for cooking purposes, adding that eating the crop was "absolutely not" harmful.

Peru's violent past—and its links with the illegal drugs trade—continued to reverberate, however. García called for the death penalty to be imposed on those individuals who killed eight people, including five police officers, on 16 December during an ambush on a police operation against illegal coca cultivation. The ambush took place in a coca field in the Ayacucho region of PERU. No group claimed responsibility for the attack, but some officials blamed members of the Shining Path (Sendero Luminoso), the Maoist guerrilla movement which had in the 1980s and 1990s led a 12-year insurgency in which up to 70,000 people died or disappeared. Although the insurgency was brought to an end in the early 1990s, the authorities in Peru believed that some factions of the Shining Path remained active in the illegal drug trafficking trade. Meanwhile, a civil court in the city of Callao on 13 September sentenced the founder of Shining Path, Manuel Rubén Abimael Guzmán Reynoso, to life in prison in Peru for "aggravated terrorism" committed during the insurgency. Judges also sentenced Elena Reboredo Iparaquirre, the Shining Path's second-in-command and Guzman's former lover, to a life sentence, whilst 10 associates received prison terms ranging between 24 and 35 years. Lesser figures sentenced in 2006 included, on 15 March, Alvaro Espejo Sebastian and Wilfredo Guzman, two leaders of the People's Aid (Socorro Popular)—a faction of the Shining Path—who were sentenced to 30 years in prison for terrorism and associated crimes; and on 21 March, Víctor Polay Campos and Miguel Rincon, two leaders of the Tupac Amarú Revolutionary Movement (MRTA), a left-wing guerrilla group, who were sentenced to 32 years in prison. The court convicted Polay Campos and Rincon of 29 crimes committed between 1987 and 1995, including kidnappings, assassinations, and attacks on property. The MRTA had in December 1996 staged a 126-day siege of the Japanese embassy in Lima.

The 42-year civil war in Colombia continued to claim lives in 2006, despite President Uribe's tough security policies, as rebels from the Colombian Revolutionary Armed Forces (FARC), Colombia's largest leftist guerrilla organisation, stepped up their attacks against government security services ahead of the legislative elections in March and the presidential election in May (see above). Attacks launched by FARC rebels in March included the explosion of land mines which killed five soldiers in the department of North Santander and three in the province of Putumayo. FARC rebels were also blamed for planting a bomb in a house in San Vicente del Caguan, in the department of Caqueta, on 6 March, which was detonated when an army patrol passed by and which killed three people. FARC rebels on 31 July also killed 18 soldiers and injured 27 others in three separate attacks, according to military officials. Officials said that 15 soldiers were also killed in July when rebels ambushed an army patrol in the department of North Santander; one soldier was killed and 21 were injured when a car bomb exploded in Bogota; and two soldiers died and six others were injured in another bomb attack in the port city of Tumaco in south-western Colombia. The military launched an investigation in September after the commander of the armed forces, General Mario Montoya, revealed his suspicions that soldiers had staged the discovery of car bombs in Bogota as part of a plan to claim rewards from the government for preventing FARC bomb attacks. The investigation included the questioning of two soldiers in connection with a fatal car bomb attack in August, which had, at the time, been blamed on FARC rebels. It was alleged that the two soldiers had recovered a series of unexploded bombs which they had themselves planted.

Meanwhile, a US judge presiding over the trial on kidnapping charges of Ricardo Palmera (also know as Simón Trinidad), a senior FARC commander, on 21 November declared a mistrial after jurors failed to agree on a verdict. Also in November, FARC published a letter appealing to the "people of the United States" to apply pressure on President Bush to support rebel attempts to reach an agreement with Uribe over a humanitarian exchange of rebel-held hostages for government-held rebel prisoners. Palmera was amongst the government-held prisoners whom FARC wished to be included in any exchange. FARC spokesperson Raúl Reyes announced in February that Ingrid Betancourt, a dual French-Colombian citizen who had been abducted by FARC in February 2002 whilst campaigning as a candidate in the Colombian presidential elections, remained alive and in good health (a unilateral attempt by the French government to rescue Betancourt in July 2003 had failed, see AR 2003, p. 54).

Despite the continued rebel attacks and the failure to reach agreement over an exchange of prisoners, Uribe did secure some nominal victories in 2006, including the release on 25 March of two police officers who had been taken hostage in November 2005, and the release on 4 April of Lothar Hintze, a German businessman, who was kidnapped in March 2001 from his business premises in Prado, 130 km south of Bogota. Exploratory talks over the terms of a possible peace process between the government and the leftist National Liberation Army

(ELN), which had commenced in December 2005, continued in 2006 with a second round of talks in February and a third round in April, both of which were held in Havana, the capital of Cuba.

The right-wing paramilitary organisation, the United Self Defence Forces of Colombia (AUC), also presented Uribe with a series of difficult challenges during 2006. Government peace commissioner Luis Carlos Restrepo announced in April that more than 30,000 AUC members had demobilised under the terms of the Santa Fe de Ralito (demilitarisation) agreement of July 2003 (see AR 2003, pp. 207-08), adding that the paramilitary organisation had, therefore, been effectively ended. In June, however, the media revealed that the Administrative Department of Security (DAS), Colombia's intelligence service, had information regarding the presence of "unconventional right-wing armed groups" in 25 of Colombia's 32 provinces, prompting speculation that the AUC was rearming.

Adding to Uribe's woes, the Constitutional Court on 18 May rejected key elements of the Justice and Peace Law, which was approved by the Chamber of Deputies (the lower house of the Colombian bicameral legislature) in June 2005 (see AR 2005, p. 165) and which had led to the demobilisation process. According to the ruling, which was irreversible, it was unconstitutional to limit to eight years the prison sentences of paramilitaries who had been accused of serious crimes and to reduce sentences for time spent in negotiations. Some 59 AUC leaders, many of whom were trying to avoid extradition to the USA on drug trafficking charges, on 7 December threatened to expose public officials who had collaborated with their illegal fight against FARC rebels. The threat followed a government decision to transfer the former paramilitary leaders to a high-security prison, a move which the AUC leaders described as a "betrayal of confidence". On 9 November the Supreme Court had ordered the arrest of Alvaro Garcia, Jairo Merlano, and Erik Morris, three legislators representing parties allied to Uribe, on charges of financing former paramilitaries.

CORRUPTION AND HUMAN RIGHTS DEVELOPMENTS. The authorities in PERU in November issued an international arrest warrant against the country's former president, Alberto Fujimori, on charges that he had ordered the killing of 20 members of the Shining Path during a prison uprising in 1992. Fujimori had been detained in CHILE since his arrest in November 2005 and was also wanted in Peru on a series of human rights and corruption charges (see AR 2005, p. 161). The Supreme Court in Santiago, Chile, on 19 May granted bail to Fujimori, pending completion of an investigation into Peru's request for his extradition, but the court also prohibited Fujimori from leaving Chile. Meanwhile, Alejandro Toledo, the former Peruvian president who left office in July, also became embroiled in corruption allegations when he was charged on 18 December with falsification of public documents. The charges related to allegations that he had participated in an illegal scheme to forge signatures to register his Peru Possible (PPP) party for elections held in the 1990s. Toledo, who was in the USA when the charges were brought against him, strongly denied the allegations.

A court in Ascunción, the capital of PARAGUAY, on 5 June sentenced the former Paraguayan president, Luis González Macchi (1999-2003), to six years in prison for embezzling some US$16 million of public money arising from the sale of two state-owned banks which had collapsed between 1994 and 1998. On 4 December González was also sentenced to eight years in prison for illegal enrichment and providing false testimony, after public prosecutors argued that he fraudulently obtained some US$1 million, which he had deposited in a Swiss bank account during his presidency. The same court on 29 December ruled that González could remain under house arrest pending his appeal against the conviction.

The former president of URUGUAY, Juan Maria Bordaberry, and his then foreign minister, Juan Carlos Blanco, were arrested on 17 November and charged in connection with the abduction and murder in 1976 of four government opponents. Their detentions were ordered after a judge determined that crimes committed outside Uruguay during the country's "dirty war" era (1973-85) were not covered by amnesty laws. The charges related to the discovery in May 1976 of the bodies of Uruguayan legislators Zelmar Michelini and Hector Gutierrez Ruiz, and Tupamaro guerrillas Rosario del Carmen Barredo and William Whitelaw Blanco, in Argentina, where they had been living in exile prior to their death. Also in Uruguay, a judge on 7 December approved the extradition of five retired soldiers and a police officer to face human rights charges in Argentina. All six men, who had been detained by the authorities in Uruguay since their arrest in May, were wanted in Argentina in connection with the disappearance of 11 Uruguayan citizens (see p. 167).

FOREIGN AND REGIONAL RELATIONS. Relations between ECUADOR and the USA faltered in May after the former annulled the contract of Occidental Petroleum (OP), a US-based oil company, following a protracted legal dispute. The Ecuador government claimed that the sale by OP of a 40 per cent stake in its oil concession to Canadian oil company EnCana was a breach of contract. The US government responded by suspending talks with Ecuador over a proposed free trade agreement (FTA).

The tense and often sour diplomatic relations between VENEZUELA and the USA showed no signs of warming in 2006. In January José Vicente Rangel, Venezuela's vice-president, claimed to be in possession of intelligence which proved that staff at the US embassy in Caracas were operating an espionage ring in Venezuela. The allegations prompted President Chávez to threaten US officials with imprisonment if they were caught "trying to obtain information about our armed forces". Venezuela's attempts to purchase new military equipment, however, were frequently complicated by US attempts to veto such deals. In October Venezuela cancelled a contract to buy 12 military aircraft from Spain because it was financially unfeasible to replace the US technology contained in the aeroplanes. The cancellation followed a decision by the US government in January to exercise its right under the US Arms Export Control Act, preventing the sale of US military technology by foreign companies (see p. 65). Chávez did on 27 July sign a contract to buy 24 Sukhoi Su-30 fighter jets and 53 helicopters, thought to be worth around US$1.6 billion, from Russia. The deal was strongly condemned by the US government, which had "encouraged" Russia to "reconsider" selling military equipment to Venezuela.

In September Chávez told the opening session of the 61st UN General Assembly in New York that "US imperialism" threatened the "survival of the human species" and described President Bush as "the devil" (see p. 121). Chávez also called on the UN to end the "anti-democratic veto power" wielded by permanent members of the UN Security Council, including the USA. Nicolás Maduro Moros, Venezuela's foreign minister, on 28 September accused the USA of making a distinction between "good terrorists and bad terrorists", after a US judge had recommended the release from US custody of Luis Posada Carriles, a Cuban-born Venezuelan national who had escaped from prison in Venezuela in 1985 after being convicted on charges related to the bombing of a Cuban airliner. On 3 August Chávez also criticised the Israeli government, recalling Venezuela's ambassador to the country in protest at the Israeli military campaign in Lebanon (see pp. 197-203). Chávez said that he was forced to recall the ambassador because "nobody does anything to stop this horror". Israel responded on 7 August by withdrawing its ambassador from Venezuela, prompting Chávez to say that he had "no interest in maintaining diplomatic relations with a state like Israel, which every day increases its offensive".

A souring of relations between BOLIVIA and the USA, which had been widely predicted since Morales was elected president in 2005, was also evident in 2006. In March the US government terminated a counter-terrorism training and aid agreement with Bolivia after Morales appointed Colonel Rory Rodriguez as head of the country's Joint Counter-Terrorism Task Force (JCTF). The appointment of Rodriguez was unpopular amongst US officials because they suspected that he had leaked information to Morales during his election campaign about the arrival of 30 Bolivian missiles in the USA for decommissioning. Morales on 20 June claimed that US military personnel, disguised as tourists and students, had entered Bolivia to gather intelligence. The US embassy in La Paz denied the charges as "unfounded". Also in June, US officials criticised the impending election of Bolivia's constituent assembly, describing it as a "potentially anti-democratic" reform, prompting Bolivian Foreign Minister David Choquehuanca Céspedes to remind US officials that the assembly was intended to strengthen democracy.

COLOMBIA, meanwhile, continued to enjoy cordial relations with the USA in 2006, culminating on 22 November in the signing of the United States-Colombia trade promotion agreement (CTPA), in Washington DC, which was designed to "eliminate tariffs" and "other barriers to trade" between the two countries. There were serious doubts, however, that the agreement would be ratified by Congress (the US bicameral federal legislature), after it emerged that US Democrats, who had won control of the US legislature in mid-term elections in November (see pp. 130-39), were concerned about Colombia's labour and human rights laws.

Colombia's relations with neighbouring Ecuador were damaged in February and March following incursions into Ecuador's airspace by the Colombian airforce. Colombia defended the incursions by claiming that its aircraft had been deployed to pursue FARC rebels, who had mounted attacks in Colombia before fleeing to Ecuador. General (retd) Oswaldo Jarrin, Ecuador's defence minister, resigned unexpectedly in August after asking the Colombian authorities for an official explanation for the firing on 24 August of a mortar bomb from Colombia, which landed in the Ecuadorian town of Puerto Nuevo, near the Ecuadorian-Colombian border, injuring three people.

Relations between Peru and Venezuela also soured when outgoing President Alejandro Toledo in April accused President Chávez of interfering in Peru's presidential elections, leading to the recall of their respective ambassadors. Chávez responded by saying that Venezuela could not maintain diplomatic relations with a government led by Alan García, describing the then Peruvian president-elect as a "lap dog" of the USA.

V MIDDLE EAST AND NORTH AFRICA

ISRAEL

OFFICIAL LANGUAGE: Hebrew   POLITICAL SYSTEM: multiparty republic
HEAD OF STATE: President Moshe Katzav (since July '00)
RULING PARTIES: Kadima leads coalition, with Labour party, Sephardic Torah Guardians (Shas), Pensioners of Israel to the Knesset (Gil), and Yisrael Beiteinu
HEAD OF GOVERNMENT: Ehud Olmert (Kadima), Prime Minister (since April '06)
CURRENCY: shekel (end-'06 £1=Sh8.17530, US$1=Sh4.18720)
GNI PER CAPITA: US$18,620, US$25,280 at PPP ('05)

Two events dominated the year. On 4 January Prime Minister Ariel Sharon suffered a severe stroke and, overnight, he was removed from the domestic and international political stage. A highly controversial figure, Sharon had in recent years been the dominant force in Israeli politics and his sudden departure led many commentators to talk of a "vacuum". Israeli newspapers featured pictures of Sharon's empty chair during the weekly cabinet meeting in Jerusalem, and it appeared that his stroke had had not only a political impact but, in the words of one report, a "personal and psychological impact" upon the country. The second major event occurred on 12 July when Hezbullah guerrillas crossed the Lebanese border into Israel and captured two Israeli soldiers, Ehud Goldwasser and Eldad Regev. Israel responded with a massive military offensive against Lebanon, but when a truce was agreed 34 days later, the two Israeli soldiers remained in enemy hands and a triumphant Hezbullah was fully intact, having fired thousands of rockets into Israel, killing 44 civilians and wounding almost 1,500 others (for more detailed analysis of the war see pp. 197-203). That the war had been prosecuted by two men with no military background—new Prime Minister Ehud Olmert and Defence Minister Amir Peretz—led some Israelis to question whether the outcome would have been better for Israel under the leadership of the stricken Sharon, a war hero to many Israelis, who had fought in Suez and the Six-Day and Yom Kippur wars

After Sharon, who had suffered a mild stroke in December 2005, was more severely stricken on 4 January, he was declared "temporarily incapacitated" and power was handed over on an interim basis to Olmert, hitherto deputy prime minister and minister of finance, and a member of Sharon's recently formed Kadima (Forward) party (see AR 2005, p. 172). Olmert quickly moved to reassure the country of political continuity and stability and it was announced that a general election would be held, as scheduled, on 28 March. The election had been called in November 2005 by Sharon after the newly-elected leader of the Labour Party, Amir Peretz, had said that he intended to withdraw his party from Sharon's Likud-led coalition government. Sharon had responded by resigning from the Likud and forming Kadima to contest the election. Sharon's term as prime minister formally came to an end on 11 April when he was declared "permanently incapacitated"; he remained in a coma throughout the year.

Elections to the 120-member Knesset (the unicameral legislature) were thus duly held on 28 March. During the campaign, Olmert described the election as a referendum on his plan to draw Israel's borders, unilaterally if necessary, by 2010. Olmert said that the boundary would run along, or close to, Israel's security barrier in the West Bank. He would wait a "reasonable time" to see if the radical Islamist Hamas—which had won the Palestinian legislative elections in January (see p. 186)—was willing to recognise Israel, disavow violence, and accept previous Israeli-Palestinian agreements. However, if Hamas was not willing to accept such principles, Israel "would need to begin to act", Olmert said.

Olmert's Kadima won the largest number of seats in the new Knesset (29), but the less than decisive victory meant that he was forced to enter into coalition negotiations with the Labour party and other smaller groups. The Labour party, under new leader Peretz, had stressed its preference for bilateral negotiations with the Palestinians and emerged as the second strongest party with 19 seats. The right-wing Likud was shown to be in virtual meltdown, winning only 12 seats. Olmert negotiated a coalition agreement with Peretz and with the ultra-Orthodox Sephardic Torah Guardians (Shas) and the Pensioners of Israel to the Knesset (Gil), and the new government won the approval of the Knesset on 4 May. The most controversial appointment was that of Peretz as defence minister. The Moroccan-born Peretz, a former head of the Histadrut trade union confederation, had no military experience. Tzipi Livni, Israel's most prominent female politician, was appointed as vice prime minister and minister of foreign affairs. Veteran former Labour leader Shimon Peres was given charge of developing the Negev and Galilee and was given the courtesy title of vice premier, junior to Livni.

In late October Olmert broadened his coalition by adding the far-right Yisrael Beiteinu ("Israel, Our Home"), which held 11 seats in the Knesset. Yisrael Beiteinu was led by 48-year-old Avigdor Lieberman, a Soviet immigrant who had been dismissed as minister of transportation in June 2004 because of his opposition to Sharon's Gaza disengagement plan (see AR 2004, p. 180). Lieberman was appointed as deputy prime minister with responsibility for strategic threats against Israel, primarily those presented by Iran's nuclear ambitions. Lieberman's appointment was highly controversial. He was best known in Israel for his "population exchange plan", under which the Arab-populated "meshulash" ("triangle") area of the Wadi 'Ara region—transferred to Israel by Jordan as part of the 1949 Armistice Agreement—would return to Arab sovereignty in exchange for keeping large Jewish-populated settlement blocs in the West Bank. The plan drew sharp criticism from both left and right: from the former for its discriminatory overtones, and from the latter for the notion of ceding parts of "Eretz Yisrael" (the "Land of Israel").

Ophir Pines-Paz was the only cabinet member to vote against Yisrael Beiteinu's entry into the coalition government, and he immediately resigned as minister of science and technology. Pines-Paz, a member of the Labour party, said that Yisrael Beiteinu had a platform with "racist ingredients" and that its leaders were tainted "by racist declarations and declarations that harm the democratic character of Israel". In his resignation speech, Pines-Paz asked whether Lieberman was "the answer to the government's loss of direction after the second Lebanon war". Indeed, the war against Hezbullah raised a storm of outrage in Israel following the UN-brokered ceasefire that took effect on 14 August. The conflict killed 158

Israelis, mostly soldiers, and an estimated 1,300 Lebanese, mostly civilians.

Whilst Israel and the USA declared that Hezbullah had lost the war, the more widely accepted verdict concluded that merely by surviving a concerted attack by the region's strongest military power, the Shi'ite militia had effectively emerged with a military and political victory. Hezbullah fighters not only managed to sustain their defences in southern Lebanon, but also inflicted a constant barrage of rocket attacks on Israel in the face of a punishing air and land campaign. Moreover, Israel conspicuously failed to accomplish its two stated aims upon entering the conflict: the retrieval of its two captured soldiers and the destruction of Hezbullah's military capability. As soon as the 14 August ceasefire came into effect, calls were heard in Israel for military and political leaders to take responsibility for the failures of the war. A group of demobilised reservists and parents of soldiers killed in the fighting started a movement calling for the resignation of Olmert and the establishment of a state commission of inquiry. Olmert admitted to the Knesset that mistakes had been made, but refused demands for an independent state or governmental commission of inquiry. Instead, he approved two internal inspection probes, one military and the other political. Critics accused the government of a whitewash, and in September it was agreed to replace the two internal probes with a single governmental commission, headed by retired judge Eliyahu Winograd.

Furthermore, despite a growing clamour for his resignation over the war, Lieutenant-General Dan Halutz, the chief of staff of the Israeli Defence Forces (IDF), remained in post at the end of the year. However, two senior officers did resign. Major-General Uri Adam, the Israeli army commander of Israel's northern front, including the Lebanon border, stood down on 13 September. Adam had suffered weeks of criticism for his apparent hesitancy and caution during the campaign. On 12 November Brigadier-General Gal Hirsch, commander of Division 91, followed suit. Hirsch resigned under protest after an inquiry headed by reservist Major-General Doron Almog had issued an interim report, which contained severe criticism of the conduct of Division 91, the regular division in the Galilee, for failing to prevent the 12 July abduction of Goldwasser and Regev by Hezbullah.

Olmert's difficult year ended in further controversy when in an interview with a German television station on 11 December he apparently acknowledged, inadvertently, that Israel possessed nuclear weapons, thereby ending Israel's decades-long policy of "strategic ambiguity". Olmert's aides said after the broadcast that there was no change in Israel's policy of refusing to confirm or deny that it possessed nuclear weapons.

Domestically, other notable events included the resignation on 20 August of Haim Ramon as justice minister following allegations that he forcibly kissed an 18-year-old female soldier during a party at defence ministry headquarters. On 15 October the justice ministry and the police recommended that Israeli President Moshe Katsav face charges of raping and sexually assaulting women. Katsav vehemently denied any wrongdoing and he remained in post at the end of the year. A separately unfolding scandal saw Omri Sharon, the eldest son of Ariel Sharon, sentenced on 14 February to nine months' imprisonment for illegal fund-raising during his father's 1999 campaign for leadership of the Likud.

PALESTINE—EGYPT—JORDAN—SYRIA—LEBANON—IRAQ

PALESTINE

ADMINISTRATIVE CAPITAL: Ramallah INTENDED CAPITAL: East Jerusalem AREA: 5,970 sq km for West Bank territories; 365 sq km for Gaza POPULATION: 3,626,000
OFFICIAL LANGUAGES: Arabic POLITICAL SYSTEM: multiparty republic under partial Israeli occupation
HEAD OF STATE AND GOVERNMENT: President Mahmoud Abbas (since Jan '05)
RULING PARTY: Hamas (since Jan '06)
PRIME MINISTER: Ismail Haniyeh (Hamas) (since March '06)
CURRENCY: Jordanian dinar (end '06 £1=JD1.38430, US$1=JD0.70900); and Israeli shekel (end-'06 £1=Sh8.17530, US$1=Sh4.18720)
GNI PER CAPITA: US$1,120 ('05), -

THE militant Sunni Islamist group, Hamas, won an overall majority in the Palestine Legislative Council (PLC, the Palestinian legislature) in elections held in the Palestinian territories on 25 January. Hamas won 74 seats in the enlarged 132-seat PLC, against 45 for Fatah, and 13 for smaller parties and independents. The first PLC, elected in January 1996, had been dominated by Fatah, which had won 55 of the 88 seats (see AR 1996, p. 204). Subsequent elections had been repeatedly postponed because of the ongoing Israeli-Palestinian conflict. The victory stunned even Hamas leaders, who had mounted a well-organised campaign and had made serious gains in recent local elections but, nonetheless, had no experience in government. Fatah's inability to provide basic services, the numerous corruption scandals in the Palestine National Authority (PNA, the government), and Hamas's successes in providing services to the many poor and unemployed were all significant reasons for the victory. Analysts also noted that Fatah had been beset by serious internal unrest during the months leading up to the elections. The so-called "young guard" had levelled charges of corruption and incompetence against President Mahmoud Abbas and the Fatah leadership and had formed their own party list (see AR 2005, p. 177). However, in late December 2005 the two factions had agreed to submit a single Fatah list to voters, although the two groups remained at loggerheads.

Hamas's victory was greeted with alarm in Israel and the West. A statement issued by the Israeli government ruled out contacts with Hamas, saying: "Israel will not negotiate with a Palestinian power of which a part comprises an armed terrorist organisation which calls for the destruction of Israel". The US president, George W. Bush, made it clear that the USA would not deal with Hamas so long as the group "articulates the destruction of Israel". The Middle East quartet—the USA, the EU, the UN, and Russia—which had formulated the stalled "road map" peace plan, met in London in late January and set three conditions for official contact with Hamas: recognition of Israel; renunciation of violence; and adherence to previous Palestinian-Israeli agreements.

In the wake of the election result, Prime Minister Ahmed Qurie and his cabinet of technocrats formed in February 2005 (see AR 2005, p. 174) resigned and, at the opening of the new PLC on 18 February, President Abbas invited Hamas to form a new government. Hamas named Ismail Haniyeh, who had headed the group's national list in the elections, as its choice for prime minister. Haniyeh and his cabinet were sworn in on 29 March. Most of the new ministers were members of Hamas, although a few were independents. Prime Minister Haniyeh, Foreign Minister Mahmoud al-Zahar, and Interior and National Security Minister Sa'id Siyam were part of Hamas's collective leadership in Palestine formed after the assassinations of Shaikh Ahmad Yassin and Abdel Aziz al-Rantisi in March-April 2004 (see AR 2004, p. 185). Other key figures in the leadership included Khaled Meshal, the Syrian-based chairman of the Hamas political bureau.

In mid-February the Israeli government froze the transfer of tax and customs receipts to the PNA. Ehud Olmert, who had recently taken over as prime minister of Israel after Ariel Sharon had been incapacitated by a severe stroke (see p. 183), said that Hamas's election victory meant that the PNA had become "a terrorist authority". The PNA relied on a combination of tax and customs transfers from Israel, domestic revenue, and foreign budget support to meet a monthly US$100 million wage bill for some 135,000 public employees. Once the Haniyeh government had been sworn in, the international community formalised its inevitable response to Hamas's electoral success with the effective imposition of political and economic sanctions. Notwithstanding US and EU commitments to continue to direct humanitarian aid at impoverished Palestinians, the imposition of what was, in effect, an economic blockade of the PNA meant that the Palestinian territories went into economic meltdown during 2006.

In December the largest-ever appeal for emergency aid—amounting to US$453.6 million—for the occupied Palestinian territories was initiated by 12 UN agencies together with 14 non-governmental organisations. (The aid package sought for the Palestinian territories in 2007 was exceeded only by the US$1.2 billion requested for Sudan and US$687 million for the Democratic Republic of the Congo.) Announcing the appeal in Jerusalem, UN humanitarian co-ordinator Kevin Kennedy said that two-thirds of Palestinians in the West Bank and the Gaza Strip were "now living in poverty". Growing numbers of people were unable to cover their daily food needs, and agencies reported that basic services such as healthcare and education were deteriorating and likely to worsen much further. Most of the funding would go towards addressing poverty through emergency employment programmes, and expanding food and agricultural aid. The rapid deterioration was directly linked with the fiscal crisis facing the PNA that had been unable to pay its public employees. In addition, Palestinians had been subject to increasing restrictions on their freedom of movement through Israeli security measures, limiting their access to jobs, markets, health services, and schools. Reports from the Palestinian territories showed that the Israeli and Western boycott of the PNA had cut deep: shops were often empty and streets deserted as Palestinians scraped by on dwindling savings.

In an attempt to bring much-needed money into the finance ministry, Hamas officials were forced to travel to friendly countries and physically haul cash back into Gaza. In June foreign minister Zahar visited Indonesia, Malaysia, Brunei, China, Pakistan, Iran, and Egypt and returned to the Gaza Strip with an estimated US$20 million packed in 12 separate suitcases. In December, Prime Minister Haniyeh made his first official foreign trip—visiting Syria and Iran, amongst other countries—and returned to Gaza with a promise of US$250 million from Iran, and suitcases stuffed with US$35 million in cash. On this occasion, the Israelis did not allow the cash into Gaza and Haniyeh was forced to bank it in Egypt. One positive note for the Hamas government came on 12 November when the secretary general of the League of Arab States, Amr Moussa, announced that Arab countries would offer financial and material aid to the PNA regardless of the political and financial blockade by Western powers. Foreign Minister Zahar welcomed the decision, describing it as "extremely important" and said that it meant that Arabs would use the "usual means" to send aid to the Palestinians.

Hamas's rise to power was accompanied by the collapse of the facade of Palestinian unity. Two opposing sides emerged: one associated with the presidency (Fatah-dominated, backed by Israel and the West), and the other with the legislature (Hamas-dominated, opposed by Israel and the West, supported by Iran). A situation whereby the president did not belong to the ruling parliamentary bloc was foreign to Palestinian politics, and initially the tone between the two sides was civil. Hamas tried not to alienate President Abbas, who was seen as vital if the PNA was to achieve any semblance of international respectability. For his part, Abbas, as leader of Fatah, feared that he would lose domestic credibility if he was perceived as trying to bring down the government of a rival party. However, wrangling over control of the security forces quickly laid bare the deep enmity between the rival factions. Abbas held the title of general commander of the 80,000-strong security force, which consisted of five branches. Three of these were under the control of the Hamas-run interior ministry, while two reported directly to the president. In April Abbas appointed a loyalist, Rashid Abu Shbak, as commander of one of the Hamas-controlled branches, the Preventative Security Service. In the 1990s, Abu Shbak had organised a crackdown on Hamas, and his appointment was seen by the organisation as a major provocation. Hamas responded by announcing the creation of a special unit, to consist of some 4,000 of its militants, headed by Colonel Jamal Abu Samhadana, a leader of the umbrella Popular Resistance Committees (PRC) and number two on Israel's most-wanted list. Abbas annulled the decision, but Hamas refused to back down, and the standoff led to fighting between rival Hamas and Fatah factions in Gaza City in May. (Abu Samhadana was later killed on 8 June when Israel carried out an air-strike on a PRC training camp in the southern Gaza town of Rafah.)

In an address to a "national dialogue" of all Palestinian factions in Gaza on 25 May, President Abbas issued a dramatic ultimatum to Hamas to endorse within 10 days a document drawn up by Palestinian prisoners that recognised Israel, or face a referendum on the issue. Amid growing concern that gunmen for the rival factions were squaring up for a major confrontation, Abbas issued a decree on 10 June for the referendum to be held on 26 July. Hamas described the referendum as a coup against its government and said that it would boycott it. Abbas declared a state of emergency on 12 June after Hamas fighters fired anti-tank rockets into the (Fatah) Preventative Security headquarters in Gaza during the heaviest fighting yet between the two factions. Television footage showing the attack prompted Fatah loyalists to storm the PLC building in the West Bank city of Ramallah, setting it alight.

The factional infighting was overshadowed by a daring Palestinian attack on Israel on 25 June. A group of seven or eight Palestinian fighters—members of the military wing of Hamas, the Izz al-Din al-Qassem Brigades, the Popular Resistance Committees, and a previously unknown group, the Army of Islam—entered Israel through a tunnel underneath the fence that surrounded the Gaza Strip. The fighters emerged at an Israeli army outpost near the Kerem Shalom kibbutz and attacked an Israeli armoured personnel carrier and a tank. Two Israeli soldiers were killed in the attack and one other was seriously injured. Two of the Palestinian attackers were killed. The remaining Palestinian fighters escaped back into Gaza, carrying with them an injured Israeli soldier, 19-year-old Corporal Gilad Shalit. Israeli Prime Minister Ehud Olmert said that Israel viewed the Palestinian presidency and government jointly responsible for the attack, "with all that implies". He ordered the Israeli army to be on stand-by for a massive operation in Gaza. President Abbas ordered a mobilisation to search for the missing soldier. The factions involved in the attack issued a statement for the first time on 26 June, demanding the release of Palestinian prisoners in Israel in exchange for information on Shalit.

The Israeli Defence Forces (IDF) responded to Corporal Shalit's abduction on 28 June with "Operation Summer Rains", its first major offensive in the Gaza Strip since Israel's unilateral disengagement plan had been implemented in August-September 2005 (see AR 2005, pp. 170-72; 175-76). At the start of the military operation, four Israeli fighter jets flew low over the residence of President Bashar al-Assad of Syria, near the coastal town of Latakia, drawing Syrian fire. An Israeli army spokeswoman said that the fly-by constituted a warning to Syria. A number of Israeli politicians had claimed that the 25 June attack on Israel had been ordered by high-ranking Hamas figure Khaled Meshal who was based in Damascus. The Egyptian government deployed some 2,500 policemen to the border of Egypt and the Gaza Strip in order to prevent the possible transfer of Shalit into Egypt, as well as to prevent an influx of refugees out of the Palestinian territory. The Israeli army also detained at least 64 Hamas representatives, 38 of them members of the Palestinian legislature, including eight ministers, in the West Bank.

"Operation Summer Rains" began with a series of air-strikes that hit Gaza's only power station—cutting off all electricity in the territory—as well as bridges connecting the north and south of the Strip, and a Hamas training ground. Israeli tanks and ground forces consolidated positions in the south, which they had entered overnight, and took up strategic positions aimed at preventing Palestinian militants from launching rocket attacks on Israel. On 30 June the IDF began to hit the Gaza Strip with a variety of targeted bombardments. However, on 4 July Palestinian militants set off a two-engine high-trajectory Qassam rocket which travelled 12 km and hit the centre of the city of Ashkelon. No-one was injured, but Prime Minister Olmert described the attack as "an escalation without precedent" and the Israeli cabinet issued a statement threatening to "bring about a change in the rules of the game".

Meanwhile, on 12 July, Israel launched a ground and air assault on Lebanon after the militant Hezbullah organisation captured two Israeli soldiers and killed others (see pp. 197-203). While most international attention was focused on the heavy conflict in Lebanon, Israel also escalated its operations in Gaza and at least 20 Palestinians were killed, including a family of nine, when the airforce dropped a massive bomb on a house in a residential area of Gaza City. The Israelis said that they had targeted Mohammed Deif, leader of the Izz al-Din al-Qassem battalions, who was wounded in the attack. Israel continued to carry out substantial military strikes into Gaza from July until October.

The IDF conducted another major military operation ("Operation Autumn Clouds") in and around the town of Beit Hanoun in the north-east of the Gaza Strip on 1-7 November. At least 50 Palestinians, including a number of civilians, were killed during the operation. Israel claimed to have uncovered large amounts of weapons and to have destroyed nine "rocket-launching cells" from which Palestinian militants had attacked Israeli border towns. Palestinian agencies condemned the destruction of homes, orchards, water pipes, and electricity cables during the raid. Israeli artillery shells killed 19 Palestinians, including eight children and seven women, in a residential area of Beit Hanoun on 8 November. It was reported that 13 of the dead belonged to one family, the Athamnehs. Prime Minister Olmert said that a "technical failure" was to blame for the deaths and stated that he was "very uncomfortable with this event". There was widespread international condemnation of the attack and this prompted renewed efforts to forge a ceasefire agreement. Eventually, on 26 November President Abbas announced that he had managed to broker a truce. Israeli troops withdrew from the Gaza Strip and Abbas ordered his security chiefs to monitor the Gaza border area to stop militants from launching rocket attacks. With the ceasefire intact, Israeli Prime Minister Olmert sought to maintain the momentum on 27 November by holding out the prospect of a "real...dialogue" aimed at the creation of "an independent and viable Palestinian state". Olmert declared: "I hold out my hand in peace to our Palestinian neighbours in the hope that it won't be returned empty." In the first such declaration by an Israeli prime minister, Olmert said that there were "positive points" in the Saudi-sponsored March 2002 Beirut Declaration, which promised recognition of Israel by the Arab states in return for an Israeli withdrawal to pre-1967 borders (see AR 2002, pp. 206-07).

Despite such talk of peace, casualty figures released in late December by B'Tselem, the Israeli human rights group, made depressing reading. According to B'Tselem's research, from 1 January to 27 December Israeli security forces killed 660 Palestinians in the occupied territories and in Israel, including 141 minors. At least 322 of those killed were not taking part in the hostilities at the time of their death. Another 22 were targets of assassinations. In the Gaza Strip alone, since the capture of Corporal Shalit on 25 June, Israeli forces had killed 405 Palestinians, including 88 minors. Of these, 205 were not participating in the fighting when killed. Palestinians killed 17 Israeli civilians in 2006, both in the West Bank and inside Israel. In addition, Palestinians killed six members of the Israeli security forces.

Abbas's threat to hold a referendum on the recognition of Israel in July failed to materialise after the upsurge of violence in Gaza and the war in Lebanon. In mid-December Abbas tried another gambit aimed at ending the political crisis which had led to increased fighting between the rival Palestinian factions, announcing that he intended to call early legislative and presidential elections. The announcement drew a defiant response from Hamas officials, who said that the movement would not accept early elections to the PLC and challenged Abbas's right to call an early vote. In the short-term the ploy also led to intensified violence in the Gaza Strip, as rival militias organised rallies and violent clashes erupted. Abbas's election proposal received the enthusiastic support of visiting UK Prime Minister Tony Blair, who also reportedly suggested to Abbas that the UK help to fund his presidential security guard. At the end of the year reports indicated that Israel had allowed Egypt to deliver a large consignment of guns and ammunition to further shore up Abbas's guard.

Abbas and Olmert met for talks at the latter's residence in Jerusalem on 23 December. It was their first official meeting since Olmert had assumed the premiership in January. After the meeting the Israeli prime minister approved the removal of 27 of the 400 military checkpoints in the West Bank and also said that Israel would take immediate steps to improve the flow of goods in and out of the Gaza Strip. Israel also agreed to release 20 per cent of the Palestinian funds which it held (around US$100 million), but only for what were described as humanitarian purposes. The Israeli moves were undoubtedly part of a package of concessions aimed at strengthening President Abbas in his ongoing power struggle with Hamas, which had shown little sign of abating during the period of intense Israeli military involvement in Gaza.

EGYPT

CAPITAL: Cairo AREA: 1,001,000 sq km POPULATION: 74,033,000
OFFICIAL LANGUAGE: Arabic POLITICAL SYSTEM: multiparty republic
HEAD OF STATE: President Mohammed Hosni Mubarak (since '81)
RULING PARTY: National Democratic Party (NDP)
PRIME MINISTER: Ahmad Mahmud Mohammed Nazif (since July '04)
MAIN IGO MEMBERSHIPS (NON-UN): AL, OAPEC, AU, COMESA, OIC, NAM, Francophonie
CURRENCY: Egyptian pound (end-'06 £1=E£11.1471, US$1=E£5.70930)
GNI PER CAPITA: US$1,250, US$4,440 at PPP ('05)

CONSTITUTIONAL reform was the dominant theme on the Egyptian government's political agenda in 2006, but its proposals for change fell way below the demands of its opponents in the Muslim Brotherhood (MB) and amongst the liberal intelligentsia. The Egyptian economy, meanwhile, reaped the benefits of the efforts made since the change of government in July 2004 to improve conditions for business, and 2006 set a new record for inflows of foreign direct investment.

The first of a series of political clashes during the year came in February when the government passed a law to extend the term of Egypt's local councils by two years, thereby, in effect, postponing municipal elections, which were scheduled to be held that month. The government claimed that the move was necessary in order to allow for the reform of municipalities before the election of new councillors. However, the MB criticised the postponement as a blatant ploy to halt its electoral advance. The Islamist movement had secured 88 of the 454 seats in the

People's Assembly (the lower house of the bicameral Parliament) in elections held over three increasingly fractious rounds in November and December 2005 (see AR 2005, p. 179), and it was also buoyed up by the success of the main Palestinian Islamist group, Hamas, in the elections in the West Bank and Gaza in January 2006 (see p. 186).

The controversy over Egypt's legislative elections continued into the early months of 2006, owing to the decision of the justice minister to press for disciplinary action to be taken against two judges who had alleged that some of their colleagues had been implicated in electoral fraud. The Judges' Club mobilised its members, numbering some 8,000, in support of the two judges in question—Hesham Bastawisi and Mahmoud Mekki—and staged protests outside the High Court in Cairo during hearings in April and May. The disciplinary tribunal decided in June to take no action against Mekki, and let Bastawisi escape with a reprimand. Following the verdict, the government pushed through legislation amending aspects of the law covering the judiciary. This went some way towards meeting longstanding demands from the Judges' Club for safeguarding the independence of the judiciary through lessening the powers of the justice ministry and enhancing those of the Supreme Judicial Council (the body responsible for most appointments and judicial affairs). However, the Judges' Club's recommendation that the Council's members be elected by their peers, rather than appointed by the government, was not included in the law.

At the end of August the justice minister, Mahmoud Abu Leil, resigned, citing poor health. He was replaced by Mamdouh Marei, a former head of the Constitutional Court who had also chaired a commission that had barred independent monitors from entering polling stations during the presidential election of 2005. One of the first actions taken by Marei was to withdraw state funding for the Judges' Club, making clear that his appointment did not presage any reduction in the tensions between the judiciary and the government.

The handling of the judges' revolt through a mixture of repression and limited concessions was characteristic of the government's general approach to political reform. The September congress of the ruling National Democratic Party (NDP) provided a platform for President Hosni Mubarak to present his plans for further constitutional reform after his 2005 initiative to allow a contested vote for the presidency, under extremely restrictive conditions. In his address to the congress Mubarak pledged that more reforms were on the way in 2007, although he provided little detail. NDP officials indicated that the reforms would involve increasing the power of the legislature with regard to the government, and devolving more authority from the president to the cabinet. It was also suggested that the rules for proposing candidates to stand for president should be modified to allow any party with at least one member in either house of Parliament to put forward a candidate. The 2005 amendment specified that a party needed to have at least 5 per cent of the seats in the lower house to propose a candidate. There was no provision for independents to stand for president, which blocked the MB from putting up a candidate, as the law prohibited the licensing of any party based on religion. There was also no mention of limiting the number of terms that a president could serve: Mubarak announced later, in his speech to the opening session of Parliament in November, that he would remain in office "as long as there is in my chest a heart that beats and I draw breath". This was taken as a sign that he had not ruled out standing for a sixth term in 2011.

The NDP congress was also notable for the announcement by Gamal Mubarak, the president's second son (and presumed heir apparent), that the government had decided to revive plans for the development of nuclear power. The initiative had political overtones, in light of the highly charged issue of Iran's nuclear programme (see pp. 280-83). However, the government made clear that there was no question of Egypt's seeking to develop the capacity to produce nuclear fuel, and that it would co-operate fully with the International Atomic Energy Agency (the IAEA). Egypt had dropped plans to develop nuclear power in the early 1990s owing to the Chernobyl disaster and the rapid increase in Egypt's natural gas output. It turned back to nuclear power because of the strain of supplying enough gas both to meet rising domestic demand and to satisfy export commitments.

The rise in electricity demand stemmed from the strong performance of the Egyptian economy in recent years. Real GDP growth in the fiscal year that ended on 30 June was 6.9 per cent, and advanced to 7.1 per cent in the first quarter of fiscal 2006-07. The balance of payments showed steadily increasing surpluses, resulting from rising foreign investment, buoyant oil and gas exports, and a thriving tourism sector, the latter unaffected by periodic terrorist attacks such as the bombing of three hotels in the Sinai resort of Dahab on 24 April, which left 23 people dead (most of them Egyptians). Investments in Egypt in 2006 included two landmark privatisation deals: the sale of Bank of Alexandria to Italy's IMI San Paolo Bank, and the sale of the Omar Effendi department store chain to Anwal, a Saudi Arabian company. The government also landed a US$2.9 billion windfall with the sale of a third mobile telephone licence to Etisalat of the UAE. The main cloud on the economic horizon was rising inflation, which reached 11.8 per cent in October. Prices were driven up by increased consumer demand, the removal of some subsidies, and the effects of an outbreak of avian influenza at the start of the year, which necessitated the slaughter of a large part of the country's poultry flock.

JORDAN

CAPITAL: Amman AREA: 89,000 sq km POPULATION: 5,411,000
OFFICIAL LANGUAGE: Arabic POLITICAL SYSTEM: multiparty monarchy
HEAD OF STATE AND GOVERNMENT: King Abdullah ibn al-Husain (since Feb '99)
PRIME MINISTER: Marouf Bakhit (since Nov '05)
MAIN IGO MEMBERSHIPS (NON-UN): AL, OIC, NAM
CURRENCY: Jordanian dinar (end-'06 £1=JD1.38430, US$1=JD0.70900)
GNI PER CAPITA: US$2,500, US$5,280 at PPP ('05)

JORDAN had a relatively uneventful year, despite the political turbulence all around it. The victory of Hamas, a radical Islamist party, in the elections in the West Bank and Gaza to the Palestine Legislative Council (see p. 186) put the Jordanian government on its guard, in light of the large Palestinian population in Jordan and the strength of support in the country for radical Islam. However, the impact of the Hamas victory was diluted by the lingering effects of the bombings of three hotels in Amman in November 2005 by followers of the Jordanian-born leader of al-Qaida in Iraq, Abu Musab al-Zarqawi. The strong popular revulsion at these attacks had prompted Jordan's Islamist political forces to adopt a low profile in a bid to dissociate themselves from these actions.

Tensions between the government and the Islamist opposition resurfaced in June following the killing of Zarqawi by US forces in Iraq (see p. 208). Four members of the House of Representatives (the lower chamber of the bicameral legislature) representing the Islamic Action Front (IAF) were arrested after they visited the al-Qaida leader's family to offer their condolences; they were charged with fuelling national discord and stirring up sectarian strife. Two of them were subsequently convicted and received jail sentences; the other two were acquitted. In October King Abdullah II issued a royal pardon to the two jailed legislators, although their convictions still stood. The political skirmishes between the IAF and the government took place in the context of the approach of legislative elections scheduled for 2007.

The Jordanian government remained largely unchanged in 2006, in contrast to the previous year which witnessed three major cabinet reshuffles. Marouf Bakhit, a former general who was appointed prime minister after the November 2005 attacks, remained in his post throughout the year.

The Jordanian economy continued to prosper, mainly as a result of strong inflows of capital from the Gulf Arab states and from Iraq. A large portion of these funds was invested in real estate, prompting a surge in property prices in Amman, as well as in Aqaba, where a number of new tourism projects were under way. The government had some success in reviving its moribund privatisation programme, with the sale of a 37 per cent stake in Jordan Phosphate Mines Company to the Brunei Investment Agency for some US$100 million and the divestment of most of the state's remaining holdings in Jordan Telecom, which raised about US$700 million.

SYRIA

CAPITAL: Damascus AREA: 185,000 sq km POPULATION: 19,043,000
OFFICIAL LANGUAGE: Arabic POLITICAL SYSTEM: multiparty republic
HEAD OF STATE AND GOVERNMENT: President Bashar al-Assad (since July '00)
RULING PARTIES: Baath Arab Socialist Party and six allies in the National Progressive Front
PRIME MINISTER: Mohammed Naji al-Atri (since Sept '03)
MAIN IGO MEMBERSHIPS (NON-UN): AL, OAPEC, OIC, NAM
CURRENCY: Syrian pound (end-'06 £1=S£101.937, US$1=S£52.2100)
GNI PER CAPITA: US$1,380, US$3,740 at PPP ('05)

DURING 2006 the Syrian government managed to improve its regional political position after the setback of the previous year when it was forced to withdraw its troops and intelligence agencies from Lebanon. Syria's gains owed much to the efforts of its regional allies—Iran, Lebanon's Hezbullah, and the Palestinian Islamist groups, Hamas and Islamic Jihad—in challenging US and Israeli power. Towards the end of the year, influential voices were raised in the USA, Europe, and Israel calling for engagement with Syria, in the hope of weakening its ties with Iran and drawing it into a regional peace settlement. However, the US administration and most European governments remained resolutely opposed to making any initiative towards Syria, because of their conviction that the regime of President Bashar Assad was seeking to undermine the elected government in Lebanon, as well as contributing to the violence in Iraq and the Palestinian Territories.

At the start of the year, the government had to deal with one of the most significant defections from within the regime. Abdel-Halim Khaddam, vice-president until 2005, gave a series of interviews to the Arab media from his exile in Paris harshly criticising the Assad regime, and strongly implying that he believed that its intelligence services had been responsible for the assassination of Rafiq Hariri, the former Lebanese prime minister, in February 2005 (see AR 2005, pp. 181-83). Khaddam subsequently joined the National Salvation Front, an opposition alliance that included the banned Muslim Brotherhood. The Front held an inaugural meeting in June 2006, calling for the abolition of Syria's 1963 emergency laws (which gave the authorities sweeping powers of arrest and detention) and for the establishment of a free multi-party system.

The government reacted to the Khaddam defection by impounding his assets and denouncing him as a traitor. President Assad also shored up his internal political front with a limited cabinet reshuffle in February, including the promotion of Farouq al-Shara, the long-serving foreign affairs minister, to the post of vice-president, which had remained vacant since Khaddam's removal at the June 2005 congress of the ruling Ba'ath party. Walid Muallim was elevated from deputy foreign minister to full minister, and his previous post was filled by Faisal Mekdad, Syria's former ambassador to the UN. The reshuffle also saw the post of interior minister filled: it had remained vacant since the death of Ghazi Kenaan, who reportedly committed suicide in his office in October 2005, apparently linked with the Hariri assassination affair (see AR 2005, p. 182). His replacement was Bassem Abdel-Majid, a military intelligence officer. One month after the reshuffle, Assad appointed Najah al-Attar, a former culture minister, as a second vice-president: she was the first woman to attain such an elevated position.

One of the most significant events of the first half of the year was a four-day state visit to Damascus by Mahmoud Ahmadinejad, the newly elected president of Iran. During the visit, Ahmadinejad held a series of meetings with the leaders of Hezbullah, Hamas, and Islamic Jihad, as well as with his Syrian hosts. He had earlier indicated his interest in developing Iran's alliance with Syria in its broader regional context by appointing as the new ambassador to Syria Mohammed Hassan Akhtari, who had been closely involved in backing Hezbullah's operations against Israeli forces in Lebanon while serving as an envoy to Damascus between 1989 and 1997. Over the next few months, tension mounted in the Gaza Strip, as Israel responded with steadily increasing intensity to military operations by Islamic Jihad and Hamas. A cross-border raid by Hezbullah on 12 July, resulting in the capture of two Israeli soldiers, then sparked off a 34-day war, as Israel unsuccessfully sought to inflict a crushing blow on the Lebanese group through massive air bombardments and a limited ground invasion (see pp. 189-90; 197-203). The extent to which Syria and Iran were involved in orchestrating these events was a matter of debate. However, President Assad made clear in his comments after the 11 August ceasefire in Lebanon that he considered the war to have been a decisive victory for Hezbullah, as well as a demonstration of the importance of applying coercive pressure on Israel, rather than making concessions and waiting in vain for Israel to respond. Assad also spoke harshly of the role of the Lebanese prime minister, Fouad Siniora, accusing him and his political allies of colluding with Israel in both the lead-up to and the conduct of the war.

These comments reflected the irritation of the Syrian government at Siniora's efforts to enlist international help in redefining Syrian-Lebanese relations. On 17 May the UN Security Council passed a resolution (1680) calling on Syria to respond positively to the request from Lebanon for co-operation in delineating the common border and in establishing normal diplomatic relations. (Syria claimed a special relationship with Lebanon, obviating the need for embassies in their respective capitals.) A number of Lebanese and Syrian intellectuals signed a "Beirut-Damascus Declaration" supporting the UN resolution. Several of the Syrian signatories, including Michel Kilo, a prominent campaigner for press freedom, and Anwar al-Bunni, a well-known human rights lawyer, were arrested and charged with plotting with a foreign power to undermine their own government.

On 12 September, Syrian guards outside the US embassy in Damascus foiled an apparent attempt by followers of al-Qaida to storm the diplomatic mission in an effort to commemorate the fifth anniversary of the 11 September attacks on New York and Washington DC. The US administration issued a terse statement of thanks to the Syrian forces for their action, but there was no further contact between the two sides. The question whether the USA should attempt to reopen diplomatic channels to Syria was revived towards the end of the year, when the bipartisan Iraq Study Group recommended that engagement with Syria should be part of the overall strategy of seeking to restore stability in Iraq (see pp. 137-38). Five US senators visited Damascus, and were received by Assad, who expressed his readiness to enter into peace negotiations with Israel. However, the US administration showed no interest in pursuing this track, but rather accused Syria of being intent on staging a coup to bring down the Siniora government in order to prevent the establishment of an international tribunal for the Hariri assassination. Assad continued to deny that Syria had anything to do with the murder, and claimed that the tribunal issue was being used as a means to attack Syria politically.

LEBANON

CAPITAL: Beirut AREA: 10,000 sq km POPULATION: 3,577,000
OFFICIAL LANGUAGE: Arabic POLITICAL SYSTEM: multiparty republic
HEAD OF STATE AND GOVERNMENT: President Emile Lahoud (since Nov '98)
RULING PARTY: 14 March movement
PRIME MINISTER: Prime Minister Fouad Siniora (since June '05)
MAIN IGO MEMBERSHIPS (NON-UN): AL, OIC, NAM, Francophonie
CURRENCY: Lebanese pound (end-'06 £1=L£2,952.10, US$1=L£1,512.00)
GNI PER CAPITA: US$6,180, US$5,740 at PPP ('05)

LEBANON was plunged back into existential crisis in 2006 as a result of the 34-day war in July and August between Hezbullah, the country's dominant Shi'ite Muslim political/military organisation, and Israel. The conflict left some 1,300 Lebanese dead, and Israeli air raids destroyed thousands of homes and caused severe damage to the country's infrastructure. Almost one million people, one-quarter of the Lebanese population, were displaced during the fighting. The overall effects on the economy were also dire, with GDP declining by about 6 per cent in real terms over the year, after recording annualised growth of some 5 per cent in the period preceding the war. However, the most powerful impact of the war was on Lebanon's political stability, as it sharpened divisions between the country's diverse sectarian and social groups, sparking fears of a slide back into civil war.

Political tension had been building up in Lebanon for some time before the July-August war. The critical event was the decision made in September 2004, under pressure from Syria, to extend the term of President Emile Lahoud by three years. This prompted the USA and France to push through a UN Security Council resolution (1559) demanding the withdrawal of foreign forces from Lebanon and the disarming of militias. The passage of the resolution was followed by an (unsuccessful) attempt in October 2004 to assassinate a prominent anti-Syrian Lebanese cabinet minister, Marwan Hamade, the first significant act of political violence inside Lebanon for several years (see AR 2004, p. 193). Over the next two years there were more than a dozen similar attacks, the most dramatic of which was the huge explosion on 14 February 2005 on the Beirut seafront, resulting in the death of former Prime Minister Rafiq Hariri and 22 of his companions. The Hariri assassination spawned a new political movement, known as 14 March after the mass demonstration staged on that day in 2005 calling for Syrian forces to leave the country. The 14 March movement, comprising the leading Sunni Muslim, Christian, and Druze political forces in the country, went on to secure political power in the legislative elections held after Syria pulled out its forces at the end of April 2005. However, it faced a potent opposition bloc made up of Hezbullah, its fellow Shi'ite Amal movement, and the Free Patriotic Movement (FPM) of Michel Aoun, a Christian former army commander who had returned to Lebanon in May 2005 after being driven into exile by Syria 15 years previously. Aoun had decided to throw in his lot with Hezbullah, despite his earlier record of hostility towards Syria—an ally of the Shi'ite movement—because of his refusal to accept a political role that was subordinate to other Christian parties.

Hezbullah and Amal (though not the FPM) agreed to join the government formed by Fouad Siniora, a close associate of the late Hariri, after the 2005 election. However at the end of that year, the two Shi'ite parties withdrew their ministers from the government owing to the refusal of Siniora to issue a statement describing Hezbullah's military wing as a "national resistance" movement and thereby exempt it from the requirement laid down in UN Security Council Resolution 1559 (2004) for its disarmament. The claim to be a resistance movement was based on the continued Israeli presence in the Shebaa Farms, a 40-sq km enclave lying at the intersection of the borders between Lebanon, Israel, and the Israeli-occupied Syrian Golan Heights. Israel held on to this area after its withdrawal from south Lebanon in 2000, on the grounds that the enclave fell within Syria's territory, not that of Lebanon. The UN examined the issue and upheld Israel's position. Following Syria's withdrawal from Lebanon by April 2005, the Siniora government sought to negotiate an agreement with Syria for the establishment of normal diplomatic relations—the two countries did not have respective embassies, owing to their special relationship—and for the formal delineation of the border. Syria indicated that it was ready to discuss these issues, but only on condition that the Shebaa Farms was not included. The UN Security Council attempted to put pressure on Syria to take a more co-operative stance, passing a fresh resolution (1680) on 17 May 2006, calling upon Syria to respond positively to the Lebanese government's requests, and reiterating previous demands for the disarmament of Lebanese militias.

The Shi'ite ministers had in the meantime agreed to return to the government, and took part in a process of national dialogue. Aoun also participated in these talks, which ultimately yielded no positive results, and claimed to have secured a commitment from Hezbullah to disband its military forces. These discussions among Lebanese parties were affected by an array of external actors. Syria was most directly concerned, given the strong suspicion that its agents had been responsible for the Hariri assassination. A UN commission, established in 2005 to investigate the assassination, stated in its first report that "converging evidence" pointed towards Syrian involvement (for text see AR 2005, pp. 490-92). The commission's reports took on a more circumspect tone after the appointment of Serge Brammertz, a Belgian prosecutor, as its new chairman at the end of 2005, replacing Detlev Mehlis. Nevertheless, the investigation posed a threat to Syria, as its purpose was to amass sufficient evidence to mount a criminal prosecution in an international tribunal. Syria, therefore, had every reason to seek to undermine the efficacy of the 14 March alliance, which was led by Saad Hariri, a son of the assassinated former prime minister, and to promote forces more sympathetic to Syria.

Iran was also deeply involved in Lebanon, having been instrumental in the rise of Hezbullah in the 1980s and in enabling the Lebanese movement to accumulate a large arsenal of missiles capable of striking Israel. That arsenal had taken on added significance in light of the developing dispute over Iran's nuclear programme (see pp. 280-83), as it provided Iran with the wherewithal to retaliate in the event of an attack on its nuclear facilities by Israel and/or the USA.

At the other end of the spectrum, the USA, France, and Saudi Arabia were also heavily involved in Lebanese affairs, supporting the Siniora government in a way that was regarded as partisan by Lebanon's opposition groups. Finally, Israel provided constant reminders of its presence through regular invasions of Lebanese airspace.

The Palestinian question had played a central part in the earlier civil war in Lebanon, which started in 1975 after a Lebanese Christian militia attack on a bus carrying Palestinians. In the 2006 conflict, the Palestinian issue was also a factor. The trigger for the Israeli assault on Lebanon was a raid carried out by Hezbullah guerrillas over the border on 12 July, resulting in the capture of two Israeli soldiers. A further eight Israelis were killed in that raid and in an attempt by Israeli forces to pursue the Hezbullah unit inside Lebanon. Hezbullah stated that its operation was intended to support the Palestinians in Gaza, who had been subjected to heavy Israeli attack after a unit from the armed wing of Hamas, the largest Palestinian Islamist group, had captured an Israeli soldier, Corporal Gilad Shalit, in a raid across Gaza's border with Israel on 25 June (see pp. 189-90). Hezbullah's leader, Sayyed Hassan Nasrallah, said that the objective of the capture of the two soldiers was to secure the release of Lebanese and Palestinian prisoners held by Israel and to force Israel to withdraw from the Shebaa Farms and cede the territory to the Lebanese government.

The Israeli government responded to the Hezbullah raid by launching a series of air strikes against the southern suburbs of Beirut and on the nearby airport. Nasrallah, in turn, announced in a defiant statement carried by al Jazeera television that he would demonstrate his forces' capacity to reply in kind. Hezbullah launched missile strikes on a swathe of northern Israel, stretching from Safad to the port city of Haifa. An Israeli naval vessel was also hit by a land-to-sea missile, resulting in the death of a number of sailors. The ability of Hezbullah to inflict casualties on Israeli civilians and military personnel won the movement strong popular support across the Arab world, although this sentiment was not shared by a number of Arab governments. King Abdullah of Saudi Arabia, for example, condemned Hezbullah's "adventurism", and a number of Gulf Arab government officials expressed the view, off the record, that if Israel were to succeed in eliminating Hezbullah's military capabilities, it would be a positive development, as this would curb the advance of Iranian-backed radical Shi'ite forces in the Arab world.

The perception that Israel was being encouraged to finish off Hezbullah was fortified by the reluctance of the major Western powers—notably the USA and the UK—to press for an early ceasefire as the conflict intensified, with increasingly heavy Israeli aerial bombardments being met by more barrages of Hezbullah missiles. The Lebanese government focused its efforts on trying to make the international community impose a ceasefire, and carefully avoided making any direct criticisms of Hezbullah, recognising the depth of the popular outrage at the destruction wrought by Israel's air raids. These raids, however, signally failed to stop Hezbullah from continuing to rain missiles down on northern Israel, including Haifa, and the Israeli government and military command were forced to acknowledge that they would not be able to achieve their objectives without a ground offensive.

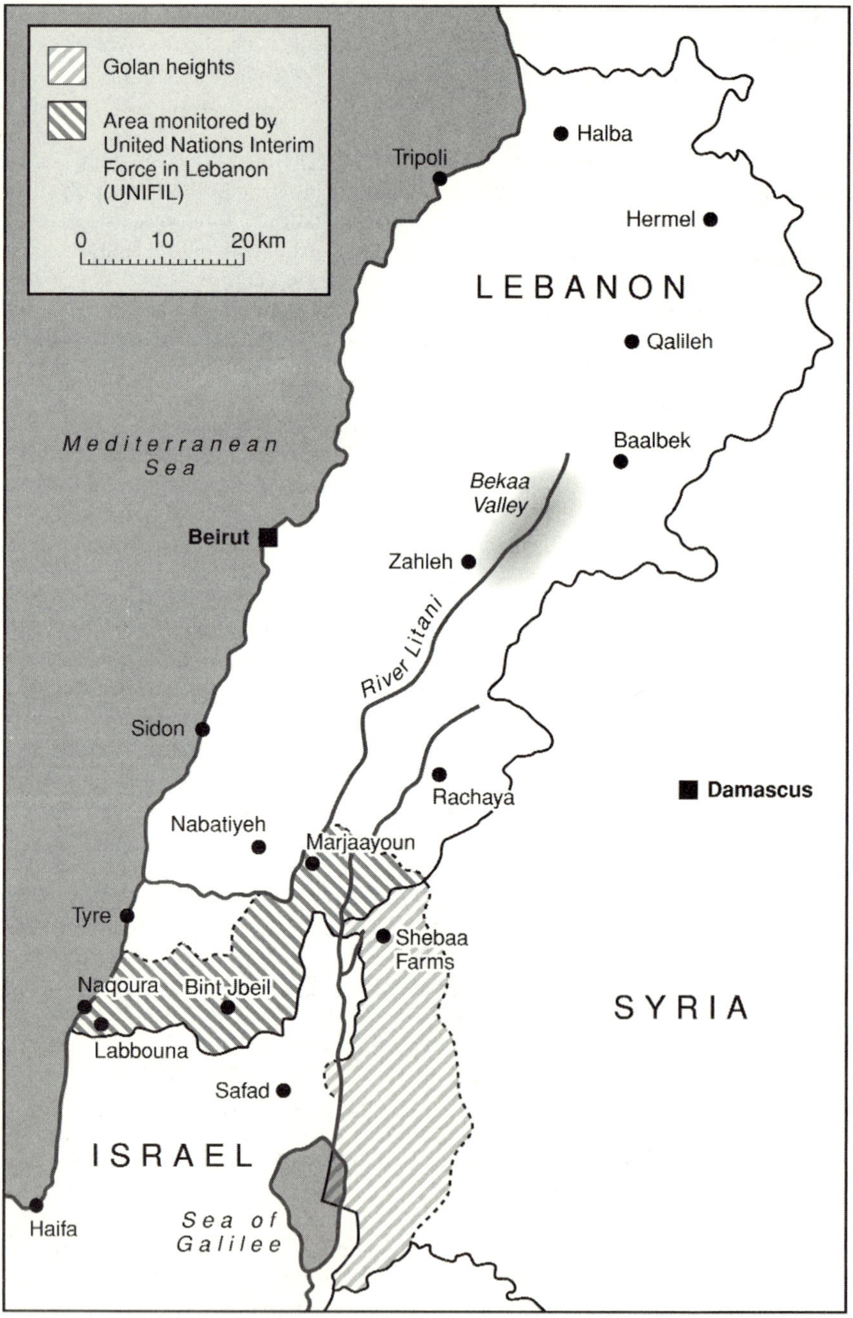

Golan heights
Area monitored by United Nations Interim Force in Lebanon (UNIFIL)
0 10 20 km
Tripoli
Halba
Hermel
LEBANON
Qalileh
Mediterranean Sea
Baalbek
Bekaa Valley
Beirut
Zahleh
River Litani
Sidon
Rachaya
Damascus
Nabatiyeh
Marjaayoun
Tyre
Shebaa Farms
Naqoura
Bint Jbeil
Labbouna
SYRIA
Safad
ISRAEL
Haifa
Sea of Galilee

Two weeks into the conflict, some 10,000 Israeli land forces crossed the border, but their advance was checked by Hezbullah's highly effective use of anti-tank missiles. By early August, as Lebanese civilian casualties were mounting, pressure for a halt to the conflict became difficult for the international community to resist. President George W. Bush of the USA and the UK prime minister, Tony Blair, in particular, were heavily criticised in the Arab world and in the Western media for their refusal to countenance an immediate ceasefire, and the two leaders were accused of seeking to string out the conflict in order to enable Israel to complete its mission. However, it became increasingly clear that Israel had badly misjudged the challenge it faced in neutralising the threat from Hezbullah, and subsequent inquiries by the Israeli armed forces were critical of the planning and execution of the campaign, prompting Lieutenant General Dan Halutz, the chief of staff of the Israel Defence Forces, to resign his post in January 2007 (see p. 185).

The diplomatic moves to put an end to the conflict were painfully slow. The Siniora government in late July secured cabinet approval for a seven-point plan, which included provisions for the disarmament of Hezbullah (if only by implication) and for the resolution of the Shebaa Farms question. Siniora sought to emphasise the significance of the fact that the cabinet's approval included that of the two ministers representing Hezbullah. In early August France and the USA started work on a draft ceasefire resolution to present to the UN Security Council. Siniora said that he was deeply disappointed with the terms of this draft, which omitted any reference to Israel being obliged to withdraw from positions it had occupied inside Lebanon since 12 July. He pleaded his case to a delegation of three Arab foreign ministers, who went on to New York to joint the deliberations on the resolution. Siniora also sought to bolster his position through ordering the deployment of 15,000 Lebanese army troops in the border area, a zone from which they had hitherto been excluded at Hezbullah's insistence. Another difficulty was the reluctance of France to commit itself to contributing significant numbers of troops to the proposed peacekeeping force (see p. 45).

These problems were eventually overcome, and on 11 August the UN Security Council passed Resolution 1701 (2006), calling for an immediate ceasefire and laying out a plan of action to sustain it (for text see pp. 528-31). The resolution stopped short of demanding an immediate withdrawal of Israeli forces, but rather called on Israel to pull out "in parallel" with the deployment of Lebanese army and UN forces in the border area. In dealing with the issue of Hezbullah's weapons, the resolution used the Siniora plan's formula, stating that there should be "no weapons without the consent of the government of Lebanon". It called for increasing the strength of the existing UNIFIL force in south Lebanon by up to 15,000 troops, but it did not give it the explicit task of disarming Hezbullah. It requested the secretary-general to report back to the Security Council on border questions, including the Shebaa Farms. The passage of the resolution had the desired effect of stopping the fighting, and the new UN troops began to arrive in the following weeks, with France and Italy making the largest contributions. By the end of 2006, UNIFIL's numbers had swelled to about 12,000.

The final casualty toll of the war on the Lebanese side was estimated by the government at 1,300, the vast majority of them civilians. There was no definitive figure published for Hezbullah military casualties. On the Israeli side, 158 people were killed, of whom 119 were military personnel and 39 civilians.

Nasrallah, the Hezbullah leader, pronounced the war a resounding victory for the Lebanese and a uniquely humiliating defeat for Israel. On 22 September, in his first public appearance since the war, he told a rally in Beirut that Hezbullah had restocked its military supplies, and that the group now possessed 20,000 missiles, despite having launched 4,000 at Israel during the conflict; six weeks later he boasted that the arsenal had reached 33,000 missiles. He also called, for the first time, for the establishment of a government of national unity, strongly implying that Hezbullah's share of seats should be larger than previously. He added that measures should be taken to make the electoral system more fair. The 2005 election had left the 14 March alliance with 72 of the 128 seats in the National Assembly (unicameral legislature), with 35 going to the Shi'ite alliance of Hezbullah and Amal, and the remaining 21 seats held by Aoun's FPM. The speech marked the start of a campaign by Nasrallah and Aoun to change the balance of power in Lebanon. However, they found Siniora and the 14 March alliance to be a tenacious adversary.

After several weeks of inconclusive talks between the two sides, Hezbullah and Amal in early November pulled their six ministers out of the cabinet, leaving the government with no Shi'ite representatives. This mass resignation came as the government was considering a law to approve the establishment of an international tribunal to investigate the Hariri assassination. Siniora's supporters, notably the USA, detected a clear connection between the efforts to destabilise the government and the establishment of a tribunal. The US government issued a statement alleging that Syria and Iran were conspiring with Hezbullah to bring down the Lebanese government by unconstitutional means in order to block passage of the statute for the tribunal. The possible involvement of Syrian agents in the Hariri assassination was a central focus of the UN investigation into the affair. Hezbullah warned that it would stage mass protest demonstrations if Siniora did not accept the opposition's terms for a united government by 13 November. The principal demand was that the opposition should have at least one-third of the portfolios, which would give it the power to block legislation. Siniora ignored the threat, and his government duly passed the law on the tribunal, based on a text already approved by the UN Security Council. The law still needed to be ratified by the president, or, failing that, by the National Assembly.

The political scene took a violent turn once more on 21 November when unidentified gunmen shot dead Pierre Gemayel, the industry minister, and grandson of the founder of the Phalangist party, the Christian nationalist party that played a central role in the 1975-76 civil war. Leaders of the 14 March alliance made clear that they were in no doubt that the assassination was a fresh instance of Syrian-inspired intimidation of the legitimate Lebanese government; newspapers close to the opposition suggested that the killing was orchestrated to discredit Syria and the anti-government forces. The UN agreed to help the Lebanese authorities in their investigation of Gemayel's assassination. After a brief hiatus, the political conflict resumed, as Hezbullah on 1 December mobilised a mass demonstration outside the National Assembly buildings in the Beirut city centre. Tens of thousands of demonstrators remained in place for the rest of the month. In the meantime, Amr Moussa, the secretary general of the Arab League, shuttled between the two sides, and came up with a proposal for a government in which one or two neutrals would hold the balance of power, with the opposition having just under the one-third representation that they were demanding. Neither side explicitly rejected the idea. However Moussa left Beirut at the end of December acknowledging that little real progress had been made.

The year ended with the Siniora government putting the finishing touches to an economic recovery programme to be presented to an international donor conference, scheduled to be held in Paris on 25 January 2007. The government aimed to raise at least US$5 billion in grants and concessionary loans to help it meet the challenge of servicing its US$41 billion debt (about half of which was owed to external creditors) and to finance reconstruction and development. This programme became yet another bone of contention between the government and the opposition. The aid, which was likely to be forthcoming owing to the strong support expressed for Siniora by the main Western and Arab powers, would strengthen the government's position in 2007. However, there appeared to be little prospect of any lessening of the political tensions in the new year, with confrontations over the Hariri tribunal and over who would become Lebanon's next president primed to escalate.

IRAQ

CAPITAL: Baghdad AREA: 438,000 sq km POPULATION: 28,100,000 (UN '04 est)
OFFICIAL LANGUAGES: Arabic and Kurdish POLITICAL SYSTEM: multiparty republic under military occupation
HEAD OF STATE: President Jalal Talabani (since April '05)
RULING PARTY: United Iraq Alliance (UIA)
HEAD OF GOVERNMENT: Jawad (Nouri) al-Maliki (UIA, Da'wa Party), Prime Minister (since April '06)
MAIN IGO MEMBERSHIPS (NON-UN): AL, OPEC, OAPEC, OIC, NAM
CURRENCY: New Iraqi dinar (end-'06 £1=NID2,585.04, US$1=NID1,324.00)
GNI PER CAPITA: US$876-US$3,465 ('05 est), -

THE year ended in the most dramatic of circumstances when Saddam Hussein, the former Iraqi president ousted by US-led forces in April 2003 (see AR 2003, pp. 229-48), was executed by hanging on 30 December (for obituary see pp. 594-95). He had been sentenced to death on 5 November after being found guilty of crimes against humanity for ordering the execution of at least 143 people in the mostly Shi'ite village of Dujail, 55 km north of Baghdad, in the aftermath of an attempt on his life in July 1982. An appeal panel upheld the death sentence on 26 December. The panel also announced that the death sentence had been upheld for two of Saddam's associates, his half-brother Barzan Ibrahim Hasan al-Tikriti and former judge Awad Hamad al-Bandr al-Saadun. Former Vice-President Taha Yasin Ramadan al-Jizrawi had been sentenced to life imprisonment, whilst three other defendants received 15-year prison sentences. One defendant had been acquitted. The Dujail trial had opened in October 2005 (see AR 2005, p. 193). The separate trial had opened in August of Saddam and six other defendants on charges of genocide and crimes against humanity for their role in the 1988-90 Anfal campaign against the Kurds.

Saddam, aged 69, was hanged at around 6.00 am (03:00 GMT) on the day upon which Sunni Muslims began celebrating Eid ul-Adha, the Feast of Sacrifice. The timing of the execution—at the dawn of what was considered a day of mercy and feasting in the Islamic world—angered Sunni Muslims across the Middle East and fuelled perceptions that the death of the former president was more about Shi'ite retribution and less about justice, fears that seemed borne out by an amateur recording of Saddam's last moments (see below). Shortly before the execution, the US military had handed over "physical control" of Saddam to the Iraqi government. The execution took place at the Iraqi army base, Camp Justice, located in the mainly Shi'ite northern Baghdad suburb of Kadhimiya. It was reported that previously the base, then known as Camp Banzai, had been used by Saddam as his military intelligence headquarters, and that numerous Iraqis had been tortured and executed there.

Iraqi television later showed footage of Saddam being placed in a noose by hangmen, but the picture cut away just before his execution. The former president appeared calm, talking to his hangmen as they wrapped his neck in black cloth and steered him towards the gallows. Iraqi television later showed footage of his body. On the evening of 30 December a US helicopter flew Saddam's body to Tikrit, where it was delivered to local dignitaries. His body was later driven to Awja, his birthplace, in a police vehicle and was buried in a cemetery beside his two sons, Qusay Hussein and Uday Hussein, who had been killed in July 2003 in a gun battle with US forces in Mosul in northern Iraq (see AR 2003, pp. 244-45).

More images of Saddam's death, apparently filmed on a mobile telephone, were widely circulated on the Internet on 31 December. The grainy images and muffled sounds contrasted sharply with the officially-sanctioned pictures broadcast by Iraqi television, and showed Saddam trading insults with his Shi'ite executioners and other witnesses. One of the guards was heard to shout at Saddam: "You have destroyed us. You have killed us. You have made us live in destitution." "I have saved you from destitution and misery and destroyed your enemies, the Persians and Americans," Saddam responded. "God damn you," the guard said. "God damn you," came the reply. The assembled witnesses to the execution, gathered below the gallows, were heard ignoring appeals for propriety as a man shouted out "Muqtada, Muqtada, Muqtada", a reference to the powerful young Shi'ite firebrand Muqtada al-Sadr, whose father, the revered Shi'ite cleric Grand Ayatollah Mohammed Mohammed Sadeq al-Sadr, had been killed on Saddam's orders in 1999. Saddam answered back: "Do you consider this bravery?" The former president was eventually hanged mid-way through his second recitation of the Muslim profession of faith, the Shahada.

Sh'ite Muslims in Iraq celebrated the execution while Sunni towns saw protests. In Sadr City—Baghdad's sprawling Shi'ite slum—and Basra and Najaf, people danced in the streets and fired celebratory gunshots. In Tikrit, Samarra, and Ramadi, however, there were reports of protests and demonstrations in support of Saddam "the martyr". In a statement, Iraqi Prime Minister Nouri al-Maliki (a Shi'ite) said: "Justice, in the name of the people, has carried out the death sentence against the criminal Saddam, who faced his fate like all tyrants, frightened and terrified during a hard day which he did not expect." In the USA, President George W. Bush issued the following statement: "Bringing Saddam Hussein to justice will not end the violence in Iraq, but it is an important milestone on Iraq's course to becoming a democracy that can govern, sustain, and defend itself." Iran's deputy foreign minister, Hamid-Reza Asefi, said that Saddam's execution amounted to "a victory of the Iraqi people". Saddam's regime had been overthrown because the Iraqi people did not support him, Asefi said, and it was "crystal clear that the United States should not misinterpret his fall and take the credit for itself". Leaders and governments of many European countries expressed strong disapproval of the use of capital punishment. There was also strong opposition to the execution in the Arab world. President Hosni Mubarak of Egypt said that carrying out the execution on the first day of Eid ul-Adha had been "unthinkable". Saddam, he said, had been turned into a martyr and the problems in Iraq remained unresolved.

INTERNAL POLITICAL DEVELOPMENTS. The Independent Electoral Commission of Iraq on 20 January announced the final results of the December 2005 elections to the 275-member Council of Representatives (the unicameral legislature) (see AR 2005, pp. 186-88). As expected, Iraqis cast their ballots largely along ethnic and sectarian lines and consequently cross-sectarian groups and independents performed poorly. The United Iraqi Alliance (UIA), the Shi'ite Muslim religious alliance representing the largest community in Iraq, won 128 seats, fewer than the 140 seats which it had won in elections to the previous legislature, the transitional National Assembly, held in January 2005 (see AR 2005, p. 185). The main changes in the Shi'ite alliance—originally put together under the auspices of Grand Ayatollah Ali al-Sistani—were the success of Muqtada al-Sadr, leader of the Mahdi army militia; the failure of former interim Prime Minister Ayad Allawi; and the departure from the coalition of Ahmed Chalabi, the US-backed leader of the Iraqi National Congress, the umbrella opposition to Saddam, whose list failed to win a single seat. The results left the UIA short of the two-thirds majority it required to form a government, a gap it could bridge if it worked in concert with its old coalition partner, the Kurdistan Alliance, which won 53 seats. The two predominantly Sunni Arab groupings—the Iraqi Consensus Front and the Iraqi National Dialogue Front—took 44 and 11 seats, respectively, making them a more powerful force in the new legislature. Sunnis had held only 17 seats in the transitional National Assembly.

On 12 February the UIA decided that Ibrahim al-Jaafari should continue in his position as prime minister. Al-Jaafari, a moderate Islamist and leader of the (Shi'ite) Da'wa party, had served in the post since April 2005 (see AR 2005, pp. 185-86). However, he had been criticised for failing to curb sectarian violence and therefore came under increasing pressure from Sunnis, Kurds, and secular leaders to make way for another candidate. President Jalal Talabani, a Kurd, led the charge against Jaafari, demanding his replacement and accusing him of reneging on agreements with the Kurds. Talabani, and the Kurds in general, had been particularly enraged when Jaafari had paid a surprise visit to Turkey in May 2005 shortly after his appointment as interim prime minister, without informing any of his Kurdish colleagues. Given the constant Kurdish fear of Turkish military involvement in northern Iraq, Jaafari could not have done anything more likely to anger the Kurds.

The Council of Representatives held its first session on 16 March, but wrangling over the appointment of a prime minister continued to delay the formation of a new national unity government. The deadlock was eventually broken on 20 April when Jaafari agreed to allow the UIA to reconsider his candidacy. The UIA convened on the following day and selected Nouri al-Maliki (a Shi'ite) as its new candidate for prime minister, a choice that received the swift support of the main Sunni and Kurdish factions. Al-Maliki, aged 56, was a close ally of Jaafari, having served as his chief aide, and a member of the Da'wa party. He had developed a reputation as a strongman and disciplinarian while in exile for more than two decades in Syria. Because he had spent most of his time in exile in Syria, rather than in Iran like many of his Shi'ite associates, Maliki was not too closely associated with the Iranian regime. "This is someone with whom we can work", said US Secretary of State Condoleezza Rice, greeting the appointment with enthusiasm.

The Council of Representatives reconvened on 22 April and voted to re-elect Jalal Talabani as president. He had first been elected to the post by the transitional National Assembly in April 2005. Adel Abdul Mahdi, a Shi'ite, retained the post of vice-president, whilst Tariq al-Hashemi, a Sunni whose nomination as speaker had earlier been opposed, was also elected as a vice-president. The Council eventually elected Mahmud al-Mashhadani of the (Sunni) Iraqi National Dialogue Front as speaker.

After weeks of negotiation, the Council of Representatives on 20 May approved a new "national unity" cabinet headed by Maliki. The formation of the cabinet was hailed by US President Bush as "a new day for the millions of Iraqis who want to live in peace". The UK's prime minister, Tony Blair, made a surprise visit to Baghdad on 22 May to meet Maliki and offer his support to his new government. Maliki's tenure as prime minister did not get off to an auspicious start: he was unable to negotiate the appointment of three key portfolios, and opted to delay the appointment of the ministers of the interior, defence, and national security, a move which was attacked by the Sunnis. The Council of Representatives eventually agreed the three appointments on 8 June, ending a stalemate among Iraq's religious and ethnic groups over the crucial posts. General Abdul-Qader Mohammed Jassim al-Mirfaji, a Sunni Arab who was not affiliated to any party, was appointed as minister of defence. Jawad al-Bolani, a Shi'ite and an independent member of the UIA, was appointed as interior minister. (The interior ministry was regarded as extremely sensitive because of accusations that the ranks of its security forces had been infiltrated by Shi'ite militias responsible for much of the sectarian violence against Sunnis.) Sherwan al-Waili, another Shi'ite, was appointed as minister of national security. Al-Waili was a member of the Iraqi Da'wa party—which was not the same as Prime Minister Maliki's Da'wa party—and he had been imprisoned after the Shi'ite uprising of 1991 in Basra. Remaining ministerial posts in the new cabinet were divided among political blocs to reflect the percentage of Council of Representative seats won in the December 2005 elections.

The Council of Representatives on 11 October approved by a slim majority a law that laid out a mechanism for forming autonomous federal regions. The controversial law would allow Iraq's 18 provinces to hold referendums on whether to amalgamate into federal regions, similar to the Kurdish autonomous region in the north. Critics of the legislation—principally the main Sunni bloc but also from within some Shi'ite parties—had argued that the legislation would set in motion the disintegration of Iraq along sectarian lines. Specifically, they had warned that the nine southern provinces might merge into one Iranian-controlled Shi'ite entity. The main Sunni coalition, the Iraqi Consensus Front, and two Shi'ite parties (the Sadrist movement and Fadhila party) had tried to prevent a vote on the federalism bill by boycotting the session, thereby preventing the 275-member body from reaching the quorum of 50 per cent. However, the quorum was just reached with 140 members present, who voted on each of the bill's 200 articles individually, passing them all unanimously.

SECTARIAN VIOLENCE. The fault lines dividing the Sunnis, Shi'ites, and Kurds widened during 2006, leading some commentators to compare Iraq to Lebanon at the start of its bloody civil war in 1975. The Iraqi sectarian violence, akin to civil war, was ignited by the 22 February bomb attack on the al-Askariya shrine in Samarra, a Sunni-dominated town some 100 km north of Baghdad. The golden-domed shrine was one of Shi'ite Islam's holiest sites—the remains of the 10th and 11th Shi'ite imams, Ali al-Hadi and his son Hassan al-Askari, rested there—exceeded in veneration only by the shrines of Najaf and Karbala. No-one was injured in the Sunni attack on the shrine, which brought down the golden dome, but the political impact was enormous. One commentator said that it was as if, 400 years ago, during the religious wars in Europe, militant Protestants had blown up St Peter's basilica in Rome. Iraq's main Shi'ite religious leader, Grand Ayatollah Sistani, issued a call for restraint, but it was ignored.

A line had been crossed and the Shi'ite majority was in a strong position to retaliate with brutal force. The Shi'ites controlled not only the interior ministry and most of the police force in southern and central Iraq, but also the two main Shi'ite militias, Muqtada al-Sadr's Mahdi army and the Badr brigade of the

Supreme Council for the Islamic Revolution in Iraq (SCIRI), both of which were powerful forces in Shi'ite areas. In the days following the bombing as many as 1,300 bodies, mostly Sunni, were found dumped in and around Baghdad. Many had been tortured. Some 50 Sunni mosques were attacked and burned.

Sectarian tensions in Baghdad and elsewhere in Iraq increased dramatically during March, as Shi'ite and Sunni Muslims carried out retaliatory killings on a massive scale. On 19 March, the eve of the third anniversary of the US-led invasion of Iraq, the former interim prime minister, Ayad Allawi, told reporters that Iraq was indeed "in a civil war". The country, he said, was losing each day, as an average, 50 or 60 people and "if that is not a civil war, then God knows what civil war is". The sectarian violence spurred tens of thousands of Iraqis to flee from mixed Sunni-Shi'ite areas. The developing new pattern of settlement led to further separation of the Shi'ite and Sunni communities, moving the country towards a de facto partitioning along sectarian and ethnic lines. A report published by the Red Crescent Society in early May said that more than 100,000 people had fled their homes in the two months since the destruction of the al-Askariya shrine.

The unrest was not halted by the death of Abu Musab al-Zarqawi, the Jordanian-born leader of al-Qaida in Iraq, in a US air-strike on a remote house in a village in Diyala province, north of Baghdad, on 7 June. With a US$25 million bounty on his head offered by the USA, Zarqawi had been the most wanted man in Iraq for his leadership of a group that had carried out many of the most brutal attacks of the Sunni insurgency, including a large number of suicide bombings, kidnappings, and beheadings. The raid that killed Zarqawi took place in an area known as the Hibhib, close to the town of Baquba, the site of a new wave of sectarian killings in early June. A message posted by the al-Qaida Organisation for Holy War in Iraq on one of its websites on 8 June confirmed Zarqawi's death, but vowed to continue "the holy war". On 12 June the group posted another message announcing that Zarqawi had been replaced as leader by Shaikh Abu Hamza al-Muhajir. Al-Muhajir was believed to be Egyptian and had fought in Afghanistan and against US forces during the battle of Fallujah in November 2004 (see AR 2004, p. 200).

The death of Zarqawi did little to stem the Sunni insurgency. Attacks on the US military continued throughout the year, and on 28 December 22-year-old Dustin R. Donica was shot dead in Baghdad, taking the toll incurred by US troops since the start of the invasion in March 2003 to the landmark 3,000 figure. The cycle of sectarian violence steadily worsened as the year progressed. Reports of barbarous acts of brutality became commonplace. On 6 June police in Baquba found nine severed heads, wrapped in plastic bags and left in a fruit box by the side of a road. At least 50 people were killed in Baghdad on 11 July, in what the *International Herald Tribune* described as "a stunning array of violence" that included a double suicide attack near entrances to the heavily fortified Green Zone government compound, beheadings, shootings, a series of car bombs, mortar attacks and the ambushing of a bus carrying Shi'ite mourners returning from a funeral. The violence was relentless. On the next day gunmen stormed a bus station in Muqdadiya, 90 km north-east of Baghdad, seized 24 Shi'ites after separating them from the crowd and shot dead all but four of them.

A report issued in early September by the US defence department (the Pentagon) confirmed that the "core conflict" in Iraq had changed from a battle against Sunni insurgents, such as Zarqawi, to an increasingly bloody fight between Shi'ite and Sunni Muslims. The report concluded, however, that "the current violence is not a civil war, and movement toward a civil war can be prevented." Casualty figures suggested otherwise. Figures released by the UN Assistance Mission for Iraq (UNAMI) for the whole of 2006 estimated that nearly 35,000 civilians had been killed during the course of the year, a sharp increase from the estimate of just over 12,000 reported previously by the Iraqi government. When asked about the difference, Gianni Magazzeni, the UNAMI chief in Baghdad, said that the UN figures were solid and had been compiled from information obtained through the Iraqi health ministry, hospitals across the country, and the Medico-Legal Institute in Baghdad. The UNAMI report concluded that the "root causes of the sectarian violence lie in revenge killings and lack of accountability for past crimes as well as in the growing sense of impunity for ongoing human rights violations". The agency called on the Iraqi government to step up efforts to restore law and order.

In the USA, the Bush administration came under intense pressure throughout the year to deal with the mounting sectarian violence in Iraq, and rising criticism of the war at home (see pp. 125-39). In a sombre assessment of the situation, President Bush said on 25 October that he shared the dissatisfaction of his countrymen with the intensity of the fighting, but insisted that Iraq was crucial to US security. He said that mounting US casualties in Iraq were a "serious concern", but again refused to set a timetable for pulling out US troops. "A fixed timetable for withdrawal, in my judgement, means defeat," he said. In mid-term legislative elections in the USA, held on 7 November, the opposition Democrats gained control of both houses of Congress. Polls had indicated that a substantial proportion of voters were primarily worried about the war in Iraq and were unconvinced that the Bush administration had devised a credible policy to end the insurgency and sectarian violence. US Defence Secretary Donald Rumsfeld, one of the main neo-conservative architects of the Bush administration's military adventure in Iraq, paid the price for the Democrats' success and resigned on 8 November. One of his last actions as defence secretary was to pay a surprise visit to Iraq on 10 December to bid farewell to members of the US military serving there.

Rumsfeld was replaced as defence secretary by former CIA director Robert Gates, a close friend of the Bush family. In his confirmation hearing, Gates was asked if he thought the USA was winning the war in Iraq, and responded: "No, Sir." He then went on to say that he did not think the USA was losing the war either. Gates had been a member of the bipartisan Iraq Study Group (the Baker-Hamilton commission), appointed by Congress to reassess strategy in Iraq, which delivered its final report on 6 December (for summary see pp. 539-41). The most significant of the recommendations proposed a change in the "primary mission" of US combat forces, which would allow a "responsible" withdrawal of those forces. Whilst the report did not set a detailed timetable, it contended—subject to unexpected developments—that the bulk of US combat forces "could" be withdrawn from Iraq by the first quarter of 2008. The report's authors also recommended that the Bush administration should open direct negotiations with Iran and Syria in order to build an international consensus for stability in Iraq and the region. Furthermore, the report recommended that it should be made clear to the Maliki government that if it failed to make "substantial progress" on reconciliation and security in the coming months, by such measures as confronting the armed militias, the USA would be forced to reduce its political, economic and military support.

Apparently unprepared to take on board these recommendations, the Bush administration at the end of 2006 seemed to be ready to alter its tactics in Iraq by increasing—rather than preparing to reduce—its military involvement in the country, and little change could be detected in the administration's overall strategy towards the Middle East.

SAUDI ARABIA—YEMEN—ARAB STATES OF THE GULF

SAUDI ARABIA

CAPITAL: Riyadh AREA: 2,150,000 sq km POPULATION: 24,573,000
OFFICIAL LANGUAGE: Arabic POLITICAL SYSTEM: non-party monarchy
HEAD OF STATE AND GOVERNMENT: King Abdullah ibn Abdul Aziz (since Aug '05), also Prime Minister
HEIR APPARENT: Crown Prince Sultan ibn Abdul Aziz (since Aug '05), also Deputy Prime Minister
MAIN IGO MEMBERSHIPS (NON-UN): AL, OPEC, OAPEC, GCC, OIC, NAM
CURRENCY: Saudi riyal (end-'06 £1=SR7.32300, US$1=SR3.75070)
GNI PER CAPITA: US$11,770, US$14,740 at PPP ('05 est, based on regression)

KING Abdullah ibn Abdul Aziz's first full year as Saudi Arabia's ruler saw a consolidation of his early efforts to modernise Saudi politics and flesh out its economic buoyancy with a more aggressive push for reform. Developments in 2006 fell short of the high expectations of Saudi liberals, though the continuation of the stability enjoyed in 2005 allowed greater space for the Saudi leadership to modernise the apparatus of power and widen participation beyond the clique of al-Saud princes. The oil-fired economic boom dissipated much of the insistence for change. Massive waves of liquidity fuelled investment in public services and infrastructure, providing for a general "feel good factor" that took the edge off political stresses and strains. Furthermore, with the situation in Iraq deteriorating rapidly, the leadership's attention was diverted elsewhere for much of the year.

The Saudi leader continued in his efforts to quell radical Islamism and ensure a far more equitable distribution of the oil bounty in a conscious attempt to tackle Jihadism's root causes. In this effort he proved successful, encouraging consensus support for his strategy, and being greatly assisted by his own reputation for probity and fairness.

The main focus of political reform was manifested in the process of formalising the leadership succession. This issue was not only central to the future of the kingdom, but also reflected Abdullah's vulnerable position within the House of Saud. To buttress his own strength vis-a-vis the royal family's Sudeiri branch—the sons of the kingdom's founder, King Abdul Aziz al-Saud, by his favoured wife

Hessa bint Ahmed al-Sudeiri—Abdullah instituted a series of reforms that culminated in October in the creation of the Allegiance Committee. This body was to be composed of the sons and grandsons of King Abdul Aziz, and would decide the eligibility of future kings for power, thereby representing a curb on the Sudeiri influence by putting all of Abdul Aziz's many sons on an equal footing as potential successors to Abdullah. (Abdullah himself was the fifth of Abdul Aziz's sons to succeed to the throne).

The formation of the committee in effect weakened the king's position. Hitherto, the monarch had chosen his successor, but that prerogative now passed to the committee, which would have the right to endorse the nomination of a crown prince proposed by the king. Moreover, if neither the king nor the crown prince were deemed fit to rule, a transitory council made up of five members of the Allegiance Committee would take over the affairs of state for a maximum of one week.

Abdullah ensured that his own leadership was unchallenged in 2006, assisted by the poor health of the two main Sudeiri princes, Crown Prince Sultan ibn Abdul Aziz and Interior Minister Prince Naif ibn Abdul Aziz. He also kept the flame of political participation alive, promising elections to the Majlis al-Shura, the consultative council. However, this was a long-term aim, and the strong showing of Islamists in all Gulf elections meant that there would be no haste in pressing ahead with this programme.

The king signalled his intent to unify the kingdom, visiting the country's poverty-stricken south-western province in early November to dispense development funds and make a number of gestures towards minority communities represented in the region. Abdullah ordered the release of 77 Ismailis imprisoned for their involvement in a riot in Najran in 2000. The move had symbolic resonance, given the kingdom's traditional antipathy towards religious minorities, and echoed the renewed emphasis that Abdullah placed on the "national dialogue" programme, using public debate to improve relations between Shi'ites, Ismailis, and Sunni Saudis (see AR 2005, p. 195). Meanwhile, the Majlis al-Shura convened more regularly. A more liberal outlook was evident, with the Muttawa religious police deployed in a more subtle manner.

Prince Naif's security forces continued with their effective efforts to draw the poison from the Jihadist movement. State forces mopped up militants with sporadic raids on terrorist hideouts and arms caches. In recognition of the increased danger of Jihadist influence from Iraq, the defence and aviation ministry announced in May a tender to build a major security fence along the entire length of its border with Iraq, expected to be 900 km long with fence-mounted ultraviolet intruder detection sensors. The project was subsequently shelved, pending the appointment of a consultant, but tightening security remained a key strategic ambition.

The Saudi leader stressed his intention to bolster the country's regional priorities. The most obvious manifestation of this was the robust Saudi challenge to resurgent Iran. Saudi Arabia signalled that it would no longer accept the Islamic Republic's expanding influence in Iraq, and made clear to the US administration that it would not countenance a US troop withdrawal, which would allow Iranian-linked Shi'ites to cement their domination of Iraq. A Saudi adviser based in Washington DC hinted in a newspaper article in late November that Saudi Arabia might start to fund Iraq's Sunni insurgents, if the USA left a power vacuum in Iraq.

One side effect of Saudi Arabia's position as a bulwark of Sunni influence in the region was to improve the country's relations with the USA. In stark contrast to the situation in 2001, Saudi Arabia was now regarded as a force for regional stability, rather than for division and religious intolerance. The kingdom found itself central to diplomatic efforts to stem the region's slide into further violence. This had the effect of emboldening the Saudi leadership, which became more vocal in its criticism of the US administration, and distanced itself from US foreign policy, particularly over the USA's support for Israel in the Israel-Palestine conflict.

There was a rapid increase in Saudi defence spending, which also drew the country into international controversy, while providing further affirmation of the country's renewed sense of self-confidence. This was demonstrated at the close of the year when the UK's Serious Fraud Office was forced by Prime Minister Tony Blair to abandon a two-year long investigation into allegations that BAE Systems had paid kickbacks to members of the Saudi royal family from a £40 billion arms contract. Senior Saudi officials had applied strong pressure on the UK, threatening to pull out of a new multibillion-dollar contract for British-made Eurofighter Typhoons if the investigation was not halted. British diplomats confirmed that Saudi sources had threatened to end all security contacts, including intelligence sharing on al-Qaida. This made it easier for Blair to justify the climb-down politically, while providing testament to Saudi Arabia's revived international clout. Such a situation could not have been imagined in 2003-04, when the country was assailed by a wave of domestic terrorism and its international reputation lay in tatters.

YEMEN

CAPITAL: Sana'a AREA: 528,000 sq km POPULATION: 20,975,000
OFFICIAL LANGUAGE: Arabic POLITICAL SYSTEM: multiparty republic
HEAD OF STATE AND GOVERNMENT: President (Lt-Gen.) Ali Abdullah Saleh (GPC) (since May '90)
RULING PARTY: General People's Congress (GPC)
PRIME MINISTER: Abd al-Qadir Abd al-Rahman Bajammal (since April '01)
MAIN IGO MEMBERSHIPS (NON-UN): AL, OIC, NAM
CURRENCY: Yemeni rial (end-'06 £1=YR387.532, US$1=YR198.485)
GNI PER CAPITA: US$600, US$920 at PPP ('05)

HAVING promised to step down from office at the outset of the year (see AR 2005, p. 197), the incumbent president, Ali Abdullah Saleh, once more stood for election, winning the 20 September poll with a convincing 77 per cent of the vote. Despite allegations that the vote was rigged in his favour, there was little doubt that Saleh resoundingly defeated his main opponent, Faisal Bin Shamlan.

Observers from the EU who monitored the poll described the election process as "an open and genuine political contest", despite shortcomings such as the overwhelming use of state resources to back Saleh's campaign. Saleh's decisive victory prompted speculation that he would hold onto power until 2013, when he would seek to hand over to his son, Ahmed Ali Abdullah Saleh, thereby potentially starting another Middle Eastern political bloodline.

Saleh's re-election also ensured the continued confidence of large donors. Western donors had been closely monitoring the ballot, deeming that it was key to proving Yemen's democratic credentials and improving its chances of obtaining much-needed aid. The fact that Yemen held an openly contested presidential election—a rarity in the Arab world—helped to improve the international community's disposition towards the country. Indeed, the commitment of US$4.7 billion in support for Yemen at a consultative group meeting in London in November confirmed the international community's support for Saleh's programme.

That reputation for political freedom came under threat with further crackdowns on media organisations in the early part of 2006. In February, the editor of the Socialist party organ, *Al-Thori*, was banned from writing for six months for filing articles critical of the government over corruption, healthcare, and other failings.

Other prosecutions appeared more opportunist. Saleh curried favour with Islamists, supporting the prosecution of the editor of the *Yemen Observer*, which on 4 February had carried "thumbnail" images of three of the cartoons of the Prophet Mohammed first published in Denmark (see pp. 54-56), all of which were crossed out. On 11 February, the paper's chief editor, Mohammed Al-Asadi, was arrested on charges of offending Islam. The *Yemen Observer* had its licence to publish suspended, but its staff continued to produce material and publish it on the paper's website. In December, Asadi was found guilty of denigrating Islam and fined half a million Yemeni riyals.

The authorities claimed a number of successes in combating Islamist militancy as the year progressed, though they suffered an embarrassment with the escape in early February of 23 al-Qaida members from a high-security jail, including Jamal Badawi, the alleged mastermind of the bombing of the US warship, the *USS Cole*, in 2000 (see AR 2000, p. 214).

On 15 September, security forces revealed that they had thwarted two simultaneous attempts to blow up oil facilities in different parts of the country. One attack targeted a Canadian-Yemeni oil storage facility in Dubba port in Hadramawt province, and the other an oil refinery in Marib in the north-east of the country. One security guard was killed. The Yemeni interior ministry said that security officers succeeded in exploding the bombers' cars, killing the four suicide bombers before they could do any damage. On 5 December the US embassy in Sana'a was attacked by a lone agent, just days after prosecutors began the questioning of 22 Yemenis accused of the oil installation attacks in Marib and the Hadramawt.

Cross-border movements between Saudi Arabia and Yemen continued, with Yemen proving a potent source of arms shipments into its northern neighbour. These activities prompted a concerted cross-border response from the two governments, a sign that Saudi-Yemeni relations had improved significantly. Reports of the Saudi Border Guards Directorate General suggest that the amount of high explosives entering Saudi Arabia from Yemen had decreased amid tighter border controls.

ARAB STATES OF THE GULF

United Arab Emirates (UAE)

CONSTITUENT REPUBLICS: Abu Dhabi, Dubai, Sharjah, Ras al-Khaimah, Fujairah, Umm al-Qaiwin, Ajman
CAPITAL: Abu Dhabi AREA: 77,000 sq km POPULATION: 4,533,000
OFFICIAL LANGUAGE: Arabic POLITICAL SYSTEM: non-party republic, comprising federation of monarchies
HEAD OF STATE AND GOVERNMENT: Shaikh Khalifa Bin Zayed al-Nahyan (Ruler of Abu Dhabi), President of UAE (since Nov '04)
PRIME MINISTER: Gen. Sheikh Mohammed bin Rashid al-Maktoum (ruler of Dubai), Vice-President and Prime Minister of UAE (since Jan '06)
MAIN IGO MEMBERSHIPS (NON-UN): AL, OPEC, OAPEC, GCC, OIC, NAM
CURRENCY: UAE dirham (end-'06 £1=Dh7.17090, US$1=Dh3.67280)
GNI PER CAPITA: US$23,770, US$24,090 at PPP

Kuwait

CAPITAL: Kuwait AREA: 18,000 sq km POPULATION: 2,535,000
OFFICIAL LANGUAGE: Arabic POLITICAL SYSTEM: non-party monarchy
HEAD OF STATE: Sheikh Sabah al-Ahmad al-Jabir al-Sabah (since Jan '06)
PRESIDENT ELECT: Crown Prince Sheikh Nawwaf al-Ahmad al-Jabir al-Sabah
PRIME MINISTER: Sheikh Nasser al-Mohammad al-Ahmad al-Sabah (since Feb '06)
MAIN IGO MEMBERSHIPS (NON-UN): AL, OPEC, OAPEC, GCC, OIC, NAM
CURRENCY: Kuwaiti dinar (end-'06 £1=KwD0.56450, US$1=KwD0.28910)
GNI PER CAPITA: US$24,040, US$24,010 at PPP ('05 est, based on regression)

Oman

CAPITAL: Muscat AREA: 300,000 sq km POPULATION: 2,567,000
OFFICIAL LANGUAGE: Arabic POLITICAL SYSTEM: non-party monarchy
HEAD OF STATE AND GOVERNMENT: Shaikh Qaboos bin Said (since July '70)
MAIN IGO MEMBERSHIPS (NON-UN): AL, GCC, OIC, NAM
CURRENCY: rial Omani (end-'06 £1=RO0.75170, US$1=RO0.38500)
GNI PER CAPITA: US$9,070, US$14,680 at PPP ('05)

Qatar

CAPITAL: Doha AREA: 11,400 sq km POPULATION: 813,000
OFFICIAL LANGUAGE: Arabic POLITICAL SYSTEM: non-party monarchy
HEAD OF STATE AND GOVERNMENT: Sheikh Hamad bin Khalifa al-Thani (since June '95)
HEIR APPARENT: Crown Prince Shaikh Tamin Bin Hamad al-Thani (since Aug '03)
MAIN IGO MEMBERSHIPS (NON-UN): AL, OPEC, OAPEC, GCC, OIC, NAM
CURRENCY: Qatar riyal (end-'06 £1=QR7.10930, US$1=QR3.64120)
GNI PER CAPITA: US$10,726 or more ('05 est), -

Bahrain

CAPITAL: Manama AREA: 685 sq km POPULATION: 727,000
OFFICIAL LANGUAGE: Arabic POLITICAL SYSTEM: constitutional monarchy
HEAD OF STATE: Sheikh Hamad bin Isa al-Khalifa (since March '99)
HEAD OF GOVERNMENT: Sheikh Khalifa bin Sulman al-Khalifa, Prime Minister (since Jan '70)
MAIN IGO MEMBERSHIPS (NON-UN): AL, OAPEC, GCC, OIC, NAM
CURRENCY: dinar (end-'06 £1=BD72670, US$1=BD0.37700)
GNI PER CAPITA: US$14,370 (not '05), US$21,290 at PPP ('05)

KUWAIT endured a turbulent year, experiencing three separate emirs, a controversial parliamentary election, and unprecedented media attention on allegations of corruption and financial mismanagement.

The death of the emir, Sheikh Jaber al-Ahmad al-Sabah, in January (for obituary see p. 597) prompted a wave of expectation that the government would show a more decisive hand. Indeed, the smooth succession, in which the ailing crown prince, Sheikh Saad al-Salem al-Sabah, was quickly passed over in favour of the former prime minister, Sheikh Sabah al-Ahmad al-Jaber al-Sabah, suggested that Kuwait would be ready for a unified government more certain of its purpose. Those expectations were soon to be disappointed as the executive and legislative arms of state resumed their infighting. Furthermore, the government reneged on promises to engage in reform of the constituencies.

Disillusion was evident in the outcome of the 29 June legislative election, which handed Islamists a decisive victory. The election result represented a rebuff for senior government figures, such as the energy minister, Sheikh Ahmed al-Fahd al-Sabah. The legislators' main weapon remained their ability to subject ministers to questioning and remove them from their posts, a power which they continued to exercise in 2006.

The election enabled candidates committed to the electoral reform agenda of the opposition Group of 29/Alliance for Change to take 34 of the elected seats in the National Assembly. The Islamic Constitutional Movement (ICM), the Kuwaiti strand of the Muslim Brotherhood, and its allies were the single biggest winners. Voters gave short shrift to pro-government candidates, who were punished for pulling back from promises to persevere with reform. At least 11 loyalist members of the National Assembly lost their seats. Kuwaiti women exercised the right to vote for the first time, but no female candidates made it into the chamber in one of the Gulf's most conservative societies

The results of the election ensured the perpetuation of the rivalry between the government and the Assembly. As if to reinforce the sense of instability infecting the Kuwaiti state, the country was hit by a series of water and power cuts during August. Poor planning had left one of the richest per capita nations in the world with insufficient electricity and water generation to meet a peak in demand.

BAHRAIN shared a boisterous political culture with Kuwait, but the executive still appeared to have the upper hand over the legislature in the tiny island state. Despite a stronger showing in legislative elections by Bahrain's main Shi'ite group, Al-Wefaq National Islamic Society, the second round election results in early December confirmed Sheikh Hamad bin Isa al-Khalifa as the main winner, his alliance of Sunni Islamists and independents retaining a small majority in the National Assembly. Al-Wefaq swept to the top of the poll, with 45 per cent of the total vote and 17 of the 40 seats, 16 gained outright on the 25 November first round of voting, but it found itself in the unusual position of lacking sufficient strength in the Assembly to make its presence felt.

The final results saw Sheikh Hamad emerge as the biggest winner, having retained his grip on the legislature and seen the former abstentionist Shi'ite groups come into the fold. The onus was now on Al-Wefaq to demonstrate to its support base that its decision to end its boycott of the electoral process would reap dividends, in terms of improved services. One big bonus for the Shi'ite bloc was that they succeeded in gaining control of key parliamentary committees. Khalil Marzooq, deputy leader of the Wefaq parliamentary caucus, was elected to chair the crucial legislative and legal affairs committee; while Dr Aziz Abul, an independent Wefaq ally, gained the chairmanship of finance and economic affairs. Another Wefaq leader captured the chairmanship of public utilities and environment. Pro-government groups took two committee posts.

Unlike Kuwait, Bahrain was pushing the pluralism agenda. Among the 40 members of the Shura council (the nominated upper house of the legislature), were 10 women including a Christian and a Jewish human rights activist.

The UAE, unencumbered by obstreperous parliamentarians, enjoyed a smoother political process. Prime Minister Sheikh Mohammed bin Rashid al-Maktoum, who took power in December 2005, moved swiftly to stamp his authority. A new federal cabinet, announced on 9 February, saw the creation of several new portfolios, the removal of others, and eight new faces joining the cabinet. The administration saw a number of senior Dubai business figures and close associates of Sheikh Mohammed appointed, all committed to a pro-reform agenda. With leading Dubai business figures in the highest ranks of cabinet, the expectation was that the federal government would prove even more streamlined and "Dubai like" in its operations. Prime among these new appointees was Mohammed al-Gergawi, chief executive of Dubai Holding, the corporate entity that had overseen many of Dubai's major real estate projects. The new ministers had a mandate to overhaul the outmoded political processes of the federation.

This yielded fruit in the focus on the Federal National Council (FNC), for which the new government promised to hold democratic elections. In the event, the electoral process for the FNC disappointed those anticipating a more extensive plebiscite. Only half of the council would be elected, and these delegates would be selected by electoral colleges (25 per cent of whom were women) rather than via a direct popular vote. Elections to the FNC finally took place on 15 December, with 20 of the 40 members voted in, including one woman.

The UAE's external relations with its two most important allies, the USA and Saudi Arabia, suffered a series of setbacks. In March, a political controversy in the USA over Dubai Ports World's takeover of the UK's P&O, thereby granting the Dubai company control of six US port operations, ended with Dubai Ports World selling off its US operations in the face of political uproar. Relations between the UAE and the USA were strained, despite the attempts by the US government to support the deal.

Ties with Saudi Arabia, strained since the death of the UAE president, Sheikh Zayed al-Nahyan, in 2004, worsened during the year. In July, the Saudi government told shareholders of the US$3.5 billion Dolphin gas pipeline project between Qatar and the UAE that a section of the 370 km undersea link would pass through the kingdom's waters, requiring official consent, yet to be granted. The move did nothing to stop work on the pipeline project but confirmed the heightened tensions between the two largest Gulf states.

SUDAN—LIBYA—TUNISIA—ALGERIA—MOROCCO—WESTERN SAHARA

SUDAN

CAPITAL: Khartoum AREA: 2,500,000 sq km POPULATION: 36,233,000
OFFICIAL LANGUAGE: Arabic POLITICAL SYSTEM: multiparty republic
HEAD OF STATE AND GOVERNMENT: President (Gen.) Omar Hasan Ahmed al-Bashir (since Oct '93), previously Chairman of Revolutionary Command Council (since June '89)
RULING PARTIES: government of national unity comprising mainly the National Congress Party (NCP) and the Sudan People's Liberation Movement (SPLM) (since Sept '05)
MAIN IGO MEMBERSHIPS (NON-UN): AL, AU, COMESA, OIC, ACP, NAM
CURRENCY: Sudan dinar (end '06 £1=SD393.087, US$1=SD201.330)
GNI PER CAPITA: US$640, US$2,000 at PPP ('05)

THE opposition in the country's troubled western region of Darfur—the Sudan Liberation Movement/Army (SLM/A) and Justice and Equality Movement (JEM)—joined forces in January to form the Allied Revolutionary Forces of Western Sudan. But this unity was short lived, as a faction of the SLM/A, led by Minni Minnawi, concluded the Darfur Peace Agreement (DPA) with the Sudanese government in May in Abuja, Nigeria, including a ceasefire, disarming the Janjawid militia, and giving the SLM/A faction a majority in Darfur's regional legislature. This piecemeal agreement proved to be ineffective and divided the opposition in Darfur. Fighting broke out between rival factions of the SLM/A, and Minnawi met US President George W. Bush in July to broaden the peace process, but without a positive outcome. The opposition groups to the DPA formed the National Redemption Front (NRF) to continue their rejection of the peace agreement with the Sudanese government.

Meanwhile, violence against civilians and residents of displacement camps continued to be inflicted by the government-backed militia, the Janjawid, and rebel groups, to the horror of the international community. Sudan's campaign for the chair of the AU was blocked at a summit in Khartoum in January due to the continuing conflict in Darfur, and the Democratic Republic of Congo (DRC) was elected chair instead (see p. 425). In September thousands of people from various parts of the world marked a "global day for Darfur" in protest against the killings, sexual violence and rape, and displacement of people. In March the UN Security Council approved the extension of UN Mission in Sudan (UNMIS); but in June, the Sudanese government suspended the work of UNMIS as it was accused of providing transportation for Sulaiman Adam Jamous, a leader opposed to the DPA. In October, the UN secretary-general's special envoy in Sudan, Jan Pronk, was asked by the Sudanese government to leave the country because he had stated that the national army had suffered defeats by the rebels in the Darfur region. In spite of support for the Sudanese government from the Arab League, mounting pressure by the international community and the threat of sanctions led the government at a meeting in December in Addis Ababa, the Ethiopian capital, to accept a 20,000-strong hybrid force, comprising existing African Union (AU) peacekeepers—who would have the dominant role—assisted by UN troops, to be sent to

Darfur to prevent further destruction and atrocities. Nevertheless, in December the UN began a mass evacuation of humanitarian workers from Darfur because of growing threats from Sudanese government troops and the opposition. Both Oxfam, which provided water, and Action Contre la Faim, which delivered food, stopped their operations. Libya allocated US$4.5 million to the UN to help feed people in Darfur.

Relations between Sudan and Chad to the west were strained, each accusing the other of supporting opposition groups in order to create political instability. Diplomatic relations were broken off when Chad accused Sudan of bombing Chad's capital, Ndjaména, and backing Chadian rebels in Darfur (see p. 254). Relations were resumed when Sudanese President Omar Hasan Ahmed al-Bashir paid a visit to Chad in August. However, incursions and attacks by the Janjawid and Chadian rebels into Chad continued, and UN officials reported in October that villages in southern Chad had been attacked with more than 100 killed. Amnesty International criticised Chad for lack of action against the Janjawid who were carrying out attacks in eastern Chad. Chad declared a state of emergency in December as a result of clashes between Arabs and non-Arabs.

The policy of piecemeal conflict resolution adopted by the Sudanese government in Darfur was also applied in eastern Sudan. In October, the Beja and Rashaida opposition groups concluded the eastern Sudan peace agreement (ESPA) resulting in the cessation of hostilities.

The implementation of the comprehensive peace agreement (CPA) of 2005 (see AR 2005, pp. 201-03) in southern Sudan had been slow and not without problems. A report was published in April which stated that pilot error was to blame for the helicopter crash that killed the former first vice-president, John Garang, in July 2005, although this was disputed by some elements within the Sudan People's Liberation Movement (SPLM), the main southern rebel group led by Garang. As a positive sign, in January the southern militia, the South Sudan Defence Force, headed by Major-General Paulino Matiep, agreed to disband at a meeting in Juba between Matiep and the first vice-president of Sudan and president of the government of Southern Sudan, Lieutenant-General Salva Kiir Mayardit, Garang's former deputy. In April Sudan People's Liberation Army (SPLA) forces (the military wing of the SPLM) began to withdraw from eastern Sudan and relocate to the south. SPLA forces began to lay down their arms and southern Sudanese refugees living in the DRC and Ethiopia started to return to the south as a result of the CPA. The Interim Political Bureau (IPB) of the SPLM held its first meeting in the south in April, under its chairman, Mayardit: discussions covered many issues, including the transformation of the SPLM into a political party, the implementation of the CPA, a review of security at local and national levels, and the SPLM's relations with various political groups in the north. In addition, the government of Southern Sudan, under its vice-president, Riek Machar, mediated between the Ugandan government and the rebel Lord's Resistance Army (LRA) under its leader, Joseph Kony, to end the civil war in Uganda but no final agreement was reached (see p. 237).

The economic and political situation in Sudan remained precarious. Supporters of the political opposition—the Umma Party (UP), the Democratic Unionist Party (DUP), the Communist Party (CP), New Democratic Forces, and trade unions—protested against the rising prices of petrol and sugar while salaries remained stagnant. The security forces violently dispersed the demonstration and one man was suffocated to death and a number of others arrested. Dr Hasan al-Turabi, a rival of President al-Bashir for the leadership of the ruling National Congress Party (NCP), was accused of apostasy by clerics supporting the regime when he advocated the right of Muslim women to marry outside their religion, to pray alongside men, and to adopt a more liberal attitude to the veil.

A first meeting was held in Paris in March of the Sudan Consortium, which comprised Sudan's first vice-president and 12 ministers and state ministers from the government of Sudan and the government of Southern Sudan, together with 130 partners from the international community (including eight ministers of international development). The meeting aimed to discuss the implementation of the CPA, the situation in Darfur, and measures to improve economic performance and development. Nearly US$1.8 billion was pledged in support for development and ongoing humanitarian needs. Turkey sent a delegation in March to discuss ways of assisting Sudan in prospecting for oil and natural gas. China hosted a summit in November of 48 African leaders, including Sudan's, to strengthen its economic co-operation with the continent, and particularly its interest in oil. China imported half of Sudan's oil exports, and it continued to block the imposition of sanctions against Sudan at the UN Security Council, which were being demanded in view of the human rights abuses in Darfur. Opposing China's blocking of sanctions, US President Bush in October signed an executive order which stipulated "blocking property of and prohibiting transactions with" the government of Sudan.

LIBYA

CAPITAL: Tripoli AREA: 1,760,000 sq km POPULATION: 5,853,000
OFFICIAL LANGUAGE: Arabic POLITICAL SYSTEM: one-party republic
HEAD OF STATE: Col Moamar Kadhafi, "Leader of the Revolution" (since '69)
HEAD OF GOVERNMENT: Al-Baghdadi Ali al-Mahmoudi, Secretary General of General People's Committee (since March '06)
MAIN IGO MEMBERSHIPS (NON-UN): AL, OPEC, OAPEC, AMU, AU, OIC, NAM
CURRENCY: Libyan dinar (end-'06 £1=LD2.49520, US$1=LD1.27800)
GNI PER CAPITA: US$5,530 ('05), -

LIBYA'S international rehabilitation continued during 2006. In May the US state department announced that the USA was re-establishing full diplomatic relations with Libya and that a US embassy would be opened in Tripoli. Libya would also be removed from the US list of states supporting terrorism. A new era in bilateral relations would allow "meaningful discussions" on defence of human rights, promoting free expression, and economic and political reforms.

In March France and Libya had signed an agreement to co-operate in the peaceful use of nuclear technology, the first of its type since Libya had abandoned its weapons of mass destruction programme. In December Russian companies were successful in bidding in the third international tender for oil exploration agreements.

Tension with the West remained evident, however. In February, more than 1,000 demonstrators attacked and set fire to the Italian consulate in Benghazi in protest against caricatures of the Prophet Mohammed which had been published earlier in a Danish newspaper (see pp. 54-56). The action against Italy came after an Italian minister, noted for his anti-Islamic stance, had worn a T-shirt on which the cartoons were printed. At least 11 people were killed and many others wounded as police intervened to disperse the protesters. Witnesses stated that some protesters had denounced Moamar Kadhafi's regime, but officials denied this. In March Kadhafi stated that the violence of the anti-Italian demonstration was due to the fact that Italy had not compensated Libya for its actions during the colonial period and he did not exclude further attacks on Italian interests and nationals unless compensation was paid. During talks with Kadhafi in Tripoli in September, the new Italian premier, Romano Prodi, reiterated that Italy's relations with Libya were a priority for his government and in November his foreign minister announced that agreement had been reached with Kadhafi about more specific negotiations on the "complicated problems" of compensation. Agreement was also reached to allow patrols near the Libyan coast by the European Agency for the Management of Operational Co-operation at the External Borders of the Member States of the European Union (Frontex), aimed at curbing illegal migration, on condition that these were conducted by Italy and Malta with Libyan collaboration.

The new trial of the Bulgarian nurses and Palestinian doctor accused of infecting Libyan children with the HIV virus (see AR 2005, p. 204) opened in Tripoli in May and in December they were once again found guilty and sentenced to death, despite scientific evidence from international experts proving that the virus was present before the medics began working at the hospital. Bulgaria, the EU and the USA strongly condemned the verdict.

Kadhafi continued to mediate in the conflict in Darfur and sought to end the resulting tensions between Sudan and its neighbours, Chad and the Central African Republic (see pp. 218; 254). He stated that "it was vital to avoid foreign interference and keep the door shut to outside machinations" and condemned all rebel groups. However in late January UN experts had reported that Libya was one of the states continuing to supply arms and ammunition as well as financial and political support to rebel groups in Darfur despite a UN embargo. On a visit to Mali in April, the Libyan leader called on the Tuareg tribes of the Sahel region to unite and form a "greater Sahara". Although Kadhafi condemned attacks by Tuareg rebels against military bases in northern Mali the following month (see p. 248), questions were raised about Libya's involvement.

Meeting in March, the General People's Congress announced a major cabinet reshuffle. Shukri Ghanim, secretary general of the General People's Committee, was replaced by his deputy, Dr al-Baghdadi Ali al-Mahmoudi, and left the cabinet. Seven new secretariats were created and 13 new ministers appointed. Al-Mahmoudi stated that he would continue the programme of reforms adopted three years earlier and that the new government's priorities were to end unemployment and improve efficiency in the public services. Also in March some 130 political prisoners were released, including all members of the Muslim Brotherhood held in detention (see AR 2005, p. 205) and cyber dissident Abdel Raziq al-Mansuri.

In a speech to youth organisations and associations in late August, Seif al-Islam Kadhafi, the leader's son, outlined his vision of "the Libya of the future". He denounced the "mafia" of public officials opposed to political and economic reforms, stated that "people power" did not truly exist, and deplored the absence of press freedom. He called for a permanent constitution for the next 100 years and for the privatisation of businesses to be pursued in a determined way. Shortly afterwards, addressing revolutionary committees on the anniversary of the revolution, the Libyan leader urged his countrymen to crush the political dissidents and treat them as enemies but also insisted that it was time to engage in self-criticism. He denounced corruption in Libyan society, urged transparency in dealing with public funds, and declared that 1 million Libyans had to be lifted out of poverty. In November official sources stated that Seif al-Islam Kadhafi was leaving the country "to work in an international economic institution" but gave no explanation.

At the beginning of the year Human Rights Watch released a rare report on the situation in Libya. Based on a three-week visit, it stated that the country was undergoing gradual change but that scores of individuals were imprisoned for peacefully expressing criticism of the government or alternative political views. Libya remained a closed and tightly controlled society with no independent press or civil society and no political organisations that were not officially sanctioned. Promised reforms on matters such as freedom of expression and association had been blocked and the claim of "direct democracy" through the People's Congresses was a sham because of the all-pervasive security apparatus. The use of torture also remained a serious problem. Similar conclusions were reached by Reporters sans frontières following a visit to Libya in September. The organisation reported that thanks to satellite television stations such as al Jazeera and the Internet, Libyans were no longer as isolated from the rest of the world as in the past, but the regime still controlled the media and there were no independent press outlets. It was as dangerous as ever to criticise Kadhafi and his family or to tackle issues that were off limits, such as high-level corruption. The revolutionary committees movement maintained its monopoly of power with the press continuing to be simply a propaganda tool.

TUNISIA

CAPITAL: Tunis AREA: 164,000 sq km POPULATION: 10,022,000
OFFICIAL LANGUAGE: Arabic POLITICAL SYSTEM: multiparty republic
HEAD OF STATE AND GOVERNMENT: President (Gen.) Zine el-Abidine Ben Ali (since Nov '87)
RULING PARTY: Constitutional Democratic Rally (RCD)
PRIME MINISTER: Mohammed Ghannouchi (since Nov '99)
MAIN IGO MEMBERSHIPS (NON-UN): AL, AMU, ICO, AU, OIC, NAM, Francophonie
CURRENCY: Tunisian dinar (end-'06 £1=TD2.53390, US$1=TD1.29780)
GNI PER CAPITA: US$2,890, US$7,900 at PPP ('05)

IN January opponents of President Zine el-Abidine Ben Ali announced the creation of a new "democratic coalition" which included Ettajdid, two small left wing parties, and independent personalities, but insisted that there would be absolutely no joint action with the Islamists of the banned an-Nahdah, declaring that "no political parties can speak in the name of Allah". In contrast, Moncef Marzouki, exiled leader of the Congress for the Republic, called for a more inclusive opposition "democratic front" to prepare for a "peaceful revolution" which would exclude only those Islamists who called for violence, the introduction of sharia law, and were opposed to equal rights for women. In October, in an interview with the al-Jazeera television station, he again appealed for peaceful resistance to the government as the only answer for a population tired of repression and corruption. He returned to Tunisia from exile in France shortly afterwards, despite court proceedings against him for incitement to violence and civil disobedience.

President Ben Ali pardoned 1,298 prisoners in February and granted a conditional release to another 359. They included more than 70 members of an-Nahdah and the young "cyber-dissidents" sentenced in 2004. One of the Islamists who was pardoned, Hamadi Jebali, a former member of an-Nahdah's political bureau, later supported demands by the secular opposition for a general amnesty and freedom of expression and association, insisting that Islamist parties were not opposed to democracy. A further 55 Islamist prisoners were released in November.

The authorities remained concerned, however, about the influence of Islamic fundamentalism. In October Ben Ali and the ruling Constitutional Democratic Rally (RCD) called for the mobilisation of the state, political parties, and civil society to combat the growing trend for Tunisian women to wear the hijab (Islamic headscarf), apparently as a result of the influence of certain charismatic preachers on Arab satellite television stations. They stressed their commitment to promoting "the noble values of Islam" as a fundamental element of Tunisian identity but condemned the hijab as something foreign to Tunisian traditions which posed a threat to the state's achievements since 1956 in advancing rights for women. However, the authorities denied claims by local human rights groups that girls were being forced to remove their headscarves in schools and universities. Exiled an-Nahdah leader, Sheikh Rached Al-Ghanoushi, declared that the state had no right to interfere with such matters of personal choice, and some observers argued that the hijab was being used not only as a symbol of Islamic identity but also as an act of defiance against autocratic rule.

The state of human rights within Tunisia was an issue throughout the year. In March celebrations were held across the country to mark the 50th anniversary of independence and included a ceremony in memory of Tunisia's first president, Habib Bourguiba, praised as "the father of independence". Addressing a public meeting organised by the ruling RCD, Abdelwahab Abdallah, the foreign minister, outlined the country's achievements, highlighting the fact that young Tunisians were well educated, that per capita income had quadrupled, and that women were well-represented in all key sectors. He insisted that there were no political prisoners and that freedom of opinion and expression were guaranteed for all citizens. The police dispersed a small group of opponents who gathered in Tunis to demand respect for freedom of association and expression and the release of the remaining 300 political prisoners.

Furthermore, the foreign minister stated in June that Tunisia's election to the new UN Council for Human Rights reflected the international community's confidence in President Ben Ali's efforts to preserve and defend human rights. However, earlier police had prevented the Tunisian League for Human Rights (LTDH) from holding its national congress in Tunis and assaulted several delegates as they attempted to enter the organisation's headquarters. At the same time the International Federation of Journalists highlighted the "grotesque reality" of press freedom in Tunisia, arguing that journalists were driven to acts of desperation while the government issued pious statements about its commitment to press rights. In September Reporters sans frontières included Tunisia on its list of the "15 enemies of the Internet".

In November Ben Ali paid lip service to political reform, stating that he wanted a system of fair competition between the opposition parties and the ruling RCD, and urged political parties, national organisations, and intellectuals to provide him with their views and proposals. He also announced that the country's official human rights organisation would be allowed to make unannounced prison inspections.

In terms of foreign relations, the year was a quiet one. In February Habib Ben Yahia, a former foreign minister, replaced Habib Boulares as secretary-general of the Arab Maghreb Union (UMA). In March US Secretary of Defence Donald Rumsfeld visited Tunis as part of a tour of Maghreb states, for discussions on military co-operation and counter-terrorism. In October the Tunisian ambassador was withdrawn from Qatar amidst accusations that Doha-based al-Jazeera was broadcasting programmes hostile to Tunisia. On a visit to Tunis at the end of October, the Italian premier, Romano Prodi, praised Tunisia, stating that through the interdependence of its cultural relations with Europe, the country was becoming "irreversibly secular and modern". A symbol of this progress was discernable in December when May Eljeribi was elected secretary-general of the Progressive Democratic Party (PDP), thereby becoming the first woman to lead a political party in Tunisia.

Economically, Tunisia remained a success story. The World Economic Forum ranked it as the most competitive Arab and African economy and attributed its success to large-scale institutional reforms, growing investment in human capital, high command of developed technology, and an annual growth in GDP of 6 per cent.

ALGERIA

CAPITAL: Algiers AREA: 2,382,000 sq km POPULATION: 32,854,000
OFFICIAL LANGUAGE: Arabic POLITICAL SYSTEM: multiparty republic
HEAD OF STATE AND GOVERNMENT: President Abdelaziz Bouteflika (since April '99)
RULING PARTIES: National Liberation Front (FLN) heads coalition which also includes National Democratic Rally (RND), and Movement for a Peaceful Society (MSP)
PRIME MINISTER: Abdelaziz Belkhadem (FLN) (since May '06)
MAIN IGO MEMBERSHIPS (NON-UN): AL, OPEC, OAPEC, AMU, AU, OIC, NAM
CURRENCY: dinar (end-'06 £1=AD138.016, US$1=AD71.6000)
GNI PER CAPITA: US$2,730, US$6,770 at PPP ('03-'05)

IN February a presidential decree setting out measures to implement the provisions of the "charter for peace and national reconciliation" (see AR 2005, pp. 209-10) was approved by the cabinet, thereby bypassing debate in parliament. Under its terms, members of armed Islamist groups who surrendered within six months would receive a presidential pardon and would be reintegrated into Algerian society. All members of the security forces and state-armed militias were given immunity from prosecution for actions carried out "while protecting and safeguarding the nation and preserving its institutions". Families of the disappeared and those of terrorists killed by the security forces would be eligible for compensation; both were considered "victims of the national tragedy". The decree explicitly banned any person responsible for the manipulation of religion that had led to the "national tragedy"—i.e. members of the former Islamic Salvation Front (FIS)—from taking part in any form of political activity. Furthermore, anyone who exploited "the wounds of the national tragedy to harm or weaken the state or to tarnish its image abroad" could be punished by imprisonment and a fine.

Leading international human rights organisations immediately issued a joint statement insisting that the decree amounted to a denial of truth and justice to the victims of abuses and to their families and contravened Algeria's obligations under international law. It noted that the decree threatened to penalise families of the disappeared who continued their campaign to discover the truth about the fate of their relatives and to muzzle open debate by criminalising all public discussion about the tragic events of the 1990s. The decree enraged families of the disappeared and local human rights activists who strongly denounced the new measures. Many families of victims insisted that they would never abandon their campaign for truth and justice even if this meant prison sentences, and demanded that the charter be annulled.

In March the authorities began releasing Islamist prisoners, with Ali Benhadj, the second-in-command of the former FIS, and Abdelhak Layada, one of the founders of the Armed Islamic Group (GIA) and its second emir, among the first of some 2,200 prisoners released under the terms of the charter. In September, Rabah Kebir, head of the executive bureau of the former FIS abroad, returned after 14 years' exile in Germany and later, at a press conference, insisted that no one had the right to exclude former FIS officials from political activity. In November the authorities reiterated that there would be no return of the FIS and that its officials would not be allowed to take part in any form of political activity.

Soon after the deadline for the surrender of armed Islamists had expired, the interior minister announced that the results of the charter were "satisfactory but not enough", but failed to give precise details of its progress. In late August, however, he had reported that between 250 and 300 terrorists had surrendered with their weapons to the security forces and that some 800 were still active. The leading daily newspaper described the results of the charter as "derisory". In mid-September the interior minister declared that the state would not close the door to those armed Islamists who surrendered after the deadline of 28 August and indicated that they would still benefit from the provisions of the charter. Meanwhile, the Salafist Group for Preaching and Combat (GSPC) reaffirmed its allegiance to al-Qaida and its determination to pursue jihad in Algeria. It stepped up its attacks on the security forces and police stations, targeting once again the suburbs of the capital, Algiers. In December the group carried out a bomb attack against Western oil workers.

At the end of May Ahmed Ouyahia resigned the premiership. President Abdelaziz Bouteflika appointed the secretary-general of the National Liberation Front (FLN), Abdelaziz Belkhadem, one of his most loyal allies, as Ouyahia's successor. The council of ministers remained virtually unchanged. In June the FLN put forward proposals for a revision of the constitution which would place no limits on the number of times that a president could stand for re-election and would extend the presidential mandate from five to seven years, thereby paving the way for Bouteflika to stand for a third term in 2009. Bouteflika promised a referendum on the revision of the constitution before the end of the year but this was later postponed to 2007.

Earlier, in July the president met a delegation from the Co-ordination of Aarchs, Dairas, and Communes (CADC), a citizens' movement representing the troubled Berber-speaking Kabylia region. He was reported to have reaffirmed the state's commitment to put in place the movement's demands set out in the El-Kseur platform (see AR 2005, p. 208). A degree of stability had returned to much of Kabylia, but in September a spokesman for the citizens' movement stated that only 20 per cent of their demands had been satisfied.

In May Bouteflika declared that France must offer an official apology to the Algerian people for the years of French colonisation before negotiations on the treaty of friendship could resume and continued his bitter diatribes against French colonial rule. However, in October Algeria announced its decision to join the Organisation Internationale de la Francophonie (OIF). Visiting Algiers in November, French Interior Minister and presidential candidate Nicolas Sarkozy announced measures to speed up the processing of visa applications and spoke of the "necessary and indispensable friendship between Algeria and France". When the Russian president visited Algiers in March the two countries signed a major arms agreement, and Russia cancelled an Algerian debt to the former Soviet Union estimated at US$4.7 billion. The sale of the most modern Russian combat aircraft to Algeria caused disquiet among its neighbours and concern in the US and French governments. In June Algeria and the UK finally signed a memorandum on extradition, and Bouteflika made an official visit to London in July.

By December, foreign exchange reserves stood at US$75 billion as a result of high oil and gas prices and foreign debt had fallen to below US$5 billion. Critics of the regime pointed to the lack of transparency in the management of this windfall and growing corruption among state officials. In November the energy and mines minister announced a tax on windfall foreign oil company profits.

MOROCCO

CAPITAL: Rabat AREA: 447,000 sq km POPULATION: 30,168,000
OFFICIAL LANGUAGE: Arabic POLITICAL SYSTEM: multiparty monarchy
HEAD OF STATE AND GOVERNMENT: King Mohammed VI (since July '99)
RULING PARTIES: Socialist Union of Popular Forces (USFP) heads broad coalition
PRIME MINISTER: Driss Jettou (non-party), since Oct '02
MAIN IGO MEMBERSHIPS (NON-UN): AL, AMU, OIC, NAM, Francophonie
CURRENCY: dirham (end-'06 £1=D16.4955, US$1=D8.44860)
GNI PER CAPITA: US$1,730, US$4,360 at PPP ('05)

IN a televised speech to the nation in January, King Mohammed VI announced that the Royal Consultative Council on Human Rights (CCDH), an advisory body created by King Hassan II, would be put in charge of implementing the recommendations of the Equity and Reconciliation Commission (IER) (see AR 2005, p. 210). All public authorities were required to co-operate with the move which was designed to ensure that violations of human rights would never occur again. In his speech the King chose to emphasise continuity rather than innovation, declaring that his work was part of a process begun by his late father. He offered his sympathy to the families of victims but made no apologies for the past. At the end of the month the minister of justice announced that the security forces had arrested 31 members of the police and prison administration on charges of torture and that they would face prosecution under new legislation. In May the CCDH and interior ministry signed an agreement to co-operate in a national action plan to promote a "culture of human rights" in education and training. Meanwhile, the CCDH continued the IER's investigations, locating the graves of another 100 people who had disappeared during the dark years of King Hassan's reign.

At the end of May, in response to a campaign launched by the leading Islamist movement, Al Adl wa-'l Ihsan, to recruit new members ("operation open doors"), the authorities arrested 500 activists and seized books, CDs, posters, and computer equipment in raids carried out across the country. The new interior minister, Chakib Benmoussa, declared that the movement had "placed itself outside the law" and that it was necessary to prevent citizens from being manipulated. Nadia Yassine, the movement's spokesperson, insisted that it was the victim of blind repression. In June the King visited some of the poorest parts of the country, where Al Adl wa-'l Ihsan had been particularly active, and announced a series of important public works projects in an effort to undermine the appeal of the Islamist movement.

At the end of August the interior minister announced that over 50 people had been arrested as part of the dismantling of a well-organised terrorist network, known as Jama'at Ansar al Mahdi, that was planning to declare jihad in Morocco, targeting military bases, foreign embassies, and tourist facilities. He stated that five soldiers, three gendarmes, and a police officer were among those arrested but strongly denied any systematic infiltration of the security forces by Islamists. Meanwhile, a notorious drugs baron arrested in the Rif region revealed the names of several high ranking officers in the police and gendarmerie in the north-west of the country who had given him "protection" over the years; 12 officers were subsequently suspended including the head of palace security. In September the King removed General Hamidou Laanigri, a powerful figure in the regime for many years, from his post as head of national security, demoting him to inspector general of auxiliary forces.

In December Parliament adopted new electoral laws that the interior minister stated would allow parliamentary elections scheduled for September 2007 to take place "in a climate of transparency and responsibility" and included measures to put in place an electoral system "in harmony with the objectives of the law on political parties". However, the smaller opposition parties argued that the measures were likely to eliminate many of them from representation in the new Chamber of Representatives (the lower chamber of the bicameral Parliament).

The Moroccan government described a visit by the Spanish prime minister to Ceuta and Melilla in February—the first since 1980—as "inopportune", reiterated that both towns (which were Spanish enclaves) belonged to Morocco, but stated that the visit would not prejudice the excellent relations between the two countries. In July Spain and Morocco co-sponsored a Euro-African ministerial conference on illegal immigration held in Rabat, but without Algeria's participation. At the beginning of August thousands of people took part in a national demonstration in Casablanca in solidarity with the Lebanese and Palestinian peoples who were under attack from Israel (see pp. 189-90; 197-203). In September Vladimir Putin became the first Russian president to make an official visit to Morocco. The new EU-Morocco fisheries accord was finally signed by the EU Council of Ministers in July and ratified by Morocco's Parliament in December.

WESTERN SAHARA

CAPITAL: Al Aaiún AREA: 284,000 sq km POPULATION: 267,405 ('04 est)
STATUS: regarded by Morocco as under its sovereignty, whereas independent Sahrawi Arab Democratic Republic (SADR) was declared by Polisario Front in 1976
MAIN IGO MEMBERSHIPS (NON-UN): AU
CURRENCY: Moroccan dirham (de facto)
GNP PER CAPITA: n/a

KING Mohammed VI of Morocco made another visit to the Western Sahara in March where he opened a series of development projects in the capital, Al Aaiún, and other towns and pardoned 216 Sahrawi prisoners. The Moroccan press reported that enthusiastic crowds greeted the King. By contrast, Polisario described the visit as a "provocation" and claimed that despite a massive police and military presence Sahrawis chanting slogans in favour of independence had taken to the streets of the capital to protest against the visit before being brutally dispersed by security forces. A local human rights group also reported that a series of arrests of Sahrawi activists had been made before and during the visit.

Khelli Henna Ould Errachid, a former minister for Saharan affairs under King Mohammed's father, King Hassan II, was named as head of the re-activated

Royal Council Charged with Saharan Affairs (CORCAS), composed of 140 newly appointed members, which held its first meeting in April. Its stated priorities included setting out its view of the form that autonomy for the territory should take and creating a united front against Polisario. Delegations were dispatched to several European countries and the USA to promote Morocco's autonomy proposal and to counter Polisario propaganda. Critics of the new council argued that it was undemocratic and unrepresentative and firmly under the control of Morocco's intelligence services.

In his report to the UN Security Council in mid-April, Secretary-General Kofi Annan stated that he and his personal envoy, Peter van Walsum, were convinced that allowing the current impasse to continue was a recipe for violence that would not lead to an independent Western Sahara. They saw no advantage in drafting a new UN plan and the only option was, therefore, direct negotiations without preconditions between Morocco and Polisario to work out a compromise between international legality and political reality that would produce a just, lasting and mutually acceptable political solution and provide for self-determination. Annan insisted that it should be made clear to the interested parties that the UN was taking a step back from the problem and that responsibility for a settlement now rested with them. He expressed the belief that the parties could arrive at a compromise if they engaged in constructive dialogue, and he urged that Algeria and Mauritania be invited to participate in the negotiations. He stated that members of the Security Council should do everything in their power to facilitate the negotiations and he recommended extending the mandate of the Mission for the Referendum in Western Sahara (MINURSO) for another six months. He also announced that all parties had accepted a mission by the Office of the UN High Commissioner for Human Rights that would visit the Western Sahara and the Tindouf refugee camps in May to investigate alleged human rights abuses. Polisario immediately rejected the secretary-general's proposals for direct negotiations and threatened to resume armed struggle if the report was adopted. Algeria also rejected the report stating that any negotiations should concern implementation of the revised Baker plan (see AR 2003, p. 266).

At the end of April the UN Security Council unanimously adopted a resolution that merely reaffirmed its commitment "to assist the parties to achieve a just, lasting and mutually acceptable political solution that will provide for the self-determination of the people of Western Sahara". MINURSO's mandate was extended to 31 October. Both Polisario and Morocco declared that the resolution supported their stance and the impasse continued.

The confidential report of the UN delegation to the Western Sahara and the refugee camps, leaked to the press in early October, confirmed human rights violations by Morocco in the Western Sahara and concluded that the Sahrawis' right to self-determination must be ensured and implemented without delay. It also questioned Polisario's monopoly of power in the camps and the absence of any dissident views. Morocco rejected the report as completely erroneous and biased in favour of Algeria and Polisario.

Reporting to the Security Council in mid-October, Secretary-General Annan stated that the continuing impasse did not benefit either Morocco or Polisario and once again called upon both parties to begin negotiations (without preconditions) aimed at securing self-determination for the people of the Western Sahara. He also said that MINURSO's presence in the territory was indispensable for the maintenance of the ceasefire and its mandate should be renewed for a further six months. Meeting at the end of October the Security Council unanimously adopted a new resolution that made no new proposals but simply reaffirmed the points made in its previous resolution and extended MINURSO's mandate until 31 April 2007. Polisario claimed that the resolution failed to refer to the violation of human rights in Western Sahara by Morocco because of opposition from France.

In November King Mohammed declared that independence for the Western Sahara would risk destabilising the region and create a haven for terrorists and criminal gangs. In early December CORCAS presented its long awaited autonomy proposal to the King. Its president declined to disclose details and merely stated that it guaranteed Sahrawis all their political, economic, social and cultural rights within the framework of Moroccan sovereignty and represented "a final and definitive package to close the dossier". At the end of the month the Moroccan minister of communications stated that the autonomy project would be presented to the UN "very soon".

VI EQUATORIAL AFRICA

HORN OF AFRICA—KENYA—TANZANIA—UGANDA

ETHIOPIA—ERITREA—SOMALIA—DJIBOUTI

Ethiopia

CAPITAL: Addis Ababa AREA: 1,104,000 sq km POPULATION: 71,256,000
OFFICIAL LANGUAGE: Amharic POLITICAL SYSTEM: multiparty republic
HEAD OF STATE: President Girma Woldegiorgis (since Oct '01)
RULING PARTY: Ethiopian People's Revolutionary Democratic Front (ERPDF)
HEAD OF GOVERNMENT: Meles Zenawi, Prime Minister (since Aug '95)
MAIN IGO MEMBERSHIPS (NON-UN): AU, COMESA, ACP, NAM
CURRENCY: birr (end-'06 £1=Br17.2202, US$1=Br8.81980)
GNI PER CAPITA: US$160, US$1,000 at PPP ('05 est, based on regression)

Eritrea

CAPITAL: Asmara AREA: 118,000 sq km POPULATION: 4,401,000
OFFICIAL LANGUAGES: Arabic & Tigrinyam POLITICAL SYSTEM: transitional government
HEAD OF STATE AND GOVERNMENT: President Isayas Afewerki (since May '93)
RULING PARTY: People's Front for Democracy and Justice (PFDJ)
MAIN IGO MEMBERSHIPS (NON-UN): AU, COMESA, ACP, NAM
CURRENCY: nakfa (end-'06 £1=N26.3581, US$1=13.5000)
GNI PER CAPITA: US$220, US$1,010 at PPP ('05 est, based on regression)

Somalia

CAPITAL: Mogadishu AREA: 638,000 sq km POPULATION: 8,228,000
OFFICIAL LANGUAGES: Somali & Arabic POLITICAL SYSTEM: transitional government
HEAD OF STATE AND GOVERNMENT: President Colonel Ahmed Abdullahi Yusuf (since Oct '04)
PRIME MINISTER: Ali Mohammed Gedi (since Nov '04)
MAIN IGO MEMBERSHIPS (NON-UN): AL, AU, ACP, OIC, NAM
CURRENCY: Somalia shilling (end-'06 £1=Ssh2,696.33, US$1=Ssh1,381.00)
GNI PER CAPITA: US$875 or less ('05 est)

Djibouti

CAPITAL: Djibouti AREA: 23,000 sq km POPULATION: 793,000
OFFICIAL LANGUAGES: Arabic & French POLITICAL SYSTEM: multiparty republic
HEAD OF STATE AND GOVERNMENT: President Ismail Omar Guelleh (since April '99)
RULING PARTIES: the Union for a Presidential Majority (UMP) (coalition of the Popular Rally for Progress (RPP), the Front for the Restoration of Unity and Democracy (FRUD), the People's Social Democratic Party (PPSD), and the National Democratic Party (PND)) (since Jan '03)
PRIME MINISTER: Dilleita Mohamed Dilleita (since March '01)
MAIN IGO MEMBERSHIPS (NON-UN): AL, AU, COMESA, ACP, OIC, Francophonie, NAM
CURRENCY: Djibouti franc (end-'06 £1=DFr341.093, US$1=DFr174.700)
GNI PER CAPITA: US$1,020, US$2,240 at PPP ('05 est, based on regression)

ON 18 January, Hilary Benn, the UK's secretary of state for international development, told the Ethiopian prime minister, Meles Zenawi, that the UK was suspending indefinitely its annual £50 million budgetary support to the government of ETHIOPIA, following the brutal treatment of protesters in November 2005, when 129 members of the opposition—including journalists and human rights activists—had been detained (see AR 2005, p. 214). The money would instead be distributed through aid agencies. Later in the year the World Bank and the UK jointly channelled £200 million to Ethiopian districts and civil society groups, thus bypassing the government.

The trial of the 129 opposition activists on charges of treason and attempted genocide opened in Addis Ababa on 24 February. All but three of the defendants refused to enter a plea and 38 were charged in their absence. On 22 March the High Court dropped charges against 18 of the 129. On 8 May the Federal High Court in Addis Ababa began hearing prosecution evidence against 76 of the defendants.

On 18 March the Political Parties Registration Office rejected the requests of three opposition parties—All Ethiopia Unity Party (AEUP), Ethiopia Democratic League (EDL), and Rainbow Ethiopia: Movement for Democracy and Social Justice (RE: MDSJ)—to form a unified Coalition for Unity and Democracy Party (CUDP). However, in May a new political Alliance for Freedom and Democracy (AFD), which incorporated a number of opposition parties, was formed.

Relations with neighbouring ERITREA remained uneasy and often hostile throughout the year. On 7 March bombs exploded at four sites in Addis Ababa, wounding four people, and were attributed to Eritreans and their supporters. On 27 March five more bombs were exploded, killing one person and injuring 17. A further eight bombs exploded in the capital on 12 May killing four and injuring 40. The government announced on 26 June that its forces had killed 111 members of the "anti-peace forces" in the Amhara regional state, who it claimed had entered the country from Eritrea. Talks between Ethiopia and Eritrea, held in London during May, failed to reach any agreement about their border dispute. On 10 August about 150 Ethiopian troops and a senior commander defected to Eritrea. Their leader, Brigadier-General Kemal Gelchin, was an ethnic Oromo and he said that he and his men would join the Oromo Liberation Front (OLF) and fight the government, which was dominated by Tigreans. Further OLF-supporting soldiers, including two senior commanders, defected during September.

Devastating floods in July and August killed 600 people. On 25 August the Disaster Prevention and Preparedness Agency appealed for US$61 million in emergency relief for 199,000 affected people. In October a report by the UK newspaper, *The Guardian*, claimed that the government had suppressed an official inquiry into the killing of unarmed demonstrators in May.

Border tension with Ethiopia increased during January when ERITREA imposed a number of restrictions on the UN Mission in Ethiopia and Eritrea (UNMEE). There followed bellicose and provocative rhetoric from both sides, and border clashes increased as the two countries stepped up troop movements. On 10 March members of the Eritrea-Ethiopia Boundary Commission (EEBC) met in London for the first time in three years. (The EEBC had been established in December 2000.) On 14 March the UN Security Council extended the UNMEE mandate to 15 April. The Eritrean government ordered three international charities—Concern Worldwide, Mercy Corps, and Acord—to leave the country. The UN Security Council on 13 April again extended the UNMEE mandate for a further month and called upon

Eritrea to lift the restrictions that it had imposed upon it. Then in May the UN extended the UNMEE mandate to 30 September, although reducing the maximum strength of the force following the breakdown of the London EEBC talks. UNMEE numbers were reduced to a maximum of 2,300 troops including 230 military observers, instead of the 4,200 troops permitted previously. In September the UNMEE mandate was extended to 31 January 2007. In a speech at Georgetown University, USA, on 30 October, UN Secretary-General Kofi Annan warned that war between Ethiopia and Eritrea could reignite unless meaningful talks were held.

In SOMALIA the rift between President Colonel Ahmed Abdullahi Yusuf and the speaker of the transitional legislature, Sharif Hasan Sheikh Aden, was patched up on 5 January when they met in Aden, southern Yemen. Their quarrel was about the siting of the government, then in Jowhar, some 90 km north of the Somali capital, Mogadishu. They agreed that the government should move to Baidoa (an alternative site favoured by Yusuf) and then on to Mogadishu. On 26 February, 200 of the 275 members of the transitional legislature which had been selected in August 2004 in Kenya (see AR 2004, p. 230), met for the first time in Somalia, in Baidoa. President Yusuf told the legislature: "Somalis are fed up with hostilities, displacement and endless violence. The people want peace, freedom and to live under the rule of law."

Instead, over 22-25 March, heavy fighting took place in Mogadishu, resulting in some 93 deaths. The fighting was between the Islamic Courts' militia and a newly created coalition of warlords and businessmen, the Alliance for the Restoration of Peace and Counter-Terrorism (ARPCT). The Islamic Courts' militia was led by Sheikh Sharif Ahmed Siyar, who was accused of having links with the al-Qaida organisation. His militia numbered 1,500 well-armed fighters, who appeared to be better disciplined than those of the other militias. The ARPCT, meanwhile, included warlords and controlled the greater part of Mogadishu. According to the Islamic Courts, the ARPCT was funded by the USA's Horn of Africa counter-terrorism force, the Djibouti-based Combined Joint Task Force-Horn of Africa (CJTF-HOA). There was fierce fighting in Mogadishu throughout May between the Islamic Courts' militia and the ARPCT, with some 170 people being killed during the month.

By early July the Islamists had come out on top when the last warlord fighting in Mogadishu surrendered after two days of battles in which 140 people were killed. The Islamists now controlled most of Mogadishu and a moderate Islamic leader, Sheikh Sharif Ahmed, said: "From today onwards, we promise the world that this city is safe. We need to overcome tribalism and the Somali enemies. There are so many enemies and in order to defend ourselves against them we need to unite." The prime minister, Ali Muhammad Gedi, called for international peacekeepers to help the government restore stability, but the Islamic Courts rejected the idea of foreign troops in Somalia. Although moderates within the Islamic Courts claimed that they only wanted to bring law and order to Somalia, in June the Union of Islamic Courts (the UIC) had named as its chairman Sheikh Hassan Dahir Aweys, who the US government claimed had links with al-Qaida.

Tensions were heightened dramatically on 20 July when troops from ETHIOPIA crossed the border into SOMALIA to support the Yusuf government in Baidoa and threatened to crush the UIC. The Islamists then threatened to take Baidoa, prompting Ethiopia's information minister, Berhan Hailu, to say that his country would use "all means at our disposal to crush the Islamist group" if it tried to attack Baidoa. By this time, it seemed, the Baidoa-based government had little power and less authority, while the Islamists had created a semblance of law and order in the capital and had taken down the security checkpoints which the warlords had used to exact money, with the immediate result of lowering food prices.

The chairman of the UIC, Sheikh Aweys, called for a holy war against Ethiopia and said that Ethiopia was bolstering the puppet regime of Somalia's President Yusuf, whom he described as a "servant of Ethiopia". About 5,000 Ethiopian troops had crossed into Somalia though neither the USA nor any other member of the UN Security Council condemned the intervention. Observers linked the Ethiopian invasion with the US-led "war on terror" and claimed that the US government supported the Ethiopian move. The leader of al-Qaida, Osama bin Laden, in a tape recording, had backed the UIC, whose leader, Aweys, was on the USA's "most wanted" list of terrorists. At the end of July the UK's foreign office gave its unequivocal backing to the Yusuf government. Then 19 members of the Yusuf government resigned at the same time that the Islamists took over the presidential palace in Mogadishu. The outgoing ministers accused the government of taking orders from Ethiopia. By early August, effective power in Somalia appeared to lie with the Islamic Courts while the Yusuf government in Baidoa was on the verge of collapse.

By November, peace talks between Somalia's transitional national government (TNG) and the UIC had broken down and observers were predicting an all-out war as Ethiopia moved between 6,000 and 8,000 troops to the border and seemed determined to prevent an Islamist government coming to power in Somalia. According to the TNG foreign minister, Ismael Mohamoud Hurreh, a war would erupt if the Islamic Courts were "not checked definitively". In October, Ethiopia's prime minister, Meles Zenawi, had admitted that a few hundred Ethiopian soldiers were in Somalia as "military advisers" while Hurreh claimed that Ethiopia would come to the assistance of the TNG in Baidoa, should the UIC move against it. Meanwhile, ERITREA was reported to have sent 2,000 troops to Somalia to support the UIC.

The situation came to a climax during December. Despite Ethiopian denials, by mid-December an estimated 8,000 Ethiopian troops were fighting alongside the forces of the TNG in Baidoa, while the leader of the UIC, Sheikh Aweys, claimed that Somalia was at war with Ethiopia. The Ethiopian forces prevailed and TNG Prime Minister Gedi, from being all but irrelevant, rode triumphantly into Mogadishu while the UIC forces melted away. By the end of the year, as UIC forces fled southwards, Ethiopia's Prime Minister Zenawi was calling for an international peacekeeping force to be sent to Somalia without delay. Meanwhile, Ethiopian troops would remain in Somalia to help the victorious government pacify the Horn of Africa, after what had turned out to be only a two-week war to oust the UIC. Kenya, as opposed to an Islamist government in Somalia as was Ethiopia, moved troops to its border with Somalia to prevent fleeing Islamists entering the country. However, given the history of endless guerrilla warfare in Somalia, the apparent collapse of the UIC probably signalled the beginning of a new phase in the struggle rather than a clear victory for the interim government, while any lengthy occupation by Ethiopian troops would be more likely to unite Somalis against them than achieve any measure of long term stability.

On January 10, DJIBOUTI gave to the International Court of Justice in The Hague jurisdiction over a long-running dispute (since 1995) with France, covering the alleged violation by France of its "international obligations in respect of mutual assistance in criminal matters" in connection with the investigation into the killing of the French judge, Bernard Borrel, in Djibouti in 1995. France had failed to pass on to Djibouti details of its investigation of the murder. According to Radio France International, the Borrel affair had been "poisoning relations" between Djibouti and France for 10 years.

Two US CH-53E helicopters crashed off the coast of northern Djibouti on 17 February, killing eight US Marines and two members of the US Air Force. Two injured crew were rescued. The US forces were serving with the Djibouti-based US-led Combined Joint Task Force-Horn of Africa (CJTF-HOA), established in 2002 to combat terrorism in Djibouti, Eritrea, Ethiopia, Sudan, Kenya, Tanzania, Uganda, and Somalia in Africa, and Yemen.

On 6 April a Djibouti ferry capsized, killing 113 people, though many more were reported missing.

KENYA

CAPITAL: Nairobi AREA: 580,000 sq km POPULATION: 34,256,000
OFFICIAL LANGUAGES: Kiswahili & English POLITICAL SYSTEM: multiparty republic in British Commonwealth
HEAD OF STATE AND GOVERNMENT: Mwai Kibaki (NARC) (since Dec '02)
RULING PARTY: National Alliance Rainbow Coalition of Kenya (NARC-K)
MAIN IGO MEMBERSHIPS (NON-UN): AU, COMESA, ACP, CWTH, NAM
CURRENCY: Kenya shilling (end '06 £1=Ks135.305, US$1=Ks69.3000)
GNI PER CAPITA: US$530, US$1,170 at PPP ('05)

IN presenting his "something for everyone" budget in June, Amos Kimunya, the new finance minister, projected a growth rate of at least 6 per cent and said that development expenditure would be increased by 38 per cent. Though fuel would cost more, the annual road licence was abolished and several tax and import duty exemptions were announced. The loss-making Telkom Kenya and the profitable Kenya Reinsurance Corporation were scheduled to be privatised.

Allegations of high level corruption dominated the year's news. At its centre was the 2004 Anglo Leasing scandal which concerned government plans to pay the (allegedly fictitious) company £20 million for a sophisticated passport equipment system and another £29 million for forensic services. The investigation into the scandal was revived by John Githongo, the country's former senior corruption official who, from his exile in London, submitted a 36-page dossier to President Mwai Kibaki and Aaron Ringera, head of the Kenya Anti-Corruption Commission

(KACC). In January, shortly before the story hit the press, the KACC summoned 30 people for questioning about the scandal, including the vice-president, two cabinet ministers, several junior ministers, top civil servants, and businessmen. David Mwiraria, the finance minister, protested his innocence and resigned early in February to clear his name. So, too, did George Saitoti, the education minister who, as minister of finance under former President Daniel arap Moi, was accused of being involved in the massive Goldenberg financial scandal of 1990-93 (see AR 1993, p. 250; AR 2004, p. 232). No politician had faced charges over this scandal, but a judicial report submitted in February raised the question of bringing criminal charges against Saitoti. The beleaguered president reshuffled his cabinet.

The government's credibility was further affected by wasteful expenditure on a £7 million vehicle fleet and by evidence in March that it was attacking media freedom. The arrest of three journalists working for *The Standard* newspaper over an allegedly fabricated story about the president was followed by masked police raids on the newspaper's printing press and a private television station, causing extensive damage. The government admitted responsibility, justifying the police action on national security grounds. Despite these setbacks, in July the ruling National Alliance Rainbow Coalition of Kenya (NARC-K)—formed the previous month to replace the faction-divided ruling party, NARC—easily won three of the five National Assembly (unicameral legislature) seats in the north east following the death of five Assembly members in an air crash. These victories, a growing economy, and a split opposition nominally united under the banner of the Orange Democratic Movement, suggested that NARC-K might even win the December 2007 general elections.

Developments on other fronts included severe drought in the north early in the year and the urgent need for food aid; the three-day visit of Hu Jintao, the Chinese President, in April, when an oil exploration deal was signed; the trial, beginning in September, of Thomas Cholmondeley, heir to the Fifth Baron Delamere, on a charge of murdering a suspected poacher on his estate; and, in Nairobi in November, the convening of an international conference on global warming.

TANZANIA

CAPITAL: Dodoma AREA: 945,000 sq km POPULATION: 38,329,000
OFFICIAL LANGUAGES: Kiswahili & English POLITICAL SYSTEM: multiparty republic in British Commonwealth
HEAD OF STATE AND GOVERNMENT: President Jakaya Kikwete (CCM) (since Dec '05)
RULING PARTY: Chama Cha Mapinduzi (CCM)
PRESIDENT OF ZANZIBAR: Amani Abeid Karume (since Oct '00)
PRIME MINISTER: Edward Lowassa (since Jan '06)
MAIN IGO MEMBERSHIPS (NON-UN): AU, SADC, ACP, CWTH, NAM
CURRENCY: Tanzanian shilling (end-'06 £1=Tsh2,499.14, US$1=Tsh1,280.00)
GNI PER CAPITA: US$340 (mainland Tanzania only), US$730 at PPP ('05)

EARLY in January Jakaya Kikwete, who had been elected president in December 2005 on a "new vigour, new enthusiasm, new speed" slogan (see AR 2005, pp. 218-19), made radical changes to the structure of government, establishing some new ministries, including a ministry of public safety and security, and dropping others; 22 ministries emerged in place of the former 19. His 60-strong government (29 cabinet members and 31 junior ministers) blended new appointees with a sprinkling of veterans; many former ministers lost office. Edward Lowassa, the former minister of water and livestock development, became prime minister and Amani Abeid Karume continued as president of Zanzibar. The number of women in the cabinet was increased from four to six and, for the first time in the country's history, two of these women headed the key ministries of finance and foreign affairs; 10 of the junior ministers were also women. Many regional commissioners were dropped and the others moved to different regions. The Civic United Front (CUF), with 31 seats, all from Zanzibar, formed the official opposition in a National Assembly (legislature) dominated by the ruling Chama cha Mapinduzi (CCM), and pressed for new elections in Zanzibar under international supervision.

In presenting the budget in June, Zakia Meghji, the newly appointed finance minister, said that high fuel prices and drought had increased inflation, but the growth rate still exceeded 6 per cent. Donor funding, at 39 per cent of the national budget, remained essential to reduce poverty and to achieve development: 26 per cent of domestic revenue was to be spent on the latter. Large hydropower facilities were to be created and the electricity generation capacity improved. A further 36 corporations were to be restructured, adding to the 11 corporations privatised in 2005.

Unexpectedly, in mid-October, the president, who officially took over the chairmanship of CCM in June, carried out a major cabinet reshuffle. Possibly responding to Assembly members' criticisms, this "wake-up call" entailed moving 10 ministers and eight junior ministers to other ministries. It did not significantly affect the ministries of finance, foreign affairs, and education, each of which continued to be headed by the same woman who held office before these changes were made.

UGANDA

CAPITAL: Kampala AREA: 241,000 sq km POPULATION: 28,816,000
OFFICIAL LANGUAGE: English POLITICAL SYSTEM: multi-party republic in British Commonwealth
HEAD OF STATE AND GOVERNMENT: President Yoweri Museveni (since Jan '86)
RULING PARTY: National Resistance Movement (NRM)
PRIME MINISTER: Apollo Nsibambi (since April '99)
MAIN IGO MEMBERSHIPS (NON-UN): AU, COMESA, ACP, CWTH, OIC, NAM
CURRENCY: new Uganda shilling (end-'06 £1=Ush3,431.43, US$1=Ush1,757.50)
GNI PER CAPITA: US$280, US$1,500 at PPP ('05 est, based on regression)

THE finance minister, Ezra Suruma, admitted in his June budget speech that it had been a difficult year with crippling power shortages and prolonged drought adversely affecting agriculture and causing a sharp rise in food prices. He listed priority areas as rural development, support for the urban poor, industrial development, and the rehabilitation and reconstruction of northern Uganda. In its fight against HIV/AIDS, the importance of using condoms was again stressed; they were exempted from VAT. Uganda itself would finance about 59 per cent of the budget; the UK remained the leading donor, but, like a number of other

Western countries, cut its aid in protest at the way that the presidential election was conducted.

This and legislative elections—the first multi-party elections for 25 years—were held on 23 February. President Yoweri Museveni—allowed to stand for a third term by virtue of a 2005 constitutional amendment (see AR 2005, pp. 219-20)—appealed to voters on the basis of the stability which he had brought to the country, his control of the army, and his economic record: a growth rate of some 6 per cent per year for the past 10 years. His main opponent was Kizza Besigye, leader of the Forum for Democratic Change (FDC), who had opposed him in 2001 (see AR 2001, p. 264) and who accused him of becoming increasingly authoritarian. Besigye's campaign was disrupted by his frequent summonses to court to answer spurious rape and treason charges. Though electoral irregularities did occur, however, the margin of Museveni's victory was not in doubt: he won 59 per cent of the vote as against 37 per cent for Besigye. The ruling National Resistance Movement (NRM) won 191 of the directly elected seats and the FDC 37, while the other parties shared 19 seats between them. Of candidates standing as independents, 36 were successful. The NRM's losses were heaviest in the north. Voters rejected 17 former ministers, underlining the extent of the decline in the government's popularity. The president reappointed Apollo Nsibambi as prime minister to head a top-heavy 69-member government with a vice-president, three deputy premiers, 22 full ministers, and over 40 ministers of state; one of the latter was Museveni's half-brother Lieutenant-General Salim Saleh. The appointees included six women and a number of technocrats.

Always sensitive to external criticism, President Museveni accused Western donors of interfering in internal affairs. He blamed them for recent power shortages and with attempting to curb Uganda's military spending. During a visit to Tanzania and Uganda in June Wen Jiabao, the Chinese prime minister, offered assistance in the agricultural, infrastructural, and other fields. The many problems that the government faced included tackling poverty—one-third of Ugandans still lived on less than one US dollar per day—and fighting HIV/AIDS, which was on the increase.

A pressing problem was to restore peace in northern Uganda, where the rebel Lord's Resistance Army (LRA) ravaged the towns and villages, raping and killing local people and abducting children for use as soldiers or sex slaves. In May Joseph Kony, the LRA leader, requested peace talks; protracted negotiations followed in Juba, southern Sudan, with a senior minister from the Southern Sudan government acting as intermediary (see p. 218). The International Criminal Court (ICC) opposed these talks and insisted that its October 2005 warrants (originally requested by the Ugandan government) for the arrest and prosecution for war crimes of Kony and three other LRA commanders should be respected. In July President Museveni, acting in defiance of the ICC, offered a total amnesty to Kony in exchange for ending the damaging 19-year old conflict. With Kony moving between hideouts in Sudan and the Democratic Republic of Congo, the peace talks made slow progress. A ceasefire agreement was eventually reached, but broke down when the LRA failed to move its troops to designated assembly points. In October the Ugandan Defence Force resumed military operations against the LRA, though Kony still insisted that he wanted an end to the fighting.

NIGERIA—GHANA—SIERRA LEONE—THE GAMBIA—LIBERIA

NIGERIA

CAPITAL: Abuja AREA: 924,000 sq km POPULATION: 131,530,000
OFFICIAL LANGUAGE: English POLITICAL SYSTEM: multiparty republic in British Commonwealth
HEAD OF STATE AND GOVERNMENT: President (Gen. retd) Olusegun Obasanjo (since May '99)
RULING PARTY: People's Democratic Party (PDP)
MAIN IGO MEMBERSHIPS (NON-UN): AU, ECOWAS, OPEC, ACP, OIC, NAM, CWTH
CURRENCY: naira (end-'06 £1=N250.402, US$1=N128.250)
GNI PER CAPITA: US$560, US$1,040 at PPP ('05 est, based on regression)

POLITICAL manoeuvres ahead of the 2007 elections and growing violence in the Delta region were the two most obvious Nigerian concerns during 2006. Political issues could be solved through the ballot box but the harsh realities of the Delta discontent showed little sign of being adequately addressed by the government and threatened to continue as a running sore that demonstrated how oil had proved a mixed blessing for Nigeria.

Unrest in the Delta grew throughout the year. On 11 January armed militants kidnapped four Western expatriate oil workers—a US citizen, a Briton, a Honduran, and a Bulgarian—when they boarded a support vessel serving the international energy group Shell's EA field. The following day the Shell pipeline to the Forcadas export terminal was blown up, forcing Shell to halt the 120,000 barrels per day (b/d) production of the EA field, equivalent to one-tenth of the country's oil output. A new group—the Movement for the Emancipation of the Niger Delta (MEND)—claimed responsibility. MEND warned all Western oil companies to quit the Delta. On 17 January MEND attacked the Benisede flow station and in the fighting which followed at least 17 Nigerian soldiers were killed as well as an unknown number of militants and Shell workers, causing Shell to evacuate vulnerable sites. The government placed the security forces on high alert. MEND demanded US$1.5 billion compensation for environmental damage in Bayelsa state and called for the release of two indigenous Ijaw leaders: Niger Delta People's Volunteer Force (NDVF) leader, Alhaji Mujahid Dokubo-Asari, and the governor of Bayelsa state, Diepreye Alamieyeseigha. On 24 January boatloads of gunmen stormed the offices of the Italian energy company, Agip, in Port Harcourt, killing eight police and one civilian. They stole money from the bank on the premises. At the end of this violent month MEND freed the four hostages that it had seized, on humanitarian grounds, but issued a statement that it would ensure a "February target of a 30 per cent reduction in Nigeria's export capacity".

In mid-February MEND fighters kidnapped nine foreign oil workers in a number of attacks upon Shell installations (six of the kidnapped men were released on 1 March, while the other three were held until later in the month), forcing Shell to shut off 455,000 b/d production. What was seen as a major victory for the Ijaw people occurred on 24 February when the Federal High Court in Port Harcourt ordered Shell to pay US$1.5 billion damages for polluting the Niger Delta. Disturbances continued through to 2 June when eight foreign workers were abducted from an offshore oil platform in the Gulf of Guinea, 60 km from Warri: six were British citizens, one US, and one Canadian. Ransoms were paid for the release of the kidnapped men. On 7 June five South Korean gas workers were kidnapped and 10 security guards killed in an attack on a natural gas plant. MEND repeated its demand for the release of Dokubo-Asari, who however appealed to MEND to release the kidnapped men. By August the kidnapping of oil workers had become standard practice: the men would be released a few days later following the payment of ransoms. President Olusegun Obasanjo ordered a crack down with the response of "force for force" and some 100 arrests were made in the Port Harcourt region over 21-22 August. A new wave of violence followed in October with gunmen linked to MEND attacking boats supplying the oil fields in Rivers State when another 10 soldiers were killed and 25 contractors were abducted. The unrest continued to the end of the year by which time it was reckoned that over the 50 years since oil exploitation began some 1.5 million tons of oil had been spilt in the ecologically unique Delta region. The militants—MEND or other groups—claimed, simply enough, that what belonged to them (the oil wealth) did not come to them. During May, the government issued 17 new oil-drilling licences to companies from China, India, the UK, and Nigeria. One block was reserved for a company linked to the militant activists in the Delta, Niger Delta Limited. Also in May, China agreed to make a loan of US$1 billion to Nigeria for the improvement of its railway system.

In domestic politics, conflict erupted between the president and his deputy. On 6 April the office of the vice-president, Atiku Abubakar, issued a statement calling on President Obasanjo to resign for pursuing an attempt to alter the constitution to enable him to seek a third term. A presidential spokesman invited Abubakar, if unhappy, to step down as vice-president. On 16 May the Senate (the upper house of the bicameral legislature) rejected by voice vote a proposed constitutional amendment that would have paved the way for Obasanjo to seek a third term; Obasanjo accepted the decision and called on the ruling People's Democratic Party (PDP) to plan for the 2007 elections on the basis of the constitution as it stood. On 1 June five cabinet ministers resigned to "enable them to pursue their ambitions for elective office in 2007". Obasanjo found immediate replacements for them. In August General (retd) Ibrahim Babangida (military ruler 1985-1993) announced that he would run for the presidency in April 2007. On 7 September, Obasanjo sent the Senate a report detailing fraud allegations against his vice-president, Abubaker. If proven, Abubaker could be impeached since, as vice-president, he was immune from ordinary prosecution. Abubaker responded to these allegations by claiming that he would produce a list of impeachable offences committed by Obasanjo. At the end of September the PDP national executive suspended Abubaker from the party for three months for anti-party activities.

On 3 August the foreign minister, Ngozi Okonjo-Oweala, resigned following Obasanjo's abrupt termination of her remaining responsibilities for economic reforms. She had formerly been finance minister and was widely credited with masterminding the cancellation of Nigeria's US$18 billion of debt. Her anti-corruption campaign, which had led to the jailing of Nigeria's most senior police officer and the dismissal of a number of judges and senior customs officials, had brought her into conflict with some of the most powerful interests in the country (see AR 2005, p. 222). Joy Ogwu of the Nigeria Institute of International Affairs was named foreign minister.

Early in the year violent protests occurred in the northern, mainly Muslim states of the country at the publication in a Danish newspaper during 2005 of satirical cartoons of the Prophet Mohammed, leading to between 55 and 80 deaths (see pp. 54-56). The protests led to fighting between Muslims and Christians in Maiduguri, Katsina, Bauchi, and Onitsha. The Sultan of Sokoto, Muhammadu Maccido, was killed in an air crash at the end of October. A direct descendant of Usman dan Fodio, Maccido, as sultan, was president of the Supreme Council of Islamic Affairs in Nigeria. He was one of the most influential traditional rulers in Africa.

On 19 October, President Obasanjo declared a state of emergency in Ekiti state and appointed Brigadier-General (retd) Tunji Olurin to administer and maintain security for six months. The president suspended both the state legislature and the governor, Ayodele Fayose. Prior to this, on 16 October, the legislature had voted to impeach Fayose after he had been indicted on charges of corruption. However, the impeachment proceedings were ruled unconstitutional and Obasanjo intervened to prevent the state descending into chaos.

The year ended with a major oil-related tragedy when hundreds of Nigerians in Lagos were killed after fuel from a broken pipeline exploded to burn many people alive and leave bodies scattered over the streets. In the previous 10 years some 2,000 Nigerians had been killed in similar circumstances as people desperate for oil took jerry cans to the site of a spill to scoop oil from puddles below the pipeline.

GHANA—SIERRA LEONE—THE GAMBIA—LIBERIA

Ghana

CAPITAL: Accra AREA: 239,000 sq km POPULATION: 22,113,000
OFFICIAL LANGUAGE: English POLITICAL SYSTEM: multiparty republic in British Commonwealth
HEAD OF STATE AND GOVERNMENT: President John Agyekum Kufuor (since Jan '01)
RULING PARTY: New Patriotic Party (NPP)
MAIN IGO MEMBERSHIPS (NON-UN): AU, ECOWAS, ACP, CWTH, NAM
CURRENCY: cedi (end-'06 £1=C18,009.5, US$1=C9,224.08)
GNI PER CAPITA: US$450, US$2,370 at PPP ('05 est, based on regression)

Sierra Leone

CAPITAL: Freetown AREA: 72,000 sq km POPULATION: 5,525,000
OFFICIAL LANGUAGE: English POLITICAL SYSTEM: multiparty republic in British Commonwealth
HEAD OF STATE AND GOVERNMENT: President Ahmad Tejan Kabbah (since March '96)
RULING PARTY: Sierra Leone People's Party (SLPP)
MAIN IGO MEMBERSHIPS (NON-UN): AU, ECOWAS, OIC, ACP, CWTH, NAM
CURRENCY: leone (end-'06 £1=Le5,806.48, US$1=Le2,973.94)
GNI PER CAPITA: US$220, US$780 at PPP ('05)

The Gambia

CAPITAL: Banjul AREA: 11,300 sq km POPULATION: 1,517,000
OFFICIAL LANGUAGE: English POLITICAL SYSTEM: multiparty republic in British Commonwealth
HEAD OF STATE AND GOVERNMENT: President (Col) Yahya Jammeh (APRC) (since Sept '96)
RULING PARTY: Alliance for Patriotic Reorientation and Construction (APRC)
MAIN IGO MEMBERSHIPS (NON-UN): AU, ECOWAS, ACP, CWTH, OIC, NAM
CURRENCY: dalasi (end-'06 £1=D54.2782, US$1=D27.8000)
GNI PER CAPITA: US$290, US$1,920 at PPP ('05 est, based on regression)

Liberia

CAPITAL: Monrovia AREA: 97,750 sq km POPULATION: 3,283,000
OFFICIAL LANGUAGE: English POLITICAL SYSTEM: multiparty republic
HEAD OF STATE AND GOVERNMENT: President Ellen Johnson-Sirleaf (since Jan '06)
RULING PARTY: Unity Party
MAIN IGO MEMBERSHIPS (NON-UN): AU, ECOWAS, ACP, NAM
CURRENCY: Liberian dollar (end-'06 £1=L$97.6225, US$1=L$50.0000)
GNI PER CAPITA: US$130 ('05), -

IN a major cabinet reshuffle of 28 April, President John Kufuor of GHANA dropped several key ministers, including those who had declared their intention to contest the 2008 presidential elections, the most prominent of whom was the minister for education and sports, Yaw Osafo-Maafo. The president, serving his second and final term, would not be eligible to stand in 2008. He made four new appointments while nine other ministers took over new responsibilities. The president completed his ministerial changes on 13 May, when he nominated a further six ministers. Forty deputy ministers were also appointed.

On 24 October a report in *The Ghanaian Chronicle* claimed that Kufuor had accused former President Jerry Rawlings of "going round the globe, soliciting funds to destabilise the nation". Kufuor suggested that Rawlings had visited an "oil rich country" and asked its leader to give him money to help overthrow the Kufuor government. Rawlings denied the story and called upon Kufuor to provide proof of the allegation.

By the end of the year New Patriotic Party (NPP) delegates were preparing to hold a congress to elect their presidential candidate for the 2008 elections and were entertained by a series of parties given by presidential hopefuls. The most important question was whether the vice-president, Aliu Mahama, was going to stand; his decision was likely to prove of decisive importance for the NPP's chances in 2008.

Other developments during the year included the death, in February, of Peggy Appiah, the daughter of Sir Stafford Cripps (the UK chancellor of the exchequer, 1947-50). Her marriage in 1953 to Joe Appiah, a leading politician then and for years to come, predictably caused controversy in Britain at that time. In Ghana she produced a number of books retelling Ashanti stories.

On 8 April there was a disaster on Lake Volta when a packed ferry capsized and 120 people were drowned.

At the very end of 2005 SIERRA LEONE witnessed the withdrawal of the last of 17,500 UN peacekeeping forces (the UN Mission in Sierra Leone, UNAMSIL) that had been in the country for three years; as the new year began the government had to rely upon its own army and police for the maintenance of law and order in a country still deeply troubled after 11 years of civil war. The UN operation had been seen as one of Africa's success stories. Meanwhile, perhaps prematurely, London-based travel companies were beginning to market Sierra Leone as a tourist destination for off-season sun and surf vacations.

On 18 January Radio UNAMSIL reported that Sierra Leone and China had signed a military pact under the terms of which a Chinese surveillance vessel would patrol Sierra Leone waters to prevent illegal fishing and smuggling. China also undertook to train the maritime wing of the Republic of Sierra Leone Armed Forces.

Preparations began for the presidential elections due in 2007 at the expiration of President Ahmad Tejan Kabbah's term. On 11 April Radio Democracy reported that the Political Parties Registration Commission had registered the People's Movement for Democratic Change (PMDC) as a political party. The PMDC, led by its interim chairman, Charles Margai, then announced its intention to field candidates in the 2007 presidential and legislative elections.

On 11 May state prosecutors charged a former US soldier, Michael Chemidlin, and two Sierra Leonians, Felix Rogers and Collins Kamara, with conspiracy against the state through an alleged plot to help the former president of LIBERIA, Charles Taylor, escape from detention at the Special Court for Sierra Leone set up with UN backing as a war crimes tribunal. Taylor, who was first brought before the court in April, was later transferred to The Hague for trial (see p. 463).

Also in May, the IMF approved a three-year arrangement for Sierra Leone under its Poverty Reduction and Growth Facility (PRGF) for a total of SDR31.1 million. The facility was in support of the government's 2006-08 economic programme. A first instalment of SDR4.7 million was immediately available.

Although 2006 saw much welcome progress, Sierra Leone continued to face formidable problems. Thus, four years after President Ahmad Kabbah declared the civil war over, Sierra Leone remained the second poorest country in the world in which, for example, more children died before the age of five than anywhere else. Much of the capital, Freetown, remained without electricity or proper water supplies. As a young man, who would not give his name for fear of retribution, said to the UK's *The Independent* newspaper: "This country is like a tinderbox, it will only take one spark." The biggest problem concerned the large number of unemployed and disenchanted youth. It was widely feared that the elections due in June 2007 could provide the spark to set off a new wave of unrest. Meanwhile, the victims of war violence had not received compensation and the ongoing disarmament programme was causing resentment. On the brighter side, a massive programme to vaccinate all under-fives against measles and provide them with free mosquito nets was underway and making some progress.

In THE GAMBIA, on 22 March, the president's office announced that the security forces had uncovered a coup plot on the previous day by a group of army officers who intended to overthrow the government. Colonel Ndure Cham, chief of the defence staff, was its leader, but he escaped capture while a number of other officers were arrested. Colonel Lang Tombong Tamba was appointed new chief of staff. The plot was uncovered when President Yahya Jammeh was out of the country on an official visit to Mauritania. On his return the president vowed to set an example that would put an end to what he described as "ruthless, callous and shameless acts of treachery and sabotage". He referred to "possible outside influence" though he did not name any country or group. However, one of the plotters later appeared on television and said that he had been instructed to liaise with neighbouring Senegal, and it was believed that Cham had fled to that country. On 2 May, 16 people who had been arrested in March in connection with the plot were charged with conspiracy and treason. They included the former head of the National Intelligence Service, Adulaye Kujaby, the former chief of immigration services, Tamsir Jassy, and the former treasury director, Alieu Jobe.

Presidential elections held on 22 September saw Jammeh, of the ruling Alliance for Patriotic Reorientation and Construction (APRC), re-elected for the third time. He obtained 67 per cent of the vote as opposed to his nearest rival, Ousainou Darboe, of the United Democratic Party (UDP), who polled 27 per cent. On 28 September an Economic Community of West African States (ECOWAS) observer mission reported that the elections had been "generally peaceful, free, fair and transparent" although Darboe claimed that there had been some intimidation of voters.

Following his election victory the president announced a cabinet reshuffle on 19 October, with further changes on 25 October. The new cabinet was sworn in on 27 October.

Ellen Johnson-Sirleaf was sworn in as president of LIBERIA on 16 January, thereby becoming the first female head of state in Africa. In her inaugural address she promised a "fundamental break" with the country's violent past. The ceremony was witnessed by a gathering of thousands of Liberians as well as foreign dignitaries, including President Olusegun Obasanjo of Nigeria and President Thabo Mbeki of South Africa. Johnson-Sirleaf's first task was to appoint a new cabinet, the members of which required confirmation by the newly elected legislature, which was also sworn in on 16 January. Edwin Snowe, an independent and former son-in-law of former president Charles Taylor, was elected speaker of the House of Representatives (the lower chamber). He defeated Dusty Wolokollie from the ruling Unity Party, by 48 votes to 13, a reminder for the president that she would face substantial opposition from forces associated with the past. Snowe was especially controversial since he was subject to a UN travel ban.

On 14 February Johnson-Sirleaf appointed Frances Johnson Morris as justice minister; she had formerly been chair of the National Election Commission (NEC) and her elevation led George Weah's opposition Congress for Democratic Change (CDC) to portray the appointment as a "reward for doctoring the elections". Having pledged to tackle corruption, the president dismissed the staff of the ministry of finance in February while saying that employees could reapply for their jobs. However, she instructed the finance minister, Antoinette Sayeh, to screen all employees "to reflect honesty, transparency and efficiency".

In an attempt to come to terms with the country's dark past, Johnson-Sirleaf was under growing pressure to bring Charles Taylor to justice. On 17 March Liberia requested that Nigeria extradite Taylor who had been indicted for war crimes by the UN's Special Court for SIERRA LEONE. Following an attempt to escape, Taylor was captured by Nigerian police on 29 March near the Cameroon border and sent to Monrovia from whence he was transported to the Special Court in Freetown, the capital of Sierra Leone. In June the UN Security Council authorised his transfer to the International Criminal Court at The Hague in the Netherlands. In a further attempt to heal the wounds of the past, on 10 October Liberia's Truth and Reconciliation Commission (TRC) began hearings from victims and perpetrators of the civil war.

On 31 March the UN Security Council extended the mandate of the UN Mission to Liberia (UNMIL) to 30 September, and on 29 September extended it again until 31 March 2007. In June the UN lifted various sanctions that had been imposed on Liberia in 2001 and 2002, including the arms embargo, so that this would not apply to the Liberia Special Security Services (SSS).

On 6 June the army began to recruit women into the new post-war force in order to achieve a gender balance. On 1 August the president carried out a cabinet reshuffle following a fire in the presidential mansion that had begun in the office of the minister of state for presidential affairs, and the minister, Morris Dukuly, was dismissed. It transpired that the fire had started shortly after a visit to Dukuly's office by Sekou Damate Conneh, leader of the disbanded rebel Liberians United for Reconciliation and Democracy (LURD).

In October Johnson-Sirleaf signed into law new forestry legislation, which was a precondition for ending sanctions on timber exports, to ensure an accountable, transparent, government-controlled forestry sector.

Like its neighbour Sierra Leone, Liberia faced a long, hard path to a better life in the aftermath of its brutal civil war. The government was often unable to pay the official wage of US$30 a month and much medical care depended upon the international aid agency, Merlin, which ran almost half of the country's fragile health service. Many donors, believing that the emergency (of the civil war) was over, were beginning to leave. The economy, however, had been all but destroyed and Liberia would need external assistance for a long time to get back on its feet.

WEST AFRICAN FRANCOPHONE STATES—CENTRAL AFRICAN FRANC ZONE

SENEGAL—MAURITANIA—MALI—GUINEA—CÔTE D'IVOIRE—BURKINA FASO—TOGO—BENIN—NIGER

Senegal

CAPITAL: Dakar AREA: 197,000 sq km POPULATION: 11,658,000
OFFICIAL LANGUAGE: French POLITICAL SYSTEM: multiparty republic
HEAD OF STATE AND GOVERNMENT: President Abdoulaye Wade (since April '00)
RULING PARTY: Front for Changeover (FAL) coalition
PRIME MINISTER: Macky Sall (since April '04)
MAIN IGO MEMBERSHIPS (NON-UN): AU, ECOWAS, UEMOA, ACP, OIC, NAM, Francophonie
CURRENCY: CFA franc (end-'06 £1=CFAFr970.576, US$1=CFAFr497.107)
GNI PER CAPITA: US$710, US$1,770 at PPP ('05 est, based on regression)

Mauritania

CAPITAL: Nouakchott AREA: 1,026,000 sq km POPULATION: 3,069,000
OFFICIAL LANGUAGES: French & Arabic POLITICAL SYSTEM: multiparty republic under military rule
HEAD OF STATE AND GOVERNMENT: Colonel Ely Ould Mohamed Vall (since Aug '05)
RULING PARTY: Coalition of Forces for Democratic Change (CFCD) (since Dec '06)
PRIME MINISTER: Sidi Mohamed Ould Boubacar (since August '05)
MAIN IGO MEMBERSHIPS (NON-UN): AU, UEMOA, AMU, AL, ACP, OIC, NAM, Francophonie
CURRENCY: ouguiya (end-'06 £1=O529.701, US$1=O271.300)
GNI PER CAPITA: US$560, US$2,150 at PPP ('05 est, based on regression)

Mali

CAPITAL: Bamako AREA: 1,240,000 sq km POPULATION: 13,518,000
OFFICIAL LANGUAGE: French POLITICAL SYSTEM: multiparty republic
HEAD OF STATE AND GOVERNMENT: President Gen. (retd) Amadou Toumani Touré (since June '02)
RULING PARTY: Alliance for Democracy in Mali (ADEMA) is main party in presidential majority
PRIME MINISTER: Ousmane Issoufi Maiga (since April '04)
MAIN IGO MEMBERSHIPS (NON-UN): AU, ECOWAS, UEMOA, AL, ACP, OIC, NAM, Francophonie
CURRENCY: CFA franc (see above)
GNI PER CAPITA: US$380, US$1,000 at PPP ('05)

Guinea

CAPITAL: Conakry AREA: 246,000 sq km POPULATION: 9,402,000
OFFICIAL LANGUAGE: French POLITICAL SYSTEM: multiparty republic
HEAD OF STATE AND GOVERNMENT: President (Gen.) Lansana Conté (since Dec '93); previously Chairman of Military Committee for National Recovery (from April '84)
RULING PARTY: Party of Unity and Progress (PUP)
PRIME MINISTER: Fodé Bangoura, Minister of State for Presidential Affairs and Co-ordination of Government Action (since May '06)
MAIN IGO MEMBERSHIPS (NON-UN): AU, ECOWAS, ACP, OIC, NAM, Francophonie
CURRENCY: Guinean franc (end-'06 £1=GFr10,845.9, US$1=GFr5,555.00)
GNI PER CAPITA: US$370, US$2,240 at PPP ('05)

Côte d'Ivoire

CAPITAL: Yamoussoukro (official) Abidjan (de facto) AREA: 322,000 sq km POPULATION: 18,154,000
OFFICIAL LANGUAGE: French POLITICAL SYSTEM: transitional government under international supervision
HEAD OF STATE AND GOVERNMENT: President Laurent Gbagbo (since Oct '00)
RULING PARTIES: Ivorian Popular Front government controls south; rebel New Forces control north
PRIME MINISTER: Charles Konan Banny (since Dec '05)
MAIN IGO MEMBERSHIPS (NON-UN): AU, ECOWAS, UEMOA, ACP, OIC, NAM, Francophonie
CURRENCY: CFA franc (see above)
GNI PER CAPITA: US$840, US$1,490 at PPP ('05)

Burkina Faso

CAPITAL: Ouagadougou AREA: 274,000 sq km POPULATION: 13,228,000
OFFICIAL LANGUAGE: French POLITICAL SYSTEM: multiparty republic
HEAD OF STATE AND GOVERNMENT: President (Capt.) Blaise Compaoré (CDP) (since Dec '91); previously Chairman of Popular Front (from Oct '87)
RULING PARTY: Congress for Democracy and Progress (CDP)
PRIME MINISTER: Paramanga Ernest Yoli (since Nov '00)
MAIN IGO MEMBERSHIPS (NON-UN): AU, ECOWAS, UEMOA, ACP, OIC, NAM, Francophonie
CURRENCY: CFA franc (see above)
GNI PER CAPITA: US$400, US$1,220 at PPP ('03-'05)

Togo

CAPITAL: Lomé AREA: 57,000 sq km POPULATION: 6,145,000
OFFICIAL LANGUAGES: French, Kabiye & Ewem POLITICAL SYSTEM: multiparty republic
HEAD OF STATE AND GOVERNMENT: President Faure Gnassingbé (RPT) (since May '05)
RULING PARTY: Rally of the Togolese People (RPT)
PRIME MINISTER: Prime Minister Yaovi (Yao) Agboyibo (Action Committee for Renewal (CAR)) (since Sept '06)
MAIN IGO MEMBERSHIPS (NON-UN): AU, ECOWAS, ACP, OIC, NAM, Francophonie
CURRENCY: CFA franc (see above)
GNI PER CAPITA: US$350, US$1,550 at PPP ('05 est, based on regression)

Benin

CAPITAL: Porto Novo AREA: 113,000 sq km POPULATION: 8,439,000
OFFICIAL LANGUAGE: French POLITICAL SYSTEM: multiparty republic
HEAD OF STATE AND GOVERNMENT: President Yayi Boni (since April '06)
RULING PARTY: Union for the Benin of the Future (UBF)
MAIN IGO MEMBERSHIPS (NON-UN): AU, ECOWAS, UEMOA, ACP, OIC, NAM, Francophonie
CURRENCY: CFA franc (see above)
GNI PER CAPITA: US$510, US$1,110 at PPP ('05)

Niger

CAPITAL: Niamey AREA: 1,267,000 sq km POPULATION: 13,957,000
OFFICIAL LANGUAGE: French POLITICAL SYSTEM: multiparty republic
HEAD OF STATE AND GOVERNMENT: President Mamadou Tandja (since Dec '99)
RULING PARTY: National Movement for a Society of Development (MNSD)
PRIME MINISTER: Hama Amadou (since Jan '00)
MAIN IGO MEMBERSHIPS (NON-UN): AU, ECOWAS, UEMOA, ACP, OIC, NAM, Francophonie
CURRENCY: CFA franc (see above)
GNI PER CAPITA: US$240, US$800 at PPP ('05 est, based on regression)

IN SENEGAL, as in several African countries in 2006, preparation for elections, both presidential and parliamentary, dominated the country's political life. Having already postponed legislative elections due early in the year for 12 months, much of 2006 was taken up with preparations for the contest. President

Abdoulaye Wade demonstrated his ambition to remain in office—despite officially turning 80 (some believed him older)—and run for another seven-year term. Manoeuvring among Senegal's multiple opposition parties continued, although Wade's autocratic policies meant that his blandishments for a government of national unity were largely refused. By the end of the year two main coalitions had emerged, the Alternance '07 included the Alliance of the Forces of Progress (AFP) of Moustapha Niasse and a number of minor parties, and the Rewmi, which combined the Socialist Party of Ousmane Tanor Dieng and the supporters of Wade's former closest lieutenant, former prime minister Idrissa Seck. He had fallen out with his boss in 2005 and was still under threat of legal proceedings, and his candidacy was uncertain.

The president was increasingly preoccupied with the pursuit of his "grands projets" which he intended to be a part of his legacy, but which were only just beginning to get underway. These included a new international airport, on which construction had begun; and a new toll-paying motorway to connect to the airport, a "university of the future", and a new administrative capital city, which were still at the drawing-board stage. Also included among these plans was an Islamic summit, at which Wade hoped to launch a dialogue between the West and the Islamic world. This had to be postponed until 2008, just as a planned arts festival—successor to the pioneering Negro Arts Festival of 1966—was further delayed.

One constraint on the "projets" was cost, as Senegal was not resource rich, and was one of the biggest recipients of donor aid per capita in Africa. The economy had, however, been doing a little better under Wade's liberal policies, and had registered real GDP growth of over 5 per cent in the previous three years

The low intensity conflict in the rebellious southern province of Casamance, which had been quiescent for months following a tentative peace agreement with a faction of the Movement of Democratic Forces of Casamance (MFDC), flared up again in August, when government troops launched an offensive against the wing of the movement that had not accepted the peace. There was more concern in October when Salif Sadio, leader of the dissident wing, escaped from detention in the regional capital, Ziguinchor, and disappeared from view. The assassination at the end of the year of Oumar Lamine Badji, president of the regional council of Casamance, threatened further to inflame the situation.

While preparations for presidential elections in Mauritania in March 2007 continued, the economy was experiencing an oil boom of 20 per cent growth (although the World Bank had originally forecast 28 per cent), whereas growth in 2005 had been only 5.4 per cent. It was expected that oil exports, which began early in 2006, would reach 18.6 million barrels. In the context of the world energy situation there was no shortage of buyers: the first 1 million barrels went to China, with a further supply contracted. A dispute with Woodside Energy, the Australian operator of the Chinguetti offshore oilfields, was resolved in April with an increase agreed in royalties payments, although details remained secret. Increased government revenues meant that as of April the number of government workers was officially doubled.

Elections to the National Assembly (the lower house of the bicameral legislature) in November and December showed the strength of the former opposition to the regime which had been overthrown by a coup in 2005 (see AR 2005, pp. 229-30). The former opposition consisted of a coalition of parties, led by Ahmed Ould Daddah, the half-brother of Mauritania's first president, Moktar Ould Daddah, who was overthrown by the military in 1978. His group, the Coalition of Forces for Democratic Change (CFDC), obtained the largest number of seats, but there was also confusion because of the large number of successful independent candidates. These were, in some cases, political figures who had once been part of the presidential majority. It was alleged that these candidates had been encouraged by the military, and had some links to former President Maaouyia Ould Taya, overthrown in the coup of 2005. President Colonel Ely Ould Mohammed Vall, who had staged the coup, remained officially above politics and seemingly intent on handing over power by June 2007.

Some of the independents were identifiable Islamist candidates. Islamic parties, however, were officially banned, the argument being that all Mauritanians were Muslims (it was, after all, one of Africa's few Islamic republics), so Islamic parties were unnecessary. There had in the past been concerns over ties between Mauritanian Islamic groups and Middle Eastern radicals, from Ba'athists to suspicions of the presence of al-Qaida.

It was for the most part a quiet year in MALI, though again preparations for presidential elections in 2007 began to raise political tensions, even if President Amadou Toumani Touré seemed confident of returning for a second five-year term.

In May, the northern desert capital of Kidal, and Mekaka, another nearby base, suffered attack by a group of Touareg rebels believed to be army deserters. They were demanding better economic conditions for their people, and withdrew after a day's occupation. The surprise attack showed the continual potential for trouble in the whole Sahara-Sahel area, especially in the light of the mounting crisis in the Middle East and its echoes in Africa.

GUINEA's year was dominated by the long drawn-out twilight of President Lansana Conté, in office since 1984. Though virtually incapacitated by diabetes in his home village, Wawa, he was not too ill for occasional sorties into the political arena. He was able, for example, suddenly to intervene to dismiss the reforming prime minister, Cellou Dalein Diallo, disagreeing with the latter's sweeping cabinet reshuffle in which Conté loyalists had been removed. The sacking was followed by a reconstitution of the former government in which one of the president's closest allies, Fodé Bangoura, returned with more powers. He had already exercised considerable power as secretary-general to the presidency, and in May was made minister of state for presidential affairs responsible for co-ordinating defence, security, and economic and financial policy, effectively replacing the post of prime minister, which was abolished.

President Conté was out of the country for medical treatment in Geneva from August to October, and left Bangoura in charge. There was further political tension in December when the president got up from his sickbed to release from detention a rich business colleague, El Hadj Mamadou Sylla, who had been jailed on Bangoura's instigation—following donor pressure—on corruption charges. The release outraged Guinean public opinion, already in a febrile condition.

Meanwhile the country's economic disintegration, worsened by the lack of any firm governmental control, was of increasing concern. Throughout the year there had been a series of country-wide general strikes protesting at the galloping cost of living, food shortages, and the decline in public services such as education and health. International agencies reported a heavy fall in school registration and a rise in malnutrition, especially among children. In one strike in early June, 11 demonstrators were killed and many more injured, and there were increasing disturbances towards the end of the year. There was speculation that the army, headed by General Kerfalla Camara, although apparently supporting the government, might be forced to intervene politically, as it was being increasingly deployed to support an extreme unpopular regime.

The year 2006 in CÔTE D'IVOIRE was a strange echo of the previous one in which "no war no peace" was the prevailing slogan and the political stalemate, however bitter, never deteriorated into open conflict. The basic parameters of crisis remained unchanged: the country was de facto partitioned between north and south, and peace was maintained by a buffer zone between the two, manned principally by 4,000 French troops, under the umbrella of a UN force which, with the French, totalled over 10,000.

Political tensions erupted almost immediately, with four days of violence that hit Abidjan and other towns in the south in January. This was for the most part organised by the Young Patriots, a militia connected to the ruling Ivorian Popular Front (FPI) which often controlled the streets. The demonstrations were officially against the actions of the United Nations in calling for the dissolution of the National Assembly (legislature), whose mandate, the UN said, had been wound up in the last Security Council resolution, and targeted particularly UN personnel and property. The protesters were also complaining over the threat of UN sanctions made at the renewal of the arms embargo in November 2005, but in fact appeared to have also been a test of the will of the new prime minister, Charles Konan Banny. He had been appointed the previous December, again with the blessing of the UN as well as the African Union (AU) and the Economic Community of West African States (ECOWAS), in succession to Seydou Diarra who had been criticised for ineffectiveness (see AR 2005, p. 232). Banny's authority had been reinforced, but the division of powers with President Laurent Gbagbo remained vague. The violence ended as suddenly as it had begun, suggesting a certain remote control from on high. Although the National Assembly was allowed to survive, its role was not recognised internationally, and it was felt that it might be difficult to mount such protests too frequently.

In the course of the year Banny defended his patch, despite persistent criticism, but there was little progress in areas that mattered: the registration of voters for the elections, which depended on the vexed issue of Ivorian "identity" or Ivoirité, and the disarmament of the northern rebel "New Forces" (see AR 2005, p. 231). The rebels said that until the identity issue was clarified, as would happen in the registration exercise, it was difficult for them to disarm, even if some token steps were made on all three issues. The year moved to its predictable denouement at the end of October when, as in the previous year, planned presidential elections were postponed for a further year, with an even more biting UN Security Council resolution (1721 (2006)) at the beginning of November, which had been carefully rehearsed at summits of both ECOWAS and the AU in the preceding weeks.

So the year ended as it had begun, except that the resolution defined powers more clearly, and was more definitely rejected by the Gbagbo camp. A crisis over toxic waste deposits, which caused a serious health scare in Abidjan in September, further poisoned the situation, with Banny having to take measures to dismiss officials in Abidjan close to the FPI. This led to a further confrontation with Gbagbo in November, when the president reinstated the officials, and then sacked the heads of media organisations which had criticised the reinstatement.

Meanwhile, the economic situation continued to deteriorate, in spite of growth in the oil and gas sector. Reports from the north indicated a further damage to infrastructure, in a country that had once been the best endowed with infrastructure in west Africa.

It was an ominous year for BURKINA FASO, especially at the end, when, in December, the capital, Ouagadougou, was subjected to two days of fighting between the army and the police in which five people died. Because of the security situation, planned summits of ECOWAS and the francophone West African Economic and Monetary Union (UEMOA) had to be cancelled at the last minute. Apart from the loss of regional prestige incurred at a time when President Blaise Compaoré was trying to establish himself as an elder statesman (as mediator in TOGO and Chad), there were new concerns about the effectiveness of his control over his own armed forces.

The fighting, triggered by an accusation that soldiers had killed a gendarme, meant that the city was a zone of insecurity until order was restored. Concerns over security featured in demonstrations earlier in December, when the annual protest march over the unsolved murder of journalist Norbert Zongo attracted more demonstrators than usual because of wider concerns over the way impunity was used by the authorities. The strength of opposition to Compaoré would be tested in legislative elections due in 2007, but there was also apprehension that the 20th anniversary of the death of Thomas Sankara, Compaoré's predecessor, in the coup which brought the present president to power, might be a focus for further anti-regime demonstrations.

TOGO continued its slow attempt to pursue national reconciliation, which was also the key to the consolidation of the regime of Faure Gnassingbé, who had come to power in an unorthodox manner after the death of his father in 2005, even if confirmed by a form of elections (see AR 2005, pp. 232-34). The main progress towards this objective came after the middle of the year when, following a political accord in Ouagadougou attended by all parties and brokered by BURKINA FASO'S President Blaise Compaoré, the EU agreed to a qualified end to the suspension of its aid which had been enforced since 1993. This was hailed as a major step forward.

Even so, when the candidate for prime minister proposed by opposition leader Gilchrist Olympio's Union of Forces for Change (UFC) was turned down, and another opposition leader, Yaovi Agboyibo of the Action Committee for Renewal (CAR), was appointed, a true government of national union remained in doubt, although it was still being insisted upon by the EU. Since the UFC was much the most influential opposition party, talks continued through to the end of the year. There was little progress, however, as all the parties already had an eye on the all-important legislative elections, scheduled for "before June". These would be the last hurdle before the full resumption of EU aid. There were still expectations that this would bring, for example, a poverty reduction strategy programme and entry to the IMF and World Bank HIPC scheme for debt relief for the highly indebted poor countries, from both of which TOGO had been excluded. The depressed state of the economy over recent years bore testimony.

The major event of the year in BENIN was the presidential election in March. This took place over two rounds, on 5 and 19 March. Twenty-five candidates stood, but in the first round only four obtained over 8 per cent of the vote. Yayi Boni, a political outsider who had been head of the West African Development Bank in Togo's capital, Lomé, was ahead with 35.6 per cent, and his main rival, Adrien Houngbédji, a veteran politician and former prime minister, was in second place with 24.23 per cent. In the second round Yayi obtained a convincing lead of 75.51 per cent, having attracted most of the votes from other candidates, while Houngbédji only slightly increased his vote to 35.49 per cent.

This convincing win was hailed as a triumph for democracy in one of the world's smallest and poorest countries. Although the outgoing president, Mathieu Kérékou, had shown signs of trying to delay his departure (pleading lack of financial resources), he eventually agreed to apply the constitution, which prevented those over 70 (which included not only himself but also his old rival Nicéphore Soglo) from standing. Some extra election support funds were made available from the EU.

The government that Yayi formed included mostly technocrats and no former ministers or party leaders. Although his extensive foreign travel earned some domestic criticism, he was able to record a tripling of aid commitments, as well as some promises of more foreign investment. He was also engaged in building up his own political support, forming an alliance of small parties called Kauri, rather than launching a new party of his own.

NIGER continued to be dominated by the struggle for survival in the face of persistent drought in the Sahara following one of the worst rainfall deficiencies in 2005, which put Niger in the world headlines. In July 2006 heavy rains avoided the worst difficulties of the previous year, but flooding in September brought different problems to some regions. This did not preclude the annual problem of the "hungry season", for which Niger needed assistance every year, as a poor country of 14 million where the Food and Agriculture Organisation estimated that there were 3.8 million under-nourished people.

A minor flurry occurred in August when the government threatened to expel members of the community of Mahamids (nomadic Arabs originating from both sides of the Chad-Sudan border in the Biltine area). It emerged that the numbers had been wildly exaggerated, and that the original community had been there since the drought of the mid-1970s, and had only been added to by refugees from the current Darfur-Chad fighting (see p. 218). The threat was eventually rescinded, but the affair illustrated the difficulties of maintaining the nation state in a region, such as the Sahel, populated by nomads.

CAMEROON—CHAD—GABON—CONGO—CENTRAL AFRICAN REPUBLIC—EQUATORIAL GUINEA

Cameroon

CAPITAL: Yaoundé AREA: 475,000 sq km POPULATION: 16,322,000
OFFICIAL LANGUAGES: French & English POLITICAL SYSTEM: multiparty republic in British Commonwealth
HEAD OF STATE AND GOVERNMENT: President Paul Biya (since Nov '82)
RULING PARTY: Cameroon People's Democratic Movement (CPDM)
PRIME MINISTER: Ephraim Inoni (since Dec '04)
MAIN IGO MEMBERSHIPS (NON-UN): AU, CEEAC, ACP, OIC, CWTH, NAM, Francophonie
CURRENCY: CFA franc (end-'06 £1=CFAFr970.576, US$1=CFAFr497.107
GNI PER CAPITA: US$1,010, US$2,150 at PPP ('05)

Chad

CAPITAL: Ndjaména AREA: 1,284,000 sq km POPULATION: 9,749,000
OFFICIAL LANGUAGES: French & Arabic POLITICAL SYSTEM: multiparty republic
HEAD OF STATE AND GOVERNMENT: President (Col.) Idriss Déby (MPS) (since Dec '90)
RULING PARTIES: Patriotic Salvation Movement (MPS), Union for Renewal and Democracy (URD), & National Union for Development and Renewal (UNDR)
PRIME MINISTER: Pascal Yoadimnadji (since Feb '05)
MAIN IGO MEMBERSHIPS (NON-UN): AU, CEEAC, ACP, OIC, NAM, Francophonie
CURRENCY: CFA franc (see above)
GNI PER CAPITA: US$400, US$1,470 at PPP ('05)

Gabon

CAPITAL: Libreville AREA: 268,000 sq km POPULATION: 1,384,000
OFFICIAL LANGUAGE: French POLITICAL SYSTEM: multiparty republic
HEAD OF STATE AND GOVERNMENT: President Omar Bongo (PDG) (since March '67)
RULING PARTY: Gabonese Democratic Party (PDG)
PRIME MINISTER: Jean Eyeghe Ndong (since Jan '06)
MAIN IGO MEMBERSHIPS (NON-UN): AU, CEEAC, ACP, OIC, NAM, Francophonie
CURRENCY: CFA franc (see above)
GNI PER CAPITA: US$5,010, US$5,890 at PPP ('05)

Congo

CAPITAL: Brazzaville AREA: 342,000 sq km POPULATION: 3,999,000
OFFICIAL LANGUAGE: French POLITICAL SYSTEM: multiparty republic
HEAD OF STATE AND GOVERNMENT: President Denis Sassou-Nguesso (since Oct '97)
RULING PARTIES: Congolese Labour Party (PCT) heads United Democratic Forces alliance
MAIN IGO MEMBERSHIPS (NON-UN): CEEAC, ACP, NAM, Francophonie
CURRENCY: CFA franc (see above)
GNI PER CAPITA: US$950, US$810 at PPP ('05)

Central African Republic

CAPITAL: Bangui AREA: 623,000 sq km POPULATION: 4,038,000
OFFICIAL LANGUAGE: French POLITICAL SYSTEM: transitional government
HEAD OF STATE AND GOVERNMENT: President Gen. François Bozizé (since March '03)
RULING PARTIES: National Convergence "Kwa Na Kwa" (KNK) coalition
PRIME MINISTER: Elie Doté (since June '05)
MAIN IGO MEMBERSHIPS (NON-UN): AU, CEEAC, ACP, OIC, NAM, Francophonie
CURRENCY: CFA franc (see above)
GNI PER CAPITA: US$350, US$1,140 at PPP ('03-'05)

Equatorial Guinea

CAPITAL: Malabo AREA: 28,000 sq km POPULATION: 504,000
OFFICIAL LANGUAGES: Spanish & French POLITICAL SYSTEM: multiparty republic
HEAD OF STATE AND GOVERNMENT: President (Brig.-Gen.) Teodoro Obiang Nguema Mbasogo (since Aug '79)
RULING PARTY: Equatorial Guinea Democratic Party (PDGE)
PRIME MINISTER: Miguel Abia Biteo Borico (since June '04)
MAIN IGO MEMBERSHIPS (NON-UN): AU, CEEAC, ACP, NAM, Francophonie
CURRENCY: CFA franc (see above)
GNI PER CAPITA: US$3,466-10,725 ('05 est), US$7,580 at PPP ('05 est, based on regression)

THE year 2006 was the year in which CAMEROON seemed at last to begin to tackle its poor reputation on corruption: in 1998 and 1999 Transparency International, the international corruption monitoring non-governmental organisation, had named it as Africa's most corrupt country. The tone for improvement was set in January, when President Paul Biya announced that he was setting up a commission on the subject, with himself at its head. This followed serious lobbying by donors and international companies operating in Cameroon, such as Shell and Standard Chartered Bank. In February the minister of energy and water resources, Alphonse Siyam Siewe, was dismissed and detained for corrupt practices. After a warning from the IMF that corruption could affect debt relief, several senior officials were also dismissed for embezzlement, and on 1 May, it was duly announced that Cameroon had met the completion point for debt relief under the scheme for highly indebted poor countries (HIPC). This meant that the country was now eligible for relief on bilateral debt worth US$1.267 billion, and also opened up the possibility for relief on multilateral debt. Pressure on corruption continued, and later in the year a number of senior officials of the ruling party were also interrogated on embezzlement charges.

Speculation about the succession to Biya, because of the president's remoteness and possible illness, continued, but was muted for fear of the demons that it might launch of regionalism in both the north and the anglophone west, and ethnic particularism. There were, however, rumours of a possible pact with the north. By the time of the next election in 2011, Biya would be 78.

A major success for Cameroon came in June, with a definitive agreement with Nigeria for the handing over of the Bakassi peninsula on the coastline of the Gulf of Guinea between the two countries, where there were both petroleum and fishing resources. This was in accordance with a 2002 decision of the International Court of Justice in The Hague, which had found against Nigeria on the disputed peninsula (see AR 2002, pp. 471-72). But there had been many months of negotiation in which protection for the rights of the inhabitants was sought. The final transfer of territory happened in an orderly fashion in mid-August.

It was a turbulent year for CHAD, as the repercussions from the conflict beyond the Sudan border in Darfur continued to make waves (see p. 218). In March there was an alleged coup plot against President Idriss Déby while he was in the air returning from a central African summit. Then, on 13 April came the news that a column of rebels, who had penetrated from Sudan, was advancing on the capital, Ndjaména, having briefly captured towns on the way. The column was halted by a pitched battle in the capital with the Chad army, but there was reportedly logistical support from Chad-based French troops. The rebels, who came from a Sudan-based group called the United Front for Change (FUC), claimed that they had been strafed by French aircraft.

In spite of uncertainties, and a call for a boycott by opposition parties, the presidential election of 3 May went ahead. The results, announced at the end of the month, gave Déby 64.67 percent of the vote, whereas the initial figure announced had been over 77 per cent. Likewise the turnout was just over 52 per cent, whereas 60 per cent had originally been stated. Of several other candidates, the nearest was former Prime Minister Kassiré Koumakoyé with 15.13 per cent. The elections scarcely seemed to consolidate Déby's position, however. Having accused Sudan of supporting rebel attacks from Darfur (with Sudan making similar accusations) he went to Libya in July for a Kadhafi-brokered detente. This did not stop Sudan from switching its support to another more powerful umbrella group, the Union of Forces for Democracy and Development (UFDD), which scored a number of successes over the next few months, including attacks on the cities of Am Timan in October and Abéché in November. The presence of 250,000 refugees from Darfur in camps in Chad, and the mounting international concern over the wider regional impact of the Darfur situation, added to tensions. Continued French military involvement became more conspicuous when Chad, with French support, sent military assistance to the CENTRAL AFRICAN REPUBLIC, also faced with a Sudan-backed rebellion.

CHAD's growing oil exports, which began flowing in 2003, also put it in the international spotlight. There was a row during the year with the World Bank, which suspended aid in January following the breach of complicated monitoring agreements on the developmental use of oil revenues. This was temporarily resolved in July, but Déby, anxious to make nationalist capital from the affair, turned his attention to Chevron and Petronas, two of the oil companies involved in the pipeline consortium. Threats to expel the companies, made in September, led to a tough renegotiation of their position. The de-recognition of Taiwan in

August, and the opening of relations with mainland China was also oil-related, as China in its quest for energy had already been granted prospecting licenses and was offering aid.

The Darfur effect was also felt in the CENTRAL AFRICAN REPUBLIC, still in a fragile and poverty-stricken condition following the 2003 coup by General François Bozizé, who became president in 2005 after a democratic transition. For some years there had been a small African peace-keeping force in the CAR, funded by France and the EU, because of a permanent risk of instability (parts of the CAR had been described as "ungoverned space"), but the capture by Sudan-based rebels of the key north-eastern town of Birao, apparently in co-ordination with CHAD rebels, necessitated a more direct response. Government troops fought to recapture the town throughout November, but French aircraft from their Ndjaména (Chad) base regularly bombing rebel units reportedly made a decisive difference. An observation by France's President Jacques Chirac on the need to support "friends" was perceived as an old style Gaullist response, but it was possible that the branding of Sudan as a pariah state could lead to a situation in which France would come under further pressure to intervene, especially if the CAR began to look like another failed state.

As in a number of African countries, GABON was beginning to contemplate the succession to its president, the 71-year-old Omar Bongo Ondimba. This was partly because he had been in power since 1967, making him Africa's longest serving head of state.

He himself tried to quash all speculation by announcing that it was premature to talk of succession as he would be a candidate for yet another seven-year term in the presidential elections of 2012, at which date he would be 77. There was some speculation that he was increasingly impatient with the warring barons of his own party, the Gabonese Democratic Party (PDG). This was seen in the greater leeway allowed to opposition candidates in legislative elections in December. Ondimba was also said to be encouraging one of the main opposition leaders, the long-standing critic of his regime, Pierre Mamboundou, but this was a long way from anointing any successor.

For President Denis Sassou Nguesso of the CONGO REPUBLIC it was not an easy year. This was in spite of the prestige that accrued in January from his unexpected accession at the Khartoum summit of the African Union to the chairmanship of the organisation, because of the need to find an alternative to the host, Sudan, embroiled in the Darfur crisis (see p. 425). Nguesso's profile was undoubtedly raised internationally, but the demands on his time from the AU meant that he had some difficulty controlling domestic political considerations, especially relations with two former dissident leaders, Bernard Kolelas, who returned from exile in 2005, and former Prime Minister Pascal Lissouba (still in exile, but willing to negotiate). He also had to face aggravated relations with international donors because of problems of transparency over oil revenues.

Interest in EQUATORIAL GUINEA continued to be divided between its phenomenal oil-based economic expansion and its more unattractive political sphere. Although the growth of the past 10 years had stabilised at around 7 per cent, the economy was still booming, with further growth expected. A new capital, Malabo II, was under construction, and a US$1.2 billion liquefied natural gas project was due to come on stream in 2007, even if accords with neighbouring states that were needed to make the project function had yet to be concluded. A border dispute with GABON over the oil rich Mbanié area was still to be resolved, despite mediation efforts.

No elections were held in 2006, but the oil-enriched political system of President Teodoro Obiang Nguema Mbasogo continued to attract international criticism. Attention particularly focused on the extravagant lifestyle of the president's son, Teodorin Nguema Obiang, often spoken of as the heir. The president, still only aged 64, after 28 years in power, was reportedly seriously ill, although he denied this strongly in October, asking "do I look like a sick man?"

GUINEA-BISSAU—CAPE VERDE—SÃO TOMÉ & PRÍNCIPE

Guinea-Bissau

CAPITAL: Bissau AREA: 36,000 sq km POPULATION: 1,586,000
OFFICIAL LANGUAGE: Portuguese POLITICAL SYSTEM: multiparty republic
HEAD OF STATE AND GOVERNMENT: President João Bernardo "Nino" Vieira (since Oct '05)
RULING PARTIES: African Party for the Independence of Guinea-Bissau and Cape Verde (PAIGC) with the support of the Social Renewal Party (PRS)
PRIME MINISTER: Aristides Gomes (PAIGC) (since Nov '05)
MAIN IGO MEMBERSHIPS (NON-UN): AU, ECOWAS, UEMOA, ACP, OIC, NAM, CPLP, Francophonie
CURRENCY: CFA franc (end-'06 £1=CFAFr970.576, US$1=CFAFr497.107)
GNI PER CAPITA: US$180, US$700 at PPP ('05)

Cape Verde

CAPITAL: Praia AREA: 4,000 sq km POPULATION: 507,000
OFFICIAL LANGUAGE: Portuguese POLITICAL SYSTEM: multiparty republic
HEAD OF STATE: President Pedro Pires (since March '01)
RULING PARTY: African Party for the Independence of Cape Verde (PAICV)
HEAD OF GOVERNMENT: José Maria Pereira Neves, Prime Minister (since Feb '01)
MAIN IGO MEMBERSHIPS (NON-UN): AU, ECOWAS, ACP, NAM, CPLP, Francophonie
CURRENCY: CV escudo (end-'06 £1=CVEsc162.639, US$1=CvEsc83.3000)
GNI PER CAPITA: US$1,870, US$6,000 at PPP ('05 estimate, based on regression)

São Tomé & Príncipe

CAPITAL: São Tomé AREA: 965 sq km POPULATION: 157,000
OFFICIAL LANGUAGE: Portuguese POLITICAL SYSTEM: multiparty republic
HEAD OF STATE AND GOVERNMENT: President Fradique de Menezes (since Sept. '01)
RULING PARTIES: Democratic Movement Force for Change-Party of Democratic Convergence (MDFM-PCD) coalition
PRIME MINISTER: Prime Minister Tomé Soares da Vera Cruz (MDFM) (since April '06)
MAIN IGO MEMBERSHIPS (NON-UN): AU, CEEAC, ACP, NAM, CPLP, Francophonie
CURRENCY: dobra (end-'06 £1=Db113,227.8, US$1=Db6,775.00)
GNI PER CAPITA: US$390 ('05), -

THESE three Lusophone countries continued to play active roles in the Community of Portuguese-Speaking Countries (CPLP). When that organisation met in GUINEA-BISSAU in July in Bissau, President "Nino" Vieira of the host country was elected as its chair (see p. 395). That the meeting could be held in Guinea-Bissau reflected the return of a measure of stability to the country after decades of unrest. Guinea-Bissau's politics nevertheless remained fractured and its economy very weak.

The former ruling party, the African Party for the Independence of Guinea-Bissau and Cape Verde (PAIGC), had split in late 2005, and Vieira had appointed a prime minister from among those PAIGC members who supported him, without the consent of the National Assembly (the unicameral legislature) (see AR 2005, pp. 238-39). In January the country's Supreme Court ratified this, much to the dismay of the PAIGC, but political tensions died down later in the year, allowing the prime minister to get legislation and a budget through the Assembly.

Eighty percent of the population continued to live on less than US$2 per day. In March and again in August schoolteachers who had not been paid salaries went on strike, and later in the year the bottom dropped out of the world market for cashew nuts, by far the country's main export. As many of the smallholders who produced the nuts were unable to sell them, they were not able to afford to buy rice, the staple food, most of which had to be imported. After many postponements, Guinea-Bissau's main donors—the EU, Spain, Portugal, and Japan—finally met in Geneva in November and agreed to contribute US$266 million to the country, mainly for poverty reduction programmes and security reforms.

In legislative elections held in January, the African Party for the Independence of CAPE VERDE (PAICV), under the leadership of the prime minister, José Maria Neves, won 41 of the 72 seats in the National Assembly (the unicameral legislature). Then in February Cape Verde's incumbent president, Pedro Pires, also of the PAICV, won another five-year term by narrowly beating Carlos Veiga of the main opposition party, the Movement for Democracy (MPD), who had lost to Pires even more narrowly five years before. The MPD claimed electoral fraud, but the Supreme Court threw out the case. Of the 325,000 citizens registered to vote, 20 percent lived abroad, mainly in Portugal and the USA, and they swung the result to Pires.

He pledged to tackle poverty and unemployment on the 10 mostly mountainous islands of the archipelago—one-quarter of the population was unemployed—and to push for associate status for Cape Verde with the European Union. After an IMF team commended Cape Verde for achieving GDP growth of nearly 6 per cent in 2005, owing largely to infrastructural projects and construction for the tourism sector, the government promised to press ahead with its privatisation programme. Cape Verde remained burdened by a large external debt, and was heavily dependent on international aid—it received one of the highest levels of aid per capita of any country—food imports, and remittances from the 700,000 Cape Verdeans in the diaspora.

In SÃO TOMÉ & PRÍNCIPE's legislative elections in March, the historic ruling party, the Movement for the Liberation of São Tomé and Príncipe-Social Democratic Party (MLSTP-PSD), won fewer seats than the coalition of the Movement of Democratic Forces (MDFM) and the Party of Democratic Convergence (PCD), which obtained 23 seats in the 55 seat National Assembly (unicameral legislature). The MDFM-PCD then formed a minority government, with the support of the president, Fradique de Menezes. At the end of July, in the presidential election, de Menezes won a second five-year term. He gained 60 per cent of the vote, thereby eliminating the need for a run-off, in what international observers agreed was a free poll. Then, in August, the MDFM-PCD won the municipal elections decisively. That the government and the president worked together brought new political stability to the country, but the accord that the MLSTP-PSD signed in August with the third largest party, Independent Democratic Action (ADI), gave them 31 seats in the Assembly and great potential to obstruct.

De Menezes began his last term by promising that he would reduce unemployment and tackle health and education issues. More than half the population remained poor, and 30 per cent of the working-age population was unemployed. The country carried a debt burden of US$300 million. The oil that had been discovered offshore, however, promised a future bonanza. The USA and other Western countries, seeking new sources of petroleum, strengthened links with the archipelago, strategically placed in the Gulf of Guinea. It remained to be seen whether, when significant new wealth from oil arrived, it would spread to those who currently relied on remittances from abroad to survive.

VII CENTRAL AND SOUTHERN AFRICA

DEMOCRATIC REPUBLIC OF CONGO—BURUNDI AND RWANDA—MOZAMBIQUE—ANGOLA

DEMOCRATIC REPUBLIC OF CONGO

CAPITAL: Kinshasa   AREA: 2,345,000 sq km   POPULATION: 57,549,000
OFFICIAL LANGUAGE: French   POLITICAL SYSTEM: multiparty republic
HEAD OF STATE AND GOVERNMENT: President Maj.-Gen. Joseph Kabila (since Jan '01)
RULING PARTY: Alliance for the Presidential Majority (AMP) coalition
PRIME MINISTER: Antoine Gizenga (since Dec '06)
MAIN IGO MEMBERSHIPS (NON-UN): AU, SADC, COMESA, CEEAC, ACP, Francophonie, NAM
CURRENCY: Congo franc (end-'06 £1=CFr1,056.28, US$1=CFr541.000)
GNI PER CAPITA: US$120, US$720 at PPP ('03-'05)

IN February, clearing the way for elections, the Supreme Court confirmed the results of the December 2005 constitutional referendum (see AR 2005, p. 241), with 84 per cent of votes in favour. Ten months later, on 6 December, 35-year-old Joseph Kabila was inaugurated as the DRC's first democratically elected president in 40 years, promising "good governance, democracy and respect for human rights". Elections for provincial governorships and the Senate (the upper chamber of the bicameral legislature) were postponed, prolonging the democratisation process into early 2007.

The presidential and legislative elections were held on 30 July, with 33 names on the presidential ballot and nearly 10,000 candidates competing for 500 National Assembly (lower house) seats. Incumbent President Kabila won 45 per cent of the vote, short of the majority necessary for outright victory, followed by Jean-Pierre Bemba of the Congolese Liberation Movement (MLC) with 20 per cent. This made a second round necessary. The legislative elections did not produce a clear majority either: Kabila's People's Party for Reconstruction and Democracy (PPRD) won 111 seats, followed by the MLC with 64 seats; altogether 132 parties won representation. The new National Assembly was installed on 22 September.

The elections were generally peaceful, and international observers pronounced them free and fair despite some irregularities. Turnout was high, with 17 million of the 26 million registered voters going to the polls. There was some violence in Mbuji-Mayi, a stronghold of Étienne Tshisekedi's Union for Democracy and Social Progress (UDPS), which boycotted the elections. The announcement in August of the results of the first round of the presidential election provoked armed conflict involving heavy weaponry on the streets of Kinshasa between the private militias of the two candidates, with over 60 people killed and many wounded in three days of fighting. In September, two television stations belonging to Bemba were burned by rioters.

In the run-off between Bemba and Kabila, held on 29 October, Kabila won 58 per cent of the vote to Bemba's 42 per cent. The Carter Centre in Atlanta reported that although irregularities occurred, they did not affect the result. Bemba initially rejected the outcome, and a mob of his supporters set fire to the Supreme Court as it considered his complaints of fraud on 21 November. On 27 November the Court confirmed the Kabila victory, and after some uncertainty, Bemba eased tension by promising to act within the constitutional framework "in the national interest".

Outbreaks of preventable diseases continued as a result of poor sanitation, a collapsing healthcare system, and constant population movement. There were cholera epidemics in Katanga in January and South Kivu in March. There was an avian influenza scare in Kasai Occidental in March, and deaths from a meningitis-like disease in Bandundu in April. An outbreak of pulmonary plague in Ituri caused fatalities in June, and the water-borne hepatitis E variety killed 13 people and threatened thousands in Equateur in October. The HIV prevalence rate varied between 1.7 per cent and 7.6 per cent of the population, according to region, and was rising, according to UNAIDS data; among the country's many rape survivors it may have been as high as 20 per cent.

Sporadic violence contributed to continuing population displacement across the country. In January, 100,000 people in Katanga fled government campaigns against Mayi Mayi militias, and by May the number of displaced persons had increased to between 165,000 and 200,000. However, thousands of people began to return home in June as fighting died down in the so-called "triangle of death". Fighting between government forces and militias in North Kivu, South Kivu, and Ituri in January, March, July, and December provoked short-term flows of tens of thousands of people to such sanctuaries as Bunia, or Kasenyi in Uganda. The UN High Commissioner for Refugees stated in December that there were 1.2 million displaced persons inside the DRC and 410,000 refugees in neighbouring countries. The UN estimated that US$687 million was needed to deal with the post-conflict aftermath, but thousands of displaced people were receiving no support of any kind, according to humanitarian organisations. MONUC, the UN mission in the DRC, remained the UN's largest military operation, peaking at just under 20,000 troops in June.

In November hopes were raised of an end to fighting in Ituri, when the government signed an agreement with three militia groups: the Forces of Patriotic Resistance in Ituri (FRPI), the Nationalist and Integrationist Fronts (FNI), and the Revolutionary Congolese Movement (MRC). Under the accord, 3,500 militiamen were to be disarmed. However, at the end of the year there were still several thousand armed militiamen in both the Ituri and Kivu regions, loyal to local warlords, rebel groups, and foreign militias. As some of the militias began to lay down their arms, the scale of human rights abuses in the DRC emerged, especially the use of rape as a weapon of war by government soldiers and militiamen alike. Rape survivors in areas that had been cut off began to seek help: in South Kivu, some 42,000 women received treatment for rape in local clinics, and the national figures were estimated in the hundreds of thousands.

New investment rules and the reopening of internal trade networks across much of the country contributed to an overall economic growth rate of around 7 per cent for the year. The economy benefited from the high price of copper, although production levels appeared to drop slightly early in the year. Manufacturing, agriculture, and construction also played their part. Although donor funds continued to flow, the government's inability to control large-scale unbudgeted expenditure attracted criticism and strained relations with the IMF and the UN at mid-year, and pushed inflation into double figures. An IMF Poverty Reduction and Growth Facility failed in March, and a UN Security Council delegation that visited Kinshasa in June also censured fiscal indiscipline and lack of transparency.

BURUNDI AND RWANDA

Burundi

CAPITAL: Bujumbura AREA: 28,000 sq km POPULATION: 7,548,000
OFFICIAL LANGUAGES: French & Kirundi POLITICAL SYSTEM: multiparty republic
HEAD OF STATE AND GOVERNMENT: President Pierre Nkurunziza (CNDD-FDD) (since Aug '05)
RULING PARTY: National Council for the Defence of Democracy-Forces for the Defence of Democracy (CNDD-FDD) (since July '05)
MAIN IGO MEMBERSHIPS (NON-UN): AU, COMESA, CEEAC, ACP, NAM, Francophonie
CURRENCY: Burundi franc (end-'06 £1=BrF1,915.67, US$1=BrF993.810)
GNI PER CAPITA: US$100, US$640 at PPP ('03-'05)

Rwanda

CAPITAL: Kigali AREA: 26,000 sq km POPULATION: 9,038,000
OFFICIAL LANGUAGES: French, Kinyarwanda & English POLITICAL SYSTEM: multiparty republic
HEAD OF STATE AND GOVERNMENT: President Paul Kagame (RPF) (since April '00)
RULING PARTIES: Rwandan Patriotic Front (RPF) heads five party coalition
PRIME MINISTER: Bernard Mazuka (since April '00)
MAIN IGO MEMBERSHIPS (NON-UN): AU, COMESA, CEEAC, ACP, NAM, Francophonie
CURRENCY: Rwanda franc (end-'06 £1=RFr1,071.52, US$1=RFr548.806)
GNI PER CAPITA: US$230, US$1,320 at PPP ('05 est, based on regression)

UN Secretary General Kofi Annan characterised the situation in BURUNDI as "fragile" in his 18 December report to the Security Council, warning of challenges ahead for the democratically-elected government. Nevertheless, the UN Operation in Burundi (ONUB) closed down on 31 December when the last 2,500 blue helmets left the country. The demobilisation of government and rebel soldiers continued throughout the year, under the auspices of the National Commission for the Demobilisation, Reintroduction, and Reintegration of ex-combatants (CNDRR). ONUB was to be replaced by the UN Integrated Office in Burundi (BINUB), but some South African troops would remain in the country.

In a broadcast on 7 March, President Pierre Nkurunziza announced the discovery of a coup plot involving senior police and army officers as well as political leaders. An army spokesperson denied knowledge of any conspiracy, however, and the opposition demanded that the allegations be withdrawn or evidence produced. After a delay, in August the government arrested former Vice-President Alphonse Marie Kadege of the opposition Union for National Progress (UPRONA), four members of the National Freedom Forces-Icanzo (FNL-Icanzo), two from the Front for Democracy in Burundi (FRODEBU), and Colonel Damien

Ndarisigaranye, on coup-related charges. Former transitional President Domitien Ndayizeye was taken into custody after his parliamentary immunity was controversially revoked. Seven accused, including Kadege and Ndayizeye, appeared in court in November—after four months in jail—but proceedings were halted when lawyers challenged the bench's impartiality. On 17 December, Defence Minister Major General Germain Niyoyankana added to the uproar by stating that military intelligence had no evidence that a coup plot existed.

In March, Agathon Rwasa, leader of the Hutu People Freedom Party-National Forces for Freedom (Palipehutu-FNL)—the only rebel group not to have joined the peace process—signalled willingness to enter into negotiations. Talks began in May in Dar es Salaam (Tanzania), with South Africa's Safety and Security Minister Charles Nqakula as facilitator. The two sides apparently reached an accord in June, but returned to the table and only achieved final agreement on a ceasefire in early September. Meanwhile, sporadic attacks continued in Bubanza province, near Bujumbura. In December, the government granted temporary immunity to FNL members.

The food situation in Burundi remained difficult, especially in the north and east. In January over 100 people died and over 2,500 fled to Tanzania because of drought-related food shortages in the eastern Ruyigi and Muyinga provinces. In Muyinga, 80 per cent of the population faced crop failure and hunger. In late January, in an appeal to donors, the government declared that 13 of the country's 17 provinces needed food aid, and announced a US$75 million emergency programme for 460,000 families, about 30 per cent of the population. In late April, heavy rains and flooding made thousands homeless in Cibitoke province; in May another 5,000 were made homeless in Bururi. In December the UN's Food and Agriculture Organisation predicted that this drought-and-flood pattern would be repeated, since the September rains were poor, affecting the planting of beans and maize, and flooding recurred in November. Population pressure on land, and plant viruses attacking such staples as cassava, exacerbated the situation.

The coffee harvest for the 2005-06 season, ending in April, totalled only 5,500 tonnes, and export revenues for the first six months were low. Donor income fell, and an extremely negative balance of trade was registered at mid-year, with under 10 per cent of imports covered by export earnings. The government failed to meet the deadline for a poverty reduction strategy paper (PRSP), an important step towards eventual acceptance in the IMF and World Bank's heavily indebted poor countries (HIPC) debt-relief programme.

In Rwanda in November, conflict over gacaca (traditional court) tribunals for genocide suspects erupted into deadly violence in Rukumberi and Mwulire sectors, raising concerns about increasing ethnic tensions. (The gacaca system, based on traditional courts, was established in 2001 for lower category genocide cases, see AR 2001, p. 292.) In one episode a relative of a gacaca judge was murdered, provoking the revenge slaying of eight others. Elsewhere, a gacaca judge was killed and three suspects were allegedly executed after being arrested.

Meanwhile, the International Criminal Tribunal for Rwanda (ICTR) in Arusha, Tanzania, acquitted a former mayor, Jean Mpambara, and a former government minister, André Rwamakuba, bringing unsuccessful prosecutions to five. The sensitive relations between the government and the ICTR were further strained in September over the tribunal's failure to dismiss or prosecute Calixte Gakwaya, a defence lawyer accused of genocide crimes. Altogether 28 people were on trial, but the ICTR's mandate would expire in 2008, when the government anticipated taking over remaining cases. In a move towards that end, the ruling Rwandan Patriotic Front announced in October that it would abolish the death penalty. On the last day of the year, four genocide suspects living in the UK under assumed identities were remanded by a British court after police swoops.

The government responded touchily to foreign disapproval of corruption, poor governance, and the silencing of criticism contained in reports by the World Bank, the African Union (AU), and Transparency International. The AU's African Peer Review Mechanism report faulted the lack of political freedom and the harassment of the media, but was later toned down. The World Bank's conclusion in a September evaluation that government performance had declined in six key areas since 2004 drew strong reactions from government supporters, mainly on methodological grounds. In November, Transparency International ranked Rwanda 121st out of 163 countries in its Corruption Perception Index, drawing a strong protest from the government ombudsman, who stressed government commitment to eliminating corruption. The government did draw praise from the US ambassador in October for the rollout of anti-retroviral drugs to HIV-positive people, for participation in the Darfur peace-keeping operations where Rwanda had 254 soldiers serving with the UN Mission in Sudan (UNMIS), and for improved relations with the Democratic Republic of Congo (DRC).

The presence of Rwandan militias in the eastern DRC continued to contribute to regional tension. The Democratic Forces for the Liberation of Rwanda (FDLR), with several thousand men and alleged links to Congolese intelligence, included both ex-Rwandan army and Interahamwe (Hutu militia) fighters. Relations with Uganda showed signs of improvement with a high level meeting between heads of security services and the armed forces taking place in Kigali in November.

Freedom of the press and expression remained problematic. In August two independent journalists who had criticised the government, Bosco Gasasira and Bonaventure Bizumuremyi, complained of government threats and surveillance, and Bizumuremyi went into hiding. A Catholic priest, Father Jean-Marie Vianney Uwizeyeyezu, was sentenced to 12 years by the ICTR in October for genocide denial, which became a punishable offence in 2003.

The government's draft budget for 2007, approved by the legislature in October, forecast a growth rate of 7 per cent on the estimated GDP for 2006 of around US$2.5 billion. Coffee and tea remained Rwanda's principal export crops, and government policy emphasised improvements in the quality of the harvest produced by the country's half-million coffee farmers, including the construction of coffee washing stations. Coffee production for the 2006-07 season was expected to reach 25,000 tonnes.

In November, a row erupted when a French judge said that President Paul Kagame should be tried for involvement in the downing of President Juvenal Habyarimana's aircraft in 1994 (see AR 1994, pp. 292-93). The French jurist issued warrants for the arrest of eight Rwandan officials. In a television interview Kagame accused France of training soldiers for the genocide and called the French remarks "the justice of bullies". The Rwandan ambassador was recalled from Paris, and the lycée (secondary school) and Alliance Française in Kigali were closed. In December it was announced that Rwanda intended to apply, with Ugandan support, to join the British Commonwealth.

MOZAMBIQUE

CAPITAL: Maputo AREA: 802,000 sq km POPULATION: 19,792,000
OFFICIAL LANGUAGE: Portuguese POLITICAL SYSTEM: multiparty republic in British Commonwealth
HEAD OF STATE AND GOVERNMENT: President Armando Emílio Guebuza (Frelimo) (since Feb '05)
RULING PARTY: Front for the Liberation of Mozambique (Frelimo)
PRIME MINISTER: Luisa Diogo (since Feb '04)
MAIN IGO MEMBERSHIPS (NON-UN): AU, SADC, ACP, CWTH, OIC, NAM, CPLP
CURRENCY: metical (end-'06 £1=M50.9589, US$1=M26.1000)
GNI PER CAPITA: US$310, US$1,270 at PPP ('05 est, based on regression)

DURING its second year in power, the administration of President Armando Emílio Guebuza of the Frelimo party adopted a generally more hard-line style than that of his conciliatory predecessor, Joaquim Chissano, also of Frelimo. A case in point was the government's refusal either to charge or release 14 supporters of the main opposition party, Renamo (Mozambican National Resistance), who had been detained after the Mocimboa da Praia rioting in September 2005 (see AR 2005, pp. 246-47), a case seen by some as a manifestation of Frelimo's new tough line. Renamo deputies protested formally in October, and the group's lawyer alleged political interference.

A resurgent Frelimo, the ruling party since independence in 1975, continued to dominate national politics. In September, Renamo showed its organisational weakness by postponing its fifth congress, scheduled for 2006 in Nampula, until early 2007. In contrast, Frelimo's ninth congress took place in Quelimane, a Renamo stronghold, from 10 to 14 November, attended by 1,300 delegates and fully a year ahead of schedule. The congress was held early to prepare for a tough timetable of provincial elections in 2007, local elections in 2008, and legislative and presidential elections in 2009. The debates focused almost exclusively on what were seen as key social issues, such as poverty and crime.

In April, the ad hoc commission set up in March 2005 to propose electoral reform reported that it had been unable to reached consensus over the central issue of membership of the National Elections Commission (CNE), with Renamo insisting that it be enlarged and that it continue to be composed mainly of party representatives, and Frelimo wanting to professionalise the body. The Assembly of the Republic (the country's unicameral legislature) then closed down the commission, and in June an Assembly committee began work drafting electoral legislation under normal majority voting procedures. In September, however, Frelimo admitted that the provincial elections scheduled for 2007 depended on the new legislation to define the powers of the new provincial assemblies, raising fears of postponement.

Several events were held throughout the year to mark the 20th anniversary of the death of President Samora Moisés Machel and other political figures in a plane crash in October 1986 (see AR 1986, pp. 249-51), and both South Africa's President Thabo Mbeki and his security minister, Charles Nqakula, promised early in the year to reopen enquiries into what Mbeki called a "dastardly crime". On 19 October, the actual anniversary, President Guebuza reiterated his determination to discover the truth. Machel's image also appeared on new currency notes issued during the year.

Economic growth for 2006 was close to 8 per cent, according to a report issued by the ministry of planning and development in December. Commodity exports for the first three-quarters of the year topped US$1.7 billion, an increase of 40 per cent over the figures for the previous year. Aluminium from the Mozal smelter, electricity generated by the Cahora Bassa dam, and natural gas from Inhambane made up about 70 per cent of export value, with agricultural and fisheries products such as prawns, tobacco, sugar, cotton, and cashew nuts constituting the remainder. Good rains during the 2005-06 agricultural season also allowed for sharp growth in grain production (over 2 million tonnes), in pulses (over 360,000 tonnes), and in the staple food crop, cassava (7.5 million tonnes), all increases of 10 per cent or more.

The Poverty Reduction and Growth Facility, running from July 2004 to July 2007, continued to define the government's economic policy objectives, with an emphasis on overall economic stability and better social services. Spending on public sector wages, social services, and poverty alleviation programmes increased sharply in 2006, financed mainly by donor funds and debt relief. In October the government signed the formal agreement with the Portuguese government to transfer ownership of the company which ran the Cahora Bassa hydroelectric scheme—a major foreign exchange earner—from Portugal to Mozambique, as agreed in 2005 (see AR 2005, p. 247).

In mid-March Health Minister Ivo Garrido told Assembly members that HIV/AIDS was the single most serious threat to Mozambican development, and had lowered overall life expectancy to 38 years. Prevalence based on surveys of pregnant women was calculated at 16.2 per cent. Access to anti-retroviral drugs was available at 35 health centres, with another 30 scheduled to open during the year.

In May, the public prosecutor charged Nyimpine Chissano, the son of former President Joaquim Chissano, with murder in the long-running case of journalist Carlos Cardoso, gunned down in November 2000 (see AR 2003, p. 307). It was unclear when or even whether a trial would begin, however, as a judge was still required to rule if the charges needed to be answered.

An earthquake struck rural Machaze district in Manica province on 23 February, killing four villagers and injuring several others. The shock registered 7.5 on the Richter scale, making the quake—felt as far away as Lusaka in Zambia and Johannesburg in South Africa—the strongest ever recorded in southern Africa.

ANGOLA

CAPITAL: Luanda AREA: 1,247,000 sq km POPULATION: 15,941,000
OFFICIAL LANGUAGE: Portuguese POLITICAL SYSTEM: multiparty republic
HEAD OF STATE AND GOVERNMENT: President José Eduardo dos Santos (since Sept '79)
RULING PARTY: Popular Movement for the Liberation of Angola-Workers' Party (MPLA) heads nominal coalition
PRIME MINISTER: Fernando da Piedade Dias dos Santos (since Dec '02)
MAIN IGO MEMBERSHIPS (NON-UN): AU, COMESA, SADC, CEEAC, ACP, NAM, CPLP
CURRENCY: readj. kwanza (end-'06 £1=Kw154.743, US$1=Kw80.2774)
GNI PER CAPITA: US$1,350, US$2,210 at PPP ('03-'05)

IN 2006 Angola continued to recover from the war that had ended in 2002 with the death of Jonas Savimbi, the leader of the Union for the Total Independence of Angola (UNITA) (see AR 2002, pp. 284-86), but the long-awaited presidential and legislative elections—the first since 1992—were again postponed. Voter registration proceeded slowly but the year ended without it becoming clear whether presidential and legislative elections would be held together or separately, and whether in 2007 or later. President José dos Santos, who said in April that it was "an open question" whether he would run again, insisted that major infrastructural work must be done before any election could be held. Every indication was that the governing Popular Movement for the Liberation of Angola (MPLA) would easily win any such election, for UNITA, its main rival, was far from united. With some UNITA members of the National Assembly (unicameral legislature) enjoying state patronage, the UNITA leader, Isaias Samakuva, battled to hold the party together and was not in a position to press hard for an early election.

After Savimbi's death, fighting had continued with rebels in the northernmost province of Cabinda, which was separated from the mainland by a strip of land belonging to the Democratic Republic of Congo (DRC). In July an agreement was reached in Brazzaville, capital of the Republic of Congo, with the rebels, providing for a cessation of hostilities and amnesty for rebel fighters, who were to be demobilised and integrated into the Angolan military. A "special status" was to provide some form of political and economic autonomy for Cabinda. Angola's richest province, Cabinda produced more than half of the oil that came from the offshore wells, and the end of the conflict there opened the way for exploration for onshore oil.

Angola's oil revenues almost doubled from those of the previous year, thanks to increased production and rising prices. The country remained sub-Saharan Africa's second largest oil producer after Nigeria, and output reached almost 1.5 million barrels per day (b/d). This was expected to increase to 2 million b/d in 2007, although in November Angola announced that it would join the Organisation of the Petroleum Exporting Countries in March 2007 and it was possible that OPEC would impose production caps. The Angolan government rejected calls by the World Bank and IMF for greater transparency in respect of the revenue derived from oil.

China, the second-largest importer of Angolan oil after the USA, was the largest foreign investor in the reconstruction of the country, and by the end of 2006 an estimated 50,000 Chinese citizens had entered Angola. Diamond production continued to increase and was worth US$1 billion annually. Only a small Angolan elite benefited from the vast new wealth, however. State social spending was very limited, and Angola remained 160th out of 177 countries on the UN Human Development Index. A cholera epidemic had caused over 2,000 deaths in the south in the 2005-06 rainy season, and cholera returned in November 2006.

ZAMBIA—MALAWI—ZIMBABWE—BLNS STATES

ZAMBIA

CAPITAL: Lusaka AREA: 753,000 sq km POPULATION: 11,668,000
OFFICIAL LANGUAGE: English POLITICAL SYSTEM: multiparty republic in British Commonwealth
HEAD OF STATE AND GOVERNMENT: President Levy Patrick Mwanawasa (since Jan '02)
RULING PARTY: Movement for Multi-Party Democracy (MMD)
MAIN IGO MEMBERSHIPS (NON-UN): AU, COMESA, SADC, ACP, CWTH, NAM
CURRENCY: Zambian kwacha (end-'06 £1=Kw7,936.72, US$1=Kw4,065.00)
GNI PER CAPITA: US$490, US$950 at PPP ('05)

RECOVERING from the mild stroke which he had suffered in April, and for which he received treatment in London, President Levy Mwanawasa took advantage of the death in May of Anderson Mazoka—the leader of the largest opposition grouping, the United Democratic Alliance (UDA), and the man whom many Zambians believed had won the 2001 presidential election—to dissolve the National Assembly (unicameral legislature) and announce that presidential, parliamentary, and local elections would be held in late September. He did this after the Supreme Court had rejected a petition by the Law Association of Zambia to stop him from doing so on the grounds that election dates should be decided by the independent Electoral Commission of Zambia and not the president, because he was an interested party.

Mwanawasa was praised by Western donors for promoting privatisation and taking action against corruption. Much of Zambia's US$7 billion foreign debt was written off, thereby reducing the debt burden to US$500 million by the end of the year. In October it was announced that Zambia's first oil and gas had been discovered in the north west, near the Angolan border. Though the government tried to encourage diversification of the economy into tourism and agriculture, copper remained the chief export. On the back of demand from China and India the copper price reached six times what it had been five years earlier. Zambia recorded economic growth of over 5 per cent and in June inflation fell to a single digit for the first time in three decades. Instead of having to import food, there was a food surplus and some was exported to Zimbabwe.

Yet two-thirds of Zambia's people subsisted on less than US$1 per day and only 400,000 Zambians were in formal employment. About 1.6 million were infected with HIV, and only 60,000 had access to anti-retroviral drugs. There were only 600 registered doctors in the public and private health sectors.

Mwanawasa's caps on wages angered workers, who supported Michael Sata of the Patriotic Front (PF) in the presidential elections. He ran a populist campaign in which he criticised the government's privatisation programme and the role of Chinese and Indian business. The trial of former President Frederick Chiluba, who was accused with two businessmen of stealing hundreds of thousands of dollars of state funds while serving as head of state (1991-2001), was postponed, and Chiluba was allowed eventually to go to South Africa for medical treatment. He accused Mwanawasa of using his trial to bolster his presidential campaign, and urged Zambians to vote for Sata, who promised to drop the corruption charges if he were elected.

Although Mwanawasa had failed to provide Zambia with a new constitution containing a requirement that a presidential candidate had to win at least 50 per cent of the vote, new rules were introduced to help reduce electoral tensions. These provided for transparent ballot boxes to allay fears of vote-rigging, the use of voters' fingerprints on their registration cards to prevent fraud, and for the media to be barred from announcing the results before the official declaration by the Electoral Commission.

The outcome of the presidential election was that Mwanawasa won a second and final five-year term, by gaining 43 per cent of the vote to Sata's 29 per cent, while businessman Hakainde Hichilema, who had assumed leadership of the UDA after Mazoka's death, took 25 per cent of the 2.52 million votes cast. International observers said that the September poll was the most transparent since multiparty elections had been re-introduced in 1991, but Sata claimed that Mwanawasa and his Movement for Multiparty Democracy, which won a narrow majority in the legislature, had rigged the results. When Sata threatened to run a rival "people's government" in those municipalities won by his Patriotic Front in Lusaka, the capital, and the copperbelt, the country's industrial hub, Mwanawasa denounced this as treasonable. With the president not in good health, the government was clearly concerned by Sata's level of support, and when he was charged with false declaration of assets, some saw this as a means of disciplining him. Mwanawasa's apparent choice as his successor was his new vice-president, the veteran politician and diplomat Rupiah Banda, a former foreign minister and ambassador to the UN.

MALAWI

CAPITAL: Lilongwe AREA: 118,000 sq km POPULATION: 12,884,000
OFFICIAL LANGUAGE: English POLITICAL SYSTEM: multiparty republic in British Commonwealth
HEAD OF STATE AND GOVERNMENT: President Bingu wa Mutharika (DPP), since May '04
RULING PARTY: Democratic Progressive Party (DPP)
MAIN IGO MEMBERSHIPS (NON-UN): AU, COMESA, SADC, ACP, CWTH, NAM
CURRENCY: Malawi kwacha (end-'06 £1=Kw272.152, US$1=Kw139.390)
GNI PER CAPITA: US$160, US$650 at PPP ('05)

MALAWI hit the headlines in October when, on a brief visit, the pop-singer Madonna and her film-director husband Guy Ritchie adopted a one-year old boy amid a glare of publicity and soon whisked him out of the country. When questions were asked about whether the usual procedures for adoption had been followed, it was pointed out that David Banda's life-chances in Malawi were extremely poor (see p. 123). The draft poverty and vulnerability assessment compiled by the Malawi government and the World Bank and released in June 2006 compared the 1998 and 2005 household surveys and concluded that there had been little or no progress in reducing poverty and inequality. It found that one-fifth of all Malawians were not able to meet the daily recommended food requirements. With 60 per cent of the population aged under 20, more than half of the poor were children, many of them AIDS orphans, and many stunted because of malnutrition. Of the 1 million people infected with HIV, only 50,000 were receiving anti-retroviral drugs.

Political tensions remained high throughout the year, although the opposition did drop its attempt to impeach president Bingu wa Mutharika. His ailing predecessor, Bakili Muluzi, who had become Mutharika's leading opponent, had to remain in the UK for months recovering from a back operation. Mutharika appealed for unity in an address to the nation marking the end of two years in office, but his critics accused him of poor leadership and of not providing the good governance he had promised. They charged that he was using the Anti-Corruption Bureau to persecute his political opponents, and claimed that he had wrongly used public funds to launch his own political party. They condemned the arrest of the owner, the editor, and a reporter on *The Chronicle* newspaper on criminal libel charges as another sign of the government's creeping authoritarianism.

In April the country's vice-president, Cassim Chilumpha, who was a member of Muluzi's United Democratic Front, was arrested on a charge of treason. Mutharika had tried to sack him in 2005, but the Constitutional Court had ordered his reinstatement and ruled that only the National Assembly (unicameral legislature) could dismiss him. He was now alleged to have asked a leading businessman to hire a professional assassin to kill Mutharika, and promised him millions of dollars-worth of government contracts once he (Chilumpha) became president. Chilumpha's defence argued that he was immune from prosecution while in office, but he was kept in custody when other opposition figures and businessmen arrested in connection with the case were released for lack of evidence, then placed under house arrest until the High Court ordered that he be freed.

Mutharika meanwhile invited Robert Mugabe, whom he praised as an African hero, to make a state visit in May, during which the Zimbabwe president opened a new road, named after him, between Blantyre and the tea-growing district of Mulanje, in the south east. The following month a founder of the pro-democracy movement against former President Hastings Kamuzu Banda, Chakufwa Chihana, who had supported Mutharika's presidential bid, was given a state funeral but was refused burial in the Heroes Acre where Banda was interred.

Mutharika had built up his Democratic Progressive Party by using state patronage to entice members of other parties to defect to it. In November the country's highest court upheld the requirement in the constitution that members of the National Assembly who defected to other parties had to leave the Assembly and seek re-election. As the president refused the opposition's demand that he immediately recall the Assembly to put this into practice, the implications of the ruling would only become clear in 2007.

ZIMBABWE

CAPITAL: Harare AREA: 391,000 sq km POPULATION: 13,010,000
OFFICIAL LANGUAGE: English POLITICAL SYSTEM: multiparty republic in British Commonwealth
HEAD OF STATE AND GOVERNMENT: President Robert Mugabe (since Dec '87); previously Prime Minister (from April '80)
RULING PARTY: Zimbabwe African National Union-Patriotic Front (ZANU-PF)
MAIN IGO MEMBERSHIPS (NON-UN): AU, COMESA, SADC, ACP, NAM
CURRENCY: Zimbabwe dollar (end-'06 £1=Z$488.113, US$1=Z$250.000)
GNI PER CAPITA: US$340, US$1,940 at PPP ('05)

At the start of the year Zimbabwe's inflation rate was 613 per cent, the highest in the world. By March it had risen to 782 per cent, and the following month to 918 per cent. A monthly consumer basket of items for the average Zimbabwean family now cost Z$28 million, and doubled every two months. While the price of essential foodstuffs was tightly controlled by government, rent, postal services, and school fees had increased by well over 1,000 per cent in a year. By the end of July inflation was reported at 1,184 per cent, and on 1 August the government knocked three zeros off the nation's currency by creating a "kilo-dollar", in effect devaluing the Zimbabwe dollar by 60 per cent. The intention was to rationalise the circulation of trillions' worth of small denomination banknotes, and return the currency to the 15-digit capacity of banking software. Independent economists criticised the measure for ignoring the true causes of inflation: the excessive printing of money, the collapse of commercial agriculture, and rampant corruption within the government and civil service.

In March Gideon Gono, governor of the Reserve Bank of Zimbabwe (the country's central bank), attacked draft legislation prepared by the ruling Zimbabwe African National Union-Patriotic Front (ZANU-PF) government which would facilitate the compulsory acquisition of a majority share in leading mining companies, the last significant foreign-currency earners in the country. Gono, who had wrongly predicted an upturn in the country's economic fortunes after March, remained the only official whose criticism of government policy was tolerated. He clashed repeatedly with Herbert Murerwa, the finance minister, on issues of monetary policy. Later in the year he was said to be positioning himself as a possible successor to the 82-year-old president, Robert Mugabe, and came under personal attack by other groups in the succession struggle. Gono's endeavours to secure financial backing from first the IMF, then Russia, China, and Iran gave him protection, but by the end of the year no external investment was in sight.

Attempts by Mugabe to root out corruption through the efficient but feared Central Intelligence Organisation drew particular attention to illegal activity among his own ministers. In July Bright Matonga, the deputy minister of information, was arrested on suspicion of bribery. In November both Gideon Gono and the agriculture minister, Joseph Made, were questioned in relation to a fertiliser importation scam. Even Mugabe's vice-president, Joice Mujuru, was linked to reported improprieties at Ziscosteel, the near-bankrupt state iron and steel company. The same month Mujuru's husband, the former army general Solomon Mujuru, was implicated in exchange control irregularities. Obert Mpofu, minister of industry and international trade, who sought to raise public concerns about the Ziscosteel collapse, was threatened with contempt of Parliament. A powerful ZANU-PF kleptocracy appeared ready to help itself to the country's resources at the expense of the unemployed and impoverished majority. In August Mugabe himself moved into a 26-bedroom "retirement palace", built in suburban Harare at a cost of US$26 million. Fifteen months earlier his government had rendered thousands homeless in its forced eviction programme, "operation murambatsvina" (see AR 2005, p. 252).

At the annual ZANU-PF party conference in Goromonzi, outside Harare, in mid-December, plans to amend the constitution and extend Mugabe's presidential term—purportedly to "synchronise" with legislative elections in 2010—encountered clear opposition. The issue temporarily united the two factions competing for the presidency, that of the Mujurus on one hand, and of the former parliamentary speaker and current rural housing minister, Emmerson Mnangagwa, on the other. Rather than receiving spontaneous acclaim, the plan was referred to the party's central committee for further discussion. By late December a "stop Mugabe campaign" had been launched by ZANU-PF members of Parliament, the first open resistance to Mugabe in his 26 years as Zimbabwe's leader.

Squabbling within ZANU-PF represented the only sustained challenge to Mugabe's government. The opposition Movement for Democratic Change (MDC), fractured since the previous November over the issue of elections to the Senate (the newly-created second legislative chamber), continued to confront itself rather than the government (see AR 2005, p. 252). On 25 February the pro-Senate MDC faction elected as its leader a former student activist and academic, Professor Arthur Mutambara, a new figure in Zimbabwe's political life. The following month Mutambara's rival, the long-time MDC leader Morgan Tsvangirai, appeared to raise his game by declaring that "the dictator must brace himself for a long bustling winter". Through the mediation of a Christian action group, the Christian Alliance, the competing leaders met on 29 July. They embraced, engaged in discussion and committed themselves to work together to oppose Mugabe's administration. But despite repeated evidence of government incompetence and an avalanche of financial misdemeanours towards the end of the year, the MDC made little impact, being described by the *Zimbabwe Independent* as "asleep at the watch".

With unemployment at 80 per cent, public despair was manifested by instances of brave and spontaneous small-scale protest. In September the Zimbabwe Congress of Trade Unions demonstrated against the harsh effects of the declining economy, and in November student activists marched through central Harare. A public protest to mark International Women's Human Rights Defenders' Day the same month led to 34 arrests. Outside the country the 3 million exiled Zimbabweans were increasingly vocal. In London Free Zimbabwe Youth campaigned during the state visit of Mozambique's President Armando Guebuza against his government's failure to tackle the Zimbabwe issue. South Africa's foreign minister, Nkosazana Zuma, was heckled by Zimbabwean students on similar grounds during a debate at the Oxford Union.

In April a report from the World Health Organisation noted that the average life expectancy of Zimbabwean women had fallen to 34, the lowest in the world, while that for Zimbabwean men was 37. As the country's civil infrastructure deteriorated, rumours surfaced that the government would not have the money to pay the army, police force, or civil service. By December inflation had risen to 1,281 per cent. The president had misjudged the tolerance of his crippled nation, and his influence was ebbing away.

BOTSWANA—LESOTHO—NAMIBIA—SWAZILAND

Botswana

CAPITAL: Gaborone AREA: 582,000 sq km POPULATION: 1,765,000
OFFICIAL LANGUAGES: English and Setswana POLITICAL SYSTEM: multiparty republic in British Commonwealth
HEAD OF STATE AND GOVERNMENT: President Festus Mogae (since March '98)
RULING PARTY: Botswana Democratic Party (BDP)
MAIN IGO MEMBERSHIPS (NON-UN): AU, SADC, SACU, ACP, CWTH, NAM
CURRENCY: pula (end-'06 £1=P11.7685, US$1=P6.10500)
GNI PER CAPITA: US$5,180, US$10,250 at PPP ('05)

Lesotho

CAPITAL: Maseru AREA: 30,000 sq km POPULATION: 1,795,000
OFFICIAL LANGUAGES: English & Sesotho POLITICAL SYSTEM: multiparty monarchy in British Commonwealth
HEAD OF STATE: King Letsie III (since Jan '96)
RULING PARTY: Lesotho Congress for Democracy (LCD)
HEAD OF GOVERNMENT: Bethuel Pakalitha Mosisili, Prime Minister (since June '98)
MAIN IGO MEMBERSHIPS (NON-UN): AU, SADC, SACU, ACP, CWTH, NAM
CURRENCY: maloti (end-'06 £1=M13.4827, US$1=M6.90550)
GNI PER CAPITA: US$960, US$3,410 at PPP ('05)

Namibia

CAPITAL: Windhoek AREA: 824,000 sq km POPULATION: 2,031,000
OFFICIAL LANGUAGES: Afrikaans & English POLITICAL SYSTEM: multiparty republic in British Commonwealth
HEAD OF STATE: President Hifikepunye Pohamba (SWAPO), since March '05
RULING PARTY: South West Africa People's Organisation (SWAPO)
HEAD OF GOVERNMENT: Nahas Angula, Prime Minister (since March '05)
MAIN IGO MEMBERSHIPS (NON-UN): AU, SADC, COMESA, SACU, ACP, CWTH, NAM
CURRENCY: Namibian dollar (end-'06 £1=N$13.4827, US$1=N$6.90550)
GNI PER CAPITA: US$2,990, US$7,910 at PPP ('05 est, based on regression)

Swaziland

CAPITAL: Mbabane AREA: 17,350 sq km POPULATION: 1,131,000
OFFICIAL LANGUAGES: English & Siswati POLITICAL SYSTEM: non-party monarchy in British Commonwealth
HEAD OF STATE: King Mswati III (since '86)
HEAD OF GOVERNMENT: Absalom Themba Dlamini, Prime Minister (since Nov '03)
MAIN IGO MEMBERSHIPS (NON-UN): AU, COMESA, SADC, SACU, ACP, CWTH, NAM
CURRENCY: lilangeni/pl. emalangeni (end-'06 £1=E13.4827, US$1=E6.90550)
GNI PER CAPITA: US$2,280, US$5,190 at PPP ('05)

BOTSWANA, Lesotho, Namibia, and Swaziland faced a number of common issues, notably challenges in respect of economic development, food insecurity, poverty, and the HIV pandemic.

In Botswana annual inflation stood at 8.6 percent in 2005, but rose steeply at the beginning of 2006, reaching a 13-year record in February, as a result of rising oil prices and the effects of currency devaluations in 2004 and 2005. In addition, after 20 years of free provision, the government had introduced school fees for secondary education, a controversial measure in a country renowned for the quality and accessibility of social services. By December, however, year-on-year inflation had fallen to 8.5 per cent, although this was still above the government's objectives of 4-7 percent.

Botswana was the world's largest producer of diamonds by value. Botswana and the mining company, De Beers, agreed to establish a Diamond Trading Company Botswana (DTCB), which would sort and value all of Debswana's diamonds (a diamond mining partnership between De Beers and the Botswana government). Botswana furthermore remained committed to beneficiating (cutting and polishing) diamonds, as opposed to having this done elsewhere.

The position of Botswana's minority San (Bushman) ethnic group was highlighted by the conclusion of a long-running case in the country's High Court that centred on the eviction of some 1,000 San from their ancestral home in the central Kalahari game reserve. The San had accused the Botswana government and De Beers of having evicted them to clear the land for mining. The government said that the San had agreed to leave the reserve voluntarily, and that they had been paid compensation. In December, the San won the right to return to the land. In a majority decision, the court found that the San were dispossessed unlawfully and without their consent.

Some 24.1 per cent of Botswana's population between the ages of 15 and 49 was estimated to be HIV-positive, according to a report by UNAIDS. People infected with the virus, were, however able to access anti-retroviral drugs from the government: some 70,000 people, including 6,000 children, were being treated on this programme.

In Lesotho GDP grew by some 2.9 per cent in 2005. The country's agricultural production had been subjected to disruption by a drought between 2002 and 2005, and by heavy rains in the early part of 2006, which destroyed some 35 per cent of crops planted.

The country's textile industry, buffeted by competition from producers in China, was making a recovery. This was due to a concerted campaign by the country's government and industry to become "a destination of ethical choice", as well as to the lower costs of production.

HIV/AIDS remained a major challenge, with 23.2 per cent of adults between 15 and 49 being HIV positive. The problem was exacerbated by a shortage of healthcare workers. Lesotho was engaged in a "know your status campaign", aimed at providing testing and counselling, with the objective of reaching all households by 2007. Of the 180,000 orphaned and vulnerable children (OVCs) in the country, some 100,000 were estimated to have lost their parents to the disease. Early in 2006, the government approved a policy for caring for OVCs, offering care, education, and future opportunities.

Controversy continued in relation to the Lesotho highlands water project, a large dam construction endeavour. Several officials and firms had been implicated in corruption, but Lesotho received praise from many quarters, including from the president of the World Bank, Paul Wolfowitz, for its perseverance in instituting prosecutions.

In late 2006, Lesotho began its active participation in the African Peer Review Mechanism, in terms of which it would conduct a broadly consultative internal self-assessment, and submit to review by a continental panel of eminent persons and African heads of state. The country assumed the chairmanship of the Southern African Development Community (SADC) from Botswana in August.

In NAMIBIA, the economy grew by some 4.2 per cent in 2005, and the IMF estimated that growth would be marginally higher in 2006. However, the country's land reform programme was a source of concern, as dissatisfaction grew with its slow pace. It was run on a "willing buyer-willing seller" principle, and the government asserted that not enough properties were being offered at reasonable prices. By 2006, some 150 commercial farms had been acquired, and some 10,000 people resettled. Beneficiaries were also frequently unable to run the farms on a successful commercial basis. The minister of land and resettlement, Jerry Ekandjo, said that Namibia had received some 240,000 applications for resettlement since the start of the programme, although many people had made repeated applications. A government report estimated that Namibia would have to spend some N$3.7 billion in the next 15 years to acquire 10.3 million hectares of commercial farmland to resettle some 6,727 families.

Namibia, which earned some 60 per cent of its foreign exchange from its diamond-mining industry, was at odds with De Beers over the renewal of a five-year sales contract. The Namibia government disagreed with the manner in which diamonds were marketed, and wanted to reduce its contribution to De Beers' marketing arm, the Diamond Trading Company. Like BOTSWANA, NAMIBIA wanted to promote local beneficiation of diamonds. After lengthy negotiations, an agreement was reached under which De Beers would sell a certain portion of its diamonds in Namibia, and a Namibian Diamond Trading Company would be established to handle distribution of diamonds.

Government-sponsored research conducted on Namibian households indicated that some 28 per cent were either poor or severely poor, as measured by the food-consumption ratio. Some 22 per cent of the Namibian workforce was seeking work, while a further 15 per cent was without work but not actively seeking any. In November 2006, the country's National Society for Human Rights said that respect for human rights had deteriorated. It cited unemployment, food insecurity, and poverty, as well as human rights violations: 123 people had lodged complaints about torture or other cruel or inhuman treatment with the society. It also noted that the backlog of cases in the nation's courts (some 93,552 in the lower courts) compromised the right to a fair trial.

The government established a ministry for veterans of the conflict for Namibia's independence, a demand of former participants in the conflict.

Mozambique had a similar ministry, while the demands of Zimbabwe's war veterans (or those claiming to be veterans) was a significant factor behind violence and land invasions in the late 1990s in that country.

Namibia continued to contend with the HIV/AIDS pandemic. Some 19.6 per cent of its adult population was infected with the virus, producing a growing number of orphans and vulnerable children (OVCs), and contributing to the malnourishment of around one-quarter of children in Namibia. A programme including government, the UN's World Food Programme, and NGOs was initiated to provide adequate nutrition to OVCs and to register participating orphans for government financial support. However, the WFP noted that a shortage of funding was retarding their efforts. In November 2006, the WFP said that it was "extremely difficult" to secure funds for small countries like NAMIBIA, LESOTHO, and SWAZILAND, and that since opening offices in Namibia in 2005, no donations had been received.

A new constitution entered into force in SWAZILAND, sub-Saharan Africa's last absolute monarchy, in January 2006. The product of a lengthy drafting process, it was regarded by observers as politically conservative, as it did not significantly temper the absolute rights of the king, Mswati III, but as socially enlightened (by granting women equality with men). In October a woman, Constance Similane, was appointed as Swaziland's deputy prime minister.

Opposition groups, such as the Swaziland Coalition of Concerned Civic Organisations, rejected the constitutional process as being dominated by the monarchy. Of particular concern was that the constitution did not specifically protect the right to form political parties. In March police dispersed a demonstration by the People's United Democratic Movement, a banned opposition group, in the town of Manzini. Prince Mangaliso Dlamini, brother of the king and head of the Constitutional Review Commission, had warned that the constitution did not allow political parties to operate. There appeared to be some ambiguity about this, however, as a royalist party—Sive Siyinqaba, which had formerly existed as a cultural organisation and had defended the powers of the monarch—launched itself as a political party in August.

Swaziland's GDP grew at 2.3 per cent in 2005, and the IMF estimated that growth would be slightly lower (at around 2 per cent) in 2006, which was insufficient to match population growth of some 2.9 per cent per year. Economic difficulties continued to dog the country: its textile industry continued its decline owing to Asian competition and the rising strength of the lilangeni (the Swazi currency, pegged to the South African rand), sugar exports suffered as the EU downscaled its preferential trade agreement with Swaziland, and little foreign investment was forthcoming. Estimates of employment in the country suggested that the number of formal-sector jobs had declined by at least 50 per cent between 2002 and 2006, while in 2001 (the latest period for which data were available), some 29 per cent of the workforce was unemployed. Chronic drought hit subsistence farming particularly hard, forcing thousands of families to depend on food aid. In 2005, Swaziland suffered disinvestment to the value of some US$14 million.

At 33.4 per cent, Swaziland's HIV infection rate was among the highest in the world. The government announced a plan of action to provide some US$243.7 million for the needs of the large number of orphaned and vulnerable children, in part a product of the HIV/AIDS epidemic. By October, however, it announced that it was unable to make payments as the money had been depleted. Swaziland's health services were meanwhile under severe pressure, owing to a shortage of staff. Emigration and the impact of HIV/AIDS meant that 44 per cent of physicians' posts and 19 per cent of nurses' were unfilled.

SOUTH AFRICA

CAPITAL: Pretoria AREA: 1,221,000 sq km POPULATION: 45,192,000
OFFICIAL LANGUAGES: Afrikaans, English & nine African languages POLITICAL SYSTEM: multiparty republic in British Commonwealth
HEAD OF STATE AND GOVERNMENT: President Thabo Mbeki (since June '99)
RULING PARTY: African National Congress (ANC)
MAIN IGO MEMBERSHIPS (NON-UN): AU, SADC, SACU, CWTH, NAM
CURRENCY: rand (end-'06 £1=R13.4827, US$1=R6.90550)
GNI PER CAPITA: US$4,960, US$12,120 at PPP ('05 est, based on regression)

DURING 2006, South Africa was dominated by speculation about, and jockeying for, the presidency of the country. Local government elections were held and the country continued to struggle with extensive socio-economic and security challenges. On the foreign policy front it pursued an expansive and active agenda, and achieved a long-sought goal of election to the UN Security Council as a non-permanent member.

The controversy surrounding the former deputy president, Jacob Zuma, continued. He stood trial on two charges, one concerning the rape of a family friend and the other of corruption in respect of a large arms deal: he was alleged to have been aware that his former financial adviser, Schabir Schaik, had tried to arrange for large annual payments from a foreign arms company in exchange for shielding the deal from corruption investigations. Zuma was acquitted on the rape charge in May, while the second case was struck off the roll (the prosecution having requested a postponement, which the court denied) in September.

Zuma's apparent vindication was heralded as a major victory for him, bolstering his chances of assuming the presidency of the ruling African National Congress (ANC) at its national congress in December 2007, and, consequently, the presidency of the country when the present incumbent, Thabo Mbeki, left office in 2009. Zuma appeared to hold widespread support from the left of the ANC (in particular from its allies, the South African Communist Party and the Congress of South African Trade Unions). This was seen as a reflection of discontent with Mbeki's perceived aloofness and autocratic leadership style, as well as a belief that Zuma would prioritise the concerns of the poor, a perceived weakness of Mbeki, who was regarded as focusing on macro-economic stability at the expense of poverty alleviation and job creation.

Zuma's allies called for his reinstatement as deputy president after the corruption case was struck off. However, the announcement by the National Prosecuting Authority soon afterwards that it might charge him again, sparked renewed tensions, with the Young Communists League warning that "hell will be unleashed in South Africa", should this happen, and other supporters echoing the YCL's sentiment that Zuma was being victimised and humiliated.

On 1 March South Africa held elections to the country's municipal governments. These were held in the context of the municipalities' difficulties in terms of a lack of resources against the extensive responsibilities assigned to them. The ANC took some 66 per cent of the total vote, the Democratic Alliance (DA) 15 per cent, the Inkatha Freedom Party (IFP) 8 per cent, and the Independent Democrats (ID) 2 per cent. The results suggested that the ANC had retained its position as the country's dominant party, and that no opposition groups had made significant progress in attracting disaffected ANC voters.

Preparations continued for hosting the 2010 Football World Cup, amid doubts that the country would be ready in time. Reports in the foreign media indicated that executives of the International Football Association (FIFA) had privately expressed concerns that South Africa could handle the event and were discussing contingency plans to stage the event elsewhere. Subsequently, FIFA denied the existence of such plans.

As a signatory to the African Peer Review Mechanism (under which countries agreed to conduct self-assessments of governance and developed plans of action to address shortcomings), South Africa underwent most of its review process during 2006. A widely-held belief that the government was trying to control the process characterised much of the self-assessment aspect and caused considerable dissatisfaction among civil society participants. This was aggravated by the final self assessment report from which a great deal of politically sensitive material had been excised. The country review team, headed by Nigerian economist Adebayo Adedeji, conducted its country review visit in July 2006, and completed its report in November. This discussed a number of issues which had been removed from South Africa's self-assessment report, thus implicitly criticising it.

South Africa continued to grapple with the challenges of HIV/AIDS. The infection rate stood at some 18.8 per cent of people in the 15 to 49 age bracket. The government's response to the disease continued to be perceived as inadequate and embarrassing. South Africa received considerable derision following the biennial International Aids Conference in Toronto in August, where the South African stall emphasised the role of herbal and nutritional remedies in dealing with the disease. In September and October, press reports said that the minister of health, Dr Manto Tshabalala-Msimang, widely associated with and blamed for the deficiencies of South Africa's approach to AIDS, would no longer be at the forefront of the country's AIDS efforts. The president announced that the deputy president, Phumzile Mlambo-Ngcuka, would assume the chair of the South African National AIDS Council; and the deputy minister of health, Nozizwe Madlala-Routledge, began to play a more active role on AIDS policy issues. At the end of September there were some 213,800 people on anti-retroviral drugs, only one-quarter of the number thought to need the treatment.

Violent crime remained a serious concern. During the course of the year, there was a marked spike in serious and violent crime in many provinces, leading to an announcement by the department of safety and security of a six-month national offensive against crime. There were 18,545 cases of murder between April 2005 and March 2006, a small improvement over the same period in 2004-05 (18,793 cases), and a significant improvement when compared to the same period in 2001-02 (21,405 cases). The government did not always appear to acknowledge the depth of public concern about the issue, or deal with it with sensitively. In particular, the commissioner of police, Jackie Selebi, had not communicated government plans for fighting crime adequately; and the minister for safety and security, Charles Nqakula, said in Parliament that people who "whinged" about crime should emigrate, although he subsequently retracted the statement. In addition, Selebi was embroiled in controversy over his relationship with a person allegedly prominently involved in organised crime, Glenn Agliotti. While admitting to a friendship with Agliotti, Selebi denied any wrongdoing. However, the perception of very poor judgement on Selebi's part did his reputation, and that of the police, much harm. Agliotti was arrested in December on suspicion that he had been involved in the murder of a businessman, Brett Kebble, in September 2005.

There were a few high profile cases which suggested favouritism or laxity in the penal system: Tony Yengeni, former ANC chief whip, was imprisoned on corruption charges, but was moved from the notorious Pollsmoor prison to Malmesbury prison, on the instructions of the correctional services minister; while an inmate, Annanias Mathe, being held in the maximum security facility in Pretoria (C-Max), escaped and somewhat embarrassingly was apprehended by a private security firm rather than by the police service.

Corruption in the public service and within the ruling party continued to plague the political establishment. In the "oilgate" scandal, an amount of R12 million was still owing to PetroSA, a South African parastatal company, by Imvume Management, which had diverted funds earmarked for paying Glencore, its foreign supplier for oil condensate, to the ANC in the run-up to the national election in 2004 (see AR 2005, p. 259). The "travelgate" scandal—relating to collusion between travel agents and members of Parliament (MPs) to get Parliament to pay for expensive airline tickets, which were not used but converted to cash—continued during 2006. Several MPs entered plea bargains, and a few resigned from Parliament. Around 200 current and former MPs had been implicated in the scandal.

South Africa continued to wrestle with its economic predicament: a generally sound economy, which was not producing adequate opportunities to deal with extensive unemployment. Real annual GDP growth in 2005 was 5.1 per cent, and was predicted by the Treasury to fall to around 4.4 per cent in 2006. This was below the 6 per cent level which would enable the economy to make a serious dent in unemployment. Some 25.6 per cent of the workforce was unemployed in 2006, around 0.9 of a percentage point lower than the previous year. Average inflation for 2005 was 3.4 per cent and 4.7 per cent for 2006.

In the realm of foreign policy, South Africa assumed the leadership of the Group of 77 (G-77) in January, where it committed itself to enhancing its role in relations with the developed world, supporting development goals for the developing world, implementing UN agreements, improving global governance challenges, and improving scientific and technological capacities in developing countries. South Africa continued its assistance to other African states. The deployments of South Africa troops in various African countries (Burundi, Côte d'Ivoire, Democratic Republic of Congo (DRC), and Sudan) were extended to March 2007, while a contingent was dispatched to the Comoros ahead of presidential elections. South Africa also signed a military co-operation pact with the DRC, among the provisions of which were to assist in integrating the various armed factions into one army. South Africa provided substantial support for the DRC presidential and legislative elections, including printing and distributing ballot papers, deploying police personnel, and dispatching a mission to observe the process (see pp. 259-60).

South Africa's intervention was less well-received in Côte d'Ivoire, where Mbeki had been mediating between the government and rebels at the request of the AU (see pp. 249-50). Mbeki was viewed by some as being too close to the incumbent government. In September, Senegalese President Abdoulaye Wade publicly criticised his role, and the following month a report by the Economic Community of West African States (ECOWAS) called for Mbeki to be removed as mediator. Mbeki subsequently announced that South Africa would step down from its mediation in Côte d'Ivoire to avoid any conflict of interest with its new role as a non-permanent member of the UN Security Council, a position to which it was elected in October (see p. 362).

VIII SOUTH ASIA AND INDIAN OCEAN

IRAN—AFGHANISTAN—CENTRAL ASIAN STATES

IRAN

CAPITAL: Tehran AREA: 1,633,000 sq km POPULATION: 70,000,000 (preliminary census results, Nov '06)
OFFICIAL LANGUAGE: Farsi (Persian) POLITICAL SYSTEM: multiparty republic, under religious leadership
SPIRITUAL GUIDE: Ayatollah Seyed Ali Khamenei (since June '89)
HEAD OF STATE: President Mahmoud Ahmadinejad (since Aug '05)
MAIN IGO MEMBERSHIPS (NON-UN): OPEC, ECO, CP, OIC, NAM
CURRENCY: Iranian rial (end-'06 £1=IR18,023.10, US$1=IR9,231.00)
GNP PER CAPITA: US$2,770, US$8,050 at PPP ('05)

THE government appeared in the first half of the year to have slipped markedly into the hands of the Islamists as President Mahmoud Ahmadinejad injected his fundamentalist beliefs into official policy. Most affected were foreign affairs, where cautious defence of the country's interests—particularly the furtherance of its nuclear programme—and above all concern for the survival of the Islamic regime had previously dictated an independent, low key approach.

Iranian involvement in the Islamic world's confrontation with Israel, opposition to the growth of US military interests in the Persian Gulf, and the management of Iran's links with the UN on nuclear development were dramatically changed. President Ahmadinejad moved towards open support of policies designed to stiffen the Islamic stand against Israel and to frustrate the Western powers in the Middle East, particularly the USA. Overt Iranian financial backing for Hamas in Palestine increased, as did direct encouragement to militant Shi'ite groups like Hezbullah in Lebanon, which could act as proxies for Iran. Co-religionists in the shape of the Ba'ath regime in Syria and the Shi'ite sector in Iraq were natural allies for Iran as it pursued this line.

The Iranian government pursued a collision course with the USA, the EU, and the International Atomic Energy Agency (IAEA) over the rapid expansion of its nuclear development programme into production of enriched uranium that could be used for manufacture of nuclear weapons. An IAEA-brokered suspension of Iranian research in 2005 was short lived (see AR 2005, pp. 262-63), and confrontation hardened on 3 January, when Iran made known that it was to resume nuclear research activities.

The Iranian authorities argued that their programme was for peaceful purposes and that the advance into research on uranium enrichment was not in contravention of the Nuclear non-Proliferation Treaty (NPT). IAEA seals at a nuclear facility in Natanz were removed on 10 January with the justification that the action was a "national right". Iranian talks continued with the EU troika (Germany, France, and the UK) but with a warning to Iran that the matter would be referred to the UN Security Council. The dispute worsened when, on 14 February, Ahmadinejad announced that experiments on uranium enrichment had begun.

The US and European groups lost patience and pushed for referral of the case to the Security Council, which on 29 March called on Iran to accept the IAEA's request to cease development of enrichment facilities. The option for other than diplomatic sanctions against Iran, however, was ruled out when permanent members of the Security Council failed to secure support from China and Russia for more swingeing penalties. The impasse was made more serious when, in a nationally televised address, President Ahmadinejad announced on 11 April that small quantities of enriched uranium had been successfully produced and proclaimed that Iran had "joined the club of nuclear countries" (for text see pp. 549-51).

During the summer, attempts at a compromise settlement were made by Russia, which offered to enrich Iranian uranium and by the EU troika, which proposed an aid programme for the civil development of the Iranian nuclear industry. US Secretary of State Condoleezza Rice intimated that, if a moratorium on uranium enrichment were agreed, the USA would take part in direct talks with the Iranian regime.

The Iranian side used this period covertly to accelerate its nuclear programme. On 14 November the Iranian president claimed that Iran would soon possess the means to run the full nuclear fuel cycle. On 21 December he stated that Iran would "go nuclear" by the start of the anniversary of the revolution in February 2007. Finally, the Security Council reached a unanimous decision in late December, with Resolution 1737 (2006), to impose sanctions on Iran in response to its failure to comply with the earlier resolution of 31 July (1696 (2006)) which had ordered Iran to halt uranium enrichment. The December resolution banned the export to and imports from Iran of nuclear equipment and materials, froze some Iranian bank accounts, and constrained travel by named individuals (for text see pp. 542-48).

Iran's insistence on developing the potential to construct nuclear weapons, and the muscle flexing by the Iranian president, attracted followers at home, made neighbouring states anxious, and incensed the USA. The determination of the Iranian government to become a member of the nuclear club dominated foreign policy, and gave added importance to President Ahmadinejad's close support of Hezbullah in Lebanon and Hamas in the Palestine territories in their struggle against Israel, a country which, Ahmadinejad had declared in October 2005, should be "wiped off the map". The successes claimed by Hezbullah during the war in Lebanon (see pp. 197-203) gave the appearance of an Iranian-orchestrated challenge by the Shi'ite communities of the Middle East to Israel, the Western powers, and the orthodox Sunni populations of the region. The divide between Sunni and Shi'ite versions of Islam was exacerbated by the internecine strife in Iraq, and Iran seemed, by the end of the year, to be politically in the ascendant in large areas of the Near and Middle East.

Oil revenues in recent years had been extremely high, providing the government with the financial resources to import goods and services with little constraint and to spend abroad to make allies and influence poorer countries. Iran graduated from a posture of comparative quietism in religious and foreign affairs to being a significant manipulator of events in the region, seeking political hegemony in the Persian Gulf and, in religion, active leadership of the major Shi'ite communities world wide. It was apparent too, during the course of the year, that the influence of President Ahmadinejad on the foreign policy of the Islamic Republic had resulted in a very aggressive stance towards the West.

On the Palestine question he overturned the principle that Iran should be no more radical than the Palestinians themselves. There was evidence that the supply of arms and financial subventions to Shi'ite militias in Iraq and Lebanon was much augmented, while anti-Israeli organisations such as the Hamas government in Gaza also received funds from Iran. Ahmadinejad's engagement in battles in the Levant was, however, far from universally popular within the Iranian regime or among the Iranian people, whose ambitions lay in economic progress and new employment opportunities at home.

In domestic politics the key events were the elections on 15 December for the Assembly of Experts (which had the power to appoint the country's supreme leader), local councils including Tehran City Council, and the elections for seats in the Majlis (the legislature). The president and his supporters suffered a set back in a good (64 per cent) turnout of voters. The progressive core of the regime represented by former President Ali Akbar Hashemi Rafsanjani and his allies improved its position; the mayor of Tehran, Mohammed Baqer Qalibaf, and other reformists such as Mehdi Chamran, who led the Tehran council, were also successful.

The election results proved Ahmadinejad to be less popular than expected. His undoing appeared to have arisen from fears that Iran was being dragged into uncertain ventures in Iraq, Lebanon, and Palestine. The international conference on the Holocaust, attended by numerous established Holocaust deniers, held in Tehran on 11-12 December and sponsored by the president, succeeded in gratuitously alienating world opinion and was not to the taste of many Iranians.

The preliminary results of the sixth national census, published in November, showed a total population of 70 million, with unemployment at 12 to 15 per cent. The fighting in Iraq and Afghanistan caused major movements of refugees into Iran, possibly totalling 3 million individuals, who joined the lower paid workforce and pushed down both job opportunities for Iranian nationals and their wage rates. The task of diversifying the economy away from oil dependence, which was a priority of the Islamic regime, was complicated by the rise in international oil prices and the growth by 16 per cent in Iran's annual oil income (estimated at US$70 billion). The oil, petrochemicals, and natural gas industries performed well but, other than a surge in the growth of small private sector enterprises and a tenacious adherence to cultivation of the farming community, growth rates were mediocre. The economy as a whole was characterised by the IMF as inefficient, inflation prone, and inflexible. Distortions were induced by huge subsidies on basic food items and fuel, while privatisation of the considerable industrial holdings of the state was slow and lacking conviction. Inflation rose to 20 per cent.

Part of the difficulty with initiating economic development was political, since the central role of the Management and Planning Organisation was under attack by the office of Supreme Leader Ayatollah Khamene'i, which obstructed the implementation of the proposed five-year and 20-year plans. In the place of the planned development was a poorly conceived "justice share" programme that called for the distribution to the underprivileged of shares in state owned commercial entities slated for privatisation. This predictably failed to reduce the decline in the welfare of the poorer groups in society.

AFGHANISTAN

CAPITAL: Kabul AREA: 650,000 sq km POPULATION: 28,766,000 ('03)
OFFICIAL LANGUAGES: Pushtu, Dari (Persian) POLITICAL SYSTEM: multiparty republic
HEAD OF STATE AND GOVERNMENT: President Hamid Karzai (since Dec '04)
MAIN IGO MEMBERSHIPS (NON-UN): ECO, CP, OIC, NAM
CURRENCY: afgani (end-'06 £1=Af94.9536, US$1=Af49.2600)
GNI PER CAPITA: US$875 or less ('05 est), -

THE year began with a symbol of optimism when on 2 January, in one of its first measures since legislative elections in September 2005 (see AR 2005, p. 264), Afghanistan's new democratic National Assembly (bicameral legislature) ordered the removal of the concrete security barriers surrounding foreign compounds that had been erected after the US-led invasion in 2001 to protect offices and homes from attack. Hope was short-lived, however. Just three days later a Taliban suicide bomb attack—the latest in a series over the previous three months—killed 10 and wounded 50 at a bazaar in Uruzgan province, increasing fears that Iraqi influence was shaping the escalating insurgency. By late December, it had become evident that Afghanistan had suffered its most violent year since 2001.

Stepping up their attacks dramatically, the Taliban made their comeback in the south of the country, crossing the borders from Pakistan to fight with unexpected ferocity and firepower. By the end of the year a total of around 200 coalition soldiers had been killed, more than the total for both of the previous years combined; casualties among Afghans, including the Taliban, government forces, and civilians, ran into the thousands. The engagement of coalition forces in battle was joined by a spate of roadside bombs and suicide bombings, tactics previously unheard of in the country.

A conference of international donors in London during February saw countries pledging US$10.5 billion in reconstruction aid over a five-year period, as well as setting targets for improvements in human rights, economic development, and security. President Hamid Karzai subsequently claimed that Afghanistan had been offered just a fraction of what was needed to rebuild the country.

On 26 January the UK announced that it was to deploy around 6,000 troops during 2006 in its largest and most dangerous military operation since the invasion of Iraq in 2003. The majority of troops were sent to the volatile Helmand province, in a three-year mission that included suppressing the escalating opium industry in that region. Other forces were designated to form the headquarters of the NATO-led and UN-mandated International Security Assistance Force (ISAF) in Kabul.

US-led air strikes on Taliban targets near Kandahar on 22 May resulted in the deaths of 16 civilians when homes and a school apparently sheltering insurgents were also bombed. Just seven days later, a US military vehicle crashed into traffic in Kabul, killing five Afghans. In the ensuing violence, which included the setting alight of cars and foreign aid agency offices, the looting of businesses, and the stoning of US soldiers, 16 people were killed and 142 injured. The unrest served to underline the population's growing resentment towards the foreign military presence.

A major anti-Taliban offensive, "Operation Mountain Thrust", was launched by coalition forces on 15 June. By the end of the month it had resulted in the death of more than 250 people. The operation deployed around 11,000 Afghan, British, Canadian, and US troops throughout four of the most troubled provinces in the south, and continued into July, as the coalition neared the end of its command before transferring the command of coalition operations in the six southern provinces of Day Kundi, Helmand, Kandahar, Nimroz, Uruzgan, and Zabul to NATO.

Although more than 600 Taliban militants were killed during July, and despite US claims that the operation had been successful, the UK commander of NATO forces in the country, General David Richards, warned that the situation was "close to anarchy", with six British soldiers killed in the space of a few weeks. The upsurge in fighting continued throughout August, with the deaths of a further eight British soldiers. On 1 August, insurgents killed three British troops in an ambush the day after NATO took over operations in the region. General Richards compared the intense fighting in Helmand to the Korean War and World War II.

The challenge facing British troops was underlined when it was revealed on 16 August that Afghan opium cultivation had soared, with a record poppy harvest up by more than 40 per cent from 2005. The sharp increase came despite costly coalition measures, with the largest rise in production occurring in British-patrolled Helmand province.

Relations with Pakistan became progressively more strained by the year's end as the two countries tried to assign responsibility for cross-border insurgency. Although Pakistani President General Pervez Musharraf and President Karzai met in September for talks which they described in a joint news conference as "highly fruitful", relations were later damaged by comments attributed to Musharraf implying that Karzai was weak and incapable of defeating the Taliban. In an attempt to smooth relations, US President George W. Bush hosted a dinner in honour of the pair at the White House on 28 September, with plans made to establish tribal councils to resolve the violence. However, on 13 December Karzai contributed to a further cooling of relations, claiming that Pakistan wanted to "enslave" Afghans, but that the country would "never yield".

In the month in which NATO assumed control of coalition forces in the east from the US-led alliance—giving NATO control of operations throughout Afghanistan—a NATO bombing raid near Kandahar on 24 October resulted in as many as 31 civilians killed. Karzai appointed a special committee to investigate the air strike, while a number of organisations criticised the tactics of NATO, whose supreme commander, General James L. Jones, publicly apologised for the deaths. In November, NATO heads of state and government agreed to a small increase in the number of alliance troops in Afghanistan, of just 5 per cent. The leaders also agreed to abolish a number of national restrictions on troop movements and activities which had prevented some countries from deploying both personnel and equipment to the more volatile regions in the south and east.

By the end of 2006 many observers saw NATO's mission as a formidable one: to rebuild the country's infrastructure and win over support from Afghans for their elected government rather than for the resurgent Taliban, all in the context of fierce fighting and a growing civilian death toll.

KAZAKHSTAN—TURKMENISTAN—UZBEKISTAN—KYRGYZSTAN—TAJIKISTAN

Kazakhstan

CAPITAL: Astana AREA: 2,717,000 sq km POPULATION: 15,146,000
OFFICIAL LANGUAGES: Kazakh & Russian POLITICAL SYSTEM: multiparty republic
HEAD OF STATE AND GOVERNMENT: President Nursultan Nazarbayev (since Feb '90)
RULING PARTY: Nur-Otan People's Democratic Party
PRIME MINISTER: Daniyal Akhmetov (since June '03)
MAIN IGO MEMBERSHIPS (NON-UN): CIS, PFP, OSCE, OIC, ECO
CURRENCY: tenge (end-'06 £1=T246.868, US$1=T126.440)
GNI PER CAPITA: US$2,930, US$7,730 at PPP ('05)

Turkmenistan

CAPITAL: Ashgabat AREA: 488,000 sq km POPULATION: 4,833,000
OFFICIAL LANGUAGE: Turkmen POLITICAL SYSTEM: multiparty republic
HEAD OF STATE AND GOVERNMENT: acting President Gurbanguly Berdymukhammedov (since Dec '06)
RULING PARTY: Democratic Party of Turkmentistan (DPT)
MAIN IGO MEMBERSHIPS (NON-UN): CIS, PFP, OSCE, OIC, ECO, NAM
CURRENCY: Turkmen manat (end-'06 £1=M10,152.7, US$1=M5,200.00)
GNI PER CAPITA: US$876-US$3,465 ('05 est), -

Uzbekistan

CAPITAL: Tashkent AREA: 447,000 sq km POPULATION: 26,593,000
OFFICIAL LANGUAGE: Uzbek POLITICAL SYSTEM: multiparty republic
HEAD OF STATE AND GOVERNMENT: President Islam Karimov (since March '90)
RULING PARTY: People's Democratic Party (PDP)
PRIME MINISTER: Shavkat Mirziyoev (since Dec '03)
MAIN IGO MEMBERSHIPS (NON-UN): CIS, PFP, OSCE, OIC, ECO, NAM
CURRENCY: sum (end-'06 £1=S2,421.16, US$1=S1,240.06)
GNI PER CAPITA: US$510, US$2,020 at PPP ('05)

Kyrgyzstan

CAPITAL: Bishkek AREA: 199,000 sq km POPULATION: 5,156,000
OFFICIAL LANGUAGES: Kyrgyz & Russian POLITICAL SYSTEM: multiparty republic
HEAD OF STATE AND GOVERNMENT: President Kurmanbek Bakiev (since March '05)
RULING PARTY: Democratic Movement of Kyrgyzstan heads coalition
PRIME MINISTER: Feliks Kulov (since Sept '05)
MAIN IGO MEMBERSHIPS (NON-UN): CIS, PFP, OSCE, OIC, ECO
CURRENCY: som (end-'06 £1=S74.0467, US$1=S37.9250)
GNI PER CAPITA: US$440, US$1,870 at PPP ('05)

Tajikistan

CAPITAL: Dushanbe AREA: 143,000 sq km POPULATION: 6,507,000
OFFICIAL LANGUAGE: Tajik POLITICAL SYSTEM: multiparty republic
HEAD OF STATE AND GOVERNMENT: President Imomali Rahmonov (since Nov '92)
RULING PARTY: People's Democratic Party of Tajikistan
PRIME MINISTER: Akil Akilov (since Dec '99)
MAIN IGO MEMBERSHIPS (NON-UN): CIS, OSCE, OIC, ECO, PFP
CURRENCY: somoni (end-'06 £1=6.73790, US$1=3.42650)
GNI PER CAPITA: US$330, US$1,260 at PPP ('05)

THERE were no major upheavals in the Central Asian states during 2006. However, the situation in KYRGYZSTAN was far from stable. A year after the "Tulip revolution" of March 2005 (see AR 2005, p. 267), some of the leaders of the popular uprising that had removed President Askar Akayev from power openly condemned the new government for failing to implement reform. Moreover, corruption—one of the most powerful charges laid at the feet of the former regime—had increased exponentially and known criminals were flaunting their links with high-ranking officials. Relations between government and the legislature (the Supreme Assembly) deteriorated into open confrontation. There was also friction between Prime Minister Feliks Kulov and President Kurmanbek Bakiev. Protest rallies were held throughout the year, some demanding the resignation of Kulov, others criticising Bakiev. There was a tense showdown in early November, during which opponents of the government demanded constitutional reform and a curbing of presidential powers. In response, a revised constitution was hurriedly pushed through the legislature. However, this was later rejected owing to procedural lapses. In mid-December, Prime Minister Kulov and the entire cabinet resigned. President Bakiev refused to accept their resignation, creating more confusion. Further revisions to the constitution were proposed, but rejected by the legislature. The year ended with the standoff still unresolved.

By contrast, the situation in TAJIKISTAN was calm; the presidential election was held in an orderly fashion, as scheduled, on 6 November. Apart from the sitting president, Imomali Rahmonov, there were four other contenders. Press coverage focused on the incumbent leader, but the other candidates were given the legally required amount of access to broadcast and print media. The Islamic Rebirth party, whose long-standing leader, Said Abdulla Nuri, had died in August, chose not to field a presidential candidate. Two other opposition parties, the Democratic and the Social Democratic, boycotted the election. As anticipated, President Rahmonov was re-elected, though with a somewhat reduced majority, receiving 76.4 per cent of the vote (compared with 97 per cent in 1999).

In KAZAKHSTAN, the year began with Nursultan Nazarbayev, re-elected in a landslide victory in December 2005 (see AR 2005, p. 269), taking the presidential oath as he embarked on a new seven-year term of office. Setting out future goals, President Nazarbayev highlighted Kazakhstan's plans to join the World Trade Organisation in the near future and to chair the Organisation for Security and Co-operation in Europe (OSCE) in 2009. Domestically, the authorities appeared to be adopting a more conciliatory line towards the opposition, as evidenced by the granting of parole to the jailed leader, Ghalymzhan Zhaqiyanov. However, in early February Altynbek Sarsenbayev Sarsenbayuly, a prominent opposition figure, was murdered, along with his driver and bodyguard. Once a political ally of the president, Sarsenbayev had later joined the opposition party Bright Path (Ak Zhol) and subsequently was a cofounder of the splinter group, Naghyz Ak Zhol (formed in April 2005). Some claimed that the government was implicated in Sarsenbayev's murder, but others insisted that it was part of a smear campaign to discredit Nazarbayev. An official investigation was undertaken with assistance from the US Federal Bureau of Investigation; 10 members of the state administration and National Security Committee were eventually arrested and put on trial. Charges against the defendants included the allegation that they had plotted a coup d'etat against President Nazarbayev; all were found guilty and prison sentences ranging from three to 20 years were handed down.

In December, the president of TURKMENISTAN, Saparmurat Niyazov, who had led the country since independence and had been confirmed in office for life, died of a heart attack (for obituary see p. 589). He was known to have a serious heart condition, but did not appear to be at immediate risk. Yet contrary to the predictions of some commentators, his sudden demise did not cause a political upheaval. Health Minister and Deputy Prime Minister Gurbanguly Berdymukhammedov took over as acting head of state. After the state funeral, which was attended by high-ranking international delegations, it was announced that presidential elections would be held on 11 February 2007; six candidates were registered. Leading members of the exiled opposition announced that they intended to return to Turkmenistan to take part in the elections.

In UZBEKISTAN, the security clampdown that had been introduced following the violence in Andijan in May 2005 (see AR 2005, pp. 267-68) was maintained. Western governments continued to call for an independent enquiry into the Andijan events and the EU renewed the sanctions that it had imposed in May 2005. However, in an unexpected turn of events, refugees from Andijan who had been given asylum in the USA and in Europe began to petition the Uzbek government for permission to return home. By the end of the year around a hundred (approximately one-quarter) of those who had fled the country in 2005 had either returned or were waiting for their applications to be processed. Several claimed that they had never intended to seek asylum abroad but had been caught up in the confusion; some hinted that they had been misled by foreign officials.

There was a noticeable improvement in relations between the Central Asian states. A milestone event was President Nazarbayev's official visit to Tashkent at the end of February. Commenting on the Andijan events, the Kazakh leader said that Uzbek President Islam Karimov had acted to protect not only the peace of UZBEKISTAN, "but also that of Kazakhs, Kyrgyz and Tajiks". He added, "Today, it is known for certain through the intelligence services that groups of trained extremists had entered Uzbekistan with the aim of destabilising not only you but also us." He went on to call for closer bilateral co-operation to combat terrorism and drug trafficking. In September, President Karimov made a reciprocal visit to KAZAKHSTAN. The two leaders agreed to set up a co-ordination council under their joint patronage, aimed at speedily resolving bilateral issues. Several other measures to facilitate trade, communications, and investment were adopted.

There were also signs of greater co-operation between KYRGYZSTAN and UZBEKISTAN, particularly in the fight against "international terrorism" and "religious extremism". Relations between Kyrgyzstan and TAJIKISTAN, however, were more strained, exacerbated by ongoing, though small-scale, border incidents. There was also ongoing friction along the Tajik-Uzbek border; the Tajik authorities complained that the lives of innocent civilians were being put at risk by trigger-happy Uzbek border guards. Tension between the two states was further heightened when the Tajik security services arrested people on charges of spying for Uzbekistan; three of the accused received heavy prison sentences, despite their protestations of innocence.

Throughout the region, concern over militant Islamism increased. Dozens of suspected extremists were arrested, some of them for alleged involvement in cross-border terrorist attacks. In April, the National Security Committee of KAZAKHSTAN announced that it had broken up a terrorist group that was planning attacks on public places. Weapons had been found, as well as subversive books and tapes promoting radical religious views and propagating the idea of an Islamic caliphate. Similar arrests were made in UZBEKISTAN, also in KYRGYZSTAN and TAJIKISTAN. Most of the accused received long prison sentences. Yet despite the tough approach of the authorities, radical Islamist movements such as Hizb-ut Tahrir (Liberation Party), the Islamic Movement of Uzbekistan (also known as Islamic Movement of Turkestan), and the Jihadi Union seemed to be attracting a growing number of adherents.

On 8 September, the foreign ministers of KAZAKHSTAN, KYRGYZSTAN, TAJIKISTAN, TURKMENISTAN, and UZBEKISTAN signed a treaty creating a nuclear-weapon-free zone in Central Asia. The ceremony took place in Semipalatinsk, the former Soviet nuclear test site, the venue itself highlighting the symbolism of the event. The document was prepared over several years, under the aegis of the UN, and with input from several international partners, particularly Japan. This joint action, unprecedented in recent years, was an extraordinary sign of solidarity among the Central Asian states.

Involvement with the West also progressed. All the Central Asian states (including TURKMENISTAN) continued to participate in NATO's Partnership for Peace programme, but KAZAKHSTAN was the first to sign up to an individual partnership action plan (IPAP); this came into force in January. Several NATO-sponsored events were held in Kazakhstan during the year. In September, as part of the Kazakhstan-British Military Co-operation Programme (under the aegis of NATO), the regular anti-terrorist exercise "Steppe Eagle 2006" took place. However, the relationship between the government of KYRGYZSTAN and the US-led coalition forces involved in the campaign in Afghanistan and based at Manas (near Bishkek) deteriorated somewhat (see AR 2005, pp. 269-70). The Kyrgyz authorities demanded a 100-fold increase in rent for the use of the base. Negotiations continued throughout most of the year; details of the sum that was finally agreed were not disclosed in full, but it was clear that it was substantially less than the Kyrgyz were anticipating. A further cause of resentment was the conduct of US personnel. There were at least two serious incidents, one of which resulted in the death of a Kyrgyz citizen.

Central Asia's oil and gas resources continued to attract attention. In KAZAKHSTAN, it was announced that proven reserves in Kashagan, the offshore mega-oil field that was being developed by a Western consortium of international energy companies, were considerably larger than had originally been anticipated; however, owing to the extraordinarily difficult technical and environmental conditions, full-scale production would be delayed until 2009 or 2010. In June, Kazakhstan officially announced that it would join the Baku-Tbilisi-Ceyhan (BTC) oil pipeline, initially with a quota of 7.5 million tonnes, eventually rising to 25 million tonnes. This would allow Kashagan oil to be shipped directly to the Mediterranean.

Chinese acquisitions in Kazakhstan increased, but were still comparatively small scale and mostly involved joint deals with KazMunaiGaz, the Kazakh state oil and gas company. In July, the Chinese energy company, CNPC, sold a 33 per cent stake of PetroKazakhstan, the previously Canadian-owned company that it had acquired in October 2005, to KazMunaiGaz. On 31 December, China's International Trust and Investment Corporation (CITIC) acquired the Karazhanbas deposit from the Canadian-registered company, Nations Energy; again, the deal included offering KazMunaiGaz the option to buy a stake in the project. Energy ties between China and Kazakhstan were strengthened by the inauguration of a cross-border oil pipeline from Atasu (Kazakhstan) to Alashankou (China) in May. Preparatory work was already beginning on a cross-border gas pipeline.

In TURKMENISTAN, the government severely restricted the presence of foreign energy companies. However, Malaysia's national oil company, Petronas, which had concluded a 25-year production sharing agreement with the Turkmen government in 1996, expanded output. In April, during President Niyazov's visit to Beijing, he and China's President Hu Jintao signed an agreement whereby China would receive 30 billion cu m of Turkmen gas per annum from 2009, to be supplied via a new pipeline that was to be constructed from Turkmenistan to China. The convoluted dispute over Turkmenistan's supply of gas to Ukraine was partially resolved in March, when agreement was reached over the settlement of Ukraine's debt for shipments of Turkmen natural gas in 2003-05. However, there were also disagreements between Turkmenistan and Russia's Gazprom. Since Turkmen gas exports were transported through the Russian pipeline network, this also affected supplies to Ukraine. There were further problems in June, when the Turkmen government demanded a substantial price increase for its gas. Gazprom finally agreed to the price rise in September. This left Ukraine in a weakened position. Negotiations were still in progress at the end of the year.

The Central Asian presidents made a number of important official visits abroad. Apart from consolidating personal relationships and allowing for a frank exchange of views with foreign counterparts, these occasions provided opportunities for the signing of inter-governmental agreements and for developing public and private sector ties in areas of mutual interest. A notable outcome of Kazakh President Nazarbayev's visit to Washington DC in September was the signing of a joint statement with US President George W. Bush on the future of the strategic partnership between the two countries. In November, Nazarbayev visited the UK, where he met Queen Elizabeth II and held talks with Prime Minister Tony Blair and leaders of trade and industry. Following Egyptian President Hosni Mubarak's visit to KAZAKHSTAN earlier in the year, President Nazarbayev made a reciprocal visit to Egypt in December. Talks covered regional issues as well as trade and investment.

Security matters were high on the agenda during Uzbek President Karimov's visit to Pakistan in May. President General Pervez Musharraf spoke of closer co-ordination between the two countries in the fight against al-Qaida. Karimov also visited Seoul, where he signed a strategic partnership declaration with South Korea's president, Roh Moo Hyun. A number of economic agreements were signed, and the Korean National Oil Corporation and Korean Gas Corporation inked a memorandum of understanding with Uzbekneftegaz (Uzbekistan's national oil and gas company) on prospecting and developing oil and gas deposits in UZBEKISTAN. President Rahmonov of TAJIKISTAN visited Delhi in August and had meetings with the Indian president and prime minister. The two sides discussed co-operation in such fields as hydroelectric power generation and transport infrastructure, also the joint processing of Tajik aluminium.

INDIA—PAKISTAN—BANGLADESH—SRI LANKA—NEPAL—BHUTAN

India

CAPITAL: New Delhi AREA: 3,288,000 sq km POPULATION: 1,094,583,000
OFFICIAL LANGUAGES: Hindi & English POLITICAL SYSTEM: multiparty republic in British Commonwealth
HEAD OF STATE: President A.P.J. Abdul Kalam (since July '02)
RULING PARTIES: Congress (I)-led United Progressive Alliance (UPA) coalition (since May '04)
HEAD OF GOVERNMENT: Manmohan Singh (INC), Prime Minister (since May '04)
MAIN IGO MEMBERSHIPS (NON-UN): SAARC, CP, CWTH, NAM
CURRENCY: Indian rupee (end-'06 £1=Rs86.6107, US$1=Rs44.3600)
GNI PER CAPITA: US$720, US$3,460 at PPP ('05 est, based on regression)

Pakistan

CAPITAL: Islamabad AREA: 796,000 sq km POPULATION: 155,772,000
OFFICIAL LANGUAGE: Urdu POLITICAL SYSTEM: military regime with elected legislature in British Commonwealth
HEAD OF STATE AND GOVERNMENT: President (Gen.) Pervez Musharraf (since June '01), formerly Chief Executive Officer of National Security Council (since Oct '99)
RULING PARTIES: coalition led by Pakistan Muslim League—Quaid-i-Azam (PML)
PRIME MINISTER: Shaukat Aziz (PML) (since August '04)
MAIN IGO MEMBERSHIPS (NON-UN): OIC, SAARC, ECO, CP, NAM, CWTH (suspended)
CURRENCY: Pakistan rupee (end-'06 £1=PRs118.904, US$1=PRs60.9000)
GNI PER CAPITA: US$690, US$2,350 at PPP ('05)

Bangladesh

CAPITAL: Dhaka AREA: 144,000 sq km POPULATION: 141,822,000
OFFICIAL LANGUAGE: Bengali POLITICAL SYSTEM: multiparty republic in British Commonwealth
HEAD OF STATE: President Iajuddin Ahmed (since Sept '02)
RULING PARTIES: Bangladesh Nationalist Party (BNP) BNP-led coalition
HEAD OF GOVERNMENT: President Iajuddin Ahmed, chief adviser of caretaker government (since Oct '06)
MAIN IGO MEMBERSHIPS (NON-UN): SAARC, CP, OIC, CWTH, NAM
CURRENCY: taka (end-'06 £1=Tk133.535, US$1=Tk69.2750)
GNI PER CAPITA: US$470, US$2,090 at PPP ('05)

Sri Lanka

CAPITAL: Sri Jayawardenapura (Kotte) AREA: 66,000 sq km POPULATION: 19,582,000
OFFICIAL LANGUAGES: Sinhala, Tamil, English POLITICAL SYSTEM: multiparty republic in British Commonwealth
HEAD OF STATE: President Mahinda Rajapakse (SLFP) (since Nov '05)
RULING PARTIES: Sri Lanka Freedom Party (SLFP) heads United People's Freedom Alliance (UPFA) coalition (since April '04)
HEAD OF GOVERNMENT: Ratnasiri Wickremanayake, Prime Minister (since Nov '05)
MAIN IGO MEMBERSHIPS (NON-UN): SAARC, CP, CWTH, NAM
CURRENCY: Sri Lankan rupee (end-'06 £1=SRs210.181, US$1=SRs107.650)
GNI PER CAPITA: US$1,160, US$4,520 at PPP ('05)

Nepal

CAPITAL: Kathmandu AREA: 147,000 sq km POPULATION: 27,133,000
OFFICIAL LANGUAGE: Nepali POLITICAL SYSTEM: multiparty monarchy
HEAD OF STATE: King Gyanendra (since June '01)
RULING PARTIES: Seven-Party Alliance
HEAD OF GOVERNMENT: Prime Minister Girija Prasad Koirala (NCP) (since April '06)
MAIN IGO MEMBERSHIPS (NON-UN): SAARC, CP, NAM
CURRENCY: Nepalese rupee (end-'06 £1=NRs138.577, US$1=NRs70.9760)
GNI PER CAPITA: US$270, US$1,530 at PPP ('05)

Bhutan

CAPITAL: Thimphu AREA: 46,500 sq km POPULATION: 918,000
OFFICIAL LANGUAGES: Dzongkha, Lhotsan & English POLITICAL SYSTEM: non-party monarchy
HEAD OF STATE: Dragon King Jigme Khesar Namgyel Wangchuck (since Dec '06)
HEAD OF GOVERNMENT: Prime Minister (rotates among cabinet) Lyonpo Khandu Wangchuck (since Sept '06)
MAIN IGO MEMBERSHIPS (NON-UN): SAARC, CP, NAM
CURRENCY: ngultrum (end '06 £1=Nu85.4062, US$1=Nu44.3070)
GNI PER CAPITA: US$870 ('05), -

INDIA'S rise as a major world power continued during the year, although its own internal political processes were not always smooth. NEPAL saw what amounted to a political revolution. Elsewhere in the region, ethnic and regional conflict dominated the political scene. The regional economy showed strong performance with overall growth of around 8.2 per cent, although there were some country variations. Inflation, however, averaged nearly 8 per cent and poverty levels declined only modestly.

INDIA. The United Progressive Alliance (UPA) coalition government, led by Dr Manmohan Singh and dominated by his Congress party, successfully completed its second full year in office. In March there was a minor crisis when Sonia Gandhi, the widow of Rajiv Gandhi, who had declined the opportunity to become prime minister (see AR 2004, p. 294) but remained in many ways the most powerful figure in the Congress as well as acting as chair of the UPA, was forced to resign her parliamentary seat over a technicality, but a by-election held in May returned her to Parliament with a huge majority in a constituency that had always been closely identified with the Nehru-Gandhi family. The presence on the campaign trail of her two children, Rahul and Priyanka, born in 1970 and 1972 respectively, indicated that the next generation of the family was being readied to enter the political arena. The important post of minister for external affairs, vacant since K. Natwar Singh was forced to resign in November 2005 on corruption charges (see AR 2005, p. 275), was filled in October by the veteran Congress leader, Pranab Mukherjee, who moved sideways from the ministry of defence.

State assembly elections were held in five states in April and May, each with a very different set of dynamics. Overall, the results confirmed the status quo. The Congress lost a little ground but without seriously threatening its position, and the Communist Party of India (Marxist) (CPI(M))—an external ally of the Congress at national level while still critical of many of its policies—did well. In West Bengal, the CPI(M) won a record seventh term in office, with the result never in any doubt. The incumbent chief minister, Buddhadeb Bhattacharya, who had held office since 2000, continued with the pragmatic policies of his predecessor, Jyoti Basu, and looked to private sector and external investment to stimulate economic growth in the state, as well as pursuing his party's welfarist policies that had kept it in power for so long. The CPI(M), heading a coalition of other left and centrist parties, also secured an additional prize by taking the south Indian state of Kerala from the Congress party.

In the south Indian state of Tamil Nadu, where for 40 years power had been held by one or other faction of the Dravidian movement, there was a change of guard, with J. Jayalalithaa of the All-India Anna Dravida Munnetra Kazhagam (AIADMK) being ousted by M. Karunanidhi of the Dravida Munnetra Kazhagam (DMK). Both parties were committed to similar programmes of economic development alongside the protection of Tamil rights against what was often defined as an alien north Indian culture. The DMK was an ally of the Congress at the national level, so that its victory at the state level—where Congress had, in fact, contested separately—did not disturb the position in the national Parliament in New Delhi.

In Pondicherry (officially renamed Puducherry in September)—a small union territory adjacent to Tamil Nadu—the Congress-led coalition retained power. In the north-eastern state of Assam, where a number of different ethnic groups had been at odds, often violently, for many years, the Congress also managed to retain its position at the head of the ruling coalition. It had succeeded in displacing the Asom Gana Parishad as the voice of the local Assamese population, fearful of migration from other parts of India and BANGLADESH, on the one hand and local tribal militancy on the other. The coalition attempted peace talks with the militant United Front for the Liberation of Assam, which during the year carried out several targeted attacks on Hindi-speaking migrants from northern India, but these talks soon broke down, and towards the end of the year the Front was blamed for a series of bomb explosions in the state capital.

Overall, the opposition to the ruling UPA coalition remained fragmented and largely ineffective. The principal opposition party on the right, the Hindu nationalist Bharatiya Janata Party (BJP), had acquired a new leader at the beginning of the year, Rajnath Singh. He and his predecessor, L.K. Advani, attempted to generate support through concentrating on the status of the Muslim minority and the role of PAKISTAN in allegedly sponsoring terrorist acts in India, but they achieved only a muted response. However, in the south Indian state of Karnataka, local political differences led to the BJP participating in a coalition government with another party, the Janata Dal (Secular), and it also did well in local elections in Uttar Pradesh, especially in the cities. The BJP's ally in Maharashtra, the Shiv Sena, which had lost power in the state in 1999, split in March when Raj Thackeray, the nephew of its founder, set up his own Maharashtra Navnirman Samiti (Maharashtra Reconstruction Association).

As a coalition with a broadly centrist approach, the UPA had to take account of the interests of its various constituents, which were sometimes at odds with each other, or with the reforming thrust of the prime minister. The central government was forced, for example, to suspend the planned privatisation of the Neyveli lignite mines in Tamil Nadu in response to pressure from the DMK, which was concerned about the impact on employment. It was evident from her public statements that Sonia Gandhi, as chair of the coalition, was pressing the government to be more active in addressing poverty issues directly. In certain states suicides by small farmers, unable to cope with low prices for crops such as cotton, continued to increase, and it was estimated that there had been more than 8,000 such deaths in the past decade. The compulsory acquisition of land for factories or for special economic zones provoked opposition in several areas. In West Bengal, it was a prominent local political leader, Mamata Banerjee, who led a powerful movement against the CPI(M)'s decision to acquire agricultural land near Kolkata for a car manufacturing plant.

An issue that had featured in Indian politics since the 1950s and which achieved renewed prominence during 2006 was the mandating of quotas in employment and educational institutions for members of underprivileged groups, very often defined in terms of their status in the caste system. A senior Congress minister often seen as close to the Gandhi family, Arjun Singh, initiated moves to reserve seats for members of such groups in India's most prestigious educational institutions, the Indian Institutes of Technology and of Management, and this proposal provoked the anticipated backlash from upper caste groups, anxious about their own prospects, although not on the same scale as in 1990 when similar measures had been introduced. Many of his colleagues clearly felt that he was pushing the matter too fast and too far in order to bolster his own political position. There were even more concerns over a recommendation from a government committee in November that more needed to be done for the Muslim minority, whose economic condition in certain areas was worse than that of some of the groups who had already benefited from government action. The report of the committee was endorsed by the prime minister but it was clear that implementation of its recommendations would be difficult.

In March there was a series of bombings in the major religious centre of Varanasi in which 15 people died. In July the country suffered a major terrorist attack when co-ordinated bomb explosions took place on suburban rail services in Mumbai in which nearly 200 people were killed and many more injured. The attack attracted widespread national and international condemnation. Suspicion fell on one or more radical Islamic groups, and arrests were subsequently made of a number of individuals claimed by the police to be linked to the Lashkar-e-Toiba, a PAKISTAN-based group that had been prominent in Kashmir. Claims were also made that Pakistani official intelligence agencies were involved in helping to plan and direct the operation, but this was vigorously denied by the Pakistan government. A link was also suggested with the Students Islamic Movement of India (SIMI), which was banned by the government in April. In September there was a further terrorist outrage in the city of Malegaon in Maharashtra, where 37 were killed in a bomb attack. Members of SIMI were eventually arrested but it was also suggested that the Bajrang Dal, an extreme Hindu group seeking revenge for the July bombings, could have been responsible.

In Kashmir too there were occasional violent actions attributed to militant groups, including in May an episode in which 32 Hindus were massacred. The prime minister visited Srinagar (summer capital of Jammu and Kashmir) in May in order to engage with pro-autonomy groups but the main group, the All Parties Hurriyat Conference, refused to meet him. A similar initiative in February had also been rebuffed, although some less public contacts continued.

The government faced a dilemma in respect of the conviction of Afzal Guru, who had been arrested in connection with the lethal attack on the Indian Parliament building in 2001 (see AR 2001, p. 334). Mainstream opinion, orchestrated by the BJP and others, was strongly in favour of his execution, but it was recognised that this would have an adverse effect on many sections of Muslim opinion in Kashmir and elsewhere, and by the end of the year no decision had been made. Doubts were also raised by some human rights activists about the reliability of the evidence against him.

In Nagaland, where there had also been a longstanding militant movement aimed at securing independence for the state, the National Socialist Council of Nagaland extended its ceasefire at the beginning of the year and in September it was announced that oil and gas exploration, suspended for more than a decade, would resume. However, smaller dissident groups continued to enact sporadic acts of violence.

During the year several scandals embarrassed the government but without significantly damaging its position. In December, the federal coal minister, Shibu Soren, who had had a controversial political history (see AR 2005, p. 274), was sentenced to life imprisonment for the murder of a political aide during the 1990s. Many other members of the Parliament and state assemblies were also facing serious criminal charges, a reflection of the often violent character of local politics. In December, however, Laloo Prasad Yadav, the railways minister and a key figure in the UPA coalition because of his support among large sections of the rural electorate in north India, especially his home state of Bihar, was acquitted of 10-year old corruption charges.

PAKISTAN. Politics during the year were conducted in the shadow of the elections scheduled for 2007. In May the leaders-in-exile of the two major opposition parties in Pakistan, the Pakistan Muslim League (N) (PML(N)) and the Pakistan People's Party (PPP), Nawaz Sharif and Benazir Bhutto, signed a "charter of democracy" in London. Despite this show of unity, there were persistent and plausible rumours that the PPP was in discussion with President General Pervez Musharraf (through his advisors) about a political deal that would preserve the latter's position for a further period of years while allowing Benazir Bhutto to return to Pakistan. Such a deal would imply that President Musharraf would jettison his political supporters grouped under the Pakistan Muslim League (PML) banner, and could dispense with his support from the parties of the religious right, grouped together as the Muttahida Majlis-e-Amal (MMA), although this latter, in any case, became increasingly tenuous during the course of the year.

In the provinces, Punjab, the largest, remained under the control of the PML. The Muttahida Quami Movement (MQM), whose power base lay in Karachi and other urban centres of Sindh, began to establish a foothold in Punjab, using the argument that it stood for the people against the so-called feudal elite who formed the government. In Sindh, the ruling coalition showed signs of stress between its landlord-based rural elements, grouped under the PML banner, and the MQM, as well as between factions of the PML.

In North-West Frontier Province (NWFP) the MMA remained in power, although there was a divide between those who wanted to hold on to power, even at the cost of some compromise with the Musharraf government, and those who wanted a more confrontational approach, even at the cost of resignation from the government. In November, despite strong opposition from many quarters, the NWFP government pushed through the Hasba bill, authorising the enforcement of Islamic morality in people's private lives, although its implementation was stayed by a Supreme Court order.

In Balochistan, a PML-MMA coalition remained intact but was largely irrelevant to the armed struggle between the federal government and separatist forces, which claimed many lives on both sides. In April the government banned the Balochistan Liberation Army. This struggle intensified during the year, especially after government forces at the end of August killed a prominent tribal leader, Nawab Akbar Bugti. There was an intense debate among political parties and government over how best to bring peace, which embraced not simply Balochistan but the broader question of devolution of power to all the provinces, but no major initiatives had been taken by the end of the year.

One major concern of the government, in which domestic and international factors overlapped, was the ongoing resentment in the tribal areas along the Afghanistan border. Since the 19th century no government in the region had attempted to administer them, and it was generally believed that members both of al-Qaida and of the Taliban had sought refuge there, banking on cross-border solidarity among the Pathan tribes. From shortly after the US invasion of Afghanistan, the Pakistan army had been attempting to penetrate the region but encountered fierce resistance, with many casualties on both sides. In September, in a reversal of policy, the government announced that an agreement had been reached with tribal leaders in the North Waziristan area, where the fighting had been fiercest. However, this agreement was widely criticised internationally, especially by the USA, as a sell-out to the militants, who, under the terms of the agreement, were allowed to remain in the area. At the end of October, opposition to government policy was intensified after an air attack on a madrassah in the tribal area of Bajaur killed over 80 people. While the government asserted that it was carried out by Pakistani forces, it was widely believed to have been a cross-border attack by US forces. The following month, there was a suicide attack on a Pakistan army base which killed 40 soldiers and 20 civilians. This was generally seen as a revenge attack.

Sectarian killings continued to occur. In April a bomb killed almost all the top leadership of a religious group, the Sunni Tehrik, and many others at a meeting in Karachi. Suspicion fell on rival religious groups although no conclusive evidence was produced. In July a prominent Shi'ite cleric, Allama Hasan Turabi, was also assassinated in the city, although there was no necessary connection between the two events.

A longstanding problem in Pakistan was the perverse consequences of legislation passed under General Mohammed Zia-ul-Haq in the 1980s to implement Islamic provisions on sexual misconduct. Thousands of women spent years in prison without their cases being resolved and often on the basis of dubious or non-existent evidence. During 2006, the government introduced legislation to remedy the situation, but this was fiercely opposed by some elements of the MMA and also by some ruling party legislators. Eventually a watered down version was passed in November. It had the support of the PPP and MQM, but not the PML(N).

BANGLADESH. The political deadlock that had been a characteristic of Bangladesh's politics for many years became even more entrenched as the scheduled 2007 elections approached. In April two general strikes organised by the Awami League under Sheikh Hasina Wajed brought the economy to a virtual halt, and in July the party organised national protests calling for electoral reform. In October, the Bangladesh Nationalist Party (BNP) government, led by Begum Khaleda Zia, handed over to a caretaker government, which, under the constitution, was expected to hold the elections and to guarantee to domestic and international opinion that they had been conducted fairly. However, the first nominee as head of the interim government, a retired chief justice, refused to accept the assignment. President Iajuddin Ahmed, who had originally been the BNP's nominee for the position, then chose to make himself the caretaker head. Although within the letter of the constitution, this act was regarded as a partisan move by the Awami League, and a large-scale national protest campaign, which turned violent on occasion, was launched. Besides the question of who was to lead the caretaker government, the Awami League also demanded the revision of the country's electoral rolls, which were claimed to be out of date and padded with fictitious names.

The political battle was primarily between the two main political parties, both attempting to occupy the broad centre of the political spectrum. However, each was prepared to accept alliances with smaller Islamist groups, and to promise concessions to them on religious matters. The BNP faced defections at the end of October, when a group of its legislators, led by former President A.Q.M. Badruddoza Chowdhury, broke away to form the Liberal Democratic Party and started discussions with the Awami League. The Awami League was also in alliance with the former military ruler of the country, General H.M. Ershad, and argued strongly for his right to contest, despite continuing corruption charges against him. At the end of the year the deadlock continued, and it seemed doubtful that the elections would be held on schedule.

Bangladesh received a welcome boost when Professor Muhammad Yunus, founder of the Grameen Bank, whose micro-finance model was hugely influential throughout the world, was awarded the Nobel Peace Prize (see p. 441).

SRI LANKA. In Sri Lanka, the struggle between the Sri Lanka Freedom Party-led government and the Tamil Tigers (Liberation Tigers of Tamil Eelam, LTTE), which had begun to intensify at the end of 2005, rapidly grew more violent during the year. Over 3,400 deaths were reported by official sources, adding to the more than 65,000 fatalities since the conflict began in 1972 over the Tamil minority's demand for an autonomous or independent state in the north and east of the island. An estimated 250,000 more people were forced to flee their homes. In April the LTTE carried out an attack in Colombo in which the army chief was injured, and there were other attacks in the commercial capital during the year. LTTE forces began to lose ground, however, to considerable military pressure, especially in the eastern areas. In August the army blocked the road linking Jaffna, the major Tamil city, to the rest of country, leading to severe food shortages. It was regularly reported that children were being kidnapped to serve as soldiers. In June a bomb attack on a bus, presumed to be by Tamil militants although this was denied by the LTTE, caused more than 60 deaths.

Talks between the two sides resumed in February, as in the past with the assistance of Norwegian mediators. However, there was so little progress, even on procedural matters, that proposed talks in Oslo in June were cancelled and the process ground to a halt in October, with most observers feeling that there was little real political will on either side to reach an agreement, even though theoretically the 2002 ceasefire remained in force. One major sticking point was the LTTE demand that the road to Jaffna be reopened, and another was the LTTE demand that the dissident Tamil group, led by Colonel Karuna Amman, be disarmed by the government. While the international community continued to encourage peace talks, there was evidence of growing reluctance to overlook Tamil acts of violence. The USA had for a number of years banned the LTTE. In April Canada placed the LTTE on its list of terrorist organisations, as did the EU the following month. The LTTE responded by insisting on the withdrawal of European ceasefire monitors.

The LTTE's chief spokesman and ideologue, Anton Balasingham, often seen as a moderate within the movement, died of cancer in December. Earlier in the year he had appeared indirectly to accept, and to regret, the Tigers' involvement in the assassination of Rajiv Gandhi in 1991.

The country's president, Mahinda Rajapakse, consolidated his position as the country's principal Sinhalese leader after local elections at the end of March, although elections in the Tamil areas generally had to be postponed because of the security situation. In October he was able to sign an agreement with the main opposition party, the United National Party, to facilitate a common approach to negotiations with the LTTE, although he remained under pressure from smaller coalition partners to take a harsh and rigid line towards the Tigers.

NEPAL. The year was one of great political turmoil and saw the effective sidelining of the monarchy in favour of a party-based government, which in turn reached out to the Maoist rebels and brought them into the fold, ending, at least for the time being, the civil war that had cost over 12,000 lives since 1996.

At the beginning of the year King Gyanendra continued to exercise direct executive authority, following his dismissal of the government in February 2005 (see AR 2005, p. 278). An attempt to organise local elections in order to rebuild support for his government failed. This was followed in April by a popular uprising and confrontation, especially in the capital. The Maoist rebels played a major role in these events. The king was forced to enter into talks, and at the end of the month agreed to the restoration of parliamentary democracy, with the veteran leader, Girija Prasad Koirala, leader of the Nepal Congress party, as prime minister. In June, the reinstated House of Representatives (the lower house of the bicameral legislature) passed a measure that abolished the power of royal veto, thus reducing the king to a largely ceremonial role. A few days later, negotiations began between the prime minister and Prachanda, leader of the Maoists. These led to the Maoists' agreement to end their rebellion and to take part in an interim assembly, pending elections and the framing of a constitution. INDIA had initially attempted to mediate between the two sides in order to maintain some influence in the country, but to no effect. It also encouraged Prachanda to enter into dialogue with the mainstream political parties.

BHUTAN. In Bhutan, King Jigme Singye Wangchuck had already announced in 2005 that he would permit elections in 2008 and at that point abdicate in favour of his son Jigme Khesar Namgyel Wangchuck (see AR 2005, p. 278). In December that year, however, he announced that he was abdicating ahead of schedule and duly did so, 12 months later, in December 2006. By August 2006 the electoral commission had been able to prepare a draft electoral roll containing some 400,000 names and preparations for the elections were initiated thereafter.

In October there was an announcement by the USA that it would accept up to 60,000 refugees from Bhutan currently living in camps in NEPAL, giving hope that, with similar offers from Canada and Australia, this longstanding refugee problem might be resolved. The refugees came from the Lothsampa ethnic group, who were originally of Nepali origin, although settled in Bhutan for a long period.

REGIONAL RELATIONS. The Indo-Pakistan dialogue stuttered along in the early part of the year, with official-level talks on a variety of issues, as well as exchange of visits by various non-official groups, but no major outcomes other than a limited and largely symbolic extension of transport links. However, the Mumbai bomb blasts in July (see p. 294) were blamed by INDIA on PAKISTAN-based militant groups, and for a little while it looked as though the whole peace process was going to end. In September, however, Prime Minister Singh and President Musharraf met on the sidelines of the Non-Aligned Movement meeting in Havana, Cuba (see pp. 396-97), and agreed to resume the dialogue. In November the two foreign ministers met in New Delhi. At the beginning of December President Musharraf stated in an on-the-record interview what had presumably already been discussed in back-channel discussions: that a way forward would be for the disputed territory in Kashmir to be demilitarised. If this were done, and the Kashmiris allowed self-government, then Pakistan would be prepared to give up its territorial claims. On the Indian side, the argument being advanced was that while boundaries could not be changed, they could be made irrelevant. India was evidently hoping that discussions with "moderate" sections of the separatist groups (see p. 295) might provide an alternative to negotiations with Pakistan over what it had always claimed to be a purely internal affair. India also insisted that Pakistan be more co-operative on terrorism issues, for example by handing over suspects claimed to be sheltering in Pakistan, although the Pakistan government insisted that they were not in the country. Other irritants between the two countries were discussed during the official-level talks, such as the military stand-off on the Siachen glacier in Kashmir and a disputed maritime boundary, but nothing major had been achieved by the end of the year.

Pakistan-Afghanistan relations deteriorated during the year, mainly over claims and counterclaims about where Taliban and al-Qaida leaders were based, and about alleged continuing support for the Taliban by elements of Pakistan's intelligence services (see p. 284). On several occasions the Afghan president, Hamid Karzai, openly accused PAKISTAN of harbouring militants, while Pakistan saw these statements as attempts to divert attention from the Afghan government's internal weakness. The Afghan position received some support from the NATO allies in the country, especially at the time of the agreement between the Pakistan government and the militants in North Waziristan (see p. 296).

There was no summit meeting of the South Asian Association for Regional Co-operation (SAARC) during the year, but regular ministerial and official-level meetings were held. In April it was agreed to add the USA and South Korea to the list of observer countries, and preparations continued for Afghanistan to join as a full member in 2007. The South Asian Free Trade Area (SAFTA), announced in 2004 (see AR 2004, p. 413), came into being at the beginning of the year, on the basis that customs duties would be gradually reduced over a 10-year period. However, PAKISTAN refused to apply the first round of reductions to INDIA, on the grounds that its manufacturing sector would not be able to compete.

THE USA AND SOUTH ASIA. US President George W. Bush visited both INDIA and PAKISTAN in March. In Pakistan his visit appeared to be intended to keep pressure on Pakistan to stay in line over the "war on terrorism". Although an agreement was announced to establish a "strategic partnership", the USA evidently regarded Pakistan as an unreliable ally. In India, however, the Bush visit was truly part of a new relationship that had emerged between the two countries in the previous few years. A central part of this was US acceptance of India's nuclear status, and thereby of India's role as one of the world's major powers (see pp. 121-22). The first announcement of a nuclear deal had come the previous year (see AR 2005, p. 281) but given how strongly the USA had criticized the Indian nuclear tests in 1998 it was not surprising that there was a lot of persuasion to be done both by the US administration and by the powerful Indian lobby in the USA before the deal was finalised. Eventually, however, the agreement was ratified by the US Senate in November and signed into law the following month by President Bush (although further negotiations were to be held to operationalise the agreement and to overcome any difficulties with the international Nuclear Suppliers Group). The agreement gave India access to US nuclear technology and to nuclear fuel while allowing eight of its 22 nuclear reactors to remain unsafeguarded and able to produce military material. India in effect had become one of the world's accepted nuclear powers. It had also, without actually being able to sign, acceded to the Nuclear non-Proliferation Treaty regime in that capacity. Although warmly welcomed by the Indian government, there was significant opposition to the agreement from other political groups, who pointed to the limitations it placed on India's nuclear ambitions, particularly if it were to want to hold further nuclear tests. The references in the US legislation to common action against Iran, even if not binding, were also a source of concern. However, India was extremely anxious to obtain uninterrupted supplies of fuel for its nuclear programme and to expand its nuclear power capacity, both of which would now be possible. Towards the end of the year, the largest business delegation ever sent abroad by the USA visited India to discuss future co-operation and investment, thus complementing the diplomatic and strategic elements of the relationship.

CHINA AND SOUTH ASIA. There was a major visit to the South Asian region in November by the Chinese president, Hu Jintao, which followed a visit the previous year by the Chinese premier, Wen Jiabao (see AR 2005, p. 282). China had emerged as a major trade partner with the region, with cheap manufactured goods achieving a dominant position in many sectors. In PAKISTAN, where there was a long history of friendly relations dating back to the 1960s, the two countries signed a free trade agreement. While there was a great emphasis on China's longstanding links with Pakistan, there was no formal agreement on co-operation in the nuclear field beyond what was already taking place. In INDIA, the emphasis was also on economics, with trade between the two countries planned to double to US$40 billion by 2010. The longstanding question of resolving the border disputes that had taken the two countries to war in 1962, and on which there appeared to have been progress following then Indian Prime Minister Atal Behari Vajpayee's visit to China in 2003 (see AR 2003, p. 340), was not addressed; indeed, public statements by China's ambassador to India, in which his country's claim to the remote Indian state of Arunachal Pradesh was reiterated, suggested that the dialogue had gone backwards.

At the beginning of the year the Muslim population of the whole region took strong exception to the publication of cartoons in a Danish newspaper, which included offensive representations of the Prophet Mohammed. Large-scale demonstrations occurred in many places, especially in PAKISTAN (see pp. 54-56).

An Indian candidate, Shashi Tharoor, a senior UN official, was backed by his government for the secretary-generalship. While he was regarded as a serious contender, he ultimately failed in his bid; press reports suggested that he had not been supported by the USA. INDIA'S campaign to be included as a permanent member of the UN Security Council continued, and gained verbal support from many world leaders, but an actual result would be dependent on a broader restructuring of the Council.

ECONOMIES. Growth throughout the region continued to be strong, with a regional growth rate of around 8.2 per cent. However, none of the South Asian countries approached self-sufficiency in energy, so that the sudden upturn in oil prices during the year was a challenge, even though by the end of the year there had been a marked decline from the peak reached in July.

INDIA'S GDP growth during the year was estimated at 8.7 per cent, second only to China among the major economies of Asia, thus continuing the trend of recent years. Private investment and resource mobilisation through taxation both increased significantly, although still below levels reached by other successful economies in Asia. Foreign trade continued to play an ever greater role, with exports in 2005-06 increasing by 27.5 per cent, the fourth successive year in which the increase exceeded 20 per cent. Although imports continued to rise at least as fast, increased invisible exports—mainly in the information technology (IT) sector—and substantial inward remittances from overseas workers, together with privatisation and other receipts, ensured that foreign exchange reserves at more than US$150 billion hit record levels. The growth of the economy was echoed by the record performance of the stock market. Inflation at 6.7 per cent, however, was a danger signal for the future. The economy was also constrained, as it had been for many years, by acute shortages of power and by other infrastructural factors such as a limited network of good roads.

Per capita income grew at 7 per cent during the year, but the benefits of growth went disproportionately to the upper strata, with the percentage of people below the poverty line remaining at around 25 per cent. Regional disparities also continued to increase, with the southern, western, and north-western states outstripping the heavily populated northern and eastern areas. Compared to China and other emerging Asian economies, manufacturing was still a relatively small part of the total economy, so that it had yet to generate a large number of employment opportunities.

One of the healthiest sectors of the economy was the export-focused IT sector, embracing a wide range of services from software development to call centres serving the developed economies worldwide. The total value of IT-based exports in the financial year 2006 was placed at US$23.6 billion, a 33 per cent increase on the previous year, and the latter part of 2006 saw continuing strong growth. India's largest IT companies were increasingly part of the global economy, with Infosys, for example, the second largest, included in the Nasdaq-100 index. India's IT industry found itself looking outside the country for some of its skilled manpower needs.

A sign of the growing maturity of India's manufacturing sector was its ability to launch high profile takeover bids for companies abroad. The most striking of these was a US$7.7 billion bid by Tata Steel, India's largest producer, for Corus, an Anglo-Dutch company and the EU's second largest steelmaker. By the end of the year, however, Tata Steel was still in competition with another emerging economy producer from Brazil. Indian companies, in turn, became the target of takeover bids from global players. A two-thirds stake in the fourth largest

Indian telecommunications company, Hutchison Essar, became the subject of hectic bidding from both Indian and international players. Some of the bids put the total valuation of the company at over US$20 million. India had 136 million mobile phone users during the year, with the numbers increasing by nearly 10 million per month.

Overall, therefore, the modern sectors of the Indian economy became increasingly integrated into the global economy. India's largest firms, several of them the product of the last few years of economic growth, grew very fast both through expansion of existing activities and by moving into new areas. The year saw the establishment of additional special economic zones to encourage large scale industrial investment through relaxed regulatory regimes and tax incentives. Another sign of India's entry into the global market was its efforts to acquire stakes in the oil sector, especially in west Africa, so as to provide at least some assured sources of energy in the coming decades.

India and the EU, which was its biggest trading partner, held the latest in a series of summit meetings in Helsinki, the capital of Finland, in October. The major outcome was a decision to move towards a comprehensive trade and investment agreement over the next few years, although the agricultural subsidies issue was identified as a possible stumbling block. India's bilateral links with the UK continued to grow, with the latter being the main recipient of Indian investment abroad. During 2006 India in fact invested more in the UK than vice-versa and became the third largest foreign investor during that year.

PAKISTAN'S growth was estimated at 6.6 per cent. However, little progress was made in tackling such structural problems as low resource mobilisation, low productivity in the agricultural sector, or increasing gaps between rich and poor. The trade gap widened alarmingly during the year, with exports largely stagnant, so that the economy's ability to grow depended heavily on high remittance flows from overseas Pakistanis and one-time privatisation receipts which garnered US$6.1 billion in 2006. By the end of the year, inflation was rising at 8.8 per cent. The government and the State Bank had to tread a difficult path between dampening inflation through restraining the money supply and holding back economic growth. Concerns in some quarters about the speed with which government assets were being privatised were heightened by a Supreme Court verdict overturning the sale of Pakistan Steel Mills, the country's only integrated steel plant, to a consortium led by a Saudi concern. Pakistan's agriculture was held back by the need for new dams to increase irrigation facilities.

In BANGLADESH the constant political instability which manifested itself in frequent general strikes (see p. 297) was a significant constraint on economic growth, although growth was in excess of 6 per cent. In July INDIA'S Tata group suspended a US$3 billion investment project in steel and fertilisers, which would have been by far Bangladesh's largest foreign investment, because of a lack of government commitment. However, Bangladesh was able to increase both the volume of its textile and garment earnings and its remittances from overseas workers, thus enabling a surplus on its balance of payments after several years of deficit.

The economies of both NEPAL and SRI LANKA suffered significantly because of civil strife. In Nepal, the rate of GDP growth in 2005-06 was put at only around 2 per cent, with actual declines in both industrial and agricultural production. In Sri Lanka the effect was more limited, with the areas not directly affected by the fighting able to do reasonably well both in agriculture and in textiles. But while at the beginning of 2006 the impact of reconstruction following the 2004 tsunami (see map, AR 2005, p. 296) was still having a positive effect on the growth rate, by the second half of the year there had been a significant reversal of these trends.

One of the major issues for all the countries in the region was water, with multi-purpose big dams becoming the focus of often heated debate. In INDIA the Narmada dam in western India, which some estimated would have displaced 35,000 people by the time it was fully operational but which would have a major impact on the economic conditions of Gujarat and neighbouring areas, neared completion during the year. In PAKISTAN, it was announced that five major dams would be built by 2016, but the most controversial, at Kalabagh, would no longer be the first to be built. Instead, it was announced that this would be at Diamer-Basha, in a remote mountainous region in the north, and the foundation stone was laid in April. Protest movements against the dams in both countries focused on the negative impact on those displaced and on environmental risks, as well as on the way the benefits would be distributed between different sectors of the economy and, especially in Pakistan, between regions.

INDIAN OCEAN STATES

Seychelles

CAPITAL: Victoria AREA: 454 sq km POPULATION: 84,000
OFFICIAL LANGUAGES: Seychellois, English & French POLITICAL SYSTEM: multiparty republic in British Commonwealth
HEAD OF STATE AND GOVERNMENT: President James Michel (since April '04)
RULING PARTY: Seychelles People's Progressive Front (SPPF)
MAIN IGO MEMBERSHIPS (NON-UN): AU, COMESA, SADC, OIC, ACP, CWTH, Francophonie, NAM
CURRENCY: Seychelles rupee (end-'06 £1=SRs11.3431, US$1=SRs5.80970)
GNI PER CAPITA: US$8,290, US$15,940 at PPP ('05 est, based on regression)

Mauritius

CAPITAL: Port Louis AREA: 2,040 sq km POPULATION: 1,248,000
OFFICIAL LANGUAGE: English POLITICAL SYSTEM: multiparty republic in British Commonwealth
HEAD OF STATE: President Sir Anerood Jugnauth (since Oct '03)
RULING PARTIES: Social Alliance (AS) comprising Mauritius Labour Party (MLP), Mauritian Party of Xavier Duval (PMXD), Mauritian Socialist Militant Movement (MMSM), Republican Movement (MR), and the Greens-Fraternal Organisation (VERTS-OF)
HEAD OF GOVERNMENT: Navin Ramgoolam (MLP), Prime Minister (since July '05)
MAIN IGO MEMBERSHIPS (NON-UN): AU, COMESA, SADC, ACP, CWTH, Francophonie, NAM
CURRENCY: Mauritian rupee (end-'06 £1=MRs63.5328, US$1=MRs32.5400)
GNI PER CAPITA: US$5,260, US$12,450 at PPP ('05)

Comoros

CAPITAL: Moroni AREA: 1,860 sq km POPULATION: 600,000
OFFICIAL LANGUAGES: Arabic & French POLITICAL SYSTEM: multiparty federal republic
HEAD OF STATE: Union President Ahmed Abdallah Sambi (since May '06)
PRESIDENTS OF REPUBLICS: Anjouan President, Mohamed Bacar; Ngazidja (Grande Comore) President, Abdou Soule Elbak; Mohéli President, Mohamed Said Fazul
HEAD OF GOVERNMENT: Hamada Madi Borelo (since Nov '00)
MAIN IGO MEMBERSHIPS (NON-UN): AU, COMESA, ACP, AL, OIC, Francophonie, NAM
CURRENCY: Comorian franc (end-'06 £1=Fr727.932, US$1=Fr372.830)
GNI PER CAPITA: US$640, US$2,000 at PPP ('05 est, based on regression)

Madagascar

CAPITAL: Antananarivo AREA: 587,000 sq km POPULATION: 18,606,000
OFFICIAL LANGUAGES: Malagasy & French POLITICAL SYSTEM: multiparty republic
HEAD OF STATE: President Marc Ravalomanana (since May '02)
RULING PARTY: I Love Madagascar Party (TIM)
HEAD OF GOVERNMENT: Jacques Sylla, Prime Minister (since May '02)
MAIN IGO MEMBERSHIPS (NON-UN): AU, COMESA, OIC, ACP, Francophonie, NAM
CURRENCY: ariary (end-'06 £1=MGA3,920.52, US$1=MGA2,008.00)
GNI PER CAPITA: US$290, US$880 at PPP ('05)

Maldives

CAPITAL: Malé AREA: 300 sq km POPULATION: 329,000
OFFICIAL LANGUAGE: Divehi POLITICAL SYSTEM: non-party republic in British Commonwealth
HEAD OF STATE: President Maumoon Abdul Gayoom (since Nov '78)
RULING PARTY: Maldivian People's Party (DRP)
MAIN IGO MEMBERSHIPS (NON-UN): SAARC, CP, OIC, CWTH, NAM
CURRENCY: rufiya (end-'06 £1=R24.9914, US$1=R12.8000)
GNI PER CAPITA: US$2,390 ('05), -

THE year in SEYCHELLES was dominated by the presidential elections, which had to be held by August 2006. It was clear that this would once again be a contest between Wavel Ramakalawan of the Seychelles National Party (SNP) and the incumbent president, James Michel of the Seychelles People's Progressive Front (SPPF). The small Democratic Party, led by Paul Chow, was expected to support the SNP. The election campaign focused on the poor economic performance of the SPPF, its reluctance to devalue the rupee, and the inability of the government to reach agreement with the IMF. Shortly before the elections the government agreed a wages rise for civil servants and announced a house-building programme. This, coupled with its control of the media, meant that, once again, the presidential candidate of the ruling SPPF won a narrow majority when the election was held at the end of July.

There was an 88 per cent turnout and James Michel won 53.7 per cent against Ramakalawan's 45.7 per cent. This was an almost exact repeat of the results of the previous presidential and legislative elections in 2001 and 2002 respectively (see AR 2001, p. 347; 2002, pp. 328-29), suggesting that the SNP under its current leader had reached a ceiling of support.

James Michel made few changes to his cabinet, though he himself took over the economic planning portfolio. The policies of his government remained largely unaltered: a refusal to devalue, subsidies for essentials to control inflation, a gradual privatisation programme, and the encouragement of environmentally-conscious tourism. A key change was the decision to relax foreign exchange controls from October. Michel also announced his intention to rejoin the Southern Africa Development Community (SADC) from which Seychelles had resigned in 2003.

In October violence erupted outside the National Assembly when police broke up a demonstration by the SNP against a law that would have prevented the establishment of a private radio station. Wavel Ramakalawan was injured in the violence and the president ordered an inquiry into police conduct. This was an issue of importance as the government's control of the media was a major factor in its continued electoral success.

In MAURITIUS after serious setbacks in legislative and local elections in 2005, the political alliance between the Mauritian Militant Movement (MMM), led by former Prime Minister Paul Bérenger, and the Mauritian Socialist Movement (MSM), led by the son of the president, Pravind Jugnauth, who lost his seat in the elections, broke up in April. As a result Bérenger had to give up his position as official leader of the opposition to Nando Bodha, the new leader of the MSM in the National Assembly (unicameral legislature). However, the MSM suffered a setback when Ashock Jugnauth, uncle of Pravind, quit the party to form a new political movement called National Union. Both opposition parties entered into negotiations with the ruling Labour party with a view to joining the government. However, these proved unsuccessful and a rapprochement between MMM and MSM was once again envisaged.

In June the finance minister, Rama Sithanen, produced his first budget. This proposed sweeping economic reforms and was adopted without amendment. The strategic objective was to reposition Mauritius in the global economy by the time the protection enjoyed in Europe by its traditional sugar and textile industries was phased out. However, legislation to strengthen the Commission against Corruption (ICAC) had to be abandoned when it was opposed by both the opposition and the legal profession.

In May the High Court in London ruled that the British government's action to prevent the Chagos Islanders returning to their homeland was unlawful. The British government announced that it would appeal, but this ruling was considered to be another success for the islanders and indirectly for Mauritius, which maintained its claims to the islands.

The constitution of the COMOROS, which was agreed in 2000, made provision for the head of state (the Union president) to be elected from each of the three islands in turn. In 2006 the elections were for a Union president from the island of Anjouan. The process began in April with an eliminating round in which the electors of Anjouan chose three candidates to go forward to the second round. The three successful candidates were Ahmed Abdallah Sambi, Ibrahim Halidi, and Mohammed Djaanfari. The very experienced Caabi El-Yachroutu Mohammed, who was a candidate favoured by aid donors, came fourth and failed to make the cut. In May the voters of all three islands made their choice and Ahmed Abdallah Sambi, who was publicly supported by all three island presidents, was elected with a decisive 58 per cent of the vote.

President Sambi was thought to hold Islamist views as he was a founder member of the National Justice Front (FNI) and talked about the election result being a "green revolution", but he quickly made it clear that he wanted to follow the aid donors' agenda and tackle corruption and the dependence of the islands on imports. Soon after his election the anti-corruption commission began investigations into 36 officials connected with the previous regime of Colonel Azali Assoumane, including a former prime minister, three former cabinet ministers, and the director-general of the Customs and Excise.

The islands' economy, fragile at the best of times, was weakened by the fall in the price of vanilla and a decline in tourist numbers, but financial support from the IMF was agreed and in June negotiations were opened for a full Poverty Reduction and Growth Facility (PRGF).

President Sambi also announced that he would reopen the issue of the status of Mayotte, the fourth island of the archipelago which had remained, since 1974, under French administration. This followed a rise in deportations of illegal immigrants from Mayotte. Relations with France were not improved by a court decision in France giving the French mercenary leader, Bob Denard, only a suspended prison sentence for his part in the 1992 coup in the Comoros (see AR 1992, pp. 326-27).

The date of the presidential elections in MADAGASCAR, which were to have been held in January 2007, were brought forward to 3 December 2006 and for most of the year political speculation was concerned with which leading politicians would challenge the incumbent president, Marc Ravalomanana. The veteran radical, Albert Zafy, who was the moving spirit behind the Three National Forces (3FN) coalition, declared he would not stand while Pierrot Rajaonarivelo, the leader of Arema, the party of the previous president, was still in exile and in August was convicted in absence of further corruption offences. Visits from Kofi Annan, secretary-general of the UN, and the president of Germany, while underlining support for President Ravalomanana, also made it clear that the international community expected fair and transparent elections and proper freedom of the press. However, the president resisted calls for the establishment of an independent electoral commission. The president suffered some haemorrhage of support with the dismissal of the speaker of the National Assembly, Jean Lahiniriko, whose political power base was in the south of the island. This dismissal followed the speaker's openly-expressed support for Iran.

The elections took place as planned with 14 names on the ballot sheet and a 61.9 per cent turnout. Ravalomanana won a decisive victory in the first round of voting and embarked upon another five-year term. He polled 54.79 per cent of the vote, his nearest rivals, Jean Lahiniriko and Roland Ratsiraka, polling just 11.65 per cent and 10.14 per cent respectively. Observers from southern Africa and the EU declared the elections fair and the Constitutional Court confirmed the results.

Ravalomanana was concerned to play a high profile role in both the Indian

Ocean Commission—by hosting the ministerial council—and the SADC which Madagascar joined in 2005. At the same time he was concerned to maintain his reputation for sound economic management. In June a development plan, "Plan d'action Madagascar" (MAP), was approved, followed in July by a programme to attract a Poverty Reduction and Growth Facility (PRGF). The priority given to rural development, health, and education, and the decision to privatise Jirama, the parastatal responsible for water supply, were thought to be appropriate. Both these plans proved immediately successful on the international stage, attracting major flows of funding from the World Bank and the African Development Bank.

The MALDIVES had been ruled since 1978 by Maumoon Abdul Gayoom, who was re-elected unopposed for the sixth term of office in 2003. Throughout 2006, however, there was growing pressure for political reform after 19 candidates of the opposition Maldives Democratic Party (MDP) won seats as independents in the 50-seat legislature (Majlis) in January 2005. In December 2005 a group of government ministers, calling themselves New Maldives (apparently in imitation of New Labour), gave a press conference in Colombo, Sri Lanka, setting out the government's commitment to democratic reform, while admitting that an earlier promise that a new constitution would be produced in January 2006 would not be realised. The reform programme was given impressive detail in March with the publication of a "road map" setting out a range of reforms, including legislation to allow political protest and freedom of assembly.

On 23 June the New Maldives ministers (Foreign Minister Dr Ahmed Shaheed and Attorney General Hassan Saeed) met representatives of the MDP at Westminster House, the British High Commissioner's residence in Colombo. A further meeting took place on 17 July. A series of agreements was reached whereby the government agreed to implement specific reforms, including the removal of Adam Zahir, the chief of police, in return for the opposition scaling down public protest. As a result, a number of high profile political prisoners were released, including Jennifer Latheef and Mohamed Nasheed (known as Anni), the leader of the MDP. The agreement seemed to confirm the influence of the New Maldives group in the government. As further progress seemed to be blocked, and the date of the publication of a new constitution was delayed until November 2007, the opposition announced a major demonstration which would bring the capital to a halt on 10 November. Before the event the MDP legislators issued a letter condemning the proposed demonstration, which was duly cancelled. This very public split in the MDP was seen to strengthen the hard line supporters of Gayoom and the government responded by arresting 100 MDP activists.

IX SOUTH-EAST AND EAST ASIA

SOUTH-EAST ASIAN STATES

BURMA (MYANMAR)—THAILAND—MALAYSIA—BRUNEI—SINGAPORE—VIETNAM—CAMBODIA—LAOS

Burma (Myanmar)

CAPITAL: Yangon (Rangoon); administrative capital Pyinmana AREA: 677,000 sq km POPULATION: 50,519,000
OFFICIAL LANGUAGE: Burmese POLITICAL SYSTEM: military regime
HEAD OF STATE AND GOVERNMENT: Gen. Than Shwe, Chairman of State Peace and Development Council (since April '92)
PRIME MINISTER: Lt-Gen. Soe Win (since Oct '04)
MAIN IGO MEMBERSHIPS (NON-UN): ASEAN, CP, NAM
CURRENCY: kyat (end-'05 £1=K12.3752, US$1=K6.42000)
GNI PER CAPITA: US$875 or less ('05)

Thailand

CAPITAL: Bangkok AREA: 513,000 sq km POPULATION: 64,233,000
OFFICIAL LANGUAGE: Thai POLITICAL SYSTEM: multiparty monarchy under martial law
HEAD OF STATE: King Bhumibol Adulyadej (Rama IX), since June '46
HEAD OF GOVERNMENT: Gen. (retd) Surayud Chulanont, interim Prime Minister (since Oct '06)
MAIN IGO MEMBERSHIPS (NON-UN): ASEAN, CP, APEC, NAM
CURRENCY: baht (end-'06 £1=Bt69.4194, US$1=Bt35.5550)
GNI PER CAPITA: US$2,750, US$8,440 at PPP ('05)

Malaysia

CAPITAL: Kuala Lumpur AREA: 330,000 sq km POPULATION: 25,347,000
OFFICIAL LANGUAGE: Bahasa Malaysia POLITICAL SYSTEM: multiparty monarchy in British Commonwealth
HEAD OF STATE: King Mizan Zainal Abidin ibni Al-Marhum Sultan Mahmud Al-Muktafi Billah Shah, Sultan of Terengganu (since Nov '06)
RULING PARTY: United Malays National Organisation
HEAD OF GOVERNMENT: Abdullah Ahmad Badawi, Prime Minister (since Oct '03)
MAIN IGO MEMBERSHIPS (NON-UN): ASEAN, APEC, CP, OIC, CWTH, NAM
CURRENCY: ringgit Malaysia (end-'06 £1=RM6.85800, US$1=RM3.51250)
GNI PER CAPITA: US$4,960, US$10,320 at PPP ('05)

Brunei

CAPITAL: Bandar Seri Bagawan AREA: 5,765 sq km POPULATION: 374,000
OFFICIAL LANGUAGES: Malay & English POLITICAL SYSTEM: sultanate in British Commonwealth
HEAD OF STATE AND GOVERNMENT: Sultan Sir Hassanal Bolkiah (since '67)
MAIN IGO MEMBERSHIPS (NON-UN): ASEAN, APEC, OIC, CWTH, NAM
CURRENCY: Brunei dollar (end-'06 £1=Br$2.96070, US$1=Br$1.53600)
GNI PER CAPITA: US$10,726 or more ('05 est), -

Singapore

CAPITAL: Singapore AREA: 1,000 sq km POPULATION: 4,351,000
OFFICIAL LANGUAGES: Malay, Chinese, Tamil & English POLITICAL SYSTEM: multiparty republic in British Commonwealth
HEAD OF STATE: President S.R. Nathan (since Sept '99)
RULING PARTY: People's Action Party (PAP)
HEAD OF GOVERNMENT: Lee Hsien Loong, Prime Minister (since August '04)
MAIN IGO MEMBERSHIPS (NON-UN): ASEAN, APEC, CP, CWTH, NAM
CURRENCY: Singapore dollar (end-'06 £1=S$2.99310, US$1=S$1.53300)
GNI PER CAPITA: US$27,490, US$29,780 at PPP ('05)

Vietnam

CAPITAL: Hanoi AREA: 332,000 sq km POPULATION: 82,966,000
OFFICIAL LANGUAGE: Vietnamese POLITICAL SYSTEM: one-party republic
HEAD OF STATE: President Nguyen Minh Triet (since June '06)
RULING PARTY: Communist Party of Vietnam (CPV)
PARTY LEADER: Nong Duc Manh, CPV secretary general (since April '01)
HEAD OF GOVERNMENT: Nguyen Tan Dung, Prime Minister (since June '06)
MAIN IGO MEMBERSHIPS (NON-UN): ASEAN, APEC, NAM, Francophonie
CURRENCY: dong (end-'06 £1=Vnd31,346.6, US$1=Vnd16,055.0)
GNP PER CAPITA: US$620, US$3,010 at PPP ('05)

Cambodia

CAPITAL: Phnom Penh AREA: 181,000 sq km POPULATION: 14,071,000
OFFICIAL LANGUAGE: Khmer POLITICAL SYSTEM: multiparty monarchy
HEAD OF STATE: King Norodom Sihamoni (elected Oct '04)
RULING PARTIES: Coalition of the Cambodian People's Party (CPP) and the United National Front for an Independent Neutral, Peaceful, and Co-operative Cambodia (Funcinpec)
HEAD OF GOVERNMENT: Hun Sen, Prime Minister (since July '97)
MAIN IGO MEMBERSHIPS (NON-UN): ASEAN, CP, Francophonie, NAM
CURRENCY: riel (end-'06 £1=R7,880.09, US$1=R4,036.00)
GNI PER CAPITA: US$380, US$2,490 at PPP ('03-'05)

Laos

CAPITAL: Vientiane AREA: 237,000 sq km POPULATION: 5,924,000
OFFICIAL LANGUAGE: Laotian POLITICAL SYSTEM: one-party republic
HEAD OF STATE: President (Lt.-Gen.) Choummaly Sayasone (since June '06)
RULING PARTY: Lao People's Revolutionary Party (LPRP)
HEAD OF GOVERNMENT: Bouasone Bouphavanh, Prime Minister (since June '06)
MAIN IGO MEMBERSHIPS (NON-UN): ASEAN, CP, Francophonie, NAM
CURRENCY: new kip (end-'06 £1=K18,891.9, US$1=K9,676.00)
GNI PER CAPITA: US$440, US$2,020 at PPP ('05)

THE consolidation of democracy in THAILAND was interrupted by events culminating in a military coup on the evening of 19 September. Although this was the 18th coup in Thailand since the introduction of a written constitution in 1932, it was the country's first since 1992.

The intervention by the military, which was carried out without any loss of life, occurred while the prime minister, Thaksin Shinawatra, was attending a meeting of the United Nations in New York. The prime minister proved unable to assert control over events and, following the cancellation of his scheduled address to the UN General Assembly, he flew to London where he had a residence.

The coup appeared to win broad support, particularly in the capital, Bangkok, where images were broadcast of soldiers receiving flowers from members of the public. Support for the military's takeover of power was further ensured by expressions of loyalty given by its leading figures to Thailand's king, Bhumibol Adulyadej. The military's support for the king was reciprocated, as he swore in the new leadership on 9 October while instructing them to make repair of the country's international image, damaged by the coup, a top priority.

Prime Minister Thaksin's difficulties stemmed at least in part from the sale in January by his family of its holdings in a Thai telecommunications company, Shin Corporation, to Temasek, an investment arm of the government of SINGAPORE. Anger over the sale of an important national asset to foreign ownership was augmented by resentment over the profit gained by the Thaksin family and subsequent disclosures that the sale had been arranged so that no tax on the profit would need to be paid.

Ongoing demonstrations and rallies against the government, focusing on alleged corruption, led the prime minister to dissolve the legislature on 24 February and call fresh elections. Although this would have given the Thai public the opportunity to decide for themselves whether the prime minister and his Thai Rak Thai party should continue in power, the attempt to resolve matters through new elections failed when the three main opposition parties announced that they would not take part. The legislative elections went ahead in April nevertheless, with the Thai Rak Thai party winning an easy victory, gaining 57 per cent of the vote. Millions of Thais boycotted the elections or cast protest votes, depriving the government of legitimacy and the election of credibility. On 4 April, two days after the election, the prime minister announced that he would be taking a break from office.

Prime Minister Thaksin's decision to step aside in a bid to restore national unity and quell the ongoing protest was viewed by many, correctly, as only a temporary measure. The opposition's boycott meant that the lower house, the House of Representatives, lacked the full 500 lawmakers required to convene, and by-elections held in late April to fill legislative vacancies failed to resolve matters. On 25 April the king called on Thailand's courts to solve what he described as a "mess" and, two weeks later, on 8 May, the country's Constitutional Court invalidated the election. In July a Thai court sentenced each of the country's three election commissioners to four years in prison for failures of supervision in relation to the April elections. The men resigned their posts, were released on bail, and announced their intention to appeal.

In August police intercepted a car near Prime Minister Thaksin's house, which was being driven by a military officer. The vehicle contained a large bomb, and Thaksin responded by accusing military officers of plotting to assassinate him. There had been anger in the military over some of Thaksin's personnel decisions, involving promotions and appointments, and the military, with traditionally strong loyalty to the king, was also reportedly unhappy about what was considered to be disrespectful behaviour by Thaksin towards the monarch.

These events were only part of a turbulent year for Thailand, entirely out of keeping with what the country's 77-year-old king had hoped to enjoy as he marked the 60th anniversary of his reign. That occasion was celebrated on 9 June, which was declared a national holiday. The anniversary of the king's accession to the throne was also celebrated in mid-June through a gathering representing most of the globe's reigning royal houses.

The political upheaval in Bangkok was in some ways the least of the king's concerns. More troubling was the increasingly violent insurgency taking place in the largely Muslim south of the country. During 2006 there were hundreds of deaths due to terrorism, including terrorist incidents that took place in the capital, far from the Muslim-majority southern provinces. In late January, for instance, a small bomb exploded in a park next to Thailand's justice ministry in suburban Bangkok, injuring four people. Nevertheless most of the violence was concentrated in the south, where efforts by the military and the police were unable to make much headway.

In March there were arson attacks in 18 locations in Pattani and Songkhla provinces. In June approximately 50 bombs went off in a single day, targeting government offices and police stations. In August, 22 small bombs exploded simultaneously in banks in Yala province. In September, on the day before the coup, there was a series of bomb blasts in the commercial centre of Hat Yai, in Songkhla province, injuring at least 60 people.

There was no denying the sectarian nature of the violence, with Buddhist teachers and school principals among the targets. In one incident, insurgents ambushed a military convoy that was protecting teachers on their way to school, killing five security officers. The failure of the government to end the insurgency, and to protect the public from terrorist attack, was a factor further eroding Prime Minister Thaksin's authority.

The September coup also reflected personal resentment against Thaksin—a wealthy businessman—as well as concerns among some in the capital about his popularity in the north and among the rural poor. The Thai Rak Thai party had been expected to win its fourth successive victory at the elections, scheduled for 15 October, which the coup served to avert. In its aftermath a newly established nine-member governing Council for Democratic Reform (CDR) dissolved the legislature, cabinet, and the Constitutional Court; repealed the 1997 constitution; and declared that the leadership of the country's main political parties were to be banned from politics for a five year period. A statement from coup leaders urged workers and farmers—Thaksin's key constituents—to remain calm. Unauthorised gatherings of more than five people were punishable by six months in prison under martial law. The army commander-in-chief asserted that the goals of the coup were "to resolve the conflict and bring back normalcy and harmony", with the CDR motivated by a desire to end intensifying conflicts in Thai society, corruption in government, insults to the king, and attempts by Thaksin to destroy democratic institutions. On 3 October Thaksin resigned from the Thai Rak Thai party in a letter sent from London. More than 200 of the party's members had already quit and, with the departure of its leadership, the Thai Rak Thai party was dissolved.

A new 242-member National Legislative Assembly was installed on 12 October, dominated by military leaders and technocrats. The assembly, endorsed by the king, featured 60 military officers and a total of 76 generals, including members of the police. Anyone who had been a member of a political party or had held political office during the previous two years was banned from participating in the drafting of a new constitution. The disdain for politicians was apparent in the composition of the cabinet, which comprised civil servants, military officers, and corporate executives.

On 1 October a former army commander, Surayud Chulanont, considered close to the king, was appointed interim prime minister, with the CDR promising a new constitution and elections in about a year. In October the new prime minister travelled to all of Thailand's immediate neighbours and he was able to meet other Asian leaders at regional meetings later that month. Western countries were critical of the coup, expressing disappointment and calling for a rapid return to democracy. The USA reduced military aid to Thailand, exempting only assistance in the field of counter-terrorism.

The UN secretary-general, Kofi Annan, observed mildly that the coup was "not a practice to be encouraged", expressing himself as confident that Thailand would be able to "go back to a democratic system as soon as possible". The coup doomed the candidacy of Surakiart Sathirathai, who had served in the past both as deputy prime minister and foreign minister and had been hoping (with support from Association of South-East Asian Nations (ASEAN) member countries) to succeed Annan as the UN's next secretary-general.

In late October former Prime Minister Thaksin was warned against seeking to return to Thailand without prior permission from the CDR. That same month Thailand's Supreme Administrative Court allowed a lawsuit to proceed intending to revoke Shin Corporation's telecommunications licences, a move reflecting ongoing anger over the sale of the conglomerate to Temasek. The transaction was also being investigated by the police following allegations of the illegal use of proxies to evade Thailand's limit on foreign shareholding in telecommunications companies. The new prime minister, visiting SINGAPORE, assured that country's prime minister, Lee Hsien Loong, that there would be no intervention by the Thai government in the probe.

In late December the Bank of Thailand announced that it would be filing corruption charges against Thaksin for his alleged involvement in the purchase of overpriced equipment for Bangkok's new Suvarnabhumi airport, and for his role in a controversial land deal in 2003. Although Thaksin was apparently prepared to return to Thailand to defend himself against the charges, his return required permission from the new government, which remained concerned both about his popularity and the possibility of violence and civil disorder. On 29 December the government responded to a request from Thaksin, seeking to return to Thailand, that he would be able to do so once investigations into his business and political affairs were completed.

The coup leader, General Sonthi Boonyaratglin, had been appointed army commander in October 2005 by Thaksin, as the first Muslim to be chosen commander-in-chief of the mostly Buddhist Thai military. Despite this, General Sonthi's initial proposal for the government to hold talks with the Islamic insurgents was not accepted by the Thaksin government. The failure of the Thaksin regime to resolve either the insurgency in the south or the political impasse in Bangkok led General Sonthi and other military leaders, both prior to and after the coup, to stress that their loyalties were to the king, rather than to the government or the constitution. In choosing to intervene, the country's generals characterised their involvement as necessary in order to "relieve" the king of his anxieties and restore peace and order to the country.

Following the coup General Sonthi said that he would hold the first talks with Muslim rebels since the insurgency began in 2004. He agreed to meet the leaders of rebel factions, who had contacted an army commander to request talks. Prime Minister Surayud travelled south to apologise to Muslims for the government's harsh actions. His government went on to drop charges against Muslim protesters, while agreeing to pay compensation to families of Muslims who had died in custody. These steps did little to stem the tide of violence and bombings, however. While the coup introduced new opportunities to deal with the insurgency, efforts by the military regime to resolve matters through dialogue proved fruitless. The military was unable to accept demands to allow the southern provinces to separate from Thailand and nor were they receptive to the introduction of Islamic law in the region. By the end of the year, approximately half of the country remained under martial law. The post-coup government lifted martial law in Bangkok and nearby provinces in November in a move intended to deflect local criticism, as the initial enthusiasm for the coup began to wane.

The security situation deteriorated suddenly and sharply on 31 December with a series of bomb blasts in Bangkok, leading to troops patrolling the capital for the first time since the coup. The eight co-ordinated bombs killed three people, injured more than 30, and forced the cancellation of the planned end-of-year celebrations. The first round of six explosions in the early evening killed two men and wounded more than 20, one of whom died later. A second series of blasts went off just before midnight, injuring 11 people, most of them foreign tourists. The source of the bomb blasts was in dispute, with claims that the bombings were linked to the political upheaval (and, by inference, to pro-Thaksin forces) rather than to the Muslim separatist unrest in the south. Following the explosions soldiers returned to the streets to patrol key intersections, and security was stepped up at the airport and the city's light rail network.

The coup in Thailand added a further element of awkwardness to attempts by ASEAN states and others to induce the regime in BURMA to move towards greater democracy. Thai Prime Minister Thaksin and General Sonthi had visited the country's rulers in their new capital, Naypyidaw, in August, with Thaksin the first foreign head of government to do so. On 11 September, little more than a week prior to the coup in THAILAND (see above), General Sonthi made another visit to Burma, holding talks intended to strengthen military co-operation between the two countries. The Burmese government ended the year by adjourning its protracted and intermittently convened constitutional conference, with only a few additional "principles" having been completed. Construction at the country's new capital, however, continued to move forward, with Naypyidaw effectively absorbing the adjacent town of Pyinmana.

In February the head of the ruling junta, General Than Shwe, moved to his new residence in the capital, which was then named "Naypyidaw" in the country's state-run media. The new capital's name—translated as "royal city"—gave further insight into the regime's motivation in deciding to transfer the country's administrative institutions there, as Than Shwe gave evidence of seeking to identify himself as the founder of a new dynasty. The following month celebrations of the country's armed forces day were held in Naypyidaw for the first time, thus in a sense officially inaugurating the site as Burma's new capital. The visit in May by UN Under Secretary-General Ibrahim Gambari also lent credibility to the move, as he became the first high-ranking representative of the UN to visit. The construction projects required by the relocation of the country's capital, funded in part by multi-million dollar loans from banks in China and THAILAND, were providing new business opportunities for local companies, although there were also allegations about government confiscations of land and the use of forced labour.

The visits to Burma by Gambari, in May and November, provided him with an opportunity to hold talks with government officials and to visit opposition leader Aung San Suu Kyi, currently in her third consecutive year of detention. Despite Gambari's claim to have held "frank and extensive" talks with General Than Shwe on political and humanitarian issues, there were no signs that these discussions had had any effect whatsoever. In New York, the USA succeeded in gaining approval for the situation in Burma to be placed on the agenda of the UN Security Council, a small step in the direction of greater international scrutiny, but not one that committed the UN or its members to any sort of action.

In other ways, too, Burma's relationship with the international community continued to deteriorate. In February the country's regime suspended prison visits by the International Committee of the Red Cross, notwithstanding UN estimates that there were over 1,100 political prisoners in the country. Gambari's comments about Aung San Suu Kyi, now 60 years old, focused on her health and her need for regular access to medical care.

In late April the government threatened to dissolve Aung San Suu Kyi's National League for Democracy (NLD), claiming that it had links with terrorist groups and exiled dissident organisations. The threat came after a series of bombs went off in Rangoon. MALAYSIA'S Foreign Minister Syed Hamid Albar, a persistent critic of the Burmese government, warned that banning the NLD would reduce the credibility of the regime's "roadmap to democracy". His own influence on events in Burma seemed minimal, however. In March he left Rangoon without meeting any members of the opposition, despite the fact that his trip had been regarded as an opportunity for ASEAN to gain information about what it optimistically characterised as Burma's "democratic transition". The Malaysian foreign minister succeeded in meeting with the country's Prime Minister General Soe Win, but not with anyone from the NLD.

In October the government announced the arrest of five former student dissidents, ostensibly to prevent unrest and terrorist attacks. The military linked the arrests to the decision to place Burma on the agenda of the UN Security Council, which allowed the Security Council to ask for briefings by UN officials and to consider resolutions on the matter. In September the official *New Light of Myanmar* newspaper derided the initiative, accurately predicting that "friendly nations among the permanent members" would "oppose the efforts" of the USA to bring about a UN resolution. The regime denied that anyone was detained for political reasons, describing Aung San Suu Kyi as being "restricted at home" under a law safeguarding the state "from the danger of destructive elements". The regime also chose to characterise the Nobel Peace Prize laureate as a "traitor" who helped Burmese "terrorists", and as "hindering the democratisation process".

In mid-November the International Labour Organisation (ILO) decided to pass its dossiers about forced labour in Burma on to the International Criminal Court. The ILO indicated that it was seeking the prosecution of members of the military government for crimes against humanity. The ILO also resolved to report its concerns about Burma both to the UN Security Council and to the International Court of Justice.

In SINGAPORE the governing People's Action Party (PAP) was easily able to retain power, winning endorsement as it had done at every election held in the country since independence in 1959. The party won 82 of the 84 seats in Parliament (the unicameral legislature) in the 6 May election, failing to win the "clean sweep" that it had anticipated but clearly maintaining its pre-eminence over the country's political and economic life. Meetings of the World Bank and the IMF were held in Singapore in September, with outdoor demonstrations against the meetings banned by the government for security reasons.

In VIETNAM the 10th National Party Congress, held every five years, convened in Hanoi on 18-25 April, setting social and economic goals for the next five years and selecting a new Politburo. The Party Congress nominated a new state president, prime minister, National Assembly chairman, and deputy prime minister, choices that were confirmed in June by the National Assembly. The Communist Party's general secretary, Nong Duc Manh, 65, was not replaced, however, being appointed to a second five-year term.

The new government brought the deputy prime minister, Nguyen Tan Dung, to the position of prime minister, succeeding Phan Van Khai. The new president, Nguyen Minh Triet, the Communist Party leader in Ho Chi Minh city (or Saigon), replaced Tran Duc Luong. The changes reflected a move towards a somewhat younger leadership. Phan Van Khai was 72 and Tran Duc Luong was 69, as was the National Assembly chairman, Nguyen Van An. By contrast the new prime minister, Nguyen Tan Dung, was 56; President Nguyen Minh Triet was 63; and the Hanoi party chairman, Nguyen Phu Trong, who became the new chairman of the National Assembly, was 62.

In other ways, too, there was an accelerated pace of change in Vietnam, as the country's economy continued to expand. Vietnam became the 150th member of the World Trade Organisation in November, the announcement occurring just prior to the Asia-Pacific Economic Co-operation (APEC) meeting hosted by Vietnam and held in the country's capital, Hanoi. In December the US Congress enacted legislation restoring "permanent" normal trade relations between the USA and Vietnam. On 29 December US President George W. Bush signed a proclamation formally extending full and normal trade relations with Vietnam and also clearing the way for Vietnam to qualify for US military aid.

The gathering in Hanoi for the APEC summit on 18-19 November further raised Vietnam's profile internationally. The communiqué was read out by President Nguyen Minh Triet, offering a consensus view on terrorism, avian influenza, HIV/AIDS, corruption, energy and other topics. As ever, the APEC meeting focused on measures to promote economic growth and trade liberalisation, with US concerns about Iran's and North Korea's nuclear ambitions also being discussed (see pp. 430-31).

In LAOS, the president, Khamtay Siphandone, 82, retired from the presidency as well as his position as head of the governing Lao People's Revolutionary Party (LPRP). The announcement came at a meeting in March of the party congress which, as in VIETNAM, occurred every five years. In June a newly elected National Assembly, with 115 members (113 LPRP and two independents), elected Choummaly Sayasone as president. A new prime minister was also chosen, with Bouasone Bouphavanh replacing Boungnang Vorachit. The elections promised little change, with the government publicly committed to retaining one-party governance by the LPRP, promoting economic growth, and enforcing anti-corruption policies.

In July further tentative steps were taken in CAMBODIA to bring surviving Khmer Rouge leaders to trial for their crimes against humanity and for acts constituting genocide against their own people. Members of a joint 25-member UN-Cambodian international tribunal were sworn in at Phnom Penh in July, even as one of the few Khmer Rouge figures in custody, Ta Mok, nicknamed "the butcher" for his crimes, died without having faced trial.

The royalist Funcinpec party, a junior coalition partner in the government, removed former co-prime minister Prince Norodom Ranariddh (a son of retired King Norodom Sihanouk) as its leader in October. The party voted to replace him with Keo Puth Ramsey, son-in-law of the former king, a move intended to strengthen the party for the 2008 elections.

In BRUNEI, likewise, political and family rivalries were seemingly hopelessly intermingled. In mid-February the sultan, Hassanal Bolkiah, failed in his attempt to have his younger brother, Prince Jefri, jailed in the UK. Their feud over financial affairs, stemming from accusations of multi-billion pound embezzlement, had seen legal and financial representatives of the sultan and his brother involved in years of litigation. In February the sultan ended a contempt of court action against his brother, arising out of the prince's refusal to disclose information about his financial affairs. Subsequently Prince Jefri was ordered by Brunei's Court of Appeal, and by the country's chief justice, to hand over properties and other assets worth billions of pounds, though there was little sign that the prince, resident in London, was in any way inclined to do so.

The financial dispute had no apparent effect on the lavish birthday celebrations organised on the sultan's behalf, as he celebrated his 60th birthday in July with a dinner for approximately 10,000 people at his 1,788-room palace. The sultan had ascended the throne in 1967 and in 2006 was the third longest-reigning monarch, after Thailand's King Bhumibol and the UK's Queen Elizabeth II. The Sultan also used the occasion of his birthday to provide a pay increase for government workers, the first to have been granted to them in 22 years.

MALAYSIA, too, experienced fraternal discord of a sort, as former Prime Minister Mahathir Mohamad continued his attacks against his hand-picked successor, Abdullah Ahmad Badawi. In June Mahathir observed that while he had chosen Prime Minister Badawi to succeed him, "I'm in the habit of choosing the wrong people." A meeting in mid-June of the council of the ruling party, the United Malays National Organisation, gave the prime minister its full backing, but also refrained from criticising his predecessor for his repeated and widely publicised efforts to undermine Badawi. Further criticisms led to a private meeting between the two men, which accomplished little as it was followed by a press conference in which Mahathir made further allegations against his more mild-mannered successor. Subsequently the prime minister responded, characterising Mahathir's renewed attack on him as "stronger doses of venom".

Malaysia widened its participation in regional and Islamic affairs, contributing about 500 troops and police to East Timor in May following disturbances there (see pp. 321-22), and sending 360 peacekeepers to Lebanon in the aftermath of the Israel-Hezbullah war (see pp. 197-203). The Malaysian government reacted to publication of the Danish cartoons of the Prophet Mohammed in a newspaper in Sarawak, in north Borneo, suspending the newspaper (see pp. 54-56). The prime minister also cautioned about the merits of interfaith dialogue in Malaysia, urging one such group to halt its forums, stressing the risks of such discussions within the context of Malaysia's multi-ethnic, multi-religious population.

The country's ties with neighbouring SINGAPORE likewise remained sensitive. These were hardly strengthened by the failure of the two countries' governments to agree on plans to erect a new bridge across the Johor Strait linking the two countries. The proposal became entangled with other issues, including efforts by Singapore to obtain supplies for land reclamation projects and approval for overflights by its air force during training missions.

INDONESIA—EAST TIMOR—PHILIPPINES

Indonesia

CAPITAL: Jakarta AREA: 1,905,000 sq km POPULATION: 220,558,000
OFFICIAL LANGUAGE: Bahasa Indonesia POLITICAL SYSTEM: multiparty republic
HEAD OF STATE AND GOVERNMENT: President Gen. (retd) Susilo Bambang Yudhoyono (since Oct '04)
RULING PARTIES: Nationhood Coalition comprising the PDI-P and Golkar
MAIN IGO MEMBERSHIPS (NON-UN): ASEAN, APEC, CP, OIC, OPEC, NAM
CURRENCY: rupiah (end-'06 £1=Rp17,513.5, US$1=Rp8,970.00)
GNI PER CAPITA: US$1,280, US$3,720 at PPP ('05)

East Timor

CAPITAL: Dili AREA: 153,870 sq km POPULATION: 976,000
OFFICIAL LANGUAGES: Portuguese, Tetum and Bahasa Indonesian POLITICAL SYSTEM: transitional government overseen by UNTAET
HEAD OF STATE: President José Alexandre (Xanana) Gusmão (since April '02)
HEAD OF GOVERNMENT: José Ramos-Horta, Prime Minister (since July '06)
MAIN IGO MEMBERSHIPS (NON-UN): NAM, G-77, CPLP
CURRENCY: US dollar (end-'06 £1=1.95250)
GNI PER CAPITA: US$750 ('05), -

Philippines

CAPITAL: Manila AREA: 300,000 sq km POPULATION: 83,054,000
OFFICIAL LANGUAGE: Filipino POLITICAL SYSTEM: multiparty republic
HEAD OF STATE AND GOVERNMENT: President Gloria Macapagal-Arroyo (since Jan '01)
RULING PARTY: Lakas ng EDSA-National Union of Christian Democrats (Lakas-NUCD)
MAIN IGO MEMBERSHIPS (NON-UN): ASEAN, APEC, CP, NAM
CURRENCY: Philippine peso (end-'06 £1=PP95.4358, US$1=PP48.8800)
GNI PER CAPITA: US$1,300, US$5,300 at PPP ('05)

THE year 2006 in INDONESIA saw significant movement in the always fraught area of territorial politics, a perennial preoccupation for the huge and diverse archipelagic country. Islamism and its terrorist extremes also occupied much national attention. The context in which these challenges presented themselves was for once, however, one of relative governmental stability, not a familiar characteristic of the Indonesian narrative over the previous decade.

In January the national legislature debated a draft law on the autonomy of the strongly Muslim province of Aceh, in northern Sumatra. This was part of the 2005 agreement between the central government and the separatist Free Aceh Movement, GAM (see AR 2005, pp. 297-98). The new law was formally adopted in April. As well as allowing for far-reaching—at least by Indonesian standards—local self-government, including the introduction of a form of Muslim Shariah law, the new Aceh administration was to have control over the expenditure of the larger part of the region's promised oil and gas revenues. Confidence in the adoption of the agreement had already, in April, seen the senior leadership of GAM return to Indonesia from their exile in Sweden for the first time in three decades. Election planning for the new autonomous administration got underway, with a team from the EU—which had already performed a range of monitoring functions in the province—being asked to supervise the process. On 11 December, largely incident-free elections were held for governor, town mayors, and district-level representatives who together would lead the new autonomous administration.

Developments were less positive in Papua (formerly Irian Jaya), another restive province at the opposite end of the national archipelago. In March there were widespread violent protests against a US-owned copper mine in the interior of the province. The trouble began when police forced out local independent miners from the site, but the protest was soon directed at the larger issue of the environmental damage inflicted on Papua's unique eco-system by the huge Freeport-McMoRan venture. Underlying everything were simmering discontents over the alienation of traditional land rights by large foreign ventures, which enriched a Javanese elite but brought little or no economic benefit to the indigenous Melanesian population.

The Islamist challenge, which had been a major source of concern for both the Indonesian government and the Western powers leading the so-called "war on terror", continued in 2006, though it showed signs of internal fragmentation. At the beginning of the year one of the chief suspects in the 2002 Bali bombings still at large, the Malaysian Noordin Mohammed Top, was reported to have split from the main south-east Asian movement, Jemaah Islamiah (JI), to form a new movement, the Organisation for the Basis of Jihad (TQJ). Divisions within JI had already been reported, with a significant part of its membership becoming concerned at popular hostility to the deaths and injury of local people caused by the organisation's bombs (see AR 2005, p. 299).

Some encouragement could be taken by the Islamists from the noisy demonstrations in the country in February against the publication in Denmark of cartoons depicting the Prophet Mohammed (see pp. 54-56). The disturbances were not as violent or sustained in Indonesia as in other parts of the Muslim world, however. Muslim protests also took place in April following the launch of an Indonesian edition of *Playboy* magazine. Inoffensive by the jaded standards of the West, the publication enraged sections of Islamic opinion and publication was discontinued. Responding to the clamour, the government brought charges against the magazine's editor for publishing "indecent material" and a trial began in December. Although quite trivial in itself, the affair marked the shifting balance in what had been a largely secular society between the forces of westernisation and the power of political Islam.

There was some concern in the West at the release from prison in June of JI's spiritual leader, Abu Bakar Bashir. Although there was no evidence of his direct involvement, he had been convicted of conspiracy charges relating to the Bali and Jakarta bombings of 2002 and 2003 (see AR 2002, p. 340; 2003, p. 362). It was unlikely, though, that the ailing and closely monitored Bashir would pose any major practical threat. The Indonesian government also pointed out that it had been denied access by the USA to the man suspected of masterminding the devastating Bali attacks of 2002, who was being held in custody at the US naval base in Guantánamo Bay, Cuba. In the meantime, in May, four alleged JI members went on trial for the Bali bombings of the previous year. (see AR 2005, pp. 298-99) and in September were sentenced to various prison terms. Some Indonesian

Christians drew unfavourable comparisons between these sentences and the fate of three Christians who, in the same month, were executed for inciting violence against Muslims during the inter-religious riots of 2000 (see AR 2000, p. 324).

Despite the caution and "creative ambiguity" of the government's response to Islamist violence, Indonesia was still regarded by the West as a key ally in the "war on terror". The year saw the arrival of a procession of western leaders anxious to underpin the position of President Susilo Bambang Yudhoyono and his administration. As well as visits from US Secretary of State Condoleezza Rice and from Defence Secretary Donald Rumsfeld during the year, Indonesia received the UK prime minister, Tony Blair, who included the country in an Asian regional tour in March, the first visit by a British head of government since the time of Margaret Thatcher. A visit by US President George W. Bush in November was of only limited symbolic value after it was downgraded to a six-hour stopover amidst US security fears.

At the end of May a devastating earthquake struck southern Java, badly damaging the ancient cultural centre of Yogyakarta. Around 6,000 lives were lost and about half a million people were made homeless. At the same time the nearby volcanic Mount Merapi had been in a state of apparently incipient eruption, further stretching emergency services (scientists were unsure whether the two events were linked). Two months later, in July, a tsunami struck the southern Javanese coast killing about 300 people and destroying several villages. The disaster inevitably brought memories of the devastating regional tsunami of 2004 (see AR 2004, p. 319; for map see AR 2005, p. 296). In contrast to these natural events, human agency had a hand in the loss of about 400 lives at the end of December when a crowded ferry *en route* from Borneo to Java sank in the Java Sea.

The year 2006 was a bad one for EAST TIMOR, Asia's newest state. Having navigated its way through chaos and violence to independence in 2002, East Timor had recently been showing signs of increased political stability and social normality. These proved to be fatally fragile, however, when, in March, the capital, Dili, experienced once again the disorder and factional violence that had followed its assertion of independence in 1999.

The trigger for the violence was the dismissal by the defence minister, on the orders of Prime Minister Mari Alkatiri, of about 600 members of the country's 1,400-strong paramilitary force. Although the move was ostensibly designed to impose some economic rationality on government spending, there appeared to be ethnic and political factors at play as well. The demobilised troops were almost entirely ethnic Loromonu, from the west of the country. This left the defence force dominated by the eastern Lorosau ethnic group. The Lorosau had been prominent in the guerrilla army of the Fretelin movement, which had fought the Indonesian occupation between 1975 and 1999, and which after independence had dominated the officer ranks of the defence force. Already resentful at what they regarded as Lorosau bullying in barracks, newer Loromonu recruits now found themselves out on the street. Making common cause with Dili's pool of jobless and disaffected youth, the aggrieved former soldiers caused mayhem. The situation was complicated by the fact that the civilian police—nominally responsible for law and order—were seen by the Lorosau-dominated military as sympathetic to the dissident Loromonu.

The violence reached a peak at the end of April and, at the request of the government, an Australian-led international force was once again deployed on the streets of Dili. It soon became clear that the crisis was interwoven with a serious power struggle within the ruling elite. A long-smouldering hostility between Alkatiri and President Xanana Gusmão now caught fire and pressure grew for the prime minister's resignation. Fatally for Alkatiri, he had also incurred the hostility of the foreign minister, José Ramos-Horta. Between them, Gusmão and Ramos-Horta embodied the national struggle in the minds and hearts of the East Timorese, and their combined wrath could not long be resisted. Alkatiri resigned at the end of June amidst claims that he and his supporters had been engaged in a violent clandestine campaign against their political rivals. He was replaced by Ramos-Horta.

Tensions remained high, particularly in the capital, however, and although the actual death toll was relatively low (about 40 fatalities were confirmed during the trouble), the international force (by the end of the year composed of Australian and Portuguese personnel) remained in place. Responding to the crisis, the UN authorised a new agency for the country, the Integrated Mission in East Timor (UNMIT), which included a substantial civilian police element though no military personnel.

The violence and instability of the year was the more unfortunate as East Timor's prospects on the broader international and economic fronts had seemed to be improving. In January Foreign Minister Ramos-Horta and his Australian counterpart, Alexander Downer, had reached an agreement to what had been a bitter wrangle over the distribution of revenues from oil and gas production in the Timor Sea (see AR 2004, p. 319). At issue was the international maritime boundary which East Timor had wished to be set at the midway point between the two countries (the conventional arrangement) but which Australia sought to have fixed at a point more favourable to itself. In return for an agreement to leave the boundary issue under a 50-year moratorium, Australia accepted a gas revenue sharing deal which would potentially be worth several billions of dollars to East Timor, sums which, at a stroke, could transform the country's dismal economic situation.

In 2006 the PHILIPPINES saw the presidency of Gloria Macapagal-Arroyo beleaguered from a range of directions. Claims of coup attempts and draconian government reaction to them gave a sense of crisis to the year. In the meantime guerrilla challenges, from Islamists, separatists, and communists, suggested that, in contrast to the circumstances of its neighbours elsewhere in south-east Asia, the Philippines state remained as fragile as it had been at any time in the previous two decades.

At the end of February the Arroyo government declared a state of emergency in response to claims that senior military figures had just narrowly averted a coup. The leader of the plot was said to be former Senator and army Colonel Gregorio

"Gringo" Honason, a veteran hero of the anti-Marcos agitation of the 1980s and still a potent force among some sections of the military. The basis of the alleged coup was opaque, with both renegade right-wingers and communist elements supposedly involved. Honason himself had disappeared after his plot was foiled. In the meantime the police were given extraordinary powers of arrest and detention until the lifting of the state of emergency at the beginning of March.

Typically in the Philippines, the government's narrative of threat and conspiracy was greeted with considerable scepticism. The self-preservatory instincts of Arroyo's presidency—which had been beset by mounting challenges to its legitimacy—were detected behind the heavy-handed response. Many, including such influential national figures as former Presidents Corazon Aquino and Fidel Ramos, suspected that the coup threat, if not wholly manufactured, had been exaggerated to enable Arroyo to move against political opponents. About 50 individuals were charged in relation to the alleged coup, including military officers, members of Congress (the bicameral legislature), and communists. "Gringo" Honason himself eluded capture until November, when he was detained in Manila.

Although an impeachment attempt against President Arroyo was heavily defeated in the House of Representatives (the lower chamber of Congress) at an early stage in August, the affair represented another step in the decline of Arroyo's once considerable reputation at home and abroad. Perhaps by way of restoring her earlier liberal credentials, she formally abolished the death penalty in June (which in fact had been in abeyance for some considerable time already). She also made a number of public gestures designed to distance herself from the growing epidemic of extra-judicial killings of local political activists which had spread across the country during her time in power. It was unclear, however, whether she had the authority to end these crimes by renegade elements in the security apparatus.

Unsteadiness at the centre of national power vitiated efforts against both Marxist and Islamist insurgencies. The year began with fighting to the north of the capital between security forces and the New People's Army (NPA), the armed wing of the Philippines Communist Party, which had been a thorn in the side of the state for decades. Evidently unaffected like other Marxist insurgent groups by the end of the Cold War, the NPA persisted as a formidable military force throughout the 1990s and had consistently rejected offers of a political settlement, most recently after talks in 2004 which had seemed at the time to offer an end to the conflict (see AR 2004, p. 321).

Of greater international concern was the threat posed by Islamism, both fundamentalist and separatist. News emerged during the year that the two Muslim separatist movements based on the southern islands, the Moro National Liberation Front (MNLF) and the Moro Islamic Liberation Front (MILF), were negotiating their reunification (having split in the mid-1980s). This was alarming news, as the MNLF had reached a settlement with the government in 1996 and the MILF had observed a de facto ceasefire for the previous two years (see AR 1996, pp. 325-26). June saw bombings in Mindanao, followed by fighting between the army and the MILF. In September the army began a large scale offensive against the even more hardline Abu Sayyaf group (AS) in Sulu province. The AS was a particular concern for the USA because of its apparent links to the al-Qaida network. More than 6,000 government troops were involved in the operation as were US special forces units.

The climatic effects of global warming continued to take their toll on the Philippines during 2006. In February several hundred people died in mudslides in Southern Leyte province following extreme levels of rainfall. At the other end of the year even more died in more mudslides in the east of the country following Typhoon Durian, with the country's largest island, Luzon, particularly badly hit.

EAST ASIAN STATES

PEOPLE'S REPUBLIC OF CHINA—HONG KONG—TAIWAN

People's Republic of China

CAPITAL: Beijing AREA: 9,597,000 sq km POPULATION: 1,304,500,000
OFFICIAL LANGUAGE: Chinese POLITICAL SYSTEM: one-party republic
HEAD OF STATE: President Hu Jintao (since March '03)
RULING PARTY: Chinese Communist Party (CCP)
PARTY LEADER: Hu Jintao (since Nov '02)
CCP POLITBURO STANDING COMMITTEE: Hu Jintao, Wu Bangguo, Wen Jiabao, Jia Qinglin, Zeng Qinghong, Huang Ju, Wu Guanzheng, Li Changchun, Luo Gan
CCP CENTRAL COMMITTEE SECRETARIAT: Zeng Qinghong, Liu Yunshan, Zhou Yongkang, He Guoqiang, Wang Gang, Xu Caihou, He Yong
CENTRAL MILITARY COMMISSION: Hu Jintao, chairman (since March '04)
PRIME MINISTER: Wen Jiabao (since March '03)
MAIN IGO MEMBERSHIPS (NON-UN): APEC, SCO
CURRENCY: renminbi (RMB) denominated in yuan (end-'06 £1=Y15.2391, US$1=Y7.80510)
GNP PER CAPITA: US$1,740, US$6,600 at PPP ('05, based on 1986 bilateral comparison of China and USA)

Hong Kong Special Administrative Region

CAPITAL: Victoria AREA: 1,000 sq km POPULATION: 6,944,000
STATUS: Special Administrative Region of People's Republic of China (since 1 July 1997)
CHIEF EXECUTIVE: Donald Tsang Yam-Kuen (since June '05)
ADMINISTRATIVE SECRETARY: Rafael Hui (since June '05)
MAIN IGO MEMBERSHIPS (NON-UN): APEC
CURRENCY: Hong Kong dollar (end-'06 £1=HK$15.2031, US$1=HK$7.78670)
GNP PER CAPITA: US$27,670, US$34,670 at PPP ('05)

Taiwan

CAPITAL: Taipei AREA: 35,981 sq km POPULATION: 22,876,527 ('06)
OFFICIAL LANGUAGES: Chinese POLITICAL SYSTEM: multiparty republic
HEAD OF STATE AND GOVERNMENT: President Chen Shui-bian (since May '00)
RULING PARTY: Democratic Progressive Party (DPP)
PRIME MINISTER: Su Tseng-chang (DPP) (since Jan '06)
MAIN IGO MEMBERSHIPS (NON-UN): APEC; Taiwan is not a member of UN or associated IGOs
CURRENCY: New Taiwan dollar (end-'06 £1=NT$63.2692, US$1=NT$32.4050)
GNI PER CAPITA: US$26,700 ('05 est), -

THE People's Republic of CHINA, the PRC, continued to enjoy rapid economic growth in 2006, but this growth generated tensions both within the country and with China's main economic partners. The political system remained stable with the "fourth generation" leadership under President Hu Jintao firmly in control and preparing for the important Chinese Communist Party (CCP) congress that was expected to convene in 2007. China's key bilateral relationships all remained stable and secure, although the North Korean nuclear test had important repercussions for Chinese diplomacy.

Official figures stated that the Chinese economy grew at 10.7 per cent in 2006, and claimed an inflation rate for the year of 2.2 per cent. Indications that the economy was overheating saw the leadership attempt to slow down the economy through a series of monetary and administrative measures. Compared with similar attempts in 2004, observers commented that the macro-economic policy was better co-ordinated and more effective in 2006. The interest rates on loans was raised by 0.27 of a percentage point in April, and the reserve ratio on bank deposits was raised by half a percentage point in July, and again in August. Other measures to soak up liquidity and reduce investment demand were also introduced. Analysts suggested that the central bank, the People's Bank of China (PBC), was becoming more activist in its approach to macro-economic policy. Local and overseas commentators differed on the possible impact of the interest rate changes, some claiming that they might smother a stock market recovery, others claiming that powerful local governments and cash-rich state-owned enterprises could fill the gap in liquidity and undermine the central strategy.

Linked to the issue of tackling the economy's overheating was a gradual appreciation of the renminbi (RMB) against the US dollar over the course of the year: the appreciation averaged 0.2 per cent per month from March 2006, giving an appreciation of just under 5 per cent for calendar year 2006, or an appreciation of 6.4 per cent against the US dollar since July 2005 when the decade-old link between the dollar and the RMB was lifted (see AR 2005, p. 304). The slow appreciation of the RMB was a result of both a desire to cool the overheating economy and of significant pressure placed on China from overseas, by the USA in particular. In September the US treasury secretary, Henry Paulson, visited China with the currency issue at the top of his agenda

The fourth session of the 10th National People's Congress (NPC, the unicameral legislature) was held in Beijing in March. The trend towards paying greater attention to the negative social consequences of the economic reforms was palpable. Prime Minister Wen Jiabao acknowledged a number of "long-standing and deep-seated" problems, including difficulties in raising rural incomes and grain output; excessive growth, and "irrational" investment growth in fixed assets; problems with social welfare, especially the cost of education and medical treatment; problems with safety at work, especially in the mining industry; and deficiencies in local government. Wen stated that the government would tackle these issues through pursuing a policy of "steady but fast" economic growth, stimulating domestic demand through consumption (rather than investment), increased spending on the countryside aimed at enhancing rural infrastructure, and reducing inequalities between the countryside and the cities. The need to deal with the issues of rural poverty and inequalities between the urban and rural areas was highlighted again later in the year, and was perhaps becoming a defining feature of the Hu Jintao era. The concept of "new socialist rural areas" was frequently advanced during the year along with calls for a greater role for the urban and industrial sectors in promoting development and improving health and education in rural areas. In a speech in September, Wen stressed the abolition of the agricultural tax—a small but regressive and deeply unpopular levy—as a key step in improving the wellbeing of Chinese farmers.

The year 2006 was the first year of the 11th five year plan; the official targets for 2006 were an 8 per cent growth in GDP along with a 4 per cent reduction in energy consumption (per unit of GDP), inflation to be below 3 per cent, and equilibrium in China's balance of payments. Stronger environmental protection measures and more co-ordination of regional development projects were also stressed. The major goals for the five year plan were stated as (i) average annual GDP growth rate of 7.5 per cent; (ii) per capita GDP in 2010 to be double that of 2000; and (iii) energy consumption per incremental unit of GDP to fall by 20 per cent. The importance of good governance and combating corruption and related "unhealthy practices" was highlighted, and Wen stated that greater transparency was the key to improving government performance in these areas. China's troubled banking sector appeared to be improving, at least according to official figures. The People's Bank of China reported that non-performing loans owed to commercial banks had fallen to a record low of 8.8 per cent in 2005 (from 13.2 per cent in 2004 and 17.9 per cent in 2003).

The importance of social stability, and the "fourth generation" leadership's mantra of "creating a harmonious socialist society" were also significant and were stressed in Wen's speech to the NPC when he touched on the need for China to accelerate the establishment of a more comprehensive social security system. Wen announced that re-employment support for workers laid off by state-owned enterprises would be extended to three years and pilot projects for individual insurance schemes were being implemented. The prime minister repeated previous comments on the importance of the "five guarantees" for the destitute: food, clothing, medical care, housing, and burial expenses.

Referring to data from 2005, the ministry of public security announced a 6.6 per cent increase in disturbances to public order in 2005 over 2004, including an 18.9 per cent increase in crimes which "interfered with government business", a 13 per cent increase in mass gatherings which "disturbed public order"; and an 11.8 per cent increase in "provocation and stirring up trouble". The report claimed that the major sources of public disorder were rural unrest over compensation for land, migrant workers complaining about unpaid wages, and unemployed workers demanding welfare payments. Hong Kong media reports further claimed a significant increase in police injuries and fatalities.

Zhang Weiqing, the head of the National Population and Family Planning Commission, cautioned that a "mini baby boom" was likely, as the first generation of children born since the inauguration of the population and family planning strategy (the so-called "one-child policy")—estimated at approximately 100 million people—reached child-bearing age. The government stated that its population growth targets (keeping the population below 1.5 billion over the next 15 years) were being met, but tensions within China's "one-child policy" were also apparent when the government announced figures indicating that the male-female sex ratio at birth was 119:100. Furthermore, the Chinese government began to recognise the potential danger of an aging society and began exploring ways in which it could meet the significant increase in the costs of caring for the elderly after 2030. Estimates suggested that by 2051 almost one in three citizens would be over 60.

In June the government issued a white paper on "environmental protection in China", highlighting the difficult tensions between environmental protection and promoting economic growth. The report was strongly critical of the failure of local governments, especially in "remote and backward areas", to enforce environmental regulations. On 1 July the official rail link between the Tibetan capital, Lhasa, and the rest of mainland China was formally inaugurated. The railway was the highest in the world and was celebrated as massive achievement of Chinese engineering prowess, although some foreign critics complained that it would lead to environmental damage and to fundamental changes to Tibetan culture.

Elite level politics in the PRC appeared stable in 2006, but there was considerable speculation in domestic and international media as the Chinese Communist Party prepared for its 17th party congress, scheduled for 2007. Speculation was especially noticeable with regard to the eventual successors to President Hu Jintao and the rest of the "fourth generation" leadership. The emerging formal and informal rules over leadership succession in the PRC suggested that Hu and his leadership cohort would retire in 2012, and no obvious successors had as yet been identified. The detention on corruption charges of Chen Liangyu, head of the Shanghai's CCP municipal committee, the city's former mayor, and a former Politburo member, marked the highest profile corruption case in China since the arrest of Beijing mayor Chen Xitong in 1995. Chen Liangyu, along with several of his relatives and friends, was accused of using Shanghai's pension fund for personal gain. Foreign media speculated that his arrest could be related to high-level political manoeuvring ahead of the 2007 party congress. Chen Liangyu was regarded as not adhering properly to central government directives to slow the Shanghai economy, and also as being too close to the previous Chinese president, Jiang Zemin.

The Chinese leadership strongly criticised the government of Chen Shui-bian on TAIWAN following its decision in March to abolish the National Unification Council (the body designated to promote reunification with mainland CHINA) and for stating that the "guidelines for national unification" would no longer apply (see p. 333). The PRC also criticised Chen Shui-bian's calls for constitutional reform on Taiwan as an attempt to push the island toward independence. However, the PRC remained silent regarding the many problems that beset President Chen over the year, perhaps reasoning that an intervention into the politics of Taiwan might increase support for the beleaguered president. The Chinese leadership continued to pressure the US government over the issue, however, making it clear that the PRC would not accept Taiwanese independence and calling on the USA to rein in those on Taiwan who pursued this objective.

Political relations between the PRC and the USA were solid through the year, but were troubled by uncertainty over Korea (see below) and by continued persistent disagreements over the trade imbalance, protection of intellectual property in China, and the value of the Chinese currency. President Hu visited the USA in April, but the welcome ceremony was marred by a serious diplomatic blunder (the wrong Chinese title—the "Republic of China", i.e. Taiwan—was announced before the PRC national anthem was played) and a member of the Falun Gong religious group exploited press credentials to stage a public protest during the welcome ceremony.

The PRC's relations with Africa received considerable attention over the course of the year. In January China's first "African policy paper" was issued, stating China's ambition to establish a strategic partnership with African countries. This was followed through the year by a series of high profile visits to various African nations by senior Chinese leaders promoting both trade and improved political relations. In April President Hu visited Morocco, Nigeria, and Kenya, and Premier Wen Jiabao made a high profile tour of Africa in June, which included visits to Egypt, Ghana, the Republic of Congo, Angola, South Africa, Tanzania, and Uganda. The Chinese side paid special emphasis to their desire to create "a new type of strategic partnership" rooted in principles of equality and respect for sovereignty. The various visits resulted in trade and other financial agreements with estimated values of several billions of dollars. The diplomatic initiatives culminated in November when Beijing hosted the "China Africa summit" at which the PRC pledged to double its aid to Africa by 2009. Some Western commentators criticised the PRC's approach as ignoring issues of human rights and governance, but the Chinese side claimed that it was respecting sovereignty and maintaining principles of peaceful co-existence and non-interference.

The growing significance of natural resources issues for China was marked not only by the increased emphasis on relations with African states, but also by high level meetings between the Chinese and Saudi Arabian officials. In January, King Abdullah ibn Abdul Aziz made the first ever visit to China by a Saudi king, and in April President Hu made a state visit to Saudi Arabia. Saudi Arabia had emerged as China's largest supplier of crude oil and its second largest export market in west Asia and Africa, with bilateral trade expected to reach US$40 billion by 2009-10.

Sino-Russian relations saw a series of high-level meetings, related in part to China's "year of Russia". Russia's President Vladimir Putin visited Beijing in March and President Hu Jintao welcomed the final resolution of disagreements over boundary issues between the two countries and called for a deepening of strategic co-operation in the political and economic fields. A series of agreements related to oil and gas co-operation was signed. Hu visited St Petersburg in July to attend the outreach aspects of the G-8 (Group of Eight) summit, and as well as dealing with matters related to Sino-Russian relations he engaged in a number of bilateral and multi-lateral meetings with other countries. In September Premier Wen addressed the fifth prime ministerial meeting of the Shanghai Co-operation Organisation (SCO) at its meeting in Dushanbe, the capital of

Tajikistan, and called for collective and concerted action to combat ethnic separatism, terrorism, and religious extremism. Wen attended the Sixth Asia-Europe Meeting (ASEM 6) in Helsinki, the Finnish capital, in September: he re-stated longstanding Chinese objections to the EU arms export ban against the PRC.

The characterisation of the Sino-Japanese relationship as "economically hot, politically cold" remained accurate, at least until the departure of Japanese Prime Minister Junichiro Koizumi removed an important obstacle for the Chinese side and the North Korean nuclear crisis provided an issue over which a common position could be agreed. Until September senior level relations with Japan were in a holding pattern as the Chinese government awaited Koizumi's departure. In February, China's former Foreign Minister Tang Jiaxuan told Noda Takeshi, a visiting pro-China member of Japan's ruling Liberal Democratic Party (LDP), that he did not expect anything from the China-Japan relationship for the next eight months. Koizumi was deeply distrusted by the Chinese leadership because of his repeated visits to the controversial Yasukuni shrine in Tokyo, which commemorated Japan's war dead, including convicted war criminals. Koizumi's final visit to the shrine as prime minister, on 15 August, the anniversary of Japan's surrender in World War II (see p. 337), brought the expected condemnation from China. The Chinese leadership maintained a cautious but clear public position that visits to the shrine by any of Koizumi's putative successors were unacceptable and that the issue of visits to the Yasukuni shrine was a litmus test of Japanese goodwill and the key to improving the political relationship between the two states.

The eventual election of Shinzo Abe as Japan's prime minister in September was initially a cause of concern, given his supposed sympathy with Taiwan and his nationalist background; but the Chinese side accepted his ambivalent public position on Yasukuni, and the North Korean nuclear test which quickly followed Abe's appointment presented both leaderships with a matter of high importance that helped to put other differences to one side. Abe travelled to Beijing in early October for a summit with Hu Jintao and Wen Jiabao where they reaffirmed the importance of the six party talks for peace and stability on the Korean peninsula (see pp. 337-38).

The acutely sensitive issue of TAIWAN also troubled the relationship between the PRC and Japan, with Japanese Foreign Minister Taro Aso referring to Taiwan as a "country" and praising the impact of Japanese colonial rule over the island. Aso made a series of statements over the course of the year on issues such as the Yasukuni shrine, China's military build-up, and the need for China to learn from Japan. The comments were not well received. Disagreement between China and Japan over their maritime border in the East China Sea and ownership of potential natural resources continued throughout the year. Little progress was made in talks addressing the possibility of joint exploration and exploitation of resources in the disputed areas, but a positive change in atmosphere was reported following the election of Prime Minister Abe.

After early indications that the PRC's relations with North Korea were well established and that the Chinese leadership was able to exercise some influence over the North Koreans, the relationship suffered significant setbacks. In January the North Korean leader, Kim Jong Il, made a week long visit to China, touring coastal areas and generating considerable speculation about possible economic reform in North Korea. However by the summer goodwill declined rapidly, and by the end of the year relations between the PRC and North Korea were at perhaps their most hostile since the two communist regimes were founded in the 1940s. The PRC had been unable to persuade North Korea to return to the six party talks, and in July a North Korean missile test was criticised by the Chinese government. To the surprise of many observers, China signed UN Security Council resolution 1695, which condemned the missile test (for text see pp. 552-53). The North Korean nuclear test in October damaged the relationship still further. While the Chinese leadership refused to accede to some of the more punitive sanctions called for by Japan, its public condemnation of North Korea was worded in the strongest terms and it signed UN Security Council resolution 1718 and agreed to participate in sanctions against North Korea (see p. 345; for text see pp. 554-58). Although the North Korean government alerted China immediately before the test, the Chinese government's credibility was damaged: the PRC had not been able to exercise the influence over North Korea which many foreign governments hoped it could.

Relations with South Korea, meanwhile, remained on a firm economic footing, but a series of low-level disagreements, such as the abuse of diplomatic privilege by a Chinese diplomat in Seoul and minor trading disputes, in addition to the general uncertainty generated by North Korea's nuclear test, dogged the diplomatic relationship

After the turbulent events of the previous year, 2006 was relatively quiet and stable in HONG KONG. The chief executive, Donald Tsang, reacted to the defeat of his reform proposals in 2005 (see AR 2005, p. 307) by presenting a more modest agenda, and in January he announced that his priorities would be issues related to the economy and to people's livelihoods. Evidence for this was seen in changes to the working week for civil servants and the introduction of a voucher system for pre-school education. Tsang's administration suffered a small setback in March when it was forced to abandon proposals for the development of the West Kowloon cultural district in the face of opposition from developers and various activist groups. A large committee under Chief Secretary Rafael Hui Si-yan was formed to address the issue.

Albert Ho Chun-yan, a member of the Legislative Council (LegCo, the unicameral legislature) and chairman of the Democratic Party, was attacked in August after attending a demonstration against the introduction of a goods and service tax (GST). It was unclear whether the attack was related to the demonstration, to Ho's political position, or to a number of controversial legal cases in which he was involved in his capacity as a lawyer. The issue of the GST remained very divisive and in December the government announced that it would withdraw the planned levy.

In September former Chief Secretary (head of the colonial civil service) Anson Chan announced that she would not contest the chief executive election scheduled for 2007, but would instead focus on proposals for constitutional and governance reforms to the former colony. Candidates identified with a "pro-democracy" position did very well in functional constituency sub-sector elections in December, enabling more of their candidates to appear on the list for the 2007 elections.

The Hong Kong economy did well over the year, with the Hang Seng index posting a record high of 20,001 points in December and the government reporting a surplus of HK$10 billion. Total employment in Hong Kong reached a record level of more than 3.47 million, and unemployment fell to its lowest rate in over five years (4.8 per cent). The economic success, however, did not immediately generate into a greater sense of security within society at large. Social order received considerable attention throughout the year. Hong Kong Disneyland generated chaotic scenes in February when serious overcrowding forced the theme park to ban entry to pre-paid ticket holders, and there were widespread complaints of a decline in standards of public administration after confusion in a mortuary over the identity of two bodies, and the mistaken release of confidential information by the Independent Police Complaints Council. The remarkable popular cultural hit of the year, though, was a video of an elderly man berating a younger passenger over his behaviour on a bus. Civic activism was very much in evidence, as well, in public demonstrations against the demolition of the Star Ferry terminal.

There were two high profile visits to the Special Administrative Region by senior politicians from mainland CHINA. In March Jia Qinglin , chairman of the Chinese People's Political Consultative Conference (CPPCC, a political advisory body), visited; he was followed in December by Wu Bangguo, chairman of the National People's Conference (NPC, the unicameral legislature).

In TAIWAN President Chen Shui-bian and the ruling Democratic Progressive Party (DPP) endured a very difficult year, with the administration rocked by corruption allegations, levelled initially against the president's family and later against the president himself. This in turn saw a collapse in public support, and massive anti-government demonstrations paralysed the capital in September and October. Some respite appeared toward the end of the year, when the DPP narrowly won the mayoral election in Taiwan's second city, Kaohsiung. Chen also took an antagonistic approach toward relations with the People's Republic of CHINA (PRC), abolishing symbolically important state bodies responsible for managing the relationship. This generated concern in the USA over a possible change to the status quo in the Taiwan Straits.

Accusations of corruption dominated Taiwan in 2006. In May, following lengthy speculation and negative press coverage of the issue, President Chen's son-in-law, Chao Chien-ming, was arrested over allegations of insider trading. In addition, President Chen's wife, Wu Shu-chen, continued to be dogged by accusations that she had received significant financial rewards from a Taipei department store after intervening in a dispute over the store's ownership. In April, Chen Che-nan, President Chen's former deputy chief-of-staff, was arrested over allegations of accepting a NT$7 million bribe to help to settle charges against a business associate. This followed a series of ongoing charges against Chen Che-nan with regard to manipulating bids for infrastructure projects.

At the end of May President Chen announced that he would relinquish all of his governmental and party authority other than the direct powers granted to the president under the constitution, and would delegate government and party policy-making authority to the prime minister and to the DPP chairman. This concession failed to appease his many opponents, who called for Chen's resignation; opposition legislators attempted to recall the president, but the attempt fell short of the two-thirds majority required. In June the situation became much more difficult for the president, when the ministry of audit called for an investigation after it revealed that around NT$37 million of the president's budget (around 77 per cent of the total) was not properly accounted for. The presidential office claimed that around NT$24 million of that budget was classified, and on that basis declined to submit documentation. However the impact on public opinion was incendiary and Chen's approval ratings fell below 20 per cent. In November First Lady Wu Shu-chen and three senior members of the presidential office were indicted for involvement in false accounting over receipts for a sum of NT$14.8 million. As the serving president, Chen himself could not be prosecuted until he left office.

The most dramatic and visible sign of Chen's unpopularity came from a series of massive anti-Chen protests that occupied the capital in September and October. Estimates of the size of the crowds varied from 90,000 to over 300,000. The protests were organised and co-ordinated by Shih Ming-teh, a former DPP chairman and one of Taiwan's most prominent pro-democracy activists. The demonstrations were specifically designed not to present a party position but to be a campaign against corruption and against the president: all protestors were encouraged to wear red, to demonstrate their non-partisan stance. The demonstrations against Chen at the time of the national day celebrations on 10 October were regarded as acutely embarrassing for the president, who later stated that he was considering terminating the public celebrations in the future.

In January Frank Hsieh stood down as prime minister, to take responsibility for the DPP's poor performance in the 2005 local elections (see AR 2005, pp. 308-09). He was replaced by Su Tseng-chang. Hsieh's resignation enabled him to run as the DPP candidate in the Taipei mayoral election in December. He was unsuccessful, but commentators suggested that he was likely to seek the DPP's nomination to run as its presidential candidate for 2008. Some optimism returned to the ruling party in December, however, when it narrowly succeeded in winning the mayoral elections in the southern port of Kaohsiung, but by a margin of just 1,114 votes, or 0.14 per cent.

Opposition leader Ma Ying-jeou enjoyed a successful year, at least until December, in part benefiting from the president's problems and also from his own reputation as an honest politician. As mayor of Taipei he was confronted with a difficult issue with regard to the anti-Chen demonstrations, given that he clearly opposed Chen's tenure but still needed to maintain law and order in the city. He squared the circle by supporting the demonstrations in a private capacity, while the mayor's office attempted to maintain order and stability. In December Ma was accused of misuse of public funds, related to receipts being substituted by one of his staff. Ma denied the charges and stated that, if indicted, he would resign as chairman of the opposition Kuomintang (KMT).

In February President Chen announced that the National Unification Council (the body designated to promote reunification with mainland CHINA) was to be abolished and stated that the "guidelines for national unification" would no longer apply. The next day Chen gave an interview to a Japanese newspaper in which he stated that he would drive an initiative either to change Taiwan's constitution, or create a new statute for the island. Chen and other politicians remained ambiguous, or perhaps contradictory, over whether the issue was one of reforming the existing constitution or creating an entirely new one. The move was widely criticised by Chen's opponents as an attempt to distract the public from the corruption issue and also a dangerous move that damaged Taiwan's international position. The call for a new constitution or constitutional revision generated significant anger in the PRC and concern in the USA. The PRC leadership feared that this was a step towards independence for Taiwan, while the US government criticised Chen for going back on earlier pledges not to change the constitution and also for potentially damaging the delicate political and military balance in north-east Asia. Despite the criticism, Chen continued to push the idea of constitutional change, and in October called for the foundation of a "second republic". His call led to a strong rebuke from several US state department officials who urged the Taiwanese not to alter the status quo in cross-Straits relations.

Whilst the political relationship across the Straits remained frosty, economic exchanges continued to grow. Bilateral trade between Taiwan and China in the nine months to September rose by 16.9 per cent from the same period in 2005 to US$64.44 billion. Taiwan's trade surplus for January to September was estimated at US$28.32 billion, up by 9.4 per cent from a year earlier. In the first 10 months of 2006 there was an 18.3 per cent increase in so called "three mini-link" exchanges over the same period in 2005. The "three mini links" referred to the postal, transport, and trade links between Taiwan's outlying islands of Kinmen and Matsu, and Xiamen and Fuzhou harbours in China's Fujian province. This growth occurred despite attempts by the ruling DPP and its pro-independence ally, the Taiwan Solidarity Union (TSU), to block opposition proposals to ease restrictions on trade and investment with China. The size of Taiwan's economic relationship with China was highlighted with the publication in March of a WTO report, which noted that Taiwan enjoyed the world's largest trade surplus with China, at US$58 billion.

In September the government launched its 14th bid to re-enter the UN as the Republic of China (ROC). The bid received only modest support from Taiwan's small number of formal diplomatic allies, and was rejected by the UN General Assembly's general committee. This led President Chen to call for any future applications for UN membership to be carried out under the name of "Taiwan" instead of the ROC. The Taiwanese government attempted to counter the PRC's high profile diplomatic initiatives in Africa (see p. 328), and Minister of Foreign Affairs Huang Chih-fang toured Taiwan's diplomatic partners in Africa in July, but failed to stem the on-going decline in support: Chad switched recognition to the PRC in September (see pp. 254-55).

JAPAN

CAPITAL: Tokyo AREA: 378,000 sq km POPULATION: 127,760,000 (official estimate, Oct '06)
OFFICIAL LANGUAGE: Japanese POLITICAL SYSTEM: multiparty monarchy
HEAD OF STATE: Emperor Tsugu no Miya Akihito (since Jan '89)
RULING PARTIES: Liberal Democratic Party (LDP) in coalition with the New Komeito party
HEAD OF GOVERNMENT: Shinzo Abe, Prime Minister (since Sept '06)
MAIN IGO MEMBERSHIPS (NON-UN): APEC, CP, OECD, G-8
CURRENCY: yen (end-'06 £1=Y233.054, US$1=Y119.365)
GNI PER CAPITA: US$38,980, US$31,410 at PPP ('05)

THERE were three major developments in Japan during 2006: the retirement of Junichiro Koizumi as prime minister in September; the birth of a son to Princess Kiko; and North Korea's nuclear weapons test in October which affected Japan's security.

The year started calmly, however, with Koizumi securely in office thanks to the overwhelming victory for his Liberal Democratic party (LDP) in the September 2005 general election and its continuing coalition with the small Komeito party. Since he came to power in April 2001, Koizumi had achieved his long-standing goal of passing legislation for breaking up the Post Office into several divisions and thus destroying its political significance (see AR 2005, p. 311). He had moulded the LDP in his own image and reduced the internal faction-fighting. He had inherited a country with massive bad debts on the part of its banks and presided over an economic revival after the stagnant years of the 1990s. With positive and severe economic policies he put the country back on its feet and steered through a series of drastic banking reforms. Economic expansion in 2006 marked a new postwar record, thanks largely to expanding trade with China. But there were still concerns over the slow revival in personal consumption and the impact that the uncertain future of the US economy would have on Japan.

In January Japan was rocked by financial scandals on a grand scale, the most serious in the history of the Japanese stock markets. Takafumi Horie, a young entrepreneur from the Internet services company, Livedoor, who had gained notoriety when he fought a constituency unsuccessfully in the September 2005 general election, was arrested along with other executives of his Internet empire. The accusation was false accounting by overstating the earnings of the company. The Tokyo Stock Exchange, besieged by shareholders wishing to sell off the company's stock, had to suspend trading. The Tokyo Prosecutor's Office charged the executives with distorting company accounts in order to conceal a deficit. Owing to the vast publicity which the case attracted, Horie—who pleaded not guilty—was hounded by the press. Another scandal in June, when the Bank of Japan's governor apologised for having invested in a fund administered by fund manager Yoshiaki Murakami, who had admitted to insider trading, was similarly unsettling for the markets. The outcome of these cases—which remained unresolved at the end of the year—was expected to have great significance for regulatory mechanisms in Japan.

On the question of the imperial succession, the government, which in November 2005 had received a report from a commission recommending that female heirs should be acceptable on the Japanese throne (see AR 2005, pp. 313-14), promised that it would introduce legislation to that effect. It was, however, announced in February that 173 members of the Diet (the bicameral legislature) had expressed their opposition to any legislation that would revise the Imperial Household Law to allow females and their descendants to ascend the throne. This was followed almost immediately by the announcement that Princess Kiko, the wife of Prince Akishino, the younger brother of the crown prince, was pregnant. Since there was the possibility that the offspring would be male, the governing LDP changed course, announcing that it was inappropriate to reconsider the country's tradition of restricting the imperial succession to a male heir and abandoning its intention to introduce amending legislation. On 6 September a son was born to Princess Kiko, the first boy to be born in the imperial family since the birth of the child's father, Prince Akishino, in 1965. The young prince was named Hisahito and became third in line to the throne, after Crown Prince Naruhito, the current Emperor's first son, and Prince Akishino. The implication seemed to be that Princess Aiko, the four-year old daughter of the crown prince, might be passed over.

The year saw the withdrawal of Japan's ground troops from coalition forces in Iraq. When the new Iraqi government came to power in the spring, after long wrangling over posts (see pp. 205-07), the Japanese announced on 20 June the withdrawal of the 600 soldiers of their Ground Self-Defence Forces (SDF), who had served for two years with the coalition in Samawah, southern Iraq, as the Japanese Iraq Reconstruction and Support Group. They were engaged in humanitarian and reconstruction efforts for the rehabilitation of the country, such as ensuring water supply and medical assistance, but were constitutionally forbidden from undertaking combatant activity. The mission, which was a rare example of Japanese forces serving overseas, had been remarkably successful. The evacuation was completed on 17 July. Japan, which was one of the most generous donors of relief to the Iraqi administration, went on to offer substantial official development aid to Iraq. Japan's foreign minister, Taro Aso, visited the country in August and promised further aid. But, even if the Ground SDF were no longer in Iraq, the air wing continued to be involved in air transport activities there and the Maritime SDF in supplying fuel to US and other vessels engaged in anti-terrorism activities in the northern reaches of the Indian Ocean.

For Japan the relationship with the USA was crucial, especially in the field of defence. For some years the two countries had been working towards a realignment of US forces in Japan. In May they published a plan calling for the relocation of Futenma airbase within Okinawa prefecture, the transfer of 8,000 marines to Guam, and the relocation of US aircraft to Iwakuni in Yamaguchi prefecture in western Japan. But Okinawan residents were opposed to the first of these proposals by a substantial margin. The government secured agreement with the mayor of Nago in Okinawa for the construction of two runways to cater for aircraft being transferred from elsewhere in the islands. On 8 April the governor of Okinawa expressed opposition to the proposal, although he agreed to continue discussion on this prickly subject. The US-Japanese plan provided for the implementation of these changes gradually by 2014 in the interest of closer defence co-operation. But the issue was far from settled, since it involved a constitutional struggle between Okinawan politicians and the government in Tokyo.

There was a heavily publicised dispute between Japan and the USA on a different issue in January when Japan re-imposed a ban on US beef imports after meat was found to contain prohibited spinal column material. The ban, imposed two years previously and only eased in December 2005, was an attempt to prevent BSE (bovine spongiform encephalopathy, or "mad cow disease") from entering domestic herds. It required top-level diplomacy to resolve the problem and was a major issue discussed between US President George W. Bush and Prime Minister Koizumi. Japan lifted its ban after inspection of 35 US meat-packaging plants but the first consignment did not reach Japan's shores until August.

Japan suffered from a series of territorial disputes with four of its neighbours. South Korea sent gunboats to the disputed islet of Takeshima (known to Koreans as Dokdo, and administered by South Korea) whose sovereignty had long been at issue with Japan. Both sides put forward claims to incorporate the islets in their "exclusive economic zones". In June, when officials met to discuss the issue, Japan asked South Korea not to conduct a maritime survey in the area. But South Korea went ahead with the survey and Japan threatened to send a similar oceanographic team to these waters. Another old issue came to the fore in the summer with China: who would take advantage of the development of gas fields off islands in the East China Sea? In particular there was the long-standing dispute over the Senkaku Islands (known to China as the Diaoyu islands). They were administered by Japan but claimed by China. Direct talks on the islands proceeded throughout the year. Despite these territorial differences, Japan was anxious to keep on good terms with her neighbours because of the need for a common front against North Korea.

With Japan's other neighbour, Russia, there were acrimonious cases of Russian military aircraft violating Japanese airspace. Meanwhile the disputed Northern Territories—islands that Japan claimed but which Russia had occupied as the southern Kuriles since 1945—came to the fore in August when Russian coastguards shot dead a Japanese man on a fishing vessel that was fishing for a rare species of crab in Russian territorial waters. The Russians apologised but claimed that the Japanese fishermen were poaching.

North Korea's nuclear activities were on a more significant scale than these issues, however. While the other countries concerned were anxious to restart the six party talks, the North Koreans imposed conditions which were unacceptable to the USA and Japan. In July North Korea conducted test launches for seven ballistic missiles, which fell in the Japan Sea. Japan took this very seriously and reacted by banning the North Korean ferry from Japanese ports for six months. But it was left for the new Japanese administration that took over from Koizumi in September to deal with the major crisis in relations caused by North Korea's underground nuclear test carried out in October (see below).

Koizumi, in the last throes of his premiership, continued his hectic travels. On 26 May he presided at a meeting of 16 countries attending the Japan-Pacific Islands Forum in Okinawa. He pledged Y45 billion in development aid to the region. In a bid to woo the Central Asian republics, he paid visits in August to Mongolia, Kazakhstan, and Uzbekistan in order to meet their leaders. Koizumi had earlier travelled to the USA where he and President Bush signed the prospectus for a new US-Japanese alliance for the 21st century and reaffirmed their scheme for a next generation missile defence system, on which they had conducted a joint interceptor missile test in Hawaii. Koizumi then visited Middle Eastern countries before attending the St Petersburg summit of the G-8 (Group of Eight) most industrialised countries in July.

Controversial to the last, Koizumi visited the Yasukuni shrine in Tokyo to pay his respects to the war dead on 15 August, the anniversary of the day that Japan had surrendered in the Pacific War. This action had not been taken by a prime minister for two decades and was a snub for China and Korea, which renewed their protests (see pp. 329; 343). The visit was all the more controversial because it followed an important revelation in July that the Emperor Hirohito (1926-89) had disclosed that he believed that the management of Yasukuni shrine had made a mistake in including Class A war criminals from World War II among those honoured there. Although the emperor had visited the shrine prior to 1975, he had ceased doing so when they took this step. Emperor Akihito (Hirohito's son) had not visited Yasukuni.

As promised, Koizumi resigned in September as president of the LDP and also as prime minister after serving for five-and-a-half years. On domestic issues he had been relatively successful with his reform programmes and left his successors a substantial parliamentary majority. In foreign affairs his legacy was less secure. He was consistently loyal to Japan's major partner, the USA, and travelled obsessively in order to promote his country. He was prominent at international meetings of high profile organisations such as the UN and the G-8 summits. But his relations with his neighbours were less successful. His stubborn determination to pay annual visits to the Yasukuni shrine prevented a substantial discussion with China when summit-level dialogue was desirable on a number of issues. His attendance at Yasukuni also antagonised the South Korean government.

The LDP held its leadership election for Koizumi's successor in September. As had been widely predicted for months, Shinzo Abe was successful by a large margin, gathering 464 votes from party members, or 66 per cent of votes cast. Abe had been chief cabinet secretary in the outgoing cabinet and was Koizumi's favoured candidate. He was a member of a leading political family, being the grandson of Nobusuke Kishi, Japan's prime minister in 1957-60. His election as prime minister was confirmed by a vote of both houses of the Diet on 26 September, in which he gained a total of 475 out of 716 votes cast. At 52, Abe became the youngest head of government since World War II and the first to have been born after 1945.

For his cabinet Abe generally chose politicians who had supported his leadership campaign. Yasuhisa Shiozaki, a known moderate and Harvard university graduate, was given the key post as chief cabinet secretary; Taro Aso, who had opposed Abe in the leadership contest, continued as foreign minister; while

Bummei Ibuki from the conservative wing of the LDP was selected for the critical role of education minister.

In his first policy speech to the House of Representatives (the lower house) on 29 September, Abe emphasised the urgency of restructuring education with an emphasis on the need for patriotism and a departure from the existing educational structure which had been laid down during the US occupation in 1947. He promised to promote economic growth through innovation. He proposed also to continue Koizumi's reformist policies and to seek economies by reducing the bureaucracy and by reining in the debts of local governments. The general tenor of his policies was conservative with "a tilt to the right". Abe was less confrontational inside the LDP itself. Indeed, one of his early controversial acts was to welcome back into the LDP fold 11 members who had been excluded by Koizumi for their opposition to his postal reform bills.

A controversial bill revising the existing educational law of 1947 passed through both houses of the Diet in December in sessions boycotted by the opposition. This was merely the first stage in fundamental reforms which Abe initiated by forming an education rebuilding council, with himself in the chair. Its task was to assess the state of current public education with a view to recommending radical changes.

Soon after taking office, Abe embarked on two important, but unexpected, visits to China and South Korea. Constructive bilateral talks with China had been going on for some time at official level, and in March President Hu Jintao of China had told a visiting delegation that he was prepared to return to summit meetings with Japanese leaders as soon as they discontinued visiting the Yasukuni shrine (see p. 329). Assuming that China would welcome a visit from a new face from Japan, Abe visited Beijing on 8 October for talks. In spite of many enquiries from the media about his stance on Yasukuni, he stated that he had not yet decided where he stood. Chinese Premier Wen Jiabao was expected to make a return visit to Tokyo in April 2007.

Abe flew on to South Korea and tried to sort out differences with President Roh Moo Hyun. Japan and South Korea had for some time been at odds over the need for punitive measures to be taken against the North. But their discussion took on a new urgency when North Korea announced, on the day of Abe's visit to the South, that it had conducted an underground nuclear weapons test (see p. 345). This was immediately condemned by both leaders. They also took the opportunity to set up a joint Korean-Japanese commission to re-examine the sensitive issue of historical interpretation.

On his return to Tokyo, Abe took steps to implement sanctions against North Korea. These took the form of prohibiting entry by North Korean citizens, North Korean ships, and North Korean imports for a six-month period. Japan also backed the USA in trying to persuade the UN Security Council to pass a resolution imposing strict sanctions on North Korea. This must have pleased Abe, whose path to power had benefited from his strong line on North Korea in the past, especially over the issue of returning family members of Japanese abductees in North Korea. The Chinese leadership succeeded in bringing US and North

Korean representatives together for a resumption of the six party talks on North Korea's nuclear programme, which had been stalled for more than a year because of a North Korean boycott. They were formally reopened on 18 December. But the meeting ended with no apparent result and without fixing a date for a further meeting. Bilateral talks between the six parties continued, however, in the context of international sanctions against North Korea (see p. 345).

Japan's economy continued to expand steadily during the year. The unemployment rate (seasonally adjusted) dropped to slightly above 4 per cent; Abe called for a squeeze on government expenditure at both the central and local levels; the Bank of Japan dropped its policy of zero per cent interest rates. A worrying trend was found in population statistics. The census estimate was that 21 per cent of Japan's population was aged 65 or over, the highest proportion in the world. Japan's population in October, according to estimates released by the ministry of internal affairs and communications, stood at 127.76 million, with population falling on an annual basis by about 20,000 because of high survival rates and the declining birth rate.

Worried about the consequences of rising oil prices, Japan was active in Asian trade diplomacy. It sought economic partnership agreements (EPAs) with a number of emerging countries, having already concluded EPAs with Singapore, Mexico, Malaysia and, most recently, the Philippines. Talks had also begun with India and Australia with that objective.

It was not clear how far and how fast Abe would go with his conservative agenda. There was opposition within his own party to some of the steps which he had inherited from Koizumi. There were political problems connected with any changes he might make over taxation and retrenchment, which could damage some of his initial popularity. Over defence, he steered through a bill increasing the status of the Defence Agency to a full ministry within the cabinet. This reform seemed justified because of the greater role which the SDF was taking in operations abroad and the need to take decisions over troop deployment without bureaucratic delays. Whether the government would embark on a comprehensive reform of the peace constitution of 1947 before a general election was doubtful.

At the end of the year, the political climate was unpredictable. The LDP benefited from the honeymoon period of Prime Minister Abe who seemed to be as energetic in travelling and pursuing foreign contacts as had been his predecessor. It won two important by-elections. Against this, its reputation was damaged by two high-profile scandals which surfaced in December, one involving the tax commission chairman, the other the important state minister for administrative reform, whose role in the programmes of the new government was to have been vital. The prime minister's popularity rating in the opinion polls dropped accordingly. For its part, the leading opposition party, the Democratic Party of Japan (DPJ), had mixed fortunes since its modest electoral performance in 2005. Its president resigned because of a parliamentary blunder but the experienced statesman, Ichiro Ozawa, took over the job.

All was set for a battle for half of the seats in the House of Councillors (the upper chamber of the Diet) which was due to take place in June 2007. The result was by no means a foregone conclusion for Abe—who did not come to power in a general election—and for his party. The LDP would not have the charismatic and idiosyncratic leadership of Koizumi, who carried it through in 2005. Nor could it rely any longer on the traditional support of the agricultural vote which had been sacrificed in favour of the urban electorate.

Ryutaro Hashimoto, a leading LDP politician who had been in the House of Representatives since 1963 and became prime minister in 1996-98), died on 1 July aged 68 (for obituary see p. 580).

SOUTH AND NORTH KOREA

South Korea

CAPITAL: Seoul AREA: 99,000 sq km POPULATION: 48,294,000
OFFICIAL LANGUAGE: Korean POLITICAL SYSTEM: multiparty republic
HEAD OF STATE AND GOVERNMENT: President Roh Moo Hyun (since Feb '03)
RULING PARTY: Uri Party
PRIME MINISTER: Prime Minister Han Myong Suk (Uri Party) (since April '06)
MAIN IGO MEMBERSHIPS (NON-UN): APEC, CP, OECD
CURRENCY: won (end-'06 £1=W1,808.16, US$1=W926.100)
GNI PER CAPITA: US$15,830, US$21,850 at PPP ('05)

North Korea

CAPITAL: Pyongyang AREA: 123,370 sq km POPULATION: 22,488,000
OFFICIAL LANGUAGES: Korean POLITICAL SYSTEM: one-party republic
HEAD OF STATE: Kim II Sung, Eternal President, died 1994
RULING PARTY: Korean Workers' Party (KWP)
PARTY LEADER: Kim Jong Il, KWP general secretary (since Oct '97)
PRIME MINISTER: Pak Pong Ju (since Sept '03)
MAIN IGO MEMBERSHIPS (NON-UN): NAM
CURRENCY: won (end-'06 £1=W248.100, US$1=W142.450)
GNP PER CAPITA: US$875 or less ('05 est)

IN the Republic of Korea (ROK—SOUTH KOREA), the year saw no letup in President Roh Moo Hyun's political problems. A cabinet reshuffle in January was widely criticised. It brought back into the cabinet two ruling Uri Party ("Our Party") possible contenders for the 2007 presidential election, while a number of new ministers were seen as leftwing. In particular, Lee Jong Seok, a former academic who had been deputy director of the National Security Council, came under fire as too favourable to the Democratic People's Republic of Korea (DPRK—NORTH KOREA), and too hostile towards the USA. Although some commentators noted that his academic writings had, in fact, been critical of North Korea, the charge stuck.

Further problems came in March. Prime Minister Lee Hai Chan, with a national rail strike in the offing, went golfing in the company of business leaders who were under suspicion of trying to use their links with politicians for their own advantage, instead of attending the commemoration of the 1 March 1919 anti-Japanese uprising. It was not the first time that Lee had put golf before duty, but this proved one occasion too many. Roh replaced Lee with South Korea's first female prime minister, Han Myong Suk, a political dissident from the 1970s. She did not have as much power as her predecessor, but she sailed through the National Assembly (unicameral legislature) approval process.

A further ministerial reshuffle in July did little to enhance either the president or the party's position. It began to go wrong very quickly, when the new minister for education, Kim Byong Joon, resigned in August following claims that he had once published the same paper twice in different academic journals. A final reshuffle in December followed the appointment of a new foreign minister to replace Ban Ki Moon, who succeeded Kofi Annan as UN secretary-general (see p. 361). Even this did not help President Roh's popularity, which, according to some polls, fell to below 10 per cent, and there was a widespread belief that his professed policy of "participatory politics" had made the country more polarised than ever before.

The Uri Party was not alone in having problems. A female journalist from the *Dong-a Ilbo* newspaper accused secretary general Choi Yun Hee of the opposition Grand National Party (GNP) of sexual harassment at a party. His claim that he had mistaken her for a waitress did not go down well, and he resigned. However, he refused to give up his parliamentary seat despite an almost unprecedented—though unbinding—National Assembly resolution. The GNP also brought actions in April against two of its members for alleged bribe taking in advance of the May local elections. None of this affected the GNP's success in those elections, when it took 12 of the 16 provincial governor and city mayor positions, and over 75 per cent of the local council seats. The GNP's cause was helped by a attack on its chairwoman, Park Geun Hye, whose face was slashed by two drunken men while she was campaigning. Chung Dong Young, the Uri Party general secretary, appointed at the beginning of the year and widely seen as a likely candidate in the 2007 presidential election, took responsibility for the defeat and resigned. He was succeeded by Kim Geun Tae, whom he had defeated in February. The Uri Party trailed the GNP in opinion polls, leaving it in a poor position as the country geared up for the 2007 presidential election.

Scandals added to the government's image problem, even if most of them were outside its control. In January, the journal *Science* withdrew papers published in 2004 and 2005 by the alleged pioneer of stem cell research, Hwang Woo Suk (see AR 2005, pp. 315-16; 405). Seoul National university sacked him in March and he lost his state-awarded "Supreme Scientist" title. In May, he was charged with fraud and embezzlement. The chairman of the Samsung Group, Lee Kun Hee, returned in February from the USA, where he had gone after being acquitted of making illegal political donations. He refused to admit wrongdoing but announced that he would donate US$850 million for charitable purposes. Samsung had further troubles in the USA, where it was fined US$300 million for price fixing. Hyundai, another leading business group, was in trouble over alleged fraudulent practices. Hyundai apologised in April for the scandal and pledged to donate assets worth over US$1.1 billion to charity, but later that month its chairman, Chung Mong Koo, was arrested and charged with embezzling US$109 million and creating slush funds worth over US$100 million with which to bribe politicians. In May the founder of the Daewoo group, Kim Woo Choong, received a 10-year prison sentence and a fine for accounting fraud. Strikes and labour disputes, together with protests over the proposed free trade agreement with the USA and the move of US forces south from Seoul (see below)—protests which were often accompanied by violence—added to the sense of crisis. Even South Korea's vaunted claim to be a world information technology (IT) leader seemed under threat with the news in April that Iceland had surpassed South Korea as the country with the highest proportion of broadband Internet connections.

Yet despite claims that the country was in a terrible state and that the middle class—to which most South Koreans thought they belonged—was in terminal decline, the economy did well, with GDP growth of almost 5 per cent. Total GDP was estimated at US$768.5 billion, with per capita GDP at US$24,200. Strong export growth was the main driving force, despite the steady appreciation of the won: the US dollar fell back from just over W1,000 at the end of 2005, to W926 by December 2006. Exports rose 13 per cent, with good sales of semi-conductors and steel products. Inflation, at around 3 per cent, remained low. Unemployment was also low, at 3.4 per cent, but it remained high among younger workers. Although the OECD predicted that growth in 2007 would drop back, it was still forecasting over 4 per cent growth. Government sources regularly claimed that there would be a level playing field for all companies regardless of nationality, but the foreign business community's doubts about South Korea's commitment to globalisation were reinforced by the continued investigation of the US investment group Lone Star's takeover of the Korea Exchange Bank in 2003.

Negotiations on a free trade agreement with the USA began in February. The government pledged that they would be completed within a year, though this looked unlikely. Free trade negotiations with Japan, stalled in 2005, were not resumed, but talks were underway with Canada, India, and Mexico, as well as with the Association of South East Asian Nations (ASEAN). An EU -South Korea summit in Helsinki, the Finnish capital, in September reaffirmed the continuation of preliminary talks for a similar agreement. None seemed likely to come to an early fruition. The government promised that no deal would threaten agriculture or service industries, while at the same time saying that it would establish a fund to protect groups adversely affected.

South Korea maintained its military presence in Iraq. Various issues related to the US forces stationed in Korea loomed large, although some of the heat went out of earlier quarrels with a joint statement by US Secretary of State Condoleezza Rice and Ban Ki Moon in Washington DC, in which the two sides agreed on an expanded role in Asia for the US forces in Korea. Other issues included continued efforts to relocate US forces out of the capital to sites further south, especially at Pyongtaek. The US forces were eager to go, and the South Korean government was keen to have a source of tension removed from the capital, but there was much local opposition, including violent demonstrations, to the takeover of farmland that such a move would require. The withdrawal of US forces from Korea, to supplement forces in Iraq, was less contentious, although some conservative commentators expressed worries that it would send the wrong signal to NORTH KOREA. Conservative critics also continued to argue against government moves to reclaim wartime command over South Korean forces, which, in one form or another, had been assigned to the commander of US forces in Korea since the 1950-53 Korean War. Although the issue had been raised originally in the 1990s, and seemed welcome to both the US military and politicians, former military officers and defence ministers protested on the streets at what they called a dangerous move that would undermine South Korea's security.

The dispute with China over the status of the ancient Koguryo kingdom remained quiescent. There was increasing South Korean concern at the growth of Chinese influence in NORTH KOREA, however, with major increases there in Chinese trade and investment. The dispute with Japan over the Dokdo islands (called Takeshima in Japan) bubbled up from time to time. Relations were further affected by what the government saw as an over heavy Japanese response to the North Korean missile test in July (see below). The change of prime ministers in Japan was watched cautiously. Shinzo Abe's decision not to attend the Yasukuni shrine was welcomed, but fears remained about his hardline approach to North Korea (see pp. 337-38).

In the first presidential visit to Africa since 1982, President Roh visited Egypt, Nigeria, and Algeria in March. As well as signing trade agreements, Roh announced a massive increase in aid, to reach US$100 million by 2008. A further sign of South Korean interest in Africa was the first "Korean-African forum" held in Seoul in early November. A presidential visit to Mongolia, Azerbaijan, and the United Arab Emirates in May was seen as designed to secure much needed resources, especially oil.

In NORTH KOREA, domestic matters were again overshadowed by security issues. The continued movement of people into China, despite the dangers, indicated that economic problems continued, and also perhaps that more North Koreans were becoming aware of the poor state of their country. The North reported heavy flooding in the summer, with some outside observers claiming that the damage was far greater than the authorities stated. The flooding and reduction of international food aid as a result of the North's decision in 2005 to accept only development aid, led to fears of a return to famine conditions (see AR 2005, p. 317). However, under a new agreement with the World Food Programme, the latter was still able to operate within North Korea, although on a reduced basis. Until the autumn, food supplies from China and SOUTH KOREA seemed to be meeting the shortfall. According to the small number of Western businesses operating in North Korea, US economic sanctions, imposed in 2005 as a result of North Korean counterfeiting of US currency and goods, hit legitimate trade as well. This was especially the case when US pressure led the Macao-based Banco Delta Asia to suspend North Korean-related accounts. North Korea made it clear that failure to lift these sanctions would hinder negotiations on other issues.

The failure of the reconvened six party talks in 2005 and US economic sanctions cast a shadow over SOUTH KOREA'S continued wish to engage with the North, but contacts continued. When Kim Jong Il visited China in January, he seemed once again interested in economic development. The level and apparent warmth of his reception by senior Chinese leaders indicated that rumours of Chinese willingness to support a US sanctions' regime were unfounded (see pp. 329-30). In March, military talks between North and South resumed after two years. Also in March, talks between the two Koreas and Russia looked forward to linking the North Korea railway system to the Trans-Siberian railway, and the parties agreed to continue the discussions. The same month, South Korea formally opened new checkpoints along the demilitarized zone (DMZ). Cross-DMZ travellers totalled 400,000 in 2005, a tenfold increase since 2003. Much of this traffic was the result of the growth of the special economic zone at Kaesong, just across the DMZ, although the tourist project in the Kumgang (Diamond) Mountains at the eastern end of the DMZ enjoyed something of a revival. In addition, 2006 saw an increase in both flights and ships' visits. The originator of South Korea's engagement policy, former President Kim Dae Jung, announced that he would make a second visit to the North, though this was abandoned because of the South Korean elections. In May, an exhibition of art treasures from the North opened in Seoul, and later went to the city of Taegu.

It was not all smooth however. In March, South Korean reporters withdrew en masse from covering Red Cross (ICRC) talks in the Kumgang Mountains on the question of missing South Korean POWs and civilians, after a North Korean censorship attempt. In May, the North Korean side cancelled plans for a test of a through train on the North-South railway. South Korea still had to contend with much US opposition to its engagement policy, condemned for propping up the regime in the North.

From May onwards, there were signs that North Korea was preparing for missile tests. There were numerous international warnings, including one from Chinese Premier Wen Jiabao, not to do so, but on 4 July North Korea launched a series of missiles. Most were short or medium range, but one was apparently a Taepodong-2, similar to one launched in 1998. Although the launches broke no international agreement, and the Taepodong was apparently a failure, there was international outcry. On 7 July, the UN Security Council backed a Japanese-sponsored resolution calling for sanctions, although China and Russia argued for a softer approach and refused to go along. Eventually a unanimous resolution—which did not make sanctions legally binding although it required UN member states to prevent the transfer of missile-related materials, technology, and finances to North Korea—was adopted on 15 July (for text see pp. 552-53). The South Korean government, while condemning the missile launches, attacked the Japanese government for a heavy handed approach. The North Koreans condemned all sanctions, and broke off cabinet-level talks with SOUTH KOREA. They also ignored a Chinese protest by Vice-Foreign Minister Wu Dawei, who travelled to Pyongyang soon after the launches.

The missile launch showed that there was no united international approach to dealing with North Korea, and that apparently little pressure could be brought to bear to make it change its policies. This became even more apparent as evidence mounted from mid-August that the North might also be preparing for a nuclear test. North Korea had claimed since 2003 that it had nuclear weapons, but hitherto it had not tested whatever devices it had. Despite appeals, the North announced on 3 October that it would conduct a nuclear test. International pressure proved unavailing, and on 9 October some form of test took place. Exactly how successful it was remained uncertain. It seemed to have been much smaller than other countries' first nuclear tests, and there remained a strong suspicion that it was a failure. Nevertheless, it was carried out in defiance of international opinion. The UN Security Council unanimously condemned the North Korean action, and even China and SOUTH KOREA said that they would impose sanctions, as set out in UN Security Council Resolution 1718 in October (for text see pp. 554-58).

Yet the apparent international agreement began to break up almost immediately, as China and South Korea indicated that, while opposing North Korea's nuclear activity, they would not become involved in measures such as the proliferation security initiative, involving the searching of North Korean ships. At the Asia Pacific Economic Co-operation (APEC) meeting in November, the USA found reluctance on the part of several participants to raise pressure on North Korea. By the end of the year, North Korea had agreed to return to the six party talks, but the eventual outcome was as uncertain as ever.

MONGOLIA

CAPITAL: Ulan Bator AREA: 1,564,116 sq km POPULATION: 2,554,000
OFFICIAL LANGUAGE: Halh (Khalkha) Mongolia POLITICAL SYSTEM: multiparty republic
HEAD OF STATE: President Nambariyn Enkhbayar (MAHN) (since June '05)
RULING PARTY: Mongolian People's Revolutionary Party (MAHN)
HEAD OF GOVERNMENT: Prime Minister Miyeegombo Enkhbold (MAHN) (since Jan '06)
MAIN IGO MEMBERSHIPS (NON-UN): NAM, EBRD
CURRENCY: tugrik (end-'06 £1=T2,274.60, US$1=T1,165.00)
GNI PER CAPITA: US$690, US$2,190 at PPP ('05)

MONGOLIA celebrated 800 years of statehood in 2006, but the turbulent political situation saw Prime Minister Tsakhiagiyn Elbegdorj's coalition government dismissed in a move that critics called unconstitutional and motivated by worries over the scope of an anti-corruption drive which the prime minister had initiated. In January members of the Mongolian People's Revolutionary Party (MAHN), along with a small number of members of the Democratic Party (AN), to which Elbegdorj belonged, withdrew from the ruling coalition leaving many cabinet post unfilled. Large protests followed the collapse of the government but by the end of January, helped by defections from the AN, the MAHN had formed a new government under Miyeegombo Enkhbold as prime minister.

Protesters returned to the capital again in April, demanding the resignation of the new prime minister and accusing him of corruption dating from the time when he was mayor of Ulan Bator. The protesters also alleged that a series of recent agreements with foreign companies over the exploitation of Mongolia's natural resources was not in the national interest. The delicate political situation eased a little in September, when the MAHN won a by-election by a comfortable margin (56.74 per cent of the total vote, against 40.65 percent for the Democratic Party candidate), giving the MAHN an absolute majority in the Great Hural (the unicameral legislature). The opposition accused the MAHN of extensive and systematic electoral fraud.

In October opposition AN legislators launched a vote of no confidence against Prime Minister Enkhbold citing corruption and misconduct. He survived the vote, which went along party lines, by 46 to 22, with eight members not in attendance. As in the April protests, Enkhbold was accused of inappropriate land sales while serving as Ulan Bator mayor, accusations that had to be set in the context of a property boom within the capital.

In the international arena, Mongolia received a visit from the Dalai Lama in August. He had a high profile in Mongolia, a predominately Buddhist country, but his visits were always controversial given the sensitivities of his status and the importance of Mongolia's ties with the People's Republic of China, the PRC. Sino-Mongolian ties were nonetheless said to be on a sound footing by both sides later in the year when Prime Minister Enkhbold visited Beijing in November and during a reciprocal visit in December by Jia Qinglin, chairman of the Chinese People's Political Consultative Conference (CPPCC, an advisory political body in the PRC). The Japanese Prime Minister, Junichiro Koizumi, visited Ulan Bator in August in what some regarded as a drive by Mongolia to weaken its reliance on its two giant neighbours, China and Russia. Koizumi attracted some criticism for his decision to pray at a memorial for Japanese soldiers who had been detained in Mongolia after World War II.

X AUSTRALASIA AND THE PACIFIC

AUSTRALIA—PAPUA NEW GUINEA

AUSTRALIA

CAPITAL: Canberra AREA: 7,741,000 sq km POPULATION: 20,321,000
OFFICIAL LANGUAGE: English POLITICAL SYSTEM: multiparty system in British Commonwealth
HEAD OF STATE: Queen Elizabeth II (since Feb '52)
GOVERNOR-GENERAL: Maj.-Gen. Michael Jeffery (since August '03)
RULING PARTY: Liberal-National coalition
HEAD OF GOVERNMENT: John Howard, Prime Minister (since March '96)
MAIN IGO MEMBERSHIPS (NON-UN): APEC, PC, PIF, CP, ANZUS, OECD, CWTH
CURRENCY: Australian dollar (end-'06 £1=A$2.46040, US$1=A$1.26020)
GNI PER CAPITA: US$32,220, US$30,610 at PPP ('05)

AUSTRALIA suffered one of its worst droughts for a century, with little relief until the last few days of the year. Water conservation became a major political concern and the Australian government reversed its previous scepticism about global warming. Discussion of the development of nuclear energy to limit greenhouse gases was initiated by the government. Australia had major reserves of uranium but was also the largest coal exporter in the world. The political situation remained stable, with the national government in the hands of Prime Minister John Howard and his coalition of the Liberal and National parties. Control of the six states and two territories, however, remained with the Australian Labor Party (ALP) which was re-elected in four state contests. Despite the drought, the economy continued buoyant with an unemployment level below 5 per cent.

A modest military contribution (fewer than 1,000 men) continued in Iraq, but popular support for the war declined throughout the year. Australia played an active role in the affairs of the Solomon Islands, Afghanistan, East Timor, and Fiji, with police or military forces in place to preserve stability. However both the Solomons and Fiji removed the powers of their Australian police commissioners during the year. The Australian high commissioner in the Solomons was asked to leave Honiara for alleged interference in domestic politics. Australia criticised the military coup in Fiji on 5 December and relations were consequently strained (see p. 357).

The prime minister continued to be active in international affairs, making seven overseas visits to India, China, East Timor, Malaysia, the USA, Canada, and Ireland, and to the Pacific Islands Forum (PIF) in Fiji in October and the Asia Pacific Economic Co-operation (APEC) summit meeting in November in Vietnam (see pp. 430-31).

The South Australian Legislative Council and House of Assembly were both elected on 18 March, using different electoral systems. In the Legislative Council (the upper house), the Australian Labor Party (ALP) won four seats;

the Liberals three; independents two; and the Greens, and Family First one seat apiece. Family First was a new party, supported largely by Pentecostals and other Christian fundamentalists and gaining 5.9 per cent of the lower house vote. In the House of Assembly (the lower house) the Australian Labor Party won 28 seats; the Liberals 15; independents three, and the National Party one seat.

The Tasmanian House of Assembly was also elected on 18 March, using proportional representation. In this contest, the ALP won 14 seats; the Liberals seven, and Greens three. As at the last national election in 2004 (see AR 2004, pp. 340-41), the timber industry remained at the heart of Tasmanian politics. Claims that a religious minority, the Exclusive Brethren, had been giving assistance to the Liberals were being investigated at the end of the year.

The Queensland state election on 9 September confirmed the ALP government of Peter Beattie with a large majority in the only house of the state Parliament. The Liberals were hampered by the overthrow of their leader, Bob Quinn, only two days before Beattie called the election. The results gave the ALP 59 seats; the National Party 17; the Liberals eight; One Nation one seat, and other parties four. The Greens failed to win any seats.

Both houses of the Victoria Parliament were elected on 25 November. The result confirmed the strong following for the ALP government of Steve Bracks, with 55 seats in the Legislative Assembly (the lower house). The Liberals won 23 seats, the Nationals nine, and an independent gained one seat. The Greens, with 10 per cent of the vote, failed to gain a seat and polled best in ALP inner Melbourne districts. In the upper house, the Legislative Council, the ALP won 19 seats, with the Liberals winning 15; the Greens three; the National Party two; and Democratic Labor one. The victory of the Democratic Labor party on a variety of second preferences revived a party which had broken away from the ALP over 50 years before and had been regarded as dead for years. It represented conservative Catholics and potentially held the balance of power in the house.

A major problem for the national government was presented by an inquiry into UN claims that the monopoly Australian Wheat Board had, in 1999 and later, given almost A$300 million to a transport company owned by the government of Saddam Hussein, in return for wheat purchases by Iraq. This was in breach of UN sanctions against Iraq. While the Board had been privatised, its dealings were still a concern of the department of foreign affairs and trade. The official inquiry, by Terence Cole QC, began on 18 January and reported on 27 November. Its terms of reference concerned only officials of the Board and exempted consideration of ministerial actions. Despite this, several ministers were summoned to give evidence and on 13 April the prime minister appeared. In his evidence he accused the Wheat Board of "deceiving the government and trading on the trust it enjoyed". The eventual report exonerated the government from any illegality, but put the blame on several Wheat Board executives. They were expected to be tried in due course, following a task force enquiry into their culpability. The Wheat Board monopoly was threatened with termination by the government. The department of foreign affairs and trade was criticised for failing to exercise supervision, although the minister, Alexander Downer, remained in office.

While there were no terrorist attacks in Australia, there was continuing anxiety about the threat of terrorism. Public and media opinion was concerned throughout the year with the fate of Australian citizen David Hicks, who had been detained in the US naval base at Guantánamo Bay, Cuba, for more than four years without trial, following his capture in Afghanistan. Another Australian Muslim convert, Jack Thomas, was convicted in March of offences under anti-terrorism legislation introduced in 2001, but this was later dismissed on the grounds of coerced evidence. He was placed under a strict control order and a retrial was ordered in December. The most important case during the year was that of Faheem Khalid Lodhi, a Pakistani engineer accused of planning to attack various strategic targets on which he had collected information. He was sentenced to 20 years in prison on 23 August.

The ALP once again changed its national leadership. In a contested vote, Kim Beazley, who had been elected in 2005 (see AR 2005, p. 321), was replaced by Kevin Rudd of Queensland on 4 December. Rudd had previously been shadow foreign minister and was from a moderate Catholic background. Julia Gillard, from Melbourne, was elected as his deputy leader. The party immediately improved its position in the polls, becoming a serious contender for winning office at the next election.

Among those who died during the year were folk hero and conservationist Steve Irwin, aged 44 (for obituary see pp. 582-83); architect Harry Seidler (82); the founder of the Australian Democrats, Don Chipp (81); popular artist Pro Hart (77); former senator John Wheeldon (76); Justice Rae Else-Mitchell (90); Sydney underworld figure Abe Saffron (86); and veteran racist Eric Butler (90).

PAPUA NEW GUINEA

CAPITAL: Port Moresby AREA: 463,000 sq km POPULATION: 5,887,000
OFFICIAL LANGUAGES: Pidgin, Motu & English POLITICAL SYSTEM: multiparty system in British Commonwealth
HEAD OF STATE: Queen Elizabeth II
GOVERNOR-GENERAL: Sir Paulias Matane (since May '04)
RULING PARTY: National Alliance Party (NAP)
HEAD OF GOVERNMENT: Sir Michael Somare (NAP), Prime Minister (since August '02)
MAIN IGO MEMBERSHIPS (NON-UN): APEC, CP, PC, PIF, ACP, CWTH, NAM
CURRENCY: kina (end-'06 £1=K5.79860, US$1=K2.96990)
GNI PER CAPITA: US$660, US$2,370 at PPP ('05 est, based on regression)

DEPRESSINGLY, the year 2006 saw business as usual in Papua New Guinea (PNG) with governmental instability, endemic corruption, uncontrolled crime, and factional violence dominating the national agenda.

In March Arthur Somare, the planning minister and son of the veteran prime minister, Sir Michael Somare, was referred to the public prosecutor for misuse of public funds. Health Minister Melchoir Pep was similarly referred during the year, as was the deputy prime minister, Sir Moi Avei. Sir Michael Somare's own close relationship with Chinese timber interests also came under scrutiny. As in the past, however, regardless of the strength of evidence against national leaders, there was little prospect that any of them would suffer any setback to their careers, let alone face successful prosecution. The younger Somare, in fact, was promoted to the key state enterprise and communications portfolio by his father in a government reshuffle in July.

In August a state of emergency was declared in the Southern Highlands province, long a location of civil disorder and inter-group conflict extreme even by Papua New Guinea standards. The following month the provincial governor, Hami Yawari, faced a raft of charges of corruption and misconduct in office. In contrast to the experience of politicians accused of misbehaviour at national level, there was some prospect that Yawari would be held to account by the courts. The jailing of the Madang governor, James Yali, for 12 years for rape at the beginning of the year gave at least some grounds for hope that not every PNG politician was above the law.

A corrective to too much optimism in this regard, and a marker of the tensions inherent in regional relations, came in October when the Australian government cancelled a planned visit by Sir Michael Somare and other ministers after his government was judged to have helped a Solomon Islands politician evade extradition to Australia where he was facing prosecution for sexual offences. At the end of the year the new foreign affairs minister, Paul Tientsen (who had taken over the portfolio from Sir Michael Somare himself, who had combined it with the premiership), moved to resolve the crisis in relations with the country's most important neighbour.

Former PNG Prime Minister Bill Skate, who had been instrumental in bringing an end to the conflict with the island of Bougainville, died in January (for obituary see pp. 597-98).

NEW ZEALAND—PACIFIC ISLAND STATES

NEW ZEALAND

CAPITAL: Wellington AREA: 271,000 sq km POPULATION: 4,110,000
OFFICIAL LANGUAGE: English POLITICAL SYSTEM: multiparty system in British Commonwealth
HEAD OF STATE: Queen Elizabeth II (since Feb '52)
GOVERNOR-GENERAL: Anand Satyanand (since April '06)
RULING PARTIES: New Zealand Labour Party (NZLP) & Progressive Coalition Party (PCP)
HEAD OF GOVERNMENT: Helen Clark, Prime Minister (since Dec '99)
MAIN IGO MEMBERSHIPS (NON-UN): ANZUS (suspended), APEC, PC, PIF, CP, OECD, CWTH
CURRENCY: New Zealand dollar (end-'06 £1=NZ$2.76300, US$1=NZ$1.41510)
GNI PER CAPITA: US$25,960, US$23,030 at PPP ('05)

PRIME Minister Helen Clark's narrow election victory in September 2005 (see AR 2005, p. 325) meant that her government, now in its third three-year term, was almost certain to be challenged more forcefully in Parliament than in previous years. This proved to be the case, with a strengthened National Party providing strong criticism of the Labour-led coalition.

In March there were new allegations against a cabinet minister who had previously faced charges that he had mistreated pupils while a school teacher (see AR 2005, p. 326), with the prime minister eventually conceding that the minister, David Benson-Pope, had made an "error of judgement" in advising Parliament that he had been unaware of complaints made against him as a teacher. The new allegations included accusations of bullying another teacher and of using inappropriate disciplinary measures against students, including claims that the minister had gone into girls' dormitories and showers while on a school camp in 1997. The minister did not offer his resignation and nor was it sought, as his responses moved from denials to attacks against the complainants to eventual admissions that "something clearly happened", culminating in expressions of regret "for any upset" to "some former students". The attacks against Benson-Pope, in which he was characterised at one point as a "pathological bully, liar and pervert", damaged the image both of the government and the prime minister.

Further damage was caused as a result of another Labour MP, Phillip Field, coming under investigation for allegedly accepting free or low-paid labour by illegal immigrants seeking his assistance. Field was placed on indefinite leave from Parliament in December as police investigated allegations that he had benefited financially from assistance given to constituents seeking his services.

Another cabinet minister, David Parker, the attorney-general, resigned in March when a magazine disclosed that prior to his appointment he had committed errors certifying annual returns related to a failing business venture. The prime minister accepted Parker's resignation as attorney-general, but initially retained him in his other ministerial portfolios, only agreeing to his removal from all ministerial responsibilities a day later. While the minister was praised for his decision to resign, the prime minister's hesitations about removing him from cabinet altogether were less well received. Subsequently an official investigation concluded that there was "no basis whatsoever" to prosecute Parker and he was reappointed to cabinet, but not as attorney-general.

The government's reputation was further eroded by claims made by the auditor-general—an independent official—that the Labour Party had spent significantly more money on its 2005 re-election campaign than was permitted under the Electoral Act. Whilst other political parties were also found to have breached the legal threshold, by far the largest amount of overspending had been by Labour. More damaging still for the prime minister was the fact that most of the overspending had occurred through expenditure on two items paid for from a budget provided to party leaders for non-political purposes. The prime minister's response to criticism—a refusal to accept that errors had been made, followed by attempts to shift responsibility to others—did little to reduce the political damage.

In October, following opportunities for all parties to make submissions based on the draft report circulated to them, the auditor-general issued his report, which showed not only that public money had been improperly spent but that the Labour leadership had been advised during the campaign that such spending was not permissible. As Labour celebrated the 90th anniversary of its founding, the party accepted that it would need a special fundraising effort to repay the NZ$825,000 taken from the leader's budget, with the prime minister accepting the need to do so while continuing to assert that she had not acted inappropriately.

These affairs, drawn out over many months, took their toll on the government's popularity. Nevertheless the prime minister never surrendered her lead as preferred prime minister over the National Party's leader, Don Brash, as he stumbled badly. National was also found to have erred in its election spending, failing to take tax into account in commissioning its broadcast advertising, with the result that it owed more than NZ$100,000 which it was unable to pay since doing so would take its total election spending over the legal limit.

As parliamentary conflict intensified, with National MPs describing Labour as "corrupt", the rivalry between New Zealand's two main parties became increasingly personal. The prime minister blamed National and a small religious group, the Exclusive Brethren, for a "smear" campaign against her husband, Peter Davis, following suggestions in a magazine that he was a homosexual. In Parliament a cabinet minister's interjection shortly thereafter led to disclosures that National's leader, Brash, was having an extra-marital affair, which he conceded, noting, "I've never held myself up as a morals campaigner".

The revelations eroded Brash's image as a principled leader and at least temporarily gave Labour a respite from criticisms over its electoral spending. In November Brash became embroiled in a legal dispute as he sought, and obtained, a temporary injunction against publication of a book, *The Hollow Men*, whose disclosures of Brash's links to the Exclusive Brethren appeared to contradict statements that he had made during and after the 2005 campaign. For his colleagues, this latest diversion proved one too many. In late November Brash announced his resignation as National Party leader, and he was soon followed by the departure of his deputy. The National Party's parliamentary team unanimously elected its finance spokesperson, John Key, as leader, with former leader, Bill English, as deputy. Thus as a deeply divisive political year came to a close, Helen Clark was still New Zealand's prime minister and she had outlasted yet another National leader, with Key the fourth in that role since Clark's election as prime minister in 1999.

The Clark-led government was able to score some other successes during 2006. Foreign Minister Winston Peters was able to meet US Secretary of State Condoleezza Rice in Washington DC, reflecting a warming of relations between the USA and New Zealand. The prime minister authorised the dispatch of New Zealand soldiers and armed police to three Pacific trouble spots. When rioting broke out in April in Honiara, the capital of the Solomon Islands, Clark joined with Australia's prime minister, John Howard, in sending troops to strengthen RAMSI, a regional peacekeeping force already in the country (see p. 356). Similarly, an appeal in May for help from the foreign minister of East Timor was accepted, with New Zealand forces serving under Australian command in an attempt to quell the violence there (see p. 322). In November, an outbreak of arson and looting in the Tongan capital, Nuku'alofa, brought a similar request for assistance, and again New Zealand dispatched peacekeepers to patrol and restore calm (see p. 358). New Zealand forces also continued their efforts in Afghanistan, where their work in Bamiyan province in reconstruction efforts won praise from the USA.

Efforts by the New Zealand government to avert a military coup in Fiji, including the hosting of talks in Wellington between Fiji's prime minister and the head of the country's military, proved unsuccessful. When the coup occurred in early December, the New Zealand government declined to intervene militarily (see p. 357). The coup was followed by a strong condemnation from Prime Minister Clark and the imposition of sanctions.

As in the past, so too in 2006 there were notable developments in connection with New Zealand's national identity. In April the prime minister announced that the next governor-general (whose role was to serve as the representative of New Zealand's head of state, the British monarch) would be Judge Anand Satyanand, who took office in August. Born in New Zealand, the appointee was the son of Indo-Fijian migrants to New Zealand and thus became the first New Zealand governor-general of Asian descent. The appointment continued the recent practice of using the largely symbolic position to emphasise the values of equality and multiculturalism.

PACIFIC ISLAND STATES

Fiji

CAPITAL: Suva AREA: 18,375 sq km POPULATION: 848,000
OFFICIAL LANGUAGES: Fijian, Hindi & English POLITICAL SYSTEM: multiparty republic in British Commonwealth, under military rule
HEAD OF STATE: acting President Commodore Frank (JV) Bainimarama (since Dec '06)
HEAD OF GOVERNMENT: Jona Baravilalala Senilagakali, caretaker Prime Minister (since Dec '06)
MAIN IGO MEMBERSHIPS (NON-UN): CWTH, PC, PIF, CP, ACP
CURRENCY: Fiji dollar (end-'06 £1=F$3.23680, US$1=F$1.65790)
GNI PER CAPITA: US$3,280, US$5,960 at PPP ('05)

Kiribati

CAPITAL: Tarawa AREA: 1,000 sq km POPULATION: 99,000
OFFICIAL LANGUAGES: English & Kiribati POLITICAL SYSTEM: multiparty republic in British Commonwealth
HEAD OF STATE AND GOVERNMENT: President Anote Tong (since July '03)
MAIN IGO MEMBERSHIPS (NON-UN): CWTH, PC, PIF, ACP
CURRENCY: Australian dollar (end-'06 £1=A$2.46040, US$1=A$1.26020)
GNI PER CAPITA: US$1,390 ('05), -

Marshall Islands

CAPITAL: Dalap-Uliga-Darrit AREA: 200 sq km POPULATION: 63,000
OFFICIAL LANGUAGES: English & Marshallese POLITICAL SYSTEM: multiparty republic in free association with USA
HEAD OF STATE AND GOVERNMENT: President Kessai Note (since Jan '00)
RULING PARTY: United Democratic Party (UDP)
MAIN IGO MEMBERSHIPS (NON-UN): PC, PIF
CURRENCY: US dollar (end-'06 £1=1.95250)
GNI PER CAPITA: US$2,930 ('05), -

Federated States of Micronesia

CAPITAL: Palikir (Pohnpei) AREA: 701 sq km POPULATION: 110,000
OFFICIAL LANGUAGE: English POLITICAL SYSTEM: multiparty republic in free association with USA
HEAD OF STATE AND GOVERNMENT: President Joseph Urusemal (since 10 May '03)
MAIN IGO MEMBERSHIPS (NON-UN): PC, PIF
CURRENCY: US dollar (end-'06 £1=1.95250)
GNI PER CAPITA: US$2,300 ('05), -

Nauru

CAPITAL: Domaneab AREA: 21.4 sq km POPULATION: 10,100
OFFICIAL LANGUAGES: Nauruan & English POLITICAL SYSTEM: one-party republic, special member of the British Commonwealth
HEAD OF STATE AND GOVERNMENT: President Ludwig Scotty (since June '04)
MAIN IGO MEMBERSHIPS (NON-UN): CWTH, PC, PIF
CURRENCY: Australian dollar (see above)
GNI PER CAPITA: US$5,740 (GDP per capita '04), -

Palau (Belau)

CAPITAL: Koror AREA: 460 sq km POPULATION: 20,000
OFFICIAL LANGUAGE: English POLITICAL SYSTEM: multiparty republic in free association with USA
HEAD OF STATE AND GOVERNMENT: President Tommy Remengesau (since Nov '00)
MAIN IGO MEMBERSHIPS (NON-UN): PC, PIF
CURRENCY: US dollar (end-'06 £1=1.95250)
GNI PER CAPITA: US$7,630 ('05), -

Samoa

CAPITAL: Apia AREA: 2,842 sq km POPULATION: 185,000
OFFICIAL LANGUAGES: English & Samoan POLITICAL SYSTEM: multiparty monarchy in British Commonwealth
HEAD OF STATE: Susuga Malietoa Tanumafili II (since Jan '62)
RULING PARTY: Human Rights Protection Party (HRPP)
HEAD OF GOVERNMENT: Tuilaepa Sailele Malielegaoi, Prime Minister (since Nov '98)
MAIN IGO MEMBERSHIPS (NON-UN): CWTH, PC, PIF, ACP
CURRENCY: Tala (end-'06 £1=T5.24050, US$1=T2.68020)
GNI PER CAPITA: US$2,090, US$6,480 at PPP ('05 est, based on regression)

Solomon Islands

CAPITAL: Honiara AREA: 28,000 sq km POPULATION: 478,000
OFFICIAL LANGUAGE: English POLITICAL SYSTEM: multiparty system in British Commonwealth
HEAD OF STATE: Queen Elizabeth II
GOVERNOR-GENERAL: Nathaniel Waena (since July '04)
RULING PARTY: People's Alliance Party (PAP)
HEAD OF GOVERNMENT: Manasseh Sogavare (SoCred), Prime Minister (since May '06)
MAIN IGO MEMBERSHIPS (NON-UN): CWTH, PC, PIF, ACP
CURRENCY: Solomon Island dollar (end-'06 £1=SI$14.5672, US$1=SI$7.44600)
GNI PER CAPITA: US$590, US$1,880 at PPP ('05)

Tonga

CAPITAL: Nuku'alofa AREA: 750 sq km POPULATION: 102,000
OFFICIAL LANGUAGES: Tongan & English POLITICAL SYSTEM: non-party monarchy in British Commonwealth
HEAD OF STATE: King Siaosi Tupou V (since Sept '06)
HEAD OF GOVERNMENT: Feleti (Fred) Sevele, Prime Minister (since March '06)
MAIN IGO MEMBERSHIPS (NON-UN): CWTH, PC, PIF, ACP
CURRENCY: pa'anga (end-'06 £1=P3.95310, US$1=P2.02350)
GNI PER CAPITA: US$2,190, US$8,040 at PPP ('05 est, based on regression)

Tuvalu

CAPITAL: Fongafale AREA: 26 sq km POPULATION: 11,000 ('03 est)
OFFICIAL LANGUAGE: English POLITICAL SYSTEM: non-party monarchy, special member of the British Commonwealth
HEAD OF STATE: Queen Elizabeth II (since Feb '52)
GOVERNOR-GENERAL: Faimalaga Luka (since Sept '03)
HEAD OF GOVERNMENT: Apisai Ielemia, Prime Minister (since Aug '06)
MAIN IGO MEMBERSHIPS (NON-UN): PC, PIF, ACP, CWTH
CURRENCY: Australian dollar (end-'06 £1=A$2.46040, US$1=A$1.26020)
GNI PER CAPITA: n/a

Vanuatu

CAPITAL: Port Vila AREA: 12,000 sq km POPULATION: 211,000
OFFICIAL LANGUAGES: English, French & Bislama POLITICAL SYSTEM: multiparty republic in British Commonwealth
HEAD OF STATE: President Kalkot Mataskelekele (since Aug '04)
RULING PARTIES: Union of Moderate Parties (UMP)-led coalition (since July '04)
HEAD OF GOVERNMENT: Ham Lini (NUP), Prime Minister (since Dec '04)
MAIN IGO MEMBERSHIPS (NON-UN): CWTH, PC, PIF, ACP, Francophonie
CURRENCY: vatu (end-'06 £1=V207.654, US$1=V106.355)
GNI PER CAPITA: US$1,600, US$3,170 at PPP ('05 est based on regression)

CONCERNS about a deterioration in Pacific security were strengthened in 2006 by developments in a number of Pacific Island states.

Parliamentary elections were held in the SOLOMON ISLANDS in April under the watchful gaze both of an international team of election observers and of the regional peacekeeping force, RAMSI (Regional Assistance Mission to Solomon Islands). On 18 April, the announcement that the new Parliament had elected Snyder Rini as the country's new prime minister led to rioting in the capital, Honiara. Neither police nor RAMSI were able to deter or control the arson and looting, which saw the destruction of businesses owned by Chinese residents. The attacks produced an exodus of Chinese from Honiara, with several hundred being flown back to China, whose government condemned the Solomon Islands government for its failure to protect them. In the aftermath, Australia and New Zealand dispatched additional armed personnel to Honiara in order to prevent further disturbances.

Two members of the Solomon Islands parliament were arrested after the riots, accused of involvement, and held without bail for months. This did not prevent them from voting for a new prime minister when Rini's fragile coalition collapsed eight days after he was elected. A new ballot on 4 May returned former Prime Minister Manasseh Sogavare to the position that he had held in 2001-02, but he immediately provoked criticism from Australia and New Zealand by moving to appoint the two imprisoned MPs to cabinet positions, one of them as minister of police. While these appointments were later rescinded, at least temporarily, Sogavare and the Australian government continued their criticisms of one another, with the prime minister questioning Australia's role in RAMSI and the peacekeeping force's influence over Solomon Islands politics. In September, Sogavare ordered the expulsion of the Australian high commissioner—its diplomatic representative in the country's capital—leading to travel bans being placed on Solomon Islands politicians. Matters deteriorated further in October when a lawyer, wanted in Australia for alleged sexual offences, was flown to the Solomon Islands where he was not only given refuge but was nominated to be the country's attorney-general. Sogavare dismissed the country's police commissioner, an Australian, in December.

In FIJI, likewise, parliamentary elections proved an ineffective palliative for deeper social and institutional rifts. A simmering dispute between the government of Prime Minister Laisenia Qarase and the head of the country's armed forces, Commodore Josaia Voreqe (Frank) Bainimarama, left the country seemingly permanently hovering on the brink of a coup. In March, on the final day of the parliamentary session, Bainimarama had the military stage a march through the capital. Disregarding suggestions that the head of the military should not be involved in politics, Bainimarama urged voters to reject Qarase's United Fiji Party (SDL) in the parliamentary elections held in May. The elections returned the SDL to power, however, as it won 36 seats—a bare overall majority—in the 71-seat House of Representatives (the lower chamber). The party also had the support of two independent MPs. Following provisions of the country's constitution, the second-placed party, the Fiji Labour Party, with 31 seats, was offered seats in the cabinet, which it accepted, leaving the House of Representatives with only two other MPs to comprise the opposition.

In any case it was Bainimarama, and the wider Fiji military, who constituted the true opposition to the SDL government. The military's objections centred principally on the government's willingness to take a conciliatory approach to those involved in the May 2000 coup which, though it failed, had led to Qarase's coming to power (see AR 2000, pp. 361-62). Bainimarama's hostility to the perpetrators of the coup reflected the fact that there had been an attempt to assassinate him in November 2000 from which he had only narrowly escaped.

As concerns about a new coup mounted, the police commissioner, an Australian, attempted to deny access to a shipment of ammunition imported by the military. Defying the commissioner, armed soldiers seized the shipment, leading subsequently to attempts by the police to investigate Bainimarama, including an attempt to use the resources of Interpol to apprehend him during a private visit that he made in late November to New Zealand.

Although Bainimarama equivocated, giving the government ultimatums to accept a list of demands—including the withdrawal of legislation that would have given amnesty to those associated with the 2000 coup, and of another government proposal that would have given ownership of Fiji's "foreshore and seabed" to indigenous Fijians—there seemed little that the Qarase government could do to avert a coup. In November the government appeared to accept Bainimarama's conditions, but by then all remaining trust between the two men had evaporated. On 5 December Parliament was dissolved and the following day Bainimarama appointed himself acting president. In the aftermath of the coup Qarase was flown to his remote home island of Lakeba, in the Lau group, from which he was unable to return to participate in post-coup discussions. Efforts by Fiji's prestigious Great Council of Chiefs to forestall or reverse the coup proved unsuccessful, with Bainimarama ignoring the group and, in late December, refusing to meet them.

The coup—Fiji's fourth since 1987—was conducted without any loss of life. It was accompanied by warnings against dissent, however, and rights of freedom of expression and association, guaranteed under the country's constitution, were suspended. The coup was condemned internationally and in the Pacific region, with Fiji once again being suspended from the Commonwealth and facing a loss of aid, and other sanctions, from the EU, the USA, Australia, and New Zealand. In December, Fiji's first and most famous coup plotter, Sitiveni Rabuka, responsible for the first two coups (in 1987) and Fiji's prime minister from 1987 to 1999, was acquitted of any involvement in the November 2000 events. The most visible protagonist in the May 2000 coup attempt, George Speight, jailed for life for treason, was removed from his comfortable prison on Nukulau Island and taken to a grim maximum security prison in Suva. Others convicted of involvement in the coup were also removed from the island, as Bainimarama announced the closure of the prison and Nukulau Island's return to the public for recreational purposes.

In TONGA—in some ways the most stable of Pacific polities, with the region's oldest constitution and a regime dominated by a royal family—the long-smouldering movement for greater democracy finally burst into flame. The year had begun with a new initiative, as one of the king's sons, Prince 'Ulukalala Lavaka Ata, resigned as prime minister. He was replaced by People's Representative Frederick Sevele, as the king moved to allow a "commoner" to become the head of the country's government. In September King Taufa'ahau Tupou IV, 88 years old, died after a long illness, ending 40 years on the throne.

While the king received a royal funeral, followed by 30 days' public mourning, his reign had ended as proposals for a more democratic system of government were being brought forward for consideration. His son, Prince Tupouto'a, was associated with business interests in Tonga, including ownership of Shoreline, the country's telecommunications company. On becoming King Siaosi Tupou V, he withdrew from his business involvements. Nevertheless, on 16 November, as the Tongan Parliament concluded its annual session without having completed consideration of the pro-democracy movement's proposals, a mob of young people went on a rampage in the capital, Nuku'alofa, attacking buildings associated with the government—including the prime minister's office—and with the king, and burning Shoreline's premises. The rioters also chose to burn and loot businesses owned by Chinese residents, leaving downtown Nuku'alofa in ruins. As in Honiara, so too in Tonga, hundreds of Chinese were forced to flee for their lives, being flown out of the country while the Chinese government expressed its concern. Following the riots, the Tongan military, assisted by Australian and New Zealand soldiers and police, rapidly restored order. The only fatalities were seven Tongans, apparently killed while perpetrating their arson attack on the Shoreline building. By the end of December more than 700 Tongans had been arrested for their involvement in the riots, for which pro-democracy MPs denied responsibility.

Intermittent disturbances in Pape'ete, the capital of FRENCH POLYNESIA, closed the territory's main port, blockaded roads, and disrupted government activities. In October anti-government demonstrators occupied key government buildings, including the offices of the president and vice-president as well as the Territorial Assembly. In response the French high commissioner ordered French riot police to clear the buildings. This occurred while the territory's president, Oscar Temaru, was attending the Pacific Islands Forum, seeking support for the territory's independence from France. Temaru's challenges to the legitimacy of French rule, made both within the territory and while overseas, earned him more than one public rebuke from the French high commissioner. In March he was reported as wishing to be described as "president of Tahiti Nui" rather than "French Polynesia", while the high commissioner reminded him that "independence is not on the agenda". At the same time, Temaru's hold on office weakened, and on 12 December his government was defeated on a motion of no-confidence as several of his allies deserted him. Two weeks later, on 26 December, the Assembly elected a new president, Gaston Tong Sang, the first part-Chinese to hold the office, who defeated Temaru by 31 votes to 26.

Elsewhere in the Pacific, political rivalries provoked less upheaval. In the New Zealand territory of TOKELAU, voters disdained the opportunity for a change to the territory's political status. To the disappointment of the New Zealand government and the UN, a long-awaited "act of self-determination", held in February, found the electorate unwilling to vote in sufficient numbers to alter existing ties with New Zealand. In AMERICAN SAMOA, likewise, a Future Political Status Study Commission investigating alternatives to the territory's current political status found little public interest in the possibility of change. Indeed, the national anthem of the USA, "The Star Spangled Banner", was translated into the Samoan language, 106 years after the territory became a US possession, with the Samoan version being sung in January for the first time in the American Samoan Senate.

The loyalties of residents of other territories associated with the USA were emphasised through the continual loss of life by Samoans and Micronesians serving in Iraq and Afghanistan. In September the US military announced the death of the ninth soldier of Samoan ancestry in the two conflicts, and the first to be killed in Afghanistan. Several soldiers from GUAM died in Iraq during 2006, as did another soldier from the FEDERATED STATES OF MICRONESIA, the 13th casualty from Micronesia since the invasion of Iraq in 2003.

SAMOA'S general elections in March also endorsed the status quo, with a victory by the Human Rights Protection Party and the incumbent prime minister, Tuilaepa Sailele, who retained the position which he had held since 1998. In the COOK ISLANDS, the governing Democratic Alliance Party of Prime Minister Jim Marurai was returned to power in elections held in September. On GUAM Governor Felix Camacho was re-elected in November, surviving post-election legal challenges to the result from his opponent. In TUVALU, however, the prime minister lost office, as the August general election brought to power a new prime minister, Apisai Ielemia.

The PITCAIRN men convicted of raping and assaulting women and underage girls on the island lost their final appeals, as their claim that they were not British subjects, and that British law consequently did not apply on the island, was rejected by the Pitcairn Court of Appeal and by the Privy Council, sitting in London (see AR 2004, p. 352; 2005, 332). Subsequently the UK government announced that it would send jailers to Pitcairn, which had a population of about 60 people. It was possible that their workload would be increased, as in June two further Pitcairn men, living in New Zealand, were brought before the Pitcairn Magistrates Court sitting in Auckland to face similar charges.

There continued to be rivalry between the People's Republic of China (the PRC) and Taiwan for the support of Pacific Island states. The government of the PRC supported the construction of new residences in Pohnpei for the leadership of the FEDERATED STATES OF MICRONESIA—the president, vice-president, speaker, and chief justice—which were completed in September. Financial support from Taiwan, meanwhile, allowed for the relocation of PALAU'S capital from Koror, as a complex of buildings resembling the US capitol in Washington DC was completed in Melekeok on Palau's largest island, Babeldaob.

In October the annual Pacific Islands Forum, which was held in FIJI, noted the "new summitry" in the Pacific, with "a number of the region's major donor partners", i.e. Japan, France, China, and Taiwan, organising "separate periodic leaders' summits". In 2006 these meetings included the fourth Pacific Island Leaders Meeting to be hosted by Japan; the first Taiwan-Pacific allies summit, held in PALAU, bringing together Taiwan's President Chen Shui-bian and the heads of state of the six Pacific Island states with diplomatic ties to Taiwan (Palau, Kiribati, Marshall Islands, Nauru, Solomon Islands, and Tuvalu); and a France-Oceania summit, held on 26 July, in Paris. At that meeting the French government gave its permission for both NEW CALEDONIA and FRENCH POLYNESIA to become associate members of the Pacific Islands Forum, with WALLIS AND FUTUNA given permission to seek observer status. These arrangements were approved by the Forum at its October summit (see p. 431).

XI INTERNATIONAL ORGANISATIONS

UNITED NATIONS AND ITS AGENCIES

DATE OF FOUNDATION: 1945 HEADQUARTERS: New York, USA
OBJECTIVES: To promote international peace, security and co-operation on the basis of the equality of member-states, the right of self-determination of peoples and respect for human rights
MEMBERSHIP (END-'06): 192 sovereign states; those not in membership of the UN itself at end-2006 were the Holy See (Vatican) and Taiwan (Republic of China), although all except Taiwan were members of one or more UN specialised agency
SECRETARY-GENERAL: Kofi Annan (Ghana)
SECRETARY-GENERAL ELECT: Ban Ki Moon (South Korea)

THIS was yet another eventful year for the United Nations: the General Assembly sought to fulfil the requirements of the 2005 "world summit" document (see AR 2005, pp. 334-37); new institutions had to bed down; and the organisation had to address many major issues including the war in Lebanon, the Israeli-Palestine dispute, Darfur, nuclear non-proliferation, Iraq, Afghanistan, how it could support effectively the surge in peacekeeping, and the election of a new secretary-general. The Security Council in a special meeting on 22 December paid tribute to the work of retiring Secretary-General Kofi Annan.

The United Nations gained a new member. The General Assembly on 28 June, on the recommendation of the Security Council, admitted the Republic of Montenegro as the 192nd member of the UN (see pp. 104-05).

ELECTIONS. The General Assembly on 13 October, acting on a recommendation of the Security Council, appointed by acclamation Foreign Minister Ban Ki Moon of South Korea (the Republic of Korea, ROK), to be the United Nations' eighth chief executive. He would succeed Kofi Annan who retired on 31 December after two terms. Ban was the first Asian secretary-general since U Thant of Burma (Myanmar), who left office in 1971.

In an election that was reduced to five candidates from Asia—Ban Ki Moon; Shashi Tharoor, UN under secretary-general for communications and public information, from India; Surakiart Sathirathai, deputy prime minister of Thailand; Jayantha Dhanapala, senior advisor to the president of Sri Lanka; and Zeid Ra'ad Zeid al-Hussein, ambassador and permanent representative to the UN from Jordan—there were some interesting developments. The Security Council attempted to involve the General Assembly and member states more deeply in the process than hitherto, although it was not prepared to offer more than one candidate, as desired by some members of the Assembly, because this would have diluted the Council's—and in particular the permanent members'—control of the election. The candidates with official encouragement presented themselves and their policies before regional and other groupings within the Assembly, granted interviews to the press, and had private meetings with civic and non-government organisations which were sponsored by permanent missions. Secondly, the candidates openly canvassed in national capitals, prompting rumours that deals had been struck. Thirdly, the Security Council, albeit in secret, quickly developed a consensus behind one candidate. In the three straw polls held in the Security Council, before the official recommendation, to indicate the degree of support for each candidate, Ban Ki Moon was first. This had not been the case when Annan had been elected for his first term beginning in 1997 (see AR 1996, pp. 370-71).

Although it was accepted that the election process had improved with a deeper involvement of the Assembly, open campaigning, and a degree of accountability, critics still claimed that the emphasis upon regional rotation of the post reduced the number of good quality candidates, that the quality and extent of their campaigning depended partly upon the degree to which their government could provide financial support, and that more attention was paid to the nationality of the candidate rather than his qualifications for what was sometimes described as the most impossible job in the world.

On 16 October the General Assembly, following its normal geographical formula, elected Belgium, Indonesia, Italy, and South Africa, on the first ballot, as new non-permanent members of the Security Council, replacing Denmark, Greece, Japan, and Tanzania whose two-year terms were to end on 31 December. It was unable to fill the Latin American and Caribbean regional seat until 7 November, on the 48th ballot, when Panama—a compromise candidate—was elected to replace Argentina. In the previous 47 ballots Guatemala maintained its lead over Venezuela, except for one tied vote, but never achieved the two-thirds majority required (122 votes). Both states then withdrew in favour of Panama, which they described as a bridge between the northern and southern regions of Latin America (see p. 146).

The legal counsel to the royal family of Bahrain, Haya Rashed al-Khalifa, was elected president of the 61st session of the General Assembly on 8 June. She was only the third woman to hold this post and the first elected since 1969.

IMPLEMENTATION OF THE 2005 SUMMIT DOCUMENT. In March 2006 the General Assembly established the Human Rights Council, which was intended to remedy the deficiencies of the earlier commission on human rights. The council's 47 members were elected not by regional groups but by a majority of the General Assembly. This was intended to prevent states with dubious human rights records from becoming members, and to prevent the emergence on the council of regional groups who might shield their allies from review and criticism. The council would meet for at least three sessions, totalling ten weeks, in Geneva, compared with the commission's six weeks. In 2006 it met in June, September, and November. It held special sessions in July, August, November, and December on the human rights situation in Palestine and other occupied Arab territories, in Lebanon, and in Darfur. It further established missions for Palestine and Darfur, and a commission of enquiry for Lebanon.

The Secretary-General had been asked in the Summit document to provide a report on how the management of the UN's budgetary, financial, and human resources could be made more efficient. In March Annan issued his report:

"Investing in the United Nations: For a stronger organisation world wide", which contained 23 proposals. These proposals proved controversial. In the fifth committee (administrative and budgetary), the 20-year practice of consensus collapsed when a majority of the members voted to support a Group of 77 (G-77) proposal, which was later endorsed by the Assembly, that Annan provide concrete evidence on how his suggestions would make the organisation more effective. The Secretariat provided seven detailed reports.

In July the Assembly approved a limited number of reforms by consensus, including giving the secretary-general on an experimental basis limited spending discretion of US$20 million within the biennium budget; the creation of a chief technology officer; and the upgrading of certain parts of the UN computer system. In an effort to strengthen UN procurement practices, which had been the subject of extensive criticism, the Assembly also authorised approximately US$700,000 for the recruitment of new procurement officers. (The secretary-general, in an attempt to prevent any further scandals involving UN procurement staff, announced on 22 December unprecedented employment restrictions. Staff when leaving the UN would have to wait for one year until they could be employed by any company with which they had had procurement dealings, and they would not be able to contact the UN for two years if their new post related to their former responsibilities. There would be sanctions against companies and former staff that violated these restrictions.) Action, however, was deferred until 2007 on the remaining suggested improvements.

The new peacebuilding commission, which was established by the Security Council and the General Assembly in December 2005 (see AR 2005, p. 335) and whose principal task was to help co-ordinate the rebuilding of post-conflict states, was asked by the Security Council in June to provide advice on Burundi and Sierra Leone. The commission identified key areas for attention in Burundi: promoting good governance, including human rights, strengthening of the rule of law and the security sector, and ensuring community recovery; and for Sierra Leone: youth empowerment and employment, consolidating democracy and good governance, justice and security sector reform, and capacity building.

A peacebuilding fund was established on 11 October to support post-conflict stabilisation initiatives. The fund was based on pre-pledged non-earmarked funds; the target was US$250 million and US$140 million had been pledged in October. The commission recommended that Burundi and Sierra Leone should be eligible to receive support from the fund.

The high level panel on UN system-wide coherence, co-chaired by the prime ministers of Pakistan and Norway, reported in November. It stated that the UN could save up to 20 per cent of its current costs if it eliminated duplication and consolidated certain funds and programmes, which would release more funds for humanitarian purposes. It recommended that there should be a single UN country programme, which would co-ordinate the organisation's work in each state, replacing the current fragmented approach; that there should be a development board at headquarters, which would make decisions on and co-ordinate the single UN country programme; and that there should be a funding mechanism which would provide multi-year financing for achieving the Millennium Development Goals, the targets for 2015 arising from the UN millennium summit of September 2000 (see AR 2000, p. 366). The panel recommended that the single UN country programme should start in 2007 with five pilot countries.

FINANCE. The assistant secretary-general, controller, Warren Sach, told the fifth committee on 31 October that the financial indicators for 2006 were mixed. First assessments for the regular budget and payments for the regular budget were lower than the previous year by US$73 million and US$39 million respectively; similarly only 122 states in 2006, compared with 130 in 2005, had paid their assessments in full. Unpaid assessments were down by US$58 million to US$661 million because of payments made in the last quarter of 2005, and almost 95 per cent of this sum was owed by four states: the USA, Japan, Brazil, and Argentina. The final picture for 2006 would depend largely upon the USA. If it did not pay its assessment in full, the UN might have to borrow over US$200 million from the reserve account by the end of the year; if it paid in full the organisation would have a cash balance similar to that at the end of 2005.

Sach informed the committee that peacekeeping assessments were based upon adjustments to the regular budget scale. Until a new scale was adopted to replace the existing scale, the Secretariat would be unable to issue peacekeeping assessments beyond 31 December, despite the General Assembly having approved the budgets of individual missions beyond that date. He estimated, therefore, that assessments totalling over US$1.5 billion would have to be despatched early in 2007.

Sach stated that there was more than US$2.5 billion in outstanding peacekeeping assessments, over half of which was owed by the USA and Japan. There was just over US$1.6 billion in cash available in closed and current peacekeeping accounts. However, the General Assembly had imposed restrictions on the use of this money: no current operation could be financed from another active mission. Thus, only funds available in the closed accounts was currently available for cross-borrowing.

There was expected to be US$300 million available in the closed accounts but US$259 million was due to be returned to member states for outstanding payments for troops and equipment and credits. Thus only US$41 million would be available for possible cross-borrowing for other accounts including the regular budget, the tribunals, and active peacekeeping missions.

The peacekeeping debt owed to member states was likely to increase by over US$300 million by the end of the year. UN peacekeeping costs had risen mainly because of the full deployment of troops in Côte d'Ivoire and the Democratic Republic of Congo (DRC), the expansion of the mission in Lebanon (UNIFIL), and the establishment of the UN Integrated Mission in East Timor (UNMIT). Payment for troops and equipment had been largely met until September, except for the missions in Western Sahara, Kosovo, and Georgia. The increase in peacekeeping debt to member states in the final quarter of the year was due to delays in the receipt of contributions, exacerbated by the unavailability of rates of assessment for 2007.

The international tribunals' financial position, Sach believed, had remained relatively healthy. Although payments received so far had remained somewhat lower than in 2005, the amount outstanding was US$18 million less. The final situation would depend upon the payment of assessed contributions.

The General Assembly on 23 December decided to allocate US$1,876.7 million over the period 2007-14 for the capital master plan to renovate and to improve the security of the New York headquarters buildings, which were energy inefficient, which had lacked essential upkeep, and which failed to meet current local standards. During the period 2002-06, the Assembly had authorised assessments of US$150 million for the plan, but only US$66 million had been received. Thus, timely execution of the project would require all members to pay their assessments in full and on time.

THE SECURITY COUNCIL. The Security Council met formally on 224 occasions; it adopted 87 resolutions and issued 59 presidential statements. There were Security Council missions to Sudan and Chad from 4 to 10 June; to Addis Ababa, Ethiopia, to attend a consultative meeting on Darfur on 13 November organised by the African Union (AU); and to Afghanistan in November.

The Council held thematic debates on civilians in armed conflict; the protection of journalists in conflict situations; children and armed conflict; small arms; women, peace and security; and co-operation with regional organisations.

NON PROLIFERATION OF WEAPONS OF MASS DESTRUCTION. The Council decided on 27 April to extend for two years the mandate of the "1540 committee", which was established in 2004 to address the possible acquisition of weapons of mass destruction by non-state actors.

On 5 July NORTH KOREA (the Democratic People's Republic of Korea, DPRK) announced that it had conducted a series of tests on ballistic missiles and on 9 October stated that it had carried out the testing of a nuclear bomb (see pp. 344-45). On 15 July, in Resolution 1695, the Council condemned the ballistic missile tests, demanded the reinstatement of the moratorium, and required member states to prevent the transfer of any item that might contribute to North Korea's missile or weapons of mass destruction programmes and to refrain from obtaining any such items or technology from North Korea. On 14 October, in Resolution 1718, the Council imposed sanctions upon North Korea and called upon that state to return immediately to the six party talks without precondition (for texts see pp. 552-58). Although the text was adopted under chapter 7 of the UN Charter, there was to be no automatic military enforcement under article 41. The sanctions banned sales to, or export from, North Korea of any military equipment and of any nuclear and missile related items; froze the finances and banned the travel of anyone involved in nuclear and missile programmes; and called upon member states to co-operate in allowing the inspection of cargo to and from North Korea. The Security Council did not establish a panel of experts. The sanctions committee would therefore have to depend upon the advice of the Secretariat for what was a very technical range of sanctions.

IRAN posed three problems for the Council during 2006: its nuclear enrichment programme posed proliferation risks; it had failed to meet the requirements of the International Atomic Energy Agency (IAEA) in proving full information about every aspect of its undeclared nuclear material and activities; and it had failed to met the Council's demand in Resolution 1696 of 31 July that it suspend all enrichment and reprocessing activities within one month or face the possibility of economic and diplomatic sanctions (see pp. 280-81). On 23 December, having received reports from the IAEA on 31 August and 15 November which indicated that although Iran had co-operated to a degree it had failed to comply with Resolution 1696, the Council imposed similar sanctions to those against North Korea (for text see pp. 542-48). The sanctions banned the import or export of sensitive nuclear material and equipment and froze the financial assets of any person or entities supporting the state's "proliferation" of sensitive nuclear activities or the development of nuclear weapons delivery systems. There would not, however, be a travel ban. A sanctions committee was established. The sanctions would be lifted if the IAEA could verify that Iran had met its obligations: if it did not the Council would adopt additional sanctions.

THE MIDDLE EAST. With regard to PALESTINE, the Security Council received monthly secretariat briefings on developments in the relationship between Israel and the Palestine National Authority (PNA, the government). The Council issued a presidential statement on 3 February that congratulated the Palestinian people on a free and fair and secure electoral process to the Palestine Legislative Council (see p. 186) and stated that all members of a future Palestinian government must be committed to the "road map" peace plan, previous agreements and obligations between the parties to the Israeli-Palestinian conflict, and a negotiated two state solution.

On 13 July the USA vetoed a draft resolution that would have demanded that Israel halt its two week military offensive in the Gaza Strip, prompted by the Palestinian capture of an Israeli soldier (see p. 189). On 11 November the USA again vetoed a draft resolution. The General Assembly met on 17 November in its resumed 10th emergency session and adopted a similar resolution to that which had been vetoed. This called for an immediate withdrawal of Israeli forces from the Gaza Strip and a cessation of violence by both sides. It also asked the secretary-general to establish a fact-finding mission on the 8 November incident in Beit Hanoun, in which Israeli artillery shells had killed eight Palestinian children and seven women (see p. 190). Annan later reported to the Assembly that he had been unable to fulfil his mandate.

With regard to LEBANON and SYRIA, the Security Council received regular briefings on the progress achieved by the investigation commission into the killing of former Lebanese Prime Minister Rafik Hariri in February 2005 (see p. 189; AR 2005, pp. 182-83, 490-92). Serge Brammertz, the head investigator, was able to report that Hariri had been killed by a single blast; that an RDX-based high explosive had been used; that a Mitsubishi van had carried the improvised device; and that it was likely that a person had triggered the explosion from within or immediately in front of the van, rather than via a remote controlled device. The Council renewed the mandate of the commission until mid-June 2007. The Council also requested the secretary-general to negotiate an agreement with the Lebanese government to establish a tribunal of an international character to try those found responsible for the killing of Hariri and 22 others.

On 12 July, sparked by the capture of two Israeli soldiers by Hezbullah guerrillas, ISRAEL mounted a massive military offensive against southern LEBANON and Hezbullah responded by making increased rocket attacks upon northern Israel (see pp. 197-203). Hostilities ceased on 14 August. The Secretariat provided regular briefings in which there were calls for the Council to take immediate action to halt the spiralling violence. The Council met on a number of occasions to renew the mandate of the existing UN Interim Force in Lebanon (UNIFIL), to request the Israeli government to conduct a comprehensive inquiry into the killing of four UN observers by the Israeli Defence Forces, and to call for an end to the violence. Finally—after a week of extensive diplomatic activity both within and without the organisation—the Council adopted a French-US-negotiated resolution (1701) on 11 August (for text see pp. 528-31).

This called for an immediate cessation of hostilities followed by the immediate deployment of Lebanese troops; authorised an enlarged UNIFIL (which later was to include naval craft) to assist the Lebanese forces and to be deployed as the Israeli force withdrew; called upon Israel and Lebanon to support a long-term political solution; requested the secretary-general to make proposals within 30 days on the disarming of militias and the delineation of the international borders of Lebanon (including the Shebaa Farms area); and called for an arms embargo on the transfer of arms to any entity or individual in Lebanon other than the government. Furthermore, the resolution authorised UNIFIL to use force to prevent hostile activities and to resist threats to its mandate.

The Security Council remained concerned about the range of challenges facing the government of AFGHANISTAN (see pp. 283-85). The Council renewed the mandates of the UN mission and the NATO-led International Security Assistance Force (ISAF). It received briefings from the Secretariat and sent a visiting mission to Afghanistan in November: the first for three years. The mission found that progress towards the Afghanistan compact, which provided a framework for a five-year partnership between the government and the international community to address Afghanistan's range of problems and which the Council had endorsed in February, had not been as smooth or rapid as had been hoped. Indeed it was contended that without a sustained partnership over the long haul there could be no guarantee that the country would not slide back towards conflict.

The Security Council received regular briefings on the political, humanitarian, military, and diplomatic conditions in the Darfur region of SUDAN from the secretariat, the African Union (AU), and its own visiting mission. The Security Council sought to maintain access for humanitarian organisations and to encourage the parties to negotiate and maintain an AU-mediated peace agreement. It also sought to authorise travel restrictions and financial sanctions against four named

Sudanese individuals (Resolution 1672, passed by 12 votes with three abstentions: China, Qatar, and the Russian Federation), and to obtain consent from the Sudanese government for the deployment to Darfur of an enlarged UN Mission in Sudan (UNMIS) to support the effective implementation of the Darfur peace agreement and the 2004 humanitarian ceasefire (Resolution 1706, adopted by 12 votes with the identical three abstentions). This mission would transfer peacekeeping from the AU to the UN (see pp. 217-18).

The Sudanese government was opposed to a UN operation. The AU, however, adopted a communique which endorsed a hybrid UN-AU force. On 27 December the secretary-general announced that the Sudanese president had accepted a three-phased approach leading to a hybrid force. This force could have a strength of 17,000 troops and 3,000 police, compared with the AU force's strength of 7,000.

The Security Council maintained a watching brief on IRAQ. It renewed the mandates of the multinational force and the UN Assistance Mission in Iraq (UNAMI), congratulated the Iraqi people for electing the Iraqi Council of Representatives in difficult circumstances and for the inauguration of their constitutionally elected government, but it also condemned the acts of terrorism in the country, and urged all the people to participate in the political processes peacefully (see pp. 205-10). The Council received quarterly briefings from the USA on the activities of the US-led multinational force, regular briefings from the special representative and other members of the Secretariat, and reports from the secretary-general. The secretariat briefings and reports highlighted the violence in the country, and offered advice to the government on the formidable political, security, and economic difficulties that it faced. It was feared that the violence within the country was out of control, which provoked widespread concern for the future of Iraq.

During the Security Council's consideration of the most appropriate UN presence in EAST TIMOR, after the mandate of UNOTIL ended in May, violence broke out in the new state in April and May that displaced over 100,000 people and revealed the fragility of its institutions (see pp. 321-22). The Council supported the deployment of troops from Portugal, Australia, New Zealand, and Malaysia in response to a request from the Timorese government, welcomed the initiatives of the secretary-general including sending a special envoy to help facilitate political dialogue, and extended the mandate of UNOTIL (the UN Office in Timor Leste) three times until 23 August.

Then on 25 August the Council established a new, larger mission for an initial period of six months with an authorised strength of up to 1,608 police and 34 military officers. The international security forces were called upon to co-operate with, and provide assistance to, the UN Integrated Mission in East Timor, UNMIT. The mission had an extensive mandate: to support the government in consolidating stability and facilitating political dialogue among the Timorese in their efforts to achieve national reconciliation; to support the country in holding presidential and legislative elections in 2007; to restore and maintain public security through the presence of UN police; and to assist the government in reviewing the security sector, strengthening the national capacity for promoting and protecting human rights, and promoting justice and reconciliation.

PEACEKEEPING. The level of UN peacekeeping activity during 2006 was unprecedented. There were 93,000 personnel serving in 16 peacekeeping operations and two peace support missions. This was an increase of 10,000 from 2005, and the deployments to the Lebanon and East Timor would increase the total to 112,000. (The previous peak had been in July 1993 when 78,444 personnel were deployed, almost one third of them in the UN Protection Force in Bosnia & Herzegovina, UNPROFOR.) The under secretary-general for peacekeeping, Jean Marie Guehenno, believed that there were a number of reasons for this activity: member states were addressing conflicts in a complex and uncertain environment through a collective approach; there was a greater confidence in the capacity of the UN to execute its mandates; and a better understanding of regional organisations was creating a greater demand for joint action with the UN.

There were, however, a number of challenges to face if this level of activity were to be sustained effectively. First, it was necessary to have a core of experienced civilian peacekeepers that was retained from mission to mission and which would provide essential peacekeeping services ranging from logistical support to public relations. Secondly, there was a similar need for police and military personnel. The UN operated the second largest global military deployment but there were only 12 military planners. Thirdly, the safety and security of field personnel was of concern: 17 out of 72 fatalities in five operations in 2006 were malicious acts. The peacekeeping department was working closely with the department of safety and security and through the establishment of new operation centres in the field to increase security. Yet there was still no "backstopping" capacity in the peacekeeping department to address the safety of personnel or to investigate the causes of serious incidents in the field. Fourthly, clear doctrine was the backbone of effective peacekeeping: once the new doctrine had been completed it would provide a framework for absorbing lessons learned and creating workable guidelines for best practices, as well as replacing the 1995 general guidelines. Fifthly, following recommendations from the office of internal oversight, the department was seeking to strengthen management capacity and address conduct and discipline issues by creating teams at headquarters and at eight missions (with additional teams to cover the remaining missions) and by revising the draft model memorandum of understanding with contributing governments about the provision of troops. The peacekeeping department and missions continued to take action to prevent sexual exploitation and abuse. (The Security Council had received a full briefing on this issue on 23 February, and a high level conference on eliminating sexual exploitation and abuse by UN and non-governmental organisations personnel was held in New York on 4 December.) Sixthly, the department was taking various measures to deal with resources: in particular, oversight of procurement systems was being improved, especially in light of an audit that exposed mismanagement and the risk of serious financial loss. A panel had reviewed requirements, and a dedicated office in New York advised missions on field procurement; there was increased pooling in logistics and a

UNITED NATIONS PEACEKEEPING MISSIONS 2006

Mission	Established	Present Strength	Renewal Date
UNTSO: United Nations Truce Supervision Organisation	May 1948	149 military observers; 104 international civilians; 121 local civilians. Total personnel: 374. Fatalities: 48. Appropriations for 2006: $29,961,200.	
UNMOGIP: United Nations Military Observer Group in India and Pakistan	January 1949	43 military observers; 21 international civilians; 49 local civilians. Total personnel: 113. Fatalities: 11. Appropriations for 2006: $7,919,100.	
UNFICYP: United Nations Peacekeeping Force in Cyprus	March 1964	853 military; 65 civilian police; 38 international civilians; 108 local civilians. Total personnel: 1,064 Fatalities: 176. Approved budget July 06 to June 07: $41,588,400 including voluntary contributions of one-third from Cyprus and $6,500,000 from Greece.	June 2007
UNDOF: United Nations Disengagement Observer Force	June 1974	1,023 military; 35 international civilians; 107 local civilians. Total personnel: 1,165. Fatalities: 42. Approved budget from July 06 to June 07: $41,588,400.	June 2007
UNIFIL: United Nations Interim Force in Lebanon	March 1978	8,741 military; 105 international civilians; 308 local civilians. Total personnel 9,154. Fatalities: 258. Approved budget from July 06 to June 07: $97,579,600.	August 2007
MINURSO: United Nations Mission for the Referendum in Western Sahara	April 1991	29 troops; 190 military observers; 4 civilian police; 100 international civilians; 129 local civilians; 20 UN volunteers. Total personnel 472. Fatalities: 14. Approved budget July 06 to June 07: $44,460,000.	April 2007

UNITED NATIONS PEACEKEEPING MISSIONS 2006 *continued*

Mission	Established	Present Strength	Renewal Date
UNOMIG: United Nations Observer Mission in Georgia	August 1993	127 military observers; 12 civilian police; 101 international civilians; 182 local civilians; 1 UN volunteer. Total personnel: 423. Fatalities: 11. Approved budget July 06 to June 07: $34,827,000.	April 2007
UNMIK: United Nations Interim Mission in Kosovo	June 1999	37 military observers; 1,893 civilian police; 508 international civilians; 2,049 local civilians. 144 UN volunteers. Total personnel: 4,631. Fatalities: 46. Approved budget July 06 to June 07: $227,400,400.	Established for an initial period of 12 months; to continue unless the Security Council decides otherwise.
MONUC: United Nations Organisation Mission in the Democratic Republic of the Congo	November 1999	16,630 troops; 767 military observers; 1,080 civilian police; 953 international civilians; 2,079 local civilians; 658 UN volunteers. Total personnel: 22,167 Fatalities: 98. Approved budget July 06 to June 07: $1,138,533.	February 2007
UNMEE: United Nations Mission in Ethiopia and Eritrea	July 2000	2,064 troops; 205 military observers; 144 international civilians; 197 local civilians. 61 UN volunteers. Total personnel: 2,671. Fatalities: 17. Approved budget July 2006 to June 2007: $182,237,800.	January 2007
UNMIL: United Nations Mission in Liberia	September 2003	14,434 troops; 207 military observers; 1,098 civilian police; 521 international civilians; 869 local civilians; 256 UN volunteers. Total personnel: 17,385. Fatalities: 85 Approved budget July 06 to June 07: $745,572,300.	March 2007

UNITED NATIONS PEACEKEEPING MISSIONS 2006 *continued*

Mission	Established	Present Strength	Renewal Date
UNOCI: United Nations Mission in Côte d'Ivoire	April 2004	7,845 troops; 194 military observers; 993 civilian police; 369 international civilians; 518 local civilians; 232 UN volunteers. Total personnel: 10,151. Fatalities: 26. Approved budget July 06 to June 07: $438,366,800.	January 2007
MINUSTAH: United Nations Stabilization Mission in Haiti	June 2004	6,652 military; 1,682 civilian police; 418 international civilians; 599 local civilians; 173 UN volunteers. Total personnel: 9,524. Fatalities 20. Approved budget July 06 to June 07: $510,394,700.	February 2007
ONUB: United Nations Operation in Burundi	June 2004	2,347 troops; 80 military observers; 14 civilian police; 256 international civilians; 339 local civilians; 106 UN volunteers. Total personnel: 3,142. Fatalities: 23. Approved budget July 06 to 31 December 06: $82,386,000.	Mandate ended on 31 December 2006.
UNMIS: United Nations Mission in the Sudan	March 2005	8,891 military; 695 military observers; 662 civilian police; 753 international civilian; 2065 local civilians; 165 United Nations volunteers. Total personnel: 13,231. Fatalities 15. Approved budget from July 2006 to June 2007: $1,126,295,900.	April 2007
UNMIT: United Nations Integrated Mission in Timor-Leste (East Timor)	August 2006	31 military observers; 959 police; 87 international civilians; 227 local civilians; 36 UN volunteers. Total personnel: 1,340. Fatalities 0.	February 2007

NOTES.

Different Categories of personnel serving in peacekeeping missions as of 31 October 2006:
Military troops, observers and civilian police, 80,696 (69,509 troops, 8,462 civilian police, and 2,725 military observers.)
International civilian, 4,513
Local civilian, 9,946
United Nations volunteers, 1,852
Total number of personnel serving in the 16 peacekeeping operations, 97,007
Contributing Countries, 112

Total number of fatalities from all categories in peacekeeping operations between 1948 and 31 October 2006, 2,312.

The top 10 troop contributors: Pakistan (9,790); Bangladesh (9,655); India (9,276); Jordan (3,819); Nepal (3,522); Ghana (2,674); Uruguay (2,583); Ethiopia (2,568); Nigeria (2,429); and South Africa (2,077).

Finance:
Approved budgets for the period 1 July 2006 to 30 June 2007, about $4.75 billion (excluding the mission in East Timor and the possible expansion of the mission in the Sudan).
It was anticipated that, if there were full deployment in Lebanon and the mission to Darfur took place, the budget could reach $7 billion.

Estimated total costs from 1948 to 30 June 2006, about $41.04 billion.
Outstanding contributions to peacekeeping, about $2.5 billion.

UNTSO and UNMOGIP were funded from the UN regular biennial budget. The costs to the UN of the 14 other current operations were financed from their own separate accounts on the basis of legally binding assessments on all member states.

Peacekeeping was paid for by member states according to an agreed special formula.

The current top 10 contributors: the USA (27 per cent); Japan (19 per cent); Germany (9 per cent); UK (7 per cent); France (7 per cent); Italy (5 per cent); Canada (3 per cent); Spain (3 per cent); China (2 per cent); and the Netherlands (2 per cent).

Number of peacekeeping operation since 1948, 61.

(Sources: UN background note 31 October 2006; UN current peacekeeping operations website; and UN press releases.)

UNITED NATIONS POLITICAL AND PEACEBUILDING MISSIONS 2006.

Mission	Established	Present Strength	Current Authorisation
UNPOS: United Nations Political Office for Somalia	April 1995	Representative of the Secretary-General and Head of UNPOS: François Lonseny Fall (Guinea). 15 international civilians.	31 December 2006
Office of the Special Representative of the Secretary-General for the Great Lakes Region.	December 1997	Special Representative of the Secretary-General: Ibrahimi Fall (Senegal). 8 international civilians; 7 local civilians.	31 March 2007
UNOGBIS: United Nations Peace-building Support Office in Guinea-Bissau.	March 1999	Representative of the Secretary-General and Head of UNOGBIS: Shola Omoregie (Nigeria). 10 international civilians; 2 military advisers; 1 civilian police adviser; 1 UN volunteer.	31 December 2006
UNSCO: Office of the United Nations Special Co-ordinator for the Middle East.	October 1999	Special Co-ordinator for the Middle East Peace Process and Personal Representative of the Secretary-General to the Palestine Liberation Organisation and the Palestine Authority: Alvaro de Soto (Peru). 29 international civilians; 22 local civilians.	19 September 2007
BONUCA: United Nations Peace-building Office in the Central African Republic.	February 2000	Representative of the Secretary-General and Head of BONUC: Lamine Cissé (Senegal). 18 international civilians; 5 military advisors; 6 civilian police; 44 local civilians; 3 UN volunteers.	31 December 2006
UNTOP: United Nations Tajikistan Office of Peace-building.	June 2000	Representative of the Secretary-General for Tajikistan: Vladimir Sotirov (Bulgaria). 8 international civilians; 1 civilian police adviser; 20 local civilians.	1 June 2007

UNITED NATIONS POLITICAL AND PEACEBUILDING MISSIONS 2006. *continued*

Mission	Established	Present Strength	Current Authorisation
Office of the Personal Representative of the Secretary-General for Lebanon	August 2000	Personal Representative of the Secretary-General: Geir O. Pedersen (Norway). 6 international civilians; . 6 local civilians	
Office of the Special Representative of the Secretary-General for West Africa	November 2001	Special Representative of the Secretary-General: Ahmedou Ould-Abdallah (Mauritania). 7 international civilians; 9 local civilians.	31 December 2007
UNAMA: United Nations Assistance Mission in Afghanistan	March 2002	Special Representative of the Secretary-General: Tom Koenigs (Germany). 191 international civilians; 769 local civilians; 11 military observers; 3 civilian police; 30 UN volunteers.	23 March 2007
UNAMI: United Nations Assistance Mission for Iraq	August 2003	Special Representative of the Secretary-General for Iraq: Ashraf Jehangir Qazi (Pakistan). Authorised strength: 938 (406 international civilians; 532 local civilians). Current strength (staff are based in Iraq, Jordan, and Kuwait): 228 international civilians; 352 local civilians; 11 military observers.	10 August 2007
UNIOSIL: United Nations Integrated Office in Sierra Leone.	January 2006	Executive Representative for UNIOSIL: Victor da Silva Angelo (Portugal). 66 international civilians; 184 local civilians; 9 military observers; 19 civilian police; 22 UN volunteers.	31 December 2006

NOTES.
UNAMA and UNIOSIL, although political missions, are directed and supported by the department of peacekeeping operations. All the other political and peace-building missions are directed by the department of political affairs.

The following mission was completed in 2006:
UNOTIL: United Nations Office in Timor-Leste (East Timor): May 2005-August 2006.

Current number of missions, 11

Personnel:
International civilians, 586
Military and civilian police advisers and liaison officers, 291
Local civilian personnel, 1,413
UN volunteers, 56

Total number of personnel serving in political and peacebuilding missions, 2,346.

Sources: United Nations Political and Peace-Building Missions background note 30 September 2006; and the UN website.

comprehensive review of information management had been completed. Finally, peacekeepers had to run themselves out of business. It was not possible to take on new demands without a managed reduction of the case load.

There were two dimensions to a managed reduction and a sustainable exit. National capacity had to be increased to create the conditions for withdrawal of peacekeepers. This might mean an increased political engagement by international and local actors. There was also a need to support national security institutions which were viable administratively and fiscally. The second dimension was effective partnerships with development agencies to provide long term economic regeneration and long term political reintegration.

SANCTIONS. There were three important general developments in UN sanctions. On 8 August in Resolution 1699 the Council requested that the secretary-general should increase co-operation between the UN and Interpol, which would help member states to have better tools to implement sanctions committees measures, particularly the freezing of assets, travel bans, and arms embargoes.

The Security Council in two resolutions in December attempted to address the widespread criticisms about the lack of due process and transparency in the placing and removal of individuals and entities from the lists of targeted sanctions that had been drawn up by the sanctions committees. First, the Council decided, in Resolution 1730 of 19 December, that a focal point should be established within the UN Secretariat to ensure fair and clear listing and de-listing procedures for sanctions committees. The Council also directed the sanctions committees to revise their guidelines so that only one member, rather than the whole membership, need recommend de-listing in order to place the item on the agenda. Second, in Resolution 1735 of 22 December, the Council endorsed new guidelines drawn up by the 1267 committee, which monitored the sanctions against al-Qaida, Osama bin Laden, and the Taliban; the Council called for similar action from the other sanctions committees. The new guidelines required the designating state to provide a detailed evidential statement about who was to be listed, why they were to be listed, and how much of the statement might be made available to other member states; yet there was still no provision for informing the accused or for permitting a written defence. The Council also decided that the 1267 committee should continue to develop guidelines for de-listing, taking into consideration whether there had been mistaken identity, if an individual had died, or had severed all association with the relevant groups and actors.

The Security Council on 21 December received the report of its informal working group on the general issues of sanctions. This had been meeting since April 2000 to develop general recommendations on how to improve the effectiveness of UN sanctions. The report contained "best practice" on the design, implementation, and evaluation of sanctions, on committee working methods, monitoring and enforcement, and the methodological standards and format for reporting by expert groups. The Council took note of the contents with interest and requested its subsidiary bodies to take note as well.

MILITARY FORCES. The Security Council authorised for further periods of 12 months: on 12 September (in Resolution 1216) the International Security Assistance Force in Afghanistan, (ISAF); on 21 November (in Resolution 1272) the EU Stabilisation Force (EUFOR) and a NATO headquarters in Bosnia & Herzegovina; and on 28 November, at the request of the Iraqi prime minister, in Resolution 1723, the multinational force in Iraq.

In Resolution 1725 of 6 December the Council authorised for six months a joint intergovernmental authority on development—African Union protection and training mission in Somalia (see pp. 232-34), which was mandated to protect the members of the transitional national government (TNG); to train their security forces to enable them to provide their own security; to help re-establish national security forces; to maintain security in Baidoa; to monitor progress on dialogue between the TNG and the Islamic Courts' militia; and to ensure the free movement and safety of all those involved in the dialogue process.

DEFENCE ORGANISATIONS

North Atlantic Treaty Organization (NATO)

DATE OF FOUNDATION: 1949 HEADQUARTERS: Brussels, Belgium
OBJECTIVES: To ensure the collective security of member states
MEMBERSHIP (END-'06): Belgium, Bulgaria, Canada, Czech Republic, Denmark, Estonia, France, Germany, Greece, Hungary, Iceland, Italy, Latvia, Lithuania, Luxembourg, Netherlands, Norway, Poland, Portugal, Romania, Slovakia, Slovenia, Spain, Turkey, UK, USA (total 26)
SECRETARY GENERAL: Jaap de Hoop Scheffer (Netherlands)

Partnership for Peace (PFP)

DATE OF FOUNDATION: 1994 HEADQUARTERS: Brussels, Belgium
OBJECTIVES: To provide a framework for co-operation between NATO and the former communist and neutral states of Europe and ex-Soviet Central Asia
MEMBERSHIP (END-'06): Albania, Armenia, Austria, Azerbaijan, Belarus, Bosnia & Herzegovina, Croatia, Finland, Georgia, Irish Republic, Kazakhstan, Kyrgyzstan, Macedonia, Moldova, Montenegro, Russia, Serbia, Sweden, Switzerland, Tajikistan, Turkmenistan, Ukraine, Uzbekistan (total 23)

For data on other organisations mentioned in this article, see specific entries.

NATO's summit in Riga, Latvia, in November 2006 had for long been billed as the "transformation summit", the moment at which the NORTH ATLANTIC TREATY ORGANISATION would demonstrate that it had successfully adapted its political procedures and its operational (military) capabilities to meet the increasing, and increasingly hazardous, security challenges of the early 21st century. By the time the summit took place, however, NATO's extensive and growing commitment in Afghanistan, in the form of the UN-mandated International Security Assistance Force (ISAF) (see pp. 283-85), had come to dominate the agenda. As a result, when NATO's heads of state met in Riga their discussions were more focused than might otherwise have been expected on day-to-day operational matters to do with ISAF. One such matter was the contentious subject of the size and shape of the force and the level of commitment from NATO's European members.

Some commentators had also expected that the Riga summit would address the thorny issue of NATO's strategic concept, the Alliance's "business plan". This document was last revised in 1999 and had increasingly become regarded as an obsolete reference point for the Alliance as it confronted complex new security dynamics almost 20 years after the end of the Cold War. Yet revision of the document had been carefully avoided, largely because it was considered unwise to open up one of NATO's core documents for discussion and amendment at a time when the security environment was in a state of flux, and when NATO's membership was expanding. As NATO continued to enlarge, however, with a membership that could soon be approaching 30, critics argued that the interim solution agreed at the June 2004 summit in Istanbul, Turkey, was no longer sustainable. At Istanbul, it was agreed that the 1999 strategic concept would be supplemented by a comprehensive political guidance paper and by a confidential paper known as "Vision 2020" issued jointly by NATO's military commands.

Expectation grew during 2006 that the Riga summit would initiate a review of the strategic concept, possibly with results as fundamental as the 1967 Harmel report, which set the Alliance on the twin tracks of defence and détente (see AR 1967, pp. 154-55). Some—including German Chancellor Angela Merkel—called for the process to be complete by the time of NATO's next enlargement, probably during 2008. Others argued that a new strategic concept should be prepared in time for the 60th anniversary of the founding of the Alliance in 2009. There were also those for whom concern over the strategic concept, and whether it should or could be reviewed, was indicative of a deeper malaise within NATO; rather than become bogged down in constitutional-style debates, what mattered instead was for NATO to be able to adapt to the rapidly evolving—and increasingly menacing—international strategic landscape. But behind this debate lay another, far greater challenge. Any review of NATO's strategic concept would inevitably invite some difficult questions to which there appeared to be no simple answers. What was NATO for? Were the United States and its European allies diverging in their strategic interests and concerns? Was the EUROPEAN UNION coming to be seen—in Europe at least—as a viable alternative to NATO? Did some European governments no longer consider a formal strategic relationship with the USA to be either necessary or desirable? Or could the transatlantic security partnership be maintained through securing a dynamic and efficient relationship between NATO and the EU?

Since the end of the Cold War the relationship between NATO and the EU had been neither easy nor especially productive. Progress had been made—politically, institutionally, and operationally—but usually at a frustratingly slow pace. During 2006, while some were inclined to congratulate the EU for its achievements in the security and defence field, there was in NATO a mounting sense of frustration at the scale and pace of the EU's achievement, and generally a sense of puzzlement that the NATO-EU strategic partnership should have proved so difficult to develop. In that vein, the Riga summit declaration, having noted that NATO and the EU "share common values and strategic interests" then went on to call for "improvements in the NATO-EU strategic partnership" in order to ensure "closer co-operation and greater efficiency, and avoid unnecessary duplication, in a spirit of transparency and respecting the autonomy of the two organisations". These words had a certain familiarity to them, reminiscent of the security and defence debates of the early 1990s.

The two organisations were united in many ways: by strategic vision, by a sense of responsibility for regional and international security and stability, by similarities in membership, and by vulnerability to security threats and challenges. NATO and the EU were also united by budgetary constraints; it was beyond the means of member governments to maintain two, entirely separate, security and defence organisations. Nor would it make much sense to do so. In five key areas—geopolitical burden-sharing, operational collaboration, rapid reaction force planning, resource and capability planning, and, finally, responses to terrorism—the structures and procedures for NATO/EU co-operation were largely in place. Yet in terms of practical collaboration and achievement, the results were mixed. Overall, the outcome was that the NATO-EU relationship was neither co-operative nor healthily competitive, but dysfunctional.

GEOPOLITICAL BURDEN-SHARING—territorially, functionally, or both—was an issue that had exercised NATO and the EU for many years. Both organisations had a global outlook, and both had aspirations to act in a wide variety of political circumstances. In early 2006 the chairman of NATO's military committee declared: "In order to guarantee our safety at home, we are now required to go further and further afield to promote security and stability in an ever more unpredictable world. There is now very little distinction between domestic and international security, or between homeland defence and forward defence." For its part, the EU had from its inception been a regional and global actor, in a diverse range of trade, economic, and development activities. In the December 2003 European security strategy (ESS), the EU also adopted the rhetoric of a global security actor concerned with a range of problems from proliferation in the Middle East, tension on the Korean peninsula, regional conflict in the Great Lakes region in Africa, and state failure in Somalia and Liberia, to organised crime in Afghanistan and the Balkans. The document described terrorism as a "key threat" which was "global in its scope", and the foundation for a strategic outlook which was strikingly similar to that of NATO: "In an era of globalisation, distant threats may be as much a concern as those that are near at hand."

All of this could create the impression that NATO and the EU were emulating each other and were engaged in a competition to become the preferred international security actor for the European area and beyond. There were, however, signs that some level of accommodation could be possible between the two organisations. In spite of its global ambitions, there was at least one part of the world beyond Europe where conflict was rife, yet where NATO appeared unlikely to become fully involved and content to let the EU take the lead. Since the disastrous outcome of its involvement in Somalia in 1993-94, followed by the 1998 bombings of US embassies in Kenya and Tanzania, the USA had been reluctant to become involved in military operations in Africa, a reluctance borne out in Liberia in 2003. Judgements could change, particularly as the United States became more interested in Africa, but for some time it had been thought unlikely that Africa could become a major commitment for NATO. Yet it was just as difficult to imagine the EU not becoming increasingly involved in Africa, when confronted by state failure, economic degradation, and social collapse.

There would be no straightforward division of labour between NATO and the EU, whether geographical or functional, although there could be some kind of an inter-institutional modus vivendi over Africa. But without agreement at the highest political levels that NATO and the EU should not duplicate their efforts, the trend was inevitably in the direction of competition rather than co-operation.

OPERATIONAL COLLABORATION between NATO and the EU was enabled by the so-called "Berlin Plus" arrangement, by which the EU could draw upon NATO military assets and planning capabilities (see AR 2002, p. 398). The EU mounted two operations under Berlin Plus—"Operation Concordia" in Macedonia and "Operation Althea" in Bosnia & Herzegovina—which increased the EU's operational experience considerably. European forces had also undertaken other military missions not under the auspices of NATO or Berlin Plus. Gradually, the EU was acquiring experience which many assumed could never happen in the absence of a general transatlantic security consensus. In early 2005 both NATO and the EU became involved in providing airlift support to the African Union mission (AMIS II) for its peacekeeping operations in the Darfur region of Sudan. The EU also provided military assistance in the form of technical, planning, and management support, working closely with NATO in a joint strategic air transport cell in Addis Ababa, the capital of Ethiopia. Procedurally, regular meetings took place in 2006 between the military committees of both NATO and the EU, and for planning purposes each had its own permanent liaison team embedded in the other organisation, at SHAPE (Supreme Headquarters Allied Powers Europe) and EUMS (Military Staff of the European Union), respectively.

There were some grounds for optimism as far as operational collaboration was concerned between the EU and NATO. Yet at the political level there were lingering doubts as to the wisdom of such co-operation. In its 2006 annual review, the UK-based think tank, the International Institute for Strategic Studies, found "persistent difficulties in NATO-EU co-operation", and noted that both organisations found it "difficult to strengthen their strategic dialogue". Once again, the absence of a high-level agreement on the relationship between NATO and the EU threatened to undermine practical co-operation. One suggestion which received a good deal of attention during 2006 was that of the Washington-based Centre for Strategic and International

Studies, which argued for a "Berlin Plus in reverse", whereby NATO would seek to draw upon the European Union's so-called "soft power" strengths in non-military crisis management. Yet again, however, it was clear that without high-level agreement on a robust and durable rationale for NATO-EU co-operation, the hard and soft, military and civil assets of each organisation could scarcely be exploited to best effect.

RAPID REACTION FORCE PLANNING offered a close illustration of the problem. Here, the efforts of NATO and the EU were strikingly similar, albeit on different levels of capability. Nevertheless, given compatibilities in training and operational standards, and given that there was only one pool of military manpower to serve both initiatives, there ought to have been grounds for collaboration between NATO's Response Force (NRF) and the EU's battlegroup (EUBG) project. But there were doubts as to the effectiveness of the EUBG project, even when full operating capability was reached, due to be in 2007, and it was clear that, even at full capacity, one force would in military terms have an "operational" capability (NATO), while the other would be merely tactical (EU).

At full capacity, the NRF should be in a position to deploy a brigade-sized land component (i.e., four or five battlegroups), a naval task force involving an aircraft carrier battle group, an amphibious task group, and a surface action group, enough combat aircraft to mount 200 sorties each day, and with special forces as necessary. The EUBG project, on the other hand, envisaged a reserve of 13 designated battlegroups (four national and nine multinational), each of about 1,500 troops, reaching full operating capability in 2007. From 2007, the EU's intention was to be able to mount two EUBG operations simultaneously, with two battlegroups at readiness to move on a six-month rotation. This was a much smaller scale of operations than that envisaged for the NRF, and even then doubts remained as to the military efficacy of the EUBG project. In the first place, the lack of dedicated strategic airlift was a major deficiency. Battlegroups could also vary in the quality of training, in their military capability, and in their readiness to deploy. There were even disagreements as to the basic mission of the EUBGs, and whether the primary role should be expeditionary operations or territorial defence. Most important of all, the battlegroups were mainly ground forces, with very few naval and air assets attached, although some progress was made by the EU on "naval enablers" and on a "rapid response air initiative". NRF and EUBG could not, therefore, be compared like-for-like. Deconfliction (the organisation of operations to minimise interference) between the two force structures was declared to have been achieved, but during 2006 it was clear that much more still needed to be done to generate positive and constructive co-operation in scenario and contingency planning, training and certification, and in logistics and communications.

Both organisations made slow progress in RESOURCE AND CAPABILITY PLANNING. Since neither organisation had met expectations, it would be prudent not to expect too much in terms of co-operation in this area. There was a relationship between NATO and the EU in capability development, but not one that could be described as healthy and productive. During 2006 it was evident that co-operation between NATO's 2002 Prague Capabilities Commitment (PCC) on the one hand, and the EU's 2001 European Capabilities Action Plan (ECAP) and 2004 European Defence Agency (EDA) on the other, needed much more momentum (see AR 2002, pp. 396-97; AR 2004, p. 373).

Neither PCC nor ECAP/EDA was meeting expectations, implying that co-operation between the two sides might not yet prove fruitful. The diagnosis was not entirely gloomy, however. Both organisations established liaison mechanisms on capability development and there were some successful cases of co-operation; NATO's Strategic Airlift Interim Solution (SALIS) launched in March 2006, for example, involved 16 countries, 14 of which were EU member states. In some cases collaboration had more tangible results; in the development of interoperable communications capabilities for EU forces, for example, EU agencies collaborated with NATO's Consultation, Command and Control Agency. Similarly, the European Defence Agency's project to develop a "Long Term Vision" for Europe's military requirements in the longer term (published in October 2006) was drawn up with the advice of NATO's Allied Command Transformation, International Staff, and International Military Staff, and was been closely co-ordinated with NATO's own "Future Vision", due to be published in 2007.

A working and productive relationship between NATO and the EU in capability development was surely essential. But to date, too much of the relationship was focused on procedural matters, and too little on the practical requirement for common capabilities. The capability relationship was alive in 2006, but only just. What was needed for 2007 and onwards was a focus on lower-level, but rather more achievable, targets, such as the rationalisation of airlift and sealift co-ordination centres, and the determination that NATO-EU co-operation in capability should be demand-led, rather than institution-focused.

Finally, the security relationship between NATO and the EU was least developed in arguably the most immediate and important area of security and defence policy, RESPONSES TO TERRORISM. Both organisations acknowledged the need for policy co-ordination, at the very least. High level meetings were held regularly between NATO's North Atlantic Council and the EU's Political and Security Committee, addressing such issues as counter-terrorism policy and the proliferation of chemical, biological, radiological and nuclear weapons and materials. Yet it proved difficult to move the NATO/EU counter-terrorism relationship much beyond rhetoric and process to real policy substance; one analyst described the relationship in mid-2006 as "woeful". While all could agree that there was a strong case for co-operation, it was the differences in approach—in style, focus, and tempo—that best described EU/NATO co-operation in counter-terrorism rather than the similarities. To a considerable extent, the weakness of the relationship reflected fundamental differences between the two organisations: one was a politico-military alliance with a well-developed strategic culture, while the other was a more complex civil organisation which was still uncertain about its role in security and defence policy. Even in its preferred "civil" approach to counter-terrorism, the EU was criticised for a lack of common vision and co-ordination, and for a lack of policy coherence among member states and within the institutions of the EU. In September 2006, following a meeting in Tampere, Finland, the EU's counter-terrorism and cross-border policing plans were described as being "in tatters".

During 2006 measures were considered which could improve the NATO/EU counter-terrorism relationship, such as the development of standardised warning and alert procedures between NATO and the EU, and agreement on procedures by which NATO could "back-fill" national requirements for key equipment, assist in the deployment of forces and their logistic support, and offer assistance in counter-terrorism operational planning. Steps such as these could, in time, make it possible to achieve what was most needed for effective counter-terrorism co-operation between NATO and the EU: the full and frank exchange of terrorism-related intelligence.

In many key areas of security policy and practice, the achievement of effective and efficient co-operation between NATO and the European Union was frustrated by the absence of what might be called a "grand bargain" between the two organisations, a high-level political agreement on positive and constructive co-existence. Since any such agreement on constructive co-existence would need to be validated by practical outcomes in operations and equipment, for example, the result was that the relationship between NATO and the EU became circular and self-defeating, lacking both cause and effect.

Perhaps the moment had come to break the cycle, by abandoning the reliance upon, or expectation of, a grand-strategic arrangement between NATO and the EU from which all other things would flow. Instead, in order to create a virtuous circle of efficient and mutually supportive co-existence between the two organisations, the solution might be to concentrate on the "bottom-up" achievement of what was actually required in the real world of security risks and challenges, rather than on the distant and somewhat abstract goal of an institutional accommodation between the North Atlantic Alliance and the European Union. In time, through a process of "learning by doing", practical co-operation might well lubricate the highly politicised and intractable transatlantic security debate which had for so many years proved to be an impediment to effective co-operation.

ECONOMIC ORGANISATIONS

International Monetary Fund (IMF)

DATE OF FOUNDATION: 1945 HEADQUARTERS: Washington DC, USA
OBJECTIVES: To promote international monetary co-operation and to assist member states in establishing sound budgetary and trading policies
MEMBERSHIP (END-'06): 184 members
MANAGING DIRECTOR: Rodrigo Rato y Figaredo (Spain)

World Bank (International Bank for Reconstruction and Development (IBRD) and International Development Association (IDA))

DATE OF FOUNDATION: 1945 HEADQUARTERS: Washington DC, USA
OBJECTIVES: To make loans on reasonable terms to developing countries with the aim of increasing their productive capacity
MEMBERSHIP (END-'06): 184 members
PRESIDENT: Paul Wolfowitz (USA)

World Trade Organisation (WTO)

DATE OF FOUNDATION: 1995 (successor to General Agreement on Tariffs and Trade, GATT) HEADQUARTERS: Geneva, Switzerland
OBJECTIVES: To eliminate tariffs and other barriers to international trade and to facilitate international financial settlements
MEMBERSHIP (END-'06): 149 acceding parties
DIRECTOR GENERAL: Pascal Lamy (France)

Organisation for Economic Co-operation and Development (OECD)

DATE OF FOUNDATION: 1965 HEADQUARTERS: Paris, France
OBJECTIVES: To promote economic growth in member states and the sound development of the world economy
MEMBERSHIP (END-'06): Australia, Austria, Belgium, Canada, Czech Republic, Denmark, Finland, France, Germany, Greece, Hungary, Iceland, Ireland, Italy, Japan, South Korea, Luxembourg, Mexico, the Netherlands, New Zealand, Norway, Poland, Portugal, Slovakia, Spain, Sweden, Switzerland, Turkey, UK, USA (total 30)
SECRETARY GENERAL: Angel Gurria (Mexico)

DISCUSSIONS about the functions and structure of international economic institutions grew more intense in 2006 with significant contributions from high level officials such as the governor of the Bank of England. There was a widespread sense that the institutional architecture created in the aftermath of World War II (and of the depression of the 1930s) was no longer well adapted to the present world economy, but there was much less agreement on the reform of specific institutions or how they should relate to one another. The institutions discussed in this article constituted only one part, albeit a major one, of a much larger debate that embraced the United Nations, other international institutions such as the Bank for International Settlements, as well as national regulatory authorities.

The ways in which the world of 2006 differed from that in 1946 shaped the various calls for reform from different groups and interests. First, the move from a world of fixed exchange rates, capital controls, and limited free trade to one of floating rates, free capital movements, and open economies had undermined the original role of bodies such as the IMF and led to calls for a new set of "rules of the game" to prevent or contain threats to the stability of the international financial system and to minimise the international spill-over effects of inconsistent national policies. Here, the voices of the developed countries tended to be loudest. Neo-liberal views that such matters could be left to market forces were in a minority, the emphasis in 2006 being on reform of existing institutions to handle the externalities of global economic activity. Second, the number of independent states had grown from under 80 in 1946 to over 190 and most of the "new" states were developing countries, unhappy with the control of international economic institutions by the "old" states and their influence on development policies. The increased weight of Asia in the world economy both strengthened the voice of "new" countries in demanding a more legitimate and democratic governance of these institutions and increased the willingness of the "old" countries to respond, since they needed the co-operation of countries such as China and India in handling global externalities and risks to economic stability. Third, there was growing awareness of the need to address the inter-connectedness of issues such as economic and social development, the environment, pandemic diseases, post-conflict reconstruction, and so forth. The broad objective—creating the foundations for security and a prosperous and endurable peace—was the same as in 1946, but the route had changed and was, perhaps, more complex.

INTERNATIONAL MONETARY FUND (IMF). The IMF attempted to reform itself in response to three broad and related factors: an emerging crisis in its own finances; its declining influence in many parts of the world, especially among middle-income emerging economies; and criticism from member governments about its governance and its policy record. The Fund's financial problems arose from a sharp fall in its traditional revenue as a result of pre-payment of its loans by major clients: Argentina, Brazil, and Indonesia in 2004-05, Uruguay and the Philippines in 2006; and at the end of the year Ecuador announced that it would follow suit. Pre-payment strengthened the Fund's balance sheet and left it with abundant liquidity but it was forced to draw on reserves to finance its running costs, including those for administering the poverty reduction and growth facility (PRGF) and the exogenous shocks facility (ESF). A declining loan book, from more than US$100 billion three years before to less than US$20 billion, combined with running costs of some US$1 billion, pointed to yearly deficits from 2007. An expert group was set up in May to examine ways to secure the Fund's financial future; it was due to report in early 2007. It was widely noted that the crisis underlined the inequitable nature of IMF financing: essentially, a number of middle-income developing countries were financing both assistance to poorer members and the provision of public goods, the costs of which should be borne by all members.

The reasons for pre-payment of IMF debt varied, but most of the countries involved emphasised their desire to escape from the intrusive conditionality attached to loans, which restricted their ability to adopt policies for their particular circumstances. Some of the critics from the developed countries agreed that the IMF intruded excessively on domestic policy space; the USA and the UK, for example, wanted the Fund to focus more on monitoring the macro-economic policies of systemically important countries and promoting orderly exchange rates. In April, the Fund was mandated to seek agreement among the countries most concerned on policies to reduce global current account imbalances and thus the risk of financial crisis. By the end of the year there was little agreement either on the causes of the problem or on the nature of the Fund's surveillance role.

At its annual meeting in September, the quotas of China, Mexico, South Korea, and Turkey were raised from 5.41 per cent (in aggregate) to 7.07 per cent, but those of other developing countries, including India, were reduced, while the advanced economies remained dominant. The second phase, to be agreed by spring 2008, would include a doubling of the "basic" vote to protect the existing share of low-income countries and a revision of the method for calculating quotas. The latter promised to be controversial since the redistribution of votes would depend on the definition of GDP and the other variables to be considered. The judgement of most developing countries and independent observers was that the 2006 reform was minor and when completed would still leave the advanced economies in firm control of the organisation.

THE WORLD BANK. Paul Wolfowitz's first year as president was not free of controversy. Aside from internal arguments over management structures, the more public controversy concerned the Bank's anti-corruption drive. There was some confusion about the programme in the early months—the Bank was criticised for ignoring corruption when it made two loans to Kenya in January—and at its spring meeting the Bank's board of directors called for the approach to be clarified; a new draft of the strategy was presented for approval to the annual meeting in September. Doubts concerned the definition and identification of corrupt practices, the consistency of their application across countries, and fears that the approach was too narrow.

In the meantime assistance was withheld from several countries, including India, Argentina, and Chad, but this led to mixed reactions from the board of directors, some of whom regarded political issues as outside the Bank's mandate. These concerns were highlighted by the UK's threat to withhold a £50 million contribution to the International Development Association (IDA, part of the World Bank) unless the Bank eased its loan conditions and tackled corruption in a wider framework of institutional improvement rather than risk penalising the poor. At the annual meeting in September, the Bank's governing body decided that it would have the final say in implementing the strategy, a decision interpreted by some European governments as giving the shareholders control of the Bank's governance policies. In December the UK released the £50 million to IDA after a report from the Bank claimed that it had reduced the number of conditions attached to its loans. A study commissioned by the Norwegian government concluded in November, however, that there had been little change in the conditions regarding privatisation and trade liberalisation.

Although the Bank came under a lot of criticism in 2006, this should be seen in the context of a broader debate about the effectiveness of aid in general and the appropriate conditions to be attached to it.

Concerning the Bank's own governance, the president accepted that it would have to reform its voting structure in favour of developing and transition countries. An internal study of what the changes at the IMF implied for the Bank was under way before the end of the year.

WORLD TRADE ORGANISATION (WTO). The WTO had a difficult and disappointing time in 2006. Despite persistent efforts by the director general to persuade the participating countries to narrow their differences, the Doha round of trade negotiations remained deadlocked and was finally suspended on 23 July (see AR 2005, pp. 356-57). Although there were more than 20 areas mandated for negotiation, the key stumbling blocks were—and remained—agriculture, non-agricultural market access (NAMA), services, rules (anti-dumping, subsidies, and so on), and the promised development dimension of the Doha round. Although press coverage highlighted the disputes between the USA and the EU over agriculture, the reluctance of the developing countries to accept developed country demands for greater access to their markets was also a key factor. In July, ministers from six participants—Australia, Brazil, the EU, India, Japan, and the USA—attempted to resolve the differences, but they were simply too wide. The trade negotiations committee therefore accepted the director general's suggestion to suspend the negotiations and encourage a period of reflection by member governments. Informal contacts continued and by November he was confident that the negotiations would resume early in 2007, although there was little sign that entrenched positions had changed significantly. It had also become increasingly clear that the development content of the round was negligible and that this would make it difficult for developing countries to make further concessions. A number of analysts suggested that the round had been on the wrong track from its start and that it was unlikely to produce an equitable outcome. Such views found support in the admission by the former US trade representative, Charlene Barshefsky, that there was never much enthusiasm for the round in the first place—it was mainly agreed out of solidarity with the USA after the 11 September 2001 attacks—and despite the rhetoric about a "development round", the richer countries were never in a position to deliver it.

A task force on aid for trade, established in February, issued a set of recommendations in the summer. These were intended to help developing countries overcome the obstacles that prevented them from taking advantage of more open markets. Their focus was on technical assistance, building institutional capacities, infrastructure investment, and adjustment assistance. The WTO role was not to engage directly in such activities but to promote "coherence" with funding agencies and regional banks by promoting the need for trade-promoting investments and projects as a complement to Doha.

The *WTO World Trade Report*, which reviewed trade developments in 2005, contained a lengthy analysis of subsidies, their role in correcting market failures, and their possible distortionary effects on international trade. The secretariat's November report on anti-dumping measures in the first half of 2006 confirmed a continuing decline in the number of new investigations (down 17 per cent on a year earlier), China being the most frequent object of these investigations.

The general council approved Vietnam's membership of the WTO (effective from January 2007) on 7 November. This would take the membership to 150.

ORGANISATION FOR ECONOMIC CO-OPERATION AND DEVELOPMENT (OECD). At the end of May Donald J. Johnston completed his second five-year term as secretary-general of the OECD and was succeeded by Angel Gurria, former finance minister of Mexico. Addressing the OECD council meeting in May, Gurria suggested a number of areas in which OECD co-operation should be extended. These included: reducing economic inequalities, poverty being "the ultimate systemic threat"; investing in human capital, understood to include better health and quality of life; addressing the issue of clean water supply in the context of the UN's Millennium Development Goals; and dealing with the pressing issues of climate change and energy security. In November, Gurria "strongly" endorsed "the major direction of the [Stern] report that argues that the benefits of early action [on climate change] far outweigh the costs" (for summary see pp. 561-64). He also stated that the OECD was ready to discuss the financial implications of enlarging its membership. A mechanism for identifying candidates was established in July. Extending the OECD's influence by increasing its membership and co-operating more with other countries was a priority of OECD ministers.

At their council meeting, ministers stressed the continued need for economic reforms, but it was notable that emphasis was given to the problems of implementation when economic needs clashed with social objectives. Thus, it was important to explain to electorates why particular reforms were necessary, not to obfuscate the costs and exaggerate the benefits, and to give more attention to building domestic coalitions for reform. This was a different language from the "no gain without pain" rhetoric of market fundamentalists.

Both ministers and the secretariat were broadly happy with the recent period of sustained growth without significant overheating. In its November *Economic Outlook*, the secretariat expected a mild slowdown in the global economy as growth and cyclical positions were "re-balanced", growth accelerating in the EU and slowing in the USA. The analysis was confident of a "soft landing" in the USA and was not greatly worried about adjustments in house prices: household balance sheets were strong and debt servicing burdens were moderate. There was more concern that benign economic conditions might weaken commitments to correct structural fiscal deficits and pursue reforms—in the labour markets, and in health and social security systems, for example—that were considered essential for sustaining growth over the longer term.

The OECD Forum 2006 brought together ministers and a wide range of civil society to debate the theme of "balancing globalisation", a sequel to the 2005 council meeting that focused on "enabling globalisation". The debates covered policies for growth, for enhancing social cohesion, and the need to co-ordinate national policies. The message that policy interventions and co-operation between governments were essential for making globalisation acceptable and successful partly reflected concerns about growing protectionism but also echoed the arguments for reforming the IMF and other international institutions.

The OECD was not only a "think tank": its members were also committed to a range of agreements, arrangements, guidelines, and conventions. One of these, the 1997 Convention on Combating Bribery of Foreign Public Officials in International Business Transactions, received considerable attention in December after the UK government stopped a Serious Fraud Office inquiry into allegations of bribery in UK sales of defence equipment to Saudi Arabia (see p. 212). The chairman of the OECD's working group on bribery stressed that the Convention required that such inquiries should not be influenced by considerations of national economic interest or the potential effect on relations with another state, and thus the UK action was a matter of serious concern for the credibility of the Convention. The UK's explanation and any possible action were due to be considered in March 2007.

OTHER WORLD ORGANISATIONS

THE COMMONWEALTH

DATE OF FOUNDATION: 1931 HEADQUARTERS: London, UK

OBJECTIVES: To maintain political, cultural and social links between (mainly English-speaking) countries of the former British Empire and others subscribing to Commonwealth democratic principles and aims

MEMBERSHIP (END-'06): Antigua & Barbuda, Australia, The Bahamas, Bangladesh, Barbados, Belize, Botswana, Brunei, Cameroon, Canada, Cyprus, Dominica, Fiji (suspended), the Gambia, Ghana, Grenada, Guyana, India, Jamaica, Kenya, Kiribati, Lesotho, Malawi, Malaysia, Maldives, Malta, Mauritius, Mozambique, Namibia, Nauru, New Zealand, Nigeria, Pakistan, Papua New Guinea, St Kitts & Nevis, St Lucia, St Vincent & the Grenadines, Samoa, Seychelles, Sierra Leone, Singapore, Solomon Islands, South Africa, Sri Lanka, Swaziland, Tanzania, Tonga, Trinidad & Tobago, Tuvalu, Uganda, UK, Vanuatu, Zambia (total 53)

SECRETARY GENERAL: Don McKinnon (New Zealand)

THE only region of the world without a Commonwealth member was the Middle East. It followed that, in a year dominated politically by the war in Iraq and the ever deteriorating situation in the countries of that region, Commonwealth concerns in 2006 were concentrated elsewhere. Politically, the quest for greater democracy and good governance was an ongoing priority. A setback came at the end of the year with the coup in Fiji (see pp. 356-57). The Commonwealth ministerial action group (CMAG) quickly convened in London under the chairmanship of Malta's foreign minister, Michael Frendo, and Fiji was for a second time "suspended from the councils of the Commonwealth", on 8 December. Fiji had left the Commonwealth after a coup in 1987 and returned in 1997, but a further coup in May 2000 had led to its suspension. With civilian government back in place Fiji was restored to full membership in December 2001 (see AR 2001, p. 426). Under Commonwealth rules agreed at the 1995 Commonwealth Heads of Government Meeting (CHOGM) in Auckland, New Zealand, a suspended country was barred from official meetings, but other Commonwealth activity—especially the work of the non-governmental organisations—continued. The point was always made that suspension was an act directed against governments and not the peoples of the country.

The Commonwealth's other membership problem remained Pakistan. A CMAG meeting held in New York on 23 September, during the UN General Assembly gatherings, again examined Pakistan's progress towards fully democratic rule. The CMAG repeated the Commonwealth view that the holding of both offices of head of state and chief of army staff by President General Pervez Musharraf was incompatible with the basic principles of democracy, and that until this changed "the process of democratisation in Pakistan will not be irreversible."

Although only Pakistan and Fiji remained on the CMAG agenda, several other countries were being helped under the "good offices" system. This entailed visits by special envoys, usually eminent Commonwealth figures appointed by Secretary General Don McKinnon. In 2006 former Prime Minister Joe Clark and former Foreign Affairs Minister Christine Stewart of Canada engaged with Cameroon on the reform of election management, human rights, the judiciary, and decentralisation; former Governor-General Sir Paul Reeves of New Zealand helped promote dialogue between the political parties in Guyana; former Nigerian head of state General Abdulsalami Abubakar tried to strengthen the electoral commission and judiciary in The Gambia; former Deputy Prime Minister of Malaysia Tun Musa bin Hitam tried to further electoral reform in the Maldives; and New Zealand's former justice minister, Sir Douglas Graham, was sent to Tonga. On 16-17 November McKinnon took the process further by convening the special envoys in London to discuss options, strategies, and techniques for conflict prevention and resolution.

As part of the governance programme McKinnon also convened in London a meeting of 30 international bodies (31 May-1 June) to discuss the principles of election observation. The African Union (AU), European Commission, Organisation of American States (OAS), UN Development Programme (UNDP), and the governments of Switzerland, Ireland, and Japan participated.

At Commonwealth ministerial meetings, increasing emphasis was put on the needs of youth and on the greater involvement of young people in Commonwealth activities. At the Commonwealth youth ministers meeting in Nassau, Bahamas (24- 26 May), young people from civil society organisations sat alongside ministers and made frequent interventions. The meeting put forward an enlarged 10-year plan for youth empowerment under which young people would become more involved in programmes concerned with the eradication of poverty, democracy and good governance, HIV/AIDS, and gender equality. Ministers were alarmed by the rising incidence of youth violence, pointing to high unemployment and unstable family relationships. Governments were urged to prioritise the empowerment of young people when developing policy in the economic and social spheres.

The importance of sport in easing these problems was highlighted at a meeting of Commonwealth sports ministers on 15 March, on the eve of the successful 18th Commonwealth Games in Melbourne, Australia (see p. 518). Ministers agreed to persuade sport and health ministries to work together to promote healthy living through sport programmes. Examples were quoted of the way in which football had been used in nine African countries in a "kick out AIDS" programme, and of the use of sport in Fiji and Tonga to combat obesity.

When education ministers met in Capetown, South Africa, on 11-14 December, civil society organisations again played a more visible role. Ministers heard that some member countries had achieved universal primary education, but that others were in danger of not meeting the agreed targets. On the plus side was the creation of the Virtual University of the Small States of the Commonwealth, an achievement of the Commonwealth of Learning based in Vancouver, Canada (a Commonwealth agency established to promote distance learning). At a cost of £1.5 million, the Virtual University would help small states produce, adapt, and use courses and learning materials which it would be difficult for one state to produce alone.

Increasingly, meetings of Commonwealth ministers were being convened on the fringes of international gatherings. In 2006 women's affairs ministers met in New York on 26 February on the eve of the 50th session of the UN commission on the status of women; environment ministers met on 6 February on the eve of the UN ministerial environment forum in Dubai; and health ministers met on 21 May alongside the World Health Organisation (WHO) meetings in Geneva, Switzerland, as they had done for many years. Also, in Geneva the Commonwealth Secretariat organised a meeting of 60 countries on "aid for trade" (21-22 March). The aim was to strengthen developing countries' ability to negotiate in a new World Trade Organisation (WTO) task force on aid for trade set up by its director general, Pascal Lamy (see p. 388).

FRANCOPHONE AND PORTUGUESE-SPEAKING COMMUNITIES

International Organisation of Francophonie (OIF)

DATE OF FOUNDATION: 1997 HEADQUARTERS: Paris, France
OBJECTIVES: To promote co-operation and exchange between countries wholly or partly French-speaking and to defend usage of the French language
MEMBERSHIP (END-'06): Albania, Andorra, Belgium, Benin, Bulgaria, Burkina Faso, Burundi, Cambodia, Cameroon, Canada, New Brunswick (Canada), Québec (Canada), Cape Verde, Central African Republic, Chad, Comoros, Republic of Congo, Côte d'Ivoire, Democratic Republic of Congo, Djibouti, Dominica, Egypt, Equatorial Guinea, France, French-speaking community of Belgium, Gabon, Greece, Guinea, Guinea-Bissau, Haiti, Laos, Lebanon, Luxembourg, Macedonia, Madagascar, Mali, Mauritania, Mauritius, Moldova, Monaco, Morocco, Niger, Romania, Rwanda, St Lucia, São Tomé & Príncipe, Senegal, Seychelles, Switzerland, Togo, Tunisia, Vanuatu, Vietnam (total 53 plus 2 associate members)
OBSERVER MEMBERS: Armenia, Austria, Croatia, Czech Republic, Georgia, Hungary, Lithuania, Mozambique, Poland, Serbia, Slovakia, Slovenia, Ukraine
ASSOCIATE MEMBERS: Cyprus, Ghana
SECRETARY GENERAL: Abdou Diouf (Senegal)

Community of Portuguese-Speaking Countries (CPLP)

DATE OF FOUNDATION: 1996 HEADQUARTERS: Lisbon, Portugal
OBJECTIVES: To promote political, diplomatic, economic, social and cultural co-operation between member-states and to enhance the status of the Portuguese language
MEMBERSHIP (END-'06): Angola, Brazil, Cape Verde, East Timor, Guinea-Bissau, Mozambique, Portugal, São Tomé & Príncipe (total 8)
EXECUTIVE SECRETARY: Luís de Matos Monteiro da Fonseca (Cape Verde)

A summit year saw heightened activity for the International Organisation of Francophonie (OIF). The 11th biennial summit of the organisation was held in Bucharest, capital of Romania, on 28-29 September, and was attended by over 40 heads of state and government, and delegations from all but five of its 68 members and observers. These included, apart from President Jacques Chirac at what was almost certainly his last francophone summit as France's leader, over 20 African presidents, including the chairman of the African Union, President Denis Sassou Nguesso of the Congo Republic, and African's longest serving head of state, Gabon's president, Omar Bongo Ondimba. Ivoirian President Laurent Gbagbo, whose relations with France were poor, was absent, although he sent his prime minister, Charles Konan Banny.

The prime minister of Canada, Stephen Harper, was attending his first such summit following his election late in 2005, alongside Quebec Prime Minister Jean Charest, both supporting Quebec's successful candidacy to be host of the 12th summit to be held in 2008. This decision followed the OIF ministerial conference held in the city of Winnipeg, Canada, in May, attended by 50 member countries, with the theme of human security. The president of the Swiss Confederation, Moritz Leuenberger, and the Belgian prime minister, Guy Verhofstadt, were also present, as well as important delegations from a number of east European countries, some of which (Albania and Macedonia) were attending for the first time as full members, as was Greece, and, with the new status of "associate", Cyprus. Also present with observer status were Austria, Croatia, Czech Republic, Hungary, Lithuania, Poland, Serbia and Slovenia, as well as Armenia, Georgia, and Ukraine, even if only a very small percentage of their populations spoke French, although Romania fancied itself as a bastion of French culture in the east, one reason why it was ready to host the summit. Andorra was also admitted as a full member, joining Monaco, the other sovereign mini-state existing within the French Republic.

France had made a point of wooing new members or observers (there was in practice little substantive difference in status between the two) from the former eastern bloc, partly to help in its efforts to build a stronger French sphere of influence within the European Union. Most of the eastern European members were also members of the EU, which accounted for the presence of one important guest, José Manuel Barroso, president of the European Commission, doubtless with one eye on the impending EU membership of Romania and Bulgaria, which were both full members of OIF. In the closing press conference, Chirac pointedly drew attention to the fact that when the two countries joined on 1 January 2007, the members of the OIF would be a majority within the EU (the same could not, however, be said of French-speakers). This thrust to the east, and the implications of enlargement, elicited some nervous commentaries: one headline in the French daily newspaper, *Le Monde*. spoke of a "crisis of growth".

There was, however, little reaction from the African membership which had often dominated proceedings in the past, especially as the secretary general, Abdou Diouf, former president of Senegal, was reappointed unanimously for a further four years. The official Romanian website, after listing every single European head of delegation, right down to Monaco and Andorra, simply said that African states were represented at a "very high level". However, the African participation in the OIF also increased, with Ghana becoming an "associate" and Mozambique achieving observer status. The contrast with the British Commonwealth, which did not share the OIF's linguistic preoccupation and had more or less resisted new members since 1997, could not have been more striking.

The European emphasis at the summit diverted attention to some extent from the increasing problems that the grouping was facing in the Arab world. These came to the surface in the row around the absence of President Emile Lahoud of Lebanon and that country's prime minister, Fouad Siniora. It was reported that President Chirac had put pressure on Romania's President Traian Basescu to withdraw the invitation to the pro-Syrian Lahoud, in the tense international climate which followed Israel's military assault upon Lebanon in the middle of the year (see pp. 197-203). This resulted in Siniora's declining to attend because of the tensions surrounding what some saw as an unwarranted interference in Lebanese affairs. Chirac and the Romanians were thus left in some embarrassment, especially as Lahoud, as head of state, had been the official host of the 9th summit in 2002, although the French presidential spokesman denied that any pressures had been exerted on the Romanians. Lebanon was represented by its minister of culture, Tarek Mitri. There were other symptoms of a malaise. President Abdelaziz Bouteflika of Algeria, who had attended the last two francophone summits (without his country actually being either a member or observer), was conspicuously absent, leaving only the regular members, Tunisia, Morocco, and Egypt, from that region. Mauritania was the only Arab country represented by its head of state. The Middle East, however, figured prominently in the summit's Bucharest declaration, with a call for the "integral application" of UN Resolution 1701, which called for an immediate ceasefire in Lebanon (for text see pp. 528-31). An attempt to include a strong resolution on the conflict in the Darfur region of Sudan was watered down at Egypt's insistence.

The official theme of the conference was "information technology and education", which was also the main theme in the Bucharest declaration. This dealt in particular with the "digital divide" between the rich and poor, and there was a second resolution of support for the recently established francophone digital solidarity fund. Other conference resolutions dealt with international migration and development, an issue of concern to both sub-Saharan African as well as Mediterranean countries; the issue of the unlawful depositing of toxic waste in Abidjan a month earlier (there was no agreement on a broader resolution on the Côte d'Ivoire crisis, despite French pressure); climate change (Canadian pressure reportedly limited the force of this resolution on support for the Kyoto Agreement); and support for the UN peace-keeping mission to Central African Republic.

Apart from opening and closing speeches, the main set-piece of the conference was the presentation of the report of the secretary general, which dealt with the main issues that had confronted the organisation in the previous two years. These included the continued support for democracy and human rights; cultural and linguistic diversity (in support of the UNESCO movement in that respect, strongly backed by France and the OIF); the challenges of the information society and the francophone presence in the "international media landscape"; education, higher education, training and research; and solidarity and sustainable development. Diouf claimed that the OIF was a "renewed organisation", and that an international strategy was evolving.

The conference also issued a directive to member states on the use of French in international organisations, and listened to the case for the two countries seeking to host the summit in 2010, Madagascar and Democratic Republic of Congo, whose presidents were both in attendance, although both were in the middle of election campaigns. Prior to the summit there was a meeting of the Association of Francophone Mayors.

The highlight of 2006 for the COMMUNITY OF PORTUGUESE-SPEAKING COUNTRIES (CPLP) was the staging of the sixth conference of heads of state and government. The gathering in Bissau, on 17 July (see p. 257), came exactly 10 years after the CPLP had been created. In celebration, the prime ministers of all eight member states stated their commitment to achieving the UN's Millennium Development Goals, and in particular, the eradication of extreme poverty and hunger. Time was devoted to evaluating several flagship projects including the centres of excellence in business development and public administration, located in Luanda and Maputo (the capitals of Angola and Mozambique), respectively. The role of the International Institute of Portuguese Language, in Cape Praia (Cape Verde), was also assessed and, in closing the conference, the organisation's determination to become a recognised international entity was affirmed. Executive Secretary Monteiro da Fonseca stressed the significance of the CPLP on the world stage through its member states' distribution over four continents, with a land surface area in excess of 10 million sq km and a total population of more than 220 million people.

Discussions were also held in Lisbon on 8 June when CPLP ministers assembled to determine progress in combating the use of child workers in their respective countries, and to work towards eliminating the worst forms of the phenomenon by 2016.

NON-ALIGNED MOVEMENT AND DEVELOPING COUNTRIES

Non-Aligned Movement (NAM)

DATE OF FOUNDATION: 1961 HEADQUARTERS: rotating with chair
OBJECTIVES: Originally to promote decolonisation and to avoid domination by either the Western industrialised world or the Communist bloc; since the early 1970s to provide a authoritative forum to set the political and economic priorities of developing countries; in addition, since the end of the Cold War to resist domination of the UN system by the USA
MEMBERSHIP (END-'06): Afghanistan, Algeria, Angola, Antigua & Barbuda, Bahamas, Bahrain, Bangladesh, Barbados, Belarus, Belize, Benin, Bhutan, Bolivia, Botswana, Brunei, Burkina Faso, Burma (Myanmar), Burundi, Cambodia, Cameroon, Cape Verde, Central African Republic, Chad, Chile, Colombia, Comoros, Congo, Côte d'Ivoire, Cuba, Democratic Republic of Congo, Djibouti, Dominica, Dominican Republic, East Timor, Ecuador, Egypt, Equatorial Guinea, Eritrea, Ethiopia, Gabon, the Gambia, Ghana, Grenada, Guatemala, Guinea, Guinea-Bissau, Guyana, Haiti, Honduras, India, Indonesia, Iran, Iraq, Jamaica, Jordan, Kenya, Kuwait, Laos, Lebanon, Lesotho, Liberia, Libya, Madagascar, Malawi, Malaysia, Maldives, Mali, Mauritania, Mauritius, Mongolia, Morocco, Mozambique, Namibia, Nepal, Nicaragua, Niger, Nigeria, North Korea, Oman, Pakistan, Palestine, Panama, Papua New Guinea, Peru, Philippines, Qatar, Rwanda, St Kitts & Nevis, St Lucia, St Vincent & the Grenadines, São Tomé and Príncipe, Saudi Arabia, Senegal, Seychelles, Sierra Leone, Singapore, Somalia, South Africa, Sri Lanka, Sudan, Suriname, Swaziland, Syria, Tanzania, Thailand, Togo, Trinidad & Tobago, Tunisia, Turkmenistan, Uganda, United Arab Emirates, Uzbekistan, Vanuatu, Venezuela, Vietnam, Yemen, Zambia, Zimbabwe (total 118)
ACTING CHAIRMAN: Raúl Castro (Cuba) (since Sept '06)

Group of 77 (G-77)

DATE OF FOUNDATION: 1964 HEADQUARTERS: UN centres
OBJECTIVES: To act as an international lobbying group for the concerns of developing countries
MEMBERSHIP (END-'06): Afghanistan, Algeria, Angola, Antigua & Barbuda, Argentina, Bahamas, Bahrain, Bangladesh, Barbados, Belize, Benin, Bhutan, Bolivia, Bosnia & Herzegovina, Botswana, Brazil, Brunei, Burkina Faso, Burma (Myanmar), Burundi, Cambodia, Cameroon, Cape Verde, Central African Republic, Chad, Chile, China, Colombia, Comoros, Congo, Costa Rica, Côte d'Ivoire, Cuba, Democratic Republic of Congo, Djibouti, Dominica, Dominican Republic, Ecuador, East Timor, Egypt, El Salvador, Equatorial Guinea, Eritrea, Ethiopia, Federated States of Micronesia, Fiji, Gabon, the Gambia, Ghana, Grenada, Guatemala, Guinea, Guinea-Bissau, Guyana, Haiti, Honduras, India, Indonesia, Iran, Iraq, Jamaica, Jordan, Kenya, Kuwait, Laos, Lebanon, Lesotho, Liberia, Libya, Madagascar, Malawi, Malaysia, Maldives, Mali, Marshall Islands, Mauritania, Mauritius, Mongolia, Morocco, Mozambique, Namibia, Nepal, Nicaragua, Niger, Nigeria, North Korea, Oman, Pakistan, Palestine, Panama, Papua New Guinea, Paraguay, Peru, Philippines, Qatar, Rwanda, St Kitts & Nevis, St Lucia, St Vincent & the Grenadines, Samoa, São Tomé and Príncipe, Saudi Arabia, Senegal, Seychelles, Sierra Leone, Singapore, Solomon Islands, Somalia, South Africa, Sri Lanka, Sudan, Suriname, Swaziland, Syria, Tanzania, Thailand, Togo, Tonga, Trinidad & Tobago, Tunisia, Turkmenistan, Uganda, United Arab Emirates, Uruguay, Vanuatu, Venezuela, Vietnam, Yemen, Zambia, Zimbabwe (total 130)
CHAIRMAN: Thabo Mbeki (South Africa)

THE 14th conference of heads of state or government of the NON-ALIGNED MOVEMENT (NAM) was held in Havana, Cuba. It opened on 11 September at the level of senior officials, moved to the level of foreign ministers after two days, and to the summit level on 15-16 September. It had been assumed that Cuba's President Fidel Castro Ruz would chair the summit, but he was too weak after undergoing surgery in July (see pp. 149-50) and his brother Raúl Castro Ruz took the chair. Much of the work of the summit was prepared by a ministerial meeting of the Co-ordinating Bureau in Putrajaya, Malaysia, on 27-30 May. The membership of the NAM increased from the previous summit in February 2003, with the addition of Antigua & Barbuda and Dominica at the Bureau meeting and St Kitts & Nevis and Haiti at the Havana summit. As Cyprus and Malta had left the NAM upon joining the EU, in May 2004, the net increase in membership was from a total of 116 to 118 countries.

The hostilities in Lebanon (see pp. 197-203) were of major concern at the summit. The organisation clearly took sides, with a "strong condemnation of the relentless Israeli aggression" and support for the "heroic resistance" of the people of Lebanon, but Hezbullah—the Shi'ite military organisation which had engaged Israel—was not directly mentioned. The NAM "rejected the collective punishment of the Palestinian people" for the election of Hamas in January 2006 and there was intense anger at Israeli military action in Gaza in mid-2006 (see pp. 186-91). Both the Bureau meeting and the summit endorsed "the establishment of the independent state of Palestine in all of the Palestinian Territory occupied by Israel in 1967". This was their most significant support for a "two-state solution", because the NAM had never before accepted Israel's borders.

Despite the deep hostility to the US-led invasion of Iraq in 2003, the summit expressed strong support for the new government of Iraq, resulting from the December 2005 elections. There was no suggestion of any willingness to condone the attacks on Coalition forces in Iraq. Instead, all acts of terrorism and "sectarian sedition" in the country were condemned and there was an appeal to Iran and Syria to assist the Iraqi government to defeat terrorism. Equally, the lack of sympathy for Islamic fundamentalist movements showed in the absence of any mention of Ethiopian intervention in Somalia and full support for the beleaguered Somali government (see pp. 232-34). Furthermore, in the section on Afghanistan, the former Taliban cadres were described as "terrorist groups" and Pakistan was implicitly criticised for the "protection and shelter" that the Taliban received.

Many points in the summit's declaration expressed implied hostility towards the USA and this became explicit in support for the governments of Syria, Cuba, and Venezuela in resisting US pressure upon them. However, a special statement on "Iran's nuclear issue" was notable for the absence of any direct criticisms of US policy towards Iran and for its failure to support the Iranian government, except to warn against "any attack" upon the country. In addition, the NAM insisted that all safeguards and verification questions should be resolved within the framework of the International Atomic Energy Agency (IAEA), a position that could be interpreted as being equally critical of both the USA and Iran.

The Havana meeting was the first summit of the NAM not to issue a detailed analysis of the problems of globalisation, development, international finance, and the burden of debt. None of the specific proposals from the Cuban government for co-operation on illiteracy, training health personnel, or on a project planning agency were endorsed. There was "serious concern" over the breakdown in the World Trade Organisation negotiations in July (see pp. 388-89) and developed countries were blamed for failing to demonstrate "flexibility and political will". Tensions arose within the NAM between oil producing and oil importing countries over the steady increase in the price of oil from early 2004, but this was papered over by agreement on the need for "greater stability and predictability" in the market. The publication of the *World Investment Report 2006* showed that south-south co-operation was beginning to bear fruit in a significant manner in the private sector, with transnational corporations being based in 87 developing countries and their cross-border activities being primarily in the local region.

The developing countries, operating through the GROUP OF 77 (G-77) caucus at the United Nations, came into an unprecedentedly high level of conflict with both the developed countries and the secretary-general over the question of management reform for the UN Secretariat. In May, they forced through a General Assembly resolution, using their voting majority to insist that all budgetary, procurement, personnel, and management policy decisions of the secretary-general were subject to approval by the General Assembly. Three weeks later, a special ministerial meeting of the G-77 in Malaysia, devoted solely to this subject, reviewed the outcome and rededicated the Group to the UN as an effective development institution. The NAM summit in September also endorsed a wide-ranging critique of the UN reform process. It met with success in its call for a successor to Kofi Annan, as UN secretary-general, to be chosen from an Asian country, but failed in its argument that the General Assembly rather than the Security Council should take the lead in the selection process (see pp. 361-62).

The NAM summit agreed that the next summit, in 2009, would be hosted by Egypt. Radio Havana reported that the meeting had agreed to establish a support unit in New York, aimed at overcoming the movement's lack of a secretariat, but the report was overly optimistic on this perennial question, as the issue had not been decided but only referred forward for further discussion. In June, the NAM News Network, an Internet news service, was formally launched in Malaysia, with news organisations from 35 Non-Aligned countries as the initial contributors. The leaders of the land-locked developing countries took the opportunity of their meeting in Havana to hold their first summit meeting, on the day before the NAM summit began. At the end of 2006, South Africa handed the chairmanship of the G-77 to Pakistan for 2007.

ORGANISATION OF THE ISLAMIC CONFERENCE (OIC)

DATE OF FOUNDATION: 1969 HEADQUARTERS: Jeddah, Saudi Arabia
OBJECTIVES: To further co-operation among Islamic countries in the political, economic, social, cultural and scientific spheres
MEMBERSHIP (END-'06): Afghanistan, Albania, Algeria, Azerbaijan, Bahrain, Bangladesh, Benin, Brunei, Burkina Faso, Cameroon, Chad, Comoros, Côte d'Ivoire, Djibouti, Egypt, Gabon, the Gambia, Guinea, Guinea-Bissau, Guyana, Indonesia, Iran, Iraq, Jordan, Kazakhstan, Kuwait, Kyrgyzstan, Lebanon, Libya, Malaysia, Maldives, Mali, Mauritania, Morocco, Mozambique, Niger, Nigeria, Oman, Pakistan, Palestine, Qatar, Saudi Arabia, Senegal, Sierra Leone, Somalia, Sudan, Suriname, Syria, Tajikistan, Togo, Tunisia, Turkey, Turkmenistan, Uganda, United Arab Emirates, Uzbekistan, Yemen (total 57)
SECRETARY GENERAL: Ekmeleddin Ihsanoglu (Turkey)

OIC foreign ministers convened for their 33rd session in Baku, the capital of Azerbaijan, on 19-21 June. The session was held under the banner of "harmony of rights, freedoms and justice". The "Baku Declaration", adopted on the final day of the conference, expressed "deep concern over the growing tendency towards Islamophobia" and called for "concrete efforts to enhance dialogue and broaden understanding among civilisations, cultures and religions by promoting tolerance, respect for and freedom of religion and belief". It strongly condemned terrorism "in all its forms and manifestations", and denounced any attempts to link terrorism with any religion, culture, or people.

The conference reaffirmed that "speedy peaceful settlement of the Arab-Israeli conflict" was a principal objective of the OIC and the "key problem" for the Muslim ummah (community or people). It reiterated its support for the Arab peace initiative adopted at the March 2002 Arab League summit in Beirut (see AR 2002, pp. 206-07) and the "road map" peace plan and "land for peace" principle. It called upon the Middle East quartet (the EU, Russia, the UN, and the USA) speedily to resume the peace process and not to recognise "unilateral Israeli measures contradictory to the principles of the peace process".

On Iran's controversial nuclear programme, the declaration stated that the only way to resolve the issue was to resume negotiations "without any preconditions". It reaffirmed the "basic and inalienable right of all member states to develop research, production and the use of atomic energy for peaceful purposes in conformity with their respective legal obligations". The declaration also called for the establishment of a nuclear weapons-free zone in the Middle East and demanded Israel's accession to the Nuclear Non-Proliferation Treaty (NPT).

The declaration strongly supported the sovereignty and territorial integrity of Iraq and requested the OIC secretary general to explore "practical ways" of ensuring a strengthened OIC role in promoting peace and stability in that country. It strongly condemned the "aggression" of Armenia against Azerbaijan and urged "immediate, complete and unconditional withdrawal of Armenian occupying forces from the occupied territories of Azerbaijan". It reaffirmed the OIC's "solidarity" with "our Muslim brothers and sisters in Northern Cyprus" and appealed to the international community to make "all necessary efforts to put an end to the isolation of the Turkish Cypriots". It also reaffirmed support for the people of Jammu and Kashmir for their "inalienable right to self-determination". The declaration commended the "recent positive developments to achieve peace and national reconciliation in the Sudan" and also commended the establishment of all-inclusive Somali transitional federal institutions.

OIC information ministers held their seventh session in Jeddah (Saudi Arabia) on 13-14 June. Tourism ministers held their fifth session in Baku on 11-12 September. The eighth session of the standing committee on information and cultural affairs (COMIAC) was held in Dakar (the capital of Senegal) on 13-15 November, whilst the 22nd session of the standing committee for economic and commercial co-operation (COMCEC) was held in Istanbul (Turkey) on 21-24 November.

EUROPEAN UNION

DATE OF FOUNDATION: 1952 HEADQUARTERS: Brussels, Belgium
OBJECTIVES: To seek ever-closer union of member states
MEMBERSHIP (END-'06): Austria, Belgium, Cyprus, Czech Republic, Denmark, Estonia, Finland, France, Germany, Greece, Hungary, Ireland, Italy, Latvia, Lithuania, Luxembourg, Malta, Netherlands, Poland, Portugal, Slovakia, Slovenia, Spain, Sweden, UK (total 25)
PRESIDENT OF THE EUROPEAN COMMISSION: José Manuel Durao Barroso (Portugal)

SURGING world energy prices and fears over the security of supply of energy were dominant themes for the European Union throughout the year, affecting both internal and external policy. Other major initiatives were off the agenda, as the 2005 failure to ratify the European Convention continued to overshadow EU politics and European leaders pondered the implications of that rejection (see AR 2005, pp. 368-70). It was officially described as a "period of reflection" and was expected to run at least until the French presidential elections, scheduled for 2007. Neither the Austrian nor the Finnish presidencies had any appetite to reopen the debate on Europe's future during their respective six month terms of office.

ENERGY POLICY. When the Barroso Commission took office in 2004, creation of a European energy policy was of little interest to the largest members of the Union. In the first days of 2006, however, the dispute between Russia, in the form of Gazprom, and its neighbours Ukraine and Moldova, brought home to the EU its increasing dependence on its neighbour to the east, underlining the need to forge a coherent energy policy for the whole of the Union. The three-day cut in natural gas supplies to Ukraine, with their knock-on effects on western Europe, was seen as evidence of an economically resurgent Russia's willingness to use energy supply for political leverage (see pp. 105-07).

A sense of political urgency regarding energy policy finally materialised, having been raised seriously as a topic for concern and for a co-ordinated European response by UK Prime Minister Tony Blair at the Hampton Court summit two months earlier. With the Ukraine crisis, the member of the European Commission responsible for energy policy, the Latvian Andris Piebalgs, was thrust into the spotlight and into high politics.

From the Russian perspective, the European reaction was extraordinary and somewhat bewildering, but the damage to the relationship was swift, serious and irreversible. Despite acceptance of the fact that Russia had been an exemplary supplier of energy to its European neighbours over the years, including during the Cold War, blueprints for a common European energy policy were hastily drawn up. Once again, it was external events that gave the impetus for internal EU policy.

The Commission published a green paper which identified priority areas focused on three core pillars: sustainability, competitiveness, and security of energy supply. The time for a new energy century had arrived, announced Commission President José Manuel Barroso, arguing that, "the EU cannot afford 25 different, unco-ordinated energy policies".

At their summit meeting in March, European leaders discussed the Commission's paper, but it became evident that a fully harmonised common energy policy remained little more than a vision. Commission plans to ensure full liberalisation of the internal electricity and gas markets, to shift to a low carbon economy, and to speak with a single European voice to external energy suppliers were welcomed at the summit, but cautiously.

There were deep disagreements on the level of market oversight which should be exercised by national regulators and also by the Commission, especially in relation to emergency energy stocks. One clear area of concern, however, was "high and volatile energy prices". Together with tackling climate change and an increasing dependence on external energy sources, a mandate was given for development of further policy options later in the year.

Plans to create a central role for the Commission as European negotiator with regard to foreign energy policy were actively opposed behind the scenes by the member states, typifying the inter-institutional struggles plaguing the Union during the "pause for reflection" on the Constitution, which followed the breakdown of the Convention ratification process after the French and Dutch referendums of 2005.

Certainly there was a realisation that Europe was increasingly living in a world where competition for energy resources was intensifying, but there was no political will to speak as a single bloc toward its suppliers. France, Italy, and Germany in particular continued to seek bilateral energy deals with Russia. For the first time, though, the warnings with regard to Russian energy ambitions issued by some of the new member states, such as Poland, began to resonate. Polish proposals to establish a European Energy Security Treaty along the lines of the NATO principles of mutual guarantees and solidarity were rejected, but the path towards greater energy solidarity was set, together with an appreciation of the benefits of further physical energy interconnections between member states.

Eventually, at the June summit, a joint paper from the European Commission and Javier Solana, the EU high representative for common foreign and security policy, emerged. The paper acknowledged that "an effective external policy on energy depends on being able to harness our considerable collective resources and place them at the service of shared interests".

Nevertheless, the thorny issue of EU-Russia energy relations remained. From March onwards, President Barroso and Commissioner Piebalgs had sought a new way forward, one based on "security and predictability for both sides, paving the way for...fair and reciprocal access to markets and infrastructures", as Barroso put it, but progress continued to be painfully slow.

Fears for the security of energy supplies were raised again in the middle of the year when Russia's President Vladimir Putin seemed to advocate the routing of Russian supplies eastwards rather than westwards, in calling for further energy co-operation with China. Russia demanded security of demand in exchange for EU security of supply. Whenever the Commission sought to address the increasing regulatory uncertainty for European operators in Russia, the Russians pointed to continuing protectionism within the EU internal market.

In February the European Commission published a preliminary report on the workings of the EU's internal energy market. The report alleged serious flaws in the market. It highlighted the behaviour of the national incumbent operators in continuing to dominate their home markets, to stifle newcomers, and to set prices in an opaque manner. Competition Commissioner Neelie Kroes and her team underlined their serious intentions by launching a series of dawn raids on energy firms in May to investigate possible breaches of anti-trust rules. "Energy is vital to the competitiveness of the EU economy and yet we have found evidence of serious malfunctions. I am determined to use competition law to protect European industry and consumers", she stated.

These malfunctions were once again starkly demonstrated with the intervention by national governments in two major cross-border energy sector mergers: EoN/Endesa and Gaz de France/Suez (see pp. 65; 43).

As the year drew to a close, concerns over security of supply and relations with Russia continued to dominate. During the October "energy dialogue" in Moscow, Commissioner Piebalgs urged both the EU and Russia to improve mutual understanding and trust. "Russia needs the European Union just as much as the European Union needs Russia", he said. Repeated EU attempts to persuade Russia to adopt the Energy Charter fell on deaf ears, with Russia arguing convincingly that, with its provisions to allow greater access to natural resources and pipelines, the Charter put energy-producing countries at a disadvantage compared with energy consumers. However, it was an invitation from the Finnish presidency to President Putin to join European leaders for dinner at the end of the Lahti summit in October which came dangerously close to exposing the limits of EU external foreign energy policy. EU leaders managed to finalise their common position only shortly before the guest of honour arrived.

The dinner was by all accounts a tense affair, coming as it did in the wake of the murder of the Russian journalist Anna Politkovskaya, with talk of corruption and human rights (see pp. 107-08), but on energy Putin said that the EU and Russia were natural partners. He noted that the EU got 44 per cent of its gas from Russia, but that around 67 per cent of Russian gas exports went to the 25 EU member states, thus making Russia if anything more dependent on the European Union and its consumers than the other way around.

The strained united front projected at Lahti was reinforced from an unexpected quarter, following a Russian import ban on Polish meat products. In response, Poland forced the solidarity question when it imposed a veto in November, effectively halting the finalisation of a negotiating mandate for a new EU-Russia partnership and co-operation agreement (PCA) (see p. 81). The existing PCA was due to expire at the end of 2007 and would, the EU hoped, be replaced by a strategic partnership agreement where energy issues could play a central role.

At the end of the year, Energy Commissioner Piebalgs was preparing to issue an historic energy package. There was a clearer sense of purpose with regard to external energy relations and a growing realisation that energy supply and its attendant question of climate change would remain ongoing issues requiring EU attention and common solutions. It might yet even emerge as one of those most rare but crucial creatures—a legacy issue for the Barroso presidency.

CLIMATE CHANGE. In implementing the Kyoto Protocol, the EU had introduced an emissions trading scheme for carbon dioxide (CO2), whereby each member country was allocated a CO2 allowance which would then be distributed at a national level; but in May the fledgling scheme virtually collapsed as the prices for CO2 permits crashed. It became clear that the member states had massively over-allocated the carbon dioxide emission permits to individual installations, notably in the energy generation sector and to certain energy intensive industries, such as glass and cement.

Some saw the price crash as a threat to EU efforts to curb CO2 emissions but others viewed it as teething problems in the world's first attempt to establish a price for carbon. As a result, the Commission vowed to ensure that national plans for the second round of allowance allocations would be more rigorous and would be extended to the aviation sector, thereby signalling that the scheme was there to stay.

ENLARGEMENT. Antipathy to the further enlargement of the EU was widely assumed to be a factor behind the "no" votes against the European Convention in 2005, so although the Union was already committed to the accession of Bulgaria and Romania either in 2007 or 2008, there was clear political pressure on European institutions to demonstrate that the terms of accession were rigorous ones. Accession for Balkan states such as Croatia and Serbia promised to be difficult and as the year progressed the prospect of Turkish membership looked increasingly problematic.

In March the European Parliament approved a report which called on the European Commission to analyse the "absorption capacity" of the EU in relation to the accession of new member countries. Presented by MEP Elma Brok, the report reminded ministers that enlargement was conditional on there being adequate resources and called for the drafting of a framework for a "close multilateral relationship with the EU", which all countries with recognised membership prospects should be able to join as a halfway house to full membership.

Reference to the EU's absorption capacity was perceived by some as introducing a new element into the enlargement process. It implied for the first time that even if a candidate country met all the necessary criteria for joining the Union, there must still be confirmation from the EU side that the new member country could be accommodated. The European commissioner responsible for the enlargement negotiations, Olli Rehn, warned MEPs of the dangers of dwelling on the EU's absorption capacity, however. He said that it would be utterly irresponsible to disrupt a valuable process that was helping to build stable and effective partners in the most unstable parts of Europe. "For the sake of Europe, let us not shake this foundation," he concluded.

BULGARIA AND ROMANIA. The European Commission's report on the preparedness of these two countries for membership was published in May. It anticipated entry on 1 January 2007, but in what it described as a "carefully calibrated approach", it made this conditional on substantial progress in several areas and deferred its final recommendation until September, thus seeking to sustain the pressure on the two governments to show real progress on the sensitive areas where the Commission was not satisfied. "Both countries should be able to reach the finishing line on 1 January 2007", said Commission President Barroso, "but in order to do so, efforts must be intensified, especially in the reform of the judiciary and fight against corruption. I encourage the authorities in Bulgaria and Romania to take our recommendation as an incentive to finalise their preparations".

Bulgaria came in for the strongest criticism. It would need to demonstrate clear evidence of results in the fight against corruption, in terms of investigations and judicial proceedings, said the report. It would also need further to reform the judiciary, in particular to reinforce its transparency, efficiency, and impartiality (see p. 93).

As for Romania, it should continue its efforts and demonstrate further results in the fight against corruption, consolidate the implementation of its ongoing justice reform, and further enhance the transparency, efficiency and impartiality of the judiciary (see pp. 90-91).

The Commission published its final recommendations on 26 September. It recognised that although further tangible results were needed, substantial progress had been made. It confirmed 1 January 2007 as the recommended date for accession, but also announced a mechanism for assessing progress for each country in the areas of judicial reform and corruption. Safeguard clauses would allow penalties if sufficient progress were not made in the coming years.

Newly re-elected Bulgarian President Georgi Purvanov was not happy with these safeguard clauses. He believed that Bulgaria had reached the same level of preparedness as the ten countries which had joined in 2004.

On 17 October the European Council of Ministers gave its approval to the Commission's recommendations and on 28 November the European Parliament approved the appointment of European commissioners from each of the countries, to take office on 1 January 2007.

THE BALKANS. Negotiations on the Croatian application to join the EU made progress during the year. In October, 12 months after the formal opening of talks, the Commission reported on the progress which Croatia was making in reforming its governmental and judicial structures, and although there were still concerns, the accession process remained on track (see p. 97).

It was a different story for Serbia. The Serbs' failure to work with the UN's International Criminal Tribunal for the former Yugoslavia (ICTY) in arresting suspected war criminal Ratko Mladic resulted in a suspension of the stabilisation and association agreement (SAA, the precursor to accession talks) with the EU on 3 May (see p. 103). Serbia's recognition of newly independent Montenegro was welcomed, but the report was critical of aspects of the new Serbian constitution, citing the lack of objective mechanisms free of political influence for promoting and dismissing judges and prosecutors and the ambiguous relationship between domestic and international law. The EU recognised Montenegro as a sovereign and independent state on 12 June. Negotiations on an SAA began in September (see p. 105).

An SAA was signed with Albania in June (see p. 94). Much broader military and security questions dominated relations with Bosnia & Herzegovina, although talks continued on developing an SAA for that country (see p. 97).

TURKEY. It was a fraught year for EU relations with Turkey, whose journey towards EU membership was set against the background of a grudging European public opinion, some negative developments in Turkey, and a sceptical view from some political leaders, especially in Austria, France, and Germany (see pp. 75-76). German Chancellor Angela Merkel showed no enthusiasm for Turkish accession, whilst the two main candidates for the French presidency, Ségolène Royal and Nicolas Sarkozy, both appeared to favour some other basis for relations, often described as a "privileged relationship" which would fall short of being a full EU member, a formula that the Turks had consistently rejected.

Notwithstanding ongoing reservations, the decision had been taken in November 2005 to open negotiations and in January 2006 the EU Council of Ministers followed up with agreement on the principles, priorities and conditions for negotiations. Formal negotiations with Turkey began on 12 June, with 35 policy areas to be negotiated, but the Turkish High Court's refusal to dismiss charges against Turkish-Armenian journalist Hrant Dink for insulting Turkishness worsened an already difficult diplomatic atmosphere. "I am disappointed by this judgment, which limits the exercise of freedom of expression in Turkey", Commissioner Rehn said in a statement.

The European Parliament's March report criticised Turkey, arguing that the pace of reform had slowed down. It called on the Turkish government to present as soon as possible a plan for further reforms, including a timetable and specific measures to meet the deadlines. In September a further European Parliament report said that Turkey had made insufficient progress in the areas of freedom of expression, minority rights, corruption, and violence against women, and this was followed on 8 November by a critical report from the European Commission. At the end of that month the Commission submitted its recommendations on the progress of negotiations, essentially proposing that they should be put on hold. The EU Council of Ministers approved this approach.

Talks were to be suspended on eight of the 35 chapters, due to the Turkish government's refusal to recognise the (Greek Cypriot) government of Cyprus and to offer Cypriot access to its ports and airports, as required under the Ankara protocol (see p. 74). A minor concession by Turkey was not accepted. EU negotiator Commissioner Olli Rehn said that the talks would slow down. "We will be able to return to normal speed as soon as Turkey has fulfilled its obligations related to the Ankara protocol", he said.

EUROPEAN UNION BUDGET. The hard-fought battle over the scale of the European budget for the period 2007-13 and the level of contributions from member states, which ended in a compromise agreement under the UK presidency in December 2005, still required approval at the turn of the year by the European Parliament, exercising its role as the joint budget authority of the Union. The Council of Ministers had agreed a total figure of €862 billion for the seven-year period (see AR 2005, pp. 370-72).

The Austrian presidency took office for the first six months of 2006 with the task of obtaining parliamentary approval for the budget. MEPs were pressing for an increased level of spending, which several member states were determined to resist. As negotiations reached their final phase the Parliament was demanding an additional €12 billion in spending, but this was reduced to €4 billion when agreement was reached on 4 April in negotiations between MEPs and ministers. This was finally voted in the Parliament on 17 May with the reluctant support of the three main political groupings. None was satisfied with the result, but all saw it as the best which could be achieved.

The Parliament's rapporteur, Reimer Böge, questioned whether the new budget was suitable for a Union of 25 countries, but said that "we have reached the very limits for an acceptable solution". He said that Parliament wanted reform of policy, new instruments, the cutting of red tape, guarantees for Parliament's input on foreign policy instruments, and a proper role in the 2008-09 review. "We have managed to get these qualitative aspects on board in a satisfactory way. As far as the figures are concerned, all sides have reached the pain threshold."

EUROPEAN ECONOMY. A resurgence in economic growth in Europe after several years of relative stagnation brought welcome relief to most eurozone countries during the year. Most significant was the recovery in Germany's economy with growth of up to 2.7 per cent, leading to higher budget revenues. The government deficit was expected to fall to 2.8 per cent of GNP for the year as whole, significantly below the 3 per cent target required by the Stability and Growth Pact and a one-year advance on the commitment made by the German government (see p. 39).

Less welcome to some was the strength of the euro, particularly for France and Italy, which had made much less progress in the restructuring of their economies. Whereas German politicians seemed unconcerned at the strength of the currency, the French prime minister, Dominique de Villepin, believed that it was too strong and questioned the exclusive role of the European Central Bank (ECB) in setting interest rates. There were six rate increases during the year, bringing the benchmark rate to 3.5 per cent by December as the ECB responded to the risk of mounting inflation.

The recovery in government revenues led to a big drop in the need for government borrowing across the eurozone as a whole. Government bond issuance was down by about 30 per cent over the previous year.

In July the Council of the EU adopted a decision that Slovenia should join the euro area from 1 January 2007. The euro would replace Slovenia's currency, the tolar, at the fixed and irrevocable conversion rate of 239.640 tolars to one euro (see p. 100). Plans to adopt the euro, which had been entertained by other countries such as Estonia, Hungary, and the Czech Republic which had joined the EU in 2004, faded further as they faced serious budget deficits, and 2010 became the earliest anticipated date. Poland would set no target date at all.

CHALLENGE TO THE SINGLE MARKET. The pace of financial restructuring and its impact on the economies of the EU countries led governments to show their colours as they faced up to the reality of foreign bidding for their national business champions. Despite a single European market and a European merger control mechanism, some governments used what powers they could to keep the national flag on their major companies.

The energy sector provoked the highest profile government responses. When Italy's ENEL made a bid for Gaz de France (GDF) in February, the French government intervened by proposing a merger with the Franco-Belgian group, Suez, to construct an essentially French group, announcing shortly afterwards that they intended to identify key sectors where government would have a right to intervene to protect national interests (see p. 43). This was followed by Spain, which tried to thwart the Germany company Eon's bid for Endesa by instructing the Spanish regulatory authority to impose unacceptable conditions on a merger with the German firm and inducing the Spanish firm, Gas Natural, to construct a merger (see p. 65).

For the European Commission these national actions posed a serious challenge. Its response was unequivocal. There could be no erosion of the basic EU principle of the free movement of capital and national governments could not ignore the Commission's competence for competition policy and design their own national energy markets.

In September the internal market commissioner, Charlie McCreevy, wrote to the French prime minister: "My deep conviction is that the special rights that the government is granting itself in order to control private companies is creating obstacles to direct investments and aiming to directly influence the management of companies, contrary to the single market".

While the French deal seemed likely to go ahead, Eon's bid remained on track as the Spanish government was forced to rethink its plans. Other examples of such economic nationalism were Italy's blocking of a €25 billion Spanish bid for Autostrada and the Polish government's efforts to prevent Italy's Unicredit from acquiring BPH, Portugal's second largest bank.

POLICY INITIATIVES. This was a year of reflection for European policy-makers. Neither the Austrian nor the Finnish presidencies had any wish to reopen the debate on the European constitution following the Dutch and French referendums of the previous year, so no new initiatives were forthcoming.

The Barroso Commission pursued its aims of creating a more business-friendly Europe, minimising the number of new legislative proposals, relying more heavily on assessment of the potential impact of new initiatives, and relying more heavily on consultation with business interests before putting forward new proposals. New proposals were kept to a minimum, especially in the areas of environment and employment policy. Introduction of REACH (Registration, Evaluation and Authorisation of Chemicals) was the most controversial and far-reaching piece of legislation, requiring as it did the testing of many thousands of chemicals before they could be authorised for sale on European markets.

The EU built on its capabilities to send forces to global trouble spots. It maintained troops in Bosnia & Herzegovina (EUFOR) in support of political stabilisation, and provided support in Democratic Republic of Congo (DRC) during the presidential elections there in July (see p. 259).

EUROPEAN ORGANISATIONS

THE COUNCIL OF EUROPE

DATE OF FOUNDATION: 1949 HEADQUARTERS: Strasbourg, France
OBJECTIVES: To strengthen pluralist democracy, the rule of law and the maintenance of human rights in Europe and to further political, social and cultural co-operation between member states
MEMBERSHIP (END-'06): Albania, Andorra, Armenia, Austria, Azerbaijan, Belgium, Bosnia & Herzegovina, Bulgaria, Croatia, Cyprus, Czech Republic, Denmark, Estonia, Finland, France, Georgia, Germany, Greece, Hungary, Iceland, Ireland, Italy, Latvia, Liechtenstein, Lithuania, Luxembourg, Macedonia, Malta, Moldova, Monaco, Montenegro (under application), Netherlands, Norway, Poland, Portugal, Romania, Russia, San Marino, Serbia, Slovakia, Slovenia, Spain, Sweden, Switzerland, Turkey, Ukraine, UK (total 47, including Montenegro)
SECRETARY GENERAL: Terry Davis (UK)

THE Council of Europe investigation into the existence of secret detention facilities in Europe and the so-called "extraordinary rendition" of prisoners by US authorities continued over the first half of the year. The rapporteur, Swiss Senator Dick Marty, released his report in June and presented it to the Parliamentary Assembly of the Council of Europe (PACE) for debate.

The report findings were that the USA had woven a "global spider's web" of disappearances, secret detentions, and unlawful inter-state transfers which encompassed much of Europe and other countries "notorious for their use of torture".

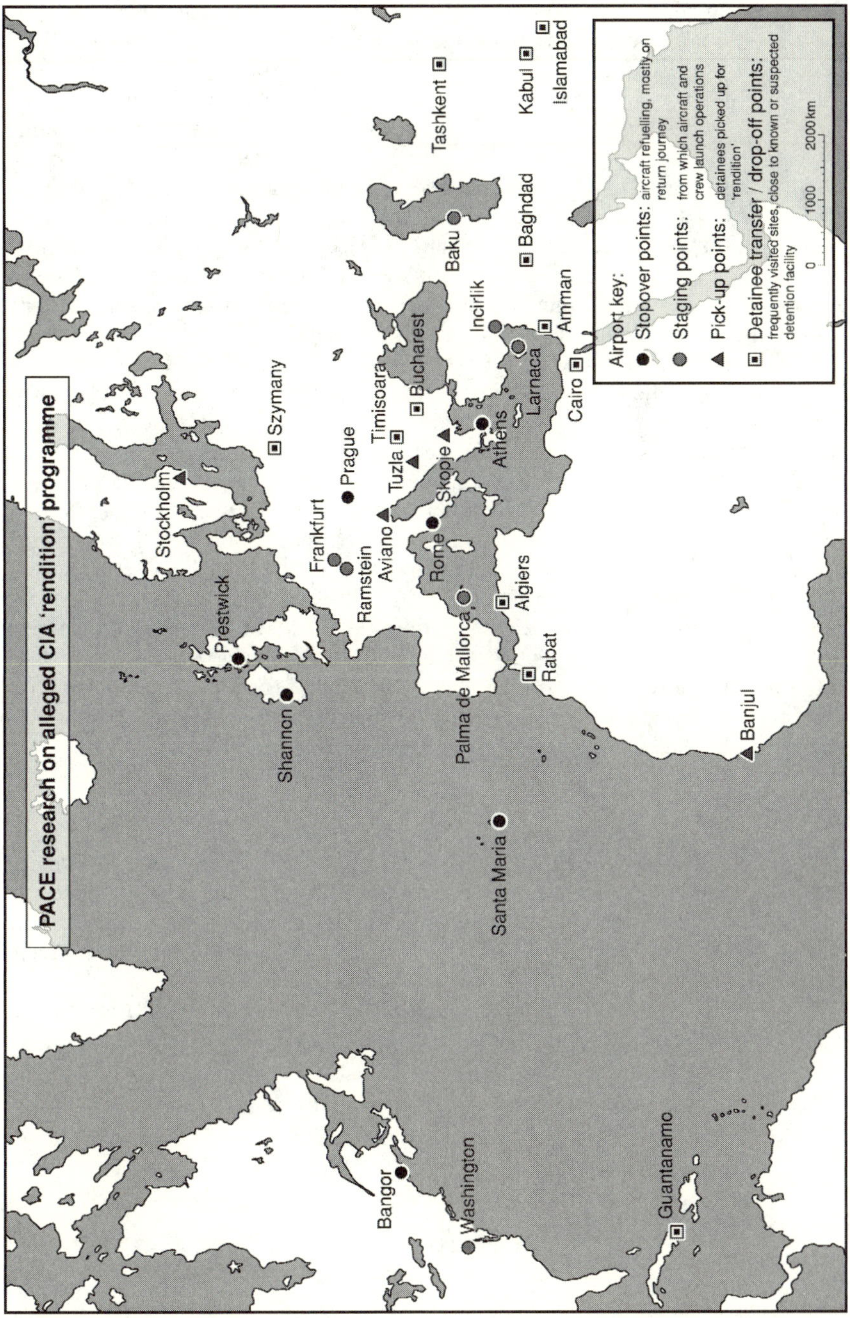
PACE research on alleged CIA 'rendition' programme
Stockholm
Szymany
Prestwick
Shannon
Frankfurt
Ramstein
Prague
Aviano
Tuzla
Timisoara
Bucharest
Skopje
Rome
Athens
Palma de Mallorca
Algiers
Rabat
Banjul
Santa Maria
Bangor
Washington
Guantanamo
Baku
Incirlik
Larnaca
Baghdad
Amman
Cairo
Tashkent
Kabul
Islamabad
Airport key:
Stopover points: aircraft refuelling, mostly on return journey
Staging points: from which aircraft and crew launch operations
Pick-up points: detainees picked up for 'rendition'
Detainee transfer / drop-off points: frequently visited sites, close to known or suspected detention facility
0 1000 2000 km

Fourteen member states of the Council of Europe were named as collaborating in these operations. Poland and Romania were cited as the "likely locations" for secret detention facilities.

A resolution adopted by the Parliamentary Assembly on 27 June called on Council of Europe member countries to review the legal framework regulating the intelligence services (for text see pp. 523-27). It urged its members to press for more investigation at the national level. Meanwhile the secretary general of the Council of Europe, Terry Davis, had used his prerogative to demand information from member countries. He said in December that they should demonstrate to their citizens that they were doing everything they could within the law to protect the safety and rights of their citizens. "Europeans know that security at the expense of freedom is neither lasting nor safe."

Measures designed to speed up the procedures of the European Court of Human Rights and allow the Court to function more effectively were blocked just before Christmas when the Russian Duma (the lower house of Russia's bicameral legislature) voted against ratification of protocol 14 to the European Convention on Human Rights. This protocol was designed to break the logjam facing the Court, which faced a caseload of 80,000-90,000 applications and was taking around six years to deal with cases. The protocol required ratification by all 46 member countries of the Council to become effective.

Budgetary constraints continued to bite on the activities of the Council. An increasing proportion of the €180 million budget had to be diverted to meet the costs of the European Court of Human Rights, so less money was available for other purposes. Campaigns were launched for the protection of children, for young people, and to protect the rights of the Roma, but these would be heavily dependent on funding from the member countries and from locally generated funds.

Luxembourg Prime Minister Jean-Claude Juncker made his recommendations for strengthening the relationship between the Council of Europe and the European Union. He proposed that by 2010 the EU should accede to the European Convention on Human Rights, recognising the Council as the "Europe-wide reference source" for human rights issues. The institutional relations between the two bodies should be strengthened, he said, and EU foreign ministers should become more involved in the Council's business.

Montenegro applied to join the Council of Europe following its declaration of independence from Serbia in June (see pp. 104-05). This would take the number of Council members to 47.

ORGANIZATION FOR SECURITY AND CO-OPERATION IN EUROPE (OSCE)

DATE OF FOUNDATION: 1975 HEADQUARTERS: Vienna, Austria
OBJECTIVES: To promote security and co-operation among member states, particularly in respect of the resolution of internal and external conflicts
MEMBERSHIP (END-'06): Albania, Andorra, Armenia, Austria, Azerbaijan, Belarus, Belgium, Bosnia & Herzegovina, Bulgaria, Canada, Croatia, Cyprus, Czech Republic, Denmark, Estonia, Finland, France, Georgia, Germany, Greece, Holy See (Vatican), Hungary, Iceland, Ireland, Italy, Kazakhstan, Kyrgyzstan, Latvia, Liechtenstein, Lithuania, Luxembourg, Macedonia, Malta, Moldova, Monaco, Montenegro, Netherlands, Norway, Poland, Portugal, Romania, Russian Federation, San Marino, Serbia, Slovakia, Slovenia, Spain, Sweden, Switzerland, Tajikistan, Turkey, Turkmenistan, Ukraine, UK, USA, Uzbekistan (total 56)
CHAIRMAN-IN-OFFICE (2006): Karel De Gucht (Belgium)

AT the annual ministerial council (Brussels, 4-5 December), the chairman-in-office, Belgian Foreign Minister Karel De Gucht, evoked two policy priorities, "tackling protracted 'frozen' conflicts and further improving OSCE efficiency," in response to the mandate for revitalisation determined by the previous year's council (see AR 2005, p. 377). Although, among such conflicts, he accepted that "it would be unwise to expect a solution in Brussels" for Nagorno-Karabakh through the "Minsk group" (see p. 117), the OSCE was actively involved in seeking settlements in Kosovo, Transdniester republic, and South Ossetia. Nevertheless, he warned, "there will be no peace or enduring security without due respect for human rights and freedoms". Responding at the Council, the secretary general of NATO, Jaap de Hoop Scheffer, assured collaboration because "NATO has broadened its agenda and it has done so in line with the objectives shared by the OSCE".

Similar liaison with the Council of Europe, pursuant to a Declaration of Co-operation of 2005 (see AR 2005, p. 378), brought a meeting in September between De Gucht and Russian Foreign Minister Sergei Lavrov, chairman of the Council's committee of ministers, on combating terrorism, trafficking in human beings, protecting national minorities, and fostering tolerance. The first collaborative outcome was an expert workshop (Vienna, 19-20 October) on how to fight incitement and related terrorist activities.

Prime among the OSCE's regular activities was the monitoring of elections and referendums in member states, through its Office for Democratic Institutions and Human Rights (ODIHR). On parliamentary elections in Azerbaijan in November 2005, it noted that "few effective sanctions were imposed on local executive authorities who interfered in the electoral process in violation of the law" (see AR 2005, pp. 111-12).

Visiting Albania in April, De Gucht urged the development of a legal framework and the modernisation of civil registration in advance of the 2009 parliamentary elections and signed an agreement to that end with the interior ministry. A conference on the role of women in the electoral process was held in Armenia in July.

The final report on the presidential election in Belarus, in March (see p. 110), concluded that it had been "severely flawed due to arbitrary use of state power and restrictions on basic rights" and condemned the arrest during the electoral campaign and subsequent trial and imprisonment of a presidential candidate, Alyaksandr Kazulin, together with many of his supporters. The head of the OSCE office in Minsk, Ake Peterson, visited Kazulin in prison.

A review of municipal elections in Georgia in October (see p. 116) accepted that they accorded with fundamental freedoms, but found that "the blurred distinction between the authorities and the governing party reinforced the advantage of the incumbents". The OSCE assessment mission to the Italian parliamentary elections in April (see pp. 45-46) made no observation of polling procedures, but monitored media coverage and the complaints and appeals process.

An ODIHR team in Kazakhstan in May pressed the authorities to bring electoral processes "into line with OSCE commitments and other international standards". In October, ODIHR monitored local elections in Kosovo and legislative elections in Latvia (see p. 83), approving its "competitive and pluralistic environment", but regretting the significant number of "non-citizens" without voting rights. At the invitation of the Dutch government, a team was deployed to monitor legislative elections in the Netherlands in November, with electronic voting of particular interest (see p. 51).

The OSCE refused to recognise constitutional referendums either in Nagorno-Karabakh in December—because that entity had not been recognised as an independent state and the Minsk process on its final legal status was ongoing (see p. 117)—or in the Transdniester republic in September, due to "the lack of basic requirements for free and fair elections" (see p. 114). The head of 900 observers (including 200 members of parliaments) from 45 countries which monitored parliamentary elections in Ukraine in March (see p. 111) enthused that they confirmed "the irreversible changes in Ukraine's democratic transformation. The door to Euro-Atlantic integration remains open."

In December the ODIHR opened an observation mission for the January 2007 parliamentary elections in Serbia. De Gucht visited Podgorica, Pristina, and Belgrade in January seeking to resolve conflict over Kosovo; Chisinau (Kishinev) in May, to assist negotiations to reintegrate the Transdniester republic into Moldova; Bucharest in June, to support the Minsk group over Nagorno-Karabakh; but "seriously regretted" the failure for "the third time in a row" of quadrilateral negotiations in Vladikavkaz in October between Georgia and separatist South Ossetia.

The OSCE police chiefs' meeting in Brussels in November launched a strategic police matters unit to pool resources on international policing assistance, and joined with the UN office on drugs and crime to avoid national duplication and increase co-ordination. Kevin Karty of Ireland was named senior police adviser. The Organisation also undertook various initiatives for protection of the environment, notably management of the Sava river basin and land degradation in Kyrgyzstan.

Montenegro became the Organisation's 56th member in June, choosing it as the first international agency which it would enter following the dissolution of its union with Serbia (which itself acceded to the former Serbia & Montenegro seat). Spain would succeed Belgium for the OSCE chairman-in-office for 2007, and Kazakhstan posed its candidacy for 2009 (see p. 287); the OSCE Parliamentary Assembly would hold its annual session there in 2008.

EUROPEAN BANK FOR RECONSTRUCTION AND DEVELOPMENT (EBRD)

DATE OF FOUNDATION: 1991 HEADQUARTERS: London, UK
OBJECTIVES: To promote the economic reconstruction of former Communist-ruled countries on the basis of the free-market system and pluralism
MEMBERSHIP (END-'06): Albania, Armenia, Australia, Austria, Azerbaijan, Belarus, Belgium, Bosnia-Herzegovina, Bulgaria, Canada, Croatia, Cyprus, Czech Republic, Denmark, Egypt, Estonia, European Investment Bank, European Union, Finland, France, Georgia, Germany, Greece, Hungary, Iceland, Ireland, Israel, Italy, Japan, Kazakhstan, Kyrgyzstan, South Korea, Latvia, Liechtenstein, Lithuania, Luxembourg, Macedonia, Malta, Mexico, Moldova, Mongolia, Montenegro, Morocco, Netherlands, New Zealand, Norway, Poland, Portugal, Romania, Russia, Serbia, Slovakia, Slovenia, Spain, Sweden, Switzerland, Tajikistan, Turkey, Turkmenistan, Ukraine, UK, USA, Uzbekistan (total 63)
PRESIDENT: Jean Lemierre (France)

THE Bank commemorated the 15th anniversary of its foundation reflecting on both its past and its future. A conference in its London headquarters in November noted that transition from planned to market economies had "brought economic growth, political freedom and a new way of life for many. But even in the most advanced countries, there are still parts of society, the country and the economy that have not prospered to the same extent as those in cities and industries that have led the transition." Those disparities were documented in the Bank's *Transition Report 2006* which showed them to be widest in the three Caucasus countries and Latvia.

The next phase in the Bank's programme would help its members to foster "political freedom and strong social structures to sustain the gains of transition". The largest single investor in the post-communist region, the Bank concentrated on private enterprises and usually partnered the capital of private investors. With complete transition to a market system signified by eight of its members having joined the European Union in 2004 and being set in 2010 to leave the Bank's recipient membership, the share in the Bank's portfolio of the other members reached 72 per cent at the start of the year. This was in conformity with its second quinquennial capital resources review (CRR2), under which, for the first time, non-sovereign loans accounted for more than half of the portfolio. Policies for CRR3 (2006-10) envisaged a cessation of lending to the EU members in the Bank (albeit coupled with monitoring whether existing projects among them were being carried out in conformity with Bank requirements); and for Bank members "at an earlier stage of transition" to have "a more active and direct policy dialogue" with other international financial institutions, such as the World Bank, the International Finance Corporation, European Investment Bank (EIB), and Asian Development Bank.

Among specific projects was the €10 million western Balkans multi-donor fund, created in May, and built upon the €88 million of new investments then under consideration for the region. The fund would develop capital markets, including securitisation, mortgage markets, and local currency financing. CCR3 would particularly address the weak capital base of enterprises and the underdeveloped infrastructure characterising those economies. An annual business volume of €3.3 billion to €3.9 billion was forecast for the period, which would be 23 per cent greater than during CRR2. Under the early transition countries initiative (see AR 2004, p. 402) donor funds alone had helped generate nearly 100 projects.

Also in May two new funds were launched: a sustainable energy initiative, whereby a €1.5 billion investment in energy efficiency and cleaner energy technologies over three years could lead to up to €5 billion in total investment, and a carbon credit fund established jointly with the EIB. The EBRD continued to extend credit to local banks for their support of small and medium enterprises (SMEs) and environmentally-friendly projects, some in collaboration with the European Commission. Among the former was a €10 million loan to a leading Bulgarian bank for local businesses involved in a wide range of products and services; while among the latter was US$7 million for mini-hydropower generation in Armenia, which would reduce that country's dependence on imported fuel.

During the year the Bank generated funds for new placements by selling some of its equity in past recipients now in successful operation. Thus, half its shares in Russia's Golden Telecom were sold, and smaller stakes sold of the Bank of Georgia. The EBRD successfully placed a 5 billion rouble (€147 million) bond with nine international and Russian banks and led its first 7.2 billion rouble (€212 million) long-term loan syndication for Moscow's power utility, Mosenergo.

The Bank came under criticism by the EU Court of Auditors for the ineffective expenditure of its loans to Romania and Bulgaria, and environmental concerns were voiced by the WWF (formerly World Wildlife Fund) over its financing of an offshore liquid natural gas pipeline on the Russian island of Sakhalin.

Revised country strategies were published for Albania, Estonia, Lithuania, Macedonia, Poland, Russia, Slovakia, and Turkmenistan, and the board of directors visited Azerbaijan, Macedonia, and Romania in advance of the formulation of country strategies.

In October Mongolia became the first non-European state to be admitted as an EBRD country of operations. As a precondition, an amendment of the Bank's founding treaty was required and was accepted by members in July.

OTHER EUROPEAN ORGANISATIONS

European Free Trade Association (EFTA)

DATE OF FOUNDATION: 1960 HEADQUARTERS: Geneva, Switzerland
OBJECTIVES: To eliminate barriers to non-agricultural trade between members
MEMBERSHIP (END-'06): Iceland, Liechtenstein, Norway, Switzerland (total 4)
SECRETARY GENERAL: Kare Bryn (Norway)

Visegrad Group

DATE OF FOUNDATION: 1991 HEADQUARTERS: rotating
OBJECTIVES: Originally, to reduce trade barriers between members with a view to their eventual membership of the European Union; since 2004, to continue developing the co-operation of the Visegrad Group countries as member states of the EU and NATO
MEMBERSHIP (END-'06): Czech Republic, Hungary, Poland, Slovakia (total 4)

Nordic Council

DATE OF FOUNDATION: 1952 HEADQUARTERS: Stockholm, Sweden
OBJECTIVES: To facilitate legislative and governmental co-operation between member states, with particular reference to proposals of the Nordic Council of Ministers
MEMBERSHIP (END-'06): Denmark, Finland, Iceland, Norway, Sweden (total 5)
SECRETARY GENERAL: Per Unckel (Sweden)

Baltic Council

DATE OF FOUNDATION: 1992 HEADQUARTERS: rotating
OBJECTIVES: To promote political, economic and social co-operation between the three Baltic republics
MEMBERSHIP (END-'06): Estonia, Latvia, Lithuania (total 3)

Central European Free Trade Agreement (CEFTA)

DATE OF FOUNDATION: 1992 HEADQUARTERS: rotating
OBJECTIVES: To promote regional stability and further membership of the EU
MEMBERSHIP (END-'06): Bulgaria, Croatia, Macedonia, Romania (total 4)

Central European Initiative (CEI)

DATE OF FOUNDATION: 1989 HEADQUARTERS: rotating
OBJECTIVES: To promote the harmonisation of economic and other policies of member states
MEMBERSHIP (END-'06): Albania, Armenia, Belarus, Bosnia & Herzegovina, Bulgaria, Croatia, Czech Republic, Hungary, Italy, Macedonia, Moldova, Montenegro, Poland, Romania, Slovakia, Slovenia, Ukraine, Serbia (total 18)
DIRECTOR GENERAL: Harald Kreid (Austria)

Black Sea Economic Co-operation Pact (BSEC)

DATE OF FOUNDATION: 1992 HEADQUARTERS: Istanbul, Turkey
OBJECTIVES: To promote economic co-operation between member states
MEMBERSHIP (END-'06): Albania, Armenia, Azerbaijan, Bulgaria, Georgia, Greece, Moldova, Romania, Russia, Serbia, Turkey, Ukraine (total 12)
SECRETARY GENERAL: Leonidas Chrysanthopoulos (Greece)

THE EUROPEAN FREE TRADE AREA (EFTA) pressed forward with efforts to broaden the range of countries with which it held free trade agreements. Upon taking up his post in September, the new secretary general, Kare Bryn from Norway, laid particular emphasis on reaching agreements with Asia and Latin America. EFTA and Peru had already endorsed a joint declaration on co-operation in Geneva in April, while in July an agreement was signed with the Southern Africa Customs Union, embracing Botswana, Lesotho, Namibia, South Africa, and Swaziland. Lesotho was the first least-developed country to become an EFTA partner. A free trade agreement with South Korea came into force in September; and, at Bogota in October, Colombia expressed an interest in launching negotiations which could lead to a free trade area agreement. As the year ended, EFTA and India agreed to launch a joint feasibility study, again with a view to negotiations over a comprehensive trade agreement. Sometimes, however, progress was frustratingly slow. Negotiations with Canada, which had started in 1998, continued but hopes of resolving the remaining issues by Christmas were disappointed.

It proved a challenging year for the VISEGRAD countries. Their former common objective had been to achieve membership of the EU and NATO. Now that this had substantially been achieved, what was to be the group's future, especially as its members were all in some measure afflicted by domestic political turbulence? Perhaps precisely because the group had not become institutionalised, but functioned mainly as a method of co-ordinating policies on remaining matters of common concern, it proved able to maintain a healthy level of activity despite "post-accession blues". One such common area of interest was energy policy, especially in the wake of Russia's clash with Ukraine over gas supplies and prices (see pp. 113; 400). In April a working group on energy discussed questions relating to research and development, emergency gas storage and facilities, construction of new gas and oil pipelines, and interconnecting power transmission systems. Other ministerial gatherings worked on common approaches to the free movement of labour, regional development, and issues arising from the EU's draft waste directive. In October the prime ministers of the four countries, marking the group's 10th anniversary, reaffirmed their commitment to working together effectively within the EU, with a particular emphasis on energy security and building relations with Benelux, the NORDIC COUNCIL, and the BALTIC COUNCIL. In November, the Visegrad and Baltic Council foreign ministers contemplated joining the Schengen area in 2007. However, it was feared that the impending enlargement of the EU would result in postponement. They also agreed to work for visa reciprocity with the USA.

In 1992 the "Visegrad four" had launched the CENTRAL EUROPEAN FREE TRADE AGREEMENT, with the aims of promoting their economic and political stability and joining the EU. They were later joined by Slovenia, Romania, Bulgaria, Croatia, and, in 2006, the Republic of Macedonia. However, the original members and Slovenia had departed upon joining the EU and Romania and Bulgaria were poised to do so, potentially leaving only Croatia and the Republic of Macedonia. In April, the South East Europe prime ministers agreed to expand CEFTA to the remaining Balkan states. These were already linked by a network of bilateral agreements as members of the 1999 Stability Pact for South-Eastern

Europe. At the prime ministers' December meeting it was formally agreed that Albania, Bosnia & Herzogovina, Moldova, the Republic of Montenegro, Serbia, and Kosovo (via the agency of UNMIK) would join the agreement in May 2007. (The Stability Pact would give way in 2008 to a Regional Co-operation Council of the countries of the region.)

Co-ordination and co-operation were also the watchwords of the CENTRAL EUROPEAN INITIATIVE (CEI), which welcomed Montenegro as its 18th member in August. The year's agenda included a projected Venice to Kiev pan-European transport corridor, how to create an innovation-friendly environment, monitoring the progress of those countries in south-eastern Europe that were working towards EU membership, and the development of e-government (electronic government) in the west Balkans. The annual summit of the Economic Forum in Tirana, Albania, in November, with the theme of innovation for sustainable growth, attracted a record attendance, with 36 countries represented. The meeting of heads of government emphasised the need for the CEI to co-ordinate with the new arrangements that would follow in the wake of the Stability Pact for South-Eastern Europe when it was phased out at the end of 2007 (see above).

With the extension of the EU's borders to the Black Sea imminent, the twelve countries of the BLACK SEA ECONOMIC CO-OPERATION PACT (BSEC) were also challenged to consider its future role. Turkey in particular argued for a comprehensive reform and restructuring of the pact, but little or no progress was made. This was not least because of tensions between countries preferring a Eurasian perspective and those favouring a more Euro-Atlantic approach. Fears were expressed about the dangers that the work of the organisation would become increasingly politicised. However, it was agreed that much could be achieved through measures to promote the security and stability of the region, to encourage democratisation and economic reforms, and to improve such areas as tourism, trade, crime, energy policy, regional transport, and environmental protection. Indeed, the length of this "shopping list" pointed to a continuing weakness in BSEC: a tendency to generate many projects in a wide variety of fields, which the organisation all too often lacked the financial resources or unity of purpose to implement successfully. Two of the most substantial advances during the year were a joint project with the United Nations Development Programme (UNDP) in November to promote economic growth and development in the region through closer economic co-operation, and a memorandum of understanding with the Eurasian Economic Community to increase co-operation between the two bodies. However, the most ambitious project under consideration was the proposed construction of a 7,000 km road network encircling the Black Sea, combined with a programme of improvement to ports and ferry services.

AMERICAN, ARAB, AFRICAN, EURASIAN, AND ASIA-PACIFIC ORGANISATIONS

AMERICAN AND CARIBBEAN ORGANISATIONS

Organisation of American States (OAS)

DATE OF FOUNDATION: 1951 HEADQUARTERS: Washington DC, USA
OBJECTIVES: To facilitate political, economic and other co-operation between member states and to defend their territorial integrity and independence
MEMBERSHIP (END-'06): Antigua & Barbuda, Argentina, Bahamas, Barbados, Belize, Bolivia, Brazil, Canada, Chile, Colombia, Costa Rica, Cuba (suspended), Dominica, Dominican Republic, Ecuador, El Salvador, Grenada, Guatemala, Guyana, Haiti, Honduras, Jamaica, Mexico, Nicaragua, Panama, Paraguay, Peru, St Kitts & Nevis, St Lucia, St Vincent & the Grenadines, Suriname, Trinidad & Tobago, USA, Uruguay, Venezuela (total 35)
SECRETARY GENERAL: José Miguel Insulza (Chile)

Southern Common Market (Mercosur)

DATE OF FOUNDATION: 1991 HEADQUARTERS: Montevideo, Uruguay
OBJECTIVES: To build a genuine common market between member states
MEMBERSHIP (END-'06): Argentina, Brazil, Paraguay, Uruguay, and Venezuela (total 5)
ASSOCIATE MEMBERS: Bolivia, Chile, Colombia, Ecuador, and Peru
ADMINISTRATIVE SECRETARY: Santiago Gonzalez Cravino (Argentina)

Andean Community of Nations (Ancom/CAN)

DATE OF FOUNDATION: 1969 HEADQUARTERS: Lima, Peru
OBJECTIVES: To promote the economic development and integration of member states
MEMBERSHIP (END-'06): Bolivia, Colombia, Ecuador, Peru (total 4)
SECRETARY GENERAL: Allan Wagner Tizón (Peru)

Caribbean Community and Common Market (Caricom)

DATE OF FOUNDATION: 1973 HEADQUARTERS: Georgetown, Guyana
OBJECTIVES: To facilitate economic, political and other co-operation between member states and to operate certain regional services
MEMBERSHIP (END-'06): Antigua & Barbuda, Bahamas, Barbados, Belize, Dominica, Grenada, Guyana, Haiti, Jamaica, Montserrat, St Kitts & Nevis, St Lucia, St Vincent & the Grenadines, Suriname, Trinidad & Tobago (total 15)
ASSOCIATE MEMBERS: Anguilla, Bermuda, British Virgin Islands, Cayman Islands, Turk & Caicos Islands
SECRETARY GENERAL: Edwin Carrington (Trinidad & Tobago)

Organisation of Eastern Caribbean States (OECS)

DATE OF FOUNDATION: 1981 HEADQUARTERS: Castries, St Lucia
OBJECTIVES: To co-ordinate the external, defence, trade and monetary policies of member states
MEMBERSHIP (END-'06): Anguilla, Antigua & Barbuda, British Virgin Islands, Dominica, Grenada, Montserrat, St Lucia, St Kitts & Nevis, St Vincent & the Grenadines (total 9)
DIRECTOR GENERAL: Len Ishmael (since May '03)

THE 36th regular session of the General Assembly of the ORGANISATION OF AMERICAN STATES (OAS) was held in June. The central theme of the meeting was "good governance and development in the knowledge-based society", a major challenge for the region. In December, environment ministers from the OAS signed the "Declaration of Santa Cruz + 10" in Santa Cruz, Bolivia, which was intended to provide a framework for hemispheric co-operation in the areas of sustainable development, environmental protection, and the management of resources and natural disasters. The document, whose title alluded to the 10th anniversary of the summit of the Americas on sustainable development, also held in Santa Cruz, contained a detailed strategic plan for improving the sustainable management of water, reducing the risks of natural disasters, and introducing truly sustainable farming, forestry, and tourism practices.

At the July presidential summit of the SOUTHERN COMMON MARKET (MERCOSUR) there was agreement to work together to increase trade, create jobs, and reduce poverty. The meeting included Mercosur's five permanent members (Venezuela formally joined the organisation at the summit, see AR 2005, p. 393) and three associate members. Venezuela's President Hugo Chávez Frías made his presence felt by urging the organisation to stand firm against US free-market policies in South America, which he argued had weakened the continent's economic standing. He also called for greater emphasis to be given to reducing poverty and creating jobs, arguing that Mercosur had much to learn from the policies of Cuban President Fidel Castro Ruz, who was attending the summit for the first time in three years. Although Cuba was not even an associate member of the group, Castro was present to sign an agreement with Mercosur on mutual trade preferences. Also at the summit Argentina's President Nestor Kirchner said he believed that Bolivia and Mexico should be allowed to join the organisation. However, this idea attracted criticism, with some commentators suggesting that Mercosur was in danger of losing its free trade focus and becoming more concerned with securing political influence.

In other developments concerning Mercosur members, Argentina strongly opposed plans by Uruguay to build two large paper pulp mills along the border. Argentina said that it feared pollution and the impact on tourism and fishing. The dispute went to the International Court of Justice, which ruled in favour of Uruguay, but Argentina pledged to continue its opposition (see pp. 168; 419).

In December, meanwhile, a Mercosur parliament was inaugurated in the Uruguayan capital, Montevideo. Its 90 members were drawn from the national parliaments of member countries, but its powers were only advisory.

The ANDEAN COMMUNITY (ANCOM/CAN) saw the departure of one of its members on 22 April when President Hugo Chávez Frías of Venezuela announced his country's withdrawal from the group. This move paved the way for Venezuela's subsequent membership of MERCOSUR (see above). Chávez argued in relation to the CAN that because Colombia and Peru had signed free trade agreements (FTAs) with the USA, the Community was "dead". He also accused fellow members of being overly aligned with the USA. In a related press release, the Venezuelan government stated that the FTAs had undermined the original purpose of the CAN by emphasising neo-liberal free trade that would lead to injustice, inequality, and exclusion. The governments of Colombia and Peru strongly disputed Venezuela's view. Nevertheless, despite Venezuela's formal withdrawal there was an understanding that it would take at least five years to bring the process to a close. Until then Venezuela would remain bound by the effects of the CAN's commercial agreements.

As expected despite an initial commitment that 12 CARIBBEAN COMMUNITY AND COMMON MARKET (CARICOM) members would join the Caribbean single market (CSM) on time, only six states were full members at the start of the year: Barbados, Belize, Guyana, Jamaica, Suriname, and Trinidad & Tobago. The official launch of the CSM was held on 30 January at the Mona Campus of the University of the West Indies in Jamaica. Then, on 3 July six countries of the ORGANISATION OF EASTERN CARIBBEAN STATES (OECS)—Antigua & Barbuda, Dominica, Grenada, St Kitts & Nevis, St Lucia, and St Vincent & the Grenadines—signed up to the single market. This was possible after an agreement was reached for the capitalisation of a regional development fund to enable the small states of the OECS to liberalise their markets in the CSM without undue harm. Membership of the single market allowed for the free movement of goods, services, capital, and persons, and the right of establishment. Three Caricom members remained outside the CSM—the Bahamas, Haiti, and Montserrat. The British Territory of Montserrat was still waiting for the UK to provide the necessary permission to become a part of the CSM; Haiti did not join the CSM because of its difficult internal political situation; and the Bahamas declined membership because of local opposition to a provision that allowed skilled workers to move freely within the CSM.

In a related development at the 43rd meeting of the Authority of the OECS held in June, heads of government signed a declaration of intent signalling their wish to form an economic union by the middle of 2007. OECS economic union was planned to complement the CSM.

Away from the CSM, Haiti was readmitted to Caricom in June after René Préval won the country's presidential elections in February (see p. 150). Haiti had suspended its membership in March 2004 after Jamaica gave temporary asylum to the ousted Haitian president, Jean-Bertrand Aristide, and Caricom refused to recognise the appointed interim government of Gerard Latortue (see AR 2004, pp. 417-18).

Meanwhile, in July Caricom heads of government agreed a US$13 million security plan for the 2007 Cricket World Cup. As part of the security package, regional leaders agreed to introduce a Caricom visa for the January to May period of 2007 to facilitate travel for visitors between the nine host countries and Dominica.

ARAB ORGANISATIONS

League of Arab States (Arab League)

DATE OF FOUNDATION: 1945 HEADQUARTERS: Cairo, Egypt
OBJECTIVES: To co-ordinate political, economic, social and cultural co-operation between member states and to mediate in disputes between them
MEMBERSHIP (END-'06): Algeria, Bahrain, Comoros, Djibouti, Egypt, Iraq, Jordan, Kuwait, Lebanon, Libya, Mauritania, Morocco, Oman, Palestine, Qatar, Saudi Arabia, Somalia, Sudan, Syria, Tunisia, United Arab Emirates, Yemen (total 22)
SECRETARY GENERAL: Amr Moussa (Egypt)

Gulf Co-operation Council (GCC)

DATE OF FOUNDATION: 1981 HEADQUARTERS: Riyadh, Saudi Arabia
OBJECTIVES: To promote co-operation between member states in all fields with a view to achieving unity
MEMBERSHIP (END-'06): Bahrain, Kuwait, Oman, Qatar, Saudi Arabia, United Arab Emirates (total 6)
SECRETARY GENERAL: Abdulrahman al-Attiya (Qatar)

Arab Maghreb Union (AMU)

DATE OF FOUNDATION: 1989 HEADQUARTERS: Casablanca, Morocco
OBJECTIVES: To strengthen "the bonds of brotherhood" between member states, particularly in the area of economic development
MEMBERSHIP (END-'06): Algeria, Libya, Mauritania, Morocco, Tunisia (total 5)
SECRETARY GENERAL: Habib Ben Yahia (Tunisia) (since Feb '06)

THE LEAGUE OF ARAB STATES (ARAB LEAGUE) held its 18th regular summit meeting in Khartoum, the capital of Sudan, on 28-29 March. As was the case at the 17th summit, held in Algeria in March 2005 (see AR 2005, pp. 383-84), the meeting was undermined by the absence of several key leaders, including President Mohammed Hosni Mubarak of Egypt, King Abdullah ibn Abdul Aziz of Saudi Arabia, President Zine el-Abidine Ben Ali of Tunisia, and Shaikh Qaboos bin Said, the ruler of Oman. In a further sign of apparent apathy, Saudi Arabia, which would hold the chairmanship in 2007, declined to host the summit, saying it preferred that it be held in Cairo, the capital of Egypt and the site of the League's headquarters. The Saudi move was seen by some as indicative of a growing impatience with the League's lack of executive power. Amr Moussa, the League's secretary general, whose term was extended for five years at the summit, sought to play down the Saudi decision, saying that Saudi Arabia and Egypt had jointly agreed to hold the next summit in Cairo.

In a major boost for President Omar Hasan Ahmed al-Bashir of Sudan, the Arab leaders pledged financial backing for the African Union (AU) Mission in the Sudan (AMIS)—the Darfur peace monitoring mission—and rejected the imposition of a UN-led force without Sudan's permission (see pp. 217-18). The Bashir regime had resisted Western pressure to let the UN take over from the 7,000 AU troops in Sudan's troubled western province, saying that this would violate Sudan's sovereignty.

In their final declaration, the leaders hailed the Palestinian legislative elections held in January, which had produced a landslide victory for the militant group Hamas (see p. 186), and called on the international community to respect the result of that vote. The leaders renewed their commitment to the Arab peace initiative ratified by the 2002 Arab League summit in Beirut, the capital of Lebanon, which offered Israel a comprehensive peace in return for a withdrawal from occupied Arab lands (see AR 2002, pp. 206-07). The leaders also addressed issues surrounding the caricatures of the Prophet Mohammed that had been published in a Danish newspaper in September 2005, causing widespread outrage among Muslims and some violent protests (see pp. 54-56). The final declaration urged the need for "co-operation, dialogue and mutual respect between peoples and cultures" and insisted that "respecting religious sanctities and beliefs is the decisive factor in building confidence and bridges of friendship between nations".

During the summit's closing session, the Iraqi foreign minister, Hoshyar Zebari, harangued fellow Arab governments, demanding firm commitments to his country, wracked by growing sectarian violence. "It is our right to tell our brothers, after decades of the authoritarian rule and wars, that we expect them to support our political march and extend any help and backing that will contribute to isolating terrorism and drying up of the sources that finance its activities", Zebari said. Arab countries, he said, should upgrade their diplomatic representation to the ambassadorial level and forgive Iraq's debts. The summit declaration said that Arab leaders had agreed to send diplomats to Baghdad, although it did not give a timeframe. Arab countries had generally been hesitant to send high-level diplomats to Baghdad since the kidnapping and murder of Algerian and Egyptian diplomats there in 2005 (see AR 2005, p. 192).

Arab League foreign ministers held an emergency, closed-door meeting on 15 July in Cairo to address Israel's military offensive in Lebanon. Israel had launched the operation on 12 July in response to the capture of two Israeli soldiers by Hezbullah fighters (see pp. 197-203). At the meeting, Saudi Arabia, supported by Jordan, Egypt, and several Gulf states, reportedly chastised Hezbullah for "unexpected, inappropriate and irresponsible acts". It was almost unheard of for Arab officials to criticise an Arab group engaged in conflict with Israel, especially as images of the widespread destruction wrought by the Israeli air force were being beamed daily into Arab homes. The willingness of some governments to defy public opinion in their own countries underscored a shift that had been prompted by the growing influence of Shi'ite Muslims and Iran in both Iraq and across the region as a whole.

After the Cairo meeting, Secretary General Moussa told journalists that the Middle East peace process was "dead" because "certain powers" had given Israel "every capacity to do whatever it wishes". Moussa said that the whole Middle East peace process "should now be sent back to the [UN] Security Council for a complete overhaul". Foreign ministers held another emergency meeting in Beirut on 7 August to voice solidarity with Lebanon. The ministers announced the immediate despatch of a delegation, headed by Shaikh Hamad Bin Jassem Bin Jabr al-Thani, the deputy prime minister and minister of foreign affairs of Qatar, to the UN Security Council in New York to negotiate changes to a draft Security Council resolution to halt the fighting in Lebanon. (A resolution was eventually approved on 11 August (for text see pp. 528-31) and a ceasefire came into effect on 14 August.)

The 27th summit meeting of the Gulf Co-operation Council (GCC) took place in Riyadh, the capital of Saudi Arabia, on 9-10 December. The summit was named the "Sheikh Jaber summit" after the emir of Kuwait who died in January (see p. 215; for obituary see p. 597). The summit was dominated by issues of regional security, especially after King Abdullah ibn Abdul Aziz of Saudi Arabia, in his opening remarks said, "our Arab region is besieged by a number of dangers, as if it was a powder keg waiting for a spark to explode". The leaders commissioned a feasibility study to investigate the development of a joint nuclear energy programme between the organisation's six, predominantly Sunni Arab, member states. Speaking to reporters after the summit, Saudi Foreign Minister Prince Saud al-Faisal ibn Abdul Aziz, insisted that the GCC states' intention to pursue civilian nuclear technology was not a "threat" to anyone. However, some analysts believed that the announcement of the study was intended to send a message to Iran that the Arab states would seek to match the Shi'ite theocracy's nuclear power if they were forced to do so (see pp. 281-82).

Habib Ben Yahia, a former minister of foreign affairs in Tunisia, took up the post of secretary general of the largely moribund Arab Maghreb Union (AMU) on 1 February. Ben Yahia replaced his compatriot, Habib Boulares, who had served since early 2002.

AFRICAN ORGANISATIONS AND CONFERENCES

African Union (AU)

DATE OF FOUNDATION: 2001 HEADQUARTERS: Addis Ababa, Ethiopia
OBJECTIVES: To promote the unity, solidarity and co-operation of African states, to defend their sovereignty, to promote democratic principles, human rights and sustainable development and to accelerate the political and socio-economic integration of the continent
MEMBERSHIP (END-'06): Algeria, Angola, Benin, Botswana, Burkina Faso, Burundi, Cameroon, Cape Verde, Central African Republic, Chad, Comoros, Congo, Côte d'Ivoire, Democratic Republic of Congo, Djibouti, Egypt, Equatorial Guinea, Eritrea, Ethiopia, Gabon, the Gambia, Ghana, Guinea, Guinea-Bissau, Kenya, Lesotho, Liberia, Libya, Madagascar, Malawi, Mali, Mauritania, Mauritius, Mozambique, Namibia, Niger, Nigeria, Rwanda, Sahrawi, São Toméí and Príncipe, Senegal, Seychelles, Sierra Leone, Somalia, South Africa, Sudan, Swaziland, Tanzania, Togo, Tunisia, Uganda, Zambia, Zimbabwe (total 53)
CHAIRMAN: Denis Sassou-Nguesso (Congo); CHAIR OF AU COMMISSION: Alpha Oumar Konare (Mali)

Economic Community of West African States (ECOWAS)

DATE OF FOUNDATION: 1975 HEADQUARTERS: Abuja, Nigeria
OBJECTIVES: To seek the creation of an economic union of member states
MEMBERSHIP (END-'06): Benin, Burkina Faso, Cape Verde, Côte d'Ivoire, Gambia, Ghana, Guinea, Guinea-Bissau, Liberia, Mali, Niger, Nigeria, Senegal, Sierra Leone, Togo (total 15)
EXECUTIVE SECRETARY: Mohamed ibn Chambas (Ghana)

Common Market of East and Southern Africa (COMESA)

DATE OF FOUNDATION: 1993 HEADQUARTERS: Lusaka, Zambia
OBJECTIVES: To establish a full free-trade area
MEMBERSHIP (END-'06): Angola, Burundi, Comoros, Democratic Republic of Congo, Djibouti, Egypt, Eritrea, Ethiopia, Kenya, Libya, Madagascar, Malawi, Mauritius, Namibia, Rwanda, Seychelles, Sudan, Swaziland, Uganda, Zambia, Zimbabwe (total 21)
SECRETARY GENERAL: Erastus Mwencha (Kenya)

Economic Community of Central African States (CEEAC)

DATE OF FOUNDATION: 1983 HEADQUARTERS: Libreville, Gabon
OBJECTIVES: To establish a full free-trade area
MEMBERSHIP (END-'06): Angola, Burundi, Cameroon, Central African Republic, Chad, Democratic Republic of Congo, Congo, Equatorial Guinea, Gabon, Rwanda, São Tomé & Príncipe (total 11)
SECRETARY GENERAL: Louis-Sylvain Goma (Congo)

Southern African Development Community (SADC)

DATE OF FOUNDATION: 1992 HEADQUARTERS: Gaborone, Botswana
OBJECTIVES: To work towards the creation of a regional common market
MEMBERSHIP (END-'06): Angola, Botswana, Democratic Republic of Congo, Lesotho, Madagascar, Malawi, Mauritius, Mozambique, Namibia, South Africa, Swaziland, Tanzania, Zambia, Zimbabwe (total 14)
EXECUTIVE SECRETARY: Tomaz Augusto Salomão (Mozambique)

Intergovernmental Authority on Development (IGAD)

DATE OF FOUNDATION: 1986 HEADQUARTERS: Djibouti city, Djibouti
OBJECTIVES: To assist member states to achieve, through increased cooperation, food security and environmental protection; peace and security and humanitarian affairs, and economic co-operation
MEMBERSHIP (END-'06): Djibouti, Eritrea, Ethiopia, Kenya, Somalia, Sudan, Uganda (total 7)
SECRETARY GENERAL: Attalla Hamad Bashir (Sudan)

Community of Sahel-Saharan States (CENSAD)

DATE OF FOUNDATION: 1998 HEADQUARTERS: Tripoli, Libya
OBJECTIVES: To work to strengthen peace, security and stability and achieve global economic and social development
MEMBERSHIP (END-'06): Benin, Burkina Faso, Central African Republic, Chad, Côte d'Ivoire, Djibouti, Egypt, Eritrea, the Gambia, Ghana, Guinea Bissau, Liberia, Libya, Mali, Morocco, Niger, Nigeria, Senegal, Sierra Leone, Somalia, Sudan, Togo, Tunisia (total 23)
SECRETARY GENERAL: Mohamed al-Madani al-Azhari (Libya)

East African Community (EAC)

DATE OF FOUNDATION: 1996 HEADQUARTERS: Nairobi, Kenya
OBJECTIVES: To promote economic integration between member states
MEMBERSHIP (END-'06): Kenya, Tanzania, Uganda (total 3)

For data on the Arab Mahgreb Union (AMU) see article on Arab Organisations

AT the sixth AFRICAN UNION summit held in Khartoum, Sudan, in January, the main issue was whether the president of the host country would take over the chairmanship, as was the usual practice. In the end, it was decided that, given the Darfur crisis, it had to be someone else, and President Denis Sassou-Nguesso of the Republic of Congo got the position instead (see pp. 217; 255).

At the seventh summit, held at Banjul, The Gambia, from 25 June to 2 July, the main topic for discussion was the integration of the eight regional economic communities that the AU recognised: the ECONOMIC COMMUNITY OF WEST AFRICAN STATES (ECOWAS); the COMMON MARKET OF EAST AND SOUTHERN AFRICA (COMESA); the ECONOMIC COMMUNITY OF CENTRAL AFRICAN STATES (CEEAC); the SOUTHERN AFRICAN DEVELOPMENT COMMUNITY (SADC); the INTERGOVERNMENTAL AUTHORITY ON DEVELOPMENT (IGAD); the Arab Maghreb Union (AMU); the COMMUNITY OF SAHEL-SAHARAN STATES (CENSAD); and the EAST AFRICAN COMMUNITY (EAC). Integration remained a remote goal, but the 14-member SADC, meeting in Lesotho in August, did go ahead with planning for a regional stand-by force and for a free trade area by 2008, and there was talk of a regional customs union by 2010, a common market by 2015, and a common currency by 2016. The six SADC members who were also members of COMESA were told that they would have to choose to which regional organisation they wished to belong in future.

In Banjul the AU promoted two further summits that were held in November: the first Africa-South America summit in Abuja, Nigeria, which talked about establishing a co-operative forum and secretariat; and the first China-Africa summit in Beijing, significant because of China's greatly increased role in Africa in recent years. The AU summit also directed Senegal to prosecute the former Chadian dictator, Hissène Habré (who lived in exile there) for human rights abuses; and it acknowledged the transitional federal government of Somalia, which allowed Ethiopia to claim AU backing when it invaded Somalia and ousted the Union of Islamic Courts from the capital, Mogadishu, in December (see pp. 232-34).

The AU's Peace and Security Council was much taken up during the year with the western Sudan issue. The talks held in Abuja led in May to the signing of a Darfur Peace Agreement between the government of Sudan and the Sudan Liberation Movement/Army, but other rebel groups failed to sign and the agreement did not end the conflict (see pp. 217-18). The Sudan government continued to refuse to allow the 7,000-member AU force in Darfur to be converted into a UN force, and the AU failed to insist that this be done. Though some predicted that the comprehensive peace agreement for southern Sudan would collapse, it remained in place as the year ended.

A stuttering peace process with rebels in northern Uganda held out the prospect of an end to conflict there (see pp. 237-38), and the elections in the Democratic Republic of Congo took place without major violence (see pp. 259-60).

Though South African troops remained in Burundi at the end of the year, under UN command, President Thabo Mbeki withdrew as AU mediator in the conflict resolution process in Côte d'Ivoire, after he had been accused of not being impartial (see p. 279). He gave as the reason for withdrawing the fact that South Africa was to serve as a non-permanent member of the UN Security Council from January 2007. No progress was made during the year on the issue of African representation on an enlarged UN Security Council (see p. 362). The AU continued to insist that at least two African countries, chosen by the AU, should become permanent members, with all the privileges of permanent membership, including the veto. African efforts to secure reform of other global multinational institutions, including the IMF and the WTO, were also ineffectual.

All AU operations were influenced by funding constraints, but when the Pan African Parliament (PAP) met in South Africa in May, it was told that its budget was exhausted, as only the host country had met its financial obligations. It managed to hold a sixth session in November, at which former South African President Nelson Mandela launched a trust fund to help finance the body. The first African Peer Review Mechanism (APRM) reports—on Ghana, Kenya, and Rwanda—were presented to the PAP in November; that on Mauritius was not completed. Set up under the AU's New Partnership for Africa's Development (NEPAD), the APRM was designed to show foreign and local investors that the countries reviewed were committed to good governance, accountability, and investor-friendly economic policies. The report on Kenya was highly critical, that on Rwanda less so, and that on Ghana mostly positive. South Africa prepared a detailed self-assessment as part of its review. Towards the end of the year it was reported that the APRM panel was critical of the lack of focus in the South African self-assessment on the seriousness of crime in the country and the impact of the HIV/AIDS pandemic (see pp. 277-78). Critics of the APRM continued to point out that there were no means to enforce the recommendations that were made.

The credibility of the AU and SADC was severely compromised by their failure to condemn the gross examples of poor governance presented by such countries as Zimbabwe and the absolute monarchy of Swaziland. The AU summit in Banjul did not discuss a report by its commission on human rights which had found that the government of Robert Mugabe in Zimbabwe had violated the AU's charter and other international legal instruments. Whether the heads of state would finally take action against Zimbabwe at the eighth AU summit, to be held in Addis Ababa, the Ethiopian capital, in January 2007, remained to be seen.

EURASIAN ORGANISATIONS

Eurasian Economic Community (EEC)

DATE OF FOUNDATION: 2001 HEADQUARTERS: Moscow, Russia
OBJECTIVES: To form a customs union and common market in the former Soviet space
MEMBERSHIP (END-'06): Belarus, Kazakhstan, Kyrgyzstan, Russia, Tajikistan, and Uzbekistan (total 6)
OBSERVER MEMBERS: Armenia, Moldova, Ukraine
SECRETARY GENERAL: Grigory Rapota (Russia)

Collective Security Treaty Organisation (CSTO)

DATE OF FOUNDATION: 2002 HEADQUARTERS: Moscow, Russia
OBJECTIVES: To further co-operation and develop joint structures in the fields of security, defence, and intelligence
MEMBERSHIP (END-'06): Armenia, Belarus, Kazakhstan, Kyrgyzstan, Russia, Tajikistan, and Uzbekistan (total 7)
SECRETARY GENERAL: Gen. Nikolai Bordyuzha (Russia)

Commonwealth of Independent States (CIS)

DATE OF FOUNDATION: 1991 HEADQUARTERS: Minsk, Belarus
OBJECTIVES: To facilitate economic and humanitarian integration between member states
MEMBERSHIP (END-'06): Azerbaijan, Armenia, Belarus, Georgia, Kazakhstan, Kyrgyzstan, Moldova, Russia, Tajikistan, Uzbekistan, and Ukraine (total 11)
EXECUTIVE SECRETARY: Vladimir Rushailo (Russia)

Shanghai Co-operation Organisation (SCO)

DATE OF FOUNDATION: 2001 HEADQUARTERS: Beijing, China
OBJECTIVES: To strengthen mutual trust and good-neighbourly relations among member states
MEMBERSHIP (END-'06): China, Kazakhstan, Kyrgyzstan, Russia, Tajikistan, Uzbekistan (total 6)
SECRETARY GENERAL: Zhang Deguang (China)

REGIONAL organisations in Central Asia and Eurasia broadened their activities during 2006. In January, the Eurasian Development Bank was created within the framework of the Eurasian Economic Community (EEC). Based in Almaty (Kazakhstan), the purpose of the bank (charter capital US$1.5 billion) was to provide credit to member states. Also in January, Uzbekistan formally acceded to the EEC, joining existing members Russia, Belarus, Kazakhstan, Kyrgyzstan, and Tajikistan. At the EEC summit in August, two projects were prioritised: the creation of a customs union and a common energy market.

The Russia-led Collective Security Treaty Organisation (CSTO), comprising Russia, Belarus, Armenia, Kazakhstan, Kyrgyzstan, and Tajikistan, also expanded its operations in Central Asia. In February, plans were announced to upgrade the Russian air base at Kant (Kyrgyzstan), established in October 2003 as part of the CSTO anti-terrorism operations; troop numbers would be increased from 300 to around 750. Joint Tajik-Russian military exercises were held in April, within the framework of the CSTO. In June, Uzbekistan announced that it was rejoining the CSTO (it had suspended its membership in 1999). This decision was motivated in large part by support for the CSTO strategy of developing a co-ordinated approach to arms trafficking and related security issues.

Kazakhstan assumed the rotating chairmanship of the Commonwealth of Independent States (CIS) in May. In this capacity the Kazakh president, Nursultan Nazarbayev participated in the July summit of the G-8 (Group of Eight) industrialised nations, hosted by Russia's President Vladimir Putin in St Petersburg. Also in July, the Kazakh, Kyrgyz, Tajik and Uzbek presidents attended the CIS Moscow summit; Turkmenistan, having withdrawn from full membership of this organisation, was not represented. Agenda items included energy security, simplification of travel procedures, better use of transport corridors, and more effective co-ordination in the fight against terrorism, extremism, and drug trafficking.

In November, a CIS summit was organised in Minsk, the Belarusian capital, timed apparently to coincide with the NATO summit in Riga, Latvia's capital (see pp. 378-80). Little resulted in the way of concrete agreements, and Nazarbayev bemoaned the fact that decisions on reforming the CIS had been delayed once again. Before the summit, he had put forward proposals to revitalise the CIS, possibly along the lines of the European Union, and suggested that topics including migration, transport, and communication could be added to the conventional agenda items of economic co-operation and anti-terrorism.

The Shanghai Co-operation Organisation (SCO) held its fifth annual summit in June in Shanghai, China. One of the achievements of the organisation had been to boost trade among member states (China, Kazakhstan, Kyrgyzstan, Russia, Tajikistan, and Uzbekistan); in 2005, a turnover of US$37.7 billion was recorded, more than double the amount in 2001, when the SCO was founded. Priorities earmarked for 2007 included the promotion of regional energy and telecommunications co-operation. Under the aegis of the SCO, in August Kazakhstan and China held a joint anti-terrorism exercise; a similar exercise was carried out between Tajik and Chinese forces in September.

Also in June, the Conference on Interaction and Confidence-Building Measures in Asia (CICA) held its second summit in Almaty, Kazakhstan. The brainchild of Kazakh President Nazarbayev, this body was envisaged as an Asian counterpart to the Organisation for Security and Co-operation in Europe (OSCE). The meeting was attended by high-ranking delegations from 18 countries. The agenda focused on such issues as regional and global security, nonproliferation, and regional conflict resolution. It was agreed that a permanent CICA secretariat should be established, based in Almaty.

ASIA-PACIFIC ORGANISATIONS

Association of South-East Asian Nations (ASEAN)

DATE OF FOUNDATION: 1967 HEADQUARTERS: Jakarta, Indonesia
OBJECTIVES: To accelerate economic growth, social progress and cultural development in the region
MEMBERSHIP (END-'06): Brunei, Burma (Myanmar), Cambodia, Indonesia, Laos, Malaysia, Philippines, Singapore, Thailand, Vietnam (total 10)
SECRETARY GENERAL: Ong Keng Yong (Singapore)

Asia-Pacific Economic Co-operation (APEC)

DATE OF FOUNDATION: 1989 HEADQUARTERS: Singapore
OBJECTIVES: To promote market-oriented economic development and co-operation in the Pacific Rim countries
MEMBERSHIP (END-'06): Australia, Brunei, Canada, Chile, China, Hong Kong, Indonesia, Japan, South Korea, Malaysia, Mexico, New Zealand, Papua New Guinea, Peru, Philippines, Russia, Singapore, Taiwan, Thailand, USA, Vietnam (total 21)
EXECUTIVE DIRECTOR: Choi Seok Young (South Korea)

South Asian Association for Regional Co-operation (SAARC)

DATE OF FOUNDATION: 1985 HEADQUARTERS: Kathmandu, Nepal
OBJECTIVES: To promote collaboration and mutual assistance in the economic, social, cultural and technical fields
MEMBERSHIP (END-'06): Afghanistan, Bangladesh, Bhutan, India, Maldives, Nepal, Pakistan, Sri Lanka (total 8)
OBSERVER MEMBERS: China, Japan
SECRETARY GENERAL: Q.A.M.A Rahim (Bangladesh)

Pacific Islands Forum (PIF)

DATE OF FOUNDATION: 1971 (as South Pacific Forum) HEADQUARTERS: Suva, Fiji
OBJECTIVES: To enhance the economic and social well-being of the people of the Pacific, in support of the efforts of the members' governments
MEMBERSHIP (END-'06): Australia, Cook Islands, Fiji, Kiribati, Marshall Islands, Federated States of Micronesia, Nauru, New Zealand, Niue, Palau, Papua New Guinea, Samoa, Solomon Islands, Tonga, Tuvalu, Vanuatu (total 16)
OBSERVER MEMBERS: Wallis & Fortuna, UN, Commonwealth Secretariat, Asian Development Bank
ASSOCIATE MEMBERS: New Caledonia, French Polynesia
SECRETARY GENERAL: Greg Urwin (Australia)

Asian Development Bank (ADB)

DATE OF FOUNDATION: 1966 HEADQUARTERS: Manila, Philippines
OBJECTIVES: To improve the welfare of the people in Asia and the Pacific, particularly the 1.9 billion who live on less than $2 a day
MEMBERSHIP (END-'06): REGIONAL MEMBERS: Afghanistan, Armenia, Australia, Azerbaijan, Bangladesh, Bhutan, Burma (Myanmar), Cambodia, China, Cook Islands, East Timor, Fiji, Hong Kong, India, Indonesia, Japan, Kazakhstan, Kiribati, Kyrgyzstan, Laos, Malaysia, Maldives, Marshall Islands, Federated States of Micronesia, Mongolia, Nauru, Nepal, New Zealand, Pakistan, Palau, Papua New Guinea, Philippines, Samoa, Singapore, Solomon Islands, South Korea, Sri Lanka, Taiwan, Tajikistan, Thailand, Tonga, Turkmenistan, Tuvalu, Uzbekistan, Vanuatu, Vietnam (total 46); NON REGIONAL MEMBERS: Austria, Belgium, Canada, Denmark, Finland, France, Germany, Italy, Luxembourg, the Netherlands, Norway, Portugal, Spain, Sweden, Switzerland, Turkey, UK, USA (total 18)
PRESIDENT: Haruhiko Kuroda (Japan)

FOREIGN ministers of the 10-member ASSOCIATION OF SOUTH-EAST ASIAN NATIONS (ASEAN) held their 39th annual meeting in Kuala Lumpur (the capital of

Malaysia) on 25 July. In order to ensure the implementation of the Vientiane Action Programme (VAP), agreed at the 10th summit meeting held in Laos in November 2004 (see AR 2004, p. 412), the ministers agreed to undertake greater efforts to enhance the "co-ordination mechanism" to help realise the goals of the ASEAN community. Furthermore, the ministers stressed the need for effective implementation of the recommendations in the report of the mid-term review of the Initiative for ASEAN Integration (IAI), which had been adopted by the leaders at their 11th summit held in Kuala Lumpur in December 2005 (see AR 2005, p. 389).

In a joint communiqué issued at the end of the meeting, the ministers "expressed concern" on the pace of the national reconciliation process in Burma (an ASEAN member state) and said that they hoped to see "tangible progress that would lead to peaceful transition to democracy in the near future". They reiterated their calls for the early release of those placed under detention and for "effective dialogue" with all parties concerned. The relatively mild communiqué contrasted with a speech made on 21 July by the meeting's chairman, Malaysian Foreign Minister Syed Hamid Albar, in which he said that Burma's intransigence was holding its neighbours hostage and that it could no longer expect ASEAN to shield it from external criticism. Albar also appealed to China and India, both of which cultivated Burma's military regime, to bring pressure on Burma to commit itself to reform (see p. 315).

A series of ministerial and senior official ASEAN meetings followed the foreign ministers' meeting. These meetings included the ASEAN+3 (China, Japan, and South Korea) foreign ministers' meeting on 26 July, and individual talks with Australia, New Zealand, Canada, Russia, the EU, and the USA on 27 July. On 28 July the 13th ASEAN Regional Forum (ARF) was held. On the sidelines of the ARF meeting, the new prime minister of East Timor, José Ramos-Horta, made a formal application for ASEAN membership, saying that he expected East Timor to need about five years to become a full member. As a preliminary step Ramos-Horta signed ASEAN's peace and security treaty.

On 25 August ASEAN signed a trade and investment framework arrangement (TIFA) with the USA. The agreement was intended to promote the development of an "ASEAN single window" to harmonise customs practices in the region in order to facilitate the flow of goods between ASEAN countries and the USA. In a related development, ASEAN Secretary General Ong Keng Yong said that member states had agreed in principle to bring forward the creation of an ASEAN single market (ASEAN Economic Community) by five years to 2015.

The 14th summit meeting of the Asia-Pacific Economic Co-operation (APEC) forum was held in Hanoi, the capital of Vietnam, on 18-19 November under the theme of "towards a dynamic community for sustainable development and prosperity". The summit was largely overshadowed by the political repercussions of North Korea's nuclear test in October (see pp. 344-45). APEC leaders were unable to agree on a written public statement condemning the North Korean action. In a declaration issued at the end of the summit, the leaders agreed to make every effort to realise APEC's goals of "free and open trade and investment" and dedicated themselves to "preventing threats to sustainable development, to building a secure and favourable business environment and to enhancing human security".

The sixth biennial Asia-Europe Meeting (ASEM) was held at the level of heads of state and government on 10-11 September in Helsinki, the capital of Finland, under the theme "global challenges—joint responses". It was agreed that by the seventh summit in Beijing, China, in 2008, the number of ASEM participants would be increased from 39—the 25 EU member states, the European Commission, the 10 ASEAN members, China, Japan, and South Korea—to 45 by the addition of Bulgaria and Romania from the EU, in addition to India, Mongolia, Pakistan, and the ASEAN secretariat.

The first meeting of interior ministers of the SOUTH ASIAN ASSOCIATION FOR REGIONAL CO-OPERATION (SAARC) was held on 11 May in Dhaka, the capital of Bangladesh. Ministers agreed to wage joint efforts against terrorism.

The 37th leaders' summit meeting of the 16-member PACIFIC ISLANDS FORUM (PIF) was held on 24 October in Suva, the capital of Fiji. The meeting was dominated by the strained relations between Australia, and the Solomon Islands and Papua New Guinea (PNG), caused by a rancorous dispute over Australia's frustrated attempts to extradite Solomon Islands Attorney General Julian Moti from PNG (see pp. 350; 356). The Solomon Islands and PNG considered that Australia had committed infringements of their sovereignty. The summit approved the application by the French territories of New Caledonia and French Polynesia for associate membership of the PIF; both countries already had observer status. Wallis & Futuna, the UN, the Commonwealth Secretariat, and the Asian Development Bank were given observer status.

The leaders of the French Pacific territories of French Polynesia, New Caledonia, Wallis & Futuna, and Vanuatu, formerly an Anglo-French condominium, on 26-27 June attended a France-Oceania summit meeting in Paris. The meeting was also attended by heads of government of all 16 PIF members. France's President Jacques Chirac pledged France's continued commitment to the Pacific region, in supporting its political stability and economic development and in protecting its environment.

The inaugural China-Pacific Island Countries Economic Development and Corporation Forum (CPICEDCF) was held in Fiji on 5-6 April. The forum was attended by Chinese Premier Wen Jiabao and representatives from Australia, the Cook Islands, the Federated States of Micronesia (FSM), New Zealand, Niue, Papua New Guinea, Samoa, Tonga, and Vanuatu. A framework agreement was signed on trade, investment, and other forms of economic co-operation.

The 39th annual meeting of the ASIAN DEVELOPMENT BANK (ADB) board of governors was held in Hyderabad, India, on 4-6 May. Governors discussed strategies for poverty reduction in the region. Delegates at the meeting also called for concrete measures by the regional financial institution to ensure the meeting of the UN Millennium Development Goals (MDGs) as scheduled by 2015.

XII THE INTERNATIONAL ECONOMY IN 2006

THE world economy grew by some 4 to 5 per cent in 2006, better than forecast and without triggering any of the instabilities that had been feared at the start of the year. (Estimates of the global growth rate varied depending on how the country or regional rates of GDP were weighted: using dollars at market prices, a standard UN practice, yielded the lower estimate, while purchasing power parity based weights, used by the IMF, produced the higher rate.) The different estimates nevertheless agreed that 2006 was the fourth consecutive year of rapid growth for the world economy and, as such, marked the longest period of sustained growth since the early 1970s.

World commodity prices continued to rise. For non-oil commodities most of the increase was due to metals and minerals for which prices rose by nearly 50 per cent during the year. Strong demand, low inventories, and supply disruptions were the principal factors behind the increase although speculative demand from hedge funds and other financial investors also played a role. Oil prices rose in the first half of the year but after peaking at nearly US$80 per barrel in August, they fell sharply and by the end of the year were heading towards US$55. The outlook for the price of the oil at the end of the year remained very uncertain.

Despite these pressures from the commodity markets, growth was still essentially non-inflationary, although there was some controversy as to whether inflationary pressures had been diverted to various asset markets, including housing. Inflation did rise in the course of 2006 in the majority of countries, largely because of higher oil prices. Their second round effects on core inflation—excluding volatile food and energy prices—and wage settlements were relatively small in most developed and developing economies. There were some exceptions due to country-specific factors, such as food shortages in some African countries or the removal of subsidies from household energy prices. A general but moderate rise in interest rates, together with the fall in oil prices in the second half of the year, strengthened confidence that inflationary pressures would ease rapidly in 2007.

Driven by strong output growth, world trade expanded rapidly, the volume of merchandise exports growing by some 10 per cent and their value by more than 15 per cent. Oil and other primary commodities played a large part in this but the volume of trade in capital goods also increased considerably as a result of the strong recovery of global fixed investment. The growth of trade in commodities and capital goods owed a lot to the rapid industrialisation of China, India, and other emerging economies, but the import demand of the USA was still the major influence. Its import demand, accounting for some 14 per cent of the world total, grew by some 6 per cent in volume. The unexpectedly strong recovery in the EU also generated a larger volume of imports (up by 10 per cent) while in Japan the increase was more moderate because of the subdued recovery of private consumption. In general, the strength of world trade growth, both for imports and exports, was broadly distributed across the global economy.

The distribution of trade deficits and surpluses continued to widen, the deficit of the USA rising to around US$770 billion by the end of the year, while the surpluses of China, Japan, and the oil-exporting countries increased. Germany continued to remain in surplus although the EU as a whole had a larger deficit. These trade imbalances accounted for most of the current account imbalances which also continued to widen. The USA's deficit at the end of the year was about US$870 billion and this was largely mirrored in the surpluses of the oil exporters (US$500 billion), East Asia—mainly China, Hong Kong, and Taiwan—(US$200 billion), Germany and Japan (US$120 billion and US$170 billion, respectively), and the Commonwealth of Independent States (CIS)—mainly Russia (over US$100 billion). At the end of 2006, the forecast pattern of regional growth rates in the world economy suggested that some narrowing in the spread of these imbalances was likely, but whether this would be sufficient to establish a more sustainable pattern remained problematic.

Two weaknesses of the global economy in 2005 were fixed investment and employment. In 2006 there was a widespread recovery of investment but labour markets were little improved. Global employment increased but given the growth in output, the improvement was small, indicating that structural factors were limiting its response to higher levels of output. Most of the improvements that did occur were in the developed economies, especially the EU. Unemployment rates fell to a five-year low in the USA and in the EU to their previous low-point in 2001. The unemployment rate also fell in Japan. Although more people were in work, the number unemployed worldwide was at an all-time high of 195.2 million or 6.3 per cent of the global labour force. Even in China, a double digit rate of output growth appeared to have a limited impact on unemployment. Unemployment, however, was only one aspect of the weak response of labour markets to economic growth; the lack of decent jobs was another. The International Labour Organisation (ILO) estimated that about half the global workforce was earning less than US$2 per day. Unemployment also bore more heavily on young people (15-24 years) who accounted for over 40 per cent of the unemployed in 2006. Thus, the robust economic growth of the last few years failed in much of the world to generate enough jobs to provide an escape from poverty. The incentives to emigrate to the richer countries of Western Europe and North America therefore remained very powerful.

A positive feature of the global economy in 2006 was that growth was broadly shared by all the major regions and by a majority of countries within them. In the developing and transition economies, GDP grew on average by just over 7 per cent, more than double the rate of the developed countries of North America, Western Europe, and Japan. A notable feature was that countries suffering adverse terms of trade were still able to sustain robust rates of growth. The reasons for this included the strength of world demand (which enabled them to expand their export volume); the recycling of financial flows from oil exporters to net importers, often in the form of foreign direct investment (FDI); and large flows of workers' remittances, including from the oil-producing countries. Official aid was also a partial offset to terms of trade losses in a number of countries in Africa. The high rates of growth in China (nearly 11 per cent) and India (nearly 9 per cent) contributed to rising levels of trade among the developing countries ("South-South" trade) as well as to stronger financial links between them. Even in the poorest countries—the 49 which were classified as "least developed" by the UN—GDP increased on average by nearly 7 per cent. Excluding China and India, the rest of the developing world, including net importers of oil, still grew by some 5 to 5.5 per cent.

Although developing countries accounted for a little over 20 per cent of global output, the developed countries nevertheless remained the major influence on movements in global activity. The latter, via US import demand, largely mirrored the profile of developments within the US economy where, for the year as a whole, GDP growth was some 3.2 per cent, approximately the same as in 2005, but through the year it decelerated from an exceptional (quarter-to-quarter) rate of 5.6 per cent in the first quarter to just over 2 per cent in the third. This reflected the impact of higher interest rates, falling investment in housing, and a sharp deceleration in the rate of increase in house prices. The consequent wealth and income effects weakened consumer spending, but this was partly offset by the buoyancy of other forms of fixed investment and the strong growth of net exports in the latter part of the year. The stabilisation of the housing market in the last few months of the year, and increasing confidence about the outlook for inflation and employment, supported hopes for only a limited slowdown in 2007 and a gradual re-balancing of the US economy. The current account deficit was a record 7 per cent of GDP in 2006 and although a depreciation of the US dollar was seen as a necessary part of the adjustment process, estimates varied widely as to how far, and how rapidly, it might have to fall. As noted above, this would depend partly on changes in the distribution of global demand, and in 2006 these began to move in the desired direction with growth in the EU and Japan starting to outpace that in the USA.

After five years of anaemic growth, activity picked up sharply in the eurozone in the first half of 2006 and, with continued expansion in Denmark, Sweden, and the UK, GDP in the EU rose by somewhat more than 2.5 per cent during the year as a whole. The recovery slowed in the third quarter but strengthened again in the fourth when most of the short-term indicators were pointing to continued strong growth in 2007. The increase in GDP was largely due to stronger domestic demand and this, together with the appreciation of the euro and other European currencies, led to a faster growth of imports. Investment in machinery and equipment was an important influence as was investment in housing, a notable development being the first increase in housing construction in Germany since the collapse of the reunification boom. Consumer expenditure, a relatively weak spot in the eurozone for a number of years, rose moderately but confidence was rising throughout the year as employment increased. Unemployment continued to fall, to some 7.9 per cent in the eurozone, although there were marked differences among countries in the rate of improvement and in some of them the rates remained well above 8 per cent. In the UK, the rate increased to 5.3 per cent.

For most of 2006 consumer price inflation in Europe was well above 2 per cent and the European Central Bank (ECB) raised its key interest rate four times to reach 3.25 per cent in October. The timing of its actions attracted criticism from some governments and international organisations which feared that a premature increase might damage the recovery of output. One of the problems facing policy-makers was the divergent performance of Germany and the other members of the eurozone, especially France and Italy. Germany's recovery (GDP growth of 2.5 per cent) was much greater than expected and its loss of competitiveness following unification was effectively reversed as a result of wage restraint, immigration from the east, and structural reforms. In France and Italy, however, growth was weaker than in Germany and the appreciation of the euro was thought to have had a greater impact on French and Italian exports. Thus the French authorities worried that euro interest rates were too high and raised again the perennial issue of the ECB's accountability to finance ministers.

The new members of the EU continued to grow rapidly, with GDP rising 5.7 per cent (against 4.7 per cent in 2005). Growth was supported by strong investment, including in public infrastructure, and by private consumption. Unemployment rates were down (in Poland from 19 per cent in early 2005 to 15 per cent) and the migration of workers to other EU members helped to ease labour market pressures. Current accounts were in deficit, largely because of net outflows of investment income, but were easily financed.

In the transition economies of south-east Europe, GDP rose by an average 5.5 per cent, against 4.5 per cent in 2005. This was largely driven by domestic demand, a reflection of the continuing process of reconstruction throughout the region. Cheap credit supported private consumption and fixed investment, while consumer and investor confidence in Bulgaria and Romania were raised by the prospect of EU accession in 2007.

Inflation increased slightly but generally remained under control. Only in Serbia did higher inflation (around 14 per cent) reflect lax and unbalanced macroeconomic policy. There were some improvements in the labour markets of Bulgaria, Croatia, and Romania, but elsewhere unemployment rates remained in double digits with little prospect of early improvement. Another element of fragility in the region was the increase in already large current account deficits.

Economic growth in the CIS countries in 2006 averaged just over 7 per cent, with most of them improving on 2005 levels. There was a marked recovery in Ukraine (from less than 3 per cent to 6.5 per cent) and a slight acceleration in Russia (to 6.6 per cent). The shape of activity in the region was heavily influenced by the commodity structure of output. The difference in average growth rates between net fuel exporters and net importers narrowed as the latter either recovered from supply-side disruptions in 2005 (Kyrgyzstan) or benefited from higher prices for cotton (Central Asia) and for metals (Ukraine). High prices for non-oil commodities generally helped to offset the effect of higher oil prices on the net oil-importing countries.

Domestic demand was behind most of the expansion in the region. Favourable terms of trade boosted national income in the oil producing countries, while migrant workers' remittances, mainly from Russia and to a lesser extent Kazakhstan, helped to ease the external constraints on many of the poorer CIS countries. Investment increased throughout the region and FDI began to flow into Russia, after years of stagnation, and from Russia to some of the other CIS members.

In most countries inflation rates were in the range of 10 to 10.5 per cent in the net fuel exporting countries and 6 to 12 per cent in the net importers. Countries dependent on Russia for most of their gas supplies (Belarus and Ukraine, for example) faced higher prices in 2006 as Russia sought to raise tariffs to world market levels. Employment growth was limited, the main source of new jobs being in the construction sectors of Russia and Kazakhstan where rapid growth attracted migrant labour from the rest of the CIS.

Current account balances improved in the oil exporting countries and in Russia there was a large addition to its foreign reserves. Except for Uzbekistan, which had a current account surplus, the oil importers had large deficits but financing them was easy. For most of the CIS, fiscal and current account surpluses and large foreign exchange reserves provided a defence against short-run instability. The need to diversify their economies was a major preoccupation of policy-makers in 2006.

In Latin America and the Caribbean the overall picture was one of strong economic growth, modest rates of inflation, fiscal and current accounts which were in surplus, and some improvement in labour markets. GDP rose on average by just over 5 per cent, the third year running that its growth exceeded 4 per cent. Moreover, with gains in the terms of trade and increased remittances from abroad, the rise in national income was over 7 per cent. The situation in Latin America was significantly different from previous cycles when economic growth was quickly brought to a halt by mounting current account deficits. Not only was national income growing more than GDP but domestic savings were rising and domestic demand was driven by fixed investment which rose by 10.5 per cent. Public outlays on both infrastructure investment and current spending increased, the boost in tax revenues simultaneously supporting smaller overall deficits (of less than 1 per cent of GDP). Increases in consumer confidence, employment and real wages added to the strength of domestic demand. Much of the inter-country variation in economic performance, particularly in gross national income, reflected differences in the commodity structure of exports

More people were drawn into paid work, the employment rate rising to 54 per cent of the working age population, its highest level in 15 years, but the average unemployment rate hardly moved and at around 8 per cent was about the same as 10 years earlier.

Many countries took advantage of their improved situation to reduce their vulnerability to possible shocks by adopting floating exchange rates, reducing external debt (through early repayment), and rebuilding their international reserves. With inflation under control, the region's monetary authorities were in a stronger position at the end of the year to support activity in the event of a slowdown in the global economy.

Economic growth in sub-Saharan Africa averaged about 5.3 per cent, the third consecutive year of expansion at over 5 per cent. There was some deceleration from 2005, mainly because of South Africa (which was afflicted by stagnant agricultural output and weak exports) and Nigeria (which suffered a fall in oil production). Excluding these two, growth was evenly distributed across the continent and averaged nearly 6 per cent, closer to 7 per cent for oil exporters and 5 per cent for oil importers. These rates, however, were still too low, according to the UN, to achieve the Millennium Development Goals: an average GDP growth rate of at least 7 per cent was needed to halve extreme poverty in the region by 2015. Between 1998 and 2006, only seven of the 52 countries in Africa had crossed this threshold.

Africa benefited from strong world demand and high prices for its exports of primary commodities (particularly of oil, metals and minerals). In contrast, manufactured exports suffered intense competition from China and India in third markets, despite quotas on Chinese exports to the EU and the USA: African exports of textiles and clothing to these two markets in 2006 fell by some 17 per cent. This commodity pattern helped to explain why the recent period of strong growth had had little impact in creating employment and reducing poverty. The unemployment rate in the region averaged just under 10 per cent but the number of working poor (those earning less than US$1 per day) increased by 14 million; eight out of 10 workers with families were living on less than US$2 a day.

East Asia and the Pacific continued to be the fastest growing region of the world economy in 2006 with an average growth in GDP of 7.6 per cent (more than 9 per cent when weighted by purchasing power parity values). Again, the Chinese economy was the driving force in the region with its GDP growing by 10.7 per cent, the largest increase in a more than a decade and the fourth year running above 10 per cent. China's growth had positive effects on other countries in the region although their growth, an average 5.5 per cent, was well below the Chinese rate.

In China, worries about overheating led to the introduction, from late April, of a number of monetary (higher interest rates and reserve ratios) and administrative measures (tighter controls on land use and on foreign investment in housing) to cool investment. These began to have an effect in the second half of 2006 and, together with a slowdown in global demand, were expected to lead to somewhat slower regional growth in 2007.

The region's current account surplus increased to some 7 per cent of GDP, but excluding China it was about 3 per cent. China's trade surplus reached US$110 billion in the first nine months of 2006, larger than for 2005 as a whole, and its reserves stood at over US$1,000 billion. China became the world's second largest exporting country in 2006.

Economic growth continued at a high rate for the fourth year running in South Asia, at an average rate of around 7 per cent. India was the driving force with GDP rising by well over 8 per cent, but most of the other economies grew above their trend rates. In general, agriculture and manufacturing (textiles and clothing) were the dynamic sectors, as were services in India. Fiscal policy was generally expansionary and fiscal deficits averaged around 7 per cent of GDP. Low real interest rates, increased household savings and a better business climate supported higher rates of private fixed investment. Monetary policy was tightened everywhere except in Iran. Strong domestic demand and higher prices for oil imports led to larger trade and current account deficits. Apart from Iran, the one net oil exporter in the region, only Nepal had a current account surplus, its trade deficit being more than offset by remittances from abroad.

Booming oil revenues led to high rates of growth in the economies of Western Asia. The average rise in GDP was a little under 6 per cent, slightly less than in 2005 because of slower growth in the oil-importing countries of the region. Growth in the six countries of the Gulf Co-operation Council (GCC) was over 6 per cent. This group accounted for 90 per cent of the region's oil revenue, the remainder going to the more populous countries of Iraq, Syria, and Yemen. The region was greatly affected by violent conflict. In Lebanon, GDP in the first half of 2006 rose by some 5 per cent but fell sharply in the wake of the July-August invasion by Israel: for the year as a whole the decline was estimated at 5.5 per cent although it could be a lot more when the full extent of the destruction wrought by the Israeli operation was accurately measured. The violence in Iraq led to the largest refugee crisis in the region since 1948, with about 2 million Iraqis fleeing mainly to Jordan and Syria and another 1.8 million being displaced within Iraq. In Israel, the economy remained buoyant, GDP growth of 4.6 per cent being supported by increases in government spending and exports.

The current account surplus of the region's net fuel exporters had risen dramatically since 2002 and was one of the key elements in the skewed distribution of global imbalances. According to UN estimates, about two-thirds of the increase in oil revenue had gone into foreign exchange reserves, oil stabilisation funds, and the repayment of domestic and external debt. A significant part of the revenue had been recycled within the region and had supported development in a number of the oil-importing countries such as Jordan and those in the Mahgreb.

The general outlook for the world economy at the end of 2006 was relatively benign: business confidence was generally high; fears of a "hard landing" in the US economy were much reduced; and there was growing confidence that the adjustment of current account imbalances could be achieved without a currency crisis and the risk of recession. Many of the downside risks identified at the start of 2006 remained, but the international economic institutions and many governments were confident about the resilience of the global economy and their own ability to handle shocks and adjustments without severe disruption. There was however an increasing number of warnings from central bankers and financial regulators about the risks involved in the boom in highly leveraged mergers and takeovers which left many of the targeted companies with very high levels of debt. The lack of transparency surrounding the operations of hedge funds and private equity companies, the widespread use of novel financial instruments that distributed individual exposures to risk in obscure ways, and the general tendency for herd behaviour in financial markets all raised concerns about heightened systemic risk.

A feature of 2006 was the much greater prominence of policy issues that were usually postponed to an undefined long-term and ignored in the analysis of short-run developments: these included climate change and energy security as well as hostility in many parts of the world to various aspects of globalisation.

There were two notable influences that greatly increased awareness of global warming as a negative externality of global economic activity, namely, the documentary film, *An Inconvenient Truth,* made by former Vice President Al Gore, and the Stern Report on the economics of climate change, commissioned by the UK government and published in October (for summary see pp. 561-64). The European Commission placed the reduction of carbon emissions among its top priorities and, despite the reticence of the US federal government, the state of California enacted legislation in August to reduce greenhouse gas emissions by 25 per cent by 2020, with other US states likely to follow with similar action. Governments were still uncertain how to deal with climate change, but it was clear by the end of the year that measures to deal with it were likely to become an important element in the future structure of macroeconomic policies, especially within fiscal policy.

Energy security was another long-term issue which came to the fore and was often closely linked to the debates on global warming. The International Energy Agency (IEA) described the prevailing structure and direction of energy demand as a recipe for serial crises and recommended increasing the supply of nuclear energy and encouraging greater energy efficiency. In Europe, worries about security increased when supplies of oil and gas to several EU members were momentarily cut as a result of Russia's disputes with Belarus and Ukraine over prices. Additional concern arose from suggestions by NATO and the IEA that the world's major gas producers might be tempted to create a cartel to co-ordinate production and support prices. As with global warming, there were disagreements as to whether energy security might best be assured by deregulated markets or by greater government intervention.

The backlash against globalisation continued in 2006, not least in the developed world. Especially notable was the growing hostility to cross-border mergers and acquisitions, particularly in sectors such as ports, energy, and banking. In the EU these gave rise to numerous challenges to the principles of the single market and there were attempts to revive notions of "national champions" and "economic patriotism". Japan resisted calls from the EU to remove its barriers to FDI and in the USA the takeover of a number of port operations by Dubai Ports World was blocked on the grounds of national security. The USA continued to bar foreign takeovers in airlines, TV networks, and any sector judged important to national security. China followed suit, introducing more controls on foreign investment in several sectors and making it more difficult for foreigners to acquire outright control of domestic companies. These reactions occurred in a year when cross-border mergers and acquisitions reached record levels.

Developing countries also started to follow Russia's example in seeking greater control over their natural resources: in Latin America, Venezuela, Bolivia, and Ecuador, for example, re-nationalised assets or insisted on re-negotiating their contracts with foreign companies. Similar action was planned by several African countries who complained that their gains from the commodity boom were disproportionately small.

Many critics dismissed such action as irrational economic nationalism and, because it tended to follow a tit-for-tat pattern, warned of a return to the 1930s. Others, however, pointed to the poor record of mergers and acquisitions in delivering the promised benefits, the fears of workers for their jobs, the lack of effective adjustment policies to help them find new ones, and the suspicion that national economic interests and those of foreign companies may not always be identical.

There was also increased resistance to the international movement of labour in 2006. The general thrust in the developed countries was to control immigration more tightly in order to ensure that their own skill needs were met while at the same time reducing the total inflow and discouraging permanent settlement. In the EU, restrictions on movements of workers from the new members from central Europe were prolonged in several states, while the UK, which had opened its labour markets to the new members in January 2005, introduced restrictions on immigration from Bulgaria and Romania in anticipation of their joining in January 2007. Popular hostility aroused by the size of the inflow of migrant workers into countries with more liberal policies, such as the UK and Sweden, was an important factor behind this more restrictive approach. In the USA, Congress approved the building of a 700 mile wall and the deployment of 6,000 national guardsmen to deter illegal migration from Mexico. In Russia, and for similar reasons to those in the EU, controls were tightened to check the inflow of workers from other parts of the CIS. The phenomenon was world-wide: in New Caledonia, workers in the aluminium sector went on strike to protest at the employment of workers from the Philippines.

Public support for globalisation declined on both sides of the Atlantic in 2006 (according to a German Marshall Fund poll) amid a growing belief that it was a threat to economic security and a cause of rising income inequality. Intra-country (excluding China) and inter-country differences in income had risen sharply in recent years, but in many of the developed countries it was the widening gap between top earners and those at both the middle and bottom of the income scale that received most attention. In the USA, authoritative voices, such as the presidents of the Federal Reserve Banks of New York and San Francisco and the former Treasury Secretary Larry Summers, warned that rising inequality and stagnation of median wages was undermining political support for free trade in particular and for globalisation in general, and that the increased exposure of families to economic risk was a threat to social cohesion and, ultimately, to the democratic system. Similar concerns were expressed in Japan and, to varying degrees, among the individual members of the EU. The possible causes of rising inequality in the developed countries remained controversial, but it was clear that it had become a major issue, as reflected in the mid-term elections in the USA when the Democrats presented their "economic fairness" agenda.

Against this background, protectionist sentiment increased throughout the global economy in 2006. Although the proximate cause of the suspension of the Doha Round of trade negotiations in July was the dispute over reducing farm subsidies in the USA and EU, the more fundamental reasons were the declining support for further trade liberalisation within the developed countries and the scepticism of developing countries that they stood to gain very much. Perhaps the fundamental issue that re-emerged in 2006 was that the stability of the global economy would ultimately depend on an acceptable distribution of its benefits: what David Ricardo identified as "the principal problem of political economy".

The Nobel Prize for Economics in 2006 went to Edmund S. Phelps, of Columbia University, for his work on inter-temporal trade-offs in macroeconomic policy and in improving understanding of the relationships between the short-run and long-run effects of economic policy. The Nobel Peace Prize also went to an economist, Muhammad Yunus, for his work on developing micro-credit as an instrument in the struggle against poverty in developing countries.

XIII THE SCIENCES

SCIENTIFIC, INDUSTRIAL AND MEDICAL RESEARCH

SPACE AND ASTRONOMY. Confirmation of water on Mars was one of many exciting findings in a year of continued space exploration. Images of the crater Victoria from the spacecraft orbiting Mars showed channels, which astronomers believed could only have been caused by torrents of water flowing on the surface within the last five or 10 years. Other evidence of major climate changes on the planet included rock and debris at the foot of tropical mountains and volcanoes, believed to be glacial deposits laid down several million years ago when there was heavy snowfall in the area. Gas geysers were found at the planet's south pole where jets of carbon dioxide blasted rock hundreds of feet into the air spraying the pole with fine sand. This was thought to explain the mysterious dark spots and other markings found at the pole.

The European lunar orbiter, *SMART-1*, was deliberately crash landed on the Moon on 3 September having been in orbit for many months sending back data on the composition of lunar soil. X-ray and infra-red spectrometer signals showed the presence of aluminium, magnesium, silicon, calcium, and iron.

On 15 January, the US National Aeronautics and Space Administration's (NASA's) *Stardust* space probe returned from a seven year, 3 billion mile journey, bringing back particles collected in 2004 when the craft flew through the tail of the Wild 2 comet. The composition of comets, which were believed to be icy remnants from the dawn of the solar system 4.5 billion years ago, was crucial to the understanding of the formation of stars and planets. Analysis of the particles showed that comets were far more complex than had been appreciated; NASA scientists examining the particles found minerals which had been formed near the sun as well as interstellar dust and ice.

The Nobel Prize for Physics was jointly awarded to US citizens John C. Mather of the NASA Goddard Space Flight Centre and George F. Smoot of the Lawrence Berkeley National Laboratory, for their discovery, using NASA's *COBE* satellite, of the nature of "blackbody radiation", the cosmic background radiation believed to stem from the Big Bang. These results provided increased support for the Big Bang theory of the origin of the universe.

After much campaigning and discussion amongst astronomers and others, the International Astronomical Union, meeting in Prague (capital of the Czech Republic) on 24 August, finally ruled that Pluto could not properly be considered to be a planet because of its elliptical orbit, which at times overlapped that of Neptune. Pluto was relegated to a new category of bodies—a "dwarf planet"—leaving only eight planets in the solar system (for document see pp. 521-22). In January NASA launched *New Horizons*, the first spacecraft to attempt to survey Pluto and its three moons. Expected to arrive there in July 2015, the craft would be unable to orbit, as Pluto's gravity was too weak, but astronomers hoped to gather information on the dwarf planet's composition before *New Horizons* continued into the Kuiper Belt.

Results were still coming in from the space probe *Cassini*, in orbit around Saturn for the last two years (see AR 2004, p. 427, AR 2005, p. 403). There was evidence that the planet's magnetic field had shifted, increasing its day length. On its moon, Titan, sand dunes measuring 100 metres high were imaged and were believed to be caused by the tidal effect of Saturn. Titan proved to have a much more interesting landscape than had been expected, with wind erosion, weather patterns, steep mountains, volcanoes, and evidence of fluid flow, probably methane.

ARCHAEOLOGY AND PALAEONTOLOGY. September saw the discovery of a crucially important new fossil when *Tiktaalik roseae* was recognised as an intermediate between fish and land vertebrates. The fossil, found in the Canadian Arctic, had features of both fish (fins and scales) and tetrapods (flat skull, neck, robust ribs, jointed limbs), proving that land-life had evolved from fish crawling out of the sea on fins, which developed into the articulated elbow and knee of land animals.

Analysis of DNA from exceptionally well preserved 38,000-year-old fossils proved that Neanderthal man was much more closely related to *Homo erectus* than had been previously recognised. Remains discovered in Gibraltar showed that Neanderthal man had survived until 28,000 years ago, living alongside humans. Some research suggested that the two species may even have interbred.

A new long-necked herbivorous dinosaur was discovered near Valencia, Spain. *Turiasaurus riodevensis*, a sauropod, was thought to have weighed over 40 tonnes and, measuring more than 30 metres from head to tail, was one of the largest creatures ever discovered and the biggest land animal yet found in Europe. Previously the largest European dinosaur fossil was the brachiosaur, which measured only 20 metres.

Analysis of fossilised remains showed that a fish common in the Devonian period (415-360 million years ago) had the most powerful bite of any creature ever discovered. Archaeologists estimated that *Dunkleosteus terrelli* could produce a pressure of 5,600 kg per sq cm from its front teeth, over four times as powerful as *Tyrannosaurus rex.*

Antikythera, a highly complex mechanical device used by the ancient Greeks and discovered in 1901, was analysed with X-ray and light imaging during the year. On 30 May scientists produced data showing that the device was able to calculate the position of the sun and moon on different dates, even reproducing subtle irregularities in the moon's orbit and accurately predicting eclipses.

PARTICLE PHYSICS AND MATHEMATICS. Particle physicists had long postulated the existence of "dark matter" to account for the force holding the solar system together. Analysis by astronomers in Arizona of a relatively recent collision of two galaxy clusters appeared to have proved this by successfully predicting the gravitational effect of the impact on light from background galaxies.

The world's brightest light source was created in July when researchers at the Diamond project in Didcot, UK, announced that tests showed that the synchrotron emitter was functioning as planned. The beam was created by firing electrons along a circular tube, generating a beam one million times more intense than a medical X-ray. The light source would be used to power giant microscopes.

The Poincaré conjecture, a complex topological (three dimensional geometry) problem relevant to understanding the shape of the universe was solved by the Russian mathematician, Doctor Grigori (Grisha) Perelman. String theory, however, which aimed to unify all the fundamental forces of nature, was under attack in 2006 by opponents in the USA, who pointed out that it had still not produced any testable predictions.

Physicists eagerly awaited the results from the Hadron collider, which was due to come on stream in 2007, hoping that it would prove the existence of the Higgs boson particle and offer some evidence of multiple dimensions. If it did not, much of the current view of the development of the universe would have to be rethought.

CHEMISTRY. Chemical solutions to global warming exercised the minds of many of the world's chemists during the year. Technology to remove greenhouse gases by scrubbing the atmosphere with hydroxides was under investigation. Very cheap photovoltaic cells were being developed, using plastics rather than silicon in order to make solar power affordable. Much research continued on biodegradable plastics and alternative fuel sources.

On 11 August, police in the UK and Pakistan thwarted an alleged plot by terrorists to smuggle onto aeroplanes the ingredients (acetone and hydrogen peroxide) for making a very sensitive explosive, triacetone triperoxide. These liquids were to be concealed in drinks containers. This led to a ban on liquids and pastes, even such standard items as shampoo and toothpaste, in airline passengers' hand luggage (see p. 17).

In March, 22 brands of soft drinks were recalled after they were found to contain levels of benzene in excess of the World Health Organisation guidelines.

Polonium-210, a radioactive isotope, which had small scale uses in industry as a heat source or to eliminate static electricity, was used in November to poison Alexander Litvinenko, a former Russian spy who defected to the UK in 2000. The isotope was highly toxic with a half life of 138 days, emitting alpha particles, which were stopped by the skin but caused extensive damage to tissue and to DNA when ingested (see pp. 22; 108).

There was controversy over the award of the Nobel Prize for Chemistry to Professor Roger Kornberg for his work on transcription and RNA (Ribonucleic acid) polymerase. This work was seen by many as being in the field of genetics rather than chemistry. The chemical societies took a different view, pointing out that chemistry crucially underpinned much bioscience. Kornberg showed the way in which the enzyme, RNA polymerase, held DNA in exactly the right position so that a precise copy was produced. The citation praised the research for "capturing the process of transcription in full flow".

Nanotechnology continued to be the fastest growing area of materials research with around 200 products on the market. Discussion about the safety of nanoparticles, both to humans and to the environment, continued during the year, with some research showing brain damage in fish exposed to water-soluble buckyballs (spherical carbon molecules).

MEDICAL AND BIOLOGICAL SCIENCES. The World Health Organisation (WHO) warned that there was a global shortage in the supply of pandemic influenza vaccine of "several billion doses". The problem was compounded by the facts that most of the pandemic vaccines in development required the administration of two separate doses to be effective, and that evidence had been found of two subtle genetic differences between outbreaks of the H5N1 avian influenza virus, thus widening the gene pool from which a form of the virus that could trigger a human pandemic might evolve. There was identification of some resistance of the H5N1 virus to osetamivir (Tamiflu), which suggested that more than one antiviral agent should be stockpiled.

A team at the Harvard School of Public Health, USA, using an analysis of the 1918 "Spanish flu" model, calculated that pandemic influenza would kill 62 million people worldwide, most of whom would be inhabitants of poorer countries who would have little or no protection in the form of vaccines or antiviral agents. Another group, working at the University of Washington, Seattle, USA, reconstructed the 1918 virus in mice and observed that there would also be a disproportionate number of deaths among healthy young adults, whose immune symptoms would be triggered by the influenza virus to produce an excess of cytokines, leading to an exaggerated inflammatory response. The predicted reaction would be similar to that which occurred when six young, healthy volunteers, taking part in a phase 1 drug trial in London, were given a drug, TGN 1412, which was a fully humanised monoclonal antibody developed for the treatment of autoimmune and inflammatory diseases and leukaemia by a German company, Te Genero. Each of the volunteers unexpectedly developed severe reactions within three hours of injection, which subsequently lead to multiple organ failure necessitating intensive care. The benefits of such trials to the volunteers were non-existent, and the risks high. Such a highly publicised disaster raised many questions, among which was the extent to which reliance could be placed on drug testing in animals before translating to humans.

Scientists from Cornell University, New York, during 2006 reported on a man who in 1984 had sustained a severe head injury, was paralysed from the neck downwards and was in a minimally conscious state (MCS). Nineteen years later (2003) he regained consciousness, which was attributed to the re-establishment of nerve tissue connections (axonal regrowth) within his brain. This "miracle" prompted intense debate about the management of similar disorders. In July, the journal *Nature* reported that a man from Massachusetts, USA, also paralysed from the neck downwards, had been fitted with a 4mm sq sensor, which read signals in the primary motor cortex of his brain, the region which would normally control the movement of his limbs. When he imagined moving his paralysed body, the implant's 100 sensors recorded activity in his brain and transmitted the signals to a computer, thus enabling him to move a cursor on a computer screen, open emails, play simple computer games, and adjust the volume of his television. He had also learnt to operate a simple robotic arm. It was suggested that this technology could later be applied to enabling similarly paralysed patients to drive wheelchairs and use prosthetic limbs.

The French woman who received the world's first (partial) face transplant in 2005 (see AR 2005, pp.405-06) gained restoration of facial sensitivity and good mobility, despite two bouts of tissue rejection. She was, nevertheless, committed to lifelong immuno-suppression. Her success enabled a British surgeon in London to gain permission to perform a full face transplant; a man who had an extensive bear injury to his face also underwent a partial facial transplant in China.

Almost 30 years after losing both her hands in a laboratory accident, a Colombian became the first woman in the world to receive a double-hand transplant. For those who had been fitted with prosthetic arms and hands, a new technique of encouraging skin tissue to bind to metal was described. The titanium prosthetic limb was osseo-integrated to the bony skeleton, thus creating a more stable and comfortable fit. A former US Marine, who lost an arm in a motorcycle accident, became the first woman to be fitted with a new prosthetic arm controlled by her original arm nerves, which had been relocated on her chest. Electrodes placed over them could, when she thought about moving her hand or arm, pick up signals which in turn sent commands to the six motors in her electronic arm.

The origin of HIV (human immunodeficiency virus) was traced to a group of chimpanzees living in southern Cameroon. Simian immunodeficiency virus (SIV cpz) was shown to be genetically very closely related to the HIV-1 virus, which caused AIDS. Professor Paul Sharp of the University of Nottingham, UK, claimed that HIV-1 had almost certainly originated in this region during the early part of the 20th century. Scientists from Seattle, USA, discovered that malaria could be contributing to the spread of HIV in sub-Saharan Africa by increasing the amount of HIV by 10 times in carriers, thus raising the chances of transmission by sexual intercourse

A woman from Devon, UK, was believed to be the first to be delivered by Caesarian section of triplets from a double womb (uterus didelphus). The larger womb contained twins and the smaller one a single foetus. Uterus didelphus was believed to affect 1 in 1,000 women but usually one womb was significantly larger than the other. This event resulted from simultaneous fertilisation by different sperm of two eggs, one in each womb.

Whereas a Danish study, which followed 420,000 mobile phone users for up to 21 years, declared that mobile phones had no effect at all on the risk of cancer, a less convincing US study found significantly lower sperm counts in men who were heavy users of mobile phones. An isolated case of a teenager who was struck by lightening whilst using her mobile phone was reported in the *British Medical Journal.* She suffered severe injuries, including deafness and complex physical cognitive and emotional problems.

A grey mouse, *Mus cypriacus*, discovered in Cyprus in October, was the first new mammalian species found in Europe for a century.

For the second time in five years the Nobel Prize for Physiology or Medicine was awarded to researchers working on the nematode *Caenorhabditis elegans*. Professor Andrew Z. Fire and Professor Craig C. Mello of the USA set out in 1998 to find why and how the artificial introduction of RNA (Ribonucleic acid) into a cell interfered with the function of its genes. It was believed that RNA interference helped to regulate the expression of genes and stabilise the genome. It could also act as a cellular defence mechanism. The technique was used by biologists to close down the activity of specific genes in cells which they wanted to study.

PUBLIC UNDERSTANDING OF SCIENCE. The battle between evolutionary theory and creationism continued during 2006. Professor Richard Dawkins, whose latest, and very successful, book, *The God Delusion*, was a direct challenge to creationists (see p. 475), set up a foundation to challenge the use of creationist literature in school science teaching.

INFORMATION TECHNOLOGY

ALTHOUGH it rarely appeared outside the pages of the technology press, an important fight to maintain the neutrality of the Internet simmered throughout the year. Historically, the Internet had never prioritised one content provider over another, but several large Internet service providers (ISPs), including AT&T, Verizon, and Comcast, made announcements in 2006 that they might try to start controlling traffic depending on its source. The ISPs argued that they needed the capacity to earn additional revenue to pay for the extensive network upgrades that they were undertaking in order to cope with increased demand for traffic-intensive services, such as peer-to-peer file sharing, Internet television, and video. In addition, they argued that the ability to prioritise some types of traffic over others would allow their customers to use their Internet connections more efficiently. Voice traffic, for example, although low in overall traffic volume, required a highly responsive connection in order to maintain high call quality. ISPs argued that they could prioritise this type of traffic over, for example, traffic such as email which could suffer delays without adversely affecting the user's experience.

Critics claimed that the proposal was designed to allow ISPs, which had increasingly also become content providers, to prioritise their own content and those of their preferred partners over others, essentially creating a "walled garden" and destroying the very feature which had made the Internet so popular: its open and democratic nature.

Interestingly, the chief protagonists in the debate were not the usual David and Goliath figures. Both sides had heavyweight supporters, with some of the Internet's largest content providers, including Microsoft, Google, and Yahoo, lobbying in favour of maintaining net neutrality. By February the subject was being actively discussed in the US Congress (the bicameral legislature). All attempts in the USA to pass legislation to enforce net neutrality, however, had proved unsuccessful by the end of the year. The last effort occurred in September, when an attempt to amend a larger communications bill to include laws preventing ISPs from prioritising their own content failed in a narrow 11-11 vote in the commerce committee of the US Senate (the upper house). With a few exceptions that were quickly remedied by the federal communications commission, no telecommunications provider appeared at the end of the year to be blocking Internet traffic and demanding payment to lift the block. The FCC also adopted a non-binding policy statement saying that US citizens were "entitled to access the lawful Internet content of their choice."

VIDEO. The ever faster speeds with which data could be moved around the Internet had seen content develop to include ever richer media. From its text-only beginnings, the Internet had become capable of delivering pictures, followed by music, and finally, in 2006, the broadcasting of video over the Internet became widespread. While content providers began to take tentative steps towards offering music video, film download, and "TV on demand" services, the runaway success of the year was YouTube, a web site that allowed users to upload and share video, which they had created themselves. Doing for film what blogs (web logs) were doing for journalism, YouTube turned consumers of content into producers. Various rival sites sprang up throughout the year, but YouTube remained far and away the most popular, serving over 100 million video clips every day. In October Google announced that it would purchase YouTube for US$1.65 billion, despite the company having yet to turn a profit (see p. 496).

WEB 2.0. The increasing richness of applications delivered over the World Wide Web (generally referred to as Web 2.0 (see AR 2005, pp. 410-11) continued to feature prominently in the technology press. Of particular interest was the emergence of web-based applications of sufficient quality and responsiveness to compete with their desktop counterparts. Often at the centre of the Web 2.0 movement, the Internet search company Google launched an online service that incorporated the functions of both a word processor and a spreadsheet application entirely within a web browser. Users could create and edit documents and spreadsheets without requiring any of the traditional desktop applications.

SOCIAL NETWORKING. Another good example of a Web 2.0 application, which became phenomenally popular in 2006, was social networking. Social networking sites facilitated the building of online communities. Typically users created a web page about themselves, incorporating several kinds of media, such as pictures, music, video, and blogs. What made social networking sites different from other personal web sites, however, was the capacity for users to describe their relationships with one another. This feature facilitated a "network effect" whereby each user was able to see themselves in a wider context and to form new relationships with other users through, for example, a mutual friend or a shared interest. It was this ability to interconnect users that led to these sites being described as social networks, and which made them compelling to members and non-members alike.

Although these types of site had enjoyed some popularity for several years, and arguably sites which brought people of similar interests together had been around almost as long as the Internet, it was in 2006 that social networking emerged as one of the biggest Internet phenomena. While sites such as Friendster blazed the trail, all were slowly eclipsed by MySpace, which by August 2006 had 100 million users and was the most visited web site on the Internet. The purchase of MySpace by The News Corporation in 2005 for US$580 million (see p. 496) reflected the continuing recognition of the Internet as an increasingly important medium for content providers and advertisers. Naturally with new technologies came new abuses of those technologies, and concerns such as the vulnerability of minors to sexual predators and the illegal publication of copyrighted material were discussed by the legislatures of many countries, including the USA and the UK.

SOFTWARE PATENTS (NOVELL & MICROSOFT). In November, software companies Microsoft and Novell announced a broad series of agreements, both business and technical, to improve interoperability between their products. The business agreement would involve the promotion of one another's products; the technical collaboration comprised a set of joint development projects designed to make Microsoft's Windows (a proprietary operating system) and Novell's Suse Linux (an operating system based largely on Open Source software, see AR 2003, p. 482) more compatible with each other. The deal soon soured, however, when serious objections were raised by the Open Source community, after it was discovered that the agreements included mutual patent protection for their respective customers. This mutual protection meant that buyers of Novell's Suse Linux received with it a covenant from Microsoft not to pursue intellectual property claims against them (with the same protection against Novell given to Microsoft's Windows customers).

The Open Source community highlighted that this protection was effectively giving credence to the idea that the Open Source software contained in Novell's Suse Linux—software created by thousands of volunteer developers from all over the world and redistributed at no cost to Novell—might contain code that was covered by patents held by Microsoft and other third parties. Their objection to this implied claim was the belief that Microsoft and other proprietary software manufacturers considered patent litigation their "weapon of last resort" against Open Source software, which continued to gain ground on them in the marketplace.

In countries where software patents were enforceable, the aggressive accumulation of patents for the sole purpose of harassing rivals was already a reality, and with typical legal costs in defending claims of patent infringement (even those widely considered trivial or nonsensical) running into several million US dollars, patent litigation had become an effective tool with which to eradicate small rivals unable to afford a legal defence.

In giving tacit consent to the idea that the Open Source software that went into making Suse Linux might contain code covered by patents, Novell were priming the weapon that could eventually be used against all Open Source software, including Novell, ironically, as their covenant with Microsoft would last only five years.

The predominant feeling within the Open Source community was a mixture of anger and pity. Many believed that the deal would ultimately marginalise Novell's Suse Linux and lead to its demise. The Open Source community feared that Novell could find themselves unable to distribute the vast majority of the Open Source software that went into making their Suse Linux product, leaving them with old versions of software and burdening themselves with the task of supporting and maintaining them.

In addition to the general feeling that the deal went against the spirit of Open Source, Eben Moglen, the attorney for the Free Software Foundation which created and oversaw the General Public Licence (GPL, the most popular Open Source licence), stated that the deal might be in violation of the GPL. Even if it transpired that there was no violation, the deal created renewed interest in the next version of the GPL (version 3), which would include provisions to prevent the distribution of Open Source software by companies party to a similar agreement.

Only a few days after the deal was announced, Novell and Microsoft had already "agreed to disagree" on whether the deal implied that there was code contained within GNU/Linux which was covered by patents held by Microsoft.

ENERGY EFFICIENCY. As worldwide energy prices continued to rise, the beginnings were seen of a concerted effort by computer manufacturers to produce more energy efficient machines. Focusing largely on server systems (typically the largest consumers of energy) manufacturers began talking less about raw processing power and more about the processing power per watt of their products. The world's two largest processor manufacturers, AMD and Intel, which had both launched so called "dual core" products in the previous year (see AR 2005, p. 409), moved from promoting their new products' greater processing power to their greater efficiency. Terms such as "flops per watt" were coined (a flop could be loosely described as the number of computations that a computer could carry out in a second). Supermicro, a manufacturer of computer systems, began fitting high efficiency power supplies to its range of server machines. Typically one of the least efficient components in a computer system, the power supply frequently lost between 40 and 50 per cent of its energy as heat: Supermicro's new power supplies ran at up to 85 per cent efficiency.

SUN MICROSYSTEMS & JAVA. Sun Microsystems became the largest contributor of Free and Open Source Software (FOSS) when, in November, they released one of their most influential software projects, Java, under the General Public Licence version 2 (the most popular licence for FOSS software).

Java, a software project consisting, in the main, of a programming language of the same name and a computer environment emulated entirely in software (known as a Virtual Machine) was popular among software developers because of its use of modern, object-oriented, programming techniques, and its capacity to run software, unmodified, on different computer hardware.

Typically software had to be modified to a greater or lesser degree before it could be made to run on a different kind of computer architecture. This often led to a significant amount of maintenance work for a large software project that was required to run on many classes of computer. Java attempted to solve that fundamental problem through the use of its Virtual Machine; software developers could write their software to run on the Virtual Machine and Sun Microsystems would ensure that the Virtual Machine ran on the different classes of hardware.

In late 2006, Java was the most widely deployed application platform in the world and it was widely held that its release under the GPL would only serve to increase its popularity.

GAMES. The year 2006 was an active one for the gaming industry, with two of the three largest manufacturers bringing out new games consoles. Sony's PlayStation 3 continued the trend of using ever greater processing power to enable richer and more detailed graphics, the same goal as Microsoft's Xbox which had been released a year earlier. Nintendo, however, surprised the industry and consumers by largely abandoning this race and, instead, opting for the more radical approach of introducing an innovative, motion-sensing controller, which allowed users to control games using actions more akin to real motions (for example, to play a tennis video game, the user would swing the controller in the same way they would a real racquet). The new controller was introduced with the stated aim of trying to make games consoles more appealing to a wider demographic, in particular to women.

THE ENVIRONMENT

HISTORIANS may remember 2006 as the year in which environmental concerns, especially those relating to climate change, became central to mainstream political discourse—if not to political action—at least in the advanced industrialised countries. The vocabulary of climate change was creeping into ordinary speech, and in the UK it became commonplace for newspapers to publish guides on how to assess (and reduce) one's "carbon footprint" (the amount of carbon dioxide emitted by an individual, through personal consumption). The media began to entertain the possibility of an end to cheap air travel, and more generally the notion that environmental responsibilities might put a brake on the imperative of consumerism.

THE POLITICS OF CLIMATE CHANGE. There was no landmark event in 2006 along the lines of the February 2005 entry into force of the 1997 Kyoto Protocol to the 1992 UN Framework Convention on Climate Change (UNFCCC) (see AR 2005, pp. 411-12). The second meeting of the parties to the Protocol, which set binding targets for industrialised states to reduce their emissions of greenhouse gases by 2012, was held on 6-17 November in Nairobi, the Kenyan capital, in conjunction with the 12th session of the conference of the parties to the UNFCCC (COP 12/MOP 2). The meeting ended with an agreement to complete a review of the

Protocol in 2008, to prepare for the setting of new targets for cutting emissions of carbon dioxide (CO2) and other greenhouse gases, which would come into effect on the expiry of the Kyoto Protocol in 2012.

Commentators noted that the emphasis of the conference was, for the first time, less on the effort to slow the pace of global warming than on the need to adapt to climate change, resulting an a ministerial agreement to establish an adaptation fund to help countries in the developing world cope with droughts, floods, rising sea levels, and changes to agricultural land. The fund would be financed through international carbon trading and implemented partly through the clean development mechanism, in which industrialised countries invested in renewable energy projects and low-carbon industry in the developing world in exchange for carbon credits.

Critics said that the agreements reached at the conference were weak, showing a failure of political will in the face of the urgency of the problem, especially following the publication in October of the Stern Report (see below). China and India, whose rapid economic growth held serious implications for the effectiveness of any strategy to reduce carbon emissions, continued to hold back from the prospect of talks to set an agenda for mandatory emissions cuts. However, it was also notable that for the first time at a UN environment conference the USA made no challenge to the science of climate change, both in its measurable reality and the causal relationship between human activities and rising temperatures.

Perhaps the two most significant political developments in relation to climate change in 2006 occurred in the two advanced industrialised countries that had refused to ratify the Kyoto Protocol, the USA and Australia.

Republican Governor of California Arnold Schwarzenegger on 27 September signed legislation imposing sweeping cuts on CO2 emissions by industry, utilities, and oil refineries, with effect from 2012, aiming to reduce the state's emissions by 25 per cent by 2020. This was in marked contrast to the position of the federal Republican administration, led by President George W. Bush, which clung to a supposed "uncertainty" in the scientific evidence of a link between the accumulation of heat-trapping gases in the atmosphere and rising temperatures, and anyway ruled out mandatory cuts in emissions because of their adverse effects on the US economy. California was the world's 12th largest producer of carbon emissions and was also vulnerable through its long coastline to rising sea levels. Schwarzenegger had also in July signed an agreement with UK Prime Minister Tony Blair, under which California and the UK undertook to participate in a joint carbon trading scheme. However, Californian voters in November rejected a measure to impose a tax on oil companies to pay for renewable energy projects.

In Australia, Prime Minister John Howard, formerly a robust sceptic on man-made climate change who was determined to protect the country's coal industry, performed an about-turn in October, telling Australian citizens that the prolonged drought that had affected southern and eastern states for five years would have serious consequences for the economy by reducing agricultural production (see p. 347). Howard also now proclaimed himself a "climate change realist", announcing a major investment in clean energy-generating technology. An inquiry commissioned by the government earlier in the year reported in November that a nuclear energy programme could fulfil Australia's energy needs while at the same time significantly cutting its greenhouse gas emissions.

A summit meeting of EU member states held in March mandated the European Commission to draw up an energy policy for Europe (EPE), for adoption in 2007, which would include "sustainability" as one of its principles. The EU's environment commissioner announced in November that in the second phase (2008-12) of the EU's emissions trading scheme (ETS) there would be a 7 per cent overall cut in member states' permitted emissions. Of 10 national plans for emissions targets submitted to the European Commission, all but that of the UK were rejected as over-generous to emitting industries. The Commission proposed in December that, from 2011, all flights within the EU should be included in the ETS and that from 2012 all flights to and from EU countries should be included in the scheme. The European Parliament had voted in July to scrap the exemption of aviation fuel from VAT, because cheap air travel was making aviation the fastest-growing source of carbon emissions, but there was little prospect that the measure would be adopted by the EU member states. Carbon emissions from aircraft—although a small proportion of total emissions—had risen by 73 per cent since 1990.

In November the International Energy Agency (IEA) published its *World Energy Outlook 2006*, which predicted that unless urgent action was taken by both governments and consumers, carbon dioxide-equivalent (cde) emissions would rise by 53 per cent by 2030, with the contribution of developing countries rising from 39 per cent in 2006 to 52 per cent, largely because China, India, and other fast-growing economies were heavy users of coal. The IEA forecast that China alone would overtake the USA in terms of carbon emissions as early as 2010. The report laid out an alternative scenario, in which effective energy-saving measures combined with increased use of nuclear power succeeded in reducing the global demand for power by 10 per cent.

A report produced by Sir Nicholas Stern, a former chief economist at the World Bank, and commissioned by the UK government, entitled *The Economics of Climate Change*, was published on 31 October, just days before the UNFCCC conference in Nairobi, the timing evidently intended to concentrate the minds of delegates. It was the first comprehensive study of the economic consequences of global warming (for summary see pp. 561-64). Stern estimated that the cost of acting quickly to reduce carbon emissions was an annual £184 billion, but that failure to take drastic action—continuing "business as usual"—would cause a permanent loss to global GDP of between 5 and 20 per cent, through the damage caused by droughts, floods, coastal erosion, water shortages, epidemics, and the increased frequency of extreme weather. The Stern review team used a combination of economic models in conjunction with the scientific data of the UN Intergovernmental Panel on Climate Change (IPCC) third assessment report (TAR) of 2001 (see AR 2001, p. 485). The report recommended that, in order to stabilise the concentration of greenhouse gases in the atmosphere at somewhere between 450 and 500 parts per million cde, a triple strategy should be pursued. Comprehensive measures of taxation, trading, and regulation should set a price on carbon emissions. Public policy should support accelerated research and development of low-carbon technologies, especially in the energy sector. The third element Stern described as "the removal of the barriers to behavioural change", through a combination of regulation and public information policies, and the inducement of a sense of collective responsibility for the environment.

ENVIRONMENTAL SCIENCE. Although there remained many areas of uncertainty in the science of climate change (related to variations in the computer models that scientists used to develop future scenarios, or to the difficulty of calculating the degree to which "positive feedback" effects would accelerate global warming), the year saw the publication of reports presenting an avalanche of evidence that changes to the Earth's climate were happening faster than previously thought, and that the window of opportunity to take action to arrest or slow the process was becoming smaller.

Several reports released during the year confirmed a continuing rise in the atmospheric levels of the main greenhouse gases—carbon dioxide (CO2), methane (CH4), and nitrous oxide (N2O)—although the results varied slightly with the different methodologies used. The US National Oceanic and Atmospheric Administration (NOAA) announced in March that the concentration of the three greenhouse gases in the atmosphere had reached 381 parts per million (ppm) in 2005, about 100 ppm higher than pre-industrial levels. The annual increase in 2005 was 2.6 ppm, which was almost double the rate of increase in the 1970s. In the same month the UN World Meteorological Organisation (WMO) released its figures for 2004, giving a concentration of CO2 of 377.1 ppm, with a rise during the year of 1.8 ppm. The WMO published its assessment for 2005 in November, with CO2 rising to 379.1 ppm, CH4 remaining stable at 1,783 parts per billion (ppb), and N2O rising to 319.2 ppb. The WMO calculated that the concentration of CO2 had risen 35.4 per cent since the late 18th century.

In September the results were announced of the latest and deepest analysis of the composition of a 3.27 km deep ice core extracted from Dome Concordia (Dome C) in eastern Antarctica by the 10-country European project for ice-coring in Antarctica (EPICA) (see AR 2005, p. 414). The results found that current concentrations of CO2 in the atmosphere were higher than for 800,000 years. EPICA scientists further calculated that hitherto the fastest rate of increase in CO2 had been of 30 ppm over a period of 1,000 years. The most recent increase of 30 ppm had taken place over the past 17 years

US government statistics released in April showed that in 2004—the last year for which figures were available—the USA released the equivalent of 16.3 billion tonnes of carbon dioxide-equivalent (cde) emissions into the atmosphere, a record level and an increase of 1.7 per cent over 2003. *Greenhouse Gas Data 2006*, a report released on 31 October by the UNFCCC secretariat on overall emissions by industrialised countries, including the first complete set of data submitted by the parties to the Kyoto Protocol, showed an overall drop in emissions in 1990-2004 of 3.3 per cent. However, this was largely accounted for by a 38.6 per cent decrease in emissions by the post-communist industrialised economies of central and eastern Europe, while the emissions of other industrialised countries rose by 11 per cent. The steepest increase in CO2 emissions was in the transport sector, where they grew by 23.9 per cent.

Perhaps the most significant findings on rising global temperatures were those contained in a report released in June by the national research council (NRC) of the US National Academies of Science in response to a request by the US Congress. A controversy had arisen over a claim made in 1999 by the climatologist Michael Mann that the warming in the last decades of the 20th century was unprecedented over the previous 1,000 years: critics had cast doubt on the reliability of Mann's research methods. The NRC report said that there was enough evidence from "proxy" data—from sediments, tree rings, retreating glaciers, ice cores, and documentary sources—to say with a "high level of confidence" that the last decades of the 20th century were indeed warmer that any comparable period for the last 400 years. However, before 1600, precise proxy evidence became sparser and the NRC would say only that the Mann team's conclusions over the period going back to 1000 were "plausible". The report noted that a documented rise in the average temperature in the northern hemisphere in the 20th century of 0.6 degrees Celsius was reflected in the detail of the contemporary proxy data.

The UK's Meteorological Office, using temperature records going back to 1659, in December released provisional figures indicating that 2006 would be the warmest year on record in the UK. The mean temperature was 10.87 degrees Celsius, 1.37 degrees Celsius above the average for the period 1961-90. A study by 19 climatologists, published in December in the US *Proceedings of the National Academy of Scientists*, which matched observable records with 80 different computer simulations, concluded that rising ocean temperatures, which caused more frequent and violent tropical storms, very likely resulted from atmospheric warming caused by greenhouse gases. Another study, by scientists at the University of Utah, USA, published in the journal *Science* in May, found that 26 years of weather satellite measurements indicated that the Earth's tropical regions, in both the northern and southern hemispheres, had expanded between 1979 and 2005 by about 2 degrees of latitude or 225 km, pushing the subtropical jet streams further away from the Equator. However, the authors stressed that they were unable to say from the evidence that the phenomenon was caused by global warming.

Studies published in *Science* on 24 March (by the University of Arizona and the US National Centre for Atmospheric Research in Colorado) identified an interglacial period between 129,000 years ago and 116,000 years ago, when sea levels rose between 4 metres and 6 metres. The researchers calculated that temperatures at that time were between 3 degrees and 5 degrees Celsius higher than current levels and therefore forecast that if these temperature rises were achieved over the next 100 years the Greenland and Antarctic ice sheets could be destabilised and substantially melt much faster than hitherto predicted.

On the replenishment of the stratospheric ozone layer protecting the surface of the Earth from harmful ultraviolet radiation, an assessment released by the UN's WMO in August forecast that the ozone layer in mid-latitudes would recover by 2049, some five years later than predicted in the previous, 2002, assessment. In the polar regions recovery would take longer, and Antarctic ozone, which had been worst affected, was not expected to recover before 2065 (15 years later than previously expected). The longer time scales were the result largely of upward revisions of the quantities of ozone depleting chemicals (principally CFCs), currently contained in refrigerators and other equipment, which would eventually be released into the atmosphere. The 1987 Montreal Protocol, which provided for the phasing out of the production and use of CFCs, was regarded as the most successful international environmental treaty ever concluded. However, it was reported in April that a study by the IPCC had found that HFCs—the family of ozone-friendly gases substituted for CFCs—were also more powerful agents of global warming than CO2.

ENVIRONMENTAL IMPACTS AND BIODIVERSITY. There was further evidence that the polar regions, which were experiencing steeper rises in temperature than anywhere else on the planet, were undergoing an accelerating loss of ice. A report published in the journal *Science* in February, based on satellite data and produced by scientists at the US National Aeronautical and Space Administration (NASA)'s jet propulsion laboratory, found that in southern Greenland the progress of the Kangerdlugssauq glacier to the sea had accelerated by 210 per cent between 2000 and 2005. In 2005 southern Greenland glaciers shed some 150 million cubic km of ice into the sea, compared with an estimated 50 million cubic km in 1996. This corresponded to a rise in air temperatures in southern Greenland of 3 degrees Celsius over the past 20 years, resulting in an accumulation of melted surface ice that trickled through crevasses to form a lubricating layer of water at the base of the glaciers. The researchers calculated that this rate of glacier melting contributed 0.5 mm to a global sea level rise of 3 mm per year. Jim Hansen, director of the NASA Goddard institute for space studies, wrote in *The Independent* newspaper that current computer predictions that the polar ice caps would take 1,000 years to melt did not take into account such acceleration of glaciers. The NASA data were reinforced by the results of a study published on 11 August in *Science* by researchers at the University of Texas. Using satellite measurements of gravitational variations in the Greenland ice sheet between 2002 and 2005, they calculated that 240 cubic km of ice was melting each year. The Greenland ice sheet totalled some 2.5 million cubic km of ice, about 10 per cent of the world's ice mass. The shrinking of the Arctic's summer sea ice had been documented in 2005 (see AR 2005, p. 415), but a study by US scientists published on 12 December in the journal *Geophysical Research Letters* forecast that, unless effective measures were taken to reduce carbon emissions, the Arctic Ocean could lose all its summer ice by 2040, some 40 years earlier than previously predicted by computer simulations.

Projected change in Arctic sea-ice and permafrost 2090

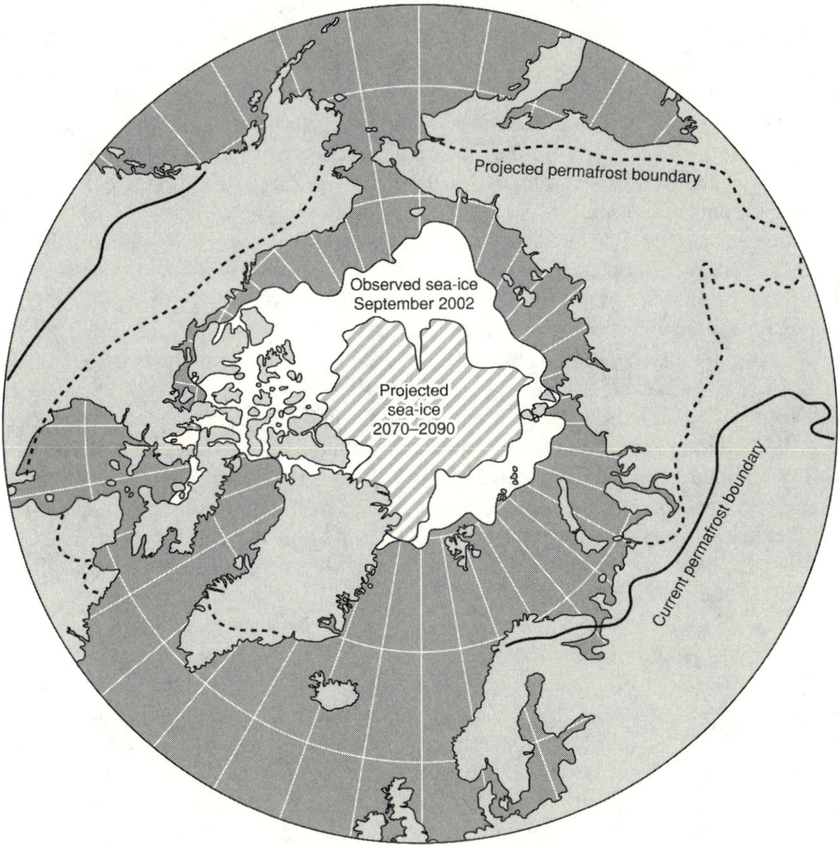

UN Environment Programme / GRID-Arendal

It was a rich irony that just as the scale of the threat to the stability of the Arctic environment was becoming apparent, so the very industries responsible for the bulk of heat-trapping carbon emissions began to envisage new opportunities in the changing environmental conditions. The countries bordering the Arctic Ocean, the USA, Russia, Norway, and Canada, all began to use the increased area of open sea to explore for hitherto inaccessible oil and gas fields. The number of new oil and gas prospecting licences granted in Greenland had tripled over the past three years. It was reported in April that the British Antarctic Survey (BAS) had expressed concern over the involvement of the US Geological Survey (USGS) with leading oil and gas companies in a proposed assessment of oil and gas reserves in the "circumarctic" area, under the auspices of the "international polar year" (IPY) due to start in March 2007. The BAS considered that the project was incompatible with the scientific and ethical guidelines underpinning the IPY, an international collaboration intended in large part to assess the impact of climate change on the polar regions.

Expectations that the Antarctic ice sheet would grow in mass because of increased snowfall appeared to be confounded by the results of a study by scientists at the University of Colorado published on 3 March in the online journal, *Science Express*. Using measurements of gravitational variations in Antarctica, taken since 2002 by two satellites, the researchers concluded that the ice sheet was losing 152 cubic km of ice each year. A study published on 4 August in the journal *Nature*, conducted by scientists from Hamilton College, New York, concluded that the collapse of the Antarctic Larsen B ice shelf in 2002 was an event on a scale unprecedented since the end of the last Ice Age, some 10,000 years ago. Also in August the BAS estimated that some 13,500 sq. km of Antarctic sea ice had been lost over the previous 50 years. In March the results of analysis of weather balloon data by the BAS showed that air temperatures in the troposphere over the Antarctic had increased by 0.7 degrees Celsius per decade over the past 30 years, an increase three times faster than the global average and a result not predicted by current climate models.

Threats to the world's biodiversity, not only from global warming and its consequences but also from the toll taken on the environment by the inexorable growth of the world's human population and its increasingly globalised economic system, were highlighted in numerous reports throughout the year. The polar bear, whose hunting grounds on the Arctic sea ice were shrinking, became the photogenic totem of global warming. In December the US department of the interior proposed to list the polar bear as "threatened" under the endangered species act, although it was unclear what this implied for US policy on carbon emissions and Arctic oil exploration. Canadian and international studies had also shown an alarming accumulation of the PBDE group of fire-retardant chemical compounds in polar bear tissue, which it was feared could seriously affect the bears' immune and reproductive systems. The polar bear was included by the International Union for the Conservation of Nature (IUCN) on its Red List published in May of the 16,119 animal and plant species under serious threat of extinction—530 more species than on the list of 2004.

The IUCN said in July that an expedition earlier in the year to Cameroon appeared to confirm that the West African black rhinoceros was extinct, the victim of poaching. It was widely reported in December that the baiji, or white-fin freshwater dolphin, unique to China's Yangtze river, included on the Red List and last seen in the wild in 2004, was thought to be extinct. Pollution, over-fishing, and the increasing volume of river traffic were all thought to have played a part in the decline of the species. The Gangetic freshwater dolphin in north India and Bangladesh was also thought to be under threat from pollution and the damming of rivers. The conservation body WWF (formerly the World Wildlife Fund) reported in July that the plight of the tiger was probably even more serious than previously thought, with the combined populations of the three surviving subspecies estimated at fewer than 5,000. There appeared to be little political will to enforce measures to protect the tiger against the chief threats to its existence: poaching and human encroachment on its habitat.

Nineteen eminent biodiversity specialists, including World Bank chief scientist Robert Watson, wrote to *Nature* in July calling for governments to establish an international political framework to arrest a steep decline in virtually all aspect of biodiversity and avert a potentially "catastrophic loss of species".

There was increasing evidence of an impending, multi-faceted crisis in the effects of human activity on the world's water resources. A report published in June, produced jointly by the UN Environment Programme (UNEP) and the IUCN, warned that damage to ocean habitats from pollution, litter, and exploitation by over-fishing would soon become irreversible. The technological capacity to exploit deep-sea environments for fishing and mining had advanced rapidly in recent years, outstripping current legal and institutional frameworks of conservation. Only international co-operation could provide effective restraint, because at least 60 per cent of the marine world was beyond national jurisdictions.

A study published in *Science* in November forecast that if levels of commercial fishing were maintained, the stocks of all fish species currently caught would collapse to 10 per cent of maximum recorded catches, a level at which commercial fishing would become unviable. In October UNEP produced two reports on the marine environment, the first focusing on the effects of land-based activities. It found that although there had been significant improvement in curbing oil and chemical leakage into the sea, there were major and increasing problems with discharges of untreated sewage, the run-off of agricultural fertiliser, industrial discharges (increasingly in developing countries), and marine litter from shipping. The number of coastal "dead zones" caused by run-off fertiliser and other pollutants had doubled every decade since the 1960s. A second report, on the effects of climate change on marine ecosystems, found a high level of correlation between coral mortality and increasing ocean temperatures. However, there was a high degree of scientific uncertainty on the long-term capacity of coral to adapt to higher temperatures.

There was consistent evidence globally of accelerated melting of the world's mountain glaciers, including research published in November by the Chinese Academy of Sciences, which found that 82 per cent of the 5,000 glaciers monitored on the Tibet-Qinghai plateau had receded by 4.5 per cent over the past 50 years. Several great river systems, including the Ganges, the Mekong, and the Yangtze, were fed by the glaciers' spring meltwaters, and scientists were concerned that a rapid melting of the glaciers as a result of climate change would initially produce catastrophic flooding in the river basins, followed by long-term aridity as the rivers' sources dried up.

The Hadley centre of the UK Meteorological Office published in October what was thought to be the first prediction of the global incidence of droughts in the 21st century, using computer climate modelling combined with historical rainfall and temperature records from 1952 to 1998, and an assumption of a continued rise in greenhouse gases. The study forecast that the incidence of moderate droughts, which had risen from 15 per cent in 1952 to 25 per cent (largely because of persistent droughts in Africa, particularly the Sahel region), could increase to 50 per cent in 2100, whilst the incidence of extreme drought could rise from 3 per cent to 30 per cent by 2100. A report produced in October by the aid agency, Tearfund, estimated that globally there were already some 25 million environmental refugees, largely fleeing from water shortages.

The WWF published in October its *Living Planet Report*, a biennial comprehensive environmental audit. It calculated that humanity's demand for natural resources had, for two decades, exceeded the Earth's capacity for self-replenishment and the absorption of CO2, and that the state of "ecological debt"—the excess of demand over renewal—in 2003 was 25 per cent. If the current global average level of consumption were sustained to 2050, two planets would be required to meet the demands of the global population, and at this point the exhaustion of natural assets was likely to precipitate large-scale ecosystem collapse. The current average "ecological footprint", expressed in terms of the area of land needed to sustain a person's consumption, was 2.23 hectares per capita (hpc), compared with a sustainable "footprint" of 1.8 hpc; this was a three-fold increase since 1961. At the top of the scale was the United Arab Emirates (11.9 hpc), followed by the industrialised countries (all of which were "in deficit"), whilst Afghanistan and Malawi lay at the bottom (0.1 hpc). The report proposed a complex strategy for moving towards a sustainable society, including a slowing of population growth, building more resource-efficient infrastructure, more accurate resource accounting to avoid environmental crises, the negotiation of schemes of "footprint allocation" that would almost certainly entail reduced rates of consumption by rich countries, and more rigorous implementation of policies to protect forests, soil, and sea resources.

XIV THE LAW

INTERNATIONAL LAW—EU LAW

INTERNATIONAL LAW

THE INTERNATIONAL COURT OF JUSTICE (ICJ) celebrated its 60th anniversary. It made rather slow progress in dealing with the 13 cases before it in 2006: it decided only one case and one request for provisional measures. In February Rosalyn Higgins (UK) was elected president, the first woman to have been elected president and the only woman on the Court; Awn Shawkat al-Khasawneh (Jordan) was elected vice-president. In presenting the Court's annual report to the General Assembly in October, Judge Higgins said that the Court's aim was to increase further its productivity.

The Court received three new cases, one of which was quickly withdrawn. The others were: first, a case by Djibouti against France concerning the scope of international criminal jurisdiction, a subject considered by the Court in several recent cases (see p. 234); second, *Pulp Mills on the River Uruguay*, a case brought by Argentina against Uruguay (see p. 168). The Court rejected Argentina's request for provisional measure in this case. Argentina claimed that Uruguay had unilaterally authorised the construction of two paper pulp mills on the river in violation of the 1975 Statute of the River Uruguay; these mills jeopardised conservation of the environment of the river and surrounding areas. It asked the Court to order Uruguay to suspend preparation for construction and halt building work, to co-operate with Argentina to preserve the aquatic environment, and to refrain from unilateral action with respect to construction which did not comply with the 1975 Statute. The Court held that these measures were not urgently required. As regarded the procedural obligations, these could be remedied at the merits stage. As to the rights of a substantive nature, there was nothing to show an imminent threat of irreparable harm to the aquatic environment or to the economic or social interests of Argentinians. The threat of pollution was not imminent as the mills were not expected to be operational before August 2007. The Court nevertheless made it clear that by proceeding with the work Uruguay bore all risks relating to any finding on the merits and that an order for destruction was still possible.

The Court held that it did not have jurisdiction in *Armed Activities on the Territory of the Congo (New Application: 2002)*, Democratic Republic of Congo (DRC) v Rwanda. Rwanda invoked 11 bases of jurisdiction and the Court went through them exhaustively, even though few offered any real prospect of success. The most controversial issue concerned the Genocide Convention: the DRC argued that Rwanda's reservation excluding the jurisdiction of the Court over disputes about the Convention was invalid under the law of treaties as the Genocide Convention contained peremptory norms. The Court accepted that the rights and obligations in the Convention were of a higher status than normal rules, but the mere fact that these rights might be at issue in a dispute would not give the Court jurisdiction.

The Court concluded hearings in the *Application of the Convention on the Prevention and Punishment of the Crime of Genocide* (Bosnia & Herzegovina v Serbia & Montenegro) on 9 May, but it did not manage to issue a judgment in this case by the end of the year. This case had started in 1993.

There were some significant developments with regard to compliance with the Court's judgments and opinions. After considerable delay Nigeria finally withdrew its troops from the Bakassi peninsula which the Court had assigned to Cameroon in its 2002 judgment (see p. 254; AR 2002, pp. 471-72). Israel had not complied with its obligations under the 2004 Advisory Opinion on the *Legal Consequences of the Construction of a Wall in the Occupied Palestinian Territory*. This determined that the construction of the wall was unlawful and violated international human rights, humanitarian law, and the right of the Palestinian people to self-determination. Israel was, therefore, under an obligation to return the land seized for purposes of construction of the wall and to make reparation for the damage caused (see AR 2004, p. 443). However, Israel had pressed ahead with construction of the wall and with new settlements in the West Bank. On 15 December the General Assembly voted overwhelmingly to establish a UN register of damage caused by the construction, to document damages for possible future adjudication. Only Israel, the USA, Australia, and four small Pacific island states voted against the resolution.

The first maritime boundary arbitration award to be decided under the 1982 UN Convention on the Law of the Sea was made in a case between Barbados and Trinidad & Tobago (see p. 154). Trinidad & Tobago contested the jurisdiction of the tribunal (at the Permanent Court of Arbitration), but it held that it had jurisdiction to delimit the continental shelf, including the outer continental shelf and the exclusive economic zone (EEZ). However, it did not have jurisdiction to issue a substantive decision on the appropriate fisheries regime. The tribunal followed well-established jurisprudence in using the equidistance line, with minor modifications in order to achieve an equitable result, in its delimitation. It rejected Barbados's argument that it should take account of the fact that Barbados fishermen had traditionally fished in waters off the island of Tobago and therefore had the right of access to fish in that area; this was outside its jurisdiction because sovereign rights with respect to living resources in the EEZ did not fall under the obligatory jurisdiction of the tribunal under the Convention. However, it nevertheless held that there was an obligation on the parties to negotiate an agreement which would give Barbados fishermen access to fisheries in the EEZ.

The INTERNATIONAL CRIMINAL COURT (ICC) began proceedings in its first case. Thomas Lubanga Dyilo, former leader of a militia group in the Ituri province of the DRC, was formally charged by the prosecutor with enlisting and conscripting children under the age of 15 and using them to participate actively in hostilities. He was the first person to be arrested and transferred to the ICC, and the first individual to be brought before an international court solely on the basis of these crimes. He was transferred from the DRC to the ICC in The Hague, the Netherlands, where the pre-trial hearing was held in November. The ICC prosecutor continued to investigate and collect evidence on the situation in the Darfur region of Sudan; he submitted a series of reports to the UN Security Council.

Charles Taylor, the former president of Liberia, was transferred to the Special Court for Sierra Leone, established with UN backing, in March (see p. 242). He had been indicted on several counts of crimes against humanity and war crimes committed through his backing for the Revolutionary United Front rebel group during the 10-year civil war in Sierra Leone. He appeared before the Court in Freetown, capital of Sierra Leone, in April. The UN Security Council then approved his transfer to The Hague for trial before a chamber of the Special Court because of fears of unrest in Sierra Leone. The trials of nine other people were also under way before the Special Court.

The INTERNATIONAL CRIMINAL TRIBUNAL FOR THE FORMER YUGOSLAVIA (ICTY) continued to make good progress; cases were closed against 100 accused out of a total of 161 indicted. All trials were scheduled to be completed by the end of 2009. However, the fact that six fugitives, including Radovan Karadzic and Ratko Mladic, were still at large meant that there was some doubt as to whether the timely completion of all trials would be possible. The ICTY continued its policy of transferring cases from The Hague for trial in the state courts of Bosnia & Herzegovina, Serbia, and Croatia.

Former Yugoslav President Slobodan Milosevic died in his cell at the ICTY detention centre in March (see pp. 102-03; for obituary see p. 588). His trial had been going on for four years, the longest war crimes trial of modern times. He was the first former head of state to be tried for war crimes before an international tribunal. The Appeals Chamber issued several important decisions. In *Stanislav Galic*, it imposed the maximum penalty of life imprisonment for the first time when it increased the sentence passed on the former Bosnian Serb army officer for terrorisation of the civilian population in Sarajevo in 1992. It reduced the sentence of *Momir Nikolic,* a former Bosnian Serb army officer, for persecution of Bosnian Muslims in Srebrenica in 1995. The Trial Chamber had made a mistake in that it took account of Nikolic's role as assistant commander for security and intelligence of the Bosnian Serb army twice, both in determining the seriousness of the crime and again as an aggravating circumstance. The Appeals Chamber confirmed the conviction of *Milomir Stakic*, a Bosnian Serb political leader, for his participation in murder, extermination, and persecution of non-Serbs in Prijedor in 1992 and sentenced him to 40 years imprisonment.

Momcilo Krajisnik, former Serb member of the Bosnian collective presidency, speaker of the legislature, and key political associate of Radovan Karadzic, was sentenced to 27 years for persecution, extermination, murder, deportation, but was acquitted of genocide. He had been involved in a joint criminal enterprise to recompose the territories ethnically by the expulsion of non-Serbs. Sentences were also passed on the former chief-of-staff of the Bosnian Muslim army for failure to take reasonable measures to prevent or punish crimes by the forces and on a Bosnian Croat commander for his involvement in the October 1993 destruction of the Bosnian village of Stupni Do.

The trials of 25 accused proceeded before the INTERNATIONAL CRIMINAL TRIBUNAL FOR RWANDA (ICTR), but 18 fugitives were still at large. In the cases of *Edouard Karemera, Mathieu Ngirumpatse,* and *Joseph Nzirorera* the Appeals Chamber made a landmark ruling that the Trial Chambers must take judicial notice as a matter of common knowledge that there was a genocide between 6 April 1994 and 17 July 1994; this was not unfair to the accused or inconsistent with the prosecutor's burden of proof. This was one of the most significant rulings of the Tribunal in that it would no longer be necessary to prove the genocide in each case.

There were three convictions for different types of criminal responsibility: *Tharcisse Muvunyi*, former commander of the Rwandan military school, was convicted of genocide and crimes against humanity as he had been responsible for the acts of junior officers under his command who had committed serious violations of international humanitarian law; he had also directly and publicly incited Hutus to eliminate Tutsis. *Joseph Serugendo*, a member of the governing board of Rwandan radio and television stations, was indicted for conspiracy and incitement to commit genocide. He had used the radio station to stir up racial hatred against the Tutsis. Despite the serious nature of the crime he was sentenced to only six years' imprisonment; the tribunal took account of the facts that he had pleaded guilty, made public expressions of remorse, co-operated with the prosecution, and was of prior good character. He later died in custody. *Paul Bisengimana* was found guilty of crimes against humanity because his presence—given his status as mayor—and his failure to stop others had encouraged attacks on Tutsis who had sought refuge in churches. The Trial Chamber also found *Athanase Seromba*, a former Roman Catholic priest, guilty of genocide and extermination.

The Appeals Chamber ruled that *Michel Bagaragaza*, as director general of the government office which controlled the tea industry, had agreed upon a genocidal plan and through his subordinates had trained and supported those carrying out massacres of Tutsi people. It upheld the acquittal of *André Ntagerura*, minister of transport and communications, and local prefect *Emmanuel Bagambiki* of genocide, for lack of evidence. It also upheld the prosecution appeal in the case of *Sylvestre Gacumbitsi* and increased his sentence for genocide and other offences to life imprisonment.

Several important human rights and humanitarian treaties were concluded or entered into force. The Optional Protocol to the Convention against Torture and Other Cruel or Inhuman Treatment or Punishment entered into force on 22 June. This enhanced the protection of persons deprived of liberty; it provided for the establishment of an international expert body, the regular monitoring of places where persons may be deprived of their liberty by regular visits by expert bodies, and national preventive mechanisms. The UN Convention on the Protection and Promotion of the Rights and Dignity of Persons with Disabilities was adopted on 13 December, after nearly two decades of work on this issue. This was the first new human rights treaty of the 21st century and marked a shift in the treatment of 650 million disabled people. It required states to guarantee freedom from exploitation and abuse. It was accompanied by an optional protocol allowing petitions by individuals and groups to an ad hoc committee after the exhaustion of domestic procedures. The UN General Assembly on 20 December adopted the International Convention for the Protection of All Persons from Enforced Disappearance; this committed states parties to criminalise enforced disappearance, to bring those responsible to justice, and to take preventive measures. It established a new monitoring body—a Committee on Enforced Disappearances—to monitor the compliance of parties, consider individual complaints, and undertake field inquiries.

The Protocol on Explosive Remnants of War came into force on 12 November. It required all parties to an armed conflict to clear all dangerous unexploded munitions on land territory and in internal waters once fighting was over. Where a state which used explosive ordnance did not control territory after the end of fighting it must provide assistance to remove and destroy these remnants of war. On 6 December the UN General Assembly voted to start the diplomatic process aimed at producing a comprehensive, legally binding instrument establishing international standards in the global trade in conventional arms. Only the USA opposed this initiative; 24 states, including Russia and China, abstained.

The International Labour Organisation Maritime Labour Convention was adopted on 23 February: this consolidated and updated more than 65 maritime labour instruments. It set minimum requirements for conditions of employment, accommodation, food, and health. The Optional Protocol to the Convention on the Safety of UN and Associated Personnel was opened for signature on 16 January. This extended the protection of the Convention to personnel delivering humanitarian assistance.

At the end of the year there were about 90,000 pending applications before the European Court of Human Rights (ECHR). About 20 per cent of the cases were against Russia, 12 per cent were against Romania, and 10 per cent against Turkey. The Court handed down 1,560 judgments, an increase of 40 per cent compared with 2005. The largest number concerned Turkey, Slovenia, Ukraine, Poland, Italy, Russia, France, and Romania. These eight states accounted for over 70 per cent of the judgments. The Court also disposed of over 28,000 other applications which they declared inadmissible or struck off. This case-load threatened the Court's ability to cope. In December the Group of Wise Persons set up in May 2005 by the Council of Europe made its final report on the long term effectiveness of the European Court of Human Rights system under the Convention and Protocol 14. The report stressed the importance of the principle of subsidiarity in the system for the protection of human rights: the national courts of member states should offer the first recourse. The Wise Persons accordingly made 10 recommendations for reform, including the establishment of a new filtering system, enhancing the authority of the Court's decisions in member states, increasing co-operation between the Court and national courts, and improving domestic remedies for violations.

The Court decided several important cases concerning the right to life, mostly against Russia and Turkey. Several arose out of deaths at the hands of security services or in custody; the Court confirmed its well-established position that government failure adequately to account for injuries, disappearances, and death could indicate violation of Article 2. There were also many cases on torture and inhumane treatment under Article 3. Several of these arose out of conditions of detention and denial of medical treatment in prison in the new states parties.

The Court continued to use Article 8 on respect for private and family life to protect the right to a clean environment. Thus in *Ledyayeva* it held that Russia had failed to take adequate steps to protect those living near to the biggest iron smelter in Russia from the dangers of serious pollution by toxic substances. In *Giacomelli* it held that Italy had failed for 14 years to follow its own procedures on environmental protection. The Court also made decisions on freedom of religion in Russia and on the scope of the right to criticise the Roman Catholic Church in France and Slovakia. It upheld the rights of civil servants to join trades unions in Turkey in several cases, and it made innovative rulings on issues arising out of DNA tests and IVF (in vitro fertilisation) treatment.

In contrast to the enormous case load of the ECHR, the American Court of Human Rights made only two judgments, one on extrajudicial executions against Venezuela and the other on psychiatric detention against Brazil.

The African Union launched the African Court on Human and People's Rights on 2 July. The 1981 African Charter had not created a court, but only a Commission with no power to make binding decisions. A 1998 protocol provided for the creation of a court; this entered into force in 2004. The Court was based in Arusha, Tanzania, using the facilities established for the ICTR. Its first 11 judges were elected in January for six-year terms. The protocol offered limited provision for individual and non-governmental organisations to bring cases, but the Court was to have wider subject matter jurisdiction than under other regional human rights treaties.

The UN General Assembly voted on 15 March to establish a new Human Rights Council to replace the commission on human rights established in 1946, regarded by some as politicised and selective in its approach (see p. 362). Forty-seven states members were elected by the General Assembly on 9 May and the Council held its first meeting on 19 June. It was hoped that this would inaugurate a new chapter in the history of the UN's work to promote and protect human rights. The Council was to conduct universal periodic reviews, a ground-breaking mechanism that would allow it to scrutinise the human rights records of all countries. It would also be possible to suspend a Council member for gross violations of human rights.

Several human rights monitoring bodies reported adversely on the situation in the US detention facility at Guantánamo Bay in Cuba, and also on the secret prisons for terrorist suspects outside the USA. Thus the UN Committee against Torture, the UN Human Rights Committee, and the five special rapporteurs of the defunct UN commission on human rights all issued critical reports asserting that the protection of human rights conventions extended to Guantánamo Bay, and that indefinite detention without charge and without access to a judicial body was unlawful. Their recommendations included a call for the end to detention at Guantánamo Bay, clarification of interrogation methods, an end to extraordinary rendition, and the identification of alleged secret US prisons. The USA did not accept these observations; it said that continuing armed conflict in the "war on terror" allowed it to detain suspects until the end of active hostilities. The Council of Europe Parliamentary Assembly report of 12 June (see pp. 408-10) also held that the CIA's secret rendition programme was unlawful and found violations of human rights by European states through co-operation with the CIA in extraordinary rendition.

EUROPEAN UNION LAW

CONSTITUTIONALLY, the EU was very quiet during 2006. The deadline of 1 November came and went and the European Convention (the treaty which would give the EU its own constitution) had still not received ratification by four-fifths of the member states, let alone by all of them. Consequently it did not come into force and the procedure in Declaration 30 (referring the treaty to the European Council of Ministers if, two years after its signature, it was still not ratified) was not initiated: but neither was the treaty discarded. Desultory discussion on its resurrection in some form took place, but without great conviction.

Enlargement to include Bulgaria and Romania was, after much hesitation, agreed for 1 January 2007 without postponement. However there was an increasing pressure to halt further enlargement, with the possible exception of Croatia. Turkey, as always, remained in a semi-limbo although official discussions on some of the enlargement "chapters" were pursued (see pp. 405-06). Attention was directed more to the "near abroad", with the adoption of a regulation on a European neighbourhood and partnership instrument. This covered those countries which formed the two main groupings: the Euro-Mediterranean (Barcelona process) countries bordering the Mediterranean's southern and eastern shores, and the partnership and co-operation agreement countries of the former Soviet Union. All of these countries were currently associated with the EU by special and quite far-reaching bilateral association agreements. The new instrument provided a framework for more proactive EU involvement. At the same time, the partnership arrangements with the Balkan countries were all updated by individual decisions to take account of political and other developments in that region.

At the other end of the EU's range of vision, Greenland, which had withdrawn from the EU many years before (in 1985)—albeit remaining a self-governing dependency of Denmark—and had been placed into the OCT category (overseas countries and territories) as regarded relations with the EU, entered into a special arrangement with the EU to provide a framework for closer partnership, with some emphasis on fisheries.

In all respects otherwise, the EU showed signs of having the bit between its teeth. In all sectors—legislative, judicial, and administrative—there was a steady flow of important texts. It seemed clear that the transition from an economic union, concentrating on developing a consistent body of mercantile law and the infrastructure necessary to support it, to a political union, concerned with the issues of the day and the exercise of power, had been successfully and definitively accomplished.

As had become clear in recent years, the centre of gravity was an increasing involvement of the EU in justice matters. The European arrest warrant system was extended to Iceland and Norway by special treaty, emphasising once again that those two European Economic Area countries were being bound closely into the EU legal system in all its aspects, in spite of remaining non-members of the Union. The same was true of the very important regulation on SIS II, the revised version of the Schengen information system, used for keeping track of aliens within the EU (except Denmark, Ireland, and the UK, under their various opt-outs) which was adopted in December. As both Iceland and Norway, and also Switzerland, had joined the Schengen system by special treaties, SIS II applied to them, and they not only were covered by the new regulation but under it they were also entitled to be represented in the SIS bodies.

Another of the EU's information databases, the visa information system (VIS), was the subject of a Commission decision laying out the standards for biometric information to be carried on the system.

The central focus of the EU concern with the justice system had long been the harmonisation of enforcement rules, principally through mutual recognition, originally by means of the Brussels convention (now regulation) on jurisdiction and the enforcement of judgments (in civil law) and latterly in the European arrest warrant (in criminal law). These extremely important texts were joined during the year by two more. One, a framework decision on the enforcement of confiscation orders, formed part of an increasingly stringent and far-reaching EU legislation on money laundering, which had been extended out of all recognition to constitute, instead, the confiscation of the proceeds of crime and even the confiscation of the assets of criminals. The new framework decision provided for the enforcement of confiscation orders issued by the criminal courts of the member states. The second such instrument was a regulation creating a European payment order whereby a national civil court, faced with an undefended claim for a fixed pecuniary amount, could issue an order for payment which would be automatically enforceable in all the other member states.

While much of the major legislation was now consistently of a constitutional nature, understood in its widest sense and including criminal law, there still remained a steady trickle of traditional law relating to the internal market. A particularly noteworthy example of this in 2006 was the adoption of the services directive. This aimed to complete the freedom to supply services, laid down in articles 49 to 55 of the European Community treaty as one of the four fundamental freedoms of the European Community. While that freedom had from very early on been directly effective on the basis of the EC treaty itself, there had been enormous scope for evasion, particularly, but not solely, through national insistence on local standards for qualification or practice. Over the years the European Court of Justice (ECJ) had settled much of this, but much scope still remained for national variation, which usually had a protectionist flavour. The new directive aimed to cut through all this by the imposition of a number of rules of general application. Originally introduced by Commissioners Henk Vredeling and then Frits Bolkestein, and hence known throughout its later gestation as the Bolkestein directive, it encountered fierce resistance from several member states and was at one time thought lost. It was revived early in 2004 in its final form and, after more hard disagreement centring on whether the rules regulating a particular service provision should be those of the state of the provider or of the recipient of the services, it was finally passed in December 2006.

Against this background, the ECJ, too, seemed to have regained its appetite for bold and challenging decisions. Several of these were of a deep constitutional nature and reflected the changed nature of the EU and its place in the world.

Perhaps the greatest success of the whole of the EC treaty was article 177 (subsequently article 234) which gave all national courts the right to ask the ECJ to give them a preliminary ruling on the meaning of an element of Community law. The whole EU legal system was based on that provision. It enshrined a principle of independence and equal respect between the national courts and the ECJ. In doing so it also provided a surprisingly effective mechanism for stimulating the national courts to apply Community law in their domestic legal orders and to apply it correctly, thereby ensuring that the member states complied with Community law.

For nearly all courts the use of that mechanism was voluntary; but it was given force by imposing on the final courts of appeal an obligation to use it, thus ensuring that, ultimately, issues involving Community law would in any case reach the ECJ. There was no sanction for a supreme court refusing to make such a reference to the ECJ except, theoretically, an action by the EU against the member state itself. But that would involve making the state responsible for the decisions of its court, which had serious implications for the independence of the judiciary under the rule of law.

The ECJ found a solution in 2003 in *Köbler v Austria*, which it reinforced during 2006 in *Traghetti del Mediterraneo SpA v Italy*. There it stated unequivocally that individuals were, under certain conditions, entitled to obtain damages from the state "when their rights are affected by an infringement of Community law attributable to a decision of a court of a Member State adjudicating at last instance". The result of the ECJ's judgment was that the low-level Italian referring court was in effect hearing, and deciding, an appeal against a judgment of the Italian Supreme Court.

Foreign relations formed the context for further significant decisions of the ECJ. The highly controversial agreement between the EU and the USA on air passenger name records (PNR) was annulled by the Court, not because of its threat to the privacy of the individuals whose data would be given to the US authorities as a result, but on technical grounds. The agreement was hastily renegotiated to adapt it to the criticisms of the Court and the new text was duly signed in October.

The freezing of funds of global terrorists was the subject of several decisions by the ECJ and the Court of First Instance (CFI) in which the ECJ had overruled the CFI, holding that where the fund-freezing order was based on EU law (and not on an individual decision of the UN sanctions committee) the individual had a right of administrative appeal to the EU Council of Ministers and also, for judicial review, to the CFI.

LAW IN THE UNITED KINGDOM

On 3 April, much of the Constitutional Reform Act 2005 came into force: Lord Chief Justice Lord Phillips replaced the lord chancellor as the head of the judiciary in England and Wales; Sir Igor Judge, in turn, replaced the lord chief justice as president of the Queen's Bench Division; Sir Andrew Morritt replaced the lord chancellor as the head of the Chancery Division of the High Court. However, the appellate committee of the House of Lords (the upper chamber of Parliament) remained, for the time being, the ultimate court of appeal in the UK, as architectural wrangling continued over the site of the new Supreme Court, which was to replace it. The initial granting of planning permission for the conversion of the Edwardian, Gothic revival Middlesex Guildhall was threatened with judicial review by the conservation group, Save Britain's Heritage. The lord chancellor maintained that the new court would open in October 2009.

Human rights cases continued to come before the courts. In *Regina (Laporte) v Chief Constable of Gloucestershire* the police turned back a coachload of demonstrators from an anti-war protest; the House of Lords held that this was a disproportionate restriction on the rights to freedom of speech and freedom of assembly under the European Convention on Human Rights (ECHR). In *Secretary of State for Work and Pensions v M*, the applicant contended that the child support legislation unlawfully discriminated against her: her assessed contribution was higher because her new partner was of the same sex, rather than a man. The legislation allowed only heterosexual partners to be taken into account, to reduce child support payments. The majority of the House of Lords dismissed the argument, observing that discrimination was not prohibited per se by the ECHR, but only when one of the substantive rights was engaged; it was not enough to show a tenuous or peripheral link (e.g. to the right to family life), since this "would be a recipe for artificiality and legalistic ingenuity of an unacceptable kind" (Lord Bingham). Moreover, the court observed, the law had now been changed to give equal recognition to same-sex partners (Civil Partnership 2004), but it could not be said that prior to 2004 it had been discriminatory to treat homosexual couples less favourably, given the prevailing mores of British society. Baroness Hale, dissenting, commented that such discrimination, like racial or gender discrimination, had always been wrong, even before society as a whole had woken up to the fact.

In *Kay v Lambeth Council*, the House of Lords had to revisit its own decision in *Harrow Council v Qazi* (2003) in the light of the European Court of Human

Rights' decision in *Connors v UK* (2004). It was acknowledged that, exceptionally, a public authority landlord's decision to seek possession of premises could infringe the right to one's home under the ECHR. The majority held, however, that such an alleged breach of the Convention could not be raised as a defence to possession proceedings. To allow such a defence would "drive a deep wedge into the domestic system for the handling of possession cases and would be a colossal waste of time and money" (Lord Hope). The House also confirmed that in the event of a conflict between one of its own decisions and those of the European Court, English courts nevertheless continued to be bound by the Lords' rulings. To hold otherwise would threaten legal chaos. On the other hand, in *Inntrepreneur v Crehan*, the House of Lords held that English courts were entitled to depart from findings of fact made by the European Commission in proceedings about anti-competitive practices, notwithstanding the "duty of loyal co-operation" which member states owed to organs of the European Union.

It was a lively year in the field of torts. An employer was held vicariously liable for the harassment of one of its employees by another, despite judicial misgivings that this might generate a flood of claims for workplace bullying (*Majrowski v Guy's Hospital*). The authors of a geological survey into the composition of Bangladeshi groundwater were not liable for having failed to analyse the water for arsenic: many villagers had been poisoned when wells were sunk under the aegis of an entirely separate United Nations initiative (*Sutradhar v National Environmental Research Council*). A bank that allowed its customer to withdraw money from an account, in breach of a "freezing order" (Mareva injunction), was not liable to creditors of the customer who suffered loss as a result (*HM Customs v Barclays Bank*). The House of Lords also provided clarification of the "*Reynolds* defence" in libel, emphasising that to protect freedom of speech, media publications on matters of public interest were "privileged" when the decision to publish accorded with standards of "responsible journalism" (*Jameel v Wall Street Journal*). On the facts, the defence was upheld since, far from being a sensationalist purveyor of gossip, the defendant newspaper had high journalistic standards, its style being "'gravely serious' (indeed some might find it seriously dull)" (Lady Hale).

Claims against employers for exposing employees to asbestos continued to cause difficulty. In one class action (*Re Pleural Plaques*), the Court of Appeal held that a benign, asymptomatic lung condition was not a "disease" for which an action in negligence could be brought. The employees' concern that they might go on to develop asbestosis or lung cancer in the future was not actionable either: the law does not compensate "mere mental distress". The House of Lords had to consider the extent of employer's liability for causing mesothelioma, pursuant to its earlier decision in *Fairchild* (2003). The court held that the employers were liable only for a share of the employees' illness, proportionate to that employer's share of the total exposure to asbestos (*Barker v Corus*). The decision meant that, in practice, mesothelioma sufferers would fail to recover full compensation, given the difficulty of tracing and suing all former employers (or their insurers) after the 40 year incubation period of the disease. As such, *Barker* came in for heavy criticism, and under pressure from its own members of Parliament, the government introduced an amendment to a bill adventitiously proceeding through Parliament, to reverse the Law Lords' decision. Thus, a statute which had initially been designed to rein in the "compensation culture" (by regulating the handlers of claims, among other things) became used to expand the liability of employers in asbestos cases.

Parliament legislated in various other fields. The Charities Act introduced a statutory definition of "charitable purpose" for the first time. The most substantial, and contentious, change was to reverse the presumption that charities designed to promote education or religion, or to relieve poverty, were for "the public benefit". Thus, elite schools (such as Eton College) would henceforth be required to show that they benefited the public as a whole, or lose their charitable status. The Identity Act provided a legal framework for a national identity register, and the power to require the carrying of identity (ID) cards. The government argued that ID cards would curb benefit fraud and illegal immigration, and improve public security (see p. 20). The Terrorism Act created various new criminal offences, such as encouraging terrorism and preparing for terrorist acts. It introduced an unprecedented power for the police to hold terrorism suspects for up to 28 days without charge, although the government had suffered an embarrassing defeat in the House of Commons (the lower house of Parliament) over its original proposals to allow such detention for 90 days (see AR 2005, p. 17).

The Fraud Act created a new offence of fraud, which might be committed by false representation, by failing to disclose information and by abuse of position. The Health Act banned smoking in enclosed and substantially enclosed public places, and in the workplace. The Climate Change and Sustainable Energy Act placed various obligations on governmental bodies to make progress towards environmentally friendly energy supplies. The Companies Act, a codifying statute with 1,300 separate sections and running to 760 pages, was the longest in British legal history.

The courts also decided that the English rules on damages were to be applied as a matter of "procedure" when deciding a tort claim arising out of an accident overseas (and so in substance governed by the law of that country): *Horton v Sadler*. The House of Lords held that when a company paid taxes which later turned out to be illegal under EU law, the company could claim the moneys back since made under a mistake of law (*Deutsche Morgan Grenfell v Inland Revenue Commissioners*).

Finally, in a case about the registration of land as a "village green", their Lordships differed over the proper definition of such an amenity. Lord Hoffmann referred to the Green at Auburn in Goldsmith's poem "The Deserted Village" (1770), quoting extensively his description of rustic characters frolicking in the shade of spreading trees. His Lordship, however, held that such an idyllic scene could not be imported as a legal requirement into the words of the Commons Registration Act 1965. Contrast Lord Scott, who had difficulty in describing the semi-aquatic scrubland in the case at hand as a "village green"; but the question was deferred for final decision on another occasion: *Oxfordshire County Council v Oxford City Council.*

LAW IN THE USA

In 2006 the US Supreme Court rendered two significant decisions on federalism: the allocation of powers between the federal and state governments. In *United States v Georgia*, the Court unanimously ruled that a state was not entitled to immunity against a law suit by disabled prison inmates. Chief Justice John G. Roberts—who replaced Chief Justice William H. Rehnquist, who, during the prior 10 years, had led in the Court's decisions that expanded the immunity of state governments from federal regulation—dissented, along with three other justices, in *Central Virginia Community College v Katz*, which held that a creditor could sue a state under federal bankruptcy legislation.

The scope of the US president's power, under the constitution and the "authorisation for the use of military force" (AUMF), the joint resolution adopted by the US Congress (the legislature) on 14 September, 2001, continued to raise the most controversial legal and policy questions in 2006. Following its decisions in 2004 and 2005 (see AR 2005, pp. 430-31), in June the Supreme Court ruled in *Hamdan v Rumsfeld* that the procedures for the trial of persons detained as enemy combatants had to comply with certain minimum standards contained within US constitutional and international law. In response to this decision, Congress enacted the Military Commissions Act in October, which established the procedures for the trial of enemy combatants and excluded from the jurisdiction of the federal courts petitions by enemy combatants for writs of habeus corpus. In December, a federal district court in Washington, DC ruled that Salim Ahmed Hamdan, the detained suspect in *Hamdan v Rumsfeld*, was barred from filing a petition for the writ of habeus corpus to challenge further the legality of his detention as a result of the new law. The ruling was appealed against. In August, in *ACUL v NSA*, the federal district court in Detroit, Michigan, ruled that the National Security Agency's practice of electronically listening to individuals' telephone conversations without first obtaining a warrant issued by the court established under the Foreign Surveillance Intelligence Act was illegal under that law and violated the First and Fourth Amendments of the constitution. On 17 January 2007 Attorney General Alberto Gonzales announced that the practice would not be re-authorised by the president.

Laws in 45 states that restricted marriage to a man and a woman continued to be challenged in the courts in several states. The highest state courts in Georgia (in *Perdue v O'Kelley*), New York (in *Hernandez v Robles*), and Washington (in *Anderson v King County*), and appellate state courts in California, Connecticut, and Maryland upheld such laws. The Eighth United States Circuit Court of Appeal, in *Citizens for Equal Protection v Bruning*, held that an amendment to the Nebraska state constitution which prohibited same-sex unions did not deny same sex couples equal protection under the US constitution. The Massachusetts Supreme Court ruling in 2003 therefore remained the sole decision of a highest state court that such a law represented a denial of equal protection.

Legislative efforts to regulate election campaign spending continued to be challenged. The Supreme Court, in *Randall v Sorrell*, held unconstitutional a Vermont campaign finance law which limited the amount that candidates could spend on their own campaigns and the amounts which individuals and political parties could contribute to campaigns. The District of Columbia Circuit Court of Appeal, in *Federal Election Commission v Wisconsin Right to Life* and *McCain v Wisconsin Right to Life*, held that the provisions in the Bipartisan Campaign Finance Reform Act of 2002, which prohibited corporate and union groups from sponsorship of broadcast advertisements that mentioned specific candidates 30 days before a federal primary election and 60 days before a federal general election, violated the First Amendment right to free speech because such advertisements addressed genuine issues. The 2002 Act was a milestone in regulation of campaign finance and had been upheld as constitutional by the Supreme Court that year in a split five-four decision. The decision in 2006 was expected to reopen the questions concerning the constitutionality of the Act. The Supreme Court was expected to examine the case under its automatic review procedure.

The Fifth US Circuit Court of Appeal decided one of the most important unresolved questions in capital punishment cases in *Panetti v Quarterman*, in which it held that Texas could execute a prisoner convicted of murder who understood the facts upon which the decision to execute him was based even though he did not appreciate that his execution was intended to seek retribution for his capital crime because, as a result of his severe mental illness, he believed the state was executing him for preaching the Gospel. The Supreme Court decided to review the case.

The tobacco companies achieved several successful results in 2006. The Supreme Court refused to review the decision of the Illinois Supreme Court, in 2005, which had overturned a $10.1 billion award (see AR 2005, p. 431). In *USA v Philip Morris*, a federal district court in Washington, DC held the tobacco companies liable for violations of the federal anti-racketeering laws; prohibited description of cigarette brands as "light", "low tar", "mild", "natural" or similar words; required the tobacco companies to correct statements previously made about the addictiveness of smoking and nicotine, the adverse health effects of smoking and secondhand smoke, and the manipulation of cigarette design; and to pay the government's costs of litigation. The judge refused the government's request in the case to require the tobacco companies to pay for a programme to help people stop smoking and to educate young people about the adverse health effects of the practice. The Florida Supreme Court overturned the $145 billion award in a class action against the tobacco companies, holding that because smokers' cases were highly individualised they did not lend themselves to class-actions.

XV RELIGION

THE following sub-sections record inter- and intra-faith issues that made headlines during the year. Some of the most colourful preaching, however, fell outside these categories, being concerned with atheism. Richard Dawkins, ethologist and popular science writer and the Charles Simonyi professor of the public understanding of science at Oxford University, stepped up his long-running tirade against all religion with the publication on both sides of the Atlantic of *The God Delusion* (Bantam Publishers and Houghton Mifflin), as well as in a BBC television series. A vocal opponent, Alister McGrath, Dawkins's sometime fellow-biologist and latterly professor of historical theology, also at Oxford, saw his critique, *Dawkins' God: Genes, Memes and the Meaning of Life* (originally published in 2005) reprinted in paperback. The debate seemed unlikely to end any time soon.

CHRISTIANITY. In the Roman Catholic Church the year began with the first Encyclical from Pope Benedict XVI, "Deus Caritas Est", which surprised some by its non-controversial subject-matter: the importance of Christian charity. Fifteen new cardinals were created in January. Restrictions on use of the Tridentine rite (the "Latin mass" or traditional Roman rite, superseded in 1969 after Vatican II) were eased. Papal journeys included trips to Poland in May, where Benedict declared his visit to Auschwitz a "duty before God"; and to Spain, which had recently passed same-sex marriage legislation and where he called for a strong married life. His main blunder of the year occurred in a lecture at Regensburg university in Germany on 12 September, when he made an unfortunate allusion to a medieval Byzantine Emperor who had accused the Prophet Mohammed of bringing "only evil" into the world and of spreading the faith "by the sword". While probably no more than ill-advised, this remark created a stir throughout the Muslim world, threatening the proposed papal visit to Turkey in November. Nevertheless the trip went ahead. Benedict was able to show solidarity with Ecumenical Patriarch Bartholomew, head of the Orthodox Church, and to celebrate mass at Ephesus for the tiny Catholic population. Although the pope twice spoke of the Christian roots of Europe, a degree of reconciliation with Islam was indicated by joint prayers in the Blue Mosque with Mustafa Cagrici, head of religious affairs in Istanbul (see pp. 61-62).

Shortly afterwards, the easing of relations between the Roman Catholic Church and the Orthodox churches was underlined with the visit of Archbishop Christodoulos of Athens to the pope. They jointly reaffirmed the "Christian character of Europe". An official dialogue between the churches resumed in Belgrade, Serbia's capital. In Jerusalem, friction continued between the state of Israel, which still recognised Patriarch Ireneos I of Jerusalem, deposed in 2005 over a property scandal (see AR 2005, pp. 432-33), and the Greek Orthodox Church.

Financial problems emerging from sexual abuse scandals again plagued the

Roman church in North America. Covington Diocese, Kentucky, was ordered to pay US$85 million damages in one settlement. Boston archdiocese faced a deficit of US$46 million. Sixty posts were cut in the national structures of the US Roman Catholic Church. On a more positive note, church leaders spoke out on a number of political issues, particularly immigration to the USA, the US treatment of detainees, and against the death penalty for the former Iraq president, Saddam Hussein.

In the Anglican Communion—the third largest denomination worldwide—the Episcopal Church of the USA met in June for its triennial general convention. In a surprise outcome the bishop of Nevada, Katherine Jefferts-Schori, was elected the new presiding bishop to succeed Frank Griswold. A committed liberal and supporter of Gene Robinson, the openly homosexual bishop of New Hampshire, she did little to dampen the internecine squabbles in the Communion. Against this backdrop, work began on developing a more coherent confessional identity for an increasingly polarised global Anglicanism. Matters were not helped when the House of Bishops in Tanzania, where the Primates were scheduled to meet in February 2007, excommunicated American liberals shortly before the end of the year.

Discussions were held in November between the pope and the archbishop of Canterbury, leader of the Anglican Communion. Both spoke of the importance of ecumenism, although as Cardinal Walter Kasper, chief ecumenical spokesman for the Vatican, had noted to the Church of England bishops in June, there were new obstacles to unity, brought about by the ordination of women as bishops as well as the issue of homosexuality.

Other churches continued to be divided over sexual ethics, although controversy in some areas was lessened. The 1 million-strong US Church of God of Prophecy, for instance, voted to allow the remarriage of divorcees. Evangelicals were shocked by the allegations in November that "Pastor Ted" Haggard, leader of the National Association of Evangelicals, had been involved in sex sessions with a former male prostitute. This may have had a modest effect on the outcome of the US congressional (legislative) elections in November (see pp. 130-37). Admitting to some of the charges, Haggard resigned to study psychology with his wife.

The World Council of Churches held its ninth general assembly with over 600 delegates in Alegre, Brazil, in February, on the theme "God, in your grace, transform the world". There were renewed calls for ecumenism, but little substantial progress.

HINDUISM. A conflict between traditional values and modernity arose in Kerala, India, over non-Brahmins functioning as temple priests. (Brahmins were, traditionally, the highest of India's castes who formed the Hindu priesthood). The dispute involved two community organisations: the Nair Service Society (NSS) and the Sree Narayana Dharma Paripalana Yogam (SNDP), which was the socio-cultural organisation of the Ezhava community. While the NSS held that appointment of non-Brahmins as priests would dilute the customs and traditions of the Hindus in Kerala, the SNDP's general secretary, Vellapally Natesan, saw the NSS view as violating a Supreme Court order. NSS delegates, meeting at its headquarters at Prunna, near Kottayam, urged the Travancore Devaswom Board (TDB) to give up plans to appoint non-Brahmins to the priesthood. The issue remained unresolved, although some Tantris (traditional Nambudri Brahmin temple priests) thought that non-Brahmins might be appointable if they were to have proper training in temple matters

Sacred to the god Shiva and worn by devotees, rudraksha beads had started to be used in the fashion industry and as jewellery. Women generally combined rudraksha and gold beads for the neck, while men tended to wear them as either a small necklace or bracelet. The beads were claimed to have beneficial health effects on wearers, including reduction of blood pressure and alleviation of heart disease. More broadly their use might be viewed as symptomatic of a growing "new age" Hinduism, which was not rooted in a particular tradition but was concerned with general "spirituality" and had developed out of the philosophy of Neo-Vedanta along with influences from the West and from Hindu diaspora communities.

In the state of Tamil Nadu, during the Pongal festival in January, the Archaeological Survey of India (ASI) opened an interpretation centre at the Tanjavur Braghadeeswarar temple. Life-size photographic reproductions were displayed of the 1,000-year-old Chola period murals from the temple . The paintings had been discovered in the 1930s. The murals comprised images of various deities, including Tripurantaka, Nataraja, and the story of Sundarar.

In the USA a 10,000 sq ft (929 sq m) Hindu temple opened in Florida. Nine deities were installed with elaborate puras (rituals). A thousand Hindus attended the event and the temple was expected to serve 70,000 Hindus in the South Florida area. Meanwhile, in the USA, the Hindu textbook controversy remained unresolved (see AR 2005, p. 435). Some Hindu communities claimed that current academic textbooks presented Hinduism in an unfavourable light. Many US scholars, for their part, opposed Hindu fundamentalist claims about history and chronology.

In the UK a temple dedicated to Lord Venkateswara was opened near Birmingham with week-long consecration ceremonies. Fifteen priests from India performed the rituals, culminating in the installation of the 3.6 m-high statue of Lord Krishna. Also in the UK, some Hindus and Sikhs petitioned the European Court of Human Rights to be allowed to conduct funerals with open pyres (currently illegal in Britain) instead of crematoria. In July an illegal open-air cremation took place in a farmer's field. Finally, in October came the gloomy news that Sanskrit was no longer to be taught at Cambridge university. To some this was a short-sighted policy, yet indicative of a broader zeitgeist in the academic world.

ISLAM. The year 2006 began with slowly-intensifying protests against the publication (on 30 September 2005) in the Danish newspaper *Jyllands-Posten* of 12 satirical cartoons depicting the Prophet Mohammed. They were accused of being blasphemous and of inciting prejudices against Europe's Muslim minority. Violent protests ensued, mainly in Pakistan and Afghanistan. Despite calls by scholars for a peaceful response, death threats followed, and a consumer boycott of Danish goods in some Middle Eastern countries resulted in an estimated €147 million decline in Denmark's annual export earnings. In September and October tensions flared again when members of the youth section of the right-wing Danish People's Party were filmed participating in a competition to draw the most insulting cartoon of the Prophet (see pp. 54-56).

Pope Benedict XVI's lecture at Regensburg (see above) provoked controversy on two matters in particular. Firstly, the pope appeared to suggest that Islam defended forced conversions. Muslims responded by pointing out that such conversions were deemed invalid under Islamic law, and by comparing Islam's record to a variety of historical incidents in which the Roman Catholic Church used constraint to impose its doctrines. Secondly, the pope advanced the view that for Muslims, "God's will is not bound up with any of our categories, even that of rationality." The apparent implication—that the Muslim God was free to act capriciously—was vigorously rejected by a group of leading Muslim theologians, who replied to the pope's claims in a long and courteous letter, published in the leading magazine *Islamica*. Non-Muslim scholars of Islam were also critical of the pope's utterance. At the close of the year the Vatican had not yet issued a reply to the *Islamica* letter to defend the pope's understanding of Muslim theology. Whatever the final resolution of the issue, it seemed to many that significant damage had been caused to Muslim-Christian relations.

A number of developments contributed to a clearer institutional definition of Islam in the West. In Germany, the Central Council of Muslims elected a new leader, 67-year old Ayyub Köhler. Speaking for Germany's estimated 3 million Muslims, Köhler immediately moved to define a moderate, integrated Muslim profile, condemning the violent protests over the *Jyllands-Posten* controversy and advocating fuller Muslim participation in German democracy. Rejected by Wahhabi activists, Köhler's appointment was regarded by the media as a sign that German Islam wished to distance itself from Middle Eastern guidance, and would seek to define a future for itself as a "European religion".

In the USA a similar mood appeared to have driven the appointment of Ingrid Mattson, a 43-year old Canadian professor at Hartford Seminary in Hartford, Connecticut, as president of the main US Muslim organisation, the Islamic Society of North America. Described by the *San Francisco Chronicle* as "arguably the most influential Muslim in America", Mattson gave an inaugural September speech in Chicago to 30,000 supporters. Although media attention focused on her status as the first convert, the first non-immigrant, and the first woman to occupy the post, her speech discussed the issues of human rights and religious education. Another prominent convert, Keith Ellison, won the Minnesota Democratic primary, thus securing a future place as the first Muslim member of Congress (see p. 136).

A conference of leading European and Middle Eastern Islamic scholars convened in Istanbul in July to issue the first general statement on the rights and obligations of Europe's Muslim communities. The "Topkapi declaration" stated that "as citizens Muslims are obliged by Islamic law to obey the legislation of their countries", and "to defend their countries against aggressors". Muslims were enjoined to "reject the cancer of terrorism", and to "work to ensure that the voice of the peaceful majority of Muslims" prevailed over that of extremists. The declaration was welcomed in the European press as a major breakthrough in defining the relationship between Muslim minorities and national states.

In Turkey the assassination in September of a popular Istanbul preacher, Bayram Ali Ozturk, was widely blamed on secularist forces opposed to the country's religious conservatives. The president of the country's established religious hierarchy, Dr Ali Bardakoglu, continued his drive for modernisation by increasing the number of female mosque preachers *(vaize)* to over 600, and by issuing a controversial new lectionary of hadiths which omitted texts that some considered demeaning to women. State Minister Mehmet Ali Sahin announced that new measures would be introduced to enforce the ban on Islamic-style clothes for men.

JUDAISM AND JEWRY. British Jews celebrated the 350th anniversary of their readmission to the country. Celebrations included a synagogue service of thanksgiving, attended by Prime Minister Tony Blair, a reception hosted by the queen, and a parliamentary debate on the Jewish contribution to Britain over the three-and-a half centuries. The accuracy of 1656 as the correct date was disputable. In 1655 the Whitehall Conference, debating the question of allowing Jews to return (following their expulsion by Edward I in 1290), failed to reach a conclusion. The Conference noted that no formal law existed excluding Jews from Britain, so technically no decision was needed. In the event, no parliamentary act was passed to permit their re-entry. This would prove advantageous a little later, since such an act might have been repealed by Charles II when he regained the throne. Instead, in 1656 some Jews already residing in London appear to have been given tacit permission to practise their religion, leading to the establishment of a synagogue and burial ground by the following year. It was these largely undocumented events that provided the basis for the anniversary.

An accompaniment to the celebrations was a poll conducted by the *Jewish Chronicle* to identify the "greatest British Jew" of history. The title was bestowed upon Rabbi Dr Louis Jacobs, viewed by some as "the greatest British chief rabbi never to have been appointed". Jacobs died in July, just days before his 86th birthday and only a few months after receiving the accolade (which he himself had characterised as "daft"). As the focus of the so-called "Jacobs affair"—a protracted set of religious controversies beginning in late 1961 and continuing in some respects to the present day— Jacobs was a figurehead for those battling against a growing religious stringency amongst orthodox Jewish authorities in the UK. A scholar by nature, and the author of some 40 books, Jacobs was a somewhat reluctant leader of religious rebellion. He was a devout Jew, trained in the bastions of British ultra-orthodox Judaism as well as in Semitics at university, who had come to question dogmas regarding divine revelation. Throughout his writings he sought to construct a rationale for sustained Jewish practice. He argued that one could maintain religious observance without becoming entangled in what he described as the genetic fallacy of the Torah's origins. In *We Have Reason to Believe* (1957) he sought to synthesise traditional beliefs in revelation with modern scholarship. The book led, however, to his ostracism from mainstream Orthodoxy. In 1961 his appointment as principal of Jews' College, Anglo-Jewry's long-established orthodox rabbinical seminary, failed to receive Chief Rabbi Israel Brodie's approval. Jacobs was subsequently barred from the ministry of a post which he had previously held in the United Synagogue, Anglo-Jewry's central synagogal institution. In 1964 his supporters established an independent synagogue in which his teachings could be expressed. This came later to be seen as marking the beginning of Masorti Judaism in the UK, a brand of conservative Judaism which questioned some of the stringent dogmas (notably on revelation) and practices (such as the exclusion of women from any officiation in synagogue services) maintained by orthodoxy.

In the USA the conservative movement of Judaism demonstrated its growing religious liberalism by permitting the ordination of homosexual rabbis and the sanctification of same-sex marriages. At the same time orthodox moves to oppose perceived feminist influence on Judaism indicated the growing polarisation of orthodox and progressive positions. A rabbinic conference scheduled for November to discuss the problem of the agunah—the "chained woman" who, for a variety of possible reasons, was unable to obtain a divorce and was therefore unable to remarry under Jewish law—was abruptly cancelled in apparent response to ultra-orthodox pressure. The conference, organised by Israel's Sephardi Chief Rabbi Shlomo Amar and the International Council of Jewish Women, was designed to consider possible resolution of difficulties caused by conflict between Jewish law and secular divorce. Some orthodox circles feared, or suspected, that devising legalistic solutions to the problem (and hence to the suffering of the women affected) even within the strict boundaries of Jewish law could be interpreted as succumbing to the influence of principles and values developed in the surrounding (non-Jewish) society.

XVI THE ARTS

OPERA—MUSIC—BALLET & DANCE—THEATRE—CINEMA—TELEVISION & RADIO

OPERA

FOLLOWING the financial cutbacks in 2005, this was a year for marking time in the operatic world. There was great relief in Italy when Romano Prodi won the general election (see pp. 45-46), but Silvio Berlusconi's 20 per cent cut in arts subsidies had already left their mark (see AR 2005, p. 439). Many opera houses curtailed both their seasons and the number of performances, and the distinguished sovrintendente of the Teatro La Fenice in Venice, Sergio Segalini, resigned in protest. In the USA the drop in audiences following the 11 September 2001 terrorist attacks was still being felt, and there were cutbacks in Houston and Chicago. In the UK the Welsh National Opera reduced its touring programme by one-third, and all arts organisations in the UK feared a standstill if not a cut in funding in the face of the successful bid for the Olympic Games of 2012.

It was also a year of anniversaries. The 250th anniversary of Mozart's birth saw many new productions worldwide, and a complete cycle of his operatic works—all 20 of them—was presented at the Salzburg festival. Shostakovich's centenary was marked by a season of all his stage works given by St Petersburg's Maryinsky Theatre (Kirov) in a guest season in London, and by revivals around the world of *Lady Macbeth of Mtsensk* and *The Nose*.

Curiously enough given general financial nervousness, it was a year of new productions of Wagner's *Ring* cycle. The Canadian Opera Company gave the first staging in their new home, the warmly welcomed Four Seasons Centre for the Performing Arts in Toronto. London's Royal Opera completed its slightly unfocused production by Keith Warner. In Lisbon, the director Graham Vick launched his cycle with a *Rheingold* staged in the auditorium, hardly a practice to maximise box-office receipts. The Royal Danish Opera performed the cycle for the first time in their new opera house. In Washington DC a new production by Francesca Zambello was set to unfold, and Flanders Opera launched their project in Ghent. An Aix festival cycle conducted by Simon Rattle (co-produced with Salzburg) was not well received at its first airing, and the new production by the playwright Tankred Dorst at the Bayreuth festival came and went with barely a murmur of either protest or praise, a rare event indeed at that particular venue. A touring production by the Maryinsky Theatre under Valery Gergiev was roundly condemned by the press when seen in Cardiff, though it had sold-out within 24 hours of the box office opening.

There were several significant changes of management. Following Stéphane Lissner's departure for La Scala, Milan, Bernard Foccroule took over at Aix.

The Australian composer Jonathan Mills succeeded Sir Brian McMaster as director of the Edinburgh festival. Peter Jonas said farewell to the Bavarian State Opera with a much-praised production of *Moses und Aron*, conducted by Zubin Mehta and directed by David Pountney. Nicolas Joel was named as successor to Gerard Mortier at the Paris Opéra, Mortier's final seasons having been a predictable series of provocative deconstructions—the film director Michael Haneke's *Don Giovanni*, set in a high-rise office block, was typical. Many felt that it was time for a change in Paris.

The biggest changes came at the Metropolitan Opera in New York. Following Joseph Volpe's departure at a celebrity-packed gala in May, the new general manager, Peter Gelb, set about changing the whole ethos of the house. The Met's production style had long been considered somewhat old-fashioned, but Gelb announced a wish-list of cutting-edge directors, starting with Robert Lepage for a new *Ring* and continuing with Richard Eyre and Willy Decker. The Met traditionally kept the press at arm's length, but Gelb instituted a high-profile publicity campaign with his season-opener, Anthony Minghella's production of *Madama Butterfly*: New York's hoardings were plastered with posters, the dress rehearsal was thrown open to the public free of charge, and the first night was transmitted live on a big screen in Lincoln Centre Plaza. At the end of the year Gelb started a series of high definition live transmissions to 150 cinemas world-wide with *The Magic Flute*.

London's Royal Opera enjoyed a solidly successful year with audience-friendly productions of *Le nozze di Figaro* and *Carmen*. Bravely, they replaced their classic, 40-year-old Zeffirelli *Tosca* with a new staging by Jonathan Kent, not greatly admired despite the presence of Angela Gheorghiu and Bryn Terfel. English National Opera's year was, as ever, mixed, but they gained a high-profile new music director in Edward Gardner and a new chairman, Vernon Ellis. Their season-opener, *Gaddafi*, by the Asian Dub Foundation, was universally condemned, but there were highly successful productions of *Jenufa* with Amanda Roocroft and *The Makropoulos Case* conducted by Sir Charles Mackerras, and they ended the year with a lively version of *The Gondoliers*.

Scottish Opera emerged from their "dark" year imposed by the Scottish Parliament (see AR 2005, p. 439) with Tim Albery's new production of *Don Giovanni*, successful revivals of *Carmen* and *Der Rosenkavalier*, and a less successful new staging of Handel's *Tamerlano*. Under their new general director John Fisher, Welsh National Opera enjoyed the presence of Bryn Terfel for their new production of *The Flying Dutchman* set, none too helpfully, in a space station. The Patrice Caurier-Moshe Leiser production of Tchaikovsky's *Mazeppa* was greatly admired; David Alden's postmodern *Return of Ulysses* less so, to put it mildly. Opera North returned to their Leeds home with an outstanding new production of *Peter Grimes* by Phyllida Lloyd, conducted by Richard Farnes.

Festival productions included Nicholas Hytner's *Così fan tutte* at Glyndebourne with an appropriately young cast directed with great, not to say disturbing, insight. There was a spectacular version by David Pountney of Zimmermann's *Die Soldaten* at the Ruhr Triennale festival in Bochum. Thomas Adès's *The Tempest* was given its first US performance at Santa Fe to universal acclaim.

The year's new operas included Tan Dun's *The First Emperor*, a bio-opera of the builder of the Great Wall of China, given at the Met with Plácido Domingo. Kaija Saariaho's *Adriana Mater*, set in Palestine, was received with respect in Paris. Glimmerglass Opera presented Stephen Hartke's *The Greater Good*, a bittersweet comedy based on Maupassant's *Boule de Suif.*

Among the year's "scandals" was a production of *The Flying Dutchman* by Peter Konwitschny, at the end of which the heroine set off an explosion that emptied the stage and silenced the orchestra: the closing bars were heard faintly on an old gramophone record. The tenor Roberto Alagna walked out in the first act of a performance of *Aida* at La Scala, Milan, having had his opening aria booed by the loggionisti (the infamous opera fans of La Scala), which hit the world's headlines. Jonathan Miller sought to put the kibosh on the Met's opening by likening the Minghella *Butterfly* to being given an enema with maple syrup. He should have been a critic.

The list of obituaries made for a melancholy year. It included the star singers Lorraine Hunt Lieberson, Anna Moffo, Elisabeth Schwarzkopf (see pp. 595-96), Léopold Simoneau, Thomas Stewart, and Astrid Varnay; the composer György Ligeti; and the impresario Sir John Drummond (see p. 576).

MUSIC

THE diversification of music by the 21st century had led to divisions in the worldwide musical culture (see AR 2004, p. 461). This was particularly noticeable in Western classical music, whose artistic and spiritual unity—once its greatest strength, symbolised by a universal musical language—was threatened in the 20th century by artistic and spiritual disunity, and aesthetic confusion. This critical, potentially destructive challenge to music, and to the public perception of it, was addressed by some leading musicians and thinkers in two ways; first, with a philosophical enquiry into music's very nature, its aesthetic foundation; secondly, with a search for reconciliation between opposing ideas, cultures, and ethnic groups.

In 2006 just such a visionary musician led the way, with a project as radical as it was idealistic and prophetic. Daniel Barenboim began to assemble his West-Eastern Divan Orchestra in Weimar in 1999, mainly from among young Jews, Palestinians, and Arabs from the Middle East and Europe. They rehearsed and played music together, under his leadership, and when they were ready they took their concert on tour—Beethoven *Fifth Symphony*, Mozart *Sinfonia Concertante*, Elgar *Nimrod*—concluding in the West Bank Palestinian city of Ramallah on 21 August 2005. The concert itself, and the events leading up to it, were recorded on CD and two DVDs (Warner Classics).

In 2006, Barenboim gave a detailed account of his project, the creative impulse behind it, the preparations for it, and the results. Never was there a clearer statement of contemporary musical aesthetics. He asked two very simple questions: first, what is music? and secondly, what stood in the way of universal public perception of music in the 21st century, when there were no generally accepted aesthetic standards whereby music was perceived and differentiated? His answers were given in the form of five lectures in five cities, in which he re-lived the creative experience of the Ramallah concert, the BBC *Reith Lectures 2006.*

1. London: *In the beginning was sound*: music is a life-force, a metaphor for life itself.
2. Chicago: *The neglected sense*: the primacy of the ear, through which we hear and learn the meaning of music. The ear was abused and assailed in 21st century culture, which tended to be visual more than aural.
3. Berlin: *The magic of music*: music is a unifying force, a continuum of past and present.
4. Ramallah: *Meeting in music*: Music makes a hierarchy of equals, expressing themselves. It leads to understanding the world, not escaping from it.
5. Jerusalem: *The power of music*: Music can transform the world. It is idealistic, proposing the unthinkable, here and now.

Barenboim was no starry-eyed dreamer. Himself Jewish, born in Argentina, he was a conductor and pianist of the highest international renown. He spoke of what he knew from 50 years' experience.

The theme of reconciliation in music, the building of bridges between cultures, was powerfully evident in 2006, and nowhere more than in the work of composers of *The Silk Road Project* (see AR 2001, p. 507). Richard Danielpour's first opera, *Margaret Garner*, on the theme of love, maintained the success of its premiere in 2005 in Michigan, USA, with further productions in Philadelphia and Charlotte, North Carolina. The composer also made a three-movement vocal suite for concert use, *Triptych from Margaret Garner*. Peter Lieberson's *Neruda Songs*, settings for voice and orchestra of the Chilean poet Pablo Neruda, were also love songs, set in a (for him) freshly simple style. The songs enjoyed a warm success when sung by the composer's wife, Lorraine Hunt Lieberson, with the Boston Symphony under James Levine. The same singer also gave Lieberson's next vocal work in May 2006, an orchestral cantata *World in flower*, with the New York Philharmonic under Lorin Maazel. It was her last performance; two months later she died.

Yo-Yo Maa's Silk Road Ensemble performed in New York *Ritmos Anchinos* by Gabriela Lena Frank, a Peruvian-US citizen concerned with discovering a bridge to her Peruvian, and before that her Chinese, ancestors. Her *Anchino Rhythms* combined a string quartet with a pipa (lute) and a sheng (mouth organ). Her *Manchey Tiempo* (*Time of Fear*) treated a Peruvian melody in a context of percussion. Also in 2006 her *Requiem for a Magical American-El Dia de los Muertos* (*The Day of the Dead*) was performed in Kansas as an instrumental requiem, without voices, blending indigenous traditions with that of Spanish Catholicism. Her *Duo* for flute and piano was equally self-explanatory: *Cuatro Bosquejos Pre-Incaicos* (*Four pre-Inca Sketches*).

Other *Silk Road* composers had a productive year in 2006. Tan Dun's multi-media project *The Map* was recorded on DVD (DG), and Bright Sheng, fresh from success in Philadelphia with his *Concerto for Orchestra-Zodiac Tales*, and *Fantasies* for violin and piano at the La Jolla Festival in California, was made the first ever composer in residence with the New York City Ballet.

Much of 2006, in Europe and the USA, was given over to the well-publicised anniversaries of the birth of Mozart (250th) and Shostakovich (100th); yet the US classical music scene still found a place, as of right, for new US composers. Ned Rorem's chamber opera *Our Town* enjoyed successful performance at the University of Indiana, while recordings included his *Flute Concerto* and *Violin Concerto*, *Auden Songs*, and *Santa Fe Songs* (Naxos). The month of April saw two important orchestral performances for John Harbison. His *Concerto for Bass Viol*, otherwise known as the double bass, was first heard in Toronto; and his *Milosz Songs* for soprano and orchestra, 10 poems by the Nobel prize winner, Czeslaw Milosz, were commissioned by a consortium of 15 orchestras, thus guaranteeing at least 15 performances, of which the first took place in New York. Another prizewinner in 2006 was Yehudi Wyner, awarded the Pulitzer Prize in Music for his Piano Concerto *Chiavi in Mano* (*Keys in hand*), a reference to the position of the hands over the keyboard. The work was given a riotous premiere in Boston with the composer as pianist in an ebullient display of sheer American energy and high spirits.

2006 was a productive year for the record industry. Indeed for British composers in the UK it was more productive than the concert season as a whole. Pride of place must go to Daniel Barenboim and the West-Eastern Divan Orchestra's recording of the Ramallah Concert, which was followed later in the year by a second recording, equally ground-breaking, in which the orchestra was joined by the German State Opera Chorus for Beethoven's *Choral Symphony* (Warner Classics). The same label also celebrated Mozart's 250th anniversary with a series of 90 discs; other labels such as Decca, Deutsche Grammophon, Harmonia Mundi, and Philips also did the same with releases from their archives, a particularly rich resource.

Notable conductors of 2006 included Charles Mackerras, who was given an award for lifetime achievement by the magazine *Gramophone*, and Bernard Haitink, whose 50 years with the Amsterdam Concertgebouw were marked with two Mahler symphonies. Other recordings of the complete Mahler cycle were those of Pierre Boulez with the Vienna Philharmonic, and Leonard Bernstein, whose understanding of the music revealed fresh aesthetic insights, from the Jewish point of view, into the 20th century.

It was a good year for British composers. Those whose music benefited from the closer scrutiny afforded by an excellent recording, included John Dowland *Flow my tears*; Benjamin Britten *Nocturnal after John Dowland*; Michael Tippett *The Blue Guitar* (James Boyd); Gustav Holst *The Planets*; Mark Anthony Turnage *Ceres* (EMI Classics); Andrzej Panufnik *Sinfonia Mistica*, *Sinfonia di Sfere* (Explore), *Sinfonia Rustica*, *Sinfonia Sacra*, *Sinfonia Concertante* (EMI Classics); Arthur Bliss *Clarinet Quintet*; Alan Rawsthorne *Clarinet Quartet*; Francis Routh *Clarinet Quintet*; (Redcliffe), *Oboe Quartet* (Oboe Classics); Alan Rawsthorne *String Quartets* (Naxos); Constant Lambert *Piano Sonata* (Dutton Express).

Those who died in 2006 included the Japanese composer Akira Ifukube, the Hungarian György Ligeti, British composers Malcolm Arnold and John Veale; the sopranos Birgit Nilsson and Elizabeth Schwarzkopf; the mezzo soprano Lorraine Hunt Lieberson; the soul singer James Brown; the writer Michael Hurd (for Arnold, Schwarzkopf, and Brown see Obituary).

BOOKS OF THE YEAR. *Deeper than reason—emotion and its role in literature, music and art*, by Jenefer Robinson; *Listening to reason*, by Peter Williams; *The singing Neanderthals—the origins of music, language, mind and body*, by Steven Mitten; *Other planets: the music of Karlheinz Stockhausen*, by Robin Maconie; *The world of South African music: a reader*, ed. by Christine Lucia; *The substance of things heard : writings about music*, by Paul Griffiths; *German Modernism : music and the arts*, by Walter Frisch; *Polish Music since Szymanowski*, by Adrian Thomas; *Edgard Varèse: composer, sound sculptor, visionary*, ed. by Felix Meyer, Heidy Zimmermann; *Perspectives on Gustav Mahler*, ed. by Jeremy Barham; *Remembering the future: Charles Eliot Norton Lectures Harvard 1993-94*, by Luciano Berio; *In the beginning was sound: BBC Reith Lectures 2006*, by Daniel Barenboim; *Sergey Prokofiev: Diaries 1907-1914, Prodigious Youth*, ed by Anthony Phillips.

BALLET AND DANCE

In 2006 two companies generally considered to be among the greatest in the world, the Bolshoi from Moscow and The Royal Ballet from London, appeared to be revitalised, presenting exciting new productions. 2006 was also a year in which reconstructions and the reworking of old ballets commanded attention, some showing greater success than others. It was also a year in which a number of dancers emerged from the ranks or consolidated their positions as new stars. In all it left a feeling of optimism for the future of dance.

Among the dancers attracting attention were Natalia Osipova who whipped up a storm as Kitri on the opening night in London of the Bolshoi's *Don Quixote* and was also memorable in solo roles throughout the Bolshoi's season. Also exciting to watch were David Hallberg who proved himself a true danseur noble as Aminta in Frederick Ashton's *Sylvia* with American Ballet Theatre in New York, and Jonathan Goddard who encapsulated the spirit of Scott Joplin's rag time music in Richard Alston's *The Devil in the Detail*. Marianela Nuñez showed new maturity, especially in Glen Tetley's *Voluntaries* with The Royal Ballet without losing her bubbling personality which gave a liveliness to so many of her performances. Also new and making a mark, Rafael Bonachela launched a company attracting the cream of British freelance modern dancers, and Siobhan Davies opened new studios in Kennington designed by Sarah Wigglesworth, a truly sympathetic and stylish space for dance.

The highlight of the year was the visit to London by the Bolshoi. The company toured for much of the season while their theatre in Moscow was being extensively refurbished. In many venues they performed their tried and tested repertoire of *Swan Lake* and *Spartacus* but for London they showed a richer, more adventurous programme. A new *Cinderella* by Yuri Possokhov gave opportunities for some fine neo-classical dancing although it suffered from being lumbered with an over complicated narrative in which Viktor Barykin played the storyteller, Serge Prokofiev (composer of the score), and represented the fairy godmother, while Svetlana Zakharova's character combined Cinderella with Ptashka (Prokofiev's wife). Roland Petit's new version of *The Queen of Spades* was overblown but redeemed by all too brief appearances by Svetlana Lukina as Lise. It was, however, programmed between two lively ballets: Alexei Ratmansky's *Go For Broke* to Igor Stravinsky's *Jeu des cartes*, and George Balanchine's *Symphony in C*. *Go For Broke* was a stylish divertissement for the younger talent of the company who were also seen to good effect in the delightful *The Bright Stream*. *The Bright Stream* both acknowledged and gently satirised the Soviet past showing the Bolshoi dancers performing exuberant choreography in a real dance comedy. The score by Dmitri Shostakovich proved to be charming and the plot of mistaken identities and muddled rendezvous, in which dancers visit an agricultural collective, was enormous fun.

Contrasting with the Bolshoi's triumph, the Kirov (Maryinsky), at the insistence of artistic director, Valery Gergiev, restricted their 10-day London season of operas and ballets to celebrating the centenary of Shostakovich's birth. Not one of the ballets was worth showing in London, even the heroic *Leningrad Symphony* lacked its former power. *Leningrad Symphony* was one of three Soviet-era creations, with Konstantin Boyarsky's simplistic *The Lady and the Hooligan* (in which Igor Zelensky gave a dramatic performance) and Leonide Jakobson's *The Bedbug*, incomprehensible even to those who knew Vladimir Mayakovsky's play on which it was based, that made up a mixed bill. Worse was *The Golden Age* hurriedly commissioned from the inexperienced Noah Gelber. The choreography was uninspired and the complex narrative, concerning the reunion of a Soviet footballer and Western gymnast, incomprehensible. Even the presence of Kirov veterans Gabriella Komleva and Sergei Berezhnoi could not redeem this fiasco.

London's Royal Ballet had a successful year beginning with the revival of Jerome Robbins's *Afternoon of a Faun* danced by Carlos Acosta and Sarah Lamb and closing with a surprisingly popular mixed bill that included two creations, *Chroma* by Wayne McGregor and *DGV* by Christopher Wheeldon. *Chroma* used the stage space to great effect with a beautifully lit architectural setting and the dancers revelling in McGregor's dynamics. *DGV* was an atmospheric work in which the dancers appeared to be spirits emerging from a crashed train.

The Royal Ballet marked the 75th anniversary of its foundation with the revival of the "Oliver Messel *Sleeping Beauty*". By Messel's *Beauty* the company meant a return to the choreographic text of the production that had re-opened the Royal Opera House, Covent Garden, in 1946, with the reconstruction of most of Messel's sets. The costumes, which lacked the individuality of the originals, were newly designed by Peter Farmer. If the designs disappointed (the costumes were improved by the second block of performances in London) the dancers were applauded both in London and during the production's tour in the USA. Alina Cojocaru made a radiant Aurora in the first cast.

A celebratory mixed bill included *The Rake's Progress* by the company's founder, Ninette de Valois. If a few details were missing from the ballet inspired by Hogarth's paintings, Johan Kobborg dramatically presented the Rake's spiral into madness. This programme included the reworking of *Homage to the Queen*, revived to mark the 80th birthday of Queen Elizabeth II: it had been premiered on the day of her coronation. The original ballet had been entirely choreographed by Frederick Ashton but only his Air section survived so three British choreographers—David Bintley, Michael Corder, and Wheeldon—were invited to created new sections for Earth, Water, and Fire respectively. Conspicuous in a solo as the Spirit of Fire was the young Australian virtuoso dancer, Steven McRea.

Homage to the Queen showed an approach to reviving a partially lost ballet which was also taken by Rambert Dance Company with *Lady into Fox*. Mark Baldwin expanded the 1939 chamber ballet for the larger stages on which the company danced but retained Andrée Howard's choreography recorded on silent film. He commissioned an effectively dramatic new score from Ben Pope (the original by Arthur Honneger had not survived) and new designs from Michael Howells (the rather more effective original designs by Nadia Benois were available). The overall result was disappointing as the dancers playing the metamorphosed Mrs Tebrick did not really capture the fox's characteristics and the central scene in which the vixen is trapped in her garden did not suggest a confined space. Generally Rambert's dancers seemed more at home with their new full company works, *bloom* by Aletta Collins and *Stand and Stare* by Darshan Singh Bhuller, both choreographers working with Rambert for the first time. *Stand and Stare* was commissioned by the Lowry Centre in Salford and inspired by L.S. Lowry's paintings, yet managed successfully to avoid making the audience think about "matchstick men". Also on the reconstruction front Suzanne Farrell brought George Balanchine's 1965 *Don Quixote* to the Edinburgh festival. This atypical Balanchine production, full of symbolism, contained a few minutes of interesting dance in Act III but it seemed a very dated work performed to a colourless score by Nicolas Nabokov.

Much more welcome visitors to the UK were Mark Morris with *King Arthur* and the Merce Cunningham Dance Company with *Ocean*. For *King Arthur* at the London Coliseum, Morris took Henry Purcell's opera, ditched the narrative and dialogue, combined his dancers with the singers from English National Opera, and increased the fun. *Ocean* at the refurbished Roundhouse in London was presented with 150 musicians at the perimeter of the auditorium, behind the spectators, enveloping them for an engrossing 90-minute experience once the distraction of the digital clocks counting down the time to the end of the performance had been overcome.

Ocean was the centrepiece of the last Dance Umbrella season to be produced by the British Umbrella's founder, Val Bourne, whose seasons had transformed the face of the British dance scene. Other highlights were the series of performances by Anne Teresa De Keersmaeker although her latest creation, *D'un soir un jour*, an ambitious project to music by Claude Debussy, Igor Stravinsky, and George Benjamin, which incorporated choreography by Vaslav Nijinsky, never really gelled. Further echoes of Nijinsky emerged in Michael Clark's reworking of his own *Mmm...Stravinsky Project Part 2*. In this exhilarating *Rite of Spring*, Amy Hollingsworth danced the taut final solo as the bare-breasted Chosen Maiden.

In 2006 the Place prize was won by Nina Rajarani's Bharatanatyam-influenced *Quick*, essentially the day in the life of an urban quartet, which incorporated video projections as well as dancers and musicians. Cross-over elements between Indian and Western dance were also seen in *Sacred Monsters* performed by Sylvie Guillem and Akram Khan. Both performers had compelling moments, particularly in their solos, but it seemed a mistake to repeat the formula of Khan's *zero degrees* of 2005 with the dancers presenting long chunks of dialogue with obviously rehearsed spontaneity. For genuine spontaneity it would be hard to better the interviews with the spry octogenarian dancers in Dayna Goldfine and Dan Geller's surprise hit film, *The Ballets Russes*, recalling their youth touring the world and taking ballet to new audiences from the 1930s to the 1960s.

THEATRE

2006 was the year in which the London theatre sang, in virtually every sense. Though business in the first six months of the year was markedly down, the year as a whole saw a sizeable upturn, not least due to the astonishing array of musicals that kept box office tills trilling, especially come the autumn. The British capital, like Broadway, had long enjoyed a good song-and-dance, but no one could remember a theatre year so rife with musicals, and of such startling variety. What did Jerry Herman's *Mack and Mabel* have in common with Stephen Sondheim and James Lapine's *Sunday In the Park With George*, beyond the fact that both musicals originated on Broadway? Nothing, except that they marked an interest in smaller-scale musicals that could coexist alongside the proverbial heavy-hitters, which in the autumn came fast and thick in the form of *Wicked*, *Monty Python's Spamalot*, *Dirty Dancing*, and *The Sound of Music*.

Of that quartet, it was the latest revival of the last collaboration between composer Richard Rodgers and lyricist Oscar Hammerstein II that most excited both the industry and the general public. For the first time, a West End leading lady had been found via television, in this case, courtesy a reality TV programme called (what else?) "How Do You Solve A Problem Like Maria?", that had been shown in prime time on Saturday night on the BBC's flagship BBC1 channel, for eight weeks starting on 29 July. The winner, voted on by more than 2 million viewers, was a young Welsh woman, 23-year-old drama school graduate Connie Fisher, who had the requisite training but not the experience many assumed to be essential in order to carry a multi-million pound musical on her untested shoulders. In the event, Fisher's tomboyish appeal and slight gaucheness turned out to be ideally suited to the evergreen tale of the trainee nun Maria's move away from the world of the convent and into the von Trapp family, first as governess to the widowed Captain's cute-as-can-be array of children and then, indeed, as his plucky, quick-thinking wife. Maria, famously, was entirely unfazed by the gathering power of the Nazis circa 1938 in the Austrian Tyrol, where the 1959 musical was set.

Billed "the people's Maria," Fisher proved more than up to the task, and it would not be until much later into the run that she started missing sizeable blocks of performances because of vocal problems that, under the circumstances, were entirely understandable. But she was just one of an astonishing array of strong women who distinguished themselves in musicals across the year. Others included another newcomer, Julie Atherton, who brought hefty vocal chops and manual dexterity to her assignment as Kate Monster and the singularly named Lucy T. Slut in the puppet-themed musical *Avenue Q*; Jenna Russell, a long-time ensemble player who finally shone as the aptly named Dot, mistress to the Impressionist painter Georges Seurat, in the West End transfer of *Sunday In the Park*; the gloriously, deliberately diva-ish Hannah Waddingham in *Spamalot*, a West End presence as considerable as she was tall; and, primus inter pares, Broadway Tony award-winner Tonya Pinkins, who crossed the Atlantic to make her London stage debut playing the title role at the National Theatre in Tony Kushner and Jeanine Tesori's revelatory *Caroline, or Change*: a show fuelled not by sentimentality, as could often be the case with musicals, but by genuine anger and fury.

Of particular interest to hordes of teenage schoolgirls was the London appearance throughout the autumn of Broadway's Idina Menzel, who, like Pinkins, came to Britain to repeat a performance that had been much heralded in New York: in Menzel's case, the part of the green-hued Elphaba, the wicked witch in the suitably titled musical behemoth, *Wicked*. (Helen Dallimore, a perky Australian newcomer, was Menzel's co-star.) Admired by some, though it left this observer totally cold, was the director Trevor Nunn's full-fledged musicalisation of the 1930s American pop opera, *Porgy and Bess*, a previous triumph for Nunn in its full operatic form but here pared down and somewhat revised in order to accommodate the needs of performers who would have to sing a demanding score eight times a week. (In the opera world, of course, performers would appear in rotating repertory, so as to safeguard their voices.) Neither lead role was ideally cast, though the part of the crippled black US southerner, Porgy, did allow US expatriate Clarke Peters another stab at West End stardom; his distaff lead, Nicola Hughes, was woefully miscast as the emotionally fraught, tremulous Bess. Bringing up the rear in every aspect except commercially was the UK debut of the stage musical of the popular Patrick Swayze film, *Dirty Dancing*, which was brought to the stage with no discernible style or flair in an entirely rote production overseen by the film's writer, Eleanor Bergstein. Again, as with *Wicked*, coach parties of women rose to the bait by arriving at the theatre (in this case, the Aldwych) en masse, this time to ogle the pectorals of Australian leading man Josef Brown and to talk along with the better-known lines from the film, which were preserved intact for the stage version. Better, more genuine, fun was to be had at south London's tiny but increasingly important Menier chocolate factory, which survived a misbegotten summertime production of Jason Robert Brown's *The Last Five Years* to mount a sweet, sassy Christmas revival of *Little Shop of Horrors*, the erstwhile long-running off-Broadway hit; Sheridan Smith was the accomplished and surprisingly touching star. Nor, amidst the year's ongoing musical panoply, could one ignore the most bizarre revival of the year: a considerable rethink of the Stephen Sondheim-James Goldman collaboration, *Follies*, a putative epic here scaled down to suit a south London pub theatre, the Landor in Clapham, that seated not many more than 50. What one lost in the show's abundant scale and sweep was made up for by a newly intense focus on the discordant human relationships at its always wounding core.

Amidst all these musicals, some complained that London was going the way of Broadway (a perennial lament), while a larger cry was raised that musicals were taking over too many West End playhouses. One response to that latter issue might be simply to ask, "So what?", since the so-called outrage brought with it an implicit snobbery that automatically, and wrongly, privileged any straight play over, apparently, any musical whatsoever. In fact, one was reminded throughout the year of the sheer breadth of work that London offered uniquely, even in comparison to New York, a theatre centre that was lucky to open in a given year half of the 150 or so major productions that made London tick.

That was partly due, of course, to the extensive level of state subsidy for the theatre in the UK, extensive, at least, by comparison with the USA if not, say, with Germany. Several state-funded theatres had banner seasons in 2006: the Royal Shakespeare Company kicked off its hugely ambitious Bardathon, in which the entire canon of William Shakespeare was due to get some kind of look-in across 17 months. Highlights of the initial wave included a feisty, funny *Much Ado About Nothing*, directed by Marianne Elliott and set in 1950s Cuba. Her leads were television actress and comedienne Tamsin Greig as Beatrice and the rangy, likeable Joseph Millson as her sparring partner, Benedick. In Stratford, *Star Trek* leading man Patrick Stewart made a highly lauded return to the canon where he had begun before Capt. Picard brought him to the attention of the world. Stewart essayed two roles: Antony opposite Harriet Walter's Cleopatra and Prospero in a Rupert Goold staging of *The Tempest* which seemed to take place somewhere near the Arctic. In the latter production, Mariah Gale impressed, as well, as a notably gawky, unformed Miranda, Prospero's sheltered, erotically and intellectually curious daughter.

A smaller but scarcely less notable theatre destination, the Royal Court, feted a half-century as the country's leading home to new writing with a series of one-night-only readings of previous hits as well as some new plays that might well themselves stand the test of time. Simon Stephens's *Motortown* took a blistering, uncompromising look at the legacy of the Iraq war as seen through the eyes of a British soldier (played by an electric Daniel Mays) newly returned from Basra. Continuing with that theme, the US dramatist Christopher Shinn scored his finest Court premiere to date with *Dying City*, the title a reference both to Baghdad and also to a grieving, grievous New York in the 21st century. *Rainbow Kiss* was a compelling, first-time play beautifully served by a veteran director in actor

Richard Wilson, though all eyes were inevitably focused on the first ever Court play from a near-legend, Sir Tom Stoppard, whose summer opening, *Rock 'n' Roll*, had its commercial transfer already in view even before the press night; Rufus Sewell—renewing a partnership with Stoppard that began with *Arcadia* 13 years previously—brought illuminating empathy and sweetness to the role of a Czech dissident and sometime spy whose own story was bound up with the tumultuous growing pains of his home country. (Many assumed the play to be an act of thinly veiled autobiography from its Czech-born author, who in fact left his homeland when he was a little boy.) Away from the Court, the year's other defining straight play success was Peter Morgan's *Frost/Nixon*, a riveting re-imagining of the 1977 television interviews between British journalist David Frost and the 37th US president, Richard Milhous Nixon. (The roles were filled, without condescension but with real skill, by Welshman Michael Sheen and two-time Broadway Tony winner Frank Langella as Frost and Nixon, respectively.)

What of Broadway, where the non-musical always had a tougher time? It was hard to get too excited about the latest from Richard Greenberg (*The House In Town*) or Paul Rudnick (*Regrets Only*), though Greenberg was responsible for the starriest event of the year: the professional stage debut on Broadway in mid-April of film star Julia Roberts, who acquitted herself passably if hardly spectacularly in Greenberg's tricky, time-shifting drama, *Three Days of Rain*. (Her co-stars were Paul Rudd and Bradley Cooper.) Also new to Broadway, if far less ballyhooed, was onetime film name Ali MacGraw (*Love Story*), who led the short lived Broadway version of the popular British play *Festen*. Indeed, though musicals like *Jersey Boys* and *The Drowsy Chaperone* did command their fair share of attention, as did Harry Connick Jr in a limited run revival of that time honoured favourite, *The Pajama Game*, it was another British export to New York that made the year's biggest noise: *The History Boys* from Alan Bennett, a playwright who was a UK household name but who had not braved the treacherous commercial waters of Broadway for some 30 years, i.e. not since his play *Habeas Corpus* had come to New York and quickly gone again.

With the capacious Richard Griffiths driving a production set amongst a group of bright state school students who were being primed for Oxbridge during the 1980s, Bennett's play seemed to chime with ongoing debates about education in the USA, as it already had in the UK. (A film version, released in the autumn, took the same cast to a wider audience.) Nicholas Hytner's Broadway staging represented easily the most successful yet in the sequence of plays taken more or less directly from Britain's National Theatre on to Broadway, courtesy of a first-look deal between the state-funded London powerhouse and two New York producers, Bob Boyett and Bill Haber. (Others had included *Democracy* and *Jumpers*, both of which flopped in New York, and *The Pillowman*, which did well.) When Griffiths ascended the podium of Manhattan's fabled Radio City Music Hall on 11 June to accept his Tony award for best actor—one of six trophies won by the production—who was there to present it to him, beaming, but a non-nominated Julia Roberts, her evident graciousness and good feeling for Broadway's finest lingering on even after her own celebrity vehicle, at least, had left town.

CINEMA

THE 2007 Oscar nominations, almost all for films produced in 2006, seemed to prove that the members of Hollywood's Academy had at last decided to go international rather than simply compliment their own films. This could be read as both a tribute to world cinema and a sign that the US commercial cinema was making fewer and fewer risk-taking and imaginative films.

There were, for instance, three British actresses (Helen Mirren, the hot favourite and winner for her performance as the Queen in the film of that name, Judi Dench, and Kate Winslet) nominated for best actress and another Briton (the veteran Peter O'Toole) for best actor. Added to that, *Babel* and *Pan's Labyrinth*, the films of two young Mexican directors, were accorded several nominations between them and won four Oscars.

Quality rather than box-office success seemed to be the watchword too, with *Little Miss Sunshine*, a small, independently-made comedy about an eccentric family's journey across the USA in order to give their small girl a chance at a talent contest in California, being nominated as best film and managing to win two Oscars. While, in the increasingly important documentary section, ex-Democratic presidential candidate Al Gore's film about climate change, *An Inconvenient Truth*, easily won the Oscar. Both these films actually did surprisingly well at the box-office, appealing especially to audiences tired of endless special effects spectaculars.

It was in this new audience, largely served by older film-makers, who had rarely ventured into the cinema in recent years, that the future of film seemed to lie. In Britain, for instance, Stephen Frears' *The Queen*, nominated as best film, initially started life as a television project which might just appeal to a few in the cinemas, and became a surprise international success. This was principally because it attracted many who remembered the furore during the aftermath of the death of Diana, Princess of Wales when the royal family seemed reluctant to acknowledge the wave of emotion felt by much of the public, and were only persuaded by Prime Minister Tony Blair to return to London and fly the Buckingham Palace flag at half mast.

The award for best film and best director, however, went to *The Departed* and Martin Scorsese. The 62-year-old Scorsese, generally considered to be the USA's outstanding film-maker, and not one closely associated with Hollywood, had previously been nominated seven times without success. If *The Departed*, a cynical if well-made thriller, with a rip-roaring central performance from Jack Nicholson as a crime boss, could not possibly be compared to such classics as *Raging Bull* and *Taxi Driver*, most felt that the award was long overdue. Surprisingly, the film was actually an American version of an even better Hong Kong thriller called *Internal Affairs* which was never nominated for an Oscar.

The fact that Forrest Whitaker won best actor for his portrait of Ugandan dictator Idi Amin in *The Last King of Scotland*, another British film, was generally thought due to the essential poverty of Hollywood's commercial vehicles during the year. It was a magnificent performance, but the absence of anything comparable from major US stars allowed it a favourite's chance to win.

Alone among his contemporaries, Clint Eastwood, now 76, increased his reputation by making two formidable films as director. They were *Flags of Our Fathers* and *Letters From Iwo Jima*. Both were about the bloody battle for the Japanese island, thought to be a key to any invasion of Japan. The former was from the American point of view, the second, almost wholly in Japanese, told the story of the Japanese defence of the island. Neither, however, attracted large audiences.

America's biggest commercial success of the year was *Pirates of the Caribbean II*. Otherwise, many of those expected to do well at the box-office failed to emulate *Casino Royale*, the new British Bond film in which Daniel Craig proved an outstanding success as a tougher, less suave than usual 007. No recent Bond had done so well.

If it was hardly a bonanza year for Hollywood, the fact remained that it still controlled the exhibition outlets of a large slice of the world, and once again one could see the same American films wherever one went in Europe and much wider afield. It did not look, whatever the Academy decided about the quality of world cinema, as if that trend would be bucked in the near future.

Defenders of this long-established position claimed it was justified by the fact that the international success of Hollywood had kept thousands of screens open and flourishing which would otherwise have closed. This was undoubtedly true, since the competition from television, the Internet, and the video and DVD business grew ever more severe. But it frequently meant that home grown films, despite some notable exceptions, were often blocked out and that the state of world cinema grew more and more precarious.

Hollywood films with well-known stars often cost in excess of US$100 million to make, and their distributors frequently spent another US$100 million on prints and publicity. That financial power produced results, though it was reckoned that a Hollywood film had to make three-and-a-half times its budget to be properly termed a success. Only India's Bollywood (commercial song and dance epics emanating from Mumbai) could regularly counteract it. These reached the Indian diaspora all over the world and could make the same kind of fortune that the most successful Hollywood films gathered.

Even so, if asked which were the three best films of the year, this critic would point to non-American films. One was Austrian director Michael Haneke's *Caché* (*Hidden*), in which a well-lined middle class French couple are made paranoid by videos and strange messages pushed through their front door from an unknown and seemingly hostile source. The film posited that the middle classes often have guilty feelings about those much poorer and less lucky than themselves and, in the case of France, about the Algerian immigrants in post-colonial days.

Just as outstanding was a relatively obscure Romanian film called *The Death of Mr Lazarescu*. Shot with hand-held cameras in Bucharest, and almost like a documentary, it showed what happens to an elderly and admittedly troublesome old man who, after a suspected heart attack, is taken by ambulance from one hospital to another before he receives adequate treatment from generally uncaring nurses and doctors. The film had lessons that reached out well beyond Romania. It suggested that if you look like a tramp, you will be treated like one by a good many of those in the medical profession who ought to know better.

The third outstanding film would be Alfonso Cuaron's *Pan's Labyrinth*, in which a small girl resorts to fantasy in order to escape the brutal attentions of the army captain who has married her mother. Set in Spain during the immediate aftermath of General Franco's triumph, the film's mixture of the real and surreal might well have satisfied the great Luis Buñuel.

Another highly successful non-American film was from Germany and won the best foreign film Oscar and the European Film Academy's award for the best European film. *The Lives of Others* is about the Stasi, the East German secret police who spied on the population to such effect that no one was safe who was not a supporter of the regime. In this case, a Stasi operative has a change of heart to save a family—a turn of events that many of those living in what used to be East Germany complained was impossible. The film was, however, an immediate success in Germany and sold all over the world.

From Spain came Pedro Almodovar's *Volver*, set in his home vicinity of La Mancha and a superbly fluent example of the art of the premier Spanish director. Employing a bevy of the actresses who had served him so well over the years, it contained a particularly watchable performance from Penelope Cruz as a housewife whose husband has left her and who finds herself alone with her child in an ever stranger world.

One of the saddest events of the year was the death of Robert Altman, the US director who came into prominence with *MASH* and went on to make classic films like the revisionist western, *McCabe and Mrs Miller*; the Raymond Chandler thriller *The Long Goodbye*; *Short Cuts*, based on the stories of Raymond Carver; and *Nashville*, a commentary on the USA of its day following 24 characters. Not all his films were successful or even good, but he proved in a long career that American films could be inventive in form and daring in subject matter (for obituary see p. 570).

Among the actors who died were Hollywood stars Glenn Ford, Shelley Winters, June Allyson, Red Buttons, Jack Palance, Anthony Franciosa, Jack Warden, and Robert Sterling; France's Philippe Noiret, India's Nadira, Japan's Tamba Tetsuro, and Italy's Alida Valli, and, from the UK, Moira Shearer (for obituary see p. 597), Tom Bell, Derek Bond, Dennis Weaver, and Jack Wild. Directors included Robert Altman, Daryl Duke, Gordon Parks, and Vincent Sherman from the USA; Japan's Imamura Shohei, Thailand's Cherd Songsri, France's Gerard Oury, Daniele Huillet, and Francis Girod, Poland's Walerian Borowczyk, Italy's Gillo Pontecorvo, Britain's Val Guest, Turkey's Atif Yilmaz, Sweden's Vilgot Sjoman and Jamaica's Perry Henzell. Among the well-known film composers were Malcolm Arnold from the UK (for obituary see p. 571), and Bollywood's Naushad.

TELEVISION AND RADIO

In broadcasting, 2006 was the year of YouTube and MySpace as a combination of the Internet and user generated content from viewers created unprecedented new competition for the professionals.

The popularity of MySpace, the online community site bought by Rupert Murdoch, chairman of The News Corporation, in July 2005 for US$580 million, continued to grow during the year. The big surprise, however, was the almost immediate impact of YouTube, an online company less than 18 months old which allowed anyone to post their video clips online, thereby making them available worldwide (see p. 448). During the year users were uploading an average of 65,000 new video clips each day and watching an astonishing 100 million videos per day.

For British broadcasters a defining moment came at a Royal Television Society conference in September when the largely middle-aged audience were shown two clips from YouTube. One was of two Chinese teenagers miming to a Western pop song in their bedroom. Another was of an American girl talking to a camera about her "lonely" life. A show of hands revealed that more than half the delegates had already seen both clips. They epitomised both the growing influence and potential danger of YouTube. It could bestow instant international fame on unknown Chinese teenagers but it could also mislead. The lonely American girl was exposed as an aspiring actress complete with an agent and the apparently spontaneous outpourings of her lonely life were largely scripted.

Nevertheless, there was no mistaking the power of the phenomenon, something well understood by the Internet content provider, Google, which bought YouTube in October for US$1.65 billion. The threat to traditional broadcasters was all too obvious. Not only were the eyes of the young going somewhere other than the television set, the greater threat was that television advertising would migrate to YouTube to follow those eyes. The response of broadcasters was varied. Some, particularly in Japan, launched lawsuits against YouTube for breach of their copyrights in areas such as sport. The majority view was that they should recognise the importance of YouTube by becoming part of it and broadcasters, including the BBC, opened talks for deals to contribute their own clips.

The Corporation may have struggled manfully to keep up with the latest technological developments—including a large increase in podcasting—but there was a threat much closer to home in the form of tough negotiations with the government on a new licence fee settlement. There was no doubt that the BBC would get a new 10-year royal charter, but by December the Treasury had leaked the news that the BBC would have to make do with a level of licence fee considerably lower than sought. The BBC asked for the settlement to be based on retail prices plus 2.3 per cent, a request later reduced, during the negotiations, to 1.8 per cent above inflation. The detailed leaks suggested a six-year deal based on a straight 3 per cent increase for two years followed by a 2 per cent rise in each of the next three years. The final year would be up to 2 per cent.

The rise was below the likely level of inflation and came with strings attached: major projects had been "ring-fenced" and would have to be paid for out of the licence fee. For example the BBC would face the short-term costs of moving a number of programme-making departments to a new media city at Salford, near Manchester. A £500 million digital transmitter system would also have to be funded by the BBC to enable all of the UK to move to digital television by 2012. The government announced that the process was to begin in autumn 2007 when Whitehaven in Cumbria would become the first town in the UK to go wholly digital. In addition the government made it clear that it wanted the BBC to pay for the £600 million cost of helping the old and poor make the transition to digital.

BBC Director General Mark Thompson expressed "disappointment" as the bad news unfolded and it became clear that the organisation would have £2 billion less than it thought it needed, a shortfall that would inevitably mean more job losses. Commercial rivals struggling with a difficult advertising market noted, however, that the BBC would still have around £20 billion of guaranteed income over the six years.

ITV, in particular had a torrid year. The broadcaster may have produced the successful film, *The Queen*, with Helen Mirren (see p. 493), but ITV 1's advertising revenue fell by 12 per cent in 2006 to £1.28 billion, only partly offset by growth coming from ITV's family of digital channels. The launch of more digital channels increased the fragmentation of the audience and was blamed for part of the decline in advertising. ITV could still claim that it remained the UK's only mass-market commercial television channel with more than 440 programmes across the year winning audiences of more than 8 million. Yet in July low ratings for the reality show *Love Island* helped to push ITV's audience share to a new record low of 16.9 per cent for the month.

The on-screen performance combined with a languishing share price to increase pressure on the ITV chief executive, Charles Allen, who finally agreed to resign in July. Allen used a swan song giving the MacTaggart lecture at the Edinburgh television festival not to defend his own record but to launch a ferocious attack on Channel 4. In his parting shot Allen accused Channel 4 of ignoring its public purposes and relying too much on reality shows such as *Big Brother*, quizzes such as *Deal or No Deal* and US imports like *Lost*. "Look at the Channel 4 afternoon schedule: quiz show, gameshow, chatshow, cartoon, soap. Or its peak schedule dominated by reality, lifestyle, US acquisitions, and 'shock docs'," said Allen.

In reply Channel 4 emphasised the amount of serious content in its schedules—the number of its documentary series *Dispatches* was greatly increased—and noted that, unlike the other terrestrial broadcasters, it had managed to maintain its audience share.

Five, now fully owned by the European broadcaster, RTL, had by way of contrast, dropped back from a share of 6.5 per cent in 2005 to 5.9 per cent in 2006 and the main programme executives were replaced to try to win back audiences.

During the year the troubles of ITV encouraged two serious attempts to take over the commercial broadcaster, the first by venture capitalists led by Greg Dyke, the former director general of the BBC. The ITV board rejected the Dyke move and then a more serious attempt materialised from the Virgin founder, Sir Richard Branson. During the year Sir Richard sold his Virgin Mobile business in a deal worth £980 million to cable group NTL, which was, in turn, in the process of merging with the other remaining large British cable company, Telewest. Sir Richard took a large minority stake in the enlarged cable group to be called Virgin Media. The new business would offer customers a "quadruple play," or as Sir Richard liked to call it, "four play". This was television, telephone, broadband, and mobile services all available on a single monthly bill. The plan was to compete head-on with Rupert Murdoch's satellite broadcaster, BSkyB. Sir Richard and Virgin Media decided to go one step further in November with a £4.7 billion bid for ITV. Murdoch, sensing danger, moved within 24 hours to buy nearly 18 per cent of ITV for £940 million. Under the 2003 Communications Act, BSkyB was prohibited from owning more than 20 per cent of ITV but the minority stake amounted to an effective mechanism to block a Branson takeover. Four days after the Murdoch swoop the ITV board rejected the Virgin Media approach. Sir Richard said that the Murdoch share purchase "has already had a material influence in the company and damaged the plurality of the British media". The issue, and the intensifying row between BSkyB and Virgin Media, seemed likely to end with the regulators.

ITV did, however, receive a major boost before the end of the year when Michael Grade, the chairman of the BBC governors, agreed to become executive chairman of ITV. The consensus view was that if anyone could turn around the fortunes of ITV it was Grade, who had spent almost all his working life in senior positions in British broadcasting. His defection meant that a new chairman had to be found for the BBC Trust, the new BBC supervisory body that would replace the governors on 1 January 2007.

Meanwhile BSkyB increased its number of satellite subscribers to 8.4 million by the end of the year. A new broadband service went from nothing to 250,000 in a few months and there was record growth in the personal video recorder service, Sky Plus, to more than 2 million boxes. BSkyB also launched high definition (HD) television in time for the football World Cup finals in Germany and subsequently signed up the first 184,000 subscribers. Sky was virtually alone with its HD service in the UK although the BBC did begin a pilot scheme.

There was one noticeable set-back for BSkyB when it was outbid by the Irish group, Setanta, for two of the packages of live English Premier League football games. In the USA, however, the BSkyB chairman, Rupert Murdoch, proved once and for all that one of his main motivations was keeping control of the company which he had created, News Corporation. For decades Murdoch had tried to build up a satellite television business in the USA. In December he let his stake in the US satellite broadcaster, DirecTV, go as part of a US$11 billion deal to see off his great rival, John Malone, and retain control of News Corporation.

On the programming front, the football World Cup was the most popular attraction, with the England v Sweden game pulling in an audience of 14.4 million.

ITV was successful with *Lewis*, an off-shoot of the *Inspector Morse* dramas, and *Heartbeat* while BBC hits included *Dr Who*, *Robin Hood*, *Strictly Come*

Dancing, and *Planet Earth*. The BBC's *Bleak House* was the big winner at both the BAFTA (British Academy of Film and Television Arts) and Royal Television Society awards.

Rather like commercial television, radio advertising came under increasing pressure. Radio executives noted the continued rise of online advertising, which headed towards £2 billion in the UK during the year and feared that radio was also suffering in the wake of ITV's problems.

Despite current revenue problems, however, the radio industry was increasingly optimistic about the future. By the end of the year there were around 5 million digital radios in the UK, a rise of 2 million in 12 months. It had previously taken five years to get to the 3 million figure. "That is a clear and unequivocal trend. It shows radio has a pretty encouraging future, albeit in a slightly different way than I would have envisaged 10 years ago," said Ralph Bernard, chief executive of GCap, the company that owned Capital Radio. The commercial sector reduced the BBC's lead in share of radio listening, partly because commercial radio was the leader in the digital sector. A further round of consolidation in commercial radio seemed likely as the Emap and Chrysalis groups were reviewing their position in radio.

There were at least three significant deaths in broadcasting during the year. David Plowright, the former chief executive of Granada television, and the man responsible for landmark programmes such as *Brideshead Revisited* and *The Jewel in the Crown*, died in August. His resignation in 1992, forced out by Granada group Chief Executive Gerry Robinson, marked the moment when ITV became less of a public service broadcaster and more of a commercial business. Marmaduke Hussey, former chairman of the BBC died (for obituary see p. 582). Lord Hussey was famous for sacking Alasdair Milne, the BBC director general. In the USA, Frank Stanton, a broadcasting pioneer and president of CBS for 26 years, died at the age of 98. He built up CBS News as a respected source of information.

The year ended as it began, with more technologically driven competition for broadcasters. In December, BT (British Telecom) launched its broadband Internet television service, BT Vision. In common with almost every telecoms operator in Europe, BT was offering an IPTV (Internet protocol television) service down the telephone line, mainly for on-demand films and entertainment. There were more than 30 IPTV operators in Europe with 3 million subscribers, mostly in France, Spain, and Italy.

There was at least some comfort for traditional broadcasters on Christmas Day when the audience deserted their new devices to watch television. The overall audience peaked at 24.8 million thanks to the demise of *EastEnders* matriarch Pauline Fowler on BBC One and an ITV comedy drama, *Doc Martin*, on at the same time. The largest individual audience that day was the 11.4 million who tuned in to see the *Vicar of Dibley*, Geraldine Granger, finally find love.

The broadcasting moment of the year had to be MP George Galloway on *Celebrity Big Brother*. Thanks to the power of the Internet, the footage of the Respect MP pretending to be a cat rubbing up against actress Rula Lenska and purring will last for ever.

VISUAL ARTS

In January the Getty museum opened its refurbished, Roman-style villa in Malibu, California, to show its antiquities collection, the celebrations dampened by the trial proceeding in Rome against former curator Marion True, accused of buying illicitly traded archaeological goods (see AR 2005, pp. 457-58). In May the museum and the Italian government announced that 21 pieces from the collection would be returned to Italy. The deal was similar to the one struck between Italy and the Metropolitan Museum, New York, earlier in the year to return an Etruscan vase, known as the Euphronios Crater, and silver, possibly illicitly excavated from Morgantina in Sicily, in exchange for comparable items to be lent from Italy. In August the Getty also agreed to return two items to Greece. In November it announced stricter guidelines governing future acquisitions of antiquities: artefacts must have left their countries of origin by 1970, the year of the UNESCO Convention, or have export documentation to be considered for purchase.

A tiny fragment of the Parthenon, measuring 8 by 11 cm, was returned by Heidelberg university to Greece. The British Museum continued to maintain the right to retain its Parthenon marbles, however, against repeated claims by Greece.

Both China and Iran launched rescue archaeology schemes at the sites of future water management projects: the former a massive scheme to divert the Yangtze along three canals running to the eastern, central, and western parts of the country; the latter at the Sivand dam, whose flooding was delayed in order to study whether it posed a threat to the tomb of Cyrus the Great. The European Court of Human Rights agreed to hear a case submitted by Turkish academics to protect the ancient city of Hasenkeyf in the south east of Turkey, which was due to be submerged by the Ilisu dam.

In April, members of the European Parliament were denied access to the Nakhichevan region of Azerbaijan to investigate claims that the Armenian Christian cemetery of Djulfa, with its intricately carved tombs dating from the ninth to the 16th centuries, had been destroyed by soldiers. The Armenians claimed that this was the final stage in the systematic cleansing of Armenian cultural heritage from Nakhichevan—a landlocked enclave of Azerbaijan, bounded by Armenia, Turkey, and Iran—mostly carried out between 1998 and 2002.

Donny George, the Christian president of the State Board of Antiquities and Heritage of Iraq, resigned in August on the grounds that Iraq was now so unsafe that the National museum, looted after the 2003 Iraq war (see AR 2003, p. 524; AR 2004, p. 479), had had to close and was completely sealed with thick concrete walls, while the State Board was under the influence of Muqtada al-Sadr, the militant Shi'ite leader: "They have no knowledge of archaeology; they are only interested in Islamic sites", said George. He went on to claim asylum in the USA. Also in August, Iran offered to help in the protection and restoration of archaeological sites in Iraq, especially Taq Kisra, the great vaulted hall at the Parthian city of Ctesiphon.

A report by Heritage Preservation in partnership with the Institute for Museum and Library Services (a US federal agency), found that nearly one-quarter of the 21 million works of art in US museums were in need of conservation. Conservation was also an issue in Turkey, where in Istanbul the 50 storage vaults of the Topkapi Palace museum were found to be in a disastrous condition, with decaying carpets, broken ceramics, and rusting weapons. The privatisation of the former sultans' palace was suggested by the Turkish minister of culture, Atilla Koc.

Istanbul also saw Turkey's first exhibition on Picasso, mounted with the support of the Sabbanci family, well known supporters of Turkey's entry into the EU. Meanwhile, in Iran, the capital, Teheran, saw an exhibition of Chagall, a Jewish Russian artist, from Iranian collections.

The rising wealth and aspirations of the Russian business elite were demonstrated at the auctions in New York and London, where they bought 19th-century Russian paintings and antiques and "impressionists" of the Soviet period, but also a US$95 million Picasso painting of his mistress, Dora Maar.

The contemporary art market continued its five-year rise, with numerous record prices at auction for artists including Damien Hirst, Andreas Gursky, and Peter Doig. In five days, the London autumn auctions had a turnover of £74 million, with Chinese artists selling particularly well. The trend-setting collector, Charles Saatchi, announced that he would be opening his new London gallery with Chinese artists.

A UNESCO report on the global trade in cultural goods showed that China had become the second largest exporter of visual arts—defined as paintings, prints and sculptures—sending out US$2.23 billion in 2002, after the UK (US$2.7 billion). While the UK also imported goods worth US$2.76 billion, being a major entrepot for the art trade, China was not among the five top art-importing nations.

In April plans for a huge cultural neighbourhood, planned as part of a property development scheme in the West Kowloon district of Hong Kong, collapsed due to the unwillingness of the developers to put up the HK$30 billion (US$3.87 billion) required to finance and operate it (see p. 330). The Pompidou centre in Paris, the Guggenheim in New York, and the Victoria & Albert Museum in London had been collaborating with rival development groups to provide outposts of their museums. Singapore announced that a new museum examining the relationship between science and art would be part of a resort complex on Marina Bay incorporating an hotel, a casino, convention and retail space, and performing arts venues, to be completed by 2009. The development company, Sands Corporation, also ran the Venetian resort hotel in Las Vegas, a reduced-size replica of Venice with an attached exhibition space for outposts of the Guggenheim museum, New York, and the Hermitage, St Petersburg.

The Gulf began to play a role in the international art world when a successful sale in Dubai of contemporary art from the Middle East, India, Pakistan, and the West fetched US$8.5 million in sales.

The Louvre museum, Paris, announced long-term paid loans from its collections to the High Museum in Atlanta, USA, the US$10 million proceeds destined to help finance the redisplay of galleries at the Louvre. The Louvre's director, Henri Loyrette was criticised by French museum professionals and some of the media for this policy.

In former East Germany, two famous museums damaged by bombing during World War II reopened. The Bode Museum on the museum island in Berlin opened to display sculpture from Byzantium to the 18th century, with particularly strong holdings of Renaissance works. The Green Vault in Dresden, which had to be almost completely rebuilt, showed the treasury of the Electors of Saxony in the 18th-century manner.

A 32,500 sq m National Museum of African-American Art, directly opposite the Holocaust memorial museum, was announced for Washington DC's "museum mile" leading up to the Capitol. Meanwhile in Paris, in June, the Musée du Quai Branly opened to display the material culture, old and contemporary, of Africa, Asia, Oceania, and the Americas. The museum had the special backing of President Jacques Chirac who said that it was "The result of a political desire to see justice rendered to non-European cultures" (see p. 44). It housed works from the former Musée de l'Homme and Musée national des Arts d'Afrique et d'Océanie. The museum attracted some vehement criticism for displaying the collections more as art than as ethnography in what the architect Jean Nouvel described as a "poetic and disturbing" environment (see p. 504).

In a landmark arbitration held in the USA, it was ruled that Austria should return five paintings by Gustav Klimt which had been stolen by the Nazis 70 years previously and were hanging in the Osterreichische Nationalgalerie. The beneficiary of the decision was Maria Altmann of California, the grand-daughter of the original owner, Ferdinand Bloch-Bauer. In June, Ronald Lauder, chairman of the US cosmetics company Estée Lauder, paid a reputed US$135 million for one of the Klimts, a gold-ground portrait of Adèle Bloch-Bauer, to show it in his New York museum, the Neue Galerie.

French billionaire François Pinault opened his new museum in the Palazzo Grassi, Venice, having abandoned plans to build one in Paris (see AR 2005, p. 459), with a show of 200 works by fashionable international contemporary artists such as Damien Hirst, Jeff Koons, and Maurizio Cattelan. The former French minister of culture, Jacques Aillagon, was the museum's director.

Art works stolen and recovered (or not), included the famous sculptural gold salt cellar by 16th-century artist Benvenuto Cellini, which had been stolen from the Kunsthistorisches museum, Vienna, in 2003 by a security-alarm salesman, and was recovered by police in January. One of two versions of Munch's *Scream* and his *Madonna*, stolen in 2004 from the Munch museum, Oslo, Norway, were recovered to national jubilation. Monumental sculpture suffered a spate of thefts, almost certainly for its scrap value: Henry Moore's two-tonne *Reclining Figure* of 1969-70 was stolen from outside his former home; Richard Serra's 38-tonne steel *Equal Parallel/Guernica-Bengasi* of 1987 disappeared from store in Madrid; while Lyn Chadwick's 1960 *The Watchers*, weighing one-third of a tonne, was taken from the grounds of Roehampton university, London.

The most visited exhibition in the world was in Japan for the third year running: the Price collection of 18th-century Japanese paintings lent from California to the Tokyo National Museum attracted 6,446 visitors per day.

Deaths in 2006 included Nam June Paik, Korean pioneer of video installations, on 29 January, aged 73; Ian Hamilton Finlay, on 27 March, aged 80, a Scottish artist and the creator of a garden called Little Sparta, full of poetical and military allusions; Allen Kaprow, on 5 April, aged 78, a US artist who staged the first "happening" in 1959 and gave the genre its name; Karel Appel, a Dutch artist, part of the CoBRa movement, on 3 May, aged 85; and Lord Thomson of Fleet, on 12 June, aged 83, a Canadian citizen, former owner of *The Times* newspaper, and major collector and benefactor of the Art Gallery of Ontario (for obituary see p. 600).

ARCHITECTURE

VITRUVIUS'S architectural trinity—firmness, commodity, and delight—slipped further into various modes of immateriality in 2006. The utopian remains of the idealised Fordism that produced the Bauhaus and subsequent expressions of modernist architecture were raked over by Professor Ricky Burdett of the London School of Economics and Political Science, curator of the Venice architecture biennale. He packed the sombre halls of the Arsenale with a vast cache of information, inferring both dystopic chaos and anarchic creativity; very little new architecture was on show. Elsewhere, Rem Koolhaas, the profession's most quoted practitioner, pursued his interest in the effects of "the violent surf of information" with increasing vigour.

Koolhaas told an audience of architects, planners, and developers at a London conference organised by the government's Commission for Architecture and the Built Environment that "we have turned the city into a surface where no square inch is left unspoken for, within the context of some kind of vision. In settings such as this, we are not supposed to misbehave, to die, to beg, to fight, to be drunk. That eerie abstraction of the generic haunts us." Architects, he said, no longer wrote manifestos: "At most, we write portraits of particular cities in the hope, not of developing a theory of what to do with them, but of understanding how cities exist currently." Koolhaas regretted the loss of utopian instincts, and the fact that "the simple commercial pressure behind almost every building these days forces eccentricities and extravagance on even the most earnest designer."

In Britain, this extravagance extended beyond bathetically excessive design. It was more crudely revealed in the hundreds of millions of pounds wasted on architecturally compromised or cancelled private finance initiative (PFI) projects in the last decade. The treasury's apparent support of the new "Smart PFI" system, sponsored by the Royal Institute of British Architects (RIBA), would, hopefully, place a greater emphasis on architectural quality, and reduce the costs associated with consortia bidding for big projects such as schools and hospitals. It currently cost individual PFI teams millions of pounds simply to compete for a single commission which, even if won, usually demanded architectural shortcuts to recoup losses. The architectural quality of the 2012 London Olympic structures was already being significantly undermined by cost and design constraints.

Postmodern architecture's continuing general collapse into an historically and culturally reductive condition recalled Hans-Georg Gadamer's comment that "the only thing that is universally familiar to us today is unfamiliarity itself, momentarily illuminated by an ephemeral glimmer of meaning." That thought was reprised by the architect Bernard Tschumi, who told a conference at RIBA that the best that architects can do now is "influence the phenomena". Pascal Schöning's Manifesto For A Cinematic Architecture, published in 2005, spoke of architecture that "aims to dissolve or expose the concept of a static material world through a buzz of constant change".

In Paris, however, Jean Nouvel's design of the Musée du Quai Branly ignored the lure of dissolution and took a distinctly polemical position, producing an architecture of typological and perceptual protest, a return, in fact, to the ruthless deconstructivism preached by Jean Baudrillard more than three decades previously. Nouvel's ethnographic museum deliberately undermined post-imperial or purely academic reactions to the tens of thousands of objects it contained. While clearly borrowing from the subtle lighting and atmospherics associated with Italian architect Carlo Scarpa, Nouvel produced extraordinarily variable viewing conditions whose precisely arranged mystery owed more to the discussion of colonialism by Joseph Conrad and André Gide—if not to Baudrillard's essay, Death to Savages—than to the contextually and polemically sterile postmodernism that dominated the urban scene in developed countries (see p. 502).

Another form of architectural sterility—the increasing quest by towns, cities, and private corporations to create so-called iconic buildings—produced examples of architecture informed by superficial rationales. A striking example of this was Foster & Partners' Pyramid of Peace in Kazakhstan. Its form was selected, according to the practice, because it could be assembled rapidly, and because it was a culturally neutral symbol; as culturally neutral, presumably, as the pyramids of Giza, or its panoptic trope on the US dollar bill.

The trivialisation or erasure of cultural, material, and historical responses in architectural forms was producing "landmark" buildings that were formal singularities rather than civil actors in, say, urban settings. Peter Eisenman, one of architecture's leading intellectuals, produced a timely essay in Log magazine, in which he argued that iconic buildings had become "the symbols for a generation that can no longer see".

The seduction of geometry continued, and was most lavishly expressed at UN Studio's Mercedes-Benz museum in Stuttgart, Germany. The Dutch practice's co-principal, Ben van Berkel, cited Frank Lloyd Wright's Guggenheim museum and the early paintings of de Chirico as inspirations. However, what ultimately confronted the viewer in Stuttgart were not shapes from the modernist or surrealist canons, but the latest example of "gigabaroque" architecture, in which the design pursued highly complex computer generated distortions of form.

There was no geometry to speak of at Renzo Piano's elegantly modernist revision of the Morgan library and museum, his first project in New York. Piano, the international market leader in museum and gallery design, said his schema drew from ideas of robber-barons, metaphysics, gravity, and the stories of Jorge Luis Borges. The new, connective architecture that infilled the portentous Madison Avenue treasure house established by Pierpoint Morgan in 1881 was straightforwardly modernist and, like its 68-year-old architect, radiated an aura of quizzical beneficence.

The ravening property developers of Moscow were less benign. Even as Lord Norman Foster delivered his design for the Moscow City Tower, which would be the tallest building in Europe, the extraordinary interlocked drums and diamond-shaped windows of the 1929 Konstantin Melnikov house remained under threat of demolition following the death of Melnikov's son, Viktor Melnikov, in 2005. The World Monument Fund was supporting attempts to save a building whose unique fusion of classical and Constructivist modes haunted Foster's brand of svelte corporate techno-modernism like an architectural version of Coleridge's albatross.

Richard Rogers Partnership's vast Barajas airport at Madrid was more a case of brightly colour-coded zones and was, in effect, Rogers' swansong building. The airport design team was led by Ivan Harbour who, with Graham Stirk, had been appointed as the practice's new co-principal. Rogers would remain as the practice's eminence grise, but it was easy to predict a bi-polar output of building types in the future: muscularly extrovert structural complexity from Harbour; and elegant, beautifully detailed post-Miesian towers from Stirk.

Rem Koolhaas's pavilion for London's Serpentine Gallery was, in every sense, hot air: an anti-architectural blog-space filled with round-the-clock debates about architecture and culture. It recalled the visionary pronouncement of the late Cedric Price that architects should not build if they could, instead, find other ways of encouraging activity that expressed "doubt, delight and change". Price's declaration that "dialogue might be the only excuse for architecture" was also well demonstrated in projects relating to the micropolitics of urban architecture which were highlighted in Talking Cities, a publication devised by Francesca Ferguson of the German Urban Drift organisation.

In the UK developers and master-planners began to appoint younger practices, committed to contextually derived architecture, to design pockets of housing on difficult brownfield sites. Three or four years previously, practices such as Lynch Architects, FAT, Buschow Henley, NORD, Witherford Watson Mann, and AOC were regarded as highly talented, but riskily polemical; today, only that degree and variety of talent could begin to make humane and coherent architectural sense of marginal sites.

The pursuit of contextual and materialist architecture was still limited, but it produced particularly notable results among Irish architects such as Sheila O'Donnell and John Tuomey. In 2005, Boyd Cody's Ruthmines House in Dublin re-wrote the end-of-terrace urban script with an intelligent vernacular asymmetry and robust materiality that was also apparent in Brendeland and Kristofferson's student housing at Trondheim, Norway. In Spain, Alberto Campo Baeza's Casa Guerrero at Cadiz re-addressed the question of the atmospherics of apparently simple spaces; and in Chile, architects such as Eduardo Castillo experimented boldly with materials and formal typologies. The distortions of his House V did not displace any sense of place, or of architecture as part of a coherent continuum. In Addis Ababa, Ethiopia, Gameren and Mastenbroek's Dutch embassy was modernist in form, yet the addition of red laterite to the rough-cast concrete produced a remarkable formal distinctiveness.

However, the dominant perception of architecture as a demonstration of amoral immateriality remained. Wolf Prix, of the Austrian practice Coop Himmelb(l)au, was interested in the architectural ramifications of amnesia. "Ours is a visual society," he told the RIBA fellows debate. "Research about memory at MIT has found that digitised images don't remain in our long term memory. This is a very important visual revolution. All the digitised images you see, you will forget in 14 days. This will change our lives dramatically. How can we plan for a joyful society that dances on a digital stage?"

His words would not have been noted in a certain penthouse apartment overlooking Rio de Janeiro's Copacabana beach. Here, Oscar Niemeyer, the last remaining great mid-century modernist architect, still drew obsessively beautiful visualisations of obdurately utopian buildings using a thick black magic marker. Niemeyer, 99, married for the second time in November.

LITERATURE

THIS was a year in which the Manichean divide between popular writing and more demanding books became especially evident in figures published at the end of 2006 concerning best-sellers. Once again authors such as Martina Cole, Stephen King, and Andy McNab easily outsold every heavyweight writer. J.K. Rowling remained the most bought novelist of her time, with the uncompleted, unpublished, untitled final book in the *Harry Potter* series already in terms of pre-publication orders outstripping any other book on the planet. There were signs, however, that apparently unassailable reputations could eventually fade. Catherine Cookson, once the most borrowed author in public libraries, lost her perch, admittedly nine years after her death. Despite the enormous popularity of Rowling, enhanced by the success of the films made from her stories, there were many critical sceptics prepared to say that her quality was not of the same class as the classic writers of children's literature. Increasingly her vast wealth, making her by some reckonings the richest woman in the world, seemed to dominate discussions of her achievements.

Much bright new talent emerged during the year, emblematised by the success of Kiran Desai in winning the Man Booker prize, the pre-eminent accolade in the UK for new fiction. Her mother, Anita Desai, had often been a serious contender for the award, but had never won it. Kiran Desai did so with only her second novel, *The Inheritance of Loss*. Another second novel which made a huge impact was *Half of a Yellow Sun*, by Chimamanda Ngozi Adichie. Like Desai, who was an Indian citizen living in the USA, the Nigerian Adichie was regarded by many as not wholly belonging to any country but part of a new global citizenry produced by the migratory flows of modern society. Indeed, peoples on the move became a feature of much of the fiction destined to be described by academics as "post-colonial": in Kate Grenville's *The Secret River*, which won the Commonwealth Writers Prize; in Christopher Hope's *My Mother's Lovers*, in which the heroine was an aviatrix; and in Thomas Pynchon's long-awaited *Against the Day*, which brought to life the busy final years of the 19th century and first two decades of the 20th.

If Pynchon's was the most anticipated novel of the year, there were others from well-established authors which did not disappoint. Among American writers, Richard Ford was thought to be at his peak in *The Lay of the Land*. Philip Roth's *Everyman* divided critics, some of whom felt his account of a dead man seeking absolution was too self-conscious whilst others saw it as an extended metaphor of modern society in the USA. John Updike hit a contemporary nerve with *Terrorist* and the witty Anne Tyler kept to form with *Digging to America*. Other internationally known novelists who brought out new work included Margaret Atwood, Peter Carey, Roddy Doyle, Per Olov Enquist, John Le Carré, Alice Munro, and C.K. Stead, though perhaps none of them hit the mark in the way that much of their earlier fiction had done.

The eyes of the informed reading public to some extent switched to a new generation. M.J. Hyland from Australia made a distinctive impression with *Carry Me Down*, her study of a 12-year-old boy's stunted emotional life. David Mitchell emerged as the leader of the pack among British novelists in their thirties, whilst Claire Messud inched towards a similar position among her US contemporaries. The Zimbabwean writer Tsitsi Dangarembga published her long awaited follow-up to *Nervous Conditions* with a brilliantly titled sequel called *The Book of Not*. The young writer, however, who captured the public's imagination and critical attention above all others actually died in 1942 at the age of 39. This was Irène Némirovsky, a Jewish Ukrainian who died in Auschwitz. Her *Suite Française*, written in her adopted language, French, lay among papers in her daughter's possession until the 1990s. It was published in 2006 in its entirety, well translated by Sandra Smith, and became an instant best-seller, with Ronald Harwood engaged to write a screen version. Many critics cited it as their book of the year.

Among the authors of world rank who published new books were three Nobel laureates, each of whom engaged with political tensions in society. Nadine Gordimer, with *Get a Life*, examined post-apartheid South Africa in a manner that suggested change might be less apparent than was often assumed. At the age of 84 José Saramago, in *Seeing*, was both satirical and meditative. Seamus Heaney, with a new collection of poems, *District and Circle*, connected with tensions arising since the attacks on the USA of 11 September 2001 whilst at the same time being impressively referential to past poets of stature.

The event of the year in the poetry world—apart perhaps from Heaney's new collection—was the publication of previously unknown poems by the great Elizabeth Bishop, who died in 1979. *Edgar Allen Poe and the Juke-Box* may not have been a major work, but it added to Bishop's reputation for unpredictability and versatility. There was also a posthumous collection from Peter Redgrove, complemented by one from his widow Penelope Shuttle, appropriately named *Redgrove's Wife*. The other key poetry volumes of the year were Michael Longley's *Collected Poems*, a summation of the great Northern Irish writer's work; Don Paterson's *Orpheus*, a superb rendition of a sequence by Rilke; and Geoffrey Hill's *Without Title*, confirming his reputation as probably the finest English poet of the day, using, as a review in *The Independent* put it, "every stop and pedal on the organ".

Among biographies there was the usual crop of political memoirs, most of which failed to make any real impression. The most publicised in advance was *The Blunkett Tapes: My Life in the Bear Pit* by former British Home Secretary David Blunkett, who had twice had to resign from government over a scandal (see AR 2004, p. 13; 2005, p. 11). There was also, as every year, a rash of "celebrity" life stories, but only one, by the actor Rupert Everett, was genuinely praised. Historical biographies were led by Antonia Fraser's much admired account of Louis XIV and the women in his life. In the field of literary biography Victoria Glendinning was thought to have tackled the slightly background life of Leonard Woolf with great acumen and sensitivity. Jenny Uglow drew attention back to the nearly forgotten figure of the engraver Thomas Bewick, whose *Book of British Birds* is famously referred to in *Jane Eyre*. Perhaps the memoir which made the biggest impression was Carmen Callil's *Bad Faith*. Callil had moved out of publishing, where she had been one of the movers and shakers for many years, to produce this remarkable account of the morally squalid Vichy collaborator, Louis Darquier. Along with Némirovsky's book, it threw light on a little understood corner of life in World War II.

Writers around the world continued to be reviled by repressive governments or hunted down by assassins. The most publicised political killing was that of the Russian journalist, Anna Politkovskaya, whose *Putin's Russia* had been published in English—but not in Russian—in 2004. Politkovskaya's investigations into events in Chechnya appeared to have made her a target (see pp. 107-08). The other renowned author to incur the wrath of the state was Orhan Pamuk, who was accused of traducing the Turkish nation because he had written about Turkey's repression of Armenians (see p. 76). He was awarded the Nobel Prize for Literature in 2006, following in the footsteps of his fellow human rights campaigner, Harold Pinter, the previous year.

The Nobel laureate of 1988, the Egyptian novelist Naguib Mahfouz, died in 2006, himself very often the victim of political attack and indeed injury (for obituary see pp. 585-86). The great Scottish novelist Muriel Spark also died. Regarded by many as the finest prose stylist in English of her time, she achieved that rarity in literature of creating an iconic character, the heroine of *The Prime of Miss Jean Brodie*, whose manner and aphorisms had subliminally entered the language (for obituary see p. 598). Sybille Bedford, another grande dame of English letters, also died. So, too, did three notable poets, the South African Mazisi Kunene, the Canadian Irving Layton, and the greatest of modern Bengali writers Shamsur Rahman. Eric Newby, author of the classic travel book *A Short Walk in the Hindu Kush*, completed his journey (for obituary see p. 589).

Popular writers who also died were the romantic novelist, Lucilla Andrews, who at the time of her death was embroiled in a plagiarism dispute whereby the novelist Ian McEwan was accused of lifting material from her work; the author of heroic fantasy David Gemmell; the American novelist William Styron (for obituary see pp. 599-600); and the flashiest and most successful of sexy potboiler thriller writers, Mickey Spillane, whose books regularly appeared with lurid dust covers showing a desperate blonde in a provocative and implicitly violent situation. Spillane at one time took seven of the top 10 places among current US best-selling authors (for obituary see p. 599). His name was a by-word for torrid passion interlaced with financial ruthlessness: in some respects he was a metaphor for what made publishing tick in 2006.

Among the books which appeared in 2006, the following are either referred to above or are of special interest:

FICTION. Chimamanda Ngozi Adichie, *Half of a Yellow Sun* (Fourth Estate); Segun Afolabi, *A Life Elsewhere* (Cape); Martin Amis, *House of Meetings* (Cape); Margaret Atwood, *Moral Disorder* (Bloomsbury); Paul Auster, *Travels in the Scriptorium* (Faber); J.G. Ballard, *Kingdom Come* (Fourth Estate); William Boyd, *Restless* (Bloomsbury); Christine Brooke-Rose, *Life, End of* (Carcanet); Peter Carey, *Theft: A Love Story* (Faber); Vikram Chandra, *Sacred Games* (Faber); Rachel Cusk, *Arlington Park* (Faber); Tsitsi Dangarembga, *The Book of Not* (Ayebia); Kiran Desai, *The Inheritance of Loss* (Hamish Hamilton); Roddy Doyle, *Paula Spencer* (Cape); Margaret Drabble, *The Sea Lady* (Fig Tree); Patricia Duncker, *Mister Webster and Chérif* (Bloomsbury); Per Olov Enquist (trans. Tina Ninnally), *The Story of Blanche and Marie* (Harvill Secker); Richard Ford, *The Lay of the Land* (Bloomsbury); Nadine Gordimer, *Get a Life* (Bloomsbury); Robert Harris, *Imperium* (Hutchinson); Kate Grenville, *The Secret River* (Canongate); Mark Haddon, *A Spot of Bother* (Cape); Christopher Hope, *My Mother's Lovers* (Atlantic); Emyr Humphreys, *The Shop* (Seren); M.J. Hyland, *Carry Me Down* (Canongate); Howard Jacobson, *Kalooki Nights* (Cape); Imre Kertész (trans. Tim Wilkinson), *Liquidation* (Harvill Secker); Daniil Kharms, *Incidences* (Serpent's Tail); Ahmadou Kourouma (trans. Frank Wynne), *Allah is Not Obliged* (Heinemann); John Le Carré, *The Mission Song* (Hodder and Stoughton); Bernard MacLaverty, *Matters of Life and Death* (Cape); Gautam Malkani, *Londonstani* (Fourth Estate); Hisham Matar, *In the Country of Men* (Viking); Patrick McCabe, *Winterwood* (Bloomsbury); Claire Messud, *The Emperor's Children* (Picador); David Mitchell, *Black Swan Green* (Sceptre); Jan Morris, *Hav* (Faber); Walter Mosley, *Fortunate Son* (Serpent's Tail); Alice Munro, *The View from Castle Rock* (Chatto and Windus); Haruki Murakami (trans. Philip Gabriel and Jay Rubin), *Blind Willow, Sleeping Woman* (Harvill Secker); Irène Némirovsky (trans. Sandra Smith), *Suite Française* (Chatto and Windus); Andrew O'Hagan, *Be Near Me* (Faber);

Thomas Pynchon, *Against the Day* (Cape); Ian Rankin, *The Naming of the Dead* (Orion); Philip Roth, *Everyman* (Cape); Edward St Aubyn, *Mother's Milk* (Picador); José Saramago (trans. Margaret Jull Costa), *Seeing* (Harvill Secker); Helen Simpson, *Constitutional* (Cape); C.K. Stead, *My Name was Judas* (Harvill Secker); Adam Thorpe, *Is This the Way You Said?* (Cape); Anne Tyler, *Digging to America* (Chatto and Windus); Barry Unsworth, *The Ruby in Her Navel* (Hamish Hamilton); John Updike, *Terrorist* (Hamish Hamilton); Sarah Waters, *The Night Watch* (Virago).

POETRY. Dannie Abse, *Running Late* (Hutchinson); Fergus Allen, *Gas Light and Coke* (Dedalus); Simon Armitage, *Tyrannosaurus Rex Versus the Corduroy Kid* (Faber); Elizabeth Bishop, *Edgar Allen Poe and the Juke-Box* (Carcanet); Leonard Cohen, *Book of Longing* (Viking); Paul Farley, *In Tramp in Flames* (Picador); Vicki Feaver, *The Book of Blood* (Cape); Matthew Francis, *Whereabouts* (Rufus); Durs Grünbein (trans. Michael Hofmann), *Ashes for Breakfast* (Faber); Seamus Heaney, *District and Circle* (Faber); W.N. Herbert, *Bad Shaman Blues* (Bloodaxe); Geoffrey Hill, *Without Title* (Penguin); Tobias Hill, *Nocturne in Chrome and Sunset Yellow* (Salt); Michael Longley, *Collected Poems* (Cape); Paul Muldoon, *Horse Latitudes* (Faber); Grace Nichols, *Startling the Flying Fish* (Virago); Don Paterson, *Orpheus* (Faber); Peter Redgrove, *The Harper* (Cape); Robin Robertson, *Swithering* (Picador); Penelope Shuttle, *Redgrove's Wife* (Bloodaxe); Brian Turner, *Here, Bullet* (Alice James); Vernon Watkins, *New Selected Poems* (Carcanet); Hugo Williams, *Dear Room* (Faber).

BIOGRAPHY AND AUTOBIOGRAPHY. John Allen, *Rabble-Rouser for Peace: The Authorised Biography of Desmond Tutu* (Rider); Kate Berridge, *Waxing Mythical: The Life and Legend of Madame Tussaud* (John Murray); David Blunkett, *The Blunkett Tapes: My Life in the Bear Pit* (Bloomsbury); Rodney Bolt, *Lorenzo Da Ponte: The Adventures of Mozart's Librettist in the Old and New Worlds* (Bloomsbury); Sarah Bradford, *Diana* (Viking); Carmen Callil, *Bad Faith* (Cape); David Cannadine, *Mellon: An American Life* (Allen Lane); Rupert Everett, *Red Carpets and Other Banana Skins* (Little, Brown); Antonia Fraser, *Love and Louis XIV: The Women in the Life of the Sun King* (Weidenfeld and Nicolson); Victoria Glendinning, *Leonard Woolf* (Simon and Schuster); Adrian Goldsworthy, *Caesar: The Life of a Colossus* (Weidenfeld and Nicolson); John Heilpern, *John Osborne: A Patriot for Us* (Chatto and Windus); Zachary Leader, *The Life of Kingsley Amis* (Cape); Tom Lodge, *Mandela: A Critical Life* (O.U.P.); Brenda Maddox, *Freud's Wizard: The Enigma of Ernest Jones* (John Murray); William Mann, *Kate: The Woman Who Was Katherine Hepburn* (Faber); E.A. Markham, *At Home with Miss Vanessa* (Tindal Street Press); Patrick Marnham, *Wild Mary: a Life of Mary Wesley* (Chatto and Windus); Anna Massey, *Telling Some Tales* (Hutchinson); Richard Reeves, *President Reagan: The Triumph of the Imagination* (Simon and Schuster); Lee Sever, *Ava Gardner* (Bloomsbury); Adam Sisman, *The Friendship: Wordsworth and Coleridge* (HarperCollins); Donald Spoto, *Enchantment: The Life of Audrey Hepburn* (Hutchinson); Tommy Steele, *Bermondsey Boy* (Michael Joseph); John Stubbs, *Donne: The Reformed Soul* (Viking); Claire Tomalin, *Thomas Hardy: The Time-Torn Man* (Viking); Jenny Uglow, *Nature's Engraver: A Life of Thomas Bewick* (Faber); Kate Williams, *England's Mistress: The Infamous Life of Emma Hamilton* (Hutchinson).

OTHER. Robert Aldrich (ed.), *Gay Life and Culture: A World History* (Thames and Hudson); Kwame Anthony Appiah, *Cosmopolitanism: Ethics in a World of Strangers* (Penguin/Allen Lane); Guy Arnold, *Africa: A Modern History* (Atlantic); Antony Beevor, *The Battle for Spain: The Spanish Civil War 1936-1939* (Weidenfeld and Nicolson); Christopher Clark, *Iron Kingdom: The Rise and Downfall of Prussia 1600-1947* (Allen Lane); Jan Dalley, *The Black Hole: Money, Myth and Empire* (Fig Tree); William Dalrymple, *The Last Mughal: The Fall of a Dynasty, 1857* (Bloomsbury); Richard Dawkins, *The God Delusion* (Bantam); Tim Flannery, *The Weather Makers: The History and Future Impact of Climate Change* (Allen Lane); Michael Frayn, *The Human Touch: Our Part in the Creation of the Universe* (Faber); Peter Hennessy, *Having It So Good: Britain in the Fifties* (Allen Lane); Simon Jenkins, *Thatcher and Sons: A Revolution in Three Acts* (Allen Lane); Tony Judt, *Postwar: A History of Europe Since 1945* (Heinemann); Thomas Keneally, *The Commonwealth of Thieves: The Story of the Founding of Australia* (Chatto and Windus); Pankaj Mishra, *Temptations of the West: How to be Modern in India, Pakistan and Beyond* (Picador); George Monbiot, *Heat: How to Stop the Planet Burning* (Allen Lane); Walid Phares, *Future Jihad* (Palgrave Macmillan); Thomas Ricks, *Fiasco* (Allen Lane/Penguin); Andrew Roberts, *A History of the English-Speaking Peoples since 1900* (Weidenfeld and Nicolson); Simon Schama, *Power of Art* (BBC); Amartya Sen, *Identity and Violence: The Illusion of Destiny* (Allen Lane); James Shapiro, *1599: A Year in the Life of William Shakespeare* (Faber); Sun Shuyun, *The Long March* (HarperCollins); Colin Thubron, *Shadow of the Silk Road* (Chatto and Windus); Marina Warner, *Phantasmagoria* (O.U.P.); Stanley Wells, *Shakespeare and Co* (Allen Lane); Lawrence Wright, *The Looming Tower* (Allen Lane).

XVII SPORT

FOOTBALL. The World Cup was an extraordinary triumph for Italy, who beat France in a dramatic final. The Italians had arrived in Germany, the host country, in the midst of a corruption scandal which had sullied the reputation of their domestic league. Unfancied by most observers, Marcello Lippi's team might easily have been knocked out early in the competition but improved with each match. The final finished 1-1 after extra time, with Italy winning 5-3 on penalties after Zinedine Zidane, the best player of his generation, was sent off in bizarre circumstances. The Frenchman, playing the last match of his career, headbutted Marco Materazzi in the chest after the Italian defender had taunted him. France were on top for most of the match but were unable to turn their superiority into goals. Italy had been lucky to beat Australia and needed extra time to see off Germany in the semi-finals. Nevertheless, the Italian defence was excellent throughout; Fabio Cannavaro was later chosen as FIFA's (the International Football Association) player of the year and received the Golden Ball award for the top player in Europe. France had struggled in the group phase but were magnificent in beating Spain and Brazil before Zidane's penalty beat Portugal in the semi-finals.

Germany were excellent hosts and the home team played attractive football (see p. 38). However, many of the other leading nations disappointed. Argentina promised much but lost to Germany in the quarter-finals after a penalty shoot-out. Ronaldo broke Gerd Müller's record of 14 goals in the finals, but Brazil's big-name players generally under-performed. The English referee, Graham Poll, embarrassingly failed to send off Croatia's Josip Simunic after showing him two yellow cards. He eventually dismissed him after his third yellow.

England lost in the quarter-finals to Portugal, who won 3-1 on penalties. It was the third time in a row that Luiz Felipe Scolari, the Portugal and former Brazil coach, had got the better of England in a major competition. England's pre-tournament preparations had been hampered by an injury to Wayne Rooney, who broke a bone in his foot only six weeks before the tournament began. Michael Owen damaged knee ligaments in the group game against Sweden and his subsequent absence highlighted England's lack of striking resources. Sven-Göran Eriksson, the England manager, stood down after the World Cup, having agreed a £2.5 million pay-off with the Football Association in January. Steve McClaren, his assistant, took over and immediately dropped David Beckham, who had stepped down as captain after the World Cup.

In the early stages of qualifying for the 2008 European Championship, England were shaken by a 2-0 defeat away to Croatia. Steve Staunton was named Republic of Ireland manager in succession to Brian Kerr, but a crushing 5-2 defeat away to Cyprus did not augur well for his reign. Wales lost 5-1 at home to Slovakia, but Northern Ireland and Scotland were heartened by wins over

Spain and France respectively. The African Cup of Nations was won by Egypt, the hosts, who beat Côte d'Ivoire in the final.

Barcelona beat Arsenal 2-1 in the Champions' League final in Paris after Jens Lehmann, the Premiership team's goalkeeper, was sent off early in the match. Arsenal, Chelsea, Liverpool, Manchester United, and Celtic all qualified for the knock-out phase of the 2006-07 Champions' League. Sevilla beat Middlesbrough 4-0 in the Uefa Cup final in Eindhoven. Internacional, who beat their fellow Brazilians Sao Paulo in the final of the Libertadores Cup, beat Barcelona in the Club World Cup final in Japan.

The match-fixing scandal in Italy ended with Juventus being relegated to Serie B and Milan, Fiorentina, Lazio, and Reggina having points deducted. Cannavaro left Juventus for Real Madrid, while Milan sold Andrei Shevchenko, their 29-year-old Ukrainian striker, to Chelsea, who successfully defended their Premiership title. Manchester United were runners-up, nine points adrift, with Liverpool third and Arsenal, who in the summer moved from Highbury to the new Emirates Stadium, a distant fourth. Overseas investors continued to buy into the Premier League, which reached a new television agreement with Sky and Setanta worth £28 million per year to each club (see p. 498). Alexander Gaydamak, the son of a controversial Russian-Israeli billionaire, Arkady Gaydamak, took over Portsmouth; Randy Lerner, the owner of the Cleveland Browns American football team, bought control of Aston Villa; and West Ham United were taken over by an Icelandic consortium. Liverpool won one of the best FA Cup finals for years, winning a penalty shoot-out against West Ham United after the match had finished 3-3. Manchester United beat Wigan Athletic to win the Carling Cup. Thierry Henry broke Cliff Bastin's record of 150 goals for Arsenal, while Alan Shearer beat Jackie Milburn's milestone of 200 for Newcastle United before retiring. Roy Keane, the former Manchester United midfielder, also ended his playing days and went into management with Sunderland. Lord Stevens, the former Metropolitan Police commissioner, reported on alleged corruption in transfers in English football. He attacked the Football Association for the way it ran the game and named 17 transfers involving eight agents which required further investigation. However, his report was criticised as a "whitewash" because it did not name names.

Celtic won the Scottish Premier League and the Scottish League Cup in Gordon Strachan's first season as manager. Alex McLeish, the manager of Rangers, was replaced at the end of the season by the former Lyon coach, Paul Le Guen. Heart of Midlothian won the Scottish Cup, beating Gretna on penalties.

CRICKET. It was a testing year for England as many of the established players struggled with injury, including captain Michael Vaughan, Andrew Flintoff, and Ashley Giles. Marcus Trescothick pulled out of the India tour with a stress-related illness and left Australia before the start of the Ashes series when it flared up again. Giles also made an early departure to be with his sick wife.

Paul Collingwood made his maiden Test century against India in Bagpur in March as England drew the series 1-1. However, they lost the subsequent one-day series 5-1. Sri Lanka, the first visitors of the English summer, came from behind to draw a three-Test series 1-1. England won the second Test at Edgbaston with a day-and-a-half to spare, but Muttiah Muralitharan took eight wickets on the last day of the final Test at Trent Bridge to give Sri Lanka victory by 134 runs. Sri Lanka won the one-day series 5-0.

Captained by Andrew Strauss in the absence of Vaughan and Flintoff, England won 3-0 in a four-Test home series against Pakistan, who then drew the subsequent one-day series 2-2. The fourth Test at the Oval ended when Pakistan, angered by accusations that they had tampered with the ball, refused to return to the field after tea on the fourth day. The umpire at the centre of the row was Darrell Hair, who after the subsequent hearings was dropped by the International Cricket Council (ICC) from its elite list. Inzamam-ul-Haq, the Pakistan captain, was cleared of ball-tampering but was banned for four one-day internationals for bringing the game into disrepute.

The rest of the year was a tale of woe for England, who had a poor Champions Trophy and then lost the Ashes as Australia won the first three Tests in the five match series. There was strong criticism of the England selectors for not picking Monty Panesar early in the tour and for keeping faith with Geraint Jones as wicketkeeper in preference to Chris Read, while the burden of captaincy seemed to affect Flintoff's game.

Australia had an ageing team. Shane Warne, Glenn McGrath, Justin Langer, and Damien Martyn all announced their Test retirements during the series, but the form of Michael Hussey, Stuart Clark, and Michael Clarke indicated that Australia's future was in good hands. Ricky Ponting led by example and was named the ICC's player of the year. The opening ball of the first Test in Brisbane proved ominous for England as Steve Harmison bowled a delivery which was so wide that it was fielded by second slip. Australia subsequently won the match by 277 runs. Collingwood scored a double century in the second Test, but when Australia went on to win by six wickets it proved a crushing blow. The Ashes-winning delivery in the third Test was bowled by Warne, who went on to become the first player to take 700 Test wickets. When Australia won the fourth Test, at the end of December, by an innings and 99 runs inside three days it was their 10th victory in 10 Tests during the year.

Australia had gone into the Ashes series having won the Champions Trophy, beating the West Indies in the final. Two Pakistan bowlers, Shoaib Akhtar and Mohammad Asif, were sent home from the tournament after failing drugs tests for nandrolone. Initial suspensions were later overturned when it was accepted that the banned steroid may have been present in supplements that they were taking.

At the start of the year Australia won home and away Test series against South Africa, though the South Africans clinched a one-day series with a remarkable win in Johannesburg. The highest one-day international total was set twice in the space of four hours as the home side successfully chased a target of 435. Pakistan's Mohammad Yousuf scored 1,788 runs in the calendar year, breaking Viv Richards's 30-year-old record. Pakistan won a home series against India, who went on to record their first series victory away to the West Indies for 35 years. Zimbabwe withdrew from Test cricket after a series of poor results following the refusal by many of the best players to represent the country because of their opposition to the country's authoritarian government.

Sussex won the County Championship from Lancashire and got the better of the same opponents in the final of the Cheltenham and Gloucester Trophy. Surrey won the County Championship Second Division title, while Essex and Gloucestershire took the NatWest Pro40 First and Second Division championships respectively and Leicestershire lifted the Twenty20 Cup.

RUGBY. France won a mediocre Six Nations' Championship, securing their fourth win from five matches when they came from behind to win their final game against Wales in Cardiff. Ireland were runners-up and took the Triple Crown. Wales, the defending champions, won only once and England lost three matches in a row after opening with victories over Wales and Italy. Scotland, who under their new coach, Frank Hadden, had opened with a 20-16 win over France, beat England at Murrayfield; France trounced Andy Robinson's men 31-6 in Paris; and Ireland won 28-24 in the finale at Twickenham.

The Rugby Football Union sacked three of Robinson's coaching staff and appointed Rob Andrew as its first elite rugby director. However, two heavy defeats in Australia were followed by more poor results in the autumn. Victories at Twickenham for New Zealand and Argentina took England's losing run to seven matches, equalling their worst ever sequence. A last-ditch win over South Africa earned a brief respite, but after a 25-14 defeat against the same opponents a week later Robinson was dismissed. Brian Ashton stepped up from assistant coach to replace him.

The Wales coach, Mike Ruddock, stepped down just two matches into the Six Nations' Championship. Nine months earlier he had led the country to their first Grand Slam for 27 years, but he had lost the support of his players. Scott Johnson took temporary charge before Gareth Jenkins, the Llanelli Scarlets coach, was appointed on a permanent basis. In the autumn Wales drew with Australia and lost to New Zealand, who also won twice in France. With Scotland losing to Australia, it was Ireland who enjoyed the best autumn campaign, beating South Africa and Australia. In the summer New Zealand won the Tri-nations trophy.

Munster finally won the Heineken Cup, beating Biarritz in Cardiff, while Gloucester beat London Irish in extra time after a thrilling European Challenge Cup final at the Stoop. Ulster won the Celtic League, Sale won the Guinness Premiership, beating Leicester 45-20 in the final at Twickenham, Wasps beat Llanelli Scarlets in the Anglo-Welsh Cup final and Pontypridd took the Welsh Cup, beating Neath in the final.

St Helens dominated rugby league. Daniel Anderson's team beat Hull in the Grand Final to record their fifth win in 11 seasons. They also won the Challenge Cup, beating Huddersfield in the final. Great Britain enjoyed one surprise victory over Australia in the Tri-Nations tournament, in which Australia overcame New Zealand in the final.

TENNIS. The introduction of instant television replay technology, enabling players to challenge line calls, was a major change within tennis, but in other respects there was little new. The men's year was again dominated by Roger Federer, who won Wimbledon, the Australian Open, and the US Open and would have become the first player since Rod Laver to win the Grand Slam had he not lost to Rafael Nadal in the final of the French Open. In total Federer won 92 matches, a record bettered only by Ivan Lendl with 106 wins in 1982, and 12 titles. Federer lost only five matches all year, four in finals to Nadal (in Dubai, Monte Carlo, Rome, and Paris) and the fifth to Britain's Andy Murray in Cincinnati. The Swiss became the first man in the Open era to reach six consecutive Grand Slam finals and in winning Wimbledon for the fourth consecutive year he beat Bjorn Borg's professional era record of 41 successive victories on grass and extended it to 48.

Nadal, however, remained dominant on clay. The Spaniard broke Guillermo Vilas's 29-year-old record of 53 unbeaten matches on the surface and extended his run to 60 with his victory over Federer in the final at Roland Garros. On his way to the Wimbledon final Nadal beat André Agassi in the American's final appearance at the All England Club. Agassi played his last matches amid scenes of high drama at the US Open, knocking out Marcos Baghdatis, the No 8 seed, before losing to Benjamin Becker. Andy Roddick, whose fortunes improved after the appointment of Jimmy Connors as his coach, reached the final in New York but was outplayed by Federer.

Murray, who succeeded Tim Henman as British No 1, won his first tournament, the SAP Open in San Jose. At Wimbledon he beat Roddick, the No 3 seed, before losing to Baghdatis, who had lost the Australian Open final to Federer. In July Murray began working with Brad Gilbert, Agassi's former coach, and soared up the rankings, finishing the year as world No 17. Henman improved after a difficult start to the year but enjoyed little success in the Grand Slam tournaments. Greg Rusedski dropped 155 places in the world rankings to No 193. Russia won the Davis Cup, beating Argentina in the final.

Women's tennis was dominated by Amélie Mauresmo and Justine Henin-Hardenne. Mauresmo lifted her first Grand Slam title when she won the Australian Open, beating Henin-Hardenne in the final after her opponent retired when trailing 6-1, 2-0. The Belgian, who complained of severe stomach pains, was criticised for spoiling Mauresmo's moment of glory. Henin-Hardenne remained the queen of clay, beating Svetlana Kuznetsova in the French Open final, but she lost to Mauresmo in the final at Wimbledon. Maria Sharapova won her second Grand Slam title when she beat Henin-Hardenne in the US Open final. Henin-Hardenne ended the year as world No 1 after beating Mauresmo in the Sony Ericsson Championships final in Madrid. Martina Navratilova retired and Serena Williams rarely played, but Martina Hingis, who had left the sport in 2002 because of injury, returned. She won two titles and ended the year ranked as the world's No 7. Italy beat Belgium in the final of the Fed Cup.

Roger Draper was appointed chief executive of the Lawn Tennis Association and promptly made a number of high-profile appointments. Gilbert led the way, joining primarily as Murray's coach. John Lloyd replaced Jeremy Bates as Davis

Cup captain, with Peter Lundgren, Federer's former coach, signing up as his assistant. Carl Maes, Paul Annacone, and Nigel Sears, the former coaches of Kim Clijsters, Pete Sampras, and Daniela Hantuchova respectively, were all brought into Draper's team.

GOLF. Europe won the Ryder Cup in Dublin in impressive style, never looking back after taking a 5-3 lead after a tight first day. They beat the USA by 19-and-a-half points to nine-and-a-half to record a third successive win for the first time. It was also the first time under the current format that either team won all five sessions. Ian Woosnam was an inspirational leader, while Darren Clarke conquered his emotions to play a vital part following the death from cancer of his wife, Heather. Every European contributed at least one point to the winning total.

Phil Mickelson won his second Masters title by a two-stroke margin from South Africa's Tim Clark. Tiger Woods, who took a break after the death of his father in May, missed the cut at the US Open at Winged Foot, where Geoff Ogilvy, a 29-year-old Australian, won his first major, taking advantage of Colin Montgomerie's double-bogey at the last hole. Montgomerie, who lost by a single stroke, finished runner-up in a major for the fifth time. Woods was back to his best for the Open at Hoylake as he became the first player to defend his title successfully since Tom Watson in 1983. Chris DiMarco finished second, two strokes adrift, with Ernie Els a further three shots back. Woods was even more dominant in the US PGA Championship at Medinah, winning by five strokes from Shaun Micheel. Padraig Harrington topped the European Order of Merit after a thrilling finish to the Volvo Masters at Valderrama. It seemed likely that Paul Casey would finish ahead of him until Sergio Garcia faltered at the final hole, enabling Harrington to claim a crucial share of second place in the tournament.

The women's majors went to four different players: Karrie Webb (Kraft Nabisco Championship), Se Ri Pak (LPGA Championship), Annika Sorenstam (US Women's Open), and Sherri Steinhauer (British Women's Open). Laura Davies was European No 1 for the seventh time. The USA beat Great Britain and Ireland by a margin of five points in the Curtis Cup in Oregon.

WINTER OLYMPICS. Once again an Olympics was overshadowed by a drugs scandal. Italian police and drug-testers raided the Austrian cross-country skiing and biathlon squad at the Turin Games, having been alerted to the presence in the Austrian camp of Walter Mayer, a banned coach. Mayer, who had been banned because of suspicion over his involvement in blood manipulation during the Salt Lake City Games, fled across the border to Austria. He eventually crashed his car 250 miles from Turin after a police chase.

Austria won a record 14 Alpine skiing medals, although the men's downhill favourite, Michael Walchhofer, was beaten by France's Antoine Deneriaz, who had not won a World Cup race for more than two years. Austria's Michaela Dorfmeister won the women's downhill. Britain won just one medal at the Games, Shelley Rudman taking silver in the women's skeleton bob.

COMMONWEALTH GAMES. The Melbourne Games were an organisational triumph. Australia's total of 207 medals was more than double that of England, who finished second in the table. Nevertheless it was not a Games that caught the public's imagination elsewhere, partly because of the absence of key performers. The distance runner Paula Radcliffe and the swimmer Ian Thorpe pulled out with a foot injury and bronchitis respectively. Thorpe's absence contributed to a poor showing by the hosts' swimmers, whose male team won just one gold medal. British swimmers won 15 gold medals and set 50 personal bests and 11 British records.

England's boxers won five gold medals and there were five British golds in the velodrome, but there were major disappointments in the athletics stadium. England failed to win a gold on the track and their final athletics tally of six golds was the worst by an England team for 40 years. Although there were some high points—most notably a first major decathlon gold medal for Dean Macey—English fortunes were summed up by the men's sprint relay team, who failed to reach the final after a mix-up when handing over the baton. Mick Gault became the most decorated English competitor at the Games when he won four shooting medals to take his career tally to 15.

ATHLETICS. Drugs once again cast their shadow over sport when Justin Gatlin tested positive for testosterone and other steroids. The Olympic and world 100m champion had equalled the 100m world record earlier in the year when he ran 9.77sec in Doha, but he was later banned for eight years and stripped of the world record. He appealed and promised to co-operate with the doping authorities. Asafa Powell, the original 100m world record-holder, equalled the mark twice during the year, firstly at Gateshead (the first 100m world record run seen in Britain) and again in Zurich. The Gateshead race was also notable for the return of the British sprinter, Dwain Chambers, after a two-year ban for drug abuse.

Russia topped the medals table at the European Championships in Gothenburg. The British team finished in 10th place, though only Russia bettered their tally of 11 medals. There was only one British gold, in the men's sprint relay, and that was tainted by Darren Campbell's refusal to join the lap of honour in protest at the inclusion in the team of Chambers following his drugs suspension. Deena Kastor, a 33-year-old Californian, and Kenya's Felix Limo won the women's and men's races at the London Marathon.

HORSE RACING. Speciosa, ridden by Micky Fenton and trained by Pam Sly, was the unlikely winner of the 1000 Guineas and while order was restored by the 2000 Guineas and Oaks victories of Aidan O'Brien's George Washington and Alexandrova, both ridden by Kieren Fallon, the Derby provided a thrilling spectacle. Sir Percy, who was trained by Marcus Tregoning and cost just £16,000 as a foal, held on after a pulsating race to enable Martin Dwyer to become the first English jockey to win since 1997. Frankie Dettori won his fourth St Leger, on Sixties Icon.

André Fabre landed his seventh Prix de l'Arc de Triomphe when Rail Link, ridden by Stéphane Pasquier, beat Pride by a neck. Ouija Board, trained by Ed

Dunlop, became the most successful horse in the history of the Breeders' Cup when she won the Filly and Mare Turf at Churchill Downs. Her jockey, Dettori, went on to record another victory for a British trainer, winning the Turf on Brian Meehan's Red Rocks.

Fallon, the six-times champion jockey, was one of 11 people charged in connection with a police inquiry into allegations of race-fixing. Under British rules he was not subsequently permitted to ride in Britain. Later in the year he was banned from riding for six months anywhere in the world after failing a drugs test in France.

The Irish dominated Cheltenham's National Hunt Festival. War of Attrition, ridden by Conor O'Dwyer and trained by Mouse Morris, led home an Irish 1-2-3 in the Gold Cup. Brave Inca, ridden by Tony McCoy and trained by Colm Murphy, won the Champion Hurdle. There was also Irish joy at Aintree, where Numbersixvalverde provided Niall Madden with victory in his first Grand National ride. Paul Nicholls won the trainers' title from Martin Pipe, who retired after saddling 4,180 winners.

MOTOR SPORT. Fernando Alonso retained his Formula One world drivers' title but was pushed all the way by Michael Schumacher, who retired at the end of the season. The seven-times world champion, the most successful driver in history with 91 race wins, trailed Alonso by 25 points in June but had an impressive second half of the season as Ferrari challenged the supremacy of Renault, who eventually won the constructors' title by just five points. Britain's Jenson Button recorded his first victory in 113 starts. Two major driver changes were announced for 2007, Alonso signing for McLaren and Kimi Raikkonen leaving McLaren to replace Schumacher at Ferrari.

France's Sebastien Loeb, driving a Citroen, again dominated the world rally championship, securing his third successive title despite missing the last four races through injury. Ford won their first manufacturers' title for 27 years. Valentino Rossi was dethroned as MotoGP champion by Honda's Nicky Hayden in a dramatic final race of the season in Valencia. Australia's Troy Bayliss, riding a Ducati, won the world superbikes championship.

BOXING. Ricky Hatton and Joe Calzaghe were again the two most successful British boxers. Calzaghe retained his World Boxing Organisation (WBO) super-middleweight title for the 18th time and took Jeff Lacy's International Boxing Federation (IBF) crown with an emphatic 12-round victory. However, the Welshman was pushed all the way by Cameroon's Sakio Bika before winning on points to maintain his 42-fight unbeaten record.

Hatton moved up to welterweight and claimed the World Boxing Association (WBA) world crown after a gruelling victory over Luis Collazo. Audley Harrison's career appeared in decline when he suffered a second successive defeat, to the unfancied Dominick Guinn (USA), but a three-round victory over Danny Williams revived his hopes. Amir Khan, the Olympic silver medallist, maintained his steady progress. Russia took a hold on all the heavyweight world titles through Nikolai Valuev (WBA), Vladimir Klitschko (IBF), Sergei Liakhovich (WBO), and Oleg Maskaev (World Boxing Council).

MISCELLANEOUS. Drugs scandals once again overshadowed the Tour de France. On the eve of the race three of the favourites—Jan Ullrich, Ivan Basso, and Francisco Mancebo—were sent home after being linked to a drugs syndicate in Spain. The race was won by Floyd Landis, who had gone into it knowing that he needed a hip replacement operation. It was an extraordinary triumph, but less than a week later it was revealed that the US cyclist had failed a drugs test. He contested the charge and the matter remained unresolved by the end of the year. Britain's Nicole Cooke won the women's Tour de France and went on to claim her second World Cup title.

Zara Phillips became only the third rider to hold both the European and world three-day event championships at the same time. Riding Toytown, the 25-year-old daughter of the Princess Royal (who herself won the European title in 1971) took the lead in the cross-country section and held on to it on the final day. Phillips was later voted the BBC's "sports personality of the year", as her mother had been 35 years previously. Australia's Andrew Hoy won the Badminton three-day event.

Britain's swimmers finished as the top nation at the European Championships in Budapest. The rowing world championships were held at Eton and there were home celebrations when Britain's men's coxless four took gold. Oxford won the Boat Race by five lengths. The British sailor, Dee Caffari, became the first woman to sail single-handedly around the world westwards, against the prevailing winds and currents.

Phil Taylor took the Professional Darts Corporation's World Championship for the 13th time; Graeme Dott won his first world snooker title; and Beth Tweddle secured Britain's first gold medal at a world gymnastics championships when she won on the asymmetric bars in Aarhus, Denmark. Britain's Tim Don won the triathlon world championship, but was later banned for three months for missing three drugs tests.

In the USA, the Pittsburgh Steelers joined the San Francisco 49ers and the Dallas Cowboys as five-times Super Bowl winners after beating the Seattle Seahawks in Detroit. The St Louis Cardinals beat the Detroit Tigers to win baseball's World Series. The Miami Heat lost the first two games of the National Basketball Association finals to the Dallas Mavericks but recovered to win 4-2.

XVIII DOCUMENTS AND REFERENCE

INTERNATIONAL ASTRONOMICAL UNION GENERAL ASSEMBLY CLASSIFICATION OF PLUTO AS "DWARF PLANET"

Published below are the resolutions adopted by the 2006 General Assembly of the International Astronomical Union (IAU) at its closing session, on 24 August, in Prague, distinguishing planets from "dwarf planets". The IAU reclassified Pluto as a dwarf planet, a new distinct class of objects.

The IAU members gathered at the 2006 General Assembly agreed that a "planet" is defined as a celestial body that (a) is in orbit around the Sun, (b) has sufficient mass for its self-gravity to overcome rigid body forces so that it assumes a hydrostatic equilibrium (nearly round) shape, and (c) has cleared the neighbourhood around its orbit.

This means that the Solar System consists of eight "planets" Mercury, Venus, Earth, Mars, Jupiter, Saturn, Uranus and Neptune. A new distinct class of objects called "dwarf planets" was also decided. It was agreed that "planets" and "dwarf planets" are two distinct classes of objects. The first members of the "dwarf planet" category are Ceres, Pluto and 2003 UB313 (temporary name). More "dwarf planets" are expected to be announced by the IAU in the coming months and years. Currently a dozen candidate "dwarf planets" are listed on IAU's "dwarf planet" watchlist, which keeps changing as new objects are found and the physics of the existing candidates becomes better known.

The "dwarf planet" Pluto is recognised as an important proto-type of a new class of trans-Neptunian objects. The IAU will set up a process to name these objects.

Results:
Resolution 5A: "Definition of Planet" was not counted but was passed with a great majority.
Resolution 5B: "Definition of Classical Planet" had 91 votes in favour, but many more against so there was no count.
Resolution 6A: "Definition of Pluto-class objects" was passed with 237 votes in favour, 157 against and 17 abstentions.
Resolution 6B: "Definition of Plutonian Objects" had 183 votes in favour and 186 votes against.

Below are the planet definition Resolutions that were passed.

RESOLUTIONS:
Resolution 5A is the principal definition for the IAU usage of "planet" and related terms.
Resolution 6A creates for IAU usage a new class of objects, for which Pluto is the prototype. The IAU will set up a process to name these objects.

IAU Resolution: Definition of a Planet in the Solar System:
Contemporary observations are changing our understanding of planetary systems, and it is important that our nomenclature for objects reflect our current understanding. This applies, in particular, to the designation "planets". The word "planet" originally described "wanderers" that were known only as moving lights in the sky. Recent discoveries lead us to create a new definition, which we can make using currently available scientific information.

RESOLUTION 5A

The IAU therefore resolves that "planets" and other bodies in our Solar System, except satellites, be defined into three distinct categories in the following way:

(1) A "planet"[1] is a celestial body that (a) is in orbit around the Sun, (b) has sufficient mass for its self-gravity to overcome rigid body forces so that it assumes a hydrostatic equilibrium (nearly round) shape, and (c) has cleared the neighbourhood around its orbit.
(2) A "dwarf planet" is a celestial body that (a) is in orbit around the Sun, (b) has sufficient mass for its self-gravity to overcome rigid body forces so that it assumes a hydrostatic equilibrium (nearly round) shape[2], (c) has not cleared the neighbourhood around its orbit, and (d) is not a satellite.
(3) All other objects[3] except satellites orbiting the Sun shall be referred to collectively as "Small Solar-System Bodies".

[1]The eight "planets" are: Mercury, Venus, Earth, Mars, Jupiter, Saturn, Uranus, and Neptune.
[2]An IAU process will be established to assign borderline objects into either dwarf planet and other categories.
[3]These currently include most of the Solar System asteroids, most Trans-Neptunian Objects (TNOs), comets, and other small bodies.

IAU Resolution: Pluto

RESOLUTION 6A:

The IAU further resolves:

Pluto is a "dwarf planet" by the above definition and is recognized as the prototype of a new category of trans-Neptunian objects.

(Source: IAU press office.)

PACE RESOLUTION ON ALLEGED SECRET DETENTIONS AND UNLAWFUL INTER-STATE TRANSFERS OF DETAINEES

Published below is Resolution 1507 (2006) of the Parliamentary Assembly of the Council of Europe (PACE), adopted on 27 June 2006, on the basis of the report (Document 10957) of the PACE Committee on Legal Affairs and Human Rights (Rapporteur Dick Marty, Switzerland), which analysed information from air traffic control authorities and other sources to investigate the CIA's "rendition" programme of terrorist suspects [for map see p. 409]. The PACE Resolution condemned Council of Europe member states and the USA for their part in these disappearances and secret detentions.

PARLIAMENTARY ASSEMBLY OF THE COUNCIL OF EUROPE

Resolution 1507 (2006)

Alleged secret detentions and unlawful inter-state transfers of detainees involving Council of Europe member states

1. The Council of Europe is both the point of reference and the guardian for human rights, democracy and respect for the rule of law in Europe. It draws its legal and moral authority from, *inter alia*, the common standards of human rights protection embodied in the European Convention on Human Rights (ECHR - ETS No. 5) and the European Convention for the Prevention of Torture and Inhuman or Degrading Treatment or Punishment (ETS No. 126), to which all of its 46 member states subscribe.

2. The Parliamentary Assembly of the Council of Europe places human rights at the heart of its work. It is the duty of the Assembly to raise the alarm internationally whenever human rights are set aside, or when established standards for their application are undermined.

3. The Assembly clearly reaffirms the absolute necessity to prevent and combat the threat of terrorism, and its commitment to do so; but it must equally speak out in the strongest possible terms against the numerous and systematic human rights abuses committed in the pursuit of the so-called "war on terrorism". It considers that such violations play into the hands of the terrorists and ultimately serve to strengthen those who aim to destroy the established political, legal and social order.

4. The United States of America finds that neither the classic instruments of criminal law and procedure nor the framework of the laws of war (including, *inter alia*, respect for the Geneva Conventions) have been apt to address the terrorist threat. As a result, the United States has introduced new legal concepts, such as "enemy combatant" and "rendition", which were previously unheard of in international law and stand contrary to the basic legal principles that prevail on our continent.
5. Thus, across the world, the United States has progressively woven a clandestine "spiderweb" of disappearances, secret detentions and unlawful inter-state transfers, often encompassing countries notorious for their use of torture. Hundreds of persons have become entrapped in this web, in some cases merely suspected of sympathising with a presumed terrorist organisation.

6. The spiderweb has been spun out with the collaboration or tolerance of many countries, including several Council of Europe member states. This co-operation, which took place in secret and without any democratic legitimacy, has allowed the development of a system that is utterly incompatible with the fundamental principles of the Council of Europe.

7. The facts and information gathered to date, some of which are still in the process of being brought to light, clearly indicate that the key elements of this spiderweb include, among others: a worldwide network of places of secret detention on CIA "black sites" and in military or naval installations; the CIA's programme of renditions, under which persons suspected of terrorism are transferred from one state to another on civilian aircraft, outside of the scope of any legal protections, often to be handed over to states who customarily resort to degrading treatment and torture; and the use of military airbases and aircraft to transport detainees as human cargo to Guantánamo Bay in Cuba or to other detention centres.

8. The Assembly condemns the systematic exclusion of all forms of judicial protection and regrets that, by depriving hundreds of suspects of their basic rights, including the right to a fair trial, the United States has done a disservice to the cause of justice and has tarnished its own hard-won reputation as a beacon of the defence of civil liberties and human rights.

9. Some Council of Europe member states have knowingly colluded with the United States to carry out such unlawful operations; others have tolerated them or simply turned a blind eye. They have also gone to great lengths to ensure that such operations remained secret and protected from effective national or international scrutiny.

10. This collusion with the United States of America by some Council of Europe member states has taken several different forms. Having carried out a legal and factual analysis on a range of cases of alleged secret detentions and unlawful transfers, the Assembly has identified instances in which Council of Europe member states have acted in one or several of the following ways, wilfully or at least recklessly in violation of their international human rights obligations, as explained in the explanatory memorandum of the report (see Doc. 10957) which led to the present resolution:

    10.1. secretly detaining a person on European territory for an indefinite period of time, whilst denying that person's basic human rights and failing to ensure procedural legal guarantees such as habeas corpus;

    10.2. capturing and handing a person over to the United States whilst knowing that such a person would be unlawfully transferred into a US-administered detention facility;

    10.3. permitting the unlawful transportation of detainees on civilian aircraft carrying out rendition operations, travelling through European airspace or across European territory;

    10.4. passing on information or intelligence to the United States whilst being fully aware that such material would be relied upon directly to carry out a rendition operation or to hold a person in secret detention;

    10.5. directly taking part in interrogations of persons subjected to rendition or held in secret detention;

    10.6. accepting or making use of information gathered in the course of detainee interrogations, before, during or after which the detainee in question was threatened or subjected to torture or other forms of human rights abuse;

    10.7. making available civilian airports or military airfields as "staging points" or platforms for rendition or other unlawful detainee transfer operations, and facilitating the preparation and take off of an aircraft on its operation from such a point; and

10.8. making available civilian airports or military airfields as "stopover points" for rendition operations, whereby an aircraft lands briefly at such a point on the outbound or homebound flight, for example to refuel.

11. Attempts to expose the true nature and extent of these unlawful operations have invariably faced obstruction or dismissal from the United States and its European partners alike. The authorities of most Council of Europe member states have denied their participation, in many cases without actually having carried out any inquiries or serious investigations.

12. In other instances such attempts have been thwarted on the grounds of national security or state secrecy. The Assembly takes the view that neither national security nor state secrecy can be invoked in such a sweeping, systematic fashion as to shield these unlawful operations from robust parliamentary and judicial scrutiny.

13. The Assembly highlights the widespread breach of the positive obligation of all Council of Europe member states to investigate such allegations in a full and thorough manner. It has now been demonstrated undeniably, through numerous well-documented and convergent facts, that secret detentions and unlawful inter-state transfers of persons deprived of their rights and involving European countries have taken place, such as to require in-depth inquiries and urgent responses by the executive and legislative branches of all the countries concerned.

14. While the Assembly has been seized in this instance with looking into allegations concerning very specific facts, it cannot ignore other allegations surrounding the existence of other secret detention centres in Europe, apparently also set up in the context of the war on terrorism. In particular, the Assembly expresses its deep concern at the continued reports of secret detentions in the North Caucasus. The European Committee for the Prevention of Torture and Inhuman or Degrading Treatment or Punishment (CPT) issued a public statement on this subject in 2003, which was recently supplemented by new, detailed testimony by victims and credible allegations from non-governmental organisations. Further serious investigation and analysis of secret detentions in the North Caucasus is clearly required.

15. The Assembly also regrets that detention centres in Kosovo were not accessible, until very recently, to the CPT. The lack of access seems all the more unacceptable in light of the fact that the international community intervened in that region with the declared aim of restoring order, peace and the respect for human rights. In that context the Assembly wishes to commend the repeated efforts of the Secretary General of the Council of Europe and his clear line taken on the matter.

16. The Assembly believes that broader rights should be attributed to the institution of the Commissioner for Human Rights of the Council of Europe, in order for it to be more closely involved in any investigation on violations of human rights the Assembly might carry out in the future. It encourages the Commissioner for Human Rights to play an active role in this respect.

17. The Assembly's main objective is to prevent violations of the sort described in this resolution from occurring in the future.

18. The Assembly therefore commends the Secretary General of the Council of Europe for the swift and thorough use of his power of inquiry under Article 52 ECHR.

19. The Assembly calls upon the member states of the Council of Europe to:

    19.1. ensure that unlawful inter-state transfers of detainees will not be permitted and take effective measures to prevent renditions and rendition flights through member states' territory and airspace;

    19.2. ensure that no one is arbitrarily detained, secretly or otherwise, on a member state's territory or any territory within the member states' effective control;

    19.3. undertake a critical review of the legal framework that regulates the intelligence services, with the dual objective of enhancing their efficiency and strengthening accountability mechanisms against abuse; clear regulations must also govern co-operation with foreign services and the activities of foreign services on national territory;

    19.4. ensure that all international co-operation and mutual legal assistance is carried out only in circumstances that respect human rights and international conventions in the field;

    19.5. ensure that the laws governing state secrecy protect the whistle-blowers, that is persons who disclose illegal activities of state organs from possible disciplinary or criminal sanctions;

    19.6. undertake a review of bilateral agreements signed between Council of Europe member states and the United States, particularly those on the status of US forces stationed in Europe and on the use of military and other infrastructure, to ensure that these agreements conform fully to applicable international human rights norms;

    19.7. urge the United States to dismantle its system of secret detentions and unlawful inter-state transfers and to co-operate more closely with the Council of Europe in establishing common means of overcoming the threat of terrorism in line with international human rights standards and respect for the rule of law;

    19.8. ensure that independent, impartial and effective investigations are carried out into any serious allegation that the territory, including airports or airspace, have been used in the context of rendition or secret detention. Such investigation should examine thoroughly any action taken by state or foreign agents linked to acts of rendition as well as laws or practices which may facilitate such acts. The scope and findings of the investigation should be made public;

    19.9. ensure that any person responsible for human rights violations in connection with renditions or secret detentions, including those who have aided or abetted these crimes, are brought to justice;

    19.10. ensure that all victims of rendition or secret detention have access to an effective remedy and obtain prompt and adequate reparation, including restitution, rehabilitation and fair and adequate financial compensation.

20. The Assembly also calls on the United States of America, which is an observer state to the Council of Europe and Europe's long-standing ally in resisting tyranny and defending human rights and the rule of law, to:

20.1. send a strong message to the world by demonstrating that terrorism can be overcome by lawful means, thereby proving the superiority of the democratic model founded on the respect of human dignity;

20.2. co-operate more closely in identifying and employing the most effective means with which to prevent and suppress the threat of terrorism in conformity with international human rights norms and the rule of law;

20.3. align its definitions of torture and other cruel, inhuman or degrading treatment with the definition used by the United Nations Committee against Torture;

20.4. prohibit the "extra-legal" transfer of persons suspected of involvement in terrorist organisations and all forcible transfers of persons from any country to countries that practise torture or that fail to guarantee the right to a fair trial, regardless of any assurances received;

20.5. issue official apologies and award compensation to the victims of illegal detentions or renditions, and bring to justice those responsible for secret detention or human rights violations in the course of renditions;

20.6. refrain from prosecuting any former or current public servants or journalists who, by providing testimony or other information, have helped to bring to light the system of unlawful detentions and mistreatment;

20.7. review, together with European states, their bilateral agreements in order to avoid creating direct or indirect *de jure* or de facto exemptions in applying European conventions to which Council of Europe member states are parties.

21. The Assembly invites its Committee on Legal Affairs and Human Rights to continue following up the issues raised in the present resolution and to report back to the Assembly as appropriate.

22. The Assembly further urges its members to call for rigorous inquiries in their respective national parliaments, especially in those states from which no or insufficient information has been forthcoming. The Secretary General's inquiry under Article 52 ECHR should be a first basis of information which member states should build upon.

23. The Assembly recognises, in the context of the present inquiry into secret detentions, that it lacks appropriate investigative powers akin to those provided to parliamentary inquiries in member states, including the powers to subpoena witnesses and compel the disclosure of documents, and calls for consideration of this issue.

24 Finally, the Assembly expresses its appreciation to the relevant European Union institutions (European Commission, European Parliament and EU Satellite Centre), as well as to Eurocontrol, for their valuable contributions to this inquiry, whilst reiterating the Council of Europe's role as the guardian of human rights, democracy and respect for the rule of law, throughout Europe.

(Source: Council of Europe official website.)

UNSC RESOLUTION 1701 ISRAEL-LEBANON CEASEFIRE

Published below is the text of the UN Security Council Resolution 1701 (2006) calling for an immediate ceasefire in the Israel-Hezbullah conflict in Lebanon, adopted on 11 August 2006.

Resolution 1701 (2006)

Adopted by the Security Council at its 5511th meeting, on 11 August 2006

The Security Council,

Recalling all its previous resolutions on Lebanon, in particular resolutions 425 (1978), 426 (1978), 520 (1982), 1559 (2004), 1655 (2006) 1680 (2006) and 1697 (2006), as well as the statements of its President on the situation in Lebanon, in particular the statements of 18 June 2000 (S/PRST/2000/21), of 19 October 2004 (S/PRST/2004/36), of 4 May 2005 (S/PRST/2005/17), of 23 January 2006 (S/PRST/2006/3) and of 30 July 2006 (S/PRST/2006/35),

Expressing its utmost concern at the continuing escalation of hostilities in Lebanon and in Israel since Hizbollah's attack on Israel on 12 July 2006, which has already caused hundreds of deaths and injuries on both sides, extensive damage to civilian infrastructure and hundreds of thousands of internally displaced persons,

Emphasizing the need for an end of violence, but at the same time *emphasizing* the need to address urgently the causes that have given rise to the current crisis, including by the unconditional release of the abducted Israeli soldiers, *Mindful* of the sensitivity of the issue of prisoners and *encouraging* the efforts aimed at urgently settling the issue of the Lebanese prisoners detained in Israel,

Welcoming the efforts of the Lebanese Prime Minister and the commitment of the Government of Lebanon, in its seven-point plan, to extend its authority over its territory, through its own legitimate armed forces, such that there will be no weapons without the consent of the Government of Lebanon and no authority other than that of the Government of Lebanon, *welcoming also* its commitment to a United Nations force that is supplemented and enhanced in numbers, equipment, mandate and scope of operation, and *bearing in mind* its request in this plan for an immediate withdrawal of the Israeli forces from southern Lebanon,

Determined to act for this withdrawal to happen at the earliest,

Taking due note of the proposals made in the seven-point plan regarding the Shebaa farms area,

Welcoming the unanimous decision by the Government of Lebanon on 7 August 2006 to deploy a Lebanese armed force of 15,000 troops in South Lebanon as the Israeli army withdraws behind the Blue Line and to request the assistance of additional forces from the United Nations Interim Force in Lebanon (UNIFIL) as needed, to facilitate the entry of the Lebanese armed forces into the region and to restate its intention to strengthen the Lebanese armed forces with material as needed to enable it to perform its duties,

Aware of its responsibilities to help secure a permanent ceasefire and a longterm solution to the conflict,

Determining that the situation in Lebanon constitutes a threat to international peace and security,

1. *Calls for* a full cessation of hostilities based upon, in particular, the immediate cessation by Hizbollah of all attacks and the immediate cessation by Israel of all offensive military operations;

2. Upon full cessation of hostilities, *calls upon* the Government of Lebanon and UNIFIL as authorized by paragraph 11 to deploy their forces together throughout the South and *calls upon* the Government of Israel, as that deployment begins, to withdraw all of its forces from southern Lebanon in parallel;

3. *Emphasizes* the importance of the extension of the control of the Government of Lebanon over all Lebanese territory in accordance with the provisions of resolution 1559 (2004) and resolution 1680 (2006), and of the relevant provisions of the Taif Accords, for it to exercise its full sovereignty, so that there will be no weapons without the consent of the Government of Lebanon and no authority other than that of the Government of Lebanon;

4. *Reiterates* its strong support for full respect for the Blue Line;

5. *Also reiterates* its strong support, as recalled in all its previous relevant resolutions, for the territorial integrity, sovereignty and political independence of Lebanon within its internationally recognized borders, as contemplated by the Israeli-Lebanese General Armistice Agreement of 23 March 1949;

6. *Calls on* the international community to take immediate steps to extend its financial and humanitarian assistance to the Lebanese people, including through facilitating the safe return of displaced persons and, under the authority of the Government of Lebanon, reopening airports and harbours, consistent with paragraphs 14 and 15, and *calls on* it also to consider further assistance in the future to contribute to the reconstruction and development of Lebanon;

7. *Affirms* that all parties are responsible for ensuring that no action is taken contrary to paragraph 1 that might adversely affect the search for a long-term solution, humanitarian access to civilian populations, including safe passage for humanitarian convoys, or the voluntary and safe return of displaced persons, and *calls on* all parties to comply with this responsibility and to cooperate with the Security Council;

8. *Calls for* Israel and Lebanon to support a permanent ceasefire and a longterm solution based on the following principles and elements:
   - full respect for the Blue Line by both parties;
   - security arrangements to prevent the resumption of hostilities, including the establishment between the Blue Line and the Litani river of an area free of any armed personnel, assets and weapons other than those of the Government of Lebanon and of UNIFIL as authorized in paragraph 11, deployed in this area;
   - full implementation of the relevant provisions of the Taif Accords, and of resolutions 1559 (2004) and 1680 (2006), that require the disarmament of all armed groups in Lebanon, so that, pursuant to the Lebanese cabinet decision of 27 July 2006, there will be no weapons or authority in Lebanon other than that of the Lebanese State;
   - no foreign forces in Lebanon without the consent of its Government;
   - no sales or supply of arms and related materiel to Lebanon except as authorized by its Government;
   - provision to the United Nations of all remaining maps of landmines in Lebanon in Israel's possession;

9. *Invites* the Secretary-General to support efforts to secure as soon as possible agreements in principle from the Government of Lebanon and the Government of Israel to the principles and elements for a long-term solution as set forth in paragraph 8, and *expresses* its intention to be actively involved;

10. *Requests* the Secretary-General to develop, in liaison with relevant international actors and the concerned parties, proposals to implement the relevant provisions of the Taif Accords, and resolutions 1559 (2004) and 1680 (2006), including disarmament, and for delineation of the international borders of Lebanon, especially in those areas where the border is disputed or uncertain, including by dealing with the Shebaa farms area, and to present to the Security Council those proposals within thirty days;

11. *Decides*, in order to supplement and enhance the force in numbers, equipment, mandate and scope of operations, to authorize an increase in the force strength of UNIFIL to a maximum of 15,000 troops, and that the force shall, in addition to carrying out its mandate under resolutions 425 and 426 (1978):
    (a) Monitor the cessation of hostilities;
    (b) Accompany and support the Lebanese armed forces as they deploy throughout the South, including along the Blue Line, as Israel withdraws its armed forces from Lebanon as provided in paragraph 2;
    (c) Coordinate its activities related to paragraph 11 (b) with the Government of Lebanon and the Government of Israel;
    (d) Extend its assistance to help ensure humanitarian access to civilian populations and the voluntary and safe return of displaced persons;
    (e) Assist the Lebanese armed forces in taking steps towards the establishment of the area as referred to in paragraph 8;
    (f) Assist the Government of Lebanon, at its request, to implement paragraph 14;

12. Acting in support of a request from the Government of Lebanon to deploy an international force to assist it to exercise its authority throughout the territory, *authorizes* UNIFIL to take all necessary action in areas of deployment of its forces and as it deems within its capabilities, to ensure that its area of operations is not utilized for hostile activities of any kind, to resist attempts by forceful means to prevent it from discharging its duties under the mandate of the Security Council, and to protect United Nations personnel, facilities, installations and equipment, ensure the security and freedom of movement of United Nations personnel, humanitarian workers and, without prejudice to the responsibility of the Government of Lebanon, to protect civilians under imminent threat of physical violence;

13. *Requests* the Secretary-General urgently to put in place measures to ensure UNIFIL is able to carry out the functions envisaged in this resolution, *urges* Member States to consider making appropriate contributions to UNIFIL and to respond positively to requests for assistance from the Force, and *expresses* its strong appreciation to those who have contributed to UNIFIL in the past;

14. *Calls upon* the Government of Lebanon to secure its borders and other entry points to prevent the entry in Lebanon without its consent of arms or related materiel and *requests* UNIFIL as authorized in paragraph 11 to assist the Government of Lebanon at its request;

15. *Decides* further that all States shall take the necessary measures to prevent, by their nationals or from their territories or using their flag vessels or aircraft:
    (a) The sale or supply to any entity or individual in Lebanon of arms and related materiel of all types, including weapons and ammunition, military vehicles and equipment, paramilitary equipment, and spare parts for the aforementioned, whether or not originating in their territories; and
    (b) The provision to any entity or individual in Lebanon of any technical training or assistance related to the provision, manufacture, maintenance or use of the items listed in subparagraph (a)

above; except that these prohibitions shall not apply to arms, related material, training or assistance authorized by the Government of Lebanon or by UNIFIL as authorized in paragraph 11;

16. *Decides* to extend the mandate of UNIFIL until 31 August 2007, and *expresses its intention* to consider in a later resolution further enhancements to the mandate and other steps to contribute to the implementation of a permanent ceasefire and a long-term solution;

17. *Requests* the Secretary-General to report to the Council within one week on the implementation of this resolution and subsequently on a regular basis;

18. *Stresses* the importance of, and the need to achieve, a comprehensive, just and lasting peace in the Middle East, based on all its relevant resolutions including its resolutions 242 (1967) of 22 November 1967, 338 (1973) of 22 October 1973 and 1515 (2003) of 19 November 2003;

19. *Decides* to remain actively seized of the matter.

(Source: UN Security Council.)

NATIONAL INTELLIGENCE ESTIMATE "TRENDS IN GLOBAL TERRORISM"

Published below are the key judgments contained in the US National Intelligence Estimate (NIE): "Trends in Global Terrorism: Implications for the United States", dated April 2006. The 30-page NIE warned that the situation in Iraq was contributing to the risks felt by the USA, rather than helping to minimise them, as claimed by President George W. Bush in his 11 September anniversary speech (see below). As a result of the publication of leaked extracts from the report by the New York Times *on 24 September, Bush ordered the declassification of parts of the NIE, which were then released to the press by the Office of the Director of National Intelligence on 26 September.*

DECLASSIFIED KEY JUDGMENTS OF THE NATIONAL INTELLIGENCE ESTIMATE "TRENDS IN GLOBAL TERRORISM: IMPLICATIONS FOR THE UNITED STATES" DATED APRIL 2006

KEY JUDGMENTS

United States-led counterterrorism efforts have seriously damaged the leadership of al-Qa'ida and disrupted its operations; however, we judge that al-Qa'ida will continue to pose the greatest threat to the Homeland and US interests abroad by a single terrorist organization. We also assess that the global jihadist movement—which includes al-Qa'ida, affiliated and independent terrorist groups, and emerging networks and cells—is spreading and adapting to counterterrorism efforts.

- Although we cannot measure the extent of the spread with precision, a large body of all-source reporting indicates that activists identifying themselves as jihadists, although a small percentage of Muslims, are increasing in both number and geographic dispersion.

- If this trend continues, threats to US interests at home and abroad will become more diverse, leading to increasing attacks worldwide.

- Greater pluralism and more responsive political systems in Muslim majority nations would alleviate some of the grievances jihadists exploit. Over time, such progress, together with sustained, multifaceted programs targeting the vulnerabilities of the jihadist movement and continued pressure on al-Qa'ida, could erode support for the jihadists.

We assess that the global jihadist movement is decentralized, lacks a coherent global strategy, and is becoming more diffuse. New jihadist networks and cells, with anti-American agendas, are increasingly likely to emerge. The confluence of shared purpose and dispersed actors will make it harder to find and undermine jihadist groups.

- We assess that the operational threat from self-radicalized cells will grow in importance to US counterterrorism efforts, particularly abroad but also in the Homeland.

- The jihadists regard Europe as an important venue for attacking Western interests. Extremist networks inside the extensive Muslim diasporas in Europe facilitate recruitment and staging for urban attacks, as illustrated by the 2004 Madrid and 2005 London bombings.

We assess that the Iraq jihad is shaping a new generation of terrorist leaders and operatives; perceived jihadist success there would inspire more fighters to continue the struggle elsewhere.

- The Iraq conflict has become the "cause celebre" for jihadists, breeding a deep resentment of US involvement in the Muslim world and cultivating supporters for the global jihadist movement.

Should jihadists leaving Iraq perceive themselves, and be perceived, to have failed, we judge fewer fighters will be inspired to carry on the fight.

We assess that the underlying factors fueling the spread of the movement outweigh its vulnerabilities and are likely to do so for the duration of the timeframe of this Estimate.

- Four underlying factors are fueling the spread of the jihadist movement: (1) Entrenched grievances, such as corruption, injustice, and fear of Western domination, leading to anger, humiliation, and a sense of powerlessness; (2) the Iraq "jihad;" (3) the slow pace of real and sustained economic, social, and political reforms in many Muslim majority nations; and (4) pervasive anti-US sentiment among most Muslims—all of which jihadists exploit.

Concomitant vulnerabilities in the jihadist movement have emerged that, if fully exposed and exploited, could begin to slow the spread of the movement. They include dependence on the continuation of Muslim-related conflicts, the limited appeal of the jihadists' radical ideology, the emergence of respected voices of moderation, and criticism of the violent tactics employed against mostly Muslim citizens.

- The jihadists' greatest vulnerability is that their ultimate political solution—an ultra-conservative interpretation of *shari'a*-based governance spanning the Muslim world—is unpopular with the vast majority of Muslims. Exposing the religious and political straitjacket that is implied by the jihadists' propaganda would help to divide them from the audiences they seek to persuade.

- Recent condemnations of violence and extremist religious interpretations by a few notable Muslim clerics signal a trend that could facilitate the growth of a constructive alternative to jihadist ideology: peaceful political activism. This also could lead to the consistent and dynamic participation of broader Muslim communities in rejecting violence, reducing the ability of radicals to capitalize on passive community support. In this way, the Muslim mainstream emerges as the most powerful weapon in the war on terror.

- Countering the spread of the jihadist movement will require coordinated multilateral efforts that go well beyond operations to capture or kill terrorist leaders.

If democratic reform efforts in Muslim majority nations progress over the next five years, political participation probably would drive a wedge between intransigent extremists and groups willing to use the political process to achieve their local objectives. Nonetheless, attendant reforms and potentially destabilizing transitions will create new opportunities for jihadists to exploit.

Al-Qa'ida, now merged with Abu Mus'ab al-Zarqawi's network, is exploiting the situation in Iraq to attract new recruits and donors and to maintain its leadership role.

- The loss of key leaders, particularly Usama Bin Ladin, Ayman al-Zawahiri, and al-Zarqawi, in rapid succession, probably would cause the group to fracture into smaller groups. Although like-minded individuals would endeavor to carry on the mission, the loss of these key leaders would exacerbate strains and disagreements. We assess that the resulting splinter groups would, at least for a time, pose a less serious threat to US interests than does al-Qa'ida.

- Should al-Zarqawi continue to evade capture and scale back attacks against Muslims, we assess he could broaden his popular appeal and present a global threat.

- The increased role of Iraqis in managing the operations of al-Qa'ida in Iraq might lead veteran foreign jihadists to focus their efforts on external operations.

Other affiliated Sunni extremist organizations, such as Jemaah Islamiya, Ansar al-Sunnah, and several North African groups, unless countered, are likely to expand their reach and become more capable of multiple and/or mass-casualty attacks outside their traditional areas of operation.

- We assess that such groups pose less of a danger to the Homeland than does al-Qa'ida but will pose varying degrees of threat to our allies and to US interests abroad. The focus of their attacks is likely to ebb and flow between local regime targets and regional or global ones.

We judge that most jihadist groups—both well-known and newly formed—will use improvised explosive devices and suicide attacks focused primarily on soft targets to implement their asymmetric warfare strategy, and that they will attempt to conduct sustained terrorist attacks in urban environments. Fighters with experience in Iraq are a potential source of leadership for jihadists pursuing these tactics.

- CBRN capabilities will continue to be sought by jihadist groups.

While Iran, and to a lesser extent Syria, remain the most active state sponsors of terrorism, many other states will be unable to prevent territory or resources from being exploited by terrorists.

Anti-US and anti-globalization sentiment is on the rise and fueling other radical ideologies. This could prompt some leftist, nationalist, or separatist groups to adopt terrorist methods to attack US interests. The radicalization process is occurring more quickly, more widely, and more anonymously in the Internet age, raising the likelihood of surprise attacks by unknown groups whose members and supporters may be difficult to pinpoint.

- We judge that groups of all stripes will increasingly use the Internet to communicate, propagandize, recruit, train, and obtain logistical and financial support.

(Source: Office of the Director of National Intelligence.)

ADDRESS BY US PRESIDENT ON ANNIVERSARY OF 11 SEPTEMBER 2001

Published below is the address to the nation broadcast by US President George W. Bush on the fifth anniversary of the terrorist attacks on the USA on 11 September 2001. Linking the US campaign in Iraq to the safety of the USA and to efforts to suppress the al-Qaida terrorist network, Bush expressed confidence that US forces in Iraq would be successful.

THE PRESIDENT: Good evening. Five years ago, this date — September the 11th — was seared into America's memory. Nineteen men attacked us with a barbarity unequaled in our history. They murdered people of all colors, creeds, and nationalities — and made war upon the entire free world. Since that day, America and her allies have taken the offensive in a war unlike any we have fought before. Today, we are safer, but we are not yet safe. On this solemn night, I've asked for some of your time to discuss the nature of the threat still before us, what we are doing to protect our nation, and the building of a more hopeful Middle East that holds the key to peace for America and the world.

On 9/11, our nation saw the face of evil. Yet on that awful day, we also witnessed something distinctly American: ordinary citizens rising to the occasion, and responding with extraordinary acts of courage. We saw courage in office workers who were trapped on the high floors of burning skyscrapers — and called home so that their last words to their families would be of comfort and love. We saw courage in passengers aboard Flight 93, who recited the 23rd Psalm — and then charged the cockpit. And we saw courage in the Pentagon staff who made it out of the flames and smoke — and ran back in to answer cries for help. On this day, we remember the innocent who lost their lives — and we pay tribute to those who gave their lives so that others might live.

For many of our citizens, the wounds of that morning are still fresh. I've met firefighters and police officers who choke up at the memory of fallen comrades. I've stood with families gathered on a grassy field in Pennsylvania, who take bittersweet pride in loved ones who refused to be victims — and gave America our first victory in the war on terror. I've sat beside young mothers with children who are now five years old — and still long for the daddies who will never cradle them in their arms. Out of this suffering, we resolve to honor every man and woman lost. And we seek their lasting memorial in a safer and more hopeful world.

Since the horror of 9/11, we've learned a great deal about the enemy. We have learned that they are evil and kill without mercy — but not without purpose. We have learned that they form a global network of extremists who are driven by a perverted vision of Islam — a totalitarian ideology that hates freedom, rejects tolerance, and despises all dissent. And we have learned that their goal is to build a radical Islamic empire where women are prisoners in their homes, men are beaten for missing prayer meetings, and terrorists have a safe haven to plan and launch attacks on America and other civilized nations. The war against this enemy is more than a military conflict. It is the decisive ideological struggle of the 21st century, and the calling of our generation.

Our nation is being tested in a way that we have not been since the start of the Cold War. We saw what a handful of our enemies can do with box-cutters and plane tickets. We hear their threats to launch even more terrible attacks on our people. And we know that if they were able to get their hands on weapons of mass destruction, they would use them against us. We face an enemy determined to bring death and suffering into our homes. America did not ask for this war, and every American wishes it were over. So do I. But the war is not over — and it will not be over until either we or the extremists emerge victorious. If we do not defeat these enemies now, we will leave our children to face a Middle East overrun by terrorist states and radical dictators armed with nuclear weapons. We are in a war that will set the course for this new century — and determine the destiny of millions across the world.

For America, 9/11 was more than a tragedy — it changed the way we look at the world. On September the 11th, we resolved that we would go on the offense against our enemies, and we would not distinguish between the terrorists and those who harbor or support them. So we helped drive the Taliban from power in Afghanistan. We put al Qaeda on the run, and killed or captured most of those who planned the 9/11 attacks, including the man believed to be the mastermind, Khalid Sheik Mohammed. He and other suspected terrorists have been questioned by the Central Intelligence Agency, and they provided valuable information that has helped stop attacks in America and across the world. Now these men have been transferred to Guantanamo Bay, so they can be held to account for their actions. Osama bin Laden and other terrorists are still in hiding. Our message to them is clear: No matter how long it takes, America will find you, and we will bring you to justice.

On September the 11th, we learned that America must confront threats before they reach our shores, whether those threats come from terrorist networks or terrorist states. I'm often asked why we're in Iraq when Saddam Hussein was not responsible for the 9/11 attacks. The answer is that the regime of Saddam Hussein was a clear threat. My administration, the Congress, and the United Nations saw the threat — and after 9/11, Saddam's regime posed a risk that the world could not afford to take. The world is safer because Saddam Hussein is no longer in power. And now the challenge is to help the Iraqi people build a democracy that fulfills the dreams of the nearly 12 million Iraqis who came out to vote in free elections last December.

Al Qaeda and other extremists from across the world have come to Iraq to stop the rise of a free society in the heart of the Middle East. They have joined the remnants of Saddam's regime and other armed groups to foment sectarian violence and drive us out. Our enemies in Iraq are tough and they are committed — but so are Iraqi and coalition forces. We're adapting to stay ahead of the enemy, and we are carrying out a clear plan to ensure that a democratic Iraq succeeds.

We're training Iraqi troops so they can defend their nation. We're helping Iraq's unity government grow in strength and serve its people. We will not leave until this work is done. Whatever mistakes have been made in Iraq, the worst mistake would be to think that if we pulled out, the terrorists would leave us alone. They will not leave us alone. They will follow us. The safety of America depends on the outcome of the battle in the streets of Baghdad. Osama bin Laden calls this fight "the Third World War" — and he says that victory for the terrorists in Iraq will mean America's "defeat and disgrace forever." If we yield Iraq to men like bin Laden, our enemies will be emboldened; they will gain a new safe haven; they will use Iraq's resources to fuel their extremist movement. We will not allow this to happen. America will stay in the fight. Iraq will be a free nation, and a strong ally in the war on terror.

We can be confident that our coalition will succeed because the Iraqi people have been steadfast in the face of unspeakable violence. And we can be confident in victory because of the skill and resolve of America's Armed Forces. Every one of our troops is a volunteer, and since the attacks of September the 11th, more than 1.6 million Americans have stepped forward to put on our nation's uniform. In Iraq, Afghanistan, and other fronts in the war on terror, the men and women of our military are making great sacrifices to keep us safe. Some have suffered terrible injuries — and nearly 3,000 have given their lives. America cherishes their memory. We pray for their families. And we will never back down from the work they have begun.

We also honor those who toil day and night to keep our homeland safe, and we are giving them the tools they need to protect our people. We've created the Department of Homeland Security. We have torn down the wall that kept law enforcement and intelligence from sharing information. We've tightened security at our airports and seaports and borders, and we've created new programs to monitor enemy bank records and phone calls. Thanks to the hard work of our law enforcement and intelligence professionals, we have broken up terrorist cells in our midst and saved American lives.

Five years after 9/11, our enemies have not succeeded in launching another attack on our soil, but they've not been idle. Al Qaeda and those inspired by its hateful ideology have carried out terrorist attacks in more than two dozen nations. And just last month, they were foiled in a plot to blow up passenger planes headed for the United States. They remain determined to attack America and kill our citizens — and we are determined to stop them. We'll continue to give the men and women who protect us every resource and legal authority they need to do their jobs.

In the first days after the 9/11 attacks I promised to use every element of national power to fight the terrorists, wherever we find them. One of the strongest weapons in our arsenal is the power of freedom. The terrorists fear freedom as much as they do our firepower. They are thrown into panic at the sight of an old man pulling the election lever, girls enrolling in schools, or families worshiping God in their own traditions. They know that given a choice, people will choose freedom over their extremist ideology. So their answer is to deny people this choice by raging against the forces of freedom and moderation. This struggle has been called a clash of civilizations. In truth, it is a struggle for civilization. We are fighting to maintain the way of life enjoyed by free nations. And we're fighting for the possibility that good and decent people across the Middle East can raise up societies based on freedom and tolerance and personal dignity.

We are now in the early hours of this struggle between tyranny and freedom. Amid the violence, some question whether the people of the Middle East want their freedom, and whether the forces of moderation can prevail. For 60 years, these doubts guided our policies in the Middle East. And then, on a bright September morning, it became clear that the calm we saw in the Middle East was only a mirage. Years of pursuing stability to promote peace had left us with neither. So we changed our policies, and committed America's influence in the world to advancing freedom and democracy as the great alternatives to repression and radicalism.

With our help, the people of the Middle East are now stepping forward to claim their freedom. From Kabul to Baghdad to Beirut, there are brave men and women risking their lives each day for the same freedoms that we enjoy. And they have one question for us: Do we have the confidence to do in the Middle East what our fathers and grandfathers accomplished in Europe and Asia? By standing with democratic leaders and reformers, by giving voice to the hopes of decent men and women, we're offering a path away from radicalism. And we are enlisting the most powerful force for peace and moderation in the Middle East: the desire of millions to be free.

Across the broader Middle East, the extremists are fighting to prevent such a future. Yet America has confronted evil before, and we have defeated it — sometimes at the cost of thousands of good men in a single battle. When Franklin Roosevelt vowed to defeat two enemies across two oceans, he could not have foreseen D-Day and Iwo Jima — but he would not have been surprised at the outcome. When Harry Truman promised American support for free peoples resisting Soviet aggression, he could not have foreseen the rise of the Berlin Wall — but he would not have been surprised to see it brought down. Throughout our history, America has seen liberty challenged, and every time, we have seen liberty triumph with sacrifice and determination.

At the start of this young century, America looks to the day when the people of the Middle East leave the desert of despotism for the fertile gardens of liberty, and resume their rightful place in a world of peace and prosperity. We look to the day when the nations of that region recognize their greatest resource is not the oil in the ground, but the talent and creativity of their people. We look to the day when moms and dads throughout the Middle East see a future of hope and opportunity for their children. And when that good day comes, the clouds of war will part, the appeal of radicalism will decline, and we will leave our children with a better and safer world.

On this solemn anniversary, we rededicate ourselves to this cause. Our nation has endured trials, and we face a difficult road ahead. Winning this war will require the determined efforts of a unified country, and we must put aside our differences and work together to meet the test that history has given us. We will defeat our enemies. We will protect our people. And we will lead the 21st century into a shining age of human liberty.

Earlier this year, I traveled to the United States Military Academy. I was there to deliver the commencement address to the first class to arrive at West Point after the attacks of September the 11th. That day I met a proud mom named RoseEllen Dowdell. She was there to watch her son, Patrick, accept his commission in the finest Army the world has ever known. A few weeks earlier, RoseEllen had watched her other son, James, graduate from the Fire Academy in New York City. On both these days, her thoughts turned to someone who was not there to share the moment: her husband, Kevin Dowdell. Kevin was one of the 343 firefighters who rushed to the burning towers of the World Trade Center on September the 11th — and never came home. His sons lost their father that day, but not the passion for service he instilled in them. Here is what RoseEllen says about her boys: "As a mother, I cross my fingers and pray all the time for their safety — but as worried as I am, I'm also proud, and I know their dad would be, too."

Our nation is blessed to have young Americans like these — and we will need them. Dangerous enemies have declared their intention to destroy our way of life. They're not the first to try, and their fate will be the same as those who tried before. Nine-Eleven showed us why. The attacks were meant to bring us to our knees, and they did, but not in the way the terrorists intended. Americans united in prayer, came to the aid of neighbors in need, and resolved that our enemies would not have the last word. The spirit of our people is the source of America's strength. And we go forward with trust in that spirit, confidence in our purpose, and faith in a loving God who made us to be free.

Thank you, and may God bless you.

(Source: White House press office.)

IRAQ STUDY GROUP REPORT: EXECUTIVE SUMMARY

Published below is the Executive Summary of The Iraq Study Group Report, *published on 6 December 2006. The Iraq Study Group, commissioned in March and co-chaired by James A. Baker III and Lee H. Hamilton, examined the current and likely future situation in Iraq and the region, and how this was likely to affect US interests.*

Executive Summary

The situation in Iraq is grave and deteriorating. There is no path that can guarantee success, but the prospects can be improved.

In this report, we make a number of recommendations for actions to be taken in Iraq, the United States, and the region. Our most important recommendations call for new and enhanced diplomatic and political efforts in Iraq and the region, and a change in the primary mission of U.S. forces in Iraq that will enable the United States to begin to move its combat forces out of Iraq responsibly. We believe that these two recommendations are equally important and reinforce one another. If they are effectively implemented, and if the Iraqi government moves forward with national reconciliation, Iraqis will have an opportunity for a better future, terrorism will be dealt a blow, stability will be enhanced in an important part of the world, and America's credibility, interests, and values will be protected.

The challenges in Iraq are complex. Violence is increasing in scope and lethality. It is fed by a Sunni Arab insurgency, Shiite militias and death squads, al Qaeda, and widespread criminality. Sectarian conflict is the principal challenge to stability.

The Iraqi people have a democratically elected government, yet it is not adequately advancing national reconciliation, providing basic security, or delivering essential services. Pessimism is pervasive.

If the situation continues to deteriorate, the consequences could be severe. A slide toward chaos could trigger the collapse of Iraq's government and a humanitarian catastrophe. Neighboring countries could intervene. Sunni-Shia clashes could spread. Al Qaeda could win a propaganda victory and expand its base of operations. The global standing of the United States could be diminished. Americans could become more polarized.

During the past nine months we have considered a full range of approaches for moving forward. All have flaws. Our recommended course has shortcomings, but we firmly believe that it includes the best strategies and tactics to positively influence the outcome in Iraq and the region.

External Approach

The policies and actions of Iraq's neighbors greatly affect its stability and prosperity. No country in the region will benefit in the long term from a chaotic Iraq. Yet Iraq's neighbors are not doing enough to help Iraq achieve stability. Some are undercutting stability.

The United States should immediately launch a new diplomatic offensive to build an international consensus for stability in Iraq and the region. This diplomatic effort should include every country that has an interest in avoiding a chaotic Iraq, including all of Iraq's neighbors. Iraq's neighbors and key states in and outside the region should form a support group to reinforce security and national reconciliation within Iraq, neither of which Iraq can achieve on its own.

Given the ability of Iran and Syria to influence events within Iraq and their interest in avoiding chaos in Iraq, the United States should try to engage them constructively. In seeking to influence the behavior of both countries, the United States has disincentives and incentives available. Iran should stem the flow of arms and training to Iraq, respect Iraq's sovereignty and territorial integrity, and use its influence over Iraqi Shia groups to encourage national reconciliation. The issue of Iran's nuclear programs should continue to be dealt with by the five permanent members of the United Nations Security Council plus Germany. Syria should control its border with Iraq to stem the flow of funding, insurgents, and terrorists in and out of Iraq.

The United States cannot achieve its goals in the Middle East unless it deals directly with the Arab-Israeli conflict and regional instability. There must be a renewed and sustained commitment by the United States to a comprehensive Arab-Israeli peace on all fronts: Lebanon, Syria, and President Bush's June 2002 commitment to a two-state solution for Israel and Palestine. This commitment must include direct talks with, by, and between Israel, Lebanon, Palestinians (those who accept Israel's right to exist), and Syria.

As the United States develops its approach toward Iraq and the Middle East, the United States should provide additional political, economic, and military support for Afghanistan, including resources that might become available as combat forces are moved out of Iraq.

Internal Approach

The most important questions about Iraq's future are now the responsibility of Iraqis. The United States must adjust its role in Iraq to encourage the Iraqi people to take control of their own destiny.

The Iraqi government should accelerate assuming responsibility for Iraqi security by increasing the number and quality of Iraqi Army brigades. While this process is under way, and to facilitate it, the United States should significantly increase the number of U.S. military personnel, including combat troops, imbedded in and supporting Iraqi Army units. As these actions proceed, U.S. combat forces could begin to move out of Iraq.

The primary mission of U.S. forces in Iraq should evolve to one of supporting the Iraqi army, which would take over primary responsibility for combat operations. By the first quarter of 2008, subject to unexpected developments in the security situation on the ground, all combat brigades not necessary for force protection could be out of Iraq. At that time, U.S. combat forces in Iraq could be deployed only in units embedded with Iraqi forces, in rapid-reaction and special operations teams, and in training, equipping, advising, force protection, and search and rescue. Intelligence and support efforts would continue. A vital mission of those rapid reaction and special operations forces would be to undertake strikes against al Qaeda in Iraq.

It is clear that the Iraqi government will need assistance from the United States for some time to come, especially in carrying out security responsibilities. Yet the United States must make it clear to the Iraqi government that the United States could carry out its plans, including planned redeployments, even if the Iraqi government did not implement their planned changes. The United States must not make an open-ended commitment to keep large numbers of American troops deployed in Iraq.

As redeployment proceeds, military leaders should emphasize training and education of forces that have returned to the United States in order to restore the force to full combat capability. As equipment returns to the United States, Congress should appropriate sufficient funds to restore the equipment over the next five years.

The United States should work closely with Iraq's leaders to support the achievement of specific objectives—or milestones—on national reconciliation, security, and governance. Miracles cannot be expected, but the people of Iraq have the right to expect action and progress. The Iraqi government needs to show its own citizens—and the citizens of the United States and other countries—that it deserves continued support.

Prime Minister Nouri al-Maliki, in consultation with the United States, has put forward a set of milestones critical for Iraq. His list is a good start, but it must be expanded to include milestones that can strengthen the government and benefit the Iraqi people. President Bush and his national security team should remain in close and frequent contact with the Iraqi leadership to convey a clear message: there must be prompt action by the Iraqi government to make substantial progress toward the achievement of these milestones.

If the Iraqi government demonstrates political will and makes substantial progress toward the achievement of milestones on national reconciliation, security, and governance, the United States should make clear its willingness to continue training, assistance, and support for Iraq's security forces and to continue political, military, and economic support. If the Iraqi government does not make substantial progress toward the achievement of milestones on national reconciliation, security, and governance, the United States should reduce its political, military, or economic support for the Iraqi government.

Our report makes recommendations in several other areas. They include improvements to the Iraqi criminal justice system, the Iraqi oil sector, the U.S. reconstruction efforts in Iraq, the U.S. budget process, the training of U.S. government personnel, and U.S. intelligence capabilities.

Conclusion

It is the unanimous view of the Iraq Study Group that these recommendations offer a new way forward for the United States in Iraq and the region. They are comprehensive and need to be implemented in a coordinated fashion. They should not be separated or carried out in isolation. The dynamics of the region are as important to Iraq as events within Iraq.

The challenges are daunting. There will be difficult days ahead. But by pursuing this new way forward, Iraq, the region, and the United States of America can emerge stronger.

(Source: US Institute of Peace.)

UN SECURITY COUNCIL RESOLUTION 1737 (2006)

Published below is the text of UN Security Council Resolution 1737 (2006), adopted on 23 December 2006, which imposed sanctions on Iran for its failure to suspend its nuclear material enrichment programme.

The Security Council,

Recalling the Statement of its President, S/PRST/2006/15, of 29 March 2006, and its resolution 1696 (2006) of 31 July 2006,

Reaffirming its commitment to the Treaty on the Non-Proliferation of Nuclear Weapons, and recalling the right of States Party, in conformity with Articles I and II of that Treaty, to develop research, production and use of nuclear energy for peaceful purposes without discrimination,

Reiterating its serious concern over the many reports of the IAEA Director General and resolutions of the IAEA Board of Governors related to Iran's nuclear programme, reported to it by the IAEA Director General, including IAEA Board resolution GOV/2006/14,

Reiterating its serious concern that the IAEA Director General's report of 27 February 2006 (GOV/2006/15) lists a number of outstanding issues and concerns on Iran's nuclear programme, including topics which could have a military nuclear dimension, and that the IAEA is unable to conclude that there are no undeclared nuclear materials or activities in Iran,

Reiterating its serious concern over the IAEA Director General's report of 28 April 2006 (GOV/2006/27) and its findings, including that, after more than three years of Agency efforts to seek clarity about all aspects of Iran's nuclear programme, the existing gaps in knowledge continue to be a matter of concern, and that the IAEA is unable to make progress in its efforts to provide assurances about the absence of undeclared nuclear material and activities in Iran,

Noting with serious concern that, as confirmed by the IAEA Director General's reports of 8 June 2006 (GOV/2006/38), 31 August 2006 (GOV/2006/53) and 14 November 2006 (GOV/2006/64), Iran has not established full and sustained suspension of all enrichment-related and reprocessing activities as set out in resolution 1696 (2006), nor resumed its cooperation with the IAEA under the Additional Protocol, nor taken the other steps required of it by the IAEA Board of Governors, nor complied with the provisions of Security Council resolution 1696 (2006) and which are essential to build confidence, and *deploring* Iran's refusal to take these steps,

Emphasizing the importance of political and diplomatic efforts to find a negotiated solution guaranteeing that Iran's nuclear programme is exclusively for peaceful purposes, and *noting* that such a solution would benefit nuclear non-proliferation elsewhere, and *welcoming* the continuing commitment of China, France, Germany, the Russian Federation, the United Kingdom and the United States, with the support of the European Union's High Representative to seek a negotiated solution,

Determined to give effect to its decisions by adopting appropriate measures to persuade Iran to comply with resolution 1696 (2006) and with the requirements of the IAEA, and also to constrain Iran's development of sensitive technologies in support of its nuclear and missile programmes, until such time as the Security Council determines that the objectives of this resolution have been met,

Concerned by the proliferation risks presented by the Iranian nuclear programme and, in this context, by Iran's continuing failure to meet the requirements of the IAEA Board of Governors and to comply with the provisions of Security Council resolution 1696 (2006),

Mindful of its primary responsibility under the Charter of the United Nations for the maintenance of international peace and security,

Acting under Article 41 of Chapter VII of the Charter of the United Nations,

1. *Affirms* that Iran shall without further delay take the steps required by the IAEA Board of Governors in its resolution GOV/2006/14, which are essential to build confidence in the exclusively peaceful purpose of its nuclear programme and to resolve outstanding questions;

2. *Decides*, in this context, that Iran shall without further delay suspend the following proliferation sensitive nuclear activities:
   (a) all enrichment-related and reprocessing activities, including research and development, to be verified by the IAEA; and
   (b) work on all heavy water-related projects, including the construction of a research reactor moderated by heavy water, also to be verified by the IAEA;

3. *Decides* that all States shall take the necessary measures to prevent the supply, sale or transfer directly or indirectly from their territories, or by their nationals or using their flag vessels or aircraft to, or for the use in or benefit of, Iran, and whether or not originating in their territories, of all items, materials, equipment, goods and technology which could contribute to Iran's enrichment-related, reprocessing or heavy water-related activities, or to the development of nuclear weapon delivery systems, namely:
   (a) those set out in sections B.2, B.3, B.4, B.5, B.6 and B.7 of INFCIRC/254/Rev.8/Part 1 in document S/2006/814;
   (b) those set out in sections A.1 and B.1 of INFCIRC/254/Rev.8/Part 1 in document S/2006/814, except the supply, sale or transfer of:
   (i) equipment covered by B.1 when such equipment is for light water reactors;
   (ii) low-enriched uranium covered by A.1.2 when it is incorporated in assembled nuclear fuel elements for such reactors;
   (c) those set out in document S/2006/815, except the supply, sale or transfer of items covered by 19.A.3 of Category II;
   (d) any additional items, materials, equipment, goods and technology, determined as necessary by the Security Council or the Committee established by paragraph 18 below (herein "the Committee"), which could contribute to enrichment-related, or reprocessing, or heavy water-related activities, or to the development of nuclear weapon delivery systems;

4. *Decides* that all States shall take the necessary measures to prevent the supply, sale or transfer directly or indirectly from their territories, or by their nationals or using their flag vessels or aircraft to, or for the use in or benefit of, Iran, and whether or not originating in their territories, of the following items, materials, equipment, goods and technology:
   (a) those set out in INFCIRC/254/Rev.7/Part2 of document S/2006/814 if the State determines that they would contribute to enrichment-related, reprocessing or heavy water-related activities;
   (b) any other items not listed in documents S/2006/814 or S/2006/815 if the State determines that they would contribute to enrichment-related, reprocessing or heavy water-related activities, or to the development of nuclear weapon delivery systems;
   (c) any further items if the State determines that they would contribute to the pursuit of activ-

ities related to other topics about which the IAEA has expressed concerns or identified as outstanding;

5. *Decides* that, for the supply, sale or transfer of all items, materials, equipment, goods and technology covered by documents S/2006/814 and S/2006/815 the export of which to Iran is not prohibited by subparagraphs 3 (b), 3 (c) or 4 (a) above, States shall ensure that:
   (a) the requirements, as appropriate, of the Guidelines as set out in documents S/2006/814 and S/2006/985 have been met; and
   (b) they have obtained and are in a position to exercise effectively a right to verify the end-use and end-use location of any supplied item; and
   (c) they notify the Committee within ten days of the supply, sale or transfer; and
   (d) in the case of items, materials, equipment, goods and technology contained in document S/2006/814, they also notify the IAEA within ten days of the supply, sale or transfer;

6. *Decides* that all States shall also take the necessary measures to prevent the provision to Iran of any technical assistance or training, financial assistance, investment, brokering or other services, and the transfer of financial resources or services, related to the supply, sale, transfer, manufacture or use of the prohibited items, materials, equipment, goods and technology specified in paragraphs 3 and 4 above;

7. *Decides* that Iran shall not export any of the items in documents S/2006/814 and S/2006/815 and that all Member States shall prohibit the procurement of such items from Iran by their nationals, or using their flag vessels or aircraft, and whether or not originating in the territory of Iran;

8. *Decides* that Iran shall provide such access and cooperation as the IAEA requests to be able to verify the suspension outlined in paragraph 2 and to resolve all outstanding issues, as identified in IAEA reports, and *calls upon* Iran to ratify promptly the Additional Protocol;

9. *Decides* that the measures imposed by paragraphs 3, 4 and 6 above shall not apply where the Committee determines in advance and on a case-by-case basis that such supply, sale, transfer or provision of such items or assistance would clearly not contribute to the development of Iran's technologies in support of its proliferation sensitive nuclear activities and of development of nuclear weapon delivery systems, including where such items or assistance are for food, agricultural, medical or other humanitarian purposes, provided that:
   (a) contracts for delivery of such items or assistance include appropriate end-user guarantees; and
   (b) Iran has committed not to use such items in proliferation sensitive nuclear activities or for development of nuclear weapon delivery systems;

10. *Calls upon* all States to exercise vigilance regarding the entry into or transit through their territories of individuals who are engaged in, directly associated with or providing support for Iran's proliferation sensitive nuclear activities or for the development of nuclear weapon delivery systems, and *decides* in this regard that all States shall notify the Committee of the entry into or transit through their territories of the persons designated in the Annex to this resolution (herein "the Annex"), as well as of additional persons designated by the Security Council or the Committee as being engaged in, directly associated with or providing support for Iran's proliferation sensitive nuclear activities and for the development of nuclear weapon delivery systems, including through the involvement in procurement of the prohibited items, goods, equipment, materials and technology specified by and under the measures in para-

graphs 3 and 4 above, except where such travel is for activities directly related to the items in subparagraphs 3 (b) (i) and (ii) above;

11. *Underlines* that nothing in the above paragraph requires a State to refuse its own nationals entry into its territory, and that all States shall, in the implementation of the above paragraph, take into account humanitarian considerations as well as the necessity to meet the objectives of this resolution, including where Article XV of the IAEA Statute is engaged;

12. *Decides* that all States shall freeze the funds, other financial assets and economic resources which are on their territories at the date of adoption of this resolution or at any time thereafter, that are owned or controlled by the persons or entities designated in the Annex, as well as those of additional persons or entities designated by the Security Council or by the Committee as being engaged in, directly associated with or providing support for Iran's proliferation sensitive nuclear activities or the development of nuclear weapon delivery systems, or by persons or entities acting on their behalf or at their direction, or by entities owned or controlled by them, including through illicit means, and that the measures in this paragraph shall cease to apply in respect of such persons or entities if, and at such time as, the Security Council or the Committee removes them from the Annex, and *decides further* that all States shall ensure that any funds, financial assets or economic resources are prevented from being made available by their nationals or by any persons or entities within their territories, to or for the benefit of these persons and entities;

13. *Decides* that the measures imposed by paragraph 12 above do not apply to funds, other financial assets or economic resources that have been determined by relevant States:
    (a) to be necessary for basic expenses, including payment for foodstuffs, rent or mortgage, medicines and medical treatment, taxes, insurance premiums, and public utility charges or exclusively for payment of reasonable professional fees and reimbursement of incurred expenses associated with the provision of legal services, or fees or service charges, in accordance with national laws, for routine holding or maintenance of frozen funds, other financial assets and economic resources, after notification by the relevant States to the Committee of the intention to authorize, where appropriate, access to such funds, other financial assets or economic resources and in the absence of a negative decision by the Committee within five working days of such notification;
    (b) to be necessary for extraordinary expenses, provided that such determination has been notified by the relevant States to the Committee and has been approved by the Committee;
    (c) to be the subject of a judicial, administrative or arbitral lien or judgement, in which case the funds, other financial assets and economic resources may be used to satisfy that lien or judgement provided that the lien or judgement was entered into prior to the date of the present resolution, is not for the benefit of a person or entity designated pursuant to paragraphs 10 and 12 above, and has been notified by the relevant States to the Committee;
    (d) to be necessary for activities directly related to the items specified in subparagraphs 3 (b) (i) and (ii) and have been notified by the relevant States to the Committee;

14. *Decides* that States may permit the addition to the accounts frozen pursuant to the provisions of paragraph 12 above of interests or other earnings due on those accounts or payments due under contracts, agreements or obligations that arose prior to the date on which those accounts became subject to the provisions of this resolution, provided that any such interest, other earnings and payments continue to be subject to these provisions and are frozen;

15. *Decides* that the measures in paragraph 12 above shall not prevent a designated person or entity from making payment due under a contract entered into prior to the listing of such a person or entity, provided that the relevant States have determined that:
    (a) the contract is not related to any of the prohibited items, materials, equipment, goods, technologies, assistance, training, financial assistance, investment, brokering or services referred to in paragraphs 3, 4 and 6 above;
    (b) the payment is not directly or indirectly received by a person or entity designated pursuant to paragraph 12 above; and after notification by the relevant States to the Committee of the intention to make or receive such payments or to authorize, where appropriate, the unfreezing of funds, other financial assets or economic resources for this purpose, ten working days prior to such authorization;

16. *Decides* that technical cooperation provided to Iran by the IAEA or under its auspices shall only be for food, agricultural, medical, safety or other humanitarian purposes, or where it is necessary for projects directly related to the items specified in subparagraphs 3 (b) (i) and (ii) above, but that no such technical cooperation shall be provided that relates to the proliferation sensitive nuclear activities set out in paragraph 2 above;

17. *Calls upon* all States to exercise vigilance and prevent specialized teaching or training of Iranian nationals, within their territories or by their nationals, of disciplines which would contribute to Iran's proliferation sensitive nuclear activities and development of nuclear weapon delivery systems;

18. *Decides* to establish, in accordance with rule 28 of its provisional rules of procedure, a Committee of the Security Council consisting of all the members of the Council, to undertake the following tasks:
    (a) to seek from all States, in particular those in the region and those producing the items, materials, equipment, goods and technology referred to in paragraphs 3 and 4 above, information regarding the actions taken by them to implement effectively the measures imposed by paragraphs 3, 4, 5, 6, 7, 8, 10 and 12 of this resolution and whatever further information it may consider useful in this regard;
    (b) to seek from the secretariat of the IAEA information regarding the actions taken by the IAEA to implement effectively the measures imposed by paragraph 16 of this resolution and whatever further information it may consider useful in this regard;
    (c) to examine and take appropriate action on information regarding alleged violations of measures imposed by paragraphs 3, 4, 5, 6, 7, 8, 10 and 12 of this resolution;
    (d) to consider and decide upon requests for exemptions set out in paragraphs 9, 13 and 15 above;
    (e) to determine as may be necessary additional items, materials, equipment, goods and technology to be specified for the purpose of paragraph 3 above;
    (f) to designate as may be necessary additional individuals and entities subject to the measures imposed by paragraphs 10 and 12 above;
    (g) to promulgate guidelines as may be necessary to facilitate the implementation of the measures imposed by this resolution and include in such guidelines a requirement on States to provide information where possible as to why any individuals and/or entities meet the criteria set out in paragraphs 10 and 12 and any relevant identifying information;
    (h) to report at least every 90 days to the Security Council on its work and on the implementation of this resolution, with its observations and recommendations, in particular on ways to strengthen the effectiveness of the measures imposed by paragraphs 3, 4, 5, 6, 7, 8, 10 and 12 above;

19. *Decides* that all States shall report to the Committee within 60 days of the adoption of this resolution on the steps they have taken with a view to implementing effectively paragraphs 3, 4, 5, 6, 7, 8, 10, 12 and 17 above;

20. *Expresses* the conviction that the suspension set out in paragraph 2 above as well as full, verified Iranian compliance with the requirements set out by the IAEA Board of Governors, would contribute to a diplomatic, negotiated solution that guarantees Iran's nuclear programme is for exclusively peaceful purposes, *underlines* the willingness of the international community to work positively for such a solution, *encourages* Iran, in conforming to the above provisions, to re-engage with the international community and with the IAEA, and *stresses* that such engagement will be beneficial to Iran;

21. *Welcomes* the commitment of China, France, Germany, the Russian Federation, the United Kingdom and the United States, with the support of the European Union's High Representative, to a negotiated solution to this issue and encourages Iran to engage with their June 2006 proposals (S/2006/521), which were endorsed by the Security Council in resolution 1696 (2006), for a long-term comprehensive agreement which would allow for the development of relations and cooperation with Iran based on mutual respect and the establishment of international confidence in the exclusively peaceful nature of Iran's nuclear programme;

22. *Reiterates* its determination to reinforce the authority of the IAEA, strongly supports the role of the IAEA Board of Governors, *commends* and *encourages* the Director General of the IAEA and its secretariat for their ongoing professional and impartial efforts to resolve all remaining outstanding issues in Iran within the framework of the IAEA, *underlines* the necessity of the IAEA continuing its work to clarify all outstanding issues relating to Iran's nuclear programme;

23. *Requests* within 60 days a report from the Director General of the IAEA on whether Iran has established full and sustained suspension of all activities mentioned in this resolution, as well as on the process of Iranian compliance with all the steps required by the IAEA Board and with the other provisions of this resolution, to the IAEA Board of Governors and in parallel to the Security Council for its consideration;

24. *Affirms* that it shall review Iran's actions in the light of the report referred to in paragraph 23 above, to be submitted within 60 days, and:
    (a) that it shall suspend the implementation of measures if and for so long as Iran suspends all enrichment-related and reprocessing activities, including research and development, as verified by the IAEA, to allow for negotiations;
    (b) that it shall terminate the measures specified in paragraphs 3, 4, 5, 6, 7, 10 and 12 of this resolution as soon as it determines that Iran has fully complied with its obligations under the relevant resolutions of the Security Council and met the requirements of the IAEA Board of Governors, as confirmed by the IAEA Board;
    (c) that it shall, in the event that the report in paragraph 23 above shows that Iran has not complied with this resolution, adopt further appropriate measures under Article 41 of Chapter VII of the Charter of the United Nations to persuade Iran to comply with this resolution and the requirements of the IAEA, and underlines that further decisions will be required should such additional measures be necessary;

25. *Decides* to remain seized of the matter.

Annex

A. Entities involved in the nuclear programme

1. Atomic Energy Organisation of Iran
2. Mesbah Energy Company (provider for A40 research reactor — Arak)
3. Kala-Electric (aka Kalaye Electric) (provider for PFEP — Natanz)
4. Pars Trash Company (involved in centrifuge programme, identified in IAEA reports)
5. Farayand Technique (involved in centrifuge programme, identified in IAEA reports)
6. Defence Industries Organisation (overarching MODAFL-controlled entity, some of whose subordinates have been involved in the centrifuge programme making components, and in the missile programme)
7. 7th of Tir (subordinate of DIO, widely recognized as being directly involved in the nuclear programme)

B. Entities involved in the ballistic missile programme

1. Shahid Hemmat Industrial Group (SHIG) (subordinate entity of AIO)
2. Shahid Bagheri Industrial Group (SBIG) (subordinate entity of AIO)
3. Fajr Industrial Group (formerly Instrumentation Factory Plant, subordinate entity of AIO)

C. Persons involved in the nuclear programme

1. Mohammad Qannadi, AEOI Vice President for Research & Development
2. Behman Asgarpour, Operational Manager (Arak)
3. Dawood Agha-Jani, Head of the PFEP (Natanz)
4. Ehsan Monajemi, Construction Project Manager, Natanz
5. Jafar Mohammadi, Technical Adviser to the AEOI (in charge of managing the production of valves for centrifuges)
6. Ali Hajinia Leilabadi, Director General of Mesbah Energy Company
7. Lt Gen Mohammad Mehdi Nejad Nouri, Rector of Malek Ashtar University of Defence Technology (chemistry dept, affiliated to MODALF, has conducted experiments on beryllium)

D. Persons involved in the ballistic missile programme

1. Gen Hosein Salimi, Commander of the Air Force, IRGC (Pasdaran)
2. Ahmad Vahid Dastjerdi, Head of the AIO
3. Reza-Gholi Esmaeli, Head of Trade & International Affairs Dept, AIO
4. Bahmanyar Morteza Bahmanyar, Head of Finance & Budget Dept, AIO

E. Persons involved in both the nuclear and ballistic missile programmes

1. Maj Gen Yahya Rahim Safavi, Commander, IRGC (Pasdaran)

(Source: UN Security Council.)

SPEECH BY PRESIDENT AHMADINEJAD ANNOUNCING THAT IRAN HAD SUCCESSFULLY ENRICHED URANIUM

Published below is the text of the speech delivered by Iran's President Mahmoud Ahmadinejad, to senior military officers, government officials and foreign dignitaries, in the city of Mashhad, on 11 April 2006, and broadcast live on Iranian television, in which he announced that Iran on 9 April had successfully enriched uranium for the first time and therefore had "joined the club of nuclear countries".

In the name of God, the Merciful, the Compassionate. O God! Please advance the coming of the Lord of the Age and grant us the honour of becoming his pious companions. Peace be upon Imam Reza, the son of Ali.

O the noble and honourable nation of Iran! May God's peace and greetings be upon you. Blessed be the souls of your martyrs. And may God honour the devotion of your war-disabled and war veterans. God's salutations upon our noble young people, who are pushing back the boundaries of science through their own endeavours. These youths have taken our nation to the summit of knowledge, science and global technology. And they will continue to make progress in these spheres.

Yesterday, it was thanks to the devotion of your courageous youth [serving in the Iran-Iraq war] that our dear Iran managed to scale the heights of independence and honour. And today, the beloved young people of our Islamic homeland are pressing forwad to conquer the peaks of science and technology.

The noble Iranian people deserve to be able to study science, to conduct research and to undertake selfless scientific endeavour. This is a just demand of our dear nation.

The beloved Prophet Muhammad of Islam called upon all humans to acquire knowledge and technology. In accordance with these instructions, our fine scholars and young people began extensive efforts to acquire various modern technologies. And praise be to God, they have managed to make considerable headway in medical science, engineering, aerospace and nuclear technology.

The reason for holding this glorious ceremony today is the news concerning our major progress in the field of nuclear energy. The technical report on this progress was presented to you by [the head of Iran's Atomic Energy Organization] Mr Gholamreza Aqazadeh.

Access to nuclear fuel is a national demand of the entire Iranian people. At their gatherings in cities, villages and in all parts of the world, our people—wherever they might be—have repeatedly stressed this point.

The most important manifestation of this national demand was on previous year's 22 Bahman [11 February, the anniversary of the Iranian Islamic revolution] when the people—in their tens of millions, from the cities of Iran, districts and many villages as well as various parts of the world—responded to a call by their servant. I had asked them to express their views. They voiced their decisive support and cried out their unanimous demand.

Since then, and without exception, during any event or gathering, they have stressed this legitimate demand.

On the threshold of the birthday anniversary of the honourable prophet of Islam and beside [the shrine of] Imam Reza, peace be upon him, and at this historic juncture, I would like to announce that—thanks to the blessing of His Holiness Lord of the Age, may God hasten his noble advent, and thanks to the efforts of Iranian scientists, committed and creative young people and prayers of the brave, intelligent and omnipresent people of Iran—we have completed the nuclear fuel cycle at the laboratory level and our young people enriched uranium to the enrichment level required by nuclear power plants on 20 Farvardin [9 April] of the current year, 1385.

[Chants of: "God is great", "Khamene'i is our leader", "Down with those who oppose the rule of the supreme jurisconsult", "Down with America", "Down with Britain", "Down with Israel" and other interjections.]

I am proud to announce that currently 110 tonnes of UF6 has been produced at these important plants. The Islamic Republic of Iran is currently considered the eighth country in the world to possess the technology to process uranium in a single complex. In terms of the project to produce heavy water, this is one of the world's most complex modern technologies and only a few countries have the capability to achieve it. Currently, the initial implementation of this project has commenced and the first phase of heavy water storage has begun. This important project's final storage capacity is 16 tonnes of heavy water per annum.

As far as the uranium enrichment in Natanz is concerned, this project is one of the important and sensitive stages in nuclear fuel technology and has been set up and designed to produce nuclear fuel for nuclear power. The high degree of sensitivity attached to this technology made us employ renowned experts who were skilled in all its aspects. We sought to use the most modern industries and our country's latest achievements in the project's design, construction, components manufacture, assembly and installation which are extremely sensitive.

The 20 Farvardin of 1385 is a great day. It will be chronicled in the history of Iran. It will continue to inspire this nation and will encourage this country's youth in all their endeavours.

I find it necessary at this point to highlight some aspects of this momentous event. Science and technology should serve humanity. Science must be accompanied by faith in order to serve peace, tranquillity and progress. We have repeatedly stated that we pursue only peace and stability based on faith and justice for all people. As we have always maintained, and continue so to do, our nuclear technology is designed solely for peaceful purposes. We maintain that the only people who require weapons of mass destruction are those who are stuck in a mindset dating back to 50 years ago. These are the same people who still believe that by amassing weapons of mass destruction they can force victories in political, economic and cultural fields.

This is a civilised and cultured nation. It relies on the will of its faithful youth. In order to realise its aspirations, our nation depends solely on those noble ideals and values which are deeply rooted in the Islamic and Iranian culture. The source of our nation's strength is not a nuclear arsenal. The strength of our nation stems from its deep religious faith. We have always maintained and continue to state that all of our nuclear activities, in all repects, have been within the IAEA guidelines. The agency has closely monitored all of our activities. We would like to continue our programme while being monitored by the agency. What we have achieved and continue to achieve has been and will remain within the sphere of our nation's inalienable rights. Our achievements are in accordance with the established rules and regulations including our rights as stipulated by the IAEA and the Non-Proliferation Treaty. We will continue down this route, adhering to international law and pursuing our undeniable rights, until we have produced industrial levels of fuel which we will use in our power plants.

Unfortunately, in its voyage towards progress and development, our nation has been confronted by the anger, wrongdoings and bullying of some powers. Of course, our history is filled with such events. During the movement for the nationalisation of oil, which was our nation's undeniable right, some of these powers demonstrated their opposition and impudently stood against the Iranian nation's inalienable rights. Of course—I stress this point one hundred times—this approach bore no results other than the achievement of the everlasting emnity of the Iranian nation towards them. Today, the very same people are using the same justification, language and psychological warfare and wish to prevent the Iranian nation from exercising its undeniable and inalienable rights. I advise them not to repeat their bitter experience of the past and instead to respect the Iranian nation's rights. I advise them not to create everlasting hatred towards them in Iran and other freedom-seeking nations.

We have always maintained that the development and strength of Islamic Iran aimed to serve the interests of peace, tranquillity and stability, thereby benefiting all our neighbours and the world community. The country will continue along this same path. As the representative of the people, the government fully supports the country's ulema, researchers, scientists and our talented youth who work towards advancing the country in various fields. The government fully supports their labours. As a public servant I thank all those who have played a role in achieving this victory, especially our scientists, researchers, mangers and employees of the Atomic Energy Organisation and of course Mr Aqazadeh. I ask them to use all of their abilities to move speedily towards fully realising our goal of producing nuclear fuel for use in power plants.

The government of the Islamic Republic would like to bow down before God and thank him for this great achievement and divine blessing and I would like to ask all Iranians outside and inside the country to thank God for this great blessing. I would like to thank sincerely the academics, intellectuals, foreign and domestic guests, honourable Majlis deputies and military commanders, students and the dear young people, artists, released POWs, the honourable martyrs' families, war-disabled, people from various walks of life from various parts of our Islamic homeland, and especially the leader's special representative, for taking part in this magnificent and historic meeting. I wish all the best and ever-increasing success and dignity for you and the precious Iranian nation.

(Source: Iranian television, channel 1; unofficial translation from Persian.)

UNSC RESOLUTION 1695 NON-BINDING SANCTIONS ON NORTH KOREA

Published below is the text of the UN Security Council Resolution 1695 (2006), calling on member states to prevent the transfer of missile technology to North Korea, which was adopted unanimously on 15 July 2006 in the wake of North Korea's ballistic missile tests carried out on 4 July.

Resolution 1695 (2006)

Adopted by the Security Council at its 5490th meeting, on 15 July 2006

The Security Council,

Reaffirming its resolutions 825 (1993) of 11 May 1993 and 1540 (2004) of 28 April 2004,

Bearing in mind the importance of maintaining peace and stability on the Korean peninsula and in north-east Asia at large,

Reaffirming that proliferation of nuclear, chemical and biological weapons, as well as their means of delivery, constitutes a threat to international peace and security,

Expressing grave concern at the launch of ballistic missiles by the Democratic People's Republic of Korea (DPRK), given the potential of such systems to be used as a means to deliver nuclear, chemical or biological payloads,

Registering profound concern at the DPRK's breaking of its pledge to maintain its moratorium on missile launching,

Expressing further concern that the DPRK endangered civil aviation and shipping through its failure to provide adequate advance notice,

Expressing its grave concern about DPRK's indication of possible additional launches of ballistic missiles in the near future,

Expressing also its desire for a peaceful and diplomatic solution to the situation and welcoming efforts by Council members as well as other Member States to facilitate a peaceful and comprehensive solution through dialogue,

Recalling that the DPRK launched an object propelled by a missile without prior notification to the countries in the region, which fell into the waters in the vicinity of Japan on 31 August 1998,

Deploring the DPRK's announcement of withdrawal from the Treaty on Non-Proliferation of Nuclear Weapons (the Treaty) and its stated pursuit of nuclear weapons in spite of its Treaty on Non-Proliferation of Nuclear Weapons and International Atomic Energy Agency (IAEA) safeguards obligations,

Stressing the importance of the implementation of the Joint Statement issued on 19 September 2005 by China, DPRK, Japan, Republic of Korea, the Russian Federation and the United States,

Affirming that such launches jeopardize peace, stability and security in the region and beyond, particularly in light of the DPRK's claim that it has developed nuclear weapons,

Acting under its special responsibility for the maintenance of international peace and security,

1. *Condemns* the multiple launches by the DPRK of ballistic missiles on 5 July 2006 local time;

2. *Demands* that the DPRK suspend all activities related to its ballistic missile programme, and in this context re-establish its pre-existing commitments to a moratorium on missile launching;

3. *Requires* all Member States, in accordance with their national legal authorities and legislation and consistent with international law, to exercise vigilance and prevent missile and missile-related items, materials, goods and technology being transferred to DPRK's missile or WMD programmes;

4. *Requires* all Member States, in accordance with their national legal authorities and legislation and consistent with international law, to exercise vigilance and prevent the procurement of missiles or missile related-items, materials, goods and technology from the DPRK, and the transfer of any financial resources in relation to DPRK's missile or WMD programmes;

5. *Underlines*, in particular to the DPRK, the need to show restraint and refrain from any action that might aggravate tension, and to continue to work on the resolution of non-proliferation concerns through political and diplomatic efforts;

6. *Strongly urges* the DPRK to return immediately to the Six-Party Talks without precondition, to work towards the expeditious implementation of 19 September 2005 Joint Statement, in particular to abandon all nuclear weapons and existing nuclear programmes, and to return at an early date to the Treaty on Non-Proliferation of Nuclear Weapons and International Atomic Energy Agency safeguards;

7. *Supports* the six-party talks, calls for their early resumption, and urges all the participants to intensify their efforts on the full implementation of the 19 September 2005 Joint Statement with a view to achieving the verifiable denuclearization of the Korean Peninsula in a peaceful manner and to maintaining peace and stability on the Korean Peninsula and in north-east Asia;

8. *Decides* to remain seized of the matter.

(Source: UN Security Council.)

UNSC RESOLUTION 1718 BINDING SANCTIONS ON NORTH KOREA

Published below is the text of the UN Security Council Resolution 1718 (2006), adopted on 14 October, imposing sanctions on North Korea in response to its having conducted a nuclear test on 9 October, in defiance of international calls for it to desist. The resolution did not authorise the use of armed force to enforce the sanctions, nor did it make mandatory the inspection of cargo to and from North Korea.

Resolution 1718 (2006)

Adopted by the Security Council at its 5551st meeting, on 14 October 2006

The Security Council,

Recalling its previous relevant resolutions, including resolution 825 (1993), resolution 1540 (2004) and, in particular, resolution 1695 (2006), as well as the statement of its President of 6 October 2006 (S/PRST/2006/41),

Reaffirming that proliferation of nuclear, chemical and biological weapons, as well as their means of delivery, constitutes a threat to international peace and security,

Expressing the gravest concern at the claim by the Democratic People's Republic of Korea (DPRK) that it has conducted a test of a nuclear weapon on 9 October 2006, and at the challenge such a test constitutes to the Treaty on the Non-Proliferation of Nuclear Weapons and to international efforts aimed at strengthening the global regime of non-proliferation of nuclear weapons, and the danger it poses to peace and stability in the region and beyond,

Expressing its firm conviction that the international regime on the non-proliferation of nuclear weapons should be maintained and recalling that the DPRK cannot have the status of a nuclear-weapon state in accordance with the Treaty on the Non-Proliferation of Nuclear Weapons,

Deploring the DPRK's announcement of withdrawal from the Treaty on the Non-Proliferation of Nuclear Weapons and its pursuit of nuclear weapons,
Deploring further that the DPRK has refused to return to the Six-Party talks without precondition,

Endorsing the Joint Statement issued on 19 September 2005 by China, the DPRK, Japan, the Republic of Korea, the Russian Federation and the United States,

Underlining the importance that the DPRK respond to other security and humanitarian concerns of the international community,

Expressing profound concern that the test claimed by the DPRK has generated increased tension in the region and beyond, and *determining* therefore that there is a clear threat to international peace and security,

Acting under Chapter VII of the Charter of the United Nations, and taking measures under its Article 41,

1. *Condemns* the nuclear test proclaimed by the DPRK on 9 October 2006 in flagrant disregard of its relevant resolutions, in particular resolution 1695 (2006), as well as of the statement of its President of 6 October 2006 (S/PRST/2006/41), including that such a test would bring universal condemnation of the international community and would represent a clear threat to international peace and security;

2. *Demands* that the DPRK not conduct any further nuclear test or launch of a ballistic missile;

3. *Demands* that the DPRK immediately retract its announcement of withdrawal from the Treaty on the Non-Proliferation of Nuclear Weapons;

4. *Demands* further that the DPRK return to the Treaty on the Non-Proliferation of Nuclear Weapons and International Atomic Energy Agency (IAEA) safeguards, and *underlines* the need for all States Parties to the Treaty on the Non-Proliferation of Nuclear Weapons to continue to comply with their Treaty obligations;

5. *Decides* that the DPRK shall suspend all activities related to its ballistic missile programme and in this context re-establish its pre-existing commitments to a moratorium on missile launching;

6. *Decides* that the DPRK shall abandon all nuclear weapons and existing nuclear programmes in a complete, verifiable and irreversible manner, shall act strictly in accordance with the obligations applicable to parties under the Treaty on the Non-Proliferation of Nuclear Weapons and the terms and conditions of its International Atomic Energy Agency (IAEA) Safeguards Agreement (IAEA INFCIRC/403) and shall provide the IAEA transparency measures extending beyond these requirements, including such access to individuals, documentation, equipments and facilities as may be required and deemed necessary by the IAEA;

7 *Decides* also that the DPRK shall abandon all other existing weapons of mass destruction and ballistic missile programme in a complete, verifiable and irreversible manner;

8. *Decides* that:

(a) All Member States shall prevent the direct or indirect supply, sale or transfer to the DPRK, through their territories or by their nationals, or using their flag vessels or aircraft, and whether or not originating in their territories, of:

(i) Any battle tanks, armoured combat vehicles, large calibre artillery systems, combat aircraft, attack helicopters, warships, missiles or missile systems as defined for the purpose of the United Nations Register on Conventional Arms, or related materiel including spare parts, or items as determined by the Security Council or the Committee established by paragraph 12 below (the Committee);

(ii) All items, materials, equipment, goods and technology as set out in the lists in documents S/2006/814 and S/2006/815, unless within 14 days of adoption of this resolution the Committee has amended or completed their provisions also taking into account the list in document S/2006/816, as well as other items, materials, equipment, goods and technology, determined by the Security Council or the Committee, which could contribute to DPRK's nuclear-related, ballistic missile-related or other weapons of mass destruction-related programmes;

(iii) Luxury goods;

(b) The DPRK shall cease the export of all items covered in subparagraphs (a) (i) and (a) (ii) above and that all Member States shall prohibit the procurement of such items from the DPRK by their nationals, or using their flagged vessels or aircraft, and whether or not originating in the territory of the DPRK;

(c) All Member States shall prevent any transfers to the DPRK by their nationals or from their territories, or from the DPRK by its nationals or from its territory, of technical training, advice, services or assistance related to the provision, manufacture, maintenance or use of the items in subparagraphs (a) (i) and (a) (ii) above;

(d) All Member States shall, in accordance with their respective legal processes, freeze immediately the funds, other financial assets and economic resources which are on their territories at the date of the adoption of this resolution or at any time thereafter, that are owned or controlled, directly or indirectly, by the persons or entities designated by the Committee or by the Security Council as being engaged in or providing support for, including through other illicit means, DPRK's nuclear-related, other weapons of mass destruction-related and ballistic missile-related programmes, or by persons or entities acting on their behalf or at their direction, and ensure that any funds, financial assets or economic resources are prevented from being made available by their nationals or by any persons or entities within their territories, to or for the benefit of such persons or entities;

(e) All Member States shall take the necessary steps to prevent the entry into or transit through their territories of the persons designated by the Committee or by the Security Council as being responsible for, including through supporting or promoting, DPRK policies in relation to the DPRK's nuclear-related, ballistic missile-related and other weapons of mass destruction-related programmes, together with their family members, provided that nothing in this paragraph shall oblige a state to refuse its own nationals entry into its territory;

(f) In order to ensure compliance with the requirements of this paragraph, and thereby preventing illicit trafficking in nuclear, chemical or biological weapons, their means of delivery and related materials, all Member States are called upon to take, in accordance with their national authorities and legislation, and consistent with international law, cooperative action including through inspection of cargo to and from the DPRK, as necessary;

9. *Decides* that the provisions of paragraph 8 (d) above do not apply to financial or other assets or resources that have been determined by relevant States:

(a) To be necessary for basic expenses, including payment for foodstuffs, rent or mortgage, medicines and medical treatment, taxes, insurance premiums, and public utility charges, or exclusively for payment of reasonable professional fees and reimbursement of incurred expenses associated with the provision of legal services, or fees or service charges, in accordance with national laws, for routine holding or maintenance of frozen funds, other financial assets and economic resources, after notification by the relevant States to the Committee of the intention to authorize, where appropriate, access to such funds, other financial assets and economic resources and in the absence of a negative decision by the Committee within five working days of such notification;

(b) To be necessary for extraordinary expenses, provided that such determination has been notified by the relevant States to the Committee and has been approved by the Committee; or

(c) To be subject of a judicial, administrative or arbitral lien or judgement, in which case the funds, other financial assets and economic resources may be used to satisfy that lien or judgement provided that the lien or judgement was entered prior to the date of the present resolution, is not for the benefit of a person referred to in paragraph 8 (d) above or an individual or entity identified by the Security Council or the Committee, and has been notified by the relevant States to the Committee;

10. *Decides* that the measures imposed by paragraph 8 (e) above shall not apply where the Committee determines on a case-by-case basis that such travel is justified on the grounds of humanitarian need, including religious obligations, or where the Committee concludes that an exemption would otherwise further the objectives of the present resolution;

11. *Calls upon* all Member States to report to the Security Council within thirty days of the adoption of this resolution on the steps they have taken with a view to implementing effectively the provisions of paragraph 8 above;

12. *Decides* to establish, in accordance with rule 28 of its provisional rules of procedure, a Committee of the Security Council consisting of all the members of the Council, to undertake the following tasks:

    (a) To seek from all States, in particular those producing or possessing the items, materials, equipment, goods and technology referred to in paragraph 8 (a) above, information regarding the actions taken by them to implement effectively the measures imposed by paragraph 8 above of this resolution and whatever further information it may consider useful in this regard;

    (b) To examine and take appropriate action on information regarding alleged violations of measures imposed by paragraph 8 of this resolution;

    (c) To consider and decide upon requests for exemptions set out in paragraphs 9 and 10 above;

    (d) To determine additional items, materials, equipment, goods and technology to be specified for the purpose of paragraphs 8 (a) (i) and 8 (a) (ii) above;

    (e) To designate additional individuals and entities subject to the measures imposed by paragraphs 8 (d) and 8 (e) above;

    (f) To promulgate guidelines as may be necessary to facilitate the implementation of the measures imposed by this resolution;

    (g) To report at least every 90 days to the Security Council on its work, with its observations and recommendations, in particular on ways to strengthen the effectiveness of the measures imposed by paragraph 8 above;

13. *Welcomes and encourages further* the efforts by all States concerned to intensify their diplomatic efforts, to refrain from any actions that might aggravate tension and to facilitate the early resumption of the Six-Party Talks, with a view to the expeditious implementation of the Joint Statement issued on 19 September 2005 by China, the DPRK, Japan, the Republic of Korea, the Russian Federation and the United States, to achieve the verifiable denuclearization of the Korean Peninsula and to maintain peace and stability on the Korean Peninsula and in north-east Asia;

14. *Calls upon* the DPRK to return immediately to the Six-Party Talks without precondition and to work towards the expeditious implementation of the Joint Statement issued on 19 September 2005 by China, the DPRK, Japan, the Republic of Korea, the Russian Federation and the United States;

15. *Affirms* that it shall keep DPRK's actions under continuous review and that it shall be prepared to review the appropriateness of the measures contained in paragraph 8 above, including the strengthening, modification, suspension or lifting of the measures, as may be needed at that time in light of the DPRK's compliance with the provisions of the resolution;

16. *Underlines* that further decisions will be required, should additional measures be necessary;

17. *Decides* to remain actively seized of the matter.

(Source: UN Security Council.)

DECLARATION OF INDEPENDENCE BY THE REPUBLIC OF MONTENEGRO

Published below is the declaration of independence by the government of the Republic of Montenegro, on 3 June 2006, following the referendum (held on 21 May 2006) in which a majority voted for dissolution of the union with Serbia, the last residue of the former Yugoslavia.

3 June 2006

Declaration of the Government of the Republic of Montenegro addressed to the citizens of Montenegro

Proceeding from the unanimously adopted Decision on Calling for the Referendum on State-Legal Status of the Republic of Montenegro, and constitutional authorizations and responsibilities it has in state-creation process;

Respecting the inalienable right of citizens to the self-determination and creation of an independent state and historic continuum of the Montenegrin statehood, acquired in the century lasting fight for freedom;

Respecting fundamentals contained in documents of the United Nations Organization, Council of Europe, European Union, the Constitutional Charter of the state union Serbia and Montenegro and the Constitution of the Republic of Montenegro and in accordance with the internationally recognized standards;

The Government of the Republic of Montenegro addresses to the citizens of Montenegro

DECLARATION

Free expressed will of citizens is a basis for creation of an independent and internationally recognized State of Montenegro. It shall be the heritage of all citizens of Montenegro regardless of their political or any other choice.

Independent State is a precondition for citizens to decide about themselves and their future. It is a guarantor of the economic prosperity based on respect and protection of ownership rights and freedom of entrepreneurship, as well as realization of the rule of law principle and faster inclusion of Montenegro in the European and Euro-Atlantic Integrations.

Montenegro as a democratic State will be developed based on the respect of human rights and freedoms, respecting all internationally recognized standards, social justice and equality of all citizens. The State of Montenegro will create conditions for rational and efficient use of natural, human and all other potentials with the aim to increase the standard of living to the one adequate the Europe of the 21st Century.

With the aim of creating advanced and rich society, the state will create conditions for the provision of equal opportunities for all of its citizens, and, in particular, the promotion of the young and talented persons. In particular, it shall provide all pre- conditions for education of young people in accordance with their interests and the needs of Montenegro. The state of Montenegro will provide all regular students from Montenegro, who have initiated the studies in Serbia, with the necessary conditions for completion of their education, in the case they are put in unfavorable situation due to the change of the state legal status.

Continuing the tradition and promoting Montenegro as multi-ethnic, multi-confession and multi-cultural society, the consistent provision and protection of minority rights and freedoms will be provided for, according to the highest international standards.

Institutionally and by measures of the current policy, Montenegro will make even better the cooperation with Diaspora and create conditions for its full participation within the social and economic life of Montenegro.

As an independent state, Montenegro will continue amicable and close cooperation with Serbia. In reaching that goal, Montenegro will have an open border with Serbia, in order to provide for free flow of people, goods, services and capital, with no administrative barriers.

As part of the family of European states, Montenegro will be amicable and peaceably open toward other states and particularly toward its neighbors.

Strategic interest of Montenegro remains the European Union and NATO membership. It will be accomplished by a consistent realization of all standards at the political, economic and security plan, which are conditions to the European and Euro-Atlantic integrations.

Democratic achievement of the state independence of Montenegro is the base to overcome its historical, inherited and current divisions. The modern state of Montenegro will be a democratic community of all its citizens and equal entity in the European family of states.

(Source: Parliament of Montenegro official website.)

STERN REVIEW: THE ECONOMICS OF CLIMATE CHANGE:

Published below is the summary of the conclusions of the Stern Review: The Economics of Climate Change, *carried out by Sir Nicholas Stern, head of the UK government's economic service and former World Bank chief economist. The review, published on 30 October 2006, was commissioned by UK Chancellor of the Exchequer Gordon Brown in July 2005. The review estimated that the dangers of uncontrolled climate change could cost the equivalent of 20 per cent of global GDP annually, but that the cost of taking action to move to a low-carbon economy could be around 1 per cent of global GDP annually.*

SUMMARY OF CONCLUSIONS

There is still time to avoid the worst impacts of climate change, if we take strong action now.

The scientific evidence is now overwhelming: climate change is a serious global threat, and it demands an urgent global response.

This Review has assessed a wide range of evidence on the impacts of climate change and on the economic costs, and has used a number of different techniques to assess costs and risks. From all of these perspectives, the evidence gathered by the Review leads to a simple conclusion: the benefits of strong and early action far outweigh the economic costs of not acting.

Climate change will affect the basic elements of life for people around the world - access to water, food production, health, and the environment. Hundreds of millions of people could suffer hunger, water shortages and coastal flooding as the world warms.

Using the results from formal economic models, the Review estimates that if we don't act, the overall costs and risks of climate change will be equivalent to losing at least 5% of global GDP each year, now and forever. If a wider range of risks and impacts is taken into account, the estimates of damage could rise to 20% of GDP or more.

In contrast, the costs of action - reducing greenhouse gas emissions to avoid the worst impacts of climate change - can be limited to around 1% of global GDP each year.

The investment that takes place in the next 10-20 years will have a profound effect on the climate in the second half of this century and in the next. Our actions now and over the coming decades could create risks of major disruption to economic and social activity, on a scale similar to those associated with the great wars and the economic depression of the first half of the 20th century. And it will be difficult or impossible to reverse these changes.
So prompt and strong action is clearly warranted. Because climate change is a global problem, the response to it must be international. It must be based on a shared vision of long-term goals and agreement on frameworks that will accelerate action over the next decade, and it must build on mutually reinforcing approaches at national, regional and international level.

Climate change could have very serious impacts on growth and development.

If no action is taken to reduce emissions, the concentration of greenhouse gases in the atmosphere could reach double its pre-industrial level as early as 2035, virtually committing us to a global average temperature rise of over 2°C. In the longer term, there would be more than a 50% chance that the temperature rise would exceed 5°C. This rise would be very dangerous indeed; it is equivalent to the change in average temperatures from the last ice age to today. Such a radical change in the physical geography of the world must lead to major changes in the human geography - where people live and how they live their lives.

Even at more moderate levels of warming, all the evidence - from detailed studies of regional and sectoral impacts of changing weather patterns through to economic models of the global effects - shows that climate change will have serious impacts on world output, on human life and on the environment.

All countries will be affected. The most vulnerable - the poorest countries and populations - will suffer earliest and most, even though they have contributed least to the causes of climate change. The costs of extreme weather, including floods, droughts and storms, are already rising, including for rich countries.

Adaptation to climate change - that is, taking steps to build resilience and minimise costs - is essential. It is no longer possible to prevent the climate change that will take place over the next two to three decades, but it is still possible to protect our societies and economies from its impacts to some extent - for example, by providing better information, improved planning and more climate-resilient crops and infrastructure. Adaptation will cost tens of billions of dollars a year in developing countries alone, and will put still further pressure on already scarce resources. Adaptation efforts, particularly in developing countries, should be accelerated.

The costs of stabilising the climate are significant but manageable; delay would be dangerous and much more costly.

The risks of the worst impacts of climate change can be substantially reduced if greenhouse gas levels in the atmosphere can be stabilised between 450 and 550ppm CO2 equivalent (CO2e). The current level is 430ppm CO2e today, and it is rising at more than 2ppm each year. Stabilisation in this range would require emissions to be at least 25% below current levels by 2050, and perhaps much more.

Ultimately, stabilisation - at whatever level - requires that annual emissions be brought down to more than 80% below current levels.

This is a major challenge, but sustained long-term action can achieve it at costs that are low in comparison to the risks of inaction. Central estimates of the annual costs of achieving stabilisation between 500 and 550ppm CO2e are around 1% of global GDP, if we start to take strong action now.

Costs could be even lower than that if there are major gains in efficiency, or if the strong co-benefits, for example from reduced air pollution, are measured. Costs will be higher if innovation in low-carbon technologies is slower than expected, or if policy-makers fail to make the most of economic instruments that allow emissions to be reduced whenever, wherever and however it is cheapest to do so.

It would already be very difficult and costly to aim to stabilise at 450ppm CO2e. If we delay, the opportunity to stabilise at 500-550ppm CO2e may slip away.

Action on climate change is required across all countries, and it need not cap the aspirations for growth of rich or poor countries.

The costs of taking action are not evenly distributed across sectors or around the world. Even if the rich world takes on responsibility for absolute cuts in emissions of 60-80% by 2050, developing countries must take significant action too. But developing countries should not be required to bear the full costs of this action alone, and they will not have to. Carbon markets in rich countries are already beginning to deliver flows of finance to support low-carbon development, including through the Clean

Development Mechanism. A transformation of these flows is now required to support action on the scale required.

Action on climate change will also create significant business opportunities, as new markets are created in low-carbon energy technologies and other low-carbon goods and services. These markets could grow to be worth hundreds of billions of dollars each year, and employment in these sectors will expand accordingly.

The world does not need to choose between averting climate change and promoting growth and development. Changes in energy technologies and in the structure of economies have created opportunities to decouple growth from greenhouse gas emissions. Indeed, ignoring climate change will eventually damage economic growth.

Tackling climate change is the pro-growth strategy for the longer term, and it can be done in a way that does not cap the aspirations for growth of rich or poor countries.

A range of options exists to cut emissions; strong, deliberate policy action is required to motivate their take-up.

Emissions can be cut through increased energy efficiency, changes in demand, and through adoption of clean power, heat and transport technologies. The power sector around the world would need to be at least 60% decarbonised by 2050 for atmospheric concentrations to stabilise at or below 550ppm CO2e, and deep emissions cuts will also be required in the transport sector.

Even with very strong expansion of the use of renewable energy and other low-carbon energy sources, fossil fuels could still make up over half of global energy supply in 2050. Coal will continue to be important in the energy mix around the world, including in fast-growing economies. Extensive carbon capture and storage will be necessary to allow the continued use of fossil fuels without damage to the atmosphere.

Cuts in non-energy emissions, such as those resulting from deforestation and from agricultural and industrial processes, are also essential.

With strong, deliberate policy choices, it is possible to reduce emissions in both developed and developing economies on the scale necessary for stabilisation in the required range while continuing to grow.

Climate change is the greatest market failure the world has ever seen, and it interacts with other market imperfections. Three elements of policy are required for an effective global response. The first is the pricing of carbon, implemented through tax, trading or regulation. The second is policy to support innovation and the deployment of low-carbon technologies. And the third is action to remove barriers to energy efficiency, and to inform, educate and persuade individuals about what they can do to respond to climate change.

Climate change demands an international response, based on a shared understanding of long-term goals and agreement on frameworks for action.

Many countries and regions are taking action already: the EU, California and China are among those with the most ambitious policies that will reduce greenhouse gas emissions. The UN Framework Convention on Climate Change and the Kyoto Protocol provide a basis for international co-operation, along with a range of partnerships and other approaches. But more ambitious action is now required around the world.

Countries facing diverse circumstances will use different approaches to make their contribution to tackling climate change. But action by individual countries is not enough. Each country, however large, is just a part of the problem. It is essential to create a shared international vision of long-term goals, and to build the international frameworks that will help each country to play its part in meeting these common goals.

Key elements of future international frameworks should include:

- *Emissions trading:* Expanding and linking the growing number of emissions trading schemes around the world is a powerful way to promote cost-effective reductions in emissions and to bring forward action in developing countries: strong targets in rich countries could drive flows amounting to tens of billions of dollars each year to support the transition to low-carbon development paths.

- *Technology cooperation:* Informal co-ordination as well as formal agreements can boost the effectiveness of investments in innovation around the world. Globally, support for energy R&D should at least double, and support for the deployment of new low-carbon technologies should increase up to five-fold. International cooperation on product standards is a powerful way to boost energy efficiency.

- *Action to reduce deforestation:* The loss of natural forests around the world contributes more to global emissions each year than the transport sector. Curbing deforestation is a highly cost-effective way to reduce emissions; large-scale international pilot programmes to explore the best ways to do this could get underway very quickly.

- *Adaptation:* The poorest countries are most vulnerable to climate change. It is essential that climate change be fully integrated into development policy, and that rich countries honour their pledges to increase support through overseas development assistance. International funding should also support improved regional information on climate change impacts, and research into new crop varieties that will be more resilient to drought and flood.

(Source: UK Cabinet Office.)

UNITED KINGDOM LABOUR GOVERNMENT

(as at 31 December 2006)

Members of the Cabinet

Prime Minister, First Lord of the Treasury and Minister for the Civil Service	Rt Hon. Tony Blair, MP
Deputy Prime Minister and First Secretary of State	Rt Hon. John Prescott, MP
Chancellor of the Exchequer	Rt Hon. Gordon Brown, MP
Leader of the House of Commons, Lords Reform and Party Funding	Rt Hon. Jack Straw, MP
Secretary of State for Foreign and Commonwealth Affairs	Rt Hon. Margaret Beckett, MP
Secretary of State for Trade and Industry	Rt Hon. Alistair Darling, MP
Secretary of State for the Home Department	Rt Hon. Dr John Reid, MP
Secretary of State for Health	Rt Hon. Patricia Hewitt, MP
Secretary of State for Culture, Media and Sport	Rt Hon. Tessa Jowell, MP
Cabinet Office Minister and for Social Exclusion and Chancellor of the Duchy of Lancaster	Rt Hon. Hilary Armstrong, MP
Secretary of State for Northern Ireland and Secretary of State for Wales	Rt Hon. Peter Hain, MP
Leader of the House of Lords and Lord President of the Council	Rt Hon. Baroness Amos
Secretary of State for Constitutional Affairs and Lord Chancellor	Rt Hon. Lord Falconer of Thoroton, QC
Secretary of State for International Development	Rt Hon. Hilary Benn, MP
Secretary of State for Education and Skills	Rt Hon. Alan Johnson, MP
Secretary of State for Communities and Local Government	Rt Hon. Ruth Kelly, MP
Secretary of State for Work and Pensions	Rt Hon. John Hutton, MP
Secretary of State for Environment, Food and Rural Affairs	Rt Hon David Miliband, MP
Secretary of State for Defence	Rt Hon. Des Browne, MP
Secretary of State for Transport and Secretary of State for Scotland	Rt Hon. Douglas Alexander, MP
Minister without Portfolio	Rt Hon. Hazel Blears, MP
Parliamentary Secretary to the Treasury and Chief Whip	Rt Hon. Jacqui Smith, MP
Chief Secretary to the Treasury	Rt Hon. Stephen Timms, MP

Also attending Cabinet

Minister for Europe in the Foreign and Commonwealth Office	Rt Hon. Geoff Hoon, MP
Minister for Trade in the Foreign and Commonwealth Office and the Department for Trade and Industry	Rt Hon. Ian McCartney MP
Lords Chief Whip, and Captain of the Gentlemen-at-Arms	Rt Hon. The Lord Grocott
Attorney General	Rt Hon. The Lord Goldsmith, QC

UNITED STATES REPUBLICAN ADMINISTRATION

(as at 31 December 2006)

Members of the Cabinet

President	George W. Bush
Vice President	Richard B. Cheney
Secretary of Agriculture	Mike. Johanns
Secretary of Commerce	Carlos Gutierrez
Secretary of Defence	Robert M. Gates
Secretary of Education	Margaret Spellings
Secretary of Energy	Samuel W. Bodman
Secretary of Health and Human Services	Michael O. Leavitt
Secretary of Homeland Security	Michael Chertoff
Secretary of Housing and Urban Development	Alphonso Jackson
Secretary of Interior	Dirk Kempthorne
Attorney General and Head of Department of Justice	Alberto Gonzales
Secretary of Labour	Elaine Chao
Secretary of State	Condoleezza Rice
Secretary of Transportation	Mary E. Peters
Secretary of the Treasury	Henry M. Paulson, Jr
Secretary of Veterans' Affairs	Jim Nicholson

Cabinet Rank Members

Director of Office of Management and Budget	Rob Portman
Administrator of Environmental Protection Agency	Stephen Johnson
White House Chief of Staff	Joshua B. Bolten
United States Trade Representative	Ambassador Susan Schwab
Director of Office of National Drug Control Policy	John Walters

Other Leading Executive Branch Officials

Chairman of Council of Economic Advisers	Edward P. Lazear
Chairman of Council on Environmental Quality	James L. Connaughton
Director of Domestic Policy Council	Karl Zinsmeister
Homeland Security Adviser	Frances Fragos Townsend
Director of National Economic Council	Allan Hubbard
National Security Adviser	Stephen J. Hadley
Director of White House Office of Faith Based and Community Initiatives	Jay Hein
Director of Office of National AIDS policy	vacant
Director of White House Office of National Drug Control Policy	John P. Walters
Director of Office of Science and Technology Policy	John Marburger
Chairman of President's Foreign Intelligence Advisory Board	Stephen Friedman
Chairwoman of Privacy and Civil Liberties Oversight Board	Carol E. Dinkins
Director of USA Freedom Corps	Desiree T. Sayle
Director of White House Military Office	Rear Adml Mark I. Fox
Director of Central Intelligence Agency	Gen. Michael V. Hayden
Director of National Intelligence	John D. Negroponte

MEMBERS OF THE EUROPEAN COMMISSION

(as at 31 December 2006)

Members of the European Commission, 2004-2009

José Manuel Durão Barroso (Portugal)	*President*
Margot Wallström (Sweden)	*First Vice-President; Institutional Relations & Communication Strategy*
Günter Verheugen (Germany)	*Vice-President; Enterprise & Industry*
Jacques Barrot (France)	*Vice-President; Transport*
Siim Kallas (Estonia)	*Vice-President; Administrative Affairs, Audit, & Anti-Fraud*
Franco Frattini (Italy)	*Vice-President; Justice, Freedom, & Security*
Viviane Reding (Luxembourg)	*Information Society & Media*
Stavros Dimas (Greece)	*Environment*
Joaquín Almunia (Spain)	*Economic & Financial Affairs*
Danuta Hübner (Poland)	*Regional Policy*
Joe Borg (Malta)	*Fisheries & Maritime Affairs*
Dalia Grybauskait (Lithuania)	*Financial Programming & the Budget*
Janez Potonik (Slovenia)	*Science & Research*
Ján Figel (Slovakia)	*Education, Training & Culture*
Markos Kyprianou (Cyprus)	*Health*
Olli Rehn (Finland)	*Enlargement*
Louis Michel (Belgium)	*Development & Humanitarian Aid*
László Kovács (Hungary)	*Taxation & Customs Union*
Neelie Kroes (Netherlands)	*Competition*
Mariann Fischer Boel (Denmark)	*Agriculture & Rural Development*
Benita Ferrero-Waldner (Austria)	*External Relations & European Neighbourhood Policy*
Charlie McCreevy (Ireland)	*Internal Market & Services*
Vladimír Špidla (Czech Republic)	*Employment, Social Affairs, & Equal Opportunities*
Peter Mandelson (UK)	*Trade*
Andris Piebalgs (Latvia)	*Energy*

NOBEL LAUREATES 2006

PHYSICS

John C. Mather, USA, b. 1946, NASA Goddard Space Flight Center, Greenbelt, MD, USA (1/2 of the prize)

George F. Smoot, USA, b. 1945, University of California, Berkeley, CA, USA (1/2 of the prize)

"for their discovery of the blackbody form and anisotropy of the cosmic microwave background radiation"

CHEMISTRY

Roger D. Kornberg, USA, b. 1947, Stanford University, Stanford, CA, USA

"for his studies of the molecular basis of eukaryotic transcription"

PHYSIOLOGY OR MEDICINE

Andrew Z. Fire, USA, b. 1959, Stanford University School of Medicine, Stanford, CA, USA; and Craig C. Mello, USA, b. 1960, University of Massachusetts Medical School, Worcester, MA, USA

"for their discovery of RNA interference - gene silencing by double-stranded RNA"

LITERATURE

Orhan Pamuk, Turkey, b. 1952

"who in the quest for the melancholic soul of his native city has discovered new symbols for the clash and interlacing of cultures"

PEACE

Muhammad Yunus, Bangladesh, b. 1940, founder of Grameen Bank (1/2 of the prize); and
Grameen Bank Dhaka, Bangladesh, Founded in 1976 (1/2 of the prize)

"for their efforts to create economic and social development from below"

ECONOMICS

Edmund S. Phelps, USA, b. 1933, Columbia University, New York, NY, USA

"for his analysis of intertemporal tradeoffs in macroeconomic policy"

(Source: the Nobel Foundation official website.)

INTERNATIONAL COMPARISONS: POPULATION, GDP AND GROWTH (2006)

The following table gives population, gross domestic product (GDP) and growth data for the main member states of the Organisation for Economic Co-operation and Development plus selected other countries. (Source: World Bank, Washington DC.)

	Population		**GDP ($000mn)**		**GDP growth %**	
	2005 mn	Avg. annual % growth 1990-2004	2004	2005	2004-2005	Avg. annual % growth 2000-2004
Algeria	32.9	1.8	84.6	102.3	20.92	4.8
Argentina	38.7	1.2	153.0	183.2	19.74	-0.1
Australia	20.3	1.2	637.3	732.5	14.94	3.5
Austria	8.2	0.4	292.3	306.1	4.72	1.2
Bangladesh	141.8	2.1	56.6	60.0	6.01	5.2
Belgium	10.5	0.3	352.3	370.8	5.25	1.4
Brazil	186.4	1.5	604.0	796.1	31.80	2.0
Canada	32.3	1.0	978.0	1,113.8	13.89	2.6
Chile	16.3	1.4	94.1	115.2	22.42	3.7
China	1,304.5	0.9	1,931.7	2,234.3	15.66	9.4
Colombia	45.6	1.8	97.7	122.3	25.18	2.9
Denmark	5.4	0.4	241.4	258.7	7.17	1.1
Egypt	74.0	1.9	78.8	89.4	13.45	3.4
Finland	5.2	0.3	185.9	193.2	3.93	2.3
France	60.9	0.4	2,046.6	2,126.6	3.91	1.5
Germany	82.5	0.3	2,740.6	2,794.9	1.98	0.6
Greece	11.1	0.6	205.2	225.2	9.75	4.2
Hungary	10.1	-0.2	100.7	109.2	8.44	4.0
India	1,094.6	1.7	691.2	805.7	16.57	6.2
Indonesia	220.6	1.4	257.6	287.2	11.49	4.6
Iran	68.3	1.5	163.4	189.8	16.16	6.0
Irish Republic	4.2	1.1	181.6	201.8	11.12	5.1
Italy	58.6	0.1	1,677.8	1,762.5	5.05	0.8
Japan	127.8	0.2	4,622.7	4,534.0	-1.92	0.9
Kenya	34.3	2.5	16.1	18.7	16.15	2.7
South Korea	48.3	0.8	679.7	787.6	15.87	4.7
Malaysia	25.3	2.4	118.3	130.3	10.14	4.4
Mexico	103.1	1.6	676.5	768.4	13.58	1.5
Netherlands	16.3	0.6	579.0	624.2	7.81	0.5
New Zealand	4.1	1.2	99.0	109.3	10.40	4.0
Nigeria	131.5	2.5	72.1	99.0	37.31	5.4
Norway	4.6	0.6	250.1	295.5	18.15	1.6
Pakistan	155.8	2.4	96.1	110.7	15.19	4.1
Philippines	83.1	2.1	84.6	99.0	17.02	3.9
Poland	38.2	0.0	242.3	303.2	25.13	2.8
Portugal	10.5	0.4	167.7	183.3	9.30	0.3
Russia	143.1	-0.2	581.4	763.7	31.36	6.1
South Africa	46.9	1.8	212.8	239.5	12.55	3.2
Spain	43.4	0.7	1,040.0	1,124.6	8.13	3.0
Sweden	9.0	0.4	346.4	357.7	3.26	2.0
Switzerland	7.4	0.7	357.5	367.0	2.66	0.6
Thailand	64.2	1.1	161.7	176.6	9.21	5.4
Turkey	72.1	1.7	302.8	362.5	19.72	4.2
United Kingdom	60.2	0.3	2,124.4	2,198.8	3.50	2.3
USA	296.4	1.2	11,711.8	12,416.5	6.02	2.5
Venezuela	26.6	2.0	110.1	140.2	27.34	-1.2
Vietnam	83.1	1.5	45.2	52.4	4.97	7.2

XIX OBITUARY

Ackner, Lord (b. 1920), British barrister who became a Lord of Appeal in Ordinary. Educated at Highgate school in London and Clare College, Cambridge, he came into the public eye with a series of conspicuous libel actions and during the public inquiry into the Aberfan disaster of 1966, when a coal tip slid over a Welsh village school, killing 144 people, most of them children. Representing the families of the victims, Ackner accused the National Coal Board of callous indifference and won compensation for his clients. He was appointed to the High Court in 1971, to the Court of Appeal in 1980 and six years later to the House of Lords where, in spite of his conservative leanings, he was quick to condemn the Conservative government for actions which he believed would prejudice the administration of justice. He retired in 1992. Died 21 March.

Altman, Robert (b. 1925), US film director whose large output included some disasters as well as a number of critical and popular successes, notably *M*A*S*H.* Born in Kansas City and educated in local Jesuit schools, he served as a pilot during the war, later studying engineering at the University of Missouri. He began his cinematic career with a series of industrial films before making his first feature, *The Delinquents*, in 1955. His next, *The James Dean Story*, a documentary, was less successful but secured him a television series with Alfred Hitchcock before he returned to Hollywood where, in 1970, he directed *M*A*S*H.* An acronym for Mobile Army Surgical Hospital, the film was set in the Korean War and became Altman's first big success. It led to a long-running television series, with which he was not involved, though it enabled him to set up his own production company. In 1975 he directed *Nashville*, a pastiche set in the US city of country music, followed by a series of less memorable films until *The Player* (1990), a satire on Hollywood, and *Gosford Park* (2001), for which Altman received his fifth unsuccessful Oscar nomination. He was finally awarded an Oscar, for lifetime achievement, in 2006. Died 20 November.

al-Zarqawi, Abu Musab (b. 1966), Jordanian-born terrorist who was killed by a US air strike in Iraq. Born in a mining town north of Amman, his real name was Ahmed Fadeel Nazal al-Khalayleh and as a youth he earned a reputation as a petty criminal and street-fighter. In 1989 he went to Afghanistan for training in guerrilla warfare against the occupying Soviet forces. After returning to Jordan, he was imprisoned in 1996 on terrorism charges but pardoned in 1999 by King Abdullah II in a goodwill gesture to the king's Islamic opponents. Adopting his nom-de-guerre and reportedly financed by al-Qaida leader Osama bin Laden, al-Zarqawi operated in a number of Middle Eastern countries before ending up in Iraq as leader of Sunni terrorists responsible, among other atrocities, for the destruction of the United Nations headquarters in Baghdad and the Shi'ite shrine of Najaf. He also organised the abduction and beheading of foreign workers in Iraq and the suicide bombing of hotels in Amman. He received three death sentences (in absentia) in Jordan and at the time of his death was the "most wanted" man in Iraq. Died 7 June.

Arnold, Sir Malcolm, CBE, (b. 1921), English composer of nine symphonies, more than 100 other orchestral and choral works, some 80 film scores and many other compositions that defied classification. Born in Northampton, he was educated privately and introduced to music by his parents. He won a scholarship to the Royal College of Music in 1938 and three years later joined the London Philharmonic Orchestra, playing the trumpet. After service in the army as a bandsman he returned to the LPO, abandoning the trumpet to concentrate on composing. By the end of 1949 he had completed a clarinet concerto, a suite for the National Youth Orchestra and his first symphony. In 1952 he finished his second symphony, in 1953 a ballet for Sadler's Wells coronation season, *Homage to the Queen*, and in the course of the next few years completed three more symphonies, several concertos, three more ballets, and several operas. He also found time to write film scores (winning an Oscar for his music for *The Bridge on the River Kwai*) and some light-hearted compositions, including an overture for three vacuum cleaners, floor polisher, four rifles and orchestra. This musical virtuosity and lack of seriousness roused some critical disapproval, as sometimes did his erratic behaviour. He suffered from schizophrenia, bouts of depression, alcoholism and suicidal tendencies which led to periods in hospital and a mental institution. In his final years, cared for by his personal assistant, his circumstances improved and his music became more widely appreciated and understood. Appointed CBE in 1970, he was knighted in 1993. Died 23 September.

Babic, Milan (b. 1956), founder and leader of the Serb Republic of Krajina in Croatia, during the disintegration of Yugoslavia, who committed suicide after its failure. Born in the village of Kukor, he graduated as a dentist from Belgrade university in 1981 but later became politically involved with the creation of the Serbian Democratic Party, arming the local Serbs and setting up Krajina as a state within a state. His administration expelled thousands of Croats from the region and defied both Slobodan Milosevic and the UN until, in 1995, Croat forces finally moved in. Babic fled and retired to run a chicken farm, but was sentenced to 13 years' imprisonment. He gave evidence against Milosevic at the international war crimes tribunal in The Hague, and after returning there to give further evidence, he hanged himself in his cell. Died 5 March.

Banks, Tony (Lord Stratford) (b. 1943), Labour MP and former minister of sport and heritage whose sharp tongue and rebellious nature virtually guaranteed a swift return to the back benches. Though regularly campaigning for the abolition of the House of Lords he accepted a peerage on retiring from the House of Commons, but wished to continue to be known as Tony Banks. Born in Belfast, he was educated in England, first at a primary school in Brixton, then at a grammar school in Kennington, at York university, and at the London School of Economics. He became a member of the Greater London Council in 1970 and was its chairman 16 years later, shortly before it was abolished. In 1983 he was elected MP for Newham North West, soon making a reputation for himself by asking more questions, on more subjects, than any other MP. Appointed sports minister in Tony Blair's first government, he described the post as "not so much a job as a sending to heaven without having to die first". He resigned after two years. Died 8 January.

Badawi, Zaki (b. 1922), Muslim community leader and teacher who founded the Muslim College in London and used his position as its principal to speak out against violence and terrorism. Born in Egypt, he studied at al-Azhar university in Cairo and taught there before moving to the UK in 1951 to study at University College London. From there he took on a number of academic posts in Malaya and Nigeria until appointed director of the Islamic Cultural Centre and chief imam of the London Central Mosque. He was elected chairman of the Imams and Mosque Council of the UK in 1984, setting up the Muslim College two years later. He consistently argued that the true teachings of the Koran were incompatible with terrorism. He was awarded an honorary knighthood in 2004. Died 24 January.

Baker, Alice (b. 1898), served as a member of an all-female company of the Royal Flying Corps during World War I. Born in Costessey, near Norwich, she joined the Women's Army Auxiliary Corps in 1916 and was then attached to a Royal Flying Corps unit based in Dover where she served for most of the war assisting in the repair of aircraft. After the war she married and lived for the remainder of her life in Norfolk. She was the last surviving woman to have served in uniform in the Great War and her death left 10 known surviving veterans of the conflict. Died 27 February.

Basayev, Shamil (b. 1965), Chechen rebel leader who admitted acts of terrorism that led to the deaths of many innocent people. Born in Vedeno to a family with a history of resistance to Soviet control, Basayev was educated locally and at the Moscow Engineering Institute, from which he was expelled. After selling computers in Moscow for a time, he returned to Chechnya in 1981 when Djokar Dudayev unilaterally declared its independence. He took control of the Chechnyan forces when the Russians finally moved troops in to reassert their authority, successfully driving them out of the capital, Grozny, for a time. But when in 1999 he attacked the neighbouring territory of Daghestan he was defeated and driven out, thereafter resorting to acts of terrorism. He claimed responsibility for the theatre siege in Moscow in 2002, when 130 hostages were killed, and the Beslan school siege of 2004 when more than 300 people were killed, many of them children. Basayev was killed near the Chechen border, apparently by Russian special forces. Died 10 July.

Bentsen, Lloyd (b. 1921), US senator who, as treasury secretary in the early years of President Bill Clinton's administration, imposed financial discipline which helped to secure the country's economic strength. Born in Mission, Texas, Bentsen was educated locally and at the University of Texas, where he studied law. He served in the US Army Air Corps from 1942, becoming a Texas county judge after the war before being elected to the House of Representatives in 1948. He left Congress in 1954 to make money with a financial services business, returning to politics in 1970 when he stood successfully as Democratic Senator for Texas. He was chairman of the Senate finance committee from 1986 to 1992, and ran as the Democratic vice-presidential candidate in the unsuccessful Michael Dukakis campaign of 1988. Under pressure to run for the presidency in 1992 he decided against, campaigning instead for Clinton and being rewarded with the post of treasury secretary when Clinton was elected president. Bentsen successfully imposed a rigorous economic strategy on the new administration, based on a stringent control of the public deficit. He resigned in 1994 to become partner in a law firm. He was awarded the Presidential Medal of Freedom in 1999. He was widely remembered for his remark to his vice presidential rival in the 1988 election, Dan Quayle, who had likened himself to President John F. Kennedy in a televised debate. Bentsen's crushing response was: "Senator, I served with Jack Kennedy. I knew Jack Kennedy. Jack Kennedy was a friend of mine. Senator, you're no Jack Kennedy." Died 23 May.

Blow, Sandra (b.1925), English artist whose bold abstract paintings, many based on collages, are held in many international galleries and private collections. Born in London she enrolled at the age of 15 at St Martin's School of Art in London where she stayed for five years. Later she moved to the Royal Academy Schools and then to the Accademia di Belle Arti in Rome. Here she met the artist Alberto Burri, who introduced her to abstract art. She held her first exhibition at Gimpel Fils in London in 1952 and a solo show in New York in 1957, from which some paintings were acquired by the Museum of Modern Art. She spent a year at St Ives in Cornwall, which together with Exmoor and Dartmoor inspired some of her later work. Sandra Blow won the Guggenheim International Award in 1960 and was elected to the Royal Academy in 1971, holding a solo exhibition there in 1994. In the same year she returned to live in St Ives, holding a solo show at the new Tate St Ives in 2001. Died 22 August.

Botha, Pieter Willem (b. 1916), prime minister and state president of South Africa whose limited attempts at reform were accompanied by tough and increasingly brutal measures against blacks and other anti-apartheid protesters. Born in the Orange Free State, Botha studied law at Grey University College but had already joined the National Party and left to pursue a political career before taking a degree. He was elected to Parliament in 1948, the year when the United Party was finally defeated by the National Party, and held a number of ministerial posts before being appointed minister of defence in 1966. During his tenure in this office Botha developed a policy (which he described as involving economic, ideological and social affairs as much as military) which put him in a powerful position to win election as prime minister following the resignation of John Vorster in 1978. The reforms he introduced during his first years as prime minister and first state president—which removed some apartheid measures, legalised black trade unions and abolished the pass laws and legislation forbidding mixed marriages—were widely welcomed, but the constitution which he introduced in 1984, providing for assemblies for Indians and coloureds but not for blacks, and which retained the ban on the African National Congress, provoked violence in black townships. An indefinite state of emergency was declared, giving the police arbitrary powers of arrest and detention without trial, and imposing press censorship. After suffering a mild stroke in 1989, and under pressure from his party, Botha resigned. Died 31 October.

Brown, James (b. 1928), US singer and entertainer who became known as the "godfather of soul". Born in Barnwell, South Carolina, he was brought up in a brothel after his parents separated when he was four. Inspired by the gospel music of the local Baptist church, he learnt to play the piano, guitar and drums, and had formed his own group when he was 13. After a term of imprisonment, when he was 16, for breaking into cars, he joined a group called the Gospel Starlighters which soon became James Brown and the Famous Flames.

Signed up by King Records, Brown made his first hit single, *Please, Please, Please*, in 1956 and a second, *Try Me*, two years later. In 1962 his album *Live at the Apollo* reached No. 2 in the US album chart, and in 1965 his record *Papa's Got a Brand New Bag* is credited with the creation of funk music. Brown's athletic concert performances, the number he gave, and the fact that he had more than 800 songs to his name, gained him the title of the "hardest working man in show business". He continued to tour in the USA and in Britain and Europe throughout the 1990s and into the 21st century, interrupted only by a spell in prison following a conviction for assault and other charges. Died, of pneumonia, 25 December.

Carrier, Robert (b.1923), US-born writer and chef who came to Britain to transform attitudes to food subdued by wartime austerity. Born in Tarrytown, New York, Carrier served in the US Army during the war, ending up in Paris after its liberation to work as a cryptographer. After serving for a time as an apprentice chef in St Tropez, he moved to London in 1953 and began to write about food with cookery cards and a number of books, including *Great Dishes of the World* (1963), which sold 11 million copies, and *The Robert Carrier Cookbook* (1965). He opened his first restaurant, Carrier's, in Islington, in 1966 and a second, at Hintlesham Hall in Suffolk, in 1972, both earning two Michelin stars. During this time he also became a television chef with a series called *Carrier's Kitchen*, and set up a cookery school at Hintlesham. This proved to be more than he could cope with. Flamboyant and temperamental, he soon grew bored with teaching people whom he referred to as "Robert Carrier groupies", closed the school, sold both restaurants and retired to Marrakesh. Later he moved to Provence, where he took up painting. Died 27 June.

Chamberlain, Professor Owen (b.1920), US physicist who won the Nobel Prize for physics for his discovery of the antiproton. Born in San Francisco, he moved with the family to Philadelphia, where he was educated locally and at Dartmouth college before moving to the University of California at Berkeley for post-graduate studies. After the US entered the war he joined scientists working on the Manhattan Project, moving to Los Alamos in 1943. Returning to Berkeley after the war, Chamberlain collaborated with Emilio Segrè in seeking confirmation of the existence of the antiproton, which annihilates positive protons. Its existence had already been assumed, but could not be verified until the Bevatron atom smasher was built at Berkeley in the early 1950s. This gave Chamberlain and Segrè the chance to confirm their discovery that antiprotons existed only outside the nucleus in high energy nuclear collisions such as occurred in cosmic radiation. Firing protons of high electron volts at a copper target the two men created antiprotons and kept them in existence long enough to be identified. Chamberlain and Segrè jointly shared the Nobel award for their work in 1955. Chamberlain, appointed a full professor at Berkeley, went on to pioneer the use of polarised proton targets and to study the interactions of energetic light nuclei. Died 28 February.

Choi Kyu Hah (b. 1919), President of the Republic of Korea (South Korea) for nine months following the assassination of President Park Chung Hee in 1979. Born in Wonju, Choi was educated at high school in Seoul, at the College of Education in Tokyo and at the National Daedong Institute in Manchuria. Working first at the ministry of foreign affairs, he served at the South Korean embassy in Tokyo and was later ambassador in Malaysia. He was appointed minister of foreign affairs in 1967 and then special assistant for foreign affairs to Park, who was by then president. In 1976 Choi was appointed prime minister. When Park was killed in an attempted coup, Choi was appointed acting head of state. He at once rescinded some of Park's laws prohibiting criticism of the government, but ran into difficulties following a military coup led by the head of the defence security command, General Chun Doo Hwan. When Chun imposed martial law and crushed public demonstrations (including the notorious Kwangju massacre of 18 May) Choi resigned, and in September 1980 retired from public life. Died 22 October.

Crossfield, Scott (b. 1921), US test pilot who was the first man to fly at twice the speed of sound. Born in Berkeley, California, Crossfield made his first solo flight when he was 15. He went on to read aeronautical engineering at Washington university, interrupted by the war when he trained as a pilot in the US Navy. In 1950 he joined the National Advisory Committee for Aeronautics as a research pilot at Muroe Field in California, where on 20 November 1953, he piloted a Douglas D558-2 Skyrocket which, after launching from a Boeing Superfortress at 32,000ft, he took to 72,000ft and reached a speed of more than 1,320mph. For one month he was dubbed the fastest man alive, but lost that title when his colleague, Chuck Yeager, who had been the first man to break the sound barrier, flew at 1,612mph. Chamberlain later became chief engineering test pilot on the development of the X15 hypersonic research aircraft until it became clear that the way into space was by rocket rather than by aircraft. He then acted as consultant to the congressional committee on science and technology. Died 21 April.

Davis, Raymond (b. 1914), US chemist who was awarded the Nobel Prize for detecting and confirming the existence of neutrinos. Born in Washington DC, he was educated in local schools and the University of Maryland, where he took a master's degree before moving to Yale to take a PhD in physical chemistry. After serving in the US Army Air Force during the war he joined the Mound Laboratory of the Monsanto Chemical Company and in 1948 moved to the Brookhaven National Laboratory in New York. Here he worked on experiments to detect neutrinos from nuclear reactors, but having failed in this began trying to detect them from the sun. Having initially failed again with an underground mine in Ohio, he moved in 1961 to an underground goldmine in Dakota—filling a huge tank, nearly a mile beneath the surface, with the solvent tetrachloroethylene—and eventually succeeded in detecting solar neutrinos. He received the Nobel Prize for Physics in 2002. Died 31 May.

Dodds-Parker, Sir Douglas (b. 1909), wartime SOE officer who later became a Conservative MP. Born in Oxford, he was educated at Winchester and Magdalen College, Oxford, before joining the Sudan Political Service, where he remained until the war, when he was commissioned in the Grenadier Guards. He was seconded to military intelligence and to the Special Operations Executive when it was set up in 1940, returning to Sudan where he took part in General Orde Wingate's operation to restore Emperor Haile Selassie to the throne of Ethiopia. Subsequently Dodds-Parker was put in charge of the agency's operations in Corsica and France, and eventually in all the Mediterranean. He was mentioned in dispatches for this work, and awarded the Croix de Guerre and appointed a member of the Légion d'honneur in

France. His career in the British Parliament was less spectacular. Elected in 1945, he was a member of a number of committees and appointed parliamentary under-secretary at the foreign office in 1953, an office he continued to hold during the Suez operation in 1956, when Britain, France and Israel colluded in an attack on Egypt. By the time he learnt of the plan, the operation was underway and he decided that he could not resign while British forces were engaged. He returned to the back benches and retired from Parliament in 1959, but was subsequently re-elected and in 1973 was knighted and appointed a member of the British parliamentary delegation to Strasbourg. He retired two years later. Died 13 September.

Drummond, Sir John, CBE (b. 1934), British champion of the arts whose major posts included director of the Edinburgh festival and controller of the BBC's Radio 3. Born in London, he was educated at Canford in Dorset and at Trinity College, Cambridge, where he went in 1955 after National Service in the Royal Navy. In 1958 he joined the BBC as a general trainee and worked on a number of documentaries. In the early 1960s, in preparation for the launch of BBC2, he worked on a series of music documentaries, including six master classes with Paul Tortellier, and in 1969 produced a monthly series of music programmes, *Music Now*. Appointed executive producer for BBC2 arts features, he was later accused of lacking the "common touch" and left the corporation to take on the Edinburgh festival, which he ran from 1979 until 1983 with great panache, broadening its scope but disappointing those who looked for some more traditional arts features. He resigned in 1983 and two years later rejoined the BBC, first as controller of music and then as controller of Radio 3 (which included music and the Proms), where again he was innovative and provocative. Released in 1991 to produce an arts festival for the European Community, he continued with the Proms, but, finding himself increasingly isolated, left the BBC in 1995. He was knighted that year. Died 6 September.

Ecevit, Bülent (b. 1925), Turkish politician who was prime minister five times, saw as his country's mission the reconciliation of East and West, but sent troops to invade Cyprus. Born in Istanbul, he was educated in the city's Robert College. From 1946 he spent four years in the office of the press attaché in the Turkish embassy in London, returning to Ankara to work for the newspaper of the Republican People's Party. Elected to parliament in 1957, he was appointed minister of labour in the coalition and elected secretary of the RPP in 1966, when the party was in opposition. He later resigned to challenge Ismet Inönü for the party leadership and became prime minister for the first time in 1974, leading an uneasy coalition. In July of that year, when the government of Archbishop Makarios was overthrown in Cyprus, Ecevit sent Turkish troops to occupy the northern third of the island in order, he said, to protect the Turkish Cypriots living there. Despite the popularity of this act within Turkey, Ecevit was unable to retain control of the coalition and resigned in November. He became prime minister again for a month in 1977 and again in 1978, resigning in the following year. He was imprisoned and placed under house arrest for several short periods after the military coup in 1980. In 1987 he headed a new party, the Democratic Left, and emerged as prime minister again in 1998, with military support, and for the last time in the following year. After losing the election of 2002 he retired from politics. Died 5 November.

Figures, Sir Colin, KCMG, CMG, OBE (b. 1925), former chief of the British Secret Intelligence Service (SIS-commonly known as MI6) whose term of office included covert operations in the Falklands war. Born in Birmingham, he was educated at King Edward's school and Pembroke College, Cambridge, where he read French and Russian before becoming a career officer in the SIS. He worked in Warsaw and Vienna before returning to London in 1969, dealing mostly with Soviet operations and then, from 1973, with Northern Ireland. He was appointed deputy head of the service in 1979 and its chief in 1981. When the Argentinians invaded the Falkland Islands in the following year SIS became crucially involved when it was revealed that Argentinian naval aircraft, supplied by France, were equipped with Exocet missiles. An operation was launched to prevent the Argentinian naval procurement office from acquiring further Exocets, and subsequently against Argentinian saboteurs sent to attack British naval targets in Gibraltar. Figures was knighted shortly after the war, and when he left SIS in 1985 was appointed intelligence co-ordinator in the cabinet office, finally retiring from public service in 1989. Died 8 December.

Ford, Gerald (b. 1913), US Republican congressman who became 38th President in 1974 following the resignation of Richard Nixon. Born Leslie Lynch King Jr. in Omaha, Nebraska, he moved with his mother to Grand Rapids, Michigan, when his parents divorced two years after his birth. When she married again, to Gerald Ford, he was renamed Gerald Rudolph Ford Jr. in honour of his stepfather. The young Ford was educated at the University of Michigan and at the law school at Yale. After service in the US Navy during the war he returned to practise law in Michigan but soon became involved in Republican Party politics. He was elected to the House of Representatives in 1948 and became Republican minority leader in 1965. He became a friend of Nixon, who joined the House at the same time, but did not share Nixon's high aspirations and combative nature, hoping at best to become Speaker of the House, an ambition which was denied him as the Republicans remained in a minority even when Nixon became president in 1972. Ford's situation changed in the following year, when Vice-President Spiro Agnew was forced to resign. Ford was not Nixon's first choice as a replacement, but it soon became evident that he was the only man likely to receive the approval of the Democratic majority in Congress, and he was duly appointed. By this time revelations of the Watergate affair and Nixon's involvement in it were moving Congress towards the idea of impeachment, and in less than a year Nixon had resigned and Ford became president. His first concern was to restore the country's confidence in itself following the traumas of Vietnam and Watergate. "Our long national nightmare is over," he declared in his first address to the nation, and Americans were happy to accept this assurance until he announced that he was granting a presidential pardon to cover all offences that his predecessor might have committed during his presidency. Ford's popularity plummeted. The mid-term elections in 1974 led to increases in the Democratic majority in Congress and in his state of the union address the following year Ford conceded that its state was not good. Though he won the Republican nomination for the 1976 presidential election, he was defeated by Jimmy Carter and withdrew from politics quietly to enjoy his retirement. Died 26 December.

Friedan, Betty (b. 1921), author who wrote *The Feminine Mystique* and inspired the launch of the women's movement in the USA. Born Betty Naomi Goldstein in Peoria, Illinois, she was educated locally and at Smith College for women at Northampton, Massachusetts, where she took a degree in psychology, subsequently moving to the University of California at Berkeley with a research fellowship. Moving to New York she married Carl Friedan, a theatre producer, and worked as a reporter, but when her second child was born she was refused maternity leave and was dismissed. She continued to contribute to magazines and in 1963 was inspired to write *The Feminine Mystique* after re-visiting Smith College to conduct research into the lives of her contemporaries there. The results led her to reject the idea that women were fulfilled by being wives, mothers and housewives, which she concluded comprised the "feminine mystique". The book sold more than 2 million copies and she was much in demand for interviews and as a lecturer. She co-founded the National Organisation for Women in 1966, and was credited with redefining the place of women and of changing the life of the USA in the 20th century. But she subsequently objected to later, more radical, feminism, such as the emphasis on sexual liberation. She was in effect more political, wanting equal opportunities for employment, promotion and equal pay. Died 4 February.

Friedman, Milton (b. 1912), US economist whose championship of the free market profoundly influenced governments in the last decades of the 20th century. Born in Brooklyn, New York, he was educated at Rahway high school in New Jersey and at Rutgers and Chicago universities. In the 1930s and during the war he was employed as an economist in a number of government agencies before returning to Chicago as a professor where he began to make his name by developing monetarist theories and challenging the Keynesian doctrine of economic management by government control of taxes and spending. In 1962 Friedman published *Capitalism and Freedom*, which became a best-seller and greatly enhanced his reputation. In 1976 he was awarded the Nobel Prize for Economics and joined the Hoover Institute at Stanford University in California, travelling to many parts of the world to advocate economic freedom. He also greatly increased his popular appeal, and understanding of his theories, with many other books and a television series entitled *Free to Choose*. His influence was clearly seen in the policies of Margaret Thatcher's government in the UK and of Ronald Reagan's administration in the USA (he was a member of the President's Economic Advisory Board 1981-88), and those of other countries in the 1980s and 1990s. In the end, as he saw it, pragmatic politics got in the way of his theories and monetarism was not pursued with the rigour which he advocated. He was awarded the US Presidential Medal of Freedom in 1988. Died 16 November.

Galbraith, John Kenneth (b. 1908), US economist and adviser to Democratic politicians, Galbraith liked to be regarded primarily as a writer, his best known book being *The Affluent Society*. Born in Ontario, Canada, he was educated locally and at the Ontario Agricultural College in Guelph before taking a doctorate at the University of California at Berkeley in 1934. He then served in the department of agriculture before going to Cambridge university in England to study with John Maynard Keynes, one of the major influences of his life (though Galbraith rejected socialism). He became a US citizen in 1939 but was rejected for military service because of his height (6ft 8ins). Instead he worked in various government offices before becoming professor of economics at Harvard in 1948. Ten years later he published *The Affluent Society* in which he coined the phrase "private affluence and public squalor", criticising the USA for the poverty of its public services while flaunting the wealth of its private possessions. While at Harvard he taught and befriended the young John Kennedy and became one of his advisers when he ran for the Senate. When Kennedy became president in 1961 Galbraith was reluctantly persuaded to go to Delhi as US ambassador, but returned to Harvard after two years declaring that he was "a one-time-only diplomat". After Kennedy's assassination Galbraith continued to advise President Lyndon Johnson but gave up in protest at the Vietnam War. He continued writing books—more than 30 during his lifetime—including, in 1992, *The Culture of Contentment*, in which he returned to update his lifelong concern that even in wealthy countries such as the USA and the UK there was not a strong enough political constituency to look after the poor. He published his last book when he was 95. Died 29 April.

Gouled Aptidon, Hassan (b. 1916), first president of Djibouti after it gained independence from France in 1977. Born in what was then part of French Somaliland, Gouled took up politics after the war when Djibouti was made an independent territory of France with a local legislature and representation in the French Parliament. He began to participate in the country's independence campaign, becoming a member of the Ligue Populaire Africaine pour l'Indépendence in 1967 and ultimately its leader. When the country was granted its independence Gouled became president. After initially trying to form a balanced government between the minority Afars community and the majority Issas, he was confronted with the resignation of his prime minister, an Afar, and four other ministers. He resorted to the formation of a one-party state in which only candidates approved by his new party, the Rassemblement Populaire pour le Progrès, could stand for election. Meanwhile he promoted regional co-operation by arranging treaties of friendship with Ethiopia, Somalia, Kenya and Sudan. Confronted again at home in 1991 with an Afar revolt, he responded, after harshly putting it down, by allowing four parties to be formed to contest elections in the following year. In the event only two parties took part, Gouled's RPP winning all 65 seats. He was subsequently re-elected president for another term of six years, finally retiring in 1999. Died 21 November.

Harrer, Heinrich (b. 1912), mountaineer and adventurer who participated in the first successful ascent of the north face of the Eiger. Born in Huttenberg, in the Austrian province of Carinthia, Harrer studied geography and sports at the Karl Franzen university in Graz. On 24 July, 1938, he was a member of the four-man team, led by Anderl Heckmair, which made the first successful ascent of the notoriously difficult north face of the Eiger. A member of the SS, Harrer was part of a German expedition to the Himalayas in 1939 but was interned in India by the British colonial authorities following the outbreak of World War II. He escaped in 1944 and after a gruelling 21-month journey, which involved traversing the Himalayas with little equipment, he arrived in Lhasa, the capital of Tibet. One of only a few Westerners in the remote mountain kingdom, Harrer became a friend and tutor of the young Dalai Lama. His stay there, which he later described as the happiest time of his life, ended when he fled the Chinese invasion in 1950. Having returned to Europe he later took part in a number of ethnographic and mountaineering expeditions. He also wrote numerous books, the best known of which were *The White Spider*, which documented the Eiger expedition, and *Seven Years in Tibet*, a best seller which was translated into 53 languages and was the basis of a 1997 Hollywood film. Although Harrer was a keen advocate of human rights, his later years were dogged by the allegation that he had understated the strength of his Nazi connections. He rejected this charge, describing his membership of the SS as the biggest aberration of his life. Died 7 January.

Harris of High Cross, Lord (b. 1924), one of the founders, and its director-general for 30 years, of the Institute of Economic Affairs, a British think-tank which championed free-market ideas. Born in Tottenham, Ralph Harris was educated at the local grammar school and at Queen's College, Cambridge, where he took a First in economics. From 1940 he lectured on political economy at the University of St Andrews. He stood unsuccessfully as a candidate in two general elections, in 1951 as a Liberal Unionist and in 1955 as a Conservative, but once the IEA was founded, in 1957, and Harris became its director-general, he argued strongly against any direct political involvement, maintaining that politics "leads to compromise and deals and confusion and vote-getting and lying and cheating". Instead, he saw the IEA as an "awkward squad", publishing a series of pamphlets raising issues of public concern and pointing to free-market solutions. Its influence was most clearly seen in the early years of Margaret Thatcher's Conservative government. Harris was appointed a life peer in her first year of office, but sat as a cross-bencher. Died 19 October.

Hashimoto, Ryutaro (b. 1937), Japanese politician who became prime minister in 1996. The son of a politician, Ryutaro Hashimoto studied political science at Keio university in Tokyo, graduating in 1960 and two years later, aged 26, after joining the Liberal Democratic Party, becoming a member of the House of Representatives. After chairing the House's standing committee on social and labour affairs he was appointed minister of health and welfare and subsequently, in the government led by Prime Minister Yasuhiro Nakasone, minister of transport responsible for the privatisation of the Japanese National Railways. In 1989 he became minister of finance but was forced to resign two years later when it was revealed that one of his secretaries had been involved in some illegal financial transactions. Restored to government in 1994 as minister of international trade and industry, he was elected president of the LDP in 1995 and appointed deputy prime minister the same year. In January 1996, he became prime minister, retaining the office in the general election of October that year. He carried on his predecessor's policies of reconciliation and apology for his country's wartime behaviour and launched an ambitious programme of reform which was soon derailed when the economy collapsed into recession. Hashimoto resigned in 1998. For a time he briefly served as a minister in the government of Yoshiro Mori, but allegations of an earlier financial scandal put an end to any further political ambition. Died 1 July.

Hassanali, Noor (b. 1918), Trinidadian lawyer who became president of Trinidad & Tobago in 1987. Born in San Fernando, Hassanali was educated at the local Naparima college, graduating in 1937 and remaining there to teach until 1943, when he moved to Canada to take a BA at the

University of Toronto, subsequently being called to the Bar at Gray's Inn, London. He returned to Trinidad in 1948 to practise law, becoming a senior magistrate in 1960, a High Court Judge in 1966 and a Justice of Appeal in the Supreme Court in 1978. He retired from the law in 1985 and two years later was elected by the islands' parliament as president. Hassanali's term proved to be unusually troubled. Racial and religious tensions between the Christian, black Muslims and Indian Muslims erupted in a violent attack on the Parliament building in 1990 by black Muslim supporters of the Islamic fundamentalist group, Jamaat al Muslimeen. The building was occupied, the prime minister and eight of his ministers were taken hostage, and in the rioting that followed some 40 people were killed and many more injured before order was restored and the hostages freed. Though Hassanali was on a visit to London at the time, and his office was largely ceremonial, his legal objectivity and conciliatory skills, together with his Islamic faith, were credited on his return with helping to calm the situation, and in 1992 he was elected for a further five-year term. Died 25 August.

Haughey, Charles (b. 1925), Taoiseach (prime minister) of the Irish Republic whose three terms of office were accompanied by a series of scandals. Born in Castlebar in County Mayo, he was educated at St Joseph's Christian Brothers school and at University College, Dublin. He joined the republican Fianna Fail party and in 1951 married the daughter of its deputy leader, Sean Lemass, who became Taoiseach in 1959. Meanwhile Haughey had been elected to the Dail (legislature) and was appointed minister for justice in 1961, minister of agriculture in 1964, and minister for finance in 1966, from which post he was dismissed in 1970 for allegedly approving a shipment of guns for use in Northern Ireland (a charge on which he was acquitted in court). He returned to office in 1977 as minister for health and social welfare and began his first term as prime minister in 1979 following the retirement of Jack Lynch. Haughey made early attempts to ease relations with the UK, persuading Margaret Thatcher to agree to joint action on Northern Ireland and to become the first British prime minister to make an official visit to Dublin, but the relationship broke down when the IRA hunger strikes began. At home Haughey disappointed many of his followers by failing to cut public spending. He was defeated in the 1981 elections but returned in February 1982 with the narrowest of majorities and was forced from office later in the year when one of his backbenchers died. In the subsequent election his agent was caught voting in two different places and there were allegations that his justice minister had arranged for the tapping of journalists' phones. Haughey remained leader of his party and was returned again as Taoiseach in the election of 1987. This term of office included the Irish presidency of the European Union, when Haughey was seen at his best and won for his country EU funds which stimulated its economic boom. But in 1992 he felt compelled to resign when it was revealed that he had known about, if not authorised, the phone tapping of 1982. He spent much of his retirement trying to explain how he could afford his luxurious life style, defending himself against prosecutions, tax demands and a tribunal set up to examine donations he had received while in government. Died 13 June.

Hrawi, Elias (b. 1926), president of Lebanon who restored a period of stability to his country by accepting the dominant influence of Syria. Born in Zahle, he was educated at St Joseph university in Beirut and became a farmer until the civil war, when he turned to politics. Elected to the National Assembly in 1972 he served as minister of works in the 1980s, but when President René Mouawad was killed 17 days after taking office in 1989 Hrawi was elected to succeed him. His first task in ending the civil war was to recover the presidential palace from the general appointed to lead a military government in 1988 by President Amin Gemayel. This Hrawi was only able to do with the aid of Syrian troops, after which he implemented the constitutional amendments proposed in the Taif Accord to end the war and concluded a treaty with Syria by which the latter agreed to recognise Lebanon's independence and Lebanon undertook not to be used against Syrian interests. Under the Taif Accord the president's power was more evenly shared with the prime minister and the National Assembly speaker, but the fact that all three deferred to Damascus to resolve their differences showed how dependent on Syria the country had become. Subsequently it was suspected that Syria had prompted Hrawi's decision to extend his term of office by three years, after which he was replaced by the Lebanese army commander, General Emile Lahoud. Hrawi retired in 1998. Died 7 July.

Hussey of North Bradley, Lord (b. 1923), chairman of the BBC Board of Governors who imposed financial controls that led to great unrest within the corporation. Born Marmaduke James (generally known as Duke), he was educated at Rugby and Trinity College, Oxford, winning a cricket Blue before leaving to join the Grenadier Guards during the war. Landing on the Anzio beachhead in 1943 he was badly wounded and had a leg amputated before being sent to a prisoner-of-war camp. Repatriated because of remaining serious injuries, he returned to Oxford to take a First in history and in 1949 joined Associated Newspapers. He was appointed managing director of Harmsworth Publications in 1967 and four years later became chief executive of Times Newspapers, where he successfully reduced its losses but later ran into trouble with the print unions for accepting the Labour government's voluntary wage controls. In 1978-79 publication was suspended for 11 months and soon after it had ended the proprietor, Lord Thomson of Fleet, sold the newspapers to Rupert Murdoch. Hussey remained on the new board until he was appointed to the BBC in 1986, where he was again faced with a major challenge. One of his first acts was to replace the director-general, Alasdair Milne, who was blamed for much of the disorganisation and financial indiscipline that he found there. Hussey replaced Milne with his deputy, Michael Checkland, but within a few years supplanted him with John Birt. The programme of restrictions and staff reductions which then took place led to deep resentment and many resignations. Hussey retired in 1996, having secured the renewal of the BBC's charter. Died 27 December.

Irwin, Steve (b. 1962), Australian naturalist whose exuberant and fearless handling of dangerous animals on television brought him fame and an early death. Born in Essendon, a suburb of Melbourne, Irwin was educated locally and quickly became accustomed to animals when the family moved to Queensland, where his father ran a small wildlife park, specialising in nursing sick and injured animals. Young Irwin became a crocodile trapper, taking them from inhabited areas to the park. When he took over the family business he began, in 1992, a television series, *Crocodile Hunter*, that quickly won a large audience in Australia and was syndicated to many other countries. Displaying humour, boyish enthusiasm and an abiding concern for animal welfare, he would confront crocodiles, play with boa constrictors and poisonous snakes, swim with sharks and mingle with many other dangerous creatures. Describing himself as a "wildlife warrior" he did much to support the cause of conservation, though he could on occasion cause offence, such as when he fed a crocodile while holding his infant son in his other arm. He was killed by a stingray while filming under water. Died 4 September.

Ishaq Khan, Gulam (b. 1915), president of Pakistan who dismissed two democratically elected governments during his five-year term in office. Born in the Bannu district of the North-West Frontier Province, he was educated at Islamia College, Peshawar and Punjab university. He joined the civil service in 1940, becoming cabinet secretary to the government in 1970, governor of the State Bank in the following year and secretary-general at the ministry of defence in 1975. He held a number of other posts before being elected to the Senate in 1985 and becoming its chairman soon afterwards. Under the constitution, the Senate chairman succeeded as acting president of the country if the incumbent died, and when General Zia ul-Haq was killed in an aircraft crash in 1988 Ishaq Khan took over. The constitution at that time also provided that the president could force the dismissal of a prime minister or government, and Ishaq Khan used this power to dismiss Benazir Bhutto in 1990 and Mohammed Nawaz Sharif in 1993, justifying both dismissals on the grounds of corruption. These arbitrary acts undermined the country's economy and its uneasy democracy. The Supreme Court subsequently restored Nawaz Sharif as prime minister but in 1993 both he and Ishaq Khan resigned, under pressure from the army. Ishaq Khan retired to Peshawar. Died 27 October.

Jacobs, Jane (b. 1916), US author and social critic whose book *The Life and Death of Great American Cities* challenged conventional urban planning. Born June Butzner in Scranton, Philadelphia, she moved to New York during the Depression, working as a freelance on a variety of subjects until, in 1944, she married the architect Robert Jacobs, who taught her enough about buildings and urban architecture to enable her to write on the subject. She also began to campaign against a plan to build an expressway across Manhattan, close to the apartment in Greenwich Village where she was living. She argued that there should be more density and diversity in cities. The theories she propounded in her book, published in 1961, were largely drawn from her experiences in her vibrant neighbourhood, which she saw as having developed organically, with mixed uses and a complex order, with people feeling safer because they were not often alone. Later, when she moved to Toronto she helped to fight a similar road plan in the city. Died 25 April.

Jones, Ken, OBE (b.1921), Welsh rugby football player and sprinter who won a silver medal in the 1948 Olympic Games. Born in Blaenavon, he was educated at West Monmouth grammar school in Pontypool, served with the RAF in India during the war and on return taught at Newport high school. He played club rugby for Newport on 293 occasions, scoring 145 tries, and was first capped on the right wing for Wales in 1947, playing in 44 internationals for his country and scoring 17 tries. Jones won his Olympic medal as a member of the British 4x100 metres relay team. The team was originally presented with gold medals, the winning US team having been disqualified for an illegal baton change, but ended with silver when the US team was reinstated following an appeal. Jones was appointed OBE in 1960 for services to sport, and on retirement wrote on rugby for *The Sunday Express*. He resigned as president of the Newport Rugby Club in 1995 in protest at rugby becoming a professional sport. Died 19 April.

Kirkpatrick, Jeane (b.1926), US academic and political scientist who became her country's ambassador to the United Nations in 1981. Born Jeane Jordan in Duncan, Oklahoma, she was educated in New York and at Columbia university. After some postgraduate work in Paris and Washington she married Dr Evron Kirkpatrick, a fellow political scientist, in 1955, when she worked as consultant to a number of government departments while continuing with academic work, which brought her a PhD from Columbia university in 1968 for a dissertation on Peronist politics in Argentina. Turning to US politics she supported Jimmy Carter when he became president in 1977, but turned against him two years later for his support, as she saw it, of totalitarian revolutionary regimes at the expense of pro-US right-wing autocracies. An article she wrote for the magazine *Commentary* on this theme was seen by Ronald Reagan and when he took office as president in 1981 he appointed her ambassador to the UN, a member of his cabinet and of the National Security Council. She was uncompromising in her opposition to the Soviet Union and to any acts which she regarded as anti-American. When Argentina invaded the Falkland Islands in 1982 she tried unsuccessfully to persuade the president that the US should not risk its relations with Latin America by supporting the UK in what she described as a colonial war. Kirkpatrick resigned at the end of Reagan's first term in 1984 to return to writing books and to join the US lecture circuit. Among her later books were *Legitimacy and Force* (two vols, 1988) and *The Withering Away of the Totalitarian State* (1990). In 2003 she was appointed chairman of the US delegation to the UN Human Rights Commission. Died 7 December.

Laker, Sir Freddy (b.1922), British entrepreneur who introduced cheap no-frills flights across the Atlantic. Born in Canterbury, he was educated locally and at the age of 16 joined Short Brothers, the makers of flying-boats. He worked for the Air Transport Auxiliary during the war, when he learnt to fly and how to organise air transport. In 1946 he set up Aviation Traders which dealt with war surplus material and converted Halifax bombers for carrying passengers and freight, and these played a major part in the Berlin Airlift in 1948. He started a small charter airline in the 1950s which was later merged with British United Airways. In 1960 he was appointed BUA's managing director. He resigned five years later to form Laker Airways, chartering his aircraft to tour companies and pioneering the techniques of reduced take-off thrust and higher flying to save on fuel. In 1977 he introduced the Skytrain, offering regular flights to New York for £59, about one-third of the price charged by other airlines. Laker made a profit of £1million in the first year and by 1980, when he had established services to other US cities, he was carrying one in seven of all passengers across the Atlantic and was planning new routes to other countries. His success prompted other airlines to respond and in 1982 many, including British Airways, TWA and PanAm, undercut Skytrain's fares. Laker was forced into receivership, and though his loyal customers set up a "Save Fredair Fund" and he successfully sued the airlines concerned he could not save his airline and retired to the Bahamas. Died 9 February.

Lay, Kenneth (b. 1942), US businessman, chairman of Enron who was convicted of fraud after the company went bankrupt. Born in Tyrone, Missouri, Lay was educated at the University of Missouri and the University of Houston, where he took a doctorate in economics. He joined the US Navy and served in the Vietnam War and at the Pentagon, then joined the Department of the Interior in Washington as under-secretary for energy issues. He worked successfully to deregulate the natural gas market, then moved into the private sector, becoming chief executive officer of Houston Natural Gas Corporation in 1984. He created Enron the following year after merging with Inter-North, broadening Enron's activities into trading energy futures, providing guaranteed quantities at set prices, and with the profits diversifying into other products and markets. For a short time Enron became the seventh largest company in the USA and Lay a multi-millionaire, but in effect the business was taking risks which it could not justify, and when prices went against it a complex system of accounting was employed to hide its debts. In 2001 the company was forced into bankruptcy. Lay was indicted by a grand jury on 11 counts of fraud and other charges, was found guilty on 10 of them but died, apparently of a heart attack, before sentence was passed. Died 5 July.

Litvinenko, Alexander (b. 1962), former Russian intelligence officer, with political asylum in the UK, who was mysteriously poisoned by polonium-210, a radioactive isotope. Born in Voronezh, he was educated locally before joining the Soviet army and then the KGB (subsequently the FSB) in 1988 to work in counter-intelligence, later heading the department charged with investigating corruption within the secret service. In 1998 he was dismissed from the FSB, at that time headed by Vladimir Putin, after he had publicly accused his superiors of corruption, including the ordering of assassinations. He was arrested and spent nine months in prison in 1999 before leaving the country and seeking asylum, with his family, in the UK, where he became a close associate of self-exiled Russian oligarch, Boris Berezovsky. He continued to accuse his former employers of corruption, publishing, in 2002, a book *Blowing Up Russia: Terror from Within*, alleging that the FSB had been responsible for the blowing up of an apartment block in which more than 300 people had died, and which the authorities had blamed on Chechen separatists. In November 2006 he fell ill after lunching with an acquaintance at a restaurant in London, and was taken to hospital. After his death, which he blamed on the FSB, it was found that he had left a trail of the radioactive poison at places he had visited and with people he had seen before being hospitalised. Died 23 November.

Mahfouz, Naguib (b. 1911), Egyptian novelist who was awarded the Nobel Prize for Literature in 1988, long after the publication of his Cairo trilogy of novels that brought him fame throughout the Arab world. Born in the Gamaliya quarter of Cairo, he was educated locally and at Cairo university, after which he joined the civil service, working in various departments while also beginning to write novels. His early attempts failed to get into print and his first published novel, greatly influenced by Walter Scott, was not much more successful. It was not until after the war, when he began to write novels based on contemporary Cairo, that he began to establish his reputation as a novelist. The first two, *Khan al-Khalili* (1945) and *Midaq Alley* (1947) pointed the way, but it was with the Cairo trilogy that he finally made his mark with both literary critics and the general public. *Bayn al-Kasrayn* was published in three volumes between 1956 and 1959 (translated as *Palace Walk*, *Palace of Desire* and *Sugar Street*) and followed the life of a bourgeois Cairo family from 1917 to 1944 with detailed domestic and social descriptions and political analogies that were revolutionary in Arabic fiction. Following this success, for which he was awarded the State Prize for Literature, Mahfouz worked on film scripts before running into trouble with a new novel, *Children of Gebelawi*, which was condemned as blasphemous, not published in Egypt, and eventually led, in 1994, to a knife attack by two Islamic extremists which he was lucky to survive. Died 30 August.

Maktoum bin Rashid al-Maktoum, Sheikh (b. 1943), ruler of Dubai and prime minister of the United Arab Emirates. Born in the family palace in Shindagha, he was educated by private tutors and at Cambridge university, soon becoming active as his father's assistant in pushing forward developments in Dubai, including the airport and oil wells. When the British government made clear its determination to leave the Gulf, Maktoum handled negotiations with Abu Dhabi which led to the signing of an accord between the two emirates which in turn led to the establishment of the seven-member United Arab Emirates in 1971. He was appointed its first prime minister, remaining in the position until 1979, when he stood down in favour of his father, returning as deputy in 1983 and resuming as prime minister in 1990 when he took charge of a building project designed to provide houses for poorer families in the emirates. As Ruler of Dubai, following his father's death in 1990, Maktoum continued with the programme of development which was rapidly establishing Dubai as a leading tourist, trading and business centre served by the leading Middle East airline, Emirates, which the family established. Maktoum will also be remembered for his interest in sport, in particular horse racing. He owned studs in England, in Ireland and in the USA, and along with his brothers he became one of the world's most successful racehorse owners and breeders. Died 4 January,

Masefield, Sir Peter (b. 1914) British aviation journalist and pilot who became chairman of the British Airports Authority. Born in Trentham, Staffordshire, he was educated at Westminster school, at Chillon college in Switzerland and at Jesus College, Cambridge. After a brief period with Fairey Aviation he turned to writing about aviation and when war broke out in 1939 became a war correspondent with the RAF and US Air Force, often flying on bombing raids over Germany. His journalism caught the attention of Lord Beaverbrook, who took him on as secretary of the war cabinet committee charged with planning post-war civil aviation. After a brief period at the ministry of civil aviation he joined British European Airways, becoming its chief executive in 1949 and introducing the turbo-prop Vickers Viscount to its fleet. Though this helped to make the airline profitable, Masefield did not enjoy the interference of the ministry and in 1955 left to become managing director of Bristol Aircraft, moving to Beagle Aircraft in 1960 and five years later taking on in addition the chairmanship of the British Airports Authority. During his six-year term at BAA he successfully expanded Heathrow and turned the company's loss into substantial profit, but again ran into difficulties with Whitehall over plans for a third London airport. In 1978 he joined the airline British Caledonian, becoming deputy chairman in 1980 and, while there, for two years also took on the job of chairman and chief executive at London Transport. He also served on many other boards and committees, and continued to write on aviation subjects. Died 14 February.

Merlyn-Rees, Lord (b. 1920), Labour politician who was successively Northern Ireland secretary and home secretary in the 1970s and found both jobs equally intractable. Born in Cllfynydd, Wales, he was educated locally until the family moved to London, then at Harrow Weald grammar school, Goldsmith's college and Nottingham university. He joined the RAF in 1941, serving part of the time in Italy, and after demobilisation took a degree in economics at the London School of Economics, which prompted him into politics. He stood unsuccessfully for the Harrow East constituency in several elections before finally winning South Leeds at a by-election following the death of Hugh Gaitskell in 1963. When Labour returned to power in 1964 Rees was appointed parliamentary private secretary to James Callaghan, and when Callaghan became home secretary in 1967 Rees was appointed an under-secretary. In opposition he shadowed William Whitelaw in the newly-created Northern Ireland office, and when Labour returned to power in 1974 Rees duly took over as secretary of state for Northern Ireland. During his tenure the power-sharing executive which he had inherited broke down, and in spite of his good intentions he failed to make progress with setting up a constitutional convention. When Callaghan succeeded Harold Wilson as prime minister in 1976 Rees was appointed to take over the home office. Once more he found himself in difficulties. He failed to impose pay restraint on the police and firemen, and as industrial strife escalated Labour went into opposition for such a long period that he was heard to wonder whether the party would ever return to office. Rees himself retired from the House of Commons in 1992, becoming a life peer. Died 5 January.

Meri, Lennart (b.1929), Estonian politician who as prime minister and later as president helped his country move from Soviet domination into the European Union. Born in Tallinn, the son of a diplomat, he was educated in Paris and Berlin and at Tartu university. During the war the family was deported to Siberia by the Soviet authorities, but on his return to Estonia in the 1950s Meri wrote a book about the region. He worked for the Estonian radio for some years, then for Tallinnfilm, making a film, *The Winds of the Milky Way*, which won a prize in New York but was banned in the Soviet Union. In 1990, when the leading role of the Communist party was abolished, he was appointed foreign minister, taking part in negotiations that led to the Supreme Soviet of Estonia inaugurating a period of transition to independence, which duly took place in 1991, when Meri successfully secured its membership of the UN. In April 1992 Meri was appointed ambassador to Finland, but returned home later that year upon his election as president. He was re-elected for a second term in 1996, presiding over his country's campaign to join the European Union and NATO. Precluded from standing for a third term, he retired from the presidency in 2000 but shared the national rejoicing when Estonia was formally invited to join both the EU and NATO two years later. Died 14 March.

Merrifield, Bruce (b. 1921), US biochemist who won the Nobel Prize for Chemistry for developing a new method of synthesising proteins. Born in Fort Worth, Texas, he took a degree and then a doctorate in chemistry at the University of California at Los Angeles, where for a while he taught and carried out research. In 1949 he moved to the Rockefeller Institute for Medical Research, working as an assistant to D.W. Woolley, remaining at what became Rockefeller University for the rest of his working life. It was here that he developed a method of synthesising polypeptides. Peptides are short chains of amino acids, polypeptides being peptides comprising at least 10 amino acids, and it is peptides that make up proteins. The synthesis of proteins enabled scientists to make important advances in medical and other research, but it was a laborious and uncertain process, involving liquid solutions, until, in 1963, Merrifield proposed a system of solid-phase peptide synthesis, by which amino acid building blocks would be tied to an insoluble solid surface until the protein was synthesised, after which the polypeptide could be detached. The process can be carried out by machine, which greatly eases the manufacture of drugs. Merrifield was awarded the Nobel Prize in 1984. He received many other awards, and on his retirement in 1992 was appointed emeritus professor at Rockefeller University. Died 14 May.

Milosevic, Slobodan (b. 1941), Serbian leader who precipitated the break up of Yugoslavia and sparked four wars in the Balkans that caused hundreds of thousands of deaths. Born in Pozarevac, he was educated locally, meeting at school Mirjana Markovic, daughter of a prominent Communist, whom he subsequently married. Both went on to Belgrade university. Joining the Communist party, Milosevic attached himself to Ivan Stambolic who was already making his way up the party, eventually to become president. In 1987 Milosevic was sent to Kosovo, where local Serbs were protesting against their treatment at the hands of the majority Albanian population. Pouring fuel on the flames he declared to an angry Serbian mob that "no one will ever beat you." On his return to Belgrade he organised a campaign against Stambolic, who resigned. In 1989 Milosevic was elected president, quickly revoking the autonomy given to Kosovo by Marshal Tito and making clear that he regarded himself as saviour of the Serbian people. His activities prompted Slovenia and Croatia, in 1991, to secede, giving Milosevic the excuse to invade Croatia. Serbs destroyed the town of Vukovar, attacked Dubrovnik and occupied about one-third of the country. In 1992 Bosnia also seceded, and fierce battles began between local Croats, Muslims and Serbs. The war went on for three years in spite of international attempts to bring it to an end. Centred on Sarajevo, it also involved towns like Srebrenica, where some 8,000 Muslims were massacred by Bosnian Serbs. Milosevic himself kept a low profile throughout, apparently able to persuade Western leaders that he was doing his best to put an end to such atrocities. But when, in 1999, his troops moved in to drive Albanians out of Kosovo and NATO responded by launching air strikes, his people had had enough. After losing the election which he had called in 2000 he was arrested, charged with genocide, crimes against humanity and war crimes and sent for trial at The Hague. The trial was still going on when he was found dead in his cell from apparent heart failure. Died 11 March.

Newby, Eric, CBE, MC (b. 1919), English author whose travel writing revealed a sharpness of observation generally masked in an ironic, understated and entertaining form. Born in Hammersmith, London, he was educated at St. Paul's school, leaving at the age of 16 to join an advertising agency. In 1938 he joined a four-master Finnish barque carrying grain from Ireland to Australia, later writing about his experiences in his first book, *The Last Grain Race* (published in 1956). During the war he joined the Black Watch, later volunteering for a mission to sabotage a German airfield in Sicily where he was captured and sent to a prisoner-of-war camp in Italy, again recalling his adventures in another book, *Love and War in the Apennines* (1971). He was awarded the MC for his part in the Sicily mission. After the war he confirmed his reputation as a writer with *A Short Walk in the Hindu Kush* (1958), the short walk in fact being a formidable and chaotic journey which he undertook with a friend through mountainous Afghanistan, for which they had prepared with a weekend in Wales. From 1964-1973 Newby worked as travel editor for *The Observer* and though he continued to travel and write books he seemed to have been confused by the merger of travel into tourism, his writing having become, as one critic put it, "too professional". He was appointed CBE in 1994. Died 20 October.

Niyazov, Saparmurat (b. 1940), president of Turkmenistan who was a monstrously extravagant and ruthless ruler of his country. Born in the village of Kipcak, near Ashgabat, he studied at the Leningrad Polytechnic Institute, becoming active in the Communist party on his return. He was appointed head of the party in Turkmenistan by Soviet leader Mikhail Gorbachev in 1985, and president of the Turkmen Soviet Socialist Republic in 1990. When the country became independent from the Soviet Union in 1992 Niyazov was elected president. He won a referendum two years later to remain in office for a second term and in 1999 he was declared President for Life. His rule was repressive (opposition was not tolerated and there was no freedom of expression or of the media) and extravagant (he liked to erect grandiose buildings and dotted the land with thousands of statues of himself, including one which rotated so that the sun always shone on its face). Meanwhile the country's oil reserves and natural gas deposits were left undeveloped and the country's health services run down: in 1995 all hospitals outside Ashgabat were closed. In 2002 Niyazov shut all theatres and opera houses and banned recorded music. Died 21 December.

Paniagua Corazao, Valentín (b. 1936), Peruvian lawyer and politician who briefly took over the presidency at a time of political crisis. Born in Cuzco, he was educated at the university there and in Lima, joining the Christian Democratic Party and winning a seat in the 1963 elections after the party had formed an alliance with Popular Action. He was appointed justice minister and became speaker of the lower house in 1982 and president of Congress in 2000, when the country was in political turmoil following the election of Alberto Fujimori as president for a third term, which the constitution did not allow. Following revelations of election rigging, Fujimori left the country and in his absence was declared by Congress to be "morally unfit" to be president. Paniagua was sworn in as interim president on 22 November and swiftly appointed a cabinet, headed by former UN Secretary-General

Javier Pérez de Cuéllar, set up a truth commission to investigate the cases of some 4,000 Peruvians who had disappeared during the conflict between security forces and guerrillas between 1980 and 1995, and organised elections which duly took place in 2001, when he was able to hand over to the successful candidate, Alejandro Toledo. Paniagua remained in politics and stood unsuccessfully for the presidency in 2006. Died 16 October.

Patterson, Floyd (b.1935), US boxer who won an Olympic gold medal and went on to become heavyweight champion of the world. Born in Waco, North Carolina, he had a rough childhood and was sent to a reform school in New York at the age of 10. Here he learnt to box, winning the middleweight gold medal at the Helsinki Olympics in 1952. Turning professional he won all but one of his first 36 contests before challenging Archie Moore for the heavyweight title which had been left vacant by the retirement of Rocky Marciano in 1956. Patterson won by a knockout in the fifth round, thereafter holding the title for three years until he was unexpectedly defeated by the Swede, Ingemar Johannson, who knocked him down seven times before the fight was stopped in the third round. Patterson won two subsequent contests against Johannson to regain his title, but lost it in 1962 to Sonny Liston, who was taller, outweighed him by 25 pounds, outreached him by 12 inches and knocked him out in the first round. In a re-match the following year Patterson was again knocked out in the first round. He continued to fight until 1972, however, when he was beaten by Muhammed Ali. He served as chairman of the New York State Athletic Commission until 1992, when he began to suffer from dementia. Died 11 May.

Pinochet, General Augusto (b.1915), former president of Chile who seized power in a military coup and established dictatorial rule which he justified as a war on communism. Born in Valparaiso, he determined from an early age on a military career. After gaining entry to the military academy in Santiago, at the third attempt, he graduated in 1937, served as military attaché in Washington DC, and in 1961 commanding the Seventh Infantry Regiment in the province of Antofagasta. In 1972 he was appointed commander-in-chief of the army by President Salvador Allende, a democratically elected Marxist whose radical economic reforms and close relationship with Cuba's Fidel Castro were fervently opposed by conservatives within Chile and by the US government. In 1973 Pinochet led a military coup which resulted in Allende's death and the introduction of a repressive regime during which thousands of Chileans were killed and many more tortured and imprisoned. Pinochet consolidated his power and in 1980 introduced a new constitution which confirmed his presidency for the next eight years. At the same time he reversed the economic controls imposed by Allende, privatising public enterprises (although not the copper industry), restoring expropriated land to former owners, reducing trade barriers and paving the way for rapid economic growth. Although widely applauded by advocates of free market economics such as Milton Friedman (for whose obituary see above), unemployment rose sharply, real wages declined and the proportion of Chileans living in poverty significantly increased during Pinochet's tenure. In 1988 Pinochet set up a new referendum intended to extend his presidency by another eight years. Non-Marxist political parties were allowed to campaign, both in the referendum and in elections called for the following year, and in both cases Pinochet was defeated. He handed power to an elected civilian government in 1990, though he initially remained as commander-in-chief and later became a senator-for-life. In 1998, while visiting the UK for medical treatment, he was placed under house arrest pending legal proceedings instituted in Spain. The House of Lords ultimately ruled that Pinochet was not immune from charges of torture, but in the meantime he had allegedly suffered two minor strokes and the UK government allowed him to return to Chile. In the final years of his life he was subjected to repeated legal attempts to hold him accountable for the crimes which were committed by his regime as well as in response to revelations that he had been involved in massive money-laundering during his years in power and had illegally amassed a huge private fortune. Stripped of immunity, he was placed under arrest but was admitted to hospital on 3 December after suffering a heart attack. Died 10 December.

Politkovskaya, Anna (b. 1958), Russian newspaper reporter who fearlessly investigated in Chechnya and was murdered while working on an article about incidents of torture there. Born in New York, where her parents were diplomats at the UN, she was educated at Moscow state university, graduating in 1980 and starting work on *Izvestiya*. In 1980 she went to Chechnya to begin a series of reports for the newspaper *Novaya Gazeta*, including accounts of torture and extrajudicial killings. She was declared persona non grata by Russian forces in Chechnya and expelled in 2001. In spite of this she returned, though death threats had caused her briefly to leave Moscow to live in Vienna. Her dispatches were published in two books: *A Dirty War: A Russian Reports on Chechnya* (2001) and *A Small Corner of Hell* (2003), and in 2004 she also published *Putin's Russia*, an analysis of that country which was not published in Russia. She was shot dead in the entrance of her apartment building in Moscow by an unknown assassin in what appeared to be a contract killing, thought by many to have been ordered by pro-Russian Chechen Prime Minister Ramzan Kadyrov. Died 7 October.

Pollock, Admiral of the Fleet Sir Michael, GCB, LVO, DSC (b. 1916), British First Sea Lord who won the DSO for gallantry in the battle against the German battlecruiser *Scharnhorst* in 1943. Trained at the Royal Naval College, Dartmouth, from the age of 13, he passed out in 1933 and after serving as a midshipman on the battleship *Nelson* he joined the cruiser *York*, then flagship of the West Indies station. When war broke out he became gunnery officer of the cruiser *Norfolk* which was badly damaged while engaged with the *Scharnhorst* and six German destroyers before the *Scharnhorst* was eventually sunk by the battleship *Duke of York*. After the war Pollock commanded the aircraft carrier *Ark Royal* in the Far East, and was appointed Assistant Chief of Naval Staff in 1964. Two years later, as second-in-command of the home fleet on board the cruiser *Tiger* he acted as host to Prime Minister Harold Wilson and to the Rhodesian rebel leader Ian Smith during their unsuccessful talks at sea off Gibraltar. Appointed Controller of the Navy and Third Sea Lord in 1971, he unexpectedly became First Sea Lord that year when Sir Peter Hill-Norton was made Chief of the Defence Staff. Pollock's tenure was marked by the "cod war" with Iceland's fishery protection vessels and by the laying down of the Invincible class of carriers, which 10 years later were to make their mark in the Falklands war. Pollock retired in 1974. Died 27 September.

Profumo, John, CBE (b. 1915), British secretary of state for war whose career was wrecked by scandal. Born John Dennis, but generally known as Jack, he was educated at Harrow and Brasenose College, Oxford. In 1934 he was adopted as Conservative candidate for Kettering and was elected in the following year. He was one of the 30 Conservatives who voted with Labour to bring down Neville Chamberlain's government in 1940. During the war Profumo served as a staff officer in Italy and as chief of staff on the British Liaison Mission with US General Douglas MacArthur in Japan. He also took part in the D-Day landings in Normandy. He was defeated in the 1945 election but returned as MP for Stratford-on-Avon in 1950. From 1957 to 1960 he was parliamentary under-secretary for the colonies and then minister of state for foreign affairs. In 1960 he was appointed secretary of state for war, but in the following year began an affair with Christine Keeler, a 19-year-old model who had also been sharing her bed with a Soviet attaché and spy, Yevgeny Ivanov. When rumours began to circulate, Profumo made a personal statement to Parliament denying the affair, but this was challenged by Stephen Ward, who had introduced Profumo to Keeler. Profumo confessed, first to his wife, the actress Valerie Hobson, then to his colleagues, resigning from the government and from Parliament on 5 June 1963. Subsequently he worked tirelessly for the Universities' Settlement charity at Toynbee Hall in the East End of London. In 1975 Profumo was appointed CBE for his charitable work. Died 9 March.

Puskás, Ferenc (b. 1927), Hungarian footballer widely acknowledged to have been one of the world's greatest players. Born in Kispest, near Budapest, he began playing for the local team when he was 16, winning a cap for his country two years later. Playing inside left he went on to score 83 goals in 84 international appearances. He was captain of the Hungarian team which in 1953 beat England 6-3. Puskás scored twice, as he did in the following year when England lost 7-1 in Hungary. In that year Hungary were favourites to win the world cup but lost in the final to West Germany 3-2, Puskás having had a goal disallowed in the last few minutes. In 1956, when the anti-Soviet uprising was put down by Soviet forces, Puskás was playing with a local team, now named Honved, in South America. Puskás, who sympathised with the uprising, did not return to Hungary but signed for Real Madrid, where he formed a dazzling partnership with the Argentinian centre forward, Alfredo Di Stefano. Puskás became a Spanish citizen and played for his adopted country three times during the 1962 World Cup. He retired in 1966 and went on to coach in many parts of the world. Died 17 November.

Rau, Johannes (b. 1931), German politician who was president of the Federal Republic from 1999 to 2004. Born in Wuppertal, he became a publisher's apprentice and attended a booksellers' school in Cologne before joining an evangelical publishing company in 1954. He also joined the Social Democratic Party and, in 1958, became a member of the North Rhine-Westphalian Diet (legislature) in Dusseldorf, where he spent most of his political life. Here he was chairman of the SDP parliamentary group in 1967 and minister-president from 1978 to 1998, moving to the national scene by becoming a vice-president of the SDP and, in 1987, by challenging Helmut Kohl in the federal elections. He was unsuccessful, as he was in his first challenge for the federal presidency in 1994. Five years later he won the election to become the first Social Democrat to become president for 30 years. He used this formal, non-political post to encourage his countrymen to accept a more multi-racial society and not to try to forget the past. In 2000 he visited Israel, asking the Knesset to forgive his generation for the Holocaust. Died 27 January.

Rawlinson of Ewell, Lord, PC, QC (b. 1919), British barrister who served as solicitor-general and attorney-general in two Conservative governments. Born in Birkenhead, he was educated at Downside and at Christ's College, Cambridge, until war broke out, when he enlisted in the Irish Guards, being mentioned in dispatches in North Africa. After demobilisation he was called to the Bar, but also had political ambitions, and was elected as Conservative MP for Epsom in 1955 and appointed solicitor-general by Harold Macmillan in 1962, becoming involved in the Profumo scandal when he accepted the assurances of John Profumo (for whose obituary see above) to Parliament that he had not had an affair with Christine Keeler. Subsequently Rawlinson offered his resignation, which Macmillan refused to accept. In opposition (after the election of 1964) he became chairman of the parliamentary legal committee, and when the Conservatives won the 1970 election he was appointed attorney-general by Edward Heath, adding to the post in 1972 the attorney-generalship of Northern Ireland. Soon after the government's defeat in 1974 Rawlinson became Recorder of Kingston upon Thames. He was made a life peer on retirement from the House of Commons in 1978, but did not retire from practice at the Bar until 1985, during which time he memorably and successfully defended the *Daily Mail* in a lengthy libel action brought by the Unification Church (popularly known as the "Moonies"). He published an autobiography, *A Price Too High* in 1989. Died 28 June.

Richards, Ann (b. 1933), liberal and feminist politician who became governor of Texas. Born Dorothy Ann Willis, to blue-collar parents in Lakeview, central Texas, she graduated from Baylor university and, at the age of 19, married David Richards from whom she later divorced. After a brief teaching career she concentrated on raising her four children. She entered public life in 1975 when she was elected as a county councillor. In 1982, despite fighting alcoholism, she was elected to the post of state treasurer, thereby becoming the first woman in Texas in 50 years to gain election to a statewide office. She served two successful terms and achieved national prominence when she gave the keynote address to the 1988 National Democratic Convention in which she lambasted the privileged background and stumbling articulation of George Bush, the vice president and Republican presidential candidate, with the words: "Poor George, he can't help it. He was born with a silver foot in his mouth." In 1990, after a brutal campaign, Richards was elected governor of Texas and thereafter sought to reform the prison service, give schools greater autonomy, regulate the insurance industry and encourage the promotion of women and members of ethnic minorities. After losing the 1994 gubernatorial election to George W. Bush (the son of the former vice president) she taught, worked as a lobbyist, and continued to campaign for the Democratic Party cause. Died 13 September.

Rosenthal, A.M. (b. 1922), executive editor of *The New York Times* who significantly expanded its news coverage and greatly enhanced its reputation. Born Abraham Michael in Ontario, Canada, he was educated at City college, New York, joining *The New York Times* in 1944. From 1946 to 1954 he worked in the paper's UN bureau and from 1954 to 1958, having become a US citizen, he served as a foreign correspondent, first covering India, then Poland (from which country he was expelled because, the order stated, the "Polish government cannot tolerate such probing reporting"), then Vienna, Geneva and Tokyo. He was recalled to New York in 1963 as metropolitan editor, moving up to the senior post of managing editor in 1969 and, in 1977, executive editor. He supervised the paper's expansion of news reporting, ensuring that it was in the forefront of coverage (as with the publication of the Pentagon Papers in 1971), added new sections such as culture, finance, and sport, and increased sales across the country. When he gave up the editorship in 1986 he wrote a regular column for the paper for the next 12 years, and when this was ended by his publisher he wrote a weekly column for *The New York Daily News*. He was awarded the Presidential Medal of Freedom in 2002. Died 10 May.

Rugova, Ibrahim (b.1944), president of Kosovo who met increasing Serbian control with passive resistance, believing that an independent Kosovo would help to stabilise the Balkans. Born in the Istog area of Kosovo he was educated at the University of Pristina and stayed on as a lecturer and professor until, in 1988, he was appointed president of the Kosovo Writers' Association. This was to become the focus of opposition when Serbia's President Slobodan Milosevic (for whose obituary see above) moved to abolish Kosovo's autonomy, and in 1990 Rugova became head of the non-Communist Democratic League of Kosovo, declaring Kosovo to be independent and holding secret elections in which Rugova became president of what was in effect a shadow government. There was widespread international support for a time, but when Kosovo was ignored in the Dayton peace accord of 1995 Rugova's pacifist policy was sidelined by the more aggressive Kosovo Liberation Army, leading to the war and the intervention of NATO. In 2000, when municipal elections were held to replace the UN administration, Rugova's party won a majority of the seats, and in March 2002 he was elected president. In that year he gave evidence against Milosevic in the trial at The Hague, but later revealed that he was suffering from lung cancer. Died 21 January.

Saddam Hussein, (b.1937), Iraqi president who was executed after his dictatorial regime was overthrown by the US-led military invasion. Born in al-Awja, near Tikrit, when lawlessness was such that, from his earliest days, Saddam reputedly went to school with a revolver in his pocket, he went on to law school, where he became a supporter of the Ba'ath party, taking part in the attempted coup against King Faisal II in 1956 and in the attempted assassination of General Abdul Karim Kassem three years later. He fled to Egypt, returning to Baghdad in 1963 when Kassem was overthrown, eventually succeeding in establishing the Ba'athists in power under the nominal leadership of Colonel Ahmad Hassan al-Bakr, but with Saddam in charge of security and the army, which was already acquiring arms and advisers from the Soviet Union. In 1979 al-Bakr was deposed and Saddam declared president, confirming his position by summoning senior Ba'ath party members to a meeting at which he denounced 66 as conspirators and had them taken away and shot. Other opponents were tortured or eliminated with equal ruthlessness. Saddam was supported by the USA and many Western governments as his secular regime was seen as preferable to the Islamic revolution which occurred in Iran in 1979. In 1980 Saddam invaded Iran but, after initial military successes, was forced into a defensive posture during the grim eight-year war of attrition which followed. During the war the West continued to provide him with arms and support even though the Iraqi military used chemical weapons against the enemy and against Kurdish separatists within Iraq. The war ended in 1988 with Iraq heavily indebted and its economy in ruins. In 1990 Saddam invaded and annexed his small but wealthy neighbour, Kuwait, prompting UN sanctions and, eventually, the assembly of an international force and the launching of Operation Desert Storm, in January 1991, to oust Iraqi troops from Kuwait. In February Saddam capitulated, ordering his army to withdraw. He was left with enough military strength to crush subsequent revolts in his country, reportedly once again using chemical weapons to put down rebellions by Kurds in the north and Shi'ites in the south. As part of the agreement to end the war Saddam accepted that UN inspectors should monitor the removal of Iraq's chemical, biological and nuclear weapons capability, but the work of the inspectors was frequently impeded by the Iraqi authorities in the years which followed. In March 2003 a US-led invasion swiftly conquered Iraq but found no weapons of mass destruction within the country. After the fall of Baghdad, Saddam disappeared until, in December that year, he was found hiding in a foxhole near Tikrit. He was eventually put on trial by the Iraqi government (backed by the US-led coalition) and, after a legal process that was widely seen as flawed, on 5 November he was condemned to death, and subsequently hanged, for crimes against humanity. Died 30 December.

Sainsbury, Simon (b. 1930), British businessman and philanthropist who quietly and generously supported many social, heritage and artistic projects. Born in London, he was educated at Eton and Trinity College, Cambridge, training as an accountant before joining the family grocery and supermarket business where, as a director, he was responsible for finance and personnel. He was also charged with steering Sainsbury's from a private into a public company, at that time the largest flotation on the London Stock Exchange. Shunning publicity—he would not accept any honour and refused to have an entry in *Who's Who*—he formed the Monument Trust through which to channel most of his support for charities. He was chairman of trustees at the Wallace Collection in London for 20 years and a trustee of the National Gallery for seven, to both of which he gave generously, as he did to other museums and galleries, including the British Museum, the Victoria and Albert, the Tate Gallery and the Fitzwilliam in Cambridge. It was estimated that during his lifetime he gave away some £100 million. In his later years he suffered from Parkinson's disease. Died 27 September.

Schwarzkopf, Dame Elisabeth (b. 1915), German lyric soprano celebrated for her lieder recitals and performances in the operas of Mozart and Richard Strauss. Born in Poland but subsequently settling with her Prussian parents in Berlin, she was engaged by the Deutsche Oper in 1938, making her stage debut as a Flowermaiden in *Parsifal* and subsequently singing Zerbinetta in Strauss's *Ariadne auf Naxos*. During the war she appeared in a number of the propaganda films sponsored by Goebbels and her involvement with the Nazi party might well have wrecked her career had she not been spotted by Walter

Legge, who was then looking for recording artists for EMI. Schwarzkopf at that time was singing with the Vienna State Opera, which in 1947 gave a brief season at Covent Garden, providing her with her debut there as Donna Elvira in *Don Giovanni*. In the following decade she went on to sing other roles there, including Susanna in *The Marriage of Figaro* and Mimi in *La Boheme*, but when she performed her most celebrated role, the Marschallin in *Der Rosenkavalier*, the critics were disappointed. Schwarkzopf decided not to sing at Covent Garden again, though she continued to delight audiences elsewhere, particularly at La Scala in Milan, where she performed until 1963. Meanwhile, guided by Legge, whom she married in 1953, she made a series of memorable recordings, including an interpretation of Strauss's *Four Last Songs* which became a best-seller for EMI. After retiring from the operatic stage and from lieder recitals she took up coaching and gave a series of powerful master classes. She was appointed DBE in 1992. Died 3 August.

Servan-Schreiber, Jean-Jacques (b. 1924), French journalist and politician who was co-founder of the magazine *L'Express*. Born in Paris, he was educated at the lycée Janson-de-Sailly and the lycée de Grenoble. When the Germans invaded during the war the family fled to Spain and he later trained as a pilot with the Free French. Returning to France after the war he joined *Le Monde* to write on foreign affairs. In 1953 he and his mistress, Françoise Giroud, founded and edited *L'Express*. Published initially as a weekly supplement to *Les Echos*, it began primarily as a political journal supporting Pierre Mendès-France in his campaign against Charles de Gaulle, but later developed into a more general, and more popular, news magazine. In 1967 Servan-Schreiber published *Le Défi Américain*, in which he foresaw Europe's economic and cultural decline as a result of the penetration of US goods and ideas, and called on Europe to unite to meet this "American challenge". When de Gaulle resigned in 1969 Servan-Schreiber became general secretary, later president, of the centre-left political Parti Radical, becoming a member of the French National Assembly and, for a few weeks in 1974, minister for reform. He sold *L'Express* in 1977, left the Parti Radical in 1979 and failed in an attempt to replace it with a new European party. From 1984 to 1995 he taught at the Carnegie Mellon university in Pittsburgh, USA. Returning to France to write his memoirs he later began to suffer from a mental disease. Died 7 November.

Simon of Glaisdale, Lord (b. 1911), British barrister and politician who became a Lord of Appeal in 1971. Born Jocelyn Simon, always known as Jack, he was educated at Gresham's school in Norfolk and at Trinity Hall, Cambridge. Called to the Bar in 1934 he was commissioned from the Inns of Court Regiment to the Royal Tank regiment and was mentioned in dispatches for his part in the battle of Madagascar, when a British force had to fight Vichy French forces after landing on the island to forestall a Japanese invasion. He later fought in Burma. In 1946 Simon returned to the Bar, specialising in family law, and, as Conservative candidate, won the Middlesbrough West constituency in the 1951 election. He was appointed parliamentary private secretary to the attorney-general in 1951, joint parliamentary under-secretary of state at the home office in 1957, financial secretary to the Treasury in 1958, and solicitor-general in 1959. He resigned his seat in 1962 to become president of the Probate, Divorce and Admiralty Division of the High Court and was appointed a Lord of Appeal in Ordinary in 1971. Though a Conservative politically, he was by nature a reformer, much concerned with improving matrimonial and divorce law, but his term as a Law Lord was curtailed by damaged sight and hearing. He retired in 1977. Died 7 May.

Shearer, Moira (b. 1926), British ballerina who made her name in the film *The Red Shoes*. Born in Dunfermline, Fife, she was educated at the local high school and at Bearsden Academy, before joining the Sadler's Wells School at the age of 14. She made her stage debut with the International Ballet in 1941 and joined the Sadler's Wells Ballet in the following year to dance her first leading role in *Les Sylphides*. During the war a number of roles were created for her, and at Covent Garden in 1946 she danced with Margot Fonteyn in Frederick Ashton's *Symphonic Variations* and was the first to dance the title role in his *Cinderella*. In 1948 she secured lasting popular fame in the Michael Powell and Emeric Pressburger film *The Red Shoes*, which won four Oscar nominations. She went on to make more films, including *The Tales of Hoffmann* in 1950 and *The Man Who Loved Redheads* in 1954, and continued occasionally to dance and to act, including a season with the Bristol Old Vic. But after marrying the writer and broadcaster Ludovic Kennedy in 1950, she concentrated on family life with only occasional public appearances, lecture tours and some more stage plays. She also wrote articles for the press and two biographies, one of George Ballanchine (1986) and the other of Ellen Terry (1998). Died 31 January.

Sheikh Jaber al-Ahmad al-Sabah (b. 1926), Emir of Kuwait who fled during the Iraqi invasion in 1990 but returned to rebuild his country and introduce greater democracy. Born to rule, he was educated by a series of private tutors and entered public life in the territory, then under British protection, in 1949, when he took charge of security in the oilfields. As Kuwait headed towards full sovereignty in 1962 Sheikh Jaber headed the finance department, establishing a fund (10 per cent of oil revenues) against the time when the country's wells dried up. Succeeding as Emir in 1977, he supported Iraq when it attacked Iran in 1980, a stance which led to trouble with the Shi'ite community in Kuwait. After an attempt on his life in 1985, Sheikh Jaber dissolved the national assembly. Having contributed huge amounts to Saddam Hussein's long war against Iran (for Saddam's obituary see above), Sheikh Jaber was dumbfounded by Saddam's subsequent invasion of Kuwait in 1990 and, having escaped across the border into Saudi Arabia, appalled by the reports of what the Iraqis were doing to his country. Even after his triumphant return following the UN operation to free Kuwait, he seldom appeared in public, but presided over the reconstruction of destroyed oilfields, restored the legislature, albeit with a highly restricted franchise (though women were allowed the vote in the 2006 elections), and allowed US troops to launch the invasion of Iraq from Kuwait in 2003. Died 15 January.

Skate, Sir William (b. 1953), prime minister of Papua New Guinea who succeeded in ending the conflict with the island of Bougainville. Born in Port Moresby and popularly known as Bill, he was familiar with the squatter camps of the area and often accused in later life of links with the local Raskol gangs. From his humble beginnings he gained a place at university and a degree in accountancy. He entered politics in 1992 when he was elected regional MP for the National Capital District, eventually becoming prime minister after elections in 1997 which gave his People's National Congress only five seats compared with the People's Progressive Party's 16 (with whom Skate formed a coalition). During his 18 months in office Skate used his undoubted negotiating skills to broker a peace between the government in Port Moresby and the rebel province of Bougainville, a copper-rich island which, according to its inhabitants, was being fleeced by Papua New Guinea. The uneasy peace finally led to elections to Bougainville's own Legislative Assembly in 2005. Skate also served as acting governor-general (2003-04) and speaker of the National Parliament (2002-04). He suffered a stroke in late December 2005. Died 3 January.

Spark, Dame Muriel (b. 1918), British author whose best-known novel, *The Prime of Miss Jean Brodie*, sold hundreds of thousands of copies. Born Muriel Camberg in the Morningside suburb of Edinburgh, she was educated at James Gillespie's School for Girls (where she met the teacher who became the inspiration for Miss Brodie) and at a technical college from which she fled to Southern Rhodesia, where she married Sidney Spark, a schoolteacher. She left him soon after they had had a son, returning to Britain in 1944, taking a room in a London club (which she used as a model for the boarding house in her 1963 novel *The Girls of Slender Means*). In 1947 she joined the Poetry Society and for a short time edited *Poetry Review* before publishing her first books, a volume of poetry, *The Fanfarlo and other verse* (1952), *The Letters of Mary Shelley* (1951), and *The Bronte Letters* (1953). In 1954 she was received into the Catholic Church, which she later said inspired her novel writing. Her first, *The Comforters* (1957), was described by Evelyn Waugh as a masterpiece, and it was followed in quick succession by *Robinson* (1958), *Memento Mori* (1959), *The Ballad of Peckham Rye* (1960), *The Bachelors* (1960), and *The Prime of Miss Jean Brodie* (1961), which was undoubtedly her greatest success, becoming both a film and a stage play. In 1963 Spark moved to New York, where she greatly enjoyed the literary scene as well as writing another three novels, including *The Mandelbaum Gate* (1965), which won the James Tait Black memorial prize. In 1967 she moved to Italy, where she wrote another 12 novels as well as some short stories and poetry. In 1997 she won the David Cohen literature prize for a lifetime's achievement. She was appointed DBE in 1993. Died 13 April.

Spelling, Aaron (b. 1923), US television producer of soap operas ranging from *Starsky and Hutch* to *Charlie's Angels* and *Dynasty*. Born in Dallas, Texas, he studied at the Southern Methodist University in Dallas before serving in the US Army Air Force during the war. After an unsuccessful period in New York as an actor he moved to Hollywood where he wrote scripts for the Western series *Zane Grey Theatre* and *Wagon Train*. In 1968 he had his own first production success with *The Mod Squad*, which ran for five years on the ABC network. Later, with his own company, Spelling produced an almost continuous series of successful soaps for ABC during the 1970s and into the 1980s, beginning with *Starsky and Hutch* in 1975 and concluding with *Dynasty*, which ran from 1981 until 1989. He then made a series for the Fox network, including *Beverley Hills 90210* and *Charmed*. Hugely popular, though far from critical successes, they made Spelling a wealthy man, which helped him live comfortably with charges that he was partly responsible for the "dumbing down" of US television. Died 23 June.

Spillane, Mickey (b. 1918), popular US writer of tough crime thrillers, many featuring his private eye hero, Mike Hammer. Born Frank Morrison Spillane in Brooklyn, New York, he began writing when at high school, but without noticeable success. He wrote his first Mike Hammer detective story, *I, The Jury*, in under three weeks, sending it to the New York publishers E.P. Dutton, whose chief editor recommended acceptance with the comment that it was not in the best of taste, but that it would sell. Published in 1947, the book eventually sold more than 6 million copies. Spurred by its success, Spillane followed with another six Mike Hammer novels in the next five years. None received critical approval, though Spillane professed to be alarmed when *The New York Times* gave one of them quite a friendly notice. Hating New York, he moved eventually to South Carolina, writing some children's books but fewer thrillers until, in response to continuing popular demand, he wrote another Hammer story, *The Killing Man* in 1989. He also played Hammer in a number of films. Died 17 July.

Stroessner, General Alfredo (b. 1912), dictator of Paraguay who ruled for 35 years but ended his days in exile. Born in Encarnación he was educated at the military college in Asunción and from 1932 served as an artillery officer in the three-year Chaco war against Bolivia. He worked his way slowly up through the army and by 1951 was commander-in-chief. In 1954 he led a coup against President Federico Chavez, winning the election that followed as leader of the Colorado party and thereafter maintaining himself in power by a series of rigorously controlled elections after revising a constitution which stated that no president should rule for more than two five-year terms. Once he had removed all serious resistance Stroessner allowed a token political opposition, formally allocating it one third of the seats in Congress, and for a time, as the economy prospered through a hydro-electric project on the Parana river and flourishing contraband with neighbouring countries, his rule was quite popular, but increasing opposition from the Catholic Church and from the USA led finally to a coup by the army commander, General Andrés Rodríguez, in 1989. Stroessner was arrested and sent into exile in Brazil, where he remained for the rest of his life. Died 16 August.

Styron, William (b. 1925), best-selling US novelist whose work was ambitious and often controversial. Born in Newport News, Virginia, he was educated at Davidson College, North Carolina, and Duke university, interrupted by service with the US Marines. After graduating he began work on his first novel, *Lie Down in Darkness*, an elaborate work which introduced some grandiose psychological themes to the story of a young Virginian girl's suicide. Published in 1951 to encouraging critical reviews, it won the Prix de Rome. In 1952 he was briefly recalled to the Marines to train for service in the Korean War, which inspired a magazine article, *The Long March*, published later as a short book. A time spent in Europe prompted his next novel, *Set This House on Fire* (1960), about US expatriates, but he returned to a Southern theme in 1967 with *The Confessions of Nat Turner*, the story, as told by Turner himself, of a slave rebellion led by Turner, who was one of those executed when it failed. Styron won the Pulitzer Prize for the novel, which became a best-seller, as did *Sophie's Choice* (1979), the story of a survivor of Auschwitz living in

New York, which won the American Book Award and was subsequently made into a successful film. After a long period of depression Styron wrote a non-fictional account of the experience, *Darkness Visible - A Memoir of Madness*, published in 1990. Died 1 November.

Ta Mok (b. 1926), Khmer Rouge leader who carried out many of the atrocities associated with the regime of Pol Pot in Cambodia during the 1970s. Born Ung Choeun in Takeo, he adopted the name of Ta Mok when he joined the Communist party and fought with guerrillas until the Khmer Rouge finally achieved power in 1975. Already reputed to have been responsible for a number of massacres, Ta Mok was now put in charge of south-west Cambodia, where he established a reign of terror, the "killing fields" that became associated with the Pol Pot regime. In 1979, when the Vietnamese overthrew the regime and established a new government in Cambodia, Ta Mok continued to carry out guerrilla raids against military and civilian targets. As pressure grew on the Khmer Rouge, Ta Mok turned against Pol Pot, but was himself finally captured by Cambodian troops in 1999, remaining in captivity in Phnom Penh until his death. Died 21 July.

Thomson of Fleet, Lord (b. 1923), Canadian businessman who also inherited substantial interests in the UK, including Times Newspapers. Born in Toronto, Kenneth Thomson was educated at Upper Canada College before serving in the Royal Canadian Air Force during the war, after which he went to Cambridge university. His first work experience was with his father's first Canadian newspaper, the *Timmins Daily Press*, later becoming general manager of the *Galt Reporter*. When his father moved to Scotland, Kenneth became chairman of the Thomson interests in north America, which included newspapers and magazines in Florida and the Caribbean as well as a growing portfolio in Canada, including the *Globe* and *Mail*. In 1966, when *The Times* was bought to add to the family's purchase of *The Sunday Times* and form Times Newspapers Ltd, Kenneth became chairman and, on his father's death in 1976, succeeded to the title as second Lord Thomson of Fleet, though he never took his seat in the House of Lords and never used the title in Canada. His major problem on taking over the business was with the labour disputes at Times Newspapers, and in 1978 he suspended publication of both titles. The unions did not, as he had hoped, quickly settle, and after 11 months he resumed publication without any problems solved. Shortly afterwards a strike by the journalists at *The Times*, who had been paid throughout the stoppage, persuaded him to sell the papers to Rupert Murdoch. For a time Thomson maintained his other interests in the UK, but as he gradually concentrated on building up operations in Canada these were eventually sold off, including the profitable travel business. Back in Canada he developed the Thomson Corporation as an international electronic publisher of legal and financial information, bought the Hudson's Bay Company, built up an impressive art collection and became a noted patron of the arts and music in Toronto. Died 12 June.

Trueman, Fred, OBE (b. 1931), Yorkshire cricketer who, as a fast bowler for England, became the first man to take 300 test match wickets. Born in Seven Springs, near Stainton, he was educated locally and, on leaving school at 14, took a variety of jobs that allowed him to continue pursuing his cricketing ambitions. Though the committee paid for him to be coached, he did not get a regular place in the Yorkshire team until 1951, when he took 90 first class wickets and was awarded his county cap. In 1952 he was picked to play for England in the first Test against India, and such was his speed and aggression that in India's second innings he took three of the first four wickets for no runs. His career did not take off as quickly as might have been expected, partly because of his wayward behaviour off the field during the tour of the West Indies in 1953-54, and partly because at that time England also had the fast bowling of Alec Bedser, Frank Tyson, and Brian Statham to call on. But once Trueman became Statham's regular partner in 1957 his true potential was fulfilled. He took 21 Test wickets in the West Indies tour of 1959-60, took 11 for 88 in the Test against Australia at Headingley in 1961 (including six wickets for one run to finish off Australia's second innings), and took 34 Test wickets against the West Indies in 1963. He played his last Test in 1965, ending with a lifetime score of 307 Test wickets at an average of 21.57. After his retirement he became a popular public speaker and scored a notable success in the *Test Match Special* commentary box. Died 1 July.

Van Allen, Professor James (b. 1914), US physicist who discovered the radiation belts that surround the Earth. Born in Mount Pleasant, Iowa, he was educated locally and at Iowa Wesleyan College, where he studied nuclear physics before joining the Carnegie Institute in Washington DC as a research fellow. When war came he joined the US Navy, subsequently joining Johns Hopkins university as chief of its high-altitude research facility, and for a time working on the capabilities of captured German V2 rockets. He began particular research into cosmic radiation, becoming head of the physics department at Iowa state university in 1951 and travelling with expeditions to Greenland, Baffin Island and other parts of the world in preparation for the launch of Explorer I, the USA's first successful satellite, in 1958. Van Allen had devised Geiger counters for this and subsequent Explorer rockets, and it was from these that he was able to confirm the existence of a radiation band 250 miles round the Earth, and which came to bear his name. Subsequent research revealed that there are in fact two belts, an inner one containing protons and an outer composed mainly of electrons. Van Allen published nearly 300 scientific research papers during his lifetime, and was a keen supporter of unmanned space exploration. Died 9 August.

Walcott, Sir Clyde (b. 1926), West Indian cricketer who, with Frank Worrell and Everton Weekes, provided the middle batting order of one of the world's great test match teams. Born in Bridgetown, Barbados, he was educated at Harrison College and while still a pupil played for the island cricket team. In 1946 he scored 314 not out for Barbados against Trinidad, and began to make his mark in Test matches in the series against India in 1948-49. In the following year, against England, he scored seven centuries, and in a Test career that lasted until 1960 he played in 44 matches, scored 15 centuries with a total of 3,798 runs at an average of 56.68. He moved to what was then British Guiana to coach for a few years before returning to Barbados to chair the West Indies Cricket Board of Control until 1988, and was its president from 1988 to 1993. He was appointed a Knight of St Andrew, Order of Barbados, in 1993. Died 26 August.

Weinberger, Caspar (b. 1917), US secretary of defence who presided over a huge increase in his country's military capability towards the end of the Cold War. Born in San Francisco, he was educated at Harvard and law school, enlisting in the US Army and serving in the Pacific and later on the staff of General Douglas MacArthur. After the war he became a partner in a law firm, was elected to the California state assembly in 1952 and became chairman of the Californian Republican Party in 1962. He was appointed state director of finance by Governor Ronald Reagan in 1968, chairman of the federal trade commission by President Richard Nixon in 1970, and director of Nixon's office of management and budget in 1972. Though cost-cutting was his prime activity in these posts, the opposite was true in his next appointment, as secretary of defence for President Reagan. Between 1981 and 1987 he oversaw an increase in the defence budget by more than US$100 billion, part of which was devoted to increasing the strategic nuclear deterrent, including the Strategic Defence Initiative (SDI), which became known as "star wars", though difficulties with Congress prevented Weinberger from carrying out the tests he wanted. Though his defence budgets led to huge deficits, with resultant problems for the US and world economies, he had the satisfaction of knowing that he had helped push the Soviet Union into glasnost. After his resignation in 1987 Weinberger was faced with charges arising from the Iran-Contra affair, but was given an official presidential pardon in 1992. After his retirement from politics he became publisher of, and frequent contributor to, *Forbes* magazine. In 1988 he was awarded an honorary knighthood by the UK for his support during the Falklands war. Died 28 March.

Wooderson, Sydney, MBE (b. 1914), British long-distance runner who held world records for the 800 metres, the half and three-quarter miles, and the mile. Born in Camberwell, London, he was educated at Sutton Valence school, winning the public school championship mile race at the age of 18. A solicitor by profession, and an amateur as an athlete, he could train only in his spare time, but in the Empire Games in 1934 he won a silver medal in the mile, finishing behind Jack Lovelock of New Zealand. He beat Lovelock in the following year, but failed to qualify in his heat for the 1500 metres at the Berlin Olympics of 1936, having strained his ankle. In the following year he set a new world record for the mile, at four minutes 6.4 seconds, and in 1938 set a new record for the 800 metres. After the war Wooderson returned to the track to win the 1946 European 5,000 metre race in Oslo and in 1948 he won the English cross-country title over a gruelling nine-mile course. This was his last victory. A mile handicap race was run in his honour at Crystal Palace in 1987, and he was appointed MBE in 2000. Died 21 December.

XX CHRONICLE OF PRINCIPAL EVENTS IN 2006

JANUARY

2 **Nepal:** the chairman of the rebel Communist Party of Nepal-Maoist (CPN-M), Comrade Prachanda, announced the end of the party's unilateral ceasefire, in place since September 2005.

Uganda: the high court ordered the release of opposition leader Colonel Kizza Besigye, who had been put on trial in December 2005 on charges of rape and treason.

Iran: the resumption of research from 9 January "on the peaceful nuclear energy programme" was announced in a letter to the International Atomic Energy Agency (IAEA).

4 **China:** plans were announced to lift foreign exchange quota limits for overseas investment. In theory, the move would allow the value of the yuan to rise on a daily basis.

France: President Jacques Chirac lifted the state of emergency imposed in November 2005 to deal with the wave of inner-city rioting, mainly by young Muslims of African descent.

Israel: Deputy Prime Minister Ehud Olmert became interim prime minister, after Ariel Sharon suffered a severe stroke.

Turkey: the first human cases in the country of the potentially fatal H5N1 strain of avian influenza were reported.

Ukraine: a deal was agreed with Russia over the price of supplies of natural gas in 2006, following an acrimonious dispute that had led, on 1 January, to Russia's reducing the flow of gas to Ukraine, in turn affecting supplies to much of western Europe.

Tanzania: a cabinet was formed under the new president, Jakaya Kikwete, who had been elected in December 2005.

5 **Argentina:** the IMF confirmed that Argentina had completed early repayment of outstanding obligations to the IMF, amounting to SDR (special drawing rights) 6.656 billion.

United Arab Emirates: General Sheikh Mohammed bin Rashid al-Maktoum became vice president and prime minister of the UAE, and ruler of Dubai, following the sudden death on 4 January of his elder brother, Sheikh Maktoum bin Rashid al-Maktoum.

7 **Burkina Faso:** a new cabinet was formed under Prime Minister Paramanga Ernest Yoli, who was reappointed following the re-election of Captain Blaise Compaoré as president in November 2005.

11 **Kazakhstan:** President Nursultan Nazarbayev was sworn in for a further seven year term following his re-election in December 2005. A new cabinet was appointed on 18-19 January under reappointed Prime Minister Daniyal Akhmetov.

Mongolia: all 10 ministers of the Mongolian People's Revolutionary Party (MAHN) resigned from the 18-member cabinet claiming that the government of Prime Minister Tsakhiagiyn Elbegdorj of the Mongolian Democratic Party had failed to resolve economic problems. A new cabinet was appointed on 28 January, under new Prime Minister Miyeegombo Enkhbold, chairman of the MAHN.

12 **East Timor:** Foreign Minister José Ramos-Horta signed a treaty with his Australian counterpart Alexander Downer on sharing oil and gas revenues from fields in the Timor Sea.

13 **Pakistan:** at least 18 civilians were killed in an attack by a US pilotless drone aircraft which fired missiles at a housing compound in Damadola village near the border with Afghanistan. The attack was in response to reports that the deputy leader of the al-Qaida network, Egyptian Islamist militant Ayman al-Zawahiri, was attending a meeting in Damadola, although al-Zawahiri was not among those killed.

15 **Chile:** Michelle Bachelet of the Socialist Party of Chile (PSC)—a faction of the ruling Concertatión coalition—won the second round of presidential elections with 53.49 per cent of the vote. The first round had been held in December 2005. Bachelet thereby became the first female elected president of Chile.

Kuwait: Sheikh Jaber al-Ahmed al-Sabah, the emir, died. Although Crown Prince Sheikh Saad al-Salem al-Sabah was pronounced the new emir, his ill health prompted his removal from the post on 24 January by a vote in the National Assembly. The new emir was announced as Sheikh Sabah al-Ahmad al-Jaber al-Sabah, Kuwait's de facto ruler.

16 **Italy:** a new governor of the Bank of Italy was appointed. Mario Draghi replaced Antonio Fazio who resigned after allegations of favouritism.

Liberia: Ellen Johnson-Sirleaf was sworn in as president, following her victory in elections in October and November 2005. Johnson-Sirleaf thereby became Africa's first elected female head of state.

Moldova: a deal was reached with Russia over the price of supplies of natural gas.

17 **Russia:** a controversial bill to restrict the activities of foreign and domestic non-governmental organisations became law.

USA: the American civil liberties union (ACLU) and the centre for constitutional rights (CCR) filed separate cases against the domestic spying programme, seeking to have the monitoring of international communications by US citizens declared unconstitutional.

17-18 **World Health Organisation (WHO):** a conference on avian and human influenza, convened in China's capital, Beijing, produced pledges of US$1.9 billion from 33 donor countries and institutions to combat the virus.

18 **North Korea:** it was confirmed that North Korea's leader Kim Jong Il had visited China on 10-18 January, visiting economic development projects in central and southern China and meeting President Hu Jintao.

19 **Gabon:** President Omar Bongo Ondimba was sworn in for a further seven-year term, following his re-election in November 2005. His new cabinet was appointed on 21 January.

20 **Iraq:** the Independent Electoral Commission announced the final results of legislative elections held in December 2005. The (Shi'ite Muslim) United Iraqi Alliance was the largest single group, with 128 seats in the 275-member Council of Representatives (unicameral legislature).

22 **Bolivia:** Evo Morales of the left-wing Movement Towards Socialism (MAS), who won presidential elections in December 2005, was formally inaugurated as president. A new cabinet was formed on 23 January.

Cambodia: the first (indirect) elections to the 61 member Senate (upper house of the bicameral legislature) were won by the ruling Cambodian People's Party, with 45 of the 57 seats contested.

Cape Verde: legislative elections resulted in victory for the ruling African Party for the Independence of Cape Verde (PAICV), with 41 of the 72 seats in the unicameral National Assembly.

Portugal: presidential elections were won in a first round by Anibal Cavaco Silva, candidate of the opposition centre-right Social Democratic Party (PSD), with 50.59 per cent of the vote.

Russia: a programme broadcast by the RTR television station claimed that four UK diplomats were engaged in espionage, using a fake rock that hid a transmitter on a Moscow street. The programme also alleged that one of the diplomats was channelling British funds to Russian non-governmental organisations.

23 **Canada:** in a general election, the Conservative Party of Canada (CPC) won 124 seats in the 308-seat House of Commons (lower chamber of the bicameral legislature), defeating the Liberal Party (LP) which had governed for 12 years. CPC leader Stephen Harper became Canada's new prime minister.

23-24 **African Union (AU):** the sixth summit meeting was held in Khartoum, the capital of Sudan. Allegations of human rights abuses in Sudan's Darfur region prompted the appointment of President Denis Sassou-Nguesso of Congo as AU chairman, with Sudan scheduled to assume the chairmanship in 2007.

24 **USA:** chairman of the Council of Europe's committee on legal affairs and human rights, Swiss senator Dick Marty, presented his second interim report to the Council on allegations of the practice of "extraordinary rendition" of prisoners by the USA to countries that tolerated torture.

25 **Palestine:** elections to the Palestine Legislative Council (PLC) were won by the militant Islamist group Hamas, with 74 seats in the 132-seat PLC to the former ruling Fatah's 45. The Fatah-dominated government of Prime Minister Ahmed Qurie resigned the following day.

Taiwan: Su Tseng-chang was sworn in as premier of the new Executive Yuan (Cabinet) following the resignation of the previous Democratic Progressive Party (DPP)-dominated Cabinet after the DPP's defeat in local elections in December 2005.

27 **Côte d'Ivoire:** President Laurent Gbagbo unilaterally extended the term of the National Assembly (which had expired in December 2005), in defiance of a decision to the contrary on 15 January by the UN-backed International Working Group established to implement the peace plan for Côte d'Ivoire.

Honduras: José Manuel "Mel" Zelaya was inaugurated as president following victory in elections in November. A new cabinet was sworn in the same day.

Netherlands Antilles: legislative elections—the last before the planned dissolution of the Netherlands Antilles—were held throughout the five-island archipelago to the 22-member Staten (unicameral legislature).

29 **Finland:** incumbent President Tarja Halonen was re-elected for a second six-year term in a second round of voting (the first round had been held on 15 January).

space: an unmanned space probe mission to Pluto was launched by the USA's National Aeronautics and Space Administration (NASA).

30 **Chile:** Michelle Bachelet, who won presidential elections on 15 January, announced her new cabinet. Fulfilling a campaign pledge, she appointed equal numbers of men and women to the 20-member body.

31 **USA:** the president, George W. Bush, gave his annual state of the union address to a joint session of the two houses of Congress (the legislature). The same day, the Senate (the upper house) confirmed the appointment of Samuel Alito to the US Supreme Court; and Chairman of the US Federal Reserve (central bank) Alan Greenspan stepped down after 19 years and was replaced by Ben Bernanke.

FEBRUARY

1 **Afghanistan:** a two-day conference of international donors in London ended with a pledge of US$10.5 billion in aid over five years, and the setting of targets to improve human rights, development, and security.

Arab Maghreb Union: Habib Ben Yahia (Tunisia) became the new secretary general, for a three-year term, replacing Habib Boulares, also of Tunisia.

Kenya: Finance Minister David Mwiraria—a close political ally of President Mwai Kibaki—resigned after being implicated in the Anglo-Leasing corruption scandal.

USA: the Government Accountability Office (GAO) reported on the authorities' failings in responding to Hurricane Katrina. It concluded that a lack of a clear chain of command had hampered the relief effort.

1-2 **France, Italy, Spain, Switzerland, Germany, the Netherlands:** the republication in these countries' media of one or more of the 12 caricatures of the Prophet Mohammed, first printed in Denmark's *Jyllands-Posten* newspaper on 30 September 2005, prompted protests throughout the world by Muslims angered at the depiction.

2 **Poland:** the minority ruling Law and Justice Party (PiS) averted early elections by concluding a 12-month "stability pact" with the opposition Self-Defence (Samooborona) farmers' union party and the League of Polish Families (LPR), thereby enabling the Sejm (the lower house of the bicameral legislature) to pass the 2006 budget, which it had failed to adopt by the constitutional deadline of 31 January.

4 **Iran:** the governing board of the International Atomic Energy Agency (IAEA) voted to report Iran to the UN Security Council over its nuclear activities.

5 **Costa Rica:** presidential and legislative elections produced victory for former President Oscar Arias Sánchez of the National Liberation Party (PLN). No formal winner was declared, however, because of unresolved complaints about the elections.

6 **Slovakia:** the minority ruling coalition government collapsed after the Catholic Christian Democratic Movement (KDH) left the government over a dispute about abortion. Early elections were called for 17 June.

USA: President George W. Bush presented the US$2,770 billion federal budget for fiscal year 2007 to Congress (the bicameral legislature). The budget projected a sixth consecutive deficit, of US$354 billion.

7 **Haiti:** delayed presidential elections were won by former President René Préval of the Lespwa (Hope) coalition with over 50 per cent of the vote.

Senegal: former Prime Minister Idrissa Seck was released after seven months in prison, following the High Court of Justice's dismissal of embezzlement charges against him.

UK: radical Muslim cleric Sheikh Abu Hamza al-Masri received a seven-year prison sentence, after being convicted by a jury in London on 11 of 15 charges of inciting the murder of non-Muslims and possessing a document likely to be useful to terrorists.

8 **Nigeria:** it was confirmed by the World Organisation for Animal Health that Africa's first cases of the H5N1 avian influenza virus had occurred in northern Nigeria where tens of thousands of hens had died.

9 **Bangladesh:** a court sentenced three leaders of the Islamic militant group Jamaat-ul-Mujaheddin Bangladesh (JMB) to 40 years' imprisonment after they admitted participating in a bombing attack in November 2005.

10 **Cambodia:** opposition leader Sam Rainsy returned to Cambodia from exile in France after King Norodom Sihamoni granted a royal pardon on 5 February. Rainsy had been sentenced to 18 months' imprisonment in December 2005.

Serbia & Montenegro: the legislature of the disputed Serbian province of Kosovo elected Fatmir Sejdiu as Kosovo's new president, replacing Ibrahim Rugova, who had died in January.

11 **Tonga:** Prime Minister Prince Ulukalala Lavaka Ata resigned without explanation. His brother, Crown Prince Tupouto'a, appointed Labour Minister Frederick Sevele as acting prime minister, the first commoner to hold the post.

12 **Cape Verde:** presidential elections were narrowly won by incumbent Pedro Pires of the ruling African Party for the Independence of Cape Verde (PAICV). Pires appointed a new government on 8 March.

Iraq: the United Iraqi Alliance chose Ibrahim al-Jaafari to continue as prime minister, following its victory in the December 2005 elections.

13 **Kazakhstan:** opposition leader and former cabinet minister Altynbek Sarsenbayev Sarsenbayuly was found shot dead in his car, together with his driver and his bodyguard.

14 **Greece:** the foreign and defence ministers were replaced in a major cabinet reshuffle that followed the announcement on 2 February that the mobile telephones of the prime minister and some 100 senior officials had been tapped from June 2004 until March 2005.

Israel: Omri Sharon, eldest son of stroke-affected Prime Minister Ariel Sharon, received a 14-month prison sentence for illegal fundraising in 1999 during his father's leadership campaign for the Likud.

16 **USA:** the UN Commission on Human Rights (UNCHR) issued a report concluding that interrogators at the Guantanámo Bay US naval base in Cuba had committed acts that amounted to torture in order to intimidate prisoners, and that the US military tribunals violated prisoners' right to a fair trial.

17 **Sudan:** a confidential annexe to a UN report naming 17 individuals who could be considered for UN Security Council sanctions over their alleged role in the Darfur conflict was leaked. They included senior Sudanese government members.

18 **Democratic Republic of Congo:** a new constitution was promulgated by President Joseph Kabila, following its approval by referendum in December 2005.

22 **Iraq:** the Shi'ite Muslim al-Askariya shrine in Samarra, north of Baghdad—one of the four key Shi'ite holy sites in Iraq—suffered a bomb attack that destroyed its dome and prompted retaliatory attacks across the country.

23 **Uganda:** presidential and legislative elections—the first under a multiparty system in 26 years—resulted in victory for incumbent President Yoweri Museveni and his National Resistance Movement (NRM) over his main rival, Kizza Besigye.

24 **Philippines:** a state of emergency was declared after military officers claimed to have foiled a coup attempt against President Gloria Macapagal-Arroyo. The state of emergency was lifted on 3 March.

Saudi Arabia: in the first attempted attack on an oil installation in the country, suspected Islamic militants approached the world's largest oil processing plant at Abqaiq. The militants, reportedly supporters of al-Qaida, were prevented from entering the plant when security guards fired on their explosive-laden vehicles.

26 **Somalia:** the first meeting in Somalia of the transitional legislature selected in Kenya in August 2004 met briefly in the south-eastern city of Baidoa.

27 **Taiwan:** President Chen Shui-bian disbanded the National Unification Council (NUC), an advisory body established in 1990. Chen cited heightened military threats against Taiwan by mainland China as justification for the decision.

28 **Côte d'Ivoire:** the first talks in three years of conflict to be held in Côte d'Ivoire itself opened in the official capital, Yamoussoukro. The five key figures in the dispute announced support for the UN-backed peace plan of October 2005..

MARCH

1-3 **India:** during his first visit to the country, US President George W. Bush signed an agreement with Prime Minister Manmohan Singh to allow India to purchase nuclear fuel and nuclear technology from the USA.

6 **Iraq:** the international human rights organisation, Amnesty International, released a report, *Beyond Abu Ghraib: Detention and* torture in Iraq, claiming that 14,000 prisoners were being held there without charge, in breach of international law.

Uzbekistan: opposition leader, businessman Sanjar Umarov, was sentenced to nearly 11 years in prison and fined US$8.3 million, having been convicted of theft.

7 **Uganda:** opposition leader Kizza Besigye of the Forum for Democratic Change, was cleared of a rape charge. He still faced three separate treason-related charges.

9 **USA:** the USA Patriot Act—the anti-terrorism legislation granting new powers to the federal government after the terrorist attacks of 11 September 2001—was renewed, with amendments designed to offer greater protection for civil liberties.

10 **Netherlands:** a court convicted nine members of the militant Islamist Hofstad group of membership of a terrorist organisation. Mohammed Bouyeri, already serving a life sentence for the murder of film-maker Theo van Gogh, was found guilty of leading the group.

11 **Serbia & Montenegro:** Slobodan Milosevic, the former president of Yugoslavia, was found dead in his cell at the detention centre of the International Criminal Court for the Former Yugoslavia (ICTY) in The Hague, the Netherlands.

12 **El Salvador:** victory in the legislative elections was claimed by both the ruling Nationalist Republican Alliance (ARENA) and the opposition leftist Farabundo Martí National Liberation Front (FMLN), with 39.4 per cent and 39.7 per cent of the vote respectively.

Colombia: legislative elections were won by parties allied to President Alvaro Uribe Velez in both the upper and lower houses of the bicameral legislature.

14 **China:** at the end of the fourth session of the 10th National People's Congress (NPC, the unicameral legislature), which had opened on 5 March, delegates approved China's 11th Five Year Plan for 2006-10.

Senegal: fighting erupted along the border with Guinea-Bissau between rival factions of the separatist Casamance Movement of Democratic Forces (MFDC). The army of Guinea-Bissau joined the fighting on 16 March.

South Korea: Prime Minister Lee Hai Chan offered his resignation because of public displeasure that he had played golf on 1 March, the day when transport workers began a national strike and which also marked the anniversary of a 1919 uprising against Japanese colonial rule.

15 **Chad:** a coup attempt by army officers to shoot down the aircraft of President Idriss Déby was foiled.

United Nations: the UN General Assembly voted to establish a Human Rights Council (UNHRC), replacing the discredited UN Commission on Human Rights (UNCHR).

18 **Bosnia & Herzegovina:** a package of constitutional reforms that aimed to strengthen the country's central government was approved by leaders from all three communities (Bosniak or Muslim, Serb, and Croat).

19 **Belarus:** presidential elections were overwhelmingly won by the incumbent, Alyaksandr Lukashenka, amidst accusations of fraud. Opposition protests on 25 March against the result were violently dispersed.

Benin: independent candidate Yayi Boni, chairman of the West African Development Bank (BOAD), won the second round of the presidential election with 74.6 per cent of the vote. The first round had been held on 5 March. Boni appointed a new cabinet on 8 April.

Venezuela: relations with the USA deteriorated further when President Hugo Chávez Frías described US President George W. Bush as "genocidal, alcoholic, drunk, immoral". The USA's national security strategy, released on 16 March, had accused Chavez of "seeking to destabilise the region".

21 **USA:** at a press conference, President George W. Bush acknowledged that the war in Iraq would not be concluded during his term in office (due to end in January 2009).

22 **Spain:** the militant Basque separatist organisation, ETA, announced that it would introduce a permanent ceasefire, from 24 March.

The Gambia: it was announced that a plot by army officers to overthrow the government of President Yahya Jammeh had been discovered. The chief of defence staff was replaced as a consequence.

26 **Netherlands Antilles:** a new cabinet under new Prime Minister Emily de Jongh-Elhage was sworn in, following legislative elections in January.

Ukraine: elections to the Verkhovna Rada (unicameral legislature) failed to produce an overall majority for any single party, although the opposition Party of Regions claimed victory.

28 **France:** a one-day general strike was called against proposals to introduce a "first employment contract" (CPE) which would make it easier for employers to dismiss younger people in their first job. Students and workers had mounted protests throughout March against the CPE which the government had announced by decree in August 2005.

Israel: elections to the 120-member Knesset (unicameral legislature) were won by the newly-formed Kadima (Forward) party, with 29 seats; the Labour Party came second with 19 seats, whereas the former ruling Likud received only 12 seats.

USA: the White House chief-of-staff, Andrew Card, was replaced by Joshua Bolten, the director of the office of management and budget (OMB).

29 **Palestine:** a new cabinet under Prime Minister Ismail Haniyeh was sworn in, placing the radical Islamist Hamas movement in charge of the Palestine National Authority (the government).

30 **Jamaica:** Portia Simpson Miller, leader of the ruling People's National Party (PNP), became Jamaica's first female prime minister, following the retirement of Percival J. Patterson.

UK: the terrorism bill and identity cards bill became law after lengthy and contentious passages through both chambers of Parliament.

APRIL

1 **Palestine:** Israel began shelling the Gaza Strip, using gunboats for the first time, in the largest barrage against the territory since the withdrawal of Jewish settlers in August 2005. An estimated 300 shells per day were hitting the territory by mid-April.

Venezuela: the government took control of seven oil fields that were operated by foreign companies (in two cases, without agreement from the foreign companies), under the terms of a 2001 law which replaced their service contracts by joint venture contracts with Petroleos de Venezuela (PDVSA, the state-owned oil company).

3 **Liberia:** former President Charles Taylor appeared before the UN-backed Special Court for Sierra Leone in Freetown (capital of Sierra Leone) on 11 counts of crimes against humanity and violations of the Geneva Conventions during Sierra Leone's 10-year civil war. Taylor had been extradited from Nigeria to face trial on 29 March.

4 **Thailand:** Prime Minister Thaksin Shinawatra announced that he would step down. His Thai Rak Thai (TRT) party won elections to the 500-member House of Representatives (lower chamber of the bicameral legislature) on 2 April amidst great controversy and a boycott by the main opposition parties.

5 **Guinea:** a presidential decree dismissed Prime Minister Cellou Dalein Diallo for "serious offences"; the decree also rescinded the previous day's cabinet reshuffle that had extended Diallo's powers.

6 **Nigeria:** Vice President Atiku Abubakar called on President Olusegun Obasanjo to resign for allegedly planning to amend the constitution in order to stand for a third term in the 2007 presidential elections.

7 **Bosnia & Herzegovina:** the first verdict was handed down by the War Crimes Chamber of Bosnia's State Court, when Nedjo Samardzic, a Bosnian Serb, was sentenced to 13 years' imprisonment for crimes committed during the 1992-95 war.

9-10 **Italy:** the general election produced the narrowest of victories for the opposition centre-left alliance, "The Union", over the ruling House of Freedoms Coalition, with 49.8 per cent of the vote to 49.7 per cent in elections to the Chamber of Deputies (the lower house).

10 **France:** President Jacques Chirac announced that the proposed "first employment contract" (CPE) for younger workers would be withdrawn. The decision followed weeks of strikes and student protests.

USA: a "day of action for immigrant justice" saw mass demonstrations in 60 major cities to protest against the imposition of penalties on illegal immigrants.

Australia: Cabinet ministers began giving evidence to a government-appointed commission in the scandal around alleged bribes of A$300 million paid by the former Australian Wheat Board in 1997-2003 to Iraq to secure wheat export contracts.

11 **Iran:** President Mahmoud Ahmadinejad announced on national television that Iran had succeeded for the first time in enriching uranium—a key stage in the development of nuclear fuel—and had "joined the club of nuclear countries".

Israel: Ariel Sharon was declared "permanently incapacitated", allowing his deputy Ehud Olmert to assume the post of prime minister in his stead. Sharon had suffered a stroke on 4 January.

17 **Palestine:** a suicide bomber killed nine people in a fast food restaurant in Tel Aviv. Islamic Jihad claimed responsibility for the attack.

19 **South Korea:** Han Myong Suk of the ruling Uri (Our) Party became the first woman to hold the post of prime minister, following endorsement of her nomination in the National Assembly.

21 **China:** President Hu Jintao concluded a four-day visit to the USA, his first as president.

G-7: finance ministers and central bank governors of the G-7 (Group of Seven) most advanced industrial economies, meeting in Washington DC, called on the members of OPEC (the Organisation of Petroleum Exporting Countries) to increase investment in exploration and refining capacity to maintain oil supplies, in view of concerns raised by the current record high oil price of US$75 per barrel.

Haiti: a second round of voting in legislative elections saw the Lespwa (Hope) coalition of President-elect René Préval fail to produce an overall majority in either house of the bicameral legislature. A first round of voting had been held on 7 February.

Iraq: the United Iraqi Alliance (UIA)—the Shi'ite Muslim religious alliance that had won the largest number of seats in the legislature, the Council of Representatives, in December 2004—selected Nouri al-Maliki as its new candidate for prime minister, to replace Ibrahim al-Jaafari who had come under increasing pressure to relinquish the post.

Nepal: King Gyanendra called on the seven-party alliance of opposition groups to recommend a new prime minister, signalling the end of autocratic rule that he had imposed on Nepal from 1 February 2005.

Nigeria: became Africa's first country to settle its debt with its official western lenders when it made a final payment of US$4.5 billion to the Paris Club of creditor countries.

São Tomé and Príncipe: a new government was sworn in, following the legislative elections in March, under Prime Minister Tomé Soares da Vera Cruz of the Democratic Movement Force for Change (MDFM).

22 **Andean Community of Nations (CAN):** Venezuela formally submitted its decision to withdraw from the five-nation South American trade bloc, which also included Bolivia, Colombia, Ecuador, and Peru.

Samoa: a new cabinet was announced, following the confirmation of the final results of the 31 March general election, which was won by the ruling Human Rights Protection Party. Tuilaepa Sailele remained prime minister.

22-23 **IMF/World Bank:** the spring meetings of the global financial institutions in Washington DC endorsed plans for reform of the IMF and for a broadening of World Bank strategy.

23 **Hungary:** a second round of legislative elections (the first having been held on 9 April) produced a second term for the ruling Hungarian Socialist Party (MSzP) and its junior partner, the Alliance of Free Democrats (SzDSz).

24 **Egypt:** a series of explosions in the Red Sea resort of Dahab killed at least 21 people. No group claimed responsibility.

North-South Korea: the 18th round of inter-Korean ministerial talks ended in Pyongyang, the North Korean capital, having opened on 21 April. Ministers concluded an eight-point agreement.

Philippines: 49 people, including legislators and military officers, were charged with rebellion in connection with the alleged plot to stage a coup against the government of President Gloria Macapagal-Arroyo in February.

25 **Sri Lanka:** in a further dissolution of the ceasefire between government forces and the separatist rebel Liberation Tigers of Tamil Eelam (LTTE), a female suicide bomber carried out an attack on Sri Lankan Army (SLA) headquarters in the capital, Colombo, prompting retaliatory SLA air strikes and shelling of LTTE bases in the north-east.

Sudan: under Resolution 1672 (2006) the UN Security Council imposed sanctions on four senior Sudanese commanders accused of war crimes in Darfur.

Thailand: King Bhumibol Adulyadej asked the country's highest courts to resolve the "political mess" that had resulted from the disputed 2 April elections to the lower house of the legislature, the House of Representatives, and the 19 April elections to the Senate (the upper house).

26 **Bangladesh:** security forces arrested the last two members of the ruling council of the banned militant Islamic group, Jamaat-ul-Mujaheddin Bangladesh (JMB) at liberty. Two other JMB leaders had been captured in early March.

Solomon Islands: following riots at the prospect of his appointment, Snyder Rini was obliged to resign from the post of prime minister to which he had been elected on 18 April by the new 50-member National Parliament that had been formed after a general election on 5 April.

UK: Home Secretary Charles Clarke admitted failings in the prisoner release system when he confirmed that 1,023 convicted foreign nationals had not been considered for deportation upon their release from prison.

USA: a committee of the European Parliament reported that the CIA had flown 1,000 flights over European countries since 2001 and abducted individuals from within EU countries during the "extraordinary rendition" of terrorist suspects—the process whereby individuals were transferred to custody in countries that allowed the use of torture.

28 **France:** the *Le Monde* newspaper published leaked testimony indicating that in January 2004 Prime Minister (then foreign minister) Dominique de Villepin had attempted to implicate Interior and Regional Development Minister (then economy minister) Nicolas Sarkozy in the Clearstream affair, in which bogus allegations had been made in 2004 against ministers for receiving bribes through the Clearstream International bank in connection with the sale of six French frigates to Taiwan in 1991.

Iran: the International Atomic Energy Agency (IAEA)'s head Muhammed al-Baradei reported to the UN Security Council that, because Iran had failed to co-operate fully with the IAEA, the Agency could not guarantee that Iran's nuclear programme was purely peaceful.

Nepal: the House of Representatives (lower chamber of the bicameral legislature), which King Gyanendra had dissolved in May 2002, reconvened after the King, on 24 April, reinstated the body, thereby meeting the principal demand of the seven-party alliance (SPA) of opposition groups.

29 **Italy:** Silvio Berlusconi announced his resignation as prime minister, following his narrow defeat in the 9-10 April general election by opposition leader Romano Prodi, whose victory had been upheld in a 19 April decision by the Court of Cassation, Italy's highest court.

30 **Israel:** the new Prime Minister Ehud Olmert formed a new coalition government dominated by his Kadima (Forward) party, and including the Labour Party, the Sephardic Torah Guardians (Shas), and the Pensioners of Israel to the Knesset (Gil).

Laos: elections to the unicameral legislature, the National Assembly, were won by the ruling Lao People's Revolutionary Party (LPRP) which took 113 of the 115 seats, the other two being won by independents.

MAY

1 **Bolivia:** president Evo Morales nationalised the country's hydrocarbons industry, requiring foreign-owned energy companies immediately to relinquish control to the Bolivian state of their natural gas fields.

2 **Nepal:** Girija Prasad Koirala of the Nepali Congress Party, who had been nominated as prime minister by the seven-party alliance (SPA) of opposition groups, announced a new cabinet.

3 **Chad:** President Idriss Déby of the ruling Patriotic Salvation Movement was elected for a third five-year term with 64.67 per cent of the vote.

4 **Russia:** US Vice President Dick Cheney castigated Russia for using its energy supplies to "blackmail" other countries, prompting a furious response by Russian officials.

Solomon Islands: the National Parliament elected as prime minister Manasseh Sogavare, leader of the Solomon Islands Social Credit Party (SoCred). Sogavare succeeded Snyder Rini who had been obliged to resign as prime minister in April.

USA: Zacarias Moussaoui, a French citizen of Moroccan descent, who in April 2005 had pleaded guilty to six charges of conspiracy in connection with the 11 September 2001 terrorist attacks, was sentenced to life imprisonment by a federal court in Virginia.

5 **Poland:** the ruling Law and Justice party (PiS) entered a formal coalition agreement with the right-wing nationalist and anti-EU Self-Defence (Samooborona) farmers' union party and the League of Polish Families (LPR).

Sudan: the Sudan Liberation Movement/Army—one of the main rebel groups in Sudan's western Darfur region—accepted a peace plan formulated by the African Union (AU), to which the Sudanese government had agreed on 30 April. The other main rebel group, the Justice and Equality Movement (JEM), however, maintained its rejection of the plan.

UK: a major government reshuffle followed the ruling Labour Party's heavy losses in local elections on 4 May, and saw the replacement of Home Secretary Charles Clarke by John Reid, following Clarke's admission of failures in the foreign prisoner release system.

USA: the director of the CIA, Porter Goss, resigned to be replaced on 8 May by US Air Force General Michael Hayden, subject to Senate approval.

6 **Singapore:** elections produced victory for the ruling People's Action Party (PAP), which won 82 seats in the 84 seat unicameral Parliament.

7 **Somalia:** fighting broke out in the capital, Mogadishu, between warlords and the Islamic Courts' militia and continued throughout the month.

8 **Costa Rica:** former President (1986-1990) Oscar Arias Sánchez was inaugurated for his second four-year term as president, following the February elections. He announced his cabinet the same day.

South Africa: former Deputy President (until June 2005) Jacob Zuma was acquitted of rape charges. He resumed his duties as deputy president of the ruling African National Congress (ANC) on 14 May.

Thailand: the Constitutional Court ruled invalid the controversial 2 April elections to the House of Representatives (lower house). Fresh elections were anticipated in October.

9 **Palestine:** the Middle East Quartet, meeting in New York, agreed a "temporary international mechanism" to allow Palestinians to receive aid, bypassing the Palestinian National Authority (controlled by Hamas, which the USA and the EU regarded as a terrorist organisation).

10 **China:** a ceremony marked the completion of the Three Gorges Dam, some ten months ahead of schedule.

Italy: Giorgio Napolitano was elected president in a fourth round of voting by the electoral college, succeeding president Azeglio Ciampi, whose term expired on 18 May.

11 **British Indian Ocean Territory:** the High Court in London ruled irrational and unlawful the UK government's "orders in council" of 2004 that had abolished the right of abode of the exiled Chagos islanders, who had been evicted in 1967-73 in order to allow the USA to lease Diego Garcia, the principal island, as a military base.

12 **Indonesia:** corruption charges against former president Suharto (1966-98) were dropped because of his poor health, according to the attorney general.

13 **Fiji Islands:** elections that began on 6 May produced a narrow victory for the ruling United Fiji Party (SDL) over the opposition Fiji Labour Party (FLP). On 18 May incumbent Prime Minister Laisenia Qarase was sworn in for a second term.

14 **Comoros:** elections for union president were won by Ahmed Abdallah Mohamed Sambi with 58.02 per cent of the vote.

Haiti: former president (1996-2001) René Préval was inaugurated as president, becoming the first elected leader to take office since the overthrow of President Jean-Bertrand Aristide in February 2004. Préval had won elections in February.

15 **Libya:** full diplomatic relations were restored with the USA and Libya was removed from the list of countries designated by the USA as state sponsors of terrorism.

Northern Ireland: the Northern Ireland Assembly, suspended in 2002, reconvened without power. The UK and Republic of Ireland governments had agreed in April to give Northern Ireland politicians until 24 November to reach agreement on an executive, or face direct rule from the UK.

16 **Dominican Republic:** the centrist Dominican Liberation Party (PLD)-led alliance won legislative elections to Congress (the bicameral legislature).

17 **Italy:** President Giorgio Napolitano formally appointed Prime Minister Romano Prodi and a new cabinet dominated by the left-wing parties that had narrowly won the April elections.

Turkey: Islamist lawyer Alparslan Arslan opened fire on five judges in the Council of State (the highest administrative court), killing one and wounding five, in response to the court's ruling that had banned promotion for a female teacher because she wore an Islamic headscarf on her way to work. Mass demonstrations ensued against the attack and in defence of secularism.

20 **Iraq:** the unicameral legislature, the Council of Representatives, approved a "national unity" cabinet under Prime Minister Nouri al-Maliki, a Shi'ite Muslim member of the Da'wa Party.

21 **Cyprus:** legislative elections returned the governing coalition to power, with the communist Progressive Party of the Working People (AKEL) and its junior coalition partner, the Democratic Party (DIKO), defeating the opposition Democratic Rally (DISY).

Serbia & Montenegro: a referendum to determine whether Montenegro should become an independent state resulted in a 55.53 per cent vote in favour. The EU had imposed a threshold of 55 per cent in favour for the independence proposal to be carried.

24 **Algeria:** Ahmed Ouyahia of the National Democratic Rally (RND) resigned as prime minister, and was replaced by Abdelaziz Belkhadem of the rival government party, the National Liberation Front (FNL).

Thailand: Prime Minister Thaksin Shinawatra resumed the post of acting prime minister, having stood down after the controversial April general elections.

Uganda: in the first videotape he had issued, the rebel commander, Joseph Kony, leader of the Lord's Resistance Army (LRA), requested peace talks with the Ugandan authorities.

25 **East Timor:** an advance guard of 150 Australian commanders arrived at the head of an international force numbering 2,000. Prime Minister Mari Alkatiri had requested foreign troops to quell the violence resulting from a rebellion by some one-third of East Timor's armed forces in April.

Palestine: President Mahmoud Abbas, leader of the former ruling Fatah, issued an ultimatum to Hamas (which dominated the Palestinian government) to recognise Israel within 10 days by endorsing an 18-point document drafted by Fatah and Hamas prisoners in Israeli gaols, or face a referendum on the issue.

USA: the Senate (upper house) enacted a bill intended to facilitate immigration and citizenship for illegal immigrants, although a December 2005 bill, enacted by the House of Representatives (the lower house), had advocated penalising illegal immigration.

USA: the former chief executives of the collapsed Enron Corp., Jeffrey Skilling and Kenneth Lay, were found guilty of fraud and conspiracy by a jury in Texas.

26 **USA-UK:** at a joint press conference in Washington DC, US President George W. Bush and Tony Blair, the UK prime minister, admitted that major errors had been made in the execution of the war in Iraq. Both claimed, however, that the election of a government in that country had justified the invasion.

27 **Burma (Myanmar):** the house arrest of opposition leader Aung San Suu Kyi was extended for another year. Aung San Suu Kyi had, on 20 May, held her first meeting with a foreign diplomat since March 2004, when UN under-secretary-general for political affairs, Ibrahim Gambari, was allowed to visit her.

Indonesia: an earthquake measuring 6.3 on the Richter scale hit southern Java, killing at least 5,846 people by the end of the month, injuring 30,000 and making 647,000 homeless.

28 **Lebanon:** the Israeli airforce attacked Palestinian bases inside Lebanon, after Palestinian militants had fired rockets on an Israeli army base in northern Israel.

29 **Colombia:** President Alvaro Uribe Velez won an historic second term with 62.2 per cent of the vote in the presidential election. A constitutional court ruling of November 2005 had permitted Uribe to contest a second term.

Guinea: following the dismissal of Prime Minister Cellou Dalein Diallo on 5 April, a major cabinet reshuffle rid the government of his supporters and appointed Elhadj Fodé Bangoura to the newly-created post of minister of state for presidential affairs and co-ordination of government action.

30 **EU:** the European Court of Justice (ECJ) upheld part of a challenge by the European Parliament to the legality of the EU's May 2004 agreement with the USA on the advance disclosure to the US authorities of personal data about passengers on transatlantic flights from the EU.

Japan: the cabinet endorsed a plan to realign the US military presence in Japan. It included the transfer of some 8,000 US marines from Okinawa, where their presence had been a focus of popular discontent, to the US Pacific territory of Guam.

31 **Montserrat:** elections to the nine-seat Legislative Council (unicameral legislature) produced victory for the opposition Movement for Change and Prosperity.

Lithuania: the government collapsed when the Labour Party (DP) withdrew from the coalition headed by Prime Minister Algirdas Brazauskas.

Taiwan: beset by scandals, President Chen Shui-bian ceded all powers of his office, apart from defence and foreign policy, to Premier Su Tseng-chang.

JUNE

2 **UK:** Over 250 police, some armed, raided a house in east London, arresting two brothers of Bangladeshi origin, on suspicion that they were making chemical or biological weapons for terrorist purposes. The men were released without charge on June 9, no suspicious items having been found on the premises.

2-3 **Canada:** security forces arrested 17 Canadian Muslims, on the grounds that they were preparing terrorist attacks in Canada. All the men were from the Toronto area.

2-3 **Czech Republic:** a general election produced an even distribution of seats between left and right and the prospect of months of political uncertainty.

3 **Bolivia:** a five-year land redistribution programme involving some 20 per cent of Bolivia's territory began with the award of 60 titles to 3.1 million hectares of government land to the country's poor.

Montenegro: the country was formally declared an independent state, following the May referendum on independence from Serbia.

4 **Azerbaijan:** the first oil exported from Azerbaijan's offshore fields, via the Baku-Tbilisi-Ceyhan (BTC) pipeline, left the Ceyhan shipping terminal in Turkey. The BTC had been formally opened in May 2005.

Peru: former President Alan García Pérez (1985-90) of the Peruvian Aprista Party won the second round of voting in presidential elections, defeating Lieutenant Colonel (retd) Ollanta Humala Tasso.

5 **Somalia:** the Union of the Islamic Courts—a loose alliance of Islamic militias—took control of the capital, Mogadishu, after some three months of sporadic fighting, from government-allied forces.

7 **Iraq:** Abu Musab al-Zarqawi, the leader of al-Qaida in Iraq, died in a US air strike north of Baghdad.

8 **Brazil:** a congressional investigation into corruption allegations completed its work and concluded that 79 people, including senior politicians and businessmen, should face criminal charges.

Iraq: the ministers of defence, the interior, and national security were sworn in after approval of their appointments by the legislature, thereby ending stalemate between Iraq's religious and ethnic groups over the crucial posts.

Laos: The sixth National Assembly elected as president Lt-Gen. Choummaly Sayasone (the former vice president) and as prime minister Bouasone Bouphavanh (the former deputy prime minister).

9 **Haiti:** a former prime minister, Jacques Edouard Alexis, was appointed prime minister together with a new 18-member cabinet, following the inauguration in May of President René Préval.

12 **Albania:** the country signed a stabilisation and association agreement (SAA) with the EU at a ceremony in Luxembourg.

Cameroon-Nigeria: the presidents of Cameroon and Nigeria (Paul Biya and Olusegun Obasanjo) reached agreement at a meeting in New York mediated by UN Secretary-General Kofi Annan on the disputed Bakassi peninsula, following the 2002 ruling by the International Court of Justice (ICJ) that Cameroon had sovereignty.

Turkey: negotiations formally began on the first of 35 "chapters" in the accession talks with the EU, after the EU had agreed in October 2005 to membership talks with Turkey.

14 **Indonesia:** the Islamist cleric Abu Bakar Bashir, believed to be the spiritual leader of the militant Jemaah Islamiah (JI) network, was released from prison in Jakarta, the capital, having served 26 months of a 30-month sentence for involvement in terrorist attacks.

France: a court in Paris sentenced 25 Algerian members of the Islamist "Chechen cell" to up to 10 years in prison for plotting to use chemical weapons for terrorist attacks. Two defendants were acquitted.

15 **Afghanistan:** a major anti-Taliban offensive, "Operation Mountain Thrust", was launched by US-led forces in response to the continued spring offensive by the Taliban.

Iceland: Prime Minister Halldor Asgrimsson resigned, to be succeeded, at his own request, by Foreign Minister Geir H. Haarde.

16 **Liberia:** The UN Security Council authorised the transfer of former President Charles Taylor from the Special Court for Sierra Leone (the UN-backed war crimes tribunal based in Freetown, the capital of Sierra Leone) to the International Criminal Court (ICC) in The Hague. The Special Court would retain jurisdiction over Taylor.

Nepal: the chairman of the underground Communist Party of Nepal-Maoists, Comrade Prachanda, held talks with the prime minister, Girija Prasad Koirala, which resulted in an announcement that the Maoists would join an interim government to prepare for elections to a constituent assembly.

Zimbabwe: it was reported that China had agreed energy and mining deals with Zimbabwe worth around US$1.3 billion

17 **Russia:** the leader of the Chechen separatist movement, Abdul-Khalim Sadulayev, was killed in an exchange of fire with Russian troops. Sadulayev had been appointed in March 2005 following the death of popularly-elected rebel Chechen leader Aslan Maskhadov

18 **Spain:** voters in Catalonia approved by 73.9 to 20 per cent the government's plans to grant greater autonomy to the region. Turnout was only 49 per cent, however.

18-23 **Africa:** the prime minister of China, Wen Jiabao, visited seven African states (Egypt, Ghana, Congo, Angola, South Africa, Tanzania, and Uganda) in an attempt to increase China's presence in the continent's natural resources extraction industries.

19 **Australia:** Faheem Khalid Lodhi, a Pakistani-born architect, was convicted under anti-terrorism laws introduced in November 2005 of planning an attack on the New South Wales electricity grid in 2003.

23 **Benin:** the National Assembly (unicameral legislature) approved a constitutional amendment increasing the Assembly's mandate from four years to five, thereby bringing it into line with the presidential term. The next general election was therefore postponed until 2008.

USA: the *New York Times* and other media reported concerns that the US government was obtaining large data sets of financial information from the database managed by SWIFT (the Society for Worldwide Interbank Financial Telecommunications) without judicial or legislative oversight.

24 **Philippines:** President Gloria Macapagal-Arroyo abolished the death penalty which had been abolished in 1987 but restored in 1994. A moratorium on the death penalty had been imposed in 2000 by former President Joseph Estrada.

25 **Mauritania:** in a national referendum on amendments to the constitution approved by the ruling military junta, 96.97 per cent of voters, on a 76.51 per cent turnout, voted in favour.

Palestine: militants carried out an attack on Israel, killing two soldiers and taking another prisoner, prompting reprisals by Israel including the detention of Hamas representatives—amongst whom were eight ministers of the Palestinian government—on 29 June and air raids on Gaza on 30 June.

26 **East Timor:** Prime Minister Mari Alkatiri announced his resignation, following several weeks of violent unrest, for which President Xanana Gusmão and other critics held him responsible.

27 **Vietnam:** Nguyen Minh Triet was confirmed as state president of Vietnam at the ongoing session of the 11th National Assembly, and Nguyen Tan Dung was elected as prime minister. Both were seen as economic reformers.

28 **Slovakia:** a new coalition government was announced, consisting of the centre-left Direction-Social Democracy Party (S-SD) and two right-wing parties. Robert Fico of the S-SD became the new prime minister on 4 July.

29 **Kuwait:** elections to the National Assembly (legislature) were held. For the first time, Kuwaiti women voted and competed for office: no woman won a seat in the new Assembly, but reformists were said to have made significant gains.

Netherlands: the government collapsed after the centrist Democrats 66 (D66)—the smallest party in the coalition government—withdrew its support over a controversy involving Immigration Minister Rita Verdonk and the Somali-born member of the legislature, Ayaan Hirsi Ali.

Spain: the government announced it was to begin the first direct formal peace talks with the Basque separatist group, ETA, after the group had declared a permanent ceasefire in March.

USA: in *Hamdan v Rumsfeld*, the US Supreme Court ruled by five to three that the military tribunals established to try detainees held in the US naval base in Guantánamo Bay, Cuba, were illegal, violating the US uniform code of military justice and the Geneva Conventions.

30 **France:** the government's immigration bill completed its passage. The bill aimed to restrict undesirable immigration whilst encouraging the immigration of skilled workers.

JULY

1 **China:** the Qinghai-Tibet railway line, completed in 2005, was officially opened by President Hu Jintao. The railway would increase tourism and employment in the Tibet region, according to the authorities: critics said that it symbolised China's control over Tibet.

1-2 **African Union (AU):** the seventh summit meeting of the AU was held in Banjul, capital of The Gambia. The summit stipulated which regional economic communities (RECs) in Africa it would recognise and decided to launch the African Court on Human and People's Rights.

2 **Bolivia:** elections to a 255-seat constituent assembly were won by the ruling Movement Towards Socialism party (MAS), with 137 seats. The assembly was due to convene for one year from 6 August.

Mexico: presidential elections were narrowly won by Felipe Calderón, candidate of the National Action Party (PAN); but his rival, Andrés Manuel López Obrador, candidate of the Party of the Democratic Revolution (PRD) demanded a full manual recount. Supporters of López Obrador staged rallies throughout the month in protest at the official results.

Palestine: Israel launched a helicopter attack on the office of the Palestinian prime minister and Hamas leader, Ismail Haniyeh, as part of its campaign to force Palestinian militant groups to release an Israeli soldier (Corporal Gilad Shalit) captured on 25 June. Israeli attacks on Gaza over the month to 25 July killed 120 Palestinians, including 26 children, and damaged much of the area's infrastructure. One Israeli soldier was killed.

Sudan: at the request of the UN, the African Union (AU) agreed to extend by three months, until the end of 2006, the mandate of its mission in the troubled western Sudanese province of Darfur.

3 **Cambodia:** judges were sworn in on a tribunal to try surviving members of the Khmer Rouge regime (1975-79). Of the 27 judges, 17 were Cambodian and 10 were foreign UN-appointees.

3-6 **CARICOM:** the 27th annual summit of heads of government of the 15 members of the Caribbean Community and Common Market was held in St Kitts & Nevis. Haiti, suspended since March 2004, was formally restored to full membership of CARICOM.

4 **Lithuania:** Gediminas Kirkilas of the Lithuanian Social Democratic Party (LDSP) was confirmed as prime minister by the Seimas (unicameral legislature), following the collapse of the previous government on 31 May. A new four-party minority coalition government was formed on 18 July.

North Korea: the country conducted a series of ballistic missile tests, in defiance of international warnings against such action.

Uganda: President Yoweri Museveni offered "total amnesty" to Lord's Resistance Army (LRA) rebel group leader Joseph Kony, if he responded "positively" to proposed peace talks, despite the fact that Kony had been charged with war crimes by the International Criminal Court in October 2005.

5 **Macedonia:** elections to the unicameral legislature, the Sobranje, were won by an opposition coalition led by the Internal Macedonian Revolutionary Organisation-Democratic Party for Macedonian National Unity (VMRO-DPMNE).

6 **China-India:** the Nathu La (Old Silk Route) trade pass, between Tibet and the Indian state of Sikkim, was reopened, 44 years after it was closed because of a territorial dispute that led to the Sino-Indian war of 1962.

7 **Netherlands:** a minority coalition government was formed, under Prime Minister Jan Peter Balkenende, following the collapse of his government on 29 June with the withdrawal of the Democrats 66 (D66).

8 **East Timor:** Foreign Minister and Nobel Peace Prize laureate José Ramos Horta was named as the new prime minister, replacing Mari Alkatiri who had resigned on 26 June after weeks of unrest.

9-10 **Russia:** Shamil Basayev, the most notorious Chechen field commander, was killed in an explosion in Ingushetia. Russian forces claimed that the explosion had been a deliberate assassination; Chechen and Ingush rebels claimed that it was an accident.

10-11 **Europe-Africa:** a conference in Rabat, the capital of Morocco, brought together representatives of 27 African and 30 European countries, together with regional and international organisations, to formulate a co-ordinated approach to the problem of sub-Saharan migrants desperately seeking to reach Europe.

11 **India:** seven bombs exploded within a period of 15 minutes on commuter trains and at stations in Bombay (Mumbai), causing around 180 deaths and injuring nearly 800 people. Ten men were arrested in connection with the attacks, all belonging to the banned Students' Islamic Movement of India (SIMI).

Indonesia: the legislature unanimously passed a law granting increased autonomy for the north Sumatran province of Aceh, under the terms of the August 2005 peace agreement between the government and the separatist Free Aceh Movement (GAM).

12 **Lebanon:** Israel launched an air and ground assault on Lebanon, in response to attacks on Israeli soldiers and civilians by Hezbullah militants, and the capture of two Israeli soldiers. Israel's assault drew international attention away from its simultaneous attacks on Gaza in response to the capture in June of another of its soldiers.

UK: police officers arrested Lord Levy, principal fundraiser for the Labour Party and close friend of Prime Minister Tony Blair, in the ongoing investigation into the "cash for peerages" affair. Levy was questioned, and released on 13 July pending further investigations.

14 **Germany:** the first "integration summit" convened by the government to discuss ways of integrating migrants into German society was held in Berlin.

Japan: the Bank of Japan announced the end of its zero-interest-rate policy, and raised its key interest rate to 0.25 per cent.

Poland: President Lech Kaczynski appointed his twin brother and head of the centre-right Law and Justice Party (PiS), Jaroslaw Kaczynski, as prime minister, replacing Kazimierz Marcinkiewicz.

15 **Haiti:** at least 30,000 people marched in Port-au-Prince, the capital, calling for the return from exile in South Africa of former President Jean-Bertrand Aristide and demanding the release of political prisoners.

15-17 **G-8:** a summit meeting of leaders of the G-8 held in St Petersburg, Russia, was widely regarded as a triumph for Russia's President Vladimir Putin, despite concerns over his country's economic and political path.

17 **Indonesia:** a tsunami struck Java's southern coast, leaving at least 650 people dead, 300 missing, and at least 33,000 people homeless.

19 **USA:** President George W. Bush exercised his presidential veto for the first time to halt legislation enacted by the Senate on 18 July that relaxed the restrictions on federal funding for stem cell research.

20-21 **Mercosur:** the 30th summit of heads of government of the five members of Mercosur, the South American Common Market, was held in Argentina, with the aim of integrating Venezuela into the organisation following that country's formal accession to full membership on 4 July.

EU: justice and home affairs ministers provisionally approved European Commission measures designed to combat illegal immigration into the EU from Africa.

22 **Lebanon:** Israel began a ground invasion of Lebanon as part of its assault on the country in response to the Hezbullah attacks of 12 July. Israeli forces met stiff resistance from Hezbullah fighters, particularly around the town of Bint Jbail.

24 **WTO:** 14 hours of negotiation between six key members (Australia, Brazil, the EU, India, Japan, and the USA) ended without result, prompting fears that the Doha round of trade talks would collapse over the issue of US agricultural subsidies, EU agricultural import tariffs, and developing country import tariffs.

25 **Lebanon:** an Israeli air strike on a clearly-marked UN compound in the southern Lebanese town of Khiam killed four members of the UN Interim Force in Lebanon (UNIFIL).

Thailand: the Criminal Court convicted three members of the Election Commission, including its chairman Vasana Puemlarp, of malpractice during the 2 April general election and subsequent re-elections. A royal decree on 20 July endorsed new elections for 15 October.

26 **Uganda:** the government and the rebel Lord's Resistance Army (LRA) signed a truce agreement.

27 **Italy:** a controversial amnesty for 12,000 white-collar criminals was adopted by the Chamber of Deputies (the lower house of the bicameral legislature), to ease overcrowding in the country's prisons.

Venezuela: a US$1.6 billion contract was signed to buy 24 fighter jets and 53 helicopters from Russia, prompting condemnation from the US government.

30 **Democratic Republic of Congo:** the first genuine multiparty presidential and legislative elections were held since independence from Belgium in 1960, the culmination of a UN-sponsored transition process aimed at ending decades of war.

Lebanon: an Israeli bombing raid on the southern village of Qana killed at least 28 civilians, to international outrage. Israel apologised for the deaths, but claimed that Qana was a Hezbullah rocket site.

Sri Lanka: the Sri Lankan Army launched a ground offensive intended to gain control of land held by the rebel Tamil Tigers (Liberation Tigers of Tamil Eelam), prompting the LTTE to announce that the 2002 ceasefire agreement with the government was "null and void".

31 **Afghanistan:** the US-led coalition forces formally handed control of the six southern provinces (Day Kundi, Helmand, Kandahar, Nimroz, Uruzgan, and Zabul) to the NATO International Security Assistance Force (ISAF). July saw more than 600 Taliban insurgents killed in fighting.

Cuba: President Fidel Castro Ruz ceded power on a temporary basis to his brother, Raul Castro Ruz, and three other senior officials, because he was about to undergo "complicated" surgery to halt intestinal bleeding.

AUGUST

1 **Germany:** it was revealed that two suitcase bombs had been found the previous day on commuter trains in Dortmund and Coblenz. The bombs, which had failed to explode, were believed to have been planted by two Lebanese nationals, who were later arrested in Germany and in Tripoli, northern Lebanon.

Philippines: the army launched operations against the Islamic separatist Abu Sayyaf Group in the islands of the south-western Sulu province.

Uganda: the first talks were held between government officials and Joseph Kony, leader of the rebel Lord's Resistance Army (LRA), following an offer of "total amnesty " for Kony by Ugandan President Yoweri Museveni.

3 **Tuvalu:** in a general election to the 15-seat Parliament, eight sitting MPs were defeated. On 15 August Parliament elected Apisai Ielemia as the new prime minister and a new cabinet was sworn in.

Ukraine: President Viktor Yushchenko announced that he had agreed to appoint as prime minister his rival, Viktor Yanukovych, leader of the Party of Regions, which had won legislative elections in March.

4 **Argentina:** Julio Hector Simon, the first official to be convicted for human rights violations in the "dirty war" era (1976-83) since amnesty laws were overturned in August 2005, was sentenced to 25 years in prison.

6 **Bolivia:** a constituent assembly convened for one year to rewrite the country's 1994 constitution.

7 **Afghanistan:** the legislature approved nominations to five posts in the cabinet that had been vacant since it rejected President Hamid Karzai's initial choices to fill them in April.

8 **USA:** Senator Joseph Lieberman (Democrat, Connecticut) was defeated in the Connecticut Democratic primary, by 52 per cent of the vote to 48, by Ned Lamont, a relatively unknown candidate. Lieberman's defeat was attributed to his strong support for the war in Iraq.

10 **UK:** police arrested 24 UK Muslims who were believed to be planning to carry out suicide bombings on up to 10 transatlantic airliners using liquid explosives. Exceptional security measures were imposed at airports, leading to massive disruption. On 16 August, the EU agreed additional co-operation measures against terrorism.

11 **Lebanon:** the UN Security Council approved Resolution 1701 (2006) to halt the fighting in Lebanon, and to expand the existing UNIFIL force there. The ceasefire was due to take effect on 14 August, bringing to a close the massive military assault waged against Lebanon by Israel in response to the capture of two Israeli soldiers by the militant Hezbullah group on 12 July.

14 **Cameroon:** more than 3,000 Nigerian troops withdrew from the Bakassi peninsula, under the terms of the June agreement brokered by the UN.

15 **Japan:** Prime Minister Junichiro Koizumi visited the Yasukuni shrine war memorial, which honoured among its dead a number of convicted war criminals. It was the first time the prime minister had visited the shrine on the anniversary of Japan's surrender in World War II.

16 **Czech Republic:** President Vaclav Klaus appointed as prime minister Mirek Topolanek, leader of the centre-right Civic Democratic Party (ODS), following the ODS's narrow election victory in June.

Israel: Defence Minister Amir Peretz appointed a committee of enquiry to examine the military's state of readiness in the 34-day conflict against Hezbullah fighters in Lebanon, which had ended with a UN-brokered ceasefire on 14 August.

17 **USA:** a District Court judge, in a case brought by the American Civil Liberties Union (ACLU), ruled that the government's recent programme of monitoring overseas telephone conversations and electronic communications infringed the fourth and first amendments to the constitution.

21 **Iraq:** the trial opened of Saddam Hussein and six other defendants on charges of genocide and crimes against humanity for their part in the 1988-90 Anfal campaign against Kurdish villages. Saddam was already on trial for ordering executions in the village of Dujail in 1982.

Russia: two bombs exploded at the outdoor Cherkizovsky market in Moscow, killing 11 people. On 23 August two students were reported to have confessed making and planting the bombs, motivated by racial hatred.

Sri Lanka: the Sri Lankan Monitoring Mission (SLMM) from the Nordic countries withdrew all its peace monitors from the northern Jaffna peninsula and the port city of Trincomalee because of renewed heavy fighting between government forces and the Liberation Tigers of Tamil Eelam (LTTE).

23 **Somalia:** a new Cabinet was sworn in under Prime Minister Ali Mohammed Gedi, after a series of ministerial resignations from the previous interim government in protest at the presence of Ethiopian forces, in the country to support the Somali government which was losing control of territory to militias from the Union of the Islamic Courts.

24 **France:** France announced that it would increase its troop commitment to 2,000 extra troops for the expanded UNIFIL force in southern Lebanon, agreed under the UN Security Council Resolution 1701 of 11 August. UNIFIL would be commanded by France until February 2007 (after which Italy would take charge).

space: the International Astronomy Union (IAU) concluded its 26th general assembly, which began on 14 August, in Prague. Among the closing resolutions was the demotion of Pluto—the remotest planet in the solar system—to the newly-defined status of "dwarf planet".

25 **East Timor:** the UN Security Council unanimously adopted Resolution 1704 (2006) establishing a new expanded UN Integrated Mission in East Timor (UNMIT), to replace the UN Office in East Timor (UNOTIL), the mandate of which expired that day.

28 **Guyana:** legislative elections returned President Bharrat Jagdeo's ruling People's Progressive Party/Civic (PPP/C) to power for a fourth consecutive term, with 54 per cent of the vote.

31 **Palestine:** an Israeli military court ordered that 15 Hamas officials from the Palestine Legislative Council (PLC) should stand trial for membership of an outlawed organisation. During August Israel had detained one-third of the Hamas government of Palestine and over 30 members of the PLC, as part of its campaign for the release of Israeli soldier Corporal Gilad Shalit, captured by Hamas militants on 25 June.

Sudan: the UN Security Council approved Resolution 1706 which expanded the mandate of the UN Mission in Sudan (UNMIS), so that UN troops could be deployed in the troubled western province of Darfur.

SEPTEMBER

1 **Iraq:** in its regular quarterly assessment of the security situation, the US defence department, the Pentagon, said that the conflict in Iraq had changed from a battle against insurgents to a fight between Sunnis and Shi'ites, with Iraqi casualties rising by 51 per cent in the last three months to nearly 120 per day.

2 **Russia:** race riots in the town of Kondopoga, near the border with Finland, erupted following a brawl in an Azeri-owned restaurant in the town. During the violence, Russians attacked Caucasian owned businesses.

5 **Denmark:** the security police arrested nine Danish Muslim men on suspicion that they were plotting a terrorist attack in Denmark. Two were later released.

Mexico: the seven judges of the Federal Electoral Court (TRIFE) ruled unanimously that the presidential elections of 2 July had been fair and formally declared their winner—Felipe Calderón—president-elect.

Sudan: the government ordered the 7,000 troops of the African Union Mission in Sudan, which were there to oversee the May peace agreement, to leave the Darfur region by the end of the month.

6 **Burundi:** the government and the Party for the Liberation of the Hutu People-Forces for National Liberation (the only major Hutu rebel faction offering armed opposition to the government) signed a ceasefire agreement.

Côte d'Ivoire: Prime Minister Charles Konan Banny and his cabinet resigned over a scandal involving the dumping of toxic waste in the commercial capital, Abidjan, which killed at least eight people and made thousands ill. Banny formed a new government (which included only two changes) on 16 September.

Japan: Princess Akishino gave birth to a son, named Hisahito, who was third in line of succession and the first male heir to be born in the imperial house since 1965.

USA: in the first official acknowledgement of the existence of secret CIA prisons outside the USA, President George W. Bush announced that 14 "high value" detainees had been transferred from CIA custody to the detention facility at the US naval base at Guantánamo Bay, Cuba, and that "a small number of terrorist suspects" had been questioned in secret by the CIA outside the USA in a "special programme".

7 **Lebanon:** Israel lifted its air blockade of the country—imposed on 12 July at the start of its war against Hezbullah—with the sea blockade lifted on 8 September. The blockades had hampered reconstruction efforts.

UK: Prime Minister Tony Blair finally made clear his intention to leave office within 12 months, in an attempt to end a week of unrest within his ruling Labour Party over calls for his departure by MPs unhappy with his position on the Israel-Lebanon conflict and on Iraq.

10 **Montenegro:** elections to the Parliament—the first since the referendum confirming Montenegro's secession from Serbia & Montenegro in May—were won by the Coalition for a European Montenegro, led by Prime Minister Milo Djukanovic.

Tonga: King Taufa'ahau Tupou IV died in hospital in New Zealand. On 11 September, his son, Crown Prince Tupouto'a, was crowned King Siaosi Tupou V.

11 **USA:** in a televised address on the fifth anniversary of the 11 September 2001 attacks on New York and Washington, President George W. Bush linked the administration's "war on terror" to its campaign in Iraq.

12 **Vatican:** in a speech at Regensburg university, Pope Benedict XVI said that reason was secondary to the Islamic tradition and that Muslims had accepted the use of force to convert people. On 18 September, the pope apologised for offending Muslims, following protests in Islamic areas of the world.

13 **Russia:** Andrei Kozlov, first deputy chairman of the Russian Central Bank, responsible for bank reforms to combat money laundering, was shot, dying on 14 September.

14 **Environment:** the US National Aeronautical and Space Administration (NASA) released two separate studies showing that Arctic ice had melted at an accelerating rate over the previous two years.

16 **Togo:** President Faure Gnassingbé appointed Yaovi Agboyibo of the opposition Action Committee for Renewal (CAR) as the new prime minister.

17 **Hungary:** an audiotape of a speech by Prime Minister Ferenc Gyurcsany to a closed session of his Hungarian Socialist Party (MSzP) in May was broadcast by Hungarian radio. Gyurcsany admitted lying about the country's budget deficit in order to win the election on 23 April. The broadcast triggered days of rioting in Budapest, the capital.

Sweden: the centre-right opposition four-party Alliance for Sweden narrowly defeated the ruling three-party centre-left coalition of Prime Minister Göran Persson in legislative elections. The Alliance's leader, Fredrik Reinfeldt, was formally approved as prime minister on 5 October.

18 **Gibraltar:** historic trilateral agreements between Gibraltar, the UK, and Spain were signed in Córdoba, Spain, improving communications between Spain and Gibraltar.

19 **Thailand:** while Prime Minister Thaksin Shinawatra was out of the country, six army generals, including Army Commander General Sonthi Boonyaratglin, staged a coup in the name of King Bhumibol Adulyadej, in order to "maintain peace and order".

19-23 **China:** US Treasury Secretary Henry Paulson visited China for "substantive" talks aimed at resolving a protracted economic dispute, principally involving US claims that China's currency, the yuan, was significantly undervalued.

20 **Yemen:** incumbent Lieutenant-General Ali Abdullah Saleh, of the ruling General People's Congress, comfortably won the presidential elections.

22 **The Gambia:** presidential elections resulted in victory for the incumbent Yahya Jammeh, who began his third consecutive five-year term of office.

Lebanon: Hezbullah staged a massive rally of up to 500,000 people in southern Beirut to celebrate its "great divine, historic and strategic victory" over Israel.

23 **Estonia:** Toomas Hendrik Ilves was elected president by a 345-member electoral college.

25 **China:** Chen Liangyu, the Communist Party of China (CCP) secretary and mayor of the influential city of Shanghai, was dismissed and removed from the CCP politburo before being charged with corruption.

26 **Japan:** the Diet (bicameral legislature) elected Shinzo Abe to succeed Junichiro Koizumi as prime minister. Abe had, on 20 September, won a leadership election within the ruling Liberal Democratic Party (LDP).

27 **Georgia:** four officers from Russia's military intelligence service (GRU) were detained on espionage charges, for allegedly planning a "serious provocation". Russia protested in the strongest terms. The four officers were released on 2 October.

USA: Republican Governor of California Arnold Schwarzenegger signed legislation imposing stringent controls on carbon dioxide emissions in the state, aiming to reduce them by 25 per cent by 2020.

28 **USA:** the Senate passed legislation that established rules for the interrogation and trial of terrorist suspects deemed to be "unlawful enemy combatants" rather than prisoners of war. The new law (signed by President Bush on 17 October) established new military tribunals for suspects held at Guantánamo Bay, replacing those deemed illegal by the US Supreme Court in June.

Zambia: presidential and legislative elections resulted in victory for incumbent President Levy Mwanawasa and his Movement for Multiparty Democracy (MMD).

29 **Burma (Myanmar):** the UN Security Council discussed for the first time the state of human rights in Burma, after hearing a report from the UN under-secretary-general for political affairs, Ibrahim Gambari, who had visited the country in May.

30 **Lebanon:** Jan Egeland, the UN under-secretary-general for humanitarian affairs, described as "completely immoral" the deployment of massive numbers of cluster bombs by Israel in southern Lebanon in the final days of Israel's campaign against Hezbullah, when a ceasefire was imminent.

OCTOBER

1 **Austria:** a general election produced an unexpected victory for the opposition Social Democratic Party (SPÖ) over the ruling conservative People's Party (ÖVP).

Bosnia & Herzegovina: general elections were held for the presidency and legislature of the country and its constituent republics.

Brazil: incumbent President Luiz Inácio "Lula" da Silva won 48.6 per cent of the vote in presidential elections, just short of the 50 per cent necessary to avoid proceeding to a second round. Legislative and gubernatorial elections were held the same day.

Palestine: armed clashes occurred between gunmen from the rival Fatah and Hamas factions in the Gaza Strip during protests over government wages that remained unpaid because of the international economic blockade against the Hamas-dominated government for its refusal to recognise Israel.

Thailand: General (retd) Surayud Chulanont was chosen as interim prime minister by the Council for Democratic Reform (the group of army generals who had deposed Prime Minister Thaksin Shinawatra in September).

3 **Uganda:** the army announced that it had resumed operations against the rebel Lord's Resistance Army (LRA) after the latter had failed to gather at assembly points in southern Sudan, as mandated in an August ceasefire.

5 **Afghanistan:** NATO formally assumed control of coalition forces in the east of the country, giving the NATO International Security Assistance Force (ISAF), numbering 31,000 troops, responsibility for security in the country as a whole. The USA retained control of 8,000 of its troops for counter-terrorism, training Afghan forces, and the capture of al-Qaida leader, Osama bin Laden.

6 **EU-USA:** European Commission and US negotiations concluded a revised agreement on the provision of personal data on transatlantic airline passengers from EU countries to the USA. The previous agreement had been struck down by the European Court of Justice in May.

7 **Latvia:** elections to the Saeima (unicameral legislature) strengthened the position of the three-party centre-right coalition, led by Prime Minister Aigars Kalvitis of the People's Party

Russia: investigative journalist Anna Politkovskaya was shot dead at the entrance to her apartment bloc in Moscow. She specialised in reporting on the human rights abuses of Russia's campaign in Chechnya.

8 **Japan:** Shinzo Abe, the new Japanese prime minister, visited the Chinese capital, Beijing, for talks with China's President Hu Jintao and Prime Minister Wen Jiabao, in the first formal summit between the two countries since 2001.

8-11 **China:** at the annual meeting of the central committee of the Communist Party of China, a formal strategy to tackle the social problems linked to China's rapid economic growth was adopted.

9 **North Korea:** North Korea claimed to have successfully exploded a nuclear device. US intelligence sources confirmed on 16 October that an underground nuclear test had been conducted in the mountainous north-east of the country, near Punggye, with a yield of less than 1 kilotonne.

13 **UN:** the UN General Assembly appointed Ban Ki Moon (South Korea) as the eighth UN secretary-general, from 1 January 2007.

14 **North Korea:** the UN Security Council unanimously adopted Resolution 1718 (2006) imposing sanctions on North Korea in response to that country's conduct of a nuclear test on 9 October.

15 **Ecuador:** Alvaro Fernando Noboa Pontón of the Institutional Renewal Party of National Action (PRIAN) failed to win at least 40 per cent of the vote in presidential elections, although he held a narrow lead over his closest rival, prompting a second round of voting.

Israel: the justice ministry and the police recommended that President Moshe Katsav face charges of raping and assaulting women.

19 **Ukraine:** the pro-presidential Our Ukraine faction pulled four of its ministers out of the government, after deciding not to join the ruling "anti-crisis" coalition of Prime Minister Viktor Yanukovych.

20 **European Union:** an informal leaders' summit in Lahti, Finland, was dominated by discussion of energy policy, but marred by failure to agree a common position towards Russia, whose President Vladimir Putin was guest of honour at the summit dinner.

23 **Australia:** Prime Minister John Howard announced an investment of A$500 million in clean energy-generating technology to combat global warming; the Australian government, which had not signed the 1997 Kyoto Protocol, had previously been sceptical about climate change. Australia was suffering its fifth year of drought.

Hungary: violent anti-government demonstrations marred the commemorations of the 50th anniversary of the 1956 uprising against Soviet rule.

24 **Afghanistan:** a NATO bombing raid in Kandahar province killed at least 85 civilians. NATO's supreme commander, General James Jones, publicly apologised for the deaths on 28 October

India: a cabinet reshuffle saw Prime Minister Manmohan Singh relinquish the portfolio of external affairs, which he had held since the forced resignation of Natwar Singh in November 2005 after a corruption scandal.

Pacific Islands Forum: the 37th summit meeting of the PIF in Suva, the capital of Fiji, was dominated by the acrimonious dispute caused by Australia's frustrated efforts to extradite Solomon Islands Attorney General Julian Moti (wanted in Australia for alleged sexual offences) from Papua New Guinea.

26-27 **Bolivia:** foreign energy companies signed new operating contracts, ceding majority control of their Bolivian operations to the state, in accordance with the policy of nationalising Bolivia's hydrocarbons sector announced on 1 May.

28 **Bermuda:** a leadership election of the ruling Progressive Labour Party (PLP) was won by Ewart Brown, who was sworn in as Bermuda's new prime minister (replacing Alex Scott) on 30 October.

28-29 **Serbia:** a referendum approved a new constitution for Serbia, drafted following the secession of Montenegro in May. The constitution defined the UN-administered Kosovo as "an autonomous province of Serbia".

Sri Lanka: peace talks between the government and the separatist Liberation Tigers of Tamil Eelam (LTTE) in Geneva, Switzerland, ended without fresh agreement, although both sides promised to respect the 2002 ceasefire. The last round of peace talks, in February, had been followed by steadily escalating violence.

29 **Bangladesh:** President Iajuddin Ahmed was sworn in as chief adviser (head) of a caretaker government, after the ruling Bangladesh Nationalist Party (BNP)-led coalition and the opposition Awami League had failed to agree a candidate for the post.

Brazil: in the second round of the presidential election, incumbent President "Lula" da Silva of the ruling Workers' Party (PT) defeated Geraldo Alckmin, his closest rival from the first round on 1 October, by a comfortable margin, to secure a second term in office, due to begin on 1 January 2007.

Bulgaria: incumbent pro-EU President Georgi Purvanov won the second round of the presidential election with some 75 per cent of the vote, defeating anti-EU and anti-NATO nationalist Volen Siderov of Attack party.

Democratic Republic of Congo (DRC): in the second round of presidential elections, Joseph Kabila defeated his closest rival from the first round of voting on 30 July, with 58 per cent of the vote according to results released on 15 November.

Nigeria: an airliner crashed shortly after taking off from Abuja, killing 96 people, among whom was the spiritual leader of Nigeria's mainstream Islamic community, the Sultan of Sokoto, Muhammadu Maccido.

30 **Chile:** General Augusto Pinochet Ugarte was placed under house arrest after being charged, on 27 October, in relation to an ongoing investigation into instances of torture, disappearances, and murder at the Villa Grimaldi—a political detention centre—during the period of his dictatorship (1973-90).

environment: Sir Nicholas Stern published his report, commissioned by the UK Treasury, on *The Economics of Climate Change*, which warned of a possible permanent loss of 20 per cent of global GDP if action were not taken to control global warming.

Pakistan: an air strike by the Pakistani army on a madrassa (Islamic seminary) in the border area with Afghanistan killed about 80 people. The army claimed that it was a training camp for militants.

31 **North Korea:** China announced that, following intensive diplomatic efforts, it had persuaded North Korea to return to the six-party talks on its nuclear weapons programme, suspended since September 2005.

NOVEMBER

1 **Côte d'Ivoire:** the UN Security Council approved Resolution 1721 (2006), extending the mandates of President Laurent Gbagbo and Prime Minister Charles Konan Banny for a further "new and final transition period" of up to 12 months.

Uganda: the government and the rebel Lord's Resistance Army (LRA) signed an addendum to their August truce agreement in an attempt to revive it, following the resumption of military action against the LRA in October.

1-7 **Palestine:** Israeli forces carried out a major military operation ("Operation Autumn Clouds") around Beit Hanoun in the Gaza Strip, killing at least 50 Palestinians, including civilians.

4-5 **China-Africa:** at a summit of the Forum on China-Africa Co-operation (FOCAC) in Beijing, attended by heads of state and government of 48 African countries, a total of 16 trade and investment agreements were reached, valued at US$1.9 billion. China also extended US$5 billion in loans and credits to Africa.

5 **Iraq:** former President Saddam Hussein was sentenced to death having been found guilty of crimes against humanity for ordering the execution of at least 143 people in the Shi'ite village of Dujail, in 1982.

Nicaragua: former President Daniel Ortega Saavedra (1985-90) won the presidential election, and his Sandinista National Liberation Front was victorious in elections to the National Assembly.

6 **Tajikistan:** President Imomali Rahmonov was re-elected for a third consecutive seven-year term, with over 79 per cent of the vote.

6-17 **environment:** the second meeting of parties to the Kyoto Protocol (COP/MOP 2), in conjunction with the 12th session of the conference of the parties to the UN Framework Convention on Climate Change (UNFCCC) was held in Nairobi, Kenya. Ministers agreed to review the Kyoto Protocol in 2008, in preparation for the setting of new targets for emissions cuts.

7 **Guam:** Republican Felix Camacho was elected for a second term as governor.

USA: the Democratic Party gained control of both houses of Congress—the House of Representatives and the Senate—in the mid-term legislative elections. The results were a severe reversal for Republican President George W. Bush, who described them as a "thumping".

8 **Kyrgyzstan:** eight days of mass protests in the capital, Bishkek, ended with concessions by President Kurmanbek Bakiev to limit the powers of the presidency and grant more authority to the legislature.

USA: Defence Secretary Donald Rumsfeld tendered his resignation, following the Republicans' defeat in the mid-term elections. Replacing him, subject to confirmation by the Senate (granted on 6 December), would be a former director of the CIA, Robert Gates.

9 **Russia:** the European Court of Human Rights found Russia to be in contravention of the European Convention on Human Rights, to which it was signatory, in three cases involving the deaths of civilians in Chechnya, the third and fourth such rulings against it.

WHO: the 193 member states of the World Health Organisation elected Margaret Chan of China as WHO's new director general.

10 **Montenegro:** a new government, led by former Justice Minister Zeljko Sturanovic, was approved by Parliament. Sturanovic replaced his Democratic Party of Socialists (DPS) ally, Milo Djukanovic.

12 **Georgia:** the separatist republic of South Ossetia held a referendum on independence—which was comprehensively supported—and conducted presidential elections, which were won by the incumbent, Eduard Kokoity. The international community recognised neither vote.

13 **Uzbekistan:** the EU extended for a further 12 months its arms embargo and visa restrictions on 12 senior officials, imposed in response to the government suppression of protesters in Andizhan in May 2005.

16 **Germany:** the Federal Court of Justice quashed the acquittal in August 2005 by a Hamburg court of Mounir Motassadeq (a Moroccan national) on charges of having assisted the "Hamburg cell" of al-Qaida activists plan the 11 September 2001 attacks on the USA.

USA: Nancy Pelosi (Democrat, California) was elected unopposed as speaker of the House of Representatives. Pelosi, the first woman to hold the post, which she would assume in January 2007, was an outspoken critic of President George W. Bush and the war in Iraq.

18-19 **APEC:** the 14th summit meeting of the Asia-Pacific Economic Forum (APEC) was held in Hanoi, the capital of Vietnam. Although dominated by the repercussions of North Korea's nuclear test in October, the meeting was unable to agree a common strategy towards that country.

19 **Mauritania:** the first legislative elections were held since the overthrow of President Maaouyia Ould Taya in 2005.

20-23 **India-China:** China's President Hu Jintao visited India for the first time since 1984 and agreed a 10-point programme to further co-operation in information technology, trade, science, and education.

21 **Nepal:** ending the civil war that began in 1996, a peace agreement was signed between Prime Minister Girija Prasad Koirala and Comrade Prachanda, chairman of the Communist Party of Nepal-Maoist. The peace agreement was followed on 28 November by an agreement on the disarmament of the Maoist rebel troops.

Lebanon: Industry Minister Pierre Gemayel was shot dead in his car in Beirut. Gemayel was from a leading Christian political family and opposed Syrian influence in Lebanon.

Syria: diplomatic relations with Iraq were restored. They had been broken off in 1980 when Syria sided with Iran in its war against Iraq.

22 **Netherlands:** a general election was held, following the departure in June of the Democrats 66 (D66) from the ruling coalition. The Christian Democratic Appeal of Prime Minister Jan Peter Balkenende was expected to form a coalition government.

23 **Iraq:** five car bombs and two mortar rounds hit street markets in the Shi'ite area of Sadr City, killing 215 people and wounding 257. Retaliation against Sunni targets followed.

UK: Russian former security service officer Alexander Litvinenko, who had been granted political asylum in the UK in 2001, died in hospital having apparently ingested the radioactive substance, polonium-210. In a letter published posthumously, Litvinenko accused Russia's President Vladimir Putin of wanting to silence him.

24 **EU-Russia:** an EU-Russia summit in Helsinki, Finland, left issues between the two sides unresolved, particularly over energy supply. Prior to the summit, Poland blocked the opening of negotiations on a new strategic partnership between Russia and the EU.

Northern Ireland: unionist and nationalist politicians convened in the National Assembly (the devolved Northern Irish legislature) at Stormont Castle, to try and meet the deadline set by the UK and Ireland governments for them to nominate first and deputy first ministers of a cross-community power-sharing executive.

Rwanda: diplomatic relations with France were severed after a French court issued arrest warrants against aides of President Paul Kagame in relation to the assassination in 1994 of former President Juvenal Habyarimana.

25 **Bahrain:** legislative elections, with a second round on 2 December, were held to the House of Representatives (first elected in 2002). The main Shi'ite opposition group, Al-Wefaq National Islamic Society, made significant gains.

26 **Ecuador:** the second round of the presidential elections was won by former Finance Minister Rafael Correa. He pledged to sever ties with international financial institutions and to rewrite the country's constitution.

Palestine: a ceasefire began between Israel and Palestinian militants, brokered by Palestinian President Mahmoud Abbas

27 **Iraq:** UN Secretary-General Kofi Annan said that civil war would ignite in Iraq unless action was taken "drastically and urgently" to stop it.

30 **Gibraltar:** over 60 per cent of the electorate approved a new constitution that would devolve more powers from the UK to Gibraltar.

Philippines: Typhoon Durian hit the eastern Philippines. According to Red Cross estimates on 4 December, at least 1,000 people had been killed by the resulting floods and landslides.

DECEMBER

1 **Lebanon:** up to 800,000 pro-Syrian protesters gathered in Beirut, calling for the resignation of the government of Prime Minister Fouad Siniora. The protests were organised by the Shi'ite factions, Hezbullah and Amal, whose ministers had quit the Siniora government on 11 November.

Ukraine: the Verkhovna Rada (unicameral legislature) dismissed Foreign Minister Boris Tarasyuk in its ongoing conflict with the president, Viktor Yushchenko. Reinstated by Yushchenko, Tarasyuk continued to work as foreign minister but found himself barred from cabinet meetings.

3 **Madagascar:** presidential elections resulted in an emphatic victory, in the first round, for incumbent President Marc Ravalomanana of the ruling I Love Madagascar (TIM) party.

Mauritania: a second round of elections to the legislature (following the first round on 19 November) was held, resulting in victory for the Rally of Democratic Forces (RFD), the main party in the former opposition Coalition of Forces for Democratic Change (CFCD).

Venezuela: President Hugo Chávez Frías was re-elected for a further six-year term, with more than 62 per cent of the vote.

3-14 **Palestine:** on his first foreign trip since the formation of his Hamas government in March, Prime Minister Ismail Haniyeh visited Syria, Iran, and Egypt. There was violence between Hamas forces and the rival Fatah when Israeli officials at the Rafah crossing point with Egypt refused to allow him to re-enter Palestine with US$35 million in cash collected from Syria, Iran, Qatar, and Sudan in support of the blockaded Hamas government. The money was eventually deposited in an Egyptian bank.

4 **India:** the final sentences were passed in the trial of those accused of involvement in the 1993 bombings in Mumbai (Bombay), which had killed 257 people. Of the 123 defendants, 100 had been convicted.

USA: US Ambassador to the United Nations, John Bolton, resigned. President George W. Bush acknowledged that Bolton would not secure approval from the Democratic-controlled Senate.

5 **Fiji:** a long-anticipated military coup took place, led by Commodore Josaia Voreqe (Frank) Bainimarama, commander of Fiji's military forces, after months of dispute between the armed forces and Fiji's Prime Minister Laisenia Qarase. Bainimarama appointed himself acting president on 6 December.

6 **Bulgaria:** the National Assembly adopted a bill that allowed all files kept by the former communist state security and military intelligence agencies to be declassified, and that required all files revealing public figures to have been former communist secret agents to be published.

USA: the bipartisan Iraq Study Group, a high-level panel established in March by Congress (the legislature), reported to Congress and President George W. Bush. It warned that the Iraqi state could collapse if US policy were not changed.

10 **Chile:** former dictator of Chile, General (retd) Augusto Pinochet Ugarte, died in a military hospital in Santiago, the capital, aged 91.

11 **Israel:** Prime Minister Ehud Olmert apparently inadvertently revealed Israel's nuclear weapons capability in an interview broadcast on German cable television news N24.

St Lucia: in legislative elections, the ruling St Lucia Labour Party (SLP) was defeated by the United Workers' Party (UWP), led by Sir John Compton, 82, who was inaugurated as prime minister, with his new cabinet, on 15 December.

Turkey: EU foreign ministers endorsed a proposal by the European Commission to suspend negotiations with Turkey on eight of the 35 chapters of Turkey's EU accession talks, because of Turkey's refusal to recognise Greek Cyprus.

14 **Bhutan:** King Jigme Singye Wangchuck announced his abdication in favour of his son, Crown Prince Jigme Khesar Namgyel Wangchuck.

UK: Prime Minister Tony Blair was questioned as a witness by police investigating the "cash for peerages" affair.

15 **Japan:** controversial legislative amendments were adopted by the Diet (the bicameral legislature). The first altered school curricula to instil a greater sense of patriotism in students; the second upgraded the status of the defence agency to that of a ministry.

16 **Nepal:** an interim constitution was signed, which transferred constitutional powers of governance from the monarch to the prime minister, as part of the November peace agreement of between the government and the rebel Communist Party of Nepal-Maoist.

17 **Gabon:** elections were held to the National Assembly (the lower chamber of the bicameral legislature), resulting in a comprehensive victory for the ruling Gabonese Democratic Party (PDG) led by President Omar Bongo Ondimba.

18 **India:** US President George W. Bush signed into law a bill on co-operation between India and the USA on civil nuclear energy (the Hyde Act, 2006).

18-22 **North Korea:** the six-party talks on the country's nuclear weapons programme resumed for the first time since September 2005 in China's capital, Beijing, but ended without progress.

21 **Indonesia:** the Supreme Court quashed a conviction on conspiracy charges of Islamist cleric Abu Bakar Bashir, believed to be the spiritual leader of the militant Jemaah Islamiah (JI) network. Bashir had been released from prison in June.

Russia: the foreign consortium consisting of Royal Dutch Shell and two Japanese corporations that owned the Sakhalin-2 oil and gas development in Russia's far east agreed to sell a majority stake to Gazprom, Russia's state-controlled gas monopoly.

Turkmenistan: life-long President Saparmurat Niyazov died unexpectedly of heart failure, raising questions of the succession.

23 **Iran:** the UN Security Council unanimously approved Resolution 1737 (2006) imposing sanctions on Iran for its refusal to abide by an earlier resolution demanding that it halt all uranium enrichment activities.

24 **Somalia:** Ethiopian forces in Somalia launched a major offensive against the Union of Islamic Courts (UIC)—the Islamist militia that had controlled much of the south of the country and the capital Mogadishu since June—leading to the UIC's retreat by the end of the month.

26 **French Polynesia:** Gaston Tong Sang was elected president by the Territorial Assembly, following the fall of the Oscar Temaru government on 13 December after a no-confidence vote in the Assembly.

30 **Iraq:** former President Saddam Hussein was hanged, having been sentenced on 5 November. Although official film of the execution showed Saddam apparently calm, unofficial footage, circulated on 31 December on the Internet, showed him being taunted by his Shi'ite executioners.

Spain: government peace talks with the separatist Basque ETA organisation were halted after ETA broke its nine-month ceasefire by detonating a bomb at Barajas airport in Madrid, the Spanish capital.

31 **Democratic Republic of Congo (DRC):** newly-elected President Joseph Kabila, who had been inaugurated on 6 December for a five-year term, appointed Antoine Gizenga, 80, secretary general of the Party of Unified Lumumbists (PALU), as prime minister and invited him to form a coalition government.

INDEX

Page references in bold indicate location of main coverage.